ISBN 978-1-332-29426-8
PIBN 10310311

English
Français
Deutsche
Italiano
Español
Português

www.forgottenbooks.com

Mythology Photography **Fiction**
Fishing Christianity **Art** Cooking
Essays Buddhism Freemasonry
Medicine **Biology** Music **Ancient**
Egypt Evolution Carpentry Physics
Dance Geology **Mathematics** Fitness
Shakespeare **Folklore** Yoga Marketing
Confidence Immortality Biographies
Poetry **Psychology** Witchcraft
Electronics Chemistry History **Law**
Accounting **Philosophy** Anthropology
Alchemy Drama Quantum Mechanics
Atheism Sexual Health **Ancient History**
Entrepreneurship Languages Sport
Paleontology Needlework Islam
Metaphysics Investment Archaeology
Parenting Statistics Criminology
Motivational

FOOTE FAMILY

COMPRISING THE

GENEALOGY AND HISTORY

OF

NATHANIEL FOOTE

OF WETHERSFIELD, CONN.

AND HIS DESCENDANTS

Also a partial record of Descendants of Pasco Foote of Salem, Mass.
Richard Foote of Stafford County, Va., and
John Foote of New York City

VOL. I

By ABRAM W. FOOTE

Please send additional family records, and corrections if any,
also all correspondence regarding purchase or sale
of this book, to A. W. Foote Co.,
Middlebury, Vermont

MARBLE CITY PRESS—THE TUTTLE COMPANY
RUTLAND, VERMONT
1907

TABLE OF CONTENTS

FOOTE COAT OF ARMS
As Used by Descendants of Nathaniel Foote

ONE HUNDRED DESCENDANTS OF NATHANIEL FOOTE,
WETHERSFIELD, CT., JUNE 5, 1907

LIST OF ILLUSTRATIONS

INTRODUCTION

I have been asked by the author to prepare a short introduction to the Foote Family History now in press.

I comply with this request with pleasure for the opportunity it gives me to express my gratitude to the author for having undertaken this work and carried it forward to completion.

We all know what such a work means to the author and compiler. To some extent it may be a labor of love, but, in the main, it requires infinite patience and long continued painstaking labor. Few, indeed, have the courage to undertake such a work, even where there is hope of some substantial financial reward. The sale of this book will be too limited to justify any such hope, and we must credit our author with other and more disinterested motives.

The descendants of Nathaniel Foote, the settler, now living, appreciate to the fullest extent the debt of gratitude which the family owes to Nathaniel Goodwin, who in 1849 rescued from fast approaching oblivion their pedigree and made possible the present work. Even so will the remote descendants of the members of the present generation hold in highest esteem the memory of the author of this book for doing a similar and equally important work for their benefit. And such must be his chief reward.

Accuracy is no doubt the chief desideratum in a work of this kind, but no amount of care and labor has been found sufficient in similar works to insure against all errors. Until the work appears, we cannot, of course, know how far our author has been successful in this respect, but no matter with what care and accuracy the author may have done his part of the work, we may expect to find errors due to the carelessness or mistakes of the hundreds of different individuals, of all the different degrees of accuracy and carelessness, upon whom he has been compelled to rely for much of his information.

Let us hope that on the whole this work will be found to compare favorably in respect of accuracy with other genealogical books.

I venture to suggest to all who may discover errors that they send a correction to the author promptly for use in the first new edition that may be required.

NATHANIEL FOOTE.

Rochester, N. Y., September, 1907.

PREFACE

With very few exceptions, the Footes in America all descended from either Nathaniel Foote, of Colchester, England, who came to Watertown, Mass., about 1630, or Pasco Foote, who settled in Salem, Mass., soon after, or from Richard Foote, of Cornwall, England, and later of Stafford Co., Va. That the first two were nearly related, if not brothers, there can be very little doubt.

The following legend has been handed down by many different sources: "Three brothers came from England in the brig 'Ann,' landed at Plymouth, Mass., Nathaniel, Pasco and John (or Caleb). Nathaniel settled in Watertown, Mass.; Pasco settled in Salem, Mass., and John (or Caleb) died without issue."

Emigration to New England languished for ten years after the arrival of the "Mayflower," and until the expedition by John Winthrop and Sir Richard Saltonstall, which numbered about 1,500, came over in the summer of 1630, very few colonists came over.

It is very difficult to connect these emigrants with their ancestors in the Mother Country.

In Burke's Commoners, Vol. I., page 372, is an account of the Foote Family in Kent. It is stated that the family possessed large estates in the county of Cornwall prior to 1420. Thomas Foote was Lord Mayor of London in 1650, and there are many others of the family who have distinguished themselves in the Mother Country. There are ten different armorial bearings, granted to as many different branches of the family who distinguished themselves. While it is very probable that this is all one family, yet we have not the positive proof at present.

There is a tradition that our ancestors in England lived at the foot of a mountain at the time when surnames were adopted, and they called them Foote. The name was sometimes spelled Fotte or Foot. The latter is in use at the present time by a few members of the family.

We have been compelled by lack of space to leave out several parts of the book that we had prepared for it, including lists of Revolutionary soldiers from the various States by the name of Foote, Pensioners of the Revolutionary War, College Graduates by the name of Foote, and biographical sketches of prominent members of the English branch. This material will be available for future use.

In addition to the several thousand Footes here recorded, we have received a number of family records that we could not definitely connect with any of the several branches of the family. These records are on file, and if they can later (as I have no doubt many of them can) prove their connections, we shall be glad to make the record.

In compiling this work, I have searched all of the Genealogies and Historical Works that I could find, including those at the Wordsworth Historical Library and State Library at Hartford, Ct., Vermont State Library, the Billings and Carnegie Library at Burlington, Vt., and Middlebury College Library, Middlebury, Vt.

The family data of Nathaniel Foote in Nathaniel Goodwin's Genealogy of 1849 is herein included. Without this aid it would have been impossible, at this date, to make a work as complete as this. We have also included, by permission, Miss Brainard's pamphlet and that of Rev. J. B. Foote's, on descendants of John Foote, and a large part of the data has been received direct from the living members of the family, and yet we realize that there are descendants who have not been reported. If you, dear reader, are one, and can trace your descent from any of these branches, do not fail to write at once, enclosing all the data and information you have, to A. W. Foote, Middlebury, Vt., and it matters not how many years have rolled away, someone will file the papers and it will be printed in the future in the Second Volume of this work.

The numbers in parentheses following the name of a father are the numbers of his Father, Grandfather, Great-grandfather, and so forth, and number 1 is understood to be Nathaniel Foote, the Settler. By counting the numbers you will ascertain the generation. The numbers following the name of the wife of a son are the numbers of their children.

By this system the following generations can easily be recorded and printed in the Second Volume. The children of a daughter are indicated by figures (1), her grandchildren by letters (a), the great-grandchildren by Roman numerals (i), the great-great-grandchildren by Roman numerals and figures (i1). A name in parentheses indicates the maiden name of the mother. When the birth-place is not given it is understood to be at the place given as the residence of the parents.

The following are explanations of the abbreviations used: Abt., about; ae., aged; b., born; bldg., building; ch., children; Ch., Church; dau., daughter; d., died or dead; m., married; n. f. k., nothing further known; p., page; res., residence, resided, or resides; unm., unmarried; s. p., *sine prole* (without issue); wid., widow or widower; yr., year.

I take this opportunity to thank the many friends who have assisted me in gathering this mass of family data. Miss Lucy A. Brainard, who, since publishing a pamphlet in 1886 on her own branch, has added a large amount of data in connection with her own great work, the Brainard-Brainerd Genealogy; James Hall Foote, N. Y.; John Crocker Foote, Belvidere, Ill.; Harry Foote, Springville, N. Y.; Dr. Winfield

Scott Hall, Chicago, Ill.; Rev. J. B. Foote and Wife, Syracuse, N. Y.; Rev. E. J. Foote, Trenton, N. J.; Caroline Foote Marsh, New York City; Miss J. M. Foote, Hobart, N. Y.; J. A. Foote, Pasadena, Cal.; Miss Charlotte M. Tuttle, Boston, Mass.; Chas. H. Bigelow, Findlay, O.; David Thompson Foote, Bridgeport, Ct.; Mrs. Elizabeth Jenkins, New Haven, Ct.; Misses Essie and Ellen Foote, Cleveland, O.; Chas. N. Foote, Lee, Mass.; Mrs. O. F. Sheldon, Ripon, Wis.; Mrs. Antoinette Burgoyne, Bridgeport, Mich.; Mrs. Augusta Foote, Philadelphia, Pa.; Rev. Lemuel Foote, Rochester, N. Y., and many others too numerous to mention.

And now, dear friends, get acquainted, write to the cousin you have lost track of or, perhaps, never knew of before, and give your own number, and if you receive such a letter, answer it at once, before you forget it.

The social pleasures derived from the Wethersfield meeting, and from the correspondence all over the country, have more than compensated me for the work.

Truly Yours,

Abram W. Foote

Middlebury, Vt., Sept., 1907.

THE NATHANIEL FOOTE MONUMENT.

While we know that the remains of Nathaniel Foote, the Settler, and many of his family rest in the graveyard back of the old church of Wethersfield, yet it is a lamentable fact that there is not a stone in the whole yard with the name of FOOTE on it. The stones have either been taken away or used for foundations many years ago, and we are not able to mark the exact locations of their graves.

But we can locate the old Foote homestead lot, and this property extended out into what is now a public park at the foot of Broad Street, and it is the purpose of the association to erect a monument to Nathaniel Foote and his family on this public property and at the same time mark the original property.

We hope to dedicate this monument in June, 1908.

FOOTE COAT OF ARMS

Arg. (silver), a chevron Sable (black), and in the dexter quarter a trefoil of the second (black) crest an oak tree proper (natural color). There are ten different Coats of Arms recorded in the College of Heralds to members of the Foote Family; five of these have the chevron and trefoil in the dexter quarter, with different crests. Maj. L. R. D. Fayling, Gen. Manager of the International Bibliophile Society of New York, writing under date of May 7, 1907, says:

"I have not the slightest doubt but that you have the authentic Foote Arms. In Europe, frequently the 'arms' of a family are officially 'confirmed' by the 'College of Heralds' simply on the strength of a family having 'borne' such a 'coat' for *three* or more generations."

The above Coat of Arms has been used by the Foote Family in America for two hundred and fifty years (250), as shown by the following letters:

From Dr. Nathaniel Foote, of Colchester, Ct., dated Mar. 11, 1907.

More than sixty-five (65) years ago my grandmother, Abigail Foote (No. 245), gave me a picture or fine engraving of the Foote Coat of Arms, about three inches square, which she told me was given to her by her grandfather, Nathaniel Foote (No. 25). In 1864 I had a steel plate engraved of the Coat of Arms, reduced in size, as shown on the letter head I sent you. The engravers who made it for me, and the printers who printed the stationery, are now deceased.

Extract copied from letter of Daniel Elisha Foote.

Jirah Isham Foote, Esq.   Belvidere, Ill., Dec. 11, 1894.

Dear Sir,—In regard to the Foote Coat of Arms, I have in my possession what is said to be the original, and of which the one owned by the late Rev. Henry Ward Beecher (See No. 804, 8) is a copy. I also have a paper in the handwriting of my great-grandfather, Isaac Foote (No. 247). This paper contains the following statement: "The following is the pedigree of ancient family of Footes, taken from autentic history. It appears that some time between A. D. 1630 and 1635, three brothers by the names of Nathaniel, Caleb and Pasco came to this country from Colchester, in England, and settled as follows: Pasco settled at Salem, Mass., where there is now some of his descendants. Caleb is supposed to have died in Boston, without issue. Nathaniel, the eldest, first settled at Watertown, Mass., in 1636. He, with a number of others, removed to Wethersfield, Ct., and were among the first that settled there. He had two sons, Nathaniel and Robert. Robert settled in the town of Branford, in the county of New Haven. Nathaniel, the eldest, who settled in Wethersfield, married Margaret Bliss, of Springfield, Mass. He was principal agent in getting the town of Colchester located and incorporated, and gave it the name of Colchester (the name of the town of his nativity).''

The following is the King-James tradition of the Foote Coat of Arms, which I have heard from my early youth, and has been generally believed by my relations and ancestors, so far as I am informed. It was copied by my mother from a writing of Hon. Isaac Foote (No. 247), and was found with the Coat of Arms among his effects:

''A Coat of Arms was bestowed on the family of Footes' for the following reasons: In a war between the English and the Scots, King James was in imminent danger of being killed or taken prisoner, and James Foote, a trusty officer, escorted him to a certain wood, where was a large oak tree, the trunk whereof was hollow, he concealed the King, unknown to anyone, until he obtained a safer retreat. And for that act of fortitude and fidelity the King ordered the Coat of Arms to be struck and given to the said James Foote. The chevron in the center of the card is an emblem of firmness and fidelity. We trace our ancestry from this same James Foote.''

In Hume's History of England, Vol. V, page 417-420, is a similar incident related of King Charles I., so much resembling the tradition in regard to James, his immediate predecessor, as to give rise to the query whether the tradition had not changed the name of the King in passing from memory of one to another so many times.

THE FOOTE COAT OF ARMS.

The genuineness of the Foote Coat of Arms has been held by the family from the first, and has come down to the present generation with the endorsement of our ancestors for two hundred and fifty years. Judge Isaac Foote, of Colchester, Ct., came to the present town of Smyrna, N. Y., in 1794. He was the first Judge of Chenango County. He had been Justice of the Peace and member of the Assembly for Connecticut before coming here, and was for several terms a member of the Assembly for the State of New York.

Judge Foote was born in Colchester, Ct., in 1746, and died in Smyrna in 1842. Judge Foote's grandfather, Nathaniel Foote, was born in Wethersfield, Ct., in 1682, thirty-one years after the battle of Worcester. He came to Colchester, where Judge Foote was brought up, early in the seventeenth century, and died there in 1774, at the age of 92. Judge Foote lived in Colchester until 1773, until within a year of his grandfather's death, and so lived in the same town with his grandfather twenty-seven years.

Henry Ward Beecher believed the story of the origin of this Coat of Arms. and named his country seat Boscobel, after the name of the town where the incident occurred which led to the bestowal of the honor. Mr. Beecher's family and Judge Foote's family were very closely related. The father of Mr. Beecher's mother was Eli Foote, a brother of Judge Isaac Foote.

It is manifest that Judge Foote had peculiar advantages for satisfying himself as to the truth of the story. If such a man as he accepted it as genuine, as he did, we may readily conclude that he had good reasons for accepting it. Henry Ward Beecher's biographers (his son and son-in-law, Rev. Samuel Scoville), have introduced the place of the Arms and the story into the biography. The battle of Worcester, with which the matter is associated, occurred Sept. 3, 1651· The histories, so far as ascertained, do not connect the name of Foote with the battle, nor do they mention any one being knighted for any deed performed in connection with it; nor do they mention the clover-field out of which came a part of the insignia, namely, the clover leaf. The histories narrate the story somewhat as follows:

The battle of Worcester was fought Sept. 3, 1651. Cromwell, with 30,000 men, fell upon Worcester and attacked it, meeting with little resistance. The entire Scottish army was either killed or captured. The King, Charles the Second, was obliged to fly. He fled some twenty-six miles with fifty of his friends, when it was deemed wise for him to separate from his companions. The Earl of Derby advised him to go to Boscobel. At Boscobel lived one Penderell, a farmer, to whom the King entrusted himself. Penderell, with the assistance of his four brothers, took the King, clothed him in a garb like their own, led him into a neighboring wood and pretended to employ themselves in cutting fagots. For better concealment the King climbed an oak tree, where he sheltered himself among the leaves and branches for twenty-four hours. This tree was afterwards called The Royal Oak.

The story, as it has been handed down by our *ancestors,* is that one James Foote, father of Nathaniel Foote, the settler, an officer of King Charles the Second's army, concealed the King in his flight from Cromwell, after the battle of Worcester, at a place called Boscobel, in an oak tree, which was located in a clover field: for which act of chivalry Foote was knighted, the distinct features of the Arms being an oak tree and a clover leaf. The motto of the Arms was "Loyalty and Truth."

While there are marked differences in the two stories, there is no necessary conflict between them. There is nothing in the recorded history to show that one James Foote, an officer of the Army, did not do all the latter story claims for him, or that he was not honored by the King for doing it, as the Foote family have always believed.

LEWIS RAY FOOTE.

Brooklyn, N. Y., Aug. 24, 1896.

THE FOOTE FAMILY ASSOCIATION

The first gathering of the Foote Family Association of America took place in Wethersfield, Connecticut, on June 5, 1907. The descendants of Nathaniel Foote, the settler, gathered in the old town, and formed a permanent family organization. There were over one hundred representatives of the Foote family present from all over the United States.

For some six months previous to the meeting, a vigorous correspondence had been carried on between Judge Abram W. Foote, of Middlebury, Vermont, Mr. John M. Foote, of Hartford, Connecticut, Mr. Nathaniel Foote, of New York City, and Dr. Lewis Nathaniel Foote, of Brooklyn, New York. As a result of these conferences, a letter was sent out to a few members of the family, and the responses were so hearty and enthusiastic that no doubt was left as to the desire for a reunion, and the prospects appeared bright for its success.

Later, a general invitation was scattered as widely as possible.

On Tuesday afternoon, June 4th, representatives of the family from near and far began to gather in Hartford. The Garde Hotel had been chosen as the headquarters of the clan, and on that evening an informal reception was held, which was attended by some sixty-five persons. Remarks were made by Judge Abram W. Foote touching the Foote coat-of-arms and its history. Some discussion followed, which was participated in by Mr. Nathaniel Foote, of New York, Judge Nathaniel Foote, of Rochester, New York, Mrs. Caroline Foote Marsh, of New York, Mrs. Mabel Ward Cameron, of Boston, and others. The reception was a most delightful affair.

On the morning of June 5, 1907, a special electric car conveyed the guests to Wethersfield. Arrangements had most generously been made by the members of the Grange, the Business Men's Association and the selectmen of the town to entertain the gathering in the Grange Hall.

The reunion proper opened with an informal reception from 10 to 11 in the hall, when the assemblage was called to order by Dr. Lewis Nathaniel Foote, of Brooklyn, New York.

He spoke briefly as follows:

Cousins and Friends:

It is indeed a great pleasure to be permitted to call to order this the first gathering of the Foote Family Association.

There have been other reunions of Footes here and there throughout the country but to-day marks the beginning of the national, and who knows but that it may grow into an international organization.

From Boston to Seattle have responses come wishing good success to this gathering. So it behooves us to make firm the foundations we lay to-day that the Foote Family Association may last to the end of time.

The Rev. Henry Lewis Foote, of Marblehead, Massachusetts, delivered the invocation.

Upon the declination of Mr. John Foote, of Hartford, Connecticut, to serve as presiding officer, the name of Judge Nathaniel Foote, of Rochester, N. Y., was presented, and he was unanimously chosen to fill that position.

Upon assuming the chair he addressed the gathering as follows:

Ladies and Gentlemen:

You will not expect me to be wholly free from embarrassment in the presence of so many cousins whom I have now, for the first time, the pleasure of meeting.

It was a very happy inspiration of the person or persons responsible for our meeting to-day to have conceived the plan of such a gathering, and they were equally happy in locating the place of this meeting at Wethersfield, where our common ancestor, who came to this country now more than two hundred and eighty years ago, made his fight for existence and to bring up his family, against the wilderness and the savage. To that fight and to its successful issue all who are gathered here to-day, and thousands more, are indebted for the privilege of existence and for the privilege of enjoying the many comforts and blessings which they enjoy at the present day. To that common ancestor, who lies buried in yonder churchyard, we owe a debt of gratitude too great to be stated in words or to be rightly appreciated. Let us do what little we can to honor his memory, and to that end, I hope a permanent organization of his descendants now living may be formed here, which will result in regular gatherings of the family in the future.

The address of welcome was then delivered by Rev. George L. Clark.

An historical paper was then read by Mr. Nathaniel Foote, of New York City. He said in part:

Mr. Chairman, Ladies and Gentlemen:

The genesis of the name Foote is found in the tradition that when the primitive inhabitants of the British Isles took names to distinguish one family or clan from another, a man who lived at the foot of the mountain called himself Foote. Of course, I can offer no evidence to sustain this statement, owing to the length of time which has elapsed since this occurrence took place, if it ever did. If we accept it as authentic, we must class it with the story of the escape of Charles I. after the battle of Worcester and the services said to have been rendered him by his loyal subject, James Foote of Boscobel.

You are doubtless familiar with this family tradition, for it has been generally accepted among us in one form or another for many years. The story has taken to itself a visible and permanent existence in the coat of arms and crest of the family. We have the oak tree as a crest and the clover-field on the face of the coat of arms, both to remind us of the peril of the King and the degree of Knighthood which afterward was conferred on some ancestor of ours. Unfortunately we have not been able to ascertain which king it was that honored him.

Some of us have understood that it was Charles I. of England, but English history says otherwise. The battle of Worcester and the escape of the King to Boscobel took place in 1651, or sixteen years after the settlement at Wethersfield. It is quite true that a large number of the family remained at home, and Burke's Book of Heraldry gives a description of ten different coats of arms which belonged to the various branches of the family. It is possible that the degree of Knighthood was conferred on some of those who remained in England.

The earliest record in existence of Nathaniel Foote, the Settler, in this country, is found in the records of the grants and possessions of lands in the Colony of Massachusetts Bay in 1633, when he took the oath of Freeman, and in Watertown, where he first located and where is an entry of land to him. Then came the search after a new home, and after fourteen days of travel in the wilderness he, with the rest of the company, settled in Wethersfield. We do not know the reason for this move, although it was stated at the time that the settlers in Watertown wanted "more room for their cattle." It is more probable, however, that it was the outcome of some sort of a theological dispute which led to the new settlement. Later disputes of the same kind led to the settlement of Stamford, Connecticut, in 1640; Branford in 1644, and Hadley, Massachusetts, in 1659. The records of Wethersfield show that Nathaniel Foote took title to a farm on February 21st, 1637, just 270 years ago, and the purchase of this tract made him the largest holder of adventure lands in the settlement. The word "adventure" in this case being used to describe lands the title of which did not come from the town. This settlement of Wethersfield was the beginning of what is now the State of Connecticut, so that our common ancestor was one of the founders of not only a town but a great Commonwealth as well. I say great because the term is well deserved. No student or observer of American affairs can study the history of the State of Connecticut and say otherwise. And in all the various conditions and movements which have contributed to this result our family have borne their share of the burden. I will venture to mention some of them by name: George Foote, of Bennington, Vermont, who stood by the side of Ethan Allen when he demanded the surrender of Fort Ticonderoga. He was one of the pioneer settlers of that State.

Honorable Isaac Foote, of Colchester, Connecticut, a soldier of the Revolution, and the first Judge of Chenango County, New York, to which place he had removed. He died in February, 1843, at the age of 97.

Nathaniel Foote, the projector of the settlement of Colchester, Connecticut. He was representative to the General Assembly for twenty-two successive sessions. He died in August, 1774, at the age of 92, and his son Nathaniel died in 1811 at the age of 99.

Honorable Ebenezer Foote, of Delhi, New York, another Revolutionary soldier and first Judge of Delaware County.

Honorable Samuel Augustus Foote, of Cheshire, Connecticut, Member and Speaker of the House of Representatives of Connecticut; a representative at the Congress in Washington, afterwards United States Senator; Governor of the State of Connecticut, and Presidential Elector in 1844. His son, Andrew Hull Foote, was the well-known Rear-Admiral in the United States Navy.

I will also mention Elial Todd Foote, for twenty-five years Presiding Judge of the Court of Common Pleas of the State of New York; Hon. Leverett Brainerd, former Mayor of Hartford; Frederick W. Foote, of Elizabeth, New Jersey; Right Reverend Fred Foote Johnson, the youngest Bishop in the Episcopal Church;

Honorable Nathaniel Foote, Judge of the Court of Appeals of the State of New York; and Honorable Abram W. Foote, of Middlebury, Vermont.

Judge Abram W. Foote, of Middlebury, Vermont, then addressed the gathering. He said in part:

Dear Cousins:

Two hundred and seventy years ago Nathaniel Foote came to Wethersfield, Conn., and helped settle this, the first town in this valley; he had probably come from Colchester, England, about five years before.

The same energy that prompted Nathaniel Foote to leave Colchester, England, and come to Watertown, and then push again forward to Wethersfield, was apparent in his sons, Nathaniel 2nd, who founded the town of Colchester, Conn., and Robert, who moved to Branford, Conn.; and in the next few generations we find the descendants moving to Vermont and New York State, the frontier at that time, and in the next century pushing on to Michigan and Ohio, and as the country was opened up for settlement, still farther, until to-day we find them in nearly every part of the United States and some parts of Canada.

With the publication of the Genealogy the work of the Association really begins. There is no doubt but what there are many by the name of Foote who have not been traced out; some are indifferent, others have not the means of knowing, but in a few weeks you will all be able to trace the lines just so far as I can now, and by keeping up the interest the greatest success will be attained.

Let each member of the family report any additions or corrections at any time to the Secretary and the record will be preserved for future publication.

These meetings should be held bi-annually, at least, and in different parts of the country, and thus reach a larger proportion of the family.

The object of the Association is two-fold: closer social relations and to collect and preserve the history of the family.

To accomplish these purposes, I would suggest that we have an Assistant Secretary in each State, so far as possible, and that we encourage State Associations that shall meet bi-annually, alternating with the Nathaniel Association, and, if practicable, establish an English Association.

The ties that bind us are naturally closer than that of any fraternity: "Blood is thicker than water."

As we tread the ground that was subdued and tilled by our ancestors, let us not forget that they suffered those privations and braved those dangers that our parents, ourselves, and our children should reap the benefits of living in this Glorious Republic.

This closed the literary character of the morning session.

After some informal remarks by Dr. Foote, of Brooklyn, congratulating Judge Abram W. Foote upon the success of his efforts upon the Foote Genealogy,

It was moved and carried that as an association we tender to him our most hearty thanks for the work that he has done and that some reference in the form of a resolution be placed upon the minutes of this meeting.

The following resolution was introduced and most enthusiastically endorsed by the association:

THE FOOTE FAMILY ASSOCIATION OF AMERICA.

Wethersfield, Connecticut, June 5, 1907.

Hon. Abram William Foote, Middlebury, Vermont.

At the first meeting of the Foote Family Association, held at Wethersfield, Conn., on the 5th day of June, 1907, the following resolution was proposed and unanimously adopted:

Resolved: That we extend to the Honorable Abram W. Foote, of Middlebury, Vermont, our sincere thanks and deep appreciation for the labor which he has so cheerfully given, and for the untiring efforts put forth by him in revising the Foote Genealogy to the present time, as well as to render this gathering so enjoyable to us all.

It has been ordered that this resolution be placed upon the minutes of this the first meeting of the Foote Family Association of America.

NATHANIEL FOOTE, Presiding Officer.

LEWIS NATHANIEL FOOTE, M. D., Acting Secretary.

It was moved and carried that a committee be appointed to nominate officers, draw up rules and by-laws and present some brief form of organization.

The chair appointed as such committee Mr. Julius Merrill Foote, of Newark, New Jersey, Mr. Lawrence Foote, of Canton, Mississippi, and Judge Abram W. Foote, of Middlebury, Vermont.

The benediction was then pronounced by the Rev. John Bartlit Foote, D. D., of Syracuse, New York, thus closing the morning meeting.

Owing to the rainy weather, the guests were largely confined to the Grange building, although later in the day many strolled to the Old Foote Tract and gazed upon the wonderful elm tree.

Lunch was served in the Grange dining hall at 1 o'clock. Over one hundred and fifty were seated and enjoyed a most bountiful repast which was furnished by the Grangers gratuitously.

After luncheon, a flashlight photograph of all those present at the meeting was taken. Instead of the picture being taken under the elm tree, as planned, the weather forbidding, the gathering was photographed in the Grange Hall. A short time was then spent in singing patriotic songs.

The business session was called to order with Judge Nathaniel Foote, of Rochester, New York, in the chair.

The report of the committee on the constitution and by-laws was called for and read.

It was moved and carried that the Foote Family Association of America be hereby organized, and do hereby adopt the constitution and by-laws as offered.

The report of the committee on nominations for officers was called for and the following names were presented:

For President—Hon. Nathaniel Foote, of Rochester, New York.

For Vice-Presidents—Dr. Lewis Nathaniel Foote, of Brooklyn, New York; Mr. John Crocker Foote, of Belvidere, Illinois.

For Secretary and Treasurer—Judge Abram William Foote, of Middlebury, Vermont.

For Historian—Mr. Nathaniel Foote, of New York, N. Y.

For Counselors—Mr. Julius Merrill Foote, of Newark, New Jersey; Mr. Lawrence Foote, of Canton, Mississippi; Mr. Elizur V. Foote, of New York, N. Y.

It was moved and carried that the chairman of the committee on nominations cast the unanimous ballot of the association for the proposed officers.

Judge Nathaniel Foote assumed the chair as president and addressed the association briefly.

It was moved and carried that resolutions of thanks be sent to the hosts of the day and that the resolutions be incorporated in the minutes of the Association.

The subject of a suitable memorial being placed in the town of Wethersfield to perpetuate the name of Nathaniel Foote, the Settler, was brought before the meeting by Judge Abram W. Foote.

It was moved and carried that a committee be appointed, with power to solicit subscriptions for, and to place in the town of Wethersfield, a suitable memorial to Nathaniel Foote, the Settler.

The president appointed as such committee Judge Abram W. Foote, of Middlebury, Vermont, Dr. Lewis Nathaniel Foote, of Brooklyn, New York, and Mr. John A. Foote, of Catskill, New York.

The business meeting was then declared adjourned.

Mr. Josiah G. Adams had been requested to preside at a symposium, at which addresses were listened to with much pleasure from the Wethersfield friends.

Those who spoke included Mr. Henry A. Stillman, of Hartford; Representatives E. Hart Fenn and John T. Welles, Messrs. R. R. Wolcott, George W. Harris, Robert Griswold and F. A. Griswold, of Wethersfield, and Mr. John Howard Foote, of Brooklyn, New York.

The day closed with the singing of "Blest be the Tie that Binds."

Many letters of regret and telegrams were received from those who could not be present.

During the day a telegram was sent to President Roosevelt.

Minutes of June 4 and 5, 1907.

NATHANIEL FOOTE, *President.*

ABRAM W. FOOTE, *Secretary.*

LEWIS NATHANIEL FOOTE, M. D., *Acting Secretary.*

DESCENDANTS OF NATHANIEL FOOTE OF WETHERSFIELD, CT.

1. NATHANIEL FOOTE. The first settler. He was b. abt. 1593; m. in England abt. 1615, Elizabeth Deming, sister of John Deming, who was one of the first settlers of Wethersfield. She was b. abt. 1595. He d. abt. 1644. She m. abt. 1646, Thomas Welles. He was magistrate, afterwards Governor of the Colony. He d. ~~~~~~~ She d. July 28, 1683.

I. NATHANIEL FOOTE, one of the first settlers of Wethersfield, Ct., belongs, not to that class of men who fill a large place in the world's history, because called by some great emergency into positions of power and influence,—but to that more meritorious class of pious and excellent persons, who, born to the great inheritance of labor, walk meekly along the paths of common life, perform every duty, public or private, love and help their fellow men, and act always as if in their Great Task Master's eye. It is to such men that society owes at once its peace, stability and progress, and yet history takes no note of such, and hence

"The world knows nothing of its greatest men."

His business in life was that of agriculture,—necessarily the leading pursuit of New England in its early history, when the forests were to be elled, the soil broken up, the seeds of all the grains, and plants and fruits which constitute the food of men and beasts to be sown, and its great staples of commercial exchange supplied. And in every period of society the agriculture population has proved of the highest importance to the wealth, dignity and strength of a State. It is from this class of the population that the city and the village, that commerce and the arts, are ever drawing the bone and muscle of their laborers, and much of the energy of their directing force. In no other of the leading pursuits in society are there the same facilities for cultivating bodily energy, and the force and vigor of mind consequent upon a vigorous constitution. The pure air, the rough exposure, the healthful toil, the constant call for thought and reflection, the walking with God in the open field, the study of his laws as unfolded in the circuit of the seasons, and in the growth of the seed and ripening of the harvest, the better domestic training under which children can be reared in the country,—all these things are favorable for converting the agricultural population into an element of conservation, much needed to give stability to the ever restless desire of change which animates a young community, and to uphold society in moments of danger and trial. It is the boast of Connecticut, and of Wethersfield in particular, to have had from the beginning a large population of intelligent, industrious and pious farmers in her population, and that the ranks of her merchants, her mechanics, her seamen and her professional men have been replenished by contributions drawn from this source. To this she undoubtedly owed her reputation for steady habits, and the domestic peace which has reigned so continuously in her borders. To this class of her population Mr. Foote belonged;—he was an intelligent, pious and industrious farmer, and, like all of that class of farmers, he was from time to time summoned to the discharge of public trusts by his neighbors and townsmen.

From all that we can learn Mr. Foote came from Shalford, in Colchester, Eng., and settled in Watertown, Mass. The first mention I find made of his name is in the Records of the Colony of Massachusetts Bay, in 1633, when he took the oath of freeman. In the "Records of the Grants and Possession of the Lands in Watertown," (in which town Mr. Foote first located himself) the following entry is made:

17

(2)

" Nathaniel Foote.

"1. An homstall of sixteen acres by estimation, bounded ye north and north-west wth ye highway, the south and southwest wth Jeremiah Norcross, granted to him.

"2. Two acres of marsh by estimation, bounded ye south wth ye River, the north wth Henry Curtis, the east wth John Firmin, and the west wth John Smith, granted to him."

Whether Mr. Foote was among the pioneers from Watertown, who made the first lodgment in, or before, 1635, on the banks of the Connecticut at Pyquag, is not known, but his name is found in its first Records, and among those to whom the first distribution of land was made; and he, therefore, must have shared all the dangers and privations of that long and toilsome journey through the wilderness in 1636, and have encountered all the horrors and trials of the first winter in their new home. And how difficult it is for us, in our comfortable dwellings, or traversing with every means and appliance of comfort, the distance between Wethersfield and Boston, in half as many hours as they consumed days, to realize the sufferings of that journey and of that first winter here! We never can be too thankful that courage and strength was meted out to them in proportion to their trials. For them, the trail of the Indian, too narrow for teams or herds,—for them, the unbridged stream and morass,—for them, the steep hill,—for them, the dangers from wild beasts, or from savage men, were not enough to cause them to turn back. It was not 'till winter had come down from the north to lock up the streams, 'till the fire in their temporary lodgments could not keep out the biting cold, 'till famine stared them in the face, that they turned again for food and shelter to the coast; and when spring returned, they were again on their way, with their thinned ranks recruited, to commence anew the work of settlement.

In a few years we find them, with their brethren in Hartford and Windsor, laying the foundations of a Commonwealth in which they aim "to maintain and preserve the liberty and purity of the Gospel of our Lord Jesus," and "to be governed and guided by such laws, rules, orders and decrees as shall be made, ordained and declared" by the General Court, to be appointed by the freemen of the Commonwealth. To found a State under any circumstances has ever been counted among the great works of great men, but to found a State, in which the equal rights of all men are so well recognized and guarded, in the wilderness, amid the trials of frost and famine, and with daily, hourly, constant apprehension of assault and butchery from the savage, is no common event in the world's history, and should be ever remembered by those who have enjoyed its protection.

In the original distribution of the lands of the town, as recorded in 1640, Mr. Foote had assigned him a house lot of ten acres on the east side of Broad street, near the south end of the street. A part of this lot is now owned and occupied by Mr. Josiah Adams. Mr. Foote became the owner of several other tracts of land, laying partly in the Great Meadow east of his house lot, and containing in the whole, upwards of four hundred acres. The cultivation of his land constituted his main business, although he was called by his neighbors to participate in the public trusts of the town, and in 1644 was appointed a delegate to the General Court.

Mr. Foote married in England, about the year 1615, to Elizabeth Deming, sister of Mr. John Deming, who was one of the first settlers of Wethersfield, and for many years one of the magistrates of the Colony of Connecticut, and one of the patentees named in its charter. His children were all born in England, except perhaps the youngest. Mr. Foote died in 1644, aged about 51 years, and was buried in the ancient burying ground in the rear of the Meeting House, where are gathered together the ashes of nine generations. He left behind him, surviving, a widow, two sons and five daughters. He left no will. At a Particular Court held at Hartford, November 20, 1644, the following inventory of his property and distribution of his real estate were exhibited, and an order of court granting administration on his estate and directing a distribution to be made, was passed.

An inventory of the goods and lands of Nathaniel Foote, of Wethersfield, deceased, being truly taken and indifferently prised by Richard Tratte, Samuel Smith and Nath: Dickinson.

Imprs his purse and apparrell	7.16.00
It in neat cattell and in hay	93.00.00
It in horsse fleshe	34.00.00
It in hoggs	66.00.00
It in debts	29.00.00
It in Englishe corne	70.00.00
It in goats	3.15.00
It in carts, ploughs and the furniturr belonging theretoo	6.00.00
It in nayles	1.10.00
Ite in Indian corn	8.00.00
It in old wheat and pease	6.06.00
It for certen things in the chamber	2.00.00
It ffor amunition	5.00.00
Ite for fower beds wth the furniture	13.06.08
Ie in fyne Lynnen	5.10.00
Ite 2 table boards, 2 chests, Trunke wth other Implets	5.00.00
It pewter and brasse and other useful vessell	12.00.00
It in husbandry tools	3.00.00
It in beife butter and cheese and other necessary pvision for the howse	8.14.00
Ite in poultry	1.00.00
	380.17.00

THE LAND.

Ten acres of home lots wth one dwelling house and 2 barnes wth other building thereuppon.

4 acres of home lotts.

6 acres of meadow wth an acre of swampe.

20 acres of plaine fenced in being 14 ac broke up.

7 acres of the plaine meadow plowed up.

20 acres in the great meadow of hay ground.

4 acres in the bever meadow.

27 acres of swampe ground.

81 acres of upland in the weste field.

32 rod broad beyond the River being three myles in length.

RICHARD TREAT.
SAMUEL SMITH.
NATHANIEL DICKENSON.

A debt formerly forgotten wch the said Deceased Nath: Foote did owe. 1.10.00
 Dated November the 20th, 1644.
Land devided to the Wydowe ffoote.

4 ac home lott wherr her howse is	20.00.00
The howseing	50.00.00
2 ac unsubdued	4.00.00
7 ac plaine brok	28.00.00
3½ plaine med:	20.00.00
14 ac meadow	70.00.00
3 ac plaine not broake up	5.00.00
30 ac upland in Westfield	15.00.00
	212.00.00

Land devided to the eldest sonne.

3 ac homelott next her	15.00.00
2 ac unsubdued	4.00.00
7 ac plaine broke up	28.00.00
3½ of meadow	20.00.00
3 ac in great med:	24.00.00
4 ac in beaver med:	4.00.00
27 ac swampe	1.10.00
3 ac not broke up	5.00.00
30 ac upland west field	15.00.00
Halfe the east side	10.00.00
	126.10.00

Land for the youngest sonne.

3 ac homelott	15.00.00
6 ac mea: in the swamp	30.00.00
21 ac west field	10.00.00
halfe on the east sd	10.00.00
	65.00.00

The age of the 5 children Dwelling wth their mother.

Nath: ffoote		24 years
Rob ffoote	about	17 years
Frances	about	15 years
Sarah	about	12 years
Rebecka	about	10 years

The wyddowe of the said Nath: ffoote is admitted to administer the Estate, and the eldest sonne is to have the lands before mentioned as they are valued at 126l. 10s. wch is to be made uppe 148l, and the youngest sonne the pticular landes above mentioned for him at 65l. wch is to be made uppe 74l. and the daughters disposed in marriedge are to have 30l. a peece wch they have receevede made uppe 74l. and the other children are to have 74l. a peece privded it is lefte at the dispose of their mother to detracte from any of them if shee see just cause 5l. of the portion here sett downe, and to adde yt to such of the other as best desearve yt.

 "At a Particular court holden December 12, 1644. Present,—Edward Hopkins, Esq., Governor; John Haynes, Esq., Deputy Governor, and the several Magistrates.

"Mr. Heynes and Mr. Willis are desired to consider of the estate of Nath: ffoote, deceased, and to take in what help they please from any of the neighbors to advise how yt may be Disposed of, and to report there apprehensions to the next Court."

This last vote is of many evidences which might be quoted from the Records to show the confidence reposed in the leading men of the Colony, and how naturally the people turn to such men for help when public business is to be done, or private affairs even are to be regulated.

Mrs. Foote, the widow of Nathaniel Foote, was married about the year 1646, to "Mr. Thomas Welles, Magistrate," afterwards Governor of the Colony, whom she likewise survived.

Governor Welles died Jan. 14, 1659-60, leaving a will. When in life, he gave a good estate to each of his children, except his son John, who settled in Stratford, Ct. Mr. John Welles died before his father, and in his will gave him his son Robert, then a child, to whom Governor Welles, in his will, which is dated November 7, 1659, gave the bulk of the large estate of which he died seized.

Mrs. Welles died July 28, 1683, aged about 88 years. She left a will which was exhibited to and approved by the "Particular Court," August, 1683. The following is a copy of that Instrument:

"I, Elizabeth Welles, of Wethersfield, in the county of Hartford, in the colony of Connecticut, Widdow, Being stricken in yeares & in expectation of my Solemn Change but of Good and perfect memorie blessed by allmighty God, for the setleing of the Temporall estate God hath lent me, & that peace may be continued amongst my relations when I am gathered to my Fathers, doe make, constitute & ordain & declare this to be my last will & Testament in Manor & form following, revoking & adnulling by these presents all former & other will or wills, Testament or Testaments by me heretofore made and declared by word or writeing & this to be taken onely for my last will & Testament & none other, & first I committ my soule to allmighty God my Saviour & redeemer in whome & by the merits of Jesus Christ I trust and believe to be saved & to have forgiven of my sins, & that my Soule with my body at the Generall day or resurection Shal be reunited againe, & through the meritts of Christ's death and passion possesse & Inheritt the kingdom of heaven prepared for the Elect, & my body to comely and Christian Buriall as my overseers shall see meet, & my estate I disspose as followeth. I will that all those debts I ow in right or consciens to any man or men be well and Truly contended & payd out of my estate in the first place. My fourteen acres of land in the great meadow & Thirty acres in the west field I give unto my son Robert foote and to his heirs forever prohibiting him the sale of the same, he paying for the lands forty five pounds to be payed to the children of my Daughter Sarah J deceased nine pounds, & to my foure daughters, viz. my daughter Churc y daughter Goodrich, my Daughter Barnard & my daughter Smith, to each of them Nine pownds a piece, I give unto my son Nathaniel foots Eldest son and his Brother eleven pownds, & to their children, To Daniel forty shillings, & to Elizabeth fower pownds which legacies, bothe the eleven pownd forty shillings & fower pownds shall be payed out of The money Nathaniel Graves owes me By Bill, I give and bequeth unto my Grand Son John Studder halfe my Great lott which lyes at the farther Bownds of the Towne & the other halfe of the sayd lott I give unto my Grandsons Joseph & Benjamin Churchall & theire heirs forever. The remaynder of my estate (when a legacy is pd to my overseers out of it) shall be divided into five parts one part I give to my daughter

Judsons children to be to them and their heirs for ever, & to my daughter Churchall & her children one fifth part, & to my Daughter Goodrich & her children one fift part, and to my Daughter Barnard & her children one fift part, and to my Daughter Smith & her children one fift part, it is my will that what I give my foure daughters shall be wholly at their disspose, to disspose among their children as they see Good, I do nominate & appoynt my welbeloved Captaine John Allin to be my Executor, & my beloved Brother, Mr. John Deming, senr. & my Grand Sonn Henry Beck to be the desired overseers of this my will, and as a token of my respect to them I give them Thirty Shillings a piece out of my estate, & for the confirmation of the premises I have hereunto Set my hand this 28 day of March, 1678. memorandum it is my will that the Nine pounds a peice I give my foure daughters & the fift part of my estate I give them shall be divided among the children of each of them the one halfe of it imediatly after my deccasse.

Elizabeth   Welles

E. W.   L. S.

her   mark

This signed and declared to be the last will and Testament of Mrs. Elizabeth Welles In presence of us:

Joseph Rowlandson.

John Deminge.

Memorandum: I give unto my grandson Nath: ffoott: the eldest son of my sonn Nathll; the one half of my fourteen acres of Medow & one half of my thirty acres of upland lying in the West field; wth liberty of takeing the first choice, he paying one half of the Legacyes wch were to be pd by my sonn Robt had he lived to possess ye sd land.

my will is that that part of ye eleven pownds (wch I formerly will'd to my sd grandson Nathll & his Brothr,) wch belonged to him by will, shall be equally distributed between my foure daughters above mentioned, and for the memorandum all rents of Land due to me, I will to be divided equally amongst my foure fore-mentioned daughters & their heirs;

Elizabeth   Welles

her mark

Witnessed by us

Samll Tallcott

John Deminge

The following entry appears on the back of the will:

The distribute of 17 lb:

To Samll: Foott	= 05 = 10 = 00
To Elizabeth ffoot	= 04 = 00 = 0C
To Lift: Smith	= 01 = 07 = C6
To ffrancis Barnard	= 01 = 07 = 06
To Josiah Churchall	= 01 = 07 = 06
To Lift. Tracey	= 01 = 07 = 06
To Danll: ffoot	= 02 = 00 = 00
	17 = 00 = 00

The original will of Mrs. Foote, alias Welles, from which I copy, is in the handwriting of Rev. Joseph Rowlandson, minister of Wethersfield; the codicil, or "Memorandum," in that of Samuel Tallcott, of Wethersfield, son of John Talcott, one of the first settlers of Hartford.

2. i.   ELIZABETH, b. abt. 1616; m. 1638, Josiah Churchill, of Wethersfield, Ct. He d. abt. Jan. 1, 1686. She d. Sept. 8, 1700. Ch.:
(1) Mary Churchill, b. Mar. 24, 1630; m. Samuel Church, of
Hadley, Mass. (2) Elizabeth, b. May 15, 1642; m. Oct. 31, 1660,
Henry Buck, of Wethersfield, Ct. He was b. abt 1626; d. July
7, 1712. She d. ————.' Ch.: 8. Henry, the youngest, settled
in Cohanzy, N. J. The late Henry Sheppard, of Springfield,
Mo., and ch.: (1) Mary, who. m. Oliver H. Picher, (2) Lieutenant Comdr. Francis Henry Sheppard, and (3) Miss Margaret
Sheppard, are descendants of Elizabeth through Henry
Buck 2nd. (3) Hannah, b. Nov. 1, 1644; d. before Nov.
11, 1683. (4) Ann, b. 1647; m. ———— Rice. (5) Joseph, b. Dec.
2, 1649; m. May 13, 1764, Mary ————. He d. Apr. 1, 1699.
Ch.: 9. (6) Benjamin, b. May 16, 1652; m. 1677, Mary ————.
She was b. abt. 1652; d. Oct. 30, 1712. Ch.: 3. (7) Sarah, b.
Nov. 11, 1657; m. June 11, 1673, Thomas Wickam, of Wethersfield, Ct. He was b. New Haven, Ct., Oct. 15, 1651; d. Apr. 30,
1730. He was buried in the Wethersfield burying ground. She
d. ————. Ch.: 6.

3. ii.   NATHANIEL, b. abt. 1620; m. Elizabeth Smith.

4. iii. MARY, b. abt. 1623; m. 1st, 1642, John Stoddard, of Wethersfield,
Ct. He d. Dec., 1664; m. 2nd, 1674, John Goodrich, of Wethersfield. He d. Apr., 1680; m. 3rd, Lieut. Thomas Tracy, of Norwich, Ct. He d. Nov. 7, 1685. She d. ————. Ch.: (1) Mary
Stoddard, b. May 12, 1643; m. Dec. 10, 1663, Joseph, son of
Thomas Wright, of Wethersfield. She d. Aug. 23, 1683. He m.
2nd, Mercy Stoddard, his wife's sister. He d. Jan. 1715. Ch.
by 1st wife, F., one of whom, Joseph, b. Feb. 14, 1669, d. Sept. 2,
1756; res., Colchester, Ct. (2) John, b. Apr. 12, 1646; m. May
26, 1647, Elizabeth, dau. of Thomas Curtis, of Wethersfield.
He d. Dec. 4, 1703, ae. 57. Ch.: 8. (3) Caleb, b. Sept. 12,
1648; d. in childhood. (4) Joshua, b. Sept. 12, 1648; m. Aug.
15, 1684, Berthia, dau. of Richard Smith, of Wethersfield. He
d. abt. 1725, p. s. (5) Mercy, b. Nov. 1652; m. Mar. 10, 1685,
Joseph Wright, of Wethersfield. Ch.: 2. (7) Elizabeth, b.
July, 1656; m. ———— Wright. (8) Nathaniel, b. Mar. 1661;
m. 1st, Mary. She d. Jan. 17, 1693; m. 2nd, Dec. 7, 1693, Eunice,
dau. of Thomas Standish, of Wethersfield. He d. Feb. 9, 1714.
She d. Aug. 5, 1716, ae. 52. Ch.: 1 by 1st wife, 3 by 2nd.

5. iv. ROBERT, b. abt. 1627; m. 1659, Sarah, dau. of William Potter,
of New Haven, Ct. (New Haven Land Records.)

6. v.   FRANCES, b. 1629; m. 1st, 1648, John Dickinson, of Hadley,
Mass. He d. 1676; m. 2nd, 1677, Frances Barnard, of Hartford, Ct., and Hadley, Mass. She d. ————. He d. Feb. 3,
1698, ae. 81. Ch.: (1) Hannah Dickinson, b. Dec. 6, 1648;
m. Sept. 23, 1668, Samuel Gilet, of Hadley. He was lost at
"Falls Fight," May 19, 1676. M. 2nd, May 15, 1677, Stephen
Jennings, of Hadley. She was captured by the Indians Sept.
19, 1677, and carried to Canada. She returned in 1678. Abt.

1690 they moved to Brookfield, Mass. While haying in a meadow with five neighbors they were sprung upon by Indians, and killed, July 22, 1710. She d. abt. 1705. Ch.: (a) Hannah, b. Sept. 20, 1669; d. Feb. 1671. (b) Mary, b. Dec. 1670. (c) Samuel, b. May 24, 1672. (d) Hannah, b. Sept. 5, 1673. (e) Captivity Jennings, b. Mar. 14, 1678, soon after her mother returned from captivity; m. Abijah Barlett, of Brookfield, Mass. He was slain by Indians. (f) Stephen, b. June 16, 1680. (g) Joseph, b. Aug. 23, 1682. (h) Sarah, b. Aug. 29, 1648. (2) Mary, b. m. 1674, Samuel Northam, of Hadley, both d. res. Hatfield and Deerfield, Mass., and Colchester, Ct. Ch.:(a) Samuel, b. May 4, 1675, in Hatfield. (b) Mary, b. Jan. 7, 1677. (c) Elizabeth, b. Apr. 1, 1680. (d) Jonathan, b. May 18, 1682. (3). John, b. m. Susanna, dau. of Joseph Smith, of Hartford Ct., and of his wife Lydia, dau. of Rev. Ephriam Hewett, of Winsor, Ct. She was b. June, 1667. Ch.: (a) John, b. Nov. 1, 1689. (4) Jonathan, b. d. before Mar., 1678. (5) Sarah, b. m. 1st, Dec. 11, 1677, Samuel Lane, of Suffield, Ct. He d. abt. 1690, in Suffield; m. 2nd, Feb. 27, 1691, Martin Kellogg, of Suffield; both d. Ch.: (a) Samuel, b. (b) Sarah, b. (c) Mary, b. May 7, 1684. (d) John, b. Apr. 3, 1686. (e) Elizabeth, b. (f) Joseph Kellogg, b. Nov. 8, 1691. Was captured by French and Indians at Deerfield, Feb. 29, 1704, and taken to Canada. He learned the Indian language and on his return from captivity was often employed as an interpreter. (g) Joanna, b. Feb. 8, 1693. She was captured with her brothers. She through choice remained among the Indians, marrying an Indian chief. She d. leaving ch. (h) Rebecca, b. Dec. 22, 1695. Was captured with the others. She also learned the Indian language and acted as interpreter for missionaries. (i) Jonathan, b. Dec. 17, 1698. (6) Elizabeth, b. d. before Mar., 1678. (7) Rebecca, b. 1658; m. Feb. 11, 1680, Joseph, son of Lydia and Joseph Smith, of Hadley, Mass. She d. Feb. 16, 1731. He d. 1733. Ch.: (a) Joseph, b. Nov. 3, 1682; d. Oct. 21, 1767. (b) John, b. Oct. 24, 1684; d. Aug. 27, 1686. (c) John, b. June 5, 1686; d. Aug. 14, 1686. (d) Rebecca, b. June 11, 1689. (e) Jonathan, b. Oct. 28, 1691. (f) Lydia, b. Sept. 15, 1693. (g) Benjamin, b. Jan. 22, 1696. (h) Elizabeth, b. Dec. 22, 1701; d. Feb. 14, 1728. (8) Abigail, b. m. 1st Dec. 6, 1683, Thomas Croft, of Hadley, Mass. He d. Feb. 27, 1692. M. 2nd, Nov. 30, 1704, Samuel Crofoot. He was b. 1662; d. Oct. 10, 1733; buried at Hadley, Mass. She d. 1714. Ch.: (a) John Croft, b. Nov. 8, 1684. (b) Mary, b. Feb. 2, 1686. (c) Abigail, b. Sept. 29, 1688. (d) Thomas, b. Feb. 27, 1690; d. Apr. 12, 1714. (e) Elizabeth, b. Apr. 17, 1691. (f) Benoni Croft, b. Oct. 22, 1692. (g) Sarah Crofoot, b. May 25, 1706. (9) Mercy, b. m. June 8, 1688, Joseph Chamberlain, of Hatfield, Mass., and Colchester, Ct. He d. Aug. 7, 1752, ae. 87. She d. June 30, 1735, ae. 67, in Colchester, Ct. Ch.: (a) Sarah, b. Nov. 2, 1690; d. in infancy. (b) Sarah, b. Mar. 10, 1693;

m. Ephraim Foote (26). (c) John, b. Mar. 4, 1700. (10)
Mehitabel, b. m. June 26, 1689, John Ingram, Jr., of Hadley,
and Amherst, Mass.; both d. Ch.: (a) Elizabeth, b. Mar. 15,
1691. (b) John, b. Jan. 9, 1693; d. Nov. 11, 1737. (c) Ebenezer, b. Dec. 10, 1694; d. Nov. 21, 1695. (d) Hannah, b. Oct.
19, 1697. (e) Mehitabel, b. Sept. 13, 1698. (f) Ebenezer, b.
Nov. 10, 1700; d. Jan. 6, 1702. (g) Mary, b. July 10, 1702.
(h) Rebecca, b. Nov. 5, 1704. (i) Jonathan, b. Dec. 15, 1708;
d. Jan. 26, 1709. (j) Experience, b. Apr. 17, 1714; d. Aug. 21,
1714. (k) Elisha, b. Sept. 7, 1717.

7. vi.   SARAH, b. abt. 1632; m. 1652, Jeremiah, son of William and
Grace Judson, of Stratford, Ct. Grace Judson d. Sept. 29, 1659.
William Judson, m. 2nd Feb. 8, 1660, Elizabeth Willmot, of New
Haven. William Judson is ancestor of Rev. Adoniram Judson,
the celebrated missionary; res., Burmah, East Indies.; and of
Dea. David P. Judson, of Stratford, Ct. William d. July 29,
1662, in New Haven, Ct. Sarah Judson d. 1673. Jeremiah
Judson, m. Nov. 8, 1675, Catharine Cragg, widow of Thomas
Fairchild, of Stratford. She d. May, 1706. Mr. Judson d. of
palsy, May 15, 1701. Ch.: (1) Isaac, b. Mar. 10, 1653. (2)
Mary, b. Dec. 31, 1655. (3) Elizabeth, b. Feb. 24, 1658. (4)
Sarah, b. Apr. 7, 1662. (5) Mercy, b. June 14, 1665. (6) Jere-
miah, b. Mar. 1, 1671.

8. vii.   REBECCA, b. abt. 1634; m. 1st abt. 1657, Lieut. Philip, son of
Samuel Smith, of Wethersfield, Ct., and Hadley, Mass. Rev.
Cotton Mather says he was "murdered with an hideous witch-
craft." He d. Jan. 10, 1685. She m. 2nd Oct. 2, 1688, Major
Aaron Cook, of Windsor, Ct., and Northampton, Mass.
He was b. abt. 1610 ; d. Sept. 5, 1690. She d. Apr. 6,
1701, in Hadley. Ch.: (1) Samuel Smith, b. Jan., 1658; m.
1st, Nov. 16, 1682, Mary, dau. of Samuel Church, of Hadley.
She was b. 1664; d. June 18, 1700. M. 2nd, Jan. 22, 1701, Mary
Smith, of Hadley. He was Dea. in the Ch. in East Hartford,
where he had purchased an estate. He d. 1707. She d. ———.
Ch.: (a) Mary Smith, b. Dec. 28, 1689, in Hadley. (b) Rebecca,
b. Nov. 20, 1691. (c) Samuel, b. Dec. 18, 1694. (d) Mehita-
bel, b. May 9, 1696. (e) Benoni, b. June 12, 1700. (f)
Timothy, b. June 1, 1702. (g) Edward, b. Nov. 17, 1704. (h)
Mercy, b. in East Hartford, Ct.; d. young. (2) John, b. Dec.
18, 1661; m. Nov. 29, 1683, Joanna, dau. of Joseph and Joanna
Kellogg, of Hadley. She was b. Dec. 8, 1664; d. ———. He
was Dea. in the Ch. in Hadley; d. Apr. 16, 1727. (a) John, b.
Dec. 3, 1684; m. and had 7 ch. One of them John, b. 1717,
had a son John, called Major John Smith, who lived and d. in
Hadley. Orlando Smith, town clerk of Hadley, and postmaster, was his son. Res., So. Hadley, Mass. (b) Joanna,
b. Sept. 7, 1686. (c) Rebecca, b. Aug. 5, 1688. (d) Joseph,
b. July 19, 1690. (e) Martin, b. Apr. 15, 1692; m. 1715, Sarah
Wier, of Wethersfield, Ct. Ch.: 7. (f) Elizur, b. Sept. 25,

1694. (g) Sarah, b. Nov. 18, 1696; d. Dec. 28, 1697. (h)
Sarah, b. Nov. 9, 1698. (i) Prudence, b. Mar. 15, 1701. (j)
Experience, b. Apr. 19, 1703. (k) Elizabeth, b. Oct. 12, 1705.
(l) Mindwell, b. May 25, 1708. (3) Jonathan Smith, b. 1663;
m. Nov. 14, 1688, Abigail, dau. of Joseph and Abigail (Terry)
Kellogg, of Hadley. She d. ———. He d. abt. 1737; res.,
Hatfield, Mass. Ch.: (a) Jonathan Smith, b. Aug. 10, 1689;
m. had a son Jonathan, who m. Rebecca, dau. of Dr. Nathaniel
Smith, and he had most of Nathaniel's estate, including a
large farm, in the vicinity of where the college now is. He
had one dau.; res., Amherst, Mass. (b) Daniel, b. Mar. 3,
1692. (c) Abigail, b. Apr. 20, 1695. (d) Stephen, b. Dec. 5,
1697; res., Amherst. (e) Prudence, b. May 16, 1700. (f)
Moses, b. Sept. 8, 1702. (g) Elisha, b. July 10, 1705; m. and
had 12 ch.; res., Whately, Mass. (h) Elizabeth, b. May 8,
1708. (i) Ephriam, b. Mar. 24, 1711; res., Athol, Mass. (j)
Aaron, b. Feb. 7, 1715; res., Athol, Mass. (4) Philip Smith,
b. 1665; m. 1st July 9, 1687, Mary, dau. of Samuel Bliss, of
Springfield. She was b. abt. 1670; d. Dec. 23, 1707, in Hartford. M. 2nd Sept., 1708, Mary, sister of John Robinson, of
Hartford. In 1704 he purchased lands in East Hartford, Ct.
He d. Jan. 25, 1725. She d. May 17, 1733; res., Hadley, Mass.,
Springfield, Mass., and East Hartford, Ct. Ch.: (a) Philip, b.
Hadley, May 1, 1689. (b) David, b. Hadley, Apr. 23, 1691.
(c and d) Twin girls, b. Hadley, June 11, 1693. (e) Martha,
b. Hadley, Sept. 27, 1694; m. Thomas Wiard. (f) Aaron, b.
Springfield, Feb. 14, 1697. (g) Mary, b. Springfield, Feb. 23,
1699; m. John Benjamin, Jr., of Hartford, Ct.; res.,
Stratford, Ct. (h) Samuel, b. 1702, in Spring-
field. He was Dea. of the Ch. in East Hartford, Ct.; d. Aug.
28, 1777. (i) Rebecca, b. (j) Ebenezer, b. Jan. 1, 1707, in
Hartford. (k) Nehemiah, b. Hartford, July 17, 1709. (l)
Hannah, b. Hartford, Nov. 20, 1711. (5) Rebecca Smith, b. 1668;
m. 1686, George Stillman, of Hadley, Mass., and Wethersfield, Ct.
He was b. abt. 1654; was a merchant of enterprise and wealth,
was the representative of Hadley in the General Court of
Mass., in 1698; d. Nov. 17, 1728. She d. Oct. 7, 1750; ch. all b.
in Hadley. Ch.: (a) George Stillman, b. 1686; res., Wethersfield, Ct.,
until abt. 1730, when he disappeared. Abt. the same time a
Dr. George Stillman appeared in Westerly, R. I.; they probably were identical. (b) Rebecca, b. Jan. 14, 1688; d. Oct. 19,
1712. (c) Mary, b. July 12, 1689; m. Deliverence Blinn. (d)
Nathaniel, b. July 1, 1691; m. Mar. 3, 1715, Anna Southmayd.
She d. Jan. 6, 1730. M. 2nd, 1731, Sarah Allyn. She d. Mar.
4, 1794. He d. Jan. 1, 1770. Ch.: (i) Nathaniel, b. (ii)
Allyn, (iii) Anna, (iv) Sarah, (v) Joseph, (vi) Samuel, (vii)
Mary, (viii) Rebecca, (x) George. (e) John, b. Feb. 19, 1693;
m. May 26, 1715, Mary Wolcott. She d. July 2, 1777. He d.
1775. Ch.: (i) John, (ii) Rebecca, (iii) Mary, (iv) Abigail,
(v) Martha, (vi) Sarah, (vii) Elisha, (viii) Appleton, (ix)

Huldah. (f) Sarah, b. Dec. 28, 1694; m. Jan. 18, 1715, Samuel Willard. Ch.: (i) Samuel, (ii) Sarah, (iii) Rebecca, (iv) Hannah, (v) Elisha, (vi) George, (vii) Martha, (viii) Joseph, (ix) Elisha, (x) Elisha. (g) Martha, b. Nov. 28, 1696; d. Oct. 2, 1712. (h) Ann, b. Apr. 6, 1699; m. Apr. 27, 1721, Hezekiah May. He d. Sept. 3, 1783. She d. Nov. 7, 1767. Ch.: (i) Ann, (ii) Samuel, (iii) Prudence, (iv) Hezekiah, (v) Elizabeth, (vi) Eleazur, (vii) John, (viii) William. (6) Nathaniel, b. 1671; m. Feb. 6, 1696, Mary, dau. of Nathaniel and Hannah Dickinson, of Hatfield, Mass. She d. Aug. 16, 1718, ae. 45. He d. 1740. Ch.: (a) Nathaniel, b. July 1, 1698. (b) Mary, b. Dec. 11, 1700. (c) Joshua, b. Nov. 2, 1702. (d) Rebecca, b. Apr. 4, 1705. (e) Hannah, b. Mar. 7, 1707. (f) Martha, b. Jan. 31, 1709. (g) Lydia, b. Mar. 16, 1711. (g) Jerusha, b. Jan. 9, 1713. (7) Joseph Smith, b. 1674; m. Sept. 15, 1697, Esther, dau. of Cornet Joseph Parsons, one of the first settlers of Northampton, Mass., and Springfield. She was b. Dec. 24, 1672. He was ed. for the ministry, and grad. Harvard College, 1695. He was employed as teacher at Hopkins Academy, in Hadley, Mass., and in Springfield. In 1708, Mr. Smith went to Cohanzy, N. Y., and was ordained pastor there, by Philadelphia Presbytery, May 10, 1709. Abt. 1713 he received a call from Upper Middletown, Ct., which he accepted, abt. two years preceding the time of the organization into the church. It having been organized, he was installed pastor Jan. 15, 1715. He d. Sept. 8, 1736. She d. May 30, 1760. Ch.: cess-Martha, b. Sept. 17, 1699; m. Capt. Richard Hamlin, Nc miles 1721. Ch.: (i) Mary, (ii) Esther, (iii) Nathaniel. (b) J Capt. b. 1704; m. Dec. 20, 1726, Elizabeth Bulckley. Ch.: (i) M noved (ii) James, (iii) Elizabeth, (iv) Joseph, (v) John, st of Nathaniel, (vii) Joseph, (viii) Edward. (c) Mary, b. 1709; Dec. 10, 1729, Rev. Samuel Tudor. Ch.: (i) Theophilus, (ii) Elihu, (iii) Rhoda, (iv) Samuel, (v) Mary, (vi) Ursula, (vii) Martha, (viii) Oliver, (ix) Oliver, (x) Alpheus. (8) Ichabod; b. Apr. 11, 1676; m. July 19, 1698, Elizabeth, dau. of Capt. Aaron Cook. Ichabod d. Sept. 6, 1746. She d. Oct. 10, 1751. Ch.: (a) Philip, b. May 2, 1609. (b) Aaron, b. Sept. 20, 1700; moved from Hadley. (c) Nathaniel, b. Feb. 16, 1702; res., Amherst, Mass.; was a physician; d. 1774. (d) Rebecca, b. Nov. 9, 1703. (e) Moses, b. Apr. 30, 1706; farmer. (f) Bridget, b. Mar. 15, 1708. (g) Mirriam, b. Aug. 22, 1710. (h) Elizabeth, b. Sept. 10, 1712. (i) Samuel, b. Aug. 4, 1715. (j) Experience, b. Jan. 27, 1717. (k) Elisha, b. Jan. 23, 1721; res., in Vermont.

3. NATHANIEL FOOTE, b. abt. 1620; m. 1646, Elizabeth, dau. of Lieut. Samuel Smith; res., Wethersfield, Ct., and Hadley, Mass. He d. 1655. She m. 2nd, William Gull, Wethersfield, and Hatfield, Mass. She had four ch., Mary, Anna, Esther, Marcy.

9. i. NATHANIEL, b. Jan. 10, 1647; m. Margaret Bliss.

* It was his son, No. 9, who lived in Hadley

10. ii. SAMUEL, b. May 1, 1649; m. Mary Merrick.

11. iii. DANIEL, b. 1652; m. Sarah ———; 2nd, Mary ———.

12. iv. ELIZABETH, b. 1654; m. Nov. 10, 1670, Daniel, son of William
          Belden, of Wethersfield, Ct. He was b. Nov. 20, 1648; d. Aug.
          14, 1732, in Deerfield, Mass. She was killed by Indians Sept.
          16, 1696. Ch.: (1) William, b. 1671. (2) Richard,
          b. 1672. (3) Elizabeth, b. Oct. 8, 1673; taken captive by In-
          dians, Sept. 16, 1696. (4) Nathaniel, b. June 26, 1675; d. Aug.
          21, 1714. (5) Mary, b. Nov. 17, 1677. (6) Daniel, b. Sept. 1,
          1680; slain by Indians, Sept. 16, 1696. (7) Sarah, b. Mar. 15,
          1682. (8) Esther, b. Sept. 29, 1683; taken captive by Indians,
          Sept. 16, 1696. (9) Abigail, b. 1686. (10) Samuel, b. Hat-
          field, Mass., Apr. 10, 1687; wounded by Indians, Sept. 16, 1696.
          (11) John, b. Deerfield, Mass.; d. June 25, 1689. (12) Abigail,
          b. Aug. 18, 1690; wounded by Indians, Sept. 16, 1696. (13)
          John, b. Feb. 28, 1693; slain by Indians, Sept. 16, 1696. (14)
          Thankful, b. Dec. 21, 1695; slain by Indians, Sept. 16, 1696.

The following was taken from the Hatfield Town Records:

"Elizabeth, wife to Daniel Beldenye head of the family, together
with Daniel Belden, John Belden and Thankful Belden, their chidren, were all of
them slaine by the enemie September 16, 1696."

"Sept. 16, 1696. The Indians came along from up Green River to the town,
and assaulted Mr. Daniel Belden's house; took Mr. Belden, his son Nathaniel and
daughter Esther captive, killed his wife and three children, and wounded Samuel
᷏ Abigail, but they recovered, altho' Samuel had a hatchet stuck in his head,
some of his brains came out at his wound. Samuel was born Apr. 10, 1687.

᷏rom Mather's Magnalia:

The Indians making an Assault upon Deerfield, in this Present War, they
᷏ a Hatchet some Inches into the Skull of a Boy there, even so deep that
᷏Boy felt the force of a Wrench used by 'em to get it out. There he lay a
᷏ong while Weltering in his Blood; they found him, they Dress'd him; considerable Quantities of his Brain came out from time to time when they opened the
Wound; yet the Lad recovered, and is now a Living Monument of the Power
and Goodness of God."

5. ROBERT FOOTE (1), b. 1627; m. 1659, Sarah Potter; res., Wethersfield,
Ct., Wallingford, and in 1668, Branford. He d. 1681. She m. 2nd, 1686, Aaron
Blachley, of Branford, Ct.; res., Guilford. She d. ———.

13. i. NATHANIEL, b. Apr. 13, 1660; m. Tabitha Bishop of Branford,
         Ct. He d. 1714. She d. 1715. Ch.

14. ii. SARAH, b. Feb. 12, 1662; m. 1st, Aug. 13, 1682, Isaac, son of
          Richard Curtis, of Wallingford, Ct., by Rev. John Moss. He
          d. July 15, 1712, ae. abt. 52; m. 2nd, Aug. 9, 1714, Nathaniel
          How, of Wallingford, Ct. He d. Feb. 12, 1723 She d. ———.
          Ch.: (1) Isaac, b. Nov. 6, 1683. (2) Sarah, b. June 11, 1685. (3)
          Joseph, b. July 11, 1689. (4) Ebenezer, b. Oct. 6, 1691; d. July
          20, 1717. (5) Stephen, b. Mar. 8, 1694. (6) Phebe, b. d. Aug.
          5, 1718. (7) John, b. 1698; d. July 20, 1719. (8) Elizabeth, b.
          Aug. 10, 1701. (9) Benjamin, b. Mar. 2, 1703.

15. iii. ELIZABETH, b. Mar. 6, 1666; m. Jan. 12, 1685, John, son of Dea. John and Elizabeth (Stillwell) Graves, of East Guilford, Ct. He d. Dec. 1, 1726, ae. 68. She d. May, 1730. Ch.:(1) Elizabeth, b. July 17, 1686; d. May 28, 1687. (2) Mehitabel, b. Feb. 1, 1688. (3) John, b. Feb. 9, 1690. (4) Ann, b. Aug. 29, 1692. (5) Noadiah, b. Dec. 4, 1694. (6) Mindwell, b. Nov. 4, 1696; m. Nathaniel Stephen, of Claremont, N. H. (7) Sarah, b. Apr. 14, 1699. (8) David, b. Jan. 31, 1701, d. Sept. 16, 1726. (9) Elizabeth, b. Jan. 4, 1703. (10) Ebenezer, b. July 15, 1705.

16. iv. JOSEPH, b. Mar. 6, 1664; m. Abigail Johnson, Sarah Rose, Susannah Frisbie.

17. v. SAMUEL, b. May 14, 1668; m. Abigail Barker.

—18. vi. JOHN, b. July 24, 1670; m. Mary ———, 58-64.

19. vii. STEPHEN, b. Dec. 14, 1672; m. Elizabeth Nash and Hannah Howd, 65-9.

⸱ 20. viii. ISAAC, b. Dec. 14, 1672; m. Rebecca Dickerman, 70-2.

9. NATHANIEL FOOTE, (3, 1) b. Jan. 10, 1647; m. May 2, 1672, Margaret Bliss, dau. of Thomas and Margaret (Lawrence) Bliss, of Springfield, Mass.; res., Hatfield, Springfield and d. at Wethersfield, Jan. 12, 1703. She d. in Colchester, Ct., Apr. 3, 1745.

Nathaniel Foote was born at Wethersfield, Jan. 14, 1648. He settled in Hatfield, Mass., and married, May 2, 1672, Margaret Bliss, dau. of Nathaniel Bliss, of Springfield. After residing in Hatfield two years, he removed to Springfield, like almost every householder, he was called into the service of his country against the Indians, and was actively engaged in the bloody and successful attack on their encampment at the falls in Connecticut river. a few miles above Deerfield, since called Turner's Falls, in commemoration of the brave Capt. Turner, who commanded the expedition. From Springfield, Mr. Foote removed to Stratford, where his house lot of one acre was on Main street, directly east of the old burial ground near the present Congregational Church. This lot he conveyed in March, 1680, to Benjamin Lewis, having decided to move with his family to Branford, where, in February, 1679, he was admitted ''a planter'' of the town, and a ''home lot'' was granted to him, ''on condition that it should have a tenantable house built upon it within two years, and that he come to settle amongst us, or else the lot to return to the town again.'' In pursuing his ''manifest destiny'' to migrate, Mr. Foote conveyed this lot with sundry other lots of which he had become possessed, to Jonathan Pitman, of Stratford, and moved to Wethersfield, where he continued to reside till his death, although he had, previous to that event, planned another removal to a new settlement begun under his enterprise, at ''Jeremy's Farm,'' since and now called Colchester, on the road from Hartford to New London. An order authorizing a settlement at this place was made by the General Court in October, 1698, and the new settlement was made to embrace the territory bounded north by Twenty-mile river, south by Lyme, west by Haddam and Middletown, and east and northeast by Lebanon and Norwich. This land was conveyed by Owaneco, Sachem of Mohegan, ''for the consideration of love and affection,'' to Nathaniel Foote, to be distributed by him ''according to his discretion,'' except fifty acres to be selected by himself, which he had the privilege of reserving to himself and his heirs forever. The settlement was commenced in 1701, but on account of failing health, Mr. Foote did not remove. He died Jan. 12, 1703, leaving a widow and nine children, four sons and five daughters. His widow and four youngest children, three sons and one daughter, subsequently moved to Colchester. Mrs. Foote died Apr. 3, 1745, at the age of 95. The children all married, and settled in the neighborhood of each other in the new town.

Although a house carpenter by trade, and as such was employed to repair the Meeting House at Bradford, Mr. Foote, after his return to Wethersfield, appears to have pursued the practice of the law,—his name frequently appearing on the records of the County Court as Attorney in cases before that court.

21. i. Sarah, b. Feb. 25, 1672; m. Nov., 1691, Thomas Olcott. She d. July 24, 1756. He d. Nov. 30, 1691. Ch.: (1) Abigail, b. Aug. 4, 1692; d. Aug. 17, 1710. (2) Sarah, b. Dec. 12, 1694. (3) Mary, b. Nov. 21, 1696. (4) Cullick, b. Apr. 18, 1699; d. 1732. (5) Nathaniel, b. Sept. 11, 1701. (6) Josiah, b. March 2, 1703. (7) Margaret, b. April 12, 1705. (8) Hannah, b Aug. 4, 1707. (9) Elizabeth, b. Nov. 17, 1709; d. Feb. 11, 1804. (10) Thomas, b. 1713.

22. ii. Margaret, b. Dec. 1, 1674.

23. iii. Elizabeth, b. June 23, 1677; m. June, 1701, Robert Turner. He d. abt. 1745. Ch.: (1) Mary, b. Sept. 16, 1703. (2) Habakuk, b. June 18, 1705. (3) John, b. June 7, 1707. (4) Elizabeth, b. Sept. 16, 1711. (5) Sarah, b. Nov. 13, 1713. (6) Joseph, b. June 6, 1716. (7) Samuel, b. March 26, 1719.

24. iv. MARY, b. Nov. 24, 1679; m. May 14, 1706, Daniel Rose, Jr., b. Aug. 20, 1667, son of Daniel and Elizabeth (Goodwin) Rose. Ch.: (1) Ruth, b. Oct. 14, 1706. (2) Jehiel, b. Sept. 8, 1708. (3) Daniel, b. Aug. 29, 1710. (4) Josia, b. Nov. 27, 1712. (5) Lydia, b. Oct. 1, 1714. (6) Ruth, b. March, 13, 1717. (7) Mary, b. Feb. 6, 1719; m. James Wright, and d. Nov. 19, 1797. (8) Esther, b. Aug. 3, 1721. Esther's great great grandson is A. R. Robinson; is a resident of Wethersfield, Ct.

25. v. NATHANIEL, b. Sept. 9, 1682; m. Ann Clark and Hannah Coleman, 73-82.

26. vi. EPHRAHAM, b. Feb. 13, 1685; m. Sarah Chamberlain, 83-91.

27. vii. JOSIAH, b. Sept. 27, 1688; m. Sarah Welles, 92-102.

28. viii. JOSEPH, b. Dec. 28, 1690; m. Ann Clothier and Hannah Northam, 103-7.

29. ix. EUNICE, b. May 10, 1694; m. Dec. 3, 1712, Michael Taintor, Jr., son of Michael and Mary Taintor. He was b. Sept., 1680; d. March 11, 1771. Ch.: (1) Eunice, b. Apr. 18, 1714. (2) Michael, b. Dec. 31, 1719. (3) Charles, b. Feb. 28, 1723. (4) John, b. Feb. 23, 1725. (5) Mary, b. Nov. 7, 1727. (6) Prudence, b. Dec. 9, 1729. (7) Sarah, b. Apr. 3, 1731. (8) Ann, b. Oct. 31, 1734; d. Jan. 31, 1755, unm.

10. SAMUEL FOOTE, (3, 1,) b. May 1, 1649; m. 1671, Mary, dau. of Thomas and Mary Merrick. She d. Oct. 3, 1690. He d. Sept. 7, 1689; res., Hatfield, Mass.

30. i. NATHANIEL, b. 1672; m. Mary Ward, 108-10.

31. ii. MARY, b. July 9, 1674; d. in childhood.

32. iii. SAMUEL, b. ——; killed by Indians at Deerfield, Feb. 29, 1704.

33. iv. MARY, b. Feb. 28, 1680; m. Feb. 13, 1707; Samuel Sikes. He d. 1736. She d. Feb. 8, 1752. Ch.: (1) Mary, b. Nov. 20, 1707. (2) Sarah, b. June 29, 1710. (3) Samuel, b. Oct. 21, 1715. (4) Mirriam, b. July 11, 1719.

34. v. SARAH, b. Feb. 26, 1682; m. June 21, 1706, William, son of John and Sarah (Bliss) Scott, of Springfield and Kingston, Mass. He d. Dec. 11, 1773. She d. Nov. 22, 1764. Ch.: (1) Sarah, b. June 12, 1707; m. Benj. Dickenson, Oct. 3, 1737. (2) John, b. Mar. 9, 1709. (3) Mary, b. Aug. 4, 1710. (4) Margaret, b. Aug. 2, 1712; d. Dec. 10, 1716. (5) Elizabeth, b. Jan. 20, 1714; m. Stewart Southgate. (6) Margaret, b. Dec. 25, 1720;
    .... .1707. ... . b. Nov. 2 .1723.. m..Abigal
                                                                        —,

11. Daniel Foote (3,1,) b. 1652, had a daughter, Mary Foote, b. about 1690-92, who —; married at Stratford, Conn., Dec.10,1713, Caleb Dayton, as per Stratford marriage records. Caleb Dayton came from Long Island, N.Y., to Stratford, Conn. After marriage he settled at Newtown, Conn., by 1714, where his son Josiah was born Sept. 20, 1714. Caleb died at Newtown,Conn., between the date of his will, Nov.12,1730, and the proving of it on Jan.18,1730-31.

The same Daniel's son Jehiel was born at Stratford, Conn., March 17,1685-6; he died there Sept. 2, 1740 as per his gravestone there.

The same Daniel's son Peter was born at Stratford in 1698, and died there Dec. 8, 1753, unmarried, as per his gravestone there. His will, dated Dec. 4,1753, was proved Jan. 15,1754.

Information supplied by
C. A. Hoppin.
June 15, 1938

sons and five daughters. His widow and four youngest children, three sons and one daughter, subsequently moved to Colchester. Mrs. Foote died Apr. 3, 1745, at the age of 95. The children all married, and settled in the neighborhood of each other in the new town.

Although a house carpenter by trade, and as such was employed to repair the Meeting House at Bradford, Mr. Foote, after his return to Wethersfield, appears to have pursued the practice of the law,—his name frequently appearing on the records of the County Court as Attorney in cases before that court.

21. i.   Sarah, b. Feb. 25, 1672; m. Nov., 1691, Thomas Olcott. She d. July 24, 1756. He d. Nov. 30, 1691. Ch.: (1) Abigail, b. Aug. 4, 1692; d. Aug. 17, 1710. (2) Sarah, b. Dec. 12, 1694. (3)

33. iv. MARY, b. Feb. 28, 1680; m. Feb. 13, 1707; Samuel Sikes. He d.
1736. She d. Feb. 8, 1752. Ch.: (1) Mary, b. Nov. 20, 1707.
(2) Sarah, b. June 29, 1710. (3) Samuel, b. Oct. 21, 1715. (4)
Mirriam, b. July 11, 1719.

34. v. SARAH, b. Feb. 26, 1682; m. June 21, 1706, William, son of John
and Sarah (Bliss) Scott, of Springfield and Kingston, Mass.
He d. Dec. 11, 1773. She d. Nov. 22, 1764. Ch.: (1) Sarah,
b. June 12, 1707; m. Benj. Dickenson, Oct. 3, 1737. (2) John,
b. Mar. 9, 1709. (3) Mary, b. Aug. 4, 1710. (4) Margaret,
b. Aug. 2, 1712; d. Dec. 10, 1716. (5) Elizabeth, b. Jan. 20,
1714; m. Stewart Southgate. (6) Margaret, b. Dec. 25, 1720;
d. Apr. 6, 1737. (7) William, b. Nov. 8, 1723; m. Abigal
Kibbe.

35. vi. ELEAZUR, b. Sept. 5, 1684; m. Lydia Bidwell, and Sarah ———,
111-2.

36. vii. THOMAS, b. Nov. 24, 1686; m. Abigail Seger, 113-4.

37. viii. DANIEL, b. Feb. 6, 1689; m. Mary Collyer, 115-22.

11. DANIEL FOOTE, (3, 1,) b. 1652; m. 1st Sarah ———, 2nd Mary ———;
res., Stratford, Ct.

38. i. JOHN, b. June 17, 1680; m. Sarah Prindle, 123-9.

39. ii. DANIEL, b. Jan. 10, 1682; m. Dorathy Blakeman and Abigail
Shepard, 1306.

40. iii. HANNAH, b. Feb. 13, 1684; m. Dec. 7, 1704, Richard, son of
Azariah Beach. He was b. Oct. 19, 1677. Removed to Durham 1708. Bought land in Hebron, 1730. Was an early settler in Hebron. Ch.: (1) Azariah Beach, b. New Haven, Ct.,
Sept. 3, 1705; m. Oct. 20, 1730, Lydia, dau. of Jonathan and
Mindwell (Taylor) Burt. He was a Dea. in Hebron; d. in
Hebron. Ch.: (a) Mindwell Beach, b. Aug. 11, 1731; m. Sept.
13, 1753, Ezekiel Jones, of Hebron. She d. July 8, 1799. Both
buried in Jones' burying ground.

41. iv. JEHIEL, b. Mar. 17, 1687; m. Susannah ———, 142-50.

42. v. PETER, b. ———; d. 1753; unm.

13. NATHANIEL FOOTE, (5, 1,) b. Apr. 13, 1660; m. Tabitha Bishop, of
Guilford, Ct. She d. 1715. He d. 1714; res., Branford, Ct.

43. i. ELIZABETH, bap. March, 1696; m. March 29, 1710, Joseph, son
of Michael and Mary (Loomis) Taintor, of Branford, Ct. He
was b. Nov., 1687; d. Jan., 1729. She d. about the same time.
Ch.: (1) Mary, b. July 11, 1711. (2) Joseph, b. Nov. 29, 1714;
d. Oct. 15, 1750. (3) Elizabeth, b. Oct. 28, 1716. (4) John
bap. July 16, 1719. (5) Michael, bap. June 8, 1723. (6)
Nathaniel, bap. Nov. 9, 1725.

44. ii. DORCAS, bap. Mar., 1696; m. Nov. 30, 1720, William Goodrich,
of Branford, Ct. He d. Feb. 27, 1758. She d. Feb. 23, 1752.
Ch.: (1) Nathaniel, b. Jan. 30, 1722. (2) Mary, bap. Jan. 14,
1725. (3) Dorcas, bap. Oct. 23, 1726; d. Nov. 26, 1803. (4)
Gideon, bap. Mar. 31, 1728. (5) Phineas. (6) Moses, d. 1759.
(7) Daniel, bap. May 27, 1739.

45. iii. NATHANIEL, bap. June, 1696; m. Hannah Frissell, 151-8.
46. iv. DANIEL, bap. Feb., 1697; m. Mary Barker, 159-62.
47. v. MOSES, b. Jan. 13, 1702; m. Mary Byington and Ruth Butler, 163-74.
48. vi. ABRAHAM, b. 1706; d. in childhood.
49. vii. ABIGAL, b. 1706; m. Aug. 20, 1725, John Bird. He d. abt. 1757. Ch.: (1) Mary, b. June 4, 1726. (2) Dorcas, b. Feb. 10, 1728. (3) Robert, b. June 4, 1730.

16. JOSEPH FOOTE, (5, 1,) b. Mar. 6, 1666; m. 1690, Abigal Johnson, of New Haven, Ct.; b. Apr. 9, 1670, and d. ——; m. 2nd, 1710, Sarah Rose, of Branford, Ct. She d. June 3, 1741. M. 3d, Sept. 8, 1741, Susannah Frisbie. She d. May 17, 1767. He d. Mar. 6, 1751; res., North Branford, Ct.
50. i. JOSEPH, b. June 20, 1691; m. Anna Johnson, 175-83.
51. ii. DANIEL, b. May 19, 1695; d. Nov. 19, 1695.
52. iii. SAMUEL, b. Dec. 25, 1696; d. in childhood.
53. iv. ROBERT, b. May 31, 1699; m. Mary Linsley, 184-92.
54. v. DANIEL, b. Aug. 16, 1701; m. Sarah Thompson, 193-9.
55. vi. ABRAHAM, b. Dec. 28, 1704; d. in childhood.
56. vii. ICHABOD, b. May, 1711; m. Hannah Harrison and Damaris Finch, 200-10.

17. SAMUEL FOOTE, b. May 14, 1668; m. 1694, Abigal Barker. He d. 1696; res., Branford, Ct.
57. i. THANKFUL, b. Nov. 3, 1694; m. Aug. 10, 1713, Jonathan Frisbie. He d. July 13, 1722. M. 2nd Dec. 18, 1723, Benjamin Farnam. She d. Aug. 23, 1724; res. Branford, Ct. Ch.:(1) Elizabeth, b. May 3, 1715. (2) Jonathan, b. Oct. 4, 1717. (3) Mary, b. May 7, 1720.

18. JOHN FOOTE, (5, 1,) b. July 24, 1670; m. 1696, Mary ——. He d. 1713; res., Branford, Ct.
58. i. ELIZABETH, b. 1697; m. 1720, Caleb Parmele, Jr. He d. July 14, 1750. She d. 1725. Ch.: (1) Abigal, b. Apr. 16, 1721. (2) Mary, b. Dec. 25, 1722. (3) Sarah, b. Oct. 16, 1724.
59. ii. MARY, b. 1697; m. 1st, Feb. 8, 1715, John Chedsey; m. 2nd, Nathaniel Luddington. She d. May 7, 1758; res., E. Haven, Ct. Ch.: (1) Sarah, b. Dec. 6, 1716. (2) John, b. Sept. 15, 1720. (3) Eunice, b. Mar. 21, 1723.
60. iii. THOMAS, b. 1699; m. Elizabeth Sutliff, 211-21.
61. iv. JOHN, b. 1700; m. Elizabeth Frisbie and Abigal Frisbie, 222-3.
62. v. SAMUEL, b. 1702; d. in early life.
63. vi. JONATHAN, b. 1704; m. Lydia Shutliff, 224-7.
64. vii. PATIENCE, b. 1706; m. Jan. 13, 1726, Daniel Palmer, Jr. Ch.: (1) Rebecca, b. Apr. 28, 1728. (2) Lucy, b. Jan. 18, 1733.

19. STEPHEN FOOTE, (5, 1,) b. Dec. 14, 1672; m., 1st, 1702, Elizabeth Nash. She d. Jan. 15, 1739. M. 2nd, Hannah Howd, June 27, 1739. She d. Sept. 10, 1754. He d. Oct. 23, 1762.
65. i. SUSAN, b. Oct. 4, 1706; m. 1st, Apr. 10, 1729, Joseph Harrison. He d. Jan. 13, 1785. She d. May 14, 1733. Ch.: (1) Abigail, 1765; res., Branford, Ct. Ch.: (1) Joseph, b. 1729. (2) Stephen, b. 1731. (3) Leah, b. 1732. (4) Rachel b. 1734.

TOMBSTONE OF NATHANIEL FOOTE. No. 25

TOMBSTONE OF MRS. PATIENCE FOOTE, WIFE OF
NATHANIEL FOOTE.   No. 73

TOMBSTONE OF NATHANIEL FOOTE.   No. 73

66. ii. ELIZABETH, b. Nov. 10, 1709; m. Apr. 2, 1727, John Blackstone. He d. Jan. 13 1785. She d. May 14, 1733. Ch.: (1) Abigail, b. Apr. 20, 1728; d. Sept. 15, 1810. (2) Stephen, b. Feb. 15, 1730. (3) Elizabeth, b. Dec. 18, 1731. (4) John, b. May 7, 1733; d. Aug. 10, 1818.

67. iii. LYDIA, b. Sept. 11, 1712; d. young.

68. iv. MARY, b. Sept. 21, 1715; m. Dec. 5, 1733, Orchard Guy. He d. Jan. 30, 1774. She d. abt. 1780. Ch.: (1) Sarah, b. Nov. 27, 1734; d. Apr. 12, 1742. (2) Mary, b. May 13, 1737; d. Sept. 15, 1816. (3) Elizabeth, b. Dec. 5, 1738. (4) Anna, b. July 17, 1740. (5) John, b. May 26, 1742. (6) Orchard, b. July 27, 1744. (7) Lydia, b. ———. (8) William, b. Apr. 20, 1754.

69. v. REBECCA, b. Oct. 20, 1723; m. Jan. 22, 1746, Samuel Maltbie, Jr. She d. Feb. 9, 1755. He d. Jan., 1773. Ch.: (1) Samuel, b. Nov. 15, 1746. (2) James, b. May 30, 1749. (3) Jonathan, b. Oct. 21, 1751. (4) Rebecca, b. May 25, 1754; d. May 15, 1755.

20. DR. ISAAC FOOTE, (5, 1,) b. Dec. 14, 1672; m. 1709, Rebecca Dickerman. She d. Oct. 15, 1757. He d. Feb. 11, 1758; res., North Branford, Ct.

70. i. JACOB, b. Feb. 19, 1710; d. unm., July 8, 1731.

71. ii. HANNAH, b. Feb. 28, 1712; m. Dec. 24, 1735, Rev. Philemon Robbins, of Branford, Ct.; d. June 16, 1776. He d. Aug. 13, 1781. Ch.: (1) Philemon, b. Nov. 1, 1736. (2) Chandler, b. Aug. 13, 1738. (3) Ammi R., b. Aug. 25, 1740. (4) Hannah, b. Sept. 1, 1742. (5) Rebecca, b. July 27, 1744. (6) Irene, Nov. 16, 1746. (7) Sarah, b. Jan. 11, 1749. (8) Hannah R., Apr. 18, 1751. (9) Rebecca H., b. Apr. 7, 1753.

72. iii. ISAAC, b. July 16, 1717; m. Mary Hall, 228-32.

25. NATHANIEL FOOTE, (9, 3, 1,) b. Sept., 1682; m. 1st, July 4, 1711, Ann Clarke. She d. June 25, 1726. M. 2nd Sept. 13, 1727, Mary, wid. of Joseph Hancock, of Durham, Ct. She d. 1765. He d. Aug. 20, 1774. He was a very influential man in the new town of Colchester, Ct. He held all of the principal offices in succession, and was Representative to the General Assembly for twenty-three sessions.

73. i. NATHANIEL, b. May 28, 1712; m. Patience Gates, 233-41.

74. ii. ISRAEL, b. Oct. 16, 1713; m. Elizabeth Kimberly, 242-5.

75. iii. ANN, b. Aug. 25, 1715; m. July 3, 1740, Isaac Day, son of John and Grace (Spencer) Day; d. June 22, 1760. He b. May 17, 1713; d. Mar. 7, 1765. Ch.: (1) Ann. (2) Mary. (3) Daniel. (4) John. (5) Isaac. (6) Jacob. (7) Hannah. Res., Colchester, Ct.

76. iv. DANIEL, b. Feb. 6, 1716; m. Margaret Parsons and Mary Skinner, 246-57.

77. v. CHARLES, b. Dec. 26, 1718; d. June 15, 1719.

78. vi. HANNAH, b. Apr. 17, 1720; m. Apr. 5, 1753, Samson Howe; d. Mar. 2, 1802. Ch.: (1) Allacia. (2) Hannah. (3) Perly. (4) Damaris.

79. vii. ELIZABETH, b. Feb. 15, 1722; m. Nov. 20, 1744, Joseph Baker, Jr.; d. Jan., 1809. Ch.: (1) Eunice. (2) Margaret. (3) Joseph. (4) Elizabeth. (5) Jonithan. Res., Branford, Ct.

(3)

80. viii. CHARLES, b. Nov. 10, 1723; m. Jerusha Chamberlain, 260-8.
81. ix.   ASA, b. May 4, 1726; m. Jerusha Carter, 269,74.
82. x.   JARED, b. Aug. 28, 1728; m. Hannah Buell, Hepzibah Phelps and
            Joanna Jennings, 275-83.

26. EPHRAIM FOOTE, (9, 3, 1,) b. Feb. 13, 1685; m. June, 1708, Sarah, dau.
of Joseph and Mary (Dickinson) Chamberlain; d. June 10, 1765. She b. Mar. 10,
1693; d. June 9, 1777; res., Colchester, Ct.

83. i.   MARGARET, b. May 13, 1711; m. Mar. 6, 1729, Benj. Day, bro.
           of No. 75's husband; d. Apr., 1801. He b. Feb. 7, 1704; d. Dec.
           22, 1777. Ch.: (1) Ann. (2) Benj. (3) Adonijah. (4) Asa.
           (5) Asa. (6) Margaret. (7) Aaron. (8) Amasa. (9) Lydia.
           (10) Daniel. (11) David. (12) Edith. Res., Colchester, Ct.
84. ii.   SARAH, b. Oct. 20, 1713; m. Oct. 22, 1733, Josiah Douglass. Ch.:
           (1) Joshua. (2) Sarah. (3) David. Res., Colchester, Ct.,
           and N. J.
85. iii. EPHRAIM, b. Apr. 27, 1716; m. Margaret Smith, Miss Lord and
           Lucretia Lewis, 284-97.
86. iv.   REBECCA, b. ———; m. Oct. 24, 1736, David Johnson. Ch.:
           (1) Elihu. (2) David. (3) Abner. (4) Noah. (5) Lucy.
           (6) Charles. Res., Colchester, Ct.
87. v.   IRENE, b. 1722; m. Nov. 20, 1740, Abraham Day, bro. of Isaac
           and Benj., Nos. 75 and 83; d. Aug. 7, 1809. He b. Mar. 17,
           1762; d. Mar. 18, 1791; res., Colchester, Ct. Ch.: (1) Ephraim
           Day, b. July 10, 1741. (2) Ezra Day, b. Apr. 22, 1743. (3)
           Nehemiah Day, b. Mar. 5, 1745. (4) Abraham Day, b. Sept.
           20, 1747. (5) Elisra Day, b. Jan. 30, 1749. (6) Lucy Day,
           b. May 14, 1752; m. ——— Brainard. (7) Elijah Day, Dec. 1,
           1754. (8) Irene Day, b. Mar. 7, 1757. (9) Sarah Day, b. Mar.
           26, 1759. (10) Oliver Day, b. Sept. 12, 1761.
88. vi.   LYDIA, b. m. June 15, 1746, Thomas, son of Thomas and Eliza-
           beth (Robins) Smith. He b. 1728; d. 1811. She d. 1816; res.,
           Lyme, Ct. Ch.: (1) Lydia Smith, b. Aug. 18, 1747. (2)
           Esther, b. Apr. 30, 1749. (3) Rachel, b. Mar. 6, 1752. (4)
           Sophia, b. May 16, 1754. (5) Stephen, b. Apr. 4, 1756. (6)
           Thomas, b. May 7, 1758. (7) Ithamer, b. Sept. 4, 1760. (8)
           Ephraim, b. Sept. 4, 1762. (9) Sally, b. Sept. 28, 1764. (10)
           Dudley, b. May 28, 1767. (11) Rhoda, b. June 15, 1770.
89. vii. ADONIJAH, b. 1729; m. Grace Day and Abigal Roberts, 298-306.
90. viii. DORATHY, bap. Apr. 29, 1733; m. Dec. 19, 1751, John Isham,
           2d, of Colchester, Ct.; d. Nov. 8, 1790. He d. Mar. 2, 1802, ae.
           82. Ch.: (1) Samuel Isham, b. Dec. 20, 1752; res., Malden,
           N. Y. (2) Sarah Isham, b. July 31, 1854; d. Feb. 5, 1766. (3)
           Mary Isham, b. Sept. 24, 1755; m. Aaron Foote, No. 236. (4)
           John Isham, b. June 20, 1757; res., East Haddam and Farm-
           ington, Ct.; d. at Farmington. (5) Jonathan Isham, b. July
           16, 1759. (6) Lois Isham, b. July 8, 1761. (7) Noah Isham,
           b. Apr. 4, 1764; d. at Bolton, Ct. (7) Lucy Isham, b. Apr. 4,
           1764; d. Dec. 25, 1775. (9) Dorathy Isham, b. Oct. 19, 1770;
           m. ——— Canfield; res., Malden, N. Y. (10) Ezra Isham, b.

Mar. 5, 1773; d. Feb. 8, 1835, in Manchester, Vt. (11)
Ephraim Isham, b. July 16, 1776; merchant; d. Feb. 8, 1838,
Hartford, Ct.

91. ix. ABIGAIL, bap. Aug. 18, 1734; m. Thomas Ackley. Ch.: (1)
Dau., said to have m. an Isham and removed to Ulster Co.,
N. Y., 1712.   ⟋ 1712 (?)

27. JOSIAH FOOTE, (9, 3, 1,) b. Sept. 27, 1688; m. Dec. 7, 1738, Sarah, dau.
of Lieut. Noah Wells; d. Dec., 1778. She d. Aug. 3, 1766.

92. i. JOSIAH, b. July 28, 1713; m. Sarah Chamberláin, 306 and 1-8.
93. ii. JONATHAN, b. Mar. 23, 1715; m. Sarah Fenner, 307-14.
94. iii. EUNICE, b. Sept. 26, 1716; m. May 13, 1735, Josiah Treadway,
of Colchester, Ct.; d. Oct. 22, 1801. He d. May 16, 1790. Ch.:
(1) Josiah. (2) Amos, b. Feb. 19, 1738; m. Middletown, Ct.,
June 16, 1760, Elizabeth Blade. She was b. 1735; d. Mar.
21, 1799. He d. Dec. 11, 1814, at Middletown, Ct. Ch.: (a)
Josiah Treadway, b. Nov. 12, 1761. (b) Amos Treadway, b.
Aug. 6, 1762. (c) Elizabeth Treadway, b. July 28, 1764; m.
Middletown, Feb. 1, 1785, Joseph Ward, Jr. He was b. New-
fields, Dist. Middletown, Aug. 25, 1860; d. Sept. 2, 1834, at
Middletown. She d. Jan. 31, 1850, at Newfields. Ch.: (i)
Richard Ward, b. Nov. 7, 1785. (ii) Elizabeth Ward, b. July
19, 1788; d. June 17, 1814. (iii) Truman Ward, b. June 9,
1790. (iv) Henry S. Ward, b. June 17, 1793. (v) Belinda
Ward, b. Apr. 15, 1895. (vi) Merrils Ward, b. Nov. 20, 1796;
m. 1st, Feb. 12, 1818, Moriah, dau. of Calvin and Abiah
(Roberts) Johnson. She was b. Apr. 6, 1797; d. Oct. 17, 1850.
M. 2nd, May 17, 1857, Sarah Merwin. She b. N. Y. C. Sept.
6, 1817; d. Dec. 8, 1887, at Middletown. He d. Nov. 11, 1875,
both at Middletown. Ch.: (1) Dau. still b., Dec. 29, 1818.
(2) London Bailey Ward, b. Dec. 20, 1820. (3) Harriet Wetmore Ward, b. Aug. 25, 1823; d. Mar. 2, 1824. (4) Jane Abiah
Ward, b. Feb. 8, 1825; d. July 30, 1896. (5) Harriet Moriah
Ward, b. June 15, 1827. (6) Frances Amelia Ward, b. Oct. 30,
1829. (7) Austin Merrils Ward, b. Oct. 25, 1831; m. Nov. 15,
1853, Delia, dau. of James, Jr., and Electa (Griswold) Bidwell.
(1 John, 2 John, Jr., 3 Thomas, 4 Jonathan, 5 Jonathan, Jr.
6 James, 7 James, Jr.) She was b. Hartford, Ct., July 22, 1831;
d. Apr. 19, 1901. He d. Sept. 17, 1875, both at Hartford, Ct.
Ch.: (a) Stella Ward, b. Nov. 5, 1860; d. Nov. 11, 1860, at Chicago, Ill. (b) Mabel Ward, b. Chicago, Ill.; m. Hartford, Ct.,
June 19, 1888, Charles Ernest Cameron, M. D. C. M., member
of Royal College Surgeons, England. Ch.: (i) Ward Griswold
Cameron, b. Montreal, Canada, Apr. 13, 1889. (c) Edith Ward,
b. Albany, N. Y.; m. Hartford, Ct., June 25, 1896, Henry Cecil
Dwight, Jr. Ch.: (i) Elizabeth Ward Dwight, b. Albany. (ii)
Cecil Britwall Dwight, b. Albany. (d) James Austin Ward, b. Hartford, Dec. 31, 1873; m. July 22, 1897, Edith Wiley Rice. Ch.:
(di) Hubbard Beach Ward, b. Hartford. (dii) Constance Ward,
b. Hartford. (vii) Susan Ward, b. Sept. 3, 1798; m. John
Smith. (viii) Harvey Ward, b. Jan. 29, 1800. (ix) Chauncey

Ward, b. July 26, 1803. (d) Abigail Treadway, b. Feb. 2, 1766. (e) Richard Treadway, b. Jan. 28, 1768; d. Mar. 23, 1797. (f) Molly Treadway, b. Sept. 16, 1769. (g) Elijah Treadway, b. Dec. 23, 1771. (h) Seth Treadway, b. Feb. 5, 1774. (i) Clarissa Treadway, b. Dec. 30, 1775; m. ―― Sill. (j) Harvey Treadway, b. May 8, 1778. (3) Eliphalet. (4) Eunice. (5) Sarah. (6) David. (7) Mary. (8) Charles. (9) James. (10) Alpheus. (11) Elijah. (12) John.

95. iv. DAVID, b. Feb. 24, 1718; d. Sept. 3, 1757, unm.

96. v. JOSEPH, b. May 12, 1721; m. Thankful ――, 315-6.

97. vi. HABAKUK, b. Jan. 27, 1723; m. Mary Welles, 317-21.

98. vii. MARY, b. May 22, 1726; m. Oct. 10, 1748, Jonas Wyles; d. June 19, 1811. He d. May 4, 1802; res., Colchester and Vernon, Ct. Ch.: (1) John. (2) Hab. (3) David. (4) Russell. (5) Molly.

99. viii. JOHN, b. Aug. 15, 1728; m. Anna Thompson and Maria C. Miller, 322.

100. ix. SARAH, b. Jan. 28, 1731; m. Jan. 5, 1758, Cullick, son of Richard and Margaret (Olcott, dau. of No. 14,) Ely, of Lyme, Ct.; d. Aug. 15, 1818. He was b. Jan., 1733; d. Aug. 29, 1821. Ch.: (1) David. (2) Cullick. (3) Eleazur. (4) Eunice. (5) Sarah. (6) Russell. (7) Charles. (8) Joseph.

101. x. CATHARINE, b. Apr. 13, 1733; m. July 14, 1756, Daniel Isham, of Colchester, Ct. Ch.: (1) Mary. (2) David. (3) Ellis. (4) Daniel. (5) Asa. (6) Sarah. (7) Abigail.

102. xi. NOAH, b. 1738; m. Esther Kellogg and Tabitha Shaylor, 323-35.

28. JOSEPH FOOTE, (9, 3, 1,) b. Dec. 28, 1690; m. 1st, Dec. 12, 1719, Ann Clothier. She d. Apr. 15, 1740. M. 2nd, Sept. 2, 1740, Hannah, widow of John Norton; d. Apr. 21, 1756.

103. i. AMBROSE, b. Apr. 3, 1723; d. young.

104. ii. JEREMIAH, b. Oct. 15, 1732; m. Ruhamah Northam, 336-46.

·105· iii. HOSEA, b. 1729; m. Eunice Chamberlain, 347-55.

106. iv. ANNA, bap. Oct. 15, 1732; m. Sept. 10, 1752, Samuel Bridges, of Colchester, Ct.; d. Aug. 7, 1803. Ch.: (1) Jonithan. (2) Eunice. (3) Esther. (4) Eunice. (5) Edmund. (6) Samuel. (7) Asa. (8) Ann C. (9) Amasa. (10) Molly. (11) Margaret.

107. v. EUNICE, bap. June 1, 1735; d. Apr. 28, 1755; unm.

30. NATHANIEL FOOTE, (10, 3, 1,) b. 1672; m. Nov. 5, 1707, Mary Ward; res., Hatfield, Mass.

108. i. DINAH, b. Oct. 5, 1708.

109. ii. EZRA, b. June 28, 1713.

110. iii. BENONI, b. June 28, 1713; d. July 2, 1713.

35. ELEAZUR FOOTE, (10, 3, 1,) b. Sept. 5, 1684; m. 1st, May 24, 1717, Lydia, dau. of Joseph and Mary Bidwell, of Wethersfield, Ct. She b. May 13, 1689; d. Feb. 9, 1719. M. 2nd, Sarah ――. She d. Dec.17, 1773. He d. Nov. 17, 1758; res., Springfield and Brimfield, Mass.

111. i. ELEAZUR, b. Feb. 8, 1719; d. young.

112. ii. LYDIA, b. Feb. 8, 1719.

36. THOMAS FOOTE, (10, 3, 1,) b. Nov. 24, 1686; m. Nov. 3, 1726, Abigail Seger; d. abt. 1766; res., Springfield and Monson, Mass.

113. i. SAMUEL, b. Nov. 12, 1728; m. Abigail Field, 356-64.
114. ii. JOSEPH, b. 1730; m. Rosella Chapin, Thankful Parcy and Widow Sawyer, 365-9.

37. DANIEL FOOTE, (10, 3, 1,) b. Feb., 1689; m. Nov. 19, 1718, Mary Collyer; d. July 15, 1740. She d. June, 1769.

115. i. SAMUEL, b. Oct. 4, 1719; m. Lois Loomis, 370-9.
116. ii. MARY, b. Nov. 20, 1721; m. 1st, 1737, Joel Gillett; 2nd, ——— Fillmore. Ch.: (1) Joel. (2) Lucy. (3) Abner. (4) Moses. (5) Sarah.
117. iii. DANIEL, b. Apr. 27, 1724; m. Martha Stillman, 380-91.
118. iv. JOSEPH, b. Feb. 17, 1727; m. Azubah Griswold, 392-402.
119. v. JOHN, b. 1729; m. Rosanna Humphrey and Mary Fowler, 403-8.
120. vi. RACHEL, b. 1731; d. Jan. 21, 1737.
121. vii. SARAH, b. 1732; m. June 9, 1762, Daniel, son of Timothy and Hannah (Crane) Boardman. Ch.: (1) Sarah. (2) Mary. Res., Wethersfield, Ct.
122. viii. RACHEL, b. Mar., 1736; m. June 5, 1760, Timothy Phelps. Ch.: (1) Samuel. (2) Daniel. (3) Frederick. (4) Rachel Foote. Res., Simsbury, Ct.

38. JOHN FOOTE, (11, 3, 1,) b. June 17, 1680; m. July 13, 1715, Sarah Prindle. Res., Newton, Ct.

123. i. SARAH, b. Oct. 30, 1715.
124. ii. ELIZABETH, b. May 14, 1718.
125. iii. NATHAN, b. Oct. 24, 1719; m. Abiah Gilbert, 409-10.
126. iv. JOHN, b. Nov. 29, 1721; m. Deborah Hoyt, 411-8.
127. v. PHEBE, b. 1723; m. Dec. 4, 1751, Timothy Treadwell, of Fairfield, Ct.
128. vi. PETER, b. 1725; m. Sarah Hurd, 419-31.
129. vii. HANNAH, b. 1727.

39. DANIEL FOOTE, (11, 3, 1,) b. Jan. 10, 1682; m. 1st, Jan. 2, 1705, Dorathy Blakeman. She d. Jan. 28 1722, 2nd, Abigail, w. of John Shepard, and dau. of Gideon Allen, of Milford, Ct.; res., Stratford and Newtown, Ct.

130. i. DAVID, b. July 7, 1707; m. Eleanor Blakesley, 432-8.
131. ii. JOHN, b. July 20, 1711; m. Amy ———, 439-45.
132. iii. SARAH, b. June 16, 1713.
133. iv. ABIGAIL, b. Oct. 16, 1714; d. young.
134. v. DANIEL, b. May 5, 1716; m. Sarah ———, 446-58.
135. vi. JEMIMA, b. Mar. 13, 1718; m. ———; Bristol.
136. vii. ELIZABETH, b. Aug. 1719; m. ——— Hubbard.
137. viii. EBENEZUR, b. Sept. 22, 1720; m. Christiana ———, 459.
138. ix. TABITHA, b. Jan. 1, 1722; m. Dec. 24, 1741, Timothy Hurd, of Woodbury, Ct.
139. x. SARAH, b. Sept. 8, 1723; m. James Fairchild, of Newtown. Ch.: (1) Silas. (2) James.
140. xi. GEORGE, b. Mar. 26, 1725; m. Catharine Burrit, 460-8.
141. xii. DORATHY, b. Mar. 21, 1729; m. Nov. 16, 1752, Reuben Salmon, of Fairfield.

41. JEHIEL FOOTE, (11, 3, 1,) b. Mar. 17, 1687; m. Susannah ———; d. Sept., 1740; res., Stratford, Ct.

    142. i.   JOSEPH, b. Dec. 17, 1714; m. Sarah Blakeman, 469-76.

    143. ii.   DANIEL, b. July 25, 1717; m. Sarah Whitney, 477-84.

    144. iii.   JEHIEL, b. Dec. 17, 1719; d. young.

    145. iv.   GEORGE, b. Nov. 4, 1721; m. Hannah Hurd, 485-8.

    146. v.   JEHIEL, b. Feb. 29, 1724.

    147. vi.   SARAH, b. Aug. 17, 1726; m. Feb. 19, 1744, Daniel Munroe, of Stratford.

    148. vii.   SUSANNAH, b.. Dec. 13, 1729; m. 1754, John Beers.

    149. viii.   MARY, bap. May 9, 1731; m. Dec. 10, 1753, Caleb Dayton.

    150. ix.   HANNAH, bap. Dec. 9, 1733.

45. NATHANIEL FOOTE, (13, 5, 1,) bap. June, 1696; m. Mar. 2, 1720, Hannah dau. of Joseph Frissell, of Woodstock, Mass.; d. July 4, 1771. She d. June 30, 1772; res., Branford, Ct.

    151. i.   SARAH, b. Mar. 6, 1721; m. Mar. 24, 1748, Timothy Goodrich, of Branford, Ct.; d. before 1789. He d. 1802.

    152. ii.   NATHANIEL, b. Oct. 15, 1723; m. Sarah Beers and Mary Jones, 489-92.

    153. iii.   EPHRAIM, b. ———; m. Lucy Barker, 493-500.

    154. iv.   DORCAS, b. July 4, 1727; m. Jan. 9, 1746, Amos Hitchcock, Jr., of New Haven, Ct.; d. June, 1802, in Bethany, Ct. He d. Nov. 20, 1791. Ch.: (1) Dorcas. (2) Amos. (3) Sarah. (4) Abigail. (5) Mary. (6) Abijah. (7) Amos. (8) Elihu. (9) Phineas. (10) Eli.

    155. v.   HANNAH, b. ———; m. Nov. 2, 1776, Nathaniel Wheedon, of Branford, Ct.; p. s.

    156. vi.   ABIGAIL, b. ———; m. April 28, 1758, Papillion Barker, of Durham, N. Y.; d. abt. 1809. He d. abt. 1813. Ch.: (1) Phineas. (2) Sarah. (3) Archelus. (4) Christina. (5) Submit. (6) Hannah. (7) Nathaniel.

    157. vii.   PHINEAS, bap. July 21, 1735; d. young.

    158. viii.   MARY, bap. June 18, 1736; m. 1st, June 8, 1772, Peter Baldwin, of Branford, Ct.; 2nd abt. 1777, Stephen Thompson; d. Dec. 16, 1817. He d. Nov. 10, 1808. Ch.: James. Res., East Haven, Ct.

46. DANIEL FOOTE, (13, 5, 1,) bap. Feb., 1697; m. Sept. 27, 1721, Mary, dau. of Wm. Barker; d. Oct. 23, 1774. She d. before 1741; res., N. Branford, Ct.

    159. i.   MARY, b. Dec. 8, 1724.

    160. ii.   LUCY, b. Oct. 7, 1727.

    161. iii.   HULDAH, Mar. 3, 1729; m. Nov. 4, 1762, Daniel Barker, Jr., of Branford, Ct. He d. 1781.

    162. iv.   ABIGAIL, b. ———.

47. MOSES FOOTE, (13, 5. 1,) b. Jan. 13, 1702; m. 1st, June 22, 1726, Mary, dau. of John Byington. She d. Jan., 1740. M. 2nd, Ruth, dau. of Jonathan Butler, Nov. 5, 1740; d. Feb., 1770. She d. Aug. 7, 1792, in Gill, Mass. Res., Branford and Waterbury, Ct.

Moses Foote lived in that part of Waterbury, Conn., now called Plymouth. We find that for many years before his death in 1770, he and his second wife,

Ruth, and several of their children were members of the church at .Plymouth. Among these was Obed Foote, the youngest son, born November 25, 1741. He became in love with the minister's daughter, Mary Todd, then 19 years of age. He was only 20, and they were married in 1761. Eleven children were the fruit of this happy marriage. Her father, Rev. Samuel Todd, was a graduate of Yale, pastor of the church at Plymouth for 25 years, and a chaplain in the Continental army in the Revolution, and afterwards the first pastor of the Church at North Adams, Berkshire county, Mass. Of Obed's four brothers three were in the Revolutionary service. One, David, was killed by the British in their attack on Fairfield, Conn. Another, Ebenezer, died in the army, and each of these had a son in the service. While these brothers were in the Revolutionary army, Obed, the youngest son, remained at home to care for the widowed mother, then 70 years of age, and his young family, among whom was Samuel Foote, born April 7, 1770, at Plymouth, Conn., who was in later years one of the pioneers of Sherburne and Plymouth, N. Y.

163.　i.　REBECCA, b. Apr. 10, 1727; m. Jan. 3, 1750, Josiah Butler, Jr., of Bradford and Harwinton, Ct.; d. 1802, at Charlemont, Mass.

164.　ii.　LYDIA, b. March 23, 1728; d. young.

165.　iii.　DORATHY, b. March 26, 1729; d. young.

166.　iv.　DAVID, b. Nov. 11, 1730; m. Hannah Bronson, 501-7.

167.　v.　RUTH, b. Aug. 1, 1732; d. young.

168.　vi.　MOSES, b. Aug. 4, 1734; m. Thankful Bronson and Amy Richards, 508-17.

169.　vii.　MARY, b. Oct. 9, 1736; d. Feb. 21, 1758, in Waterbury, unm.

170.　viii.　AARON, b. July 5, 1738; m. Mary Bronson, 518-25.

171.　ix.　EBENEZER, b. May 21, 1740; m. Rebecca Barker 526-32. .

172.　x.　OBED, b. Nov. 25, 1741; m. Mary Todd, 533-43.

173.　xii.　LYDIA, b. Nov. 30, 1743; m. Isaac Curtis; d. Sept. 6, 1788.　Ch.:
(1) Jonathan, b. Jan. 28, 1765.

174.　xiii.　DORATHY, b. Nov. 10, 1745; d. 1749.

50.　JOSEPH FOOTE, (16, 5, 1,) b. 1691; m. Nov. 19, 1717, Anna Johnson, dau. of Ebenezer Johnson, d. June 16, 1761. She d. Nov. 25, 1759.　.

175.　i.　SAMUEL, b. Jan. 8, 1718; d. Feb. 28, 1733.

176.　ii.　ABIGAIL, b. May 29, 1720; m. 1st, June 23, 1737, Jacob Curtis. He d. abt. Jan. 1, 1739; 2nd, Solomon Palmer.

177.　iii.　JOSEPH, b. Apr. 2, 1722; d. Aug. 1, 1727.

178.　iv.　STEPHEN, b. Aug. 20, 1724; m. Sybil Foster and Mary Frisbie, 544-9.

179.　v.　DAVID, b. May 5, 1727; d. Sept. 24, 1749, unm.

180.　vi.　ANN, b. Sept. 15, 1729. d. Oct. 31, 1730.

181.　vii.　ANN, b. Oct. 24, 1734; m. May 8, 1754, Samuel Allen, of Branford, Ct.　Ch.: (1) Mary, b. Aug. 29, 1755.　(2) Joseph, b. Nov. 18, 1757.　(3) Anna, b. Apr. 12, 1760.

182.　ix.　THANKFUL, b. Feb. 15, 1734; d. unm.

183.　x.　SILENCE, b. Apr. 2, 1737; d. Sept. 25, 1749.

53.　CAPT. ROBERT FOOTE, (16, 5, 1.) b. May 31, 1699; m. Jan. 25, 1721, Mary, dau. of John Linsley; d. June 14, 1761. She d. Apr. 1785; res., North Branford, Ct.

184. i. MARY, b. Apr. 9, 1722; m. Dec. 6, 1738, Jonathan Rogers, of Branford, Ct.; d. March 16, 1761. He d. Mar. 6, 1805. Ch.: (1) Eli. (2) Mary. (3) Lydia. (4) Sarah. (5) Mary. (6) Jonathan. (7) Abigail.

185. ii. ABRAHAM, b. June 16, 1725; m. Abigail Rogers and Mary Ponsonby, 550-7.

186. iii. LYDIA, b. Mar. 23, 1728; d. Jan. 2, 1740.

187. iv. GIDEON, b. Feb. 19, 1730; d. Apr. 1, 1730.

188. v. THANKFUL, b. Feb. 6, 1731; m. Dec. 7, 1749, Jacob Barker, of North Branford, Ct.; d. Dec. 24, 1751. He d. Oct. 31, 1751. Ch.: (1) Jacob, b. Oct. 11, 1750.

189. vi. EBENEZER, b. Jan. 7, 1734; m. Phebe Palmer, 558-9.

190. vii. ABIGAIL, b. June 15, 1737; d. Dec. 17, 1738.

191. viii. ABIGAIL, b. Dec. 22, 1739; d. Aug. 12, 1751.

192. ix. LYDIA, b. Apr. 12, 1743; m. 1st, June 26, 1771, Ebenezer Baldwin. He d. Feb. 3, 1777; m. 2d. Elisha Scoville, of Meriden, Ct. Ch.: (1) Ebenezer Baldwin. (2) Abigail.(3) Lydia; res., Turin, N. Y.

54. DANIEL FOOTE, (16, 5, 1,) b. Aug. 16, 1701; m. 1726, Sarah, dau. of John Thompson, of E. Haven, Ct.; d. Nov., 1742. She m., May 5, 1746, John Taintor; d. Sept. 6, 1774.

193. i. SARAH, b. Dec. 1, 1727; m. Sept. 25, 1747, Michael, son of Joseph and Elizabeth (Foote) Taintor, of N. Branford, Ct.; d. Oct. 27, 1776. He bap. June 8, 1723; d. Oct. 14, 1794. Ch.: (1) Abigail. (2) Michael. (3) Mary. (4) Medad. (5) Sarah. Res., Branford, Ct.

194. ii. HANNAH, b. Apr. 22, 1730; m. Nathan Porter.

195. iii. JACOB, b. Mar. 20, 1732; m. Lucy Bunnell, 560-3.

196. iv. DANIEL, b. June 5, 1734; m. Mary Ingraham, 564-77.

197. v. ASA, b. July 5, 1737; d. Oct. 31, 1776, unm.

198. vi. SAMUEL, b. May 12, 1740; m. Anna Harrison, 578-84.

199. vii. DESIRE, b. ———; d. unm.

56. DR. ICHABOD FOOTE, (16, 5, 1,) b. May, 1711; m. 1st, Mar. 4, 1734, Hannah, dau. of Isaac Harrison. She d. Sept. 2, 1748, ae. 36; m. 2nd, Damaris, dau. of Daniel Finch. He d. Sept. 11, 1773; res. N. Branford, Ct.

200. i. JARED, b. July 17, 1735; m. Submit Bishop, Sarah Stillman and Jemima Holcomb, 585-9.

201. ii. JOSEPH, b. Mar. 3, 1737; m. Abigail Winchel, 590.

202. iii. JOHN, b. Feb. 18, 1740; m. Ruth Culver, Sarah Culver and Hannah Kimberley, 591-4.

203. iv. HANNAH, b. Jan. 30, 1742; d. Oct. 31, 1751.

204. v. ABIGAIL, b. Dec. 6, 1743; d. Dec. 19, 1754.

205. vi. ICHABOD, b. Feb. 24, 1746-7; m. Jemima Smith, 595-603.

206. vii. RUTH, b. 1749; m. Nov. 29, 1773, Ebenezer Finch; d. Jan. 13, 1821. He d. Sept. 4, 1825. Res. Branford and Southington, Ct. Ch.: (1) Caleb, (2) Jessie Foote. (3) Solomon, (4) Samuel, (5) Ruth. (6) Eunice.

207. viii. ROBERT, b. 1752; m. Rachel Lewis, and Sarah Bishop, 604-8.

208. ix. HELI, b. 1755; m. Silance Harrison and Ruth Polly, 609-21.

209. x. JESSE, b. Jan. 22, 1758; m. Rachel Benedict and Elizabeth Taylor, 622-8.

210. xi. HANNAH, b. 1760; m. 1781, Mark Warner, of Waterbury, Ct.; d. Sept. 15, 1794. He d. Oct. 26, 1805. Her mother m. his father, second marriage of each. Ch.: (1) Elizabeth, (2) Noah. (3) Jared, (4) Clarissa, (5) Hannah, (6) Olive. (7) Mark. (8) Submit.

60. DR. THOMAS FOOTE, (18, 5, 1,) b. 1699; m. Elizabeth Sutliff; d. Dec. 19, 1776. She d. Nov. 16, 1789, ae. 82. Res., Branford and Plymouth, Ct.

211. i. SAMUEL, b. 1723; m. Mary Lyon, 629-36.

212 ii. JEMIMA, b. 1725; m. Apr.19, 1748, Abraham Hickox, of Waterbury, Ct.; d. May 20, 1779. Ch.: (1) Mary. (2) Lucy. (3) Jesse. (4) Jared. (5) Joel. (6) Timothy. (7) Abraham. (8) Samuel. (9) Preserve.

213. iii. ELIZABETH, b. 1728; m. May 26, 1765, Noah Griggs, of Waterbury, Ct.; d. Feb. 16, 1807. He d. Dec. 12, 1812. Ch.: (1) Jacob. (2) Noah. (3) Amos.

214. iv. EBENEZER, b. 1730; m. Martha Moss, 637-41.

215. v. TIMOTHY, b. 1735; m. Mary Garnsey and Lucy Wheeler, 642-9.

216. vi. NATHAN, b. Jan. 25, 1738; m. Mavina Selkrigg, 650-60.

217. vii. THOMAS, b. May 10, 1740; m. Rebecca Doud and Ann Adams, 661-4.

218. viii. JOHN, b. Aug. 24, 1742; m. Esther Mattoon and Mary Peck, 665-75.

219. ix. JACOB, b. Oct. 30, 1744; m. Esther Doolittle and Rhoda Saxton, 676-86.

220. x. JOSEPH, b. Apr. 3, 1747; m. Thankful Ives, 687-96.

221. xi. ISAAC, b. Mar. 25, 1750; m. Sarah Selkrigg, 697-701.

61. CAPT. JOHN FOOTE, (18, 5, 1,) b. 1700; m. 1st, Dec. 25, 1733, Elizabeth, dau. of Jonathan Frisbie. She d. Feb. 3, 1737; m. 2nd, Aug. 16, 1788, Abigail Frisbie. He d. Jan. 26, 1777. She d. May, 1779, ae. 67.

222. i. JONATHAN, b. Jan. 28, 1737; m. Lydia Baldwin, 702-8.

223. ii. JOHN, b. Apr. 2, 1742; m. Abigail Hall and Eunice Hall, 709-16.

63. JONATHAN FOOTE, (18, 5, 1,) b. 1704; m. June 14, 1727, Lydia, dau. of John Sutliff; d. June 26, 1754. She d. Sept. 27, 1768, ae. 64; res., Branford and Plymouth, Ct.

224. i. JERUSHA, b. Oct. 1, 1728; d. Mar., 1741.

225. ii. EUNICE, b. July 26, 1731; m. Mar. 22, 1750, Timothy Williams, of Waterbury, Ct.; d. Dec. 5, 1776. Ch.: (1) Jonathan. (2) Jerusha. (3) James. (4) Daniel. (5) Timothy. (6) Lydia.

226. iii. AARON, b. Dec. 8, 1734; d. Dec. 3, 1814, unm.

227. iv. LYDIA, b. ——; d. Dec. 1, 1748.

72. MAJOR ISAAC FOOTE, (20, 5, 1,) b. July 16, 1717; m. Mary, dau. of John Hall; d. Oct. 7, 1755, in Greenbush, N. Y. She d. May 6, 1792, ae. 74, in Branford, Ct.

Major Isaac Foote was b. at Branford, Ct., July 16, 1717. His father, Isaac Foote, Esq., and his mother, dau. of Abraham Dickerman, of New

Haven, were highly esteemed by their acquaintance, particularly in the duties of the Christian character. This, their only son, was early consecrated to God, and, with two sisters, was trained up with parental care, and with the best advantages for education that could be ordinarily obtained at that day. In his youth he exhibited an inclination to the military profession, which was necessarily cultivated, more or less, at that period of our history. What part he took in the war of 1745 is not well known, but it is supposed that he was an officer in the militia, and probably engaged in the important expedition to Cape Breton, which issued in the capture of the strongly fortified town of Louisburg.

The next period of peace between England and France continued but seven years. The succeeding war, commonly denominated the "French War," commenced in 1755; the same season as the defeat of the unfortunate Braddock. The regiment to which Major Foote was attached joined the Northern army under the command of Gen. Shirley. Great preparations were made that year for the approaching contest; the best troops in New England were called out, it being generally expected that the decisive conflict of war would take place in Canada. This proved to be the case in the successful battle of Quebec, with the death of Gen. Wolfe.

At this eventful occasion we have in Major Foote a striking exhibition of the Christian soldier. While this detachment was at Albany, Gen. Shirley had a dining party, of which Mr. Foote was one, on the Sabbath. He attended public worship in the morning, and then went to dinner. At the call for the afternoon exercise Major Foote rose at table and asked permission to leave the company. Gen. Shirley said, " No, Major, do not leave this company, and these choice wines." He modestly renewed his request, and was refused as before. Mr. Foote stood, but was silent. The Gen. spoke again, "No compulsion, Major, take your choice, leave if you wish." He took a respectful leave for the house of prayer.

A few extracts from his letters, written to his wife a short time previous to his decease, will give a distinct view of the Christian character of Major Foote, and may be more interesting than the remarks of another. He was in the tract of country between Albany, Lake Champlain and Lake Ontario, distinguished in our history for military achievements.

" Fort Nicholson, Aug. 15, 1755.—I am now arrived at the great carrying-place where General Lyman built a fort. I do not expect to write you any letters before we attack the fort and have an engagement; and stand or fall, live or die, as God pleases, I feel, in general, resigned to the disposal of Divine Providence; and if it should be my lot to fall in battle, or otherwise die here, let me recommend to you, as from a dying husband, to live entirely devoted to God and his service. Spend your time in doing the will of God. The great part of your care must be in bringing up the dear children, and use your utmost endeavor to instruct them in the principles of religion; pray much with them and for them. . . . I hope your heart is fixed, trusting in God, so that evil tidings shall not make you afraid. I know that, like Eli, your heart will tremble, you will want to hear and yet be afraid to hear. And when you learn that there are a number slain (for it would be very extraordinary if none should be killed), how your heart will tremble lest I should be in the number of them that fall in battle. And if it should be the case, do not mourn immoderately, for while you are mourning and weeping, through the Redeemer's merits, I shall be adoring before the throne of God."

In the next letter, dater Aug. 20th, he writes,—'' We have orders to move forward our regiment. I am not well, but resigned to the will of God. Hope you are, and will continue so. The comforts of religion are real, solid, and sometimes ravishing. O Saviour, how much do I long to be conformed to Thee. Love God, pray much, instruct the children, and if I ever come home I intend to do more for them than I have ever done. Pray for Zion's prosperity. I trust you will be faithful in the affair of religion of the family. I now have the distemper that prevails among us, though not mortal, except in two instances. But I am in safe hands. Do not be concerned about me; you may mention the case to a prayer-hearing God, and desire the prayers of my Christian friends. I trust I shall be saved from the pestilence that walketh in darkness, and the arrows and bullets that fly at noon-day. But, however it be, do you love and praise God, and join with me in ascribing praise and honor to the Lamb, to Whom be glory ever-lasting.''

In a letter of Sept. 1st, he says,—''I left the camp about a week ago on account of my ill-health. Am now pretty well recovered, and design to go to the army to-morrow. Gen. Johnson, with 1,500 men is ___

The tombstone of Major Isaac Foote, died 7 October, 1755, age "38 years, 2 months, 7 days," now (1932) lies flat in the East Greenbush Cemetery, Clinton Heights Rensselaer County, N.Y.

Tradition has it that "some years ago" the stone was removed from a burial plot near "Fort Cralo". Cemetery records may show whether the remains were also removed.

East Greenbush Cem is not at Clinton Heights but there is a cem. both places.
Information from Mr. Leech. Room 319
June 1, 1932.

___ should go home, if ever. I would have you cast all your care and roll all your burden upon God. He will support you. Is he not better to you than an earthly friend? I am sure He is to me. When dejected, He raises me up; when fainting, He gives me refreshing cordials; when thirsty, He gives me the water of life.''

'' Thursday Morning,—Slept comfortably; hope you had a good night, and freedom this morning to pour out your soul to God. I am very poor and pained to-day; but it is all well; because as to health, it is as God would have it. · · · It is now 9 o'clock; I will lay down and rest my poor body, if God pleases, and to-morrow I may perhaps write more; and so good-night to you and the children and friends.''

About this period Major Foote obtained permission to leave the army on account of his constant and increasing illness, hoping to be able to reach his home.

Haven, were highly esteemed by their acquaintance, particularly in the duties of the Christian character. This, their only son, was early consecrated to God, and, with two sisters, was trained up with parental care, and with the best advantages for education that could be ordinarily obtained at that day. In his youth he exhibited an inclination to the military profession, which was necessarily cultivated, more or less, at that period of our history. What part he took in the war of 1745 is not well known, but it is supposed that he was an officer in the militia, and probably engaged in the important expedition to Cape Breton, which issued in the capture of the strongly fortified town of Louisburg.

The next period of peace between England and France continued but seven years. The succeeding war, commonly denominated the "French War," commenced in 1755; the same season as the defeat of the unfortunate Braddock. The regiment to which Major Foote was attached joined the Northern army under the command of Gen. Shirley. Great preparations were made that year for the approaching contest; the best troops in New England were called out, it being generally expected that the decisive conflict of war would take place in Canada. This prov   ~~~~ful battle of Quebec, with the death of Gen. Wolf

At th
Christian
dining p
worship
exercise
Gen. Sh
wines.''
stood, l
your ch
prayer.

A
his dec
and ma
countr
our hi
''

place
letter
or die, as God p
ence; and if it should be my lot to run
recommend to you, as from a dying husband, to live entirely devoted
his service. Spend your time in doing the will of God. The great part of your care must be in bringing up the dear children, and use your utmost endeavor to instruct them in the principles of religion; pray much with them and for them.
. . . I hope your heart is fixed, trusting in God, so that evil tidings shall not make you afraid. I know that, like Eli, your heart will tremble, you will want to hear and yet be afraid to hear. And when you learn that there are a number slain (for it would be very extraordinary if none should be killed), how your heart will tremble lest I should be in the number of them that fall in battle. And if it should be the case, do not mourn immoderately, for while you are mourning and weeping, through the Redeemer's merits, I shall be adoring before the throne of God.''

In the next letter, dater Aug. 20th, he writes,—"We have orders to move forward our regiment. I am not well, but resigned to the will of God. Hope you are, and will continue so. The comforts of religion are real, solid, and sometimes ravishing. O Saviour, how much do I long to be conformed to Thee. Love God, pray much, instruct the children, and if I ever come home I intend to do more for them than I have ever done. Pray for Zion's prosperity. I trust you will be faithful in the affair of religion of the family. I now have the distemper that prevails among us, though not mortal, except in two instances. But I am in safe hands. Do not be concerned about me; you may mention the case to a prayer-hearing God, and desire the prayers of my Christian friends. I trust I shall be saved from the pestilence that walketh in darkness, and the arrows and bullets that fly at noon-day. But, however it be, do you love and praise God, and join with me in ascribing praise and honor to the Lamb, to Whom be glory ever-lasting."

In a letter of Sept. 1st, he says,—"I left the camp about a week ago on account of my ill-health. Am now pretty well recovered, and design to go to the army to-morrow. Gen. Johnson, with 1,500 men, is now at the Lake St. Savian, building a fort; and some things look discouraging. Yet I trust, if the reinforce-ments come seasonably, we shall proceed to some point. We have some prospect of an engagement.

I am at present in low spirits. Oh, alas, how various are my frames! Last letter I wrote you I was on the mount; and could unite with angels in adoring sovereign grace;—and now, alas, why sunk down in stupidity and sloth. Oh, cry to Heaven for me. I hope you and the few dear praying ones will continue to besiege, as you beautifully express it, the throne of Grace. You may do more than Gen. Johnson can with his army. Oh! the prayer of saints—I had almost said Omnipotent. Mr. Bellamy, in a letter, tells me all the children of God lie prostrate before the Lord for success in this enterprize. . . . Oh, amazing grace! how safe is the believer. Perils and dangers he may pass through, afflic-tions may encompass him like bees, death may stare him in the face and threaten an onset. Serene and calm he awaits the blow, and asks the monster: Where is its sting, and where its victory-boasting grave?"

"Flatts, 4 miles above Albany, Sept. 17, '55,—I am here at Colonel Schuyler's waiting for a guard, for it is not deemed safe to go alone. I am in a very feeble state of health; think it is owing to Jesuit's bark, taken to break fever and ague fits, or to the almost constant fogs that arise from the river. If I was at home I should give quite out. I am tenderly looked after, go where I will, and treated very kindly. . . . I know not when I shall go home, if ever. I would have you cast all your care and roll all your burden upon God. He will support you. Is he not better to you than an earthly friend? I am sure He is to me. When dejected, He raises me up; when fainting, He gives me refreshing cordials; when thirsty, He gives me the water of life."

"Thursday Morning,—Slept comfortably; hope you had a good night, and freedom this morning to pour out your soul to God. I am very poor and pained to-day; but it is all well; because as to health, it is as God would have it. . . It is now 9 o'clock; I will lay down and rest my poor body, if God pleases, and to-morrow I may perhaps write more; and so good-night to you and the children and friends."

About this period Major Foote obtained permission to leave the army on account of his constant and increasing illness, hoping to be able to reach his home.

But he was not able to proceed any farther than Greenbush, opposite Albany, where he died, Oct. 7, 1755, in the 39th year of his age. In the ancient burying ground, opposite the lower part of the city of Albany, he sleeps in peace, to be called by the Lord at the '' resurrection of the just.''

228. i. REBECCA, b. Apr. 25, 1739; m. 1st, Oct. 17, 1759, Rev. Caleb Smith. He was b. Jan. 9, 1724; d. 1761; m. 2nd, Rev. Azel Roe, Sept., 1763. He d. Dec. 2, 1815. She d. Sept. 1, 1794. Ch.: (1) Apollos. (2) Fanny. (3) Rebecca. (4) John. (5) Elizabeth. (6) Isaac. (7) Lucia. (8) Oliva. (9) Phebe.

229. ii. LOIS, b. Oct. 30, 1740; d. Sept. 21, 1751.

230. iii. ABIGAIL, b. ———, 1744; d. in youth.

231. iv. ISAAC, b. Dec. 4, 1747; m. Lydia Tyler and Phebe Benton, 717-25.

232. v. SALLY, bap. Nov. 8, 1753; m. Baldwin.

73. NATHANIEL FOOTE, (25, 9, 3, 1,) b. May 28, 1712; m. Apr. 15, 1736, Patience, dau. of Joseph and Elizabeth (Hungerford) Gates, of East Hadden, Ct.; d. May 9, 1811. She was b. May 21, 1712; d. Feb. 22, 1799; res., Colchester, Ct.

233. i. PATIENCE, b. June 17, 1737; m. Jan. 17, 1762, David Bigelow, Jr., son of David and Edith (Day); d. June 29, 1791. He d. Oct. 6, 1820, ae. 88. Ch.: (1) David. (2) Erastus, m. Lucy Root. (3) Patience, m. Solomon Finley. (4) John, m. Sally Buell. (5) Anna. (6) Isaac. (7) Asa. (8) Esther. Res., Glastonbury, Ct.

234. ii. ANN, b. Aug. 1, 1739; m. Apr. 6, 1758, Joshua, son of David and Jane Bailey; d. Dec. 5, 1772. She d. Sept. 1, 1809. Ch.: (1) Amos. (2) Joshua. (3) Rhoda. (4) Nathaniel. (5) Asa.

235. iii. NATHANIEL, b. Feb. 7, 1742; m. Jerusah Cadwell, Patience Skinner and Abigail Foote, 1758-60. 252-260

236. iv. AARON, b. Mar. 10, 1744; m. Mary Isham and Sarah Williams, 1761-9.

237. v. MARGARET, b. May 7, 1746; m. Mar. 26, 1767, Azariah Bigelow, of Colchester, Ct. He was b. in Colchester, Ct., Dec. 26, 1741; d. Feb. 5, 1812. She d. June 30, 1836, ae. 90 years, and is buried beside her husband in the cemetery at Marlboro, Ct. Ch.: (1) Dr. Aaron Bigelow, b. at Colchester, Ct., June 8, 1768; m. Mary Dickinson. He was a physician, and resided at Granville, Mass., where he d. Apr. 18, 1803, ae. 34 years. Ch.: (a) Margaret E.; d. May 14, 1803, ae. 5 years. (b) Aurelius H.; d. June 15, 1803, ae. 2 years. (c) Aaron A.; d. Aug. 14, 1803; ae. 6 mo. (2) Abner Bigelow, b. in Colchester, Ct., Apr. 22, 1770; m. Jan. 15, 1809, Mary Foote, dau. of Aaron and Mary (Isham) Foote; b. Jan. 13, 1777. Resided in Marlboro, Ct. She d. June 7, 1835. He d. in 1823. P. S. (3) Jesse, b. Jan. 29, 1775; d. Nov. 10, 1778. (4) Henry, b. Jan. 29, 1775; d. Oct. 8, 1775 (twins). (5) Rev. Henry Bigelow, of Middletown, Vt.; b. at Colchester, Ct. Feb. 20, 1778. He took the degree of Bachelor of Arts at Yale College in 1802, and the degree of Master of Arts in 1805. Middlebury College granted him an honorary degree of Master of Arts in 1811. He was a subject of the revival

in college in 1802, and studied theology with Dr. Charles Backus, of Somers, Ct. He became pastor of the Congregational Church in Middletown, Vt., in Sept., 1805, where he remained until his death, June 25, 1832, in the 55th year of his age—a man loved and respected by all. In 1803, he married Abigail Clark, a niece by marriage of his theological instructor, in whose family she had lived for many years. She was b. Jan. 28, 1780, and d. in Findlay, O., Apr. 10, 1852. Ch.: (a) Margaret Foote Bigelow, b. July 17, 1804; m. Aiden H. Green, of Danby, Vt., May 13, 1835. She d. Dec. 10, 1840, and is buried beside her father in Middletown, Vt. Aiden H. Green d. Nov. 1, 1860. Ch.: (i) Henry Bigelow Green, b. Sept. 30, 1837; m. Sarah Spaulding, Sept. 21, 1867; b. May 27, 1840; res., Findlay, O., where he d. Feb. 15, 1892. He was 2nd Lieut of Co. B, 161st Regt., Ohio Volunteer Infantry. His family now reside at Los Angeles, Cal. Ch.: (1) Agnes Elizabeth Green, b. Apr. 9, 1870. (2) Horace Aiden Green, b. May 1, 1874; m. Sept. 1904, Phoebe Steele. (ii) Horace Clark Green, b. Nov. 6, 1840. He was in the service of his country in Harris's Light Cavalry, and d. from a gun-shot wound in his temples, Dec. 20, 1864, and is buried beside his mother in Middletown, Vt. (b) Abigail Clark Bigelow, b. Apr. 16, 1806; m. Apr. 22, 1835, Amos Frisbie, a physician, by whom she had two children. She d. Feb. 25, 1847, and is buried at Royalton, O. Ch.: (i) Celestia J., b. Sept. 21, 1836; d. May 2, 1905. (ii) Angilicia L., b. Jan. 4, 1840; d. June 12, 1879; m. Dec. 2, 1869, Edwin R. Hay. Ch.: (ii1) Abigail Hay, b. Feb. 24, 1871; m. June 25, 1895, Dr. Franklin Bennett Entrikin. Ch.: (ii1a) Edwin Wayne Entrikin, b. Nov. 21, 1896. (ii1b) Lorain Entrikin, b. Dec. 5, 1900. (ii2) Charles Edwin Hay, b. Mar. 3, 1876. (c) Nancy Hill Bigelow, b. Apr. 23, 1808; m. 1829, Alva Paul, a physician; b. July 14, 1805; d. Feb. 23, 1875. She d. May 14, 1865, and is buried at Royalton, O. Ch.: (i) Maria, b. in Vt., Oct. 30, 1830; m. Jan. 3, 1849, Joseph W. Clement, b. Nov. 2, 1824. She d. Sept. 22, 1854. He d. June 11, 1903. Ch.: (i1) Creed Paul Clement, b. Nov. 20, 1849; m. Jan. 31, 1878, Isabell Sherman. She was b. Apr. 1, 1862. Ch.: (i1a) Helen Jane Clement, b. Feb. 8, 1878; m. Robert Stewart. (i1b) Mamie Alice Clement, b. Aug. 7, 1881; m. John Miller. (i1c) John Paul Clement, b. Oct. 2, 1883. (i1d) Grace Isabell Clement, b. Sept. 6, 1885. (i1e) May Elizabeth Clement, b. May 15, 1890. (i1f) Leonora Anna Clement, b. Jan. 17, 1893. (i1g) Vera Ruth Clement, b. Nov. 28, 1898. (i1h) Ervin Creed Clement, b. Sept. 8, 1901. (i2) Charles R. Clement, b. May 1, 1852; is a physician, and resides at Groveport, O.; m. Sept. 25, 1879, Elizabeth Freed; b. Nov. 28, 1854; no issue. (ii) Henry Bigelow Paul, b. in Vermont May 6, 1833; m. Oct. 4, 1855, Sarah Lockwood; b. Sept. 29, 1837; res., Petersburg, Neb. He d. Oct. 25, 1872. Ch.: (ii1) Alva Lockwood, b. June 20, 1856; d. Oct. 8, 1856. (ii2) Martha Helen, b. Feb. 16, 1859; d. Mar. 26, 1879. (ii3) Alfreda Leona, b. Nov. 11, 1861; m. July 20, 1887, F. W. Sullivan; b.

(ii3b) William Edwin, b. Jan. 12, 1891. (ii3c) Orville Leo, b. Nov. 5, 1893. (ii3d) Susanna Mary, b. Dec. 21, 1897. (ii3e) Henry Bigelow, b. Sept. 15, 1905. (ii4) Susan Mitchell, b. Mar. 5, 1864; d. Nov. 27, 1880. (ii5) Nancy Bigelow, b. June 14, 1867; d. Dec. 17, 1872. (ii6) Horace Edwin, b. Feb. 15, 1870; d. Dec. 24, 1872. (iii) Abigail Paul, b. in Vermont, and died, ae. 6 years. (iv) Horace A. Paul, b. in Ohio, May 20, 1841; m. 1874, Jane Ford, b. in 1858; res., Kas. Ch.: (iv1) Alva Leroy Paul, b. Jan. 14, 1875. (v) Alva Leroy Paul, b. Sept. 6, 1848; m. Oct. 27, 1875, Gertrude A. Paul; b. Sept. 18, 1850. He is a physician, and resides at Ottawa, O. Ch.: (v1) Edwin T. Paul, b. Dec. 10, 1876. (v2) Gertrude L. Paul, b. May 30, 1878; m. Oct. 12, 1896, Frank Wilson; b. Dec. 15, 1876. Ch.: (v2a) Paul Wilson, b. Feb. 27, 1898. (v2b) Reed Wilson, b. Aug. 15, 1899. (vi) Helen Paul, b. March 1850; m. Emmet Bigelow Williams; res., Portland, Ore., where she d. Feb. 20, 1899. Ch.: (vi1) Lenore Lorain Williams. Was graduated at Leland Stanford University with A. B. degree in 1905. (d) Aaron Henry Bigelow, b. July 21, 1810; was graduated at Middlebury College in 1836; m. Eliza Ann Green, of Danby, Vt., and moved to Findlay, O., where for a time he practiced law, subsequently moving to a farm near Atwood, Ind., where he d. Apr. 24, 1868. Ch.: (i) Margaret Foote. (ii) Clarinda Adelaide. (iii) Edwin Green. (iv) Nellie Vermont. (e) Philip Doddridge Bigelow, b. at Middletown, Vt., Dec. 1, 1812; m. in Erie county, Ohio, May 5, 1840, Harriet Hine Frisbie, formerly of Rutland Co., Vt.; b. Nov. 11, 1821. Removed to Findlay, O., July 4, 1841. He was a major in the Ohio Militia in 1839, and was a link in the "Underground Railway." He was a merchant in the early 40's, and later resided on Bigelow Hill, where he d. Aug. 13, 1868, and is buried in the family lot in Maple Grove Cemetery in Findlay, O. Mr. Bigelow had five children. (i) Frank Frisbie Bigelow, b. Jan. 28, 1850; m. Oct. 28, 1874, Viola A. Stephenson. He d. May 27, 1903. Ch.: (i1) Bertha B., b. Oct. 15, 1877; d. Sept. 26, 1878. (i2) Clarence C., b. Feb. 8, 1880. (i3) Edna V., b. July 21, 1883. (i4) Ethel A., b. Sept. 14, 1884. (i5) Gail I., b. April 19, 1888. (ii) Charles Henry Bigelow, b. June 5, 1854; m. Oct. 15, 1879, Flora May Vance, b. May 22, 1858, dau. of Horace M. and Flora (Shattuck) Vance. She d. Nov. 22, 1895. Ch.: (ii1) Bernard Barton Bigelow, b. Aug. 5, 1882. Was graduated at the Ohio State University with the degree of Ph. B. in 1903; and later at Yale University, with the degree of M. A., in 1905. Resides with his father on Bigelow Hill, Findlay, O. (iii) Ella Jane Bigelow; b. Jan. 15, 1858; m. June 15, 1881, George L. Cusac; b. Oct. 5, 1854. Ch.: (iii1) Inez May Cusac, b. Oct. 26, 1884. (iv) Effie Lorain Bigelow, b. July 12, 1860; d. Jan. 31, 1863. (v) Everton Bigelow, b. June 29, 1863, and d. Aug. 15, 1865. (f) Lucia Lorain Bigelow, b. Apr. 27, 1816; d. May 22, 1874; m. Apr. 23, 1845, Elijah Williams, a lawyer, b. Aug. 4' 1809; d. May 16, 1886. Moved to Salem, Ore. Ch.: (i) Helen Lorain Williams, b. June 25, 1848, in Findlay, O.; m. Nov. 9, 1870, in Salem, Ore., to Milton Adams Stratton, who was b. in Big Creek, Jefferson Co., Ind., in 1838; d. in Portland, Ore., Feb. 24, 1895. Ch.: (i1) Creed Williams Stratton, b. Sept. 16, 1872. (i2) Carroll Bigelow Stratton, b. Nov. 10, 1878. (i3) Milton Adams Stratton, b. Oct. 31, 1884. (i4) Lloyd Lorain Stratton, b. Sept. 30, 1886. All reside in Oregon City, Ore. (ii) Emmet Bigelow Williams, b. Feb. 15, 1853; m. 1st Helen Paul, who was b. Apr. 7, 1851; d. Feb. 23, 1899. They were married July 6, 1882. Ch.: (ii1) Lenore Lorain Williams, b. Oct. 25, 1883; A.B. Leland Stanford University, May, 1905. (ii2) Paul Paine Williams, b. July 10, 1886; d. Sept. 5, 1886. Mr. Williams m. 2nd June 13, 1900, Mary Eloise Combs, who was b. Aug. 11, 1856; d. Mar. 12, 1902. (g) Eliza Jane Bigelow, b. Oct 22, 1820; d. Feb. 4, 1873; m. Nov. 11, 1845, Ezra Brown, a lawyer, b. Aug. 4, 1814; d. Apr. 17, 1892; res., Findlay, O. Ch.: (i) Clark Wiltsie Brown, b. Aug. 10, 1846; d. in the service of his country at Memphis, Tenn., Apr. 13, 1863. Was a member of Co. F, 57th Regt., Ohio Volunteer Infantry. (ii) Emmet Bigelow Brown, b. Sept. 12, 1851; d. July, 1853. (iii) Emma Bigelow Brown, b. Mar. 7, 1854; m. May 4, 1877, Surrel Pearson De Wolf. Ch.: (iii1) Clark Frisbie De Wolf, b. July 21, 1880. Was a member of Co. M, 35th Regt. U. S. Volunteers, and saw service in the Phillipines. (iii2) Metta Abigail De Wolf, b. Oct. 15, 1882. (iv) Metta Clark Brown, b. Oct. 1, 1863. (6) Dr. Jesse Bigelow, son of Azariah and Margaret (Foote) Bigelow; was b. in Colchester, Conn., May 18, 1780; m. Oct. 12, 1818, Roxy Robbins. He was graduated from Yale College, and practised medicine in East Haddam, Conn., where he d. May 2, 1823. Ch.: (a) Amelia Mellicent, b. Oct. 25, 1820; m. Dec. 5, 1848, John Robert Holliday; res., Baltimore, Md., where she d. July 6, 1881. Ch.: (i) Frances Belknap, b. Sept. 3, 1857. (b) William Jesse Bigelow, b. May 21, 1823; m. Sept. 5, 1848, Elizabeth Ann Seeley; res., New York, where he d. Dec. 4, 1849, leaving one dau. (i) Amelia Jessie, b. Sept. 27, 1849; m. Nov. 5, 1885, Samuel Dibble Seelye, M. D.; res., Montgomery, Ala. Ch.: (i1) Ethel Bigelow Seelye, b. Sept. 2, 1887.

238. vi. ESTHER, b. Apr. 13, 1748; m. Oct. 17, 1775, Caleb Gates, of East Haddam, Ct.; d. Oct. 11, 1799. He d. Feb., 1822, ae. 73. Ch.: (1) Caleb. (2) Selden. (3) Russell. (4) Esther.

239. vii. LUCY, b. July 28, 1750; m. Nov. 3, 1774, Joseph, son of Joseph and Abigail (Fuller) Gates, of East Haddam, Ct.; d. May 30, 1810. He d. Sept. 3, 1832, ae. 78. Ch.: (1) Epaphroditus. (2) Lucy. (3) Olive. (4) Orrin. (5) Uri. (6) Eli.

240. viii. MARY, b. Jan. 8, 1753; m. Oct. 17, 1775, Stephen, son of Richard and Patience (Rowley) Skinner, of Colchester, Ct.; d. Apr. 14, 1785. He d. 1842, in Hamilton, Madison Co., N. Y. Ch.: (1) Mary. (2) Stephen. (3) Alfred. (4) Amasa.

241. ix. DAN, b. Aug. 16, 1755; m. Isabella Henry, 770-81.

74. ISRAEL FOOTE, (25, 9, 5, 1,) b. Oct. 16, 1713; m. Dec. 28, 1748, Elizabeth, dau. of Thomas Kimberley; d. Aug. 25, 1785. She was b. Jan. 13, 1715; d. Jan. 6, 1798.

242. i.   ELIZABETH, b. May 29, 1750; m. Nov. 5, 1778, Rev. David, son of John and Mehitable (Metcalf) Huntington; d. Oct. 25, 1845. He was b. Nov. 24, 1745; d. Apr. 12, 1812, ae. 67, in North Lyme.

243. ii. MARY, b. Apr. 3, 1752; m. Nov. 5, 1778, Nathaniel Otis, of Colchester, Ct.; d. Nov. 14, 1837. He d. Mar. 18, 1834, ae. 81, in New London. Ch.: (1) Mary. (2) Israel. (3) Asa, b. Feb. 10, 1786; d. Mar. 10, 1874. He gave nearly one million dollars to the American Board of Missions. (4) Betty.

244. iii. ISRAEL, b. Jan. 30, 1755; m. Sarah Otis, Elizabeth Worthington, Prudence Hale, 782-90.

245. iv. ABIGAIL, b. Mar. 13, 1757; m. Jan. 31, 1791, Nathaniel Foote. See No. 235-for family record.

76. DANIEL FOOTE, (25, 9, 3, 1,) b. Feb. 6, 1716; m. 1st, June 9, 1743, Margaret dau. of Ebenezer Parsons, of Springfield, Mass.; she d. July 6, 1765; m. 2nd, July 31, 1766, Mary, wid. of Rev. Thomas Skinner, of Colchester, Ct., nee Mary Thompson. She d. 1814, ae. 96. He d. Dec. 27, 1801. He was a professor of religion,—a grave and venerable man of the highest respectability; res., Colchester, Ct., and Williamstown, Mass.

246. i.   DANIEL, b. June 21, 1744; m. Elizabeth Margaret Woodcock, 791-4.

247. ii.   ISAAC, b. Jan. 4, 1746; m. Mary Kellogg, 795-802.

248. iii. ELI, b. Oct. 30, 1747; m. Roxana Ward, 803-12.

249. iv.   MARGARET, b. May 31, 1749; d. Dec. 14, 1752.

250. v.   MARTHA, b. Jan. 27, 1751; m. Dec. 8, 1768, John Barney; d. June 30, 1797; res., Colchester and Norwich, Ct., and Newburg, N. Y. Ch.: (1) John. (2) Daniel. (3) Eli. (4) Harry.

251. vi.   MARGARET, b. May 24, 1752; m. Nov. 11, 1778; Rev. Emmerson Foster, of Killingly, Ct.; she d. Jan.,-1807. Ch.: (1) Nathaniel E. (2) Margaret Parsons. (3) Isaac. (4) Hannah. (5) Whitbey. (6) Harriet.

252. vii. ANN, b. Apr. 11, 1754; m. 1773, Gen. Thompson Joseph Skinner; d. Dec. 15, 1808. He d. ———. Ch.: (1) Thompson Joseph. (2) Mary. (3) Thomas. (4) Ann. (5) Eliza. (6) George Denison.

253. viii. EBENEZER, b. Apr. 12, 1756; m. Jerusa Foote and ———. Rosekrans, 813-6.

254. ix.   STEPHEN, b. Jan. 10, 1758; m. Hannah Waterman, 817-22.

255. x.   JOHN, b. Feb. 17, 1760; m. Hannah Johnson.

256. xi.   JUSTIN, b. July 31, 1762; m. Maria Evertson.

257. xii. Child (name not given), d. in infancy.

80. CHARLES FOOTE, (25, 9, 3, 1,) b. Nov. 10, 1723; m. Oct., 1750, Jerusha Chamberlain, dau. of John Chamberlain. He was a member of the 4th Reg. Connecticut troops, and was at the Siege of Boston; d. Aug. 25, 1795. She d. April 10, 1782, ae. 50; res., Colchester, Ct.

260. i. LOIS, b. Apr. 22, 1751; m. Nov. 10, 1772, Dan Worthington, of
Colchester, Ct., and Lenox, Mass.; d. Feb. 22, 1840, in Lenox,
Mass. He d. Oct. 24, 1821, ae. 74, in Lenox, Mass. Ch.: (1)
Molly. (2) Dan. (3) Jerusah. (4) Charles. (5) Judith.
(6) Betsy. (7) John. (8) Gad. (9) Guy. (10) Robert.
(11) Laura. (12) Louisa.

261. ii. CHARLES, b. June 5, 1753; m. Sarah Day, 823-34.

262. iii. JERUSHA, b. Mar. 2, 1755; m. Feb. 25, 1779, Joseph Johnson, of
Colchester, Ct.; d. Jan. 21, 1831, in Coventry, Chenango Co.,
N. Y. He d. Nov. 17, 1808, ae. 58, in Colchester, Ct. Ch.:
(1) Demis. (2) Elisha. (3) Gurdon. (4) Clarissa. (5) Lois.
(6) Gurdon. (7) Ralph. (8) Theodosia. (9) William. (10)
Jerusha.

263. iv. ELISHA, b. Jan. 10, 1757; m. Phebe Sabin, 835.

264. v. EUNICE, b. Mar. 13, 1759.

265. vi. CHLOE, b. June 5, 1764; m. Richard Mott, of Hudson, N. Y.;
moved to Sheffield, Mass. Ch.: (1) Henry. (2) Melissa. (3)
Russell Foote. (4) Julia Ann.

266. vii. ELIAS, b. Oct. 4, 1766; m. Sally Tracy, 836-42.

267. viii. RUSSELL, b. Dec. 29, 1769; m. Anna Gillett, Sylvia Loveland,
Salome Parsons, 843-6.

268. ix. WILLIAM, b. Aug. 4, 1772; m. Mary Ann Lord, 847-52.

81. ASA FOOTE, (25, 9, 3, 1,) b. May 4, 1726; m. Apr. 26, 1752, Jerusha,
dau. of Ezra Carter; d. May 11, 1799. She d. May 15, 1770, ae. 44; res., Marlborough, Ct.

269. i. ASA, b. May 1, 1753; m. Lucy Kellogg, 853.

270. ii. JERUSHA, b. Feb. 24, 1755; m. Nov. 5, 1772, Nathaniel Cornwall,
of Portland, Ct.; d. May 30, 1793. He d. Mar., 1823, ae. 73.
Ch.: (1) Asa. (2) Jerusha. (3) Anna. (4) Sarah. (5) Asa.
(6) Ezra. (7) David.

271. iii. EZRA, b. Aug. 22, 1757; d. May 16, 1780, unm.

272. iv. DAVID, b. Oct. 5, 1760. Was graduated at Dartmouth College.
Was rector of the Episcopal Church, in Rye, N. Y., where he
d. Aug. 1, 1793, unm.

273. v. JOEL, b. June 26, 1763; m. Abigail Robbens Lord and Rachel
Lord, 854-65.

274. vi. ROGER, b. June 9, 1765; m. Eunice Bulkley, 866-77.

82. JARED FOOTE, (25, 9, 3, 1,) b. Aug. 28, 1728; m. 1st, 1753, Hannah,
dau. of Capt. Timothy and Hannah (Bradford) Buell. She b. Nov. 9, 1735, in
Marlborough, Ct.; d. Apr. 5, 1774. M. 2nd, Hepzibah, dau. of Charles Phelps, from
whom he was subsequently divorced. M. 3rd, Joanna Jennings, widow of ———
Jennings. He d. Jan. 28, 1806. She d. May 17, 1823, ae. 75.

275. i. HANNAH, b. Nov. 19, 1754; m. 1773, Philip Warner, of Stafford,
Ct., and Cornwall, Vt.; d. Sept. 27, 1822. He d. Nov. 14, 1826,
ae. 74. Ch.: (1) Philip, (2) Hannah, b. m. Collins. (3)
Jared, b. Ellington, Ct., Feb. 2, 1782; m. Bennington, Vt., Feb.
16, 1803, Anna Rockwell. She was b. Oct. 30, 1780; d.
Jan. 3, 1827, at Shoreham, Vt.; m. 2nd Mary Hamilton. He
d. Aug. 17, 1829. Ch.: (a) Horace Warner, b. Dec. 11, 1804;

(4)

m. Feb. 22, 1827, Laura Cooper. Ch.: Lester L. Warner; res., Dansville, Mich., and four others. (b) Willes Warner, b. ——; res., Sylvan, Mich. Ch.: Chas. Henry Warner, res., Dexter, Mich., and three others. (d) Dennis Warner, b. ——; res., Dexter, Mich. (e) Lucy Warner; m. Amos Wanen Davis; res., Jackson, Mich. 1 ch. (e) Anna Warner, b. ——; m. Lucius H. Cooper; res., Lansing, Mich. (f) Jared Warner, b. ——; res., Flenning, in Howell, Mich. Ch.: (i) Sarah, b. ——; m. Damon W. Boyd; res., Sylvan, Mich. (ii) Ellen A., m. Chas. P. Hill; res., Owosso, Mich.; and three others. (4) Thomas. (5) Sally. (6) Dan Warner, b. Feb. 29, 1792; m. 1st, Mary Goodrich, 2nd Nancy Gates, 3rd Mrs. Gillett. He was Dea. of Congo. Ch. of Cornwall for many years; d. and buried at Cornwall, Sept., .1881. Ch.: (a) Hannah Warner, b. Dec., 1814; m. Benjamin Wooster, of Whiting, Vt. 2 ch. (b) Philip Buel Warner, b. May 14, 1816; m. Ellen ——. Ch.: (i) Mary Warner, b. ——; m. Oriska Gillett. (ii) Susan Warner, b. ——; m. Earl Thrall. 8 ch. (c) Lucy Ann, b. 1818; m. Edwin Hayward; res., Chicago, Ill. (d) Clancliur Henry, b. Aug. 17, 1823; m. Eliza Cook. Ch.: (i) Frank H. Warner, b. Feb. 22, 1858; m. June 1, 1893, Harriet Lane. She was b. Aug. 23, 1866. Ch.: (i1) Carlton Henry Warner, b. May 7, 1894. (i2) Mary Pauline Warner, b. Aug. 6, 1901. (e) Rollin Evanchler Warner, b. May 2, 1825. (f) Mary Susan, b. Apr. 24, 1827; m. Apr. 26, 1858, Rev. Isaac Farwell Holton. He was b. Aug. 30, 1812; d. Jan. 25, 1874. She d. Sept. 7, 1901. Ch.: (i) Clara E., b. Jan. 16, 1859; d. Mar. 19, 1879. (ii) Nancy Gates, b. Cornwall, Vt., Aug. 25, 1860. (iii) Edward Payson, b. Millsgrove, Ill., Feb. 24, 1864; m. Aug. 7, 1894, Gertrude Minnie Sears. She was b. Groton, N. H., Mar. 5, 1864. He is a missionary to Manamadure, India. Ch. all b. there. Ch.: (iii1) Clara E., b. Sept. 22, 1895; d. Apr. 1, 1897. (iii2) Olive Warner Holton, b. Jan. 17, 1897; d. Dec. 17, 1902. (iii3) Henry S. Holton, b. Sept. 3, 1898. (iii4) Ruth Gladys, b. Dec. 19, 1901. (iii5) Sylvia Gates Holton, b. Oct. 16, 1903. (iii6) Faith Kirubai Holton, b. Nov. 19, 1905; d. same day. (iv) Charles Sumner Holton, b. Medford, Mass., May 4, 1866; m. Somerset, N. Y., Dec. 20, 1892, Grace Adelaid Toll. He is pastor of the First Congo. Ch. in Newburyport, Mass. No. ch. (g) Levi Gates, b. May, 1830. (h) Bushnell Miner, b. Apr., 1836. (7) Sally, b. 1796; m. Jesse Keeler. She d. 1884.

276. ii.   RHODA, b. June 3, 1757; d. 1812, unm.
277. iii.   LUCY, b. 1758; d. in infancy.
278. iv.   MERCY, b. July 6, 1760; m. June 13, 1785, Jonathan, son of Jonathan and Elizabeth (Bachelder) Porter, of Ellington, Ct.; d. Apr. 22, 1835. He d. Mar. 31, 1825, ae. 77. Ch.: (1) Sally, b. Mar. 27, 1786. (2) Louisa. (3) Marilda. (4) Lemuel, m. Lucinda Jennings. (5) Sally. (6) Betsy. (7) Jerusha. (8) Horace; d. at sea. (9) Dolly. (10) Guy. (11) Philo, b. Jan. 27, 1806; res., Windsorville, Ct.

279. v. JARED, b. 1764; d. in infancy.
280. vi. LUCY, b. Dec. 6, 1767; m. 1st, Nov. 19, 1789, Reuben Gunn, of Pittsfield, Mass. He d. Sept. 19, 1794, ae. 30. M. 2nd, Oct. 10, 1797, Cordial Jennings, of Ellington, Ct. Ch.: (1) Hannah. (2) Reuben L. (3) Lucy F. (4) Lucinda. (5) Sherburn. (6) Joel F. (7) David. (8) Betsy. (9) Chauncy. (10) Joel Bradford.
281. vii. JARED, b. Sept. 30, 1770; m. Lucinda Jennings, 878-86.
282. viii. CHILD, not named, d. in infancy.
283. ix. ASA, b. Jan. 17, 1788; m. Eunice Ingraham and Maria Tooker, 887-95.

85. EPHRAIM, (26, 9, 3, 1,) b. Apr. 27, 1716; m. Margaret Smith. She d. July 4, 1754. M. 2nd, Miss Lord; 3rd, Lucretia Lewis. He d. 1800. She d. 1815, ae. 93, at Vernon, Oneida Co., N. Y.; res., Stockbridge, Mass.
284. i. Ephraim, b. ———; m. Lydia Cushman, 896-904.
285. ii. ELIZABETH, b. ———; m. Cornelius Van Buren, of Kinderhook and Johnstown, N. Y.
286. iii. ASA, b. ———; m. ———, 905-9.
287. iv. DEBORAH, b. ———; m. Benjamin Crippen, New Concord, N. Y.; both d.; no more known.
288. v. PEGGY, b. ———; m. Selah Trowbridge, of Chatham, N. Y.; both d.; no more known.
289. vi. SAMUEL, b. ———; m. ———, 910-5.
290. vii. JOHN, b. ———; m. Elizabeth Babcock, 917-25.
291. viii. LYDIA, b. ———; m. John Darrow, of New Canaan, N. Y.; both d. Ch.: (1) Betsy. (2) Lydia. (3) Sally. (4) John. (5) Mead. (6) Rufus. (7) Daniel.
292. ix. SALLY, b. ———.
293. x. GEORGE, b. ———.
294. xi. HANNAH, b. ———.
295. xii. ADONIJAH, b. Apr. 14, 1768; m. Sabra Mott, 926-33.
296. xiii. POLLY, b. ———.
297. xiv. WILLIAM, b. ———.

89. ADONIJAH FOOTE (26, 9, 3, 1,) b. 1729; m. 1st, Oct. 24, 1754, Grace, dau. of Joseph and Esther (Hungerford) Day, of Colchester Ct. She d. Mar. 16, 1776; m. 2nd, Mar. 17, 1777, Abigail, widow of Jonathan Roberts, and dau. of Jonathan Emmons. He d. Aug. 19, 1795. She d. Dec. 30, 1811, ae. 84; res., Colchester, Ct.
298. i. JESSE, b. Dec. 25, 1756; m. Mary Skinner, 934-45.
299. ii. ADONIJAH, b. Mar. 26, 1760; m. Sarah Foster and ——— Chittenton, 946-56.
300. iii. REUBEN, b. Nov. 8, 1761; m. Lydia Emmons, 957-9.
301. iv. GRACE, b. Dec. 19, 1763; m. Dec., 1779, James Williams, of Colchester, Ct. He d. Feb. 29, 1840, ae. 84. Ch.: (1) Gilbert. (2) Grace. (3) Sally. (4) James. (5) Roderick. (6) Sophrona. (7) Anna. (8) Aristarchus. (9) Deborah.
302. iv. EPHRAIM, b. Aug. 1, 1765; m. Lydia Ackley, 960-70.
303. vi. SARAH, b. Mar. 3, 1767; m. Oct. 25, 1786, William Dunham, of Colchester and Middletown, Ct.; d. Mar. 31, 1837. He d. Mar.

6, 1837, ae. 70. Ch.: (1) William. (2) Julius. (3) Sarah. (4) Amanda. (5) Lucretia. (6) Elizabeth Green. (7) Edward. (8) Eleazur. (9) Samuel. (10) Mary.

304. vii. EPAPHRODITUS, b. Sept. 14, 1769; m. Anna Bixley, Sylvia Beebe, Mehitabel Douglass and Anna Ives, 971-81.

305. viii. DEBORAH, b. Apr. 24, 1774; m. Dec. 26, 1792, Zelotes, son of Daniel and Mary (Brainard) Bigelow, of Colchester, Ct., and of Brookfield, Vt.; d. June 14, 1846. Ch.: (1) Talitha, b. Apr. 2, 1793. (2) Deborah. (3) Zelotes. (4) Abel. (5) Nabby. (6) Mary Brainard. (7) Lucinda Malvina, b. Aug. 17, 1815.

306. ix. TALITHA, b. Mar. 16, 1776; m. Aug. 6, 1794, Roswell Chamberlain, Colchester, Ct. He d. Mar. 14, ae. 72. Ch.: (1) Talitha, b. Oct. 6, 1796. (2) Harriet. (3) Grace. (4) Clarissa. (5) Mary. (6) Roxanna. (7) Sarah. (8) William. (9) Elizabeth, b. Aug. 13, 1821.

92. JOSIAH FOOTE, (27, 9, 3, 1,) b. July 28, 1713; m. Dec. 7, 1738, Sarah, dau. of William Chamberlain, of Colchester, Ct. She d. Dec. 29, 1799, ae. 81, in Windsor, Ct. He d. Feb. 17, 1798, in Windsor, Ct.

306¹. i. JERUSHA, b. June 4, 1739; m. Dec. 16, 1760, Samuel Bancraft, of East Windsor, Ct. She d. of lung fever, Mar. 26, 1803. He d. July 1, 1830, ae. 93. Ch.: (1) Anna, b. Oct. 30, 1761; m. Joseph Newberry, of East Windsor, Ct. (2) Anson, b. Nov. 19, 1763; m. Mirriam Elmer, dau. of Timothy Elmer, of East Windsor, Ct. (3) Laysel, b. Aug. 21, 1767; m., res., Westfield, Mass. (4) Jerusha, b. Sept. 12, 1769. (5) Polly, b. June 8, 1772. (6) Sophia, b. Apr. 20, 1775; m. ―――― Hodget, of Westfield, Mass. (7) Samuel, b. Mar. 30, 1777; m. Sally, dau. of Joseph Hosmer, of East Windsor, Ct. (8) Theodocia, b. May 24, 1779; m. Capt. Owen, son of Dr. Tudor, of East Windsor, Ct. (9) Solomon, b. May 12, 1738.

306². ii. DELIGHT, b. Aug. 11, 1741; m. Phineas Drake, of Windsor, Ct. She d. of lung fever, Mar. 16, 1803. He d. 1803.

306³. iii. ELITHEA, b. July 17, 1744; m. Apr. 25, 1768, Prince Brewster, of Lebanon, Ct.. afterwards of Colchester, North Bolton, Coventry and Hartford, Ct. She d. Feb. 9, 1802, in Hartford, Ct. He d. Oct. 16, 1816, ae. 68, in Windsor, Ct. Ch.: (1) Betsey, b. Sept. 3, 1769, Colchester. (2) Josiah Foote, b. Colchester, Oct. 3, 1771. (3) Sally, b. Colchester, July 6, 1773. (4) Polly, b. Colchester, Oct. 16, 1775. (5) Hopey, b. North Bolton, Apr. 20, 1778. "(6) Pascal Paoli, b. Coventry, July 6, 1780. (7) John Emmanuel, b. Coventry, Apr. 12, 1782. (8) Fanny, b. Hartford, Jan. 22, 1784. (9) Charles Augustus, b. Hartford, Aug. 7, 1787; d. 1816, in North Carolina, where he had gone for his health.

306⁴. iv. SARAH, b. June 15, 1746; d. Nov. 7, 1747.

306⁵. v. SARAH, b. Apr. 11, 1748; supposed to have died in childhood.

306⁶. vi. BARZILLIA, b. 1750; d. Jan. 17, 1751.

306⁷. vii. SON, not named; b. Jan., 1752; d. Jan., 1752.

306⁸. viii. BETTY, bap. Oct. 27, 1754; d. in childhood.

93. JONITHAN FOOTE, (27, 9, 3, 1,) b. Mar. 23, 1715; m. May 25, 1749, Sarah, dau. of John Fenner, of Saybrook, Ct.; d. Nov. 11, 1803, in Lee, Mass. She d. 1791, ae. 61, in Lee, Mass.; res., Colchester, Ct., and Lee, Mass.

Jonathan Foote, with five sons, came from Colchester to Lee, Mass., in 1770. Sons, Jonathan, Fenner, David, Asabel, Solomon; daughter, Lovice.

The first religious service was held in Oliver West's barn, Jan. 8, 1778.

The haymow, it is said, was used as a singer's gallery, and the five sons of Jonathan Foote, with their sister, Lovice, constituted the choir, a fact commemorated by the poet and wit of the time, Nathan Dillingham:

> "David and Ase sung base;
> Jonathan and Fenner sang tenor;
> 'Vice and Sol beat them all."

307. i. FREELOVE, b. Mar. 11, 1750; m. Simeon Wright, of Rutland, Vt. Ch.: (1) Robert Wright, b. Dec. 2, 1770. (2) Simeon Wright, b. Mar. 12, 1773. (3) Freelove Wright, b. Oct. 28, 1774. (4) Lucy Wright, b. May 31, 1776. (5) Daniel Wright, b. June 6, 1778. (6) David Wright, b. July 19, 1780. (7) Wait Wright, b. May 28, 1783. (8) Sallie Wright, b. Apr. 9, 1785. (9) Jonathan Wright, b. Sept. 14, 1787. (10) Patience Wright, b. Mar. 7, 1789. (11) Rachel Wright, b. Rutland, Vt., Apr. 3, 1792; m. 1814, Ezekiel Scovel, of Rutland, Vt., in 1810; they moved to Hartford, O.; she d. Dec. 24, 1873, in St. Marie, Wis.; he d. 1834. Ch.: (a) William Franklin Scovel, b. Rutland, Vt., Oct. 28, 1815; m. May 26, 1848, Margaret Gushery, dau. of Henry Fulton, of West Moreland Co., Pa. She was b. Sewickley, Pa., Feb. 26, 1822; d. Aug. 25, 1868, in St. Marie, Wis. He was educated at Dennison College. Ch.: (i) Jane Scovel, b. Hartford, O., May 5, 1849. (ii) Ezekiel Scovel, b. Hartford, O., Jan. 21, 1851; d. Jan. 29, 1884. (iii) Mary Elizabeth Scovel, b. July 27, 1853; m. Dec. 19, 1878, Henry Gibbons, of Fayette Co., Pa. He is a graduate of Amherst College, has taught classics for thirty years; since 1894 has been prof. of Latin literature in the University of Pa. She has the old family Bible of Freelove Foote. Ch. (all born in Pittsburg, Pa.): (iii1) Alice Margaret Gibbons, b. Oct. 14, 1879; d. Nov. 5, 1883. (iii2) Helen Wilson Gibbons, b. July 14, 1881. (iii3) Howard Vernon Gibbons, b. Aug. 23, 1884. (iii4) Mary Fulton Gibbons, b. June 15, 1886. (iii5) Lois Oliphant Gibbons, b. Aug. 30, 1887. (iii6) Caroline Scovel Gibbons, b. June 3, 1889. (iv) Keziah Scovel, b. Dec. 1, 1856; d. June 10, 1875. (v) Harriet Scovel, b. Hartford, O., Feb. 24, 1858; d. Jan. 19, 1884. (vi) Franklin Scovel, b. St. Marie, O., Feb. 16, 1864. (b) Harriet Wright, b. Hartford, 1817. (c) Ezra Wright, b. Hartford, 1819. (d) Maria Wright, b. Hartford, 1824. (e) Mariette, b. Hartford, 1826. (f) Simeon Wright, b. Hartford, 1833. (12) Caroline Wright, b. Dec. 14, 1794.

308. ii. JONATHAN, b. Mar. 30, 1752; m. Deliverance Gibbs, 982-6.

309. iii. FENNER, b. Oct. 5, 1754; m. Sarah Wilcox, 987-95.

310. iv. SARAH, b. Jan. 12, 1758; m. abt. 1778, Jesse Clark, of Lee, Mass. Ch.: (1) Eli, b. Sept. 3, 1779. (2) Cynthia. (3) Jesse.

(4) Sarah.   (5) Mildred.   (6) Triphena.   (7) John.   (8)
Charles. (9) Alma. (10) Chauncey Fenner. (11) Ruth, b.
May 24, 1802.

311. v.   DAVID, b. Sept. 4, 1760; m. Betsey Hamblin, 996-1005.
312. vi.   ASAHEL, b. Apr. 22, 1763; m. Anna Abbot, 1006-13.
313. vii. LOVICA, b. 1765; d. Mar. 17, 1840, unm.
314. viii. SOLOMON, b. ———, 1788; m. Betsey Crassett, 1014-17.

96. JOSEPH FOOTE, (27, 9, 3, 1,) b. May 12, 1721; m Thankful ———.
He d. Feb., 1757; res., Colchester, Ct.
315. i.   WALTER, b. May 18, 1755, supposed to have d. young.
316. ii.   WEALTHY, b. May 18, 1755, supposed to have d. young.

97. HABAKUK FOOTE, (27, 9, 3, 1,) b. Jan. 27, 1723; m. Mar. 5, 1754, Mary,
widow of Elisah Welles, and dau. of William Chamberlain; d. 1803.. She d. May
14, 1801, ae. 80; res., Colchester, Ct.
317. i.   OLIVE, bap. Oct. 12, 1755; d. Oct. 22, 1776.
318. ii.   EUNICE, bap. Sept. 5,.1756; m. Aug. 12, 1787, William Hall, of
            Colchester, Ct., and Groton, Ct.; d. July 15, 1826, in Marietta,
            O. He d. Aug. 16, 1810, ae. 53, in Groton, Ct. Ch.: (1)
            Polly, b. June 9, 1788; m. Sidney Dodge. (2) Wyllys. (3)
            Joseph Ely. (4) Theodocia, m. Daniel H. Buell. (5) William.
            (6) Eunice, b. Sept. 3, 1804; m. David B. Anderson.
319. iii. RHODA, bap. Aug. 26, 1759; d. June 26, 1761.
320. iv.   JOHN, b. 1763; m. Elizabeth Carey, 1018-19.
321. v.   THEODOSIA, b. Jan. 20, 1766; m. 1st, John Bulkley, of Colchester,
            Ct., Apr., 1787. He d. Oct. 10, 1788, ae. 29; m. 2nd, Aaron
            Buckland, of Colchester, Ct. He d. Apr. 8, 1829, ae. 73. She
            d. Dec. 1, 1802. Ch.: (1) Roxy, b. May 14, 1788; m. James M.
            Goodwin. (2) John. (3) Sophia, b. Jan. 1, 1801; m. 1st, Dr.
            Ebenezer W. Bull; m. 2nd, George Beach.,

99. JOHN FOOTE, (27, 9, 3, 1,) b. Aug. 15, 1728; m. 1st, Anna, dau. of John
and Mary (Otis) Thompson, of New London, Ct. She d. Mar. 28, 1798, ae. 64; m.
2nd, Maria Cathrine, dau. of John Miller, of Glastenbury, Ct. She d. Nov. 5, 1845,
ae. 86, in Glastenbury, Ct. He d. Oct. 9, 1818; res. Hebron, Ct.
322. i. JOSEPH, b. Oct. 7, 1800; m. Jerusha Ann Rose, 1020-30.

102. NOAH FOOTE, (27, 9, 3, 1,) b. 1738; m. 1st, Apr. 18, 1768, Esther, dau.
of Silas Kellogg, of Colchester, Ct. She d. Dec. 18, 1771, ae. 29; 2nd, Tabitha,
dau. of Ebenezer Shaylor, of Bolton, Ct., 1774; d. Feb. 28, 1809. She d. Aug. 1,
1815, ae. 62; res., Colchester, Vernon, Hebron and Columbia, Ct.
323. i.   SARAH, b. 1769; m. Dec., 1795, Israel Thompson, of Goshen, Ct.,
            and Windham, Green Co., N. Y. Ch.: (1) Diantha, Sept., 1796.
            (2) Eli, b. Aug. 7, 1798.
323. ii.   CHILD, not named; b. Dec., 1771; d. Dec. 17, 1771.
325. iii. LUCY, b. Mar. 1, 1775; m. May, 1796, George Charters, of Elling-
            ton, Ct., res., Springfield, Mass., Richmond, Va., New York, N. Y.
            While in New York he was of the firm of Charters & Williams,
            wholesale dry goods merchants. She d. Feb. 20, 1844. Ch.: (1)
            Dau., b. ———; d. in infancy. (2) Henry, b. ———; d. 3
            years of ae.
326. iv.   CHILD, not named; b. Apr. 26, 1777; d. May 27, 1777.

327. v.   ESTHER, b. July 13, 1778, Hebron, Ct.; unm.
328. vi.   NOAH, b. Oct. 15, 1780; d. July 10, 1786.
329. vii.   WALTER, b. Sept. 29, 1782; lost at sea abt. Jan. 1, 1805.
330. viii.   JULIUS, b. Mar. 19, 1785, Hebron, Ct.; unm.
331. ix.   JOSIA, b. June 27, 1787; d. at sea abt. Jan. 1, 1805.
332. x.   POLLY, b. June 27, 1789; m. Apr. 6, 1811, William Hewlett, of Richmond, Va. He d. Jan. 21, 1840, ae. 48. Ch.: (1) Louisa Malvina, b. Feb. 12, 1812; d. May 28, 1813. (2) Lucy Ann. (3) Mary Ann Tabitha. (4) Jane Elizabeth. (5) George C. (6) Son unnamed. (7) Maria Louisa. (8) Son unnamed, b. Oct. 28, 1824; d. in infancy.
333. xi.   SON not named, b. Dec. 7, 1791; d. in infancy.
334. xii.   CHILD, not named, b. Dec. 17, 1796; d. Jan. 17, 1797.
335. xiii.   HIRAM SHAYLOR, b. Apr. 14, 1799; m. Emily Mack, 1031-40.

104. JEREMIAH FOOTE, (28, 9, 3, 1,) b. Oct. 15, 1732; m. Sept. 14, 1749, Ruhamah, dau. of John and Hannah (Pomeroy) Northam; d. May 15, 1784. She b. Oct. 15, 1727; d. Feb. 8, 1809; res., Colchester, Ct.

336. i.   AMBROSE, bap. Apr. 11, 1750; d. same day.
337. ii.   AMBROSE, b. July 15, 1751; m. Anna Foote, 1041-5.
338. iii.   BETTY, b. Jan. 17, 1753; m. Apr. 3, 1777, Joseph Foote, 347.
339. iv.   STEPHEN, b. 1755; m. Esther Clark, 1046-51.
340. v.   UZZIEL, b. 1757; m. 1st, Elizabeth Clark and Lydia W. Metcalf, 1052-5.
341. vi.   JEREMIAH, bap. Jan. 21, 1759; m. Jerusha Taylor, 1056-61.
342. vii.   RUHAMAH, b. Oct. 15, 1760; m. Sept. 15, 1777, John Birge, of Hebron, Ct., and Franklin, N. Y. He d. May 17, 1838, ae. 84. Ch.: (1) Daniel, b. Jan. 31, 1779. (2) Betsy. (3) Dudley. (4) Pamela. (5) John. (6) Alfred. (7) Polly. (8) Dimis. (9) Charlotte, b. June 6, 1803.
343. viii.   ANN, b. June 13, 1762; m. Mar. 20, 1784, Edmund Bridges, of Colchester, Ct.; d. Feb. 23, 1842. He d. Sept. 11, 1816, ae. 53. Ch.: (1) Jeremiah, b. Dec. 19, 1785. (2) Samuel. (3) Marcus. (4) Edmund. (5) William. (6) Minerva. (7) Anna. (8) Uzziel, b. Nov. 22, 1800; res., Geneseo, N. Y.
344. ix.   HANNAH, b. Apr. 4, 1766; m. Jan. 28, 1789, Gibbons Mather; d. Oct. 18, 1844. He d. Aug. 5, 1815, ae. 55. Ch.: (1) Gibbons Parsons, b. Dec. 7, 1791; m. Dec. 27, 1812, Sophia Smith. (2) Henry De Wolf. (3) Hiram F. Whitney, Gen. P., 758. (4) Ralph Colton. (5) Son, not named. (6) Daniel W., b. Jan. 1, 1807.
345. x.   MARTIN, b. ———; he was never m.
346. xi.   ESTHER, bap. Oct. 27, 1771; m. Sept. 29, 1791, Ralph Taylor, Jr. He d. Sept. 27, 1828, ae. 60. Ch.: (1) Charles, b. July 15, 1792. (2) Esther. (3) Ralph. (4) Esther. (5) Mary D. (6) Hannah P. (7) Giles B. (8) Nancy M. (9) George. (10) Caroline. (11) Gibbons Mather, b. Jan. 24, 1814.

105. HOSEA FOOTE, (28, 9, 3, 1,) b. 1729; m. Apr. 8, 1756, Eunice, dau. of John Chamberlain; d. Sept. 23, 1808. She d. May 3, 1789, ae. 51 years; res., Colchester, Ct.

347. i.   JOSEPH, b. Oct. 26, 1755; m. Betty Foot (No. 338), 1062-70.
348. ii.   EUNICE, b. 1757; d. Aug. 27, 1759.
349. iii.   ANNA, b. July 23, 1759; d. Aug. 13, 1759.
350. iv.   HOSEA, b. Sept., 1763; m. Sally Bulkley, 1071-4.
351. v.   ANNA, b. Apr. 2, 1765.
352. vi.   EUNICE, b. Nov. 24, 1766; m. Nov. 24, 1785, Ezra Clark, 2nd,
           son of Ezra and Ann (Bates), of Colchester, Ct.; d. Aug. 1,
           1851. He d. Feb. 9, 1826, ae. 66. Ch.: (1) Ezra. (2) Eunice,
           twins, b. Jan. 22, 1787. (3) Jerusha. (4) George; m. Sophia
           Taylor (No. 354-3). Ch.: (a) Sarah, b. 1831; m. John Foote
           Calvin, b. Ezra, 1834. (c) Jerusha, b. 1835. (d) Margaret, b.
           1837. (e) Leonard Chester, b. 1842. (5) Sally, b. Mar. 1, 1796.
353. vii.   MARGARET, b. ———; d. young.
354. viii.   MARGARET, b. 1775; m. 1st, Oct. 28, 1792, Daniel Taylor, of
           Colchester, Ct.; He d. May 11, 1812, ae. 45; m. 2nd, John J.
           Avery, of Groton, Ct. She d. Nov. 6, 1843. Ch.: (1) Mar-
           garet, b. June 23, 1794; m Salmon C. Foote. (2) Daniel. (3)
           Sophia, m. her cousin, George Clark. (4) Lauria, b. 1807; m.
           Elisha A. Baker.
355. ix.   OLIVE, b. Sept. 17, 1781; m. 1st, Sept. 24, 1805, Daniel Hubbard,
           of Colchester, Ct. He d. Oct. 2, 1811, ae. 30; m. 2nd, Sept. 10,
           1821, Dr. Howell Rogers. Ch.: (1) Elizabeth Perkins, b. July
           24, 1806. (2) Abby, b. Feb. 20, 1810. (3) William Henry, b.
           Nov. 9, 1822. (4) George Hammond, b. Apr. 22, 1824. (5)
           Charles Howell, b. July 24, 1826.

113. SAMUEL FOOTE, (36, 10, 3, 1,) b. Nov. 12, 1728; m. abt. 1750, Abigail
Field; d. Dec. 16, 1790. She d. Aug. 5, 1791, ae. 61. Res., Norfolk, Ct., New
Haven, Vt.
356. i.   ABIGAIL, b. ———; m. Simeon Dudley, of Spencertown, N. Y.
357. ii.   EBENEZER, b. ———; m. Prudence Brainard, 1074¼-¾.
358. iii.   HANNAH, b. ———; m. Daniel Cole, of Norfolk, Ct.
359. iv.   MARY, b. ———; m. James Hale, of Spencertown, N. Y.
360. v.   CANDACE, b. ———; d. ae. 14.
361. vi.   SAMUEL, b. abt. 1770; m. Martha Bunnell and Cathrine Mew-
           man, 1075-6.
362. vii.   THOMAS, b. abt. 1773; m. Anna Constantine, 1077-84.
363. viii.   SARAH, b. ———; d. in childhood.
364. ix.   LUCINDA, b. ———; d. in childhood.

114. JOSEPH FOOTE, (36, 10, 3, 1,) b. 1730; m. 1st, Roselle, dau. of David
Chapin. She d. in Monson, Mass., ae. 30; m. 2nd, Thankful Parcy. She d. in
Spencertown, N. Y., ae. 40; m. 3rd, Widow Sawyer. He d. 1795; she d. ———.
365. i.   JOSEPH, b. Oct. 24, 1760; m. Abigail Dudley and Dorcas
           Reynolds, 1085-9.
366. ii.   THANKFUL, b. 1762.
367. iii.   DANIEL, b. 1764; m. Violetta Mahew, 1090-4.
368. iv.   DAVID, b. ———.
369. v.   RODERICK, b. ———.

115. LIEUT. SAMUEL FOOTE, (37, 10, 3, 1,) b. Oct. 4, 1719; m. Nov. 24,
1743, Lois Loomis; d. Sept. 18, 1775. She d. ———.

370. i.   SAMUEL, b. Oct. 10, 1744; m. Hannah Bidwell, 1095-6.

371. ii. LOIS, b. Apr. 5, 1746; m. May 29, 1765, Eleazur Merrils, of Farmington, Ct. He d. May 16, 1769; m. 2nd, Oct., 1770, John Wells, of Farmington, Ct., and in 1784 he moved to ~~Jamestown~~, N. Y. Ch.: (1) Eleazur, b. Nov. 9, 1766. (2) Lois, b. Mar. 12, 1769. (3) Lindy, bap. Apr. 19, 1772. (4) Rhoda. (5) John. (6) John. (7 and 8) Lindy and Lucy twins. (9) Eleazur. (10) Clarissa. (11) Nathan Perkins, b. 1786.

372. iii. MARY, b. June 21, 1748; m. Nov. 19, 1766, James Cadwell, Jr., of Windsor, Ct.; d. Mar. 8, 1834. He d. Dec. 16, 1811, ae. 69 years. Ch.: (1) Aaron, bap. Nov. 6, 1768. (2) Mary. (3) Rhoda. (4) James. (5) Martin. (6) Anna. (7) Samuel, b. 1786.

373. iv. LUCY, b. Dec. 1, 1750; d. Jan. 29, 1753.

374. v.   TIMOTHY, b. Oct. 9, 1752; m. Abigail Barnes and Lucy Throop, 1097-1111.

-375. vi. ELIJAH, b. Mar. 14, 1755; m. Mary Lattimer and Zurvia Barton, 1112-21.

376. vii. LUCY, b. May 3, 1757; m. Nov. 7, 1777, Pelatiah Cadwell, of Windsor, Ct.; d. Aug. 10, 1781. He d. Sept. 24, 1817. Ch.: (1) Pelatiah, b. Dec. 7, 1778. (2) Levi, b. Feb. 18, 1780.

377. viii. GROVE, b. Oct. 25, 1759; m. Elizabeth Cadwell, 1122-30.

378. ix. HEPZIBAH, b. Feb. 1, 1762; m. 1st, Oct. 20, 1779, Darius Case, of Simsbury, Ct., and Johnstown N. Y. He d. May 23 1797, ae. 48; 2nd, Feb. 8, 1798, Pelatiah Hayden. She d. Apr. 9, 1836, at Pompey, N. Y. Ch.: (1) Hepzibah, b. June 10, 1780. (2) Darius. (3) Justus. (4) Polly. (5) Samuel. (6) Huldah. (7) Rufus. (8) Rhoda. (9) Roxanna, b. Aug. 12, 1797. (10) Pelatiah, b. Jan. 10, 1799. (11) Almira. (12) Lucy. (13) David E., b. Dec. 20, 1808.

379. x.   ROGER, bap. July 15, 1764; d. Jan. 1, 1766.

117. DANIEL FOOTE, (37, 10, 3, 1,) b. Apr. 27, 1724; m. Jan. 14, 1748, Martha, dau. of Dea. John Stillman, and great-grand-dau. of Lieut. Phillip Smith, of Hadley, Mass. She d. July 24, 1794; ae. 64. He removed from Simsbury, Ct., about 1764 to Washington, Mass., and cleared away the forest and made a farm. He moved next to Dalton, Mass.; purchased land and brought into cultivation a valuable farm. This he sold to Daniel, his oldest son, and moved to Middlebury, Vt., and bought one thousand acres of wild land, on which he built mills, felled the forest, and resided for many years. About 1783 he bought all of the land that is now in the village of Middlebury on the west side of the river and erected a grist mill and saw mill. This property was given by him to his sons Stillman and John, the latter selling his interest to Appleton in 1792. They built dwellings and improved the property. (See History of Middlebury.) Daniel Foote built the first bridge at Middlebury Falls. About 1801 he divided his property at Middlebury among his children, and went to Canton, N. Y., his son Stillman having moved there a short time before. In passing through Montreal, he took the small-pox and died a few days after he arrived in Canton. He was a man of great industry and indominable perseverance, and peculiarly fitted for a pioneer in a new country. He d. May 10, 1801, and was buried in an elm bark coffin. All of his twelve children were members of the church. His sons also were pioneers, and their children are now widely scattered over the United States.

380. i.   DANIEL, b. Oct. 3, 1748; m. Mary Goodrich and Prudence Knowles, 1131-8.
381. ii.   GEORGE, b. Oct. 30, 1749; m. Weltha Ann Woodward, 1139-45.
382. iii.   MARTHA, b. Mar. 30, 1751; d. Apr. 17, 1751.
383. iv.   PHILIP, b. July 29, 1752; m. Isabella Milikin, Abigail Cornish and Rebecca Spaulding, 1146-9.
384. v.   MARTHA, b. June 10, 1754; m. 1st, Aug. 14, 1772, Enoc Dewey, of Westfield, Mass. He d. Feb. 16, 1778, ae. 32; 2nd, May 20, 1779, Roger Noble. He d. Mar. 7, 1813, ae. 64. She d. Jan. 30, 1831; res., New Haven, Vt. Ch.: (1) Stillman, b. July 1, 1773. (2) Patty, b. May, 1777. (3) Electa, b. Aug. 15, 1780; m. Russel Foote (1113). (4) William. (5) Roger. (6) Anna. (7) Mary. (8) Israel, b. Dec. 17, 1792.
385. vi.   HULDAH, b. Feb. 22, 1756; m. May, 1775, George Sloane. He was a colonel in the Revolution. She d. Apr. 26, 1798; res., Washington, Mass., and Middlebury, Vt. He d. 1840, at Canton, N. Y., ae. 91. Ch.: (1) Huldah, b. abt. 1776. (2) Millesent. (3) Horace. (4) Lucretia. (5) Campbell. (6) Electa. (7) Alma, b. abt. 1790.
386. vii.   MILLESENT, b. Dec. 2, 1757; d. Nov. 10, 1762.
387. viii. FREEMAN, b. Sept. 22, 1759; m. Silence Clark and Bathsheba Morton, 1150-4.
388. ix.   MARTIN, b. Oct. 22, 1761; m. Hannah Dean and Anna Branch, 1155-62.
389. x.   STILLMAN, b. Sept. 10, 1763; m. Lovica Donaghy and Mary Pember, 1163-8.
390. xi.   JOHN, b. Nov. 12, 1765; m. Lucy Thayer and Ann Sumner, 1169-77.
391. xii.   APPLETON, b. Aug. 28, 1767; m. Mary Groves, 1178-82.

118. JOSEPH FOOTE, (37, 10, 3, 1,) b. Feb. 17, 1727; m. Dec. 8, 1757, Azubah dau. of Nathaniel Griswold, of Windsor, Ct.; d. Sept. 16, 1779; res., Simsbury, Ct. She d. Aug. 12, 1829, at Northampton, N. Y., ae. 93.
392. i.   JOSEPH, b. Oct. 26, 1758; m. Barsheba Burr, 1183-6.
393. ii.   AZUBAH, b. Apr. 13, 1760; m. 1775, Ashbel Case, of Simsbury, Ct. He d. Apr. 23, 1822, ae. 69. Ch.: (1) Chloe, b. Jan. 8, 1776. (2) Ashbel. (3) Timothy. (4) Levi. (5) James. (6) Joseph G., b. Oct. 24, 1793.
395. iii.   SARAH, b. June 21, 1762; m. Jan. 14, 1780, John Bacon, of Simsbury and Northampton, N. Y.; d. Oct. 7, 1842. He d. Mar. 1, 1847; ae. 93 years and 5 mos. Ch.: (1) Sarah, b. July 21, 1785. (2) Abiah. (3) Laura. (4) John. (5) Seth. (6) George. (7 and 8) Ashel and Asaph, twins, b. Aug. 4, 1799.
396. iv.   ELISHA, b. Aug. 26, 1764; m. Rebecca C. Miller, 1187-97.
397. v.   DELIGHT, b. Jan. 8, 1767; m. June 23, 1796, Joab Judson, of Northampton and Antwerp, N. Y.; d. Oct. 5, 1847. He d. May 9, 1836, ae. 80 years. Ch.: (1) Daniel, b. Mar. 26, 1798. (2) Delight, b. May 1, 1800.
398. vi.   AARON, b. Apr. 10, 1769; m. 1st, Apr. 7, 1799, Esther, dau. of Joseph Barber, of Windsor, Ct. She d. Aug. 3, 1820, ae. 42; 2nd, May 13, 1822, Ruhamah Schribner. He d. Dec. 8, 1842, p. s.; res., Simsbury, Ct., and Northampton, N. Y.
399. vii.   DAU. not named, b. May 6, 1771; d. in infancy.

400. viii. LEVI, b. May 10, 1773; d. Sept. 16, 1775.

401. ix. AMELIA, b. Apr. 28, 1777; d. Oct. 14, 1792.

402. x. ELECTA, b. Apr. 27, 1780; m. Jan. 15, 1797, Caleb Hitchcock, Jr., of Windsor, Ct. She d. June 15, 1848. Ch.: (1) Samuel Foote, b. Jan. 29, 1798. (2) Electa Amelia. (3) Eliza Abba. (4) Eliza. (5) Ulysses. (6) Mary. (7) Electa. (8) Julia Ann. (9) Gaylord, b. Feb. 4, 1820.

119. CAPT. JOHN FOOTE, (37, 10, 3, 1,) b. 1729; m. 1st, 1753, Rosanna, dau. of Jonathan and Mary (Ruggles) Humphrey. She d. Oct. 10, 1793, ae. 62; 2nd, Mary Fowler, of Salem, Ct. He d. Sept. 15, 1813.; res., Simsbury, Ct.

403. i. ROSANNAH, b. Oct. 14, 1754; m. Ephraim Mills, of Canton, Ct. He d. 1818, ae. 65. Ch.: (1) Rosannah, b. 1780. (2) Ephraim. (3) Phebe. (4) Simeon. (5) Simeon, b. Sept. 22, 1787. (6) Andrew. (7) Ruth. (8) Andrew. (9) Norman, b. Aug. 2, 1795.

404. ii. JOHN, b. Jan. 9, 1760; m. Lois Mills, 1198-1207.

405. iii. LUTHER, b. Mar. 5, 1761; m. Temperance Hayes and Mary Ann Bronson, 1208-14.

406. iv. LUCRETIA, b. Oct. 28, 1763; m. 1780, Elias, son of Dudley and Dorcas (Humphrey) Case, of Canton, Ct.; d. Oct. 1, 1844. He b. 1759; d. Mar. 21, 1809, ae. 50. Ch.: (1) Cadance, b. Oct. 10, 1785. (2) Dudley. (3) Noadiah. (4) Luke. (5) Harlow. (6) Sally, b. Nov. 9, 1796.

407. v. RACHEL, b. Nov. 27, 1766; m. 1782, Dan Case, bro. of Elias, of Canton, Ct.; d. Aug., 1783. He b. 1769; d. 1815. Ch.: Dan, b. 1783.

408. vi. HILPAH ROSIETTE, b. Oct. 18, 1772; m. 1795, Lawton Marcy, of Otis, Mass.; d. Mar. 1846. He d. Mar., 1846, ae. 78. Ch.: (1) Patia L., b. Sept. 27, 1796. (2) Mary F. (3) Alice. (4) John F. (5) Clarissa. (6) Luther. (7) Selinda. (8) Bradford R. (9) Calvin L. (10) Sally C., b. Oct. 27, 1815.

125. NATHAN FOOTE, (38, 11, 3, 1,) b. Oct. 24, 1719; m. July 3, 1750, Abiah Gilbert; res., Fairfield,. Ct.

409. i. ABIAH, b. Jan. 15, 1751.

410. ii. HANNAH, b. May 12, 1754.

126. JOHN FOOTE, (38, 11, 3, 1,) b. Nov. 29, 1721; m. 1750, Deborah Hoyt; d. July 28, 1791. She d. Aug. 6, 1777, ae. 53.

411. i. MARY, b. June 19, 1751; m. Noah Robinson; d. Dec., 1836; res., Hubbardton, Vt.

412. ii. DEBORAH, b. Aug. 22, 1753; m. Andrew Aiken, of Wilton, Ct.; d. May 1, 1844.

413. iii. SARAH, b. May 9, 1755; m. Isaiah Robinson; d. Oct. 8, 1833; res., Hubbardton, Vt.

414. iv. MINDWELL, b. Jan., 1758; m. John Joyce; d. Oct., 1831, p. s.; res., Hubbardton, Vt.

415. v. JOHN, b. Apr. 2, 1761; m Huldah Stone, 1215-21.

416. vi. LUCY, b. 1763; m. Robert McMahan and Isaac Trowbridge, of Danbury; d. Aug. 27, 1804.

417. vii. DAVID, b. May 28, 1765; m. Dec. 29, 1792, Elizabeth, dau. of Asa Bull, of Litchfield, Ct. At the age of 16 he was a soldier in

the Revolutionary Army. Justice of the Peace for many years, and Director and President of the Fairfield Co. Bank. Res., Danbury, Ct.; p. s.; d. Feb. 29, 1852. She d. Apr. 16, 1848.

418.　viii.　ENOCH, b. May 2, 1770; m. Abigail Brooks, 1222-4.

128.　PETER FOOTE, (38, 11, 3, 1,) b. 1725; m. July 6, 1759, Sarah Hurd; res., Newtown Ct.

419.　i.　PETER, b. ———; m. Eunice Pond, 1224¼-5.
420.　ii.　PHILO, b. ———; m. Martha Hale and Phebe Beers, 1225¼-¾.
421.　iii.　TRUMAN SHERMAN, b. ———; m. Sarah Jackson, 1226-32.
422.　iv.　JOHN BURGOYNE, b. ———; m. Sally Norton, 1232½-7.
423.　v.　NEWTON, b. ———; m. ———. Beers, sister of David Beers, who m. 430; moved to Vt.
424.　vi.　GRANDISON; d. young.
425.　vii.　CLARISSA, b. Apr. 14, 1760; m. Amos Williams, and settled below. Newton, Ct., near Greenfield; had two sons and a dau.—Pricella, who m. Samuel Wooster, and lived at Oxford, Ct., in 1875, near Zoar Bridge.
426.　viii.　PAURILLIS, b. Apr. 7, 1762; m. ———. Hubbel. Ch.: Philena, m. ———. Judson, of Newton, Ct.
427.　ix.　SYLVANEY, b. Apr. 3, 1764.
428.　x.　EXPERIENCE.
429.　xi.　POLLY ANN.
430.　xii.　PHEBE ANN; m. David Beers. } Twins.
431.　xiii.　CLOTILDA.

130.　DAVID FOOTE, (39, 11, 3, 1,) b. July 7, 1707; m. 1735, Eleanor Blakesley; d. 1797. She d. 1783; res., Washington, Ct.

432.　i.　DAVID, b. ———; m. Esther Averill, 1238-45.
433.　ii.　ISAAC, b. Jan. 4, 1741; m. Anna Hurlbut, 1246-52.
434.　iii.　AARON, b. ———; m. Content Hurd, 1253-8.
435.　iv.　ESTHER, b. ———.
436.　v.　MARY, bap. Sept. 3, 1749; d. Jan. 7, 1820; unm.
437.　vi.　ELEANOR, bap. May 28, 1751; m. Joseph Rood.
438.　vii.　DORATHY, b. ———.

131.　JOHN FOOTE, (39, 11, 3, 1,) b. July 20, 1711; m. 1731, Amy ———. He d. Dec., 1762; res., Newton, Ct.

439.　i.　MARY, b. Oct. 17, 1732; m. Oct. 24, 1756, Lemuel Thomas, of Newton, Ct.
440.　ii.　AMY, b. Mar. 16, 1735.
441.　iii.　LUCY, b. abt. 1736.
442.　iv.　RUTH, b. abt. 1738.
443.　v.　ELIJAH, b. abt. 1740; m. ———, 1259-65.
444.　vi.　EZRA, b. abt. 1748.
445.　vii.　ISAAC, b. abt. 1753.

134.　DANIEL FOOTE, (39, 11, 3, 1,) b. May 5, 1716; m. 1744, Sarah ———. She d. Dec. 14, 1803. Res., Taunton, Ct.

446.　i.　ABIGAIL, b. Oct. 6, 1745.
447.　ii.　JAMES, b. June 20, 1747; m. Adah Stillson, 1266-78½.
448.　iii.　MEHITABEL, b. Jan. 20, 1749; d. Jan. 31, 1749.

449. iv.   SAMUEL, b. Jan. 24, 1750.
450. v.   MEHITABEL, b. Nov. 30, 1752.
451. vi.   GEORGE, b. Nov. 18, 1754.
452. vii. DORATHY, b. Jan. 4, 1756.
453. viii. WILLIAM, b. Jan. 5, 1758; m. Martha Janes, 1279.
454. ix.   DINAH, b. Jan. 7, 1760.
455. x.   JEHIEL, b. Apr. 23, 1762.
456. xi.   DEBORAH ANN, b. Mar. 22, 1764.
457. xii. MARY, b. Mar. 11, 1766.
458. xiii. SARAH, b. Sept. 27, 1770.

137. EBENEZER FOOTE, (39, 11, 3, 1,) b. Sept. 22, 1720; m. Christiana
————; res., N. Stratford, Ct.
459. i.   DANIEL, b. Nov. 26, 1749; m. Abigail Hurd, 1280-7.

140. GEORGE FOOTE, (39, 11, 3, 1,) b. Mar. 26, 1725; m. 1742, Catharine
Burrit; d. Apr. 12, 1818, and buried in Zoar village; res., Newton, Ct.
460. i.   EDWARD, b. July 1, 1743; m. Anna Prindle, 1288-1301.
461. ii.   JOSIAH, b. ab. 1746; d. 1803; unm.
462. iii. DANIEL, b. abt. 1748; m. Lucia Byington, 1302.
463. iv.   ABIJAH, b. abt, 1751; d. May 29, 1810; unm.
464. v.   ABEL, b. abt. 1754; m. Anna Daw, 1303-5.
465. vi.   SARAH, b. abt. 1757; m. ————. Curtis.
466. vii. BETSEY, b. abt. 1760; m. Samuel Hughes.
467. viii. CLOTILDA, b. Feb. 23, 1763; m., 1788, Lockwood Winton.
468. ix.   SYBIL, b. abt. 1765; m. Edon Stevens.

142. JOSEPH FOOTE, (41, 11, 3, 1,) b. Dec. 17, 1714; m. Nov. 24, 1737,
Sarah Blakeman. He d. Mar. 14, 1791; res., Stratford Ct.
469. i.   ISAAC, b. Sept. 13, 1738.
470. ii.   MARTHA, b. Feb. 7, 1741; m. John Fairfield, of Newton, Ct.
            Ch.: (1) Agnes, b. Nov. 5, 1768. (2) Electa, b. Aug. 6, 1770.
471. iii. RACHEL, b. July 8, 1744; d. unm.
472. iv.   HANNAH, b. Dec. 26, 1746; m. ————. Brice, of Newton.
473. v.   JOSEPH, b. Dec. 6, 1748; m. Hepzibah Sherman, 1306-15.
474. vi.   SARAH, b. Feb. 27, 1750; m.
475. vii. JEHIEL, b. Feb. 15, 1756; m. ————. Blakeman and Abigail
            Shepard, 1316-22.
476. viii. POLLY, b. ————; m. abt. Mar. 1, 1779, Moses Gillet, of New-
            town, Ct.; d. abt. 1827. He d. May, 1835. Ch.: (1) Samuel. (2)
            Joseph. (3) John. (4) Lamira. (5) Nehemiah. (6) Polly Ann.

143. DANIEL FOOTE, (41, 11, 3, 1,) b. July 25, 1717; m. Nov. 6, 1746,
Sarah, dau. of Samuel and Ann (Laboree) Whitney; res., Stratford and Newton,
Ct.; d. June 28, 1790. She d. Nov. 2, 1794.
477. i.   ABIGAIL, b. Nov. 4, 1747.
478. ii.   ANNA, b. June 14, 1749; d. Nov. 17, 1827; m. Stephen, son of
            John S. Shepard, of Newton, Ct.; d. July 24, 1830. Ch.: (1)
            William. (2) Allen. (3) Oliver. (4) Joannah. (5) Parsons.
            (6) Ann Maria, b. June 9, 1793.
479. iii. CHARITY, bap. June 21, 1752; m. 1st, Elias Bristol, of Newtown,
            Ct. He died before 1785; m. 2nd, Samuel Sanford, of Newtown,

Ct.; d. Nov. 13, 1826. He d. Nov. 26, 1817. Ch.: (1) Anna
Bristol, b. Oct. 13, 1773; m. Feb. 10, 1790, Isaac, son of Samuel
and Abiah Denning; she d. June 25, 1825. (2) Jerusha Bristol,
b. July 25, 1776; m. Reid Wheeler; res., Balston, N. Y. (3)
Abiah Ann Sanford, b. Jan. 10, 1790, Clemet Northrop. (4)
Josiah, b. June 9, 1793; m. Polly Johnson; res., Elyria O. (5)
(Philo, b. July 11, 1796; m. Aug. 21, 1826, Martha B.
Burgess.)

480. iv.   DANIEL, b. 1762; m. Bettey Northrup, 1323-½.
481. v.   PETER, b. 1768; m. Naomi Gillett, 1324-30.
482. vi.   SUSANNAH, b. ———; m. 1st, Amos Griffin, of Newtown, Ct.
           He d. Aug., 1791; m. 2nd, Enoch Lacy, of New York. Ch.: (1)
           Amos, b. 1781. (2) Lucy. (3) John. (4) Susanna, b. 1789.
483. vii. JERUSHA, b. ———; m. David Curtis, Wainwright.
484. viii. LEMUEL, b. ———; m. Charity Beers, 1330½-2.

145. GEORGE FOOTE, (41, 11, 3, 1,) b. Nov. 4, 1721; m. 1745, Hannah, dau.
of James Hurd. He d. at sea abt. 1755; res., Stratford, Ct.

485. i.   BETTEY, b. Aug. 7, 1746.
486. ii.   GEORGE, b. Oct. 11, 1749; m. Charity Stillson, 1333-9.
487. iii. JAMES, b. Mar. 5, 1752.
488. iv.   JOHN, b. July 14, 1754; m. Ruth Searl, 1339½-49.

152. NATHANIEL FOOTE, (45, 13, 5, 1,) b. Oct. 15, 1723; m. 1st, Jan. 5,
1747, Sarah Beers. She d. ———; m. 2nd, Jan. 26, 1768, Mary Jones. He d. Feb.
6, 1785; res., Branford.

489. i.   SAMUEL, b. Feb. 19, 1759; d. unm.
490. ii.   JARED, b. Mar. 12, 1762; d. unm.
491. iii. SYBIL, b. Jan. 24, 1765; d. unm.
492. iv.   SARAH, b. Feb. 13, 1767; d. unm.

153. EPHRAIM FOOTE, (45, 13, 5, 1,) b. ———; m. July 31, 1760, Lucy,
dau. of Jonithan and Hannah (Benton) Barker; d. Mar 24, 1791. She d. 1830.

493. i.   REBECCA, b. May 6, 1761; m. Nov. 17, 1778, John Blackstone,
           of Branford, Ct. Ch.: (1) Ransom. (2) Augustus. (3) Lucy.
494. ii.   PHINEAS, b. Oct. 26, 1763; m. Irene Hoadley, 1350-2.
495. iii. LUCY, b. May 28, 1766; d. July 24, 1775.
496. iv.   CLARISSA, b. Feb. 10, 1769; d. Aug. 17, 1775.
497. v.   JONATHAN, b. Mar. 13, 1772; m. Martha Frisbie, 1353-7.
498. vi.   EPHRAIM, b. Sept. 1, 1775; m. Polly Hobart, 1358-65.
499. vii. LUCY CLARISSA, b. Feb. 24, 1778; d. May 27, 1797.
500. viii. SAMUEL, b. May 16, 1780; d. abt. 1815; unm.

166. DAVID FOOTE, (47, 13, 5, 1,) b. Nov. 11, 1730; m. Feb. 28, 1752,
Hanna, dau. of John Bronson, Jr. She was. b. Mar. 6, 1734; d. 1795. He was
killed by the British troops at Fairfield, Ct., 1779.

501. i.   TYPHENA, b. Feb. 13, 1754.
502. ii.   RUTH, b. Oct. 8, 1756; m. Aner Wooden, of Watertown, Ct.
503. iii. Dau., not named, b. Apr. 15, 1760; d. May 13, 1760.
504. iv.   MARY, b. Sept. 4, 1761.
505. v.   HANNAH, b. Dec. 16, 1763; m. Jacob Mallory, of East Haven,
           Ct.; d. Mar. 27, 1830. Ch.: (1) Isaac. (2) Sarah. (3) Jesse.
           (4) Fanny. (5) Emily. (6) Jacob.

506. vi. COMFORT, b. June 23, 1769; m. Aaron Curtis, of Burlington, Ct.

507. vii. REBECCA, b. Nov. 3, 1773.

168. MOSES FOOTE, (47, 13, 5, 1,) b. Aug. 4, 1734; m. 1st, Aug. 12, 1756, Thankful, dau. of John Bronson, Jr. She was b. Sept. 6, 1736; d. Sept. 5, 1757; m. 2nd, May 17, 1759, Amy, dau. of Jonah Richards, of E. Hartford and N. Hartford, Ct. She d. at Clinton, N. Y., Aug. 13, 1813, ae. 76. He commanded a Company in the 27th Reg. of Ct. Vol. (D. A. R. Records).

Moses Foote, the son of Moses Foote, was born in that part of Waterbury now Plymouth, Ct., where he resided until soon after the close of the Revolutionary War, when he moved with his family to commence a settlement in the western wilderness of New York. He was accompanied in this movement by the families of his sons and his sons-in-law—making altogether a neighborhood of his own. With Mr. Foote to lead and direct the enterprise, the party were admirably fitted to commence a new settlement. They were all charged with Yankee ingenuity, energy and perseverance, and Mr. Foote was endowed with an iron frame, six feet high, and of a temperament and muscular texture which admirably fitted him for a pioneer life. They took up a temporary residence at German Flatts, on the Mohawk River, then the very boundary of civilization on the west. In the autumn of 1786 they determined on a location sixty miles beyond, at a place now called Clinton, and there erected log huts, preparatory to an early removal in the succeeding spring. Accordingly, with the other families, Mr. Foote commenced the settlement of the new town in March, 1787, when scarcely the smoke of a log cabin inhabited by a white family could be discerned for twenty miles round. The town was called Paris, by the Legislature, on the petition of the inhabitants, in commemoration of the liberality of a merchant at Fort Plains, on the Mohawk, who supplied the infant settlement with corn and other provisions at a low price and a long credit, at a season when the crops, affected by the unfavorable weather, had nearly failed. The purchase made in 1788, by George Clinton and other Commissioners appointed by the Legislature, from the Oneida Indians, of all their land, except some small reservation, gave a new and powerful impetus to the settlement of all this section of country, and in the course of a few years the germs of from twenty to thirty towns were planted in the region round about Mr. Foote's settlement. Mr. Foote lived to see his own settlement expand and strengthen into a beautiful and flourishing village, bearing the honored name of Clinton, and the seat of a University, called after the no less honored name of Hamilton. During his life the wilderness through which he and his companions cut their way with the axe was converted into fields of grass and corn and wheat —and the stupendous work of connecting the waters of Lake Erie and Hudson river, by a navigable canal, was devised and completed, and his own crops were borne on its bosom to the Atlantic markets along the very route on which he made his slow and toilsome progress, through tangled forests, on foot, forty years before. He died Feb 9, 1819, at the age of 84. In the upper end of the park at Clinton is a granite monument, with this inscription on the south side, "Moses Foote, Esq., with seven other families, commenced the settlement of this town March 3, 1787." On the opposite side is the names, viz.: "Moses Foote, Luther Foote, Ira Foote, Ludim Blodget, James Bronson, Bronson Foote, Barnabas Pond, Levi Sherman."

508. i. BRONSON, b. Sept. 5, 1757; m. Thankful Pond, 1366-73.

509. ii. IRA, b. Nov. 13, 1759; m. Polly Pond, 1374-80.

510. iii.   THANKFUL, b. Jan. 30, 1762; m. Barnabas, son of Timothy
              and Sarah (Munson) Pond; d. Oct. 8, 1814. He was b. Oct. 29,
              1755; d. May 9, 1814. Res., Clinton, N. Y. He was a farmer,
              and lived and died on the farm he cleaned up. His name is on
              the monument, where they cut the first tree and built the first
              meeting house. He was a major in the Revolutionary War.
              While Lafayette was passing through the thousands of the hardy
              yeomanry of the country anxious to express their gratitude to
              the French General and joy at meeting him as the nation's honored
              guest at Utica, N. Y., the General's keen military eye caught the
              figure and form of the venerable Barnabas Pond, and rising up
              in his carriage, pointed him out and addressed him as ''Major
              Pond.'' They met, embraced, while the tears of joy mingled as
              they coursed down the venerable cheeks. Major Pond d. May
              9, 1841, at Clinton, N. Y. She d. Oct. 8, 1814, at Clinton, N. Y.
              Ch.: (1) Lewis Pond, b. Plymouth, Ct., Sept. 26, 1784.   (2)
              Andrew Storrs Pond, b. German Flatts, N. Y.   (3) Julius C.
              Pond, b. Clinton, N. Y., July 26, 1789. (4) Mary Pond, b. 1791;
              m. Gad Crokley Wankesha, Wis. (5) Chas. H. Pond, b. Clinton,
              N. Y., May 17, 1797.
511. iv.   LUTHER, b. Oct. 4, 1764; m. Sally Pond, 1381-8.
512. v.   AMY, b. Feb. 13, 1767; d. Sept., 1775.
513. vi.   ANNA, b. Feb. 13, 1767; m. ———. Dewey. Ch.: a dau., m.
              Wm. Olcott, of Mich.
514. vii.   MOSES, b. Jan. 4, 1770; m. Martha Brown, 1389-91.
515. viii.   ARUNAH, b. Sept. 28, 1772; drowned in a well Sept. 15, 1779.
516. ix.   JARIUS, b. Sept. 2, 1777; m. Susan Holt; d. 1829; p. s.
517. x.   BETSEY, b. Sept. 2, 1777; m. Sept. 30, 1801, Dea. Gould, son of
              Dea. Isaac and Jane (Reynolds) Benedict; d., p. s., Apr. 22, 1846.
              He d. Aug. 7, 1868, ae. 92½ years.

170. AARON FOOTE, (47, 13, 5, 1,) b. July 5, 1738; m. Nov. 13, 1760, Mary,
dau. of John Bronson, Jr., of Waterbury, Ct.; d. Feb. 23, 1822. She was b. Feb.
2, 1739; d. Feb. 10, 1824; res., Harwinton and Sheffield, Ct.
518. i.   BERIAH, b. Dec. 16, 1761; m. Hannah Rossiter and Phebe Mills,
              1392-8.
519. ii.   MARY, b. Dec. 10, 1763; m. Feb. 10, 1798, Samuel Harrald, of
              Sheffield, Mass.; d. Sept. 25, 1829; several ch.; res., Clinton, N. Y.
520. iii.   JOHN, b. Mar. 26, 1766; m. Huldah Rossiter, 1399-1409.
521. iv.   AMOS, b. Jan. 20, 1768; m. Adah Frisbie; 1410-18.
522. v.   AARON, b. Apr. 24, 1771; m. Jedidah Sherman, 1419-27.
523. vi.   DORCAS, b. May 6, 1773; m. 1806, John McLish, of Sangerfield,
              N. Y.; d. Mar. 21, 1847; p. s.
524. vii.   SAMUEL, b. May 25, 1775; d. unm.
525. viii.   CYRENE, b. Aug. 7, 1760.

171. EBENEZER FOOTE, (47, 13, 5, 1,) b. May 21, 1740; m. July 1, 1761,
Rebecca dau. of Uzel Baker of Waterbury Ct.; d. June, 1778, at Mud Fort, Horse
Neck, Ct.; res., Harwinton, Ct. A soldier in the Revolutionary War. She d. Apr. 26,
———, at Dryden, N. Y., ae. 84.
526. i.   DARIUS, b. Apr. 10, 1762; m. Lurinda Ann Preston, 1428-35.

527. ii. SIMEON, b. Sept. 22, 1764; m. Lovisa Bacon, 1436-45.
528. iii. GIDEON b. Nov. 6, 1766; drowned at Troy, N. Y.; unm.
529. iv. DAVID, b. Aug. 7, 1768; m. Irene Lane, 1446-57.
530. v. UZEL, b. Aug. 26, 1772; d. young.
531. vi. LUCY, b. Aug. 19, 1774; m. Isaac Church.
532. vii. LOWLY, b. Jan. 19, 1778; m. 1st, Ebenezer Clauson, of Dryden,
    · N. Y.; m. 2nd, J. Richardson.

472. OBED FOOTE, (47, 13, 5, 1,) b. Nov. 25, 1741; m. Dec. 3, 1761, Mary,
dau. of Rev. Samuel Todd, son of Samuel and Mercy (Evans) Todd of Northfield,
Ct. She b. Sept 11, 1742; m. 2nd, Mar. 26, 1798, Rev. Jonathan Leavitt, of Heath,
Mass.; d. May 16, 1815. Mr. Foote d. Sept. 21, 1797; res., Plymouth, Ct., and Gill,
Mass. In May, 1780, Obed Foote, with his mother and his young family, removed
to Rowe, Mass., where he purchased a large tract of land (about 1,000 acres). In
1784 he removed to Gill, Mass., where he purchased the farm on which he lived until
his death in 1797. His mother, Ruth Foote, died at Gill in 1792, aged 86. Obed
Foote's wife survived and was afterwards married to Rev. Jonathan Leavitt, of
Heath, Mass., whom she also survived. She died in 1815, at the home of her daughter, Mrs. Judge Goodale, at Bernardston, Mass., and was buried at Gill, a few miles
distant.

533. i. ASENATH, b. Sept. 19, 1762; m. June 20, 1791, Eliphaz, son of
    Simeon Alexander; d. Nov. 18, 1713. He was b. Mar. 8, 1764;
    res., Northfield, Mass., and Burlington, N. Y. Ch.: (1) Laura, b.
    July 4, 1792; d. July 8, 1842, at Moravia, N. Y., unm. (2)
    Almira, b. Mar. 21, 1794; d. June 11, 1835, unm. (3) Amanda,
    b. Nov. 26, 1795; m. Jan. 20, 1818, Wm. H. Alexander. Ch.:
    (a) Wm. Henry, b. May 4, 1819. (b) Laura, b. Feb. 14, 1822;
    m. Aug. 17, 1842, H. G. Mattison, of Syracuse, N. Y. (c)
    Sarah, b. May 8, 1824; m. Oct. 16, 1844, Wm. Smart, of Brock-
    ville, Can. (d) Caleb. (e) Francis Elizabeth, and three others,
    all d. young. (4) Mary Ann, b. July 12, 1797; m. Feb. 24, 1820,
    Isaac W. Skinner, of Brasher, N. Y. Ch.: (a) Mary Ann. (b)
    Elizabeth. (5) Eliphaz, b. Apr. 17, 1799; d. 1802. (6) Lydia,
    b. Apr. 1, 1801; d. Jan. 3, 1835. (7) Sarah, b. Feb. 21, 1805.
534. ii. MARY DOROTHEA, b. June 11, 1764; m. Dec., 1783, Rev. Amasa
    Cook, of Barnardstown; d. Apr. 17, 1835. He was b. June, 1750;
    d. June, 1816. Ch.: (1) Amasa, b. Feb., 1788. (2) Amanda, b.
    Mar., 1790; d. 1794. (3) Peypton Randolph, b. Jan., 1792.
535. iii. BERNICE, b. June 5, 1766; m. Melinda Field, 1458-64.
536. iv. SEDATE, b. Mar. 5, 1768; m. June 11, 1809, Josiah Jones, of
    Brockville, U. C.; d. Dec. 8, 1837. He was b. 1765; d. Mar. 4, 1839.
    Ch.: Emeline Sedate, b. Nov. 29, 1810; m. Jan. 17, 1839, Rob.
    Bell, of Brockville, Upper Canada.
537. v. SAMUEL, b. Apr. 7, 1770; m. Sibbil Doolittle and ——— Parker,
    1465-75.
538. vi. CHLOE, b. Mar. 21, 1772; m. Isaac Pierce, of Preston, Ct.; d. 1829.
539. vii. LYDIA, b. May 15, 1774; m. Apr., 1794, Judge Job Goodale. He
    founded Goodale Academy, in Barnardstown, and d. there Oct. 25,
    1833. Ch.: (1) Feronia, b. Feb. 9, 1795. (2) Maria, Dec. 22, 1796.
540. viii. ERASTUS, b. Sept. 19, 1777; m. Susan Carlton and Eliza Carlton,
    1476-82.

(5)

541. ix. PHILENA, b. Sept. 22, 1779; m. 1st, 1802, Israel, son of Israel Jones, Sr. He d. 1811, ae. 33; m. 2nd, Nov. 7, 1816, Rev. Wm. Smart, of Brockville, Upper Canada. Ch.: (1) Alathea Foote, b. Aug. 3, 1803; m. A. Morris. (2) Israel Foote, b. July 5, 1805; m. and d. at Prescott, U. P. (3) Charles, b. Aug. 1, 1809. (4) William, b. Mar. 19, 1818.

542. x. RHODA ANN, b. Jan. 1, 1781; m. July 7, 1806, Nathaniel Martin, of Camden, Me.; d. Jan. 14, 1837. He was b. Nov. 25, 1775; d. Mar., 1841. Ch.: (1) Nathaniel William, b. 1808. (2) Mary Emily, b. 1809. (3) Edward Byam, b. Apr., 1811. (4) Erastus Foote, b. Aug. 12, 1812.

543. xi. OBED, b. Apr. 27, 1787; m. Ann G. Wallpole ana Mary Davis, 1483-91.

178. STEPHEN FOOTE, (50, 16, 5, 1,) b. Aug. 20, 1724; m. 1st, Nov. 5, 1747, Sybil, dau. of John Foster, of Southampton, L. I. She d. ———; m. 2nd, Mary, wid. of Lieut. Timothy Frisbie. She d. Jan. 26, 1832, ae. 92 years. He d. Aug. 26, 1802.

544. i. KETURAH, b. Nov. 19, 1748; d. Sept. 1, 1773, unm.

545. ii. DAVID, b. Nov. 1, 1750; m. and d. in Newburn, N. C. Ch.

546. iii. SILENCE, b. Apr. 28, 1753; m. 1st, Benj. Stedman; m. 2nd, Samuel Linsley; d. June 21, 1805.

547. iv. THANKFUL, b. Oct. 12, 1755.

548. v. SYBIL, bap. Aug. 28, 1757.

549. vi. STEPHEN, bap. Apr. 24, 1763; m. Mary Pardee, 1485-91.

185. CAPT. ABRAHAM FOOTE, (53, 16, 5, 1,) b. June 16, 1725; m. 1st Apr. 15, 1745, Abigail Rogers. She d. ———; m. 2nd Mary Ponsonby. She d. 1817, ae. 85. He d. Dec. 6, 1823, in Woodbury, Ct. He commanded a company in the old French War, and was also in the Army of the Revolution; res., Branford, Ct.

550. i. JERUSHA, b. Oct. 22, 1746; m. Samuel Palmer; d. in Middlebury, Ct.

551. ii. MARY, b. Oct. 15, 1748.

552. iii. ABIGAIL, b. June 25, 1752; d. Dec. 20, 1775.

553. iv. LURINDA, b. June 30, 1754; m. Benjamin Bates; d. in Middlebury, Ct.

554. v. ELSIE, b. Oct. 19, 1756; m. Asahel Ives; d. in Woodbury, Ct.

555. vi. CYNTHIA, b. Sept. 25, 1759; d. Jan. 16, 1774.

556. vii. ACTIVE, b. Aug. 6, 1764; m. Israel Frisbie; d. Aug., 1791, in Middlebury, Ct.

557. viii. ROBERT ABRAHAM EBENEZER, b. Sept., 1766; m. Lucy Orton, 1492-1501.

189. EBENEZER FOOTE, (53, 16, 5, 1,) b. Jan. 7, 1734; m. July 8, 1755, Phebe Palmer; d. ———. She d. Dec. 1788; res. North Branford, Ct.

558. i. THANKFUL, b. Sept. 24, 1759; m. Apr. 1, 1779, Isaac Smith, of North Branford, Ct. Ch.: (1) Betsey, b. Nov. 15, 1779. (2) Augustus, b. July 12, 1782.

559. ii. LUCRETIA, b. 1765; bap. Sept. 24, 1775, ae. 10; m. James Butler, Aug., 1788.

195. LIEUT. JACOB. FOOTE, (54, 16, 5, 1,) b. Mar. 20, 1732; m. Mar. 23,

1768, Lucy Bunnell; d. Apr. 25, 1818. She d. Jan. 12, 1838, ae. 94. He d. Apr. 25, 1818. Res., Branford and Canton, Ct.

560.   i.   LUCY, b. Jan. 17, 1769; m. May 11, 1790, Thomas F. Bishop, of Avon, Ct. He was b. Oct. 27, 1763, in Farmington, Ct. He was four years and four months in the War of the Revolution. Served at Yorktown under Col. Hamilton, and was engaged in several skirmishes. Is a pensioner, and attended the celebration of Independence, at Hartford, July 4, 1848. Ch.: (1) Stella F., b. Oct. 21, 1790. (2) Benjamin, b. Aug. 25, 1792. (3) Delia, b. Sept. 23, 1794. (4) Samuel, b. Mar. 20, 1797. (5) Jeffrey A., b. Apr. 15, 1799. (6) Jacob, b. Jan. 23, 1801. (7) Lucy F., b. Dec. 17, 1802. (8) Thomas N., b. June 2, 1804. (9) Gedor P., b. May 2, 1806. (10) Sarah A., b. Dec. 15, 1807. (11) Joseph, b. May 30, 1810.

561.   ii.   JACOB, b. Mar. 20, 1771; m. Sarah Wilcox, 1502-11.

562.   iii.   HANNAH, b. May 26, 1773; m. Mar. 27, 1794, Ezekiel Hosford, of Canton, Ct.; d. Dec. 7, 1843. He d. Mar. 6, 1838, ae. 64. Ch.: (1) Delinda, b. Dec. 28, 1794. (2) Uriah. (3) Lucy. (4) Amon. (5) Dan. (6) Ezekiel. (7) Maria. (8) Clarissa, b. Mar. 2, 1812.

563.   iv.   JOSEPH, b. Oct. 4, 1775; m. Cynthia Hosford and Rhoda Olcott, 1512-16.

196. DANIEL FOOTE, (54, 16, 5, 1,) b. June 5, 1734; m. Feb. 13, 1755, Mary, dau. of Isaac and Hannah Ingraham; d. Mar. 6, 1797. She d. June 23, 1822, ae. 85.

564.   i.   DANIEL, b. Mar. 23, 1756; d. Aug. 7, 1756.

565.   ii.   ELIHU, b. Aug. 19, 1757; m. Lucy Williams, 1517-20.

566.   iii.   EDWIN, b. Aug. 20, 1759; d. Nov. 13, 1776.

567.   iv.   DANIEL, b. Dec. 7, 1760; m. Hannah Potter, 1521-2.

568.   v.   JOHN, b. Jan. 30, 1763. —

569.   vi.   JACOB, b. June 30, 1764; m. Sally Bunnel, 1523-31.

570.   vii.   ISAAC, b. Mar. 15, 1766; d. Apr. 2, 1766.

571.   viii.   SARAH, b. Oct. 1, 1767; m. Jan. 1, 1795, Reuben Harrison, of Branford, Ct.; d. Aug. 22, 1874. He d. Sept. 19, 1845, ae. 76. Ch.: (1) Elisa, b. Oct. 29, 1796; d. Apr. 13, 1808.

572.   ix.   ISAAC, b. Sept. 7, 1769; m. Peggy Fitchet, 1532.

573.   x.   RUFUS, b. Mar. 24, 1771; m. Elizabeth Harrison, 1533-40.

574.   xi.   ASA, b. Dec. 28, 1773; m. Olive Linsley, 1541-2.

575.   xii.   DAVID, b. Mar. 28, 1776; m. Elizabeth Smith, 1543-7.

576.   xiii.   BENJAMIN, b. Aug. 1, 1778; m. Sally Parmele Hall, Betsy Hall, Harriet Homiston, 1548-54.

577.   xiv.   POLLY, b. May 17, 1780; m. 1st, Jan. 17, 1814, Joel Doolittle, of Wallingford, Ct. He d. ———; m. 2nd, Russell Hill, of North Guildford and East Haven, Ct. Ch.: Eliza, b. ———; m. a Church.

198. SAMUEL FOOTE, (54, 16, 5, 1,) b. May 12, 1740; m. Dec. 28, 1764, Anna Harrison. She was b. May 12, 1743. He d. Dec. 12, 1798. She d. Sept. 30, 1819. Res., Brandon, Ct.

578.   i.   SAMUEL, b. Dec. 25, 1765; m. Submit Foote, 1554-9.

579.   ii.   ANNA, b. Sept. 25, 1769; m. Jan. 1, 1794, Deacon Munson Linsley, of Branford, Ct.; d. Feb. 11, 1842. He d. June 13, 1845, ae. 76. Ch.: (1) Samuel, bap. May 20, 1799. (2) Esther Lois, bap. May 20,

1799. (3) Angelina, bap. May 20, 1799. (4) Cleora D., bap. Dec. 1, 1799. (5) Marcus, bap. Aug. 2, 1801. (6) Alfred, bap. July 3, 1803. (7) Mary, bap. Mar. 30, 1805. (8) Lucy Ann, bap. Feb. 28, 1813.

580. iii. ENOS, b. Mar. 4, 1772; m. Roxanna Perkins, 1560.
581. iv. LOIS, b. Nov. 26, 1774; d. May 14, 1790.
582. v. EUNICE, b. July 14, 1777; m. Dr. Joseph Foote, of North Haven, Ct.; d. Nov. 12, 1833.
583. vi. URIAH, b. Jan. 15, 1780; m. Esther Goodyear, 1561-4.
584. vii. THADDEUS, b. Dec. 1, 1783; m. Polly Forward, 1565-71.

200. DR. JARED FOOTE, (56, 16, 5, 1,) b. July 17, 1735; m. 1st, May 12, 1763, Submit Bishop. She d. June 11, 1810, ae. 72; m. 2nd, Nov. 13, 1812, Sarah Stillman; she d. Apr. 28, 1858, ae. 58; m. 3rd, Aug. 11, 1815, Jemima Holcomb; she d. Oct. 5, 1816; m. 4th, May 20, 1817, Hannah Kimberly. He d. Oct. 11, 1820. She d. ———. Res., Branford Ct.

585. i. OLIVE, b. ———; m. Nov. 23, 1791, Jude Smith, of North Haven, Ct.
586. ii. SUBMIT, b. Feb. 7, 1766; m. Samuel Foote, Jr., of Branford, Ct.
587. iii. ANNA, b. Nov. 5, 1769; d. Aug. 25, 1786.
588. iv. JOSEPH, b. May 12, 1770; m. Mary Bassett and Eunice Foote, 1572-7.
589. v. LUCY, b. ———; m. Feb. 29, 1796, John Vills, of North Haven, Ct.

201. JOSEPH FOOTE, (56, 16, 5, 1,) b. Mar. 3, 1737; m. Feb. 26, 1761, Abigail Winchel; d. Nov. 19, 1762; she d. Aug. 14, 1774, ae. 43; res., North Branford, Ct.

590. i. ABIGAIL, b. 1762; m. Sept. 10, 1782, John Plyment, of Cheshire, Ct.; d. Feb. 15, 1802; he d. Mar. 13, 1826, ae. 63. Ch.: (1) William Champlin, b. May 2, 1783. (2) John. (3) Sarah. (4) Harriet. (5) Joseph. (6) Abigail, b. May 14, 1793.

202. JOHN FOOTE, (56, 16, 5, 1,) b. Feb. 18, 1740; m. 1st, Nov. 7, 1771, Ruth, dau. of Caleb Culver, of Wallingford, Ct.; she d. Aug. 7, 1812, ae. 61; m. 2nd, 1789, Sarah, dau. of Samuel Culver, of Wallingford, Ct.; he d. Feb. 15, 1830; res., North Branford, Ct.

591. i. JOHN, b. July 25, 1772; m. Huldah Fowler, 1578-9.
592. ii. JOSIAH, b. June 25, 1775; m. Lydia Lyme.
593. iii. HANNAH, b. Feb. 19, 1784; m. Albert Todd, of North Branford, Ct.
594. iv. POLLY, b. Dec. 26, 1789; m. Chas. E. Thompson, of Guilford, Ct.

205. ICHABOD FOOTE, (56, 16, 5, 1,) b. Feb. 24, 1746; m. Aug. 21, 1767, Jemima, dau. of Dea. Stephen Smith, of E. Haven, Ct.; d. Feb. 26, 1830, in Franklin, N. Y. A Revolutionary soldier. She d. 1840, ae. 92; res., N. Branford, Ct., and Johnstown, N. Y.

595. i. REBECCA, b. Dec. 17, 1768.
596. ii. JEMIMA, b. Nov. 25, 1771.
597. iii. STEPHEN, b. Jan. 23, 1774; m. Mary Wilson, 1584-7.
598. iv. JAIRUS, b. June 5, 1776; m. ———, dau. of Noah Willson, of Torrington, Ct.; res., Franklin, N. Y.
599. v. ANSON, b. Mar. 11, 1779; d. May 12, 1781.

600 vi. ANSON S., b. Aug. 27, 1784; m. Clarissa Buel, 1588-93.

601. vii. SON, not named, b. and d. in infancy.

602. viii. JARED, b. Jan. 22, 1789; m. Sally Scott, 1594-1600.

603. ix. ICHABOD C., b. Dec. 9, 1791; m. Harty Kingsley, 1601-7.

207. CAPT. ROBERT FOOTE, (56, 16, 5, 1,) b. 1752; m. 1st, Nov. 17, 1774, Rachel Lewis; she d. Nov. 27, 1820; m. 2nd, Apr. 11, 1822, Sarah Bishop; she d. Jan. 23, 1844, ae. 88. He d. Apr. 10, 1836; res., Southington, Ct.

604. i. ASAHEL, b. Oct. 22, 1775; m. Elsie Barret and Rosehannah Barnes, 1608-10.

605. ii. ROBERT, b. Sept. 22, 1779; m. Diadena Hitchcock and Lucina Dunham, 1611-12.

606. iii. LUCY, b. Jan. 6, 1783; m. Feb. 28, 1805, Quartus P. Newell, of Southington, Ct.; she d. Mar. 20, 1853. Ch.: (1) Sophia, b. Mar. 27, 1806. (2) Lydia. (3) Lucy. (4) Janette. (5) Jane, b. Aug. 15, 1816.

607. iv. LEWIS, b. Sept. 26, 1789; m. Orra Newell and Catharine F. Adams, 1613-6.

608. v. LEONARD, b. Apr. 8, 1791; m. Beda Wright, 1617-22.

208. HELI FOOTE, (56, 16, 5, 1,) b. 1755; m. 1st, 1780, Silence, wid. of John Harrison, and dau. of Joseph Frisbie. She d. abt. 1709; m. 2nd, abt. 1793, Ruth, dau. of Hiram Polley; she d. 1832 or 1833 in Fredonia, N. Y. He d. Oct. 30, 1827; res., North Branford, Ct., Johnstown and Deerfield, N. Y.

609. i. BETSY, b. Aug. 19, 1781; m. Jan. 18, 1798, David Butler, of N. Branford, Ct., until 1829, and then of Atwater, O. Ch.: (1) Rufus, b. July 16, 1799. (2) Luther. (3) Mary. (4) Fanny. (5) Harriet E. (6) Jane. (7) John Lester. (8) Elizabeth. (9) Tryphena. (10) Lydia. (11) Martha Ann. (12) William D. (13) Sarah, b. Aug. 19, 1825.

610. ii. ANSON, b. July 5, 1783; m. Clarissa Gould and Eunice Hutchinson, 1623-8.

611. iii. SALLY LAMENT, b. July 12, 1786; m. June 19, 1805, Philander, son of John Walker, of Guilford, Ct., by the Rev. Nathaniel Burgess. She d. 1832 at North Branford, Ct.; res., Guilford, Ct. Ch.: (1) James Walker, b. Oct. 21, 1805; res., Guilford, Ct.; unm. (2) Abigail Walker, b. Mar. 24, 1807; m. Dec. 26, 1826, Adolphus Palmer; res., Branford, Ct. (3) Sarah W. Walker, b. Nov. 24, 1808; m. June 26, 1826, John S. Small; she d. Apr., 1876, at Colfax, Ia. Ch.: (a) Henry J. F. Small, b. Mar. 18, 1828; res., (Longwood) Chicago, Ill. (b) William J. Small, b. ———; res., Colfax, Ia. (c) Elizabeth Small, b. ———; m. ———. Benton; res., Colfax, Ia. (4) George Walker, b. Oct. 26, 1810; m. Orange, 1831, Minerva Ford, moved to Watertown, N. Y. Ch.: (a) Edward, b———, and several others. (5) John Walker, b. Feb. 24, 1812; m. Mar., 1834, Ann W. Boardman; 4 ch., 2 sons who d. in infancy, 2 daus. who res. in New Haven 1875. (6) Fanny W. Walker, b. July 31, 1814; m. Nov. 9, 1835, Sidney A. Thomas; res., New Haven, Ct.

612. iv. HARVEY, b. 1795; m. Amy Northrop, 1629-32.

613. v. SUSANNAH, b. 1797; m. Henry Heard; she d. 1831.

614. vi. POLLY, b. 1798; m. Ezekiel Foster.
615. vii. HIRAM, b. 1800; d. 1817.
616. viii. HELI, b. 1800; m. Catharine Nichols, 1633-7.
617. ix. CLARISSA, b. Oct. 11, 1805; m. Apr., 1829, Jacob C. Space, of Utica, N. Y. Ch.: (1) Edward Heli. (2) Susannah Foote.
618. x. HENRY, b. Mar. 4, 1808; m. Harriet Northrop and Jane Champlin, 1638-50.
619. xi. PROSPER P., b. 1814; m. Delia Metcalf, 1651-3.
620. xii. WILLIAM, b. Aug. 7, 1816; m. Clarinda Dickinson, 1654-6.
621. xiii. THOMAS, b. 1818; m. Mary Ann Somyer, 1657-8.

209. JESSE FOOTE, (56, 16, 5, 1,) b. Jan. 22, 1758; m. 1st, 1777, Rachel, dau. of Jabez and Charity (Booth) Benedict; she was b. 1754, d. Aug. 3, 1803, ae. 49; m. 2nd, 1804, Elizabeth Taylor; d. June 24, 1842. She d. Aug. 17, 1844, ae. 87; res., Danbury, Ct., and Johnstown, N. Y. He was a Soldier of the Revolution.
622. i. ANNA, b. Aug. 5, 1778; m. 1801, ——. ——, of Mayfield, N. Y.
623. ii. JABEZ, b. Dec. 26, 1779; m. Ann Carey, 1659-62.
624. iii. RUTH, b. Dec. 26, 1779; d. 1820.
625. iv. CHARITY, b. Feb. 20, 1784; d. 1810.
626. v. DAMARIS, b. May 23, 1786; m. 1st, John Sands; m. 2nd, Albertus Day, of Shemo Bay, N. Y.
627. vi. JESSE FINCH, b. Aug. 11, 1788; m. Angelca Van Buren, 1663-73.
628. vii. HANNAH, b. Feb. 21, 1791; d. Sept. 30, 1811.

211. SAMUEL FOOTE, (60, 18, 5, 1,) b. 1723; m. June 5, 1750, Mary, dau. of John Lyon, of Haddam, Ct.; d. June 9, 1776; res., Watertown, Ct.; she m. June 6, 1780, Timothy Judd, of Watertown, Ct., and d. Oct., 1782.
629. i. MARY, b. Jan. 10, 1751; d. Apr. 9, 1768.
630. ii. DAVID, b. Jan. 24, 1753; m. Mary Scovel, 1674-81.
631. iii. ELIZABETH, b. July 1, 1755; m. Roger Avery, a soldier of the Revolution.
632. iv. ANNA, b. Oct. 16, 1757; m. Benj. Avery, a Soldier in the Revolution.
633. v. SAMUEL, b. May 2, 1760; m. Sarah McDonald, 1682-3.
634. vi. HULDAH, b. Feb. 13, 1762; m. James McDonald, of Watertown, Ct.; d. Feb. 7, 1796.
635. vii. LUCY, b. Oct. 8, 1764; d. May 7, 1767.
636. viii. ABRAHAM, b. 1766; d. Sept. 5, 1777.

214. EBENEZER FOOTE, (60, 18, 5, 1,) b. 1730; m. June 17, 1752, Martha, dau. of John Moss, of Wallingford, Ct.; she was b. Sept. 1733. He d. Dec. 23, 1763, at Cornwall, Vt. She m. John Hart, of Cornwall, Vt.; he d. and she m. John Thompson, of Goshen, Ct.; she d. there Dec. 18, 1804.
637. i. MARTHA, b. Aug. 25, 1753; m. Mar. 15, 1769, Aaron, son of Col. Ebenezer Norton, of Goshen, Ct.; in Feb., 1796, they moved to East Bloomfield, N. Y.; he d. there Nov. 30, 1828, ae. 85. She d. the same year. Ch.: (1) Huldah, b. Jan. 24, 1770; m. May 7, 1793, Cyrus Collins (his bro. m. No. 641). (2) Betsy, b. July 12, 1771; m. Aug. 17, 1792, Roswel Humphrey; d. 1841. (3) Ebenezer F., b. Nov. 7, 1774; m. Dec. 21, 1798, Abigail Kibbe. (4) Aaron, b. May 12, 1776; m. Abigail Fyler; d. June 1, 1825, in O. (5) Patty, b. Jan. 24, 1780; m. Oct. 23, 1823, Peter Brown; d. Oct. 24, 1844. (6) Elisha, b. Aug. 6, 1781; m. Apr. 3, 1803, Margaret

Clarke. (7) Reuben, b. June 15, 1783; m. Dec. 5, 1805, Clarissa
Steele. (8) Philo, b. June 20, 1785; m. Charlotte Shepard; d.
June 1, 1830. (9) Harvey, b. Dec. 18, 1786. (10) Mavana, b.
Mar. 15, 1792; m. Apr. 30, 1815, Harvey Hobart. (11) Olive, b.
Feb. 28, 1794; m. J. Wadhams. (12) Miles, b. Apr. 9, 1799; m.
Vina Dibble.

638. ii.   HANNAH, b. Feb. 26, 1758; m. Aug. 13, 1772, Berwin Baldwin,
of Goshen, Ct.; d. June 10, 1823. He d. Sept. 6, 1833, ae. 81.
Ch.: (1) Mary Ann, b. Nov. 29, 1773; m. Amos Tolles, of Colebrook, Ct.; d.; had six ch. (2) Timothy, b. Oct. 16, 1775; d.
Colebrook, Ct., Feb. 12, 1817; 9 ch. (3) Asahel, b. Oct. 23, 1777;
d. Dec. 7, 1777. (4) Nancy, b. Jan. 25, 1779. (5) Jonathan, b.
Apr. 17, 1781; d. Sept. 4, 1793. (6) Sylvester, b. Dec. 14, 1783;
m. Candace, dau. of Levi Ives; 10 ch. (7) Birdsey, b. Feb. 3,
1786; m. Lucia, dau. of Daniel Baldwin; res., Goshen, Ct.; 7 ch.
(8) Betsy, b. May 18, 1788; m. Nov. 11, 1811, Allen Maltbie.
(9) Ammi R., b. Feb. 3, 1791; m. Sarah Sears, Sandsfield, Mass.;
3 ch. (10) Martha, b. May 9, 1793; m. Halsie Bigelow; 3 ch.
She d. Mar. 16, 1826. (11) Jonathan, b. abt. 1795; m. Laura
Wilton, of Goshen, Ct.; 5 ch. (12) Laura, b. Jan. 18, 1798; m.
Jesse Maltbie; she d. Apr. 19, 1824, leaving one child.

639. iii.   OLIVE, b. Mar. 6, 1758; d. July 31, 1759.

640. iv.   OLIVE, b. July 12, 1760; d. Apr. 24, 1762.

641. v.   OLIVE, b. July 24, 1762; m. Nov. 3, 1782, Philo Collins, of
Goshen, Ct.; d. Feb. 7, 1838. He was b. Jan. 5, 1761, and d.
May 8, 1833. Ch.: (1) Olive, b. Sept. 19, 1783; m. July 9, 1809,
Benj. Sedgwick, of Cornwall, Ct. (2) Martha, b. Sept. 1, 1786.
(3) Betsey, b. Aug. 22, 1795; m. Jan. 6, 1824, Julius Bell, of
Cornwall, Ct.; 1 ch. (4) Harriet, b. Mar. 9, 1798; m. William
Miles, of Goshen, Ct. They have 11 ch. (5) Emily, b. Sept. 13,
1801; m. Oct. 30, 1837, O. M. Hogeland; she d. July 8, 1846,
leaving 3 children.

215. TIMOTHY FOOTE, (60, 18, 5, 1,) b. 1735; m. 1st, June 5, 1755, Sarah,
dau. of Dea. Jonathan Garnsey, of Waterbury, Ct.; she d. Oct. 22, 1777, ae. 41; m.
2nd, Mar. 11, 1778, Lucy (Parks), wid. of Preserved Wheeler, of Woodbury, Ct.;
she d. Mar. 6, 1815. He d. May 8, 1799.

642. i.   SARAH, b. Mar. 29, 1756; m. Samuel Reynolds, of Plymouth, Ct.

643. ii.   TIMOTHY, b. Nov. 4, 1757; d. June 15, 1762.

644. iii.   JEMIMA, b. Nov. 9, 1759; m. Thomas R. Reynolds, of Plymouth,
Ct.

645. iv.   LEWIS, b. Oct. 5, 1761; m. Lois Wentworth, 1683-8.

646. v.   ABIGAIL, b. Oct. 15, 1764; m. 1st, Michael Dayton, of Water.
town, Ct.; he d. Feb. 9, 1805, ae. 58; m. 2nd, ———. Church.

647. vi.   TIMOTHY, b. Apr. 5, 1768; m. Abigail Stoddard, 1689-93.

648. vii.   JONATHAN NORTHRUP, b. May 17, 1774; d. Nov. 16, 1776.

649. viii.   LUCY ROSANNAH, b. Apr. 29, 1779.

216. DR. NATHAN FOOTE, (60, 18, 5, 1,) b. Jan. 25, 1738; m. June 12,
1759, Mavina, dau. of Wm. Selkrigg, of Waterbury, Ct. Dr. Foote came from

Waterbury, Ct., in 1774, and was the first settler in the town of Cornwall, Vt. He was driven back by the Indians, and went to Watertown, Ct., for five years, returning to Cornwall, Vt., after the war, with his family. He d. July 25, 1808. She d. Sept. 26, 1814, ae. 74.

650. i.   DANIEL, b. Apr. 3, 1760; m. Sarah Johnson and Ellen Scott, 1694-7.

651. ii.   NATHAN, b. Nov. 16, 1761; m. Sarah Sutherland and Hester Hunt, 1698-1703.

652. iii.   MILLESCENT, b. Nov. 6, 1763; m. 1783, Jedediah Durfay, of Cornwall, Vt.; d. Aug. 15, 1802, at Lincoln, Vt. Ch.: (1) Olive, b. May 9, 1784. (2) Eli, b. Apr. 21, 1786. (3) Electa, b. Aug. 25, 1788. (4) Lovica, b. Nov. 7, 1790. (5) Nancy, b. Mar. 17, 1793. (6) Truman, b. Sept. 19, 1796.

653. iv.   ABIJAH, b. Mar. 23, 1766; m. Polly Bronson, 1703-½.

654. v.   URI, b. July 12, 1768; m. Rhoda Pierson, 1704-½.

655. vi.   JESSE, b. in Williamstown, Mass., Sept. 17, 1770; d. Dec. 7, 1772, at Clarendon, Vt.

656. vii.   MARIAN, b. in Clarendon, Vt., Nov. 6, 1772; m. Feb., 1795, Asher Omstead, of Cornwall, Vt.; d. Apr. 4, 1798. Ch.: (1) Lucius F., of Cayuga, N. Y.; he has ch.

657. viii. JESSE SELKRIGG, b. in Cornwall, Vt., May 17, 1776; m. Abby Hosley, of Salisbury, Vt.; she d. at Southfield, N. Y., 1819; m. 2nd, 1821, at Chittenango, N. Y., Eliza Denis, 1705-11.

658. ix.   THOMAS, b. in Rutland, Vt., July 9, 1778; lost at sea Sept. 3, 1819; unm.

659. x.   WILLIAM, b. Sept. 5, 1780; m. Patty Janes, 1711¼-½.

660. xi.   PARTHENIA M., b. at Cornwall, Vt., May 5, 1784; d. unm.

217. THOMAS FOOTE, (60, 18, 5, 1,) b. May 10, 1740; m. 1st, May 17, 1762, Rebecca dau. of John Doud, of Middletown, Ct.; she d. Apr. 22, 1799, ae. 58; m. 2nd, Anna (Baldwin), wid. of Eli Adams; d. Feb. 18, 1803; she d. Oct. 2, 1824, ae. 65; res., Watertown, Ct.

661. 1.   AMOS, b. Jan. 15, 1763; m. Anna Seymour and Eunice Daley.

662. ii.   RACHEL, b. June 18, 1764; m. 1st, Matthew, son of Dea. Thomas and Anna (Rice) Dutton; he d. June 18, 1783; m. 2nd, Stephen Turner. She d. June 18, 1783; res., Watertown, Ct. Ch.: (1) Keziah, b. 1783; m. June 1, 1800, Allyn Merriam, of Watertown, Ct. He d.; m. 2nd, May 8, 1814, David Hickox; m. 3rd, Elam Beardslee. He m. 2nd No. 679.

663. iii.   REBECCA, b. 1769; m. Daniel Matthews, of Watertown, Ct.; d. Jan. 26, 1794.

664. iv.   A son, not named, b. ———; d. Feb. 8, 1773.

218. CAPT. JOHN FOOTE, (60, 18, 5, 1,) b. Aug. 24, 1742; m. 1st, July 26, 1764, Esther, dau. of David Mattoon, of Waterbury, Ct. She d. Mar. 10, 1769, ae. 26; m. 2nd, July 20, 1769, Mary, dau. of Gideon Peck, of Harwinton, Ct. He was a Revolutionary soldier; he d. July 5, 1809. She d. Nov. 22, 1822, at Ogdensburgh, N. Y., ae. 77; res., Waterbury, Ct.

665. i.   EBENEZER, b. Apr. 16, 1765; d. Feb. 16, 1768.

666. ii.   JOHN, b. Dec. 17, 1766; d. Aug. 13, 1772; killed by the kick of a horse.

667. iii. ESTHER MATTOON, b. July 30, 1770; m. June 26, 1788, Isaac Edwards, of Watertown, Ct. Ch.: One dau. and six sons, all heads of families.

668. iv. RUTH, b. Aug. 29, 1771; m. 1792, Thomas John Davies, of Watertown, Ct. He d. 1845. Six ch. For complete record see Davies Gen.

669. v. EBENEZER, b. July 6, 1773; m. Elizabeth Colt, 1712. / 8 / 2.

670. vi. JOHN, b. Apr. 25, 1775; d. 1806, in Watertown, Ct.; unm.

671. vii. MARY, b. Jan. 24, 1778; m. 1st, Samuel Howes; he d. Jan. 3, 1799, ae. 25; m. 2nd, 1806, Amos Lane, Esq., Counselor-at-Law, of Ogdensburgh, N. Y. Ch.: Four sons and two daus.

672. viii. SABREA, b. June 29, 1779; d. Jan. 27, 1780.

673. ix. SABREA, b. Mar. 11, 1781; m. Jan. 1, 1802, Silah Scovill; he was b. Dec. 4, 1776; d. Sept. 7, 1847. She d. Apr. 12, 1854. Ch.: (1) Hubert Scovill, b. Nov. 19, 1802; m. May 18, 1831, Eliza Porter; she d. Nov. 29, 1895. He d. Feb. 7, 1891. Ch.: (a) Marion Foote Scovill, b. Apr. 11, 1832; m. ———. Burr; d. Oct. 29, 1878. Ch.: Prof. W. H. Burr, 151 West 74th St., N. Y. (b) Alfred Foote Scovill, b. Oct. 12, 1833; d. Jan. 14, 1849. (c) George Marshall Scovill, b. Sept. 2, 1835; d. Mar. 24, 1837. (d) Henry Hubert Scovill, b. July 13, 1841; d. Oct. 14, 1844. (e) Alfred Hubert, b. Nov. 15, 1849; m. Oct. 22, 1879, Lucy Toune Johnson; she d. Oct. 22, 1903. Ch.: (i.) Charlotte Eliza Scovill, b. Dec. 6, 1880. (ii) Marion Foote Scovill, b. Apr. 13, 1882. (iii) Sabrea Scovill, b. June 4, 1884. (iv.) Helen Johnson Scovill, b. Dec. 31, 1887. (v.) Alfred Hubert Scovill, Jr., b. Nov. 29, 1890. (2) Edward Augustine Scovill, b. Mar. 27, 1810; d. Dec. 25, 1810. (3) Sarah Lavinia Scovill, b. Mar. 24, 1813; m. Sept. 18, 1834, William H. Marshall; res., Ogdensburgh, N. Y. Ch.: (a) John H., b. Aug. 1, 1842; m. Nov. 10, 1875, Nellie Hubbard, of Cheshire, Ct. Ch.: (i.) Sarah Lucilla. (ii.) Louise Benton. (b) Eveline L., b. Oct. 10, 1849; m. H. E. Fenton, of New Haven, Ct. (c) George D., b. ———, 1851; m. Lilla Gove, of Lock, Cal. Ch.: (i.) Luverne Leathe. (ii.) Warren; res., Shanghai, China.

674. x. LAVANIA, b. Apr. 29, 1787; m. Joseph York, of Ogdensburgh, N. Y. He d. 1829. Ch.: (1) Mary Elsie, b. ———; m. David M. Chapin; she d. Apr. 8, 1891, at Ogdensburgh, N. Y. Ch.: (a) Mary Lavina, b. July 17, 1840; m. Sept. 3, 1862, Capt. George Berneut Bacon, U. S. N.; res., 13 St. Felix St., Brooklyn, N. Y. Ch.: (i) Mary Chapin Bacon, b. Aug. 2, 1863; m. Sept. 3, 1885, Silas Edgar Brown, M. D.; res., 22 Greene St., Ogdensburgh, N. Y. Ch.: (i1) Josephine Chapen Brown, b. Oct. 20, 1887. (i2) Marion Hastings Brown, b. July 12, 1889. (i3) George Bacon Brown, b. Apr. 9, 1893. (ii) Sophia Louise Bacon, b. Jan. 27, 1866; m. Oct. 5, 1893, Morton Voorkes Brokan; res., Bound Brook, N. J. Ch.: (ii1) Elizabeth Bacon Brokan, b. Mar. 24, 1898, at Brooklyn, N. Y. (ii2) Mary Virginia Brokan, b. Oct. 15, 1900, at Brooklyn, N. Y. (iii) Fanny Hastings Bacon, b. Jan. 24, 1872, at Brooklyn, N. Y.; m. June 4, 1896, Will Walter Jackson; res., 13 St. Felix Street, Brooklyn, N. Y. Ch.: (iii1) Morris

Bacon Jackson, b. May 27, 1898. (iii2) George Berneut Jackson, b. Apr. 4, 1900. (iii3) Katherine King Jackson, b. Apr. 15, 1906. All b. at Brooklyn, N. Y. (b) Joseph York Chapin, b. Aug. 4, 1843; res., 22 Greene St., Ogdensburg, N. Y.; unm. (c) Sophia Elizabeth Chapin, b. Dec. 29, 1847; m. Jan. 27, 1876, Jacob B. Wells. Ch.: (i.) Elsie Bogert Wells, b. Mar. 18, 1880; d. Jan. 6, 1888. (ii.) Theodore Bassett Wells, b. Oct. 11, 1883; res., 14 So. Elliott Place, Brooklyn, N. Y. (d) Louise Elsie Chapin, b. Nov. 7, 1853; m. Jan. 26, 1885, Melancthon H. Seymore, of Montreal, Que.; res., 25 Chomedey St., Montreal, Que. Ch.: (i.) David Chapin Seymore, b. Dec. 22, 1885. (ii.) Allyn Olmsted Seymore, b. Aug. 14, 1887. (iii.) Louise Elsie Seymore, b. Jan. 21, 1889. (iv.) Howard York Seymore, b. Sept. 2, 1891. (e) David John Chapin, b. July 25, 1858; d. Jan. 13, 1861. (2) Joseph York, Jr.

675. xi.   SAMUEL ALFRED, b. Dec. 17, 1790; m. Mariam Fowler and Jane Campbell, 1713-23.

219. JACOB FOOTE, (60, 18, 5, 1,) b. Oct. 30, 1744; m. Dec. 25, 1776, Esther Doolittle. She d. Aug. 30, 1790, ae. 46, in Watertown, Ct.; m. 2nd, May 26, 1791, Rhoda Saxton; d. Apr. 6, 1810. She d. in Whitesborough, N. Y.; res., Watertown, Ct., and Harpersfield, N. Y.

676. i.   ABIAH, b. Aug. 31, 1767; d. Jan. 13, 1774.
677. ii.   REUBEN, b. July 16, 1769; d. Nov. 14, 1769.
678. iii.   REUBEN, b. Dec. 4, 1771; m. Silence Hitchcock, 1724-6.
679. iv.   LUCY, b. Sept. 7, 1772; m. 1795, Daniel Matthews his 1st wife was No. 663) of Watertown, Ct. In 1804 moved to Harpersfield, N. Y., and in 1837 to Meriden, Mich. Ch.: (1) Rebecca. (2) George.
680. v.   MILES, b. Sept. 13, 1774; m. Polly Hitchcock and Esther Northrup, 1727-34.
681. vi.   JACOB, b. June 14, 1776; d. June 22, 1776.
682. vii.   ABIAH, b. Aug. 22, 1777; d. Jan. 13, 1797.
683. viii.   EUNICE, b. May 3, 1779; m. Samuel Hendry, of Carlisle, N. Y.
684. ix.   BETSY, b. Mar. 9, 1782; m. Abraham Jones, of Jefferson, N. Y.; 3 ch.
685. x.   SYLVIA, b. June 18, 1783; m. Samuel Clark, of Eden and Boston, Erie Co., N. Y.
686. xi.   JACOB, b. Apr. 21, 1789; m. Amanda Givens, 1735-42.

220. JOSEPH FOOTE, (60, 18, 5, 1,) b. Apr. 3, 1747; m. Nov. 6, 1768, Thankful, dau. of Stephen Ives, of Wallingford Ct. She was b. July 15, 1744; d. Feb. 3, 1792. He d. June 29, 1789; res., Watertown, Ct.

687. i.   MARY, b. Aug. 12, 1769; d. Sept. 7, 1771.
688. ii.   JOSEPH, b. Sept. 4, 1772; m. Abigail Baldwin, 1743-9.
689. iii.   STEPHEN, b. Jan. 24, 1774; m. Rhoda Hand, 1750-7.
690. iv.   JAMES, b. Sept. 27, 1776; d. May 3, 1795.
691. v.   THANKFUL, b. ——; d. unm. abt. 24 years old.
692. vi.   ASENATH, b. Nov. 20, 1780; m. Ruliff Perry, of Scipio, N. Y.
693. vii.   PHEBE, b. Oct. 8, 1782; d. Apr. 5, 1807.
694. viii.   ROXANA, b. Sept. 9, 1784; d. Oct. 30, 1804.
695. ix.   MARY, b. Apr. 17, 1787; d. Oct. 27, 1806.

696. x. EZRA, b. Feb. 12, 1789; d. abt. 1806.

221. ISAAC FOOTE, (60, 18, 5, 1,) b. Mar. 15, 1750; m. Aug. 21, 1770, Sarah, dau. of John Selkrigg; she was b. Mar. 12, 1751; d. Oct., 1815; he d. June, 1834; res., Watertown, Ct., and Windsor, N. Y.

697. i. ALLEN, b. Jan. 22, 1771; m. Betsey Andrus.

698. ii. ANNA, b. July 30, 1772; m. 1st, Rufus Goff, of Chatham, Ct.; 3 ch.; m. 2nd, March 24, 1799, Reuben, son of Orlando Bridgeman, of Bainbridge, N. Y, Ch.: (1) Amelia Bainbridge; m. Aaron Myers. (2) William, m. Nancy Seymour (Rev.). (3) Peter Goff, unm. (4) Electa, m. Cyrus McMaster. (5) Laura, m. Ebenezer Stowell. (6) Paulina, m. Ebenezer Stowell. (7) Lewis Hunt. (8) Miranda.

699. iii. ISAAC, b. Jan. 16, 1774; m. Esther Andrus.

700. iv. SARAH, b. June 20, 1779; m. Dan Todd, of Woodbridge, Ct.; removed to Homer, N. Y.

701. v. TITUS, b. Aug. 25, 1781; m. Elizabeth Bronson, Patience Bills, Hannah Bills, 1758-60.

222. JONATHAN FOOTE, (61, 18, 5, 1,) b. Jan. 28, 1737; m. Nov. 19, 1761, Lydia, dau. of Noah Baldwin. He d. Jan. 11, 1801. She d. May 9, 1825, ae. 89.; res., North Branford, Ct.

702. i. JONATHAN, b. June 24, 1762; d. June 25, 1762.

703. ii. JONATHAN, b. May 3, 1765; m. Esther Russell, 1761-3.

704. iii. ELIZABETH, b. Sept. 5, 1767; m. Chauncey Hall, of Cheshire, Ct.

705. iv. LYDIA, b. June 11, 1770; d. Nov. 24, 1791, unm.

706. v. SAMUEL, b. May 21, 1773; m. Lydia Baldwin, 1764-70.

707. vi. JOHN, b. Jan. 26, 1775; d. young.

708. vii. NOAH BALDWIN, b. Mar. 6, 1777.

223. REV. JOHN FOOTE, (61, 18, 5, 1,) b. Apr. 2, 1742; m. Nov. 19, 1767, Abigail, dau. of Rev. Samuel Hall, of Wallingford, Ct. She d. Nov. 19, 1788, ae. 39; m. 2nd, Apr. 28, 1791, Eunice, dau. of John Hall, Esq., of Cheshire, Ct. Mr. Foote was graduated at Yale College, 1765, studied Divinity, and succeeded Rev. Mr. Hall as pastor of the Congregational Church in Cheshire; d. Aug. 31, 1813. She d. Jan. 31, 1819.

709. i. ABIGAIL SARAH HALL, b. Jan. 2, 1769; d. Jan. 20, 1775.

710. ii. MARY ANN, b. Sept. 21, 1770; m. ———.

711. iii. LUCINDA, b. May 19, 1772; m. July 29, 1790, Thomas T. Cornwall, M.D., of Middletown, Ct.; d. Aug. 23, 1834. He d. Feb. 16, 1846, ae. 79. Ch.: (1) Matilda, b. Oct. 5, 1791; d. July 12, 1794. (2) Lucinda. (3) Abigail Hall. (4) Lucinda. (5) John Alfred. (6) Child, not named. (7) Mary Ann. (8) William Roderick. (9) Edward Augustus. (10) Grace Ann Elizabeth, b. Sept. 10, 1811; d. Feb. 12, 1816.

712. iv. JOHN ALFRED, b. June 2, 1774; d. Aug. 23, 1794.

713. v. ABIGAIL MARY ANN, b. Sept. 16, 1776; d. Aug. 23, 1794; unm.

714. vi. WILLIAM LAMBERT, b. Oct. 10, 1778; m. Mary Scovill, 1771-6.

715. vii. SAMUEL AUGUSTUS, b. Nov. 8, 1780; m. Eucodia Hull, 1777-82.

716. viii. MATILDA, b. May 6, 1785; d. Oct. 9, 1787.

231. CAPT. ISAAC FOOTE, (72, 20, 5, 1,) b. Dec. 4, 1747; m. 1st, Apr. 24, 1768, Lydia, dau. of Peter Taylor, of Branford, Ct. She d. ———; m. 2nd, Sept. 20, 1796, Phebe Benton. He d. Mar. 14, 1818; she d. Dec., 1846, ae. 80; res., North Branford, Ct.

717. i.   ISAAC, b. Dec. 17, 1769; d. June 25, 1796; unm.

718. ii.   MALICHI, b. Apr. 14, 1771; m. Martha Rockwell and Melissa ———, 1783-9.

719. iii. LYMAN HALL, b. June 29, 1773; m. Lucretia Page, 1790-7.

720. iv.   REBECCA, b. in Northford, Ct., Dec. 8, 1775; m. 1st, Dr. Benjamin Rockwell, of New York City, N. Y., Nov. 27, 1796. Dr. Rockwell d. April 1, 1815; m. 2nd, John McComb, widower, of New York City, June 24, 1821. Mr. McComb was the leading architect of that day, and built the now celebrated New York City Hall. There were no children by this marriage. Rebecca Foote McComb died at the home of William Rockwell, her grandson, at Plainfield, N. J., Mar. 31, 1870. Her children by her first husband are:

(1) William Rockwell, of New York City, b. July 18, 1800; m. Maria Gale at Goshen, N. Y., May 23, 1821. Mrs. Rockwell was born at Goshen, N. Y., Dec. 11, 1800. Both died at Long Branch, N. J., during the year 1867. They had no children William Rockwell was one of the leading physicians of New York, having been Health Officer of that Port. He served under General Banks in the Civil War.

(2) Darwin Foote Rockwell, b. Sept. 28, 1807; m. Lucille S. Downer, dau. of Samuel Downer, of Westfield, N. J., Oct. 5, 1830. She was b. at Westfield, Nov. 22, 1810, and d. at Plainfield, N. J., Nov. 16, 1878. Mr. Rockwell engaged first in Rail Road affairs, and was later, for many years, Superintendent of the Jersey City Ferry to New York City. He died at Jersey City May 31, 1849. Ch.: (a) James Burnet, b. at Jersey City, N. J., July 27, 1833; d. Feb. 2, 1843. (b) William, b. at Westfield, N. J., Apr. 12, 1837; m. Eleanora W. Locke, dau. of Ira Locke, at Glens Falls, N. Y., Jan. 13, 1870. Mrs. Rockwell was b. at Glens Falls Oct. 7, 1846. Mr. Rockwell is cashier of State Bank at Newark, N. J., having aways held financial positions. He resides at Plainfield, N. J. Ch.: (i.) William Locke, b. at Plainfield, Dec. 18, 1870; m. Lavinia Shivers, dau. of David Shivers, at Woodbury, N. J., Sept. 1, 1897; Mrs. Rockwell was b. Feb. 3, 1874. Mr. Rockwell is a lawyer at Newark, N. J. (ii.) Albert Vincent, b. at Plainfield, Oct. 31, 1872. (iii.) Harriet Roberts, b. at Plainfield, July 1, 1874. (iv.) Nora Locke, b. at Plainfield, N. J., Dec. 20, 1876. (v) Bertram Stanley, b. Newark, N. J., Jan. 7, 1879. (vi.) Lucille Downer, b. at Newark, Apr. 23, 1880. (vii.) Sidney Jerome, b. at Plainfield, Oct. 30, 1888. (c) Lucille Stanley, b. at Jersey City, May 30, 1839; m. 1st, Abraham Van Nest, of New Brunswick, N. J., May 30, 1864; he died May 17, 1865; childless; m. 2nd, Robert Dod, of 159 Littleton Ave., Newark, N. J., Nov. 25, 1874. Their ch. were: (i.) Lucilla, b. at Newark, May, 1877; d. Feb. 22, 1878. (ii.) Lydia,

b. at Newark, Jan. 26, 1879; d. May 3, 1887. (d) Rebecca, b. at Jersey City, Oct. 5, 1841; d. at Plainfield, N. J., Jan., 1903; unm. (e) Eliza De Forest, b. at Jersey City, May 7, 1844. (f) Harriet Downer, b. at Jersey City, May 3, 1846. (g) George Schuyler, b. at Jersey City, Dec. 4, 1848; m. Mattie Conkling, dau. of James H. Conkling, of Bellevale, N. Y., Feb. 26, 1891. Ch.: (i.) Raymond L., b. Sept. 10, 1896; d. Apr. 15, 1900.

(3) Benjamin Rockwell, b. June 26, 1813; m. Lavinia Bigelow Fenton, dau. of Joseph Seneca Fenton, banker, of. Norwich, N. Y., at Palmyra, N. Y., July 15, 1835. Mrs. Rockwell was b. Sept. 20, 1811, and d. at Yonkers, N. Y., Sept. 19, 1887. Mr. Rockwell d. at Yonkers, Feb. 4, 1887; he followed mercantile pursuits. Ch.: (a) Sarah Fenton, b. at Flint, Mich., Feb. 8, 1837, d. at Brooklyn, N. Y., 1853. (b) Fenton, b. at Flint, Mich., Apl. 28, 1839; m. Rebecca J. Dwight, dau. of Theo. Dwight, of Brooklyn, N. Y., Oct. 8, 1867. Mrs. Rockwell was b. at New York City, Mar. 1, 1843. Fenton Rockwell, LL.B., Columbia University, N. Y., served in the Civil War from 1861 to 1866, and was Judge Advocate in the Department of the South. Since the war he has practiced law at Brooklyn, N. Y. Ch.: Benjamin Fenton, b. at Minneapolis, Minn., Sept. 17, 1868; m. Minnie Tracy Case, dau. of Joseph Silleck Case, a banker, Brooklyn, N. Y., Oct. 25, 1893. Mrs. Rockwell was born at Brooklyn, Jan. 1, 1869. Ch.: (1) Rodmond Case Rockwell, b. Mar. 4, 1895, at Brooklyn. (2) Helen Rockwell, b. May 4, 1896, at Brooklyn. (ii.) Theodore Dwight, b. at Brooklyn, N. Y., Jan. 8, 1874; d. Mar. 21, 1878. (iii.) Rebecca Dwight, b. at Brooklyn, Jan. 21, 1879.; (iv.) Dwight, b. at Brooklyn, Jan. 8, 1881; m. Virginia Tompkins, of and at Brooklyn, N. Y., Feb. 8, 1904; Mrs. Rockwell was b. April 29, 1883, at Brooklyn. (v.) Kate Bowers, b. at Brooklyn, June 22, 1883; d. July 21, 1885. (c) Julia Fenton, b. at Flint, Mich., Oct., 25, 1841; m. Thomas Astley Atkins, LL.B., Harvard University, 1860, at Brooklyn, N. Y., Oct. 25, 1860. Mr. Atkins was admitted to practice at the Bar of the State of New York, May, 1860. They moved to Yonkers, Westchester Co., N. Y., April, 1862, and Mr. Atkins in 1866 was elected Judge of the Court at that city, holding Court in the Old Phillipse Manor House. He has been Clerk of the Vestry of St. Paul's Church, Yonkers; Member of the Association of the Bar, N. Y. City; of the Union League Club, N. Y. City; of the Harvard Club, N. Y. City; President and Vice-President of the Yonkers Historical and Library Association; Member of the Harvard Law School Association; Trustee and Honorary Trustee of St. John's Hospital, Yonkers; Founder 1867 and now Honorary Member of the Palisade Boat Club of Yonkers, and an active participant in politics from the Lincoln campaign to date, having been in turn a representative in every Convention from the fraction of a City Ward to a National Convention. Their ch. were: (i.) Astley, b. Aug. 11, 1861, at

Bloomfield, N. J.; m. Alice Kindred Hyde at Newton, Mass., July 4, 1891, dau. of Albert Hyde. Mrs. Atkins was b. at New York City, Mar. 13, 1864. Mr. Atkins is engaged at Boston, Mass., in mercantile pursuits. Ch.: (i.1) Bowman Shepard, b. July 9, 1893, at New London, Ct. (i.2) Arthur Kindred, b. Oct. 6, 1895, at Melrose Highlands, Mass. (i.3) Josephine, and (i.4) Kate, b. Jan. 6, 1900, at Winthrop, Mass. (i.5) Alice, b. Nov. 12, 1904, at Newton Lower Falls, Mass. (ii.) Julia, b. Nov. 4, 1864; d. Nov. 17, 1864. (iii.) Fenton, b. Feb. 21, 1866; d. March 15, 1866. (iv.) Kate, b. Jan. 10, 1869, at Yonkers, N. J. (d) Benjamin Fenton, b. at Brooklyn, Jan. 29, 1847; d. at Brooklyn, N. Y., Sept. —, 1861.

721. v.   WILLIAM, b. Oct. 11, 1799; m. Cathrine Picket, 1798-1802.

722. vi.   LOIS, b. Mar. 13, 1784; bap. Apr. 25, 1784; a farmer; m., 1804, Luzone Bartholomew, b. July 31, 1781, in Northford, Ct. Ch.: (1) Rockwell, b. Dec. 7, 1805; res., Fair Haven, Ct. (2) Darwin Foote, b. Dec. 16, 1807; d. 1860 in Mendon, Ill. (3) Mary Jane, b. Sept., 1810; m. 1st, John Frisbie; m. 2nd, Lewis Elliott; res., Fair Haven, Ct.

723. vii. LYDIA, b. Dec. 15, 1785.

724. viii. ISAAC, b. aMy 21, 1799; m. Caroline Hall, 1803-7.

725. ix.   FREDERICK, b. Nov. 7, 1806; m. June 25, 1840, Sibyl Celestia Tuttle, 1808-13.

235. NATHANIEL FOOTE, (73, 25, 9, 3,) b. Feb. 7, 1742; m. 1st, Mar. 28, 1769, Jerusha Cadwell; she was b. Dec. 22, 1747, and d. Dec. 30, 1777; m. 2nd, July 16, 1778, Patience, dau. of Israel Skinner, of Colchester, Ct. She d. Mar. 12, 1790, ae. 35; m. 3rd, Jan. 31, 1791, Abigail, No. 245, dau. of Israel Foote, his cousin, of Colchester, Ct. He d. Jan. 22, 1829. She d. Jan. 2, 1852, ae. 94, at Colchester, Ct.

750. i.   HULDA, b. Dec. 15, 1769; m. June 18, 1789, Oliver Usher, of Chatham, Ct. She d. Sept. 21, 1791. Ch.: (1) Jerusha, b. ———; m. James Wakeman. They lived and d. at Macon, Ga.; p. s.

751. ii. NATHANIEL, b. June 8, 1779; d. Dec. 30, 1799, in New York City; unm. With him was lost the old family appellative, which had been continued for seven generations without interruption.

752. iii. JERUSHA, b. Feb. 1, 1783; m. Stephen Skinner (son of No. 240), of Colchester, Ct.; they moved to Western N. Y. and Maitland, Canada. She d. Nov. 11, 1846, at Burford, Ontario, Canada. Ch.: (1) Jira, was a doctor; res., Brantford, Canada; 3 children d. young. (2) Jerusha Skinner, b. ———; m. a widower, Dr. Church, of Marrickville, Canada. He was a Member of Parliament when he d. abt. 1830. She d. soon, leaving a dau., and was buried in Maitland. The dau. was brought up by her grandparents, and m. Mr. Hall.

753. iv. PATIENCE, b. Feb. 1, 1783; m. Oct. 31, 1797, William, son of William Brainard, of Westchester, Ct.; d. June 19, 1859. He d. Mar. 18, 1844. For complete family record see Brainard Genealogy. Ch.: (1) Jerusha, b. Aug. 31, 1800; m. May 6, 1823, Alfred Kellog, of Chatham, Ct.; p. s. (2) Nathaniel, b. Aug.

PATIENCE (FOOTE) BRAINERD.

HULDAH (FOOTE) BRAINARD.

From Brainerd-Brainard Genealogy.

20, 1801; m., Mar. 25, 1834, Lucy Brainard. (3) Lucy Day, b.
Nov. 4, 1804; m. Sept. 16, 1824, William Brainard, of East
Haddam, Ct. (4) Abigail Lucinda, b. Sept. 27, 1807; m. Sept.
26, 1832, Samuel Ackley Brainard, of East Hamilton, N. Y.; she
d. Mar. 26, 1864. He d. Mar. 26, 1864; p. s. (5) William, b.
Feb. 23, 1810; m. 1st, July 13, 1837, Eliza Carrier; she d. Aug.
22, 1852; m. 2nd, Rhoda Staples, May 4, 1853. (6) Margaret, b.
July 6, 1812; d. Apr. 11, 1860. (7) Clarissa Loomis, b. July 19,
1814; m. Nov. 27, 1834, Stephen Brainard Day, of Colchester, Ct.
(8) Asa, b. Dec. 24, 1816; m. Mar. 15, 1846, Susan Elizabeth
Buell, of Colchester. (9) Harriet Atwood, b. Sept. 23, 1819; m.
Mar. 7, 1866, Seymour Kellog, of Colchester, Ct. (10) Samuel
Newell, b. Apr. 14, 1822; m. May 22, 1853, Charlotte Fidelia
Williams, of Chatham, Ct.

754 v. ASA, b. Jan. 31, 1785; m. Betsey Gates, Esther Ann Ferry, and
Christina Brisban, 1825-33.

755. vi. LUCINDA, b. Apr. 24, 1788; m. Amasa Skinner; d. Nov. 10,
1790; p. s. He d. abt. 1875.

756. vii. ABSALOM, b. Mar. 1, 1790; d. Mar. 1, 1790.

757. viii. HULDAH, b. Dec. 4, 1791; m. Mar. 29, 1824, Amaziah, son of
William and Lucy (Day) Brainard, of Colchester, Ct. He was b.
June 12, 1780; d. Apr. 1, 1841. She d. at Hartford, Ct., Aug.
9, 1881, ae. 89 yrs., 8 mos., 5 ds. She was buried in the cemetery
in the Southwest district in Westchester, Ct., by the side of her
husband. She was of a quiet and gentle disposition, social and
pleasing in her manners, and much respected and beloved by her
relatives and friends. If the poor needed a helper or a friend,
she was ever ready to sympathize with them and to render such
aid as time and strength would permit her to do. The following
words of King Lemuel in Proverbs, Chapter 31, are applicable to
her: ''She layeth her hands to the spindle, and her hands hold
the distaff. She stretcheth out her hands to the poor: yea, she
reacheth forth her hands to the needy. She openeth her mouth
with wisdom: and in her tongue is the law of kindness. She
looketh well to the ways of her household, and eateth not the
bread of idleness.'' She was blind the last eight years of her
life. Amaziah Brainard's life was spent in his native town,
Colchester, Westchester Soc. In his earlier years he taught school
for several seasons with success; later he occupied many positions of honor and trust. He was acting justice of the peace
from 1828 to 1835, inclusive, and in 1839. He represented his
town in the legislature during the sessions of 1829 and 1830 with
much credit to himself and satisfaction to his constituents. He
was a man of large and commanding figure, being six feet and
one inch in height and correspondingly heavy. Possessing more
than an ordinary degree of intelligence and of strict integrity, he
enjoyed the honor and respect of his associates during life and
was lamented at death. He was a farmer, having built his house
at the time of his marriage on the site where his grandfather
built when he settled in the southwest district, Westchester

Society. Ch.: (1) Leverett, b. Feb. 13, 1828, in Westchester, Ct.; m. Mary Jerusha Bulkeley, of Hartford, Ct. (2) Albert, b. June 26, 1832, in Westchester, Ct.; unm. (3) Lucy Abigail, b. June 26, 1832, in Westchester, Ct.; unm. She is the compiler of the Brainard—Brainard Genealogy, which can be consulted for further information of William and Amaziah Brainard's families.

758. ix.   ISRAEL, b. May 29, 1794; m. Lucy Brainard and Clarissa Ely, 1834-39.

759. x.   DAVID, b. Apr. 22, 1796; m. Dorothy Shattuck, 1840-41.

760. xi.   ABIGAIL, b. June 26, 1798; m. Apr. 6, 1826, Alfred Isham, son of David and Clarissa (Williams) Loomis, of Westchester, Ct. He b. Nov. 3, 1796, and d. Mar. 25, 1882. She d. June 6, 1899. Ch.:

(1) Abigail, b. Feb. 11, 1827; m. Nov. 25, 1852, Charles Edward Brownsell, of East Haddam, Ct. Ch.: (a) George L., b. July 13, 1854; m. Elizabeth M. Reed. Ch.: (i) Leroy. (ii) Carl Reed. (b) Edward Cole, b. Jan. 27' 1856; m. Leila J. Alexander. Ch.: (i) Edward A. (ii) Abigail Foote. (iii) Sylvia Judd. (c) Charles Howe, b. July 7, 1859; m. Annie Wentz. Ch.: (i) Helen. (ii) Roger Wentz. (d) Mary Hammond, b. Apr. 15, 1861; d. Apr. 6, 1879. (e) Abigail Foote, b. July 13, 1863; d. 1879.

(2) Alfred Isham, b. Nov. 2, 1829; d. Apr. 21, 1866.

(3) Jane Clarisse, b. July 31, 1832; m. Apr. 9, 1863, Philo, son of Isaac and Annie (Avery) Bevin. He d. 1893. She occupies the res. at East Hampton with his son, Chas., by first wife. No Ch.

(4) George Champion, b. Jan. 31, 1835; d. June 31, 1847.

(5) Emily Harvey, b. Mar. 20, 1837; m. Apr. 4, 1861, Edward Augustus Bliss. Ch.: (a) Edward Milton, b. Jan. 6, 1863; m. Ada Richards. (b) Alfred Lumis, b. Aug. 17, 1866; m. Francis L. Smith. (c) Jennie Louise, b. June 11, 1871; d. 1884. (d) Helen Augusta, b. Sept. 22, 1872; m. Cushman H. Case.

(6) Israel Foote, b. Nov. 8, 1839; m. Nov. 8, 1866, Elizabeth MacFadden. Ch.: (a) Alfred Israel, b. 1868; d. 1893. (b) Charles Brownell, b. Nov. 3, 1869. (c) Mary Abigail, b. Aug. 28, 1871; m. John MacDonald; res., Greenfield, Mass. 10 ch.

(7) Milton Lathrop, b. July 16, 1842; m. Nov. 11, 1869, Sarah E. Tracy. Ch.: (a) Geo., b. July 17, 1871; m. Gladys Jones. Ch.: (i) Emeline Tracy. (b) John Robbins, b. Aug. 23, 1873; m. Amelia Jones. (c) Caroline Buell, b. May 23, 1882.

236. CAPT. AARON FOOTE, (73, 25, 9, 3, 1,) b. Mar. 10, 1744; m. Jan. 3, 1774, Mary, dau. of John Isham, formerly of Barnstable, Mass., now of Colchester, Ct. She d. Oct. 26, 1804, ae. 49; m. 2nd, June 29, 1807, Sarah, widow of Thomas William Wate, of Chatham, Ct. He d. July 13, 1824. She d. Apr. 16, 1818, ae. 72.

761. i.   DORATHY, b. Dec. 28, 1774; m. Nov. 18, 1792, James, son of John and Prudence (Taintor) Otis, of Colchester, Ct.; b. June 6, 1767; she d. Feb. 24, 1849.

762. ii.   MARY, b. Jan. 13, 1777; m. Jan. 15, 1809, Abner Bigelow, of Marlborough, Ct.; she d. June 7, 1835.

ABIGAIL (FOOTE) LOOMIS.

From a photograph taken on her one hundredth birthday. The one hundred roses were a gift from the Wadsworth Chapter of Middletown, Conn., of which she was a member as a real daughter.

763. iii. MARGARET, b. Mar. 19, 1779; m. Dec. 25, 1807, Isaac Bigelow, of Marlborough, Ct.; he d. May 7, 1832; she d. Apr. 24, 1841.

764. iv. AARON, b. May 16, 1781; d. Feb. 4, 1857; res., East Haddam, Ct.; unm.

765. v. AMASA, b. July 7, 1783; m. Lydia Worthington Tracy, 1842-51.

766. vi. LOVICA, b. June 18, 1786; d. June 7, 1831; unm.

767. vii. DYER, b. July 29, 1788; m. Sally Maria Miller, 1852-59.

768. viii. DAN, b. Aug. 9, 1792; d. June 22, 1823, in Cincinnati, O.; unm.

769· ix. LUCY, b. July 18, 1798; m. Feb. 28, 1821, Merrit Bradford, of Canterbury, Ct. They removed to Newsburge, N. Y., where he taught in the Academy. He d. Jan. 28, 1846.

241. DR. DAN FOOTE, (73, 25, 9, 3, 1,) b. Aug. 16, 1755; m. 1784, Isabella, daughter of Malcom Henry of Blanford, Mass. He read medicine with Dr. Percival, of Haddam, Ct., and was Surgeon in the Revolution (in the Navy three years),—practiced medicine in Pittsfield, Mass., ten years, and then removed to New Berlin, Chenango Co., N. Y., then a wilderness country, and had an extensive practice during his life, and was much esteemed. He d. Feb. 6, 1820. She d. Sept. 13, 1840, ae. 76.

Doctor Foote read medicine with Doctor Percival, of East Haddam, Ct. During the war of the Revolution he was three years in the naval service as surgeon. He practiced medicine in Pittsfield, Mass., some nine to ten years, and removed from thence to New Berlin, Chenango Co., N. Y., at a very early period in the settlement of this part of this county, and had an extensive practice during his life and was much esteemed. During the first few years of his residence in New Berlin, in common with the few neighbors who had emigrated to this wilderness, his courage, decision and perseverance were often severely tested by the hardships and conflicts he was compelled to endure. Notwithstanding his title to the land he had purchased was valid in the law, yet the beasts of the forest, holding a claim by right of discovery, refused to yield him peaceable possession. Having, however, just had some experience in settling the claims which the British Lion pretended to have upon the lands and tenements of this country, he thought he could safely and successfully prosecute this matter of dispute with the American Bear. Accordingly, as neither party seemed disposed to relinquish his claims, and both feeling confident in the justice of their cause and of their superior physical force, an appeal to arms was made. A bear seizing a hog belonging to one of the neighbors of Doctor Foote, the tocsin of war was sounded, and the little band, comprising only three men, Doctor Foote, old Mr. Marvin, and his son Elisha, Spartan like, were ready for the conflict. They took up their line of march in the trail of the bear, and pursued on until they reached the spot where the bear had slain his prize and made a delicious meal of his blood. The bear, and his place of rendezvous not being distinctly known by them, they followed on a short distance further and made a halt. A rustling among the leaves was soon heard at a little distance from where they stood. In a moment the bear was in sight. The Doctor at once levelled his piece and gave him a broadside. A large dog then sprang at the bear and was instantly overpowered. It soon became evident from the treatment the dog received while prisoner of the bear that the bear was waging a war of extermination. Their ammunition exhausted, and but one gun in the company, and the dog suffering pains and penalties worse than those of a Romish Inquisition, conspired to create a moment of disagreeable suspense. At length the Doctor mounted the log under which his dog was confined by the bear and commenced beating him with the breech of his gun, hoping by this manoeuvre at least to liberate his dog from the very unkind embrace of the bear. But the bear, indignant at such an interference when he was contending with the champion of the canine race, rose in all his brutish majesty, and at one fell swoop brought the Doctor to the ground. The dog, acting on the principle that discretion is the better part of valor, made good his escape to the house, and was unhesitatingly entered on the list of killed and wounded. While the Doctor was on the ground being mangled and torn by the bear, Mr. Marvin, the younger, undertook to save the Doctor's life at the risk of his own. He seized the bear, thinking that he could not only separate the bear from the Doctor but escape himself from being hurt. But no sooner had he touched the animal than he himself was in the same dangerous situation, the bear having him down, mangling and tearing his limbs with, if possible, increased ferocity. While the Doctor was revolving in his mind their situation and danger, the thought of his little pocket Barlow knife, the only weapon now left with which there was any chance of dispatching their more than troublesome antagonist. But before he could get his knife from his pocket and open it, his hands and arms being badly wounded, Mr. Marvin, the elder, seeing his son in such imminent danger, rushed into the arena for his rescue. The father made a pass at the ears of old Bruin, with the expectation of drawing him back-wards beyond the reach of his son, and not only relieve his son but escape him-self. It is thought he would have remained a spectator of the tragedy had it not been for his strong paternal feelings. But the bear had been too long the forest king to permit such familiarity from an invader of his dominions. He, therefore, as quick as thought turned upon him, and with one blow of his paw felled him to the ground. No sooner had the bear laid him prostrate than he proceeded to gnaw his head and mangle his limbs with great cruelty. By this time the Doctor had succeeded in opening his knife, and he walked up to the bear, threw his arm over on the opposite side of him, thinking that as soon as the bear felt the thrust of his knife he would wheel about in an opposite direction from him. The Doctor stabbed the bear twice over the region of the heart, when he turned suddenly round as was anticipated, and set off in a tangent for the swamp at the foot of the hill, mortally wounded. Just at the moment the bear started to leave the field of action he met a Mr. Franklin, who had been sent by the wives of Doctor Foote and Mr. Marvin as a kind of reinforcement to their husbands. The moment Franklin came in sight of the bear, supposing the bear in pursuit of him, he wheeled and took to his heels down the hill, running with the speed of the wind. Upon looking back, after coming in sight of the women, he then for the first time ascertained that the bear was not, and never had been, in pursuit of him, but was making his way, with all necessary speed, to the swamp, to slake his thirst, created by loss of blood. Franklin came up to where the women stood, and on their anxious inquiry after the fate of their husbands and son, Franklin faintly ejaculated, 'Dead! all dead!'' ''Go call Elder Camp'' they quickly rejoined. Franklin, somewhat recovered from his fatigue and fright, started off. Upon arriv-ing at the bank of the Unadilla, opposite to Elder Camp's house, he screamed at the top of his voice, ''Elder Camp! Elder Camp!'' On hearing such unearthly cries the Elder hurried out of his house and asked ''What's wanted?'' ''There are four men dead,'' replied Franklin. ''Four men dead,'' echoed the Elder, ''who are they?'' ''They are,'' says Franklin, in a piteous tone, ''Doctor Foote, old Mr. Marvin, his son Elisha, and myself. All are dead and gone!''

770. i.   LAURA, b. Nov. 12, 1784, in Becket, Mass.; m. 1805, Elisha, son of Enoch and Ruth (Ely) Marvin, of Butternuts and Carroll, N. Y. She d. Aug. 20, 1851; b. in Kintone, N. Y. Ch.: (1) Chauncy S., b. June 4, 1806; m. Res., Mich. (2) Minerva, b. June, 1808; m. Edson Hall, of Busti, N. Y. He was b. May 23, 1810; d. Mar. 9, 1843. She d. Nov. 29, 1844. Ch.: (a) Robert Hall; enlisted in May, 1861, as a private in the celebrated Bucktail Regiment; was in the Seven Days' Fight, was taken prisoner, released, and in second Bull Run and Antietam and Fredericksburg; became Lieutenant, and was killed in Gettysburg on the third day. He d. July, 1863; was later brought home and buried in Stillwater Cemetery. (b) Isabella C. Hall, b. Aug. 31, 1840; d. Mar. 18, 1864, and was buried beside Robert. (3) Elisah, b. 1813; m. Loraine Jones, of Ellicott, N. Y.

771. ii.   ADRIAN, b. Apr. 2, 1787; m. Sally Sole and Philomela Alden, 1860-64.

772. iii.   MINERVA, b. May 13, 1789.

773. iv.   BETSEY, b. May 30, 1791; m. Feb. 3, 1808, Alpheus Jeffords, of Oxford, Mass. He d. Nov. 19, 1857. She d. Jan. 19, 1879; res., Pittsford, N. Y. Ch.: (1) Mary Ambrosia, b. June 11, 1809; m. Apr. 7, 1830, Henry Angell, of New Berlin, N. Y. Ch.: (a) Horatio Pratt, b. Apr. 8, 1831. (b) Malcom H. (c) Ruth. (d) Mary Ambrosia. (e) James Matterson. (f) Ruth Ann. (g) Sarah Elizabeth, b. June 25, 1845. (2) Alpheus McDonough, b. July 30, 1815; m. 1st, Mary Arnold, she d.; m. 2nd, Mary Jenkins. (3) Laura Lavona, b. Oct. 22, 1819; m. Sept. 10, 1839, Chas. A. Matterson, of New Berlin, N. Y. Ch.: (a) James, b. Feb. 9, 1841. (b) George J., b. May 5, 1844.

774. v.   HENRY, b. Apr. 14, 1794; m. Adah Vail, 1865-9.

775. vi.   NATHANIEL, b. Sept. 3, 1796; m. July 25, 1830, Betsey, dau. of Asa Angell. He d. Oct. 17, 1841. She d. 1881. Res., New Berlin, N. Y.

776. vii.   LUCY, b. May 25, 1798; d. Mar. 11, 1803.

777. viii.   DAN, b. Apr. 19, 1800; d. July 10, 1808.

778. ix.   POLLY, b. Apr. 26, 1802; d. July 15, 1815.

779. x.   ESTHER, b. Sept. 27, 1804; d. 1882.

780. xi.   ISABELLA, b. June 19, 1807; m. June 9, 1827, Rev. Horatio Pratt, of Jamestown, N. Y., Pastor of the Baptist Church in that town. He was b. 1801, in Clarendon, Vt.; d. Apr. 20, 1829, at Jamestown, N. Y.; m. 2nd, June 11, 1837, Capt. Alvin Babcock, of New Berlin, N. Y. Ch.: (1) Linn, b. Apr. 22, 1838. (2) Sidney. (3) Adrian, b. Dec. 24, 1844.

781. xii.   DAN, b. Feb. 9, 1810; m. Sarah C. Gordon, 1872-76.

244. ISRAEL FOOTE, Jr., (74, 25, 9, 5,) b. Jan. 20, 1755; m. Nov. 5, 1778, Sarah, dau. of John and Prudence (Taintor) Otis, of Colchester, Ct. She was b. May 24, 1755; d. Feb. 1, 1781; m. 2nd, Mar. 17, 1782, Elizabeth, dau. of Capt. Elija Worthington, of Colchester, Ct. She d. Apr. 6, 1795, ae. 39; m. 3rd, Feb. 1, 1797, Prudence, dau. of David and Mary (Wells) Hale, of Glastenbury, Ct. She died Dec. 25, 1819, ae. 59. He d. May 18, 1826.

782. i.   SARAH, b. Aug. 2, 1779; m. Dec. 14, 1801, Roger Hale, son of
           Dea. David and Mary (Mills) Hale. She d. Apr. 25, 1804. Ch.:
           (1) Titus, b. Oct. 14, 1802. (2) Israel, b. Apr. 21, 1804.
783. ii.   ISRAEL, b. Jan. 19, 1783; m. Sarah Taintor, 1877-82.
784. iii. ELIJAH, b. Sept. 14, 1784; m. Betsy Strong and Lois Worth-
           ington, 1883-89.
785 iv.·   BETSY, b. May 2, 1786; m. July 19, 1826, John Hollister, of
           Glastonbury, Ct. They moved to Hamilton, Licking Co., Ohio.
786. v.   ERASTUS, b. Feb. 28, 1788; res. with his sister Betsy; unm.
787. vi.   JUSTIN, b. Apr. 1, 1790; d. in Natchez, unm.
788. vii. Son, not named, b. Mar., 1795; d. May 27, 1795.
789. viii. MARY, b. Mar. 25, 1795; m. Jan. 27, 1825, Benjamin Childs, b.
           Dec.· 18, 1789; d. Aug. 4, 1882 (7300, Childs Gen.). Ch.: (1)
           George Dexter, b. Sept. 17, 1831; m. Cordelia Lombard; res.,
           Chicago, Ill. Ch.: (a) Mary Ellen, b. Apr. 28, 1852.
790. ix.   SOPHIA, b. Nov. 9, 1800; m. Jan. 13, 1827, Jonathan, son of
           Joseph and Molly (Allen) Dexter. He was b. June 6, 1797; d.
           Mar. 6, 1876. Ch.: (1) Mary, b. Sept. 28, 1828. (2) Edward, b.
           Aug. 22, 1831.

246. DANIEL FOOTE, (76, 25, 9, 3,) b. June 21, 1744; m. Elizabeth Margaret Woodcock; d. Feb., 1825.
791. i.   MARGARET, b. abt. 1775; m. Joseph Talmadge, of Williamstown,
           Mass. They moved to Scipio and New York, N. Y.
792. ii.   DANIEL, b. 1777; m. Mrs. Bradley, of Aurora, N. Y.; was a
           merchant. He d. 1804. Ch.: two, Daniel and a dau. He was a
           very intelligent and enterprizing man and his business prospects
           of the first.
793. iii. HANNAH, b. 1779; m. Elijah Miller, Esq., of Auburn, N. Y.
           She d. Mar., 1811, in Williamstown, Mass., at her father's
           home.
794. iv.   JUSTIN, b. 1781; d. Oct., 1811, in Williamstown, Mass.

247. JUDGE ISAAC FOOTE, (76, 25, 9, 3,) b. Jan. 4, 1746; m. Mary Kellogg
at Colchester, Ct., May 31, 1768. She was the daughter of Jonathan Kellogg, Jr.,
of that place, and she was a descendant in the fourth generation of Joseph
Kellogg, first of Farmington, Ct., and afterwards of Hadley, Mass. She died in
Smyrna, Nov. 15, 1826, aged 82. In the common schools of that town and in his
early puritan home, he received that sound, but plain elementary instruction and
that religious training which fitted him for a long life of practical usefulness, of
strict integrity, and the most consistent piety.

"In May, 1773, he removed from Colchester to what was called Square Pond
Settlement, being within the limits of East Winsor, and bounding on West
Stafford, Ct. In May, 1778, he removed to Stafford, and in the year 1779 he was
by united application of the people appointed Justice of the Peace, which office he
continued to hold until he removed from that state. He was frequently elected
to represent the town of Stafford in the General Assembly of Connecticut, and
was a delegate to the convention to consider the adoption of the Constitution of
the United States.

This was the character Judge Foote had attained at an early day in his native
state. That he was a soldier in the Revolution is evidenced by the following
extract from a letter written by him in the 87th year of his age, in 1832, to Hon.

Elial T. Foote, and still preserved by a son of the latter, H. A. Foote, Esq., of New York, who has furnished the writer of this sketch with a copy of the same. He says: There was a mistake in the account that Rennsalaer (Foote) gives about Ebenezer's (Judge Foote's younger brother, who was afterwards a prominent citizen of Delhi, Delaware County, where he was successively Member of Assembly, District Attorney, State Senator and County Judge,) swimming across the Hudson river in the winter. He was taken prisoner by the enemy at the evacuation of New York, I think in September (1776). I was there at the same time as a militiaman.

He was taken by the Hessians in that retreat, but he got away from them and fled to the river, and he, with three others who made their escape, collected some logs and withed them together and shoved out into the river with setting poles, and the tide being going out then it wafted them toward the British shipping. Some people from the Jersey side seeing their condition manned a boat and went out and took them across to the Jersey side, and the next day they crossed back again and came into camp where I was.'' No further evidence than this is needed of the fact that he was a patriot soldier in the stormy days of the Revolution.

But to give a little further retrospective glimpse of the honorable ancestry of Judge Foote, we quote again from his letter above referred to, as follows: ''Grandfather (Nathaniel Foote 3rd) was the first magistrate in Colchester, and sustained that office to a very advanced age; and my father (Daniel Foote), who was the third son, and always lived with him, succeeded him in that office, and held it about the same length of time.'' The Judge in his worthy career was simply following on in the line of those who had preceded him.

The graphic account of the removal of the family of Isaac Foote to what was then denominated the town of Sherburne, and of their movements for a few years prior thereto, is herewith given from the pen of Isaac Foote, Jr.: ''My father (Judge Foote) at an early day seemed to have an unconquerable desire to settle in some part of the then western country. In pursuance of this desire he joined a company in 1788 in the purchase of a very desirable tract of land adjoining the Susquehanna river in Wyoming County, Pa., but after spending two or three seasons at work preparatory to settle thereon with his family, the title proved insufficient, and he lost his land and all his labor, and several hundred dollars which he advanced in payment. Having sold his farm in Stafford, Ct., he purchased an hundred acres in Franklin, now Delaware County, N. Y., on which there was a log house and about 35 acres of cleared land, on to which he proposed to move his family and look for a better location. The fall after I was fourteen years old (1790) my father took me with a hired man and a team and a few cattle and set off for Franklin, intending to return for the family in the winter following. There was about 50 miles between Catskill and Franklin, where the State road was not cleared out so that a wheeled carriage could pass. We therefore left the wagon and took a few light articles on a sled and went through to Franklin. The first sleighing we returned to our wagon, put our goods on a sled and started back for Franklin—then a very new place. There was one place where there was ten miles between houses, and it was so that the day we passed over the ten miles was an uncommon cold one, and it was eight o'clock at night before we got through. Consequently I became so benumbed that I could hardly walk. My father hurried through about a mile and a half to the first house. My feet, hands and ears were badly frozen, so that coming to the fire put me in extreme pain. I will only add that we got to Franklin the next day.

"My father left me with a friend and returned for the family. But our misfortunes did not end here. When my father got home he found one of my sisters very sick, so that she could not be moved until the sleighing was gone; and then the neighbours, who were unwilling that my father and his family should move away, prevailed upon him to purchase a farm which was for sale at a low rate in that vicinity.

"My father consequently returned to Franklin early in the spring, made arrangements for me to stay until June, and then take a pair of oxen and the horse, and as many articles as the team could draw on a sled and go to where the wagon was left and take as many things as the team could draw from there and so return home. I got home safe and had the credit of performing a service unusual for a boy of my age.

"My father being still bent on getting into some part of the western country, after improving his new farm awhile took a journey to Chenango; found the 8th township (present Smyrna) with but a very few settlers; made a contract for about 700 acres of land, returned home and made preparations for removing the family on to the 100 acres which he had previously purchased at Franklin, and there abide until he could complete arrangements for moving to the 8th township, (then part of Sherburne).

"In the year 1794, in August, my father hired a man to cut the timber on five acres, and sent me to cook and do what I could in the way of making preparations for removing the following winter, and he was to join us in two or three weeks and help roll up the logs for a house, and leave me to finish it as best I could. At this time there was a poor wagon road from Franklin to Oxford, and my father sent by a person going through with a wagon, a barrel with some meat, and some utensils for cooking, and also a bag of flour, to be left at Mr. Hovey's till called for by myself or his order. These articles were soon called for, and Col. Hovey sent the man who stored them to deliver them to me. They were put upon a sled, and supposed to be all right, (I had not seen the barrel which was sent from Franklin,) and we set forward. There was no road from Oxford to Sherburne excepting through what is now Norwich village, other than marked trees, and the underbrush cut out so that we could only get along with a sled, and we designed to get to a house four miles from our lot before dark; but in this we failed. Soon after sunset it grew very dark, and a heavy rain fell during nearly the whole of the night. We had a pair of oxen and a cow. We chained the oxen to a tree, secured our flour as well as we could, and waited for daylight. As soon as we could see to travel we set forward, and after travelling about one and a half miles we reached the house where we had contemplated arriving the night before.

"After drying our clothes and getting breakfast, we set forward again and arrived at Mr. Joseph Porter's, adjoining our lot, where we made our home. But judge of our surprise, when on opening our barrel, instead of meat, we found a quarter of a barrel of hayseed! A blunder justly imputable to Col. Hovey's man and myself. But what must be done? It must immediately be carried back, and I must do it. I had to travel sixty miles on bare ground, but the business was soon done.

"After a while my father came and helped to roll up the body of a log house, and then returned to Franklin, leaving me to finish it, which I did by changing works with a man who was doing a job of chopping about two miles distant. The house was finished and was called a good one. I remained on the lot until the latter part of December, and then went home to help move the family.''

As to the exact date of Judge Foote's arrival at his new home in the then town of Sherburne, present Smyrna, there are different statements, but Judge Foote himself, in a record made by him in the album of his grandson, John J. Foote, Esq., now of Belvidere, Ill., written at Smyrna, in the spring of 1832, says: ''In February, 1795, I removed to this place.'' And that may be taken as the absolutely correct date.

The following further data is copied from the same record above noted: ''In the year 1798 I was elected Member of the Legislature of the state, and procured the incorporation of the County of Chenango and was appointed First Judge of the Court of Common Pleas and General Sessions of the Peace, and in 1800 I was elected Senator for four years. And in 1806 I resigned the office of First Judge and retired from all public office.''

In the above memorandum Judge Foote omits to state that in 1796, and the next year after his arrival, he was chosen as the first Supervisor of Sherburne, representing the town that year at the annual meeting of the Board held at Herkimer. And in the following year, 1797, he was appointed a Justice of the Peace for the town of Sherburne. Also he omits to state that his retirement from the office of Judge was by reason of his having reached the then constitutional limitation of sixty years of age, and not because of any inability on his part to discharge the duties of that office. Such promotion to public office and such oft repeated honors bestowed, and so soon after his arrival in that town and county, are remarkable and indubitable evidence of his ability and character, and that reputation was well maintained throughout his long and useful life. In fact, Judge Foote was a unique representative character of those early times, one of the best type of the sturdy sons of rugged New England who wrought well whenever work was to be done, and who helped to lay the foundations of the state and the nation.

His religious faith was the strongest, most potent and controlling force of his life, and everything else was made subservient to it. While he was State Senator and County Judge he was active in the formation of the Society and Church on Sherburne West Hill, when the old records, largely preserved through his instrumentality, showed that he served as Trustee and Deacon and Clerk, some of the time filling all three offices. He was interested in every object which promised to conserve the best interests of the community where he lived, chief and first among which he evidently considered the Church, and to that he gave his strong and steady support. It is said of him that he was given ''much to reading and writing, and especially to the study of the Sacred Scriptures, and commenting on the same, until wholly deprived of sight.''

The following quaint certificate of Judge and Mrs. Foote's early church membership is here given:

Stafford, 20th October, 1796.

This certify, whom it may concern, that Isaac Foote, Esq., and Mary, his wife, were members in full communion in the church under my care and in good standing when they left this place. Esq. Foote was chosen a Deacon in this church and served in that office for a number of years before he left us, to universal acceptance. And is hereby with Mrs. Foote recommended to any Christian society or church wherever Providence may cast them.

Attest, Isaac Foster, of the First Congregational Church, Stafford.

The above letter is doubtless the one presented by Judge Foote and his wife when they united with the Old Church on Sherburne West Hill, where they remained members until Mar. 4, 1831, when they, together with their sons, Isaac, Jr., Amasa, and Hiram, also Harriet, Sally Irene, Harriet (2nd), and Sally Kellogg (Mrs. Amasa) Foote, withdrew to join the Congregational Church at Smyrna.

Judge Foote only had the benefit of the common school education of those primitive times, but that he improved it well there is abundant evidence. He was not an orator, but on occasion he was called upon to make public address.

795.   i.   MARY, b. Feb. 27, 1769; m. Dea. Joseph Adams, first of Hamilton, N. Y., afterwards of Sherburne, N. Y., Feb. 22, 1801. He was b. in New Ipswich, N. H., Dec. 13, 1765; d. at Sherburne, N. Y., Oct. 11, 1849. She d. Feb. 2, 1844. Ch.: (1) Isaac, b. Dec. 4, 1801, at Hamilton, N. Y.; Congregational clergyman; m. Laura Austin, Nov. 9, 1831; A. B., Hamilton College; he d. at Norwich, N. Y., Nov. 23, 1876. Ch.: (a) Charles S., b. Apr. 22, 1834, at Columbus, N. Y.; d. at Lahaina, Hawaii, June 21, 1861. (b) William P., b. Mar. 6, 1836; m. Jennie Dunning, of Manlius, N. Y., April 17, 1865; d. at Woodstock, Ill., Dec. 23, 1869. (c) John Milton, b. Nov. 19, 1837; d. at Eaton, N. Y., Aug. 11, 1840. (d) Joseph Henry, b. Dec. 21, 1839; m. ———; d. at Horseheads, N. Y., Aug. 16, 1864. He was orderly sergeant of 38th Regt., N. Y. State Volunteers in Civil War. 1 dau. (e) Emily R., b. Mar. 1842; m. William C. Korthals at Shanghai, China, Nov., 1870; d. at Heidelberg, Germany, Oct. 23, 1900. Ch.: (i) John, residing in Nice, France. (ii) Gertrude, m. and living in Heidelberg, Germany. (iii) William, d. ———. (f) Mary Alice, b. July 15, 1844; now living (July, 1906) at Battle Creek, Mich.; m. G. L. Marsh, June 9, 1886. (2) Hiram, b. Oct. 25, 1803, at Hamilton, N. Y.; physician; Fabius, N. Y.; m. Emily Rexford, of Sherburne, N. Y., Oct. 25, 1827. He d. at Fabius, N. Y., Mar. 9, 1865 Ch.: (a) Homer, b. Nov. 15, 1828; d. Aug. 3, 1867. (b) Mary, b. Sept. 8, 1832; d. Aug. 30, 1851. (c) Franklin, b. July 20, 1837; d. May 24, 1861. (d) Minerva, b. Aug. 21, 1839; m. Rial W. Talbot, Jan. 9, 1866; d. June 3, 1882. Ch.: (i) Maud E. Talbot, b. Jan. 10, 1870. (ii) Mary A. Talbot, b. Dec. 28, 1872; d. ———. (iii) Fannie E. Talbot, b. Oct. 20, 1874; d. Jan. 21, 1875. (iv) Edmund R. Talbot, b. Sept. 7, 1880. (Maud E. and Edmund R. Talbot are now (July, 1906,) living at Penn Yan, N. Y.) (e) Emily R., b. Sept. 22, 1847; m. Rev. Edmund M. Mills, Aug. 23, 1873; d. at Elmira, N. Y., Mar. 14, 1904. (3) Mary, b. Feb. 15, 1808, at Sherburne, N. Y.; m. Benjamin Pierce Johnson, of Rome, N. Y., Mar. 1, 1838, and d. at Albany, N. Y., Dec. 1, 1862. Benjamin P. Johnson died at Albany, N. Y., 1869. Graduated at Union College, class of 1815; attorney-at-law; secretary of New York State Agricultural Society. Ch.: (a) Benjamin William, b. at Rome, N. Y., June 16, 1844; m. to Mary H. Bennett, dau. of Lorenzo Bennett, of Homer, N. Y., Nov. 11, 1868. Graduated at Hamilton College, class of 1865; now (July, 1905) assistant treasurer Albany Savings Bank, Albany, N. Y. Ch.: (i) Harriet Bennett Johnson, b. Oct. 31, 1869; res., Albany, N. Y. (ii) Florence Bennett Johnson, b. Sept. 16, 1872;

res., Albany, N. Y. (iii) Benjamin Robert Johnson, b. Dec. 30, 1874; graduated at Hamilton College, class of 1897, and at the law school of Georgetown University, Washington, D. C., 1902; is practising law in Washington, D. C. (b) Gerrit Smith, b. at Albany, N. Y., Sept. 7, 1849; d. at Albany, N. Y., Jan. 22, 1851. (4) Minerva, b. at Sherburne, N. Y., July 7, 1811; d. at Norwich, N. Y., Mar. 30, 1887.

796. ii. MARGARET PARSONS, b. Dec. 29, 1771; m. Jan., 1794, Henry G. Cady, of Monson, Mass. She d. 1862. Ch.: (1) Martin, b. ———. (2) Henry. (3) John Parsons. (4) Willard. (5) Isaac. (6) Sabra Green. (7) Mary Kellogg. (8) Julia. (9) Lucilla Stanley.

797. iii. ISAAC, b. Feb. 22, 1774; d. in infancy.

798. iv. ISAAC, b. Apr., 1776; m. Harriet Hyde, 1890-6.

799. v. AMASA, b. Mar. 23, 1778; m. Sally Kellogg, 1897-1903.

800. vi. ASHAEL, b. Aug. 19, 1783; d. Feb. 26, 1790.

801. vii. JOHN, b. Apr. 30, 1786; m. Mary B. Johnson, 1904-14.

802. viii. HIRAM, b. Aug. 22, 1789; m. Mary G. Strong, 1915-19.

248. ELI FOOTE, (76, 25, 9, 3,) b. Oct. 30, 1747; m. Oct. 11 1772, Roxanna, oldest dau. of Gen. Andrew and Diana (Hubbard) Ward, of Guilford, Ct.; d. Sept. 8, 1792, in North Carolina. She b. Jan. 7, 1751; d. Oct. 31, 1840, in Guilford, Ct. He was a man of fine person, polished manners and cultivated taste. He was educated for the bar and practiced a little in Guilford, but eventually became a merchant and traded at the south.

803. i. HARRIET, b. July 28, 1773; d. Apr. 19, 1842, unm.

804. ii. ROXANNA, b. Jan. 10, 1775; m. Sept. 19, 1799, Dr. Lyman Beecher. He was b. Sept. 2, 1775; d. Jan. 10, 1863, at Brooklyn, at his son's residence (Henry Ward Beecher). She d. Sept. 24, 1816. Nine very remarkable ch. were the result of this union. Ch.:

(1) Catherine, b. Sept. 6, 1800; d. ———.

(2) Rev. William Henry Beecher, b. Jan. 15, 1802; m. Catherine Edes, of Boston, Mass.; d. June 23, 1889, at Chicago, Ill.

(3) Rev. Edward Beecher, D. D., b. Aug. 27, 1803; m. Isabella Jones, of Wiscasset, Maine. He was pastor of a Congo. Ch. in Boston, Mass. He was the third child and second son of Dr. Lyman Beecher, and was born during the pastorate of his father on the east end of Long Island from 1798 to 1810. Catherine, who died last year, was the oldest child. She spent her years and efforts in advancing female education, founding schools and seminaries for girls and teaching and writing for their benefit. She was born in 1800. William was the second child. He has served his day and generation in the ministry and now lives a retired life in Chicago. Then comes Dr. Edward Beecher, third in the line of a remarkable family. He graduated at Yale College in 1822, and studied theology at Andover and New Haven; became tutor in Yale College in 1825, and pastor of Park Street Church, Boston, in 1826, which post he held until 1831, when he went to Jacksonville, Ill., and was mainly instrumental in establishing the college at that place, of which he became its first president, and

labored not only as president and professor, but also as financial
agent for it. After fourteen years' service there he returned to
Boston and took charge of Salem church, in the North End, where
he remained twelve years and labored not only there but in revi-
vals in other churches, and also edited the *Congregationalist,* the
denominational organ.   After this the doctor returned to Illinois
and organized a church in Galesburg, the seat of Knox College, and
took charge of it, at the same time giving lectures in the theological
seminary in Chicago.   When he resigned that charge eight years
ago he settled down in Brooklyn, and has lived in that city ever
since. After the doctor in the family order came George, who,
while in the ministry in Wellsville, Ohio, lost his life by accident.
A son of his is still in the ministry.   Then comes Henry Ward
Beecher, Thomas K., next, then Charles, who was for many years
a pastor at Georgetown, Mass; then James, who is a pastor in the
western part of New York State. Mrs. Perkins and Mrs. Stowe
follow in succession. The father of this family was married twice,
so that the children had not all one mother.

(4) Mary F. Beecher, b. July 19, 1805; m. Hon. Thomas C. Perkins, of Hartford, Ct., where they reside.

(5) Harriet Beecher, b. Feb. 11, 1808; d. same year.

(6) Rev. George Beecher, b. East Hampton, N. Y., May 6, 1809;
m. July 13, 1837, Sarah Sturges Buckingham, of Zanesville, O. He
graduated from Yale College 1828; was pastor of Pres. Ch. in
Chillicothe, O. He was an affectionate son, a warm-hearted brother,
an earnest Christian, a faithful minister. He d. July 1, 1843, at
Chillicothe, O.

(7) Harriet Elizabeth Beecher, b. June 14, 1811; m. Rev. Prof.
Calvin E. Stowe, of Lane Seminary, Cincinnati, O.   She is the
author of ''Uncle Tom's Cabin,'' and other works. Ch.: (a)
Harriet Stowe, b. Sept. 29, 1836, in Cincinnati, O.; d. Jan. 25,
1907; unm.   (b) Eliza Stowe, b. Sept. 29, 1836, in Cincinnati, O.;
res., Simsbury, Ct.; unm.   (c) Henry Ellis Stowe, b. in Cincinnati,
Jan. 14, 1838.   Drowned at Hanover, N. H., July 9, 1857, while a
student at Dartmouth College.   (d) Frederick William, b. at Cincinnati, May, 1840. He enlisted in the Civil War as private, Co. A,
1st Mass. Vol.; rose to be captain; wounded in the head at the
battle of Gettysburg, July 11, 1863, from which he never recovered. After a sea voyage around the Horn to San Francisco, he
disappeared, and the date of his death is unknown; unm. (e)
Georgiana May, b. May 25, 1843; m. 1866, Rev. Henry Freeman,
son of Freeman and Harriet (Reed) Allen. He graduated at Harvard in 1860, and studied at Andover Theological Seminary. He
was rector of the Episcopal Ch. at Stockbridge, Mass., also of the
Ch. of the Messiah at Boston, later of St. Stephen, Boston. He
was rector of the American Ch. at Lucerne; res., Florence, Italy.
Ch.: (i) Freeman Allen, b. Sept. 27, 1870. Studied at Noble's
School at Boston; graduated at Harvard Academic, A.B., 1893; from
the Harvard Medical School 1899, M. D.; is a practising physician in
Boston, Mass.   (f) Samuel Charles, b. Jan., 1848; d. July 26,

HON. ERASTUS FOOTE. No. 540

HARRIET BEECHER STOWE.   No. 804 (7)

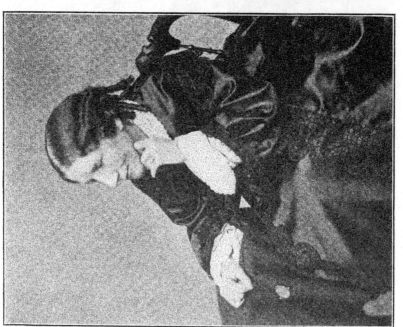

HENRY WARD BEECHER.   No. 804 (8)

1849, of cholera, in Cincinnati, O. (g) Charles Edward Stowe, b. July 8, 1850, at Brunswick, Me.; m. 1879, Susan Mitchell, dau. of Charles W. and Susan (Hall) Munroe. She was b. in 1853. He is a Congo. clergyman, and has had charge of parishes in Saco, Me., Hartford and Simsbury, Ct., and has been some years at Bridgewater, Mass. Ch.: (i) Lyman Beecher Stowe, b. Dec. 22, 1880. (ii) Leslie Munroe Stowe, b. Mar. 14, 1883; d. Mar. 29, 1887. (iii) Hilda Stowe, b. Jan. 19, 1887.

(8) Henry Ward Beecher, clergyman, b. in Litchfield, Ct., June 24, 1813; m. Eunice White, dau. of Dr. Arbemas Bullard, of West Sutton, Mass. He d. at Brooklyn, N. Y., Mar. 8, 1887. He was the fourth son of Lyman and Roxana (Foote) Beecher. His mother died when he was but three years old; his stepmother, under whose guardianship his childhood days were spent, was an Episcopalian. Both parents were devoted Christians, his father one of the most influential of New England pastors is an important transition period of her history. Graduated from Amherst College, 1834, in his twenty-first year. From there he entered Lane Theological Seminary, Cincinnati. At the same time he engaged in Christian work as a Bible class teacher, and in journalistic work in connection with a Cincinnati paper in which he took an active part as an ardent abolitionist in the anti-slavery campaign then fairly begun. His first parish was the Presbyterian Church at Lawrenceburg, Ind., on the Ohio river. On Jan. 13, 1893, a tablet in honor of its famous preacher was dedicated and unveiled in the vestibule of Plymouth Church. The tablet is of brass and enamel, mounted on a panel of antique oak, 64 x 47 in. in size. A border of interlaced oak leaves surrounds the tablet, upon which appears a medallion bust in bronze. The inscription is: "In memoriam Henry Ward Beecher, first pastor of Plymouth Church, 1847-87. 'I have not concealed thy loving kindness and thy truth from the great congregation.'" Ch.: (a) Harriet Eliza Beecher, b. May 7, 1838; m. Rev. Samuel Scoville. He was b. Dec. 21, 1835, at West Cornwall, Ct. Graduated at Yale, in 1857. Was pastor of Cong. Ch., Norwich, N. Y., 1861-1879, Stamford, Ct., 1879-1899. He d. Apr. 15, 1902. Ch.: (i) Harriet Beecher Scoville, b. Sept. 13, 1862; m. June 19, 1888, Spencer Cone, son of Thomas H. and Emma (Clark) Devan, M. D. and D. D. He was b. Mar. 18, 1856; d. Feb. 3, 1893. She was a graduate of Wellesley College. Ch. b. in Buffalo, N. Y. Res., Stanford, Ct. Ch.: (i1) Scoville T. Devan, b. Aug. 18, 1889. (i2) Harriet Beecher Devan, b. Mar. 7, 1891. (ii) Annie Howard Scoville, b. Norwich, N. Y., Jan. 27, 1866. She graduated at Wellesley and Oxford University. Is a teacher at Hampton Institute and Catharine Aiken School. (iii) Samuel Scoville, Jr., b. June 9, 1872; m. Katherine Gaulbadet, dau. of H. Clay Trumbull, lawyer; res., Philadelphia, Pa. Ch.: (iii1) Samuel Scoville, b. Feb. 19, 1902; d. Mar. 8, 1904. (iii2) Gurdon Trumbull, b. Nov. 1, 1904. (iii3) William Beecher Scoville, b. Jan. 13, 1906. (iv) William Herbert Scoville, b. Aug. 25, 1873; m. Louise Hopkins, dau. of Gen. S. C. Armstrong. Graduate from Yale in

1895, Hampton Normal Institute. Ch.: (iv1) Anne Beecher Scoville, b. May 11, 1903. (iv2) Samuel Armstrong Scoville, b. Sept. 14, 1905. (b) Henry Barton Beecher, b. ———; m. Harriet J. Benedict. Ch.: (i) Kate Beecher, b. ———; m. ——— Harper; d. ———. Ch.: (i1) Barton Harper, b. ———. (ii1) Henry Ward Beecher, b. ———; m. Mary Beecher; they have 3 ch. (iii1) Margaret Humphreys; m. Arthur White; they have 2 ch. (iv1) Susan Sage, b. ———; d. ———. (v1) Edith, b. ———; d. ———. (c) William Constantine Beecher, b. Brooklyn, N. Y., Jan. 26, 1848; m. Nov., 1881, Jessie H. Bigelow, of Brooklyn. He was at the famous Gunn School and then fitted at Northampton, Mass., under Prof. Josiah Clarke; graduated at Yale in 1872, and at Columbia Law School, 1875, and admitted to N. Y. bar. In Jan., 1881, he was appointed assistant district attorney for N. Y. county. In association with his brother-in-law, Rev. Samuel Scoville, he published a biography of his father, Rev. Henry Ward Beecher, and the second volume of the "Life of Christ," which his father had left unfinished at his death. Associated with Mr. Austin Abbott, he edited and prepared Abbott's Trial Brief of Criminal Causes, 1890. He is counsel for the N. Y. "Society for the Prevention of Vice." Ch. (i) Gertrude, b. Nov. 4, 1882. (ii) Bertha, b. Dec. 10, 1885. (iii) Eunice A., b. Mar. 10, 1892. (d) Herbert Foote Beecher, b. ———; m. Harriet Foster. Ch.: (i) Henry Ward; m. Mary Eunice. Ch.: (i1) Beatrice. (4) Bernice.

Beecher and the Reporter.—"What name do you give your place, Mr. Beecher?"

"Oh, it's got a new name every year. What is its name this year, ma?" he called out to Mrs. Beecher, who was in the library.

"Beecher's Farm," she replied.

"I don't mean that; I mean its English name."

"Boscobel."

"Yes, that's it, Boscobel," continued Mr. Beecher, addressing the reporter. "I don't know exactly what it means, though, perhaps, it might mean beautiful bosc or woods; but I'll tell you how I came to give it this name. You remember that Charles II., after being defeated in battle, concealed himself from the enemy by hiding in the trunk of a hollow tree. That tree stood on an estate belonging to an ancestor of mine on my mother's side named Foote, who called his place Boscobel. He assisted Charles II. to escape, and the latter, on his restoration to the throne, gave my ancestor the right to wear a coat-of-arms. I have, as you see, adopted the name of the ancestral home and have also adopted the Foote coat-of-arms."

"Then you have a coat-of-arms?"

"Oh, I have two—the Beecher and the Foote," replied the eminent divine, with a smile; "one for winter and the other for summer wear."

"How long have you occupied Boscobel?"

"It's twenty-three years since I bought the ground. God made that, but I put the hair on it. I've planted between 6,000 and

.7,000 ornamental and fruit trees, in all about 450 different varieties. About eight years ago I built this house from the profits of my lecturing. Sometimes I call it my air castle, since it is built from wind.''

(9) Rev. Charles Beecher, b. Oct. 7, 1815; m. July 23, 1840, Sarah, dau. of Nathaniel and Mary (Porter) Coffin, of Wiscasset, Me. He was pastor of the Second Pres. Ch. in Ft. Wayne.

805. iii. ANDREW WARD, b. Nov. 9, 1776; d. Sept. 29, 1794.

806. iv. WILLIAM HENRY, b. Sept. 8, 1778; d. Oct. 7, 1794.

807. v. MARTHA, b. Sept. 23, 1781; d. Sept. 23, 1793.

808. vi. JOHN PARSONS, b. June 26, 1783; m. Jane Warner, 1920-24.

809. vii. MARY WARD, b. Aug. 7, 1785; m. Sept. 1, 1803, John James Hubbard, of the Island of Jamaica, West Indies. She d. Sept. 1, 1813.

810. viii. SAMUEL EDMONDS, b. Oct. 2, 1787; m. Elizabeth B. Elliot, 1925-28.

811. ix. GEORGE AUGUSTUS, b. Dec. 9, 1789; m. Eliza Spencer, 1929-38.

812. x. CATHRINE, b. June 23, 1792; d. Aug. 27, 1811.

253. JUDGE EBENEZER FOOTE, (76, 25, 9, 3,) b. Apr. 12, 1756; m. Oct. 10, 1779, Jerusha Purdy, of Westchester Co., N. Y. She d. Nov., 1818; m. 2nd, 1791, ———. Rosekrans. He d. Dec. 28, 1829, in Delhi, N. Y.

At nineteen Ebenezer was found with the Minute men at Bunker Hill; made sergeant of the Second Conn.; was at Trenton and Valley Forge; taken prisoner at the battle of Fort Washington, and confined to the old Bridewell, managed to escape, and by means of a plank found on the shore swam the Hudson in the month of December, but the exposure brought on a severe illness, and he never again could engage in active service. His patriotism, however, would not allow him to remain an outsider, and we next find him in the Commissary Department at General Washington's headquarters on the Hudson, where he remained until his health again forced his resignation just before the close of the war. He saw much of Washington; was temporarily on his Staff, and retired with the rank of Major.

One of the most interesting events of his life is well related by Mr. Abbatt, in his delightful work entitled ''The Crisis of the Revolution,'' when Capt. Foote, in the early morning of Sept. 22, 1780, for a few moments held the fate of that gallant soldier, Major Andre, in his hands. As officer in command at Crompond, Capt. Foote scanned the pass produced by Andre, but knowing Benedict Arnold and his writing well, and seeing that his appended signature was correct, allowed the party to proceed.

After the war Major Foote engaged in a large mercantile and shipping business at Newburgh, N. Y., with his brother Justin, who later married Marie Evertson, whose sister had just married Governor Smith of Ct.

Major Foote, whose duties at headquarters caused him to ride much and far, had met and married the charming young Jerusha Purdy, of Yorktown, Westchester, N. Y., and from old tales and letters she appears to have remained a fascinator until her death.

Mr. Foote was for a long time Member of Assembly from Ulster, and was largely instrumental in procuring the setting off of Delaware Co., where he came to reside in Aug., 1797. He was Co. Clerk for a number of years, conducted an extensive land agency, and three times was appointed First or Presiding Judge, as well as acting for a short time as puisne on the bench. He represented the old Middle District for four years in the Senate of the State; was nominated for Congress, but other duties forced him to decline; sat in the Council of Appointment with Gov. Jay, and enjoyed his friendship and confidence. (See Jay Gould's History.)

In 1798 the Co. town was erected, and Judge Foote, as chief citizen, was appointed by the Legislature to name it. Not particularly desiring the honor, he said to his intimate friends at Albany, the Patroon, Gen. Schuyler, etc., ''I think I shall decline.'' They all belonged to a small club, each member bearing some fanciful name; Senator Foote's was ''The Great Mogul,'' and his fellow members said, ''We will name it for you, and call it after your city, 'Delhi','' which was done, to the great annoyance of Gen. Root, a prominent man and politician, who had also come to reside in the place, and wished much to have the privilege of giving the name.

As Speaker of the House in 1801, he gained great credit for his ''dignity and courtesy.'' At Delhi he assisted in organizing St. John's Church and an Academy, which for many years enjoyed a wide reputation; of the one he was made the first Senior Warden, of the other, the first President of the Board of Trustees.

In the issue of Jan. 7, 1830, ''The Commercial Advertiser,'' New York City, (See Life of Samuel Foote) in an extended notice of his death, speaks of his integrity, of his prominence in the State, and of his beautiful mansion, Arbor Hill, on the banks of the Delaware, and of the long list of eminent men who enjoyed from time to time its hospitality. A man refined, honest and honorable in all his ways.

His niece, Roxana, married Lyman Beecher, and became the mother of Henry Ward and Mrs. H. B. Stowe. A grand-niece married William Seward, Governor and Secretary of State.

    813. i.   FREDERICK PARSONS, b. Mar. 15, 1783; m. Charlotte Welles. 1939-41.

    814. ii.   CHARLES AUGUSTUS, b. Apr. 15, 1785; m. Maria Baldwin, 1942-6.

    815. iii.   HARRIET, b. ———; m. Dr. Ambrose Bryan, Clerk of Delaware Co., N. Y. He d. p. s.; m. 2nd, John Foote, Esq., of Hamilton, Madison Co., N. Y., being his 2nd wife. *p. 197.*

    816. iv.   MARGARET PARSONS, b. ———; m. Rev. Ebenezer Maxwell, Pastor of the First Presbyterian Church in Delhi, N. Y. He d. July, 1840. She d. 1840. Ch.: (1) Ebenezer Foote, who lives in Delhi, on the place which belonged to his Grandfather Foote, and on which he died.

    254. STEPHEN FOOTE, (76, 25, 9, 3,) b. Jan. 10, 1758; m. Nov. 16, 1786, Hannah, dau. of Nehemia Waterman, of Bozrah, Ct. He d. Mar. 23, 1843. She d. Jan. 20, 1844, ae. 82. Res., Colchester, Ct.

    817. i.   ALFRED b. Dec. 8, 1787; d. June 23, 1867, in Colchester, Ct.; unm.

    818. ii.   DANIEL, b. Sept. 23, 1789; m. Sarah Ann Scovelle, 1947-8.

    819. iii.   SARAH ISHAM, b. May 4, 1791; m. Oct. 10, 1819, Erastus Watrous, of Montpelier, Vt. She d. July 4, 1831. Ch.: (1) Sarah Foote, b. Aug. 15, 1820. (2) Daniel Foote, b. May 10, 1823.

820. iv. ELI, b. May 7, 1793; m. Marana Lyons, 1949-55.

821. v. WILLIAM HENRY, b. Dec. 20, 1794; m. Eliza Wilson Glasse and Arabella Gillman, 1956-8.

822 vi. SUSANNAH WATERMAN, b. Aug. 18, 1796; d. June 23, 1867, in Colchester, Ct.; unm.

255. JOHN FOOTE, (76, 25, 9, 3,) b. Feb. 17, 1760; m. Hannah, widow of Dr. Johnson. He d. abt. 1805. She d. ———. Res., Colchester, Ct., and Williamstown, Mass.

256. JUSTIN FOOTE, (76, 25, 9, 3,) b. July 31, 1762; m. Maria Evertson. They resided some years in Brooklyn, N. Y. He d. in Saybrook or Guilford, Ct. He was a merchant, a man of business and of integrity, and highly respected.

261. CHARLES FOOTE, Jr., (80, 25, 9, 3,) b. June 5, 1753; m. Dec. 17, 1778, Sarah, dau. of Capt. Noah Day. He was in the Conn. Vols., and marched to the relief of Boston in Apr., 1775; d. Mar. 11, 1833. She d. Apr. 4, 1813. Res., Colchester, Ct., Richmond and West Stockbridge, Mass., and Mendon, Monroe Co., N. Y., where he died.

823. i. SARAH, b. Sept. 17, 1779, in Colchester, Ct.; m. Isaac Barnes in West Stockbridge, Mass., Mar. 17, 1802, by the Rev. Oliver Ayers, and removed some years later to a farm at Allen's Creek, near Brighton, N. Y. Isaac Barnes d. Dec. 30, 1863, and his wife d. May 24, 1866. Both were buried in Brighton. Ch.:

(1) Isaac M. Barnes, b. Dec. 12, 1803, West Stockbridge, Mass.; m. Charlotte Squires, of Brighton, N. Y., and settled in Batavia, N. Y. He d. without children June 20, 1890. He and his wife were buried in Batavia.

(2) Sarah E. Barnes, b. Aug. 14, 1806, West Stockbridge, Mass., was m. to Charles West, Dec. 30, 1830, and removed to Ridgeway, N. Y. He d. Apr. 8, 1884; she d. Oct. 27, 1884, and both were buried in Ridgeway. Ch., all born in Ridgeway: (a) Daniel M., b. Oct. 27, 1831; d. Apr. 15, 1859. (b) Isaac B., b. June 21, 1833; m. Emma Case; d. Apr. 13, 1869. Ch.: (i) Charles Case. (c) Elisha Y., b. Nov. 28, 1835; d. Mar. 25, 1849. (d) Charles H., b. Feb., 1839; d. Aug. 25, 1864; buried in Reames, Fla. (e) Elisha Y., b. June 2, 1850.

(3) Charles Milo Barnes, of West Stockbridge, Mass., b. May 5, 1811; was m. to Hannah M. Palmer, of West Stockbridge, June 10, 1840. He was a millwright by trade, and settled in Brighton. He d. Dec. 16, 1884, and was buried in Brighton. She d. Nov. 4, 1885, in West Stockbridge. Ch.: (a) Charles P., b. in West Stockbridge, Mass., Mar. 10, 1843; m. to Mary J. Waldron, and lives in Brighton, N. Y., where he is postmaster. Ch.: (i) Frank Erwin, (ii) Harry Palmer, (iii) Clarence Waldron, (iv) Charles Milo, (v) Bessie Maria. (b) Frances M. Barnes, of Brighton, N. Y., b. June 9, 1848; m. Horace B. Strowger. Ch.: (i) Ernest Palmer, (ii) Frances Grace, (iii) Charles William, (iv) Jessie Maria.

(4) Mary E. Barnes, of West Stockbrige, Mass., b. Oct. 13, 1813; m. to William N. Shepard, of Brighton, N. Y., Oct. 16, 1838. He d. Aug. 5, 1885; she d. Dec. 9, 1889. Res., Pittsford,

N. Y. Ch., all b. at Pittsford: (a) Mary E., b. July 28, 1840; m. Oscar Stoutenburg, of Mendon, N. Y., and lived in Pittsford. Ch.: (i) William A., b. in Pittsford, Sept. 10, 1867. (ii) Charlotte E., b. in Wayanett, Ill., April 3, 1869. (b) Sarah F., b. May 22, 1842; m. Abram Culver, of Pittsford, May 1, 1867. Ch.: (i) Nellie B., b. in Superior, Mich., Aug. 3, 1870. (ii) Cora M., b. in Superior, Feb. 22, 1872. (c) Lucy K., b. May 8, 1844; m. George W. Farnham, of Scipio, N. C., Dec. 19, 1866. Ch., all b. in Pittsford, N. Y.: (i) Mary A., b. Oct. 2, 1868. (ii) Frank L., b. June 12, 1870. (iii) Alfred H., b. Sept. 7, 1872. (d) William M., b. June 2, 1846; m. to Sarah A. Sharp of Farmington. He d. Nov. 19, 1889. Ch.: (i) Josephine May, b. in Rochester, June 16, 1874; d. Aug. 27, 1894. (ii) Jessie, b. in Pittsford, 1876. (iii) William, b. in Brighton, N. Y., 1882. (e) Charlotte M., b. May 1, 1848; d. Apr. 17, 1881; buried in Pittsford. (f) Isaac B., b. Dec. 1, 1852; m. Dec. 3, 1879, Jessie Heacock, of Rochester, N. Y. Ch., all b. at Pittsford: (i) Lottie, b. Sept. 13, 1881. (ii) Katherine, b. Feb. 20, 1883; (iii) Ada, b. April 2, 1887. (iv) Ralph, b. May 21, 1889. (g) George N., b. June 27, 1854; d. Mar. 13, 1855; buried in Pittsford.

(5) Milan D. Barnes, of Brighton, N. Y., b. June 15, 1819; m. Ann Eliza Servis, of Victor, N. Y., May 11, 1848. He d. June 3, 1859; she d. Sept. 5, 1897, and both were buried in Brighton. Ch., all b. in Brighton: (a) Ira S., b. Feb. 22, 1849; m. Aug. 31, 1871, to Lucy M. Wright, of Rochester, N. Y. Ch.: (i) Albert W., b. in Tidiout, Pa., June 2, 1872; m. Caroline Bennett, Aug. 30, 1895; d. Aug. 20, 1898. (ii) George M., b. in Brighton, N. Y., Apr. 27, 1874. (iii) William C., b. in Brighton, Apr. 2, 1878. (b) Albert M., b. Nov. 20, 1853; d. Mar. 9, 1900. (c) Edwin, b. May 5, 1855; d. May 22, 1855.

(6) Edwin M. Barnes, b. Sept. 29, 1822; m. Julia A. Arnold, of Lee, Mass. He d. July 10, 1869; she d. Feb. 22, 1863. Both were buried in Brighton. Ch.: (a) Dwight F., b. 1854; d. Sept. 5, 1855. (b) Nellie M., of Fulton, Ill., b. ———; m. Frank M. Palmer, Oct. 6, 1880. She d. Dec. 8, 1892. Res., Stockbridge, Mass. Ch.: (i) William, b. Dec. 25, 1883. (ii) Mabel, b. June 27, 1891. (iii) Louise, b. May 11, 1892. (c) Edwin A., of Brighton, N. Y., b. Dec. 9, 1859; graduated from the University of Rochester, Class of 1882; m. Mabel L. Appleton, of Boston, Mass., Apr. 25, 1888. Res., Charleston, West Va. Ch.: (i) Arnold A., b. in Charleston, Feb. 12, 1889. (ii) Bernard E., b. in Charleston, May 16, 1890.

824. ii. CHARLES, b. Feb. 4, 1781, at Colchester, Ct.; m. Betsy Wilson and Sophia P. Foote, 1959-68.

825. iii. JERUSHA, the third child of Charles Foote, was b. in Colchester, Ct., Nov. 30, 1783; and removed with her father's family to Mendon, N. Y., about 1800. She m. Enos Blossom, Nov. 6, 1806, and resided in Brighton, N. Y., where she d. Dec. 10, 1865. She was buried in Brighton. Ch.: (1) Mary M., of Brighton, was b. Aug. 13, 1807; m. David Ald-

rich, of Uxbridge, Mass., Oct. 25, 1838, and removed to Fredonia, Mich.; she d. Jan. 18; 1866, in Marshall, Mich., and her husband d. Oct. 11, 1888. Both were buried in Marshall. Ch., all born in Fredonia, Mich.: (a) Mary Eliza, b. Sept. 22, 1839. (b) Nathan P., b. Nov. 21, 1840; m. Mary A. Perry, of Tecumseh, Mich., May 14, 1867. He d. Sept. 9, 1871, and was buried at Marshall, Mich. (c) Judith Jerusha, b. Oct. 3, 1843; m. Melville H. Bardwell, Nov. 29, 1876. Res., Marshall, Mich. Ch.: (i) Reid, B., b. in Madison, Neb., June 29, 1881; res., N. Ontario, Cal. (d) Harriet Emily, b. Apr. 9, 1846; m. Victory C. Wattles, Feb. 7, 1877; res., Battle Creek, Mich. Ch.: (i) David A., b. Oct. 28, 1879; d. Sept. 28, 1901; buried in Battle Creek. (ii) V. Howard, b. June 11, 1881. (e) Sarah M., b. July 8, 1848; m. Azariah Robinson, June 11, 1893. They reside in Battle Creek.

(2) Alice S., b. in Brighton, Jan. 26, 1809; d. May 4, 1813; buried in Brighton.

(3) Noble F., b. in Brighton, Jan. 26, 1812; m. Tryphena White, of Bellevue, Mich., Oct. 20, 1836; she d. Apr. 7, 1837, and was buried in Bellevue; m. 2nd, Mar., 1866, Mrs. Elizabeth Gifford, nee Ferguson, of Marshall, Mich. He d. Oct. 8, 1875; p. s.; and was buried in Fredonia, Mich. She d. Oct. 22, 1903, and was buried in Fredonia.

(4) Eliza D., of Brighton, b. Aug. 13, 1815; m. Marshfield Parsons, Nov. 1, 1837. She d. Apr. 8, 1880. Ch.: (a) William Marshfield, of Brighton, N. Y., b. Dec. 7, 1838; m. Arilla Lord, Oct. 9, 1873. Res., Brighton. Ch.: (i) Jane L., b. Sept. 12, 1879. (b) Enos B., b. in Brighton, Sept. 1, 1840; m. Augusta Barton, Mar. 20, 1877; d. May 6, 1897. (c) Tirza M., of Brighton, N. Y., b. Dec. 7, 1842; m. Henry E. Boardman, Sept. 6, 1865, and removed to Rochester, N. Y., where her husband d. Mar. 14, 1897, and was buried in Mt. Hope Cemetery. Ch.: (i) E. Smith, b. in Rochester, Aug. 1, 1866; m. Alice Saunders, ———. (ii) Hattie P., b. in Rochester, Mar. 28, 1872; d. Mar., 1874. (d) Mary Eliza, of Brighton, N. Y., b. Apr. 29, 1845; m. Frank J. Amsden, of Rochester, N. Y., Feb. 23, 1865. Ch.: (i) Mary B., b. June 15, 1872; d. 1876. (ii) Frank P., b. May 12, 1874. (e) Augusta P., born in Brighton, Apr. 2, 1847; m. Anson L. Beardsley, Sept. 10, 1884; he d. Aug. 14, 1896. Her res., Fairport, N. Y. No. ch. (f) Hattie L., born in Brighton, July 20, 1849; m. James D. Shelmire, Sept. 15, 1880; res., Brighton, N. Y.

(5) George D., of Brighton, N. Y., b. Aug. 13, 1815; m. Phebe Sibley, of Rochester, N. Y., Oct. 7, 1841. He d. Apr. 15, 1889, and was buried in Mt. Hope Cemetery, Rochester, N. Y. Ch.: (a) Florence, b. in Rochester, May 9, 1843; m. Chas. M. Allen, a lawyer, of Rochester, Jan. 1, 1869; she d. July 25, 1897. Ch.: (i) Newell B., b. Jan. 28, 1871. (ii) Florence, b. June 19, 1872. (iii) Gertrude S., b. Dec. 16, 1873. (iv) Charles M., b. July 22, 1876; (v) Phebe B., b. Dec. 3, 1877. (vi) Henry H., b. Mar. 3, 1881. (b) Benjamin Blossom, b. Brighton, N. Y., Apr. 4, 1817; d. Aug. 6, 1820; buried in Brighton.

(7)

826. iv.   DAN, b. Richman, Mass., Mar. 6, 1785; m. Patience Orcrett and Patience Gosnell, 1969-76.

827. v.   LOIS, b. West Stockbridge, Mass., Feb. 13, 1788; m. Gaius Lane, and lived in Mendon, N. Y., and afterwards in Rochester, N. Y., where she d. in 1814. Ch.: (1) Susan, d. unm. (2) Sophia, b. ————; m. Schuyler Moses, and removed to Cala. before 1850.

828. vi.   LYDIA ANN, b. West Stockbridge, Mass., Dec. 6, 1790; m. Edward Ball, a connection of Mary Ball, the mother of George Washington, and removed with him to Sandusky, Ohio. Mr. Ball served his country in the war of 1812, and the example thus given was followed by his family, for no less than 24 of his male descendants and men who married into the family enlisted in the Civil War. Both Mr. and Mrs. Ball d. and were buried in Iowa City, Ia. Ch.:

(1) Sandford Ball, of Freedom, N. Y., b. Sept. 18, 1807; m. Lavinia Lock, of Norwalk, O.; he d. in Clyde, Ohio. Ch.: (a) Charles Ball, is living at Sand Beach, Mich. (b) Lois, and (c) William, are both dead.

(2) Mary L. Ball, of Freedom, N. Y., b. Sept. 29, 1811; m. Joseph Burt, of Barrington, Mass. Mrs. Ball d. at Courtland, Ill., in 1900, and was buried at Malta, Ill. Ch.: (a) One dau., is now Mrs. Kate Cherry. (b) Charles B., d. at Battle Creek, Mich.

(3) Sarah Foote Ball, of Freedom, N. Y., b. May 9, 1819; m. Mr. Noble, having one son by him. After his death she m. Francis Barnes. They had one son. Mrs. Barnes d. in Lincoln, Nebraska, at an advanced age. Ch.: (a) William Paul Noble. (b) Marshall Barnes.

(4) Eunice Foote Ball, of Freedom, N. Y., b. May 9, 1819; m. Mr. Sparling, of Sandusky, Ohio. Ch.: (a) George, d. a prisoner in Libby Prison during the Civil War. (b) Emily.

(5) Maria L. Ball, of Freedom, N. Y., b. July 30, 1820; m. George Young, of Sandusky, Ohio. Mr. Young d. July 15, 1863, in the Civil War at Jackson, Miss. Mrs. Young d. in 1892, There were nine children of this marriage, four of whom died in infancy. The others are: (a) Celia S., b. in Ohio, Aug. 27, 1841; m. Clark Wood, at Batavia, Ill., Nov. 2, 1869. Mr. Wood d. Feb. 2, 1888. (b) Gilbert W., b. in Ohio, Aug. 27, 1843; m. Martha Brockway, at Batavia, Ill., Dec. 23, 1868. He d. May 30, 1882. They had two children, Charles and Celia M. (c) Nelson M., b. in Ind., Apr. 2, 1848; d. in Ill., May 5, 1862. (d) Edward R., b. in Ind., Apr. 4, 1852; m. Martha Young at Chesterton, Ind., May 4, 1872. They had one child, dying in infancy. (e) Frankie M., b. in Batavia, Ill., Feb. 27, 1863; m. Clarence Haley, Feb. 11, 1880. They have had three children, named Fern, Herbert and Bernice. Herbert d. in 1889.

(6) Edward Ball, of Freedom, N. Y., b. June 29, 1822; served in the Union Army from 1861 to 1866. He was twice married, 1st to Miss Smith, and after her death to Miss Foster. He d. near Saltille, Nebraska.

(7) Bernard A., b. July 10, 1824; served in the army throughout the Civil War; he was a carpenter by trade. He was twice m., first to Maria Stroking, of New London, O.; and May 21, 1879, to Sophia E. Stanton, of London, England. Res., Batavia, Kane Co., Ill.; p. s.

(8) John W. Ball, of Freedom, N. Y., was married in Hartland, Huron Co., O., Feb. 11, 1851, to Betsey Striker, of Clyde, N. Y. Mrs. Ball d. June 2, 1884, and was buried in Olena, O. Ch.: (a) John J. b. in Olena, O., Mar. 17, 1853; m. Delia Filkins, Mar. 17, 1889. They have one son, Cassius G. Ball, b. Feb. 17, 1889. John J. Ball d. Dec. 22, 1902, and was buried in Olena Cemetery. (b) George G., b. in Olena, O., Jan. 15, 1855.

(9) Dan M., b. in Freedom, N. Y., May 27, 1830; m. Miss Cambridge, of Iowa City. He enlisted in the army and died, in consequence, in a hospital in Cairo, Ill., in 1861.

829. vii. JOHN, b. West Stockbridge, Mass., Jan. 17, 1792; m. Sophia Palmer Rogers, 1977-9.

830. viii. EUNICE, b. West Stockbridge, Mass., Nov. 26, 1794; m. Zacharias Noble about 1820, and removed with him from Mendon, N. Y., her father's home at the time, to Olean, N. Y. Ch.: (1) Seymour J., b. Mar. 31, 1821, in Olean, N. Y.; m. Maria C. Mills, of Olean, N. Y., Jan., 1846, and engaged in farming and lumbering in Olean. Later he settled on a farm near Batavia, N. Y., and in 1871 he purchased a flour mill in Williamsport, Pa., which·he operated till his death, Oct. 15, 1890. He was buried in Williamsport. Mrs. Noble d. in Williamsport 189—. Ch.: (a) Charles S., b. in Olean in 1849; d. in 1858; and was buried in Olean. (b) Edward F., b. in Olean, Dec. 8, 1852, engaged in milling with his father; m. Nov. 4, 1886, Mary E. Mudge, of Williamsport; d. Dec. 25, 1899, and was buried in Williamsport. Ch.: (i) Frances C., b. Apr. 7, 1892. (ii) Josephine F., b. May 1, 1897. (c) Mary Belle, b. in Olean, Nov. 6, 1861; res., Muskegon, Mich.

831. ix. ELISAH, b. West Stockbridge, Mass., Feb. 26, 1796; m. Betsey Simonson, 1980-90.

832. x. ELIAS, b. West Stockbridge, Mass., May 15, 1799; m. Matilda Thorp, 1991-6.

833. xi. MARIA, b. Litchfield, N. Y., July 5, 1801; d. Feb., 1839; unm.

834. xii. EBENEZER BARNARD, b. Bloomfield, N. Y., Feb. 1, 1805; m. Mary Skidmore, 1997-9.

263. ELISHA FOOTE, (80, 25, 9, 3,) b. Jan. 10, 1757; m., 1782, Phebe Sabin, of Colchester, Ct.

835. i. ELISAH b. 1783; m. Mary Squier, Eliza J. Blague, and Sarah Beemis, 2000-2.

266. ELIAS FOOTE, (80, 25, 9, 3,) b. Oct. 4, 1766; m. Mar., 1809, Sally, dau. of Ezekiel Tracy, of Otego, N. Y.; d. July 5, 1855. She d. 1857. Res., Franklin, N. Y.

836. i. RUSSELL, b. Dec. 14, 1810; m. Sylvia Loveland, 2003-5.

837. ii. DAVID, b. Mar. 24, 1812; m. Oct. 1, 1857, Mary, dau. of Thomas Parsons; she d. 1886; he d. Oct. 29, 1897. Res., N. Franklin, N. Y.

838. iii. LOIS, b. Oct. 19, 1814; m. June 8, 1863, Jonathan Fitch, of N. Franklin, N. Y. She d. Dec. 14, 1882; he d. June, 1871.

839. iv. ASA, b. Sept. 3, 1816; m. Ophelia Brown, 2006-7.

840. v. EZEKIEL, b. May 26, 1818; m. Elizabeth Parish, 2008-11.

841. vi. JANE, b. Mar. 6, 1820; d. Aug. 20, 1889, at Franklin, N. Y.; unm.

842. vii. ESTHER, b. April 16, 1822; d. at Franklin, N. Y.; unm.

267. RUSSELL FOOTE, (80, 25, 9, 3,) b. Dec. 29, 1769; m. Jan. 14, 1802, Anna, dau. of Ezekiel Gillett of Hebron, Ct. She d. Apr. 16, 1808, ae. 32; m. 2nd, Feb. 9, 1809, Sylvia, widow of Abner Loveland, of Marlborough, Ct., and Franklin, N. Y. She d. Dec. 26, 1823, ae. 52; m. 3rd, May 29, 1825, Salome, widow of Peter Parsons, of Enfield, Ct., and Franklin, N. Y. She d. Sept. 23, 1844, ae. 64. Res., Franklin, N. Y.

843. i. CLARISSA A., b. June 21, 1804.

844. ii. CHARLES, b. Feb. 27, 1806; d. July 14, 1841.

845. iii. Child, not named, b. Mar., 1808; d. in infancy.

846. iv. Child, not named, b. Mar., 1808; d. in infancy.

268. WILLIAM FOOTE, (80, 25, 9, 3,) b. Aug. 4, 1772; m. Mary Ann, youngest dau. of James Lord, of Middletown, Ct. Res., Colchester, Glastenbury, and Middle Haddam, Ct., and then to Michigan, where they both died.

847. i. MARY, b. ———; d. Feb. 7, 1836, in East Haddam, Ct.

848. ii. HENRY, b. ———; m. ———; res., Commerce, Mich.

849. iii. CHARLES, b. ———; d. unm.

850. iv. HARRIET, b. ———; m. ———.

851. v. JERUSHA, b. ———; d. June 20, 1831, in East Haddam, Ct.

852. vi. SARAH LOUISE, b. Jan. 18, 1800; m. 1821, John S. Taylor, of New York, N. Y. She d. Aug. 2, 1836, in East Haddam, Ct. Ch.: (1) Cornelius Stewart, b. Jan. 29, 1833. (2) George Tracy, b. July 15, 1835.

269. ASA FOOTE, Jr., (81, 25, 9, 3,) b. May 1, 1753; m. June, 1779, Lucy, dau. of Elijah Kellogg, of Marlborough, Ct. He d. June 8, 1781. She d. Oct., 1825, ae. 65. Res., Marlborough, Ct.

853. i. LUCY, b. June, 1780; m. Aaron Porter, of Hebron, Ct.

273. JOEL FOOTE, (81, 25, 9, 3,) b. June 26, 1763; m. 1st, Oct. 28, 1787, Abigail Robbins, dau. of Elisah Lord, of Colchester, Ct. She d. Jan. 8, 1795, ae. 25. M. 2nd, Nov. 15, 1796, Rachel, dau. of Samuel Philips Lord, of East Haddam, Ct. She d. Oct. 6, 1843, ae. 73. He d. July 12, 1846, ae. 83. He was a man of extensive information, of great urbanity of manner, and held a conspicuous station in Town and State. For many years he represented the town in the State Legislature, and during the most of his active life was Justice of the Peace. He was remarkably active and retained the powers of his mind and body to an uncommon degree till within a few days of his death (when he took his coat down from the peg where it hung he remarked that the coat had been fourteen times to the Legislature. I have heard my mother make that statement. You must remember Connecticut at that time had two sessions a year, one session held in Hartford and one in New Haven).

Joel Foote, Esq., son of Asa and Jerush (Carter) Foote, and fourth in descent from Nathaniel Foote, of Wethersfield, was b. June 26, 1763, in that part of the town of Colchester which was set off to Marlborough. He was liberally educated and was probably as good a type of an old school gentleman as any resident of the town.

His uprightness was proverbial, and his service in places of trust was constantly sought. He represented the town in the General Assembly twentytwo successive years, and from his general prominence won the title of the "Duke of Marlborough."

He was twice married, his first wife being Abigal Robbins Lord, daughter of Elisha Lord of Marlborough, who died at an early age, leaving four children.

His second wife was Rachel Lord, daughter of Samuel P. Lord, of East Haddam. Eight children were born of this marriage. His death occurred at Marlborough July 12, 1846, at the age of 83 years.

854. i. JERUSHA, b. Jan. 4, 1789; d. Mar. 2, 1876, Andover, Ct., unm.

855. ii. ASA, b. Apr. 26, 1791; d. Nov. 24, 1791.

856. iii. ABIGAIL, b. Dec. 15, 1792; m. Dec. 15, 1814, Cyrus Bingham, of Hebron, Ct. Ch.: (1) William, b. Mar. 9, 1816. (2) Caroline Elizabeth, b. May 8, 1818. (3) Edward, b. Jan. 21, 1821. (4) Joel, b. Oct. 11, 1827.

857. iv. ROBBINS, b. Jan. 4, 1795; d. Jan. 12, 1795.

858. v. ASA, b. Mar. 20, 1798; m. Caroline Hale, 2012-6.

859. vi. EDWIN, b. Nov. 15, 1799; m. Ann Lindsley and Lydia Boydon, 2017-28.

860. vii. GEORGE, b. Oct. 5, 1801; d. Oct. 7, 1801.

861. viii. GEORGE, b. Oct. 22, 1802; m. Rachel C. Jones, 2029-32.

862. ix. EMILY, b. Apr. 25, 1805; m. 1st, Apr., 1828, Dr. Royal Kingsbury, of Marlborough, Ct. He d. Nov. 21, 1836, ae. 38; m. 2nd, Sept., 1839, Jedediah Post, of Glastenbury, Ct. She d. Mar. 13, 1859, in South Glastenbury, Ct. Ch.: (1) Emily, b. Feb. 25, 1831; m. 1st, Sheldon Hollister, a lawyer; he d. two weeks later in Minn.; m. 2nd, Virginia Cheney; res., Hartford, Ct.

863. x. WILLIAM LORD, b. Mar. 27, 1807; m. Emeline T. Foster, 2033-7.

864. xi. RACHEL LORD, b. Jan. 25, 1809; d. May 5, 1809.

865. xii. SAMUEL PHILIPS LORD, b. Aug. 10, 1811; d. Sept. 20, 1812.

274. ROGER FOOTE, (81, 25, 9, 3,) b. June 9, 1765; m. May 26, 1790, Eunice, dau. of Daniel Buckley, of Colchester, Ct. He d. June 10, 1823. She d. Jan. 22, 1846, ae. 74, in Great Barrington, Mass.

866. i. EUNICE, b. May 12, 1791; res., Great Barrington, Mass.

867. ii. EZRA, b. Oct. 30, 1792; d. July 29, 1793.

868. iii. EZRA, b. Jan. 7, 1795; m. Sarah Louisa Bowler, 2038-42.

869. iv. DOLLY OLMSTEAD, b. Mar. 3, 1797; m. David Shepard, of Geneseo, N. Y. Ch.: (1) Caroline Foote, b. Geneseo, N. Y., Apr. 2, 1821; d. June 27, 1878; unm. (2) Roger Foote, b. Geneseo, June 16, 1823; d. July 17, 1825. (3) Sarah Louisa, b. Geneseo, Dec. 15, 1825; m. 1849, Henry V. Colt, of Geneseo, N. Y. She d. Feb. 27, 1900; 5 ch. (4) David C. Shepard, b. Feb. 20, 1828; m. Frances Aurelia (Alvord), adopted daughter of Chauncey Parsons. She was b. May 1, 1830; d. Nov. 9, 1902. Ch.: (a) Frank Parsons Shepard, b. Oct. 30, 1853; m. Sept. 1, 1880, Anna W. McMillan. She was b. Aug. 29, 1856. Ch.: (i) David Chauncey, b. July 30, 1881; m. June 4, 1907, Sadee Nichols Smith. She was b. Dec., 1881. (ii) Samuel McMillan, b. April 4, 1883. (iii) Roger Buckley, b. Sept. 14, 1885. (iv) Frank Parsons, b. May 16, 1895. (b) Caroline Shepard, b. Nov. 12, 1861; m. Dec. 12, 1883,

Alvin W. Kreck. She d. Mar. 14, 1892. Ch.: (i) Alvin Shepard Kreck, b. June 14, 1887; d. Nov. 11, 1900. (ii) Shepard Kreck, b. Feb. 2, 1891. (4) Helen Maria, b. Geneseo, Mar. 28, 1831; d. Nov. 26, 1849; unm. (5) Horace Foote, b. Geneseo, Apr. 3, 1834; d. Mar. 16, 1864; unm. (6) Charles Roger, b. Geneseo, Dec. 28, 1837; res., Geneseo, N. Y.; unm. (7) William Henry, b. Geneseo, June 24, 1843; m. 1st, Mary Miller; m. 2nd, Mary Elizabeth Doland; res., Belmar, N. J. Ch.: 1, by his first wife.

870. v.   HORACE, b Mar. 21, 1799; m. 2040¹⁻⁵; res., Cleveland, Ohio. Graduated at Yale in 1820. Is an Attorney and Counsellor at Law.

871. vi.   AMEILA, b. July 15, 1801; m. Ralph C. Foote, of Colchester, Ct.

872. vii. CARTER, b. June 10, 1804; res., Perry, Ohio.

873. viii. CAROLINE, b. Sept. 7, 1806; m. Dec. 31, 1829, Luke Risley, of St. Louis, Mo.

874. ix.   DAVID, b. Aug. 15, 1809; m. Caroline Taylor, 2042¼-½.

875. x.   MARINA, b. Jan. 16, 1812; d. Apr. 16, 1812.

876. xi.   LINUS, b. July 12, 1813; res., Great Barrington, Mass.; unm.

877. xii. CHARLES, b. July 1, 1817; res., Fort Wayne, Ind.

281. JARED FOOTE, (82, 25, 9, 3,) b. Sept. 30, 1770; m. Nov. 25, 1790, Lucinda, dau. of Cordial Jennings. He resided in Pittsfield, Mass., with his parents, until 1798, when he removed with them to Cornwall, Vt. From there he removed to Scipio, N Y., and on the organization of a Church there, was appointed Deacon. After ten years' stay at Scipio, he was invited to take the office of Steward of the Theological Seminary at Auburn, N. Y., which he accepted, and removed to that place. He there became an Elder in the First Presbyterian Church. In 1830 he removed to Rushville, N. Y.

878. i.   JARED, b. July 12, 1795; m. Eliza Clark, 2043-8.

879. ii.   DAVID, b. Oct. 13, 1797; m. Maria Champlin, 2049-50.

880. iii. LUCINDA, b. Sept. 29, 1799; a successful teacher.

881. iv.   ANNA, b. Mar. 8, 1801; d. Nov. 11, 1801.

882. v.   ELI, b. Oct. 8, 1803; m. Lucy Olmsted, 2051-3.

883. vi.   OTIS CLARK, b. Dec. 11, 1806; m. Mary Aldrich, 2054.

884. vii. ANNA, b. Feb. 6, 1809; m. John P. Gillam, of Rushville, N. Y. Ch.: (1) Otis Henry, b. Apr. 10, 1831. (2) George, b. Nov. 1, 1836. (3) Anna Maria, b. Feb. 20, 1839.

885. viii. BETSY, b. Aug. 4, 1811; m. Lewis Van Anden, of Auburn, N. Y. Ch.: (1) Lewis Jennings, b. June 27, 1836. (2) Betsey Maria, b. Jan. 10, 1839.

886. ix.   LOVINA, b. Apr. 11, 1815; m. L. C. Wiswall, of Rushville, N. Y.

283. ASA FOOTE (82, 25, 9, 3,) b. Jan. 17, 1788; m. 1st, Nov. 23, 1809, Eunice, dau. of Jacob Ingraham, of Cornwall, Vt.; she d. Sept. 27, 1837; m. 2nd, Nov. 13, 1838, Maria, wid. of Shepard Tooker of Auburn, N. Y., and dau. of John B. Tibbals; she d. Dec. 13, 1873; res., Cornwall, Vt., Homer, N. Y., Ledyard, N. Y., and Rushville, N. Y. He d. Aug. 1, 1861, Ft. Atkinson, Wis.

887. i.   JOEL B., b. Apr. 21, 1811; m. 1837, Mary Thorp. He d. Mar. 25, 1841. Ch.: two, d. young. Res., Rushville, N. Y.

888. ii.   SALLY MINERVA, b. June 26, 1813; d. Dec. 23, 1815.

889. iii. MINERVA ANN, b. Aug. 18, 1816; m. 1st, Jan., 1835, David Jaycox; he d. Sept. 21, 1863; m. 2nd, abt. 1868, St. Paul Seeley;

she d. Feb. 20, 1903. Ch.: (1) Henry Jacox, b. at Rushville, N. Y., Oct. 26, 1835; d. Sept., 1902; was twice married; 1st, to Kate Bovee, Nov. 4, 1857. Ch.: (a) Lafayette Jacox, b. Sept., 1858; d. Jan., 1859. (b) Henry Jacox, b. May 13, 1861; m. Rosa ————; d. May 19, 1901; 2 ch., Larne and Erlus, children of Henry Jacox, No. 801-1, and 2nd marriage with Jennie Howley, 1875. (c) Louise Jacox, b. ————; m. 1st, John Clark, Sept. 15, 1869; m. 2nd, Edward Payne, Jan. 1, 1874. Ch.: (i) Edward Payne, Jr., b. Dec. 18, 1875; m. June 1st, 1898, Kate Sanborn; have one ch., Helen, b. May 18, 1902. (d) Ione, b. ————. (e) Mammie, b. ————. (2) Eunice Jaycox, b. Aug. 6, 1837, at Rushville, N. Y.; d. Mar. 1, 1838. (3) Hattie Jaycox, b. Nov. 13, 1839, at Rushville, N. Y.; d. Sept. 14, 1840. (4) Rosella A. Joycox, b. Jan. 10, 1841, at Rushville, N. Y.; m. Nov. 6, 1862, Samuel Austin Bridges, son of Alford and Martia (Brown) Bridges, of Moretown, Vt; they reside at Fort Atkinson, Wis. Ch.: (a) Isadene, 801-17, b. at Fort Atkinson, Wis., Mar. 30, 1866; m. Nov. 18, 1885, Louis F. Slaker; res., St. James, Minn. Ch.: (i) Raymond Slaker, b. Jan. 21, 1887. (ii) Ruth Slaker, b. Apr. 18, 1892. (iii) Louis F. Slaker, b. Feb. 14, 1902. (b) Justus Guy Bridges, b. at Fort Atkinson, Wis., Mar. 20, 1868; m. at Walla Walla, Wash., Feb. 24, 1897, Millicent Leone Merrill. (c) Inez May Bridges, b. at Fort Atkinson, Wis., July 26, 1872; m. April 27, 1893, Warner Whitney Cornish, son of Oscar S. Cornish and Elizabeth Whitney, of Fort Atkinson, Wis. Ch.: (i) Harry B. Cornish, b. at Fort Atkinson, May 11, 1896. (ii) Paul W. Cornish, b. at Fort Atkinson, Wis., Nov. 12, 1897. (5) Lavina Jaycox, b. July 13, 1843, at Eagle, Wis.; m. Nov. 8, 1860, James Payne. Ch.: (a) Ella L. Payne, b. Sept. 6, 1861; d. Nov. 14, 1882. (b) Pearl Ione Payne, b. Apr. 10, 1867; m. Apr. 18, 1904, Arthur Huntley. (c) Edna A. Payne, b. April 11, 1876; m. Aug. 28, 1900, Tom W. Conklin; one ch., Marion Conklin, b. May 8, 1902. (d) Arthur L. Payne, b. Mar. 25, 1880; d. Mar. 11, 1905. (6) Mortimer Jaycox, b. Feb. 18, 1846; d. Mar. 21, 1878; m. Mar. 24, 1868, Mary Seeley; one ch., Herbert M. Jaycox, b. June 6, 1873; m. and res. at Lake Mills, Wis. (7) Louise Jaycox, b. Aug. 2, 1850, at Eagle, Wis. (8) Ozias Pitts Jaycox, b. Feb. 23, 1853, at Eagle, Wis. (9) Oscar Jaycox, b. Apr., 1854; d. Sept. 2, 1855. (10) Asa Jaycox, b. Jan. 13, 1857 at Eagle, Wis.; d. Mar. 1, 1868.

890. iv.   DR. OZIAS P., b. May 27, 1819; graduate of Union College; d. at Rushville, N. Y., June 6, 1847; unm.

891. v.   ELISHA L., b. Aug. 30, 1821; m. Ellen Cordelia Symonds, 2055-8.

892. vi.   EUNICE LOUISA, b. Aug. 22, 1824; m. at Rushville, N. Y., Dec. 31, 1846, to Lafayette Seamans; they had 4 ch. Mrs. Seamans now res. at Walla Walla, Wash. Ch.: (1) Annis Seamans, b. at Middlesex, N. Y., Mar. 31, 1848; m. Charles Spencer Salisbury, Dec. 22, 1869; d. at Walla Walla, Wash., July 27, 1892; they had one ch., Lillian Edna Salisbury, b. Apr. 8, 1877, at West River, N. Y. (2) Eunice Adelaide Seamans, b. at Middlesex, N. Y., June 2, 1851; d. Mar. 26, 1854, at Middlesex, N. Y. **(3)**

Lillian Seamans, b. at Middlesex, N. Y., Oct. 9, 1854; m. Apr. 14, 1892, Alvin Zaring; they reside at Walla Walla, Wash.; have two ch., Robert Seamans Zaring, b. Apr. 6, 1896, and Edward Little Zaring, b. July 10, 1898. (4) Effie May Seamans, b. May 13, 1861; d. Mar. 16, 1863, at Middlesex, N. Y.

893. vii. JOANNA MARIA, b. May 1, 1840; m. May 21, 1862, John C. Damuth, of Fort Atkinson, Wis. Ch.: (1) Grace Elizabeth, b. Aug. 11, 1863; m. 1st, Aug. 16, 1882, Eugene Westcott; m. 2nd, Dec. 22, 1903, Charles Brown; res. at Fort Atkinson, Wis. (2) Louis Foote Damuth, b. Oct. 13, 1865; m. June 10, 1903, Anna Pagel, of Carroll, Iowa. Ch.: (a) John Carl Christian, b. May 13, 1904.

894. viii. JOHN WARD FOOTE, b. Nov. 4, 1844; m. Nora Berry, 2059-61.

895. ix. SARAH VICTORIA, b. Aug 11, 1847; m. Exist Ferron; res., San Diego, Cal.

- 284. EPHRAIM FOOTE, (85, 26, 9, 3, 1,) b. ———; m. Lydia, dau. of Allerton and Alethea (Stone) Cushman. She was a descendant of Robert Cushman, b. in Eng., 1580. He preached the first Protestant sermon in America; m. Fear, dau. of Elder Wm. Brewster. Mrs. Lydia Foote d. in New Concord, N. Y., 1778. He d. in Troy, N. Y., 1799.

896. i. FREELOVE, b. 1764; m. Jacob, son of Theophilus Jackson. He b. at Canaan, N. Y., 1756. She d. Fairfield, N. Y., Apr., 1821. He d. Fairfield, 1832. Ch.:

UNTOWN, CT.
APR. 6, !

(1) Lydia, b. May 28, 1782; m. Phillip Crist, b. Feb. 7, 1783, and d. Jan. 19, 1872. She d. Oct. 5, 1860. Ch.: (a) Abram Crist, b. 1815; m. Irena, dau. of Hepestead Bradford. He d. 1840. No ch. (b) Jacob, b. 1819; m. Mary Boyle. He d. 1892. No ch. (c) Morgan Cornelius, b. 1822; m. Maria Louise, dau. of Daniel and Lydia Brayton, b. 1827. He d. 1905. Ch.: (i) Daniel Brayton, b. 1856; m. Nettie M. Jackson. Ch.: (i1) Forest Jackson, b. 1884. (i2) Everet Brayton, b. 1886. (i3) Cornelius Washington, b. 1894; d. 1896. (d) Hawley, b. 1827; d. 1852, unm.

(2) Samuel, b. 1783; m. Anna Brown, b. 1791; d. 1859. He d. 1863. Ch.: (a) Julia Etta, b. 1810; m. John Wood, 1835. She d. 1856. Ch.: (i) Annie., b. 1837, Spring Green, Wis.; m. Damon C. Reed, b. 1828, and d. 1897. Ch.: (i1) Grace Annie, b. Spring Green, Wis. (b) Julia Ann. (c) Jerome Bonaparte, b. 1813; d. 1880. Ch.: (i) Rev. Geo. Anson, b. 1846; res., 43 Mt. Vernon street, Boston. (ii) Annie B., b. ———; res., 6 Quincey street, North Adams, Mass. (d) Clarissa, b. ———; m. Levi Houghton. (e) Calfernia, b. ———; m. Daniel Stewart. (f) Sarah, b. ———; m. Loomis. (g) Nathaniel, b. 1824; m. Emeline Veber. He d. 1897. Ch.: (i) Edith L., b. 1851; m. Willis J. Ball. Ch.: (i1) Flora Vista Ball, b. 1892. (ii) Maud A Jackson, b. 1854; m. Russel Wood, P. O. Herkimer, N. Y. (iii) Dora E. Jackson, b. 1858; m. Albert J. Hodge. Ch.: (iii1) Fred B. Hodge, b. 1887. (iii2) Hazel Q. Hodge, b. 1899. (iv) Blanche C., b. 1864; m. Henry E. Benjamin.

(3) Jacob, b. 1787; m. Sally Sheldon, b. 1794; d. 1869. He d. 1873. Ch.: (a) Maria Amy, b. 1817; m. Cephus Farrington. She d. 1855. Ch.: (i) Grove M. Farrington, b. d. at Fillmore, Minn., 1900. Ch.: (i1) Chas. Alten, b. 1867; res., Wykoff, Minn. (i2) Burton D., b. 1869; res., Wykoff, Minn. (i3) Clarence H., b. 1871; res., Byron, Minn. (i4) Ralph M., b. 1878; res., Dickinson, N. Dak. (ii) Romain, b. res., Chatfield, Minn. (b) Samuel H. Jackson, b. 1819; m. Emily S. Farrington, 1841. He d. 1895. Ch.: () Henry Grove, b. 1842; d. 1845. (ii) Eluella Roselia, b. 1847; d. 1853. (iii) Florence Elnora, b. 1849; d. 1853. (iv) Helen Emogene, b. ———; d. 1897; m. W. W. Richards. Ch.: (iv1) Emily Richards, b. 1874; d. 1891. (iv2) Warren W., Jr., b. res., Newport, N. Y. (iv3) Lulu M., b. res., Newport, N. Y. (v) Grove, d. 1904. (vi) Hedding, d. 1905. (c) Duane E. Jackson, b. 1823; m. Margaret Lints. He d. 1906. Ch.: (i) Clarinda E. Jackson, b. 1851; m. Levi Rinkle. She d. 1897. (ii) Seymour W., b. 1863; d. 1877. (d) Dwight Jackson, b. 1826; m Mary Lints; d. 1886. Ch.: (i) Remain, b. res. Frankfort, N. Y. (e) Lydia Ann Jackson, b. 1828; m. Dr. John Mower, 1851. She d. 1853. (f) James S., b. 1820; d. 1839. (g) Rhoda C., b. 1831; m. Rev. L. Judson Cooper, 1855. She d. 1889. Ch.: (i) Judson L., b. 1855; res., Verona, N. Y. Ch.: (i1) Lydia M. Cooper, b. 1875; m. Geo. M. Cogwin, of Rome, N. Y. Ch.: (ia) Ester A. Cogwin, b. 1898. (ib) Dorothy P., b. 1904.. (ii) Stocton D. Cooper, b. 1871; res., Seneca Falls, N. Y. Ch.: (ii1) Duane E., b. 1900. (h) Guilford H., b. 1835; d. 1852.

(4) Elijah, b. 1789; m. Elizabeth Hermis, b. 1798; d. 1876. He d. 1874. Ch.: (a) Henry M., b. 1821; m. Achsah Ann Helmer, b. 1824; d. 1883. He d. 1856. Ch.: (i) Geo. W., b. 1851; res., Herkimer, N. Y.; m. 1st, Alace Eccles, b. 1852; d. 1882; m. 2nd, Addie L. Jackson; b. 1859. Ch.: (i1) Grace A., b. 1874; res., Auburn, N. Y. (i2) Fred H., b. 1875; m. Ada J. Desermaux. Ch.: (ia) Alace E., b. 1901. (ii) Fred E., b. 1853. (b) Andrew G. Jackson, b. 1831; m. Mary Petrie. He d. 1894. Ch.: (i) Chas. A., b. 1865; d. 1868. (ii) Henry Eugene, b. 1857; m. Emma Jane Mosher; res., Middleville, N. Y. Ch.: (ii1) Earl Mosher Jackson, b. 1882. (ii2) Mary Elizabeth, b. 1885. (iii) Irving E., b. 1855; m. Jennie Enos, res., Middleville, N. Y. (iv) Delville G., b. 1859; m. 1st, Harriet Mosher, b. 1864; d. 1894; m. 2nd, Ella Pickert. Ch.: (iv1) Elberta, b. ———. (iv2) Elda, b. ———. (c) Varnum C., b. 1823; m. Mary Keller, b. 1823. He d. 1899. Ch.: (i) Willard E., b. 1853; res., Herkimer, N. Y. (ii) Anna Eliza, b. 1859; res., Herkimer, N. Y. (iii) Emma E., b. 1856; res., Herkimer, N. Y. (iv) Leander D., b. 1860; m. Sally Weiberg. Ch.: (iv1) Chas. E., b. 1892. (iv2) Varnum C., b. 1894. (iv3) Willard E., b. 1897. (iv4) Emogene, b. 1898. (v) Ella, b. 1866; m. Chas. E. Bunnell; res., Herkimer, N. Y. Ch.:(v1) Mildred I., b. 1900.

(5) Elsie, b. 1791; m. Geo. Wood, b. 1788; d. 1868. She d. 1884. Ch.: (a) Anson J., b. 1809; m. Susan E. Cobb; m. 2nd, Maria Watson. He d. 1881. Ch.: (i) Wells Wood. (ii) Simeon. (iii) Walter. (iv) Velma. (v) Almira; m. Van Pickert. (b) George

W., b. 1816; m. Mary Orenderf. He d. 1886. Ch. (i) Annette,
b. 1848; res., Middleville, N. Y. (ii) Fred, b. 1852. (iii) Helen
M., b. 1841; d. 1842. (c) Walter W., b. 1823; m. Mary E. Brown.
He d. 1879. Ch.: (i) Alace, b. 1851; m. Frank Plasteredge; res.,
Mohawk, N. Y. (ii) Silas W., b. 1853; m. Cora Kelsey. (d)
Erastus, b. ———. (e) Redney, b. ———; m. Harriette Mains.
Ch.: (i) George. (ii) James. (iii) Lottie. (f) Rosell, b. ———;
m. ———. Ch.: (i) Corneliam Walter Elliot. (ii) Chas. Wood;
d. ———. (g) Wm., m. Jane Perkins. Ch.: (i) Chas. (ii)
Ellen, m. Nelson Morey. (iii) Henry M. (iv) Stedman. (h)
Chas., m. Mary Fenner. Ch.: (i) Frank, b. ———. (i) Louisa
Wood, b. ———; m. Geo. Walker. Ch.: (i) Alta, b. ———; m.
Chas. Hendrix. Ch.: (i1) Reba Hendrix, b. ———. (j) Eme-
line, b. ———; m. Albert Ford. Ch.: (i) Adney, b. ———; m.
E. W. Corey; res., Middleville, N. Y. (k) Alexander, b. ———.
(l) John, b. 1824; d. 1831.

(6) Sibyl, b. 1792; m. Benjamin Harvey, b. and d. unknown.

(7) Asa, b. 1794; m. Lydia Sheldon, b. 1807; d. 1861. He d.
1861. Ch.: (a) Walter Washington, b. 1829; m. Helen L. Tabor,
b. 1833. He d. 1892. Ch.: (i) Albert L., b. 1857; m. Minnie
Aschenbach. He d. 1899. (ii) Addie L., b. 1859; m. George W.
Jackson. No ch. (iii) William W., b. 1860; unm.; res., Little
Falls, N. Y. (iv) Ira E. Jackson, b. 1862; m. Blanche Kent;
res., Herkimer, N. Y. Ch.: (iv1) Leon. (iv2) Lillian. (v)
Nettie M., b. 1864; m. Daniel Brayton Crist. (vi) Howard J., b.
1866; res., Auburn, N. Y. (vii) Helen M., b. 1869; m. Thomas
Griffis. (vii1) Harold J. (vii2) Helen Mary. (b) William
Wellington, b. 1829; m. Alace Sanderson; d. 1901. He d. 1899.
Ch.: (i) Fred H., res., Buffalo. (ii) Grace, b. ———; m. 1st,
Holly Petrie; m. 2nd, Frank Green. (c) Daniel Josiah, b. 1832;
m. Louisa E. Morris. He d. 1876. She b. 1840. Ch.: (i) Emma
Louisa, b. 1858; m. J. B. Fenner, res., Dolgville, N. Y. Ch.: (i1)
Jackson. (i2) Catherine Fenner. (ii) Morris Daniel, b. 1860.
(iii) Adelaide Helen, b. 1864; m. E. K. LaDue, res., Herkimer,
N. Y. Ch.: (iii1) Edna, b. 1890. (iv) Chas. Bennet, b.
1869, res., Herkimer, N. Y. (d) Asa Lafayette, b. 1833;
d. 1850. (e) John Manchester, b. 1835; m. Rebecca Jones.
He d. 1874. Ch.: (i) Thomas Varnum, b. 1863. (ii) Daniel W.,
b. 1865, res., Denver, Col. (iii) Annie Louisa, b. 1867; d. Lon-
don Eng., Sept. 14, 1891. (f) Louesa Maria, b. Oct. 12, 1837; m.
Jan. 19, 1860, Peter H. Klock. She d. Apr. 17, 1905. Ch.: (i)
Edgar Jackson Klock, b. 1863; m. Mary C. Smith, b. 1869, res.,
Frankfort, N. Y. Ch.: (i1) Mary Louesa, b. 1897. (i2) Cleore
Alzadya, b. 1899. (g) Jacob J., b. 1843; d. 1846.

(8) Prudence, b. 1795; m. Samuel A. Cahoon, b. 1790; d. 1885.
She d. 1833. Ch.: (a) Delia M., b. 1830; d. 1903, unm. (b)
Jackson Benjamin, b. 1824; d. 1906; unm. (c) Lorenzo Dow, b.
1827; m. Mary Smith. He d. 1903. Ch.: (i) Benjamin L., b.
1862; m. 1st, Clara Johnson; 2nd, Mrs. Cromwell; res., Middleville, N. Y. (ii) Ella Mary Cahoon, b. 1866; m. Tymothy Hayes;
res., Windsor, Ct. Ch.: (ii1) Francis, b. 1895. (ii2) Raymond,

b. 1896. (ii3) James, b. 1900. (d) Samuel S., b. 1833; d. 1834.
(9) Freelove, b. 1797; d. 1884; m. Daniel Wood; b. in R. I., 1792;
d. at Herkimer, N. Y., 1866. Ch.: (a) Rodman, b. 1816; d. 1901;
m. Amy Jane Fenner. Ch.: (i) Orin, b. 1844; m. Ellen Petrie.
Ch.: (i1) Mabel. (i2) Harry. (i3) Iva. (ii) Emily, b. 1854;
m. Henry M. Quackenbush. She d. 1895. Ch.: (ii1) Camilla;
m. Frank Crisman; res., Herkimer, N. Y. (ii2) Paul; m. Louisa
M. M. Atwell. (ii3) Annie, d. young. (b) Daniel R., b. 1820;
m. Lydia Fenner. He d. 1896. Ch.: (i) Albert D., b. ———.
(ii) Ellen A., b. ———; m. Chas. Lawrence. (iii) Russel L.; m.
Maud A. Jackson. (iv) Frances B., b. ———; m. Robt. Kirkland. (v) Addie E., b. ———; m. William McCarrall. (vi)
Mattie L., b. ———; m. Frank Dale. (vii) Geo. L., b. ———;
m. Nellie Garside. (viii) Minnie M., unm. (ix) Robert H.,
b. ———; m. Hattie Lynch. (c) Freelove Charrill, b. 1822; d.
1866, unm. (d) Eliza, b. 1825; m. William B. Fenner. She d.
1904. Ch.: (i) William Daniel, b. 1858; m. Addie E. Farmer.
Ch.: (i1) Harry, b. 1882. (i2) Ray Brown, b. 1884. (i3) Ralph
Geo., b. 1885. (i4) Mabel Jenette, b. 1889; d. 1906. (i5) Karl
Wm., b. 1899. (i6) Marion Frances, b. 1904.
(10) Margaret (Peggy), b. 1802; d. unm., 1885.
(11) Gertrude, b. 1804; d. 1889; m. Brayton Wood, b. 1804; d.
1885. Ch.: (a) Alma, b. 1834; m. Erastus Smith. She d. 1870.
Ch.: (i) Stanley, b. 1866. (b) Ann Eliza, b. 1838; res., Little
Falls, N. Y. (c) Harrison, b. 1841; m. Clara Spaulding. Ch.:
(i) Fannie, b. 1869; m. Frank Pickert. Ch.: (i1) Harold, b. 1896.
(ii) Jessie, b. 1872.
(12) Fanny, b. 1806; m. Stillman B. Sanders, b. 1803; d. 1890.
She d. 1846. Ch.: (a) Byron J., b. 1830; d. 1839. (b) Loeza M.,
b. 1834; d. 1839. (c) Ruth A., b. 1836; d. 1839. (d) Alfred
Devillo, b. 1845; d. 1859. (e) Helen C., ., b. 1840; d. 1848. (f)
Ardelia, b. 1831; m. Marcus Potter. She d. 1857. (g) Mary
Ette, b. 1832; m. 1st, Lucius Gardiner; m. 2nd, Joseph Gardiner.
Ch.: (i) Lucius, Jr. (ii) Fanny. (iii) Howard. (g) Gertrude, b.
1841; m. Thomas Petrie. Ch. (i) Dora I., b. 1870; m. Edward
Jones. Ch.: (i1) Clarence P. (i2) Claud E. (i3) Everett
Thomas. (ii) Maud Ethleen, b. 1873; m. William Goodell. Ch.:
(ii1) Gleneita, b. ———. (iii) Mabel R., b. 1875. (iv) Grace
Ione, b. 1882.

897. ii. OLITON CUSHMAN, b. ———; m. Thina Bull, 2062-5%.
898. iii. ZILPAH, b. ———; m. Elijah Hurlbut, of New Concord, N. Y.
          She d. at Chatham, N. Y.; p. s.
899. iv. ASA, b. ———; m. Cathrine Davis, of Albany, N. Y. Moved to
          Baltimore, Md. After his wife's death he m. 2nd in Baltimore
          and died there.
900. v.   MARGARET, b. ———; m. Hunn Beach, of Johnstown, N. Y.
          He d. ———; m. 2nd, Horatio Waldo of the same town.
901. vi. EPHRAIM, b. ———; m. ———; d. at Baam, near Long Point,
          Can., 1844, leaving two sons, Jairus and Ephraim.
902. vii. WILLIAM, b. Mar. 21, 1773; m. Eve Butler, 2066-76½.

903. viii. JACOB, b. ——; res., Albany, N. Y.; d. 1806 near Boston while
         on a journey.
904. ix. JOHN, b. ——; d. 1812 in Johnstown, N. Y.

286. ASA FOOTE, (85, 26, 9, 3,) b. ——; m. ——; he d. 1828 in Salina,
N. Y.
905. i. WARREN, b. ——.
906. ii. BETSY, b. ——.
907. iii. ASA, b. ——; d. 1830 in Salina, N. Y.
908. iv. AMASA, b. ——; d. 1830 in Salina, N. Y.
909. v. ALMIRA, b. ——.

289. SAMUEL FOOTE, (85, 26, 9, 3,) b. ——; m. ——.
910. i. JOSEPH, b. ——; res., North Canaan, Columbia Co., N. Y.
911. ii. ELIZABETH, b. ——.
912. iii. SAMUEL, b. ——, 2077-½.
913. iv. SALLY, b. ——.
914. v. PEGGY, b. ——.
915. vi. CORNELIUS, b. ——; res., Penfield, Monroe Co., N. Y.

290. JOHN FOOTE, (85, 26, 9, 3,) b. ——; m. Dec. 30, 1784, Elizabeth
Babcock. He d. Dec. 13, 1833, in Vernon, N. Y. She d. Apr. 10, 1832, ae. 72, in
Vernon, N. Y. Res., Chatham, N. Y.
917. i. ZILPHA, b. Mar. 24, 1786; d. Apr. 17, 1875; res., Vernon, N. Y.;
         unm.
918. ii. OLIVER, b. Dec. 7, 1787; m. Ruth Hungerford, 2078-82.
919. iii. AVERY, b. Aug. 9, 1791; m. Joanna Osgood, 2083-7.
920. iv. JOHN, b. Oct. 28, 1793; m. Mary Lull, 2088-96.
921. v. EPHRAIM, b. May 9, 1796; m. Almira Harmon and Electa
         Osgood, 2097-103.
922. vi. CLARISSA, b. Jan. 30, 1798; m. Ira Bronson, of Vernon, N. Y.,
         and after his death Deacon Ira Hills, of Vernon, N. Y.
923. vii. SEELEY T., b. Mar. 8, 1800; m. Content Babcock, 2104.
924. viii. DANIEL, b. Sept. 11, 1802; m. Eliza Yale, 2105.
925. ix. IRA, b. Aug. 26, 1804; d. Apr. 14, 1814.

295. ADONIJAH FOOTE, (85, 26, 9, 3,) b. Apr. 14, 1768; m. 1791, Sabra
Mott. She was b. Nov. 1, 1771; d. June 4, 1855; he d. Mar. 17, 1855; res., West
Stockbridge, Mass., and Vernon, N. Y.
926. i. MARY ANN, b. 1791; m. Alva Lloyd, of Lisbon, Ill.
927. ii. PELA, b. 1795; m. Julius ——, of Lisbon, Ill.
928. iii. POLLY LODEMA, b. Oct. 26, 1788; m. John Cook, of Syracuse,
         N. Y.
929. iv. GEORGE, b. Mar. 12, 1801; m. Hannah Wetmore, 2106-7½.
930. v. EMELINE, b. Dec. 11, 1803; m. Bryan Gaylord, of Lisbon, Ill.
931. vi. MORGAN, b. Sept. 28, 1806; m. Harriet Moyer; res., Lisbon, Ill.
932. vii. ELIHU, b. Apr., 1809; m. M. Cook, 2108-¼.
933. viii. ALMIRA M., b. May 5, 1811; m. 1835, Gardner Richmond; res.,
         Stockbridge, N. Y.

298. JESSE FOOTE, (89, 26, 9, 3,) b. Dec. 25, 1766; m. Mar. 12, 1778,
Mary, dau. of Noah Skinner, of Colchester, Ct. He d. Mar. 16, 1822; she d. Feb.
17, 1828, ae. 69; res., Colchester and Stafford, Ct.
934. i. JESSE, b. Feb. 11, 1779; d. Dec. 13, 1817.
935. ii. ADONIJAH, b. Oct. 22, 1780; m Clarissa Woodworth, 2109-13.

936. iii.   OLIVE, b. Oct. 11, 1782.

937. iv.   CYRUS, b. Aug. 3, 1784; res., Springfield, Mass.

938. v.   NOAH, b. July 12, 1786; d. Dec. 29, 1829.

939. vi.   MARY, b. May 20, 1788.

940. vii.   GRACE, b. Mar. 31, 1790; m. Noah Strong, (No. 845-6, Strong Gen.). Ch.: (1) Albert H., (2) Harriet, (3) Calista, (4) Clementa, (5) Kathryn G., (6) Mary R., (7) Col. Emery Foote, (8) Emery Judson, (9) Harriet E.

941. viii.   ROSETTE, b. Jan. 23, 1792; d. Apr. 19, 1794.

942. ix.   ERASTUS, b. July 25, 1794; m. Nancy Dimmick, 1818-24.

943. x.   ROSETTE, b. Feb. 14, 1797; m. William Usher, b. Sept. 5, 1799, of East Hamilton, N. Y. He d. Feb. 5, 1875, in Colchester, N. Y. Ch.: (1) Cordelia R., b. Jan. 4, 1827; unm.; lives in Hamilton, N. Y. (2) Devereaux William, b. Dec. 18, 1830; m. Jan. 23, 1861, Fidelia Kinney, b. Nov., 1840, dau. of Edwin and Lucinda (Hubbard) Kinney. She d. Oct. 5, 1890, ae. nearly 50 yrs. Ch.: William D., b. Oct. 28, 1866. He m. 2nd, Dec. 16, 1891, Rose Howe, dau. of Stillman and (Colson) Howe. Ch.: (1) Ambrosia, b. ———; d. in infancy; he d. Feb. 26, 1901.

944. xi.   SOPHRONIA, b. Jan. 22, 1799.

945. xii.   RALPH, b. Jan. 11, 1802.

299.   ADONIJAH FOOTE, (89, 26, 9, 3,) b. Mar. 26, 1760; m. 1st, June 19, 1782, Sarah Foster, of Long Island, N. Y.; she d. July, 1804, ae. 40; m. 2nd, ———. Chittenden, of Hartford, Ct., a widow. She d. Apr., 1836, ae. 76. He d. Sept., 1836; res., Colchester, Ct., and Granville, N. Y.

946. i.   FOSTER, b. 1783.

947. ii.   ERASTUS, b. Apr. 21, 1785; m. Edith Day, 2114-5.

948. iii   ORRIN, b. 1787.

949. iv.   HARRIET, b. Oct. 3, 1789.

950. v.   TALITHA, b. 1791.

951. vi.   MATILDA, b. 1793.

952. vii.   PHEBE, b. 1795.

953. viii.   ELECTA, b. 1797.

954. ix.   BETSEY, b. 1799.

955. x.   JAMES, b. 1801.

956. xi.   ADONIJAH, b. 1803.

300.   REUBEN FOOTE, (89, 26, 9, 3,) b. Nov. 8, 1761; m. June 10, 1787, Lydia dau. of Joseph Emmons, of East Haddam, Ct. She d. Mar. 19, 1841, ae. 78; res., Colchester, Ct., and East Hamilton, N. Y.

957. i.   LYDIA, b. Dec. 27, 1792; d. Mar. 10, 1845.

958. ii.   ELIHU, b. May 29, 1794.

959. iii.   HURON, b. Nov. 20, 1798.

302.   EPHRAIM FOOTE, (89, 26, 9, 3,) b. Aug. 1, 1765; m. Oct. 10, 1792, Lydia, dau. of John Ackley, of East Haddam, Ct. He d. 1838; she d. June, 1845, ae. 75. Res., Eagle, N. Y.

960 i.   ZELONA, b. Dec., 1793; m. Betsey E. Manchester, 2115½-25.

961. ii.   PHILA, b. Apr., 1796.

962. iii.   MILTON, b. Aug. 8, 1798; m. Jestina ———, 2126-9.

963. iv.   ADONIJAH, b. Apr., 1800.

964. v.   ALMEDA, b. Mar., 1802.

965.   vi.   CEMANTHA, b. Jan., 1804.
966.   vii. DIANTHA, b. Sept., 1805.
967.   viii. SAPPHINA, b. Apr., 1807.
968.   ix.   POLLY, b. Dec., 1808.
969.   x.   CELESTIA, b. Mar., 1810.
970.   xi.   LUCINDA, b. Apr., 1812.

304. EPAPHRODITUS FOOTE, (89, 26, 9, 3,) b. Sept. 14, 1769; m. Jan. 5, 1791, Anna, dau. of George Bixbey, of Colchester, Ct. She d. Dec. 10, 1796, ae. 26; m. 2nd, Sylvia, dau. of Silas Bebee, of Colchester, Ct.; she d. June 27, 1798, ae. 24; m. 3rd, Dec. 15, 1798, Mehitable, dau. of John Douglass, of Hamilton, N. Y.; she d. Aug. 27, 1804, ae. 28; m. 4th, Jan. 5, 1805, Anna, widow of Joel Ives, of Brookfield, N. Y., and dau. of Isaac Goodwin, of Torrington, Ct. He d. July 15, 1845, in Brookfield, N. Y. Res., Colchester, Ct., and Brookfield, N. Y.

971.   i.   EPAPHRODITUS, b. July 19, 1791.
972.   ii.   FREDERICK, b. Jan. 22, 1793; m., 2129¹-29².
973.   iii. ADONIJAH, b. July 12, 1799; d. Sept. 8, 1809.
974.   iv.   ANNA, b. May 4, 1801; m. ———. Schroley. Ch.: (1) Richard,
             b. ———; res., Richfield Springs, N. Y.
975.   v.   SYLVIA, b. May 8, 1803; d. July 16, 1843.
976.   vi.   SOPHIA, b. Sept. 19, 1806; m. ———. Hall; she d. Aug. 31,
             1831 Ch.: (1) Joel, b. ———; m. ———. Ch.: (a) Glenn Hall,
             b. ———; res., Watertown, N. Y.
977.   vii. JOEL, b. Aug. 8, 1808; d. Dec. 9, 1814.   Inglehart
✝ 978. viii. EMELINE, b. Feb. 18, 1810; m. ———. Tuglehart. Ch.: (1)
             Hiram, b. ———; d. ———. (2) Rufus, b. ———; d. ———.
             (3) Sophie, b. ———; d. ———.
979.   ix.   LEONARD, b. Mar. 18, 1812; d. Apr. 12, 1814.
980.   x.   LEONARD, b. May 16, 1814; m. Hannah Clarke, 2129³-29⁵.
981.   xi.   RUFUS, b. Aug. 21, 1817; m. Emily Hall, 2129⁶.

308. JONATHAN FOOTE, (92, 27, 9, 3,) b. Mar. 30, 1752; m. Dec. 23, 1773, Deliverance, dau. of Sylvanus Gibbs, of Sandwich, Cape Cod, Mass.; d. May 26, 1837. She d. Apr. 28, 1828, ae. 77. Res., Lee, Mass.

982.   i.   ELISHA, b. Jan. 22, 1775; m. Delia Battle, 2130-42.
983.   ii.   ALVAN, b. May 29, 1777; m. Sarah Percival, 2143-50.
984.   iii. JERUSHA, b. Dec. 29, 1781; d. May 20, 1832; res., Lee, Mass.;
             unm.
985.   iv.   SYLVANUS, b. Apr. 12, 1785; m. 1804, Abigail Bradley, 2150-1-7.
986.   v.   JONATHAN, b. Feb. 11, 1788; graduated at Yale College, 1811;
             m. Huldah, dau. of Edward Lyman, of Windam, Ohio. He d.
             Jan. 25, 1846. Res., Windham, Ohio; p. s.

309. FENNER FOOTE, (92, 27, 9, 3,) b. Oct. 5, 1754; m. Mar. 11, 1779, Sarah, dau. of Peter Wilcox, of Lee, Mass. She d. Jan. 14, 1840, ae. 76. Res., Lee, Mass.

Fenner Foote was a member of Col. Ethan Allen's Regiment, "Major Brown's detachment." The regiment was originally known as General Arnold's Regiment, "Green Mountain Boys," and was first heard of at Quebec in 1776, where it took part with great distinction in that campaign. The regiment afterwards came to New York State and went through the campaign at Plattsburg. He d. at Lee, Mass., from old age and a fall, Apr. 27, 1847, aged 92 years. A soldier of the Revolution.

987. i.   LUCINDA, b. Sept. 8, 1780.

988. ii.   CALVIN, b. Dec. 15, 1782; m. Phebe West, 2151-6.

989. iii.   OLIVE, b. Feb. 2, 1786; m. Sept. 15, 1808, Bemseley Carpenter, of Sandisfield, Mass.

990. iv.   DANIEL, b. Feb. 17, 1784; d. Sept. 4, 1840.

991. v.   JERUSHA, b. Oct. 20, 1789; m. Dea. Smith, of Winsted, Ct.

992. vi.   FENNER, b. Oct. 10, 1794; m. Cynthia Ann Lester and Almira Wright, 2162-71.

993. vii.   ERASTUS, b. Sept. 4, 1795; m. Fanny A. Jones, 2157-61.

994. viii.   ASENATH, b. Oct. 18, 1796; d. abt. 1833; unm.

995. ix.   CYRUS, b. June 18, 1800.

311.   DAVID FOOTE, (92, 27, 9, 3,) b. Sept. 4, 1760; m., at Lee, Mass., Jan. 12, 1785, Betsy, dau. of Job Hamblin, of Lee, Mass., formerly of Falmouth, Mass. She d. Jan. 10, 1844, ae. 80. Res., Lee, Mass., and Dover, Ohio.

996. i.   BETSY, b June 23, 1786; d. Nov. 16, 1860; m. Nov. 3, 1806, Noah Crocker, Jr. Ch.: (1) Roxey, b. July 7, 1807. (2) Sophia, b. Mar. 10, 1809. (3) Alma, b. Aug. 6, 1811.

997. ii.   THOMAS, b. May 21, 1788; m. Dama Perry, 2172-6.

998. iii.   DAVID, b. July 11, 1790; d. Oct. 4, 1790, in Lee, Mass.

999. iv.   SILAS, b. Aug. 18, 1791; m. Emeline Smith, 2177-9.

1000. v.   DELIA, b. May 3, 1794; m. Oct. 7, 1818, Elisah Taylor, of Lee, Mass.; she d. Jan. 6, 1852.

1001. vi.   LOVICA, b. Nov. 29, 1796, in Lee, Mass.; m. Aug. 22, 1815, Benjamin Stevens. Ch.: (1) John b. Lee, Mass., Dec. 23, 1816; m. ———. Ch.: (a) Sarah, b. ———; m. ———. Darry. (2) Ransom Foote Stevens, b. Lee, Mass., May 20, 1820; m Apr. 8,
,Mich.
n, O.;
rts, of
v. 18,
rts, b.
on F.
verse
active
[arion
ak O.
(b)
ig. 5,
vens,
right,
1876,
. 12,

(Correction, v. 1, p. 110, no.978)

* Emeline Foote, born Feb. 18, 1813 married Mr. Inglehart 𝕴𝖓𝖌𝖑𝖊𝖍𝖆𝖗𝖙 not "Tuglehart".

Mrs. George Ackerman
Hackensack, N.J.
Feb. 20, '23

, ———. (13) Cyrus Ben-jamin, b. Nov., 1901. (i4) Marian Minerva, b. July, 1903. (i5) Guy, b. Apr., 1905. (i6) Clara, b. Nov. 16, 1906. (ii) Lillian C. Stevens, b. Sept. 13, 1877. (iii) Alan Maxwell Stevens, b. Oct. 1, 1880. (iv) Nora Finetta Stevens, b. Feb. 6, 1833; m. ———. Wickman. Ch.: (iv1) Estella Wickman, b. June 16, 1903. (v) Guy Worthington Stevens, b. Apr. 14, 1885. (vi) Robert Lee Stevens, b. Nov. 12, 1886. (vii) Howard Delos, b.

965. vj.   CEMANTHA, b. Jan., 1804.
966. vii.   DIANTHA, b. Sept., 1805.
967. viii. SAPPHINA, b. Apr., 1807.
968. ix.   POLLY, b. Dec., 1808.
969. x.   CELESTIA, b. Mar., 1810.
970. xi.   LUCINDA, b. Apr., 1812.

304. EPAPHRODITUS FOOTE, (89, 26, 9, 3,) b. Sept. 14, 1769; m. Jan. 5, 1791, Anna, dau. of George Bixbey, of Colchester, Ct. She d. Dec. 10, 1796, ae. 26; m. 2nd, Sylvia, dau. of Silas Bebee, of Colchester, Ct.; she d. June 27, 1798, ae. 24; m. 3rd, Dec. 15, 1798, Mehitable, dau. of John Douglass, of Hamilton, N. Y.; she d. Aug. 27, 1804, ae. 28; m. 4th, Jan. 5, 1805, Anna, widow of Joel Ives, of Brookfield, N. Y., and dau. of Isaac Goodwin, of Torrington, Ct. He d. July 15, 1845, in Brookfield, N. Y. Res., Colchester, Ct., and Brookfield, N. Y.

971. i. ' EPAPHRODITUS, b. July 19, 1791.
972. ii.   FREDERICK, b. Jan. 22, 1793; m., 2129¹⁻²⁹².
973. iii. ADONIJAH, b. July 12, 1799; d. Sept. 8, 1809.
974. iv.   ANNA, b. May 4, 1801; m. ———. Schroley. Ch.: (1) Richard,
           b. ———; res., Richfield Springs, N. Y.
975. v.   SYLVIA, b. May 8, 1803; d. July 16, 1843.
976. vi.   SOPHIA, b. Sept. 19, 1806; m. ———. Hall; she d. Aug. 31,
           1831 Ch.: (1) Joel, b. ———; m. ———. Ch.: (a) Glenn Hall,
           b. ———; res., Watertown, N. Y.
977. vii. JOEL, b. Aug. 8, 1808; d. Dec. 9, 1814.
✝ 978. viii. EMELINE, b. Feb. 18, 1810; m. ———. Tuglehart. Ch.: (1)
           Hiram, b. ———; d. ———. (2) Rufus, b. ———; d. ———.
           (3) Sophie, b. ———; d. ———.
979. ix.   LEONARD, b. Mar. 18, 1812; d. Apr. 12, 1814.
980. x.   LEONARD, b. May 16, 1814; m. Hannah Clarke. 21293-295
981. xi.   RUFUS. b. Aug 21, 1817

308. JONAT
1773, Deliverance,
26, 1837. She d. A
   982. i.   ELI
   983. ii.   AL
   984. iii. JEI
            un
   985. iv.   SYI
   986. v.   JON
            m.
            Jar

309. FENNER
Sarah, dau. of Peter
Mass.
   Fenner Foote wa   ─, ──── ─────── ─────── 's
detachment.'' The regiment was originally known as General Arnold's Regiment, ''Green Mountain Boys,'' and was first heard of at Quebec in 1776, where it took part with great distinction in that campaign. The regiment afterwards came to New York State and went through the campaign at Plattsburg. He d. at Lee, Mass., from old age and a fall, Apr. 27, 1847, aged 92 years. A soldier of the Revolution.

987. i. LUCINDA, b. Sept. 8, 1780.

988. ii. CALVIN, b. Dec. 15, 1782; m. Phebe West, 2151-6.

989. iii. OLIVE, b. Feb. 2, 1786; m. Sept. 15, 1808, Bemseley Carpenter, of Sandisfield, Mass.

990. iv. DANIEL, b. Feb. 17, 1784; d. Sept. 4, 1840.

991. v. JERUSHA, b. Oct. 20, 1789; m. Dea. Smith, of Winsted, Ct.

992. vi. FENNER, b. Oct. 10, 1794; m. Cynthia Ann Lester and Almira Wright, 2162-71.

993. vii. ERASTUS, b. Sept. 4, 1795; m. Fanny A. Jones, 2157-61.

994. viii. ASENATH, b. Oct. 18, 1796; d. abt. 1833; unm.

995. ix. CYRUS, b. June 18, 1800.

311. DAVID FOOTE, (92, 27, 9, 3,) b. Sept. 4, 1760; m., at Lee, Mass., Jan. 12, 1785, Betsy, dau. of Job Hamblin, of Lee, Mass., formerly of Falmouth, Mass. She d. Jan. 10, 1844, ae. 80. Res., Lee, Mass., and Dover, Ohio.

996. i. BETSY, b June 23, 1786; d. Nov. 16, 1860; m. Nov. 3, 1806, Noah Crocker, Jr. Ch.: (1) Roxey, b. July 7, 1807. (2) Sophia, b. Mar. 10, 1809. (3) Alma, b. Aug. 6, 1811.

997. ii. THOMAS, b. May 21, 1788; m. Dama Perry, 2172-6.

998. iii. DAVID, b. July 11, 1790; d. Oct. 4, 1790, in Lee, Mass.

999. iv. SILAS, b. Aug. 18, 1791; m. Emeline Smith, 2177-9.

1000 v. DELIA, b. May 3, 1794; m. Oct. 7, 1818, Elisah Taylor, of Lee, Mass.; she d. Jan. 6, 1852.

1001. vi. LOVICA, b. Nov. 29, 1796, in Lee, Mass.; m. Aug. 22, 1815, Benjamin Stevens. Ch.: (1) John b. Lee, Mass., Dec. 23, 1816; m. ———. Ch.: (a) Sarah, b. ———; m. ———. Darry. (2) Ransom Foote Stevens, b. Lee, Mass., May 20, 1820; m Apr. 8, 1846, Finetta M. Ruple, of Euclid, O.; d. Sept. 8, 1890, at Byron, Mich. Ch.: (a) Mary Ann Stevens, b. Feb. 22, 1847, at Brighton, O.; graduated Oberlin 1871; m. Aug. 8, 1871, Judge Lorin Roberts, of Gustavus, O. He was a veteran of the Civil War; d. Nov. 18, 1905, at Traverse City, Mich. Ch.: (i) Alice Taylor Roberts, b. May 12, 1873; m. Traverse City, Mich., Sept. 20, 1904, Leon F. Titus. (ii) William Ransom Roberts, b. June 28, 1876, Traverse City. He served in the Spanish War, having been in active service in both Cuba and the Philippines; unm. (iii) Marion Stevens Roberts, b. Aug. 22, 1878; m. Aug. 30, 1905, Frank O. Balch. Ch.: (iii1) Lorin Roberts Balch, b. Nov. 11, 1906. (b) Cyrus Benjamin Stevens, b. Avon, O., Jan. 9, 1850; m. Aug. 5, 1875, Addie Drisdall, of Byron, Mich. (c) Elihu Burritt Stevens, b. Avon, Mich., Apr. 29, 1854; m. Feb. 10, 1875, Estella Albright, of Byron, Mich. Ch.: (i) Lorin Burritt Stevens, b. Jan. 30, 1876, Hart, Mich.; m. ———. Ch.: (i1) Lorin Ransom, b. Oct. 12, 1898. (i2) Isaiah Burritt, b. Apr. 17, 1900. (i3) Cyrus Benjamin, b. Nov., 1901. (i4) Marian Minerva, b. July, 1903. (i5) Guy, b. Apr., 1905. (i6) Clara, b. Nov. 16, 1906. (ii) Lillian C. Stevens, b. Sept. 13, 1877. (iii) Alan Maxwell Stevens, b. Oct. 1, 1880. (iv) Nora Finetta Stevens, b. Feb. 6, 1833; m. ———. Wickman. Ch.: (iv1) Estella Wickman, b. June 16, 1903. (v) Guy Worthington Stevens, b. Apr. 14, 1885. (vi) Robert Lee Stevens, b. Nov. 12, 1886. (vii) Howard Delos, b.

July 24, 1888. (viii) Donald Albright, b. Aug. 1, 1893. (ix)
Bonnibel Stevens, b. July 20, 1894. (3) Mary Ann Stevens, b.
Apr. 9, 1822, Lee, Mass. (4) Delia Taylor Stevens, b. Lee,
Mass., Nov. 30, 1824; d. Dec. 25, 1887. (5) Benjamin Franklin
Stevens, b. Lee, Mass., June 5, 1827. (6) Chauncey Barnum
Stevens, b. Sept. 20, 1833, Avon, O. (7) Sarah Bigelow Stevens,
b. Mar. 17, 1840, Avon, O.; m. 1871, Horace Braman, of Avon,
O. He was b. 1833, at Avon, O.; res., Elyria, O. Ch.: (a)
Hattie, b. 1873, at Avon. (b) Otis, b. 1875, at Avon. (c)
Frank, b. 1880, at Avon; m. 1906, Ruth Edson, of Cleveland, O.

1002. vii. TEMPERANCE, b. Nov. 7, 1800, in Lee, Mass.; m. July 3, 1821,
John Broughton Robertson, b. at Ballston Spa., N. Y., Dec. 26,
1797; d. at Amherst, Ohio, Mar. 7, 1875. She d. at Amherst,
Ohio, Dec., 1894. Ch.: (1) Sarah M., d. unm. (2) Ebenezer, d.
ae. 10. (3) Theodore H., m. 1st, Laura Johnson. Ch.: (a) Florence. M. 2nd, Harriet Hogeboom. Ch.: (a) Richard. (b) Elizabeth. (c) John. (4) John B., Jr., b. Omaha, Neb.; m. 1850, Eliza
Belden. Ch.: (a) Ellen. (b) Edith. Both d. in childhood. He
d. at Amherst, O. (5) Franklin Nelson, b. Omaha, Neb.; m.
Louise Crellin. Ch.: (a) John B. (b) Nellie, both d. in childhood. (c) Marie L., b. Amherst, Ohio, June 13, 1856; m. Charles
Keith, Nov. 25, 1903, at Merriam Park, Minn. (6) Mary L., m.
Parks Foster, of Elyria, Ohio. Ch.: (a) Sarah M., m. S. L. Kent,
of New York City. (b) Burton P., m. Mayme Cannon. (c) Mary
L., m. Arthur W. Walker. (d) Florence M., m. Theodore Luskey.

1003. viii. RANSON, b. Feb. 15, 1803; m. Cathrine Porter, 2180-90½.

1004. ix. LAURA, b. Jan. 6, 1807; m. Sept. 3, 1824, John D. Taylor, of
Lee, Mass.

1005. x. CAROLINE, b. Aug. 5, 1809; m. Jan. 14, 1830, Alexis Miller, of
Lee, Mass.

312. ASAHEL FOOTE, (92, 27, 9, 3,) b. Apr. 22, 1763; m. Aug. 21, 1793,
Anna, dau. of Seth Abbot, of Cornwall, Vt. She d. Jan. 21, 1820, ae. 49; he d.
Mar. 8, 1841. Res., Colchester, Ct., and Lee, Mass.

1006. i. SARAH ANN, b. Apr. 2, 1794; m. Sept., 1819, Henry Chapman,
of Becket, Mass.

1007. ii. ELIZABETH, b. Dec. 25, 1795; m. Oct. 7, 1823, Lucius Crocker,
of Lee, Mass.; d. Feb., 1831. Ch.: (1) Mary, b. Sept. 3, 1824.

1008. iii. LYMAN, b. July 9, 1798; m. Emily Fairchild, 2191-5.

1009. iv. CHARLES, b. May 12, 1800; m. Marcia Hunter, 2196-2203.

1010. v. AMANDA, b. Jan. 13, 1803; m. Sept., 1844, Spelman Pelton; he
was b. Oct. 8, 1789, and d. at Clarksfield, O., Feb. 10, 1875; no
ch.; farmer; well educated; res., Wellington, O.

1011. vi. ASAHEL, b. Dec. 16, 1804; m. Mary Smedly.

1012. vii. ANNA, b. Dec. 16, 1804; m. May, 1825, Daniel Whiton, Esq.,
Judge of County Court; res., Galena Co., Ohio.

1013. viii. LYDIA, b. Sept. 13, 1807; m. Dec. 29, 1829, Isaac Bennett, of
Lee, Mass. Ch.: (1) Alfred Henry, b. June 30, 1833. (2) Charlotte Mills, b. Sept. 1, 1836.

314. DR. SOLOMON FOOTE, (92, 27, 9, 3,) b. ———; m. 1798, Betsy,
dau. of Archibald Crosset, of Pelham, Mass. She d. Aug. 13, 1845, ae. 74. He
d. Oct. 26, 1811; res., Cornwall and Rutland, Vt.

HOMER NASH KIMBALL.   No. 1242 (2bi)

No. 1014

1014. i. SOLOMON, b. at Cornwall, Vt., Nov. 19, 1802; m. 1st, 1839, Emily, dau. of William Fay, of Rutland, Vt. To them was b. a dau., Ellen Eliza, who died Mar. 14, 1841, ae. 10 months. The mother d. May 2, 1842, ae. 26. He m. 2nd Mary Ann, wid. of William Dana, and dau. of Henry Hodges, of Clarendon, Vt. She was b. Apr. 16, 1805; d. Aug. 5, 1881.

Solomon Foote, Senator, representative in Congress for nineteen years, like Bradley and Edmunds long president *pro. tem.* of the Senate, and among the greatest of the succession of remarkable men Vermont has kept in the Senate, with hardly an exception, from the beginning, was a native of the State. His father died when young Solomon was only nine years old, and the boy was left to the training of an intelligent and prayerful mother. With intermissions of farm work and teaching of district schools to earn money, he fitted for college and graduated from Middlebury in 1826. For the next five years, except one year while he was a tutor at Middlebury, he was preceptor of Castleton Academy, and Professor of Natural Philosophy at the Vermont Medical School at that place. He reestablished the Academy on a broader basis, erected a handsome and spacious edifice, and, indeed, achieved a large success as a pedagogue, as he did with everything he took hold of in life.

But while teaching he had pursued the study of law; was admitted to the bar in 1831, and established himself in practice at Rutland. He at once plunged into politics, attracted attention the next year with an address which he issued in favor of Clay for President and against the re-election of Jackson, and from this time until his death he was almost constantly before the public. Rutland sent him to the Legislature in 1833, again in 1836-'37-'38, he being Speaker in the last two sessions, and freshly enhancing his reputation by the ease and ability with which he discharged the duties. From 1836 to 1842 he was State's Attorney for Rutland County, and in the latter year was elected representative in Congress as an ardent Whig, a follower of Clay, and a repudiator of Tyler. His first appearance on the floor was to present a petition for the "protection of American producers against the unfriendly and ruinous competition of foreign nations."

His first speech, June 4, 1844, was in the same line, and this was his position as long as he was in Congress. He was one of the Republicans to vote against the low tariff bill of 1857. He, of course, fought the Walker tariff bill of 1846 strenuously. He earnestly opposed the admission of Texas and the Mexican War, whose purpose he declared to be simply to obtain more territory for slavery, and denounced the measures of the Polk administration almost uniformly, and especially its construction of the Oregon boundary question. He made a hot speech Feb. 10, 1847, full of "scornful defiance" of the President for his intimation that those who censured the conduct of the Executive in carrying on the war were guilty of constructive treason. He was one of the three intrepid men who came to the rescue of Giddings of

Ohio when Dawson of Louisiana, supported by four other South-
erners, pistol in hand, threatened to shoot him for his denun-
ciation of the "brutal coarseness" and "moral putridity" of
slavery, and when it looked for a time as if the floor of Congress was to be a general shooting ground.

He served in the House two terms, and refused a re-election in
1841 to return to the practice of law. But he was the next fall
sent to the Legislature by Rutland, and reelected in 1848, and
again was Speaker of that body, and in 1850 he was elected to
the Senate to succeed Judge Phelps, and this was the arena
where he won his largest fame. He was prominent in the de-
bates over the Kansas question against the admission of the
state under the Lecompton constitution. He opposed the scheme
for the acquisition of Cuba, justified the action of Commodore
Paulding in the arrest of William Walker, whose filibustering
expedition to South America he recognized as a scheme of the
slavery extensionists. He was a participant in the discussion of
all Central American matters, and strenuous in insisting that
England should give up her protectorate over the Mosquito territory. He served with Jeff Davis as a commissioner to reorganize
the course of study and discipline at West Point. He was a
strong advocate of governmental construction of a railroad to
the Pacific coast. He carried through the bills for the erection
of a custom house at Burlington and court houses at Windsor
and Rutland, and for the improvement of the breakwater at
Burlington. He served industriously on the committees on pensions, post-offices and post roads, revolutionary claims, public
lands, pensions, contingent claims and foreign relations, rising
steadily by the care and thoroughness of his work to a position
of leadership. He supervised the enlargement of the capitol and
the erection of other government structures. He was chairman
of the committee of arrangements for the inauguration of
President Lincoln.

When the extra session of Congress was convened on account
of the war, July 4, 1861, Mr. Foote was unanimously elected
president *pro tempore*, and through the whole of this, the whole
of the Thirty-seventh and a part of the Thirty-eighth Congress
he continued in this position. During the trying days of the
war he did not appear on the floor so much as he had before
done, evidently regarding speech-making as a needless waste of
energy when there was so much work to be done, and the party
in power had things all their own way anyhow. On several important occasions, however, he kicked out of party traces. He
voted against the Legal Tender Act because he regarded it as
clearly unconstitutional, and against Sumner's Bill in 1861 to
wipe out slavery in the proposed new state of West Virginia as
a prerequisite to its admission. He was a delegate to the Republican National Convention in 1864. One of his last speeches
in the Senate was that of Jan. 12, 1865, in favor of terminating
the Canadian reciprocity treaty. He was with the leaders of his
party in sharp antagonism to President Johnson and his policy,

but died Mar. 28, 1866, before the crisis in that struggle came, though he clearly foresaw it.

In the name of God Amen. I Solomon Foote of Rutland in the County of Rutland and State of Vermont, being of sound and deposing mind and memory though infirm and weak in health, do make and declaim this to be my last will and testament.

I give and bequeath all my property and estate, both real and personal, to my beloved wife, Mary Ann, to be hers forever, subject to the following conditions: it is my will and desire that the money I have loaned to my brother Jonathan Foote, and which is embraced in two notes, executed by him to me, one for $9,000.00 and the other for $3,000, be suffered to remain in his hands so long as he lives, he paying the interest thereon of 8 per cent. per annum stipulated in semi-annual instalments to my said wife after the liquidation of the payment of which said interest is pledged, and if the said Jonathan shall survive my wife I give and bequeath to him the money so loaned to him. And order and direct said notes to be canceled.

And whereas I have procured and deposited on my lot in the Cemetery in East Rutland the material for a monument it is my will and desire that a monument be constructed from said material on said lot in conformity with a plan prepared by U. S. Walker, U. S. architect, now in the care of I. I. R. Randall, that the said lot be suitably prepared and that the remains of my former wife and child be removed and interred herein. And I appoint my esteemed friend, John B. Page, of said Rutland, executor of this my last will and testament.

In witness whereof I have hereunto set my hand and seal this 14th day of March, A. D. 1864.

SOLOMON FOOTE.　　(L. S.)

The monument referred to above is situated on the highest point of ground in Evergreen Cemetery, Rutland, Vt. It is built from Barre granite. The inscription on the south side of the monument is: "Solomon Foote, born in Cornwall, Vt., Nov. 19, A. D. 1802. Died in Washington, D. C., March 28th, 1866, in the third term of his service as a Senator of the United States from his native State." North side: "Expiring, he raised his eyes towards Heaven and exclaimed: 'I see it! I see it! the gates are wide open; beautiful! beautiful!'"

1015. ii.　JONATHAN, b. Cornwall, Vt., Oct. 31, 1804; m. Robina Dow, 2204-8.

1016. iii.　LUCIUS ARCHIBALD, b. Rutland, Vt., July 29, 1806; m. Emily Pamelia Smith, 2209-12.

1017. iv.　ELIZA CROSSET, b. Rutland, Vt., Sept. 21, 1808; m. Ebenezer Collins, of Port Henry, N. Y.; d. at Rutland, Vt., Aug. 4, 1877; buried at Port Henry, N. Y.

320.　JOHN FOOTE, (97, 27, 9, 3,) b. 1763; m. Feb. 15, 1799, Elizabeth, dau. of Ebenezer Carey, of Mansfield, Ct. He d. May 15, 1803; res., Hartford, Ct.

1018. i.　OLIVE, b. Tolland, Ct., Nov. 2, 1799; m. July 26, 1821, George W. Lay, of Batavia, N. Y. He was formerly U. S. Charge to

Stockholm, Sweden, and a Member of Congress from the State of New York. He d. Aug., 1848, at Avon Springs, N. Y., of paralysis. Ch.: (1) John Foote, b. May 1, 1822, and graduated at Yale College 1841. (2) George W., b. Sept. 1, 1823. (3) Albert Tracy, b. June 18, 1825.

1019. ii. JOHN, b. Hartford, Ct., Oct. 15, 1861; m. Georgianna Hyslop Bebee, 2212½-4¾.

322. JOSEPH MILLER FOOTE, (99, 27, 9, 3,) b. Hebron, Ct., Oct. 7, 1800; m. Sept. 4, 1823, Jerusha Ann, dau. of Silent and Jerusha (Clark) Rose, of Saybrook, Ct. She was b. So. Glastonbury, Ct., Feb. 9, 1804; d. Aug. 8, 1873; res., Saybrook and Tooryton, Ct.

1020. i. MARY JANE, b. Feb. 12, 1826; d. Aug. 29, 1827, in Glastonbury, Ct.

1021. ii. JOHN CLARK, b. Mar. 29, 1828. He was in the Civil War, army and navy, in Co. H, 25th Ct. Vol. Infantry. After the Civil War he enlisted in the navy, and during a fight at Ft. Fisher performed an act of bravery which would have won for him a Victoria Cross had he been in the English service. Throughout his life he was known as an upright, honest man and as good as he was a brave soldier. He was a member of the old Commodore Foote family. He d. Nov. 19, 1900, at Essex, Ct.

1022. iii. ASA HIRAM, b. Aug. 25, 1830; he was in the Civil War, 12th Regt. Ct. Vols.; d. Oct. 19, 1902; res., Glastonbury, Ct.

1023. iv. ELLEN ELMINA, b. Apr. 23, 1833; m. Louis Rounsavelle, a returned soldier. She d. Mar., 1894; p. s.

1024. v. TEMPERANCE LEONORA, b. Apr. 20, 1836; m. Luther Bacon. Ch.: (1) Imogene Bacon, B. S., b. Mar. 2, 1852. After graduating from a Seminary course she taught a number of years and then went to Mt. Holyoke College, graduating in Class of 1894. She is the only grandchild of this loyal family.

1025. vi. WILLIAM ALMERIN, b. July 7, 1837; drowned Aug. 19, 1860; unm.

1026. vii. LEVERET WILSON, b. Aug. 17, 1839; drowned Aug. 19, 1860; unm.

1027. viii. TRUMAN, b. May 30, 1841; killed by sharpshooters at Petersburgh, Va., Sept. 19, 1864.

1028. ix. HERMAN, b. Oct. 9, 1842; killed before Richmond, Va., Mar. 25, 1865.

1029. x. SAMUEL MILLER, b. Jan. 27, 1845; d. Oct. 9, 1845.

1030. xi. AMBROSE PRATT, b. May 2, 1846; d. in Florence Prison Feb. 25, 1865.

335. HIRAM SHAYLOR FOOTE (102, 27, 9, 3,) b. Apr. 14, 1799; m. Nov. 8, 1829, Emily, dau. of Stephen Mack, of East Haddam, Ct. She d. Nov. 1, 1848. Res., Hebron, Ct.

1031. i. SARAH ANN, b. Aug. 21, 1830.

1032. ii. HENRY A., b. Dec. 12, 1831.

1033. iii. CHARLES E., b. Aug. 28, 1833; d. Mar. 8, 1835.

1034. iv. MARY, b. Mar. 1, 1835.

1035. v. EDWIN, b. Apr. 16, 1837.

1036. vi. JANE, b. Apr. 13, 1839.

1037. vii. CHARLES, b. Apr. 27, 1841.
1038. viii. JOHN C., b Dec. 12, 1842.
1039. ix. GEORGE, b. Dec. 21, 1844.
1040. x. ALBERT, b. Sept. 13, 1846.

337. AMBROSE FOOTE, (104, 28, 9, 3,) b. July 15, 1751; m. Dec. 13, 1781, Anna, dau. of Hosea Foote, of Colchester, Ct. She d. Feb. 26, 1833, ae. 68. He d. Apr. 3, 1836. Res., Colchester Ct. He was a soldier in the Revolution.

1041. i. DAVID, b. Sept. 30, 1782.
1042. ii. JUSTIN, b. June 23, 1786.
1043. iii. RALPH, b. Nov. 7, 1788.
1044. iv. EUNICE C., b. Dec. 8, 1790.
1045. v. OLIVE A., b. July 2, 1803; d. Oct. 2, 1845; unm. Left property by will (Probate Rec. Bk. II. p. 258) to parents and brothers, also to Louisa Coleman, Lucretia and Mary Ann Foote, Sophia Park and Sophia Bulkely.

339. STEPHEN FOOTE (104, 28, 9, 3,) b. 1755; m. Apr. 29, 1779, Esther, dau. of Ezra Clark, of Colchester, Ct. She d. Mar. 30, 1842, ae. 84. He was a soldier in the Revolution; d. Sept. 11, 1798; res., Colchester, Ct.

1046. i. STEPHEN, b. May 9, 1780; m. Clarissa Foote (widow of 1062), 2215-6.
1047. ii. EZRA, b. ———; d. in the 14th year of age.
1048. iii. ESTHER, b. Sept. 28, 1787; m. John C. Cone, of Colchester, Ct.
1049. iv. ERASTUS, b. Mar. 25, 1791; m. Betsey Crouch, 2217-23.
1050. v. RALPH C., b. Aug. 11, 1793; m. Amelia Foote, 2224-9¼.
1051. vi. SALLY, b. Nov. 29, 1798; m. Enos Foote, of Great Barrington, Mass. No. 1057.

340. UZZIEL FOOTE; m. 1st, 1793, Elizabeth, dau. of Elihu Clark, of Colchester, Ct. She d. Feb., 1819, ae. 56; m. 2nd, Sept. 19, 1819, Lydia W., dau. of Reuben Metcalf of Lebanon, Colchester, Ct. He d. Mar. 1, 1829.

1052. i. ELIZABETH, b. July 20, 1820; m. May 30, 1843, Michael Crippen, of Great Barrington, Mass.
1053. ii. REUBEN METCALF, b. Nov. 1, 1821; m. ———, dau. of David Taylor; res., Omaha, Neb.
1054. iii. ASA, b. Aug. 4, 1824; lost on a man-of-war.
1055. iv. AARON, b. Aug. 25, 1826; d. abt. 21 years of age.

341. v. JEREMIAH FOOTE (104, 28, 9, 3,) bap. Jan. 21, 1759; m. Oct. 16, 1791, Jerusha, dau. of Joseph Taylor, of Colchester, Ct. She d. Aug. 6, 1825, ae. 53. He d. Mar. 27, 1836, at Great Barrington.

1056. i. JEREMIAH, b. Aug. 3, 1798; m. Betsy Little, 2229½.
1057. ii. ENOS, b. May 6, 1794; m. Sally Foote, No. 1051; res., Great Barrington, Mass.
1058. iii. CHARLES, b. Aug. 20, 1796; m. Nov. 22, 1820, Esther, dau. of Joseph Taylor, of Colchester, Ct.
1059. iv. DR. HENRY, b. Aug. 26, 1798; m. Ariette Waite, of Spencertown, N. Y. Was a celebrated physician and surgeon; d. in Spencertown, N. Y.; p. s.
1060. v. CLARISSA PAMELA, b. May 26, 1800; m. Roger Griswold Isham, of Colchester, Ct.
1061. vi. MARY, b. Apr. 21, 1806; m. Feb. 27, 1828, Gad C. Foote, No. 2230.

347. JOSEPH FOOTE, (105, 28, 9, 3,) b. Oct. 26, 1755; m. Apr. 3, 1777, Betty, dau. of Jeremiah and Rúhama Foote, of Colchester, Ct. He d. July 29, 1834. She d. Feb., 1844. Res., Colchester, Ct.

1062. i. JOSEPH, b. Nov. 18, 1788;.m. Clarissa Taylor, 2230-4.
1063. ii. BETSEY, b. Jan. 24, 1780; m. William Clark, of Colchester, Ct. She d. Apr. 11, 1813.
1064. iii. SOPHIA, b. Mar. 24, 1781; d. Feb. 13, 1782.
1065. iv. SOPHIA, b. Oct. 21, 1782; m. Nov. 2, 1797, Oliver Bulkley, of Colchester, Ct. Ch.: (1)·William E., b. Oct. 4, 1798. (2) Daniel, b. May 16, 1800. (3) Oliver, b. Jan. 4, 1802; d. June 7, 1813. (4) Lois, b. Aug. 9, 1803. (5) Benjamin, b. June 13, 1806; d. Jan. 22, 1819. (6) Sophia, b. Jan. 21, 1808. (7) Salmon, b. Feb. 23, 1810. (8) Calvin, b. Oct. 19, 1811. (9) Dorothy L., b. May 28, 1814. (10) Betsy F., b. Jan. 27, 1816. (11) Joshua, b. June 27, 1819. (12) Lucy, b. May 21, 1824.
1065½. v. LUCY, b. May 2, 1784; d. Oct. 13, 1789.
1066. vi. LOIS, b. Nov. 5, 1785; d. Jan. 30, 1816; unm.
1067. vii. PRUDENCE, b. May 8, 1788; m. Enos Clark, of Colchester, Ct.
1068. viii. CALVIN, b. Mar. 1, 1790; Pastor of the Cong. Church, E. Parish, Mass., 1831-5; at Feeding Hills, W. Springfield, Mass., 1836, and Middle Granville, Mass., 1841.
1069. ix. SALMON, b. Mar. 6, 1792; m. Margaret Taylor, 2235-47.
1070. x. LUCY, b. Mar. 27, 1795; m. William Clark, of Colchester, Ct.

350. HOSEA FOOTE, (105, 28, 9, 3,) b. Sept., 1763; m. Nov. 6, 1798, Sally, dau. of Joseph Buckley, of Colchester, Ct. She d. June 20, 1817, ae. 49. He d. May 6, 1846. Res., Colchester, Ct.

1071. i. HOSEA, b. Apr. 22, 1800.
1072. ii. SOLOMON BULKELY, b. Aug. 26, 1802 ; m. June 27, 1847, Lucinda, wid. of Talman Rider, and dau. of John Holt, both of Willington, Ct.; d. p. s.
1073. iii. LUCY SOPHIA, b. Sept. 8, 1804.
1074. iv. ELIZA ANN, b. Mar. 20, 1808; m. May 12, 1836, Dan T. Foote, and d. Sept. 30, 1839.

357. EBENEZER FOOTE, (113, 36, 10, 3, 1,) b. ———; m. Prudence, dau. of Josiah and Hannah (Spencer) Brainard, of Haddam Neck, Ct. He moved to Spencerport, N. Y. She d. there Mar. 10, 1789. He m. twice after she d. He d. Feb. 14, 1814.

1074¼. i. EBENEZER, b. Feb. 1, 1782.
1074½. ii. PRUDENCE, b. July 3, 1784; m. Mr. Walkeley.
1074¾. iii. SUSANNAH, b. Dec. 3, 1785; m. Mr. Wetmore.

361. SAMUEL FOOTE, (113, 36, 10, 3,) b. abt. 1770; m. 1st, ———; m. 2nd, Martha, wid. of Daniel Bunnell. Her maiden name was Hughes. She was b. June 14, 1781; d. May 20, 1838; m. 3rd, Cathrine, dau. of David Mewman, of Virgina. Res., New Haven, Vt., 1791; Marietta, Ohio, 1794; Ridgefield, Ohio, 1800; Montgomery Co., 1839; Ind. Xenia, Ohio, 1847. Ch. by 2nd wife.

1075. i. MARTHA, b. Apr. 17, 1802; m. 1820, Thomas Venard, of Montgomery Co., Ind.; d. 1837. Ch.: (1) Mary Ann. (2) Aaron. (3) Moses. (4) Cathrine.
1076. ii. SHUBAEL, b. 1804; d. 1806.

362. THOMAS FOOTE, (113, 36, 10, 3,) b. abt. 1773; m. Aug. 14, 1796, Anna, dau. of Jacob Constantine, of Ashburnham, Mass. She d. Feb. 15, 1848, ae. 74; res., New Haven, Vt.

    1077. iii. FREEMAN, b. July 5, 1797; d. 1817.

    1078. iv. BETSEY, b. Sept. 3, 1799; m. Oct. 15, 1816, Walter Spaulding, of New Haven, Vt. Res., Island Pond, Vt. Ch.: (1) Henry. (2) Eliza. (3) Harvey. (4) Cervilla. (5) Julia. (6) Betsey. (7) George.

    1079. v. SALLY, b. July 9, 1802; m. New Haven, Vt., Feb. 1, 1825, Ira, son of Jonathan Eastman, of Bristol, Vt. He was b. Bristol, Vt., Oct. 16, 1802. He d. in Mich. Ch.: (1) Albert C. Eastman, b. Aug. 1, 1825; m. Addison, Vt., Apr. 13, 1852, Mary E. Summer. He d. July 25, 1883. Ch.: (a) Frank L. Eastman, b. July 11, 1853; m. Charlotte, Vt., Jan. 5, 1881, Lillie L. Sherman. Ch.: (i) Albert S. Eastman, b. Jan. 24, 1882. (ii) Laura M. Eastman, b. Dec. 18, 1883; graduated from Bristol High School in 1902, from Castleton Normal School, June, 1906. (iii) Anna L. Eastman, b. Apr. 5, 1885; graduated from Bristol High School in 1902, from Castleton Normal School, June, 1906. (b) Lizzie C. Eastman, b. July 5, 1856; m. New Haven, Vt., Nov. 19, 1878, George W. Brooks. Ch.: (i) Philip E. Brooks, b. Dec. 10, 1879. (2) William D. Eastman, b. Feb. 16, 1828; m. Jackson, Mich., Helen Hurd. He d. Apr. 2, 1866. Ch.: (a) Ida Eastman, b. ———; m. Henrietta, Mich., George H. Gibbens. 3 ch. (3) Ira T. Eastman, b. Oct. 3, 1831; m. Bristol, Vt., Desire Palmer; no ch.; res., Montpelier, Vt. (4) Henry F. Eastman, b. Sept. 23, 1835; d. 1848.

    1080. vi. FIDELIA, b. Mar. 26, 1805; d. Mar. 30, 1806.

    1081. vii. HARVEY, b. Mar. 13, 1807; m. Julia M. Sumner, 2248-52.

    1082. viii. MANFRED C., b. Sept. 26, 1816; m. Rhoda A. Smith, 2253-5.

    1083. ix. WEALTHY, b. May 4, 1813; m. June 10, 1834, Samuel Smith, of Waterford, Vt. Ch.: (1) Manfred. (2) Ellen. Res., California.

    1084. x. CERVILLA, b. Feb. 29, 1817; m. June 4, 1842, Luke W. Parmele, of Bristol, Vt. Ch.: (1) Mary. (2) Charlotte. (3) Herman.

365. JOSEPH FOOTE, (114, 36, 10, 3,) b. Oct. 24, 1760; m. Mar. 25, 1786, Abigail, dau. of Simeon Dudley, of Spencertown, N. Y. She d., ae. abt. 31; m. 2nd, abt. 1795, Dorcas, wid., dau. of William Nicholson, of Ridgefield, Ct. Res., Spencertown, N. Y.

    1085. i. APOLLUS, b. Mar. 25, 1787; m. Amelia Nicholson, of Hillsdale, N. Y.

    1086. ii. ABIGAIL, b. ———; m. Simeon Coville; res., "Far West."

    1087. iii. LOUISA, b. ———; d. ae. 8.

    1088. iv. SALLY, b. ———; m Charles Hicks, of Spencertown, N. Y.

    1089. v. ALANSON, b. ———; m. Miss Henman, of Cairo, N. Y.

367. DANIEL FOOTE, (114, 36, 10, 3,) b. 1764; m. Oct., 1803, Violetta Mahew, of Spencertown, N. Y. He d. Dec. 22, 1833. Res., Butternuts, N. Y.

    1090. i. AUGUSTUS, b. Dec. 18, 1808; m. Phila Tracy, 2256-66.

    1091. ii. TERESSA, b. Aug. 12, 1813; m. Sylvester Houlette, of Auburn, N. Y. Ch.: (1) Cornelia Ann, Nov. 29, 1835. (2) Lewis Fletcher, b. June 7, 1837. (3) Violetta Wadsworth, b. Sept. 27, 1839.

1092. iii. DANIEL, b. Oct. 30, 1817; m. Oct. 6, 1847, Eliza Tibbets, of Butternuts, N. Y.; p. s.

1093. iv. WILLIAM, b. Aug. 23, 1820; m. Hannah Ann Jean, 2267-9.

1094. v. AMELIA, b. Mar. 11, 1822; m. May 2, 1842, Henry S. Goodrich. Ch: (1) Charles, b. Feb. 9, 1844. (2) Eugene, b. Aug. 27, 1846.

370. SAMUEL FOOTE, (115, 37, 10, 3,) b. Oct. 10, 1744; m. Mar. 27, 1766, Hannah, dau. of Jonathan and Hannah (Hubbard) Bidwell, of that part of Windsor now called Bloomfield, Ct. He d. July, 1770; she was b. Oct. 11, 1741, and d. Apr. 4, 1804; res., Torrington, Ct.

1095. i. ROGER, b. Dec. 27, 1766; m. Rhoda Dutton, 2270-7.

1096. ii. SAMUEL, b. Mar. 27, 1771; m. Lucy Lord, 2278-84.

374. TIMOTHY FOOTE, (115, 37, 10, 3,) b. Oct. 9, 1752; m. Dec. 12, 1771, Abigail Barnes, of Windsor and Bloomfield, Ct. She d. Apr., 1786; m. 2nd, Lucy Throop, dau of Josiah Throop, of Jamestown, N. Y. Res., Jamestown, N. Y.

1097. i. TIMOTHY, b. Mar. 13, 1773; bap. Mar. 22, 1773; m. Lucy Fiske, 2285-95.

1098. ii. SAMUEL, b. Feb. 11, 1776; left home unm., nothing more known.

1099. iii. EBENEZER, b. Mar. 12, 1778; bap. Mar. 22, 1778; m. Lydia Gage and Elizabeth Reynolds, 2296-2305.

1100. iv. ABIGAIL, b. 1780; m. Edmund Seymore, of Fairfield, O. Ch.: 1 dau., Rhoda.

1101. v. LOIS, b. 1783; m. 1806, Asa Child, of Johnstown, N. Y. He was b. May 21, 1780, in Woodstock, Ct. He d. 1828 in New York, N. Y. She d. 1875, in Chicago. Ch.: (1) Olive Pease, b. 1808, Waterloo, N. Y.; m. 1843, Dr. Jones, of Bristol, Mich. (2) Caroline, b. Jan. 18, 1810, in Johnstown, N. Y.; d. Oct. 4, 1812. (3) Chauncy, b. May 27, 1812, Johnstown, N. Y.; m. Julia Peck. (4) Wm. Chauncy, b. Aug. 16, 1817; m. Dec., 1846, Phebe W. Sanford. (5) Louisa, b. Nov. 9, 1819; m. Nelson Stillman, of N. Y. City. (6) Asa Barnes b. Mar. 1824; d. Feb. 25, 1826, in N. Y. City.

1102. vi. LUCY, b. 1786; m. ——, of Fairfield, N. Y. Ch.: 6 sons and 3 daus.

1103. vii. LYMAN, b. Apr., 1788; m. Sarah Hodge, 2306-6½.

1104. viii. POLLY, b. 1789; m. ——.

1105. ix. ROXANNA, b. 1791; d. 1794.

1106. x. PRISCILLA, b. 1793; m. ——, of Skeneateles, N. Y.; d. 1832.

1107. xi. ISAAC, b. 1795; d. 1795.

1108. xii. GEORGE, b. 1799; lived in Ohio; d. 1832.

1109. xiii. HEPZIBAH, b. 1799; m.; lived in Peru, Ohio.

1110. xiv. HEZEKIAH, b. 1801; d. 1804.

1111. xv. LUCINDA, b. 1803; d. 1804.

375. ELIJAH FOOTE, (115, 37, 10, 3,) b. Mar. 14, 1755; he served three years in the 8th Regt. Ct. Vols. (D. A. U.); m. 1st, Dec. 12, 1771, Mary Lattinmer. She d.; m. 2nd, Zurviah Barton, of Norwich, Vt. She d. 1827, in Shelby, N. Y. He d. 1828. Res., Simsbury, Ct., New Haven, Vt., Middlebury, Vt., Fairfield, Vt., and Gaines, N. Y.

1112. i. ELIJAH, bap. July 13, 1775; d. in childhood.

1113. ii. RUSSELL, bap. Mar. 2, 1777; m. Electa Noble, 2307-13.

1114. iii. ELIJAH, bap. June 20, 1779; m. Ruth Spencer and Nancy Dana, 2314-9.

1115. iv. JUSTUS, b. Simsbury, Ct., June 24, 1782; m. Harriet Swan Graham, 2320-7.

1116. v. MARY, bap. Aug. 29, 1784; m. E. Cutler.

1117. vi. IRA, b. ———; m. Sally Payne, 2328-37.

1118. vii. SAMUEL, b. ———; m. Jenny Campbell, 2338-42.

1119. viii. ALDEN, b. 1798; m. Pricilla Foote, 2343-7.

1120. ix. ORANGE, b. Sept. 9, 1800; m. Lydia Cook, 2348-54.

1121. x. ALMA, b. ———; m. Joseph L. Cook, of Orleans Co., N. Y., where both d. Ch.: (1) Chauncy.

377. GROVE FOOTE, (115, 37, 10, 3,) b. Oct. 25, 1759; m. 1783, Elizabeth Cadwell. He d. Sept. 5, 1826. Res., Simsbury, Ct., and Johnstown, N. Y. She d. Rochester, Mich., Dec., 1835.

1122. i. GROVE, b. 1784; d. 1828; unm.

1123. ii. ELIHU, b. 1786; d. 1808; unm.

1124. iii. HORACE, b. 1790; m. Mary Simmons, 2355-7½.

1125. iv. CHAUNCY, b. 1792; m. Achsah Cook, 2358-9.

1126. v. NANCY, b. 1794; m. Friend Cook, of Salisbury, N. Y.; d. Oct. 31, 1838, near Little Falls.

1127. vi. ELIZA, b. 1796; d. 1827, in Johnstown, N. Y.; unm.

1128. vii. CELESTIA, b. 1799; m. Borden Hart; d. Sept. 2, 1838.

1129. viii. FRIEND, b. Dec. 5, 1801; m. Mary Inman, 2360-2.

1130. ix. SELINA, b. 1806; m. Adolphus Shottenkirk; res., Johnstown, N. Y.

380. LIEUT. DANIEL FOOTE, (117, 37, 10, 3,) b. Oct. 3, 1748; m. July 28, 1774, Mary, dau. of Josiah Goodrich, of Wethersfield, Ct. She d. Feb. 27, 1778; m. 2nd, Nov. 11, 1779, Prudence, wid. of James Knowles, of Wethersfield, Ct. He d. Jan. 1, 1832. She d. Aug. 17, 1839.

1131. i. POLLY, b. May, 1775; d. May 7, 1775.

1132. ii. POLLY, b. Feb. 17, 1778.

1133. iii. JAMES, b. Apr. 25, 1781; m. Roxanna Dewey, 2363-75.

1134. iv. LUCY, b. Feb. 22, 1783; m. Richard Campbell; d. July 21, 1814. Ch.: (1) John.

1135. v. SAMUEL, b. June 2, 1784; m. Sally Roberts, 2376-81.

1136. vi. DANIEL, b. 1786; d. Sept. 18, 1790.

1137. vii. PATTY, b. Nov. 25, 1788; m Charles Kellogg. Ch.: (1) Charles. (2) Nathaniel. (3) Daniel. (4) Lydia. (5) Lucy. (6) Hannah. (7) Martha.

1138. viii. JOHN B., b. June 17, 1790; d. Nov. 22, 1803.

381. GEORGE FOOTE, (117, 37, 10, 3,) b. Oct. 30, 1749; m. 1776, Wealthy Ann Woodward, of Canterbury, Ct. He was one of the pioneer settlers of Vermont, first of Castleton, afterwards at Bennington. He was of the party of Green Mountain Boys who applied the Beach Seal to the settlement of Yorkers at Vergennes, and stood by the side of Col. Ethan Allen when, on the 10th of May, 1775, he demanded the surrender of Ticonderoga in the name of the Continental Congress. A humble but devoted Christian from his youth up, he was permitted to close a life of endeavored obedience to his Divine Master in the

enjoyment of the precious consolations of the faith he had professed. He d. May 12, 1830, in Canton, N. Y. She d. Oct. 18, 1835, áe. 79; res., Castleton and Bennington, Vt.

 1139. i. ALVAN, b. Castleton, Vt., Oct. 23, 1778; m. Priscilla Rice and Caroline Sanger, 2382-5.

 1140. ii. LORENZO, b. Castleton, Vt., 1780; was graduated at Dartmouth College, 1797. Was mate of a merchant vessel in 1805, which was last heard of him.

 1141. iii. MASON, b. Castleton, Vt.; m. 2386.

 1142. iv. WEALTHY ANN, b. 1786; m. Maj. Heman Fay; 8 ch.

 1143. v. ALTHA, b. 1788.

 1144. vi. LUTHER, b. Castleton, Vt., Apr. 17, 1791; m. Rosa Hutchins, 2387-8.

 1145. vii. LUMAN, b. Hanover, N. H., 1794; was graduated at Vermont University, Burlington, Vt., and is Rector of St. James' Parish Church, Arlington, Vt.

 383. PHILIP FOOTE, (117, 37, 10, 3,) b. July 29, 1752; m. 1st, Jan., 1778, Isabel, dau. of William Milikin, of Washington, Mass.; she d. Jan. 9, 1785, ae. 25; m. 2nd, 1787, Abigail Cornish, of Lanesborough, Mass. She d. Mar. 5, 1813, ae. 60; m. 3rd, June, 1813, Rebecca Spalden, of Middlebury, Vt. She was b. in Townsend, Mass. He d. Aug. 27, 1827. She d. Oct. 29, 1841, ae. 77. Res., Middlebury, Vt.

 1146. i. PATTY, b. Washington, Mass., Oct. 24, 1778; m. Lyman Yale, of Charlotte, Vt. Ch.: two sons and five daus.

 1147. ii. NANCY, b. Dalton, Mass., July 27, 1780; m. John Angel, of Champlain, N. Y. Ch.: two sons.

 1148. iii. WILLIAM, b. Middlebury, Vt., Aug. 27, 1783; m. Lucy W. Berthrong, 2389-2399.

 1149. iv. ORRILL, b. Middlebury, Vt., Jan. 9, 1785; m. Henry Manchester, of Malone, N. Y. Ch.: three sons and one dau.

 387. FREEMAN FOOTE, (117, 37, 10, 3,) b. Sept. 22, 1759; m. Oct. 5, 1788, Silence Clark, of Attlebury, Mass. She d. Sept. 22, 1832, ae. 69; m. 2nd, 1833, Bathsheba, wid. of Ichabod Morton, of Middlebury, Vt., and dau. of Seth Morton, of Middlebury, Mass. Mr. Foote was a Revolutionary soldier; served under Col. Ethan Allen 15 months. He belonged to the Vermont Volunteers. He d. Sept. 30, 1842. Res., Middlebury, Vt.

 1150. i. CLARK, b. Dec. 16, 1791; m. Hannah Boardman, 2400-6.

 1151. ii. CLARISSA, b. Feb. 17, 1795; m. 1814, Alfred Wainwright, of Salisbury, Vt. She d. Apr. 22, 1822, in Plattsburgh, N. Y. Ch.: one son and three dau.

 1152. iii. DAROXA, b. Sept. 23, 1797; m. Beriah Green, of Brandon, Vt. Present res., Whitesboro, N. Y. Ch.: two sons and four daus.

 1153. iv. ALLEN, b. Jan. 5, 1801; m. Bathsheba Morton, 2407.

 1154. v. DELIA, b. Sept. 29, 1803; m. Alfred Wainwright, of Middlebury, Vt., widower of No. 1151; res., Montpelier, Vt. Ch.: one son and one dau.

 388. MARTIN FOOTE, (117, 37, 10, 3,) b. Oct. 22, 1761; m. 1st, Mar. 6, 1788, Hannah, wid. of Benjamin Dean, of Monkton, Vt., and dau. of Jonathan Nicholas, of Trumbull, Ct. She d. Feb. 9, 1838, ae. 75; m. 2nd, Mar. 13, 1838, Anna, wid of Asa Branch, of Middlebury, Vt., and dau. of James Howard, of

Benson, Vt. Mr. Foote was a Revolutionary soldier, and served under Col. Ethan Allen 10 months. He was one of the Vermont Volunteers. Res., Middlebury, Vt.

    1155. i.   MARTIN, b. June 1, 1791; m. Betsy Boardman, 2408.

    1156. ii.   MARY, b. ——; m. Elizur Boardman, of Rutland, Vt. Ch.: (1) Dr. Elijah. (2) Horace, b. at W. Rutland, Vt., May 18, 1835; d. Feb. 26, 1888.

    1157. iii. RUHAMA, b. ——; d. in early life.

    1158. iv. CEMANTHA, b. ——; m. ——; d. p. s.

    1159. v.   ALMIRA, b. 1798; d. Apr. 1, 1817, at Litchfield, Ct.

    1160. vi. MARTHA, b. ——; m. ——; d. p. s.

    1161. vii. CHARLOTTE, b. ——; m. Ch.: 3.

    1162· viii. ALTHA, b. ——; m. ——; d. ——. Ch.: one dau.

    389. STILLMAN FOOTE, (117, 37, 10, 3,) b. Sept. 10, 1763; m. Feb. 6, 1787, Lovica Donaghy, of Sheffield, Mass. She d. Feb. 28, 1811; m. 2nd, June 10, 1811, Mary Pember. He d. Dec. 21, 1834. After dividing the mill property with his brother Appleton, which their father had left them at Middlebury, he continued to run the upper mills. His property included the College campus. Res., Middlebury, Vt., and Canton, N. Y.

    1163. i.   CHAUNCEY, b. May 9, 1780; m. Julia E. Bird, 2409-13.

    1164. ii.   HENRY, b. Oct. 12, 1791; m. Amelia Bird, 2414-21.

    1165. iii. LOVICA, b. May 11, 1793; m. Oct. 20, 1816, Cephas L. Rockwood; he was b. Mar. 12, 1786, at Bellingham, Mass.; d. May 3, 1844, in Pewaukee, Waukesha Co., Wis. He was a graduate of Middlebury College, Vt.; lawyer. She d. July 30, 1872, at Cairo, Ill. Ch.: (1) Eunice S. Rockwood, b. Chester, Vt., Nov. 12, 1819; m. Apr. 19, 1861, Daniel F. Melindy. Ch.: (a) Aphos John Melindy, b. ——. (b) Ellen R. Melindy, b. ——. (c) Harry R. Melindy, b. ——. (2) Elma L. Rockwood, b. Chester, Vt., Oct. 2, 1821; d. Aug. 27, 1830, in Canton, N. Y. (3) Aaron L., Rockwood, b. Chester, Vt., Aug. 29, 1823; m. May, 1849, Anna L. Napes; was a Captain of Cavalry, from Ill., in war of 1861; res., Cal. (4) Mary Emma Rockwood, b. Nov. 15, 1825; m. May 13, 1847 Americus W. Rowess d. Apr., 1858, in Cal. Ch.: (a) Sarah Rowess, b. (b) Cephas R. Rowess, b. (c) Celia S. Rowess (twins). (5) Sarah Ellen Rockwood, b. Nov. 15, 1825; m. Feb. 7, 1848, Jos. L. Moore, d. Aug. 14, 1854, at Sheboygan, Wis. Ch.: (a) Mary Moore, b. (b) Frank R. Moore, b. (c) Frederick M. Moore, b. (6) Catherine L. Rockwood, b. May 31, 1828; m. Oct. 20, 1852, Henry F. Eastman; res., Chicago, Ill. Ch.: (a) Myra K. Eastman, b. (b) William H. Eastman, b. (c) Louise F. Eastman, b. (d) Mary F. Eastman, b. (e) Horace R. Eastman, b. (f) Ellen E. Eastman, b. (g) Cephas W. Eastman, b. (7) Delia L. Rockwood, b. July 6, 1832; m. Feb. 15, 1858, Dr. Horace Wardner; res., Cairo, Ill.

    1166. iv. DELIA, b. Nov. 25, 1813; m. Sept. 16, 1827, Leonard Sears. He d. Feb. 20, 1859, at Maway, Ia. Ch.: (1) Elizabeth Sears, b. Aug. 1, 1830; d. Aug. 10, 1830. (2) Mary P. Sears, b. May 29, 1835; d. Sept. 29, 1835. (3) Caroline L. Sears, b. May 11, 1835; m. Dec. 2, 1855, Andrew J. Poppleton; res., Omaha, Neb. Ch.: (a) Ellen Elizabeth Poppleton, b. Sept. 11, 1856; graduated from

Vassar College, 1876. (b) Zada M. Poppleton, b. Apr. 4, 1859; d. Nov. 17, 1862. (c) William Poppleton, b. Apr. 7, 1866. (d) Mary D. Poppleton, b. July 23, 1843. (4) Charles W. Sears, b. July 12, 1857; d. Feb., 1870. (5) Stillman F. Sears, b. Sept. 6, 1839; d. Dec. 9, 1840. (6) Stillman V. Sears, b. June 29, 1842; m. Oct. 16, 1864, Margaret A. Searls; res., Maway, Ia. Ch.: (a) Leonard C. Sears, b. Aug. 2, 1865. (b) Melom L. Sears, b. Oct. 13, 1866. (c) Charles W. Sears, b. May, 1871. (7) Mary R. Sears, b. June 29, 1844; m. Dec. 2, 1860, Chas. Atkins. Ch.: (a) Carrie M. Atkins, b. Nov. 25, 1861. (8) Joseph L. Sears, b. July 1, 1846. (9) Millan F. Sears, b. Nov. 25, 1848. (10) Delia L. Sears, b. Jan. 18, 1857. (11) Elizabeth W. Sears, b. Apr. 23, 1853; d. Aug. 23, 1854.

1167. v.   STILLMAN, b. Mar., 1817; m. Mary P. Chipman and Elizabeth A. Guest, 2422-7.

1168. vi.   MARY PEMDER, b. Mar. 6, 1819; m. Nov. 30, 1836, Elam Rust, of Canton, N. Y. He was a lawyer; res., Illinois. He d. at Decatur, Illinois, Mar. 7, 1857. Ch.: (1) George Washington, b. at Waddington, N. Y., Feb. 22, 1838; m. at Baraboo, Wisconsin, 1865, Carrie C. Maxwell. Ch.: (a) Daughter, b. fall of 1866; d. 1866. (b) Melvin W., b. July 31, 1868. (c) Nellie, b. July 31, 1868, at Chicago, Ill. (d) Mary, b. at Chicago, 1870. (e) Carrie, b. at Chicago, 1874. (2) Melvin Will, b. at Waddington, N. Y., Nov. 10, 1843; a private in the 138th Ill. Regiment of Infantry; d. at Nashville, Tenn., Aug. 13, 1865. (3) Delia L., b. at Waterloo, Ill., Nov. 22, 1845. (4) Mary F., b. at Granville, Ill, June 7, 1849; d. June 27, 1850. (5) Stillman F., b. at Decatur, Ill., Apr. 18, 1856; m. Aug. 3, 1882, Clara Louisa Kniffin, b. 1855, at Kilbourne, England. He was a prominent lawyer; res., Belvidere, Waterloo, Alton, Greenville, Ill., and d. at Decatur, Ill., Nov. 7, 1857. (6) Delia L.; m. Nov. 28, 1871, Dr. William C. Wardner; res., Hornelsville, N. Y.; he was a dentist. Ch.: (a) William R., b. at Hornelsville, N. Y., Sept. 8, 1873. (b) George H., b. Mar. 3, 1876, at Hornelsville, N. Y.

390.   JOHN FOOTE, (117, 37, 10, 3,) b. Nov. 12, 1765; m. 1st, Feb. 19, 1789, Lucy, dau. of William Thayer, of Richmond, Mass., formerly of Salisbury, Ct. She d. Oct. 30, 1827; m. 2nd, Ann Sumner, wid. of William B. Sumner, and dau. of Charles Harrison, of New York, N. Y. She d. Feb. 28, 1858. He erected a hotel at East Middlebury, also a grist mill, saw mill and works for dressing cloth and carding wool and died there in 1849.

1169. i.   SARAH, b. Dec. 28, 1789; m. James Pierce.
1170. ii.   DANIEL H., b. May 12, 1792; m. Sarah Weaver, 2425-7.
1171. iii.   HARRIET, b. Nov. 4, 1795; m. Nov., 1816, Chauncey Fuller.
1172. iv.   LORAEN, b. Feb. 4, 1797; d. Mar. 25, 1798.
1173. v.   LAURA, b. Feb. 23, 1799; m. Sept. 12, 1846, Reuben Piper.
1174. vi.   DELIA, b. May 3, 1801; d. Aug. 21, 1802.
1175. vii.   JOHN C., b. Nov. 6, 1803; d. June 6, 1804.
1176. viii.   JOHN NELSON, b. July 4, 1805; m. Rebecca, dau. of Jesse Farwell; res., Mich.
1177. ix.   CHAUNCEY, b. Feb. 14, 1815; d. Mar. 13, 1816.

391. APPLETON FOOTE, (117, 37, 10, 3,) b. Aug. 28, 1767; m., 1790, Mary Groves; she was b. May 31, 1772; he d. Nov. 27, 1831, at Malone, N. Y.; she d. May 20, 1839. In 1794 he and Stillman divided their property on the west side of Middlebury Falls and Appleton, built the lower saw and grist mills on the site of the present saw mill electric light plant; he also built his residence on the site of the Sheldon Museum. Res., Middlebury, Vt., and Malone, N. Y.

1178. i. ABIGAIL, b. July 18, 1791; m. Feb. 5, 1810, William Slade, of Middlebury, Vt.; he was b. May 9, 1786, at Cornwall, Vt. He was a graduate of Middlebury College 1807; M. C. 1831 to 1843, and Governor of Vermont 1844 and 1845; was until his death Corresponding Secretary and General Agent of the Board of National Popular Education. He d. Jan. 16, 1856. Ch.: (1) Esther, b. Nov. 22, 1810; d. Aug. 13, 1811. (2) James Madison, b. Sept. 8, 1812. (3) Mary Groves, b. July 4, 1815; d. Apr. 5, 1816. (4) William, b. June 28, 1817. (5) Jane Maria, b. Sept. 9, 1819; d. Sept., 1838. (6) Henry Clay, b. Dec. 25, 1825; d. July 29, 1826. (7) Samuel, b. Jan. 14, 1827; d. May 20, 1827. (8) Charles, b. Feb. 23, 1828. (9) Henry Martyn, b. Dec. 16, 1829.

1179. ii. WILLIAM BOTT, b. July 25, 1781; m. Pamelia Orton (she was b. Apr. 29, 1794; d. Feb. 15, 1827) and Aug. 1, 1832, Amanda Greeg, b. Mar., 1801.

1180. iii. MARIA, b. Mar. 10, 1796; m. 1811, Almon Wheeler, of Malone, N. Y. He d. Jan. 5, 1827; she d. July 7, 1812. He was an eminent lawyer. Ch.: (1) Jane Maria, b. July 3, 1812.

1181. iv. EVELINA, b. Mar. 2, 1801.

1182. v. RICHARD GROVES, b. June 2, 1803; m. Sarah Doty, 2428-32.

392. JOSEPH FOOTE, (118, 37, 10, 3,) b. Oct. 26, 1758; m. Oct. 20, 1778, Barsheba Burr, of Simsbury, Ct. He d. May 27, 1789. Res., Simsbury, Ct., and Johnstown, N. Y.

1183. i. LEVI, b. Simsbury, Ct., May 10, 1779; m. Amelia Allen, 2433.

1184. ii. JOSEPH, b. Simsbury, Ct., Oct. 14, 1781; m. Hannah Wallahon, 2450-5.

1185. iii. BARSHEBA, b. Simsbury, Ct., 1784; m. ———.

1186. iv. CHESTER, b. Apr. 27, 1789; m. Fanny Hooscott, 2456-62.

396. ELISHA FOOTE, (118, 37, 10, 3,) b. Aug. 26, 1764; m. Dec. 28, 1783, Rebecca Clark, dau. of Jonathan Miller, of Avon, Ct. Mr. Foote, who was 15 years old when his father died, remained with his mother and younger brother, Aaron, and was the principal instrument of keeping the family together until they grew up to manhood, and he had settled and had a family of six children when he and his brother, Aaron, together with their mother, emigrated to Northampton, N. Y., in 1797; d. Dec. 16, 1853.

1187. i. ELISAH, b. Feb. 26, 1786; m. Pamelia Kennicott, 2463-72.

1188. ii. REBECCA G., b. Oct., 1787; d. Nov. 29, 1845.

1189. iii. JULIA, b. June 15, 1789; m. May 15, 1811, Joseph W. Kennicott, of Northampton, N. Y. Ch.: (1) Julia Foote Kennicott, b. Nov. 29, 1812; m. Sept. 8, 1841, Noah Denton; he was b. 1810; d. Mar. 28, 1878. She d. Feb. 3, 1891. Ch.: (a) J. Frank Denton, b. Aug. 10, 1847; m. Jan. 29, 1873, Frances A. Hurst; she d. Nov. 19, 1899. Ch.: (i) Mattie L. Denton, b. Jan. 15, 1874. (ii) Fannie A. Denton, b. Mar. 27, 1880; d. Sept. 21, 1881. (iii)W. Bert

Denton, b. Mar. 28, 1881. ( ) Edward K. Denton, b. Nov. 17, 1850; m. Fannie Mellen. Chb: (i) Nellie Rose Denton, b. May 7, ———; d. (ii) Lelia Denton, b. (iii) Frank Denton, b. (iv) Lizzie Denton, b. (2) Harriet B. Kennicott, b. Sept. 11, 1814; m. Nov. 26, 1833, William E. Spires. Ch.: (a) Lidia Spires, b. (b) Ellen Spires, b. (c) Sarah Spires, b. (d) William F. Spires, b. (e) Ammon Spires, b. (3) Emily M. Kennicott, b. May 23, 1816; m. Sept. 10, 1839, Chester Butler; he was b. Feb. 12, 1810; d. Apr. 4, 1895; she d. Dec. 5, 1883. Ch. (1) Erwin Butler, b. Dec. 22, 1846; m. Aug. 2, 1876, Cornelia A. Van Ness. (ii) Ella Butler, b. Apr. 10, 1856. (4) Sylvester Allen Kennicott, b. June 7, 1818; m. Feb. 27, 1854, Emma K. Reynolds. Ch.: (i) Addison Reynolds Kennicott, b. (5) George E. Kennicott, b. July 17, 1821; d. Sept. 6, 1822. (6) Martha A. Kennicott, b. Apr. 24, 1826; m. Oct. 12, 1858, Dr. E. Kies; she d. July 12, 1873. Ch.: (a) Anna J. Kies, b. Aug. 13, 1862; m. Jan. 26, 1885, John W. Thayer. Ch.: (1) Emilie K. Thayer, b. Nov. 26, 1885. (2) Martha K. Thayer, b. Dec. 10, 1886. (7) Edward Kennicott, b. May 9, 1827; m. (8) Mary C. Kennicott, b. Aug. 31, 1832; m. Oct. 8, 1857, Clement S. James. He was b. Sept. 27, 1832; d. Jan. 27, 1895. Ch.: (a) Burton K. James, b. Aug. 16, 1861; m. Mar. 7, 1888, Mabel E. Shatto; she was b. Mar. 18, 1863. Ch.: (i) Florence L. James, b. Feb. 10, 1889. (ii) Mabel D. James, b. May 15, 1891. (iii) Hazel D. James, b. Mar. 20, 1893. (iv) Hellen James, b. Mar. 8, 1896. (v) Baby (not named), b. Feb. 11, 1901. (b) Arthur D. James, b. July 26, 1869; m. Dec. 15, 1897, Frankie Hayatt; she was b. July 31, 1869.

1190. iv. HENRY, b. Apr. 19, 1791; m. Anna Hooscoot, 2473-81.

1191. v. AMELIA, b. Nov. 13, 1793; m. Mar. 10, 1817, William Morse, of Cranesville, N. Y. He d. Apr. 14, 1849. Ch.: (1) Polly Caroline, b. Oct. 1, 1818; m. Aug. 20, 1838. Ch.: 3. (2) Lucy Emeline, b. Oct. 23, 1820; m. Jan. 20, 1846. (3) Elisha F., b. Aug. 1, 1823. (4) Julia Ann, b. July 28, 1825. (5) William Henry, b. Feb. 16, 1828; d. Aug. 25, 1828. (6) John Clark, b. Apr. 4, 1834.

1192. vi. AARON, b. Dec. 25, 1795; m Dec. 8, 1825, ———. Freeman, wid.; res., Saratoga Springs, N. Y.; p. s.

1193. vii. SARAH MILLER, b. Apr. 8, 1798; m. Jan. 14, 1823, Rev. John E. Clark, an itinerant minister of the Methodist Episcopal Church. He was presiding Elder in that Church, and later Professor in Yale College; res., Lansingburgh, N. Y., and New Haven, Ct. Ch.: (1) Mary, b. Nov. 11, 1823, in Glens Falls, N. Y.; d. in Plattsburgh, N. Y., Aug. 16, 1829. (2) Helen Amelia, b. Dec. 19, 1829, in Plattsburgh, N. Y.; d. Sept. 26, 1834, at Ft. Brady, Sault de St. Marie. (3) John Emery, b. Aug. 8, 1832, in Northampton, N. Y.; m. Aug. 20, 1856, Caroline Camilla Doty, of Ann Arbor, Mich. Ch.: (a) Mary Caroline, b. Aug. 20, 1858, at Ann Arbor, Mich.; d. Dec. 13, 1860, at Boelia, Prunia. (b) John Frederick, b. Aug. 16, 1860, at Munich, Bavaria; m. Mar., 1882, Georgia Drusilla Smith; res., Tokonas, Colo. Ch.: (i) Emory Ellison, b. Nov. 22, 1883. (ii) John, b. May 14, 1885; d. Oct. 15, 1885. (iii) Alice, b. July 20, 1886. (iv) Helen, b. Nov. 5, 1888. (v) Louise

Ann, b. May 7, 1890. (vi) Clay Armour, b. Oct. 6, 1892. (vii) Jane England, b. Sept. 30, 1894. (viii) Thomas Smith Clark, b. Aug. 6, 1897. (ix) Caroline Clark, b. Jan. 20, 1900. (c) Helen, b. Feb. 2, 1866, at Ann Arbor, Mich.; m. Nov. 8, 1894, Rev. Harry R. Miles; res., Brattleboro, Vt. Ch.: (i) Margaret, b. Dec. 19, 1896. (ii) John Shepley, b. Dec. 21, 1899. (d) William Russel, b. Mar. 2, 1868, at Yellow Springs, Ohio; m. Nov. 27, 1894, Ella Lucia Treat, of New Haven, Ct.; res., New Haven, Ct.; with the Winchester Repeating Arms Co. Ch.: (i) Lucia, b. Mar. 31, 1896. Res., New Haven, Ct. (e) Alice Tucker, b. Mar. 17, 1870, at Yellow Springs, Ohio; unm.

1194. viii. LUCY, b. Apr. 10, 1800; d. Apr. 16, 1892; m. Dec. 17, 1820, Simeon Criste, Jr.; b. Nov. 11, 1796; d. July 17, 1884; of Mayfield, N. Y. Ch.: (1) Lydia Maria, b. Oct. 30, 1821; m. Sept. 21, 1846, William Jackson, of Mayfield, N. Y. (2) Jacob, b. Jan. 20, 1824. (3) James, b. May 4, 1828. (4) Harriet Jane, b. Sept. 14, 1831. (5) Child, not named, b. Feb. 7, 1836; d. in infancy. (6) William Henry, b. Feb. 18, 1840.

1195. ix. JOSEPH, b. Mar. 1, 1803; m. Angelina Spier and Cathrine Green, 2482-6.

1196. x. LYDIA, b. July 22, 1805; m. Aug. 6, 1828, Joseph Spire, of Northampton, N. Y. He is a merchant of long standing and a man of more than ordinary business habits. He likewise possesses respectable talents as a Local Preacher in the Methodist Episcopal Church.

1197. xi. JOHN WESLEY, b. Mar. 30, 1808; m. Harriet Bell and Elizabeth Slocum, 2487-½.

404. JOHN FOOTE, JR., (119, 37, 10, 3,) b. Jan. 9, 1760; m. Lois, dau. of Dea. Benjamin and Hannah (Humphrey) Mills, of Canton, Ct. She d. Dec. 23, 1802, ae. 39; he d. June 13, 1803; res., Canton, Ct.

1198. i. CHILD, not named, b. ———; d. in infancy.

1199. ii. CLARA, b. Jan., 1784; d. May 11, 1789.

1200. iii. LAURA, b. Jan. 8, 1786; m. Oct. 10, 1805, Lewis M. Norton, of Goshen, Ct. She d. 1855. Ch.: (1) Eliza, b. Sept. 3, 1807. (2) John Foote, b. Sept. 8, 1809; m. Hannah Ferancis Jenkins, of Falmouth, Mass., Aug. 19, 1839. (3) Mills, b. June 22, 1813; d. Feb. 1, 1829. (4) Henry, b. Nov. 10, 1815. (5) Maria, b. Dec. 17, 1817. (6) Edward, b. Feb. 20, 1820. (7) Robert, b. Feb. 18, 1822. (8) Laura, b. June 25, 1827; d. Aug. 18, 1828. (9) Marana, b. Mar., 1830.

1201. iv. MILES, b. Apr. 1, 1788; m. Clarinda Barber, 2488-92.

1202. v. LANCEL, b. Feb. 28, 1790; m. Laura Humphreys, 2493-2500.

1203. vi. HERSCHEL, b. Oct. 22, 1793; m. Pamela B. Townsend, 2501-3.

1204. vii. CLARA, b. Mar. 19, 1795; m. 1816, Luke Barbar, of Canton, Ct.; she d. Dec. 20, 1837. Ch.: (1) Elizabeth, d. at ae. of one year. (2) Elizabeth. (3) Helen. (4) Jane. (5) Julia.

1205. viii. STILES, b. Mar., 1797; d. Nov. 27, 1798.

1206. ix. STELLA, b. Mar. 1, 1799; m. Nov. 16, 1823, Chester Wadsworth, of Becket. She d. Aug. 7, 1839. Ch: (1) Oliver Chester, b. July

14, 1824. (2) Ellen Eliza, b. Dec. 3, 1828. (3) Laura Isabella,
b. June 12, 1834. (4) George Francis, b. Oct. 31, 1837.
1207. x. JOHN STILES, b. Oct. 2, 1805; m. Margaret Todd, 2504-6.

405. LUTHER FOOTE, (119, 37, 10, 3,) b. Mar. 5, 1761; m. Sept., 1783,
Temperance, dau. of Dea. Samuel Hayes, of Granby, Ct. She was b. Dec. 14, 1761;
d. Jan. 8, 1787; m. 2nd, Jan. 12, 1789, Mary Anne, wid. of Hosea Bronson, and
dau. of Asahel Phelps, both of Hebron, Ct. She d. Apr. 26, 1833, ae. 68. He d.
Sept. 11, 1834.

 1208. i. CALVIN, b. Feb. 28, 1785; m. Polly Burton, 2507-11.
 1209. ii. TEMPERANCE, b. Jan. 5, 1787; m. 1807, in Norfolk, Thomas,
    son of Joseph and Anna (Hoyt) Terry, of Danbury, Ct. He was
    b. Apr. 4, 1786, in Washington, Ct.; removed 1845 to Richville,
    Pa., where he d. Jan. 27, 1873. She d. Oct. 14, 1850. Ch.: (1) Milo
    Hayes Terry, b. Apr. 21, 1812, in Reading, Pa.; m. Jane Good-
    fellow; she d. 1851; he d. Oct., 1847, in New Orleans, La. Ch.:
    (a) Milton, (b) David, (c) Joseph, (d) Mary. (2) Caroline
    Terry, b. Dec. 8, 1814; m. 1835, Edward Green, of Bradford, Pa.
    Ch.: (a) Milo, (b) Emma. (3) Mary Ann Terry, b. Oct. 7, 1817;
    res., Riceville, Pa.; unm. (4) Emmeline Terry, b. Oct. 1, 1820;
    d. Aug. 20, 1847, at Riceville, Pa.; unm. (5) Huldah Terry, b.
    Nov. 10, 1826; m. in Riceville, Nov. 2, 1877, Reuben B., son of
    Benjamin B. and Abigail (St. John) Westgate. He was b. Jan.
    9, 1822; d. Aug. 30, 1874, at Riceville; she d. June 21, 1866.
    Ch.: (a) Clara Belle, b. Sept. 16, 1851. (b) Arthur Hayes, b.
    Mar. 6, 1854; m. Nov. 28, 1875, Anna Brainard. Ch.: (i) Eva
    Centennial Westgate b. 1876. (ii') Charles Reuben Westgate, b.
    1878. (c) Theodore Beecher Westgate, b. July 13, 1858. (d)
    Mary Emma Westgate, b. May 16, 1862.
1210. iii. PLINY, b. Dec. 18, 1789; m. Dorinda Mills, 2512-4.
1211. iv. ANN, b. Feb. 28, 1791; m. Feb. 2, 1814, Pomroy Baldwin, of
    Goshen, Ct. She d. Sept. 21, 1828, at Massillon, Ohio; he d.
    Aug. 31, 1817; m. 2nd, 1824, Arvine Wales. Ch.: (1) Pomroy, b.
    Mar. 19, 1818; wealthy bookseller; res., Massillon, Ohio. (2)
    Arvine, b. May, 1827.
1212. v. JOHN, b. Apr. 17, 1793; m. Laura Mills, 2515-7.
1213. vi. MARY, b. Feb. 2, 1795; m. ———. Oviatt, of Richfield, Ohio.
1214. vii. LUTHER LYMAN, b. Sept. 18, 1804; was an attorney-at-law;
    left for South America; no more known.

415. JOHN FOOTE, (126, 38, 11, 3,) b. Apr. 2, 1761; m. Nov. 28, 1781,
Hulda, dau. of Nathaniel Stone, of Carmel, N. Y. He d. Oct. 24, 1808, in New York
City. She d. Apr. 30, 1849, ae. 85, in Danbury, Ct.; res., Danbury, Ct.

 1215. i. SALLY, b. Aug. 31, 1783; m. John Simmons, of New York, N. Y.
 1216. ii. DAVID, b. June 15, 1785; m Cathrine Cobb, of New London;
    after she d. Betsy Beard, of Granville, N. Y.
 1217. iii. PHILA, b. Apr. 11, 1787; m. James McCully, of New York, N. Y.
 1218. iv. ELIJAH, b. May 2, 1789; res., Danbury, Ct.; unm.
 1219. v. JOHN, b. May 13, 1791; m. Clarisa Knapp, 2518-27.
 1220. vi. BETSY, b. May 28, 1793; m. Samuel McCully, of New York,
    N. Y.
 1221. vii. ANSON, b. Nov. 14, 1795; d. ———.

418. ENOCH FOOTE, (126, 38, 11, 3,) b. May 2, 1770; m. 1791, Abigail Brooks, wid.; she d. June 6, 1836; res., Bridgeport, Ct.

1222.   i.   ELANSON, b. July 4, 1792; lost at sea 1812.

1223.   ii.   CHARLES, b. Dec. 21, 1793; m. Ann S. Burr and Jane S. Thompson, 2528-36.

1224.   iii.   MARY ANN, b. May 26, 1797; m. Apr. 8, 1821, George, son of Capt. Ezekiel Hubbell, of Bridgeport, Ct.; she d. Dec. 29, 1841. Ch.: (1) George W. Hubbell, b. Nov., 1824; d. 1859, in New Orleans, La.

419. PETER FOOTE, (128, 38, 11, 3,) b. ———; m. Eunice Pond; res., Woodbury, Ct., and Vt.

1224.   i.   PETER, b. ———; d. ———.

1224¹.   ii.   CHLOE, b. ———; m. ———. Brown, of Williston, Vt., and d. there.

1224².   iii.   ANNA, b. ———; m. Gates Taylor, of Williston, Vt., and d. there.

1225.   iv.   ISAAC NEWTON, b. 1782; m. Abigail Bass, 2537-42.

420. PHILO, (4419) b. ———; m. Martha Hale, of Derby, Ct.; m. 2nd, Phebe Beers, of Woodbury, Ct.; lived and d. in Newtown, Ct., and was buried there.

1225¹.   i.   SABRINA, b. ———; m. David Sherman; res., Sandy Hook, Ct.

1225².   ii.   POLLY ANN, b. ———; m. Garry Miner, of Woodbury, Ct. Ch.: (1) Son, who lived in Newtown, Ct., in 1875.

1225³.   iii.   BEAMAN, b. ———; m. Naomi, dau. of Jonithan and Phebe Betts (Hawley).

421. TRUMAN SHERMAN FOOTE, (128, 38, 11, 3,) b. Nov. 15, 1778; m. Jan. 11, 1801, Sarah, dau. of David Jackson, of Woodbury, Ct. He d. at Bristol, Ct., Oct. 25, 1841.

1226.   i.   CAROLINE, b. Dec. 1, 1801, at Woodbury, Ct.; m. Feb. 5, 1818, in Woodbury, William Castle, stone mason, son of John Masters and Charlotte (Hayes) Castle, of Roxbury, Ct. He was b. June 19, 1797, in Woodbury, Ct. They dwelt in Woodbury, Bethlehem, and Sharon, Ct.; Attlebury, N. Y., and New Milford and Roxbury, Ct. They settled June 3, 1851, at Tryonville, Pa., and were living there in Sept., 1875. He served in the war of 1812, in 37th Regt. U. S. Infantry, for which he enjoyed a pension. Ch.:
(1) Don Esteran Castle, b. Aug. 28, 1818, at Woodbury, Ct.; m. in Titusville, May 27, 1845, Mary Ann Barker, Tryonville, Crawford Co., N. Y., in Sept., 1875. Ch.: (a) Ellen Lavinia Castle, b. Mar. 31, 1846, at Rome, Pa. (b) Charles Eugene Castle, b. at Memphis, Tenn., Apr. 12, 1847. (c) Flora Amanda Castle, b. at Steuben, Pa., Apr. 12, 1851. (d) Joseph Barber Castle, b. at Steuben, Pa., Jan. 18, 1854. (e) Don Estevan Castle, b. at Steuben, Pa., Nov. 22, 1856.
(2) McDonald Castle, b. Mar. 13, 1820, at Woodbury, Ct.; d. Dec. 25, 1833, at Roxbury, and was buried there.
(3) Emeline Rosetta Castle, b. Oct. 9, 1821, at Bethlehem, Ct.; m. July 20, 1849, Isaac Gillette, at Bristol, Ct.; res., Mercer, Mercer Co., Pa., Sept., 1875. Ch.: (a) Ella Gillette, b. at Bristol, Ct.; Feb. 14, 1851. (b) David Seymour Gillette, b. at Bristol,

Ct., May 15, 1854. (c) Abby Gillette, b. at Mercer, Mercer Co., Pa., Mar. 15, 1863. (d) William Gillette, b. at Mercer, Mercer Co., Pa., Nov. 10, 1865.

(4) Almer Donato Castle, b. Feb. 7, 1824; m. Aug. 20, 1849, Cornelia Farrel, at New Haven, Ct. They settled in Bristol, Ct., where they died; she d. July 5, 1853; he d. Oct. 18, 1853. They were buried in the West Cemetery in Bristol. Ch.: (1) Almer Rockwell Castle, b. at Bristol, Ct., May 11, 1853; d. Aug., 1872, at New Haven, Ct., and was buried at Westville Ct.

(5) Sarah Maria Castle, b. Nov. 28, 1825, at Attlebury, N. Y.; d. at Bristol, Ct., Feb. 15, 1847, and was buried in Bristol cemetery.

(6) Thomas Foote Castle, b. Apr. 9, 1827, at New Milford, Ct.; was drowned in the Bay of San Francisco, Cal., Jan. 28, 1850; unm.

(7) Beeman Milan Castle, b. Dec. 17, 1828, at Roxbury, Ct.; d. there Feb. 16, 1829, and was buried there.

(8) Eliza Jane Castle, b. May 6, 1830, at Roxbury, Ct.; m. Oct. 14, 1847, at Farmington, Ct., by Rev. David McAllister, Methodist Episcopal, Charles Crittenden, a farmer, son of Amos and Melissa (Phelps) Crittenden, of Southington, Ct., where he was b. Feb. 25, 1821. They settled in Bristol, Ct., and were living there in Sept. 1875, Forestville, Post Office. He enlisted at Bristol, Sept. 9, 1862, as a private in Co. I, 25th Regt. Ct. Vol. Infantry, and served one year. Ch.: (a) Thomas Castle Crittenden, b. at Farmington, Ct., Feb. 9, 1848; m. May 13, 1874, at Tryonville, Pa., Vesta Baugher; in Tryonville, Pa., Sept., 1875. (b) Sarah Isinella Crittenden, b. at Bristol, Ct., June 4, 1850; m. Feb. 24, 1873, at Springfield, Mass., by Rev. Oscar F. Stafford, Episcopal, Henry Kelly Paul, son of Timothy and Lucy Ann (Beck) Paul. He enlisted Oct. 30, 1861, in Co. K, 24th Regt. Mass. Vols., and was discharged Oct. 29, 1864, at Boston, Mass., having been wounded at Deep Run, Va., Aug. 16, 1864. They were living at Bristol, in 1875, without children. (c) Charles Crittenden, b. at Bristol, Ct., July 9, or Jan. 15, 1853. (d) Carrie Edith Crittenden, b. at Bristol, Ct., June 25, 1858. (e) Effie Jane Crittenden, b. at Bristol, Ct., Dec. 26, or 23, 1867.

(9) Carrie Ophelia Castle, b. Dec. 16, 1831, at Roxbury, Ct.; m. Feb. 23, 1870, at Franklin, Pa., John McGinnis; res., White Rock, Nevada, in Sept., 1875.

(10) William Sherman Castle, b. Sept. 2, 1833, at Roxbury, Ct.; d. on board a transport in New York Harbor, June 24, 1864, from a wound in the head, received in the battle of the Wilderness, May, 1864. He was buried in Cypress Hills Cemetery. His son. L. Herbert William Castle, b. May 4, 1859, at Tryonville, Pa.

(11) Margaret Susan Castle, twin, b. Feb. 12, 1835, at Roxbury, Ct.; m., at Steuben, Pa., July 15, 1854, Solomon Winegar Snow, a farmer, son of Josephus and Hannah (Winegar) Snow, of Tryonville, Pa. He was b. at Parma, N. Y., July 22, 1828. They settled at Steuben, where she d. May 8, 1861. She was buried at Tryonville. He m. 2nd, June 20, 1862, Sarah Ann Nebson, and was living

at Tryonville in Sept., 1875. Ch. of Solomon Winegar and Margaret Susan (Castle) Snow: (a) Almer Snow, b. at Steuben, Pa., Aug. 18, 1855. (b) Ernest Clifford Snow, b. at Steuben, Pa., Jan. 22, 1858. (c) Eva Margaret Snow, b. at Steuben, Pa., June 5, 1860.

(12) Maryette Castle, twin, b. at Roxbury, Ct., Feb. 12, 1835; d. Jan. 8, 1838, at Roxbury, and was bured there.

(13) Olive Marietta Castle, b. Dec. 20, 1837, at Roxbury, Ct.; m. Mar. 14, 1865, at Jamestown, N. Y., by Rev. N. Norton, Pastor of the Methodist Episcopal Church, Mar. 14, 1865, John Selden Gabriel, a carpenter and joiner; b. at Dayton, O., Oct. 6, 1822, son of Abraham and Keziah (Wolf) Gabriel, natives of Maryland. They dwelt for nine years in Tryonville, Pa., then moved to Meadville, Pa., and were living there in Sept., 1875. Ch.: (a) Flora Nina Gabriel, b. at Tryonville, Pa., Jan. 21, 1866. (b) Mary Patterson Gabriel, b. at Tryonville, Pa., Sept. 2, 1868; d. May 28, 1871, at Tryonville, Pa., and buried there. (c) Alice Gertrude Gabriel, b. at Tryonville, Pa., Dec. 3, 1869. (4) Lida Ellen Gabriel, b. at Tryonville, Pa., Sept. 26, 1873.

(14) Julia Catherine Castle, b. Apr. 27, 1839, at Roxbury, Ct.; m. at Limesville, Pa., James Warren Beeman. He served in Co. H, 150th Regt. Pa. Vols., and d. in Washington, D. C., Nov. 6, 1862. She m. 2nd, July 2, 1865, at her father's house in Tryonville, Pa., (her mother says Steuben) Jairus Chadwick, a carpenter and joiner, son of Samuel P. and Emily (Warner) Chadwick, of Greene, N. Y., where he was born. They were living at Tryonville, Pa., in Sept., 1875. Ch.: (a) James Warren Beeman, b. at Steuben, Pa., Feb. 15, 1863. (b) William Samuel Chadwick, b. at Steuben, Pa., June 15, 1866. (c) Elbert Warner Chadwick, b. at Steuben, Pa.,.Dec. 3, 1868. (d) Ellen Leona Chadwick, b. at Steuben, Pa., Aug. 23 or 28, 1870. (e) Don Eugene Chadwick, b. at Steuben, Pa., Oct. 11, 1872. (f) Berdenia (or Birdienia) May Chadwick, b. at Steuben, Pa., Oct. 2, 1874.

(15) Angeline Theresa Castle, b. Apr. 2, 1842, at Roxbury, Ct.; m. July 4, 1864, at Townville, Pa., Wallace Beeman, Tryonville, Crawford Co., Pa. Ch.: (a) Eva Beeman, b. Townville, Pa., July 14, 1862. (b) Carrie Virginia Beeman, b. at Steuben, Pa., May 29, 1866. (c) Florence Adelia Beeman, b. at Steuben, N. Y., June 30, 1870.

1227. ii.   EMELINE FOOTE, b. May 11, 1804, at Woodbury, Ct.; m. John Kirk, b. Apr. 12, 1803, in Southington, Ct., a farmer, son of Thomas and Lapelia (Barnes) Kirk, of Southington, Ct., Dec. 23, 1829, at her father's house in Bethlehem, Ct., by Rev. Paul Couch, Pastor of the Congregational Church of Bethlehem. They dwelt in Bethlehem till Apr., 1830, in Bristol, Ct., till Nov., 1833; then settled in Candor, N. Y., and were living there in Aug., 1875. Thomas Kirk was a Revolutionary soldier. Ch. of John and Emeline (Foote) Kirk:

(1) Mary Ann Kirk, b. Sept. 19, 1831, at Bristol, Ct.; d. Oct. 10, 1831, at Bristol, and was buried there.

(2) John Henry Kirk, b. Sept. 19, 1832, at Bristol, Ct.; a farmer; m. Jan. 7, 1855, at Caroline, N. Y., by Rev. Mr. Whit-

beck, Dutch Reformed, Rachel Jane Quick, dau. of Philip and
Ann Eliza (Myers) Quick, of Caroline, N. Y., where she was born
Jan. 8, 1833. He enlisted at Candor, N. Y., Sept., 1864, in Co.
D, 6th Regt. N. Y. S. Vol. Heavy Artillery, and died of chronic
diarrhœa, Nov. 16, 1864, at Winchester, Va., and was buried in
Candor, N. Y. She m. 2nd, May 13, 1867, Bradford B. Cook, and
was living at Ithaca, N. Y., in Aug., 1875. Ch.: (a) Francis Jay
Kirk, b. at Candor, N. Y., Oct. 23, 1856; a farmer; was living at
Dryden, N. Y., in 1875.

(3) Sarah Jane Kirk, b. Mar. 7, 1834, at Candor, N. Y.; was m.
at her father's house in Candor by Rev. W. H. Hayward, Pastor
of the Cong. Ch. of Candor, Sept. 20, 1859, to Ira Persanius; a
farmer; son of Ephraim and Catherine (Bush) Persanius, of
Caroline, N. Y., where he was b. Aug. 18, 1831. They settled in
Candor, and were living there in Sept., 1875. Ch.: (a) Melvin
Personius, b. at Candor, N. Y., Jan. 30, 1862; d. Oct. 29, 1864, at
Candor, and was buried there. (b) Ervin Personius, b. at Candor, N. Y., Sept. 22, 1865. (c) Estella Personius, b. at Candor, N. Y., Dec. 6, 1869; d. July 23, 1875, in Candor, and was
buried there.

(4) Truman Sherman Kirk, b. July 12, 1837, at Candor, N. Y.;
a farmer; m. at Caroline, N. Y., by Rev. F. S. Chubbuck, Pastor
of the Methodist Episcopal Ch. at Caroline Centre, Jan. 1, 1861,
Mary Antoinette Johnson, b. May 31, 1841, at Candor, dau. of
Richard and Hester (Hover) Johnson, of Candor. They dwelt in
Candor till Feb. 1, 1869; in Illinois till Mar. 7, 1870; in Missouri
two months; in the Indian Territory thirteen months; in Kansas
ten months; then settled in West Danby, N. Y., and were living
there in Sept., 1875. Ch.: (a) Frances Emeline Kirk, b. at Candor, N. Y., Nov. 17, 1861. (b) Mary Amelia Kirk, b. at Candor,
N. Y., Sept. 10, 1863. (c) Ida Mary Kirk, b. at Candor, N. Y.,
Oct. 10, 1865. (d) John Henry Kirk, b. at Candor, N. Y., June
26, 1868; d. at Elk City, Kansas, Oct. 15, 1873, and was buried
in Elk City Cemetery.

(5) Mariette Kirk, b. Oct. 16, 1838, at Candor, N. Y.; d. at
Candor, N. Y., Oct. 31, 1838, and was buried there.

(6) Margaret Adelaide Kirk, b. Nov. 1, 1842, at Candor, N. Y.;
was m. at Spencer, N. Y., by Rev. Eli F. Roberts, Methodist,
Aug. 27, 1870, to Charles Frederick Baylor, of Candor, where
he was b. Dec. 18, 1844. They settled at Candor, Tiago Co.,
N. Y., and were living there in Aug., 1875. He was a blacksmith and farmer; son of Daniel H. and Lydia (Evans) of Candor. Ch.: (a) John Daniel Baylor, b. at Candor, N. Y., May
24, 1870.

1228.   iii.   SARAH MARIA FOOTE, twin, b. July 21, 1807, at Woodbury,
Ct.; m. Nov. 9, 1826, at Bethlehem, Ct., Charles Goodwin Edwards, b. Jan. 28, 1804, in Huntington, Ct.; a shoemaker; son of
Sherman and Rebecca (Clark) Edwards, of Roxbury, Ct. They
dwelt in Roxbury, Ct., for a few years, then moved to Watertown, Ct., where they died; she d. Aug. 10, 1857; he d. Nov. 12,
1867. They were buried in Watertown, Ct.

(1) Elvira Maria Edwards, b. Apr. 20, 1828, at Roxbury, Ct.; a builder; m. at Watertown, Ct., Jan. 10, 1848, William Brace Judd, b. May 28, 1820, at Bethlehem, Ct., son of Ezra Hubbard and Lucy (Green) Judd, of. Bethlehem, Ct. · They settled at New Haven, Ct. She d. July 4, 1896; he d. July 1, 1897. Ch.: (a) William Brace Judd, b. at New Haven, Ct., Nov. 8, 1848; d. there Nov. 9, 1861, and was buried there. (b) Sarah Elizabeth Judd, b. at New Haven, Ct., Sept. 1, 1850; d. July 18, 1880; m. Dec. 2, 1873, at New Haven Ct., Charles Pearson Fountain, proprietor of dyeworks, son of Henry and Ruth Johnson (Rich) Fountain, of Middletown, Ct., where he was b. Dec. 2, 1852. Res., Middletown, Ct. Ch.: (i) Louise Judd, b. Sept. 22, 1874. (c) Charles Edwards Judd, b. at New Haven, Ct., Apr. 15, 1853; was living at Centreville, Col., in Aug., 1875, unm. (d) Ella Maria Judd, b. at New Haven, Ct., Apr. 13, 1861; d. Mar. 3, 1864, at New Haven, Ct., and was buried there. (e) George Edwards, b. Dec. 1, 1857. (f) Elvira Maria Judd, b. at New Haven, Ct., Oct. 3, 1862; d. Oct. 8, 1862, at New Haven, and was buried there. ((g) Nellie Maria Judd, b. at New Haven, Ct., Mar. 29, 1866; d. Apr. 4, 1866, at New Haven, Ct., and was buried there. (h) Henry Green Judd; d. at New Haven, Ct., July. 31, 1869. (i)William Brace Judd, b. at New Haven, Ct., Nov. 1, 1871.

(2) Elizabeth Amelia Edwards, b. May 5, 1830, at Watertown, Ct.; d. Oct. 25, 1857, at New Haven, Ct., and was buried at Watertown.

(3) Samuel Sherman Edwards, b. July 15, 1834, (he says 1835) at Watertown, Ct., a photographer; m. at Northwood, Iowa, July 2, 1871, Bertha Maria Lunde, dau. of ———, Aadal's Ministry, near Christiana, Norway, where she was b. Sept. 5, 1849. He dwelt from 1855 to 1858 in New Haven, Ct.; travelled in Ct., Mass., N. Y., and Iowa till Jan., 1864, when he reached Minn., and soon settled in Albert Lea, Minn., where they were living in Sept., 1875. Ch.: (a) Mary Elvira Edwards, b. Apr. 2, 1872; m. June 20, 1894; d. Feb. 24, 1901. (b) Charles Goodwin Edwards, b. Feb. 4, 1878. (c) Russell Sherman Edwards, b. Apr. 2, 1886.

(4) Sarah Rebecca Edwards, b. July 29, 1836, at Watertown, Ct.; d. Mar. 7, 1850, at Watertown, and was buried there.

(5) Catherine Cornelia Edwards, b. June 8, 1841, at Watertown, Ct.; m. at Watertown, Apr. 8, 1863, William Henry Lewis, a clergyman of the Episcopal Ch., son of William Henry and Emeline Julia (Bartow) Lewis, of Watertown. He was b. at Brooklyn, N. Y., Aug. 4, 1842. After living at Watertown and Winsted, Ct., South Orange, N. J., Philadelphia, Pa., and Brooklyn, N. Y., they were living at Woodbury, N. J., in Sept., 1875. He enlisted as a private, and was mustered July 28, 1862, as First Lieutenant in Co. D, 19th Regt. Ct. Vol. Infantry, afterward the 2nd Regt. Heavy Artillery; promoted Captain Nov. 20, 1863; wounded in second battle of Winchester, Va., Sept. 19, 1864, and discharged Jan. 25, 1865. He graduated at Trinity

College, Hartford, Ct. Ch.: (a) Robert Edward Lewis, b. Nov. 27, 1864, in Watertown, Ct.; m. Maud Wyman Mallory, Nov. 23, 1899, in Bridgeport. (b) Edward Gordon Lewis, b. Mar. 4, 1869, in Winsted, Ct.; m. Mabel Wellington, of England, in Baltimore. (c) William Barton Lewis, b. in South Orange, 1871; d. Nov. 1, 1871, in South Orange. (d) John Williams Lewis, b. Oct. 31, 1872, in South Orange. (e) Charles Hopkins Lewis, b. Feb. 24, 1878, in Woodbury, N. J.; d. July 2, 1878, in Philadelphia. (f) George Barton Lewis, b. June 29, 1881, in Philadelphia.

(6) Charles Goodwin Edwards, b. July 25, 1844, at Watertown, Ct.; a photographer; was m. at Rushford, Minn., by Rev. W. W. Snell, Congregational, June 14, 1866, to Martha Ann Blanchfield, dau. of Edward and Mary Ann (Bigley) Blanchfield, of Rushford, formerly of Claremont, N. H., where she was b. May 3, 1850. They settled in Rushford; m. 2nd, Elsie Georgiana Wetherell, July 26, 1876; b. Aug. 18, 1849, Pomfret, Ct. Ch.: (a) Truman Ward Edwards, b. July 10, 1867, Rushford, Minn. Was m. Apr. 25, 1894, at Albert Lea., Minn., to Joe Greene, b. May 31, 1873. Ch.: (i) Truman Ward Edwards, Jr., b. June 29, 1895, St. James, Minn. (ii) Pauline Edwards, b. May 21, 1897, St. James, Minn. (b) Ella Pearl Edwards, b. at Rushford, Minn., Aug. 21, 1870; d. at Rushford, Mar. 29, 1871, and was buried in Rushford Cemetery. (c) George Clark Edwards, b. Dec. 19, 1873; m. Aug. 22, 1904, Julia Kate Lauer, b. Sept. 26, 1881, Denver, Ia. Ch.: (i) Jay Phillips Edwards, b. May 14, 1905, Albert Lea, Minn. (ii) George Clark Edwards, Jr., b. May 15, 1905, Albert Lea, Minn. (twins).

(7) George Clark Edwards, b. June 29, 1846, at Watertown, Ct.; m. Adelia Holmes, of Waterbury, Ct., b. May 6, 1848. Res., Bridgeport, Ct. Ch.: (a) George Holmes Edwards, b. Feb. 26, 1881.

(8) Mary Foote Edwards, b. June 6, 1848, at Watertown, Ct.; d. Aug. 9, 1855, at Watertown, and was buried there.

(9) Truman Foote Edwards, b. Mar. 20, 1853, at Watertown, Ct.; d. Jan. 13, 1873, at Philadelphia, Pa., and was buried at Watertown.

1229. iv.   TRUMAN SHERMAN FOOTE, twin, b. July 21, 1807; m. Mary Dana, 2542½-3.

1230. v.   OLIVE ELIZA FOOTE, b. Nov. 30, 1809, at Woodbury, Ct.; m. Mar. 4, 1829, Ashbel Mix, at Bethany, Ct., a farmer, son of Ashbel and Hannah (Byington) Mix, of Bristol, Ct., where he was b. May 11, 1801. They settled May 18, 1829, at Bristol, Ct., where he d. Mar. 26, 1851, and was buried there, and in Oct., 1874, was removed to Evergreen Cemetery, New Haven, Ct. She removed May 11, 1865, to New Haven, and d. there 1895.

(1) Sarah Jane Mix, b. Feb. 20, 1830, at Bristol, Conn.; d. Sept. 27, 1831, at Bristol, and was buried there, but was moved in Oct. 1874, to Evergreen Cemetery, New Haven, Ct.

(2) Martha Eliza Mix, b. Jan. 4, 1832, at Bristol, Ct.; m. at Bristol, Hiram Harrison Fenn, a merchant, of Jersey City, N. J., who was b. in Plymouth, Ct. They were living at No. 9, Orange

Street, New Haven, Ct., in Aug., 1875; members of the Cong. Ch. Ch.: (a) Lyman Mix Fenn, b. at Jersey City, N. J., Aug. 27, 1852, and was living at No. 109 Orange Street, New Haven, Ct., in Sept., 1875; employed on railroad.

(3) Mary Louisa Mix, b. Nov. 21, 1833, at Bristol, Ct.; was living with her mother at No. 109 Orange Street, New Haven, Ct., in Aug., 1875; unm.; a member of the Cong. Ch.

(4) Olive Amelia Mix, b. at Bristol Aug. 26, 1835; m. at Bristol, Ct., Apr. 22, 1858, Herrick Payne Frost, a merchant, son of Sylvester and Philinda (Tuttle) Frost, of Southington, Ct., where he was b. Jan. 12, 1835. They were living at No. 235 Orange Street, New Haven, Ct., in Aug., 1875; a merchant; members of the Baptist Ch. He was an Alderman of the city. He was the founder of the first Telephone Exchange in the world. He also established all the telephones in the State. He established the electric light in New Haven, Ct., and Boston, Mass.; the steam heat in New Haven, Ct. At the time of his death in 1888 he was a director in 34 Telephone and Electric Light Companies throughout the United States. Ch.: (a) Louie Hyatt Frost, b. New Haven, Ct., Sept. 2, 1860; m. 1894, Clara Drake, a direct descendant of Sir Francis Drake. Res., New Haven, Ct. (b) Helen Louise Frost, b. New Haven, June 28, 1866; d. Sept. 29, 1871; buried in Evergreen Cemetery, New Haven, Ct. (c) Pauline Amelia Frost, b. New Haven, Nov. 7, 1867; m. Oct. 23, 1889, Archbald Ward, son of Rollin and Alvira (Barnes) Ives; he was b, Bristol Ct., July 26, 1864; res., West Roxbury, Mass. Ch.: (i) Paul Frost Ives, b. Aug. 12, 1893. (ii) Olive, b. July 5, 1896. (d) Dwight S. M. Frost, b. 1879; m. 1906, Helena Marsh Hills.

(5) Emerette Ann Mix, b. June 9, 1837, at Brstol, Ct.; m. at Bristol, Jan. 18, 1855, Walter Lewis, a clock maker, son of Sheldon and Lucinda (Hills) Lewis, of Bristol, where he was b. Nov. 13, 1833. They were living at No. 462 Howard Ave., New Haven, Ct., in Aug., 1875; members of the Congregational Church. Ch.: (a) George Sheldon Lewis, b. at Bristol, Ct., July 4, 1857; d. unm. (b) Arthur Brainerd Lewis, b. at Bristol, Ct., Aug. 28, 1861; m. Ch.: Geo. Sherman; unm. (c) Elsie May Lewis, b. at Bristol, Ct., May 8, 1865; d. (d) Minnie Lewis, b. at No. 462 Howard Ave., New Haven, Ct., Apr., 1875.

(6) Ashbel Mix, b. at Bristol, Ct., Nov. 12, 1842; unm.; d. at No. 109 Orange Street, New Haven, Ct., Sept. 19, 1871, and was buried in Evergreen Cemetery.

(7) Jennie Foote Mix, b. at Bristol, Ct., Oct. 20, 1848; m. Oct. 27, 1868, Truman Sherman Foote.

1231. vi. JANE ABIGAIL FOOTE, b. May 23, 1813, at Woodbury, Ct.; m. Jeremiah Tryon, at Bethlehem, Ct., she d. in Albany, N. Y., Jan. 30, 1846, and was buried in one of the State Street Cemeteries, ''where is now the Park.'' He m. a second time, and was living at Tryonville, Pa., in Aug., 1875, a Deacon, ae. 82 years. Jeremiah Tryon, of Tryonville, Crawford Co., Pa., is represented as a son, but may possibly be the husband. T. H. Tryon, her son, Hydetown, Crawford Co., Pa.

1232. vii. MARGARET FOOTE, b. Dec. 7, 1819, at Woodbury, Ct., m. Mar. 25, 1840, at Bristol, Ct., Frederick Allen, b. at Bethlehem, Ct., son of Amos and Sarah (Gilbert) Allen, of Bethlehem. They dwelt in Bethlehem nine years; in Watertown, Ct., one year; in Bristol, Ct., 22 years; then moved to New Haven, Ct., and were living there in Sept., 1875. He was then a City Missionary. Ch.: (a) Sophia Eliza Allen, b. at Bethlehem, Ct., June 19, 1841; m. Jan. 30, 1861, at Bristol, Ct., William Robinson, of Collinsville, Ct.; she d. at Collinsville, Apr. 22, 1864, and was buried at Bristol. (b) Elvira Maria Allen, b. at Bethlehem, Ct., Dec. 24, 1843; d. at Bethlehem, Jan. 6, 1846, and was buried at Bristol, Ct. (c) Margaret Sarah Allen, b. at Bethlehem, Ct., Feb. 7, 1847; d. Feb. 16, 1852, at Bristol, Ct., and was buried there. (d) Mary Foote Allen b. at Watertown, Ct., Apr. 20, 1849; m. May 14, 1874, in New Haven, Ct., Frederick Peabody Hardy, son of Isaac and Phinett (Kimball) Hardy. (e) Frederick Alonzo Allen, b. at Bristol, Ct., Jan. 24, 1856.

1232¹. viii. ROSETTA FOOTE, b. at Woodbury, Ct.; d. Sept. 15, 18—; ae. 7 years.

422. JOHN BURGOYNE, (128, 38, 11, 3,) b. 1778; m. Sally, dau. of George Norton, of Roxbury, Ct. He was a blacksmith; d. in Woodbury, Ct.; buried in Lower Cemetery; she was b. 1777; d. Jan. 30, 1836; he d. Apr. 20, 1836.

1232¹. i. STARR, b. in Woodbury, Ct.; a blacksmith; m. ——; d. in Albany, N. Y.; left a dau. in New York, N. Y.

1233. ii. HORACE, b. ——; m. Sarah French, 2544·

1233¹. iii. FANNY, b. ——; m. Horace Cheneray, of Roxbury, Ct., a blacksmith, who d. 5 months after m. She m. 2nd, Harvey Perkins; res., Chicago, Ill. Ch.: (1) Fanny; res., Chicago, Ill., and one son who d.; two daus.

1232². iv. SUSAN, b. Nov. 18, 1805; m. 1st, June 1, 1827, Birow Doolittle, a wagon maker, son of Benjamin Doolittle, of Wallingford, Ct. He was b. abt. 1803. She lived with him two years and left him; m. 2nd, Feb., 1836, Abner Harris Monroe, a farmer, son of Ebenezer and Sarah (Throp) Monroe, of Roxbury, Ct. He was b. Feb. 16, 1810, in Southbury, Ct. Res., Woodbury, Ct. Ch.: (1) Elizabeth, b. in Woodbury, Feb. 15, 1828; m. (2) Charles, b. in Woodbury, Mar., 1830, a blacksmith. (3) Sarah, b. at Roxbury, Ct., June 12, 1837; m. William Thorp, of Southington; res., Hamburgh, Iowa. (4) Chauncy, b. Woodbury, Ct., Feb. 1, 1840; a farmer; res., Woodbridge, Ct.

1233³. v. JOHN, b. Woodbury, Ct.; m. and d. in Chicago, Ill. Ch.: 3 sons. Res. unknown.

1234. vi. GEORGE, b. ——; m. twice; res., New Canaan, Ct.; a shoe maker.

1234¹. vii. CHAUNCY (twin), b. Woodbury, Ct.; m. 2545.

1234². viii. NANCY (twin), b. in Woodbury, Ct.; m. Andrew Bartis, a blacksmith, of New Canaan, Ct. She d. abt. 1856. Ch.: 1 son, b. 1856.

1235. ix. JENETTE, b. Woodbury, Ct.; m. Edward Booday, a hatter, of Woodbury, Ct. She d. June 12, 1873, in Brooklyn, N. Y. Ch.: 11.

1236. x. MARIA, b. Woodbury, Ct.; m. David Hoyt, of New Canaan, Ct. Ch.: (1) Frank, b. ———; d. in war of 1861. (2) Dau., b. ———; d. ae. 7 yrs. (3) Charles, b. ———; m. Ch.: 1. Res., Missouri.

1237 xi. DAVID PETER, b Woodbury, Ct.; a blacksmith; m.

432. LIEUT. DAVID FOOTE, (130, 39, 11, 3,) b. ———; m. Esther Averill, of New Preston, Ct. She d. Mar. 1, 1825, in Peru, Mass. He was a Lieutenant in the Army of the Revolution, and was in the battles of Stillwater, N. Y., and Danbury, Ct. Res., Washington, Ct., and Peru, Mass.

1238. i. ESTHER, b. 1770; d. in Peru, Mass.

1239. ii. DORATHY, b. 1772; m. Nathan Miner; d. 1802.

1240. iii. DAVID, b. Mar. 13, 1775; m. Betsy Minor, Eliza Gardner and Rhoda Waterbury, 2546-55.

1241. iv. LEMAN, b. June, 1776; m. Ruah Scofield, 2556-67.

1242. v. CHARLOTTE, b. July 1, 1779; m. Lemuel, son of Captain William and Judith (Mason) Frissell, of Peru, Mass., Apr. 16, 1806; d. in Peru, Mass., Oct. 8, 1859, ae. 78 (?). Mr. Frissell was a prominent resident of Peru and represented that town in the Legislature in 1844. He d. in Peru, Aug. 1, 1863, ae. 83. Ch.:

(1) Esther, b. in Peru, Mass., Sept. 8, 1807; m. in Abington, Feb. 25, 1873, Benjamin, son of Benjamin and Catherine Norton, of Abington, Mass., Oct. 30, 1844. Mr. Norton was b. in Abington in 1796; he d. in Abington in 1873. Ch.: (a) Benjamin Francis, b. in Abington, Mass., Sept. 4, 1848; m. Ella C. Morton, July 17, 1872. Mrs. Norton was b. in Halifax, Mass., June 19, 1851; res., Springfield, Mass.

(2) Charlotte, b. in Peru, Mass., Oct. 10, 1811; d. in Hinsdale, Mass., July 3, 1863; m. Edward Taylor Nash, of Hinsdale, Mass., Aug. 25, 1837. Mr. Nash was the son of Rev. Jonathan Nash, of Middlefield, Mass., and was b. in Middlefield, May 11, 1802. He removed from Peru to Hinsdale in 1842, and during many years served as deacon in the Hinsdale Congregational Church. He was twice m. He d. in Hinsdale, Mass., Apr. 21, 1859. Ch.: (a) Betsey, b. in Peru, Mass., July 12, 1838; d. in Hinsdale, Mass., Sept. 26, 1848, ae. 10 yrs. (b) Caroline Nash, b. in Peru, Mass., Feb. 22, 1841; m. Lemuel Hastings, son of Abel and Philena (Hastings) Kimball, of Madison, Ohio, Oct. 18, 1866; res., Madison. Mr. Kimball was b. in Madison, Jan. 20, 1833, and has always taken a prominent and active part in all town and church affairs. He has been for 35 years President of The Exchange Bank of Madison. Ch., all b. in Madison, O., and live there now: (i) Homer Nash, b. Oct. 11, 1867; d. in Madison, Aug. 31, 1904; unm. He was b. on the farm near Madison, O., where his parents and grand-parents had lived since 1812. The Kimball family is one of the oldest in the · Western Reserve, coming west when the country was only sparely settled and living on the same farm continuously. They came from New Hampshire, and the whole family, fathers and mothers, are of New England birth and training, and those of every branch have descended from Revolutionary stock. He was educated in the public school and high school of Madison, and graduated from

Oberlin College in 1890. In 1892 he was chosen superintendent of the village schools at Madison, where his excellent management and scholastic attainments have contributed much to make them the best in that part of the State. Mr. Kimball served since 1891 continuously as Clerk, Councilman and Mayor of Madison, and also for a term of eight years on the County Board of School Examiners for Lake County. He was a Republican in politics. His father and grandfather were among the staunch adherents of that faith in a section that has always been known as the Gibraltar of Republicanism in Ohio. Being busily engaged in his duties as teacher and superintendent, Mr. Kimball had but little time to work in politics, but at the urgent request of his home people he accepted the nomination for Representative in 1901. He was elected in the fall of that year by a very large majority, and re-elected in 1903. While a member of the Seventy-fifth and Seventy-sixth General Assemblies, Mr. Kimball had an active part in the codification of the municipal and school laws of the State. He had been engaged in several business enterprises, had served on the Board of Directors of two banks, and was one of the owners of the Madison "Review," a weekly paper of quality published in Madison. (ii) Abel, b. Dec. 19, 1869. (iii) Leila Helen, b. Mar. 16, 1873. (iv) Carl Russell, b. July 3, 1876; m. Ethel Felice Sutton, dau. of Warner P. Sutton; was b. under the United States flag at Matamoras, Mexico, Dec. 9, 1880, while her father was stationed there as U. S. Consul, July 30, 1903. Ch.: Warren Hastings, b. June 24, 1904. (v) Elizabeth Seaton, b. Jan. 11, 1880. (c) Homer, b. Feb. 22, 1841.

(3) Sarah Frissell, b. in Peru, Feb. 22, 1814; m. John Milton, son of Colonel David and Esther (Ross) Tuttle, of Peru, May 23, 1836. Mr. Tuttle was b. in Peru, Dec. 10, 1812. Their res. was Hinsdale, Mass., and he represented that town in the Legislature in 1855. He held the various town offices, and during a term of years occupied a position under the Government as Assessor of Internal Revenue. He d. in Hinsdale, Mass., July 14, 1871, ae. 58. Colonel David Tuttle, a descendant of William and Elizabeth Tuttle, who emigrated to New England in the ship "Planter" in 1635, was b. in 1783, and d. in Peru, Mass., Apr. 1, 1838, ae. 55. He was twice m. His first wife was Esther, dau. of Amasa and Sarah Ross, of Peru. They were married Apr. 15, 1810, and had two sons and one dau. Mrs. Esther Tuttle d. in Peru, Mass., Nov. 17, 1815, ae. 29. Mr. Tuttle was a prominent and energetic business man of that period. He held the various town offices, taught the district school, and during a long term of years controlled the stage route which conveyed the United States Mails (and also travellers) through that section of the country before the construction of the Boston and Albany Railroad. In 1812, or thereabout, he was engaged in a commercial business with a firm in Rochester, N. Y. (Tuttle & Thompson), transporting the goods (previously consigned to him from Boston) by team to that then distant point. Mr. Tuttle represented

the town of Peru in the Legislature during the sessions of 1828, 1829, and 1830. He served in the Militia of the Commonwealth of Massachusetts from 1823 to 1830. Ch.: (a) An infant son, b. in Peru, Mass., Mar. 6, 1838; d. in Peru, Mar. 9, 1838. (b) David Milton, b. in Peru, Mass., Aug. 27, 1839; d. in Peru, Sept. 10, 1840, ae. 1 yr. (c) Mari, b. in Peru, Mass., Aug. 22, 1841; m. Otis Sprague Taylor, son of Otis and Pamelia (Clapp) Taylor, of Chester, Mass., Oct. 22, 1867. Mr. Taylor was b. in Chester, June 4, 1829; res., Springfield, Mass. (d) Helen, b. in Hinsdale, Mass., Aug. 27, 1845; m. Lyman Mack Payne, son of Lyman and Emily (Emmons) Payne, of Hinsdale, Oct. 22, 1872; res., Hinsdale. Mr. Payne was b. in Brighton, N. Y., Feb. 4, 1847, and during a period of years was connected with the New England Mutual Life Insurance Company of Boston, Mass. He d. in Boston, Feb. 5, 1906, and was buried in Hinsdale, Mass. (e) Charlotte Elizabeth, b. in Hinsdale, Mass., Dec. 6, 1847; res. in Hinsdale until 1891. At that date removed to Boston, Mass., and occupies a position in the State House at Boston. (f) Merritt Hoffman Tuttle, b. Sept. 13, 1854; m. Effie D. Bogert, dau. of Samuel J. and Louise M. (Seeber) Bogert of Iowa, Sept. 13, 1887. Mrs. Tuttle was b. in Fayette, Iowa, June 6, 1860; res., DeVoe, Faulk County, Dakota, until 1890; res., Springfield, Mass. Ch.: (i) Sarah Louise, b. in DeVoe, Faulk County, Dakota, July 10, 1888; res., Springfield, Mass. (ii) Elizabeth Mari, b. in Springfield, Mass., July 21, 1894.

(4) Franklin Frissell, b. Sept. 2, 1816; m. Martha Emeline Cady, dau. of Abial Cady, of Hinsdale, Mass. Mrs. Frissell was b. in 1818, and d. May 24, 1857. He d. at Peru, Mass., Oct. 27, 1862. Ch.: (a) Sarah Eliza, b. in Peru, Mass., Oct. 1, 1845; m. Charles H. Phelps, of Newburg, N. Y., Aug. 12, 1873; Mrs. Phelps d. Jan. 26, 1875. Ch., b. in Baltimore, Md.: (i) William A., b. Oct. 21, 1874; m. Lena W. ——, June 6, 1903; res., Newburg, N. Y. (b) Charles Melancthon Frissell, b. May 30, 1847; m. Margaret Elizabeth Poulton, Oct. 20, 1875; Mrs. Frissell was b. Mar. 20, 1853; res., Baltimore, Md. Ch.: (i) Clarence R., b. July 19, 1877; d. in Baltimore, Md., Nov. 10, 1900; unm. (ii) Martha Almira, b. Nov. 11, 1878; m. Harvey Merryman, of Baltimore, Oct. 14, 1903. (iii) Charles Melancthon, Jr., b. Dec. 23, 1880; d. in Baltimore, Jan. 7, 1884. (iv) Laura Edna, b. Feb. 26, 1883; res., Baltimore. (v) Mary Elizabeth, b. Apr. 24, 1886; m. Charles Hollingsworth Spencer, of Baltimore, June 7, 1905; res., Baltimore. (vi) Grace Evelyn, b. July 1, 1889. (vii) Carroll Mason, b. Nov. 15, 1892. (c) Mary Elizabeth, b. Oct. 15, 1849; res., Baltimore, Md. (d) George Lemuel, b. Jan. 27, 1852; m. Louisa Noris, Nov. 24, 1875. Mrs. Frissell was b. Sept. 1, 1851. Mr. Frissell d. in Baltimore, Md., June 8, 1900. Ch., all b. in Baltimore, Md., and live there now: (i) Maud Estelle, b. Sept. 1, 1876. (ii) George Franklin, b. Sept. 26, 1879. (iii) Sara Elizabeth, b. Sept. 17, 1882.

1243. vi.   CHARLES, b. July 1, 1779; d. 1810, in Litchfield, Ct.
1244. vii. DANIEL A., b. May 12, 1783; m. Mary D. Prior, 2568-74.

1245. viii. LUCY ANN, b. 1784; m. Increase Ross; lived in Cambridgeport, Crawford Co., Pa. Ch., all b. in Peru, Mass.: (1) Charles,
unm. (2) John, m. (3) Bartlett; m. Harriet ———; res.,
Meadville and Cambridgeport, Pa. Ch.: (a) Dixie; res., British
Columbia. (b) Mowbray; res., Brooklyn, N. Y. (c) Grace; res.,
Cambridgeport; m. and had 2 ch. (twins); d. soon after the birth
of her ch., and they were taken into the family of Bartlett Ross.

433. ISAAC FOOTE, (130, 39, 11, 3,) b. Jan. 4, 1741; m. Anna Hurlburt, of
Washington, Ct. She was b. May 3, 1745; d. Nov. 9, 1815, in Charlotte, Vt. He
d. 1826 in Charlotte, Vt. Res., Washington, Ct., and Charlotte, Vt.
    1246. i.   ISAAC SALMON, b. Jan. 11, 1768; m. Esther Parker, 2575-80.
    1247. ii.   GIDEON, b. Mar. 22, 1770; m Susannah Parker, Abigail Parker
and Nancy McCune, 2581-8.
    1248. iii. SIMEON, b. Mar. 12, 1772; m. Phoebe Beach, 2589-95.
    1249. iv.   CALEB M., b. Sept. 24, 1779; m. Clarinda Newell, 2596-2600¾.
    1250. v.   NEWELL, b. Sept. 29, 1784; m. Clarissa Hill and Mary Goulden,
2601-2.
    1251. vi.   ORSON, b. Oct. 14, 1786; d. Feb. 20, 1804.
    1252. vii. JOHNSON, b. Dec. 19, 1787; m. ——— and Belsie Reed, 2603-4.

434. AARON FOOTE, (130, 39, 11, 3,) b. ———; m. Dec. 28, 1780, Content,
wid. of Ashel Hurd, of Washington, Ct. Res., Washington and Middlebury, Ct.
    1253. i.   SALLY, b. Oct. 1, 1781; m. 1808, James Ford; he d. She res.
Hudson, N. Y. Ch.: (1) Emily L., b. May 5, 1809; m. Apr. 29,
1831, Richard Gage, of Hudson, N. Y. (2) Juliette, b. July 22,
1812; m. Apr. 23, 1836, Henry Green. (3) Jane Ann, b. Nov. 22,
1813; m. Apr. 7, 1835, George Hitchcock. (4) George W., b. Apr.
9, 1816; m. Dec. 9, 1847, Ann Van Duesen. (5) William H., b.
Sept. 19, 1821. (6) James A., b. Oct. 29, 1824.
    1254. ii.   POLLY, b. ———; m. Oct., 1808, Benjamin Allen, of Berlin, Ct.
She d. July 10, 1821.
    1255. iii. EPHELIA, b. July 3, 1787; m. Sept. 8, 1811, Ephraim Fairchild.
Ch.: (1) Jane J., b. Jan. 15, 1818.
    1256. iv.   CHARLOTTE, b. ———; m. Henry L. Goodsell; p. s.
    1257. v.   RODERICK R., b. ———; m. Olivia Hurlburt, 2605.
    1258. vi.   BARNUM, b. ———.

443. ELIJAH FOOTE, (131, 39, 11, 3,) b. abt. 1740; m. ———; he d. Oct.
15, 1813; res., Newtown, Ct., and Virginia.
    1259. i.   JOHN, b. ———.
    1260. ii.   JOSEPH, b. ———.
    1261. iii. ANDREW, b. ———.
    1262. iv.   AMOS, b. Feb. 14, 1776; m. Mary Curtiss and Abby ———,
2606-14.
    1263. v.   ANER, b. ———.
    1264. vi.   PHEBE, b. ———.
    1265. vii. EUNICE, b. ———.

447. JAMES FOOTE, (134, 39, 11, 3,) b. June 20, 1747; m. Apr. 25, 1774,
Adah Stillson, of Newton. He d. Feb. 28, 1831. She b. 1754; d. Aug. 9, 1834, ae.
80.
    1266. i.   HANNAH H., b. Oct. 31, 1774; d. Aug. 15, 1800.
    1267. ii.   RHESA, b. Apr. 1, 1776; d. Sept. 5, 1777.

1268. iii. RUTH, b. Dec. 11, 1777; d. July 11, 1824.

1269. iv. LAMYRA, b. Oct. 13, 1779; d. Jan. 7, 1817.

1270. v. RHESA, b. July 5, 1781; m. Polly Hawley, 2615-25.

1271. vi. DAVID STILLSON, b. Mar. 20, 1783; d. Apr. 1, 1847.

1272. vii. VINE, b. Oct. 10, 1785.

1273. viii. HEBER, b. Dec. 5, 1787; m. Lucy Stillson, 2626-33.

1274. ix. MILTON, b. Sept. 15, 1789; m. Lois Briscoe, 2634-43.

1275. x. ANNA, b. Aug. 31, 1791; d. Jan. 31, 1824.

1276. xi. AURELIA, b. July 7, 1793.

1277. xii. ARSINOE, b. Jan. 7, 1796; d. Feb. 16, 1873.

1278. xiii. ABBA, b. Mar. 7, 1798; d. Apr. 28, 1830.

1278¹. xiv. JAMES, b. June 29, 1801; d. Nov. 17, 1854.

453. WILLIAM FOOTE, (134, 39, 11, 3,) b. Jan 5, 1758; m.

1279. i. WILLIAM, b. 1780; m., 2644-5.

459. DANIEL FOOTE, (137, 39, 11, 3, 1,) b. Nov. 26, 1749; m. Nov. 17, 1771, Abigail, dau. of Benajah Hurd, of Stratford, Ct. He d. Nov. 30, 1831, in Woodbury; she d. Mar. 11, 1842, ae. 82 years.

1280. i. EBENEZER, b. July 9, 1774; m. Mabel Banks, 2646-51.

1281. ii. BENAJAH ELLIS, b. Apr. 18, 1777; m. Mary E. Wooden, 2652-61.

1282. iii. ABIAH C., b. June 7, 1779; m. John Platt, of West Haven, Ct.

1283. iv. ELIAS B., b. Nov. 10, 1788; m. Catharine Peck (No. 334, Peck Gen.), of Bristol, Ct., b. Oct. 12, 1788; d. Dec. 16, 1856.

1284. v. POLLY, b. Sept. 26, 1785; m. Oct. 5, 1800, Daniel, son of Theophilus and Dollie (Bidwell) Botsford, b. Aug. 21, 1782. She was b. in Newton, Ct., Sept. 26, 1782, and d. in Otto, N. Y., in 1853, and he d. in Otto in 1876. He was among the last pensioners of the war of 1812. They left their home in Windsor, Ct., in 1824 and came with six children to Otto, N. Y. Ch.: (1) Luzon Marcena, b. June 4, 1802; d. 1869 (?). (2) Lucius Daniel, b. Aug. 14, 1804; d. 1872. (3) Charlotte Abigail, b. June 28, 1807; d. Apr. 4, 1876. (4) Polly Almina, b. June 19, 1809; d. 1880. (5) Urania Ursula, b. Nov. 5, 1813; d. 1843. (6). Marvin Sadocea, b. Aug. 5, 1817; d. Feb. 11, 1899. (7) Wiley Stacey, b. Mar. 3, 1826; d. Nov. 26, 1892.

(1) Luzon, m. Polly Beckwith, of Windsor, Ct. Ch.: (a) Theophilus, had several ch. (i) Daniel Botsford, of Little Valley, N. Y. (ii) Simeon. (b) Luzon. Ch.: (i) Marcena, (ii) Almina. (c) Marian, m. Stephen Herrick, of New Albion; d. in 1879, leaving 5 boys, Edwin, Emory, Marvin, William and Glenn. Of these only the following are alive: Marvin Herrick, of Kennedy, N. Y.; William Herrick, of Cattaraugus, N. Y.; and Glenn Herrick, b. in 1872, Professor of Botany and Zoology in the Agricultural College of Miss. Glenn graduated at Cornell and studied for a second degree at Harvard. He has two sons, Marvin and Stephen. (d) Clarissa Ann, m. David Whipple; she is a widow and lives at Little Valley, N. Y. She has 4 ch., Morgan, Emmeline, Frederick and Alida. Emmeline is dead, but the others are m. and live in Little Valley, N. Y.

(2) Lucius Daniel Botsford m. Mary Norton, of Union, Ct. He came to N. Y. with his father, and d. in Cattaraugus two years before his wife d.; p. s.

(3) Charlotte Abigail Botsford, b. Jan. 28, 1867; d. Apr. 4, 1876; m. Walter Willits, of Union Springs, N. Y. They removed to Delhi, Mich., where both d. Ch.:(a)Edwin Willits, b. Apr. 24, 1830; d. 1896; graduated at Ann Arbor, and was for years a Member of Congress. Later he was President of Michigan Agricultural College; later he was Assistant Secretary of Agriculture of U. S. Department of Agriculture. He had one son, George, a corporation lawyer of high standing in Chicago, and who d. in 1899 in Porto Rico. George left one ch., Ruth.   (b) Elizabeth Willits, m. Rev. Crooks, a Wesleyan Methodist preacher and editor, and d. childless. (c) Adeline Willits, m. William Wing, of Elgin, Ill. She has two ch., both living: Kate Sprawls, of Los Angeles, Cal., and Edwin Wing, of Elgin, Ill. (d) Helen Willits, m. Dorr B. Chaffee, of Egin, Ill., and now res. in Garden Grove, Cal., and has no living ch. (e) Eugene Willits lives in Detroit, Mich. He has two ch., Charles and Charlotte, both unm.

(4) Polly Almina Botsford m. for her first husband Stacy Smith, a Methodist preacher in Cattaraugus Co., N. Y. Ch.: (a) Fidelia Smith, m. John Hillabrant, of Elmira, N. Y. She d., leaving one child living, Mrs. Arthur Pratt, of Elmira, New York. (b) Finetta, m. Augustus Cochrane, of Springville, N. Y. She d., leaving ch. as follows: Stacy, lawyer and editor in Brookings, S. D. Stacy m. Miss Floy Little, of Gowanda, N. Y. They have one child, Sarah. Edwarl Cochrane, of Ipswich, S. D., Mina, Marvin and Orson Cochrane. All are m. and living in S. D. (c) Lovisa Smith, m. Larman Foote, her second cousin, and they died leaving two dau., who have since died; p. s. For her second husband Polly Almina Botsford m. Daniel Ball. (d) George Ball. (e) Lucius Ball, m. Sylviette Ballard, of Otto, N. Y. Three ch., all m. (f) Henry Ball has two daus., both m. The youngest, Anna, is the wife of her second cousin, Wiley Botsford Sherman, and they have several daus.

(5) Urania Ursula Botsford m. Harvey Little, of Otto, N. Y. Ch.: (a) Catherine, m. Ezera Eames, of Pigeon Cove, Mass., and d. without issue. (b) Eliza Little, m. Edward McCutcheon, of Gowanda, N. Y. Ch.:(i)Mrs. Bertha Bard, of Gowanda, N. Y., wife of Frank Bard. They have one dau., Catherine. (ii) Dr. Guy L. McCutcheon, 45 Harvard Place, Buffalo, N. Y.

(6) Marvin Sedocea Botsford m. Phebe King (nee Irish), of Collins, N. Y. Ch.: Anna Botsford Comstock, b. Sept. 1, 1854; m. 1878 to Professor John Henry Comstock of Cornell University. She has no ch.

(7) Wiley Stacey Botsford m. Eliza Ballard, of Otto, N. Y. Ch.: (a) Urania, m. George Sherman, of Otto, N. Y., and they have 3 ch.: Lilly, wife of Adrian Root, of Otto, N. Y., who has one son, Artie; Lizzie, who married her second cousin, Simeon Botsford (see Theophilus), and who has four ch., two boys and

two girls; Wiley Sherman, the youngest, m. his second cousin, Anna Ball. (b) Lenora Botsford, m. Walter Taft, of Otto, N. Y. They have one son, Dr. Raymond Taft, b. 1880, of Cattaraugas, N. Y., who m. Madge Holbrook, of Otto, N. Y. They have one dau., Marguerite.

1285. vi. MELISSA, b. Nov. 10, 1788; m. John Strickland. Ch.: (1) Pamelia Emmitt; m. (2) Abiah Jennette Strickland, b. Feb. 18, 1813, in Watertown, Litchfield Co., Ct. In her early youth she removed with her parents to Cette, N. Y. In 1838 she m. Hon. John P. Darling, who was a man of prominence in Western N. Y. In 1850 he was Postmaster in Otto; in 1851 he was elected Treasurer of Catt Co., which office he held for three years; in 1856 he was elected a member of the State Legislature by a majority of 8,000 from the 32nd District; State Assessor in 1864; and d. June 17, 1882. She d. Feb. 15, 1889. Ch.: (a) ———; m. ———. Straight. Ch.: (i) C. D. Straight, is Editor of the ''Olean Morning Times'' and also County Treasurer. He has two ch., a son, Alan G., aged 20 years, and a dau., Emily, aged 18. The younger son (ii), John P. Straight, is a clerk in Government employ, residing at Washington, D. C. Ch.: (ii1) George Adelbert, b. Jan. 24, 1906. (b) Martha E., b. Apr. 13, 1849; m. May 23, 1871, Matthew Griswold Elliott; res., Cattaraugus, N. Y. (3) Walter Hurd Strickland, b. Feb. 4, 1816; m. July 13, 1843, Stativa, dau. of Hon. Dan and Esther Allen. She d. Dec. 16, 1852. He d. June 21, 1904; m. 2nd, Nov. 5, 1854, Harriet Borden. He taught school for 18 years; graduated Zima, N. Y., about 1836; was School Commissioner for several years; held the usual town offices. Res., Otto, N. Y. Ch.: (a) Laura Ann, b. Nov. 6, 1844, in Otto, N. Y.; m. Nov. 11, 1868, John Amaza Smith; he d. in Silverdale, Cowley Co., Kansas, Oct. 26, 1888. Ch.: (i) James C., b. May 16, 1873; d. June 5, 1875. (ii) Elbert C., b. Mar. 9, 1875; with ''Brooklyn Daily Eagle.'' (iii) Walter, b. Oct. 25, 1877, at Silverdale, Kansas. (iv) Dan A., b. Jan. 23, 1879; d. 1892. (v) Lester R., b. June 14, 1881, at Silverdale, Kansas. (vi) Bernard M., b. Nov. 6, 1883, at Silverdale, Kansas. (vii) Alice M., b. July 31, 1886, at Cattanangacs, N. Y. (b) John Platt, b. June 23, 1846, Otto, N. Y.; m. Oct. 4, 1865, Ellen E. Stebbins; she d. June 10, 1870; m. 2nd, Clara L. Stebbins, May 21, 1877. Ch.: (i) Nellie E., b. June 6, 1870; m. Dr. Hodson, Youngstowe, Ohio. (ii) Stativa Alta, b. Jan. 21, 1880; teaching in Youngstone, Ohio. (iii) Alice M., b. July 24, 1885. (iv) Laura F., b. Dec. 1, 1890. (v) Helen J., b. June 8, 1894. (c) Dan Allen, unm.; d. May 21, 1882. (d) Channing Walter, b. Nov. 5, 1854, in Otto, N. Y.; m. Lutia Scott. Ch.: (i) Burt. (4) Abi Alsina Strickland, b. Sept. 26, 1819; m. Sept. 27, 1840, James Madison Smith. He d. Apr. 30, 1872; she d. Apr. 1, 1906. Ch.: (a) Melissa Lovina Smith, b. Jan. 18, 1842; m. Elbert P. Cook; she d. Dec. 21, 1869; p. s. (b) John Amasa Smith, b. Feb. 6, 1844; m. Nov. 11, 1868, Laura A. Strickland. Ch.: 7 (see No. a above). (c) Alida Cordelia Smith, b. Sept. 1, 1852; m. Jan. 24, 1873, Elbert. He was a banker; was shot in Buenos Ayres, S. A.; m.

2nd, Sept., 1887, H. F. MacKern; he d. in New Mexico. Ch.: 3 by first husband, 2 by second. (5) Samuel B. Strickland, b. ———; m. Maria Ingham. Ch.: (a) G. M. Strickland, b. ———; res., Cattaraugus, N. Y. (6) Martha Ann Strickland, b. at Watertown, Ct., Aug. 21, 1825; m. Sidney Niles DeLapp, at Otto, N. Y., Sept. 21, 1847; she d. at Iola, Kansas, Nov. 12, 1894. He was b. in Vt., Aug. 21, 1825, and d. at Seymore, Mo., Feb. 11, 1898. Mr. De Lapp was the owner of the machine shops at Meadville, Pa., also oil man for years in Oil City, Pa. Ch.: (a) Nellie De Lapp. (b) John Frank De Lapp, b. in Mansfield, N. Y., May 27, 1855. He is a farmer; keeps blooded stock; m. Clara Estella, dau. of Morgan Barber, Linesville, Pa., Dec. 18, 1879. Ch.: (i) Frank Burtney De Lapp, b. at Iola, Kan., July 1, 1886. (c) Alice Minnie De Lapp, b. in Mansfield, N. Y., Sept. 15, 1865; m. Edward A., son of Henry Brightly, of Iola, Kan., Dec. 13, 1888. Ch.: (i) Florence Sarah Brightly, b. at Iola, Kan., Dec. 28, 1889. (ii) Edna Alice Brightly, b. at Iola, Kan., June 20, 1894; d. at Iola, Kan., Nov. 25, 1897. (iii) Lulu Amy Brightly, b. at Birch Tree, Mo., Sept. 24, 1897. (iv) Clara Estella Brightly, b. at Iola, Kan., Aug. 31, 1900. (v) Mable Adeline Brightly, b. at Elsmore, Kan., May 12, 1906. (7) Laurica Maria Strickland, b. Dec. 1, 1827; m. 1859, John Charles Hartwell; she d. Nov. 30, 1905. Ch.: (a) Cornie Hartwell, b. July 17, 1860; teacher in the Normal School at Flagstaff, Arizona. (b) Belle Hartwell, b. Jan. 24, 1864; m. 1886, Burdette J. Elliott; res., 45 Plum St., Detroit, Mich. Ch.: (i) William Farrand Elliott; he was b. 1887.

1286. vii. RANSFORD, b. Nov. 9, 1791; m. ———, in Richmond.

1287. viii. LUZON, b. Apr. 26, 1796; m. ———. Judson, Woodbury, Ct.

460. EDWARD FOOTE, (140, 39, 11, 3,) b. July 1, 1743; m. Oct. 23, 1769, Anna, dau. of Jehosaphat Prindle, of Newtown, Ct. She d. Nov., 1826, ae. 79. He d. Oct. 14, 1835. Res., Newtown.

1288. i. OLIVE, b. Nov. 26, 1770; m. Ira Starr, of Dansbury, Ct.; they moved to Cooperstown, N. Y. She d. 1827. Ch.: (1) Harriet, b. ———; m. ———. Mason, of Wisconsin.

1289. ii. AUSTIN, b. Mar. 14, 1773; d. Sept. 12, 1773.

1290. iii. HULDA, b. July 12, 1774; m. Andrew Johnson; res., Ct. and Wis.

1291. iv. ANNA, b. Dec. 3, 1775; res., Newtown, Ct.

1292. v. LUCINDA, b. Sept. 22, 1777; m. 1804, William Taylor; she d. 1835. Ch.: (1) Charles; graduated at Yale College 1835; went to Mexico with Gen. Taylor's army; no more known. (2) Theodore; res., Wis.

1293. vi. CATHRINE, b. July 18, 1779; d. Oct. 31, 1793.

1294. vii. AUSTIN, b. June 1, 1781; m. ———; d. in New Orleans, leaving a wife and five ch. Res., Demerara, South America, and the State of New York.

1295. viii. EDWARD ALLEN, b. May 12, 1783; m. in Perryville, N. Y. He d. Oct., 1846. Ch.: 1 dau.

1296. ix. ZIBA, b. July 20, 1785; was graduated at Yale College 1805. Soon after he graduated he started for Cincinnati, under the employment of Col. Mansfield, as land surveyor. He d. Apr. 30, 1806, in attempting to swim a pond while surveying.

1297. x. WINTHROP, b. Nov. 30, 1787; res., Bedford, Ind.

1298. xi. NISAN, b. May 9, 1790; m. Miss Smith, of Derby, Ct., and after her death m. again in Philadelphia, where it is supposed he d.

1299. xii. PROSPER ALONZO, b. July 16, 1792; m. Aug. 7, 1813, Clarinda, dau. of Thaddeus Williams, of Bethel, Ct.; moved to Wabash, Apr. 15, 1831, where he d. Sept. 10, 1831. Ch.: 6.

1300. xiii. CATHRINE MARIA, b. Aug. 17, 1794; m. 1812, ———. Baldwin, of Derby, Ct.; moved to "Cave in the Rock," Ill., where he d. 1822. She m. 2nd, 1824, Capt. Abraham Hawkins, of the U. S. Army. He d. 1833; m. 3rd, ———. Story. Ch.: 7.

1301. xiv. CHARLOTTE, b. May 13, 1797; m. ———. Barnum, of Bethel, Ct. Ch.: 6.

462. DANIEL FOOTE, (140, 39, 11, 3,) b. abt. 1748; m. Lucina Byington; he d. 1819; res., Newtown, Ct.

1302. i. ARNOLD, b. ———; m. Anna Parks, 2662.

464. ABEL FOOTE, (140, 39, 11, 3,) b. 1761; m. 1st, 1786, Anna, dau. of Isaac Daw, of Danbury, Ct. She d. 1791; m. 2nd, Jane ———, b. 1768; d. Oct. 8, 1825. He d. Sept. 9, 1826. Res., Newtown, Ct.

1303. i. PHILO, b. Mar. 27, 1787; m. Eunice Lewis, 2663-7.

1304. ii. OLIVE, b. 1789; m. and settled in New Jersey.

1305. iii. ANNA, b. 1791; m. and settled in Pittsburg, Pa.

473. JOSEPH FOOTE, (142, 41, 11, 3,) b. Dec. 6, 1748; m. Aug. 21, 1771, Hepzibah Sherman. He d. Dec. 31, 1800; she d. 1842, ae. 89. Res., Newtown, Ct.

1306. i. ABIAH, b. Feb. 13, 1772; m. Zalmon Storrs, of Newtown, Ct.; she d. Ch.: 1.

1307. ii. CHARITY, b. Mar. 13, 1774; m. Ebenezer Ferry, of Danbury, Ct.

1308. iii. DAVID, b. May 17, 1776; m. Sukey Underhill, 2668-72.

1309. iv. HANNAH, b. Aug. 17, 1778; m. Richard Shepard, of Newtown, Ct.; both Ch.: (1) Ambrose, who res. in Newtown, Ct. (2) Nancy. (3) Phebe. (4) Delia. (5) Susan.

1310. v. POLLY, b. May 19, 1781; m. Silas Camp, of Newtown, Ct. Both d. Ch.: (1) Marietta, b. ———; m. Amos Hurd, of Newtown, Ct. (2) Emma. (3) Edson.

1311. vi. ANNE, b. July 20, 1783; m. Hawley Stillson, of Newtown, Ct. Ch.: (1) Polly. (2) Laura. (3) Orrin. (4) Edson. (5) Harriet.

1312. vii. ISAAC, b. Oct. 5, 1785; m. Anna Johnson, 2673-80.

1313. viii. LUCY, b. Mar. 15, 1788; m. Luther Camp, of Newtown, Ct. Ch.: (1) Miranda.

1314. ix. ALMIRA, b. Sept. 19, 1791; d. July 6, 1800.

1315. x. JULIA, b. Mar. 8, 1796; m. Edward Blakeman, of Weston, Ct. Both d. Ch.: (1) Lucinda. (2) Susan. (3) Polly Ann. (4) Sherman.

475. JEHIEL FOOTE, (142, 41, 11, 3,) b. Feb. 15, 1756; m. Jan. 1, 1781, ———. Blakeman. She d. 1785; m. 2nd, Aug., 1787, Abigail, dau. of John Shepard, of Newtown, Ct. She was b. Apr. 16, 1759, and d. Aug. 18, 1836. He d. June 24, 1798; res., Newtown, Ct.

(10)

- 1316. i.   JOSEPH, b. Oct. 1, 1781; d. Oct., 1793.
  1317. ii.   JAMES, b. ———; d. in infancy.
  1318. iii. STEPHEN, b. Sept. 1, 1788; m. Elizabeth Wood and Doras Barr, 2681-3.
  1319. iv.   LUMUEL, b. July 28, 1790; m. Lucretia Garnsey, 2684-7.
  1320. v.   SARAH ANN, b. Nov. 7, 1792; m. 1st, Dec. 20, 1823, William Garnsey, of Barker, N. Y. He d. July 20, 1825; m. 2nd, Jan. 8, 1831, Obadiah Stephens, of Barker, N. Y. Ch.: (1) Polly, b. Dec. 21, 1834.
  1321. vi.   `PHILO, b. Apr. 30, 1795; d. Apr. 23, 1796.
  1322. vii. NIRAM, b. Apr. 4, 1797; m. Amanda Dunham and Azubah Boardman, 2688-98.

480. DANIEL FOOTE, (142, 41, 11, 3,) b. Hobart, N. Y., 1762; m. Betty, dau. of John Northrup, b. July 3, 1764; d. Aug. 9, 1852; he d. July 27, 1840; res., Hobart, N. Y.

  1323. i.   NANNIE, b. July 31, 1784; m. Isaac Bennet; she d. Feb., 1851. Res., Stanford, N. Y.
  1323¹. ii. LUCIA, b. Oct. 18, 1791; m. Mar. 18, 1831, Jabez Foote; res., Wattsburgh, Pa.
  1323². iii. DAVID, b. Sept. 10, 1802; d. Feb. 4, 1805.
  1323³. iv. BETSEY, b. Sept. 28, 1806; m. June 13, 1832, John, son of Heth and Betsey (Baldwin) Griffin, b. Sept. 18, 1802; d. Mar. 19, 1867. She d. Oct. 4, 1886. Res., Hobart, N. Y. Ch.: (1) Heth, b. Sept. 29, 1833; unm.; on the old Daniel Foote farm. (2) Mary Elizabeth, b. May 31, 1839; d. Oct. 28, 1883; unm.

481. PETER FOOTE, (142, 41, 11, 3,) b. Newton, Ct., 1768; m. 1788, Naomi, dau. of Samuel Gillet, b. 1764; d. 1843. He was a weaver, and came to Stanford, N. Y., in 1805, and took up a farm, cleared the land, and endured the hardship of a pioneer life. He was blind for the last twenty years of his life; d. Apr. 26, 1846.

  1324. i.   WILLIAM, b. Newton, Ct., May 20, 1790; m. Marie Bailey, 2699-2706.
  1325. ii.   LUTHER, b. Newton, Ct., July 10, 1792; m. Pheba Judson, 2707-9½.
  1326. iii. JERUSHA, b. Newton, Ct., Feb. 17, 1795; m. Harry Newell, of Davenport, N. Y. Ch.: (1) Edward.
  1327. iv.   HENRY, b. Newton, Ct., Mar. 23, 1797; m. Losina Taylor, 2710-4.
  1328. v.   MARY ANN, b. Newton, Ct., May 6, 1799; m. July 20, 1834, James P. Grant; d. Mar. 20, 1860; she d. 1886; res., Hobart, N. Y.; p. s.
  1329. vi.   SARAH, b. Newton, Ct., May 21, 1803; m. 1842, Joseph Betts; res., Pittsfield, O.
  1330. vii. SHERMAN, b. Newton, Ct., Apr. 5, 1805; m. Emily Richmond, 2714-1-6.

484. LEMUEL FOOTE, (142, 41, 11, 3,) b. ———; m. Charity Beers; he d. Mar. 7, 1812.

  1330¹. i.   ABIGAIL, b. ———; m. Samuel Pullings.
  1331. ii.   CHARLES, b. Sept. 30, 1802; m. Abagail Augusta Marvine, 2715-⅛.

1332.   iii.   DAVID, b. ———; m. Julia Kelly, 2715¼-½.

486.   GEORGE FOOTE, (145, 41, 11, 3,) b. Oct. 11, 1749; m. Dec. 2, 1773, Charity, dau. of John Stillson, of Newton, Ct. She d. July 28, 1817; he d. June 27, 1820.

1333.   i.   BAILEY, b. Aug. 21, 1774; m. Jerusha Glover, 2716-20.

1333¹. ii.   REBECCA, b. June 11, 1776; m. Nov. 26, 1799, Joshua H. Brent, of Harpersfield, N. Y. He was b. July 10, 1752; she d. Jan. 16, 1817; he d. Dec. 24, 1822. Ch.: (1) Avaritta Caroline, b. Sept. 27, 1800; res., New York, N. Y. (2) George Howard, b. Dec. 28, 1802. (3) Morgan Lewis, b. Jan. 7, 1805; d. Jan. 20, 1808. (4) Louiza, b. Jan. 25, 1807; d. Mar. 27, 1825. (5) Jane Ann, b. Jan. 26, 1800; d. Feb. 2, 1809. (6) Morgan Lewis, b. Aug. 22, 1810. Res., Ohio. (7) Jane Rebecca, b. Aug. 26, 1812; d. Aug. 7, 1814. (8) Cyrenius Foote, b. May 25, 1815; res., Ill.

1334.   iv.   CYRENIUS, b. Jan. 31, 1781; m. Volusha Booth, 2721-5.

1335.   v.   JOHN, b. May 24, 1783; m. Sally Wainwright and Polly Sturges, 2726-31.

1336.   vi.   JABEZ BOTSFORD, b. Oct. 13, 1785; m. Lucia Foote, 2732-7.

1337.   vii.   ADAH, b. Jan. 18, 1788; m. May 11, 1817, George Sherman, first of Hobart, and afterwards of Delhi, N. Y. He was b. Aug. 2, 1787; d. Apr. 8, 1829. Ch.: (1) George Bronson, b. Mar. 27, 1820; res., New York, N. Y. (2) Elizabeth, b. Feb. 20, 1822; d. June 7, 1842. (3) John Wood, b. Oct. 12, 1823; res., Delhi, N. Y. (4) Walter, b. May 29, 1825; res., New York, N. Y. (5) Child, not named, b. Jan. 16, 1828; d. Feb. 23, 1828.

1338.   viii.   BETTY ANN, b. Mar. 1, 1790; m. Nov. 10, 1811, Edmund Meigs, of Holland Patent, N. Y. He was b. Oct. 3, 1786. Ch.: (1) Elizabeth Ada, b. Aug. 13, 1812; d. ———. (2) Amelia Ann, b. Mar. 7, 1814. (3) Lucretia Augusta, b. Apr. 19, 1817. (4) Benjamin Rich, b. Jan. 11, 1819. (5) Caroline Lovisa, b. Feb. 24, 1821; d. Jan. 12, 1838. (6) Edmund Foote, b. Sept. 2, 1823. (7) Maria Louiza, b. Aug. 11, 1825. (8) Helen, b. Apr. 18, 1828. (9) Mary, b. May 18, 1830. (10) George Forsyth, b. Aug. 16, 1833.

1339.   ix.   JEREMIAH, b. June 29, 1794; m. Maria Wood, 2738-.

488.   JOHN FOOTE, (145, 41, 11, 3,) b. July 14, 1754; m. 1775, Ruth Searl; she was b. Oct. 9, 1756; d. Jan. 29, 1846. He d. June 16, 1826; res., Arlington, Vt. His mother's maiden name was Hannah Hard, and she had a sister, Ann, who m. Andrew Hawley, with whom he spent his early years. Ch. all b. in Arlington, Vt.

1339¹. i.   IRA, b. Mar. 4, 1777; d. 1799; unm.

1340.   ii.   BETSEY, b. Dec. 25, 1778; m. 1801, Elihu, son of Rev. Elihu Bartlit; d. May 4, 1860, in Jay, Essex Co., N. Y. He d. June 1, 1824; res., East Guildford, Ct. Ch.: (1) Statira, b. Nov. 23, 1802, in Sunderland, Vt. (2) Maria, b. Jan. 14, 1804, in Jay, N. Y.; d. July 2, 1836. (3) John Foot, b. Aug. 21, 1805, in Jay, N. Y. (4) Betsey, b. Dec. 1, 1806, in Jay, N. Y. (5) Elihu Hall, b. July 6, 1808, in Jay N. Y. (6) Hannah Meigs, b. June 18, 1810, in Jay, N. Y.; d. Feb. 24, 1813. (6) Samuel, b. Nov. 16,

1811, in Jay, N. Y.; unm. (8) Adoniram, b. May 21, 1814, in Jay, N. Y.; d. Dec. 30, 1814.

(1) Statira m. Jared Pond, of Poultney, Vt., Sept. 25, 1825; he d. at Ann Arbor, Mich., Apr. 12, 1856. Ch.: (a) Elihu Bartlit, b. July 15, 1826, in Wilmington, N. Y. (b) Ashley, b. Nov. 23, 1827, in Wilmington, N. Y. (c) Jared, b. June 23, 1829, in Wilmington, N. Y.; Sergeant of Co. A, 16th Mich. Infantry; killed in battle at Gaines' Mills, Va., June 27, 1862. (d) Samuel, b. Aug. 25, 1830, in Wilmington, N. Y. (e) Ann Maria, b. Oct. 3, 1832, in Newburgh, Ohio; d. July 5, 1841. (f) Son, not named, b. Feb. 15, 1836, in Branch, Mich.; d. Mar. 26, 1836. (g) Amanda Foot, b. May 19, 1840, in Coldwater, Mich. (h) George Albert, b. Apr. 13, 1845, in Coldwater, Mich.; d. Dec. 27, 1845.

(3) John Foot Bartlit m. Sept. 11, 1828, Ann Sanford, of Jay, N. Y.; banker; he d. 1893; res., Columbus, Ohio. Ch.: (a) Mary, b. Dec. 6, 1829; d. Dec. 23, 1833. (b) Eliza, b. Oct. 9, 1831; d. Jan. 2, 1834. (c) Reuben S., b. Mar. 21, 1834; d. July 7, 1848. (d) Ann Maria, b. Apr. 14, 1836; d. Sept. 23, 1843. (e) John H., b. Feb. 2, 1841; d. Sept. 25, 1852. (f) Augusta Emeline, b. Nov. 7, 1843; d. Aug. 7, 1855. (g) Mattie, b. July 22, 1847. (h) Frank S., b. Oct. 5, 1850; d. Sept. 23, 1852. (i) Emma Amanda, b. Oct. 15, 1853.

(4) Betsey Bartlit m. Mar. 1, 1838, Lewis Pollay; he d. Nov., 1838; she d. June 10, 1904; res., Canal Winchester, Ohio. Ch.: (a) Eliza Maria, b. Dec. 6, 1838; m. Oct. 1, 1863, Col. Chas. H. Town, Col. 1st Mich. Cavalry; he d. May, 1865.

(5) Elihu Hall Bartlit m. Aug. 17, 1832, Sarah B. Martyn; she d. Apr. 7, 1854, at Jay, N. Y.; he d. Oct. 5, 1884; res., Jay, N. Y. Ch.: (a) Wilbur Fisk, b. Sept. 18, 1833, in Jay, N. Y.; d. Mar. 16, 1846. (b) Amanda Maria Bartlit, b. in Jay, N. Y., July 6, 1835; m. Dec. 14, 1857, Henry D. Boynton; she d. Feb. 15, 1904, in St. Clair, Mich. Ch.: (i) Herbert Eugene, b. Jay, N. Y., Jan. 29, 1864. (ii) Elihu Hall, b. May 2, 1874; d. Nov. 2, 1898, at Tuoxorlle, Tenn. (c) LeGrand Cannon Bartlit, b. Sept. 22, 1837; m. May 11, 1864, Mary Elizabeth Frye, at Canal Winchester, O. Ch., all b. in Canal Winchester, O. Ch.: (i) Samuel, b. Dec. 18, 1865. (ii) Emma, b. Apr. 7, 1867; d. July 19, 1867, at Canal Winchester, O. (iii) Grace Tallman, b. May 26, 1868; d. Mar. 25, 1875. (iv) Mary L., b. Nov. 12, 1870. (v) William Frye, b. Aug. 6, 1872. (vi) Ralph Hall, b. Aug. 14, 1874. (vii) John Foote, b. Aug. 28, 1876. (viii) Arthur Cowan, b. Mar. 31, 1878. (ix) Helen, b. Feb. 11, 1881. (x) Clarence Potter, b. Feb. 4, 1884. (d) Wilbur Fiske Bartlit, b. Oct. 10, 1839; d. July 7, 1865, at Ann Arbor, Mich. (e) Mary Louise Bartlit, b. Nov. 22, 1841; m. Nov. 4, 1868, in Jay, N. Y., Henry Malcolm Prime. Ch., all b. in Jay, N. Y.: (i) Wilbur Peter, b. Aug. 18, 1871; m. May 24, 1905, Katharine M. Stevens, in Keeseville, N. Y. (ii) Grace Sarah, b. Jan. 27, 1874; m. Nov. 17, 1904, George Nelson Kingsland, in Keeseville, N. Y. (iii) Anna M., b. Mar. 7, 1876. (f) Sarah Elizabeth Bartlit, b. June 8, 1844; m. in Jay, N. Y., Apr. 11, 1866, LeRoy

N. Southmayed. Ch., all b. in Virginia City, Mont.: (i) LeRoy Southmayed, M. D., b. July 19, 1869; m. at Salt Lake City, June 6, 1900, Edith Elsa Forest, of San Francisco, Cal.; d. in Feb., 1904, in Great Falls, Mont. (ii) Lula Bartlit, b. Jan. 18, 1872. (iii) Virginia, b. Nov. 11, 1873; d. Jan. 11, 1878, in Virginia City, Mont. (iv) Florence Bartlit, b. May 23, 1881. (g) Elihu Hall Bartlit, b. in Jay, Nov. 3, 1845; d. Nov. 14, 1845, in Jay, N. Y. (h) Elihu Hall Bartlit, b. in Jay, Jan. 18, 1847; m. Nov. 15, 1876, Jennie E. Holcomb; res., Haroey, Ill. (i) Bessie A. Bartlit, b. Jan. 30, 1850; m. Feb. 8, 1901, at Butte,, Mont., Hon. Orlando B. Barber.

(1a) Elihu Bartlit Pond m. Nov. 20, 1849, Mary Barlow Allen, dau. of Stephen and Deborah Allen, of Madison, Lenawee Co., Mich. He was editor and proprietor of ''The Michigan Argus,'' published at Ann Arbor, where he res. Ch.: (i) Mary Louise, b. Sept. 28, 1852, at Coldwater, Mich. (ii) Stephen Allen, b. Aug. 9, 1854, at Madison, Mich.; d. Oct. 2, 1855. (iii) Irving Kane, b. May 1, 1857, at Ann Arbor, Mich. (iv) Allen Bartlit, b. Nov. 21, 1858, at Ann Arbor, Mich. (v) Amanda, b. Mar. 9, 1863, at Ann Arbor, Mich.

(1b) Judge Ashley Pond m. May 29, 1866, Hattie L. Pearl, of Nashville, Tenn. He was Professor of Law in Mich. University. Res., Detroit, Mich. (1bi) Florence Louise, b. May 1, 1867. (1bii) Stanley Bartlit, b. Mar. 28, 1869; d. Dec. 13, 1873. (1biii) Ashley, b. July 6, 1872; m. 1903, Hazel Hallet, of Detroit, Mich. Ch.: (1) Margaret, b. Dec. 1, 1903. (2) Dorothy, b. May 30, 1906.

(1d) Samuel Pond m. Mar. 31, 1857, Maggie Jane Ewing, of Lancaster, Ohio. He d. at Canal Winchester, Ohio, Aug. 9, 1857. Ch.: (i) Jessie Statira, b. Apr. 17, 1858.

(1g) Amanda Foot Pond m. Jan. 29, 1862, Delos C. Wiley. Res., Lansing, Mich. Ch.: (i) Ashley Pond, b. Feb. 25, 1863. (ii) Lloyd Adams, b. Mar. 18, 1864; d. Aug. 6, 1864. (iii) Charles Delos, b. Jan. 30, 1866.

1341. iii. ADONIRAM, b. July 10, 1780; m. Nancy Doty and Emily Brainard, 2739-50.

1342. iv. LEMUEL THOMAS, b. June 5, 1782; m. Lucy Clark, 2751-61.

1343. v. GEORGE, b. Apr. 18, 1784; d. July 30, 1803; accidentally shot.

1344. vi. TIMOTHY TODD, b. May 16, 1786; m. Bathsheba Livingston, by whom he had one son, Ira, who d. one week old. After the death of his first wife he res. in Baltimore, Md, where he m. a 2nd wife, by whom he had one dau., Ruth Ann, of whom nothing is known. He is supposed to have been murdered in 1839 somewhere between Baltimore and Washington, D. C.

1345. vii. BELUS HARD, b. July 15, 1788; m. Betsey Hawley, 2762-71.

1346. viii. AMANDA, b. Mar. 10, 1791; m. Nov. 9, 1848, Ephraim Hunt, of Denmark, Lewis Co., N. Y. He d. Oct. 6, 1852; she d. Apr. 13, 1881, at Rome, N. Y.; p. s.

1347. ix. LINUS, b. Nov. 26, 1793; m. Laura Palmer, 2772-83.

1348. x. RUTH ANN, b. Nov. 18, 1795; d. June 5, 1817.

1349. xi. CHARLES, b. Nov. 28, 1797; m. Rebecca Wellman, 2784-9.

494. PHINEAS FOOTE, (153, 45, 13, 5,) b. Oct. 26, 1763; m. Apr. 28, 1791, Irene, dau. of Abraham and Abigail (dau. of No. 66) (Blackstone) Hoadley, of Branford, Ct.

1350. i. ABIGAIL, b. May 3, 1792; m. Jan. 12, 1817, Daniel Averill, Jr., of Branford, Ct.; d. July 24, 1876. Ch.: (1) Ralph, b. abt. 1819. Mr. Averill and Ralph were lost at sea 1837. (2) William Hoadley, b. July 10, 1821; m. Myrtie Fowler; he d. Apr. 16, 1891. (3) Samuel, b. July 12, 1824; d. Apr. 22, 1896. (4) Irene, b. Jan. 10, 1828; m. Henry Palmer, of Branford, Ct., the son of Ami Palmer and Abigail Kimberly, Jan. 15, 1846. He was b. Apr. 5, 1822, and d. Jan. 2, 1907. During his early days he remained at home helping on the farm. He soon had a calling for the sea, and was captain of his own vessel before long. He remained in the trading business until 1883, when he entered the oyster business under the firm name of Luddington & Palmer. He retired in 1900. Res., Fair Haven, Ct. She d. Jan. 11, 1907. Ch., all b. in Branford, Ct.: (a) Ralph, b. Dec. 1, 1846. (b) Abbie, b. Dec. 27, 1848. (c) Marietta, b. Aug. 6, 1851. (d) Helen, b. Feb. 10, 1854. (e) Emma Rebecca, b. June 10, 1859.

(a) Ralph Averill Palmer m. Sarah Arms Kinney, dau. of William Lewis Kinney and Jane March Bedell, of Elizabeth, N. J., in that city, Dec. 24, 1868. She was b. Dec. 4, 1847. He res. in Meriden, where he was connected with the Parker Bros. Co. until about 1901, when he went South to oversee his orange plantation at Bradentown, Fla., where he now resides. Ch.: (i) Harry Albert Palmer, b. in New York, Oct. 4, 1869; m. Nov. 30, 1894, Florence Eva Bennett, in Meriden, Ct. (ii) Florence Abbie Palmer, b. in Meriden, June 27, 1871; d. in six weeks. (iii) Ray Kinney Palmer, b. in Meriden, May 7, 1874; m. June 21, 1905, Florence Horton Swan, dau. of Wm. Baker Swan and Etta Frances Albright, in Bradentown, Fla. (iv) Guy Ammi Palmer, b. in Meriden, Feb. 14, 1877; m. Dec. 9, 1898, Jennie E. Dryhurst, in New Haven, Ct. (v) Charles Scranton Palmer, b. Sept. 3, 1878, in Meriden; m. Maud Elizabeth Hendy, in Torrington, Ct., Oct. 18, 1905, dau. of Clara and Henry John Hendy. (vi) Emma Irene Palmer, b. June 3, 1880, in Meriden, Ct. (vii) Alice Palmer b. in Meriden, Ct., May 17, 1885; m. William Henry Vanderipe, Feb. 3, 1904, in Bradentown, Fla., the son of William H. Vanderipe and Eliza Burts.

(b) Abbie Palmer m. Franklin D. Hadley, June 3, 1868, and 2nd, Smith Granniss, May 2, 1889. Res., Morris, Ct. Ch.: (i) Etta May Hadley, b. Nov. 5, 1870, in Branford, Ct.; m. Daniel Everton Judd, Oct. 30, 1895, at Morris, Ct. Ch.: (i) Irene Averill Judd, b. Feb. 9, 1897, in Litchfield. (ii) Hulda Hadley Judd, b. Oct. 2, 1898, in New York. (iii) Helen Palmer Judd, b. Oct., 1901, in Bethlehem.

(c) Marietta Palmer m. in Branford, Charles Woolsey Scranton, Sept. 23, 1869. He is the son of Sereno Hamilton Scranton and Susan Dowd, of Madison, Ct. In early life he was associated with his father in the shipping produce business. He is now engaged in the Investment Securities business in New Haven,

Ct. (established since 1861). Sereno and Susan Scranton are both direct descendants from Robert Foote (No. 5) through No. 13. Ch.: (i) Minnie Irene Scranton, b. Nov. 13, 1870, in Branford, Ct.; m. Edgar Everest Conover, in Madison, July 14, 1898. He is the son of William E. Conover, of Greenwich, Ct. Ch.: (i1) Helen Scranton Conover, b. July 14, 1900. (i2) Woolsey Scranton Conover, b. July 27, 1902. (ii) Alice Palmer Scranton, b. Mar. 24, 1872, in Branford, Ct.; m. Robert Edgar Milligan, in New Haven, Ct., Nov. 18, 1896. (iii) William Dowd Scranton, b. in New Haven, Ct., June 10, 1875; m. Katharine Frances Brown, in New Haven, Apr. 12, 1904, dau. of Robert A. Brown and C. Alene Brown. (iv) Helen Woolsey Scranton, b. in New Haven, Feb. 15, 1878. (v) Charles Woolsey Scranton, Jr., b. in New Haven, Sept. 24, 1883; d. Jan. 13, 1897.

(d) Helen Palmer m. Benjamin Francis Cook, Kingston, Mass., Dec. 25, 1871. He d. at Memphis, Tenn.

(e) Emma Rebecca Palmer m. William Ranson Hendrick, in Fair Haven, Ct., May 12, 1881. He is associated with the "New York Evening Sun." Ch.: (i) William Henry Hendrick, b. Dec. 7, 1882, in Waterbury, Ct.; d. Dec., 1884. (ii) William Ranson Hendrick, b. May 2, 1884, in Waterbury, Ct.; d. Aug. 9, 1885. (iii) Wallace Mather Hendrick, b. Nov. 11, 1886, in New Haven, Ct. (iv) Irene Palmer Hendrick, b. Mar. 1, 1890, in Brooklyn, N. Y.; d. ———.

1351. ii.   REBECCA, b. July 11, 1794.
1352. iii. LUCY CLARISSA, b. May 28, 1797.

497. JONATHAN FOOTE, (153, 45, 13, 5,) b. Mar. 13, 1772; m. Dec. 8, 1808, Martha, dau. of Samuel and Elizabeth (Taylor) Frisbie, of Branford, Ct. Martha was b. Dec. 28, 1779; d. July 31, 1866. He d. Nov. 12, 1851; a cabinet maker. Res., Branford, Ct.

1353. i.   LUCY, b. Dec. 1810; d. Feb. 20, 1848; unm.
1354. ii. JONATHAN, b. Jan. 28, 1814; m. Sarah R. Stephens, 2790-1.
1355. iii. ELIZABETH, b. Mar. 6, 1816; d. July 29, 1824.
1356. iv. MARTHA, b. Apr. 21, 1818; d. July 29, 1824.
1357. v.   CLARISSA LYDIA, b. June 12, 1821; m. Dr. Isaac P. Leete, of Guilford, Ct. He d. Oct. 20, 1902. Ch.: (1) Lucy Gertrude, b. May 18, 1848; m. Addison Lyman Abell, of Agawam, Mass., Dec. 3, 1872. Ch.: (a) Gertrude Ethleyn, b. Mar. 28, 1880; m. Jan. 5, 1905, Arthur Snow Baldwin, of Branford, Ct. (2) Emma Evangeline, b. Sept. 6, 1852; d. July 5, 1886; m. Virgil Malachi Cooke, of Springfield, Mass., Apr. 25, 1874; he d. Aug. 31, 1887. Ch.: (a) Gertrude Evangeline, b. Aug. 23, 1875; d. Feb. 17, 1894. (b) Florence Frisbie, b. Nov. 22, 1877; d. July 30, 1878. (c) Virginia, b. June 21, 1879; d. Apr. 23, 1880. (d) Ella Maud, b. June 28, 1881; m. July 21, 1904, William Higley. (3) Clarissa Martha, b. June 14, 1858; m. George Francis Reynolds, of New Haven, Ct., June 17, 1880. Ch.: (a) Grace Louise, b. July 25, 1882; m. Jan. 27, 1901, Harry James Broadhurst. Ch.: (i) Doris Reynolds, b. Aug. 12, 1903. (4) Nellie Elizabeth, b. Apr. 4, 1861;

m. Nathan Augustus Miller, Sept. 29, 1887. Ch.: (a) Earle
Leete, b. Oct, 7, 1889. (b) Nellie Evangeline, b. Oct. 1, 1893.
(c) Irving Platt, b. Nov. 15, 1895.

498. EPHRAIM FOOTE, (153, 43, 13, 5,) b. Sept. 1, 1775; m. Sept. 15, 1802,
Polly Hobart, of Branford, Ct. She was b. Mar. 19, 1784; d. Oct. 11, 1876. He
d. Jan. 15, 1846. Res., Branford, Ct.

1358 i.   HARRISON, b. May 27, 1803; m. Jan. 27, 1839, Mercia Miller;
            d. Sept. 9, 1840; p. s.
1359. ii.   JOHN, b. Dec. 23, 1805; m. Fanny Blackstone, 2792-3.
1360. iii. MARY, b. Mar. 31, 1808; m. Willis Beach, of Branford, Ct.; d.
            July 7, 1845; p. s.
1361. iv.   SALLY, b. May 14, 1810; d. Apr. 20, 1817.
1362. v.   SAMUEL, b. Sept. 18, 1812; m. Sarah Elizabeth Russel, 2794-9.
1363. vi.   BETSY, b. Feb. 27, 1816, at Brandon, Ct.; m. Harry Stedman,
            son of Benjamin Stedman, of Branford, Ct., Sept. 26, 1839.· He
            was b. in Branford, Apr. 4, 1812; a carpenter; d. Mar. 29, 1872.
            She d. in Branford, Ct., Jan. 20, 1899. Ch.: (1) Henry Harrison,
            b. at Branford, Ct., Apr. 24, 1840. He was Town Clerk and
            Town Treasurer of the town of Branford from 1877 and Judge
            of Probate from 1878 until the time of his death, which occurred
            Jan. 10, 1891. (2) Mary Foote, b. at Branford, Mar. 4, 1842; d.
            Oct. 3, 1863. (3) Hannah, b. at Branford, Ct., Nov. 7, 1844; m.
            Ebenezer T. Bradley, son of Gurdon Bradley, of Branford, Ct.,
            Dec. 29, 1866; he d. Sept. 14, 1875; they had 2 ch. (4) Grace
            Rogers, b. at Branford, Ct., Aug. 20, 1845; m. Lewis F. Shepard,
            son of Jared Shepard, of Branford, Ct., Jan. 29, 1873; they have
            1 ch. (5) Ellen, b. at Branford, Ct., July 19, 1847; m. George
            T. Benton, son of Osmar Benton, of New York City, June 19,
            1873, at Branford, Ct. They have had 7 ch. (1 living). Mr.
            Benton was b. at New York City, Oct. 13, 1846. They res. in
            Branford, Ct. (6) Charles Foyer, b. at Branford, Ct., June 14,
            1850; d. at Branford, Feb. 14, 1875. (7) Wilson Miller, b. at
            Branford, Ct., Nov. 7, 1852; d. at Branford, Apr. 5, 1875. (8)
            Hattie Frisbie, b. at Branford, Ct., Nov. 23, 1854; m. Charles
            S. Thompson, son of Hiram Thompson, of New Haven, Ct.,
            Feb. 7, 1878; he d. Oct. 23, 1897. They had 3 ch. (2 living).
1364. vii. SALLY, b. Oct. 23, 1818, ; at Branford, Ct. ; m. Elizur
            Rogers, son of Abraham Rogers, of Branford, Ct., Apr.
            20, 1843 ; he was b. at Branford, Ct., Nov. 2, 1816.
            He was a merchant and held several town offices.
            He was Town Clerk of the town of Branford from Oct., 1867, to
            Oct., 1870. She d. at New Haven, Ct., Sept. 15, 1902; he d. at
            New Haven, Ct., Oct. 21, 1903. Ch.: (1) Mason, b. at Branford,
            Ct., Apr. 25, 1844; d. Sept. 9, 1864, in Newbern, North Carolina,
            while in the U. S. Service; he was a Sergeant in Co. B, 15th
            Regt. Ct. Vols.; unm. (2) Frank Abraham, b. at Branford, Ct.,
            May 6, 1848; d. at Branford, Jan. 21, 1866.
1365. viii. HANNAH, b. Feb. 7, 1821, at Branford, Ct. ; m.
            George W. Taylor, son of John Taylor, of New Haven,
            Ct., May 27, 1851 ; he was b. in Guilford, Ct., Sept.

7, 1815. Mr. Taylor was one of the original members
of the firm of Tuttle Morehouse & Taylor, Printers and
Publishers, of New Haven, Ct. He d. at New Haven, Ct., Aug.
1, 1891. Ch.: (1) Charles, b. at New Haven, Ct., Sept. 10, 1852;
d. at New Haven, Ct., Sept. 15, 1856. (2) Edward, b. at New
Haven, Ct., June 6, 1855. (3) John, b. at New Haven, Ct., Aug.
31, 1859; d. at New Haven, Ct., Sept. 7, 1859. (4) Edward
Taylor, of New Haven, Ct.; m. Fanny Randolph, dau. of Dr.
Lewers Dixon Gray, of 88 Trumbull St., East Orange, N. J.,
Jan. 3, 1898; she was b. at Elizabeth, N. J., Feb. 25, 1870.

508. BRONSON FOOTE, (168, 47, 13, 5,) b. Sept. 5, 1757; m. May 7, 1782,
Thankful Pond, of Woodbury, Ct.; she was b. Feb. 16, 1757; d. June 9, 1843. He
d. Aug. 30, 1836; res., Clinton, Ct. N. Y.

   1366. i.   HITTY, b. Woodbury, Ct., Feb. 28, 1783; m. Jan., 1802, Joseph
                Bennet.

   1367. ii.   ORANGE, b. Woodbury, Ct., Nov. 2, 1784; m. Marilla Ives,
                2799-2802.

   1368. iii. SILAS, b. German Flats, N. Y., Jan. 30, 1787; d., unm., Clinton,
                N. Y., July 8, 1846.

   1369. iv. HORACE, b. Clinton, N. Y., Mar. 5, 1789; m. 1820, Permilla
                Burr; she d. Westport, Ct., Mar. 27, 1837. Ch.: 3.

   1370. v.   BETSEY, b. Clinton, N. Y., June 26, 1792; m. May 6, 1816,
                Erastus Johnson. Ch.: (1) Saphronia Foote Johnson, b. May 6,
                1819; m. Hiram Burgdoss, of Morrisville; he d. Apr. 2, 1847.
                (2) Mary Abigail Johnson, b. Nov. 6, 1821; m. Feb. 5, 1845,
                Spencer Johnson; res., Columbus, Wis. (3) Emeline Bearcett
                Johnson, b. Apr. 29, 1825; m. Apr. 24, 1850, Hiram Lewis; she
                d. Sept. 11, 1854. (4) Bronson Johnson, b. in Clinton, and d.
                at Little Falls. (5) Edward Porter Johnson, b. in Clinton, and
                d. at Little Falls.

   1371. vi. CHESTER, b. Clinton, N. Y., Nov. 26, 1795; d., unm., Clinton,
                Jan. 17, 1839.

   1372. vii. NOEL, b. Clinton, N. Y., Sept. 28, 1797; m. Emily Gridley,
                2804-6.

   1373. viii. DOPHRONIA, b. Clinton, N. Y., Mar. 19, 1799; d. Feb. 19, 1812.

509. CAPTAIN IRA FOOTE, (168, 47, 13, 5, 1,) b. Nov. 13, 1759, of Ellis-
burgh, N. Y.; m. Polly Pond, of Clinton, N. Y. He d. 1815; she d. ———.

   1374. i.   DAVID, b. ———; m. ———; d. ae. 30, 2807-8.

   1375. ii.   EMMA, b. ———; m. ———; d. ae. 30. Ch.: 3.

   1376. iii. ALEXANDER, b. ———; d. ae. 30; unm.

   1377. iv. SYLVIA, b. ———; m. J. Powell; d. ae 30. Ch.: 2.

   1378. v.   MERICK, b. ———; d. young.

   1379. vi. MARTIN, b. ———; d. young.

   1380. vii. MARTIN, b. Dec. 20, 1792; m. Nancy Avery, 2808-11.

511. LUTHER FOOTE, b. Oct. 4, 1764, of Clinton, N. Y.; m. Sally Pond;
he d. in the Army near Buffalo, N. Y., 1842; he was out in the Militia as a
volunteer. She d. ———.

   1381. i.   CLINTON, b. ———; d. ae. 19; unm.

   1382. ii.   DAN, b. ———; m. twice; res., Weston, Ct.

1383. iii.   SEDATE, b. May 30, 1795; m. Feb. 22, 1814, Russell H. DeWolf; she d. Nov. 11, 1814.
1384. iv.   HARRY, b. ———; d. ae. 22; unm.
1385. v.   FREEMAN, b. ———; m. Lydia Nelson. Ch.: 1 (dead).
1386. vi.   ORNAN, b. ———; d. ae. 14.
1387. vii.   SARAH, b. ———; m. 1st, S. Curtis; m. 2nd, A. G. P. Colbourn. Res., New Jersey.
1388. viii.   LUCY, b. ———; m. ———; d. ae. 35.

514.   MOSES FOOTE, (168, 47, 13, 5,) b. Jan. 4, 1770; m. 1802, Martha Brown; she was b. Feb. 9, 1781; he d. Dec. 29, 1840; res., Clinton, N. Y.
1389. i.   HELEN, b. Dec. 23, 1803; d. Sept. 26, 1844; unm.
1390. ii.   ADELIA, b. Oct. 5, 1805.
1391. iii.   THOMAS MOSES, b. Aug. 9, 1808; m. Margaret St. John, 2812-3.

518.   BERIAH FOOTE, (170, 37, 13, 5,) b. Dec. 16, 1761; m. Dec. 24, 1784, Hannah Rossiter, of Harwinton, Ct.   She was b. July 15, 1765; d. July 11, 1811; m. 2nd, Phebe Mills, wid. of Zachariah Mills; she was b. May 19, 1771; d. Feb. 14, 1843.   He d. May 1, 1841, in Galen, N. Y.   Res., Harwinton, Ct., Sheffield, Mass., Galen, N. Y.
1392. i.   CYRENE, b. 1785; m. 1810, John Robertson, of Sheffield, Mass. She d. 1813.   Ch.: 2, both d. in childhood.
1393. ii.   SAMUEL, b. Sept. 26, 1786; m. Nov. 15, 1826, Susan, wid. of Jarius Foote.   Res., Clinton, N. Y.; p. s.
1394. iii.   MILLESCENT, b. Aug. 3, 1792; m. Nov., 1812, Robert Parks; she d. Mar. 15, 1825.   Ch.: (1) Julia Ann, b. Aug. 2, 1814.   (2) James R., b. Aug. 2, 1814.   (3) Henry, b. Aug. 12, 1816.   (4) Mary A., b. Feb. 12, 1818.   (5) Jerome B., b. Oct. 27, 1820.   (6) Caroline E., b. Oct. 30, 1832.
1395. iv.   ALBERT, b. May 18, 1796; m. Mary Ann Gipson and Phebe Gillett, 2814-8.
1396. v.   ALVIN, b. Nov. 3, 1797; m. Mary Ann Palmer, 2819-22.
1397. vi.   MARY, b. Dec. 10, 1802; res., Cairo, N. Y.; unm.
1398. vii.   AARON, b. May 5, 1806; m. Isabella McMillain, 2823-.

520.   JOHN FOOTE, (170, 37, 13, 5,) b. Mar. 26, 1766; m. Hulda Rossiter, of Harwinton, Ct.   He d. Nov. 29, 1832; res., Sheffield, Mass., and Huron Co., Ohio.
1399. i.   AMANDA, b. ———; d. ae. 20.
1400. ii.   JOHN STANLEY, b. ———; m. ———.
1401. iii.   VELONA, b. ———; res., Iowa.
1402. iv.   WALTER, b. 1801; m. Jamezin Ford.
1403. v.   HENRY JARVIS, b. Aug. 22, 1805; m. Maria Wilkinson.
1404. vi.   MINERVA, b. ———; d. ae. 3.
1405. vii.   MARY, b. ———; d. ae. 2.
1406. viii.   HENRY, b. ———; d. in childhood.
1407. ix.   MINERVA, b. ———.
1408. x.   ANNA, b. ———; m. Philander Austin.
1409. xi.   MOSES R., b. Ct., Oct. 19, 1812; m. Maria Palmer and Mary Lockwood.

521.   AMOS FOOTE, (170, 37, 13, 5,) b. Jan. 20, 1768; m. Oct. 2, 1791, Adah Frisbie; she was b. Dec. 10, 1769; d. Apr. 19, 1830, in Great Barrington, Mass.; he d. May 1, 1840, in Portage Co., O.; res., Sheffield, Mass., and Freedom, O.

1410. i.   BEDA, b. July 22, 1792; d. Mar. 1, 1829, in Sheffield, Mass.; unm.

1411. ii. ORVIS, b. May 28, 1794; m. Nancy D. Shed, 2843-44½.

1412. iii. MILO, b. Dec. 19, 1796; m. Eliza Clark, 2845-45½.

1413. iv. WYLLYS, b. Nov. 25, 1798; m. Elizabeth S. Warner, 2846-50.

1414. v.   CLARRISSA, b. Jan 15, 1801; m. Apr. 28, 1831, John Hanners; he was b. July, 1802; she d. June 19, 1844.

1415. vi. AMOS, b. Mar. 15, 1803; d. July 17, 1829.

1416. vii. LEWIS, b. Apr. 8, 1805; d. Aug. 5, 1828.

1417. viii. ADAH S., b. Feb. 25, 1810; m. Oct. 23, 1832, Benjamin Bosworth; He was b. Apr. 11, 1809; d. Aug. 6, 1838; she d. Dec. 11, 1832.

1418. ix. CHARLES B., b Nov. 7, 1812; d. Sept. 17, 1814.

522. AARON FOOTE, (170, 37, 13, 5,) b. Apr. 24, 1771; m. Apr. 10, 1798, Jedidah, dau. of Deacon Elihu Sherman, of Williamstown, Mass.; he d. Aug., 1839; she d. 1843; res., Williamstown, Mass., Adams, Mass., and Geauga Co., Ohio.

1419. i.   POLLY, b. Williamstown, Mass., May 21, 1799; d. in early life.

1420. ii. AARON HUBBARD, b. Williamstown, Mass., Jan. 2, 1801.

1421. iii. ELISAH, b. Williamstown, Mass.; d. young.

1422. iv. ELIHU SHERMAN, b. Adams, Mass., Oct. 10, 1809; d. in early life.

1423. v.   SHERMAN, b. Adams, Mass., Sept. 21, 1804; m. Margarette D. Grey, 2851-3.

1424. vi. JOHN BRONSON, b. Adams, Mass., Feb. 10, 1807; m. Mary Patten, 2854-8.

1425. vii. ALMIRA, b. Adams, Mass., Feb. 10; d. ae. 35; unm.

1426. viii. ELIZABETH, b. Adams, Mass.; m. John W. Sherman.

1427. ix. JEDIDAH ANN, b. Williamstown, Mass., Oct. 12, 1813; m. Nov. 14, 1833, Isaac Newton Thompson, of Batavia, Ohio. He is a son of James Thompson, of Middlefield, Ohio, and was b. June 18, 1805. Ch.: (1) John, b. May 29, 1837. (2) Henry, b. Oct. 20, 1840. (3) Sarah Thompson, b. Jan. 6, 1844.

526. DARIUS FOOTE, (171, 47, 13, 5,) b. Apr. 10, 1762; m. 1777, Lurinda Ann, dau. of Caleb Preston, of Wallingford, and Plymouth, Mass. She d. Mar. 17, 1836; he d. Mar. 19, 1846. Res., Harwinton, Ct.

1428. i.   REBECCA, b. 1787; m. 1st, David Pond, of Harwinton, Ct.; he d.; m. 2nd, David Delano, of Palermo, N. Y. She d. 1853; he d. Mar. 25, 1880, ae. 87. Ch.: 7.

1429. ii. LURINDA ANN, b. May 8, 1789; m. May 23, 1841, Darius Stevens, of Burlington, by Rev. Charles Bentley, Harrington, Ct.; d. Aug. 3, 1880; he d. May 27, 1866, ae. 82; p. s. Res., Harwinton, Ct.

1430. iii. LEWIS, b. Nov. 6, 1792; d. Apr. 4, 1885; unm.

1431. iv. AURELIA, b. Oct. 1, 1794; m. Nov. 30, 1820, Gaylor, son of Abel and Ann (Fuller) Case, of Simsbury, Ct. He was b. Oct. 9, 1794; d. 1875. She d. July 31, 1862; both buried in the old South Cemetery, Harwinton, Ct. Ch.: (1) Maria L., b. Oct. 20, 1821. (2) Emery L., b. Dec. 6, 1823; m. Mar. 20, 1867, Ellen E. Pond, of New Hartford, Ct. She was b. May 23, 1842; d. Mar. 17, 1903. He d. Aug. 20, 1901. Res., Burlington, Ct. Ch.: (a) Eliza M., b. July 22, 1879. (3) Lurinda Ann, b. Aug. 16,

1826; m. Elisah Lines, of Waterbury, Ct. (4) Salmon D., b. Jan. 11, 1830. (5) Amy A., b. Mar. 25, 1832; d. Nov. 4, 1834. (6) Lucy A., b. Jan. 7, 1836; d. Jan. 29, 1844.

1432. v.   ABNER P., b. Dec. 25, 1800; m. Lucy Cluff and Eunice Mix, 2859.

1433. vi.   DARIUS, b. Sept., 1802; m. Rhoda Lewis; she d. May. 7, 1849; he d. Feb. 26, 1874; res., Simsbury, Ct.; p. s.

1434. vii.   DAVID, b. 1806; m. Mindwell Jones; d. Aug. 5, 1883; she d. Jan. 23, 1879, ae. 72; res., Harwinton, Ct., and Oswego Co., N. Y.

1435. viii.   ELIZA, b. Sept. 30, 1806; m. Sept. 21, 1824, Timpson R. Gates, of Simsbury, Ct. He was b. Sept. 28, 1801; d. ———; she d. Feb. 6, 1846; res., Simsbury, Ct. Ch.: (1) Dwight, b. June 27, 1825. (2) Esther, b. Oct. 21, 1827. (3) Rhoda, b. June 23, 1831. (4) Mary, b. July 17, 1835; d. July 17, 1840. (5) George W., b. Nov. 23, 1837. (6) Mary, b. Feb. 23, 1842. (7) Alice, b. Dec. 9, 1844.

527. SIMEON FOOTE, (171, 47, 13, 5,) b. Sept. 22, 1764; m. Sept. 2, 1784, Lovisa, dau. of Timothy and Mary Bacon, of West Britain, Ct. He was a Revolutionary soldier. Res., West Britain, Ct., New Lebanon, and Windsor, N. Y.

1436. i.   POLLY, b. West Britain, Ct., Mar. 15, 1786; m. James Greek, of Windsor, N. Y.

1437. ii.   SALLY, b. New Lebanon, N. Y., Sept. 22, 1787; m. James Stewart, of Pittsburg, Pa.

1438. iii.   EBENEZER, b. Watertown, Ct., Dec. 15, 1789; m. Rebecca Philips, 2860-4.

1439. iv.   ANNA, b. Windsor, N. Y., Feb. 6, 1793; d. Dec. 23, 1836; unm.; in Nicholson, Pa.

1440 v.   MARTHA, b. Windsor, N. Y., Mar. 18, 1795; m. 1813, Harry S. Bebee, of Windsor, N. Y.

1441. vi.   GIDEON, b. Great Bend, N. Y., Apr. 17, 1799; m. Lavinia Gillett, 2865-71.

1442. vii.   NATHAN B., b. Windsor, N. Y., Feb. 26, 1801; m. Elizabeth Robinson, 2872-80.

1443. viii.   SIMEON, b. Windsor, N. Y., Dec. 13, 1803; m. Ann Fergurson, 2881-5.

1444. ix.   LOVISA, b. Windsor, N. Y., Nov. 12, 1805.

1445. x.   NATHANIEL, b. Windsor, N. Y., Sept. 15, 1807; d. July 21, 1810.

529. DAVID FOOTE, (171, 47, 13, 5,) b. Aug. 7, 1768; m. in 1791, Irene, dau. of Nathan and Dorcas Lane. She was b. in Chesterfield, Mass., Nov. 2, 1774, and d. Mar. 5, 1846; he d. Aug. 22, 1845, in Hancock, Ill.; both buried at Nauvoo, Ill.

1446. i.   LAURA, b. Apr. 23, 1792, in Windsor, N. Y.; m. Elihu Allen, in Dryden, N. Y. he d. Oct. 17, 1824. After her death he m. Loly Clauson, a cousin to his first wife. She d. in Salt Lake City, Utah Ter., in 1849. He d. in Salt Lake City, Utah Ter., Nov., 1850. Ch., by 1st m.: (1) Lucinda Allen, b. Nov., 1812, in Dryden, Tompkins Co., N. Y.; d. young. (2) George Allen, b. Nov., 1815, in Dryden, Tompkins Co., N. Y.; m. Almira, and was drowned in the Missouri River in 1837 or 1838. (3) Franklin Allen, b. Apr. 15, 1818, in Dryden, Tompkins Co., N. Y.; now lives in Bertram, Lynn Co., Iowa. He m. Rebecca Myers; has a large family. (4) Caroline Matilda Allen, b. Apr. 16, 1825, in Dryden, Tompkins Co., N. Y.; m. Wm. Weeks, and now lives in Los Angeles, Cal.; has several children.

1447. ii. BETSEY, b. Feb. 8, 1794, in Windsor, N. Y.; m. Thomas Clement, b. Apr. 1, 1792, son of Darius Clement, of Dryden, N. Y., Mar. 15, 1812; he d. abt. 1848 in Dryden, N. Y.; she d. Nov. 8, 1846, in Pottawattamie Co., Iowa. Ch.: (1) Marilla Clement, b. Dec. 12, 1813, in Dryden, N. Y., Tompkins Co.; d. unm. in Dryden. (2) Nancy Clement, b. Oct. 31, 1815, in Dryden, N. Y., Tompkins Co.; m. George A. Smith in Nauvoo, Ill.; d. at Werster Quarters, New Florence, Neb., 1848. (3) Louisa Clement, b. Nov. 22, 1817, in Dryden, N. Y., Tompkins Co.; d. unm. in Dryden. (4) Albert Clement, b. Feb. 9, 1820, in Dryden; d. unm. in Pottawattamie Co., Iowa, Nov. 2, 1846. (5) Alvah Clement, b. Dec. 19, 1822, in Dryden; d. unm. in Dryden. (6) Sarah Loretta, b. Mar. 13, 1821, in Dryden; m. Daniel Lewis, of Dryden; a dau., Sarah Jane. Mrs. Lewis d. ae. 17. (7) Laura Elizabeth Clement, b. Apr. 23, 1828, in Dryden; d. in Hancock Co., Ill., in 1845. (8) Darius Salem Clement, b. Nov. 24, 1834, in Dryden; m. Louisa Kelsey, in Union, Salt Lake Co., Utah, Nov. 27, 1859; now lives in Fairview, Sanpete Co., Utah. (9) Mary Irene Clement, b. July 23, 1837, in Dryden, Tompkins Co., N. Y.; m. John F. Sanders, in Union, Utah, July 15, 1855; she d. in Fairview, Sanpete Co., Utah, Aug. 19, 1875; she had 8 ch. (10) Thomas Alma Clement, b. Mar. 24, 1842, in Dryden, Tompkins Co., N. Y.; m. Elizabeth Shoemaker, now lives in Plain City, Weber Co., Utah; had 8 ch., all dead but 3.

1448. iii. NANCY, b. May 19, 1797; m. Jonathan Bouker, of Grotton, Tompkins Co., N. Y., son of John Bouker, of Lansing, N. Y. He was b. Nov. 18, 1797; she d. Dec. 5, 1823, in Grotton, N. Y. He was living in 1882 in Grotton, N. Y. Ch.: (1) Irene Bouker, b. 1817, in Grotton, Tompkins Co., N. Y.; m. and d. in 1835. (2) Albert Bouker, b. Oct. 11, 1823, in Grotton; was twice m.; both wives dead; had 4 ch. He now lives in Clinton Co., Mich.

1449. iv. MELINDA, b. Feb. 21, 1800, in Windsor, N. Y.; m. Hiram McLean, in Dryden, N. Y. She d. in Dryden, Feb. 20, 1838; he was b. Dec. 4, 1795, and with his widowed mother and brother John came to Dryden from Orange Co., N. Y., about 1812. He m. Melinda Foote, Feb. 21, 1821, in Dryden, N. Y., by Parley Whitmore, Esq. Hiram McLean was a cooper by trade and followed that business all his life, making pork and cider barrels, and farming during the summer seasons; d. July 1, 1871, at Milan, Rock Island Co., Ill., at the home of his younger dau., Helen Eliza Johnson, and was buried in Chippianoch Cemetery, Rock Island, Ill., July 3, 1871. Ch.: (1) Nancy McLean, b. July 11, 1822, in Dryden, N. Y.; m. Darius Gaines (or Givins) in Dryden, where they still live; have 6 ch. (2) Mary McLean, b. Mar. 17, 1824, in Dryden, N. Y.; d. July 3, 1840, in Dryden. (3) Irene McLean, b. Mar. 29, 1826, in Dryden, N. Y.; d. Nov. 13, 1828, in

Dryden. (4) Almira McLean, b. Dec. 1, 1828, in Dryden, N. Y.; m. Robert Seager, in Dryden, where they still live; have 2 ch. living, 1 dead. (5) Harriet Augusta McLean, b. July 20, 1831, in Dryden, N. Y.; m. Laisdel Seager, in Dryden, N. Y., where they still live; 2 ch. (6) Warren McLean, b. Apr. 20, 1834, in Dryden, N. Y.; m. and lives in Dryden; no ch. (7) Helen Eliza McLean was b. at Dryden, Tompkins Co., N. Y., May 12, 1836. At the age of 17 months her mother (Melinda Foote McLean, d. Feb. 20, 1838) d. leaving her at home with her father, 4 sisters and 1 brother. The following year her father m. the widow Mary Johnson. She lived at home with her father and step-mother until the age of 14 years and attended the Hiles School while at home. At the age of 14 she went to live with her older sister, Almira McLean Seager (Almira McLean Seager was an invalid at that time and was for three years, being finally cured by earnest prayer and a Methodist minister who was a faith doctor), where she lived until she was m. to Matthew Thomas Johnson, Mar. 31, 1857. Matthew T. Johnson was b. in Dryden, N. Y., Aug. 4, 1834. At the age of 4 years his father, Joseph Johnson, d., leaving him with his mother (a weaver) and two sisters, Catherine and Harriet, at home to fight life's battles. At the age of 8 years he went to live with his brother-in-law, Jesse Trapp, on a farm about three miles northwest of Dryden, attending the "Gee School" winters and farming summers. At the age of 15 he went to live with his brother, Jacob Johnson, on a farm, where he remained until the age of 21, when he and his brother Jacob and family moved to Rock Island, Ill. In Mar., 1857, he returned to Dryden, and on Tuesday, Mar. 31, was m. to Helen Eliza McLean in Courtland, N. Y. The first four years of married life was spent on rented farms. Three years in Rock Island Co. and one year at Big Rock, Iowa. In 1861 he bought a farm of 40 acres about one mile east of Milan, increasing it to 400 acres in the course of 18 years. He was a member and elder of the Methodist Epis-copal Church at Milan, Ill., from 1860, to Mar. 1, 1900, and Superintendent of the same Sunday School from May, 1869, to Mar. 1, 1900, when he retired from farming and moved to Rock Island, Ill., where he now res. They celebrated their golden wedding anniversary on Easter Sunday, Mar. 31, 1907, having been m. 50 years on that date at Courtland, Tompkins Co., N. Y., by Rev. Albert S. Graves, a minister of the M. E. Church. The couple immediately came to Milan, then known as Camden Mills, and started their married life on a farm about 2½ miles south of Milan, on the Hoover farm. A notable feature of the dinner was the two roast geese that laid golden eggs for the honored couple. Another was the bride's cake, a surprise for the bride from her son and daughter, Mr. and Mrs. George H. Johnson, of Beaumont, Tex. This cake was unique in view of the fact that the frosting which covered the dainty golden con-fection was incrusted with gold dollars set into the iceing, one for each year of married life of the couple. These were all of

rare coinage and all bore the date of the year of the wedding
fifty years ago.   In addition there were other gold dollars,
souvenirs for each of the guests about the table, which will
serve to keep the memory of this gathering green. With the
dessert there were other golden gifts showered on the couple
honored on this occasion. Among these was a new gold wedding
ring to take the place of the worn band that has graced the
worn hand for half a century. All of the living descendants of
the couple, their children with their husbands, wives and
children, 16 in all, were present as follows: Mr. and Mrs. Collins
Dysart and son George, of Dixon, Ill., also their dau., Ruth, who
is a student at the Northwestern University at Evanston; Mr.
and Mrs. W. E. Johnson, of Rock Island; Mrs. Eva Forte and
daus., Nina and Margaret, who reside at the home of Mr. and
Mrs. Johnson; Mr. and Mrs. George H. Johnson, of Beaumont,
Texas, and Mr. and Mrs. H. P. Brown and dau., Marion, of Rock
Island. Ch.: (a) Ida Mary Johnson was b. April 25, 1860, at
Camden Mills, Ill. She attended the public and high school at
Milan, and Cornell College, Mt. Vernon, Iowa. Jan. 10, 1883, she
was m. to Collins Dysart, b. Nov. 7, 1858, of Nachusa, Lee Co.,
Ill. Ch.: (i) Ruth Helen, b. May 13, 1887, at Nachusa, Ill.;
graduated at Dixon High School in June, 1902, and is now in
the Northwestern University, Evanston, Ill. (ii) George Harold,
b. Jan. 25, 1892, at Nachusa, Ill.; in Dixon High School. (b)
William Edgar Johnson, b. in Milan, Ill., Apr. 21, 1864; he
attended the public and high school at Milan, and Normal
school at Dixon, Ill.; m. Bell Bernhard, at Orion, Ill., June 22,
1887. Merchant at Beatrice, Neb., one year; then farmer on
the old homestead until 1902, when he moved to Rock Island,
Ill., where he took a position as Inspector in the Rock Island
Plow Co.'s shops, and is now (Jan., 1907) Superintendent and
Master Mechanic of the factory. (c) Eva Lucy, b. Dec. 19,
1870, at Milan, Ill.; he attended the public and high school at
Milan, Ill.; res. with her parents. (d) George Hartt, b. May 31,
1867, at Milan, Ill.; educated at the public and high school at
Milan, and the Davenport Business College, Davenport, Iowa.
At the age of 23 he found employment with the War Department
of the United States on the Illinois and Missisippi Canal at
Milan, Ill., as timekeeper and clerk. He was almost continuously
employed with the United States, having spent two months of
the winter of 1894 in California, and the year 1897 as Inspector
with the Engineering Department of the United States in
Chicago, on the Chicago River; he assisting on the farm at home
during the time not employed by the U. S. He was transferred
to the U. S. Assistant Engineer's office on the Ill. and Miss.
Canal at Sterling, Ill., in Oct., 1898, and was there continuously
employed, and wrote life insurance in the evenings or on the side
when not busy with official duties, until his resignation in Jan.,
1902, to accept a position as Secretary and Manager of the
Illinois Oil Company located at Beaumont, Texas. After successfully holding that position for one year, he was one of three

parties who organized the Texas Drilling Co., of Beaumont, Texas, which has been and is now a very successful company in drilling and operating oil wells in Texas. After spending a year in Texas he returned to Illinois and m. Grace E. Lord, b. Sept. 26, 1871, of Dixon, Ill., and are now (Jan., 1907) living a happy and prosperous life at Beaumont, Texas. He is the founder of the first oil field in the State of Iowa, discovered at Maquoketa, in Jackson Co. (e) Stella Elizabeth Johnson, b. at Milan, Ill., Nov. 26, 1872; educated at the public and high school at Milan, Ill.; m. Apr. 17, 1895, Herman, P. Brown, b. June 17, 1871, of Rock Island, Ill., formerly of Milan, Ill. Agent of the Adams Express Co.; on Sept. 1, 1905, he resigned this position and accepted a position with the Rock Island Plow Co., where he is now employed. Ch.: (i) Marion, b. Dec. 9, 1901. (f) Nettie Adeline Johnson, b. Apr. 19, 1876. During the 11th year of her age, while attending school at Milan, Ill., she contracted the dreaded disease diphtheria, and d. at 9.10 a.m., Nov. 26, 1887. She was a very bright and beautiful girl; buried in Chipianoch Cemetery, Rock Island, Ill. (g) Roy Johnson, b. May 23, 1879. On the evening of Dec. 4 he was taken sick with convulsions and d. Dec. 5, 1879; he was buried in Chipianoch Cemetery, Rock Island, Ill.

1450. v.   IRENE, b. June 20, 1803, in Dryden, N. Y.; m. William Ferguson, in Dryden, N. Y., Jan. 15, 1824. He was b. in Fabeus, Onondaga Co., N. Y., Nov. 30, 1802. He d. in Mercer Co. Ill., Nov. 8, 1865. She is still living (1882) in Saline, Ill, with her dau. Ch.: (1) Louisa Ferguson, b. Oct. 28, 1825, in Dryden, Tompkins Co., N. Y.; m. Samuel Wagoner, in Chester, Geauga Co., Ohio. He was b. May 26, 1820, in Delaware, son of Christian and Elizabeth (Measle) Wagoner. He d. Nov. 4, 1868, in Mercer Co., Ill. They had 6 ch. She (in 1882) is living in Aleda, Ill. (2) Harrison Ferguson, b. Nov. 19, 1827, in Dryden, N. Y.; m. Lyma Harriet Coring, June 17, 1848, in Kirtland, O.; 1 ch. They now live in Davenport, Iowa. (3) William Emery (a twin), b. Oct. 7, 1838, in Chester, Geauga Co., O.; unm.; lives (in 1882) in Mercer Co., Ill. (4) Irene Emily Ferguson (a twin), b. Oct. 7, 1838, in Chester, Geauga Co., O.; m. Charles Francis Hunt, June 6, 1867; now live in Maline, Ill.; have 7 ch.

1451. vi.   DORCAS, b. Jan. 9, 1806, in Dryden, N. Y.; d. Apr. 2, 1806.

1452. vii. ALMIRA, b. Feb. 25, 1808, in Dryden, N. Y.; m. Isaac Ferguson, in Adams Co., Ill., June 27, 1839. He was b. in Sciota Co., O., Sept. 4, 1810. She d. Feb. 16, 1867, in South Cottonwood, Salt Lake Co., Utah. He d. Nov. 24, 1880, in the same place. Ch.: (1) Warren Haskel Ferguson, b. Mar. 22, 1840, in Adams Co., Ill.; m. Elizabeth Nickerson, in S. Cottonwood, Salt Lake Co., Utah. Now (in 1882) lives in Utah, and has 6 ch. (2) Nancy Augusta Ferguson, b. July 17, 1842, in Adams Co., Ill.; m. John Tanner, in Salt Lake City, Utah. They live in South Cottonwood, Salt Lake Co., Utah, and have 8 ch. (3) Orson Nephi, b. Mar. 30, 1844, in Adams Co., Ill.; d. in 1845. (4) Clarrissa Irene, b. July 30, 1845, in Hancock Co., Ill.; d.

DR. WINFIELD SCOTT HALL. No. 2485 (1)

FRANK FOOTE. No. 4214

MAJOR FRANK M. FOOTE. No. 4219

MATTHEW and HELEN McLEAN JOHNSON. No. 1449 (7)

ROBERT FOOTE HALL. No. 1552 (4)

(5) Isaac David, b. June 10, 1848, near Bighorn R. in the now state of Nebraska; m. Mary Jane Green, in South Cottonwood, Salt Lake Co., Utah, May 29, 1868; where he now resides; has several ch. (6) Almira, b. 1857, in South Cottonwood, Salt Lake Co., Utah; m. Tarlton (or Tarltou) Lewis; have 3 ch. living, 3 dead.

1453. viii. CLARISSA, b. June 16, 1810, Dryden, N. Y.; m. Apr., 1838, George Gates, in Chester, O.; she d. Nov. 5, 1840, in Hancock Co., Ill.; 2 ch., both d. in infancy.

1454. ix. DAVID, b. Aug. 24, 1812, Dryden, N. Y.; m. Mary Bidwell, 2886-94.

1455. x. GEORGE LANE, b. Apr. 16, 1815, Dryden, N. Y.; m. Mary Ann, Gillette, 2895-8.

1456. xi. WARREN, b. Aug. 10, 1817, Dryden, N. Y.; m. Artemisia S. Myers and Eliza Maria Ives, 2899-2915.

1457. xii. HARRISON, b. July 5, 1819, in Dryden, N. Y.; d. Sept. 5, 1820.

535. BERNICE FOOTE, (172, 47, 13, 5,) b. June 5, 1766; m. Melinda Field, of Northfield, Mass. She was b. July 20, 1770; he d. of apoplexy, Jan. 23, 1831; res., Northfield, Mass., Burlington, N. Y.

1458. i. HARRIET, b. July 20, 1792; m. May 29, 1821, Rev. Alexander B. Corning, of Manchester, Mich., at Burlington, N. Y. Ch.: (1) Erastus, b. Oct. 22, 1822; d. in infancy. (2) Alexander Foote, b. June 3, 1824. (3) Erastus B., b. Mar. 3, 1826; d. in infancy. (4) Benjamin T., b. July 23, 1829. (5) Harriet W., b. Oct. 10, 1834.

1459. ii. HORATIO, b. Northfield, Mass., Feb. 10, 1796; m. Abigail Kirkland, 2916-9.

1460. iii. LUCIUS, b. Northfield, Mass., Aug. 3, 1798; m. Electa W. Harwood, 2920-2.

1461. iv. HIRAM, b. Burlington, N. Y., Dec. 15, 1801; d. July 13, 1803.

1462. v. FERONIA, b. Burlington, N. Y., Oct. 16, 1804.

1463. vi. HIRAM, b. Burlington, N. Y., Aug. 21, 1808; m. Elizabeth Church, 2923-27.

1464. vii. HORACE, b. Burlington, N. Y., Dec. 27, 1811; m. Harriet N. Batcheder, 2928.

537. DEA. SAMUEL FOOTE, (172, 47, 13, 5,) b. Apr. 7, 1770; m. Aug. 8, 1794, Sibbil, dau. of Oliver Doolittle, of Hinsdale, N. H. She was b. Dec. 9, 1777; d. Mar. 4, 1832, in Waterboro, N. Y.; m. 2nd, Widow Parker, 1833.

Samuel Foote and Sibbil Doolittle were m. at Hinsdale, near Northfield, Aug. 8, 1794. About three years later (1797) they removed from Gill with their only child (Elial Todd Foote) to the Chenango country, then almost a wilderness, and settled in the west part of Sherburne, afterwards called Smyrna. Mr. Samuel Foote did not long remain in the west part of the town, but, as stated by his son, Elial T. Foote, "soon after 1800, he bought at Sherburne West Hill, and moved there; built and opened a country tavern opposite Lansing's (afterwards Lynde's) store. In 1806 he built his large front addition (the present Sexton house). I recollect in June, 1806, at the time of the great eclipse, I was with father at Lathrop's sawmill for a load of boards to finish that house. I remember Mr. Lansing well. He boarded with our father while there, and so did both of the Lyndes (Tilly and Charles W.) for years."

(11)

Again, in speaking of the old Sherburne West Hill Church, of which Samuel Foote and Sibbil, his wife, and Sedate, his sister, were early members, Elial T. Foote says: "I recollect the erection of the meeting house there, and the installation of the Rev. Joshua Knight. Our father (the letter from which this is an extract was directed to his brother Erastus, then living in Milwaukee, Wis.), from his hard labor did much to build that meeting house and sustain the society." And again: "Our father was the first postmaster in Sherburne, appointed by General Granger in 1803. The mails from Cooperstown to Homer, and from Utica to Oxford crossed at West Hill." That made it an important business centre, and showed its growing interest, for prior to 1803, the post office, as Hatch's history informs us, had been located at the James Elmore store on the east side of the river, he having been, according to the same authority, "the first postmaster appointed in the place, his commission bearing date of January, 1801," which accordingly antedates Mr. Foote's appointment, though doubtless he was the first postmaster at Sherburne West Hill. As the result of Mr. Foote's unwillingness to submit to the rules of the church, which inhibited dancing, as stated in the history of the Old Church, he received a dismissal therefrom in July, 1811, and soon after that time disposed of his inn, which afterwards came into the possession of the late Frederick Sexton, by whose descendants it is still occupied as a residence.

In 1817 Mr. Samuel Foote removed to Plymouth, Chenango Co., where with a few others he was instrumental in building the First Congregational Church, and settling the first minister. He was elected deacon of this church. About the year 1828 he and his wife removed to Chautauqua Co., where most of their children had settled.

In 1832 his wife, Sibbil Doolittle, died at their home near Jamestown, N. Y. He was deacon of the First Presbyterian Church in Jamestown for some fifteen years prior to his death, which occurred while on a visit to the home of his son, Obed Foote, at Grand Rapids, Mich., Jan. 25, 1848, at the age of 78. He was a warm hearted, sincere Christian, devoted in his love for his Saviour. He was buried at Fulton St. Cemetery, Grand Rapids. Res., Gill, Mass., Sherburn, N. Y.

1465. i.   ELIAL TODD, b. Gill, Mass., May 1, 1796; m. Ann Cheney and Amelia Stiles Leavitt Jenkins, 2929-33.

1466. ii. SAMUEL, b. Sherburne, N. Y., Aug. 22, 1798; m. Laura Holbrook, 2934-5.

1467. iii. ERASTUS, b. Sherburne, July 1, 1800; m. Aurilla Gallup, 2936-42.

1468. iv. MARY DOROTHEA, b. Sherburne, N. Y., Apr. 17, 1802; m. June 25, 1826, Elisha Hall, of Jamestown, N. Y., and St. Louis, Mo. He was the son of William Hall, and was b. Dec. 19, 1799, in Dover, Vt. He d. Nov. 1, 1853, in Warren, Pa. She d. July 14, 1861, in Allentown, Mo., near St. Louis. Their remains were interred in Lot 18 in Olivet Section in Lake View Cemetery in Jamestown, Chautauqua Co., N. Y. Ch., all b. in Jamestown, N. Y.: (1) Verro Vernandico Hall, b. Oct. 3, 1830 ; m. Nov., 1857, Martha Bates Masterson, of Palmyra, Mo. She was b. July 14, 1835. Ch.: (a) Edward Hall, b. Palmyra, Sept. 14, 1858; m. Sept. 1, 1886, Nellie S., dau. of Levi and Elizabeth Wilcox, of Bradford, Idaho. She was b. Marson City, Ill., Dec. 23, 1866. Ch.: (i) Laura

ALBERT ELISHA HALL. No. 1468 (2). AND WIFE.

JUDGE RUFUS B. COWING.   No. 1472 (2)

May Hall, b. Bradford, Idaho, May 30, 1887. (ii) Verro Vernandico Hall, b. Bradford, Idaho, Jan. 31, 1891. (b) Laura C.
Hall b. Palmyra, Sept., 1864. (c) Cora Edna Hall, b. Opha,
Utah, Apr. 3, 1874. (2) Albert Elisha, b. in Jamestown, N. Y., June
8, 1833;. removed with his parents to St. Louis, Mo., Mar., 1844;
entered the army May 10 1861, at St. Louis, Mo.; served under
General Lyons in South West Compaign. Mustered out of service in fall of 1861 and received a Captain's commission in
the 11th Regt. May Militia; resigned in 1862, and received a
First Lieutenant and Regimental Quartermaster commission in
10th Regt. Cavalry Mo. Volunteers; served three years. Remained in Alabama three years after the close of the war and
grew cotton. He was the first person to grow cotton under the
Free Labor System in the State of Alabama, if not in the
United States. Returned to St. Louis, Mo., in 1868; m. Ella
Webster Whiting (b. at Winsted, Ct., Oct. 5, 1848), Oct. 5, 1870,
at Terra Haute, Ind. They removed to Glyndon, Minn.,
1878, Washington Territory in 1887, Long Beach., Cal.,
June 20, 1898. A member of Long Beach Post, G. A. R. Ch.:
(a) Mary Ellen Hall, b. Glyndon, Minn., June 20, 1877; m.
Ontario, Cal., June 22, 1897, Frank L., son of John R. and Lydia
Burr; he was b. St. John's, Glinn Co., Cal.; res., Long Beach,
Cal.; no ch. (b) Albert E. Hall, Jr., b. Glyndon, Minn., Mar.
22, 1883; d. Apr. 19, 1890, at Tacoma, Wash. (3) Julia Clarissa
Hall, b. Jamestown, N. Y., Sept. 21, 1835; m. Aug. 6, 1856, in St.
Louis, Mo., James D., son of Dennis and Jane Leonard. Ch.:
(a) Frank Hall Leonard, b. St. Louis, Mo., Aug. 1, 1857. (b)
Clarence Leonard, b. St. Louis, Mo., Apr., 1861. (c) Cora Sophia,
b. St. Louis, Mo., May 20, 1863; m. Charles Overmeyer, 1884;
they reside. at No. 11, East 9th St., Topeka, Kansas. Ch.: (i)
Dorathea Overmeyer, b. 1894. (4) Erastus Foote Hall, b. Feb.
15, 1839; m. ———; d. ———. (5) Mary Dorathea Hall, b. Nov.
13, 1843; m. Feb. 5, 1872, St. Louis, Mo., Thomas Corwin, son
of Norton Case, of Granville, O. He was b. Feb. 2, 1840; d.
June 30, 1878, at St. Louis, Mo.; a veteran of the Civil War.
Ch.: (a) Norton Elisah Case, b. St. Louis, Mar. 7, 1873. (b)
Carroll Hall Case, b. St. Louis, Dec. 4, 1874. (c) Maud Case, b.
St. Louis, Dec. 31, 1876; d. July 16, 1877. (d) Janette Case, b.
St. Louis, Jan. 7, 1878; d. May 20, 1880, at St. Louis, Mo.

1469. v.   LYDIA, b. Sherburne, N. Y., Feb. 4, 1804; d. Feb. 3, 1805.
1470. vi. PHILENA, b. Sherburne, N. Y., Feb. 10, 1806; d. July 26, 1829.
1471. vii. CHLOE, b. Apr. 10, 1808; m. June 17, 1829, Smith Seayour, of
           Jamestown, N. Y. He was b. Dec. 17, 1803; she d. Oct. 11, 1840.
           Ch.: (1) Emeline Sedate, b. Mar. 31, 1830; m. A. J. Weeks, of
           Jamestown, N. Y. (2) Sibbil, b. Aug. 20, 1833; d. May 29,
           1841. (3) Burritt Grey, b. Feb. 18, 1837. (4) Chloe Foote, b.
           Oct. 8, 1840; d. Oct. 12, 1840.
1472. viii. SEDATE, b. Apr. 14, 1810, at Sherburne; m. 1837, John K. See "Additions
            Cowing, of Jamestown. He was a merchant, largely engaged in and Corrections"
            lumbering. He was son of Calvin and Emily (Bissell) Cowing, ile at Desk.
            and was b. Feb. 6, 1810. He d. Nov. 18, 1845, in Dexterville,
            N. Y. She d. in New York, May 3, 1874. Ch.: (1) James R., b.

May 25, 1838; d. May 19, 1840. (2) Rufus Billings Cowing, b.
May 25, 1840, in Jamestown, N. Y.; m. at Sing Sing, N. Y.,
June 27, 1866, Hester Ann Tugnot; m. 2nd; at Detroit, Mich.,
Apr. 23, 1901, Marie Antoinette Ling, of New York City. Mr.
Cowing graduated at Harvard Law School 1863; has held several
positions in New York City of a public and private nature; has
represented the City for one term as Alderman at Large, and
for the past 27 years has held the position of City Judge of the
City of New York, and has presided in the highest Court of
Criminal Jurisdiction in the City; has been twice elected for two
terms of 14 years each, and on both occasions was elected by
both parties (Republican and Democrat); at the last election
he polled 272,000 votes of 282,000 cast; has been Vice-President
of the Union League Club of the City, and for 12 years President of the New York Homeopathic College. Ch.: (a) Edward
K. Cowing, b. Aug. 19, 1868. (b) Rufus Billings Cowing, b. Dec.
12, 1869. (c) Charlotta L. Cowing, b. July 5, 1872. (d) James
Foote Cowing, b. Oct. 2, 1874; d. in infancy. (e) Percy Foote
Cowing, b. May 27, 1879. (f) Albert Rufus Billings Cowing, Jr.,
b. Jan. 14, 1903. (3) Frances Adalade, b. Sept. 28, 1842; d.
Nov. 25, 1843. (4) Kirkland Newton, b. Oct. 3, 1843; killed at
the battle of Chicamauga, while serving his country in the
Union Army; unm.

1473. ix.   CHARLES DOOLITTLE, b. Sherburne, N. Y., Dec. 25, 1812;
            m. Laura Ann Holbrook and Mary Daulton Arnold, 2943-51.
1474. x.   OBED HYATT, b. Plymouth, N. Y., May 18, 1817; m. Lucy
            Moore Crosby, 2952-8.
1475. xi.   OLIVER DOOLITTLE, b. Plymouth, N. Y., July 28, 1821; d.
            Feb. 2, 1822.

540. COL. ERASTUS FOOTE, (172, 47, 13, 5,) b. Sept. 19, 1777; m. 1812,
Susan, dau. of Col. Moses Carlton, of Wiscasset, Me. She was b. Jan. 28, 1796, and
d. June 28, 1817; m. 2nd, July 9, 1820, Eliza, dau. of Col. Moses Carlton, of Wiscasset, Me. She was b. July 1, 1798; d. June 27, 1880. Res., Wiscasset, Me. He
was admitted to the Bar at Northampton, Mass., and begun his professional
career at Camden, Maine. He was successively County Attorney, Senator of the
Massachusetts Legislature, Senator of the Maine Legislature immediately after
the organization of Maine into a State, and Attorney General of Maine. This
last office he held for twelve successive years, and gave a tone and character to
the Criminal Jurisprudence of the State which were alike honorable to him and
highly appreciated by the public. He d. July 14, 1856, at Wiscasset, Me.

1476. i.   MARY WOOD, b. Dec. 20, 1813; d. Jan. 13, 1814.
1477. ii.   ERASTUS MILES, b. Aug. 31, 1815; d. Feb. 16, 1816.
1478. iii. SUSAN ELIZA, b. Jan. 1, 1817; d. Oct. 5, 1887, at Wiscasset,
            Me.; unm.
1479. iv.   ERASTUS, b. Sept. 6, 1821; m. Sarah Page Wood, 2954-63.
1480. v.   MARY TODD, b. Dec. 25, 1823, in Wiscasset, Me.; m. Apr. 24,
            1850, in Wiscasset, Me., Isaac Henry Coffin. She d. in Chicago,
            Ill., Mar. 18, 1892; he d. in Wiscasset, Me., Oct. 12, 1890. Ch.:
            (1) Isabella Wood, b. Oct. 4, 1852; m. in Wiscasset, Me., Dec. 3,
            1873, Charles Evelyn Fargo, of Chicago; d. July 25,

1874. Ch. : (a) Charles Evelyn Fargo, b. July 15, 1874; res., 6758 Lafayette Avenue, Chicago, Ill. (2) Anna Foote, b. Jan. 21, 1856; m. in Wiscasset, Me., John Cowles Grant, of Chicago, Ill., Aug. 11, 1886. Ch.: (a) Mary Foote, b. in Chicago, Ill., Oct. 30, 1891. (3) Henry Isaac, b. Feb. 19, 1858; d. Sept. 19, 1858. (4) Mary Eliza, b. July 31, 1860; d. July 11, 1876. (5) Florence Carleton, b. Oct. 25, 1864, in Wiscasset, Me.; m. David Bunting Fraser, of Glasgow, Scotland, at Wiscasset, Me., Sept. 9, 1891. Ch.: (a) Albert Averell, b. Apr. 21, 1896. (b) Florence Carleton, b. Sept. 4, 1899. (c) David Bunting Fraser, Jr., b. Dec. 13, 1903.

1481. vi. ABIGAIL, b. Aug. 31, 1825; d. Sept. 7, 1826.
1482. vii. ANN BUTLER, b. Oct. 8, 1827, in Wiscasset, Me. (at present living in Chicago); m. at Wiscasset, Me., July 4, 1852, Albert James Averell, of Chicago, Ill. He was b. in Alna, Me., Mar. 20, 1823; d. in Chicago, Sept. 6, 1896.

543. OBED FOOTE, (172, 47, 13, 5,) b. Apr. 27, 1787; m. July 24, 1823, Ann G., dau. of Luke Walpole, of Indianapolis, Ind. She was b. Sept. 16, 1800, and d. July 24, 1824; m. 2nd, June 23, 1831, Mary, wid. of Francis Davis. He d. of Scer. Maligna, Sept. 24, 1833. He was an Attorney at Law and Justice of Peace. Res., Indianapolis, Ind.

1483. i. OBED, b. Apr. 19, 1824; m. Mary Grey McOuat, 2964-7.
1484. ii. CYNTHIA ANN, b. Jan. 28, 1833.

549. STEPHEN FOOTE, (178, 50, 16, 5,) bap. Apr. 24, 1763; m. Sept. 24, 1784, Mary Pardee, of East Haven, Ct. He d. Sept. 23, 1798. She d. Apr. 26, 1814, ae. 49. Res., Branford, Ct.

1485. i. KETURAH, b. 1785; d. Sept. 19, 1798.
1486. ii. FOSTER, b. 1788; m. Polly Monroe, 2968-70.
1487. iii. MARY E., b. Mar. 19, 1790; m. Jan. 31, 1810, James Woodhull; d. May 6, 1826. Ch.: (1) William S., b. Nov. 22, 1810. (2) John F., b. Jan. 14, 1812; m. July 26, 1848, Sarah F. Squire. (3) James N., b. Dec. 20, 1813; d. Oct. 13, 1819. (4) Mary E., b. Apr. 11, 1817. (5) Evander, b. Nov. 9, 1819; d. in infancy. (6) George G., b. Jan. 16, 1821; d. July 1, 1845. (7) Charles W., b. Dec. 23, 1822.
1488. iv. SALLY, b. 1791; d. Sept. 10, 1798.
1489. v. GEORGE, b. 1793; d. Sept. 19, 1798.
1490. vi. ESTHER, b. 1796; d. Sept. 20, 1798.
1491. vii. SARAH ALMIRA, b. Aug. 4, 1798; m. May 22, 1843, Orin D. Squire, of Branford, Ct.

557. ROBERT ABRAHAM EBENEZER FOOTE, (185, 53, 16, 5,) b. Sept. 17, 1776; m. Dec., 1788, Lucy Orton, of Woodbury, Ct. She d. June 25, 1858; he d. Nov. 29, 1848.

1492. i. LUCRETIA, b. Sept. 30, 1789, in Woodbury, Ct.; m. Oct. 30, 1811, Ransley Tolles. He was b. Jan. 5, 1788; res., Woodbury, Ct. Ch.: (1) Alza I., b. Oct. 6, 1812. (2) Lucretia M., b. Sept. 30, 1815; m. Apr., 1839, Joseph R. Sherman; res., Dubuque, Ia. Ch.: (a) Adolphus F., b. Feb., 1840. (3) Julia A., b. Feb. 10, 1818; res., N. Y. (4) Robert I., b. Apr. 3, 1820; res., Woodbury, Ct.; m. Sept. 21, 1841, Emeline Whitlocke. Ch.: (a) Sarah I.,

b. Mar. 16, 1843; d. Apr. 2, 1843. (5) Lucinda F., b. July 1, 1822; d. Mar. 7, 1842. (6) Chester F., b. Mar. 7, 1825; m. Feb. 25, 1846, Martha P. Homeston; res., Woodbury, Ct. Ch.: (a) Elizabeth A., b. Feb. 23, 1847. (b) Elsey L., b. Aug. 30, 1848. (7) Elsey M., May 12, 1827; res., Woodbury. (8) Franklin B., b. Oct. 1, 1829; res., Woodbury. (9) Wellington R., b. Feb. 10, 1833; res., Woodbury. (10) Frederick O., b. Nov. 4, 1835; res., Woodbury, Ct.

1493. ii. CHESTER, b. Oct. 30, 1791; m. Rebecca Sherman, 2971-9.

1494. iii. CYNTHIA, b. Jan. 2, 1794, in Woodbury, Ct.; m. Jan. 8, 1815, in Woodbury, Ct., Beach Bassett; res., Randolph, O. Ch.: (1) Lucy M. Bassett, b. Oct. 11, 1815; m. July 26, 1837, Horace S. Doty, of Randolph. Res., Ohio. Ch.: (a) Francis A., b. Jan. 23, 1841. (b) Henrietta S., b. June 24, 1842; d. July 25, 1848. (c) Ellen A., b. Aug. 30, 1844; d. Aug. 4, 1848. (2) Stiles M., b. Oct. 27, 1817; res., Ohio. (3) Nathan E., b. Apr. 28, 1820; m. Mar. 22, 1849, Emily Barron; res., Long Island, N. Y. (4) Francis M., b. June 2, 1822; m. Nov. 10, 1842, Heman H. Harrison, of Randolph, O.; res., Elkhorn, Wis. Ch.: (a) Gertrude A., b. Nov. 21, 1845. (5) Cynthia F., b. Sept. 15, 1822; m. Jan. 18, 1844, Squire Stamford, of Ohio. Res., Elkhorn, Wis. (6) Andrew H., b. Sept. 23, 1825; res., Elkhorn, Wis. (7) Beach, b. Jan. 7, 1828; res., Ravenna, O. (8) Amelia Antoinette, b. Oct. 31, 1830; res., Randolph, O. (9) Adelia Henrietta, b. Oct. 31, 1830; res., Randolph, O.

1495. iv. CHARLES, b. Mar. 16, 1796; m. Anna Lorence, of Alford, Ct.; res., Ohio.

1496. v. CHAUNCY, b. May 29, 1798; m. Eliza Bicknell; res., Ohio.

1497. vi. ELIADEE ORTON, b. July 4, 1806; m. Eliza Wooster, 2980-6.

1498. vii. LUCINDA, b. Mar. 26, 1801; m. 1st, James Hitchcock; m. 2nd, David Lang, of Huntington, O.

1499. viii. WILLIAM CLAIBOURNE, b. Nov. 2, 1803; m. Sally Bromley; res., Oswego, N. Y.

1500. ix. LUCY MINERVA, b. Jan. 10, 1810, in Woodbury, Ct.; m. Jan., 1829, Albert Robenson; she d. Nov. 2, 1836. Ch.: (1) Asiba, b. Mar. 14, 1830. (2) Albert, b. Apr. 15, 1831. (3) George, b. May 28, 1832. (4) Child, b. ———; d. in infancy.

1501. x. ABIGAIL LUGENA, b. Aug. 14, 1812; m. John Baird; res., Ohio.

1501¹. xi. ALMA ELISA, b. July 2, 1815.

561. JACOB FOOTE, (195, 54, 16, 5,) b. Mar. 20, 1771; m. Apr. 21, 1790, Sarah, dau. of James Wilcox, of Avon; d. Sept. 12, 1843. She d. Feb. 3, 1848. Res., Burlington, Ct.

1502. i. LUCY, b. Oct. 18, 1790; d. Dec. 19, 1808.

1503. ii. LUMAN, b. Sept. 27, 1792; d. Dec. 23, 1808.

1504. iii. AMELIA, b. Mar. 1, 1795; m. Grandison Dailey, of Burlington, Ct. Res., Hudson, O., where both d.

1505. iv. IRA, b. May 27, 1797; m. Nancy C. Mix, 2987-91.

1506. v. JAIRUS C., b. Aug. 16, 1799; d. Aug. 3, 1823, at Alexandria, Va.; unm.

1507. vi. SHUBAEL, b. Mar. 11, 1802; m. Marilla Pettibone, dau. of Theophilus Pettibone, of Burlington, Ct. Both d. in the South.

1508. vii. DR. ASAHEL, b. July 16, 1804; m. Caroline, dau. of Flavel Beckwith, of Burlington, Ct. She was b. Sept. 14, 1803. Res., Nelson, Ohio.

1509. viii. ARIEL, b. May 12, 1807; m. Julia Ann Webster, 2992-3½.

1510. ix. LUCY, b. Jan. 3, 1810; m. John Thompson, of New Haven, Ct.; res., Unionville, Ct.

1511. x. UNECIA, b. Aug. 25, 1812; m. Allen Wiston, of Bristol, Ct. Res., Bristol, Ct.

563. JOSEPH FOOTE, (195, 54, 16, 5,) b. Oct. 4, 1775; m. Mar. 27, 1794, Cynthia, dau. of Ezekiel Hosford, of Farmington, Ct. She d. Apr. 8, 1816, ae. 40; m. 2nd, June 2, 1816, Rhoda, dau. of James Olcott, of Litchfield, Ct.

1512. i. AMANDA, b. Sept. 27, 1795; m. Feb. 11, 1813, Richard Seymore, of Hartford, Ct. He d. July 5, 1840, ae. 53. Ch.: (1) Reuben, b. Aug. 20, 1815; d. Mar. 17, 1808. (2) Julius, b. Feb. 20, 1817; d. Oct. 19, 1822. (3) Sylvester, b. July 25, 1818. (4) Cynthia, b. Nov. 14, 1819; m. Nov. 31, 1838, William G. Collins, of East Windsor, Ct. (5) Eliza, b. Apr. 30, 1821. (6) Richard, b. July 12, 1823; m. Mary Robbins, of Wethersfield, Ct. (7) Amanda, b. Dec. 17, 1824. (8) Harriet, b. Oct. 17, 1826; d. Dec. 10, 1827. (9) Chauncey, b. Nov. 9, 1828. (10) Daniel, b. July 7, 1831. (11) Delia Jane, b. Nov. 12, 1834.

1513. ii. ABRAHAM, b. July 2, 1797; m. Mary Ransom, 2994-6.

1514. iii. REUBEN, b. Oct. 18, 1799; d. Aug. 20, 1801.

1515. iv. DANIEL, b. Jan. 10, 1802; d. May, 1829, at St. Jago de Cuba; unm.

1516. v. REUBEN, b. Dec. 31, 1808; m. Elizabeth Bebee, 2997.

565. ELIHU FOOTE, (196, 54, 16, 5,) b. Aug. 19, 1757, in Northford, Ct.; was a soldier and pensioner of the Revolutionary War; m. Lucy Williams, Nov. 11, 1789, dau. of Warham Williams, first minister in Northford, Ct., and Anne Hall, dau. of Rev. Samuel Hall, first minister in Cheshire, Ct. Samuel Hall m. 1727, Ann Law, third child of Governor Jonathan Law, of Milford, Ct. He m. Ann Eliot, grand-daughter of Rev. John Eliot, Apostle to the Indians, of Roxbury, Mass. Rev. Samuel Hall's son, Lyman, was a signer of the Declaration of Independence, from Georgia. Rev. Warham Williams, son of Rev. Stephen Williams, of Long Meadow, Mass., and grandson of Rev. John Williams, of Deerfield, Mass., and his wife, Eunice Mather, dau. of Rev. Eleazer Mather, of Northampton, Mass., was of Welsh origin. His father, Rev. John Williams, with his family, were captured by the Indians and taken to Canada, Feb. 29, 1703-4. His wife and two children killed by them. She, Eunice Mather Williams, on her mother's side was grand-daughter of Rev. John Warham, of Windham, Ct., formerly of Exeter, England. He d. June 1, 1840; she d. Dec. 21, 1839.

1517. i. EDWIN, b. Dec. 2, 1790; m. Selina Maltby, 2998-3000.

1518. ii. DELIA, b. June 23, 1792; m. Elijah, son of Solomon L. Linsley, of Northford, Ct., Jan. 27, 1813. Res., Branford, Ct., 1816. She d. Nov. 18, 1834. Ch.: (1) George Washington, b. May 11, 1815; m. 1845, Rosette Gaywood, of Fair Haven; d. in Philadelphia, Pa., 1891. She d. 1850. Ch.: (a) Winfield Scott, b. Sept. 4, 1846; m. May 14, 1868, Alice Gertrude, dau. of Willis Blakeslee and Nancy Benjamin, of New Haven, Ct. (b) Henry Gilbert, b. 1848; m. ———. (2) Mary Thankful, b. Dec. 20, 1817; d. when

4 years old. (3) Solomon, b. June 22, 1819; m. June, 1850, Adeline Hall. Ch.: (a) Noah, b. May 6, 1859; m. Oct., 1885, Sophia James, dau. of Jared, M. D., and Catherine (Baldwin) Linsley, of New York City. Ch.: (a) Jared, b. ———; d. in infancy. (4) William, b. Feb. 3, 1823; he was Dea. of First Congregational Church of Branford, Ct., 45 years; d. Mar. 5, 1903, ae. 80 years; m. Jan. 3, 1850, Harriet, dau. of Reusallace and Nancy (Averill) Carter. Ch.: (a) John Meig, b. Dec. 2, 1850; m. Nov. 15, 1876, Anna S., dau. of Barlow and Eleanor (White) Stevens, of Brooklyn, N. Y. Ch.: (i) Florence Irving, b. Jan. 7, 1879; m. Nov. 26, 1901, Albert Thomas Pate, of Brookly.., N. Y. Ch.: (i1) Beresford Linsley, b. Dec. 4, 1902; d. Jan. 20, 1905. (i2) Howard Albert, b. Oct. 8, 1904. (b) Ralph Irving, b. Oct. 11, 1853; m. Feb. 26, 1885, Eleanor White, dau. of Edwin and Harriet (White) Hall, of New York. Res., Metuchen, N. J. He d. Aug. 25, 1903, Bradford, Ct. Ch.: (i) Harriet Irving, b. Feb. 12, 1886. (ii) Gertrude Isabella, b. Feb. 14, 1888. (c) Maria Isabella, b. Sept. 4, 1857. (5) Henry, b. Mar. 20, 1825; m. Harriet, dau. of Capt. Chester and Sally Russel Averill, of Branford, Ct. Ch.: (a) Evalena, b. Oct. 1, 1853; d. Jan. 8, 1877. (b) Carrie Gertrude, b. Nov. 29, 1859; m. Harry Linsley; she d. Feb. 26, 1869. He m. 2nd, Mary Gifford Emery, of Durant, Iowa. (6) John Hancock, b. Sept. 13, 1827; d. ae. 4 years. (7) Delia Ann, b. Oct. 28, 1829; m. Oct. 24, 1850, Edwin Granniss, of East Haven, Ct. He d. Apr. 2, 1889; she d. Apr. 21, 1889.

1519. iii. WAREHAM WILLIAMS, b. Aug. 20, 1798; m. Lucinda Harrison, 3001-13.

1520. iv. ANNA HALL, b. Dec. 28, 1804; m. Albert Harrison. Ch.: (1) Ann Delia, b. ———. (2) Philo, b. ———. (3) Nathan, b. ———. (4) Jonathan, b. ———. (5) Lucy W., b. ———. (6) Albert, b. ———.

567. DANIEL FOOTE, (196, 54, 16, 5,) b. Dec. 7, 1760; m. Hannah Potter; she d. Jan. 30, 1833; he d. in Savannah, Ga. Res., Branford, Ct.

1521. i.   RALPH, b. ———; d. in the West Indies; unm.

1522. ii. AMELIA, b. ———; m. Jesse Bunnell. Ch.: 2.

569. JACOB FOOTE, (196, 54, 16, 5,) b. June 30, 1764; m. Apr., 1790; she d. Apr. 8, 1843. Res., Branford, Ct.

1523. i.   LAURA, b. Sept. 17, 1791; m. Nov. 23, 1813, Leman, son of Jonathan and Anna (Cook) Bartholomew, of Wallingford, Ct. He was b. July 15, 1791. She d. Dec. 11, 1856. Ch.: (1) John J., b. Dec. 22, 1815; m. Aug. 24, 1820, Charlotte A., dau. of Orin D. Square, of Branford, Ct. She was b. Aug. 14, 1820. (2) Antoinette, b. Oct. 29, 1818; m. Feb. 18, 1840, Edward W., son of Levi Parsons, of West Granville, Mass. (3) Rodolphus, b. June 7, 1820; m. S. Elizabeth, dau. of Capt. Samuel and Statitan (Frisbie) Griffing. Ch.: (a) S. Daggett Bartholomew, b. ———. (b) Clifford G. Bartholomew, b. ———. (c) Robert Bartholomew, b. ———. (d) Lizzie Cook Bartholomew, b. ———; m. John Edwin Brainard, of Branford, Ct. (e) Ernest S. Bartholomew,

b. ———. (4) Worthington, b. Feb. 2, 1824. (5) David Daggett, b. Aug. 1, 1826; d. Apr. 13, 1853; unm. (6) Laura A., b. May 2, 1830.

1524. ii. AGUSTUS, b. ———; m. Statira Whitney, 3014-21.

1525. iii. DANIEL, b. Aug. 14, 1796; m. Mary Potter, 3022-5.

1526. iv. JACOB, b. May 30, 1798; m. Lavinia Moulthrop, 3026-·

1527. v. MARIA, b. May 29, 1800; m. Oct. 3, 1818, Dudley Clark, of Haddam, Ct. Ch.: (1) Henry Hobart, b. Apr. 10, 1820; m. Fanny Ventress; he d. Mar. 4, 1900. (2) George Sheffield, b. Aug. 21, 1822. (3) Lewis, b. June 7, 1825. (4) Dudley, b. Sept. 4, 1827. (5) Luzerne, b. Mar. 4, 1830; d. Apr. 16, 1835. (6) Son, not named, b. July 17, 1832; d. July 19, 1832. (7) Daniel, b. Aug., 1833; d. Apr. 8, 1834. (8) Byron, b. Mar. 6, 1835; d. July 21, 1835. (9) Caroline Eliza, b. Aug. 27, 1836; d. Nov. 6, 1842. (10) Luzerne, b. Oct. 4, 1839.

1528. vi. LUCIUS, b. Dec. 21, 1803; m. Laura Hubbard and Lois Hubbard, 3027-31.

1529. vii. LUTHUR, b. ———; m. Salina Fowler, 3032-7.

1530. viii. BELINDA, b. July 9, 1807; m. Aug. 17, 1834, Luther Barnes, of New Haven, Ct. Ch.: (1) Luzerne, b. Aug., 1835; d. Aug. 1, 1835. (2) Luzerne, b. Apr. 11, 1837; d. May 13, 1838. (3) Sarah Ellen, b. Mar. 6, 1839. (4) Luzerne, b. Feb. 1, 1841. (5) Jane Augusta, b. May 4, 1843.

1531. ix. LUZERNE, b. Aug. 12, 1814; m. Grace Fowler, 3038-9.

572. ISAAC FOOTE, (196, 54, 16, 5,) b. Sept. 7, 1769; m. Peggy Fitchet.

1532. i. MARIA, b. ———; m. ———. Houghtailing.

573. RUFUS FOOTE, (196, 54, 16, 5,) b. Mar. 24, 1771; m. Mar. 12, 1799, Elizabeth, dau. of Amos Harrison, of Branford, Ct. She was b. July 22, 1779.

1533. i. BELA, b. Jan. 31, 1800; d. July 16, 1805.

1534. ii. PAMELIA, b. Jan. 9, 1802; d. July 25, 1805.

1535. iii. ABIATHAR, b. Apr. 16, 1804; m. Aug. 27, 1826, Sally Elvira Willcox, of Stockbridge; res., Warren Co., Ohio.

1536. iv. ELIZA PAMELIA, b. June 7, 1806; d. Dec. 10, 1825.

1537. v. CELIA, b. May 14, 1809; m. Oct. 14, 1829, Joseph Austin, of Branford, Ct. Res., North Haven, Ct.

1538. vi. POLLY A., b. Aug. 16, 1811; m. Sept. 30, 1835, William H. Maltby, of Branford, Ct.

1539. vii. MARIETTE, b. Dec. 10, 1813; m. Apr., 1832, Levi Talmadge, of Branford, Ct.

1540. viii. BELA, b. June 28, 1816; m. Almira Pierpont, North Haven, Ct. Res., North Branford, Ct.

574. ASA FOOTE, (196, 54, 16, 5,) b. Dec. 28, 1773; m. June 9, 1811, Olive Linsley; she was b. Sept. 21, 1790. He d. Jan. 4, 1833. Res., Northford, Ct.

1541. i. HENRY LEANDER, b. May 5, 1812; m. Caroline Bradley, of Charleston, S. C.

1542. ii. ELIZA ANN, b. Apr. 5, 1824; m. Cyrus Cook, of Guilford, Ct.

575. DAVID FOOTE, (196, 54, 16, 5,) b. Mar. 28, 1776; m. 1803, Elizabeth Smith. She was b. July 4, 1787; he d. May 5, 1843. Res., Nappanee, Canada West.

1543. i. MARGARET ELIZABETH, b. Apr. 20, 1809; m. May 17, 1826, Slants Kimmerly. Ch.: (1) Sarah Eliza, b. June 24, 1828. (2) Mary Cathrine, b. Dec. 22, 1830. (3) Amanda, b. Oct. 12, 1832. (4) Jane, b. Sept. 4, 1834. (5) John Cartwright, b. Jan. 11, 1838.

1544. ii. DAVID, JOHN SMITH, b. Dec. 2, 1811; m. Eliza Barton, 3040-3.

1545. iii. BENJAMIN, b. Mar. 6, 1815; m. Lucy Ann Briggs, 3044-8.

1546. iv. ASA, b. Sept. 3, 1817; m. Mary Baldwin, 3049.

1547. v. JOHN EDWIN, b. Sept. 20, 1822.

576. BENJAMIN, (196, 54, 16, 5,) b. Aug. 1, 1778; m. 1st, Apr. 24, 1803, Sally Parmele, dau. of Joel Hall, of Wallingford, Ct. She d. July 24, 1804, ae. 25; m. 2nd, June 2, 1805, Betsy, dau. of Andrew Hall, of Wallingford, Ct. She was b. Feb. 3, 1788; d. Sept. 20, 1831, ae. 44; m. 3rd, May 3, 1832, Harriet, wid. of Willis Homiston, of Wallingford, Ct., and dau. of Newberry Button, of North Haven, Ct; he d. Nov. 15, 1806. Res., Wallingford, Ct.

1548. i. SALLY H., b. Feb., 1804; d. May 13, 1804.

1549. ii. ANDREW H., b. Nov. 15, 1806; m. Frances Mary Hoadley, 3050-1.

1550. iii. HENRY A., b. July 14, 1809; d. Oct. 2, 1818.

1551. iv. JAMES, b. Aug. 15, 1811; m. Emeline Slead and Martha Reynolds, 3052-4.

1552. v. SARAH HALL, b. Jan. 15, 1815; m. Oct. 1, 1835, Charles Belden, son of Peter Hall, of Wallingford, Ct. Ch.: (1) Charles Kirtland, b. Philadelphia, July 27, 1836; d. Memphis, Tenn., abt. 1875. (2) Sarah Carrington, b. Philadelphia, Jan. 4, 1840; d. Cambridge, Mass., Nov. 8, 1903. (3) Albert Barnes, b. Philadelphia, Jan. 30, 1844; d. St. Paul, Minn., Oct. 13, 1867. (4) Robert Foote Hall, b. Philadelphia, May 25, 1849. He is directly descended from the John Hall who came with Rev. John Davenport and settled the town of New Haven in 1638. The son of this John Hall, named John, moved to and was one of·the organizers of the town of Wallingford, Ct., and many of his descendants live there to this day. At Portland, Ore., he m. 1st, Aletta T., dau. of Rev. A. A. Lindsley, D. D., of that city on Sept. 16, 1879. Mrs. Hall was b. Sept. 14, 1856, and d. Apr. 13, 1897; m. 2nd, Clara, daughter of Mr. E. J. Northrup, of Portland, Ore., Feb. 5, 1903. Ch.: (a) Lindsley Foote, b. Dec. 21, 1883. (b) Kenneth Stone, b. Sept. 5, 1888. Robert Foote Hall is a hardware merchant, of Portland, Ore., where he went as a young man to seek his fortune in the Far West.

1553. vi. BENJAMIN, b. Oct. 18, 1817; m. Sarah A. Hall, 3055-6.

1554. vii. HENRY CLAY, b. June 19, 1820; m. Cathrine Hall, 3057-64.

578. SAMUEL FOOTE, JR., (198, 54, 16, 5,) b. Dec. 25, 1765; m. Jan. 1, 1792, Submit, dau. of Dr. Jared Foote, of North Haven, Ct. He d. Oct. 18, 1816; she d. July 2, 1840, ae. 74, burnt to death by her clothes taking fire. Res., North Branford, Ct.

1555. i. CHAUNCY BISHOP, b. May 4, 1793; m. Nancy B. Ives, 3065-70.

1556. ii. ANN LOUISA, b. Jan. 8, 1795; m. Dec. 14, 1831, Abel Potter, of Claremont, Mass. She d. Apr. 5, 1836. Ch.: (1) Lois.

1557. iii. ROXANA, b. Sept. 17, 1796; res., North Branford, Ct.; unm.

1558. iv.   OLIVE, b. Mar. 28, 1801; m. Oct. 19, 1825, Ruel, son of Reul
            Andrus, of East Haven, Ct. Ch.: (1) Malvina Celestia, b. Sept.
            2, 1826. (2) Francis Foote, b. Mar. 18, 1828. (3) Ann Louisa,
            b. Nov. 2, 1829. (4) Harriet Minerva, b. July 7, 1834. (5)
            Eveline Foote, b. Feb. 22, 1842. (6) Samuel Winchester, b.
            Jan. 25, 1844.

1559. v.   SAMUEL WINCHESTER, b. Jan. 1, 1804; d. Aug. 31, 1830; unm.

580. COL. ENOS FOOTE, (198, 54, 16, 5,) b. Mar. 4, 1772; m. Roxanna
Perkins; he was graduated at Yale College 1791; was a merchant in Southwick,
the Colonel of the Regiment many years; a Representative from Southwick, and
two years a Senator in the Legislature of Mass., and was the first postmaster in
the town. He d. June 20, 1840; she d. 1841. Res., Southwick, Mass.

1560. i.   EMILY, b. June 17, 1800; m. Nov. 13, 1818, Hon. John Mills, of
            Springfield, Mass., who was President of the Senate of the
            Legislature of Mass. nine years in succession, a Commissioner to
            settle the North-Eastern Boundary Line, and Treasurer of the
            Commonwealth one term. Ch.: (1) Enos, b. Mar. 30, 1820; res.,
            St. Louis, Mo.; a wholesale merchant. (2) John, b. Jan., 1824;
            res., Ga.; a Civil Engineer. (3) Isaac, b. Dec., 1825; a farmer.
            (4) Sarah, b. Feb. 22, 1829; res., Springfield, Mass.

583. URIAH FOOTE, (198, 54, 16, 5,) b. Jan. 15, 1780; m. June 21, 1809,
Esther Goodyear, of Hamden, Ct. She was b. Feb. 25, 1789. Res., Hamden, Ct.

1561. i.   MERWIN H., b. Sept. 3, 1810; m. Miss Bradley, 3071-4.

1562. ii.   FRANCIS, b. Feb. 13, 1813; d. Aug. 26, 1819.

1563. iii. ENOS, b. Feb. 26, 1819; m. 1839, Laura Griffin; res., Southbury,
            Ct.; p. s. He is a merchant.

1564. iv.   ABIGAIL, b. Mar. 30, 1822; m. Apr. 2, 1835, Leveritt Dickerman,
            of Hamden, Ct.

584. THADDEUS FOOTE, (198, 54, 16, 5,) b. Dec. 1, 1783; m. Sept., 1805,
Polly Forward, Granby, Ct. She was b. Nov. 17, 1783. He is a merchant, and
has been Representative in the Legislature of the State and a Colonel of Militia,
and has sustained at various times many other important public trusts. Res.,
Southwick, Mass.

1565. i.   EDWIN HARRISON, b. Feb. 9, 1806; m. Julia Ann Bancraft,
            3074.

1566. ii.   HARRISON, b. June 23, 1807; m. Lucy Wilcox, 3075-9.

1567. iii. THADDEUS, b. Apr. 27, 1821; m. Harriette Betts, 3080-2.

1568. iv.   JOSEPH FORWARD, b. Feb. 7, 1828; graduate of Yale.

1569. v.   MARY, b. ——; m. James H. Holcomb, of Granby, Ct.; a
            merchant at Canfield, Ohio. Ch.: (1) James Foote Holcomb; was
            a missionary. (2) Edward Payson; dead. (3) Charles.

1570. vi.   MARIA, b. ——; m. Edward S. Kirkland, of North Granville,
            N. Y.; she d. Aug. 26, 1845. Ch.: (1) Maria.

1571. vii. ELIZA, b. ——; m. Dr. Artemas Bell, of Southampton, Mass.
            Ch.: 3 daus.

588. DR. JOSEPH FOOTE, (200, 56, 16, 5,) b. May 12, 1770; m. 1st, Feb.
16, 1797, Mary Bassett, of Hamden, Ct. She d. Sept. 3, 1801, ae. 24; m. 2nd,
Jan. 26, 1803, Eunice, dau. of Samuel Foote, Branford, Ct. She d. Nov. 12, 1833,
ae. 56. He d. Apr. 24, 1836. Res., North Haven, Ct.

1572. i.   MARY, b. June 3, 1798; m. Whiting Sanford; she d. Nov. 16, 1821, in Laurel, Del.
1573. ii.   JARED, b. Jan. 2, 1800; m. Rebecca Beecher, 3083-8.
1574. iii. EMILY, b. Mar. 13, 1804; m. June 30, 1830, Rev. Abraham C. Baldwin, of Springfield, Mass. He is a native of North Guilford, Ct., and was settled as Pastor in Springfield, Mass., and afterwards in New Haven, Ct., and subsequently appointed Family Guardian in the Asylum for Deaf and Dumb at Hartford, Ct.
1575. iv.   LAVINIA, b. Sept. 16, 1806; m. Rev. William Wolcott. She d. Jan. 9, 1832. Ch.: 1 son.
1576. v.   EUNICE, b. May 1, 1809; m. Nov. 25, 1832, Rev. Orson Cowles, of Woodstock and North Haven, Ct.·
1577. vi.   WILLIAM C., b. Nov. 6, 1811; m. Hannah W. Davis, 3089-90.

591. JOHN FOOTE, (202, 56, 16, 5,) b. July 25, 1772; m. Mar. 4, 1798, Hulda, dau. of William Fowler, of North Guilford, Ct. Res., North Branford, Ct.
1578. i.   URIAH COLLINS, b. May 29, 1800; d. 1835; unm.
1579. ii.   HARRIET, b. Sept. 14, 1805; m. Benjamin Todd; res., Northford, Ct. Ch.: (1) 3.

597. STEPHEN FOOTE, (205, 56, 16, 5,) b. Jan. 23, 1774; m. Mar. 4, 1795, Mary, dau. of Noah Wilson, Torrington, Ct.
1584. i.   FLORA, b. Nov. 19, 1796.
1585. ii.   STEPHEN S., b. Aug. 29, 1802; m. Nancy A. Strong, 3091-5.
1586. iii. MARY C., b. July 27, 1805.
1587. iv.   ANN E., b. Nov. 1, 1810.

600. ANSON S. FOOTE, (205, 56, 16, 5,) b. Aug. 27, 1784; m. Apr., 1810, Clarissa, dau. of Orange Buell, of Franklin, N. Y. Res., Franklin, N. Y.
1588. i.   ALBERT C., b. Dec. 28, 1811; d. Aug. 30, 1815.
1589. ii.   NANCY L., b. July 8, 1814; d. Aug. 28, 1815.
1590. iii. NANCY D., b. Apr. 23, 1817.
1591. iv.   EMILY, b. Mar. 24, 1819.
1592. v.   ALBERTI, b. Sept. 30, 1821.
1593. vi.   WILLARD P., b. Apr. 22, 1826; d. Dec. 1, 1829.

602. JARED FOOTE, (205, 56, 16, 5,) b. Jan. 22, 1789; m. Apr. 2, 1810, Sally, dau. of Caleb Scott, of Litchfield, Ct.; d. 1881. Res., Franklin, N. Y.
1594. i.   ALFRED, b. Oct. 22, 1811; m. Margaret Grant, 3096-7.
1595. ii.   REBECCA, b. Apr. 16, 1814; d. Mar. 24, 1842.
1596. iii. JARED A., b. May 11, 1817.
1597. iv.   SALLY ANN, b. July 26, 1819.
1598. v.   LYMAN B., b. Mar. 24, 1822; m. Sarah Amanda Gleason, 3098-9.
1599. vi.   ELMINA, b. May 21, 1825.
1600. vii. JOHN B., b. Oct. 11, 1826.

603. ICHABOD C. FOOTE, (205, 56, 16, 5,) b. Dec. 9, 1791; m. May 30, 1816, Harty Kingsley, of Franklin, N. Y.; he d. Oct. 19, 1862; she b. Aug. 9, 1792; d. July 15, 1874. Res., Franklin, N. Y.
1601. i.   GORDON M., b. Apr. 27, 1817; m. Jan. 18, 1842, Jannet Grant, of Catskill, N. Y. Res., Catskill, N. Y.
1602. ii.   ERASTUS N., b. Jan. 3, 1819; m. Oct. 6, 1841, Maria H. White.
1603. iii. LUCIA R., b. Dec. 4, 1820.

1604. iv. MARTHA KINGSLEY, b. July 1, 1822; m. Horatio Clinton
Faling (or Fayling), of Franklin, N. Y., on Feb. 7, 1843. It was
a double wedding, her sister, Maria H., marrying Lloyd Woodruff on the same date. Horatio Faling was b. June 30, 1821.
After the birth of their two sons they moved to Kalamazoo,
Mich., where he engaged in business as a merchant and importer.
He made frequent trips east, though travelling was very difficult
at that early period, before a railroad was built in that section.
He was a man of literary tastes and had a good library. Although
in poor health, he volunteered during the Civil War (Company C,
28th Michigan Infantry), and after gallant service died in the
Army on Dec. 4, 1864, at Mumfordsville, Kentucky. She d. June
30, 1883, at Kalamazoo, Mich. Ch.: (1) Ichabod DeWitt Faling,
b. Franklin, N. Y., Nov. 23, 1843, and was educated in Kalamazoo, Mich., and after much experience all over the United
States as telegraph operator, train dispatcher, etc., became Superintendent of Telegraph, and finally General Superintendent, for
several Western Railroad Companies. He finally located at
Portland, Ore. He was shot and killed in the streets of San
Francisco, California, by an enemy, on Apr. 16, 1888. (2) Abram
Clinton Faling, of Kalamazoo, Mich., b. at Franklin, N. Y., Dec.
22, 1845; m. in Peru, Indiana, Celia Frances Loveland, dau. of
Hon. E. P. Loveland, of Peru, Indiana, on Nov. 12, 1867. He
was once a newspaper man, but is now an official of the Michigan
Central Railroad Company, having been in the service of that
Company for many years. He res. in Kalamazoo, Mich. He is a
Thirty-second Degree Mason, a member of the "Mystic Shrine,"
etc., and is very prominent in Masonic circles. He is a collector
of old and rare books, and his private library is a noted and
valuable one. He is frequently consulted, as an authority, by
Bibliophiles. She was b. at Peru, Indiana, Nov. 25, 1846. Ch.:
(a) Lloyd Randolph DeWitt Faling (or Fayling), b. at Kalamazoo, Mich., Feb. 5, 1875; unm. He has been in the regular
military service, but has lately returned to civil life, and is at
present the General Manager of a New York Corporation. He
has also been a newspaper man, Editor, War Correspondent, and
has travelled extensively in many countries. After participating
in several filibustering expeditions to Cuba as War Correspondent, he entered the Secret Service of the Cuban Junta, with
the rank of Lieutenant, but was soon transferred to the Line
and saw much hard fighting in Cuba in 1896-97 under General
Gomez. He was promoted to the rank of Captain for gallant
service, and later received the brevet-rank of Major. He was
twice captured by the Spanish, but escaped, the last time to the
United States, a physical wreck from the effects of hard service
in the Tropics. He soon recovered his health and raised the
first Volunteer Company for the Spanish-American War to re-
spond to the call in the State of Ohio. He held the rank of
Captain. Major Fayling was at Galveston, Texas, during the
great hurricane and flood of Sept. 8, 1900; rescued 43 persons at
the peril of his own life; took command of the city, under martial

law, and restored and maintained law and order. He f·rmed a
battalion of the handful of survivors of Battery O, 1st U. S.
Regular Artillery and Militiamen, whom he drafted into service,
and was in absolute command of the city under martial law until
relieved by the Adjutant-General of Texas, with the most of the
National Guard of that State. The authorities approved of his
work and he received the official thanks of the city of Galveston,
through the Mayor, who said officially, in a letter of thanks, that
"Major Fayling's work was the saving of the city." Major
Fayling also received a gold medal, costing several hundred
dollars, from citizens of Texas, inscribed "For Bravery," and
with an account of his services. (b) Lulu Ruth, b. at Kalamazoo,
Mich., Jan. 2, 1877; unm. She was educated at the Kalamazoo
High School, the State Normal College, at Ypsilanti, Mich., and
the University of Mich. She is at present a teacher in the
Kalamazoo High School. (c) Glenn Roy Clinton, b. at Kalamazoo,
Mich., Sept. 7, 1878. Upon graduating from the Kalamazoo
High School in 1897 he entered the service of the Michigan
Central Railroad as a telegraph operator, and continued in that
employment until 1901, when he resigned in order to study law.
In 1904 he was graduated from the Law Department of the
University of Michigan, and in the same year was admitted to
practice in the States of Michigan and Ohio and in the Federal
Courts. He has since been engaged in the practice of his profession in Toledo, Ohio, where he has offices, Numbers 315, 317 and
319, in the Spitzer Building. As a railroad man he was active
in labor organization, his work having been largely instrumental
in securing for his fellow employees increased wages and better
conditions of labor. He is the author of recent legislation re-
quiring the placing of adequate fenders on street cars, and has
been active ·in civic betterment work. (d) Abram Foote, b. at.
Kalamazoo, Apr. 8, 1880; d. Oct. 3, 1881.

1605. v.   MARIA H., b. May 6, 1824; m. Feb. 7, 1843, Lloyd L. Woodruff.
1606. vi. AMANDA N., b. June 1, 1828; m. Charles H. Eccleston. He was
            b. Trenton, N. Y., May 28, 1826. Ch.: (1) Charles Gordon
            Eccleston, b. Nov. 29, 1851; m. Wilhimena Cook. Ch.: (a)
            Robert Cooke Eccleston, b. ———. (b) Anna Foote Eccleston,
            b. ———. (2) Edson Foote Eccleston, b. Feb. 1, 1856; m.
            Clara Homer. Ch.: (a) Mabel Homer Eccleston, b. ———. (3)
            Maria Amanda, b. Mar. 7, 1861; m. Geo. Johnson. Ch.: (a)
            Paul Kimble Johnson, b. ———. (b) Harold Foote Johnson, b.
            ———. (4) Walter Lee Eccleston, b. Feb. 4, 1869; unm. (5)
            Mary McCall Eccleston, b. Aug. 19, 1873; unm.
1607. vii. ICHABOD C., b. Dec. 27, 1829; d. Nov. 2, 1830.

604. ASAHEL FOOTE, (207, 56, 16, 5,) b. Oct. 22, 1775; m. Feb. 27, 1800,
Elsie, dau. of William Barret. She d. Jan. 9, 1832, ae. 55; m. 2nd, Roseannah,
wid. of Bebee Barnes, of Southington, Ct. Res., Southington, Ct.

1608. i.   HENRY, b. May 8, 1801; res., Dover, N. H.
1609. ii. ROBERT DENNIS, b. Mar. 30, 1803; res., Southington, Ct.
1610. iii. JAMES LEWIS, b. Sept. 19, 1805; res., Lowell, Mass.

605. ROBERT FOOTE, (207, 56, 16, 5,) b. Sept. 22, 1779; m. Nov. 22, 1804, Diadema, dau. of Jason Hitchcock, of Southington, Ct.; divorced; m. 2nd, Nov. 6, 1825, Lucina, wid. of Cornelius Dunham, Jr., and dau. of Dea. Pomroy Newell, both of Southington, Ct.

    1611. i. PATIENCE MARIA, b. 1804; m. Luman Lewis, of Wolcott, Ct.; res., Southington, Ct. Ch.: 6.

    1612. ii. RACHEL HARRIET, b. 1806; m. Lucius Sutliff, of Wolcott, Ct. Res., Franklin, Lou. Ch.: 7 sons.

607. LEWIS FOOTE, (207, 56, 16, 5,) b. Sept. 26, 1789; m. 1st, Oct. 10, 1813, Orra, dau. of Isaac Newell, of Southington, Ct. She d. Apr. 10, 1842, ae. 51; m. 2nd, Oct. 18, 1843, Cathrine Francis, wid. of Benjamin Adams, of Springfield, Chicopee Falls, Mass., and dau. of Chauncey Sedwick, South Windsor. Res., Southington, Farmington, and Hartford, Ct.

    1613. i. EMILY, b. Jan. 9, 1815; m. Oct. 19, 1835, Lowry Robbins, of Wethersfield, Ct.; he d. Aug. 19, 1862. Ch.: (1) Emily S., b. Mar. 3, 1837. (2) Walter L., b. July 8, 1840; d. Aug. 21, 1844. (3) Julia N., b. May 8, 1843; d. Sept. 29, 1873. (4) Frances Arabella, b. June 3, 1845. (5) David L., b. Oct. 31, 1848; m. Oct. 19, 1876, Kate L. Woodhouse. (6) Lucy Alice, b. Mar. 5, 1855.

    1614. ii. CATHRINE, b. Apr. 29, 1818; m. June 11, 1841, Truman C. Walling, of Colebrook, Ct. Ch.: (1) Lewis C., b. Aug. 23, 1842. (2) Julia F., b. July 7, 1845. (3) Cathrine, b. Mar. 15, 1874.

    1615. iii. CORNELIA, b. June 3, 1819; m. Jan. 18, 1844, Chauncy Deming, of Wethersfield, Ct. She d. Nov. 18, 1845. Ch.: (1) Newell F., b. Oct. 31, 1845.

    1616. iv. JULIA, b. July 24, 1823; m. Jan. 17, 1842, Calvin B. Hunn, of Rochester, N. Y. She d. Aug. 4, 1843. Ch.: (1) Walter L., b. July 1, 1843; d. Aug. 15, 1843.

608. LEONARD FOOTE, (207, 56, 16, 5,) b. Apr. 8, 1791; m. Oct. 4, 1812, Beda, dau. of Enos Wright, of Southington, Ct. Res., Southington, Ct., and Oxford, Chenango Co., N. Y.

    1617. i. JANE ELIZA, b. Oct. 30, 1814; d. Jan. 15, 1815.

    1618. ii. LEONARD RALZY, b. Apr. 8, 1816; m. Feb. 26, 1839, Nancy Royce.

    1619. iii. ROBERT ENOS., b. Aug. 13, 1817; m. Feb. 4, 1840, Susan Rogers.

    1620. iv. MILES LEWIS, b. Apr. 23, 1820; m. Mar. 2, 1842, Mary Ann Jewell.

    1621. v. IRA ASAHEL, b. Oct. 8, 1823; m. Oct. 31, 1844, Louisa ———.

    1622. vi. JOSEPH HUBERT, b. May 4, 1820.

610. DR. ANSON FOOTE, (208, 56, 16, 5,) b. July 5, 1783; m. Jan. 1, 1807, Clarissa Gould, of Lowville, Lewis Co., N. Y. She was b. Feb. 1, 1787, in New Marlborough, N. H., and d. Feb. 9, 1826, in Guilford, Ct.; m. 2nd, Dec. 4, 1828, Eunice, dau. of Daniel Hutchinson, M. D., of Lebanon, Ct. She was b. June 10, 1795. At the age of abt. 14 years Dr. Foote removed from Branford, Ct., where he was b., with his father to Oneida Co., N. Y., the country being new at that time. He read medicine with Dr. Hall, of Utica, N. Y., and settled in Lowville, N. Y., from whence he removed to Branford, Ct. He d. there May 2, 1841.

    1623. i. ERASMUS DARWIN, b. Aug. 2, 1808; m. Elizabeth Sterling.

    1624. ii. JUSTIN, b. June 24, 1811; d. Jan. 19, 1840; a young man of much promise.

1625. iii. CLARISSA, b. Jan. 1, 1813; m. Dr. Sweet, of Guilford, Ct.; a
             distinguished surgeon.
1626. iv.   EMELINE, b. Apr. 3, 1815.
1627. v.   DANIEL, b. July 30, 1817; d. Aug. 30, 1817.
1628. vi.   SUSANNA THROOP, b. Sept. 13, 1830.

612. HARVEY FOOTE, (208, 56, 16, 5,) b. 1795; m. Amy, dau. of Remington
and Amy (Knowles) Winthrop. He d. 1842. Res., Oneida Co. until 1837, Cattaraugus Co., N. Y.

1629. i.   SARAH ANN, b. Sept. 22, 1829; m. Dec. 9, 1848, William T.
            Remington. He d. Oct. 11, 1876. She d. at Rochester, N. Y.,
            Feb. 12, 1904. Ch.: (1) Emma, b. Aug. 3, 1851; m. Dec. 25,
            1879, Eugene H. Howard, Rochester, N. Y. Ch.: (a) Henry
            Barrington, b. Feb. 3, 1881; grad. Amherst College 1904; m. June
            22, 1906, Sophia Knyon; he is a lawyer at Rochester, N. Y.
            Ch.: (i) Henry Eugene, b. Mar. 17, 1907. (2) Willis S., b. June
            17, 1853; m. Sept. 13, 1877, Margaret C. McKenzel; res.,
            Rochester, N. Y. Ch.: (a) Nellie M., b. Jan 27, 1879; d. Aug. 10,
            1879. (b) Ray E., b. Mar. 8, 1880; student Cambridge Divinity
            School, 1907. (c) Genevieve McKenzel, b. July 23, 1883. (d)
            Willis Eugene, b. Jan. 10, 1886. (e) Ruth, b. June 7, 1890. (3)
            Nellie R., b. Dec. 17, 1855; m. Nov. 15, 1876, Clarence V. Lodge.
            (4) Janet, b. Aug. 14, 1857. (5) Frank, b. Jan. 8, 1861; d. Feb.,
            1862. (6) Harvey Foote, b. June 28, 1863. William T. Reming-
            ton was a farmer, b. July 28, 1820, at Henrietta, N. Y.; he was
            a son of Alvah Remington, who was b. in Rupert, Vt., July 25,
            1797, and m. Mercy Gorton, dau. of Rev. Thomas Gorton, des-
            cendant of Samuel Gorton, of Rhode Island, Sept. 30, 1819.
            Alvah m. for his 2nd wife Amy Northrup, wid. of Harvey
            Foote (612). The subject of this sketch is a descendant of John
            Remington, who settled in Rowley, Mass., in 1637; he received
            his education in the common schools, Geneseo State Normal
            School, and the Law Department of Union College, receiving
            the degree of LL.B. in 1887; he at once entered upon the prac-
            tice of his profession at Rochester, N. Y., and was m. May 28,
            1889, to Agnes, dau. of Thomas and Martha Hannah Brodie.
            Mr. Remington has enjoyed a large law practice, has been some-
            what identified with politics, was a supervisor in 1891, member
            of the Rochester Board of Education in 1892, Assistant Cor-
            poration Counsel 1892 to 1896, Judge of the Municipal Court 1896
            to 1898. He is a director of and attorney for a number of
            Corporations, among them the Rochester Securities Company, a
            large financial institution, and Bastian Brothers Co., the manu-
            facturers of Advertising Novelties. He is an officer in the First
            Baptist Church of Rochester, a director of the New York State
            Baptist Convention, the State Christian Endeavor Union, and a
            member of the State and local Bar Associations, the New York
            Genealogical and Biographical Society, Sons American Revolu-
            tion, and other fraternal and social organizations. Judge Rem-
            ington has travelled extensively, and in addition to his profes-
            sional and business activities is engaged in farming at Mumford,
            N. Y., where he res. in the summer, his city home being in the

suburbs of Rochester, N. Y. Ch.: (a) William Brodie, b. June 14, 1890. (b) Thomas Howard, b. Sept. 4, 1891. (c) Agnes, b. Sept. 11, 1893. (d) Harvey Foote, b. June 25, 1895. (e) John Warner, b. Jan. 10, 1897. (f) Harriet, b. July 31, 1898. (g) Francis Kirk, b. Nov. 3, 1902. (7) Frederick, b. July 3, 1866; m. Eva Potter, Sept. 3, 1891. He is a lawyer and a physician at Rochester, N. Y. Ch.: (a) Ezra Potter, b. May 28, 1892. (b) Frederick, b. Dec. 25, 1894.

1630. ii. MARY JANE, b. Deerfield, N. Y.; m. July 13, 1851, Capt. Harrison Cheney, of Freedom, N. Y. He was in the Civil War. Ch.: (1) Burdette, b. Sept. 1, 1852; d. Feb. 15, 1853. (2) Ella Mellissa, b. Mar. 24, 1854; m. Sept. 27, 1874, Charles Cassius Wood. (3) Eleanor May, b. Freedom, N. Y., Apr. 10, 1865; m. Dec. 22, 1880, Walter N. Knight. Ch., all b. at Sandusky, N. Y.: (a) Fred Daniel, b. May 30, 1883; m. June 19, 1906, Edna May Whaling. (b) Llewellyn, b. Jan. 21, 1885; d. Jan. 3, 1886. (c) Ralph La Due, b. Oct. 22, 1886. (d) Lottie Leora, b. May 17, 1888; m. Oct. 25, 1904, Albert Baker. Ch.: (i) Raymond Eugene, b. Jan. 7, 1907. (e) Glenna M., b. Mar. 30, 1890; d. Feb. 17, 1891. (f) Mary Jane, b. Dec. 2, 1891. (g) Walter, b. Apr. 20, 1895. (h) Gordon Harrison, b. Jan. 10, 1897. (i) Selden Cheney, b. June 14, 1898. (j) Glendora, b. Apr. 25, 1904. (4) Harrie Foote Cheney, b. Aug. 15, 1867; m. May 1, 1888, Bertha Humphrey. Ch.: (a) Mildred May, b. Fish Lake, N. Y., Sept. 3, 1890; m. Jan. 17, 1907, Harved Frudenthal. (b) Georgia Anna, b. May 21, 1896. (c) Edna Onetea, b. Aug. 27, 1898. (d) Harrison Humphrey, b. June 11, 1901. (e) Theodore Allen, b. Apr. 2, 1904, at Fish Lake, N. Y.

1631. iii. HARRY P., b. Deerfield, N. Y., Dec., 1841; Hospital Steward, 4th N. Y. Heavy Artillery, Civil War; d. Oct. 6, 1864, in Rochester, N. Y.

1632. iv. RUTH MELISSA, b. Deerfield, N. Y., Feb. 23, 1838; m. Dec. 31, 1870, Walter W. Cheney; she d. June 26, 1871, Freedom, N. Y.

616. HELI FOOTE, (208, 56, 16, 5,) b. 1800; m. Cathrine Nichols, of Deerfield, N. Y. Res., Cattaraugus Co., N. Y.

1633. i. CHARLES NICHOLS, b. ———; m. Grace McGregor, 3100-2.

1634. ii. ROBERT, b. ———; m. Peddy Alfred, 3103-.

1635. iii. HIRAM, b. ———; res., Freeland, Mich.

1636. iv. DELIA, b. ———; m. George Lambert. Ch.: (1) Orlando.

1637. v. CHARLOTTE, b. ———; m. Charles Williams. Ch.: (1) Jennie. (2) Carrie.

618. HENRY FOOTE, (208, 56, 16, 5,) b. Mar. 4, 1808; m. Harriet, dau. of Remington and Amy (Knowles) Northrop, of Freedom, N. Y. She was b. Nov. 3, 1810; d. June 30, 1847, in Cattaraugus Co., N. Y.; m. 2nd, 1849, Jane W. Champlain; removed to Lansing, Mich., where he d. Jan. 16, 1877. She d. Feb. 14, 1901. Mr. Foote was one of the early settlers of Lansing, Mich., where he was for many years engaged in brick-making.

1638. i. DAN POLLY, b. Aug. 18, 1831; m. Elizabeth Graham, 3104-6.

1639. ii. ANN ELIZA, b. Nov. 10, 1833; has been for 12 years overseer of the girls in the State School for the Blind, Lansing, Mich.;

before that she was a teacher in the U. S. Indian School for 14 years. From the age of 18 she has followed this line of work and is widely known and respected.. Res., Lansing, Mich.

1640. iii. JEANNETTE, b. 1835; d. in infancy, 1835.

1641. iv. HARVEY MONROE, b. Oct. 10, 1836; m. Elizabeth Young, 3107-10.

1642. v. GEORGE FRANKLIN, b. Oct. 22, 1839; m. Mary A. Duncan, 3111.

1643. vi. CAROLINE LOUISE, b. Jan. 18, 1843; m. John H. Larabee, of N. Y. Ch.: (1) John H. (2) Hattie A., d. Mar. 3, 1882, and 7 others; all dead.

1644. vii. JULIA ANTOINETTE, b. Feb. 7, 1844; m. Mar. 25, 1864, John Burgoyne, a farmer, of Bridgeport, Mich. Ch.: (1) Anna E. C., b. May 13, 1867, in Woodhull, Mich.; graduate of Hillsdale College; teacher in the public schools of Lansing for five years; m. Arthur C. Stebbins, of Lansing, Mich., general manager of the Lansing Wheelbarrow Co. Ch.: (a) Francis Burgoyne, b. Nov. 9, 1895. (b) Chas. Rowland, b. Feb. 6, 1903. (2) Frank Henry, b. Nov. 21, 1868; d. Sept. 29, 1872. (3) M. Antoinette, b. Feb. 2, 1871, in Woodhull, Mich.; graduate of Mich. Central State Normal; teacher and fruit grower. (4) George Archie, b. Oct. 19, 1873; prominent farmer of Bridgeport, Mich.; m. Sept. 20, 1905, Alice Packett. Ch.: (a) Harriet Antoinette, b. Jan. 2, 1907.

1645. viii. MARY AMELIA, b. Oct. 10, 1845; m. Lee Moyne Smith; d. May 22, 1899. Ch.: (1) Geo. Bert., b. Jan. 16, 1869; m. Oct., 1890, Carrie Aikens; d. May 21, 1892. Ch.: (a) Ray, b. Dec., 1891. (2) Eliza A., b. Dec. 12, 1873; m. Dr. Arthur A. Scott, of Lansingburg, Mich. (3) Nin Leslie, b. Sept. 24, 1878; m. Grant Gardner. Ch.: (a) Lester Marvin, b. Aug. 11, 1902. (b) Baby, b. ———. Res., Woodhull, Mich.

1646. ix. CHAS. EDWARD, b. June 30, 1847; m. Harriet Maud Beach, 3112-4.

1647. x. CLARENCE H., b. July 22, 1852; d. Nov. 19, 1856.

1648. xi. ELLA ISABEL, b. June 22, 1854; m. Frank A. Stevens, of Lansing, Mich. Ch.: (1) Bessie.

1649. xii. CLARA, b. Dec. 1, 1856; m. J. W. Luke, of Toledo, Ohio. Ch.: (1) Helen. (2) Peter.

1650. xiii. ARCHIE HUGH, b. Apr. 8, 1864; m. Lila Morris, 3115.

619. PROSPER P. FOOTE, (208, 56, 16, 5,) b. Apr. 8, 1815; m. 1st, 1859, Delia Metcalf. She d. Dec. 28, 1842; m. 2nd, Evaline Seaman; m. 3rd, Dolly Harwick. She was b. Mar. 19, 1823; d. Feb. 24, 1890. He d. Jan. 8, 1888.

1651. i. WILLIAM, b. Nov. 27, 1840; m. Mar. 28, 1882, Martha G. Gates; carriage manufacturer. Res., Filmore, N. Y.

1652. ii. HELI, b. Feb. 18, 1842; m. Helen Reid, 3115.

1653. iii. JAMES C., b. May 5, 1867; m. Kittie R. Payne, 3115⅟-16.

620. WILLIAM FOOTE, (208, 56, 16, 5,) b. Aug. 7, 1816; m. Mar. 5, 1838, Clarinda Dickerson, of Monroe Co., N. Y. She d. Nov. 10, 1903; he d. Sept. 5, 1878; res., Utica, N. Y.

1654. i. WILLIAM, b. Utica, N. Y., Feb. 22, 1843; d. Mar. 2, 1899; p. s.

1655. ii. CULVER D., b. Mar. 28, 1849; d. Apr. 3, 1881; s. p.

1656. iii. CLARINDA E., b. Apr. 15, 1849; m. Aug. 22, 1898, Edgar K. Clark; she d. Sept. 15, 1898; he d. July 9, 1903. Ch.: (1) Archibald Foote, b. Aug. 27, 1869; m. Nov. 17, 1898, Emma Ruppertz; s. p. He is a lawyer of New York City.

621. THOMAS FOOTE, (208, 56, 16, 5,) b. 1818; m. Mary Ann Somyer; res., Cattaraugus Co., N. Y.

    1657. i. FRANCIS, b. ———.
    1658. ii. MILTON, b. ———.

623. DEA. JABEZ FOOTE, (209, 56, 16, 5,) b. Jan. 22, 1758; m. Dec. 27, 1810, Ann, dau. of Reuben Carey, of Salisbury, Ct. She was b. Nov. 9, 1791; res., Johnstown, N. Y. He was a Dea. in the Baptist Church.

    1659. i. NANCY, b. Oct. 14, 1812; she was a teacher; d. ———.
    1660. ii. SARAH, b. Aug. 27, 1815; d. June 2, 1821.
    1661. iii. SARAH ANN, b. Feb. 23, 1822; d. ———.
    1662. iv. MARY ANN, b. Feb. 23, 1822; d. ———.

627. JESSE FINCH FOOTE, (209, 56, 16, 5,) b. Aug. 11, 1788; m. Oct. 14, 1817, Angellica Van Buren, of Mayfield, N. Y. She was b. Jan. 27, 1799; res., Johnstown, N. Y.

    1663. i. ROBERT, b. in Mayfield, N. Y., Mar. 6, 1818; m. Feb. 11, 1846. Ch.: (1) Harriet. (2) Jesse. Both dead. Mr. Foote was a farmer.
    1664. ii. CATHARINE STARR, b. Dec. 30, 1820; m. 1841; d. Nov. 20, 1842; s. p.
    1665. iii. SARAH MARIAH, b. Nov. 8, 1822; m. Rev. Z. T. Hoyt, Sept. 17, 1846; d. in Saratoga in 1896. Ch.: (1) Sarah Francis, b. July 26, 1847; m. E. Irwin Scott, July, 1872. (2) James T., b. May 16, 1851; graduated Union College, 1874. (3) Emma R., b. 1854. (4) Edward H., b. Nov. 22, 1860; m. Hannah C. King, Oct., 1883.
    1666. iv. JAMES HARVEY, b. Aug. 23, 1824; m. Ann E. Titcomb and Helen Hogaboom, 3116-9.
    1667. v. BYRON, b. May 27, 1826; d. Mar. 16, 1827.
    1668. vi. DANIEL, b. Feb. 24, 1828; m. Ruth Hoyt, 3120-2.
    1669. vii. ORRILLA, b. Oct. 11, 1830; m. Elliox Thomas; d. 1858. Ch.: (1) Orilla Grace, b. 1859; m. David McFalls, July, 1883.
    1670. viii. MARY JANE, b. Nov. 29, 1832; m. Elliox Thomas, of Kingsborough, N. Y., May 3, 1860; d. July 26, 1904. Ch.: (1) Earl Goodridge, b. Mar. 24, 1862; m. Lida E. Allen, Oct. 8, 1892. (2) Charles Dennison, b. Aug. 12, 1864.
    1671. ix. WILLIAM DARIUS, b. Sept. 28, 1836; m. Mary Shults, 3123-4
    1672. x. ELLEN ELMYRA, b. Sept. 7, 1839, Mayfield, N. Y.; m. Rev. Alex. Hoyt, Oct., 1868.
    1673. xi. HARRIET GRACE, b. July 11, 1844; d. Apr. 22, 1853.

630. DAVID FOOTE, (211, 60, 18, 5,) b. Jan. 24, 1753; m. 1777, Mary Scovel, of Watertown, Ct. He was a soldier in the Revolutionary Army, and participated in the Siege of Boston. He removed from Watertown, Ct., in 1795, to Cornwall, Vt., and purchased 1,000 acres in the northwest part of the town. This property still remains in the Foote Family. He was for ten years a Selectman of the town, and Representative in the General

Assembly in 1803 and 1804. He d. Sept. 27, 1821; she d. July 11, 1838; both buried at West Cornwall, Vt.

1674. i.   ABRAM, b. May, 1778, in Watertown, Ct.; d. in Cornwall, Vt., May, 1800.

1675. ii. DAVID, b. Feb., 1780, in Watertown, Ct.; m. Mehitabel Post, 3125-9.

1676. iii. OLIVE, b. May, 1782; m. Jared Abernethy, of Cornwall, Vt. He d. Apr. 19, 1838; she lived and d. at Cornwall, Vt., July 12, 1846. Ch.: (1) Ezekiel. (2) Margaret; m. ———. Sunderlin. (3) Cyrus, m. Mary Ann Stickney; res., Cornwall, Vt. Ch.: (a) Ann. (b) Jared; both living on the old homestead in Cornwall; unm. (4) Abram Foote Abernethy, b. Feb. 15, 1813; m. Jan. 9, 1840, in Cornwall, Vt., Mary Ford Goodrich; moved to Altona, 1855. She d. Apr. 23, 1893; he d. Aug. 17, 1871. Res., Altona, Ill. Ch.: (a) Cornelia Sylvema (Nellie), b. Dec. 28, 1840; m. Nov. 9, 1865, Amos Franklin Ward; she d. Jan. 10, 1900; res., Altona, Ill. Ch.: (i) Nellie Abernethy Ward, b. June 1, 1867; d. in infancy. (ii) Fred Franklin, b. Jan. 9, 1869; m. Jan. 1, 1902, Alice Penny; res., Altona, Ill. Ch.: (ii1) Florence Alice Ward, b. May 12, 1904. (iii) Edith Mary Ward, b. Feb. 21, 1873; m. Dec. 25, 1901, Charles C., son of Alvah Reynolds; res., Oneida, Ill. Ch.: (iii1) Nellie Bernice Reynolds, b. Dec. 31, 1902. (iii2) Marlyn Ward, b. Aug. 20, 1904. (iii3) Birdice Loraine, b. Sept. 24, 1905. (iv) George Amos Ward, b. Sept. 26, 1874; m. May 21, 1902, Edith M., dau. of Douglas Tracy, of Altona, Ill. Ch.: (iv1) Marion Orlena Ward, b. May 9, 1903. (iv2) Ethel Winifred Ward, b. July 24, 1904. (b) George Franklin Abernethy, b. June 10, 1842; m. Feb. 1, 1877, Arabelle McClatchey, Altona, Ill. Res., Galesburg, Ill. Ch.: (i) Nellie Edith Abernethy, b. Nov. 25, 1880; m. Dec. 25, 1902, Walter F. Coolidge, of Galesburg, Ill. Ch.: (i1) George Francis Abernethy Coolidge, b. Sept., 1904. (ii) George Earle Abernethy, b. Dec. 15, 1883. (c) Mary Jane Abernethy, b. Jan. 12, 1844; m. Apr. 6, 1865, Frank S. Marsh, of Altona, Ill. She d. Oct. 8, 1872. Ch.: (i) Charles Dexter Marsh, b. Jan. 30, 1866; m. Dec. 15, 1887, Mary B. McLean, of Lexington, Neb. She d. Nov. 10, 1894; m. 2nd, Dec. 18, 1895, Mary McLean. Ch.: (i1) Jennie Marsh, b. Sept. 25, 1889. (i2) John Frank Marsh, b. Oct. 1, 1891. (i3) Hattie Marsh, b. June 19, 1903. (ii) Hattie Abernethy Marsh, b. Mar. 12, 1867; m. May 28, 1885, James Thomas, of Lexington, Neb. Ch.: (ii1) Frank W. Thomas, b. July 4, 1886. (ii2) Martha V., b. Nov. 27, 1888; d. in infancy. (d) Martha Olive Abernethy, b. July 22, 1845; m. June 2, 1870, Edwin M. Wales, of Moffat, Colo. She d. May, 1901. (e) David Thompson Abernethy, b. Oct. 18, 1847. m. Jan. 1, 1876, Phebe Roscoe; he d. May 10, 1886; res., Ft. Dodge, Iowa. Ch.: (i) George Harley, b. Nov., 1876; res., Eagle Grove, Ia. (ii) David Frank, b. Dec., 1879; d. June 19, 1892. (iii) Vinnie, b. 1884. (iv) Mary Pearl Abernethy, b. 1881; d. Dec. 14, 1882. (f) Annie Viola Abernethy, b. Dec. 5, 1850; m. Dec. 5, 1872, Ford Sornberger, of Victoria, Ill. She d. June 15, 1875. Ch.: (i) Viola Katie, b. 1875; d. in infancy. (g) Albert Payson

Abernethy, b. Sept. 15, 1852; m. Aug. 1, 1878, Kate, dau. of
Lyman K. Moore, of Altona, Ill. He d. Feb. 12, 1900. Ch.: (i)
Thirza Viola Abernethy, b. July 30, 1879; m. Feb. 19, 1902,
Harry, son of James McGaan, of Altona, Ill. Ch.: (i1) Mildred
McGaan, b. Dec. 2, 1902; d. in infancy. (i2) Mary Gladys, b.
Nov. 23, 1903. (i3) James Albert, b. Feb. 8, 1907. (ii) Milo
Abram Abernethy, b. Nov. 20, 1882; m. Jan. 17, 1906, Etta,
dau. of Thomas Sheahan, of Altona, Ill; res., Victoria, Ill. Ch.:
(ii1) Howard Albert Abernethy, b. Oct. 29, 1906. (iii) Ray
Albert Abernethy, b. Feb. 23, 1886. (iv) Mattie Moore, b. May
12, 1888. (v) Ralph Lyman, b. Nov. 24, 1896. (h) Hattie
Goodrich, b. Dec. 18, 1854; d. Sept. 14, 1855, at Centre Point,
Ill. (5) David, d. Sept. 9, 1843, ae. 25 years.

1677. iv. POLLY, b. 1784; m. Lyman Sperry, and removed to Malone,
N. Y., where he d. in 1819.

1678. v. RUSSELL, b. May 17, 1786; m. Belinda Mead and Huldah Gibbs,
3130-40.

1679. vi. ELIJAH, b. May 10, 1788; m. Orpha Ward and Mehitabel Gale,
3141-7.

1680. vii. MARENDA, b. 1785; m. Ezra Mead, of Cornwall, Vt. They
removed to Somerset, Niagara Co., N. Y., where she d. Mar.,
1844.

1681. viii. HULDAH, b. Feb., 1798; m. Sept., 1818, Augustus Finney, of
Cornwall, Vt.; they removed to Michigan, where she d. Aug. 2,
1843.

633. SAMUEL FOOTE, (211, 60, 18, 5,) b. May 2, 1760; m. Mar. 27, 1783,
Sarah McDonald; she d. Mar. 27, 1840. Res., Middlebury, Vt., and Crown Point,
N. Y. In 1794 he purchased a hotel on the site of the present Congregational
Church in Middlebury. Here he kept a public house until 1803, when he removed
to Crown Point, N. Y. He was Deputy Sheriff while at Middlebury. Bought a
farm on Crown Point, N. Y., and d. there. His descendants still occupy the old
farm; among them are James and Samuel Murdock.

1682. i. SARAH, b. Sept. 23, 1784; m. Jan. 10, 1807, Samuel Murdock.
She d. Mar. 16, 1815; m. 2nd, Mehitable, wid. of No. 1675. Ch.
by 1st wife: (1) Sarah. (2) James. (3) Samuel F. Ch.: (a)
James. (b) Samuel; m. Jane ———. Ch.: (i) James; m. Emma
Parks. Ch.: 4 boys. They occupy the old home. (ii) S.
Foote Murdock.

1682¹. ii. SAMUEL, b. Jan. 4, 1786; m. Margaret Turner, 3148-9.

645. LEWIS FOOTE, (215, 60, 18, 5,) b. Oct. 5, 1761; m. Lois Wentworth;
res., Richland, Iowa.

1683. i. DANIEL, b. ———.

1684. ii. CHARLES G., b. ———; res., Merilla, Erie Co., N. Y.

1685. iii. HANNAH, b. ———; m. ———. Boyden, a printer, of Milwan-
pee, Wis.

1686. iv. ANNIE, b. ———; m. Geo. W. Carpenter, Merilla Co., N. Y. Ch.:
(1) Lewis; res., Merilla, N. Y. (2) Copela, b. ———. Res.,
Merilla, N. Y.

1687. v. JAMES WENTWORTH, b. Lebanon, N. Y., Mar. 26, 1802; m.
Lovisa Stowell, 3150-8.

1688. vi. LUCINDA, b. ———; m. ———. Darby; res., Merilla, N. Y.

647. TIMOTHY FOOTE, (215, 60, 18, 5,) b. Apr. 5, 1768; m. Oct 2, 1791, Abigail, dau. of Moses Stoddard, of Litchfield, Ct. She was b. Nov. 7, 1768; res., Litchfield, Ct.

    1689. i. LUCY MARINTHA, b. June 19, 1795; m. Alanson Kimberly, of Washington, Ct.

    1690. ii. ABIGAIL CAROLINE, b. Nov. 22, 1796; m. Benjamin Carpenter, No. 1926, of Litchfield, Ct.

    1691. iii. SALLY G., b. July 10, 1802; d. unm.

    1692. iv. CHILD, not named, b. Oct. 29, 1807; d. Dec. 21, 1807.

    1693. v. WILLIAM, b. Mar. 23, 1809; m. Jan. 10, 1836, Adeline T. French; he d. Sept. 1, 1848, of consumption.

650. DANIEL FOOTE, (216, 60, 18, 5,) b. at Watertown, Ct., Apr. 3, 1760; m. 1783, Sarah Johnson, of Rutland, Vt. She d. Dec. 6, 1790, ae. 25 years; m. 2nd, 1792, Ellen Scott, of Watertown, Ct. She d. Apr. 4, 1841. He was in the Army of the Revolution five years, and served his country faithfully, and was in many actions, taking of Burgoyne, etc. He was the first settler of Cornwall, Vt., where he lived and d. Aug. 24, 1848.

    1694. i. IRA, b. 1786; m. 3159-64.

    1695. ii. SYLVESTER SCOTT, b. 1800; m. Abigail Collins, 3165-6.

    1696. iii. SALLY, b. 1797; d. Aug. 13, 1860; unm.; res., Cornwall, Vt.

    1697. iv. ANNA, b. June 27, 1803; d. Nov. 13, 1873; unm.; res., Cornwall, Vt.

651. NATHAN FOOTE, (216, 60, 18, 5,) b. Nov. 16, 1761; m. 1790, Sarah Southerland, wid., formerly Sarah Evarts, of West Haven, Vt. She d. 1804; m. 2nd, 1805, Hester Hunt, wid., formerly Hester Goodrich, of Georgia, Vt. He d. Nov. 16, 1828-9, in Cornwall, Vt.

    1698. i. SALLY, b. Apr. 13, 1791.

    1699. ii. LINUS, b. Oct. 14, 1794.

    1700. iii. LUCIUS CHITTENDEN, b. Nov. 3, 1796, at Cornwall, Vt., and fitted with Rev. Jedediah Bushnell of that town. He read law in Granville, N. Y., 1815-1817; in Cayuga, N. Y., 1817-1818; practiced in Cayuga some years, and was then a land agent in Nunda, N. Y., till his death, of pleurisy, July 31, 1828.

    1701. iv. LUCINDA, b. July 30, 1800.

    1702. v. MILLICENT, b. Dec. 17, 1802; m. Wm. Whittlesy.

    1703. vi. MARIA L., b. ———; dau. m. Wm. Turner, of Cornwall, Vt.

653. ABIJAH FOOTE, (216, 60, 18, 5,) b. Mar. 23, 1766; m. 1792, Polly Bronson, of Cornwall, Vt. He d. Sept. 22, 1795, in Cornwall, Vt.

    1703¹. i. HENRY BRONSON, b. Feb. 7, 1794; res., Ohio.

654. URI FOOTE, (216, 60, 18, 5,) b. July 12, 1768; m. 1798, Rhoda Pierson, of Cornwall, Vt. He d. Apr. 30, 1841, in Cayuga, N. Y.

    1704. i. WILLIAM, b. ———.

    1704¹. ii. ROXY ANN, b. ———; m. R. Cook, of Auburn, N. Y. Ch.: 1 son and 2 daus.

    1704². iii. LOUISA R., b. ———.

657. JESSE S. FOOTE, (216, 60, 18, 5,) b. Rutland, Vt., May 17, 1776; m. 1796, Abby Hosley; she d. 1819, at Southfield, N. Y.; m. 2nd, 1821, Eliza Denis. Mr. Foote was a farmer by occupation. He served in the U. S. Forces in the

War of 1812. He d. 1846 in Chittenango, N. Y.; she d. before him. Res., Bridgeport and Eaton, N. Y. First 3 ch. b. at Bridgeport, N. Y., others at Eaton, N. Y.

    1705. i.   DENICE, b. ———; m. Betsey Conroyd, 3166½.

    1706. ii.   HIRAM, b. ———; m., raised a family; no more known.

    1707. iii. NATHAN, b. ———; m., raised a family; no more known.

    1708. iv. ALPHONSO, b. ———; m., raised a family; no more known.

    1709. v.   JOSEPH HOSLEY, b. Sept. 10, 1811; m. Rhoda Esther Mason, 3167-8.

    1710. vi. WILLIAM, b. ———; m. Anna Mariah Weaver.

    1711. vii. GEORGE L., b. July 15, 1818; m. Abigail A. Webb and Lydia M. Leigh, 3169-74.

    659. WILLIAM FOOTE, (216, 60, 18, 5,) b. Sept. 5, 1780; m. 1806, Patty Janes, of St. Albans, Vt.; d. there Jan. 26, 1815.

    1711¹. i. WILLIAM, b. ———; res., Montreal.

    1711². ii. MARY C., b. ———.·

    661. AMOS FOOTE, (217, 60, 18, 5,) b. Jan. 15, 1763; m. 1st, Ann Seymore, of Watertown, Ct. She d. Jan. 3, 1807, ae. 43; m. 2nd, Eunice Daley, widow of Eliel Daley; her maiden name was Woodward; of Watertown, Ct. She d. Jan. 8, 1843, ae. 67.

    669. EBENEZER FOOTE, (218, 60, 18, 5,) b. July 6, 1773; m. 1803, Elizabeth, dau. of Benjamin and Lucretia (Ely) Colt. She was b. Sept. 1, 1774; he d. July 21, 1814.

    1712. i. LUCRETIA, b. 1834; m. Lebbeus Boothe, of Ballstown Spa., Saratoga Co., N. Y. Ch.: 3.

    675. JUDGE SAMUEL ALFRED FOOTE, (218, 60, 18, 5,) b. Dec. 17, 1790; m. Aug. 17, 1818, Mariam, dau. of William Fowler, Esq., of Albany, N. Y. She d. Aug. 2, 1832; m. 2nd, July 1, 1834, Jane, dau. of Samuel Campbell, of New York. She was b. 1809; d. Jan. 30, 1867, at Geneva, N. Y.; res., Albany, N. Y., and Geneva, N. Y.

Samuel Alfred Foote res. with his parents at Watertown, Ct., until Sept. 1805, when he went to live with his elder brother Ebenezer, who then res. at Troy, Rensselaer Co., N. Y. After spending a little more than a year in his brother's law office, he was sent by his brother to school at Union College. He entered the Grammar School of that College in Dec., 1806, entered the Freshman Class in Sept., 1807, and was graduated in July, 1811. He read law for nearly a year after leaving College, which he did in Dec., 1810, with James Thompson, Esq., of Milton, Saratoga Co., N. Y., and then entered his brother's office in Albany, his brother then residing in that city. He was admitted an Attorney in the Supreme Court of the State of New York in Jan., 1813, and a Counselor in Jan., 1816. He entered into partnership with his brother on being admitted an Attorney. He practiced law in Albany until May, 1828, when he removed to the city of New York. He was appointed District Attorney for the city and county of Albany, under the administration of Governor Clinton, in July, 1819, and held the office until Feb., 1821, when he was removed to make room for the Hon. Benjamin Butler, who was appointed in his place.

In 1831 his Alma Mater, Union College, conferred upon him the honorary degree of Master of Arts, and in 1844 Geneva College also honored him with the degree of Doctor of Laws. On April 10, 1851, he was appointed by Gov. Hunt, without his knowledge or solicitation, as Presiding Judge of the Court of Appeals, to fill the unexpired term of Judge Bronson, resigned. His appointment was universally approved. The following is a comment upon his appointment by one of the leading journals of the State:

"The Hon. Samuel A. Foote has been appointed, by Governor Hunt, the successor to Judge Bronson, resigned—a very exceptionable selection. Mr. Foote is an eminent lawyer and upright man, possessing qualifications and traits of character especially adapting him to discharge the high functions of the station with great ability and approbation. Mr. Foote has been extensively engaged in his profession for over 25 years. He removed from Albany to this city in 1828, where he since practiced in the higher courts—having the last two years spent a portion of his time at Geneva. It is a subject of real congratulation when such a man as Mr. Foote is elevated to the Bench. In all his personal habits and dispositions Mr. Foote is admirably adapted for judicial service— diligent and methodical, patient and mild, constant and just—we have the best assurances that, while enlightened justice will be dispensed and the purest judicial rectitude observed, true dignity and conciliatory deportment will also be displayed by the appointee.—New York Herald, April 11, 1851."

The Whig Convention, held at Syracuse in Sept. of the same year, nominated him as their candidate for Judge of the Court of Appeals for the eight year term, commencing in Jan. of the following year, but the Whig party met with defeat at the general election.

In 1853 Hobart College likewise conferred upon him the honorary degree of Doctor of Laws. In 1855 the Republicans of Ontario Co., during his absence, and without his knowledge, nominated him as their candidate for the General Assembly. This was his first affiliation with the Republican Party, and while he preferred the quiet home life which at this age he had so well earned and richly deserved, yet he felt it his duty to accept and was elected by a large majority. He was also nominated and elected the following year. During his two terms in the General Assembly he earned the cognomen of "Watch Dog of the Treasury."

At and after this period Judge Foote devoted most of his time to the general pursuits of agriculture at his seat in Geneva, and to the rearing of his large family, appearing only in the higher Courts of the State in important cases. He d. May 11, 1878, at Geneva, N. Y.

1713. i. MARGARET, b. Albany, June 21, 1819; d. Nov. 11, 1820.

1714. ii. JOHN, b. N. Y. City, Apr. 30, 1835. He was a graduate of Williams College, and afterwards entered into what promised to be a brilliant career in the practice of law in New York City with his father, but was compelled on account of his health to go to Minnesota where, at the beginning of the Civil War, he enlisted and served a short time as Captain of 2nd Minn. Regt. (Infantry), and was in the battle of Mills Springs, Ky., one of the first engagements of the war. His health broke down at that time, and he proceeded to his father's home in Geneva, N. Y., to die, and was in the service at the time of his death. He d. Mar. 13, 1862, at Geneva, N. Y.

1715. iii. SAMUEL CAMPBELL, b. N. Y. City, June 15, 1836. Served during a part of the Civil War as executive officer on the gunboat "Stars and Stripes," and his vessel participated in several engagements; he was in the naval service at the time of his death. He d. June 12, 1862, at Milburn, N. J., of fever.

JUDGE SAMUEL ALFRED FOOTE. No. 675

GOV. SAMUEL AUGUSTUS FOOTE. No. 715

1716. iv. EUPHEMIA, b. N. Y. City, Dec. 12, 1837; m. Oct. 16, 1867, Worthington Whittredge, at Geneva, N. Y.; res., Summit, N. Y. Ch.: (1) Jeannie, b. Nov. 1, 1871; d. Mar. 19, 1873. (2) Effie, b. Jan. 27, 1874. (3) Olive, b. June 24, 1875. (4) Mary, b. Sept. 30, 1879; m. L. Emery Katzenbach, Nov. 7, 1903. Ch.: (a) William Emery, b. Aug. 30, 1904. Res., New York City.

1717. v. MARY, b. N. Y. City, Aug. 31, 1839; m. Dr. Robert Ross Roberts, of Harrisburg, Pa., June 14, 1865, at Geneva, N. Y. She d. Aug. 13, 1870, at Denver, Col. Dr. Roberts d. at Harrisburg, Pa. Ch.: (1) Edmund Willson Roberts, b. May 12, 1866; m. Mar. 30, 1896, Lena Isabel Norton. Res., Clyde, Ohio. Ch.: (a) Edmund Willson, b. Apr. 29, 1898. (b) Elizabeth Isabel, b. Jan. 12, 1901. (c) Ruth Estelle, b. Aug. 12, 1902. (2) Benjamin Leacock, b. Oct. 7, 1867. He was m. to Ida Richardson Cage, at Canton, Miss., Nov. 20, 1890; now res. Canton, Miss. Ch.: (a) Ross, b. June 8, 1891. (b) Albert Hunley, b. Dec. 22, 1895. (c) Dorothy, b. Dec. 7, 1896; d. May 6, 1897. (d) Catharine, b. Oct. 14, 1900. (e) Benjamin Leacock, b. Dec. 20, 1901.

1718. vi. ALFRED, b. Oct. 25, 1840; m. Rebecca Foster, 3175.

1718¹. vii. ROBERT, b. N. Y. City, Feb. 12, 1843; d. Sept. 9, 1845, at Springfield, N. J.

1719. viii. LAWRENCE, b. N. Y. City, July 7, 1844; m. Hannah Kenner and Mrs. Louise Garret Morey, 3176-77¹.

1720. ix. ROBERT EBENEZER, b. Oct. 13, 1845; m. Frances Hamilton, 3178-81.

1721. x. THOMAS, b. at Springfield, N. J., Apr. 18, 1847; d. Dec. 14, 1872, at Geneva, N. Y.; unm.

1721¹. xi. GEORGE, b. Geneva, N. Y., July 17, 1848; mining engineer; res., Tucson, Ariz.; unm.

1721². xii. WILLIAM, b. Geneva, N. Y., Sept. 25, 1849; d. Oct. 26, 1870, at Denver, Colo.

1721³. xiii. JANE, b. Geneva, Feb. 23, 1851; m. Feb. 23, 1876, George L. Hull. She d. Mar. 22, 1876, at Baltimore, Md. He d. ———.

1721⁴. xiv. ELIZA CAMPBELL, b. Geneva, Feb. 23, 1851; res., Lakewood, N. J.; unm.

1721⁵. xv. CATHERINE, b. Geneva, Oct. 19, 1852; a biologist of high reputation; res., N. Y. City; unm.

678. REUBEN FOOTE, (219, 60, 18, 5,) b. Dec. 4, 1771; m. 1795, Silence Hitchcock, of Bethlehem, Ct. In 1797 he removed to Jefferson, N. Y., where he res. until 1815, when he removed to Harpersfield O., where he d. Mar. 1816 She d. Apr., 1816.

1722. i. ABIAH, b. ———.
1723. ii. MERRIT, b. ———.
1724. iii. GEORGE b. ———.
1725. iv. CHESTER, b. ———.
1726. v. REUBEN, b. ———.

680. MILES FOOTE, (219, 60, 18, 5,) b. Sept. 13, 1774; m. 1st, 1797, Polly Hitchcock, of Bethlehem, Ct. She d. in Jefferson, N. Y.; m. 2nd, Esther Northrop. He d. Feb. 28, 1843, in Jefferson, N. Y.

1727. i.   ALMA, b. ———; m. Jacob Dewey; res., Jefferson, N. Y. Ch.: 9.

1728. ii.   ANDREW NORTHRUP, b. Jan. 16, 1801; m. Amanda Matilda Phillips, 3182-91.

1729. iii. ABRAHAM, b. Feb., 1803; m. Amy Avery, 3192-3202.

1730. iv.   PALUSKI, b. ———; res., Jefferson, N. Y.; unm.

1731. v.   HULDAH, b. ———; m. and has 8 daus.

1732. vi.   HESTER, b. ———; m. 1848, Lewis Burnit; removed to Wilson, Niagara Co., N. Y.   *June 19, 1815. See Vol. 2, p. 767*

1733. vii. EMMA, b. Aug., 1810.

1734. viii. ISAAC, b. 1821.

686. JACOB FOOTE, (219, 60, 18, 5,) b. Apr. 21, 1789; m. 1812, Amanda Givens; res., Watertown and Harpersfield, Delaware Co., N. Y.

1735. i.   SHELDON G., b. May 21, 1813; d. 1835, in Somerset, Niagara Co., N. Y.

1736. ii.   ALONZO D., b. Sept. 19, 1815; m. Lucy Lum and Ann Louisa Lum, 3203-4.

1737. iii. GEORGE A., b. Aug. 26, 1819; m. Lovica M. Hubbard, 3205-9.

1738. iv.   SARAH A., b. Aug. 12, 1821; a teacher in New York, N. Y.

1739. v.   DOTHA E., b. May 2, 1825; m. Nov. 13, 1845, George Green; res., Troy, N. Y.

1740. vi.   JACOB C., b. Apr. 15, 1827; d. Jan. 21, 1828.

1741. vii. JACOB CHESTER, b. June 16, 1830; m. Jane Tracy, 3210-5.

1742. viii. T. BRONSON, b. Dec. 13, 1833; m. and d. Res., Johnson Creek, N. Y., 3216.

688. JOSEPH FOOTE, (220, 60, 18, 5,) b. Sept. 4, 1772; m. 1795, Abigail, dau. of George Baldwin, of Washington, Ct. He d. Apr. 2, 1826.

1743. i.   REV. JOSEPH I., D. D., b. Nov. 17, 1796; graduated at Union College, 1821. He fitted himself for the Christian Ministry at the Theological Seminary at Andover, Mass., where he spent three years. Oct. 25, 1826, he was installed Pastor of the Congregational Church at West Brookfield, Mass.; in 1833 he was called to the charge of the church at Salina, N. Y., where he resided until 1835. While in pastoral charge of the church at Knoxville, Tenn., his reputation as a scholar and divine arrested the attention of the Corporation of Washington College, Tenn., who conferred upon him the degree of D. D., and tendered him President of that Institution, 1840.

1744. ii.   BETSY, b. Apr. 17, 1799; d. Apr. 30, 1818.

1745. iii. GEORGE, b. Sept. 1, 1800; m. Ann Fish, 3217.

1746. iv.   ROXANA, b. Jan. 16, 1806; m. Joshua J. Garret, of Litchfield, Ct. She d. June 13, 1824. Ch.: 1 son, b. Apr. 30, 1824; d. Aug. 30, 1824.

1747. v.   RHODA ABIGAIL, b. Aug. 18, 1807; d. ———; res, Tennessee.

1748. vi.   EZRA ALBERT, b. Feb. 13, 1809; m. Clarrissa Beach, 3218-20.

1749. vii. JOHN, b. Feb. 13, 1816; d. Apr. 1, 1816.

689. STEPHEN FOOTE, (220, 60, 18, 5,) b. Jan. 24, 1774; m. 1796, Rhoda, dau. of Timothy Hand, of Litchfield, Ct. He d. 1844, in Illinois.

1750. i.   RACHEL P., b. ———; m. John Ramsay. Ch.: 4.

1751. ii. TIMOTHY BRADLEY, b. Dec. 29, 1799; m. Jane Ann Russell, Nancy Jane Riley and Elizabeth Bessac. 3221-34.

1752. iii. STEPHEN V., b. 1802; unm.

1753. iv. JARVIS, b. 1804; m. ———; res., ———.

1754. v. AMANDA, b. 1806; m. George Babcock. Ch.: 2.

1755. vi. NANCY, b. 1808; d. 1810.

1756. vii. LUCIA, b. 1811; d. July 22, 1887, at Nephi, Utah.

1757. viii. REUBEN, b. 1814.

701. TITUS FOOTE, (221, 60, 18, 5,) b. Aug. 25, 1781; m. Nov. 12, 1804, Elizabeth, dau. of Thomas Bronson, of Watertown, Ct. She d. Nov. 8, 1840, ae. 60; m. 2nd, Feb. 21, 1845, Patience, dau. of Elijah Bills, of Harwinton, Ct. She d. Feb. 19, 1846, ae. 46; m. 3rd, June 8, 1846, Hannah, dau. of Elijah Bills.

1758. i. ANNA JANET, b. May 27, 1805; m. Bennit J. French, of Watertown, Ct.

1759. ii. POLLY BELINDA, b. June 24, 1810; d. June 9, 1815.

1760. iii. THOMAS BRONSON, b. Dec. 25, 1813; d. Nov. 23, 1827.

703. JONATHAN FOOTE, (222, 61, 18, 5,) b. May 3, 1765; m. Apr., 1792, Esther, dau. of Jonathan, Russell, of North Branford, Ct. He d. July 31, 1813. She d. Feb. 13, 1835; res., North Branford, Ct.

1761. i. WALTER RODNEY, b. Feb. 10, 1793; m. Sally Harrison, North Branford, Ct., 3235-7.

1762. ii. MERRITT, b. June 19, 1795; m. Betsey Palmer, 3238-42.

1763. iii. JOHN, b. Oct. 6, 1798; m. Sylvia Rose, of North Branford, Ct. He d. Jan. 6, 1835; p. s.

706. SAMUEL FOOTE, (222, 61, 18, 5,) b. May 21, 1773; m. Dec. 2, 1795, Lydia, dau. of Noah Baldwin, of North Branford, Ct. He d. Dec. 29, 1849. Res., North Branford, Ct.

1764. i. SAMUEL, b. Sept. 11, 1796; m. Clarissa Baldwin; both dead; s. p.

1765. ii. LYDIA, b. Sept. 11, 1796; m. Stephen Bradley, of East Haven, Ct. Ch.: (1) Baldwin. (2) Amanda. (3) Mary. (4) Samuel. (5) Steven. (6) Lydia.

1766. iii. ABIGAIL, b. Feb. 17, 1800; m. William Reynolds, of North Branford, Ct. Ch.: (1) Ross. (2) Elizabeth. Both dead; p. s.

1767. iv. AUGUSTUS, b. Jan. 16, 1802; d. June 7, 1802.

1768. v. AUGUSTUS, b. Sept. 13, 1804; m. Julia A. Palmer, 3243-5.

1769. vi. LODEMIA, b. May 10, 1810; m. Lester Palmer, of Branford, Ct.; he d.; m. 2nd, David Maine. Ch. by 2nd husband: (1) Henry. (2) Irvine. Res., Deruyter, Madison Co., N. Y.

1770. vii. JONATHAN, b. Feb. 16, 1815; m. Abigail Linsley, 3246-50.

714. DR. WILLIAM LAMBERT FOOTE, (223, 61, 18, 5,) b. Oct. 10, 1778; m. Mar. 18, 1801, Mary, dau. of Capt. Dan Scovill, of Saybrook, Ct. Mr. Foote has held the office of Town Clerk of Cheshire and Probate Judge of that district.

1771. i. WILLIAM SIDNEY, b. Nov. 21, 1802; m. Mary Butler, 3251-3.

1772. ii. MARY A., b. May 23, 1806.

1773. iii. ABIGAIL H., b. Apr. 28, 1808; m. July 2, 1829, Edward Doolittle, of Brooklyn, N. Y. He was b. Mar. 7, 1808, and d. Mar. 4, 1837.

1774. iv. SCOVILL D., b. Apr. 10, 1810; m. June, 1836, Martha Whiting, of Milford, Ct. She was b. 1807, in Milford; s. p.

1775. v.   ELIZA S., b. June 29, 1812.
1776. vi.   JOHN L., b. Sept. 14, 1817; d. Nov. 14, 1906, ae. 89 years. He
             was b. in Cheshire and always resided there, and was probably
             the wealthiest resident of Cheshire. He never interested him-
             self in politics and never held public office, excepting that of
             postmaster, which he filled nearly 50 years ago. It is estimated
             that his estate is worth about $450,000.

715. SAMUEL AUGUSTUS FOOTE, (223, 61, 18, 5,) b. Nov. 8, 1780; m.
Eudocia, dau. of Gen. Andrew and Elizabeth Mary Ann Hull, of Cheshire. He d.
Sept. 16, 1846. She d. Jan. 12, 1849. Res., New Haven, Ct., and Cheshire, Ct.
1777. i.   JOHN ALFRED, b. Nov. 22, 1803; m. Frances A. Hitchcock,
             3254-60.
1778. ii.   ANDREW HULL, b. Sept. 12, 1806; m. Caroline Flagg and
             Caroline Augusta Street, 3261-7.
1779. iii. RODERICK AUGUSTUS, b. Oct. 1, 1808; d. Feb. 24, 1810.
1780. iv.   AUGUSTUS EDWIN, b. Dec. 31, 1810; m. Oct. 7, 1832, Aurelia,
             dau. of Zina and Mary Post. She was b. June 30, 1813.
1781. v.   WILLIAM HENRY, b. Feb. 1, 1817; d. Mar. 6, 1827.
1782. vi.   EDWARD DORR, b. Feb. 3, 1820; d. Feb. 9, 1821.

718. DR. MALACHI FOOTE, (223, 61, 18, 5,) b. Apr. 14, 1771; m. Martha
Rockwell, of Salem. She d. abt. 1816, in Monticello, N. Y.; m. 2nd, Melissa
————. He d. abt. 1825. Res., Salem, Ct., and Bowling Green, Va.
1783. i.   THOMAS JEFFERSON, b. Oct. 3, 1796; m. Margaret Whithead,
             3268-74.
1784. ii.   CHARLOTTE, b. Oct. 3, 1796; m. Henry Onderdonk, of Monti-
             cello, N. Y. He d. ————; m. 2nd, Lebbeus Godfrey. Ch.: (1)
             Henry; res., near Byron, N. Y. (2) Darwin.
1785. iii. LYDIA, b. 1789; m. William Cady, merchant, of Monticello, N.
             Y. Ch.: (1) Henry.
1786. iv.   ISAAC, b. abt. 1805; educated as a physician. He practiced
             medicine in Virginia, and m. and d.; p. s.
1787. v.   ERASTUS DARWIN, b. ————.
1788. vi.   VIRGINIA, b. ————.
1789. vii. MELINA VICTORIA, b. ————; m. May 18, 1848, Jeremiah
             Higbee, of Medina Co., Ohio.

719. LYMAN HALL FOOTE, (223, 61, 18, 5,) b. June 29, 1773; m. Nov. 5,
1793, Lucretia, dau. of Amos Page, of North Branford, Ct. She was b. Feb. 14,
1774; d. Mar. 18, 1813; he d. Apr. 18, 1826. Res., Northford, Ct., Chatham, N. Y.,
Hudson, N. Y.
1790. i.   SELINA, b Dec. 27, 1794, in Northford, Ct.; m. Elijah Good-
             enough, of Chatham, N. Y. She d. June, 1843, in Chatham, N.
             Y. Ch.: (1) Lucretia, b. ————; m. John Wilford, of Branford,
             Ct. (2) John, b. ————. (3) Sarah Ann, b.
1791. ii.   LYMAN, b. Wallingford, Ct., Apr. 12, 1796; m. Ann Treadwell
             Platt and Mary Morris Cooper, 3275-86.
1792. iii. REBECCA R., b. Northford, Ct., Aug. 3, 1797; m. May 29, 1819,
             Enos M., son of Jonathan Peake, of Hudson, N. Y. He was b.
             June 27, 1793, in Chatham, N. Y. Ch.: (1) Dillon Rockwell b.
             Chatham, N. Y., Mar. 15, 1820. (2) John Lyman, b. Hudson,

N. Y., Nov. 22, 1828. (3) Gerard David, b. Hudson, N. Y., Mar. 4, 1835; d. in Hudson, N. Y.

1793. iv. MALACHI T., b. Northford, Ct., May 10, 1799; he d.

1794. v. DAVID AUSTIN, b. Branford, Ct., May 29, 1803; m. Mary H. Curtis, 3287-89.

1795. vi. HANNAH, b. June 24, 1807; m. Oct. 8, 1825, Roswell Page; he was b. Nov. 1, 1799; d. Oct. 8, 1877; she d. Apr. 17, 1885, in Bridgeport, Ct. Ch.: (1) Erastus, b. Oct. 29, 1827; d. Mar. 12, 1855. (2) Horace, b. Nov. 25, 1829; m. Sarah Wyatt; res., Bridgeport, Ct. Ch.: (a) Sadie Page, b. ———. (3) Edwell, b. July 23, 1831; res., Soldiers' Home, Noroton, Ct. (4) Effie, b. Aug. 21, 1836; d. Mar., 1884.

1796. vii. LYDIA, b. Chatham, N. Y., Mar. 8, 1809; m. George Whitlock, of Hudson, N. Y. She d. Jersey City, N. J. Res., Jersey City, N. J. Ch.: (1) Fanny, b. (2) George, b. (3) Theodore, b. (4) Frederick, b. (5) William, b.

1797. viii. STEPHEN GERARD, b. Feb. 17, 1811.

721. DR. WILLIAM FOOTE, (223, 61, 18, 5,) b. Oct. 11, 1799; m. Aug 9, 1804, Cathrine Picket; she d. Sept. 5, 1841; he d. Jan. 30, 1842; res., Durham, Ct.

1798. i. HEPZIBAH, b. Dec., 1805; d. Nov. 12, 1806.

1799. ii. JAMES PICKET, b. June 9, 1808; m. Mary Avery.

1800. iii. CATHRINE H., b. Mar. 22, 1811; m. May, 1830, Blynn T., son of William and Susanna (Tyler) Brainard, of Middletown, Ct. He was b. Haddam, Ct., Mar. 26, 1803; d. Aug. 3, 1882. In his earlier years he was a joiner and cabinet maker, but later in life a farmer. She d. Feb. 24, 1895. Ch.: (1) William Foote Brainard, b. Durham, Ct., Oct. 31, 1852.

1801. iv. REBECCA R., b. Jan., 1817; m. May, 1843, Franklin Johnson, of Columbia, Ga. She d. Dec., 1856. Ch.: (1) Frank K., b. July, 1852, Columbia, Ga.; m. Sept., 1878, Fanny B. Warthy, Columbia, Ga. Ch.: (a) Rockwell W., b. Mar., 1880, Columbia, Ga. (b) Helen, b. July, 1884, Columbia, Ga. (c) Gilbert F., b. Nov., 1886, Columbia, Ga. (2) Mary Jane, b. June, 1845, Columbia, Ga.; d. June, 1905, Edgewood, Ga.

1802. v. WILLIAM R., b. May, 1819; m. M. Amanda Jones, 3289-91.

724. ISAAC FOOTE, (223, 61, 18, 5,) b. May 21, 1799; m. Feb. 3, 1818, Caroline, dau. of Aaron Hall, of Wallingford, Ct. She was b. Dec. 21, 1799, and d. July, 1848, in Fair Haven. Res., North Haven and Fair Haven, Ct.

1803. i. ISAAC HENRY, b. July 10, 1819; m. Marietta Smith, 3292-4.

1804. ii. CAROLINE ELIZABETH, b. Dec. 9, 1822; m. 1st, July 31, 1843, Anson Hemingway Barnes, of Fair Haven, Ct.; m. 2nd, Oct., 1883, George Wells, of Geneseo, Ill.; she d. Dec. 15, 1896; s. p.

1805. iii. GEORGE BENTON, b. Feb. 24, 1824; m. Mary Flagler, 3295-6.

1806. iv. FRANCIS LEONIDAS, b. Nov. 11, 1826; d. 1864; unm.

1807. v. FREDERICK, b. Sept. 11, 1830; d. Nov. 25, 1835.

725. FREDERICK FOOTE, (221, 60, 18, 5,) b. Northford, Ct., Nov. 7, 1806; m. June 25, 1840, at Cheshire, Ct., Sibyl Celestia, dau. of Lyman Tuttle. She was b. at Mt. Carmel, Ct., Oct. 1, 1819; d. June 5, 1904, at North Haven, Ct. He

was a natural student, preferring study to farming. As a young man he would have liked to have entered the ministry, but his father having left a very large farm to be looked after it seemed necessary that he, the youngest child, should remain on the homestead. He was well versed in all historical literature, both ancient and modern, and knew the Bible literally by heart. While he was still a young man he journeyed on horseback for a number of winters through some of the western states, principally Ill. and Wis., preaching and helping to establish church organizations in new settlements. He lived an honorable life, well deserving the respect of all who knew him. He d. Aug. 2, 1882, at Northford, Ct.

    1808. i.   FREDERICK, b. Apr. 24, 1841; he was teaching school at the beginning of the Civil War in Illinois; he joined the Army from that State, and served through the campaign. He was made First Lieutenant of Ill. Cavalry. He d. Feb. 22, 1873, at Northford, Ct.

    1809. ii.   CELESTIA TUTTLE, b. Dec. 6, 1842; m. Jan. 16, 1868, at Northford, H. Willard Smith. She was an active member of Dwight Place Congregational Church, New Haven, Ct.; d. Dec. 29, 1891. Ch.: (1) Frederick Foote Smith, b. Nov. 20, 1872; m. 1892, Carolyn Koltarman. Ch.: (a) Celestia. (b) Albert, and two others. (2) Harrison W. Smith, b. Dec. 26, 1873; m. May 27, 1900, Mary Linsley Daniels. She was b. Aug. 20, 1872, North Haven, Ct. He possesses the old grandfather clock of his branch of the Foote Family. The clock is now nearly 225 years old, and was made for the father of Maj. Isaac Foote, of the French and Indian wars, from an old cherry tree that had grown on the homestead, by one of the trading English clock makers who visited this country about the year 1680. He served in the Spanish War, and is now Pay Clerk, U. S. A., at Marianao, Cuba. Res., Atlanta, Ga. Ch.: (a) Willard, b. Sept. 19, 1904. (b) Tuttle Foote, b. Feb. 14, 1906.

    1810. iii.   ISAAC, b. Oct. 17, 1844; m. Mary C. Neal, 3297-9.

    1811. iv.   ANNA ADELIA, b. June 13, 1849; d. Aug. 24, 1852.

    1812. v.   ELLEN MARY HALL, b. Aug. 4, 1856; m. Nov. 28, 1878, at New Haven, Ct., Charles Reed. He was a graduate of Yale, Class of 1871, and Yale Law School, Class of 1876. Res., Dorchester, Mass. Ch.: (1) Celesie Foote Reed, b. Jan. 9, 1882.

    1813. vi.   CAROLYN SIBYL, b. Apr. 5, 1864; m. Feb. 8, 1888, at New Haven, Dr. Wellington Campbell, a graduate of Yale College, Class of 1874, and the College of Physicians and Surgeons, N. Y. City, 1877. Res., Short Hills, N. J. Ch.: (1) Agnes Foote Campbell, b. Apr. 13, 1893. (2) Katharine Wade Campbell, b. July 18, 1896. (3) Wellington Foote Campbell, b. Oct. 7, 1897. (4) Ruth, b. Sept. 25, 1898; d. Dec. 20, 1898.

    942. ERASTUS FOOTE, (298, 89, 26, 9, 3,) b. July 25, 1794, Stafford, Ct.; m. June 10, 1821, Nancy Dimmick, by Rev. A. Dimmick. She was b. Aug. 15, 1801, at Stafford, Ct. The first ch. was b. in Mantua, O., and the others at Chardon, O.

    1818. i.   NANCY E., b. July 20, 1822.

    1819. ii.   SOPHRONIA M., b. July 14, 1824.

    1820. iii.   FRANCIS E., b. Aug. 26, 1826; m.; 3574-5.

1821. .iv. JULIA E., b. May 25, 1829; d.
1822. v. MARTHA J., b. Jan. 12, 1834.
1823. vi. WEALTHY C., b. Feb. 13, 1839.
1824. vii. JULIA E., b. Dec. 8, 1845.

754. ASA FOOTE, (235, 73, 25, 9, 3,) b. Jan. 31, 1785; m. 1st, Sept. 8, 1811, Betsey Gates. She was b. Sept. 19, 1792, and d. Oct. 14, 1832; m. 2nd, Feb. 28, 1833, Esther Ann Ferry. She was b. June 18, 1788, and d. Jan. 21, 1845; m. 3rd, June 12, 1845, Christina, dau. of John and Vashti (Speor) Brisban. She was b. Jan. 9, 1791, and d. Mar. 21, 1872. He d. July 4, 1859. Res., ———.

1825. i. PATIENCE DEBORAH, b May 30, 1812; d. June 28, 1812.
1826. ii. NATHANIEL, b. July 9, 1813; m. Olivia M. Knox, 3300-2.
1827. iii. ASA, b. Apr. 5, 1815; m. Almedia Ann Gale, 3303-6.
1828. iv. ISRAEL, b. Feb. 1, 1817; m. Mary Louisa Banks, 3307-8.
1829. v. ALMIRA HUNT, b. Feb. 22, 1819; m. May 28, 1843, Jonas Antle, son of Jonas and Mary White, of Whitestown, N.Y. He was a director and president of the bank at Whitestown, N.Y., also a successful farmer. Ch.: (1) Louisa Amelia, b. Jan. 7, 1845; d. Apr. 24, 1849. (2) Amelia Louisa, b. Mar. 22, 1850. (3) William Stratton, b. Nov. 18, 1855; d. Apr. 19, 1863. (4) Elizabeth Foote, b. July 13, 1857; m. Dec. 24, 1884, Hammond Evans, of Whitestown, N. Y. She d. May 28, 1885; no ch. (5) Alta, b. Jan. 20, 1860.
1830. vi. EZRA, b. Apr. 5, 1821; m. Rachel Mills, 3309-12.
1831. vii. DAVID, b. Nov. 8, 1823; d. July 5, 1849, at Syracuse, N. Y., of cholera; unm.
1832. viii. CHARLES OTIS, b. Apr. 5, 1825; d. Mar. 29, 1859, at Sherburne, N. Y.; unm.
1833. ix. BURTON, b. Feb. 15, 1829; m. Mariah Whitehead, 3313-6.

758. ISRAEL FOOTE, (235, 73, 25, 9, 3,) b. May 29, 1794; m. 1st, Oct. 13, 1819, Lucy Brainard, dau. of Bezaleel and Lydia (Deming) Brainard, of East Haddam, Ct. She was b. July 17, 1793; d. Feb. 24, 1853, at Sherburne, N. Y.; m. 2nd, Feb. 12, 1854, Clarissa Ely, wid. of Horace Ely, of Lyme, Ct., and dau. of Joseph and Phebe (Sterling) Marvin, of Lyme, Ct. She d. Apr. 7, 1881, at Sherburne, N. Y. He was clerk in a store at East Haddam Landing, and for many years a teacher, but after marriage a farmer, first in Westchester, then, abt. 1825, in Sherburne Four Corners, N. Y.; a man of fine physique, of good intellectual ability, and of commanding appearance. He was orator one 4th of July at Sherburne Celebration. In the War sympathies he was divided between North and South; his dau. m. a slaveholder who fought in the Rebel Army; his son fell in the Union Army. He d. July 3, 1884, at Sherburne, N. Y. He purchased the farm now occupied and owned by his son, Samuel M. Foote, in 1832. During his whole life, in whatever occupation engaged, he always took a deep interest in educational and religious matters.

1834. i. SAMUEL MILLS, b. Jan. 29, 1822; m. Sarah E. Hartwell, 3317-21.
1835. ii. SARAH TISDALE, b. Feb. 10, 1824; m. Aug. 22, 1848, Dr. William Jones Price, of Wilmington, N. C. He was b. Apr. 9, 1804, at Hamson Creek, N. C.; graduated from University of Pennsylvania, Medical Department. He d. June 25, 1868. She d. May 23, 1865. Ch.: (1) Caroline Louisa Price, b. Dec. 12, 1849; res., Wilmington, N. C.; unm. (2) William Kenan Price,

b. Nov. 4, 1853; drowned in Cape Fear river while trying to swim across it, Apr. 26, 1875. (3) Lucy Brainard Price, b. Feb. 6, 1857; d. Feb. 15, 1858. (4) Susan Ann Price, b. June 5, 1860; res., Wilmington, N. C. (5) John Jones Price, b. Jan. 23, 1863; d. Oct. 23, 1863.

1836. iii. CAROLINE ELIZABETH, b. Mar. 13, 1828; m. Oct. 5, 1864, Edward H. Purdy, son of William and Lucina (Lewis) Purdy, of North Norwich, Chenango Co., N. Y. He was proprietor or part owner of the "Oxford Times," N. Y., "Oneida (N. Y.) Dispatch," "Oswego (N. Y.) Advertiser and Times." He was b. Aug. 5, 1816; d. Apr. 5, 1895. Ch.: (1) Frederick Foote, b. Aug. 10, 1867; m. June 14, 1894, Ida Jay Harris. Ch.: (a) Frederick Harris, b. Mar. 23, 1896. (b) Ray Foote, b. Jan. 9, 1898. (2) Willard Barry, b. Aug. 27, 1870; d. Mar. 5, 1875.

1837. iv. LUCY ELLEN, b. Sept. 6, 1831; d. unm. at Lockport, N. Y., July 15, 1902. She was a woman of remarkable memory, who could recall instantly the date of any birth, marriage or death in the family records in two generations; of strong and winning personality, and a credit to the family.

1838. v. ISRAEL OTIS, b. Nov. 9, 1834; he was about to be admitted to the Bar when the War broke out. Enlisted at first call, as a pure matter of duty, as a patriot and Christian. Enlisted as private; promoted to Corporal before the march to seat of war from Staten Island; promoted to Sergeant for gallantry at battle of Fair Oaks in taking the standard from the hands of a fellow comrade and continuing it to the front. He was killed at the battle of Fredericksburg, Dec. 13, 1862.

1839. vi. MILTON LATHROP, b. Jan. 15, 1837; d. June 12, 1840.

759. DAVID FOOTE, (235, 73, 25, 9, 3,) b. Apr. 22, 1796; m. May 28, 1828, Dorothy Shattuck, dau. of David and Dorothy (Alcott) Shattuck, of Westchester, Ct. She was b. May 7, 1804. They lived for a number of years at Westchester, Ct., then removed to Colchester, Ct., where she d. Jan. 23, 1872. He d. at Colchester, Ct., Jan. 27, 1883.

1840. i. NATHANIEL, b. Aug. 8, 1831; m. Abby Jane Bigelow, 3322-3.

1841. ii. MARY S., b. Jan. 14, 1847; m. Mar. 22, 1866, Guy M. Bigelow (brother of her brother's wife), son of Guy and Nancy (Hurd) Bigelow, of Colchester, Ct. He was b. Feb. 22, 1843. She d. Apr. 15, 1885, of measles. Ch.: (1) William Harding, b. Feb. 10, 1867. (2) Bertie Marcelon, b. May 16, 1873. (3) Guy Otis, b. Mar. 12, 1877. (4) Nathaniel Foote, b. July 18, 1880. (5) Abby Jane, b. Feb. 22, 1883.

765. AMASA, (236, 73, 25, 9, 3, 1,) b. July 7, 1783, Colchester, Ct.; m. Mar. 5, 1820, Lydia Worthington, dau. of Daniel Tracy; she d. Jan. 17, 1841, ae. 41. He d. Dec. 17, 1848.

1842. i. LUCY MARIA, b. May 1, 1822; d. July 16, 1894; unm.

1843. ii. DAN, b. Mar. 26, 1824; m. Catharine Phelps, 3324-6.

1844. iii. JIRAH ISHAM, b. Oct. 10, 1825; m. Frances Maria Sherman and Margaret M. Ray, 3327-8.

1845. iv. SUSAN CLARISSA, b. Jan. 23, 1823; d. June 13, 1829.

1846. v. DYAR, b. Nov. 24, 1829; d. Oct. 2, 1840.

1847. vi.   EDWIN TRACY, b. Nov. 21, 1831; m. Julia Winans; res., James-
             ville, Wis.; no ch.

1848. vii. EUNICE AMELIA, b. Feb. 24, 1834; m. Joel Jones, of West-
             chester, Ct. Res., Westchester, Ct. No ch.

1849. viii. NELSON, b. May 8, 1836; m. Cornelia Lyon, 3329.

1850. ix.   HENRY EMERSON, b. Mar. 25, 1838; d. Oct. 8, 1838.

1851. x.   DYAR, b. Jan. 14, 1841; d. Oct. 16, 1860; unm.

767. DR. DYAR FOOTE, (236, 73, 25, 9, 3, 1,) b. July 29, 1788; m. Apr. 4,
1822, Sally Maria Miller, of Charlton, N. Y.; res., Ludlowville and Elmira, N. Y.
She was b. Sept. 26, 1803.

1852. i.   GUY, b. in Ludlowville, N. Y., Mar. 5, 1823; res., Jackson, Mich.

1853. ii.   MARY, b. Ludlowville, N. Y., Jan. 19, 1825.

1854. iii. HENRY, b. Ludlowville, N. Y., Apr. 28, 1827.

1855. iv.   FRANK, b. Ludlowville, N. Y., Jan. 14, 1829.

1856. v.   MARGARET, b. Ludlowville, N. Y., Dec. 10, 1830.

1857. vi.   DAN, b. Ludlowville, N. Y., June 28, 1833.

1858. vii. DYAR, b. Ludlowville, N. Y., May 23, 1835.

1859. viii. EMILY B., b. Elmira, N. Y., Mar. 20, 1841; d. May 19, 1842.

771. REV. ADRIAN FOOTE (241, 73, 25, 9, 3,) b. Apr. 2, 1787; m. Sally
Sole; she d.; m. 2nd, 1832, Philomela Alden, b. June 19, 1809; d. Feb. 10, 1899.
He was a Baptist clergyman, a graduate of Hamilton Theological Seminary; res.,
Ohio. He d. July 29, 1886.

1860. i.   ADRIAN VAN HORN, b. Feb. 8, 1833; m.; res., Knox, Stork
             Co., Ind.

1861. ii.   ELIZABETH ISABELL, b. Nov. 25, 1835; m. Dr. Grover; d.
             June 19, 1885.

1862. iii. SALLY HARRIET, b. July 19, 1836; d. Jan. 10, 1855.

1863. iv.   MARYETTA, b. Feb. 22, 1839; m. ———. Burnstead; res., Lin-
             coln, Neb. Has a family.

1864. v.   MERNIVA GABRIELLA, b. May 24, 1846; m. ———. Gould;
             res., Lincoln, Neb. Has a family.

774. HENRY FOOTE, (241, 73, 25, 9, 3,) b. Apr. 14, 1794; m. Oct. 9, 1820,
Adah Vail, dau. of Job Vail. He was a Colonel of Militia and a Deacon of the
Baptist Church. He d. 1880. Res., New Berlin, N. Y. Ch. all b. in New Berlin,
N. Y.

1865. i.   ADRIAN, b. Dec. 4, 1822; m. Mary Cornelia Beardsley, 3330-5.

1866. ii.   ANDREW, b. Sept. 4, 1824; res., Ashland, Mass.

1867. iii. JOHN, b. Apr. 24, 1827; d. Aug. 20, 1839.

1868. iv.   EDSON DAN, b. Nov. 4, 1832; d. Jan. 24, 1841.

1869. v.   JOHN, b. Apr. 12, 1841; resides on the old Homestead Farm
             settled upon by Dr. Dan Foote (No. 241) in 1792; it has never
             been out of the hands of his descendants.

781. DR. DAN FOOTE, (241, 73, 25, 9, 3,) b. New Berlin Center, N. Y., Feb.
9, 1810; m. Dec. 11, 1833, Sarah Conover, dau. of Jonathan Rhea and Jane (Conover) Gordon, of Freehold, N. J. She was b. Oct. 17, 1806, and d. Feb. 19, 1847.
He d. Mar. 16, 1888, at New Berlin Center, N. Y.

1872. i.   LAVANTIA JANE, b. May 31, 1836; m. Nov. 28, 1858, Oscar
             Cole, of Fall River, Mass., afterwards of Cedar Falls, Iowa. He

was b. June 13, 1834, at Nassau, Rensselaer Co., N. Y. She d.
May 23, 1901, at Cedar Falls, Iowa. Ch.: (1) Ella Gordon, b.
Sept. 24, 1859; m. May 21, 1897, Elmer Heskett, of Cedar Falls,
Iowa. He was b. in 1874 at Cedar Falls, Iowa. Ch.: (a) Flor-
ence, b. Feb. 28, 1898, at Cedar Falls, Iowa. (2) Georgia Anna,
b. Jan. 26, 1865; m. Jan. 9, 1889, Hugh John Miller, at Minne-
apolis, Minn. He was b. Dec. 21, 1866, at Genoa, Olmstead Co.,
Minn.; Graduate of University of Mich., 1891. City and County
Attorney, and in State Legislature. Ch.: (a) Vilroy Cole, b.
Mar. 4, 1890, at Ann Arbor, Mich.

1873. ii.   NATHANIEL GORDON, b. June 5, 1838; m. Sarah Eliza Dixon,
            3336-9.
1874. iii. WILLIAM HENRY, b. Sept. 10, 1840; d. July 19, 1842.
1875. iv.   LEWIS RAY, b. Mar. 29, 1844; m. Mrs. Harriet Amanda Cran-
            dell Wilson, dau. of Richard R. Crandell and Mary Lapaugh,
            June 12, 1873. She was b. July 17, 1838, at Durham, Greene Co.,
            N. Y.

The Reverend Lewis Ray (Rhea) Foote, D. D., had a remarkably useful and interesting career as a minister in Brooklyn,
N. Y., for a whole generation. He was the most efficient pastor
of the Throop Avenue Presbyterian Church, and a potent factor
in the life of his city for 32 years. It is a rare thing for a
clergyman to find his life work in one pastorate (as was his),
and one in which the young man and the young church grow to
maturity and great influence together.

He was the youngest son of Dr. Dan Foote and Sarah Conover Gordon, and was b. in South New Berlin, N. Y. His mother
was a descendant of the Rheas and Gordons of Monmouth Co.,
N. J., families that had lived in that section for many years
prior to the Revolution, and whose homestead farm was the
scene of the Battle of Monmouth. His mother died when Lewis
Ray was three years of age, and his lonely, motherless childhood
was spent with relatives in Sherburne, N. Y., near the place of
his birth. At 14 he became self supporting, working as a farm
laborer. This life on the farm laid the foundation of a rugged
constitution, and there was implanted the germ of a profound
love of nature which was fostered, not only by his intimate association with nature and his personal observations, but by the
reverent habit of recognizing God as the author of it all. The
memory of these early hardships gave him the power of an
intelligent sympathy with those who toil. Throughout his whole
life he found a spiritual uplift, physical and mental rest, in
God's great outdoors.

When 15 years of age he gave his heart to Christ and became a member of the Congregational Church at Sherburne.
That step was taken deliberately and at a time of no unusual
religious effort. It was a complete surrender and the logical result of his naturally spiritual temperament.

He was a tall manly-looking boy, and there was no hesita-
tion on the part of the recruiting officers to accept him when he
enlisted for the war in Sept., 1861. He served one year in the

61st N. Y. Vol. Infantry Regt., from Sept. 1861 to 1862, and was
honorably discharged because of a wound received at Fair Oaks
June 1st, 1862.

Upon recovering his health he entered Dr. Holbrook's preparatory school at Clinton, N. Y., and in the fall of 1865 matriculated in the freshman class of Hamilton College, from which he
graduated in June, 1869. He was a member of the Delta Kappa
Epsilon fraternity and was an excellent student, ranking particularly high in oratory. After his graduation from Union
Theological Seminary in 1872, he was for a year engaged in
mission work in New York City. He assumed his duties as
pastor of the Throop Avenue Church Nov. 1, 1873, and continued
till his death, Dec. 19, 1906.

This church was organized in 1862 and had but a handful
of members when Dr. Foote entered upon his work, but it was
located in a growing city where the vigorous and consecrated
young man soon saw the fruits of his efforts. During the first
25 years the annual increase in church membership averaged
close to a hundred, over half of whom were members of the
Sabbath School, and united with the church on the profession of
their faith. From 1885 to 1895 the church was famous for having
under its care the largest Sabbath School in the Presbyterian
connection in the United States. Throughout the 32 years of
Dr. Foote's pastorate the amount of money given for benevolent
purposes, on the average, exceeded that used for church expenses by about a thousand dollars annually, notwithstanding
the fact that a new, handsome edifice was erected in 1890, which
was never encumbered by a debt.

Dr. Foote was essentially a pastor. He knew his people in
their homes. A prominent minister of his city said of him: "A
truer friend never lived. He was a friend who would rebuke
but always in love; he would advise but always with deference
to the judgment and the conviction of those to whom he gave
advice. He rejoiced in the success that came to a friend and
sorrowed in his sorrow." He lived in a singular atmosphere of
love. He was absolutely permeated with his religion. He lived
it and gloried in it. .

Dr. Foote believed in civic righteousness and was a fearless
denouncer of political corruption. Next to his God he loved his
country. He was a careful student of public issues and was
always alert and ready to speak, work and cast his vote for the
promotion of good government. The following is from the pen
of one of the young men of his church and appeared in the
press at the time of his death: "Dr. Foote was a man's man—
one who, analyzed by the searching scrutiny that men are prone
to give to clergymen, stood the test grandly, and for a third of
a century was the exemplar of practical Christianity and lofty
patriotism. Men loved and trusted him, confident in his genuineness and his belief in every word that he preached."

As to theology, Dr. Foote was a conservative. Included in
the resolutions adopted by the Brooklyn Presbytery is the follow-

ing: "Dr. Foote believed with all his soul that the Scriptures are the inspired revelation of God, that the Gospel is true and is the power of God unto the salvation of men. He was sure of his faith. It was clear, strong, positive, affirmative. In the secret places of his soul he had proved it, therefore he could defend it— and he did. He stood foursquare to all the theological winds that blew. It was a tonic to faith to know him and to hear him."

1876. v. SARAH ELIZABETH, b. Sept. 6, 1846; graduate of Cottage Seminary, Clinton, N. Y.; m. Oct. 20, 1880, George Stryker, of Bound Brook, N. J. He was b. at Brooklyn, N. Y., Aug. 6, 1844, and is a contractor and builder. Ch.: (1) George Gordon, b. Oct. 11, 1883, at Bound Brook, N. J.; d. Apr. 16, 1888. (2) Russell Foote, b. Oct. 22, 1889, at Bound Brook, N. J.

783. ISRAEL FOOTE, (244, 74, 25, 9, 3,) b. Jan. 19, 1783; m. Feb. 20, 1815, Sarah, dau. of John Taintor, of Windham, Ct. He d. Sept. 21, 1871. She d. June 6, 1827, ae. 38, in Cincinnati, O. Res., New York, N. Y.

1877. i. ELIZA TAINTOR, b. Nov. 30, 1815; d. Feb. 24, 1825.
1878. ii. MARY SUMNER, b. Aug. 30, 1817; d. Feb. 9, 1818.
1879. iii. JOHN TAINTOR, b. May 27, 1819; m. Jordena Harris and Mary Swords Dumont, 3340-45.
1880. iv. WILLIAM GIBBONS, b. Nov. 10, 1820; in trade in Savannah, Ga.; d. 1865, at Funchal, Madeira; unm.
1881. v. MARY ELIZA, b. Sept. 22, 1822; m. Judge Peckham, of Albany, N. Y. Both lost at sea in the ill-fated steamship Villa De Harve in 1873.
1882. vi. CHARLES TAINTOR, b. Sept. 4, 1824; d. Nov. 7, 1824.

784. ELIJAH FOOTE, (244, 74, 25, 9, 5,) b. Sept. 14, 1784; m. Apr. 15, 1809, Betsy, dau. of Dr. Zenas Strong. She d. Apr. 7, 1810; m. 2nd, Feb. 15, 1811, Lois, dau. of Joel Worthington, of Colchester, Ct.; res., Delaware Co., O.

1883. i. JUSTIN HENRY, b. Apr. 3, 1810.
1884. ii. WALTHAM WORTHINGTON, b. Jan. 8, 1812.
1885. iii. FRANCIS EDWARD, b. June 28, 1814; d. Oct. 27, 1825.
1886. iv. SAMUEL EDWIN, b. June 23, 1816.
1887. v. GEORGE, b. Aug. 13, 1818.
1888. vi. JOEL WORTHINGTON, b. May 25, 1822.
1889 vii. ALBERT, b. Sept. 19, 1825.

798. ISAAC FOOTE, (247, 76, 25, 9, 3,) b. at Stafford, Ct., Apr. 18, 1776; m. Dec. 4, 1802, Harriet, dau. of Gen. Caleb Hyde, of Lisle, N. Y., formerly of Norwich, Ct. He d. Feb. 8, 1860; she d. Apr. 27, 1866. Res., Smyrna, N. Y.

Isaac Foote, Jr., came to the then town of Sherburne, in 1794, in company with his father, when only 18 years of age. His son, Isaac 3rd, of Norwich, in a published communication, says of him: "He remained at home until 26 years old, with the exception of a year spent in the Academy at Clinton, where he took the highest honors. He helped to clear his father's farm and at the age above named (26) he received from him the part of the farm afterwards owned by Nelson Bowers. On Dec. 4, 1802, he m. Miss Harriet Hyde, b. Feb. 18, 1784, at Lenox, Mass., dau. of Gen. Caleb Hyde, of Lisle, N. Y. When he went to Lisle to be m. he rode one horse and led another for the use of the bride on their wedding trip. After their marriage they started back for Smyrna, accompanied by a brother of my mother, who drove a cow and ten sheep, the setting out which she received from her father. It required four days to make the journey, the road then being mostly through the wilderness, and followed by marked trees. There were only occasional settlements where they could obtain food and lodgings. The last night on their way they stopped at a tavern kept by Hascall Ransford, which stood a short distance south of the Lamb place.''

The following is from a memorandum by his own hand, date of Apr. 13, 1848: ''At the age of 21 years I was chosen Constable and Collector, to which office I was appointed six or seven years in succession, and until I declined the appointment. At the age of 23 I was appointed Under Sheriff of the County of Chenango, and was the first that was so appointed after the county was organized, which office I held for nine years and under three different Sheriffs, all of a different political creed from that which I had adopted. In the year 1808 was chosen a Deacon in the Second Congregational Church (Sherburne West Hill), and subsequently chosen to the same office in the First Congregational Church in Smyrna, which office, though unworthy, I still hold. In 1803 was appointed to the office of Adjutant of the Regiment then commanded by Col. Benjamin Hovey; served five years and resigned. In the year 1810 was appointed High Sheriff of the County of Chenango, and held the office 3 years. In the year 1814 was appointed Agent for the Hon. Egbert Benson, the Executor of the Hon. John Lawrence, of New York; continued his Agent until the estate was divided between the heirs, by whom I was chosen to make the division of their lands in Chenango County, which was done to their acceptance. Also was intrusted with the making of the division between the heirs aforesaid and Daniel McCormick, Esq., of New York, who was joint owner with Judge Lawrence, of the town of Smyrna, and that division was also accepted. Was afterwards Agent for the heirs of Judge Lawrence and Daniel McCormick, Esq., also for four of the Livingston family, who owned four-fifths of the town of Otselic, which has all been sold, the purchase money paid, and my agency satisfactorily closed. The land so committed to my care in Smyrna, Plymouth, Columbus, Norwich and Otselic, I suppose in all amounted to about 30,000 acres.''

1890.	i.	JUSTIN, b. Nov. 22, 1803; m. Irene Warner, 3347-51.
1891.	ii.	HARRIET, b. May 2, 1806; d. Feb., 1866.
1892.	iii.	CHARLES HYDE, b. May 27, 1808; drowned in a cistern, Oct. 18, 1809.
1893.	iv.	CHARLES HENRY, b. Sept. 3, 1810; m. Hulda Brooks, 3352-62.
1894.	v.	DANIEL PARSONS, b. June 14, 1814; d. Dec. 30, 1826.
1895.	vi.	ISAAC, b. May 28, 1817; m. Jerusha Merrick, 3363-8.
1896.	vii.	ELIZABETH, b. Oct. 18, 1819; was a successful teacher in the Academy at Cortlandville, N. Y.; m. 1873, Dea. Lester Turner, of Norwich, N. Y. She d. June 13, 1894. He d. 1881; p. s. She was one of the most exemplary and faithful Christian workers in that vicinity.

799. AMASA FOOTE, (247, 76, 25, 9, 3,) b. Mar. 23, 1778; m. Sally, dau. of Martin and Hannah (Otis) Kellogg, of Colchester, Ct.; b. 1789; d. 1849. He d. 1869; both buried at Hamilton, N. Y.

Amasa Foote, son of Judge Isaac Foote, settled in Smyrna on the farm south of and adjoining P. D. Nearing's, where he lived until the infirmities of age incapacitated him for such work. He then sold his farm and removed to Hamilton, where he lived until his death at 92 years of age. Was eminently a Christian man, a Deacon in the Congregational Church for many years, and seemed to take more interest in upbuilding the Church than he did his own affairs. Was a man of strict integrity, was a Captain of the Militia, and frequently elected Supervisor and Justice of the

Peace. He married Sarah Kellogg, of Colchester, Ct., in Aug., 1805, in which affair it is said he got the better of Tilly Lynde, then a young merchant on Sherburne West Hill, who was enamored of her charms. They had Asahel, Sally, Mary, Edward, Betsey and William. Asahel, b. Aug. 31, 1807, who studied theology, was drowned in the river at Greene, in July, 1837, while in bathing, soon after entering the ministry. The writer has often heard the sad story from his father, who knew the young man well.

1897. i. ASAHEL DODDRIDGE, b. Aug. 31, 1807; studied theology at the Auburn Seminary, Auburn, N. Y.; drowned July 1837.

1898. ii. SALLY KELLOGG, b. Nov. 16, 1809; d. at Hamilton, N. Y., 1879; unm.

1899. iii. MARY PARSONS, b. May 15, 1813; d. at Hamilton, N. Y., 1893; unm.

1900. iv. FANNY AMELIA, b. July 28, 1816; d. in infancy.

1901. v. EDWARD WARREN, b. Mar. 5, 1819-20; m. Phebe Steere and Adeline Frances, 3369-70.

1902. vi. BETSEY NEWTON, b. July 6, 1821; m. John Waite, of Norwich, N. Y., Jan. 5, 1853. He d. Nov. 2, 1868. She d. Nov. 15, 1905. Ch.: (1) John K. Waite, b. Mar. 22, 1858; m. Mar. 18, 1889, Alice Bunyard. He d. Feb. 18, 1902. Ch.: (a) Edward B. Waite, b. Apr. 2, 1891. (b) Ruth K. Waite, b. Jan. 23, 1893. (c) Bryan Waite, b. Feb. 12, 1897. (d) Grace A. Waite, b. Feb. 18, 1899. (e) John Waite, b. Oct. 24, 1902. (2) Edward B. Waite, b. Norwich, Jan. 15, 1860; graduated at Colgate University, Hamilton, N. Y., in 1880, and at the George Washington University, Law Department, Washington, D. C., in 1883; was in the Government service at Washington and Minn. until 1897, and since then has practised law and held various official positions in Minneapolis. He was appointed principal Judge of Minneapolis, to fill a vacancy, in Dec., 1904, and elected to the same office in Nov., 1906; m. May 5, 1892, Alice Eaton. Ch.: (a) Bradford Waite, b. Sept. 4, 1900; d. Sept. 6, 1900.

1903. vii. WILLIAM SAWTRE, b. Aug. 23, 1824; m. Lucy Lovina Andrus, 3371-2.

801. JOHN FOOTE, (247, 76, 25, 9, 3,) b. in Stratford, Ct., Apr. 30, 1786; removed with his father's family to Sherburne-Smyrna, and grew up on his father's farm there. After attending school at the old Oneida Academy at Clinton, he studied law in the office of Judge Hubbard at Hamilton, commencing in 1809, and was admitted to practice in 1813, so continuing in his chosen profession until old age. He became eminent as a counsellor-at-law, and solicitor in chancery, and in the District Court of the United States. He early became pronounced in his anti-slavery sentiments, and also espoused the cause of temperance, being a life-long advocate of total abstinence. At 91 years of age he delivered an able address on the subject of temperance. He was one of the charter members of the Congregational Church of Hamilton, and for nearly 50 years was one of its Deacons and its Church Clerk. In all the ways and walks of life he was a consistent, devoted Christian. An honest man, whose integrity and uprightness were always above reproach. An inspiring life to contemplate. On Jan. 12, 1812, he was m. to Mary B. Johnson, dau. of Dr. Johnson, of New Canaan, Columbia Co., N. Y., from which happy union there were 11 ch. She d. Mar. 9, 1834; m. 2nd, Harriet (No. 815), wid. of Dr. Bryan, and dau. of Judge Ebenezer Foote. John Foote was an Attorney and Counsellor at Law, Solicitor and Counsellor

JUDGE ISAAC FOOTE. No. 247

JOHN FOOTE.
No. 801.

MARGARET PARSONS (FOOTE) WILLIAMS.
No. 1905

HARVEY FOOTE REMMINGTON.
No. 1629 (6)

JOEL FOOTE.   No. 273

in Chancery and District Court of the United States; d. July, 1884. Res., Hamilton, N. Y.

1904. i. ACSAH SOPHIA, b. Oct. 26, 1812; d. Feb. 19, 1891.

1905. ii. MARGARET PARSONS b. Apr. 17, 1814; m. Feb. 11, 1834, William Hart Williams. He was b. Berkshire, Tioga Co., N. Y., Dec. 10, 1811. He was a gold and silver smith during his entire business life; d. Albany, N. Y., June 26, 1896. He was a son of Solomon Williams, b. Stockbridge, Mass., July 21, 1763; d. 1840, and Hepsibeth Hart, b. Mar. 28, 1772, and a grandson of Azariah Williams, b. Hartford, Ct., 1728; d. Apr. 22, 1813, and Beulah Brown, b. 1736, d. 1816. Ch.: (1) Henry Smith, b. Canajoharie, N. Y., Mar. 29, 1836; d. Albany, N. Y., May 6, 1868. (2) Margaret, b. ——; d. in infancy. (3) Robert Day, b. Hamilton, Madison Co., N. Y., Feb 12, 1844; m. Albany, N. Y., Feb. 12, 1869, Anna Louise Sedam. She was b. Albany, N. Y., Feb. 11, 1846. She was dau. of Charles Sedam, b. Rensselaer Co., N. Y., Feb. 12, 1812; d. Albany, N. Y., Apr. 29, 1882, and Eliza Maria Heermance, his wife, b. Schodack, N. Y., Apr. 10, 1817; d. Albany, N. Y., Mar. 23, 1891, and granddaughter of Henry Sedam, b. Herkimer Co., N. Y., June 3, 1785; d. Little Falls, N. Y., Aug. 15, 1865, and Lucy Goodwin, his wife, b. Ashfield, Mass., Mar. 31, 1788; d. Greenbush, Rensselaer Co., N. Y., Feb. 9, 1855. Ch.: (a) Caroline Sedam Williams, b. Albany, N. Y., May 25, 1871. (b) Josephine Sedam Williams, b. Albany, N. Y., Jan. 25, 1881. (4) Margaret Steere Williams, b. Hamilton, Madison Co., N. Y., Mar. 24, 1846; m. Albany, N. Y., Feb. 12, 1872, Dexter Hunter. He was b. Valley Falls, N. Y., Mar. 15, 1843, son of Gilbert Hunter, Pittstown, Rensselaer Co., N. Y., b. Oct. 20, 1818; d. Jacksonville, Fla., June 29, 1881, and Eliza Ann Myres, his wife, b. Pittstown, N. Y., 1821; d. Valley Falls, N. Y., Nov. 24, 1843; and grandson of Robert and Ziptha (Anderson) Hunter. Ch.: (a) Dexter Hunter, Jr., b. Albany, N. Y., Nov. 4, 1875; graduate of Harvard College, 1899. (b) Mary Seelye Hunter, b. Albany, N. Y., Oct. 28, 1878; graduate of Smith College, 1901. (c) Ruth Williams Hunter, b. Jacksonville, Fla., Mar. 2, 1885; d. Jacksonville, Fla., May 5, 1886. (d) Kenneth Williams Hunter, b. Albany, N. Y., Oct. 13, 1889.

1906 iii. JOHN JOHNSON, b. Feb. 11, 1816; m. Mary Crocker, 3373-5.

1907. iv. MARY, b. ——; d. in infancy.

1908. v. MARY KELLOGG, b. Jan. 3, 1819.

1909. vi. CAROLINE DELIA, b. Aug. 26, 1820; m. John Mitchell, of Norwich, N. Y. He was b. Feb. 11, 1819; d. June, 1893. She d. May 22, 1903. Ch.: (1) Frederick Mitchell, b. Norwich, N. Y., Sept. 6, 1844; m. 1865, Nettie C. Pike. Ch.: (a) Frederick John Mitchell, b. May 16, 1869; m. Grace Mitchell. She was b. May 2, 1870. He d. Mar. 25, 1900. Ch.: (i) George Mitchell, b. Aug. 25, 1893. (b) May Mitchell, b. Apr. 5, 1872; m. John Croll. Ch.: (i) Nettie Croll, b. 1897. (ii) Fred Croll, b. 1899. (2) John Waite Mitchell, b. Norwich, N. Y., Apr. 6, 1848; m. 1876, Fanny Mason, of Providence, R. I. She d. 1877; m. 2nd, Lydia Pearce, of Providence, R. I. Ch.: (a) b. and d. in infancy. (b)

John Pearce Mitchell, b. 1880. (3) Franklin Benjamin Mitchell, b. Norwich, N. Y., Sept. 6, 1852; m. Apr. 28, 1880, Helen E. Sage, of Brooklyn, N. Y. He is a graduate of Yale in Class of 1875. Ch.: (a) Sally Sage Mitchell, b. Jan. 31, 1881. (b) Minot Sherman Mitchell, b. July 27, 1882. (4) Caroline Rowena Mitchell, b. Norwich, Mar. 26, 1856; m. Aug. 30, 1882, Robbins Little, of Norwich. He d. Dec. 13, 1888. Ch.: (a) Robbins Little, b. Jan. 27, 1887. (5) Mary Elizabeth Mitchell, b. Norwich, June 2, 1863; m. Jan. 21, 1885, at Norwich, I. Burkett Newton. He graduated from Yale in Class of 1883; d. Sept. 1, 1900. Ch.: (a) Rowena Mitchell Newton, b. Dec. 4, 1885. (b) Burkett Newton, b. Nov. 25, 1891.

1910. vii. SUSAN, b. Apr. 2, 1822; m. Aug. 19, 1848, Rev. David A. Peck, of Clifton Park, N. Y. He d. July 25, 1898, at Clifton Park. She d. Jan. 28, 1890, at Clifton Park. Ch., all b. at Dartford, Wis.: (1) Mary E. Peck, b. May 24, 1849; d. May 20, 1890, at Clifton Park. (2) George C. Peck, b. Apr. 21, 1851; d. Apr. 20, 1852, at Hamilton, N. Y. (3) Rev. John Foote Peck, b. Feb. 7, 1853; m. Aug. 18, 1881, Abbie F. Axtell, of Waupaca, Wis. Ch.: (a) Guy Axtell Peck, b. Waupaca, Wis., May 13, 1882. (b) Harrie Foote Peck, b. Belvidere, Ill., Mar. 29, 1885. (c) Glen Flora Peck, b. May 2, 1888; d. Sept., 1888, at Clifton Park, N. Y. (d) Arthur David Peck, b. Apr. 10, 1890, at Clifton Park, N. Y. (4) Harriet F. Peck, b. Waupaca, Wis., Apr. 15, 1855; d. Jan. 2, 1881, at Clifton Park, N. Y.

1911. viii. WILLIAM JOHNSON, b. ———; d. ae. 3.

1912. ix. DR. HENRY CADY, b. Aug. 28, 1825; m. Ann Elizabeth McKee, 3376.

1913. x. FREDERICK WILLIAM, b. Aug. 9, 1827; m. 3377-8.

1914. xi. GEORGE W., b. July 4, 1829; m. Harriet Morton, 3379.

802. HIRAM FOOTE, (247, 76, 25, 9, 3,) b. Aug. 22, 1789; m. June 15, 1817, Mary Young, dau. of Judge Asahel Strong. He d. Apr. 24, 1842. Res., Smyrna, N. Y. He sustained through life an irreproachable character. She d. Dec. 11, 1867.

Hiram Foote, youngest son of Judge Isaac Foote, after his marriage remained at the homestead of his father in Smyrna and took care of his aged parents until their death. He survived his father but a short time. The widow soon after removed to Belvidere, Ill., with her five children as follows: Erastus, who m. Mary Ann Collins, dau. of Rev. Levi Collins, of Smyrna, and is now living at or near Salt Lake; Martha, who m. Rev. Mr. Beecher, a Baptist minister, went to Burmah as a missionary, and died on her way home, leaving one child; Sophia and Sidney, both deceased, and Eli Foote, who was for a time engaged in business in Chicago.

1915. i. ERASTUS STRONG, b. May 16, 1818; m. Mary Ann Collins, 3380-1.

1916. ii. MARTHA, b. Oct. 8, 1820; m. Rev. Sidney Beecher in 1847, and were sent on a mission to Burmah by the Baptist Foreign Missionary Society; she d. at sea while returning to America.

1917. iii. ELI, b. Oct. 8, 1822; m. 1872, Mrs. Julia Milmine, a wid. with two ch. He d. Apr. 30, 1898; she d. 1905; p. s.

1918. iv. FANNY SOPHIA, b———; d. Dec. 8, 1879, at Belvidere, Ill., ae. 52 years.

1919. v. SIDNEY, b. 1830; m. Elizabeth Flower, 3382-7.

808. JOHN PARSONS FOOTE, (248, 76, 25, 9, 3,) b. June 26, 1783, at Guilford, Ct.; adopted by his uncle, Justin Foote; m. Sept. 26, 1811, Jane Warner, b. Feb. 22, 1789, in New York City; d. in 1864; dau. of James Warner, b. Dec. 19, 1763. He d. July 11, 1865, in Cincinnati, O.; member of the firm of J. & J. P. Foote, Merchant Marine, N. Y. Came to Cincinnati 1820. In company with a Mr. White and Oliver H. Wells, founded in 1820 Cincinnati Type Foundry, publishers of "Literary Gazette," edited by Mr. Foote. 1825, was one of company which purchased the Cincinnati Water Works, and was made and remained President until its sale to the city in 1840. A Director in Louisville (Ohio River) Canal; a Trustee of Woodward High School Fund; a Trustee of Cincinnati College; a Trustee of Common Schools; a Trustee of Ohio Medical College; President Academy of Natural Science; First President of Society for Promotion of Useful Knowledge; Vice-President Historical Society; Secretary Cincinnati Law School; President Cincinnati Astronomical Society, 1845 (its existence mainly due to his exertions); Officer, Ohio Mechanics' Institute (framed its Constitution), Chairman of first meeting of the House of Refuge (in company with J. H. Perkins, he was mainly instrumental in its establishment), one of Founders of Spring Grove Cemetery in 1844, and one of its Directors until death; one of the Organizers of Horticultural Society, member until death.

    1920. i.   MARY WARD, b. Aug. 22, 1813; m. Oct. 31, 1832, Dr. John Shotwell; she d. 1864; p. s.

    1921. ii.   HENRY WARD, b. Feb. 17, 1817; d. Sept. 17, 1822, in Cincinnati.

    1922. iii.   EDWARD WARNER, b. May 25, 1819; d. Nov. 23, 1821, in Cincinnati.

    1923. iv.   CATHRINE AMELIA, b. Oct. 26, 1824, at Cincinnati, O.; d. May 13, 1902, in Mechanicsburg, Pa; m. 1st, William Henry Comstock, May 25, 1847, at Cincinnati, O.; m. 2nd, Dr. J. A. Stayman, Feb. 15, 1868, at Carlisle, Pa. Ch. by 1st m.: (1) Mary Shotwell Comstock, b. May 3, 1848; d. June 20, 1852. (2) George S. Comstock, b. July 10, 1850; m. Oct. 18, 1877, Julia Watts. Ch.: (a) Edith Watts Comstock, b. June 3, 1879. (b) Katharine Foote Comstock, b. Nov. 5, 1880. (c) George S. Comstock, Jr., b. Nov. 10, 1884. (d) John Reed Comstock, b. Mar. 28, 1890. (3) Edward Foote Comstock, b. Apr. 1, 1852; unm. (4) William Hunt Comstock, b. Jan. 29, 1854; unm.

    1924. v.   HENRY EDWARD, b. June 26, 1825; m. Louise Agniel, 3388-90.

810. SAMUEL EDMUND FOOTE, (248, 76, 25, 9, 3,) b. Dec. 9, 1787; of Guilford, Ct., of New York; of Cincinnati for 20 years, and later of New Haven, Ct.; was m. Sept. 9, 1827, to his second cousin, Elizabeth Betts, dau. of Andrew and Katherine (Hill) Elliott, of Guilford, and granddaughter of Abigail Ward (sister of Gen. Andrew Ward) and Wyllys Elliott. She was b. Nov. 16, 1807. Mr. Foote was a sea captain at 18 years of age, having fitted himself by study and practice, and he continued to be until 1826. He was a man of wide interests and culture, "one of the best educated men of his time"; he spoke and wrote French, Spanish and Italian fluently, he had a wide knowledge of literature, made improvement in ship-rigging and building. In Cincinnati he did much for the improvement and growth of the city. Director and Secretary (without pay) of the Water Company until it was sold to the city. Director of Louisville (Ohio River) Canal, etc., etc. In the financial crisis of 1837 lost much of his fortune and became secretary of Whitewater Canal Company and later of the Ohio Life Ins. and

Trust Co. until he had gathered another fortune and retired from business to New Haven in 1850, where he d. Nov. 1, 1858. Mrs. Foote d. May 30, 1878.

1925 i.	GEORGE AUGUSTUS, b. Mar. 2, 1829; d. Oct., 1834, in Cincinnati, Ohio.

1926 ii.	FRANCES ELIZABETH, b. Oct. 6, 1835; m. July 27, 1859, Edwin Lawrence Godkin, son of James and Sarah (Lawrence) Godkin, of Moyne, Ireland. He was educated at Sillcoates School in England, and at Queen's College, Belfast, Ireland, and was admitted to the English Bar. He was War Correspondent for the London "Daily News" during the Crimean War. He came to America in the autumn of 1856 as correspondent for the "Daily News" to write a series of articles upon social and political conditions in the Southern States. He studied in New York in the office of David Dudley Field and became a member of the New York Bar. After the establishment of the "Nation," of which he became editor in 1865, he ceased to practice law and devoted himself to newspaper and literary work. He became editor and one of the proprietors of the New York "Evening Post" in 1881. He wrote a "History of Hungary" as a young man, and two volumes of his articles have been published in book form entitled "Problems of Democracy" and "Unforeseen Tendencies of Democracy." He d. at Greenway House, Brixham, Devon, England, May 21, 1902. Mrs. Francis Foote Godkin d. Apr. 11, 1875. Ch.: (1) Lawrence Godkin, of New York, prepared for college at Dr. Morris's Mohegan Lake School and at the Cambridge High School, and graduated at Harvard in the Class of 1881, and at Columbia Law School in 1883. Member of the New York Bar. He had charge of the week's summary of news for the "Nation" for a time, and has written articles for various periodicals on legal topics. He published, in collaboration with Dr. A. McL. Hamilton, "A System of Legal Medicine." He was appointed by the Governor of New York, in 1903, member of a Commission to investigate the "law's delay in New York" and suggest remedial legislation. (2) Elizabeth Elliott Godkin, b. May 3, 1865; d. May 30, 1873. (3) Ralph Godkin, b. July 10, 1868; d. Sept. 12, 1868. (All b. in New York.)

1927. iii.	CATHRINE VIRGINIA, b. Aug. 9, 1839, in Cincinnati, Ohio; m. June 20, 1865, Alfred Perkins Rockwell, son of John Arnold and Mary (Perkins) Rockwell. Mr. Rockwell was b. in Norwich, Ct., Oct. 16, 1834. He graduated at Yale in 1855; studied mining in Scientific Department, receiving degrees of P. H. B. in 1857 and M. A. in 1858. Continued study of mining later in London and Freiburg. He served for three years during the Civil War, first as Captain of 1st Ct. Light Battery from Jan., 1862, to June, 1864, then as Colonel of the 6th Ct. Infantry from June, 1864, to Feb., 1865. He took part in many battles, and was brevetted Brigadier-General at the close of the war. He was appointed Professor of Mining at the Sheffield Scientific School, and in 1868 was called to the same chair in the Massachusetts Institute of Technology. He resigned in 1873 to enter more active business management in Boston, for which he was

REV. LEWIS RAY FOOTE. No. 1875

GEORGE AUGUSTUS FOOTE. No. 811

especially fitted. For three years he was chairman of the Boston Board of Fire Commissioners. In 1879 he became President of the Eastern R. R. Co., and remained three years, then he resigned to become Treasurer of the Great Falls Manufacturing Co. He gave up all active business in 1886, traveling much, and on Dec. 24, 1903, he died. Mrs. Katharine Foote Rockwell d. Mar. 24, 1902. Ch.: (1) Mary Foote Rockwell, b. in New Haven, Ct., May 5, 1868; d. Aug. 2, 1868. (2) Frances Beatrice Rockwell, b. Jan. 25, 1872, in Boston; d. Mar. 25, 1886. (3) Samuel Edmond Foote Rockwell, b. in Boston, July 28, 1873; d. Mar. 18, 1884. (4) Katharine Diana Ward Rockwell, b. in Boston, July 28, 1873.

1928. iv. HARRY WARD, b. Cincinnati, Ohio, Aug. 6, 1844; prepared for college at Russell's Military School in New Haven, entered and graduated with the Class of 1866, Yale. During the winter of 1866-7 studied at the Columbia Law School. His health broke down in 1867 and he d. at his home in New Haven, June 28, 1873, having spent the intervening years at the various health resorts in Europe, Nassau, N. P., etc. By his will a bequest was made to Yale of $25,000 for the endowment of a graduate scholarship; unm.

811.. GEORGE AUGUSTUS FOOTE, (248, 76, 25, 9, 3,) b. Dec. 9, 1789, in Guilford, Ct.; m. Eliza, dau. of Samuel and Elizabeth (Tuthill) Spencer, also of Guilford, on May 24, 1829. She was b. Mar. 23, 1812. Mr. Foote was Colonel of Militia, held many town and county offices, and was First Representative (Whig) in the State Legislature five terms. He was Senior Warden of the Episcopal Church from 1861 to 1874, when he resigned from old age. He did all within his means toward building the church edifice. He d. Sept. 5, 1878.

1929. i. HARRIET WARD, b. June 25, 1831; m. Dec. 25, 1855, Joseph R. Hawley, son of Rev. Francis and Mary MacCleod Hawley. Mr. Hawley was b. Oct. 31, 1826. Mrs. Hawley was with her husband through the Civil War when possible, and when not with him, was nurse in the Army hospitals. Later, in Washington, where Gen. Hawley was first in the House of Representatives and then Senator, she was his Private Secretary. She was President of the Indian Society there, and one of the first members of the Woman's Aid Society in Hartford, which was their home. She d. Mar. 3, 1886. No ch. Gen. Hawley d. Mar. 13, 1905.

1930. ii. ANDREW WARD, b. Apr. 27, 1833; m. Charlotte A. Wilcox, 3391-4.

1931. iii. GEORGE AUGUSTUS, b. May 7, 1835, of Guilford; a cultivated man and farmer; enlisted in the Three Months' Men at President Lincoln's first call for volunteers in 1861, and re-enlisted as private in the 14th Ct. Vols., Aug. 7, 1862. He lost a leg at Fredericksburg, and d. Nov. 13, 1869, from the results of his wound. He received commission as Second Lieutenant "for bravery in the field and out of it." Unm.

1932. iv. CHRISTOPHER SPENCER, b. May 2, 1837; m. Hannah J. Hubbard, 3395-9.

1933. v. KATHERINE, b. May 31, 1840; m. Jan. 8, 1895, Andrew J. Coe, son of Calvin and Harriet (Rice) Coe. He was b. in Meriden, Sept. 15, 1834. Graduated at Wesleyan University, and was lawyer and farmer. He represented his town in the State Legislature in 1860 and again in 1867. He was the first Judge of City Court. He d. Feb. 25, 1897. Katherine Foote was for 15 years Washington Correspondent of the N. Y. "Independent" weekly, and a contributor of short stories and articles to the "Atlantic" and various other magazines. No. ch.

1934. vi. SAMUEL EDMUND, b. Jan. 20, 1843; m. Lucy Bullard, 3400-5.

1935. vii. WILLIAM TODD, b. Mar. 23, 1845; m. Emma Munger, 3406-7.

1936. viii. MARY WARD SHOTWELL, b. Sept 8, 1846; m. Apr. 16, 1872, James D., son of William and Mary (Moriarity) Hague. Mr. Hague was b. Feb. 24, 1836; graduate of Harvard 1854, Goettingen and Freiberg 1855-8. Mining engineer by profession. Mrs. Hague d. Feb. 14, 1898. New York is their home. Ch.: (1) Marian, b. June 17, 1873, in California. (2) Eleanor, b. Nov. 7, 1875, in California. (3) William, b. Mar. 31, 1882, in Orange, N. J.

1937. ix. ARTHUR DE WINT, b. May 24, 1849; m. Mary Ann Hallock, 3408-10.

1938. x. ELIZABETH ELLIOTT, b. Apr. 18, 1852; m. June 18, 1885, Edward H., son of John and Chloe (Thompson) Jenkins, of Falmouth, Mass. Mr. Jenkins was b. May 31, 1850. Graduated at Yale in 1872; Chem. special student in Sheffield Scientific School to 1875; Leipsic, Germany, 1876-7. Director Ct. Agricultural Station, New Haven, Ct. No ch.

813. FREDERICK PARSONS FOOTE, (253, 76, 25, 9, 3,) b. Mar. 15, 1783; m. Feb. 6, 1808, Charlotte Welles, of Kingston, N. Y. He held a command as General, on the frontier, during the Mexican War, the hardships of which so injured his health that at the close of the war he sought its restoration in the mild climate of Italy. He d. at Leghorn, Feb. 3, 1827.

1939. i. HARRIET ELIZABETH, b. Nov. 4, 1808; d. Dec. 3, 1825.

1940. ii. JUSTIN, b. Oct. 8, 1811; d. at Arbor Hill, Feb. 4, 1826.

1941. iii. MARGARET PARSONS, b. Mar. 26, 1814; m. Rev. Mr. Montieth of Fanday's Bush, N. Y.

814. CHARLES AUGUSTUS FOOTE, (253, 76, 25, 9, 3,) b. Apr. 15, 1785; m. May 10, 1808, Maria Baldwin; she d. Aug. 1, 1828. Was a graduate at Union College. Attorney and Counselor at Law. Member of Congress from the State of New York in 1824; d. 1828. Studied law at Kinderhook with Judge Van Schaack; of a number of men there at the time, who afterward became prominent in the world, it was young Martin Van Buren, who most often came out with him to Arbor Hill, and in time became an aspirant for the hand of sweet Margaret Foote, Charles' sister, but she had already secretly given her heart to the young clergyman whom she afterward married, and thus lost the opportunity of becoming a Mistress of the White House.

After leaving Kinderhook, Charles was for several years in the office of Josiah Ogden Hoffman, Esq., in New York, then returned to Delhi, began an excellent practice, and was sent to Congress in 1824, but his death ended all. Col. of Militia. He m. in 1808, Marie Baldwin, dau. of Margaretta de Hart and Jesse Baldwin, importing merchant at 161 Broadway, New York.

1942. i.   FRANCES, b. Aug. 1, 1809; m. Oct. 15, 1832, Charles Marvin, of
           Delhi, N. Y.; merchant. Ch.: (1) George Edward, b. ———; d.
           Delhi, Mar. 27, 1905. A man of culture and travel, and of quiet
           tastes. President of the Bank and other interests; m. Harriet
           Danforth Steele. (2) Margaret Maxwell, m. Isaac Horton May-
           nard, well known in politics, Judge, and in Treasury Depart-
           ment under Cleveland. Res., Stanford, N. Y. Ch.: Frances.

1943. ii. CATHRINE BRUEN, b. Sept. 14, 1811; d. Nov., 1897; never
           m., but spent her time and her money in good works.

1944. iii. RENSELLAER WILLIAM, b. Nov. 12, 1815; Captain in 6th
           Infantry U. S. Army, Brevet Major and Acting Colonel in the
           first battle in which he took part, and in which he was killed,
           Gaines' Mill. Was stationed in Arizona when war broke out.

1945. iv. CHARLES AUGUSTUS, b. Mar. 18, 1818; m. Adelia Johnson,
           3411-2.

1946. v.   JAMES BRUEN, b. Apr. 16, 1821.

818. DANIEL FOOTE, (254, 76, 25, 9, 3,) b. Sept. 23, 1789; m. Mar., 1812,
Sarah Ann, dau. of Soloman Scovell, of Colchester, Ct. Res., Westfield, Mass.
He d. Oct. 6, 1815.

1947. i.   DANIEL WILLIAM, b. Aug. 31, 1813; res., Westfield, Mass.

1948. ii. SARAH, b. Sept. 10, 1815; res., Westfield, Mass.

820. ELI FOOTE, (254, 76, 25, 9, 3,) b. May 7, 1793; m. Nov. 15, 1831,
Marana Lyons, of Lima, Livingston Co., N. Y. In 1845 he moved to Grand Blanc,
Genesee Co., Mich.; he d. June 6, 1875, at Flint, Mich.

1949. i.   GEORGE WAKEMAN, b. Lima, N. Y., Dec. 13, 1832.

1950. ii. HANNAH WATERMAN, b. Lima, N. Y., May 21, 1834; m. Nov.
           7, 1855, John W. Davison, of Flint, Mich. Ch.: (1) Irwin L.,
           b. Grand Blanc., Mich.

· 1951. iii. SARAH ELIZABETH, b. Lima, N. Y., Jan. 17, 1836.

1952. iv. WILLIAM HENRY, b. Lima, N. Y., Dec. 16, 1837; m. Abbey
           Langton, 3413-6.

1953. v.   GEORGE, b. Lima, N. Y., Aug. 20, 1840.

1954. vi. GEORGE WESTLEY, b. Lima, N. Y., Sept. 17, 1843; m. Julia
           Shepard, 3417-21.

1955. vii. CORIDON EDWARD, b. Grand Blanc, Mich., Jan. 9, 1849; m.
           Anna Heolms, 3422-3.

821. WILLIAM HENRY FOOTE, D. D., (254, 76, 25, 9, 3,) b. Dec. 20, 1794;
m. 1st, Feb. 21, 1822, Eliza Wilson, dau. of Joseph Glasse, of Winchester, Va.;
She d. Apr. 23, 1835, ae. 35; m. 2nd, Oct. 31, 1839, Arabella, dau. of Dr. Gillman,
of Petersburgh, Va. He was an eminent preacher and author in the
Presbyterian Church, South ; b. in Colchester, Ct., Dec. 20, 1794;
educated at Yale College, and for the ministry at Princeton.
Lived for the greater part of his life and d. in Romney, W. Va.; d. Nov. 22, 1869.
Author of "Sketches of North Carolina and Virginia," 3 vols., and "The
Huguenots, or Reformed French Church."

1956. i.   ANN WATERMAN, b. June 23, 1823; m. Judge James D. Arm-
           strong, of the 12th Judicial Circuit of W. Va. Wid.; res., Rom-
           ney, W. Va.

1957. ii. ELIZA WILSON, b. June 17, 1825; d. young.

1958. iii. MARY ARABELLA; res., Romney, W. Va.

824. CHARLES FOOTE, (261, 80, 25, 9, 3,) and child of Charles and Sarah Foote, was b. in Colchester, Ct., Feb. 3, 1781. He removed with his father's family, in 1801, to Mendon, Monroe Co., N. Y., and settled on a farm north of the burying ground, on the Stage Route. He was m. to Betsey Wilson, Nov. 17, 1806. They had 8 ch. Mrs. Foote d. Mar. 19, 1826, and was buried in the cemetery adjoining the farm. Charles Foote was m. for the second time, May 21, 1826, to Sophia P. Foote, wid. of his brother, John Foote. There were 2 ch. of this marriage.

Mr. Foote belonged to the New York State Volunteer Militia, and marched from Mendon to Rochester 'to meet the British who had landed at Charlotte, the port of Rochester on Lake Ontario. The British re-embarked without giving battle. He was Justice of the Peace in Mendon for 20 years. For some years he was engaged in lumbering with his brothers at Olean, N. Y., but returned to Mendon, where he resided until 1862, when he went to Batavia, and lived with his dau., Mrs. Thorpe. Later they removed to Rochester. The last years of his life were spent with his dau., Mrs. Charles H. Foote, in Ionia, Mich., where he d. at the great age of 102 years and 7 months, Sept. 1, 1883. He was buried in Ionia, Mich. His wife, Sophia, d. Sept. 10, 1884, and was buried beside her husband.

1959. i.   BETSEY, b. Mendon, N. Y., Dec. 12, 1807; m. Mar., 1830, Matthew Hubbell. Res. for a time in Mendon, and then removed to Richfield, O. She d. in Richfield, Jan. 19, 1840, and was buried there; he d. Oct. 10, 1886, and was buried in Wales, Mich. Ch.: (1) Lucy, b. in Mendon, N. Y., May 6, 1831; d. Mar., 1852, and was buried in Lamb, Mich. (2) Lois H. Hubbell, of Richfield, O., b. Apr. 7, 1833; m. Harvey Coburn, May 31, 1855; He d. Jan. 31, 1902, and was buried at Memphis, Mich. She m. 2nd, Richard Tebo, July 1, 1905. Res., Bay City, Mich. Ch., first four b. at Riley, Mich.: (a) Charles E. Coburn, b. Sept. 19, 1856; m. Mariette Whitaker, Oct. 8, 1879. Res., Croswell, Mich. Ch.: (i) Roy C., b. in Richmond, Mich., May 20, 1881. (ii) Earl, b. in Riley, Mich., Jan. 31, 1883; d. Feb. 15, 1886; buried at Memphis, Mich. (iii) Ethel, b. Richmond, Mich, July 31, 1888. (iv) Lois, b. Croswell, Mich., Oct. 4, 1900. (b) Louis O., b. Sept. 18, 1858; d. Jan. 20, 1862; buried at Memphis, Mich. (c) Lee A. Coburn, b. Mar. 20, 1861; m. Emma Andrews, Aug. 20, 1883. Res., South Branch, Mich. Ch.: (i) John, b. Memphis, Mich., June 25, 1889. (ii) Mae, b. Gooder, Mich., Oct. 6, 1893. (d) Frank M. Coburn, b. Feb. 15, 1863, of Riley, Mich.; m. Molly Euer, of Bay City, Sept. 16, 1896. Res., Bay City, Mich. Ch.: (i) Christie, b. Gooder, Mich., Aug. 23, 1897. (ii) Pearl, b. Bay City, Mich., May 25, 1900. (iii) Valma, b. Bay City, Mich., Aug. 1, 1905. (e) Beulah R., b. Sept. 12, 1867; d. Feb. 13, 1870; buried at Memphis, Mich. (f) Edward D., b. Sept. 23, 1869; d. Jan. 13, 1894; buried at Memphis. (3) Angeline, b. Richfield, O., Jan. 19, 1835; m. John Allen, who d. Feb. 4, 1901, and was buried in Lamb, Mich. She afterwards m. Peter Cantine. Res., Memphis, Mich. (4) Julia, b. Richfield, May 25, 1839; d. in infancy. (5) Rebecka, b. Richfield, July 31, 1837; m. Daniel Hollingshead, of Kingston, Ca., Sept. 15, 1868; d. in Ustick, Ill., Sept. 23, 1903. Mr. Hollingshead resides at Fulton, Ill., where he has a large

stock farm. Ch., all b. at Ustick, Ill.: (a) Delia O. Hollingshead, b. July 16, 1869; m. Frank Hollingshead, Nov. 11, 1892.
Res., Amadarko, Oklahama. Ch.: (i) Janette, b. Oct. 20, 1893;
d. Oct. 27, 1900. (ii) Thayer F., b. Oct. 11, 1895. (b) Louis H.
Hollingshead, b. Mar. 24, 1871; m. Phumia Willson, Apr. 24,
1894; he d. Mar. 8, 1901. Ch.: (i) Bayard H., b. May 28, 1895.
(ii) Gerald H., b. Apr. 17, 1896; d. May 20, 1901. (c) Daniel E.,
b. Feb. 24, 1874; m. Mrs. Phumia W. Hollingshead, Dec. 24,
1902. Ch.: (i) Archie F., b. Mar. 12, 1876; d. Dec. 5, 1881. (ii)
Charles B., b. Dec 12, 1878; is a farmer in Fulton, Ill. (iii)
Clara R., b. Mar. 5, 1886.

1960. ii. LOIS, b. Olean, N. Y., Aug. 16, 1809; m. Ebenezer Manning, Aug.,
1832, and removed to Medina, O. She d. Nov. 11, 1891. Mr.
Manning removed afterward to California, where he has since
d. Ch.: (1) Benjamin F., b. Medina, O., Dec. 8, 1833; d. Oct.
4, 1861; buried at Urbana, Ill. (2) Charles O., b. Medina, O.,
June 26, 1835; d. Sept. 28, 1847; buried at Medina. (3) Wilson
F., b. Medina, O., Oct. 21, 1837; d. Dec., 1865; buried at Urbana,
Ill. (4) Walter J., b. Medina, O., Aug. 31, 1839; enlisted in
Company H, Ohio Volunteer Infantry; killed in battle of Win-
chester, Mar. 3, 1863; buried at Medina. (5) Ann A. Manning,
of Medina, O., b. May 7, 1842; m. George B. Root, Apr. 3, 1861.
They had one ch. Mr. Root d. Aug. 23, 1874, and was buried at
Medina. Mrs. Root m. John B. Markley, June 8, 1878, and now
resides at Spencer, O. Ch.: Charles B., b. Medina, O., Oct. 25,
1862; m. Dec. 24, 1895, Helen Hartman. Ch.: (i) Donald. (ii)
Daniel. (iii) Allen. (6) Altha M. Manning, of Medina, O., b.
Sept. 3, 1844; m. A. F. Church, June 16, 1870, and resides in
Penfield, N. Y. Ch.: (a) Edith L. Church, of Penfield, N. Y.,
b. Nov. 25, 1871; m. John Green, of Scotland, July 21, 1896.
Res., for some years, in Penfield, and was in Santa Barbara,
Cal. Ch.: (i) Alexander M., b. Rochester, N. Y., May 14, 1897.
(ii) Alma C., b. Irondequoit, N. Y., May 31, 1898. (iii) Robert
C., b. Irondequoit, N. Y., Feb. 2, 1902. (b) Clara M., b. Elmira,
Mar. 31, 1873; d. Dec. 21, 1873. (c) Alice B., b. Penfield, Dec.
11, 1874; d. Sept. 27, 1875. (d) William F., b. Penfield, May 26'
1877. (e) Charles Foote, b. Penfield, Nov. 18, 1880. (7) Sarah
A. Manning, of Medina, O., b. Apr. 24, 1848; m. John R. Judson,
Apr. 24, 1873, and removed to Greenwich, O. He d. Jan. 29,
1881, at Chicago, Ill. Ch.: (a) Eva Lois, b. Greenwich, O., July
8, 1874; d. in Chicago, Apr. 20, 1882. (b) Harold N., b. Greenwich, O., Dec. 13, 1876. (c) Fred M., b. Chicago, Nov. 4, 1882;
m. Nov. 30, 1904, Beulah Lee, at Weiser, Idaho.

1961. iii. CHARLES C., b. Olean, N. Y., Mar. 30, 1811; m. Clarissa
C. Clark.

1962. iv. SARAH ANN, b. Mendon, N. Y., Aug. 12, 1813; m. Seneca
Leonard, Sept. 6, 1834. They removed to West Millgrove, Ohio.
Their married life extended over 70 years; Mrs. Leonard d.
Nov. 29, 1904; Mr. Leonard living at W. Millgrove. Ch.: (1)
Rosco, b. W. Millgrove, O., July, 1835; d. May 4, 1850; buried
at West Millgrove. (2) Sarah S. Leonard, of W. Millgrove, O.,

b. Oct. 12, 1837; m. J. F. Coder, Apr. 15, 1858, and is living at present at Osceola, O. Ch.: (a) Emerson E., b. Osceola, O., Dec. 8, 1858. (b) Nettie B., b. Osceola, O., Mar. 11, 1863; d Aug. 24, 1890; buried at Osceola. (3) Lois R. Leonard, of W. Millgrove, O., b. Nov. 15, 1839; m. George L. Ketcham, July 3, 1862; res., West Millgrove, O. Ch.: (a) John B., b. June 10, 1864; d. Sept., 1864; buried at West Millgrove. (b) William L. Ketcham, of W. Millgrove, O., b. Jan. 6, 1867; m. Alice Dubell, Aug. 16, 1894. Ch.: (i) Lois, b. Sept. 4, 1895. (ii) Howard L., b. May 1, 1898. (iii) Victor H., b. Aug. 6, 1900. (iv) Kenneth R., b. Dec. 31, 1902. (c) Gertrude M., b. May 1, 1874. (d) Richard B., b. Aug. 9, 1876. (4) Alma Leonard, of W. Millgrove, O., b. Oct. 25, 1851; m. S. W. DeWitt, Feb. 1, 1872; res., West Millgrove, O. Ch., all b. in West Millgrove: (a) Charles H., b. June 27, 1873. (b) Frank DeWitt, of W. Millgrove, O., b. June 14, 1875; m. Bessie Chilcote, Mar. 1, 1900. Ch.: (i) Grace, b. Feb. 10, 1902. (c) Altha, b. Oct. 8, 1877. (d) Herbert, b. Nov. 11, 1879. (e) Dorothea, b. Nov. 3, 1892. (5) Orloff, b. Oct., 1853; d. Jan. 2, 1856; buried at West Millgrove.

1963. v. ANGELINA, b. Mendon, N. Y., Sept. 13, 1815; m. Roswell H. Stevens, in 1841; res., Oberlin, O. She d. Dec. 9, 1851, and was buried in Oberlin. Mr. Stevens d. Feb. 1, 1897, and was buried at Lanham, Maryland. Ch.: (1) Catherine Isabelle Stevens, of Oberlin, O., b. May 14, 1843; m. Charles Macdonald, Feb. 28, 1870; res., Mansfield, O. Ch., all b. in Elyria, O.: (a) Florence Angie, b. Apr. 22, 1872; res., New York, N. Y. (b) Percy, b. Feb. 26, 1874; d. Aug., 1874. (c) Roswell, b. Feb. 26, 1874; d. Aug., 1874. (d) Ralph, b. Mar. 8, 1877; d. Sept., 1877. (2) Edward Charles, b. Oberlin, O., Apr. 24, 1845; enlisted in Mar., 1864, in Company E of the 30th Regiment of the Ohio Voluntary Infantry. He was wounded in the battle of the Wilderness, and was taken from the field hospital to the Lincoln Hospital, and then to Armory Square Hospital, where he remained till honorably discharged Sept. 4, 1865. He was m., Feb. 4, 1869, to Mary Knight, of Washington, D. C. He was for many years a Clerk in the Pension Office. He d. Apr. 24, 1904, and was buried at Arlington. No ch.

1964. vi. WILLIAM J., b. Mendon, N. Y., Sept. 10, 1817; m. Lucy M. Alcott, 3428-33.

1965. vii. SERAPHNEY, b. Mendon, N. Y., May 10, 1820; went to live with her sister, Mrs. Matthew Hubbell, in Richfield, and after her sister's death m. Mr. Hubbell in May, 1840. She d. Jan. 1, 1847, and was buried at Richfield, O. There was one ch. of this marriage. (For Mr. Hubbell's ch. by his first wife, Betsey Foote, see No. 1959.) Ch.: (1) Matthew, b. Richfield, O., Apr. 18, 1844; m. Elvira M. Denton, Dec. 25, 1882, having two ch. by her, both of whom d. in infancy. He was m. a second time to Effie A. Denton, Mar. 19, 1891, and now resides in Los Gatos, Cal.

1966. viii. ORLOFF, b. Mendon, N. Y., July 10, 1822; m. Mrs. Crans, 3434-5.

1967. ix. ALMA T., b. Mendon, Apr. 15, 1827; m. June 15, 1854, Rev. Dr. Charles H. Foote. (See No. 2819 for complete record.)

1968. x. MILTON S., b. Mendon, May 12, 1829; engaged in business in Mount Morris and Akron, N. Y. He was never m. He d. July 18, 1856, in Mendon, N. Y., and was buried in the Baptist Cemetery.

826. DAN FOOTE, (261, 80, 25, 9, 3,) b. Mar. 6, 1785, in Richmond, Mass. He removed with his father's family to Mendon, N. Y. He was m. to Patience Orcrett, Feb. 21, 1814, living for some years in Olean, N. Y., and removing to Ohio abt. 1819, and five years later to Ind., in Sept. 1851, to Jasper Co., Ill. She d. June 12, 1824, and was buried on the farm in Adams, Decatur Co., Ind.; m. 2nd, Feb. 10, 1828, Patience Gosnell, by whom he has three ch. She d. Mar. 1, 1873, and was buried in Kibler Cemetery, Jasper Co., Ind. Dan Foote d. Jan. 16, 1878.

1969. i. CHARLES W., b. Olean, N. Y., May 24, 1816; d. Nov. 25, 1858, and was buried in Kibler Cemetery, Jasper Co., Ind.

1970. ii. EMILY, b. Olean, N. Y., Apr. 25, 1818; d. Jan. 3, 1843, and was buried in Gasnell Cemetery, Rush Co., Ind.

1971. iii. ACENITH MARIA, b. North Bend, O., Aug. 9, 1820.

1972. iv. SAMUEL, b. North Bend, O., Feb. 28, 1822; m. Minerva A. Young, 3436-8

1973. v. DEBORAH ANN, b. Adams, Decatur Co., Ind., Mar. 15, 1824; m. Sept. 12, 1844, Daniel Stogsdill. Res., Dennison, Ill. Ch.: (1) William T., d. Sept., 1902. (2) Albert S., d. Feb., 1895. (3) Irvin.

1974. vi. BARNARD, b. Adams, Decatur Co., Ind., Dec. 4, 1829; m. Jane F. Bridges, 3439-45.

1975. vii. WILLIAM, b. Jan. 22, 1832; d. Dec. 27, 1853; was buried in Kibler Cemetery, Jasper Co., Ind.; unm.

1976. viii. EUNICE, b. July 6, 1835; res., Adams, Decatur Co., Ind; m. Franklin A. Kibler, Nov. 30, 1856. Ch., all b. in Wade, Jasper Co., Ill.: (1) William H., b. Dec. 15, 1857; m. Oct. 6, 1881. (2) Mary Jane, b. Apr. 7, 1859. (3) James P., b. Jan. 6, 1861; d. Aug. 29, 1889; buried in the Lutheran Cemetery. (4) Eliza A., b. Oct. 17, 1862; m. Oct. 7, 1885. (5) Missouri, b. Nov. 4, 1868; m. William C. Swank, Sept. 22, 1897.

829. JOHN FOOTE, (261, 80, 25, 9, 3,) b. Jan. 17, 1792, West Stockbridge, Mass. When he was nine years of age his father removed to Mendon, Monroe Co., and engaged in farming. He m. Sophia Palmer Rogers, of Mendon, Jan. 18, 1819, and removed to Hinsdale, Cattaraugus Co., N. Y., and engaged with his brothers in lumbering and farming. In May, 1825, he was instantly killed by the wheel of his loaded cart, which passed over him as he was returning in the night from the mill. He was found the next morning by a passing traveller. Was buried at Hinsdale. His widow, with their three young children, removed to her father's home in Mendon. (See under Charles Foote, No. 1824.)

1977. i. CATHRINE S., b. Mendon, N. Y., Aug. 22, 1819; m. Darius W. Stone, Apr. 12, 1843, and removed to Mount Morris, N. Y., where her husband was engaged in milling. They also resided in Rochester, Syracuse, and Homer, N. Y. She d. July 30, 1868, and was buried at Homer; he d. July 23, 1886, and was buried at Kinsley, Kansas. Ch.: (1) Frank R. Stone, b. Mount Morris, N.

(14)

Y., Sept. 17, 1848; m. Harriet J. Mason, of St. Louis, Mo., Feb. 21, 1877. He resided in Byron, Ill., and afterward in Chicago, where he was employed in the express business. He d. in Chicago, Oct. 7, 1900, and was buried there. Mrs. Stone still lives in Chicago, 6755 Union Ave. Ch.: (a) Charles R., b. Byron, Ill., Nov. 17, 1877; res., Chicago. (b) Emma Kate, b. Byron, Ill., Nov., 1881; d. in Chicago, Jan. 3, 1893. (c) Frank Lee, b. in St. Louis, Jan. 4, 1885. (d) Hazel H., b. Chicago, June 21, 1887. (e) Mamie E., b. Chicago, June 7, 1889. (2) Ella S. Stone, b. Rochester, N. Y., June 26, 1852; m. Oct. 24, 1876, L. G. Boies, a banker, of Marengo, Ill., and Kinsley, Kansas, and at present of Birmingham, Iowa. Ch., all b. in Kinsley, Kansas: (a) Emma Kate, b. Mar. 4, 1879; d. Nov. 25, 1888. (b) Bessie Alice, b. Jan. 2, 1882; d. May 12, 1883. (c) Anna T., b. Nov. 8, 1883; d. Mar. 24, 1905; buried in Birmingham, Iowa. (d) Grace G., b. Feb. 26, 1888. (e) Frank S., b. Oct. 13, 1889.

1978. ii.   ANN M., b. Mendon, N. Y., June 5, 1821; m. Russell Thorpe, of Batavia, N. Y., May 4, 1850. Mr. Thorpe d. May 3, 1869, and was b. at Batavia. His widow removed to Rochester, N. Y., and afterward lived with her married daughter, Mrs. Chamberlain, at Muskegon, Mich. She d. June 9, 1894, and was buried at Batavia. Ch.: (1) Emma M. Thorpe, b. Batavia, June 27, 1858; m. to D. T. Chamberlain, Nov. 25, 1874. They resided in Hastings, Minn., where Mr. Chamberlain engaged in the practice of law, and served in the State Legislature. Later they moved to Adrian, Mich., and Muskegon, Mich., the latter being their home at present. Ch., all b. in Hastings, Minn.: (a) Russell T., b. Sept. 23, 1875; d. Sept. 5, 1877; buried in Hastings. (b) Ella Kate, b. May 30, 1879; graduated from Kalamazoo College, Mich.; is now a teacher in the High School of ——, Wis. (c) Dan Thorpe, b. Apr. 25, 1884. (2) Charles Foote, b. at Batavia, June 25, 1854; d. while a student of Rochester University, Nov. 3, 1873, and was buried at Batavia.

1979. iii.   ELIAS JOHN, b. Hinsdale, N. Y., June 22, 1824; m. Eliza A. Spink, 3446-9.

831.   ELISHA FOOTE, (261, 80, 25, 9, 3,) b. Feb. 26, 1796, Stockbridge, Mass. When about five years of age he removed with his father's family to Mendon, N. Y. In 1823 he engaged with his brothers in lumbering in Hinsdale, Cattaraugus Co. He was m. to Betsy Simonson, of Tioga Co., N. Y., on Nov. 7, 1824. In June, 1840, they removed to Leroy, N. Y., where he engaged in farming. In 1844 he removed to Fredonia, Mich., then to Sherwood, Branch Co., Mich., and in 1855 he settled in Mendon, St. Joseph Co., Mich., where he resided until a few days before his death, spending his last days with his son Frederick, in Athens, Mich. He d. Nov. 23, 1882, and was buried in Laird Cemetery, on Notaway Prairie, near Mendon, Mich. His wife, Betsy, d. in Leroy, N. Y., Apr., 1844; m. 2nd, Mar. 15, 1846, Augusta Libhardt, dau. of Captain Oliver Foote, of Mendon, Mich.

1980. i.   JOHN, b. Hinsdale, N. Y., Nov. 16, 1825; m. Sept., 1865, Mrs. Clarissa Patterson. He d. July 17, 1877; p. s.; and was buried in Laird Cemetery on Notaway Prairie. She res. in Athens, Mich.

1981. ii.   SARAH MARIA, b. Hinsdale, N. Y., Mar. 21, 1828; m. John R. Lee, Nov. 26, 1845. Mr. Lee d. Nov. 25, 1885, and was buried at Sherwood, Mich. Res., Sherwood, Mich. Ch.: (1) Ira V. Lee, b. Sherwood, Mich., Sept. 4, 1846; m. Olive M. Chapman, Nov. 14, 1867. They now reside near Athens, Mich. Ch.: (a) Anna, b. Sherwood, Sept. 11, 1868. (b) John, b. Sherwood, May 9, 1880. (2) Earl D. Lee, b. Sherwood, Mich., Dec. 29, 1848; m. Mary A. Lee, Apr. 11, 1877. Ch., all b. in Athens, Mich.: (a) Mary L., b. Apr. 8, 1878. (b) Harriet S., b. Nov. 24, 1880; m. A. R. Dart, of Mason, Mich., Dec. 1, 1901. (c) Fred H., b. July 16, 1882. (d) Bessie, b. June 9, 1884. (e) Earl J., b. June 28, 1892. (3) Jay P., b. Sherwood, Mich., Apr. 11, 1859; m. Millie R. Graham, Apr. 11, 1885; lawyer; d. Apr. 8, 1900; buried at Lansing, Mich.

1982. iii.   FREDERICK S., b. Hinsdale, N. Y., Apr. 11, 1830; m. Helen R. Holcomb, 3450-6.

1983. iv.   EVAULETTE, b. Hinsdale, N.Y., Dec. 27, 1832; m. Orlando Porter, farmer, in Wakeshua, Mich., Feb. 5, 1854. Mr. Porter enlisted in Company I of the 7th Regiment of Michigan Infantry and served three years, taking an active part in all the battles in which his regiment was engaged during that term. After the war he removed with his family to Junction City, Kansas, where he d. Mar. 20, 1896, and where he was buried. Res., Junction City, Kansas. Ch.: (1) Frank D., b. Wakeshua, Mich., Dec. 15, 1854; d. Apr. 12, 1877; buried at Clyde, Kansas. (2) Jennie M. Porter, of Mendon, Mich., b. Oct. 20, 1858; m. Mr. Berggren at Belleville, Kansas, Dec. 25, 1876. Res., Junction City, Kansas. Ch.: (a) Mildred A., b. Minersville, Kas., Oct. 10, 1877. (b) Hattie S., b. Minersville, Kas., Apr. 29, 1880. (c) Frank L., b. Scandia, Kas., July 16, 1882. (d) Evaulette, b. Minersville, Kas., Apr. 15, 1885. (3) Charles E., b. July 30, 1873; res. in Lawrence, Kas.

1984. v.   ELIAS, b. Hinsdale, N. Y., Nov. 12, 1834. When his father removed in 1844 to Michigan, he went to live with his uncle Charles Foote, of Mendon, N. Y. In 1855 he rejoined his father's family in Michigan. He enlisted in the Union Army on Aug. 22, 1861, joining Co. I, 7th Regt. Michigan Infantry. He served under Gen. Banks in the Army of the Potomac in Shenandoah Valley. Later he served under Gen. McClellan, and was in the battle of Bull Run. He was sick in a hospital in Philadelphia, and after his recovery he was sent to Fredericksburg, under Gen. Hooker. Still later he was in the battle of Gettysburg under Gen. Mead. He was transferred to the Veteran Reserve Corps in Washington, D. C., till mustered out, Aug., 1864. A farmer from 1868 to 1900 at Burlingame, Kas. He was m. Jan. 26, 1868, to Henrietta Targee, of Clifton, Monroe Co., N. Y. Res., Athens, Mich. No ch.

1985. vi.   EUNICE, b. Hinsdale, N. Y., Apr. 8, 1836; resided for many years with the family of her uncle, Zechariah Noble, in Olean, N. Y.; m. Dr. Alfred Jewel Bigelow, in 1861, and resided in Morrisania, N. Y., where she d. Mar. 4, 1862. They had a son.

1986. vii. MARY ELIZA, b. Hinsdale, N. Y., Apr. 9, 1839; m. Cyril H. Tyler, of Italy, N. Y., Aug. 14, 1861, in Wakeshua, Mich.; present res., Manton, Wexford Co., Mich. Ch., b. at Wakeshua, Mich.: (1) Carrie Emily, b. Sept. 29, 1864; m. Albert W. Peck, Aug. 17, 1885, at Manton, Mich. (2) Laura Ann, b. Jan. 6, 1866. (3) Bessie Eugenia, b. June 14, 1871.

1987. viii. ELISAH, b. Leroy, N. Y., Apr. 2, 1841; m. Clara Burch, 3457-8.

1988. ix. ANN, b. Sherwood, Mich., July 13, 1847; d. young; buried in Laird Cemetery, Mich.

1989. x. GILBERT, b. Sherwood, Mich., Jan. 5, 1850; m. Mary F. Underwood, 3459-60.

1990. xi. CHARLES, b. Mendon, Mich., Nov. 1, 1850; d. young; buried in Laird Cemetery, near Mendon, Mich.

832. ELIAS FOOTE, (261, 80, 25, 9, 3,) b. West Stockbridge, Mass., May 15, 1799. He removed with his father's family to New York State the following year. After short stays in Litchfield and Bloomfield, they settled in Mendon. He m. Matilda Thorpe, of Gilbertville, N. Y., May 15, 1829, and engaged in woollen manufacture in Brighton, N. Y., and afterward in Batavia, N. Y., where he d. Jan. 23, 1875. His wife d. Nov. 8, 1888. Both were buried in Batavia. Ch.:

1991. i. ELIZABETH F., b. Batavia, N. Y., Aug. 23, 1830; m. May 6, 1852, Henry Worthington, of Lenox, Mass. He d. the same year, and was buried in Lenox. Ch.: Dau., d. young. Was m. 2nd, Mar. 24, 1884, to ——— Herrick; he d. Nov., 1897; p. s.

1992. ii. EDWARD T., b. Batavia, N. Y., Jan. 31, 1832; m. 1860, Helen Case, of Honeoye Falls, N. Y. She d. 1880, and was buried there. He d. 1870. Ch.: 2, d. in infancy.

1993. iii. CHARLES H., b. Batavia, June 28, 1834; d. May, 1856; buried in Batavia.

1994. iv. GEORGE A., b. Batavia, Mar. 6, 1836; d. the same year; buried in Batavia.

1995. v. FRANCES M., b. Nov. 23, 1839; m. 1857, Dr. Wells, of Clinton, Virginia. He d. 1890, and was buried in Stevensville, Mon., where she res. Ch.: (1) Richard, b. 1873. (2) Earnest, b. 1878. (3) Bruce, b. 1881. (4) Cora, b. 1886.

1996. vi. JENNIE, b. Batavia, Aug. 23, 1846; m. Jan. 15, 1866, Dr. James Rogers, of Sedalia, Mo., their present res. Ch.: (1) Robert Foote, b. July 4, 1870; d. Sept. 27, 1870. (2) James Foote, b. Jan. 5, 1888.

834. EBENEZER BARNARD, (261, 80, 25, 9, 3,) b. Bloomfield, N. Y., Feb. 1, 1805; m. Mar. 10, 1836, Mary Skidmore. He removed with his father's family to Mendon, and after his marriage resided in Batavia, where he was engaged in the manufacture of woollen goods with his brother Elias. He removed with his family to Richfield, Mich., in 1844, where he d. Feb. 19, 1890, and his wife, Aug. 1, 1900.

1997. i. MARIA A., b. Batavia, Dec. 16, 1837; m. Dec., 1858, Charles C. Warren, and removed to Sandusky, O., where they now reside. Ch.: (1) Halbert B. Warren, b. Litchfield, Mich., Sept. 19, 1859; m. Charlotte Brigham, Sept., 1879, and res. in Sandusky, O. Ch.: (a) Lucille, b. Vienna, Mich., May 12, 1880; m. William Lowenkamp, in 1902; res. in Sandusky, O. (b) Helen Bernice,

b. Vienna, Mich., Jan. 25, 1882. (c) Clarence C., b. St. Paul, Minn., Feb. 2, 1891. (2) Cora L., b. Three Rivers, Mich., Mar. 22, 1862; d. Nov. 24, 1884; buried in Toledo, O.

1998. ii. CHARLES B., b. May 7, 1851; m. Sept., 1875, Ellen Brewer; res., Colburn, Idaho, where he is a merchant and lumber dealer. No ch.

1999.. iii. EMILY M., b. Oct. 19, 1852; m. Sept., 1882, Richard Morrison; res., Allen, Mich.

835. ELISAH[7] FOOTE, (263, 80, 25, 9, 3,) b. 1783; m. 1807, Mary Squier. She d. 1820; m. 2nd, 1821, Eliza J., dau. of Giles Blague, of Saybrook, Ct. She d. Júne, 1829; m. 3rd, 1831, Sarah Beemis, of Cooperstown, N. Y. He was Judge of Otsego Common Pleas, N. Y. He emigrated to Warren, Herkimer Co., N. Y., abt. 1803, to Cooperstown, abt. 1804. Here he d. Feb. 22, 1842.

2000. i. HENRY J., b. ———; d. in infancy.
2001. ii. ELIZA H., b. ———.
2002. iii. HARRIET NEWELL, b. ———; m. Hon. William Marvin, of Key West, Florida, a U. S. Judge, and an able, excellent man, a native of Tompkins Co., N. Y. She d. Mar. 31, 1840. Ch.: 1.
2003. iv. MARY J., b. ———.

836. RUSSELL FOOTE, (266, 80, 25, 9, 3,) b. Dec. 14, 1810; m. Apr. 7, 1842, Sylvia Eliza, dau. of Benj. and Clarissa (Mann) Loveland, b. Apr. 31, 1820. He d. Jan. 26, 1883. Mechanic. Cong. Res., Franklin, N. Y.

Foote Genealogy, page 213.

Benjamin K. Loveland, son of Abner who came from Ct. to Franklin, N.Y., was born 1793, died 1831 aged 38. He married Clarissa Mann who died 1868 aged 76; she was from Ct. They had 5 children: Sylvia Eliza, born 1820, m. Russell Foote. Althea, died while at normal school, Albany, N.Y. Clarissa, teacher, died in middle life, 1869. Rachel, married S. Addison Wheat (see Wheat Genealogy, vol. 1, 1903). Abner B., married Rachel Chambers, both deceased before 1896.

See Biog. Review of Del. Co., N.Y., p. 389.

8-24-'23   Edwin Webb Wheat, R.D. #1, Mt. Vision, N.Y.

Dr. Edward Clarence, son of Hiram and Clarissa (Whitney) Traver. He was b. Aug. 31, 1866. She graduated from Mt. Holyoke College, South Hadley, Mass., in 1896, and taught in schools at Upton and Grafton, Mass.; no ch. (3) Vernette Lois, b. Jan. 5, 1874; graduated from Mt. Holyoke College in 1896. She has taught at Barnardston, Mass., Mt. Holyoke College and Wells College; unm. (4) Bertha Isabelle, b. Feb. 9, 1877; m. June 29,

1986. vii.   MARY ELIZA, b. Hinsdale, N. Y., Apr. 9, 1839; m. Cyril H.
              Tyler, of Italy, N. Y., Aug. 14, 1861, in Wakeshua, Mich.; pre-
              sent res., Manton, Wexford Co., Mich. Ch., b. at Wakeshua,
              Mich.: (1) Carrie Emily, b. Sept. 29, 1864; m. Albert W. Peck,
              Aug. 17, 1885, at Manton, Mich. (2) Laura Ann, b. Jan. 6,
              1866. (3) Bessie Eugenia, b. June 14, 1871.
1987. viii.   ELISAH, b. Leroy, N. Y., Apr. 2, 1841; m. Clara Burch, 3457-8.
1988. ix.   ANN, b. Sherwood, Mich., July 13, 1847; d. young; buried in
              Laird Cemetery, Mich.
1989. x.   GILBERT, b. Sherwood, Mich., Jan. 5, 1850; m. Mary F. Under-
              wood, 3459-60.
1990. xi.   CHARLES, b. Mendon, Mich., Nov. 1, 1850; d. young; buried in
              Laird Cemetery, near Mendon, Mich.

832. ELIAS FOOTE, (261, 80, 25, 9, 3,) b. West Stockbridge, Mass., May 15,
1799. He removed with his father's family to New York State the following
year. After short stays in Litchfield and Bloomfield, they settled in Mendon. He
m. Matilda Thorpe, of Gilbertville, N. Y., May 15, 1829, and engaged in woollen
manufacture in Brighton, N. Y., and afterward in Batavia, N. Y., where he d.
Jan. 23, 1875. His wife d. Nov. 8, 1888. Both were buried in Batavia. Ch.:
1991. i.   ELIZABETH F., b. Batavia, N. Y., Aug. 23, 1830; m. May 6,
              1852, Henry Worthington, of Lenox, Mass. He d. the same
              year, and was buried in Lenox. Ch.: Dau., d. young. Was
              m. 2nd, Mar. 24, 1884, to ——— Herrick; he d. Nov., 1897; p. s.
1992. ii.   EDWARD T., b. Batavia, N. Y., Jan. 31, 1832. -
              Case, of Honeoye Falls. N ʸ
              there....H~ ᵈ⁻ ⁻

1ᵒᵒᵒ

19:

834.
1, 1805;
to Mend
the manu
family to
1, 1900.
    1997.   ~ᴏᴄ., 1858, Charles C.
                         ~ ᴊᴀuᴅusky, O., where they now reside.
              ᵥ⁻ᵧ ᴍᴀlbert B. Warren, b. Litchfield, Mich., Sept. 19, 1859;
              m. Charlotte Brigham, Sept., 1879, and res. in Sandusky, O.
              Ch.: (a) Lucille, b. Vienna, Mich., May 12, 1880; m. William
              Lowenkamp, in 1902; res. in Sandusky, O. (b) Helen Bernice,

b. Vienna, Mich., Jan. 25, 1882. (c) Clarence C., b. St. Paul, Minn., Feb. 2, 1891. (2) Cora L., b. Three Rivers, Mich., Mar. 22, 1862; d. Nov. 24, 1884; buried in Toledo, O.

1998. ii. CHARLES B., b. May 7, 1851; m. Sept., 1875, Ellen Brewer; res., Colburn, Idaho, where he is a merchant and lumber dealer. No ch.

1999. iii. EMILY M., b. Oct. 19, 1852; m. Sept., 1882, Richard Morrison; res., Allen, Mich.

835. ELISAH⁷ FOOTE, (263, 80, 25, 9, 3,) b. 1783; m. 1807, Mary Squier. She d. 1820; m. 2nd, 1821, Eliza J., dau. of Giles Blague, of Saybrook, Ct. She d. June, 1829; m. 3rd, 1831, Sarah Beemis, of Cooperstown, N. Y. He was Judge of Otsego Common Pleas, N. Y. He emigrated to Warren, Herkimer Co., N. Y., abt. 1803, to Cooperstown, abt. 1804. Here he d. Feb. 22, 1842.

2000. i. HENRY J., b. ———; d. in infancy.

2001. ii. ELIZA H., b. ———.

2002. iii. HARRIET NEWELL, b. ———; m. Hon. William Marvin, of Key West, Florida, a U. S. Judge, and an able, excellent man, a native of Tompkins Co., N. Y. She d. Mar. 31, 1840. Ch.: 1.

2003. iv. MARY J., b. ———.

836. RUSSELL FOOTE, (266, 80, 25, 9, 3,) b. Dec. 14, 1810; m. Apr. 7, 1842, Sylvia Eliza, dau. of Benj. and Clarissa (Mann) Loveland, b. Apr. 31, 1820. He d. Jan. 26, 1883. Mechanic. Cong. Res., Franklin, N. Y.

2003. i. AUGUSTA, b. Apr. 16, 1843; m. Dec. 25, 1867, Marshville Gibbons. He was b. Sept. 3, 1838; d. Sept. 5, 1883. She d. at Buffalo, N. Y., May 2, 1896; res., Franklin, N. Y. Ch.: (1) Frank, b. Jan. 17, 1869; graduated from Hamilton College, Clinton, N. Y., in 1890, degree of A. B., and immediately removed to Buffalo, N. Y., where he has since resided, and began the study of the law there in the office of Fred M. Inglehart. Admitted to practice in the Courts of State of New York at General Term of the Supreme Court, held at Rochester, N. Y., in Oct., 1892, and in the U. S. Supreme Court in Nov., 1905. He remained with Mr. Inglehart until June, 1894, when he entered into partnership with Lyndon D. Wood, and has since been practicing his profession. He is now a member of the firm of Gibbons, Pottle (Henry W.), and Talbot (Harry A.). Was m. to Margaret Shankland, b. Dunkirk, N. Y., May 13, 1878, dau. of Robert and Mary Kidder Shankland, at Buffalo, Nov. 2, 1905. Business address, 5 Erie Co. Sav. Bank Bldg., Buffalo; res., 39 Granger Pl., Buffalo, N. Y. Member Queen City Lodge No. 358 F. and A. M., and of 74th Regt. National Guard, N. Y. (grade, First Lieutenant, Company H). Ch.: (a) Elizabeth, b. Sept. 10, 1906, at Buffalo. (2) Dora Bell, b. May 30, 1870; m. Dec. 11, 1900, Dr. Edward Clarence, son of Alvah and Clarissa (Withey) Traver. He was b. Aug. 31, 1866. She graduated from Mt. Holyoke College, South Hadley, Mass., in 1896, and taught in schools at Upton and Grafton, Mass.; no ch. (3) Vernette Lois, b. Jan. 5, 1874; graduated from Mt. Holyoke College in 1896. She has taught at Barnardston, Mass., Mt. Holyoke College and Wells College; unm. (4) Bertha Isabelle, b. Feb. 9, 1877; m. June 29,

1899, Dr. Alvah Harry, son of Alvah and Clarissa M. (Withey) Traver, of Poestenkill, N. Y. He was b. Dec. 25, 1875. Ch.: (a) Clarence Alvah, b. Aug. 15, 1900. (b) Ralph Franklin, b. Aug. 19, 1903; res., 865 Madison Ave., Albany, N. Y.

2004. ii.   ALBERT, b. May 26, 1845; d. June 3, 1871; unm.

2005. iii. FRANCES AMELIA, b. Nov. 15, 1855; m. Nov. 19, 1884, Austin J., son of William Jacobs, of Trout Creek, N. Y.; res., 559 Jefferson Ave., Brooklyn, N. Y. Ch.: (1) Wm. H., b. Apr. 7, 1886.

839.   ASA FOOTE, (266, 80, 25, 9, 3,) b. Sept. 3, 1816; m. Jan. 5, 1852, Ophelia Brown. He d. Aug. 25, 1878. Res., Franklin and Unadilla, N. Y.

2006. i.   MARY ESTELLA, b. Oct. 13, 1859; m. —— Bogart, of Unadilla, N. Y.

2007. ii.   GEORGE K., b. Jan. 22, 1864.

840.   EZEKIEL FOOTE, (266, 80, 25, 9, 3,) b. May 26, 1818; m. ——. Res., Franklin, N. Y.

2008. i.   ORLO T., b. Feb. 7, 1847; m. Julia Edwards, 3461-3.

2009. ii.   ANN ELIZA, b. Oct. 22, 1849; m. Jan. 12, 1870, George Kellogg, of Franklin, N. Y. Ch.: (1) Nellie, b. June 3, 1872; m. H. W. Lee; res., Oneonta, N. Y. (2) Lizzie, b. Mar. 27, 1875; m. Edgar Bartlett; res., East Sidney, N. Y. (3) Clara, b. ——; m. Frank Rollins, of Oneonta, N. Y. (4) Orville, b. ——; res., Schenectady, N. Y. (5) Josphene, b. ——; res., Oneonta, N. Y. (6) Charles, b. ——. Res., Treadwell, N. Y.

2010. iii. IDA V., b. Dec. 27, 1855; res., North Franklin, N. Y.; unm.

2011. iv.   LAVELLE, b. July 27, 1857; d. in Jan., 1893, at Binghamton, N. Y.; unm.

858.   ASA FOOTE, (273, 81, 25, 9, 3,) b. Mar. 20, 1798; m. Oct. 8, 1832, by Rev. Mr. Cornwall, Caroline, dau. of Ebenezer Hale, of Glastonbury, Ct.; d. at South Vineland, N. J., Mar. 26, 1876. She d. Apr. 9, 1877, ae. 77. She was a dau. of Sarah Cornwall Hale, and granddaughter of No. 270. Res., Marlborough, Ct., and Cleveland, O.

2012. i.   EMILY, b. May 12, 1838; d. Jan. 15, 1844.

2013. ii.   JOEL, b. Apr. 10, 1840; d. Jan. 14, 1844.

2014. iii. CAPT. EBENEZER HALE, b. May 12, 1842; m. Sarah J. Moorehouse, 3466-9¾.

2015. iv.   CAROLINE, b. Aug. 6, 1844; killed by lightning at South Vineland, N. J., Aug. 3, 1873.

2016. v.   SAMUEL SEABURY, b. Dec. 10, 1847; m. Delia I. Wilson, 3470-3.

859.   EDWIN FOOTE, (273, 81, 25, 9, 3), b. Nov. 15, 1799; m. 1st, May 20, 1821, Abby Ann, dau. of Dr. Sylvanus Lindsley, of East Haddam, Ct. She was b. Aug. 2, 1802; d. Mar. 21, 1837; m. 2nd, Nov. 10, 1838, Lydia Matilda, dau. of Daniel Boyden, of Guilford, Vt. She was b. Dec. 13, 1801; d. Oct. 11, 1881. He d. at Cleveland, O., Oct. 31, 1853. Res., Brooklyn, O. Mr. Foote came to Brooklyn, O., about 1820, when that vicinity was very sparsely settled. He was an expert civil engineer, but gave that up for farming on account of impaired eyesight. He also taught school. Mr. Foote raised a family of honorable, Christian men and women. He d. Oct. 30, 1853. The Edwin Foote family have held reunions annually for more than 25 years. They have recently formed an associa-

tion. Mrs. Sarah Foote Hinckley, being the oldest child of Edwin Foote now living is President, with Edwin Foote, next oldest, Vice-President.

2017. i. ABBY ANN, b. June 26, 1822; m. June 20, 1842, Franks, son of William Doubleday, of Brooklyn, O. She d. Feb. 15, 1843; he d. 1870; farmer. Ch.: (1) Abby Ann, b. Jan. 31, 1843; d. July 15, 1843.

2018. ii. EDWIN LINDSLEY, b. Oct. 20, 1823; m. 3474.

2019. iii. JOEL, b. July 25, 1825; m. Lydia Matilda Boyden and Catherine Julia Hungerford, 3475-86.

2020. iv. GEORGE, b. Aug. 10, 1827; d. Feb. 26, 1829.

2021. v. EMELINE, b. Sept. 25, 1829, of Brooklyn, O., now Cleveland; m. Thomas Charles, son of Thomas Hooper, of Manchester, England, Sept. 3, 1851. Mr. Hooper was b. Mar. 17, 1826, and d. June 16, 1868. He was a bookkeeper. Mrs. Hooper was known as "Auntie" to all her nephews and nieces, and endeared herself to all by her gentle ways. She d. Dec. 1, 1888. Ch.: (1) Sophia Emeline Hooper, of Brooklyn, O., b. June 11, 1852; m. William McCoy, son of Robinson Frazier, of Leavenworth, Kansas, Dec. 20, 1871. Mr. Frazier was b. Mar. 13, 1848, is a farmer, and has served two years in Atchison City Council, Kansas. Res., Atchison, Kansas, R. D. 3. (2) Charles Martin Hooper, of Brooklyn, O., now Brooklyn Heights, O., b. July 8, 1854; m. Emma, dau. of James Allen, of Albion, Mich., Feb. 1, 1882. Mrs. Hooper was b. July 29, 1862. Mr. Hooper is a market gardener, and a director in the Home Savings and Banking Co. of Cleveland, O. Ch., all b. in Brooklyn, O.: (a) Charles Allen, b. June 9, 1884. (b) Ruby, b. Oct. 19, 1890. (c) Russell M., b. Aug. 23, 1895; d. Mar. 1, 1897. (3) Edward Linsley, b. July 8, 1854; d. Apr., 1855. (4) Henry Thomas Hooper, of Washington, Kansas, b. Mar. 5, 1856; m. Florence Adaline, dau. of Alexander West, of Washington, Kansas, Aug. 22, 1893. Mrs. Hooper was b. Apr. 16, 1870. At Washington, Kansas, Mr. Hooper served as Councilman for three years. Mr. Hooper is a photographer. Res., Superior Ave., near E. 105 St., Cleveland, O.

2022. vi. SARAH, b. July 16, 1831; m. May 21, 1863, Abel S., son of Isaac Hinckley, b. Apr. 10, 1803, and d. Feb. 20, 1888. Res., Brooklyn, O.

2023. vii. ELIZA, b. June 21, 1833, of Brooklyn Heights, O.; m. John George, son of Adam Walter, of Altdorf, Germany, Feb. 2, 1860. He was b. June 13, 1825, and is a farmer now living in Brooklyn Heights. Mrs. Eliza Walter was a quiet, unassuming Christian woman, a friend to the unfortunate, never letting the left hand know what the right hand did. She d. Apr. 20, 1905. Ch.: (1) George Lindsley Walter, of Brooklyn, O., now Brooklyn Heights, O., b. May 11, 1870; m. Gertrude, dau. of Peter France, of Parma, O., Apr. 12, 1899. Mrs. Walter was b. Sept. 17, 1877. Mr. Walter is a market gardener, has been a Councilman, and is now a member of the School Board of Brooklyn Heights, O. Ch.: (a) Nelson Edwin, b. May 29, 1901. (b) Ralph, b. Dec. 15, 1903. (c) Helen Louise, b. July 21, 1905. (2) Edwin Clarke Walter, of Brooklyn, O., now Brooklyn Heights, b. May 11,

1870; m. Elizabeth Hattie, dau. of Peter France, of Parma, O., Mar. 12, 1895. Mrs. Walter was b. Aug. 27, 1871. Mr. Walter is a market gardener, and is Assessor in Brooklyn Heights, O. Ch.: (a) Robert Lindsley, b. Jan. 5, 1896. (b) Clara, b. Apr. 6, 1897. (c) Mary Eliza, b. June 30, 1899. (d) Grace, b. Jan. 18, 1904. (e) Howard Edwin, b. Apr. 29, 1906.

2024. viii. EDWIN, b. Feb. 15, 1835; m. Margaret Walsh, 3487-94.

2025. ix. ASA, b. Feb. 15, 1835; m. Eunice Amelia Boyden, 3495-7.

2026. x. CAROLINE FOOTE, of Gustavus, Trumbull Co., O., b. Mar. 15, 1837; m. Stephen Henry, son of John Howe, of Cleveland, O., June 28, 1856. Mr. Howe was a stone mason by trade, though he engaged in farming. He was b. Sept. 30, 1834, and d. Nov. 19, 1899. Mrs. Howe d. Jan. 12, 1888. Ch.: (1) Harry S. Howe, of Shalersville, O., b. Oct. 5, 1859; m. Arletta Jane, dau. of Israel Sponsler, of Three Rivers, Mich., Sept. 4, 1881. Mrs. Howe was b. July 31, 1863, and d. Sept. 26, 1905. Mr. Howe is a merchant in Drakesburge, O., his address being Freedom Sta., O. Ch.: (a) Lauretta Olga, b. at Tallmadge, O., May 21, 1882. (b) Halbert O., b. at Tallmadge, O., Feb. 29, 1884. (c) Claude M., b. at Akron, O., Mar. 26, 1886. (2) William Burton, b. 1861; d. 1862. (3) Laura Maria Howe, of Shalersville, O., was m. to Dr. Adden E., son of Caleb Haight, of Onondaga, N. Y., in 1884. Ch., all b. at Shalersville: (a) Pearl A., b. May 25, 1885. (b) Jay A., b. Mar. 5, 1887. (c) Myrtle F., b. Apr. 12, 1889; d. Sept. 4, 1902, at Middlefield, O. (4) Mary Emeline Howe, of Shalersville, O.; m. Maurice Edwin, son of David Parker, of Shalersville, O., Jan. 18, 1888. Mr. Parker was b. Jan. 18, 1869, and is a lumberman. Res., Freedom Sta., O., R. F. D. 22. Ch.: all b. at Shalersville, O., except g: (a) Hugh Maurice, b. Mar. 13, 1891. (b) Ethel Kate, b. Sept. 25, 1892. (c) Cleon Lindsley, b. Jan. 29, 1895. (d) Ruth Muriel, b. Apr. 25, 1897. (e) Audrey Caroline, b. Apr. 26, 1900. (f) Elton Edwin, b. June 12, 1902. (g) Glenn Ethelbert, b. Freedom, O., Jan. 30, 1905. (5) Charles Edwin, b. Cleveland, O., Aug. 20, 1870; d. Aug., 1871. (6) Caroline Eliza, b. Cleveland, Aug. 20, 1870; d. Jan., 1873. (7) Nellie Belle Howe, b. Copley, O., June 4, 1875; m. Eugene Walker, son of Stephen W. Hunter, of East Burke, Vt., Mar. 7, 1894. Mr. Hunter was b. Mar. 8, 1868, and is a farmer and carpenter. Ch.: (a) Clyde Howe, b. East Burke, Vt., Jan. 2, 1900.

2027. xi. MARY, b. Apr. 9, 1841; d. Mar. 28, 1863.

2028. xii. GEORGE, b. Oct. 22, 1842; m. Jennie P. Howell, 3498-3500.

861. GEORGE FOOTE, (273, 81, 25, 9, 3,) b. Oct. 22, 1802; m. Sept. 5, 1824, Rachel C., dau. of Solomon Jones, of Hebron, Ct. He d. at Marlborough, Ct., Feb. 22, 1874. Res., Marlborough, Ct. She d. May 11, 1883, ae. 77.

2029. i. RACHAEL C., b. June 22, 1825; m. C. B. Knox, of Manchester, Ct.; d. Dec. 31, 1866; p. s.

2030. ii. FRANCIS E., b. Jan. 7, 1830; m. Thomas B. Cherry, of Manchester; several ch. were b.; all d. in infancy. She d. Oct., abt. 1864; s. p.

2031. iii. MARY J., b. Nov. 30, 1832; m. Joseph Kneeland, of Marlborough, Ct., and d. abt. 1885; p. s.

2032. iv. ABBY L., b. Apr. 30, 1836; d. Sept. 26, 1852; unm.

863. WILLIAM LORD FOOTE, (273, 81, 25, 9, 3,) b. Mar. 27, 1807; m. Jan. 20, 1842, Emeline T., dau. of Michael Foster, of Brooklyn, O. He d. at Cleveland, O., May 25, 1876.

2033. i. ABIGAIL EMILY, b. Oct. 31, 1842; m. Apr. 9, 1867, George, son of George and Mary Arnold. He was b. Sept. 23, 1849, at Lewiston. Res., Cleveland, Ohio. Ch.: (1) George, Jr., b. Apr. 16, 1868; m. Dec. 28, 1894, Katherine Becker; d. Nov. 28, 1905, Birmingham, Alabama. Ch.: (a) George Frederick, b. Cleveland, O., Sept. 10, 1895. (b) Charles Becker, b. Brooklyn, N. Y., Aug. 19, 1902. (2) Fred, b. Aug. 11, 1874. (3) Bessie, b. Feb. 22, 1877.

2034. ii. JERUSHA, b. June 2, 1845; d. Aug. 27, 1848, at Cleveland, O.

2035. iii. SUSAN, b. Cleveland, O., May 12, 1847.

2036. iv. ELLEN, b. July 19, 1849; d. July 29, 1850, at Cleveland, O.

2037. v. ELLEN, b. Cleveland, O., Feb. 3, 1851; res., 868 Scranton Ave., Cleveland, O.

868. EZRA FOOTE, (274, 81, 25, 9, 3,) b. Jan. 7, 1795; m. Oct. 22, 1818, Sarah Louisa Bowler; res., Painsville, Ohio.

2038. i. MARY ANN, b. Sept. 14, 1819; m. Sept. 17, 1845, Rev. Henry Tullidge. He d. Mar. 18, 1897, in Philadelphia, Pa. She d. Mar. 31, 1899. Ch.: (1) Rev. Edward Kilbourne, b. Aug. 14, 1854; m. July 16, 1884, Elizabeth Muhlenburg Irwin, of Phila., Pa. She d. Sept. 18, 1904; m. 2nd, Dec. 26, 1906, Lillian Frances Corey, Millville, N. J. Res., 17 South High St., Millville, N. J. (2) Sarah, b. Feb. 16, 1860. (3) Dr. George Bowler, b. Feb. 16, 1860; m. Jan. 4, 1887, Katharine O'Donnell. Res., Phila, Pa. 6 ch.

2039. ii. CHARLES BOWLER, b. Sept. 10, 1821; m. Sarah Hall, 3500-2⁵.

2040. iii. CAROLINE AMELIA, b. Oct. 12, 1823; m. July 27, 1843, Edward Kilbourn, of Keokuk, Iowa. Ch.: (1) Louisa Bowler, b. Oct. 6, 1845, Ft. Madison, Iowa; m. Edwin A. Kilbourne. He d. Mar. 27, 1880; res., Chicago, Ill. (2) Charles Foote, b. Jan. 28, 1848, Keokuk; d. 1851. (3) Henry Wells, b. June 2, 1851, at Keokuk, Iowa; res., Brooklyn, N. Y. (4) Edward Foote, b. Apr. 4, 1853; d. 1854, in Keokuk, Iowa. (5) Mary Tullidge, b. Aug. 6, 1855; m. Dr. E. D. M. Lyon, of Peekskill, N. Y. (6) Alfred Lewis, b. Jan. 5, 1858, at Keokuk; res., Brooklyn, N. Y.; unm. (7) Dr. Arthur Foote, b. Jan. 5, 1858; m. 1888, Ella Donahower, Supt. State Hospital for Insane, Rochester, Minn. (8) Caroline Foote, b. May 23, 1862, Keokuk, Iowa; m. 1900, Frank A. Kellogg; res., Brooklyn, N. Y.

2040¹. iv. SARAH LOUISA, b. Apr. 26, 1826; d. Oct. 3, 1826.

2041. v. EDWARD A., b. Oct. 22, 1827; m. Sarah A. Bowler, 3502⁶⁻³⁴.

2041¹. vi. SARAH LOUISA, b. Jan. 23, 1830; d. Jan. 25, 1831.

2042. vii. ROBERT B., b. June 4, 1832; m. Louisa F. Bowler, 3500-4³.

874. DAVID FOOTE, (274, 81, 25, 9, 3,) b. Aug. 15, 1809; m. Caroline, dau. of Joseph and Esther Taylor, of Colchester, Ct., Apr. 16, 1831.

2042¹. i EDWARD, b. Mar. 10, 1834; m. Isabelle Brainard, 3505.

2042². ii. SARAH E., b. June 26, 1838.

878. DR. JARED FOOTE, (281, 82, 25, 9, 3,) b. July 12, 1795; m. 1826, Eliza Ann Clark, of Scipio, N. Y.; res., Venice, N. Y. He d. in 1848.

2043. i. MARCIA, b. Nov. 19, 1826; m. Nov., 1849, Calvin Whitman, a farmer. Ch.: (1) Myron, b. Dec., 1850; d. 1901. (2) Helen, b. Nov., 1852. (3) Benjamin, b. Aug., 1854. (4) Aaron, b. Sept., 1856. (5) Ida, b. Oct., 1858. (6) Elizabeth, b. Sept., 1860. (7) William, b. Mar., 1862. (8) Nellie, b. May, 1864. (9) Fred, b. Dec., 1866.

2044. ii. ELIZABETH, b. Mar. 25, 1828; m. 1851, Casper Fenner, a farmer. Ch.: (1) Clarke, b. May, 1853. (2) Luella, d. in childhood, 1856. (3) Casper, b. Oct., 1860. (4) Leslis, b. Nov., 1866; a college graduate.

2044¹. iii. DARWIN, b. Dec., 1829; d. 1840.

2045. iv. LOVINA, b. Sept. 15, 1831, m. Jan. 1, 1851, Wm. N. Baldwin, a farmer; res., Auburn, N. Y. Ch.: (1) Addie, b. Nov. 21, 1853. (2) May, b. Oct. 11, 1856. (3) Clarence, b. Dec. 22, 1859. Treasurer of a large manufacturing business. (4) Carrie, b. Oct. 23, 1869.

2046. v. MARY, b. Mar. 21, 1834; m. John B. Strong, a farmer, later a Revenue Collector. Ch.: (1) Inez, b. Sept., 1856; d. in childhood. (2) Frank, b. Aug. 5, 1859. He is now Chancellor of the University of Lawrence, Kansas. (3) Otis, b. July 4, 1861; Professor of Mathematics in High School. Both men Yale graduates.

2046¹. vi. CLARKE, b. in Venice; d. in childhood.

2047. vii. CAROLINE, b. Aug. 4, 1841; m. Dr. Elias Lester, Dec. 23, 1864. Res., Seneca Falls. Ch.: (1) Carrie, b. Dec. 23, 1868. (2) Fred, b. June, 1870; a physician, Seneca Falls, N. Y. (3) George, b. 1872; lawyer in New York City. (4) Mary, b. 1881; d. in childhood.

2047¹. viii. LUCINDA, d. in childhood.

2048. ix. JARED, b. in Venice, Jan. 4, 1844; d. Aug., 1853.

879. DAVID FOOTE, (281, 81, 25, 9, 3,) b. Oct. 13, 1797; m. 1825, Maria Champlin. Was Chief Officer in the State Prison for a number of years. Res., Auburn, N. Y.

2049. i. GEORGE, b. Nov. 22, 1825; graduated at Union College, 1843.

2050. ii. CHARLES, b. Dec. 24, 1830.

82 ELI FOOTE, (281, 81, 25, 9, 3,) b. Oct. 8, 1803; m. 1824, Lucy, dau. of Sylvester Olmsted; res., Auburn and Middlesex, Yates Co., N. Y.

2051. i. MARION, b. Oct. 19, 1824; d. 1830.

2052. ii. POWELL K., b. Feb. 7, 1826; m. Hannah Allen. She d. 1904; p. s.; res., Middlesex, N. Y.

2052¹. iii. JOEL B., b. Aug. 23, 1833; d. July 11, 1845.

2053. iv. MARION B., b. May 27, 1836; m. Mr. Williams; res., Port Chester, N. Y. Ch.: (1) Lewis C. (2) Joel F.; dead. (3) Lucy E.; dead. (4) Carlotte. (5) John E.

883. OTIS CLARK FOOTE, (281, 81, 25, 9, 3,) b. Dec. 11, 1806; m. May, 1844, Mary Aldrich. Res., Rushville, N. Y.

    2054. i. LUCY ROSETTE, b. Aug. 5, 1845.

891. ELISAH L. FOOTE, (283, 82, 25, 9, 3,) b. at Scipio, N. Y., Aug. 30, 1821; m. Apr. 6, 1842, Ellen Cordelia, dau. of William and Lucy Symonds, of Shoreham, Vt. He d. Feb. 10, 1892, at Ft. Atkinson, Wis., just two weeks after the death of his wife. Res., Rushville, N. Y., and Ft. Atkinson, Wis.

    2055. i. AGNES LUCY, b. Rushville, N. Y., Apr. 28, 1846; m. Nov. 9, 1865, Reuben S., son of Wm. and Jane (Shaw) White, at Ft. Atkinson, Wis. She d. Feb. 12, 1904, at St. Paul, Minn. Ch.: (1) Herbert E., b. July 14, 1867, at Ft. Atkinson, Wis.; m. June 3, 1891, Mabel A. Chapman. Ch.: (a) Hazel Chapman, b. May 31, 1893. Res., St. Paul, Minn. (2) Lillie B., b. Ft. Atkinson, Wis., Oct. 7, 1871; d. Sept. 15, 1872. (3) Arthur B., b. Ft. Atkinson, Wis., Aug. 19, 1873; now in business in St. Paul, Minn., where he res. with his father. (4) Lulu B., b. Ft. Atkinson, Wis., June 27, 1876; m. June 2, 1897, A. J. Douglas, Jr., in St. Paul, Minn. She d. Jan. 4, 1902.

    2056. ii. ASA, b. Rushville, N. Y., Aug. 12, 1848; m. Laura A. Gillman, 3506-9.

    2057. iii. FRANKLIN EDWARD, b. Oztalan, Wis., Oct. 21, 1857; d. May 31, 1859.

    2058. iv. CARRY, b. Ft. Atkinson, Wis., Sept. 25, 1865; m. Aug. 16, 1892, Arthur W. Mann, druggist at Onana, Iowa, their present res.

894. JOHN WARD FOOTE, (283, 82, 25, 9, 3,) b. Nov. 4, 1844; m. Nora Berry; res., San Diego, Cal.

    2059. i. MYRTLE, b. Apr. 2, Ft. Atkinson, Wis.; d. Dec. 10, 1893.

    2060. ii. BERNARD, b. ——; d. ——.

    2061. iii. CLARKE, b. Oct., 1878; m. —— ——, a dentist.

897. OLITON CUSHMAN FOOTE, (284, 85, 26, 9, 3,) b. ——; m. Thina Bull; res., St. Thomas, London District, Upper Canada. She d. Aug. 6, 1850; he d. Apr. 22, 1852.

    2062. i. ANGELINE, b.

    2062¹. ii. HUNN BEACH, b.

    2063. iii. JOHN L., b. Nov. 29, 1802; m. Eliza Partridge, 3510--21.

    2063¹. iv. ASA, b.

    2063². v. ELIZA, b.

    2063³. vi. MARIA, b.

    2063⁴. vii. HARRIET, b.

    2064. viii. JOSEPHINE, b. ——; m. —— Baker; she d. Mar. 28, 1863.

    2064¹. ix. CHARLOTTE, b. ——; m. —— Maines; she d. May 29, 1843.

    2064². x. JANE, b.

    2064³. xi. ELLEN, b.

    2065. xii. JAMES, b. ——; d. Feb. 28, 1887.

    2065¹. xiii. HENRY D., b.

    2065². xiv. GEORGE, b.

902. WILLIAM FOOTE, (284, 85, 26, 9, 3,) b. Mar. 21, 1773; m. Dec. 27, 1798, Eve, dau. of Peter Butler, of Shandaken, N. Y.

    2066. i. JOHN B., b. June 25, 1800; d. June 13, 1804.

    2067. ii. CATHRINE, b. Jan. 19, 1802; d. May 15, 1825; unm.

2068. iii. ELIZABETH, b. Feb. 5, 1804.

2069. iv. LYDIA, b. Dec. 22, 1805; d. Dec. 10, 1830; unm.

2070. v. SOPHIA, b. Mar. 20, 1808.

2071. vi. JACOB JACKSON, b. June 30, 1810.

2072. vii. WILLIAM, b. June 15, 1812.

2073. viii. MATILDA, b. Jan. 22, 1815.

2074. ix. MARY, b. Mar. 5, 1817.

2075. x. JANE, b. Nov. 11, 1819.

2076. xi. GEORGE W., b. June 15, 1821.

2076¹. xii. JOHN BERTON, b. Sept. 11, 1823.

912. SAMUEL FOOTE, (289, 85, 26, 9, 3,) b. ———; res., Locke, N. Y.

2077. i. SAMUEL, b.

2077¹. ii. CORNELIUS, b.

2077². iii. HARLOW, b. ———; m. ———.

918. OLIVER FOOTE, (290, 85, 26, 9, 5,) b. Dec. 7, 1787; m. 1813, Ruth Hungerford. She was b. June 15, 1791; d. Feb. 4, 1876, in Vernon, N. Y. He d. Aug. 11, 1832; res., Vernon, N. Y.

2078. i. MARY·ELIZABETH, b. Oct. 3, 1814; d. July 21, 1847.

2079. ii. ANGELINE RUTH, b. Oct. 31, 1816; d. Oct. 7, 1847.

2080. iii. ELLEN, b. Oct. 14, 1820; m. May 7, 1844, James S. Thomas; d. Nov. 4, 1859. Ch.: (1) Emily Elizabeth, b. May 13, 1846; d. Aug. 8, 1846. (2) Clara Harriett, b. Oct. 23, 1848; d. Jan. 9, 1871. (3) James Stringham, b. Aug. 4, 1850; d. Jan. 25, 1891. (4) Newell Foote, b. Feb. 12, 1851; d. Dec. 17, 1887. (5) George Francis, b. July 22, 1859.

2081. iv. SAMUEL NEWELL, b. Dec. 15, 1822; m. June 2, 1847, Mary, dau. of Daniel Rogers, of Little Falls, N. Y.; d. June 6, 1855. Ch.: (1) Cornelia R., b. 1848; d. June 14, 1850.

2082. v. CLARISSA, b. Oct. 3, 1828; m. June 29, 1854, Dr. Thomas Malcomb Flandrau, of Rome, N. Y. He d. Aug. 8, 1898. She d. May 1, 1890, in Rome, N. Y. Ch.: (1) Elizabeth Margaret, b. May 30, 1859, in Brookport, N. Y. (2) Ruth Hungerford, b. Rome, N. Y., Feb. 24, 1863; m. June 3, 1891, Henry Carrall Sutton, M. D., of Rome, N. Y.; he d. Mar. 5, 1907. (4) Thomas Foote, b. May 24, 1865, Rome, N. Y.; d. Aug. 18, 1865. (5) Julia· Suismore, b. Rome, N. Y., Nov. 12, 1872; m. Nov. 10, 1894, George Ethridge; res., Rome, N. Y.

919. AVERY FOOTE, (290, 85, 26, 9, 3,) b. Aug. 9, 1791; m. May 28, 1815, Joanna Osgood, of Vernon. She was b. Oct. 6, 1792; d. Apr. 1, 1846, in Parma, N. Y.; m. 2nd, Apr. 29, 1847, Almira Robinson. She was b. Aug. 11, 1811, and d. Apr. 12, 1887, in Parma, N. Y. He d. Dec. 25, 1867, in Parma, N. Y.

2083. i. IRA, b. Mar. 26, 1816; m. Elizabeth Smith, 3522-6.

2084. ii. BETSEY JANE, b. Feb. 26, 1819; m. 1st, Jan. 5, 1839, Phineas Reed, of Phelps, N. Y.; m. 2nd, Oct., 1861, Daniel Rhodes. Ch.: (1) Isaac Herbert Reed, b. Sept. 18, 1848; d. in infancy. (2) Avery L. Reed, b. Sept. 19, 1851.

2085. iii. WARREN, b. Jan. 7, 1821; m. Rhoda Reed, 3527-31.

2086. iv. ALTHA JOAN, b. May 16, 1848; d. Nov. 16, 1866, at the Saterlee Collegiate Institute, Rochester, N. Y.

2087. v. AVERY L., b. Nov. 19, 1853; m. Minnie Louisa Spaulding, 3532.

920. JOHN FOOTE, (290, 85, 26, 9, 3,) b. Oct. 28, 1793; m. Mar. 4, 1818, Mary Lull, of Butternuts, N. Y. He d. July 2, 1887. She d. at the home of her dau., Elizabeth F. Dwight, Brooklyn, Wis., July 20, 1874, ae. 77. Res., Clinton, N. Y.

2088. i. LUTHER RICE, b. Apr. 30, 1819; m. Mary A. Bronson, 3533-4.

2089. ii. ALMIRA BARNES, b. Oct. 20, 1820; m. Rev. A. S. Kneeland. She d. Aug. 23, 1859. Ch.: (1) Almira Elizabeth. (2) Rev. Francis Wayland, of Lyons, N. Y. (3) Rev. Ira Sprague, of 52 Princeton Place, Buffalo, N. Y.

2090. iii. SEELEY T., b. Aug. 27, 1822; m. Mariah Chapman, 3535.

2091. iv. JOHN, b. Jan. 9, 1825; m. Virginia Jenison, 3536-9.

2092. v. ELIZABETH, b. Mar. 31, 1827; m. May 11, 1848, Edward Woolsley, son of Dr. Benjamin Woolsley and Sophia Dwight, b. at Catskill, N. Y., Apr. 8, 1827. He was a farmer at Spring Prairie, Wis., for some years, but lived at Brooklyn, Greene Co., Wis., from 1857 to 1904. She d. Feb. 11, 1905. He d. Mar. 6, 1904. Ch.: (1) Mary Sophia, b. at Spring Prairie, Wis., Jan. 7, 1853; m. Oct. 16, 1879, Charles N. Akere, an Attorney at Law, St. Paul, Minn. Ch.: (a) Dwight Harman, b. Jan. 1, 1882; d. Apr. 13, 1887. (2) Delia Elizabeth, b. July 17, 1857. Res., 1541 West Minnehaha St., St. Paul, Minn. (3) Edward Foote, b. Apr. 7, 1862; m. Sept. 20, 1898, Mary Eddy Parcone, of Kennebunk, Me. He d. Jan. 25, 1903. Ch.: (a) Elizabeth Parcone. (b) Theodore William. (4) Theodore William, b. Mar. 12, 1865; res., Sioux Falls, South Dakota; m. Aug. 20, 1889, Jennie Brink. Ch.: (a) Helen, b. Feb. 6, 1895. (b) Edward Brink, b. Nov. 24, 1897.

2093. vi. EBENEZER LULL, b. June 10, 1829; m. Sept. 22, 1882, Hannah N. Hunn, of Batavia, N. Y. She d. Jan. 1, 1903, ae. 70. Res., Clinton, Mo.; p. s.

2094. vii. CHARLES BABCOCK, b. July 25, 1831; m. Celia Buell Rogers, 3540-1.

2095. viii. MARY LULL, b. Sept. 12, 1834; d. Apr. 20, 1835.

2096. ix. WILLIAM A., b. Dec. 12, 1839; m. Emma D. Wood, 3542-3.

921. EPHRAIM, (290, 85, 26, 9, 3,) b. May, 1796; m. 1821, Almira Harmon, of Clinton, N. Y. She d.; m. 2nd, Sept. 10, 1833, Electa, dau. of Dea. Luther Osgood, b. at Wendall, Mass., Mar. 7, 1809; d. at Spring Prairie, Wis., Mar. 15, 1879. He d. June 3, 1871. Res., Walworth Co., Wis., Spring Prairie.

2097. i. MARK HARMON, b. Nov. 16, 1825; m. Harriet Walbridge, 3544-51.

2098. ii. HORACE B., b.

2099. iii. ALMIRA ELECTA, b. Aug. 31, 1836; m. ——— Wheat. Res., Redlands, Cal.

2100. iv. ADDISON OSGOOD, b. Feb. 7, 1840; m. Sarah Margaret Gleason, 3552-71.

2101. v. LUCY JANE, b. Jan., 1842; unm.; res., Redlands, Cal.

2102. vi. EPHRAIM SEELY, b. July 14, 1847; m. Mattie R. Waite, 3558-61.

2103. vii. HATTIE JOANNA, b. Spring Prairie, Wis., Sept. 7, 1849; m. Apr. 2, 1872, Milton John, son of Miner J. Wilcox, of Spring

Prairie, Wis. He was b. Sept. 23, 1848. Ch.: (1) Lu Elesta, b. Aug. 21, 1875; d. Apr. 7, 1898. (2) Floy Sarah, b. Aug. 11, 1877; m. Grand Island, Neb., Mar. 1, 1900, William F. Tilley. (3) Ruth Almira, b. Dec. 13, 1882.   (4) Ethel Inez, b. Apr. 26, 1884. (5) Edith Ioan, b. Apr. 26, 1884; d. Aug. 18, 1887. (6) Walter Wilber, b. Aug. 31, 1886; d. Apr. 27, 1887. (7) Lillian Louisa, b. Apr. 27, 1889.

923. SEELY T. FOOTE, (290, 85, 26, 9, 3,) b. Mar. 8, 1800; m. Content Babcock, of New Berlin, N. Y. He d. June 30, 1830, in Vernon, N. Y.

2104. i. ZILPAH ANN, b.

924. DANIEL FOOTE, (290, 85, 26, 9, 3,) b. Sept. 11, 1802; m. Eliza Yale, of Vernon, N. Y.; both lived and d. in that place. He d. Aug. 4, 1832.

2105. i. CORNELIA, b. Dec. 30, 1831; m. Aug. 29, 1853, George Miller. Ch.: (1) Frank, b. July 31, 1860; m. Feb. 14, 1904, Elizabeth Biddlecome. (2) Nina, b. May 12, 1857; d. Nov. 2, 1873. (3) Frederick, b. Nov. 22, 1868; m. Sept. 3, 1891, Marie Antoinette Teft; physician and surgeon; res., Utica, N. Y. Ch.: (a) Charles Teft, b. Nov. 10, 1892; d. Feb. 27, 1894. (b) Frederick Munger, b. July 15, 1895.

929. GEORGE FOOTE, (295, 85, 26, 9, 3,) b. Mar. 12, 1801; m. Hannah Wetmore, of Vernon, N. Y. Res., Vernon, N. Y.

2106. i. EMERGENE, b. Oct. 24, 1828.

2107. ii. GEORGE NEWTON, b. Jan. 22, 1833.

2107¹. iii. CHARLES HENRY, b. May 4, 1835.

932. ELIHU FOOTE, (295, 85, 26, 9, 3,) b. Apr., 1809; m. Nov. 4, 1835, Mirim Malvina Cook. She was b. Mar. 4, 1808; d. Nov. 29, 1864. He d. May 2, 1866. Res., Vernon Center, N. Y.

2108. i. JOSIAH LEGRAND, b. Aug. 30, 1836; merchant at Vernon Center, N. Y.

2108¹. ii. ELLA CAROLINE, b. Oct. 7, 1839; d. Dec. 1, 1864.

935. ADONIJAH, (298, 89, 26, 9, 3,) b. Oct. 22, 1780; m. Sept. 20, 1807, Clarissa, dau. of Jesse Woodworth, of Montville, Mass. He d. Oct. 13, 1825. Res., Springfield, Mass. The ch. were all born on the Armory Grounds, or Government Arsenal, Springfield, Mass., and their father (Adonijah Foote) was superintendent of the U. S. Armory for many years, under Col. Ripley, then resident officer.

2109. i. EMERSON, b. Feb., 1809; m. Oct. 10, 1838, Maria Howe Shepard, dau. of Charles Shepard, of Northampton, Mass. She d. at Cold Spring, N. Y., Apr. 3, 1841. Ch.: 1, d. in infancy.

2110. ii. HOMER, b. July 27, 1810; m. Delia Dwight, 3562-71.

2111. iii. MABLE OTIS, b. July 16, 1812; m. Francis M. Carew, merchant, son of Joseph Carew, of Springfield, Mass.

2112. iv. MARY SKINNER, b. July 16, 1812; m. George Dwight, of Springfield, Mass., son of James Scott Dwight.

2112¹. v. HARRIET WOODWORTH, b. July 21, 1814; m. Edwin Seeger, M. D., son of Dr. Seeger, of Northampton, Mass. She d. Aug. 26, 1843. Ch.: (1) Harriet Seeger.

2112². vi. CLARISSA, b. Nov. 16, 1817; m. Capt. James B. Hatch, son of Solomon Hatch, of Springfield, Mass.

2112³. vii. ADONIJAH, b. Mar. 22, 1819; d. Mar. 12, 1822.

2113. viii. ADONIJAH, b. May 8, 1823; m. Julia Bowles and Amelia Ward, 3572-3.

947. ERASTUS FOOTE, (299, 89, 26, 9, 3,) b. at Colchester, Ct., Apr. 21, 1785. He removed with his parents to Granville, N. Y.; m. Edith Day in 1811. She was b. Feb. 26, 1787. Mr. Foote and family removed to Ontario, N. Y., in 1835, when he engaged in business of general merchandise and farming. He d. at Ontario, N. Y., May 14, 1855; Mrs. Foote d. May 15, 1865.

2114. i. HARRIET FOOTE; m. at Granville, N. Y., in 1831, to Southward Harkness, who was b. at Granville, Mar. 12, 1807. They removed to Ontario, N. Y., in 1835, thence to Salem, N. Y., in 1847. Mr. Harkness d. there May 20, 1851. Mrs. Harkness d. in Walworth, N. Y., Aug. 20, 1896, ae. 83 years. Ch.: (1) Edson J. Harkness, b. Ontario, N. Y., Aug. 31, 1843. Enlisted Aug. 8, 1862, 9th N. Y. Heavy Artillery. Mustered out Sept. 20, 1865; Captain 6th U. S. C. T. Brevet Major U. S. Volunteers Mar. 13, 1865. Res., Chicago, Illinois, since 1868. Attorney at Law. Retired since 1896; m. Jan. 19, 1870, Marianna Bates. Ch.: (a) Edith Alice Harkness, b. July 26, 1871; A. B., Smith College, 1894. (b) Frank Edgerton Harkness, b. Aug. 8, 1874; A. B., Amherst College, 1896; B. L., Harvard, 1900; Attorney at Law, Chicago. (c) Stanley Bates Harkness, b. Jan. 9, 1880; A. B., Oberlin College, 1904. (2) Luther Day Harkness, b. Ontario, N. Y., May 3, 1847; res., Oberlin, Ohio; retired; m. Jennie Wainwright, at Chicago, July 15, 1873. (3) Delia Annette Harkness, b. Salem, N. Y., Oct. 23, 1849; m. Ellison Hayslip; d. Sept. 11, 1881. They had 1 ch., Charles Hayslip.

2114¹. ii. SALLY, b. Dec. 20, 1815, at Granville, N. Y.; d. there May 24, 1825.

2114². iii. DELIA, b. Dec. 3, 1817; d. at Oberlin, O., Aug. 8, 1906; unm.

2114³. iv. JESSE, b. May 29, 1821, at Granville, N. Y.; d. there May 9, 1825.

2115. v. RUTH, b. at Granville, N. Y., July 3, 1824; m. Rev. Lyman Manley, at Ontario, in 1845. He was for many years a Presbyterian minister at Ontario, N. Y. He d. at Marion, N. Y., in 1869. Mrs. Manley d. at Oberlin, O., July 7, 1887. Ch.: (1) Edward Payson Manley, b. in Ontario, N. Y., Sept. 12, 1846; m. Serina McLain, at Granville, Ill., Sept. 28, 1871. Ch.: (a) Margaret Manley, b. Sept. 17, 1873; m. Theodore G. Pasco, Nov. 28, 1899. (b) Ella May Manley, b. Feb. 21, 1876. Mr. Manley's res., Streator, Ill., for over 25 years; is a hardware merchant. (2) M. Ella Manley, b. Richmond, N. Y., Feb. 28, 1856. Res., Oberlin, O.

960. ZELONA FOOTE, (302, 89, 26, 9, 3,) b. Dec., 1793; m. Jan. 1, 1821, Betsey Elizabeth, dau. of Ebenezer Manchester; she was b. Nov. 20, 1789; d. Nov. 29, 1863, at Dewitt, Mich. He was a farmer, and d. Aug. 14, 1860, at Eagle, N. Y.

2115¹. i. ZELONA, JR., b. Jan. 6, 1822; m. Samantha Hicks.

2116. ii. ISAAC W., b. Nov. 4, 1823; m. Caroline Ryon.

2116¹. iii. ALFRED R., b. Sept. 13, 1825; d. Sept. 13, 1865.

2117. iv. LUCINDA A., b. Aug. 21, 1827; m. Dewitt, Mich., Mar. 10, 1863, Levi Cole.

2118. v.   ASA M., b. Jan. 11, 1829; m. Matilda Heath.

2119. vi. LYDIA L., b. Dec. 15, 1830; m. Eagle, N. Y., Feb. 18, 1857, William Spencer.

2120. vii. ALVIN C., b. Mar. 7, 1833; m. Ester Eyrter. Res., Oregon, Ill.

2121. viii. LORETTA L., b. July 27, 1837; m. Olive, Mich., Nov. 9, 1864, Augustus Gillett.

2122. ix. ALPHEUS G., b. Mar. 17, 1838.

2123. x.   ANSON T., b. Aug. 21, 1840; m. Lattie L. Masier; res., Paw Paw, Mich.

2124. xi. RHODERIC D., b. June 4, 1843; m. Lucinda Cronkkite.

2125. xii. LAURA A., b. Dec. 1, 1848; m. St. Johns, Mich., July 4, 1869, Franklin Isbell.

962. MILTON FOOTE, (302, 89, 26, 9, 3,) b. Aug. 8, 1798; m. Jestina ———. He was b. in the town of Hamilton, Madison Co., N. Y. He moved from Hamilton to Gainesville Creek, N. Y., in 1832. He helped to organize Gainesville Creek Church. He lived most of the time in or near Eagle Valley, N. Y. He was one of the first in Eagle Valley Church. He drew the first stick of timber and the first load of stone to build the church with. He came there when the country was new. People lived in log houses, and neighbors were few and scattering. Though he found it difficult to live and support quite a large family, still if anything was neglected, it was something of a worldly nature, and never his God or the cause of his Savior. Indeed he was a pillar in the church; and in a religious point of view he was truly an extraordinary man. He d. Nov. 18, 1876.

2126. i.   ALONZO L., b. Jan. 10, 1822; m. Julia Smith, 3576-80.

2126¹. ii. BETSEY, m. Orlin Ward.

2127. iii. DAVID L., b. Oct. 10, 1830; m. Polly Frone, 3581-2.

2127¹. iv. ANGENETTE, m. William Ward, of Bliss, N. Y.

2127². v.   AMANDA, m. Aaron Ward, of Bliss, N. Y.

2127³. vi. CELINDA, m. Elias Ward. The four sisters m. four brothers.

2128. vii. WILLIAM, b. Dec. 7, 1840; m. Lydia Barber, 3583-8.

2129. viii. EDMOND, d. young.

972. FREDERICK FOOTE, (299 or 304, 89, 26, 9, 3,) b. Jan. 22, 1793; m. ——

2129¹. i.   ZELOTES, b.

2129². ii. CAROLINE, b.

980. LEONARD FOOTE, (299 or 304, 89, 26, 9, 3,) b. May 16, 1814; m. Hannah Clarke; d. 1869, Bridgewater, N. Y. Ch. all b. at Bridgewater, N. Y.

2129³. i.   MARY, b. 1838; m. J. S. Dickson, of Bridgewater, N. Y.

2129⁴. ii. GEORGE, b. 1840; m. Aurelia Johnson, 3588¹.

2129⁵. iii. FREDERICK, b. 1843; m. Nellie Brown and Zayela Conger, 3588²-84.

981. RUFUS FOOTE, (299 or 304, 89, 26, 9, 3,) b. Aug. 21, 1817, Bridgewater, N. Y.; m. Emily Hall, of Bridgewater, N. Y.; d. 1903, at Bridgewater, N. Y.

2129⁶. i.   WILLIAM E., b. 1840; m. Josephine ——— and Emma Hall, 3588-5.

982. ELISHA FOOTE, (308, 92, 27, 9, 3,) b. Jan. 22, 1775; m. Sept. 5, 1796, Delia, dau. of Justus Battle, of Tyringham, Mass. He d. in New York City, Apr. 8, 1746. Res., Lee, Mass., Albany and New York, N. Y.

2130. i.   CHANDLER, b. Lee, Mass., Aug. 19, 1797; m. ———.
2131. ii.   AMELIA, b. Lee, Mass., Feb. 2, 1799; m. Aug. 23, 1826, J. A. French, of Burlington, Vt.; p. s.
2132. iii. JUSTUS BATTLE, b. Jan. 25, 1801; m. Harriett Augustus Bartine, 3589-91.
2133. iv.   RANSOM HINMAN, b. Apr. 13, 1803; m. ———.
2134. v.   HENRIETTA, b. Jan. 19, 1805; m. William Shafer, of Albany, N. Y. She d. of cholera, July 21, 1832.
2135. vi.   SOPHIA, b. July 13, 1807; m. Mar. 17, 1830, James McGlashan. He d. ———; m. 2nd, Charles McGlashan.
2136. vii. ELISHA, b. Aug. 1, 1809; m. Eunice Newton, 3592-3.
2137. viii. DELIA, b. Lenox, Mass., Apr. 4, 1814; m. Samuel Johnson, of New York, N. Y.
2138. ix.   GEORGE FRANKLIN, b. Albany, N. Y., Mar. 13, 1817; m. Theda Louisa Steel, 3594-3600, Anna Maria Parsons and Elizabeth P. Parsons.
2139. x.   JULIA JERUSHA, b. Aug. 12, 1819; m. Joel N. Hayes, of New York, N. Y.; a merchant.
2140. xi.   THEODORE, b. Oct. 13, 1821; d. Jan. 14, 1826.
2141. xii. HENRY RUTGER, b. Mar. 2, 1824; m. 2nd, Linda Lucretia Lamar, 3601-6.
2142. xiii. ESTHER, b. July 12, 1826; d. Dec. 2, 1830.

983. CAPT. ALVAN FOOTE, (308, 92, 27, 9, 3,) b. May 29, 1777; m. Sept. 27, 1798, Sarah, dau. of Elisha Percival, of Lee, Mass. She was b. Lenox, 1779; d. in Lee, Jan. 24, 1867, ae. 88 years.

Of their eight ch., four sons were pioneers in the settlement of Ohio. Three daus. became teachers. One, the mother of Rev. Dr. Alvin Foote Sherrill, was chosen assistant to Mary Lyon at Mt. Holyoke. Marshall Foote was the son to remain on the farm, where his well spent life was closed in 1894 at the age of 88 years.

In 1757 Jonathan Foote came from Colchester, Ct., and secured by purchase and by grant 1,200 acres of land. He sold some of it to settlers and reserved enough for a farm for each of his three sons. To his son Alvan he gave the farm upon which the residence is located. It consists of 225 acres, including woodlands and contains extensive deposits of sand which have supplied the town for building purposes for many years. Alvan selected this place for a house which he built in 1797. It was burned in 1814 and the present house was erected in the same year. It is one of the best preserved of the old Colonial houses in this part of the State.

Alvan Foote was early in life imbued with the spirit of '76 and organized a company of militia of which he was chosen captain, and for many years he led his company at the "annual trainings," which day was a holiday enjoyed by the whole population. In 1797 he m. Sally Percival, dau. of Capt. Elisha Percival, of Lenox. On the 60th anniversary of their marriage the first golden wedding ever celebrated in Lee was attended by a large company of friends. The aged couple enjoyed seven years of wedded life after that event. Capt. Foote d. in his 96th year.

Capt. Foote was b. and always lived on the farm inherited from his father and grandfather. He was a Captain of Militia, a prominent farmer, and highly respected citizen. In 1798 he built a house, m. the dau. of Capt. Elisha Percival, of Lenox, and began a happy and useful life in a home still owned and occupied by his descendants. He d. Sept. 6, 1872.

2143. i. WILLIAM, b. Aug. 4, 1799; m. Mary Chapman, 3607.

2144. ii. ALVAN, b. June 10, 1801; m. Eliza Priscilla Winchell, 3608-11.

2145. iii. ELISAH PERCIVAL, b. Mar. 10, 1803; m. Roxana Freeman and Harriet Cossitt, 3612-8.

2146. iv. MARSHAL, b. Nov. 28, 1805; m. Sarah Cady, 3619-24.

2147. v. SARAH, b. May 22,1808; m. Oct. 1,1838, Rev. Edwin Jenner Sherrill, of Shoreham, Vt. Mrs. Sherrill was the assistant and lifelong friend of Mary Lyon at Mt. Holyoke, and afterward at the head of the Female Academy at Ipswich. She was a woman of saintly character, a mother in Israel—a devoted wife and helpmeet to her husband in his pastorate of 36 years at Eaton, Canada East. Mr. Sherrill was a graduate of Dartmouth College and of Andover Theological Seminary, and the evening of his life was spent in Lee, Mass. He d. June 13, 1877. She d. July 21, 1885. Ch.: (1) Sarah Andrews Sherrill, of Lee, Mass., b. Oct. 8, 1839; m. Mar. 15, 1887, William E. Bullock, of New York City. Mr. Bullock was a lawyer, and was connected with the Law Library of New York in a clerical capacity. He d. June 28, 1899. Mrs. Bullock resides in Lee. (2) Edwin Nathaniel Sherrill, of Lexington, Neb., b. Feb. 7, 1841; m. June 15, 1880, Stella C., dau. of Henry L. Smith, of Lee. Ch.: (a) Edwin Roberts, b. Apr. 18, 1881. (b) Alvan Foote, and (c) Mary Stella, b. Apr. 20, 1883. Mrs. Sherrill d. May 1, 1883. Mr. Sherrill was formerly engaged in the manufacture of shoes in Newburyport, Mass., but on account of ill health went to Nebraska, where he is a successful farmer. (3) Alvan Foote Sherrill, D. D., of Lee, Mass., b. Dec. 24, 1842; m. 1st, Feb. 5, 1874, Mary S. Jones, of Omaha, Neb.; m. 2nd, Elizabeth Wilcox, of Wyoming, Ill., May, 1903. Dr. Sherrill is a graduate of McGill University at Montreal, and of Andover Theological Seminary. He has had several pastorates at Omaha, Atlanta, Ga., and Gatesburg, Ill., and occupied pulpits in many other States for longer or shorter periods. He decided to retire from the ministry, purchased a small farm at Lee, Mass., but he still accepts many urgent calls to supply vacant pulpits, and spends each winter in Atlanta, Ga., where he occupies a Professor's Chair in a College. (4) Horace Dyer Sherrill, of New York City, b. Oct. 24, 1844; m. Lillie Edith, dau. of James Mills Stewart, of Troy, N. Y., June 19, 1873. Ch.: (a) Charlotte Foote, b. New York, Nov. 10, 1875. (b) Sara Marguerite, b. New York, Mar. 18, 1879. (c) Henry Wilkes, b. New York, Aug. 14, 1880. (d) Edith Stewart, b. New York, Aug. 4, 1887. Mr. Sherrill is engaged in the manufacture of solid gold and onyx society emblems, and the patented Princess diamond initial ring, having a factory and lapidary at Newark, N. J. He has been successful in the business for over thirty years, and his customers are the leading jewelry houses in all large cities of the United States. (5) Henry Wilkes Sherrill, b. Nov. 11, 1846; d. in Troy, N. Y., Sept. 28, 1875.

2148. vi. JONATHAN, b. Lee, Mass., Dec. 5, 1812; m. Laura Howk, 3625-8.

TRUMAN S. FOOTE. No. 1229

SARAH SOPHIA (FOOTE) BECKWITH.   No. 2162

2149. vii. ELIZA, b. Apr. 3, 1815; m. Sept. 4, 1834, Andrew W. Wright, b. Nov. 14, 1808; d. in Waukau, Wis. She d. in Lee, Mass., Aug. 16, 1872.

2150. viii. HULDA JANE, b. Feb. 7, 1827; m. Aug. 5, 1844, Thomas Slade Morey, merchant; res., Canada East.

985. SYLVANUS FOOTE, (308, 92, 27, 9, 3,) b. Apr. 12, 1785; m. 1804, Abigail, dau. of Col. Jared Bradley, of Lee, Mass. He d. July 22, 1845. Res., Wellington, O.

2150¹. i. LUCIAN, b. Sept. 9, 1805.
2150². ii. FRANCIS, b. Apr. 3, 1807.
2150³. iii. EMILY, b. Feb. 15, 1809.
2150⁴. iv. ABIGAIL, b. May 19, 1813.
2150⁵. v. JARED B., b. May 10, 1815.
2150⁶. vi. CATHARINE M., b. Mar. 5, 1818.
2150⁷. vii. HENRY ALEXANDER, b. Aug. 20, 1822.

988. CALVIN FOOTE, (309, 92, 27, 9, 3,) b. Dec. 15, 1781; m. Nov. 27, 1806, Pheebe, dau. of Ebenezer and Mehitable West, b. Aug. 6, 1785; d. Dec. 9, 1861; he d. Aug. 10, 1863. Res., Lee, Mass.

2151. i. HARRIET, b. June 1, 1810.
2152. ii. LUCIUS, b. Jan. 15, 1812; m. Lura ———, 3629-31.
2153. iii. JERUSHA S., b. Feb. 4, 1815; m. 1835, Jonathan D. Hall.
2154. iv. MARY ANN, b. Apr. 11, 1818.
2155. v. JOEL WEST, b. Sept. 27, 1820; m. Catherine Matilda Valentine, 3632-3¹.
2156. vi. EBENEZUR, b. Sept. 27, 1825.

992. ERASTUS FOOTE, (309, 92, 27, 9, 3,) b. Sept. 4, 1795; m. Jan., 1819, Fanny Jones. He lived in Rochester, N. Y., from 1847 to 1856.

2157. i. WILLIAM A., b. Sept. 20, 1821; res., Rochester, N. Y., in 1855, and New York City.
2158. ii. CHARLES S., b. Oct. 8, 1823; m. Jemima S. Bevin, 3633-43.
2159. iii. JOSEPHENE, b. Dec. 18, 1828.
2160. iv. HOMER, b. Aug. 13, 1832; m.; enlisted as First Lieutenant of Co. I, 13th Regt. N. Y. Vols., Apr., 1861; mustered out May 13, 1863; re-enlisted as First Lieutenant of Co. B, same regiment, July 9, 1863; made Captain of Co. C, Dec. 5, 1864, and discharged 1865.
2161. v. ISABELLA, b. May 8, 1837.

993. FENNER FOOTE, (309, 92, 27, 9, 3,) b. Oct. 10, 1798; m. Jan. 7, 1825, Cynthia Ann Lester, of Chatham, N. Y. She d. Feb. 29, 1835; m. 2nd, May, 1836, Almira Wright; he d. May 14, 1864. Res., Lee, Mass.

2162. i. SARAH SOPHIA, b. Mar. 22, 1826, Lee, Mass.; m. Nov. 2, 1847, in Rainbow, Ct., Charles Walton Beckwith, of Greenport, L. I. He was b. Greenport, L. I., Apr., 1820; card, clothing, and hand cards manufacturer. He d. Jan. 18, 1898, in Stafford Springs, Ct.; she d. Oct. 22, 1905, in Stafford Springs. Ch., all b. at Rainbow, Ct.: (1) Mary Lester Beckwith, b. Apr. 2, 1852; m. Sept. 5, 1877, at Stafford Springs, Frederick James, son of James and Jane Chandler, of England. He was b. at Stroud, Eng., Jan. 24, 1844. Ch., all b. at Stafford Springs: (a) Esther

Janet Chandler, b. Aug. 14, 1878; m. Apr. 25, 1900, Walter
Bruce, son of Daniel Shephard Robinson, of Palmyra, Me. Ch.:
(i) Dorothy Chandler Robinson, b. at New Haven, Ct., Jan. 27,
1901.   (ii) Janice B., b. Elmira, N. Y., Sept. 20, 1906.   (b)
Charles Frederick Chandler, b. Oct. 21, 1879.   (c) Maude Emily,
b. Aug. 21, 1882; m. Nov. 8, 1906, Earl R. Hall, of Simsbury,
Ct.   (d) James Beckwith, b. July 26, 1883; d. Aug. 15, 1884.
(e) Forrest, b. May 28, 1886; d. Aug. 16, 1886.   (f) Mary Foote
Chandler, b. Nov. 3, 1889.   (2) Martha Rebecca Beckwith, b.
Apr. 10, 1854; m. June 25, 1878, James Bliss, son of Daniel
Erskine Burbank, of Longmeadow, Mass. Ch., all b. at Long-
meadow, Mass.: (a) Grace Beckwith Burbank, b. Mar. 29,
1879; d. Apr. 3, 1907.   (b) Eunice Bliss, b. Nov. 9, 1880.   (c)
Daniel Erskine, b. May 29, 1882.   (d) Lulu Lester, b. May 24,
1883.   (e) Laura Colton, b. May 27, 1885.   (f) Rebecca Foote
Burbank, b. June 26, 1886; d. Nov. 2, 1886.   (3) Georgia Sophia,
b. Nov. 12, 1855. Res., Stafford Springs, Ct.   (4) Charles
Fenner Beckwith, b. June 8, 1858; m. 1st, Sept. 1, 1885, Edith
G., dau. of Luther F. Snow, of Palmer, Mass. She was b. Mar.
14, 1863, at Wales, Mass.; d. Dec. 13, 1899, in Stafford Springs,
Ct.; m. 2nd, June 12, 1901, Alice Knowlton, dau. of James
Chamberlin, of Stafford Springs. Mr. Beckwith is a card, clothing,
and hand cards manufacturer, as was his father. Ch., all b. in
Stafford Springs, Ct.: (a) Malcolm Snow Beckwith, b. Jan. 27,
1889.   (b) Louise Foote Beckwith, b. Mar. 24, 1894.   (c) Gertrude Beckwith, b. Apr. 15, 1902; d. Oct. 18, 1902.   (d) Charlotte Knowlton Beckwith, b. Jan. 25, 1904.   (5) Katharine Annie
Beckwith, b. Feb. 18, 1862; m. June 6, 1888, Timothy Chauncey,
son of Calvin Tiffany, of So. Manchester, Ct. He was b. Bark-
hamsted, Ct., May 2, 1862; graduated from the N. Y. College of
Dentistry, Mar. 14, 1894, D. D. S., and is now practising at 1496
Bedford Ave., Brooklyn, N. Y. Ch.: (a) Ruth Katharine Tiffany,
b. Willimantic, Ct., Dec. 19, 1893. (6) Rose Cynthia Foote Beckwith,
b. Dec. 12, 1866; m. Oct. 14, 1896, John Howard, son of John
Reade Tracy, of Lisbon, Ct. Res., Jewett City, Ct.

2163. ii.   CATHRINE, b. Aug. 27, 1828; d. unm.
2164. iii.   LESTER SYLVESTER, b. Feb. 5, 1830; m. Maria A. Williams,
              3635.
2165. iv.   GEORGE WASHINGTON, b. Nov. 27, 1831; m. Melissa J. Cooper,
              3636-7.
2166. v.   CHARLES H., b. Jan. 20, 1833; m. ——. Ch.: Dau., res. Bristol, Ct.
              Both d. in Minneapolis, Minn.
2167. vi.   CYNTHIA ANN, b. Feb. 29, 1835; m. Sept. 11, 1860, at Schenec-
              tady, N. Y., Joseph M. Smith. Res., Bloomfield, Ct. No ch.
2168. vii.   VOLNEY, b. Aug. 25, 1838; unm.
2169. viii. VIRGINIA E., b. Apr. 29, 1840; unm.
2170. ix.   ALPHONSO, b. July 16, 1842; m.; 2 ch. He went West. Nothing
              further known.
2171. x.   LESTER E., b. Apr. 10, 1845; no ch.

    995. CYRUS FOOTE, (309, 92, 27, 9, 3,) b. June 18, 1800, at Lee, Mass.;
m. Res., Peoria, Ill.

2171¹. i. MARIA, b.

997. THOMAS FOOTE, (311, 92, 27, 9, 3,) b. May 21, 1788; m. Mar. 12, 1812, Dama Perry, of Lee, Mass. She d. 1866. He d. July 31, 1856. Res., Dover, Ohio.

2172. i. SEMANTHA, b. Sept. 30, 1812; d. Oct. 28, 1813.

2173. ii. DAVID, b. July 18, 1814; m. Abigail Crans, 3638-41.

2174. iii. LYMAN PERRY, b. Mar. 22, 1817; m. Ruth B. Smith and Rebecca E. Tiedeman, 3642-7.

2175. iv. THOMAS, b. Mar. 29, 1819; m. May, 1840, Candace E. Park, 3648-50.

2176. v. TEMPERANCE R., b. Dec. 29, 1826; m. May 11, 1845, James M. Gardner, of Ramsey, Ill. She was a school teacher at Dover, Ohio. He was b. at Watertown, N. Y., Dec. 22, 1819; d. June 20, 1898. Ch.: (1) Mary A., b. Apr. 16, 1846, Dover, O.; m. Oct. 21, 1875, Isaac Traizer, Georgetown, Ill.; ed. at Cleveland, O. Music teacher; Methodist. Ch.: (a) George I., b. Mar. 31, 1878. She d. Apr. 4, 1878. (2) George W., b. Jan. 27, 1848, at Dover, O. Res., Ramsey, Ill.; m. Mar. 6, 1895, Florence Ballard, at Blenheim, Ontario, Canada. Ed. Cleveland, O., and Jamestown, N. Y. He was a farmer; Methodist. She was the dau. of Austin Ballard, of Norwich, Canada, and was b. Nov. 22, 1865. Ch.: (a) Wilfred Austin, b. June 6, 1896. (b) George Clifford, b. Apr. 12, 1898. (3) Dewitt C., b. Dec. 9, 1851; d. Aug., 1852. (4) Emma T., b. July 22, 1853, at Cleveland, O. Res., Ramsey, Ill.; m. Aug. 27, 1868, at Lexington, N. Y., John C. Martin. Ed. Cleveland, O., and Jamestown, N. Y. He was b. July 17, 1826, Williamsport, Pa., and d. July 31, 1892. Ch.: (a) John L., b. July 24, 1870; d. May 16, 1872. (b) Temperance R., b. Feb. 10, 1872; d. Oct. 3, 1876. (c) James M., b. Oct. 4, 1873. (d) George, b. Oct. 16, 1875; d. Oct. 17, 1875. (e) Calvin, b. Sept. 8, 1878. (f) Benjamin T., b. Aug. 30, 1880. (g) Thomas F., b. Sept. 16, 1882. (h) Lela Octavia, b. Sept. 17, 1886; d. Dec. 6, 1891. (5). Cora E., b. Oct. 8, 1855; d. Aug., 1856. (6) Susie, b. July 29, 1858; d. June 16, 1884. (7) Minnie, b. Jan. 25, 1860; d. June 15, 1878. (8) Lena, b. June 12, 1864. Res., Ramsey, Ill.; m. Aug. 14, 1883, William Hennion, at Vandalia, Ill. He was b. Aug. 11, 1859, near Pittsburgh, Pa. Ch.: (a) Thomas J., b. Jan. 1, 1886; d. Mar. 11, 1888. (b) Charles, b. Nov. 8, 1887. (c) Halford H., b. Jan. 23, 1891. (d) Henrietta, b. July 7, 1895.

999. SILAS FOOTE, (311, 92, 27, 9, 3,) b. Aug. 18, 1791; m. Aug. 4, 1822, Emeline Clark Smith. Res., Rockford, O. He was killed by lightning, July 14, 1828, in Dover, O. She d. May 28, 1882, in Melrose, Minn.

2177. i. SOLOMON, b. May 31, 1823; m. Adaline D. Stocking, 3651-58.

2178. ii. CAROLINE, b. Feb., 1825. Res., Cleveland, O.; m. Rev. Wm. H. Seely. Res. (1906), in Cleveland, O. Ch.: (1) Carrie.

2179. iii. SILAS, b. May 11, 1826; m. Julia Ann Bassett, 3659-64.

1003. RANSON FOOTE, (311, 92, 27, 9, 3,) b. Feb. 15, 1803; m. Mar. 28, 1824, Catharine Porter. She was b. Nov. 16, 1806, in Salem, Ct.; d. Apr. 6, 1886. He d. Oct. 11, 1846. Res., Dover, O.

2180. i. LAVIAS, b. May 16, 1825; m. Fayetta Lilly, 3665-68.

2181. ii. BETSEY HAMLINE, b. Oct. 30, 1826; d. Aug. 3, 1828.

2182. iii.   RANSON L., b. July 23, 1828; m. Julia B. Farr, 3669-75.
2183. iv.   ANGELINE PORTER, b. Apr. 30, 1830; m. Joseph E. LaVayea.
             He was b. Aug. 8, 1819. She d. Jan. 7, 1890, Cleveland, O. Ch.:
             (1) Ellen Statira, b. Sept. 17, 1847; m. Isaac M. Gilette. Ch.:
             (a) Dau., b.; d. in infancy. (b) John A., b.; res., New York. (2)
             Melissa Angeline, b. May 20, 1850; m. Feb. 15, 1871, at Cleveland,
             O., Major John G. Hamilton. He was b. Warrenpoint, Ireland,
             Oct. 22, 1844; is an Attorney. Ch.: (a) Helen Anne Noble
             Hamilton, b. Lexington, Ky., Jan. 3, 1872; is the first woman
             graduate from the Law School of the University of North
             Dakota; admitted to the Bar, June, 1905; is a practising Attorney
             at Grand Forks, North Dakota; unm. (b) Hasting Henry Hamil-
             ton, b. Dec. 14, 1874, at Cleveland, O. Served from May 23,
             1898, to Sept. 25, 1899, in Co. D, 1st N. Dak. Vols., with the
             U. S. Vol. Troops in the War with Spain. On above date the
             regiment was honorably discharged. Res., Grand Forks, N.
             Dakota; unm. (3) Henry Ely, b. Mar. 2, 1852; m. May 29, 1876,
             Mary Elizabeth White; res., Santa Monica, Cal. Ch.: (a) Grace
             White, b. Mar. 20, 1880. (4) George Leslie, b. Feb. 8, 1854; m.
             Victoria McKelvey; res., 2433 Dupont Ave., S. Minneapolis, Minn.
             Ch.: (a) Corinne, b.; d. in infancy. (b) George Leslie, b. (c)
             Florence, b. (d) Doris, b. (e) Marjorie, b. (5) Charles Victor,
             b. Oct. 21, 1858; m. Emma Comstock; m. 2nd, June 30, 1906,
             Mary Louise Chapin Fuller; res., 311 Electric Bldg., Cleveland,
             O. (6) Arthur Leon, b. Mar. 11, 1863; m. Lulu Day, at Cleve-
             land, O. She d.; he d. Mar. 18, 1904. Ch.: (a) Ruth, b. Cleveland,
             Aug. 27, 1889. Res. with her aunt, Beach Park, O. (7) Berton
             Ransom, b. July 5, 1867; res., Seattle, Wash.; unm.
2184. v.   LAURA ALLINE, b. in Dover, O., Jan. 14, 1832; m. in Barea,
             O., Sept. 27, 1855, Alfred Goodwin Bright. He was b. in New
             York State, July 7, 1832; d. Sept. 9, 1875. Ch.: (1) Fred Eugene,
             b. Richland Center, Wis., Oct. 30, 1856; m. Mar. 2, 1902, Mame
             Bement, New York City. (2) Louella Irene, b. Richland, Wis.,
             Aug. 25, 1858; m. 1st, May, 1878, in Cleveland, O., Henry Way-
             land Taft, of St. Louis, Mo. He d. June, 1883, Evansville, Ind.;
             m. 2nd, Dec. 24, 1892, George Sibley, of Los Angeles, Cal. Ch.:
             (a) Irene Belle Taft, b. Jan. 1, 1883, St. Louis, Mo.; m. Nov.,
             1903, Howard Lorenz; res., Ocean Park, Cal. Ch.: (i) Howard
             Taft Lorenz, b. Mar. 5, 1906, Venice, America. (3) Laura Belle
             Bright, b. Jan. 14, 1860, at Richland, Wis.; m. Dec. 25, 1884, in
             Cleveland, O., Charles W. Damerel, of St. Paul, Minn. Ch.: (a)
             Bright Spencer Damerel, b. Nov. 13, 1886, Wahpeton, N. Dak.
             (b) Verner R., b. Nov. 1, 1888; d. Nov. 5, 1894, at Los Angeles,
             Cal. (4) Hoyt Verner Bright, b. Dover, O., May 23, 1863; m.
             June 16, 1886, Lillian Oviatt, of Cleveland, O. (5) Linna May
             Bright, b. Dover, O., Aug. 5, 1867; m. June, 1894, Howard
             Aylsworth, of Los Angeles, Cal. (6) Eunice Ann Bright, b. New
             Lisbon, O., Apr. 10, 1871; m. Aug. 2, 1898, Budd Grey, of Lon-
             don, England. Ch.: (a) Gwendolen Grey, b. Dec. 26, 1900, in
             London, England.

2185.   vi.   EMELINE P., b. July 25, 1834; m. July 17, 1872, Thomas Lig-
gett, of Cleveland, O. He d. Feb. 23, 1902. Ch.: (1) Mary Emma
Liggett. (2) Minnie Ella Ligget (twins), b. Sept. 16, 1873.
Minnie d. Oct. 12, 1874. Res., Bay Village, N. Dover, O.

2186.   vii.   ASAHEL P., b. May 25, 1836; m. Anna Sutherland, 3676-78.

2187.   viii. CATHRINE P., b. Mar. 16, 1838; res., N. Dover, O., with Henry;
unm.

2188.   ix.   MARIETTA ROBINSON, b. Mar. 17, 1840; m. Dec. 22, 1864,
David F. Miller. He was b. Nov. 6, 1841, in Avon, O. Res.,
537 E. Ocean Ave., Long Beach, Cal. Ch.: (1) Louis Everett
Miller, b. Dec. 10, 1866, in Sheffield, O.; m. July 25, 1894, Mary
Kramer. She was b. E. St. Louis, Ill., Aug. 21, 1864. Res.,
Annaheim, Cal. Ch.: (a) Edwin Louis Miller, b. in Annaheim,
Cal., Aug. 18, 1895. (2) Willard Earl Miller, b. Sheffield, O.,
Aug. 24, 1868; m. Jan. 10, 1906, Grace House. She was b.
Columbus, O., Jan. 31, 1880; res., Long Beach, Cal. (3) George
Irving, b. June 13, 1874, Dover, O. (4) Arthur Clair,
b. Mar. 29, 1876, Dover, O.

2189.   x.   STATIRA, b. Mar. 8, 1842; d. Mar. 28, 1845.

2190.   xi.   HENRY P., b. Apr. 21, 1844. He and Cathrine occupy the old
home at N. Dover, O., on the shore of Lake Erie. P. O., Bay
Village; unm.

2190¹. xii.   ABIGAIL S., b. Oct. 30, 1846; m. Aug. 1, 1865, Thomas L. Niles.
He was b. Nov. 23, 1832, in Vt. Was engineer in numerous
lumber mills in N. Y. State until the Civil War broke out. He
enlisted in the 9th Mich. Cav. Vols., being one of the first in
answer to the call for volunteers. He d. Jan. 2, 1881. Res.,
Waverly, Mich., Chestona and Moncelona, Pa. Ch.: (1) Seabert
H., b. Oct., 1871; d. June 16, 1872. (2) Claud E., b. 1869; m.
July 5, 1892, Anna Pettis; res., McBrain, Mich. Ch.: (a) Charles
E., b. Jan. 10, 1894. (b) Mildred, b. Oct. 6, 1896. (3) Levern
Niles, b. 1875; m. Sept. 13, 1902, Mae MacKenzie; res., Mackinaw
Mich. Ch.: (a) Iva Mae, b. Feb. 14, 1904. (b) Leona Kathleen,
b. June 27, 1905. (4) Charles M. Niles, b. July, 1876; m. Sept.
23, 1891, Alice Fredinburg. He was an engineer in the lumbering
mills. He d. Oct. 17, 1904; res., Mackinaw, Mich. (5) Rosa M.,
b. May 3, 1880; m. Apr. 14, 1896, William Roth, of Sherman,
Mich. He d. Oct. 4, 1904. Res., Close, Mich. Ch.: (a) Gleason
E. Roth, b. Apr. 9, 1899. (b) Ione Roth, b. Oct. 6, 1902. (c)
Evangeline Roth, b. Feb. 29, 1904.

1008.   LYMAN FOOTE, (312, 92, 27, 9, 3,) b. July 9, 1798; m. Oct. 1823,
Emily, dau. of Daniel Fairfield, of Stockbridge, Mass.; res., Lee, Mass.

2191.   i.   EDWARD, b. Oct. 12, 1824; m. Emily Curtis Chapin, 3679-82.

2192.   ii.   HARRIET, b. Sept. 10, 1828.

2193.   iii.   ELIZABETH, b. Nov. 25, 1833; d. Mar. 2, 1850, in Lee, Mass.

2194.   iv.   THERON LYMAN, b. July 9, 1835; m. Abigail Lucelia Langdon,
3683-5.

2195.   v.   EMILY FAIRFIELD, b. May 21, 1837, in Lee, Mass.; m. Sept. 23,
1868, James Watson, son of Joseph and Almira Bassett, of Lee.
He was b. in Lee, Nov. 16, 1829; d. Apr. 18, 1903, in Lee, Mass.
Ch.: (1) Isabella Dodge Bassett, b. Lee, Jan. 5, 1871; res., Lee,

Mass. (2) Nellie Foote Bassett, b. Lee, Feb. 12, 1872; m. Sept. 11, 1894, Edward Lawrence, son of Rev. Thomas D. and Amelia C. Murphy. He was b. Roxbury, Ct., Mar. 17, 1871. Ch.: (a) Duncan Bassett Murphy, b. July 5, 1895, in Lee, Mass.

1009. CHARLES FOOTE, (312, 92, 27, 9, 3,) b. May 12, 1800; m. 1831, Marcia, dau. of Samuel Hunter, of Otis, Mass. He d. Aug. 9, 1888, in Cleveland, O. She d. June 12, 1885; both buried in Woodlawn Cemetery, Cleveland. Res., Wellington, O.

2196. i.   LOUISA, b. 1833; m. Samuel Close, in Wellington, O.; d. Jan. 26, 1893, in Blue Earth, Minn. Ch.: (1) Benjamin, b.; res., Waterloo, Indiana; and 9 others.

2197. ii. WALTER BLAIR, b. Dec. 5, 1835; m. Jane Tanner, 3686-8.

2198. iii. JENNY, b. 1837; m. Walker McClain; she d. Aug., 1895; buried in Galion, Ohio. Ch.

1011. ASAHEL FOOTE, (312, 92, 27, 9, 3,) b. Dec. 16, 1804; m. 1830, Mary Smedly, of Williamstown, Mass. He was a graduate of Williams College, 1827, and was a late Member of the Senate of the Legislature of Mass.; d. 1882.

2199. i.   HARRIET HILLSGROVE, b. Sept. 8, 1830; m. Nov. 17, 1853, Henry Hill, son of John and Ann (Osborn) Seys. He was b. at Ogdensburg, N. Y., Oct. 13, 1830, and d. June 17, 1904, at Springfield, O. She d. Apr. 27, 1876. Ch.: (1) Mary Ellen, b. Aug. 4, 1854; m. Nov. 23, 1875, Edwin D., son of Ezra and Sarah Martin (Buell) Buss. He was b. July 10, 1850. Res., Bakersfield, Cal. Ch.: (a) Harriet Foote Buss, b. Nov. 30, 1876. (b) Mabel Buell Buss, b. July 22, 1880. (2) John Henry Seys, b. May 30, 1857; d. June 5, 1864.

2200. ii. MARY HAINES, b. May 8, 1834. Res., Pasadena, Cal.

2201. iii. ELLEN MARIA, b. July 3, 1836; m. 1860, James Orton. He d. in 1877. Res., Sierra Madre, Cal. Ch.: (1) Anna B. Orton, b. June 23, 1862; res., Pasadena; unm. (2) Susan R. Orton, b. Jan. 27, 1865; res., Sierra Madre; unm. (3) Mary B. Orton, b. Nov. 4, 1866; d. 1885. (4) Albert L. Orton, b. Aug. 4, 1872.

2202. iv. CHARLES ROLLIN, b. June 2, 1838; m. Susan Cole. 3689-90.

2203. v.   KATHERINE L., b. Sept. 26, 1841; res., Pasadena, Cal.; unm.

1015. DR. JONATHAN FOOTE, (314, 92, 27, 9, 3,) b. in Cornwall, Vt., Oct. 31, 1804; m. Robina Dow. She was b. in Scotland; d. Sept. 3, 1884. He was a physician in Whitby, Canada, and Cleveland, O.

2204. i.   WILLIAM DOW, b. Jan. 22, 1836; m. Mary Frances Leggett, 3691-2.

2205. ii. HENRY SOLOMAN, b. ———; m. Harriet Eliza Clarke, 3693.

2206. iii. MARGARET ELIZA, b. ———; m. Sept. 28, 1864, Dr. Henry Warren; he d. July 11, 1872. Ch.: (1) William Limpson, b. Dec. 14, 1865. (2) Mary Ann Foote, b. June 17, 1867. (3) Henry Frank, b. July 24, 1872; all unm.

2206¹. iv. HELEN, b. ———; d. Sept., 1884; unm.

2207. v.   EMILY, b. Dec., 1853; unm. Res., North St., Toronto, Canada.

2208. vi. MARY ELSIE, b. ———; m. B. McQuay. Ch.: (1) Robina, b. (2) Florence, b. (3) Jonathan, b.

1016. LUCIUS ARCHIBALD FOOTE, (314, 92, 27, 9, 3,) b. Rutland, Vt.,
July 29, 1806; m. Apr. 19, 1831, Emily Pamelia Smith, of Addison, Vt. She d.
Jan. 16, 1879, in Port Henry, N. Y. He d. Dec. 22, 1870, in Port Henry, N. Y.

   2209. i.   HILAH ELIZA, b. June 2, 1832; m. Wallace Turner Foote, of
              Port Henry, N. Y. (See No. 2402 for complete family record.)
   2210. ii. MARY ELMINA, b. Apr. 24, 1835; m. Frederick D. Hodgman,
              of Fort Edward, N. Y. He d. Dec. 7, 1873; m. 2nd, Aug. 18,
              1880, Rev. Jeremiah F. Yates, of Fort Edward, N. Y. He d.
              Nov. 10, 1901. Res., Ft. Edward, N. Y.
   2211. iii. SOLOMON S., b. Mar. 18, 1841; d. Nov. 3, 1846.
   2212. iv. SEWARD ALLEN, b. May 31, 1844; m. Flora E. Hall, 3694-9.

1019. JOHN FOOTE, (320, 97, 27, 9, 3,) b. Oct. 15, 1801; m. Apr. 30, 1831,
Georgianna Hyslop Bebee, dau. of Major Ebenezer Bebee, of New York, N. Y. She
was b. May 4, 1811, on Governor's Island. Res., Batavia, N. Y.

   2212¹. i.   ELIZABETH, b. Oct. 18, 1833.
   2213. ii. GEORGE LAY, b. Nov. 13, 1835.
   2214. iii. ROBERT HYSLOP, b. Sept. 17, 1837.
   2214¹. iv. JOHN BEBEE, b. Aug. 20, 1839.
   2214². v. GEORGIANNA, b. Aug. 20, 1841.
   2214³. vi. OLIVE LAY, b. Sept. 29, 1844.
   2214⁴. vii. FREDERICK SPAULDING, b. May 24, 1848.

1046. STEPHEN FOOTE, (339, 104, 28, 9, 3,) b. May 9, 1780; m. Clarissa, wid.
of Joseph (1062). She d. Nov. 11, 1844. He d. Mar. 28, 1848. Res., Colchester,
Ct.

   2215. i.   HENRY, b. May 22, 1818; m. Mary Ann Lamb, 3700-¾.
   2216. ii. FRANCIS J., b. Sept. 19, 1825; d. Oct. 1, 1893; m. Joseph A.
              Foote. Ch.: (1) George W., b. 1850; d. 1903. Ch.: (a) Amelia
              S., m. Lawrence ———. Ch.: (1) Laura, b. 1892. (ii) Lawrence, b.
              1896.

1049. ERASTUS FOOTE, (339, 104, 28, 9, 3,) b. Mar. 25, 1791; m. Sept. 1,
1816, Betsy Crouch, of Hebron, Ct.

   2217. i.   WILLIAM, b. May 19, 1817; m. Emeline Brown, 3701-5.
   2218. ii. REBECCA E., b. July 6, 1818.
   2219. iii. ALBERT, b. July 22, 1821; m. Mary Ann Chase, 3706-10.
   2220. iv. JOAN G., b. Dec. 1, 1822.
   2221. v. ELIZABETH C., b. Sept. 13, 1826.
   2222. vi. ERASTUS, b. Jan. 17, 1832; d. Apr. 30, 1834.
   2223. vii. EMILY J., b. Sept. 9, 1835; m. David B. Strong, of Colchester,
              Ct. Ch.: (1) Herbert E. Strong, b. Hebron, Ct., Oct. 12, 1864;
              m. Oct. 20, 1891, Jennie S. Lounsbury, of Hartford, Ct. Ch.: (a)
              Helen L. Strong, b. Hartford, Ct., May 23, 1893. (2) Erastus
              L. Strong, b. Hebron, Ct., Jan. 6, 1866; m. Mary Davis, of Strong
              Creek, Ct. Res., Westerly, R. I. Ch.: (a) Mabel, b. (b) Clara,
              b. (c) Herbert, b. (d) Avis, b. (e) Lester, b.

1050. RALPH C. FOOTE, (339, 104, 28, 9, 3,) b. Aug. 11, 1793; m. Amelia
(No. 871), dau. of Roger Foote, of Marlborough, Ct. Res., Colchester, Ct.

   2224. i.   JANE E., b. Apr. 30, 1820.
   2225. ii. HORACE, b. Nov. 14, 1822; m. Lucy A. Webster, 3711-2.
   2226. iii. EUNICE A., b. Mar. 1, 1824.

2227. iv. SARAH L., b. May 10, 1826.

2228. v. RALPH CLARK, b. Oct. 22, 1828; m. Lydia Newton Harvey, 3713-20.

2229. vi. CAROLINE, b. Apr. 9, 1832; m. Jan. 29, 1856, David Hale, son of Henry and Melissa (Hale) McCall. He was b. Nov. 26, 1828. Ch.: (1) Charles Clark, b. Nov. 7, 1857. (2) Edward Hale, b. Feb. 10, 1868.

2229¹. vii. MARY E., b. July 6, 1858.

1056. JEREMIAH FOOTE, (341, 104, 28, 9, 3,) b. Aug. 3, 1798; m. 1st, Betsy Little. She d.; m. 2nd.

2229². i. CHILD, by his last wife.

1062. JOSEPH FOOTE, (347, 105, 28, 9, 3,) b. Nov. 18, 1788; m. Clarissa Taylor, dau. of Capt. Joseph Taylor, of Colchester, Ct. He d. Jan. 10, 1813. She m. 2nd, Stephen Foote (No. 1046), of Colchester, Ct. She d. Nov. 11, 1844.

2230. i. GUY, b. 1800; had ch. Res., Alabama.

2231. ii. BETSEY, b. 1802; m. Nov. 24, 1824, James H. Pease. Ch.: (1) Ellen A., b. Oct. 10, 1825; m. ——— Benton. Ch.: (a) Grace, b. (b) Clara, b. (2) Frances F., b. May 29, 1843; m. May 21, 1870, Peter Anderson. Ch.: (a) James H., b. Feb. 6, 1870; m. Sept. 18, 1901. Ch.: (i) Andrew B., b. Oct. 21, 1903. (b) Peter, b. June 11, 1877; d. June 13, 1877. (c) Wilhelm E., b. Jan. 15, 1883; d. Aug. 14, 1880. (d) George F., b. Jan. 1, 1883. (e) Charles W., b. May 24, 1887.

2232. iii. GAD C., b. 1804; m. Feb. 27, 1828, Mary Foote (No. 1061).

2233. iv. DAN, b. Feb. 27, 1808; m. Eliza Foote and Lucretia Kellogg, 3721-3.

2234. v. EMILY, b. May 2, 1812; m. Dea. William, son of Joseph Ives. She d. Apr. 23, 1896. Ch.: (1) Frank F., b. Sept. 29, 1838; d. Dec., 1875. (2) Jane K., b. Jan. 3, 1840; m. Nov. 10, 1896, Frank B. Taylor, of Colchester, Ct. (3) George H., b. Sept. 10, 1844; m. Hannah Clift, of New Haven, Ct. Res., Mystic, Ct.

1069. SALMON FOOTE, (347, 105, 28, 9, 3,) b. Colchester, Ct., Mar. 6, 1792; m. Nov. 15, 1814, Margaret, dau. of Daniel Taylor, of Colchester, Ct. She was b. June 23, 1794; d. Oct. 9, 1857; he d. May 27, 1882. Res., Colchester, Ct.

2235. i. DANIEL T., b. July 25, 1816; m. Martha Burr, 3724-6.

2236. ii. EDWARD Y., b. Dec. 2, 1817; d. Feb. 8, 1819.

2237. iii. EDWARD Y., b. May 31, 1819; m. Lucy A. Mason and Mary Clift, 3727-8.

2238. iv. JOSEPH A., b. Jan. 18, 1821; m. Frances Foote, 3729.

2239. v. JOHN C., b. June 28, 1823; m. Sarah Clark, 3730-2.

2240. vi. MARGARET, b. Dec. 28, 1824; m. Carleton Foote, of Great Barrington, Mass. She d. Mar. 9, 1904. Ch.: 4. Res., Mystic, Ct.

2241. vii. LAURA ELLEN, b. Apr. 15, 1826; m. Amos M. Keeler, of Brooklyn, N. Y.; d. Oct. 27, 1903, in Mystic, Ct. Res., Mystic, Ct. Ch.: (1) Edward F., m. Mary Hannah Packer, of Mystic, Ct., and has 2 ch. (2) Fanny, m. Nelson Baker.

2242. viii. SALMON C., b. Jan. 23, 1828; m. Julia A. Williams, 3733-40.

2243. ix. DIANNA, b. Oct. 12, 1829; d. Jan. 11, 1831.

2244. x. ELIZABETH CAROLINE, b. Mar. 5, 1831; m. Jan. 13, 1858, at Brooklyn, N. Y., Joseph Stanton Williams, b. Aug. 12, 1834, Mystic, Ct. No ch.

2245. xi. FRANK, b. Aug. 14, 1832; m. Lydia Crippen, 3741-3.
2246. xii. CHARLES, b. Feb. 1, 1834; d. Dec. 13, 1840.
2247. xiii. JANE, b. Sept. 11, 1835; d. May 18, 1837.

1081. HARVEY FOOTE, (362, 113, 36, 10, 3,) b. New Haven, Vt., Mar. 13, 1810; m. Dec. 4, 1827, at New Haven, Vt., Julia M., dau. of Samuel Sumner, of Middlebury, Vt. She was b. Middlebury, Vt., Aug. 11, 1809; d. Jan. 31, 1898, at Jackson, Mich. He d. Nov. 6, 1869; res., Jackson, Mich.
    2248. i. ORLANDER, b. Jan. 18, 1827; d. Sept. 12, 1892.
    2249. ii. WEALTHY, b. Apr. 15, 1833; d. Dec. 2, 1854.
    2250. iii. HARRIET, b. Feb. 26, 1835; d. Mar. 8, 1847.
    2251. iv. HENRY, b. Mar. 31, 1844; d. Apr. 5, 1844.
    2252. v. BYRON, b. June 12, 1845; res., Jackson, Mich.

1082. MANFRED C. FOOTE, (362, 113, 36, 10, 3,) b. Sept. 26, 1816; m. Sept. 17, 1835, Rhoda A., dau. of David Smith, of Waterford, Vt. She was b. Mar. 12, 1812; d. 1878, in Middlebury, Vt. He d. 1892, in Middlebury, Vt.
    2253. i. HENRY S., b. Aug. 30, 1837; m. Elizabeth A., dau. of William Davis, of Providence, R. I. Graduated at Middlebury College, 1857. Practised law in Middlebury until 1867. Was State's Attorney for three terms. Res., Providence, R. I., Brooklyn, N. Y. Practising law in New York City until 1883. Res. in Boston and vicinity, Mass., since 1893. No ch.
    2254. ii. EMMA, b. Mar. 12, 1840; m. Dec. 25, 1865, William H., son of Judge Harvey Button, of Wallingford, Vt.; moved to East Saginaw, Mich. He was a lawyer; graduated at Middlebury College, 1861. He d. 1870, at Middlebury, Vt. She d. Dec. 13, 1899. Ch.: (1) Frederick H., b. May 3, 1869. (2) William H., b. Mar. 23, 1871; m. Herrika M. Stevens, Aug. 16, 1898; both graduated at Middlebury College, 1890. Are practising law at No. 7 Nassau St., New York.
    2255. iii. FREDERICK MANFRED, b. Middlebury, Vt., Nov. 11, 1849; m. Frances Langworthy, 3744-5.

1090. AUGUSTUS FOOTE, (367, 114, 36, 10, 5,) b. Dec. 18, 1808; m. Apr. 15, 1825, Philena Tracy. She was b. Dec. 10, 1803; d. Aug. 29, 1876, in Morris, N. Y. He d. Mar. 5, 1868. Res., Butternuts, N. Y.
    2256. i. REUBEN, b. Mar. 11, 1826; m. Maria Benson, of Laurence, N. Y. He d. 1899 at Morris, N. Y.; p. s.
    2257. ii. ZEPHENIAH, b. June 9, 1827; m. Desire Brown, 4945-6.
    2258. iii. LUCIUS, b. Dec. 18, 1829; m. Lavina Cass and Amanda M. Clark, 4947-49.
    2259. iv. DELILAH, b. Dec. 12, 1831; m. 1851, Ransom C. Cox. She d. 1907, in Norwich, N. Y. Ch.: (1) William A., b. 1855; d. 1874, at Norwich, N. Y. (2) Phoebe M., b. 1856. Res., Norwich, N. Y. (3) James L., b. 1864; res., Milwaukee.
    2260. v. MOSES W., b. June 8, 1833; m. Mary Quimby, 4950.
    2261. vi. DANIEL H., b. Aug. 15, 1834; m. Catharine Crawford, 4951-3.
    2262. vii. SEDATE, b. June 29, 1836; m. Elizabeth Taylor, 4954-5.
    2263. viii. MARY ANN, b. Jan. 27, 1838; m. Mar. 13, 1859, Josiah Withey, of Morris, N. Y. She d. Oct. 7, 1859; p. s.
    2264. ix. ALBERT, b. Jan. 15, 1840; m. Amelia Palmatier, 4956-9.

2265. x. CYNTHIA M., b. Jan. 26, 1842; m. Jan. 1, 1861, Amasa Winton. She d. Mar. 5, 1868, at Morris, N. Y. Ch.: (1) Lysander S. Winton, b. 1861; m. Anna Dilworth; res., Morris, N. Y.

2266. xi. LOUISA, b. May 19, 1844; d. Apr. 3, 1874, Morris, N. Y.; unm.

1093. WILLIAM FOOTE, (367, 114, 36, 10' 3,) b. Aug. 23, 1820; m. July 4, 1838, Hannah Ann Jean. Res. Butternuts, N. Y.

2267. i. JOHN JAY, b. Sept. 27, 1839; m. Abbie S. Johnson and Emeline E. Perry, 4960-2.

2268. ii. RANSON ALLEN, b. July 22, 1845; res., Norwich, N. Y.; unm.

2269. iii. ALVAH EUGENE, b. Dec. 24, 1847; m. Emily Porter, 4963.

2269¹. iv. LEONA L., b. New Lisbon, N. Y., July 27, 1859; m. Jan. 1, 1877, at New Lisbon, Geo. B. Brooks, of Edmeston, N. Y.; res., Bells, Tenn. Ch.: (1) Ellen L., b. Oct. 11, 1877, at New Lisbon; m. Feb. 3, 1897, F. J. Vanbott, of Unadilla, N. Y. Ch.: (a) L. J. Vanbott, b. Jan. 1, 1898, in Unadilla, N. Y. (b) Leona M. Vanbott, b. June 1, 1902. (2) Anna May, b. New Lisbon, Aug. 22, 1879; m. Sept. 10, 1902, Stanley Root, of Wellsbridge, N. Y. (3) Leon R., b. New Lisbon, Dec. 3, 1883. (4) Geo. M., b. July 25, 1885, at Oneonta, N. Y. (5) Fay F., b. Bells, Tenn., Feb. 9, 1906.

1095. ROGER FOOTE, (370, 115, 37, 10, 3,) b. Dec. 27, 1766; m. Rhoda Dutton, dau. of John Dutton, of New Hartford, Ct. He settled in Torringford, Ct., and removed to Norfolk, Ct., where he res. a few years; removed to Morgan, O., where he d. Dec., 1844. She d. 1845.

2270. i. SAMUEL, b. ———; m. 4963¹.

2271. ii. ROGER, b. ———; m. Chloe Mather, 4964-7².

2272. iii. ROSWELL, b. ———; m. Sabra E. Holden, 4968-9.

2273. iv. JOHN, b. ———; m. 4970-70².

2274. v. ELIHU, b.

2275. vi. LAUREN, b. ———; m. Abigail Moses and Cornelia Ballard, 4971-5.

2276. vii. JULIUS, b. ———; m. Mary Hazet, 4976-7.

2277. viii. EMELINE, b.

1096. COL. SAMUEL FOOTE, (370, 115, 37, 10, 3,) b. Mar. 27, 1771; m. Feb. 17, 1794, Lucy, dau. of Elisah and Betsy (Ledlie) Lord, of Hartford, Ct. He d. Oct., 1848, in Torrington, Ct.

2278. i. LUCY C., b. Nov., 1795; m. Dea. Amasa Scoville, of Norfolk, Ct.

2279. ii. SAMUEL HART, b. Jan., 1797; m. Delia, dau. of Capt. Elihu Moore, of Torrington, Ct.

2280. iii. JULIA E., b. Jan. 11, 1807; m. Aug. 19, 1828, William Leach, of Torringford, Ct.

2281. iv. CORNELIA M., b. Mar. 22, 1809; m. Elias Hatch, of Winchester, Ct.

2282. v. WILLIAM, b. Apr. 11, 1811; m. Alvira Belden, of Wethersfield, Ct.

2283. vi. CLARISSA A., b. June 20, 1813; m. Thomas Matthews, of Torrington, Ct. She d. Aug. 4, 1848.

2284. vii. LUCIUS, b. June 22, 1815; m. Clarissa Wickwire, dau. of Oliver Wickwire, of Canaan, O.

1097. TIMOTHY FOOTE, (374, 115, 37, 10, 3,) b. Mar. 13, 1773; bap. Mar. 22, 1773; m. Apr. 28, 1797, Lucy, dau. of Jonathan Fiske, of Mayfield, N. Y. Res., Johnstown, N. Y. Of 11 ch. all lived to grow up and marry and all had ch. One thing worthy of mention is that the five brothers never drank, used profane language, or tobacco in any way. They were all Christian men, and all lived to be over 70 years old. They all owned farms within a few miles of Skaneateles. In 1806 Mr. Foote removed to Skaneateles, N. Y., where he d. Nov. 12, 1831.

2285. i. HULDAH, b. Johnstown, N. Y., Feb. 23, 1800; m. John Dimmock, of Fairfield, Ohio.

2286. ii. CLARISSA, b. Johnstown, N. Y., Dec. 17, 1801; m. John Insko, of Greenfield, Ohio.

2287. iii. HANNAH, b. Mayfield, N. Y., Aug. 18, 1804; m. William Cherry, of Fairfield, Ohio.

2288. iv. STEPHEN, b. Skaneateles, N. Y., Mar. 11, 1807; m. Nancy Watson and Elenor Tenure, 3746-9.

2289. v. RUTH, b. Skaneateles, N. Y., Apr. 22, 1809; m. Darius Cherry, of Hartland, Ohio.

2290. vi. ASA CHILDS, b. Skaneateles, N. Y., June 20, 1811; m. Lydia Hollister, 3750-6.

2291. vii. PERRY, b. Skaneateles, N. Y., Dec. 24, 1814; m. Lodema Benedict, 3757-60.

2292. viii. ABIGAIL, b. Dec. 19, 1817; m. Sept. 21, 1842, Peter, son of Cyrus Howard, of Owasco, N. Y. He was b. Owasco, N. Y., Sept. 3, 1819; d. Oct. 29, 1894, at Owasco. She was educated at Skaneateles. Baptist. She d. Sept. 16, 1873. Ch.: (1) Addie R., Howard, b. Dec. 19, 1843. (2) Emily Howard, b. July 4, 1847; d. Apr. 24, 1901. (3) Mary Jane Howard, b. Nov. 7, 1849. (4) Martha Howard, b. Apr. 7, 1854; d. Mar. 16, 1879. (5) George Washington Howard, b. Mar. 14, 1856; m. Oct. 29, 1884, Caroline Marion. Ch.: (a) Ethel Marion Howard, b. Sept. 24, 1885. (b) Vera Winchester Howard, b. Sept. 17, 1888.

2293. ix. WILLIAM, b. Skaneateles, N. Y., Aug. 30, 1819; m. Jane Stone, 3761-7.

2294. x. CHAUNCEY, b. Skaneateles, N. Y., Mar. 23, 1823; m. Charity Brinkerhoff, 3768-9.

2295. xi. CAROLINE, b. Skaneateles, N. Y., Feb. 1, 1827; res., Skaneateles, N. Y. Educated Aurora, N. Y. Baptist; m. 185—, Joseph W. Seccomb, at Sennett, N. Y.; d. Sept. 30, 1906. He was b. Dec. 6, 1823. Ch.: (1) Stella Lodema, b. Apr. 7, 1852. (2) Luella Adelaide, b. Jan. 24, 1865. (3) Joseph Charles, b. June 19, 1870.

1099. EBENEZER FOOTE, (374, 115, 37, 10, 3,) b. Mar. 12, 1778; bap. Mar. 22, 1778; m. Mar. 20, 1798, Lydia, dau. of Samuel Gage, of Johnstown, N. Y. She d. Aug. 10, 1842; m. 2nd, Elizabeth Reynolds. He d. N. Fairfield, O.

2296. i. SAMUEL, b. Dec. 22, 1798; m. Eliza Hunsiker, 3770-75.

2297. ii. BETSEY, b. Dec. 27, 1800; m. 1818, Spencer Baker, of No. Fairfield, O. Ch.: (1) Lydia, b. ———; m. Loren Barnes, of No. Fairfield. He d. in Chicago, Ill. (2) Lucinda, b. ———; m. John Smith; res., Hillsdale, Mich. (3) Lora, b. ———; m. ——— Hackett, No. Fairfield, O. (4) Lorintha, b. ———; m. Benjamin Statee, No. Fairfield; killed by a horse. (5) ———. (6) ———.

2298. iii.   ABIGAIL, b. Dec. 29, 1806; m. Elijah Price, No. Fairfield. Ch.: (1) Alexander, b. Feb. 29, 1826; m. Martha Ells, No. Fairfield; d. July 18, 1893. (2) Ebenezer, b. Oct. 3, 1827; m. Mary Kellogg, No. Fairfield; res., Rockford, Ill. (3) Sylvia J., b. Aug. 20, 1829; m. Charles Barnes. Ch.: (a) Charles, b. ———; d. Jan. 12, 1889. (4) William, b. Mar. 9, 1831; d. Apr. 28, 1831. (5) Elijah, b. Apr. 6, 1832; m. Harriet Place, of No. Fairfield. Ch.: (a) Elijah Place, b. (6) Mary, b. May 22, 1834; d. Dec. 23, 1837. (7) Louise, b. Dec. 16, 1837; m. Saul Washburn; d. Dec. 11, 1883, in Mich. (8) Grant, b. Apr. 15, 1843, at Fairfield; d. there May 23, 1844.

2299. iv.   RHODA, b. Apr. 18, 1808; m. Levi Cuddebach; m. 2nd, John Stoner, Marcellus, N. Y. Ch.: (1) Alfred Cuddebach, b. (2) Lydia Cuddebach, b.; m.; d.

2300. v.   LUCUS, b. Mar. 27, 1813; m. Mary Price, 3776-8.

2301. vi.   MARCUS, b. Mar. 27, 1813; m. Lora Kinney Gere, 3779-80.

2302. vii.   ALMA, b. Mar. 28, 1816; m. Jacob Genung; d. No. Fairfield, O.; s. p.

2303. viii.   ELECTA, b. Mar. 8, 1818; m. Sherwood Adams; d. No. Fairfield. Ch.: (1) Lyndon, b. Feb. 6, 1840; m. Oct. 8, 1861, Louise Angell. Ch.: (a) Willie, b. (2) Irving, b. Nov. 7, 1842; m. 1864, Louisa Carbine. Ch.: (a) Lena, b.

2303¹. ix.   SYLVIA, b. ———; m. David Johnson. Ch.: (1) Lyman, b.; d. unm. (2) Son, b.; d. unm.

2304. x.   VERONA, b. Jan. 17, 1820; m. David Johnson. Ch.: (1) Rhoda, b.; m. ——— Childs. (2) Lyman, b.; d. unm.

2305. xi.   EBEN, b. 1822; d. 1830.

1103. LYMAN FOOTE, (374, 115, 37, 10, 3,) b. Apr., 1788; m. Sarah Hodge, of Skaneateles, N. Y. He d. 1812, in Johnstown, N. Y.

2306. i.   LINUS, b.; res. in Mich.

2306¹. ii.   ROXANNA, b.; res. in Mich.; unm.

—1113. RUSSEL FOOTE, (375, 115, 37, 10, 3,) bap. Mar. 2, 1777; m. Jan., 1799, Electa, dau. of Roger and Martha (Foote, 384) Noble, of Westfield, Mass. She was b. Aug. 15, 1780. He d. Apr. 20, 1817, in Plattsburgh, N. Y. Res. also Simsbury and Windsor, Ct.

2307. i.   PATTY, b.

2308. ii.   ZURVIAH, b. ———; m. ——— Lamb, of LaPorte, Ind. Ch.: (1) George Lamb, b.; res., Moline, Ill. Ch.: (a) Mrs. Leslie E. Dodge. (2) Mary A., b. Dec. 28, 1828; m. Francis Whitney. He was b. Dec. 30, 1831; d. Sept. 18, 1906. She d. Aug. 19, 1899. Ch.: (a) Nellie E. Whitney, b. Sept. 27, 1858; d. Nov. 9, 1859. (b) Horace A., b. Jan. 11, 1862; m. Eva A. Phillips. She was b. Apr. 8, 1866; res., 307 Ohio St., LaPorte, Ind. Ch.: (i) Frank R., b. July 24, 1886. (ii) Nina M., b. Dec. 23, 1890. (c) Frankie E., b. July 14, 1864; d. Aug. 19, 1865. (d) Eddie M., b. Jan. 11, 1870; d. Mar. 12, 1871. (3) Morris Lamb, b.; m. No. 2310. (3) ———. (4) Janette, b. ———; m. ——— Angell. Res., LaPorte, Ind.

2309. iii.   NOBLE, b. Feb. 16, 1804; m. Emily B. Smith, 3781-6.

2310. iv. ELECTA, b. Addison Co., Vt., Mar. 14, 1806; m. Middlebury, Vt., 1829, Warren Thompson. He was b. Jan. 26, 1806; d. Oct. 18, 1883, at Osseo, Mich. She was educated at Middlebury. Methodist. She d. Mar. 7, 1865. Ch.: (1) Nelson W., b. May 7, 1830; d. Feb. 22, 1903. (2) Russell, b. Oct. 10, 1832; d. Apr. 14, 1846. (3) Eliza, b. Aug. 5, 1834; m. Osseo, Mar. 5, 1854, Morris Lamb (son of 2308). He was b. Granville, Vt., Dec. 1, 1830; d. Apr. 28, 1906, at Hillsdale, Mich. She was educated at Osseo, Mich. Universalist. Ch.: (a) Martha Lamb, b. Sept. 28, 1857; m. Oct. 18, 1882, Edward T. Beckharelt. He was b. Oct. 5, 1854. Ch.: (i) Blanche U. Beckharelt, b. Aug. 24, 1883. (ii) David Morris, b. Mar. 27, 1885. (iii) Warren Edward, b. July 27, 1886; d. Aug. 31, 1887. (iv) Joseph Stevens, b. Mar. 29, 1888. (v) Katherine Louise Beckharelt, b. Aug. 1, 1889. (4) Martha Jane, b. Jan. 22, 1836; d. Mar. 17, 1889. (5) Francis W., b. Aug. 11, 1836; res., Hillsdale, Mich. (6) George W., b. Mar. 3, 1834; res., Grand Rapids, Mich.

2311. v. ELIJAH, b. May 28, 1810; m. Olivia Luce, 3787-90.

2312. vi. MARTHA, b.

2313. vii. HENRY WILLIAM, b. May 20, 1815; m. Almira Goodrich, Mrs. Rebecca Doulap Miller and Mrs. Holley, 3791-9.

1114. ELIJAH FOOTE, (375, 115, 37, 10, 3,) b. ———; bap. June 20, 1779; m. Jan., 1801, Ruth Spencer, at Middlebury, Vt. She was b. 1779; d. Aug. 22, 1815, at Guildhall, Vt.; m. 2nd, Nov. 7, 1816, Nancy, dau. of Judge Dana, of Brattleboro, Vt. She was b. 1791; d. Oct. 9, 1835, at Guildhall, Vt. He d. May 26, 1853, at Brookport, N. Y.

2314. i. SAMUEL MILLER, b. Guildhall, Vt., Feb. 6, 1802; d. Aug. 25, 1815, in Guildhall, Vt.

2315. ii. AUSTIN SPENCER, b. Guildhall, Vt., Sept. 16, 1806; d. May 11, 1839, at Gaines, N. Y.

2316. iii. JULIUS DANA, b. Hinsdale, N. H., Aug. 17, 1817; m. Jane Eliza Merrill, 3800-2.

2317. iv. NANCY MARIA, b. Brattleboro, Vt., May 4, 1819; m. Mar. 18, 1841, Julius Bates, at Gaines, N. Y. She d. Jan. 23, 1903, in New York. Ch.: (1) Julius Austin Bates, b. Brockport, N. Y., May 1, 1842; m. Apr. 13, 1868, Helen Amanda Walter, at Chicago, Ill. Ch.: (a) Nellie Gertrude Bates, b. Nov. 19, 1869, Savannah, Ga.; d. May 3, 1872, Savannah, Ga. (b) Alice Walter Bates, b. Nov. 16, 1873, at Savannah, Ga. (c) Jule Annette Bates, b. Dec. 26, 1876, at Savannah, Ga. (d) Maria Lillian Bates, b. ———, at Savannah, Ga. Mr. Bates was a member of the firm of Ludden & Bates, for many years the leading dealers in musical instruments in the South; res. in New York City. (2) Frederick Dana, b. Brockport, N. Y., Mar. 3, 1845; d. May 10, 1864, at Pulaski, Tenn. (3) Ferdinand Foote, b. Brockport, N. Y., Mar. 3, 1845.

2318. v. ANNETTE, b. Brattleboro, Vt., June 14, 1821; d. Aug. 14, 1824, at Gaines, N. Y.

2319. vi. MARY LITTLE, b. Gaines, N. Y., May 4, 1827; d. Sept. 10, 1828, at Gaines, N. Y.

1115. JUSTUS FOOTE, (375, 115, 37, 10, 3,) b. Simsbury, Ct., June 24, 1782; m. Apr. 15, 1810, Harriet. Swan, dau. of Rev. John Graham, of Suffield, Ct. He d. June 10, 1829. She d. Apr. 30, 1865, ae. 76. They lived and d. at Middlebury, Vt.

2320. i.   MARY LATIMER, b. Feb. 26, 1812; m. Mar. 23, 1836, Prof. Daniel Sylvester Sheldon, of Rupert, Vt. She d. June 5, 1882, in Davenport, Ia. He was the first President of the Academy of Science and Professor in Griswold College. He d. June 5, 1886, in Davenport, Ia. Ch.: (1) Harriet Smith, b. Potsdam, N. Y., Sept. 26, 1837; d. Mar. 12, 1842, in Potsdam, N. Y.

2321. ii.   JOHN GRAHAM, b. Apr. 21, 1814; m. Eliza Jane Ewing and Mary Eliza Merrill, 3803-9.

2322. iii.   CHARLES KING, b. Aug. 5, 1816; m. Sarah B. Lion, 3810-5.

2323. iv.   HARRIET, b. Nov. 16, 1818; m. 1st, Apr. 22, 1835, Joseph Ç. Ketcham, in Middlebury; m. 2nd, John Henry Gear, in Burlington, Iowa, Dec. 15, 1852. Had two sons and four daus. Harriet Foote Gear d. in Burlington, Ia., Oct. 4, 1902. John Henry Gear d. in Washington, D. C., July 14, 1900. John Henry Gear, Republican, of Burlington, Ia., son of Ezekiel Gilbert Gear and Miranda Cook Gear, was b. in Ithaca, N. Y., Apr. 7, 1825; received a common school education; removed to Galena, Ill., in 1836; to Fort Snelling, Iowa .Territory, in 1838; and to Burlington, Ia., in 1843, where he engaged in merchandising. Was elected Mayor of the city of Burlington in 1863; was a member of the Iowa House of Representatives of the Fourteenth, Fifteenth and Sixteenth General Assemblies of the State, serving as Speaker for the last two terms; was elected Governor of Iowa in 1878-9, and again in 1880-81; was elected to the Fiftieth and Fifty-first Congresses; was beaten for the Fifty-second; was Assistant Secretary of the Treasury under President Harrison, and was elected to the Fifty-third Congress. Was elected, Jan. 23, 1894, a Senator in Congress from the State of Iowa, for six years, beginning Mar. 4, 1895; was re-elected in Jan., 1900, but d. before taking his seat; d. July 14, 1900. Ch.: (1) Justin Ketcham; dates and res. unknown. (2) Charles Ketcham; date of birth and death unknown. (3) Margaret Eliza Gear, b. in Burlington, Ia., Nov. 17, 1853; m. in Burlington, Ia., Oct. 15, 1877, Joseph William Blythe, Jr. Had one son. Joseph William Blythe, Jr., of Burlington, Ia., son of Joseph William Blythe and Eleanor Henrietta Green Blythe, was b. in Cranberry, N. J., Jan. 16, 1850. Mr. Blythe is a graduate of Princeton College. He is a lawyer. His present address is Burlington, Ia. Ch.: (a) Hugh Blythe, b. in Burlington, Ia., Aug. 22, 1876; graduaté of Harvard Law School; broker; present address, Chicago, Ill. (4) Harriet M. Gear, b. in Burlington, Ia., Dec. 23, 1855; d. Sept. 8, 1856. (5) Catherine Gilbert Gear, b. in Burlington, Ia., Oct. 17, 1860; d. Dec. 27, 1861. (6) Ruth Graham Foote Gear, b. in Burlington, Ia., Nov. 3, 1862; m. in Burlington, Ia., Horace Sherfey Rand, Nov. 18, 1885. Ch., all b. in Burlington: (a) Gear Rand, b. Apr. 20, 1886; d. Sept. 20, 1889. (b) Horace Sherfey Rand, Jr., b. June 14, 1887. (c) Harriet Gear Rand, b.

May 7, 1889; d. Jan. 18, 1890.   (d) Catherine Amy Rand, b.
May 7, 1889; d. Oct. 28, 1889.   (e) Ruth Gear Rand, b. Dec. 13,
1900.

2324.   v.   JUSTUS LYMAN, b. Aug. 5, 1816; d. Feb. 26, 1860, in Burlington, Iowa.

2325.   vi.   MOSES SCOTT, b. June 11, 1822; m. Laura Amba Fletcher and
Louisa J. Hunter, 3816-9.

2326.   vii. MARK SYLVESTER, b. Aug. 21, 1823; m. Mary Stella Mauro,
3820-7.

2327.   viii. CATHRINE GRAHAM, b. Oct. 28, 1828; d. Jan. 8, 1829.

1117. IRA FOOTE, (375, 115, 37, 10, 3,) b. Apr. 25, 1785; m. Dec. 29, 1814,
Sally H., dau. of Samuel and Castena (Holmes) Paine. . She was b. Mar. 9, 1794;
d. June 10, 1848; he d. Nov. 18, 1843. Res., Fairfield, Vt.

2328.   i.   HOLMES, b. Apr. 19, 1817; m. Hester Iverson, 3828-30.

2329.   ii.   ORANGE, b. Dec. 25, 1818; d. Aug. 10, 1820.

2330.   iii. ORANGE, b. Jan. 7, 1821; m. Charlotte L. Buckley, 3831-2.

2331.   iv.   IRA L., b. Dec. 10, 1822; m. Ann I. Albee and Jane Stevens,
3833.

2332.   v.   CASTENA, b. Nov. 15, 1824; m. May 16, 1847, Ansil Bailey.
He d. 1885; was an industrious farmer. She d. Jan. 14, 1901.
Ch.: (1) Winfield S., b. Mar., 1847; res., St. Albans, Vt. (2)
Ada A., b. Oct. 29, 1851.   (3) Charles W., b.

2333.   vi.   OSCAR, b. May 5, 1826; m. Francis Perley, 3834-6.

2334.   vii. LANDUS B., b. Apr. 28, 1828; d. Sept. 9, 1855.

2335.   viii. SARAH J., b. July 10, 1830; d. May 7, 1831.

2336.· ix.   NANCY C., b. Mar. 23, 1832; d. Aug. 25, 1833.

2337.   x.   CHARLES C., b. Nov. 25, 1833; m. Aug. 23, 1858, Marion
Frances Stevens; res., Hammond, La.

1118. SAMUEL FOOTE, (375, 115, 37, 10, 3,) b. Feb. 23, 1787; m. Oct. 28,
1814, Jennette Campbelle; m. 2nd, Jadida Hoyt, of Bakersfield. He was Sheriff
for many years; d. Sept. 22, 1841.

2338.   i.   NANCY, b. Apr. 3, 1815; d. Dec. 13, 1831.

2339.   ii.   SOLON, b. May 18, 1818; m. Mrs. Lovice R. (White) Baily
and Mary Sturges, 3837-8.

2340.   iii. LUCY LAMIRA, b. Nov. 10, 1821; d. Nov. 2, 1903; unm.

2341.   iv.   MERRITT CAMPBELLE, b. Feb. 12, 1823; m. Emily I. Stevens
and Lizzie (Maynard) Snow, 3839-41.

2342.   v.   JANE AMANDA, b. Mar. 26, 1826; m. Sept. 22, 1845, Thomas
E. Dimon; d. May 21, 1883; she d. Mar. 30, 1889. He was a
farmer. Ch.: (1) Jennett A., b. Jan. 16, 1847.

1119. ALDEN FOOTE, (375, 115, 37, 10, 3,) b. 1798; m. Priscilla Foote.
She d. 1835, in Ohio. He d. 1833, in Ohio. Res., Fairfield, Vt.

2343.   i.   BURTON, b. in Shelby, N. Y., Dec. 14, 1824; d. June 9, 1832.

2344.   ii.   JOSIAH, b. Shelby, N. Y., Aug. 16, 1826; res., Rochester, Mich.

2345.   iii. ARTHUSA, b. Shelby, N. Y., Jan. 3, 1828.

2346.   iv.   ALMA, b. Barre, N. Y., Dec. 17, 1829.

2347.   v.   JANE, b. Shelby, N. Y., Jan. 10, 1832.

1120. RUSSELL FOOTE, (375, 115, 37, 10, 3,) b. Sept. 9, 1800; m. Jan.
26, 1825, Lydia Cook, of Clarkson, N. Y. Res., Rochester, Mich.

(16)

2348. i. CHARITY, b. ———; d. in infancy.
2349. ii. ELIJAH, b. June 16, 1828; d. Oct. 10, 1832.
2350. iii. NANCY A., b. Dec. 14, 1830.
2351. iv. ADELINE, b. Sept. 15, 1833; d. Oct. 16, 1834.
2352. v. JEROME, b. Aug. 3, 1836.
2353. vi. ORANGE, b. July 14, 1838; d. Dec. 20, 1838.
2354. vii. MARTHA, b. Sept. 30, 1844; d. Oct. 18, 1844.

1124. HORACE FOOTE, (377, 115, 37, 10, 3,) b. 1790; m. 1822, Mary, dau. of Frederick Sammons, of Johnstown, N. Y. She was b. 1795; d. Oct., 1865, in Fenton, Genesee Co., Mich. He was a man of deep religious character, a member of the Baptist denomination. His home was the stopping place for ministers coming from distant places to hold services and preach in nearby places of worship. In 1835 he built a frame barn (a rare possession in those early days), and hired a teacher to conduct a school in it for the benefit of his own and neighbors' children. He d. Oct. 21, 1849, in Pontiac, Mich. Res., Romeo, Macomb Co., Rochester, and Pontiac, Oakland Co., all in Mich.

2355. i. JANE ELIZABETH, b. May 25, 1823, in Johnstown, N. Y.; m. Levi Leroy Hankinson, June 23, 1844. He d. in 1853 in Utica, Mich. After her husband's death Mrs. Hankinson moved to Fenton, Mich., where she opened and conducted a millinery store for 53 years. She was a consistent member of the Methodist Episcopal Church, and was very much respected by all who knew her. She d. in Fenton, Genesee Co., Mich., Jan. 6, 1906.
2356. ii. AMBROSE, b. Dec. 22, 1827; m. Ann Rebekah Sheets, 3842-8.
2357. iii. PE YU, b. Romeo, Mich., May 19, 1830; m. Sarah Ellen Carran, 3849-54.
2357¹. iv. JOHN RANDOLPH, b. Rochester, Mich., June 21, 1833; d. Apr. 10, 1836.

1125. CHAUNCEY FOOTE, (377, 115, 37, 10, 3,) b. 1792; m. Achsah Cook, of Ashfield, Mass.; res., Troy, N. Y.

2358. i. EDWARD, b. ———; was Professor in a College; d. unm. Res., N. J.
2359. ii. HENRY C., b. ———; m. Hannah Sheets, 3855-6.

1129. FRIEND FOOTE, (377, 113, 37, 10, 3,) b. Dec. 5, 1801; m. Mary Inman. She was b. Mar., 1802; d. 1874. He d. 1862. Res., Utica, Mich.

2360. i. ELIZA S., b. 1840. She was a teacher in the Detroit public Schools for 29 years; Principal of the Nicholson School at the time of her death; member of St. Johns Episcopal Church; d. Mich., Feb. 11, 1894.
2361. ii. HORACE G., b. 1842. He served in Mich. Infantry in Civil War; d. Sept. 13, 1897, at Vienna, West Virginia.
2362. iii. ELEAZER WELLES, b. 1844. He served in 7th Mich. Infantry; d. at Andersonville Prison.

1133. JAMES FOOTE, (380, 117' 37, 10, 3,) b. Apr. 25, 1781; m. Mar. 22, 1801, Roxanna, dau. of Asaph Dewey, of Richmond, Mass. She d. Jan. 5, 1853. He d. Sept. 28, 1852. Res., Dalton, Mass.

2363. i. DANIEL, b. Aug. 3, 1802; m. Laura Tracy, 3857-65.
2364. ii. JOHN, b. June 11, 1804; d. June 14, 1804.

2365. iii. ASAPH DEWEY, b. June 29, 1805; d. ———. Farmer; was a noble and respected citizen. Res., Pittsfield.

2366. iv. JAMES, b. May 1, 1807; m. Eliza Brown, 3866-7.

2367. v. ROXANNA, b. May 29, 1810; m. Sept. 13, 1841, Patrick Coleman, of Pittsfield, Mass. He d. in Richmond, Mass., May 19, 1872. She d. in Richmond, Mass., Nov. 23, 1893. Ch.: (1) Martin Wells, b. Mar. 7, 1843, in Pittsfield, Mass. (2) James Franklin, b. in Pittsfield, Mass., Apr. 24, 1847; res., Richmond, Mass.

2368. vi. PRUDENCE, b. Apr. 23, 1812; m. June 7, 1835, Nicholas Michels, of Manlius, N. Y. He d. in Cicero, N. Y., Aug. 8, 1897. Ch.: (1) Millicent, b. Nov. 30, 1836; d. in Cicero, N. Y., Jan. 7, 1876. (2) Roxanna, b. July 13, 1837, in Manlius, N. Y. (3) Mary Emily, b. Mar. 15, 1839; d. Sept. 13, 1840, in Manlius, N. Y. (4) James, b. Dec. 12, 1842; d. Feb. 14, 1847, in Manlius, N. Y. (5) Vesta, b. Nov. 24, 1845; d. Sept. 26, 1863, in Manlius, N. Y. (6) Freeman, b. in Cicero, N. Y., Sept. 22, 1850.

2369. vii. LUCY, b. Apr. 14, 1814; m. Apr. 13, 1836, Flavius Noble, of Washington, Mass. She d. in Pittsfield, Mass., Feb. 16, 1890. Ch.: (1) Mary Emily, b. in Washington, Mass., Oct. 9, 1837. (2) Frances, b. in Washington, Mass., 1841; d. in Pittsfield, Mass., June 10, 1879. (3) Rev. Charles Flavius, b. in Washington, Mass., Nov. 25, 1843. (4) John Wesley, b. in Washington, Mass., Aug. 7, 1846. (5) George Watson, b. in Washington, Mass., Nov. 28, 1848.

2370. viii. SAMUEL, b. Nov. 6, 1816; d. Nov., 1816.

2371. ix. POLLY, b. Nov. 5, 1817; m. 1st, Apr. 28, 1840, Selden Spencer, of Pittsfield, Mass. He d. Nov. 18, 1841. She m. 2nd, Jesse F. Wright, of Middlefield, Mass. She d. Mar. 7, 1898. He d. Aug. 20, 1902. Res., Pittsfield, Mass. Ch., all b. in Middlefield, Mass.: (1) Mary Frances, b. Apr. 19, 1847. (2) Edwin F., b. Aug. 25, 1848; d. July 29, 1865. (3) James Asaph, b. Sept. 6, 1852. (4) Arthur, b. July 2, 1855.

2372. x. HULDAH, b. Aug. 30, 1818; m. June 24, 1846, Freeman Bates, of Pittsfield, Mass. He d. Sept. 12, 1883. She d. Jan. 2, 1889. Res., Pittsfield, Mass. Ch.: (1) George Milton, b. June 22, 1853.

2373. xi. JOSEPH, b. Apr. 24, 1820; m. Martha M. Tracy and Sarah Barrows, 3868-9.

2374. xii. MAHALA, b. May 24, 1822.

2375. xiii. MARTHA, b. Sept. 24, 1825; m. Dec. 27, 1873, Rev. Nathaniel Kellogg, member of New York East Conference. He d. July 26, 1885. She m. 2nd, June 15, 1896, George Wells. Res., Pittsfield, Mass. Martha, at the age of 81, compiled this record of her brothers and sisters.

1135. SAMUEL FOOTE, (380, 117, 37, 10, 3,) b. June 2, 1784; m. Sally Roberts, of Dalton; d. May 29, 1813.

2376. i. PATTY, b.

2377. ii. CHARLOTTE, b.

2378. iii. JOHN, b.

2379. iv. DANIEL, b.

2380. v. SALLY, b.

2381. vi. GEORGE W., b. 1809; m. Lucy Mack, 3870-4.

1139. ALVIN FOOTE, (381, 117, 37, 10, 3,) b. Castleton, Vt., Oct. 23, 1778; m. 1st, Dec., 1815, Priscilla, dau. of Lieut.-Col. Nathan Rice, of Boston, Mass. She was b. June 11, 1786; d. Sept. 5, 1841; m. 2nd, 1845, Caroline Sanger. He graduated from Dartmouth College 1797. Lawyer; Unitarian; d. Sept. 21, 1856; res., Burlington, Vt.

2382. i. CHARLES RICE, b. Oct. 30, 1816; m. Pheba Loper, 3875-6.

2383. ii. GEORGE, b. Burlington, Vt., May 4, 1818; m. Phebe Gelston Dwight and Ellen Louisa Hungerford, 3877-85.

2384. iii. ANNA LUCIA, b. Apr. 27, 1819; m. Aug. 23, 1847, Dr. Leonard Marsh. He was b. June 13, 1799; d. Aug. 16, 1870. She d. Sept. 22, 1904. Ch.: (1) Mary Moon Marsh, b. Aug. 28, 1848; d. Nov. 10, 1869. (2) William Foote, b. Feb. 19, 1850. (3) George Foote, b. Mar. 31, 1852; m. Caroline Foote (See No. 3878 for record). (4) Charles Leonard, b. Oct. 27, 1854; m. Hildegard Lind; no ch. (5) Anna Louisa Marsh, b. Aug. 19, 1859; m. Daniel Temple Torrey. Ch.: (a) George Safford, b. Mar. 14, 1891. (b) Marian Marsh, b. Dec. 9, 1893. (c) Katharine Adelaide, b. Jan. 6, 1896. (d) Anna St. John, b. June 19, 1897. (e) Daniel Temple, b. Nov. 11, 1900; d. Aug. 10, 1904. Res., Williams St., Providence, R. I.

2385. iv. SARAH, b. May 13, 1824; res., Burlington, Vt.; unm.

1141. MASON FOOTE, (381, 117, 37, 10, 3,) b. Castleton, Vt., May 2, 1782; m. ———; farmer. Res., Griggsville, Ill.

2386. i. ALTHA E., b. ———; m. ——— Corey; res., Alton, Ill.

1144. LUTHER FOOTE, (381, 117, 37, 10, 3,) b. Castleton, Vt., Apr. 17, 1791; m. Rosa Hutchins. She was b. May 1, 1826. He settled as a merchant in Windsor, Vt. Transacts business in Boston, Mass. Res., Cambridge, Mass.

2387. i. MARY BRADFORD, b. Windsor, Vt., Mar. 26, 1827. Res., Cambridge, Mass.

2388. ii. GEORGE LUTHER, b. Oct. 13, 1828-9; m. Esther M. Young, 3886.

1148. WILLIAM FOOTE, (383, 117, 37, 10, 3,) b. Middlebury, Vt., Aug. 27, 1783; m. Oct. 18, 1807, Lucy W. Berthrong, of Middlebury, Vt. She was b. Middlebury, Vt., May 20, 1789; d. Aug. 5, 1864, at Burlington, Vt. He d. Dec. 27, 1863. Ch. all b. in Middlebury, Vt.

2389. i. ISABELL A., b. Sept. 24, 1808; m. Middlebury, Vt.; d. June 24, 1848, at Grand Rapids, Mich.

2390. ii. GEORGE M., b. July 22, 1810; d. in infancy.

2391. iii. MARIA, b. May 13, 1812; m. Middlebury, Vt.; d. July 11, 1863, at Grand Rapids, Mich.

2392. iv. GEORGE H., b. Apr. 10, 1814; m. ———; d. Feb. 27, 1870, at Boston, Mass.

2393. v. HANNAH B., b. Aug. 14, 1816; m. Middlebury, Vt.; d. Nov. 14, 1861, in Pittsford, Vt.

2393¹. vi. LUCIUS B., b. Oct. 19, 1818; d. in infancy.

2394. vii. WILLIAM A., b. Sept. 16, 1820; d. July 4, 1862, at Corinth, Tenn.

2395. viii. JAMES, b. July 25, 1822; m. Eliza Freeman, 3887-91.

2396. ix. JOHN BERTHRONG, b. July 25, 1822; m. Sarah L. Kilborn, 3892-4.

2397. x. LUCY W., b. Oct. 18, 1824; m. Middlebury, Vt.; d. Feb. 9, 1895, at Boston, Mass.

2398. xi. CATHERINE B., b. Aug. 21, 1826; m. Middlebury, Vt.; d. Aug. 26, 1861, at Burlington, Vt. Ch.: (1) Dau., m. Mark Hadley, Oakland, Cal. (2) Kate, m. ———. Res., Oakland, Cal.

2399. xii. ELIZABETH A., b. July 7, 1832; m. Burlington, Vt., Nov. 19, 1854, Charles Asa Griffin. He b. 1830; d. Oct. 29, 1857; m. 2nd, Nov. 7, 1869, at Newtownville, Mass., William Richard Sinclaise. He was b. May 15, 1819; d. Nov. 7, 1886. She d. at North Ferrisburgh, Vt., 1899. Ch.: (1) Alice Elizabeth, b. Oct. 2, 1855, at Keene, N. H.; m. Aug. 21, 1889, Stoddard Benjamin, son of John W. Martin. No ch.

1150. CLARK FOOTE, (387, 117, 37, 10, 3,) b. Dec. 16, 1791; m. 1818, Harriet Boardman, of Middlebury, Vt. She was b. 1797; d. 1881. He d. 1883. Res., Tompkins, Mich.

2400. i. HORACE BOARDMAN, b. June 21, 1819; m. Delia M. Haven, 3895-3901.

2401. ii. HENRY CRAWFORD, b. May 31, 1821; d. Mar. 16, 1887; unm.

2402. iii. WALLACE TURNER, b. Mar. 18, 1825; m. Hilah Eliza Foote (No. 2209), 3902-10.

2403. iv. HARRIET SILENCE, b. July 11, 1832; d. Feb., 1833.

2404. v. HARRIET DAROXA, b. Apr. 10, 1834; m. Dec. 16, 1852, Lewis L. Leggett, of Tompkins, Mich. He was a farmer. Ch.: (1) Hilah Louisa, b. Oct. 30, 1853; d. Sept. 8, 1857. (2) Helen A., b. Feb. 22, 1856; d. Aug. 22, 1857. (3) George Arthur, b. Oct. 28, 1858; m. Jan. 2, 1882, Lilly H. Hart, Tompkins, Mich. Ch.: (a) Lena V., b. Oct. 20, 1882. (b) Edith I., b. Sept. 18, 1884; d. Sept. 14, 1892. (c) Hilah M., b. Sept. 26, 1886. (d) Bereniece N., b. Apr. 3, 1889. (e) Louis H., b. Aug. 25, 1891. (f) Rea H., b. Aug. 20, 1894. (g) Clyfford A., b. Jan. 17, 1901. (4) Nellie E., b. Sept. 22, 1861; m. Feb. 22, 1881, William Mallock, of Pulaski, Mich. He d. 1887; m. 2nd, Jan. 1, 1899, Dr. M. A. Jordan. Res., Logansport, Ind. Ch.: (a) Harriet Foote Mallock, b. Jan. 21, 1882. (b) N. Roy Mallock, b. Mar. 25, 1885. (5) Harriet, b. Dec. 8, 1863; m. 1887, Will Stewart; d. Apr. 14, 1892. (6) Harry Curtis, b. Feb. 23, 1866; m. May 23, 1900, Jennie Cox.

2405. vi. HELEN CLARK, b. July 25, 1838; m. Nov. 26, 1868, Norman W. Boardman, Middlebury, Vt. Res., Tompkins, Mich. Ch.: (1) Lottie May, b. Oct. 30, 1870; m. 1st, Oct. 3, 1894, Thomas Richardson; m. 2nd, S. Y. Haines, May 11, 1898. Ch.: (a) Ruth Carrol, b. Nov. 29, 1905. (2) Ella May, b. Sept. 5, 1874; m. June 28, 1894, Chester Bartlett. Ch.: (a) Lucile May, b. Apr. 27, 1895. (b) Gladys M., b. Nov., 1896. (3) Howard Charles, b. July 28, 1877; m. Oct. 17, 1899, Marion Arcus. Ch.: (a) Horace Arcus, b. Oct. 15, 1902. (4) Ada Emily, b. July 28, 1877. (5) Katherine Foote, b. Apr. 17, 1882; m. William Miller, July 17, 1904; d. Feb. 4, 1906. Ch.: (a) Helen Eliza, b. Jan. 29, 1906.

2406. vii. CHARLES HOWARD, b. Aug. 26, 1842; m. Sarah Catherine Murdock and Mary Turner Smith, 3911-6.

1153. ALLEN FOOTE, (387, 177, 37, 10, 3,) b. Jan. 5, 1801; m. July 2, 1826, Bathsheba Morton, of Middlebury, Vt.

2407. i. ALLEN FREEMAN, b. ———; m. Elvira L. Fenn, 3917.

1155. DEA. MARTIN N. FOOTE, (388, 117, 37, 10, 3,) b. Middlebury, Vt., June 1, 1791; m. Betsey Boardman, of Rutland, Vt. He d. Mar. 23, 1833. Res., Middlebury, Vt. They had seven ch. All d. young except

2408. i. MARY, b. ———; m. Joseph W. Boyce, and had a family of children. Res., Middlebury, Vt.

1163. CHAUNCEY FOOTE, (389, 117, 37, 10, 3,) b. May 9, 1780; m. Feb. 23, 1813, Julia E. Bird, of New Haven, Vt. She d. Oct. 16, 1856, at Canton, N. Y. He d. Apr. 13, 1866, at Appleton, Wis. Res., Canton, N. Y.

2409. i. HENRY GUSTAVUS, b. Canton, N. Y., Oct. 27, 1816; m. 1844, Anne W. Flower. He graduated at Middlebury College, Aug., 1840. Was a lawyer at Ogdensburgh, N. Y.; d. May 9, 1865. She d. May 28, 1867; s. p. Res., Canton, N. Y.

2410. ii. LOVISA F., b. Apr. 28, 1819.

2411. iii. EDWARD C., b. Mar. 4, 1821; m. May 20, 1846, Jane M. Talcott. He d. Aug. 3, 1853, on the Isthmus of Panama.

2412. iv. CYNTHIA E., b. Nov. 1' 1823; m. June 28, 1848, Theodore Conkey, of Canton, N. Y. He was Captain of Cavalry in the 3rd Wis. Regiment in the War of 1861. Res., Appleton, Wis. Ch.: (1) Alice, b. May 21, 1849; m. Jan. 4, 1875, Alex. J. Reid, of Appleton, Wis. (2) Edward T., b. Sept. 15, 1854. (3) Helen Byrd, b. Apr. 6, 1858; m. ——— Barnes. Ch.: (a) Theodora C. (b) Thomas H. (c) Alice A., b. Sept. 15, 1885. (d) Edward Talcott.

2413. v. CHAUNCEY D., b. Apr. 29, 1833; m. Mary J. Northrup, 3918-20.

1164. HENRY FOOTE, (389, 117, 37, 10, 3,) b. Oct. 12, 1791; m. Amelia Bird, of New Haven, Vt. Res., Canton, N. Y.

2414. i. MARY ANN, b. ———; m. ———. No ch.

2415. ii. MARIA, b. ———. Ch.: (1) Ella. (2) Emma, d. ———.

2416. iii. AMANDA A., b. ———. Ch.: (1) Richard, d. (2) Jane, m. ——— Harrison. Res., N. Y. (3) William Beverly. (4) George, d.

2417. iv. EMMA, b. ———; m. Shell Winslow. Res., Seattle, Wash. Ch.: (1) Emma. (2) Elos.

2418. v. HENRY, b. ———; left home when young; nothing further known.

2419. vi. GEORGE B., b. ———; m. 39201-203.

2420. vii. CATHRINE, b. ———; m. Chas. Heth; res., Seattle, Wash.

2421. viii. HENRIETTA, b. July 14, 1842, Canton, N. Y.; m. July 10, 1866, Bishop L. R. Brewer, Canton, N. Y. She d. Mar. 17, 1903, Helena, Mont. Ch.: (1) Jennie Eliza, b. July 14, 1867, Carthage, N. Y.; m. 1886, Elward Floyd Crosby; m. 2nd, 1894, R. M. Atwater, Jr., Providence, R. I. Res., Helena, Mont. Ch.: (a) Margaret Floyd, b. June 20, 1887, Helena, Mont. (b) Leigh Richmond Brewer, b. Jan. 26, 1899. (c) Richard Meade, b. Nov. 5, 1901, Perth, Australia. (2) James Clark, b. ———; d. ———.

1167. STILLMAN FOOTE, (389, 117, 37, 10, 3,) b. in Canton, N. Y., June 13, 1817; m. 1st, Sept. 22, 1847, Mary R., dau. of John Chipman, of Waddington, N. Y. She was b. Aug. 16, 1819; d. Mar. 29, 1849, at Ogdensburgh, N. Y.; m. 2nd,

Nov. 16, 1853, Elizabeth A. Guest, of Ogdensburgh, N. Y. She d. June 15, 1900. He graduated at Middlebury College, 1838. Was a lawyer in Waddington and Ogdensburgh, N. Y.. In 1847 became editor of the "Ogdensburgh Sentinel." Was Surrogate of St. Lawrence Co., N. Y.; d. at Ogdensburgh, May 15, 1883.

    2422. i,   JOHN C., b. July 8, 1848; d. Aug. 17, 1849.

    2423. ii. MARY ELIZABETH, b. Jan. 3, 1855; d. Apr. 18, 1858.

    2423¹. iii. WILLIAM ALEXANDER, b. Dec. 13, 1857; d. Apr. 25, 1858.

    2423². iv. HENRY GUEST, b. Feb. 25, 1859; d. Jan. 1, 1862.

    2424. v.   JENNY CONVERSE, b. July 28, 1860; m. June 17, 1886, James G. Westbrook, of Ogdensburgh. N. Y. Ch.: (1) Stillman Foote Westbrook, b. May 15, 1888. (2) James Seymour, b. Dec. 15, 1889. (3) Thomas Beekman, b. Aug. 18, 1891; d. Apr. 20, 1896. (4) Elizabeth Guest, b. May 25, 1893. (5) Margaret Dumont, b. Jan. 24, 1895. (6) Edward Converse, b. July 20, 1897; d. Oct. 16, 1897. (7) Frances Guest Westbrook, b. May 2, 1900.

    2424¹. vi. LOUISE STILLMAN, b. Feb. 6, 1863; d. Sept. 28, 1864.

    1170. DANIEL H. FOOTE, (390, 117, 37, 10, 3,) b. May 12, 1792; m. Sarah Weaver, of New Haven, Vt. She was b. Oct. 22, 1795; d. Aug. 19, 1859. He d. Aug. 1, 1834. Res., Canton, N. Y.

    2425. i.   LUCY, b. Sept. 5, 1813; m. Erastus Vilas, of Ogdensburgh, N. Y. She d. Mar. 13, 1868.

    2426. ii. HARRIET, b. Dec. 30, 1816; d. Jan. 22, 1883.

    2427. iii. AZUBAH A., b. Dec. 7, 1723; m. Oct. 11, 1849, Wells Knapp, of Malone, N. Y. He was b. Dec. 4, 1812; d. July 29, 1875. She d. Mar. 4, 1891. Ch.: (1) Henry Hoit Knapp, M. D., b. Sept. 9, 1850; m. Katherine Buckman, of Chazy, N. Y. Res., Essex, N. Y. Ch.: (a) Bertha Vilas, b. ———; m. Arthur W. Towne. Res., Syracuse, N. Y. Ch.: (i) Dorothy Philmore, b. ———. (b) Harrie Curtis, b. ———. (c) Albert H., b. ———. (2) Alice Elizabeth, b. May 31, 1854; m. Jan. 16, 1890, Edward W. Knowlton, of Belfast, Me. Res., Malone, N. Y. Ch.: (a) Gladys Alice Knowlton, b. Aug. 24, 1891. (3) Harriet Rebecca, b. May 24, 1856; d. Jan. 26, 1895. (4) Lucy Vilas, b. Dec. 11, 1858; d. Oct. 11, 1868. (5) John Warren Knapp, b. June 19, 1863.

    1182. RICHARD GROVES FOOTE, (391, 117, 37, 10, 3,) b. June 2, 1803; m. Jan. 1, 1828, Sarah, dau. of David Doty, of Bangor, N. Y. He was Attorney and Counselor at Law.

    2428. i.   WILLIAM SLADE, b. Dec. 1, 1828; d. Aug. 14, 1832.

    2429. ii. CHARLES HENRY, b. Feb. 24, 1831; m. Isabel McLane, 3921-3.

    2430. iii. WILLIAM SLADE, b. Oct. 14, 1832; d. Feb. 19, 1844.

    2431. iv. SARAH PAMELIA, b. Nov. 8, 1838; m. 1859, James W. Sawyer.

    2432. v.   HENRY VAN RENSSELAER, b. Oct. 24, 1840; m. Henrietta A. Hubbard, 3924.

    1183. LEVI FOOTE, (392, 118, 37, 10, 3,) b. May 10, 1779; m. Jan. 4, 1803, Amelia Allen. He d. Sept. 19, 1841. Res., Fowler, Ohio.

    2433. i.   ABIGAIL, b. Oct. 7, 1803; d. Jan. 23, 1877; unm.

    2434. ii. LYDIA, b. July 5, 1805; m. May 4, 1829, Romanta Barber. She d. Apr. 21, 1881. Ch.: (1) Hiram, b. Oct. 4, 1830; res., Hyatt-ville, Bighorn Co., Wyo. (2) Melinda, b. Aug. 13, 1832; res.,

Hartford, O., and Nutwood, O. (3) Culverson, b. Dec. 18, 1834;
d. at Rushsyloania, Logan Co., O., Feb. 5, 1905. (4) Phebe, b.
Sept. 16, 1837; m. ——— Banning; d. Nov. 4, 1891, at Beaver
City, Neb. (5) Millie Hall, b. Feb. 11, 1840, at Towles, Trumbull Co., O. Res., Cortland, O.; dressmaker; Disciple or Christian;
m. Curtis, son of Amiza Hall. He was b. Fowler, O., Mar. 2,
1840; d. Nov. 12, 1878, at Fowler, O. Ch.: (a) Warren Curtis
Hall, b. Oct. 18, 1882; m. Jan. 15, 1901, Lucy Decker. She was
b. Dec. 18, 1879. Ch.: (i) Carlos Adolph Hall, b. Nov. 5, 1901.
(ii) Parmlee Eugene Hall, b. Feb. 25, 1903. (iii) Charles Curtis
Hall, b. Aug. 30, 1904. (iv) Elizabeth Lorain Hall, b. Sept. 23,
1906. (6) Henry, b. Jan. 30, 1843; res., Ransom, Neb. (7) Sue
Barber, b. June 2, 1845; m. ——— Mamsell. Res., 1806, 19th St.,
Boulder, Colo.

2435. iii. ASA, b. Aug. 15, 1807; m. Mary Dickinson, 3925-30.

2436. iv. LUA, b. Sept. 28, 1810; m. Sept. 1, 1830, Nelson Trew, of
Trumbull Co., O.; farmer. He d. July 5, 1868. She d. May 8,
1906. Res., West Farmington, O., after 1854. Ch., all b. in Bazetta,
O.: (1) Silas A., b. June 1, 1831; m. Mar. 28, 1854, Agnes P.
Green. She d. Apr. 2, 1858. He was a farmer; d. Aug. 10, 1857.
(2) Gilbert L., b. Jan. 1, 1833; d. July 20, 1848. (3) Frank S.,
b. Nov. 5, 1834; m. Oct. 18, 1857, Harriet E. Fuller; farmer and
banker. Ch.: (a) Mary L. Trew, b. Nov. 30, 1858; m. Sept. 13,
1886, John D. McLarem, M. D., of N. Y. City. (b) Charles N.
Trew, b. Apr. 21, 1860; miller; d. June 8, 1899, at Ageitec, New
Mexico. (c) Burley F. Trew, b. July 4, 1862; drowned at Tes-
cott, Kan., July 12, 1886. (4) Rebecca J, b. Apr. 7, 1837. (5)
Sara A., b. Apr. 27, 1839; m. Apr. 4, 1367, Rev. H. D. Rice.
Ch.: (a) Barbary Heck Rice, b. Sept. 27, 1867; d. July 31, 1868.
(b) Fredric T. Rice, b. June 1, 1869; d. Aug. 15, 1870. (c) John
M. Rice, b. May 23, 1871; d. Nov. 19, 1886, at Ciucinnati, O.
(d) Mary L. Rice, b. Dec. 22, 1872; res., Chicago, Ill. (e)
Frances B. Rice, b. ———; m. Mar. 14, 1900, Wilber Fish
Hogaboom, railroad office, Chicago, Ill. (6) John M., b. Oct. 30,
1841; m. Aug. 24, 1897, Sara Scott. (7) Nelson, b. Feb. 9, 1844;
d. Dec. 31, 1845. (8) E. Adell, b. Jan. 27, 1847. (9) Willmot
P., b. Oct. 23, 1849; m. Oct. 23, 1873, Ella M. George; res., Como,
Neb. Ch.: (a) George F. Trew, b. Sept. 21, 1874. (b) Levin B.,
b. Dec. 13, 1877. (c) Nelson W., b. Jan. 4, 1879. (d) Harley S.,
b. Jan. 17, 1882. (e) Inez Julia Trew, b. June 7, 1883. (10)
Arthur T., b. Aug. 16, 1851; m. Oct. 30, 1878, Lydia T. Loveland; res., West Farmington, O. Ch.: (a) Albert L. Trew, b.
Oct. 10, 1879; d. Oct. 12, 1892, in U. S. A. Army. (b) Philip S.,
b. Aug. 9, 1881. (c) Arthur S., b. Feb. 28, 1884. (d) Robert C.,
b. July 24, 1886; d. Oct. 20, 1899. (e) Helen M., b. Nov. 23,
1888. (f) Alice A., b. Oct. 10, 1897. (11) Lewis Trew, b. Aug.
4, 1853; d. Aug. 19, 1853.

2437. v. MALINDA, b. Apr. 22, 1814; m. Dec. 18, 1834, in Fowler, O.,
William Andrew Bacon. He was b. July 21, 1809; d. Aug. 6,
1903. She d. July 9, 1892. Ch.: (1) Homer Lee Bacon, b.
Vernon, Trumbull Co., O., Sept. 4, 1855; m. Fannie M. Cole; she

was b. Kinsman, O., Feb. 27, 1860. Farmer; educated at Vernon, O. Res., Kinsman, O., R. F. D. No. 3. Ch.: (a) Lena Pearl Bacon, b. Jan. 7, 1855; d. Oct. 12, 1887. (b) Lorene Cole Bacon, b. Feb. 17, 1889. (c) Isabelle Elizabeth Bacon, b. Oct. 12, 1894. (2) Andrew Bacon, b. Vienna, O., May 27, 1836; m. Emily Atwood, of Vernon, O. Ch.: (a) Kenneth, b. Dec. 10, 1863, Golden, Colo.; d. Mar. 12, 1882, Golden, Colo. (b) Bessie, b. Golden, Colo., Mar. 1, 1873. (c) Maggie, b. Golden, Colo., Oct. 14, 1868. (3) James W. Bacon, b. Vienna, Mar. 20, 1875; m. Jennie Davinson, of Colo. Ch.: (a) Lauren, b. June 25, 1876, Weld Co., Colo. (b) Archie, b. Weld Co., Colo., May 19, 1878. (4) Levi, b. Vienna, Jan. 5, 1839; d. Dec. 22, 1841. (5) Clinton, b. Vienna, Oct. 4, 1840; d. Sept. 26, 1863, at Nashville, Tenn., of a wound received at Chickamauga. (6) Lura, b. Vienna, Sept. 5, 1843; d. Dec. 12, 1904, at Longmont, Colo. (7) Helen, b. Vienna, Nov. 18, 1845; m. Nov. 25, 1886, Vande Reed. (8) Forest, b. Vernon, O., July 19, 1859; d. Sept. 9, 1863.

2438. vi. BETHSHEBA, b. June 16, 1817; m. 1839, Constant Rowlee Hulse. Ch.: (1) Rozetta, b. June 3, 1840; m. Mar. 8, 1858, Hampden, son of Edward Hume. He was b. Chessike, England, Sept. 25, 1831. Res., Morris, Gounda Co., Ill. Ch.: (a) Edward Constant Hume, b. Nov. 17, 1860; m. Jan. 14, 1884, Elizabeth Mary Caisley. She was b. May 6, 1864; d. Jan. 18, 1894; m. 2nd, Feb. 14, 1896, Grace Foster Meansh, dau. of Allen Horton Foster. He is a farmer; educated at Morris, Ill. Res., Verona. Ch.: (i) Clinton Edward Hume, b. Nov. 1, 1835. (ii) Florence Elizabeth, b. Jan. 2, 1894. (iii) Edna Hume, b. May 12, 1898. (b) Eber Foote Hume, b. Jan. 12, 1862; m. Nettie, dau. of David Miller Cook. He is a Presbyterian; farmer; educated at Morris, Ill. Res., Morris, Ill. Ch.: (i) Jennie Cook Hume, b. Sept. 11, 1890. (ii) Ettie Mary Hume, b. Oct. 8, 1893. (iii) Millard Eber Hume, b. Aug. 25, 1898; d. Apr. 4, 1901. (c) Nettie Jane Hume, b. Aug. 17, 1863; d. Jan. 26, 1866. (d) Frederick George Hume, b. Dec. 26, 1864; m. May, 1868, Cora Mary, dau. of Allen Horton Foster. He is a Baptist; farmer; educated at Morris, Ill. Res., Morris, Ill. Ch.: (i) Foster Hume, b. Sept. 1, 1890. (e) Albert Joseph Hume, b. Wauponsie, Ill., Jan. 13, 1866; m. Lucia, dau. of Terry Miller. He is a farmer; educated and res. at Morris, Ill. Ch.: (i) Hildegarde Hume, b. Oct. 22, 1898. (ii) Floyd Hume, b. Aug. 26, 1901. (iii) Millard Ernest Hume, b. Nov. 1, 1906. (f) Hampden Sidney Hume, b. Sept. 18, 1868; m. Sept. 9, 1896, Nellie, dau. of William Daly. She d. July 20, 1903. He is a farmer; educated and res. at Morris. Ch.: (i) Ralph Hume, b. Aug. 28, 1898. (ii) Ray Hume, b. Mar. 17, 1900. (g) Althea Cora Hume, b. Aug. 21, 1870; m. Feb. 27, 1888, Charles H., son of Marsh Moon. Ch.: (i) Gertie Moon, b. July 1, 1894. (2) Eber Ward Hulse, b. Apr. 3, 1842. (3) Zalmon Foote Hulse, b. June 11, 1844. Was shot at Murfreesboro, Tenn., Jan. 1, 1863. (4) Joseph Nelson, b. Mar. 22, 1846; d. July 23, 1864. (5) Althea Bethsheba Hulse, b. Sept. 23, 1848; m. Isaac, son of William Hedges. He was b. Apr. 27, 1849, at

Willshire, England. Ch.: (a) Mary Abigail Hedges, b. Sept. 20, 1872. (b) Rozetta May Hedges, b. Nov. 25, 1873; m. John A., son of Eric Wilson. Ch.: (i) Eric Reex Wilson, b. Mar. 4, 1903. (c) Charlotte Lenora, b. Sept. 28, 1878. (d) Millie Adell Hedges, b. May 2, 1880; m. Edmund Woodruff, son of Joseph Shinn. She was educated at Pittsburg. Res., 5620 Wilkins Ave., Pittsburg, Pa. Ch.: (i) Millie Adell Shinn, b. July 4, 1902. (ii) Edmund Hedges Shinn, b. Oct. 4, 1904.

2439. vii. JOSEPH, b. July 17, 1822; d. Sept. 19, 1841; unm.

1495. CHARLES FOOTE, (557, 185, 53, 16, 5,) b. Mar. 16, 1796; m. Anna Lawrence. Res., Wellington, Ohio.

2445. i. LUCINDA, b. Aug. 13, 1819; m. John Ealand; d. 1891, Oberlin, O|.
2446. ii. CHAUNCEY, b. Aug. 7, 18—; d. June 14, 1822.
2447. iii. WERIBAN, b. June 23, 1823; d. Sept. 11, 1842.
2448. iv. JOHN LAWRENCE, b. Oct. 11, 1825; m. Ann Morgan Brighton, 3740-3.
2449. v. WILLIAM, b. Feb. 21, 1828; d. Nov. 18, 1828.

1184. JOSEPH FOOTE, (392, 118, 37, 10, 3,) b. Oct. 14, 1781; m. Dec. 10, 1835, Hannah Wallahon, of ———. Res., Vienna, Ohio.

2450. i. JOHN, b. Apr. 7, 1837; m. and has family. Res. near Marietta, O.
2451. ii. JOSEPH, b. Apr. 25, 1839; d. unm.
2452. iii. CHESTER, b. Jan. 8, 1841; d. unm.
2'53. iv. HARRIET E., b. Mar. 11, 1843.
2 54. v. SARAH, b. July 21, 1844.
2:55. vi. ELMINA, b. Dec. 27, 1845.

1186. CHESTER FOOTE, (392, 118, 37, 10, 3,) b. Apr. 27, 1790; m. Feb. 25, 1812, Fanny Hoofcoot. She was b. 1792; d. 1858. Res., Mt. Morris, N. Y.

2456. i. MARIA, b. Dec. 31, 1815; m. Hon. Charles Read. Ch.: (1) Chester, b. ———; d. ———.
2457. ii. ELIZA, b. Nov. 8, 1816; d. Apr. 15, 1854.
2458. iii. GILES WESLEY, b. July 11, 1818; m. Harriet Bump, 3931-8.
2459. iv. CHARLES, b. Oct. 15, 1822; m. Sarah Mitcheal, 3939-41.
2460. v. NORMAN, b. Sept. 16, 1824; m. Emily Jane Jarred, 3942-6.
2161. vi. MARY, b. Sept. 14, 1826; m. Jan. 24, 1849, Robert Blood. Res., Elba, N. Y. Ch.: (1) Albert E., b. Apr. 28, 1850. (2) Frank A., b. Mar. 14, 1852. (3) F. Belle, b. Apr. 13, 1858.
2462. vii. HARRIET, b. Jan. 8, 1834; m. May 11, 1873, Philander Ford; d. Apr. 2, 1903; s. p.

1187. ELISHA FOOTE, JR., (396, 118, 37, 10, 3,) b. Feb. 26, 1786; m. Mar. 15, 1810, Pamelia Kennicott, of Mayfield, Ill. Res., Northampton, N. Y., and St. Charles, Ill. He d. 1876.

2463. i. SAMUEL ALLEN, b. Dec. 12, 1810; d. Apr. 22, 1813.
2464. ii. PAMELA K., b. Dec. 1, 1813; m. Oct. 30, 1845, Jacob Galusha, of Warrenville, Ill. She d. Mar. 14, 1871. Ch.: (1) Ezra Foote, b. Sept. 19, 1846. (2) Cora M., b. Dec. 11, 1848; m. June 23, 1871, Thomas Thance. (3) Edwin A., b. Feb. 20, 1851; m. Dec. 8, 1875, Elvira Scofield. Ch.: (a) Pamela, b. Oct. 9, 1876. (b) Edwin A., b. May 29, 1878. (c) George E., b. Mar. 4, 1880. (d) Frances M., b. Sept. 5, 1882. (e) Maud S., b. Aug. 25, 1884. (f) Gertrude G., b. July 29, 1886. (g) Florence, b. Dec. 6, 1887.

2465. iii. JANE ELIZA, b. Nov. 9, 1815; m. 1840, James Enos, formerly of Vermont. She d. Apr. 25, 1865. Res., Cal. Ch: (1) James E., b. Aug., 1841. (2) Ellen M., b. Mar., 1843. (3) Emily G., b. May, 1845. (4) Harriet A., b. Aug., 1849.

2466. iv. HARRIET A., b. Oct. 23, 1817; m. Nov. 8, 1836, John R. Baker, of Northampton, N. Y. She d. 1897. Res., Batavia, Ill., and Ashton, Neb. Ch.: (1) Helen Eliza, b. 1838; d. 1839. (2) John Emory, b. 1840; d. 1840. (3) Samuel Allen, b. 1841; d. 1857. (4) Mary Augusta, b. Aug. 2, 1845; m. Sidney C. Hollister, of Litchfield, Neb. Ch.: (a) Frances P., b. 1870. (b) John R., b. 1874. (c) Mary Ettie, b. 1885. (5) Etta Burr, b. Nov. 4, 1847; m. Eugene A. Brownell, of St. Charles, Ill. Ch.: (a) Lula May, b. 1868; m. 1888, George W. Wilcox, of Sterling, Ill. Ch.: (i) Etta Lucinda. (ii) Lyle Brownell. (iii) Ella Grace, d. (iv) Harriet Angeline, d. (b) Harriet A., b. 1870. (c) Mary Frances, b. 1875. (d) Eugene W., b. 1879. (e) Baker, b. 1888. (f) Willard F., b. 1894. (6) Charles Jason, b. 1849. (7) Harriet Angeline, b. Sept. 30, 1852; m. May 1, 1873, Jacob Y. Lehman. Ch.: (a) Charles Ernest, b. Aug. 6, 1874; d. Mar. 22, 1875. (b) Carl Clifford, b. July 17, 1876. (c) Olive Lillian, b. Feb. 19, 1878; m. W. Herbert Carolus, May 15, 1901. (d) Harriet Angeline, b. Feb. 22, 1885. (8) Nellie Foote, b. June 10, 1855. (9) John Randolph, b. 1857; d. 1878. (10) James Watson, b. 1859; m. Isabelle Glover, b. 1862. Res., Burwell, Neb. (11) Walter Benjamin, b. June 2, 1863; m. June 12, 1895, Sophia Nowak, b. Feb. 26, 1870; res., Ashton, Neb. Ch.: (a) Edwin Ray, b. Apr. 7, 1896. (b) Mildred Angeline, b. Feb. 9, 1898. (c) Evelyn Lucile, b. Apr. 8, 1901. (12) William Aaron, b. May 31, 1866; m. Oct. 6, 1898, Etta B. Glover, b. Dec. 1, 1869. Ch.: (a) Lester Randolph, b. Oct. 31, 1899. (b) Lawrence Wayne, b. Aug. 9, 1901.

2467. v. ELISHA MILTON, b. Apr. 23, 1820; d. Sept. 3, 1822.

2468. vi. MARY CAROLINE, b. Aug. 29, 1823; m. June 21, 1849, J. L. Warner, of Salisbury, Ct., and Geneva, Ill. He d. Apr. 11, 1872. She d. in New York City, 1902. Ch.: (1) Helen, b. Aug. 9, 1850; m. Lucius Henry Nutting, of 118 E. 16th St., N. Y. City, June 21, 1877. Ch.: (a) Helen, b. Apr. 11, 1878. (b) Mary, b. June 21, 1881; d. Apr. 14, 1882. (c) Ruth, b. Apr. 8, 1884. (d) Lois, b. Jan. 22, 1889. (2) Mary Evelyn, b. Jan. 28, 1858; d. Apr. 30, 1883. (3) Lydia A., b. Mar. 13, 1859; d. Sept. 24, 1859. (4) Jessie May, b. Apr. 9, 1862; d. Sept. 2, 1862. (5) Grace Pamela, b. July 16, 1865; d. Sept. 15, ——.

2469. vii. ELISHA F., b. Feb. 26, 1826; m. Lucy Prindle, 3947-54.

2470. viii. LYDIA ANN, b. Jan. 28, 1828; m. July 8, 1852, A. G. Barton. Ch.: (1) Harvey M., b. Apr. 18, 1853. (2) Ida M., b. July 3, 1856; m. June 14, 1877, James M. Enos. (3) Ira F., b. Aug. 28, 1857; m. M. Hill. (4) Fred F., b. Apr. 30, 1860. (5) Jessie F., b. July 1, 1862; m. M. Davis.

2471. ix. EUNICE A., b. Oct. 27, 1830; m. July 4, 1850, F. R. Warner. They celebrated their golden wedding at Los Angeles, Cal., their home. Ch.: (1) Carrie M., b. Jan. 24, 1854; m. Feb. 9, 1882,

—— Hammond. She d. Dec. 26, 1866. Ch.: (a) Helen Louisa, b. Oct. 28, 1882. (2) Clarence A., b. Sept. 16, 1861. (3) Emory A., b. July 5, 1871.

2472. x. SARAH HELEN, b. Mar. 3, 1835; m. Aug. 27, 1860, James F. Beach. She d. Jan. 12, 1901. Ch.: (1) Elmer E., b. May 22, 1861; m. May 27, 1884, Hilla Alice Feller. Ch.: (a) James H., b. Feb. 4, 1891. (b) Norwood, b. Feb. 22, 1894. (c) John, b. —— 18, 1899. (2) Elisha Foote, b. Mar. 27, 1863; m. ——; d. Aug., 1893. (3) Lucy Warren, b. Sept. 25, 1869. (4) Norwood A., b. Nov. 20, 1871. (5) Frank W., b. June 8, ——. (6) Bessie E., b. Sept. 4, ——.

1190. HENRY FOOTE, (396, 118, 37, 10, 3,) b. Apr. 19, 1791; m. Mar. 5, 1813, Ann Hooscoot. Res., Northampton, New York.

2473. i. AARON S., b. Apr. 19, 1816; m. Caroline Gifford and Susan Hazen, 3955-67.

2474. ii. ESTHER B., b. Apr. 13, 1819; d. ——; m. July 11, 1839, H. G. Phelps. He d. Aug. 20, 1880, at Juda, Wis. Ch.: (1) Harriet Ann, d. ae. 14. (2) Charles. (3) Helen Phelps; res., Gloversville, N. Y.

2475. iii. SUSAN M., b. Feb. 24, 1821; m. Mar. 17, 1842, Robert B., son of Ananias and Sally Prosper Gifford; d. Apr. 18, 1898. She d. Aug. 30, 1895. Res., Northampton, N. Y. Ch.: (1) Esther A., b. May, 1843; m. Dec. 27, 1860, William S. Newman. Ch.: (a) Irving G., b. May 24, 1866. (b) Susie L., b. Jan. 22, 1869. (c) Wm. Fay, b. Nov. 22, 1870. (d) Chester A., b. May 7, 1874. (e) Lois E., b. Mar. 13, 1877. (f) Samuel A., b. Sept. 22, 1880. (g) Ross B., b. Oct. 20, 1883. (2) Chester A., b. Oct., 1845; m. Jan. 24, 1866, Emma I. Hall. Res., Broadhead and Monroe, Wis. Ch.: (a) Netta L., b. Apr. 2, 1867. (b) Zua Belle, b. July 4, 1869. (c) Robert D., b. Mar. 17, 1872. (d) Fred C., b. Dec. 15, 1874. (3) Frances L., b. July, 1850; m. Dec. 29, 1869, Ezra N. Dinwiddie. Ch.: (a) Gertie M., b. June 16, 1871. (b) Charles M., b. Aug. 9, 1874. (c) Queen Esther, b. Apr. 20, 1883. (d) Robert D., b. Feb. 13, 1885.

2476. iv. CHARLES WESLEY, b. July 1, 1823; m. Jane Brooker, 3968-9.

2477. v. REBECCA MILLER, b. Mar. 29, 1825; m. —— Horsman. Res., Gloversville, N. Y. Ch.: (1) Anna.

2478. vi. JOSEPH HENRY, b. May 13, 1828; m. and went to Cal.; nothing further known.

2479. vii. JOHN CLARK, b. Mar. 22, 1830.

2480. viii. ORRIN FREEMAN, b. July 31, 1832; m. Mary Ann Failing, 3970-3.

2481. ix. WILLIAM CHESTER, b. Jan. 22, 1836; m. May 28, 1859, Sarah Ellen Whitley. She d. Jan. 26, 1867. No ch. Lived on the old homestead until 1861; then moved to Juda, Wis. Res., Medford, Wis.

1195. JOSEPH FOOTE, (396, 118, 37, 10, 3,) b. Mar. 1, 1803; m. Apr. 21, 1829, Angelina, dau. of Joseph Spier, of Northampton, N. Y. She d. Mar. 31, 1839, at Rock Island, Ill.; m. 2nd, Cathrine Greene, of Galway, N. Y. Res., Northampton, N. Y.

2482. i. LUCY ELMINA, b. Apr. 9, 1830; m. Thomas Collins, son of
James and Maria (McNamara), Meadville. He was b. Blair Co.,
Pa., July 24, 1832. Ch.: (1) Lucy P., b. Aug. 4, 1862; d. Aug. 9,
1862. (2) Mary M., b. Nov. 4, 1863; d. Nov. 6, 1864. (3) Julia
Elizabeth, b. Dec. 10, 1865; m. Thomas Elwood Stephens. He
was b. Chester, Morrow Co., O., Dec. 16, 1860. Ch.: (a) Harold
M. Stephens, b. July 8, 1890. (b) Orville L. Stephens, b. Sept.
16, 1892. (c) Ralph Elwood Stephens, b. Aug. 19, 1896. (d)
Lucy Emeline Stephens, b. Oct. 16, 1899. (4) Hattie Cook,
b. July 15, 1869; m. Florenz H. Fullriede. He was b. Ohio, 1863.
Ch.: (a) Hazel Fullriede, b. Oct. 6, 1896. (b) Mark C. Fullriede,
b. Oct. 22, 1900. (5) Joseph F., b. Jan. 28, 1871; d. Aug. 17,
1871. (6) Jennie Francis, b. Sept. 17, 1873. (7) Frank Brenner,
b. Jan. 1, 1875.

2483. ii. JOHN WESLEY, b. June 3, 1831; d. of cholera on the Missouri
River, Oct. 8, 1854; unm.

2484. iii. JAMES EDWIN, b. July 21, 1833; m. Mary F. Kennicott,
3974-7.

2485. iv. SARAH ADELIA, b. Aug. 9, 1835. She was educated in N. Y.,
where she taught school for two years, when her parents moved
to Otoe Co., Neb., in 1857. She taught a brief term in the
summer of 1858; m. at Nebraska City, Neb., Oct. 20, 1858, Albert
Nelson, son of Wesley and Lora (Hooker) Hall, of Churchville,
Canada. Res., Santa Paula, Cal.

(1) Prof. Winfield Scott Hall, b. Jan. 5, 1861, at Batavia, Ill.;
m. Oct. 11, 1888, Jeannette, dau. of William N. and Mary (Abbott)
Winter. She was b. Dec. 15, 1860. On Jan. 5, 1861, a son was
b. to Albert N. Hall and Adelia Foote Hall. When a name was
chosen, Lincoln had made his second call for volunteers, war was
in the air, and the boy was christened Winfield Scott. In a few
weeks Albert N. Hall marched away with the Fifty-second
Illinois to join Ulysses S. Grant's command in Western Kentucky. He took part in the engagements at Paducah, Fort Donelson, Shiloh and Corinth. A wound at Corinth retired him from
the firing line for the rest of the war. Returning from the war
in 1865, three years were required to so far mend his broken
fortunes that Albert N. Hall could, with his family, now increased by a second son, join the great tide of army veterans who
were going west to locate ''soldiers' homesteads.'' Locating
temporarily near Nebraska City, he later moved to the frontier,
and took a homestead near Hastings, Nebraska, where he has
remained to see a trackless plain develop into a thickly settled
and· prosperous community, with fine schools, numerous
churches, and other marks of prosperity and progress. The
pioneer life with its privations and its adventures tended to
develop the best that was in Winfield S. Hall. The names of
Lincoln and Grant were household words, and the lives of these
and others of the nation's heroes were ever held up by the
parents as examples of what may be accomplished by overcoming
difficulties. A difficulty was defined as something to be squarely
faced and promptly overcome. The word ''failure'' was not in

the vocabulary. The fact that schools were elementary in grade and accessible only in winter was no reason why one should not receive an education. With the father's encouragement and the mother's guidance, Winfield studied mornings and evenings in winter and continued the studies through the summer, carrying Latin paradigms or mathematical problems to the field and mastering them while at work. In the fall of 1881 he entered the Freshman class of the Northwestern University, choosing the course in Modern Languages, Mathematics and the Natural Sciences. At the end of the Sophomore year his success may be measured by his winning of the prize in Botany and receiving "special mention" in Mathematics. The meagre savings of his teaching all exhausted, it now became necessary for him to earn his way as he went. Having decided to enter the medical profession, he entered the Chicago Medical College, which was affiliated with the Northwestern University, and earned his first year's expenses by delivering morning papers The pittance ($3.25 per week) received for his seven-mile jaunt before breakfast every morning had to be expended very judiciously to cover the items of board, room, fuel, laundry, books and clothing. In the following spring he was put in charge of the Evanston Boat Club's house and boats, a position which brought him again into touch with the college life which he had left so regretfully and which he longed to enter again. The following year he resumed his Liberal Arts studies, and received in 1887, from Northwestern University, the degree of Bachelor of Science, graduating with general honors in scholarship. During his Senior year in college he was made instructor in Mathematics and Science in the Chicago Athenæum, teaching evening classes. This position solved the financial problem, and the opportunities for day classes and private tutoring in summer enabled him to have a bank balance of $500 at the end of his medical course. The medical studies were resumed, and in Apr., 1888, he received from the Chicago Medical College the degree of Doctor of Medicine. At graduation from the medical school he won the Ingalls Prize of $100, given by Ephraim Ingalls to the one who should pass the best examination in the whole field of Language, Literature, History, Mathematics, Chemistry, Physics, Biology, Astronomy, Geology, and the whole medical course of three years. He won also the Fowler prize of a $100 set of oculist's test lenses, for the best examination in theoretical and applied optics. He also won an internship in Mercy Hospital, Chicago. On Oct. 11, 1888, Dr. Hall m. Jeannette Winter, and entered upon his internship in Nov. During the year in Mercy Hospital he made a special study of a number of cases of Pathology, and on a thesis entitled "The Relation of Pathology to the Evolution Theory," received in June, 1889, from Northwestern University, the degree of Master of Science. About this time Dr. Hall received a call to the Chair of Biology at Haverford College, Pennsylvania. Accepting the call, he spent a semester at Harvard in special preparation for his new position. The four years spent at Haverford were years of the most intense activity. His teaching covered the whole field of Biology. Besides his work in Biology, he was Medical Director of the Athletic Work and the Medical Examiner at Haverford, and at the William Penn Charter School of Philadelphia. Anthropometric data collected in these examinations formed the basis of an extended research which occupied much of his vacation time at Haverford, and which was finally finished in Europe. In June, 1893, Dr. Hall resigned his position at Haverford, and with Mrs. Hall went to Leipzig, Germany, where both entered the University, Dr. Hall taking up a special line of work in Physiology with the great master, Carl Ludwig, while Mrs. Hall continued, under Leukhart, biological studies pursued for four years in Haverford. In May, 1894, Dr. Hall completed a dissertation entitled "Die Resorption des Carniferins," based upon his work in Ludwig's Laboratory. Having attended the clinics of Thiersch, Curschmann, Zweifel and Schoen, he came before the Medical Faculty as a candidate for a degree. Passing the examination successfully, he received in June, 1894, the degree of Doctor of Medicine from Leipzig University. He began at once, under the anthropologist Emil Schmidt, to complete the anthropological research begun four years before in Philadelphia. Choosing Anthropology as a major subject, and Zoology and Botany as minor subjects, he registered in the Department of Philosophy of Leipzig University as a candidate for the Doctor's degree, all requirements of which were satisfied, and the degree of Master of Arts and Doctor of Philosophy granted, in Nov., 1894. The dissertation entitled "Changes in the Proportions of the Human Body During the Period of Growth" was written in English for publication in London. After this, Dr. Hall studied a year in Zurich, Switzerland, where he conducted research work in nutrition, publishing at the end of that year two researches: (1) "Ueber die Darstellung eines kuenstlichen Futters"; (2) "Ueber das Verhalten des Eisens im thierischen Organismus." Having accepted a call to the Chair of Physiology in the Northwestern University Medical School, Dr. Hall came to Chicago and entered upon the duties of the position which he now occupies. He is eminently a college man, a man of great physical and mental strength, who is always ready to help students or his colleagues. Ch.: (a) Albert Winter, b. Zurich, Switzerland, Jan. 8, 1895. (b) (adopted) Ethel, b. Oct. 22, 1893. (c) (adopted) Raymond Ludwig, b. Jan. 20, 1897. (d) (adopted) Muriel, b. Aug. 11, 1902.

(2) Henry Nelson, b. Feb. 13, 1866, at St. Charles, Ill.; graduated at Chicago College of Veterinary Surgery, 1889. Practised since then in Hastings, Neb.

(3) Nettie Spires, b. ———; educated Peru State Normal, Peru, Neb., and University of Neb.; spent two years abroad, studying German and Biology in the University of Zurich, Switzerland; taught three years in the public schools of Lake Forest, Ill., and for four years in La Crosse, Wis.

(4) Charlotte Angelina, b. Nebraska City, Neb., Aug., 1870; d. Apr., 1875.

2486.   v.   FRANCES EMILY, b. Northville, N. Y., Oct. 1, 1837; m. George W. Sprott. He was b. Moran, Saratoga Co., N. Y., May 5, 1829; d. May 3, 1893. She res. 25 Rock St., Saratoga, N. Y. Ch.: (1) Son, b. May 13, 1880; d. in infancy.

1197. JOHN WESLEY FOOTE, (396, 118, 37, 10, 3,) b. Mar. 30, 1808; m. Mar. 13, 1838, Harriet, adopted dau. of the wife of his brother Aaron (No. 1192). She d. Mar. 26, 1841; m. 2nd, Elizabeth Slocum, of Northampton, N. Y.

2487.   i.   MELVILLE B., b. Jan. 7, 1840; m. Betsey M. Trowbridge, 3978-82.

2487¹. ii.   CHARLES E., b. Oct. 19, 1855; m. Clara J. Whitman, 3983-5.

1201. COL. MILES FOOTE, (404, 119, 37, 10, 3,) b. Apr. 1, 1788; m. Nov. 11, 1807, Clarinda, dau. of Jonathan Barber, of Canton; she was b. Apr. 11, 1789. He was b. in that part of the ancient town of New Hartford, now a part of the town of Canton. Early in life he enlisted in the First Regt. Cavalry Ct. Militia, rising in the ranks until 1824, when he received his commission as Colonel of this regiment, from Roger Wolcott, Governor of Ct. In 1814 he did active military duty as Captain of a Company in this Regt., stationed at Sacketts Harbor, N. Y. He d. at his home in Canton, Sept., 1878, ae. 90 years and 6 months. He was a vigorous and resolute man, an enthusiast on military matters, and a great lover of fine horses. Throughout his life he disdained to ride in any vehicle, always preferring to ride horseback; hardly a day passed in his later years that he did not take a ride on his horse. At a Centennial celebration, held at Collinsville, in the town of Canton, in 1876, he led a large procession on horseback, and was in the saddle the greater part of the day. His wife was b. in Canton, and d. there in 1866; both are buried in the cemetery at Canton Center, Ct.

2488.   i.   LAURA, b. June 24, 1809; m. Augustus H. Carrier, of Canton, Ct.; d. 1890, in West Hartford, Ct.; buried in Spring Grove Cemetery, Hartford, Ct. Ch.: (1) Lucy M., b. 1848; m. 1876, Nelson T. Hazard, of Hartford, Ct., and d. there in 1883; s. p.

2489.   ii.   HENRY, b. Sept. 15, 1815; m. Lemira Woodruff, 3986-90.

2490.   iii.   LUCIUS, b. Apr. 5, 1817; m. Sarah Barber, 3991-.

2491.   iv.   ELIZA M., b. Mar. 7, 1823; m. Augustus Fuller, of Farmington, Ct.; d. 1886, in Garrettsville, Ohio. Ch.: (1) Florence, b. 1852; m. ———.

2492.   v.   JOHN MILLS, b. Feb. 9, 1827; m. Savilla Woodruff, 3992.

1202. DEA. LANCEL FOOTE, (404, 119, 37, 10, 3,) b. Feb. 28, 1790; m. Feb. 18, 1814, Laura, dau. of Col. George Humphreys, of Canton, Ct., who served in the Revolution and War of 1812. He was the son of Capt. Ezeliel, an officer of the Revolution, and a descendant of Samuel Humphreys, of Simsbury, son of Michael, who settled in Windsor, Ct., in 1654. Lancel Foote exhibited unusual gentleness of disposition, united with much force of character, which rendered him energetic and successful in business, as well as a man beloved in the community. He possessed more than the average amount of native ability, while his intellectual attainments were great, beyond the men of his generation. He was chosen deacon of the Congregational Church in 1839. He d. at Brooklyn, N. Y., Dec. 3, 1865. Res., Canton, Ct.

2493.   i.   GEORGE HUMPHREYS, b. Apr. 15, 1815; d. Mar. 19, 1842.

2494.   ii.   EDWARD L., b. Feb. 5, 1817; d. Aug. 6, 1817.

2495. iii. CHARLES T., b. Oct. 12, 1818; m. Lydia E. Boardman, 3993-5.
2496. iv. ARTHUR WELLINGTON, b. Aug. 1, 1820; m. Elizabeth Rieggles, 3996-7½.
2497. v. ELIZUR LAMER FOOTE, b. Oct. 6, 1822; m. Mary E. Wilson, 3998-4000.
2498. vi. ELLEN ELIZABETH FOOTE, b. Oct. 15, 1824, at Canton Center, Ct.; m. 1st, Elisha C. Wilcox. He d. Mar. 9, 1859; m. 2nd, Charles Robinson. He d. in 1874. No ch.
2499. vii. EDWARD H., b. May 18, 1827; m. Francis Wetter, 4001.
2500. viii. JOHN H., b. Nov. 11, 1833; m. Eliza Cook and Bessie C. Penine, 4002-10.

1203. HERSCHEL FOOTE, (404, 119, 37, 10, 3,) b. Oct. 22, 1793; m. Apr. 10, 1821, Pamelia Bliss Townsend, of Albany, N. Y. She was b. Feb. 11, 1805. Herschel Foote was b. in Canton, Hartford Co., Ct., and was a pioneer settler in Cleveland, O., where he became a prosperous and esteemed merchant. He was thus engaged for nearly 40 years in what is now known as East Cleveland, where he was chosen by his fellow-citizens as Justice of the Peace, and also commissioned as Postmaster. He d. in Brooklyn, N. Y., in the autumn of 1870, in the 80th year of his age. His wife, by maiden name Pamelia Bliss Townsend, was a dau. of Christopher Townsend, a native of New York State. Her mother dying at the time of her birth, she became the adopted dau. of Jonathan and Hannah Bliss, of Cleveland, they having no children of their own. This most estimable lady was spared to a long life of usefulness, dying at the residence of her son in Larchmont Manor, in 1899, at the advanced age of 89 years.
    2501. i. ALFRED MILLS, b. Mar. 16, 1826; m. Ruth L. Adams and Sarah Evertson Brush, 4011-12.
    2502. ii. EDWARD BLISS, b. Feb. 20, 1829; m. Catherine Goodenough Bond, 4013-15.
    2503. iii. MARRETTE GREEN, b. Sept. 20, 1834; m. Jan. 29, 1856, George Washington, son of Josiah B. and Roxana Hall. He d. July 8, 1903. She d. Sept. 15, 1894, at Larchmont, N. Y. Ch.: (1) Ellen Kelley, b. Collamer, Cuyahoga Co., O., Aug. 16, 1857. (2) Marietta Foote, b. Delaware, Delaware Co., O., Oct. 7, 1859. (3) Lilly Pamelia, b. New York City, May 27, 1866; d. June 26, 1869, at St. Louis. (4) George Edward, b. Portland, Callaway Co., Mo., Mar. 23, 1868; d. July 13, 1869, at St. Louis. (5) Alfred Foote, b. St. Louis, Mo., Feb. 5, 1876; d. Feb. 7, 1876.

1207. JOHN STILES FOOTE, (404, 119, 37, 10, 3,) b. Oct. 5, 1805; m. Margaret Todd. Res., Pa.
    2504. i. SAMUEL L., b.
    2505. ii. JOHN G., b.
    2506. iii. MARGARET, b.

1208. CALVIN FOOTE, (405, 119, 37, 10, 3,) b. Feb. 28, 1785, in Northford, Ct.; m. Nov. 6, 1812, Polly, dau. of David Burton. She d. July 23, 1867, at Mill Creek, Pa. He removed to Erie, Pa., in 1810. In U. S. Service, 1812-13; d. June 12, 1879. Res., Erie and Mill Creek, Pa.
    2507. i. LYMAN, b. June 21, 1814; m. Apr. 19, 1838, Maria Burdick.
    2507¹. ii. JOHN, b. Apr. 12, 1816; d. Feb. 11, 1839; unm.
    2507². iii. LAURA, b. May 14, 1818; d. Mar. 20, 1827.
    2508. iv. MARY, b. June 9, 1820; d. Jan. 12, 1882; unm.

. (17)

2508[1]. v.   LUTHER, b. June 24, 1822; d. Aug. 8, 1825.
2508[2]. vi.   LUTHER, b. Dec. 4, 1826; d. June, 1842.
2509. vii.   JAMES, b. July 19, 1829; d. Sept. 22, 1875; unm.
2509[1]. viii. PHEBE, b. Sept. 13, 1832; d. June, 1842.
2510. ix.   ORLIN, b. Mar. 10, 1836; m. Rachel Cooper, 4016-16[1].
2511. x.   LESTER, b. Jan. 25, 1840; m. Susan Scott, 4017-¾.

1210. PLINY FOOTE, (405, 119, 37, 10, 3,) b. Dec. 18, 1789; m. May 2, 1815,
Durinda, dau. of Constantine Miles, of Norfolk, Ct. Res., Norfolk, Ct.
2512. i.   MILES MILLS, b. May 13, 1816.
2513. ii.   LUMAN, b. Dec. 25, 1820; m. Sept. 25, 1844, Maria Riggs, b. May
               14, 1819. Res., North Canaan, Ct. No ch.
2514. iii.   RUFUS, b. Nov. 7, 1822; d. July 19, 1847, in Tachrohah, Wis.

1212. JOHN FOOTE, (405, 119, 37, 10, 3,) b. Apr. 17, 1793; m. Laura, dau.
of Benoni Mills, of Norfolk, Ct. Removed to Austinburg, O., where he d. Sept. 5,
1824.
2515. i.   LYDIA ANN, b. 1816; d. 1866, Austinburg, O.
2516. ii.   JOHN, b. 1820; m. Elmina Fisher, 4018-22.
2517. iii.   LUTHER, b. 1823; m. Luna Hall, 4023-4.

1219. JOHN FOOTE, (415, 126, 38, 11, 3,) b. May 13, 1791; m. Sept. 8, 1812,
Clarissa Knapp, of Danbury, Ct. He d. Oct. 6, 1838.
2518. i.   JOSEPH B., b. Mar. 23, 1813; m. Maria L. Taylor, 4025.
2519. ii.   ELIZA M., b. May 11, 1815; m. Apr. 2, 1835, Francis Knapp, of
               Danbury, Ct. Ch.: (1) Francis, b. ———; m. ———. (2)
               William, b. ———; m. ———. (3) Edward, b. ———; m. ———.
               Res., Orange, N. J,
2520. iii.   SARAH ANN, b. May 4, 1817; m. June 18, 1837, Enos W. Littell,
               of Delaware, O. She d. Mar. 20, 1892. Ch.: (1) John Foote, b.
               July 1, 1842, Delaware, O.; m. Dec. 24, 1863, at Kenton, O.,
               Louisa M. Keel. Was in grocery business for years, and held
               many city offices. Ch.: (a) George Edward, b. Delaware, O.,
               Jan. 10, 1865; m. Eva, dau. of Robert Courlett. He d. May 16,
               1904, Sacramento, Cal. Ch.: (i) Daisy May, b. Feb. 11, 1891.
               (b) Margaret Alice, b. Nov. 6, 1866, Delaware, O.; m. Jan. 14,
               1892, Elmer E., son of William Bleckley, Allentown, Pa. Res.,
               148 S. Park St., Wichita, Kansas. Ch.: (i) Eva Frances, b.
               Nov. 17, 1892, at Michital; d. June 21, 1904. (ii) E. Russell, b.
               Dec. 30, 1894. (iii) George Littell, b. June 15, 1896; d. Jan. 16,
               1898. (iv) Clarence Elmer, b. Dec. 8, 1898. (c) Anna May, b.
               Mar. 3, 1868. (d) Lily Bell, b. May 18, 1870. (e) William
               Tracy, b. Oct. 22, 1877; d. Oct. 27, 1883. (f) Raymond Powell,
               b. June 6, 1886, Wichita, Kansas. (2) Mary Clarissa, b. May
               10, 1858; m. Dr. Frank Van Sant, at Delaware, O. Res., Ft.
               Recovery, O.
2521. iv.   MARY AMELIA, b. May 1, 1819; m. Dec. 1, 1845, Ezra Abbott,
               of Danbury, Ct. Ch.: (1) Mary Esther, b. ———; m. Peter
               Ambler. Res., Danbury, Ct. (2) Leander, b. ———; m. ———.
2522. v.   JOHN, b. May 29, 1821; d. June 6, 1822.
2523. vi.   DAVID AUGUSTUS, b. ———; m. Eliza M. Trowbridge, 4026-32.
2524. vii.   JOHN, b. May 22, 1825; m. Martha ———, 4033-6.

2525. viii. LEANDER P., b. Jan. 5, 1828; m. Catherine A. Holmes and Jennie Dawson, 4037-9.

2526. ix. MARGARET C., b. July 17, 1830; d. Aug. 28, 1830.

2527. x. CHARLES E., b. June 2, 1833; m. Mary ———, 4040-2.

1223. CHARLES FOOTE, (418, 126, 38, 11, 3,) b. Dec. 21, 1793; m. Sept. 8, 1822, Ann Strong, dau. of Elijah Burr, of Fairfield, Ct. She d. Aug. 12, 1832; m. 2nd, May 16, 1833, Jane Sterling, dau. of John Thompson, of Strafford, Ct. Mr. Foote was cashier of the Connecticut Bank for over 30 years, also held the office of Mayor, and held other offices of trust in the city. He was also Colonel in the State Militia. Res., Bridgeport, Ct.

2528. i. MARY ANN, b. Mar. 20, 1834; m. Charles M. Mitchell, of Waterbury, Ct., Feb. 1, 1854. Mr. Mitchell was a large manufacturer in Waterbury, Ct., and also President of the Bridgeport Brass Co. He d. Mar. 9, 1899; she d. Apr. 18, 1859.

2529. ii. CHARLES ENOCH, b. Mar. 10, 1836; d. Jan. 28, 1837.

2530. iii. CHARLES B., b. Sept. 6, 1837; m. Charlotte L. Ames, 4043-6.

2531. iv. WILLIAM H., b. Aug. 24, 1839; m. Ida Augusta Hayes, 4047-8.

2532. v. DAVID T., b. July 17, 1841; m. Mary A. Gould, 4049-53.

2533. vi. ELEANOR COIT, b. May 27, 1844; m. Geo. R., son of Peyton R. Bishop, of Bridgeport, Ct., Mar. 28, 1866. Mr. Bishop d. Mar. 1, 1880, ae. 33 years. Ch.: (1) George Randolph, b. Sept. 27, 1869; d. June 28, 1870. (2) Lottie Louise, b. July 4, 1872; d. July 25, 1872. (3) Peyton R., b. July 6, 1875; d. Aug. 31, 1876. (4) Forrester Foote, b. Aug. 3, 1877.

2534. vii. EDWARD ELANSON, b. Jan. 28, 1848; d. Sept. 8, 1848.

2536. viii. CAROLINE THOMPSON, b. July 14, 1850; d. Apr. 25, 1851.

1225. ISAAC NEWTON FOOTE, (419, 128, 38, 11, 3,) b. abt. 1782 at New Fairfield, Ct.; m. at New Fairfield, Ct., abt. 1808 or 1809, Abigail Bass. He was a farmer and cooper; d. at Fairfield, Vt., Aug. 10, 1833. She d. at St. Albans, Vt., abt. 1852.

2537. i. SPAULDING, b. abt. 1810; m. Elizabeth Oaks, 4054-6.

2538. ii. ANNA, b. abt. 1813; d. in infancy.

2539. iii. ANNA, b. abt. 1815; m. 1858 or 1859, Charles E. Smith, farmer, of Montgomery, Vt. She was a milliner at St. Albans, Vt.; d. at Montgomery, Vt., abt. 1859.

2540. iv. ANGELINE, b. abt. 1819; m. in the fall of 1851, Captain Hannibal Potter, farmer and sailor, of Potter's Island, off St. Albans, Vt.

2541. v. LAURA ABIGAIL, b. abt. 1821; d. at St. Albans, Vt., Apr., 1850 or 1851.

2542. vi. ISAAC, b. Feb. 2, 1823; m. Lucy L. Gillette, 4057-8.

1229. TRUMAN SHERMAN FOOTE, (421, 128, 38, 11, 3,) b. Woodbury, Ct., Jan. 21, 1807; m. Mary Dana, dau. of Abraham Dana, of Syracuse, N. Y., Mar. 3, 1840. Mrs. Foote was b. near Syracuse, N. Y., Mar. 31, 1820; d. in Albany, N. Y., Oct. 5, 1852. Mr. Foote d. in Albany, N. Y., May 21, 1851.

2542¹. i. MARY DANA, b. Albany, N. Y., May 4, 1841; d. May 4, 1841.

2543. ii. TRUMAN SHERMAN, b. Feb. 11, 1845; m. Jane Foote Mix, 4059-63.

1233. HORACE FOOTE, (422, 128, 38, 11, 3,) b. ———; m. Sarah French, of Watertown, Ct. He was a joiner and clock maker; d. in Waterbury, Ct., abt. 1865. She res. there in 1875.

2543¹. i. SARAH, b. ———; m. ——— Sheldon.

2543². ii. MARTHA, b. ———; m. ——— Beach.

1238. CHAUNCEY FOOTE, (422, 128, 38, 11, 3,) b. Woodbury, Ct., abt. 1818; m. in Milton, Ct., ——— Shoemaker. He d. Dec., 1884. Res., Milton, Ct.

2544. i. WILLIAM S., b. Jan. 3, 1862; m. Nora L. Raymond, 4787-93.

2545. ii. JENNIE ISABEL, b. ———.

1240. DAVID FOOTE, (432, 130, 39, 11, 3,) b. Mar. 13, 1775; m. Dec. 21, 1800, Betsy Minor, of Windsor, Mass. She d. Sept. 27, 1838, ae. 57; m. 2nd, Nov. 20, 1841, Eliza Gardner, of Chatham. She d. Feb. 13, 1844, ae. 57; m. 3rd, Oct. 21, 1844, Rhoda Waterbury, of Greenfield, N. Y. He d. Oct. 5, 1856.

2546. i. ERMINA, b. Jan. 27, 1802; m. Jan. 30, 1823, Jonathan Nash, Jr., of Peru, Mass. He d. Apr. 15, 1829. She m. 2nd, Nathaniel P. Baker, of Conway, Mass. He d.; m. 3rd, Solomon Williams. Ch.: (1) Francis Nash, b. Sept. 8, 1824; d. Apr. 23, 1848. (2) Jonathan Alvin Nash, b. Nov. 13, 1828; d. Mar. 16, 1829.

2547. ii. HARLOW, b. Jan. 31, 1804; m. Euretta Rockwell, 4064.

2548. iii. AMANDA, b. Mar. 18, 1806; m. Aug. 1, 1826, Jonathan A. Rathbone, of Conway, Mass. Ch.: (1) Lucy Ellen, d. Apr. 20, 1848, ae. 6 years.

2549. iv. ELIZA, b. Aug. 10, 1808; m. Mar. 8, 1825, William Thomas, of Peru, Mass. She d. Mar. 3, 1826. Ch.: (1) Eliza Foote, b. Mar. 3, 1826. The father and dau. moved to Pa. Nothing further known.

2550. v. DAVID AUSTIN, b. Dec. 10, 1810; m. Esther E. Hill, 4065-70.

2551. vi. AMELIA ANN, b. Apr. 25, 1813; m. Nov. 28, 1838, David C. Rogers, of Conway, Mass. She d. at Westfield, Mass., Sept. 8, 1896. He d. Jan. 1, 1886. Res., North Adams, Mass. Ch.: (1) Martha Ann, b. Holyoke, Mass., Oct. 10, 1839; m. May 18, 1864, Charles G. Parsons, of Boston, Mass. She d. Nov. 14, 1889. Ch.: (a) George E., b. Chelsea, Mass., Dec. 25, 1865. Res., Greenfield, Mass. (b) William J., b. Medford, Mass., 1867. Res., Millers Falls, Mass. (c) Martha R., b. Medford, Mass., 1869; m. July, 1881, Charles Handferet. Res., S. Pasadena, Cal. (2) Frances Nash Rogers, b. Holyoke, Mass., May 20, 1842; m. Apr. 21, 1880, W. P. St. Germain, undertaker at 1984 Lexington Ave., New York. Ch.: (a) Madeline Frances, b. Washington, Mass., Oct. 13, 1881; m. June 22, 1905, Lincoln Bonneau, of N. Y. City. Ch.: (i) Germain Rogers Bonneau, b. N. Y. City, Aug. 21, 1906. (3) George Edward Rogers, b. No. Adams, Mass., June 10, 1849; m. Oct. 1, 1873, Clara Clark. Ch.: (a) Ethel Christine, b. Millers Falls, Mass., Nov. 8, 1877. (b) Phillip, b. Greenfield, Mass., Feb. 3, 1888.

2552. vii. MARIETTA, b. Nov. 16, 1815; m. Apr. 30, 1840, Porter, son of Charles Welles, of Conway, Mass. Res., Whately, Mass. Ch.: (1) John, b. May 17, 1841; m. Sarah J. Root. (2) David Foote, b. Feb. 11, 1845; d. Aug. 11, 1846. (3) David Porter, b. Oct. 23, 1848; m. Nov. 15, 1871, Mary Jones Foster. (4) Calvin O., b. May 5, 1856.

2553. viii. EMERSON C., b. ———; m. Abigail Field, 4071-6.

2554. ix. ALDEN A. G., b. ———; m. Julia E. Wells, 4077-9.

2555. x.   JANE MARIA, b. Apr. 6, 1823; m. May 3, 1853, Asaph Critten-
           den. Res., Conway, Mass.; m. 2nd, Sept. 16, 1869, Sardis Bacon,
           of Wakefield, Mass. Congregationalist. Res., 151 W. Newton
           St., Boston, Mass. Ch.: (1) Robert Bruce Crittenden, b. June
           16, 1860.

1241. LEMAN FOOTE, (432, 130, 39, 11, 3,) b. June, 1775; m. 1801, Rush
Scofield, of Milton, N. Y. Res., Greenfield, N. Y. He was a Captain in the War of
1812.

2556. i.   ESTHER, b. Greenfield, N. Y., 1802; m. John Rockwell, of Sara-
            toga Springs, N. Y. Ch.: (1) Angeline. (2) Charles. (3)
            Charlotte. (4) Daniel. (5) Leamon.

2557. ii.   CHARLOTTE, b. Greenfield, N. Y., 1804; m. Thomas Wicks, of
            Charlton, N. Y. Ch.: (1) Rev. Emerson G., b. ———; res.,
            Ballston, N. Y. (2) Charles Theron, b. ———; m. Mary Elizabeth
            Hall. He d. ———; res., Cohoes, N. Y. Ch.: (a) Charles Hall
            Wicks, b. ———. (3) David Foote, b. ———; m. Alice Belding.
            He d. ———. Ch.: (a) Harry Lee Wicks, b. ———; d. in
            infancy. (b) David Irving Wicks, b. ———; m. Sara Hawley; res.,
            336 E. 16th St., Brooklyn, N. Y. Ch.: (i) Alice Wicks, b. ———.
            (c) Lillian Eva Wicks, b. ———; m. George I. Eddy. Res., 291
            Marlborough Road, Brooklyn, N. Y. Ch.: (i) Emerson Wicks
            Eddy, b. ———. (4) Mary Jane Wicks, b. ———. Res., Ballston
            Spa., N. Y. (5) Julia Ann, b. ———; m. Gilbert L. Hall; both
            d.; no ch. (6) Emmerette, b. ———; m. Orville Miller. She d.
            Ch.: (a) Julia F. Miller, b. ———; m. Nathan Curtis. Res.,
            Ballston Spa., N. Y.; no ch. (b) Elisha Henry Miller, b. ———;
            d. ae. 14 years. (c) Adelaide Miller, b. ———; m. Thomas C.
            Schutt. She d. Ch.: (i) Raymond C. Schutt, b. ———; res.,
            Ballston Spa., N. Y. (d) Alice U. Miller, b. ———; m. Edwin
            Trutmyer; res., Bellingham, Wash.; no ch. (e) Charlotte Eliza-
            beth Miller, b. ———; m. George H. Middlebrook; res., Brooklyn,
            N. Y.; no ch. (f) William Emerson Miller, b. ———; d. ———.

2558. iii. DAVID, b. 1806; m. Mary Ann Gleason, 4079¹⁻³.

2559. iv.   CHARLES, b. Feb. 19, 1809; m. Bethiah Gleason, 4080-4⁴.

2560. v.   LUCY ANN, b. Greenfield, N. Y., Sept. 9, 1810; m. Sept. 15, Calvin
            Benedict, of Kalamazoo, Mich. He was b. June 12, 1809. Ch.: (1)
            Jane E., b. June 25, 1832; m. Sept. 30, 1853, William Lovett; d.
            Apr. 9, 1857. (2) Lydia, b. Aug. 10, 1834; m. Apr. 11, 1860,
            Richard Fletcher. (3) Sarah, b. Apr. 9, 1841; m. June 27, 1862,
            Hiram A. Burt.

2561. vi.   MARY, b. Greenfield, N. Y., 1812; m. Richard Dedrick, of Clifton
            Park, N. Y.; d. 1843. Ch.: (1) George. (2) John. (3) Charles.
            (4) Margaret.

2562. vii. EMERETT, b. Greenfield, N. Y., 1814; m. David Davis, of Milton,
            N. Y. Ch.: (1) Barney. (2) Laura. (3) Charlotte.

2563. viii. SARAH, b. Milton, N. Y., 1816; m. Theron Soles; d. in Randall,
            N. Y., 1841. Ch.: (1) Sarah. (2) Frank.

2564. ix.   JULIETTE, b. Milton, N. Y., 1817; m. Richard Dedrick, of
            Clifton Park, N. Y. Ch.: (1) Mary. (2) Emerson.

2565. x.   DANIEL, b. Milton, N. Y., 1820; res., New Orleans.

2566. **xi.** RAVIA, b. Milton, N. Y., Jan. 9, 1822; m. Jan. 22, 1850, Jonathan Hiller, of Ballston, N. Y. He was b. July 15, 1822; d. Mar. 28, 1903. She d. Nov. 23, 1896. Ch.: (1) Isaac W., b. July 31, 1852. (2) Frederick Jonathan, b. May 19, 1858; res., Waterford, N. Y.

2567. **xii.** LAURA ANN, b. Greenfield, N. Y., 1823; d. 1843.

1244. DANIEL AVERY FOOTE, (432, 130, 39, 11, 3,) b. May 12, 1783; m. Mar. 13, 1813, Mary D. Prior, of Greenfield, N. Y. Res., Milton, N. Y. He d. July 20, 1849; she d. Jan. 8, 1861.

2568. **i.** WILLIAM E., b. Greenfield, N. Y., Feb. 3, 1814; d. May 6, 1814.

25°9. **ii.** ADELIA A., b.

2570. **iii.** WILLIAM H., b. Sept. 3, 1817; m. Jan. 8, 1841, Maria Hoit, of Greenfield, N. Y.

2571. **iv.** CAROLINE, b.

2572. **v.** DEA. DAUPHIN KING, b. North Milton, N. Y., June 25, 1823; m. 1st, Oct. 27, 1852, Eliza Emigh; she d. at Downers Grove, Ill., Feb. 8, 1894; m. 2nd, Feb. 2, 1897, Olive Van Potter, of Aylmer, Elvin Co., Ontario, Ca. She was b. Sept. 19, 1857. He went West and made his home in Ill. in 1849. When coming from Saratoga with his bride in 1852 they had the distinction of riding in the first passenger train that left Chicago on the Rock Island R. R. Res. at Downers Grove for 35 years; d. Dec. 12, 1906; buried at Aurora by the side of his first wife.

2573. **vi.** DANIEL BAILEY, b. May 31, 1825; m. Euphemia Powell, 4085-7.

2574. **vii.** JAMES S., b. May 6, 1833; m. Caroline A. Crandell, 4088-91.

1246. ISAAC SALMON FOOTE, (433, 130, 39, 11, 3,) b. Jan. 11, 1768; m. Dec. 1, 1793, Esther Parker, of Washington, Ct. She was b. Mar. 17, 1770; d. Feb. 2, 1845. He d. Mar. 6, 1837. Res., Washington, Ct., and Charlotte, Vt.

2575. **i.** FANNY, b. Apr. 3, 1794; m. Solomon Keeler. Ch.: (1) John, b. ———; res., Madrid, N. Y.

2576. **ii.** ISAAC S., b. Feb. 6, 1796; d. 1804; unm.

2577. **iii.** SIMEON, b. Apr. 15, 1798; d. July 22, 1864; unm.

2578. **iv.** AMANDA, b. Feb. 11, 1801; m. Feb. 6, 1823, Birdsey Newell. Ch.: (1) Polly A., b. Nov. 14, 1823; d. Jan. 8, 1824. (2) Abel A., b. Nov. 16, 1824; d. Sept. 29, 1883; unm. (3) Argolous B., b. July 13, 1827; m. Oct. 13, 1867, Sarah Lyman. He d. May 20, 1882; p. s. (4) Harriet F., b. June 10, 1830; m. May 18, 1858, Robert Sattley. She d. Dec. 7, 1888. Ch.: (a) Winfield Newell, b. June 19, 1859; d. May 18, 1901. (b) Marshall A., b. Oct. 27, 1860; res., Chicago, Ill. (c) Elmer C., b. Feb. 3, 1863. Res., Meresson, Pa. (5) William M., b. Nov. 14, 1832; d. June 20, 1893; unm. (6) Leenrs S., b. July 18, 1835. (7) Esther M., b. Oct. 3, 1839. Res., North Ferrisburg, Vt. (8) Isaac F., b. June 8, 1842; d. Feb. 6, 1844. (9) Winfield W., b. Feb. 7, 1844; d. Mar. 29, 1853.

2579. **v.** HARRIET S., b. Mar. 8, 1807; d. July 12, 1883.

2580. **vi.** JERUSHA ANN, b. Jan. 10, 1810; d. Mar. 15, 1883.

1247. GIDEON FOOTE, (433, 130, 39, 11, 3,) b. Mar. 22, 1770; m. Mar. 14, 1796, Susannah Parker, of Charlotte, Vt. She was b. Jan. 15, 1775; d. Feb. 9, 1808; m. 2nd, 1808, Abigail Parker, sister of his first wife. She b. Aug. 25, 1782; d. Jan. 29, 1812; m. 3rd, Nancy McCune, widow. Res., Washington, Ct., and Charlotte, Vt.

2581. i. ORLEY NEWELL, b. Aug. 25, 1797; d. Oct. 23, 1818, in New York.

2582. ii. GIDEON LEWIS, b. Feb. 28, 1799; d. 1844. Res., Dutchess Co., N. Y., and Tennessee; unm.

2583. iii. SUSANNA, b. Nov. 28, 1801; d. June 26, 1844.

2584. iv. ISAAC S., b. June 28, 1805; m. Mary L. Baisley, 4092-3.

2585. v. THOMAS WILLIAM, b. Nov. 17, 1807; d. Oct. 4, 1888.

2586. vi. CHARLES P., b. June 20, 1809; m. Lucy Ann Barton, 4094-7.

2587. vii. PHILO P., b. Oct. 17, 1811; m. Sarah Van Wyck, 4098-4105.

2588. viii. ORLEY NEWELL, b. Charlotte, Vt. Ch. by third wife.

All were b. in Washington, Ct., but No. 2588.

1248. SIMEON FOOTE (433, 130, 39, 11, 3,) b. Mar. 12, 1772, in Charlotte, Vt.; removed to Sandusky, O.; m. Phaebe Beach. She was b. Dec. 30, 1779; d. in Mt. Carroll, Ill., Dec. 22, 1873. He d. in Chatfield, O., Oct. 30, 1851.

2589. i. JOHNSON H., b. 1803; m. Sarah Alexander, 4106-10.

2590. ii. SABRINA, b. ——; m. Eliza Stearns. Res., Mt. Carroll, Ill. Ch.: (1) Adaline Cornealia, m. Samuel Camp, son of Lester Hayes, of Greene, Pa. Res. (1884), Chicago.

2591. iii. SAMUEL, b. Feb. 25, 1804; m. Mary Ann Hawley, 4111-5.

2592. iv. OPHELIA, b. ——; m. Malon Hollingsworth. Res., Mt. Carroll, Ill. Ch.: (1) Mary. (2) Hiram. (3) Helen. (4) Alice. (5) Malon.

2593. v. MILO, b. ——. Res., Savannah, Ill. 4116.

2594. vi. CYNTHIA, b. ——; m. Asa Stearns. Res., Trenton, Indiana. No ch.

2595. vii. CORNELIA M., b. St. Lawrence Co., N. Y., Aug 12, 1824; m. 1845, Chas. Norton, of Buryous, O. He d. abt. 1850 at Buryous; m. 2nd, Oct. 26, 1853, Felix O'Neal, of Mt. Carroll, Ill. He was b. July 5, 1824, in Greene Co., N. Y.; d. Sept. 23, 1904, at Aurelia, Ia. She d. Jan. 1, 1897; res., Mt. Carroll, Ill., and Aurelia, Iowa. Ch.: (1) Waldo Norton, b. Dec. 3, 1847; m. 1866, Ellen ——. Res., 2731 Jackson St., Dubuque, Iowa. Ch.: (a) Charles Norton. (b) Cornelia. (c) Harry. (d) Frederic. (e) Byron. (f) Wilbur. (g) Roy. (2) Margery Norton, b. Aug., 1849; d. in infancy. (3) Mary O'Neal, b. Feb. 6, 1855; d. July, 1855. (4) Robert S. O'Neal, b. Mt. Carroll, Ill., Jan. 28' 1857; m. Jan. 1, 1878, Martha Pradell, of Lanark, Ill. She d. Mar. 21, 1898, at Aurelia, Iowa. Ch.: (a) Edna O'Neal, b. June 14, 1880; m. Oct., 1899, W. E. Ausman, of Cherokee, Ia. Ch.: (i) Lois Ausman, b. Aug. 10, 1902. (ii) Neal Ausman, b. Oct., 1904. (b) Ethel O'Neal, b. Feb. 23, 1883; m. 1902, J. P. Conigan, of Sioux City, Iowa. Ch.: (i) Margaret Conigan, b. Apr. 21, 1907. (c) Carl O'Neal, b. June 10, 1885; m. Sept., 1905, Maud Tool. Ch.: (i), b. ——; d. ——. (d) Ruth O'Neal, b. Jan. 21, 1898. (5) Clara O'Neal, b. May 28, 1858; d. Jan., 1862. (6) Cora B. O'Neal, b. Mt. Carroll, Ill., May 20, 1895; m. Sept. 16, 1886, at Aurelia, Ia., to Albert Belen. Ch.: (a) Ada Belen, b. Sept. 8, 1892. (7) Louis O'Neal, b. Mt. Carroll, Feb. 2, 1861; m. Aug., 1893, Borlara Kane, of Aurelia, Iowa. He d. Nov. 28, 1902. Res., Top Bar, So. Dakota. Ch.: (a) Charles O'Neal, b. May, 1895. (b) Leo, b. Feb., 1896. (c) Harrold, b. May, 1898. (d) Mary, b. May, 1900; d. ——. (e) Clifford, b. Nov. 20, 1902. (8) Frederic O'Neal, b. Jan. 1,

1865; d. Sept., 1865. (9) Nellie, b. Mt. Carroll, Mar. 14, 1867. Res., Aurelia, Ill.; unm. (10) Norman, b. Feb. 22, 1870; d. Aug., 1870.

1249. CALEB M. FOOTE, (433, 130, 39, 11, 3,) b. Sept. 24, 1779; m. Aug. 7, 1803, Clarinda Newell, of Charlotte, Vt. Res., Charlotte, Vt., Madrid and Potsdam, N. Y.

    2596. i.   ALBERT S., b. Charlotte, Vt., July 19, 1804.
    2597. ii.   ELIHU L., b. Charlotte, Vt., Feb. 22, 1808; m. Elmina Russell. Res., Canton, N. Y.
    2598. iii. LUCY, b. Madrid, N. Y., Feb. 22, 1813; m. John Andrews, of Cleveland, O. Ch.: (1) Sarah L.
    2599. iv. MYRON, b. Aug. 10, 1815; m. Mary L. Gale, 4117-9.
    2600. v.   HORACE, b. Oct. 29, 1816; m. Rosanna Whittlesey, 4120.
    2600¹. vi. CLARISSA, b. Madrid, N. Y., July 14, 1819; d. Jan. 17, 1837.
    2600². vii. EMILY, b. Madrid, N. Y., Apr. 21, 1822; m. Wheeler Powell, of Willoughby, Ohio.
    2600³. viii. SARAH, b. Potsdam, N. Y., Dec. 10, 1826.
    2600⁴. ix. MARY E., b. Potsdam, N. Y., Dec. 29, 1829.

1250. NEWELL FOOTE, (433, 130, 39, 11, 3,) b. Charlotte, Vt., Sept. 29, 1784; m. Clarissa, dau. of Rhuma and Rhoda (Kilburn) Hill. She was b. 1788; d. May 20, 1821, in Keene, N. Y.; m. 2nd, Mary Goulden. She d. May 13, 1857. Res., Madrid, N. Y.

    2601. i.   FARNUM N., b. Feb. 28, 1825.
    2602. ii.   ORSON M., b. Dec. 21, 1857; m. Senna S. Jones, 4121-3.
    2602¹. iii. CORNELIUS, b. Oct. 7, 1830.
    2602². iv. CALEB, b. 1829.
    2602³. v. MEHITABLE, b. Mar. 4, 1823; m. Edward Lawrence, of Ft. Atkinson, Ia. 4 ch.

1252. JOHNSON FOOTE, (433, 130, 39, 11, 3,) b. Dec. 19, 1787; m. 1st, ———; m. 2nd, Elsie Reed. Had 7 ch. by 1st wife, names unknown. Ch. by 2nd wife:

    2603. i.   LAURA, b. ———; m. Henry Wilson. Ch.: (1) Sarah, b. (2) Fred, b.
    2603¹. ii. CHARLOTTE, b. ———; m. Valorus Wilson; res., Kimball, S. D. Ch.: (1) Estella, m. Alton Foote. (2) Clarence; res., St. Louis, Mo.
    2603². iii. JANE, b. ———; m. Charles Nelson. Ch.: (1) Charles, b. ———; res., Morley, N. Y.
    2603³. iv. AUGUSTINE, b. ———; m. George Wilson; both d.; no ch.
    2603⁴. v. CYNTHIA, b. ———; m. Charles Allen; both d.; no ch.
    2604. vi. GILBERT L., b. 1832; m. Welthia G. Smith, 4124-6.

1257. RODERICK R. FOOTE, (434, 130, 39, 11, 3,) b. abt. 1791; m. Oct. 23, 1822, Oliva, dau. of Gideon Hurlbut, of New Haven, Ct. He d. June 15, 1832, in New Haven, Ct.

    2605. i.   GEORGE HURLBUT, b. ———; printer. Res., New Haven, Ct.

    · 1262. AMOS FOOTE, (443, 131, 39, 11, 3,) b. Feb. 14, 1776; m. Mary Curtiss. She was b. Oct. 2, 1777, in Lanesborough, Mass., and d. Oct. 30, 1824, in Manlius, N. Y.; m. 2nd, Abby ———. She was b. Sept. 20, 1777, in Newtown, Mass., and d. there in 1847. Res., Lanesborough, Mass., Manlius, N. Y., and Bridgeport, Ct. Ch. all b. in Lanesborough, Mass., except 2613 and 2614.

2606. i. HARRIET, b. July 18, 1800.
2607. ii. AMOS C., b. Nov. 4, 1801; m. Lydia Tallman, 4127-8.
2608. iii. MELANCTON C., b. May 23, 1804.
2609. iv. ROLANDUS S., b. Nov. 10, 1806; m. Eliza Andrus, of Lanesborough, Mass. Was Inspector in Canal Office. Res., Buffalo, N. Y. No ch.
2610. v. PHEBE M., b. Jan. 14, 1809.
2611. vi. SARAH E., b. Nov. 18, 1810.
2612. vii. ELECTA J., b. Oct. 4, 1812.
2613. viii. ALBERTUS B., b. Nov. 3, 1818, in Manlius, N. Y.; m. Caroline Wellman Goodsell, 4129-31.
2614. ix. CHARLES PARMELE, b. Feb. 11, 1823, in Manlius, N. Y. Res., Buffalo, N. Y.

1270. RHESA FOOTE, (447, 134, 39, 11, 3,) b. July 5, 1781; m. Oct. 4, 1808, Polly, dau. of Elias and Ruth (Lewis) Hawley, of Munroe, Ct. She was b. Sept. 16, 1786; d. Dec. 21, 1827. He d. Dec. 6, 1861. Res., Newtown, Ct.
2615. i. JULIA MARIA, b. Nov. 8, 1809; m. Apr. 21, 1826, Charles L. Stillman. She d. Dec. 16, 1869. Res., Western New York.
2616. ii. CATHRINE HAWLEY, b. Jan. 31, 1810; m. Oct. 23, 1830, Beach Camp, of Newtown, Ct. Ch.: (1) William, b. May 23, 1832. (2) Julia Ann, b. June 29, 1835. (3) Jane Eliza, b. Apr. 6, 1837.
2617. iii. GEORGE L., b. Mar. 4, 1812; m. Minerva Tuttle, 4132-7³.
2618. iv. FREDERICK LEWIS, b. Oct. 15, 1813; d. May 12, 1814.
2619. v. MARY, b. July 15, 1815; d. June 14, 1816.
2620. vi. FREDERICK W., b. Oct. 23, 1816; m. Vashti B. Thompson, 4138-46.
2621. vii. MARY, b. Dec. 21, 1817; m. Apr. 19, 1846, Rev. Henry V. Gardner, of Harwington, Ct. Ch.: (1) George Edward Gardner, b. in Homer, N. Y., Oct. 19, 1856; m. Jessie, dau. of Mortimer G. Lewis, of Lowville, N. Y., Jan. 24, 1888. Graduated from Hobart College in 1880; from Berkeley Divinity School in 1883. Was ordained to the ministry of the Protestant Episcopal Church on June 14, 1884. He d. in St. Joseph, Missouri, on Nov. 5, 1891.
2622. viii. HARRIET, b. Apr. 13, 1819; m. Apr. 19, 1846, Rev. Wm. Atwell, of Kent, Ct.
2623. ix. ROBERT, b. Apr. 6, 1821; d. Apr. 5, 1830.
2624. x. HENRY HAWLEY, b. Jan. 6, 1823; physician in Roxbury, Ct.; d. Dec. 24, 1859.
2625. xi. JANE ELIZABETH, b. July 23, 1825; m. Oct. 18, 1848, Walter B. Welton. She d. Mar. 5, 1867.

1273. HEBER FOOTE, (447, 134, 39, 11, 3,) b. at Litchfield, Ct., Dec. 5, 1787; m. Dec. 9, 1809, at Reading, Ct., Lucy, dau. of Baily and Ann Stillson. She was b. at New Haven, Ct.; d. at Dryden, N. Y. He d. Dec. 23, 1852, Groton, N. Y.
2626. i. ERASTUS BAILEY, b. Newtown, Ct., Feb. 3, 1811; an Episcopal clergyman; d. Sept. 26, 1847, at Raleigh, N. C.; unm.
2627. ii. CHARLES H., b. May 18, 1812; m. Mary French, 4147-9.
2628. iii. CELIA, b. Jan. 13, 1814, at Newtown, Ct.; m. ——— Welch. Ch.: (1) Abba Ann, b. ———; m. ——— Grey. (2) Charles, b. ———; d. 1863. And one other.

2629. iv.   JUSTIN, b. ———; m. Sarah Ann Edgecomb and Anne M. Hickey, 4150-4.

2630. v.   WEALTHY, b. Groton, N. Y., Sept. 24, 1818; m. Chauncey Wilcox; d. Sept. 22, 1876, at Carbondale, Pa. Ch.: (1) Reginald, b. 1844; went to the war; d. Nov. 19, 1862. (2) Mason, b. ———; res., Carbondale, Pa. (3) Charles, b. ———; res., Carbondale, Pa.

2631. vi.   ABBA ANN, b. Mar. 2, 1821, at Groton, N. Y.

2632. vii.   HEBER, b. Dec. 4, 1822, at Groton, N. Y.

2633. viii.   LUCY, b. Dec. 18, 1824, at Groton, N. Y.; m. Luther Griswold. She d. June 12, 1862, at Dryden, N. Y. He d. May 9, 1896. Ch.: (1) Celia, b. ———. (2) Grace, b. ———; m. George E. Goodrich. Res., Dryden, N. Y.

1274. REV. MILTON FOOTE, (447, 134, 39, 11, 3,) b. in Richfield, Ct., Sept. 15, 1789; m. Aug., 1808, Lois Briscoe, of Newtown, Ct. Methodist minister. He d. Nov. 14, 1842, North Adams, Mich. She d. Oct. 15, 1882, Adrian, Mich.

2634. i.   HANNAH MARIA, b. Newtown, Ct., Dec. 18, 1809; m. Oct. 9, 1828, Pharis Sutton. He d. Mar. 6, 1895, in Dover, Lenawee Co., Mich. She d. May 1, 1897, at Clafton, Mich. Ch.: (1) Sarah Ann, b. in N. Y., Oct. 5, 1829; d. Feb. 26, 1834. (2) Lois B., b. Adrian, Mich., Mar. 20, 1832; m. Mar. 14, 1854, H. W. Hoxter, of Rome, Mich.; farmer. He d. Ch.: (a) Ella, b. ———; m. Mr. Gambee. (3) Julia Ann, b. Adrian, Nov. 19, 1834; d. Oct. 30, 1836. (4) Deborah, b. North Adams, Mich., July 6, 1837; m. Dec. 31, 1868, J. C. Gambee, in Dover, Mich.; carpenter. (5) Milton F., b. North Adams, Mar. 31, 1840; m. 1st, Jan. 6, 1870, Charlotte Barclay. She d. Aug. 7, 1887; m. 2nd, Aug. 17, 1893, Phoebe Brooks. She d. Farmer. Res., Osseo, Mich. Ch.: (a) George B., b. ———. (b) Maud, b. ———; m. Mr. Webster. He d. (6) Robert B., b. North Adams, Sept. 22, 1841; m. Mar. 30, 1871, Alice C. Pontins, in Dover. Farmer and Supervisor for a number of years. Res., Clayton, Mich. Ch.: (a) Margaret, b. (b) Florence, b.

2635. ii.   JOHN M., b. Sept. 19, 1811; m. Allida A. Jackson, 4154-61.

2636. iii.   ABBA, b. in Cayuga Co., N. Y., Apr. 12, 1814; m. 1st, Alonzo Moore. He b. Beekmantown, N. Y., June 7, 1809; d. at Rome Center, Mich., June 29, 1859; m. 2nd, Nov. 27, 1866, Sylvanus Kinney. He d. at Adrian, Mich., Oct. 28, 1899. She d. at Adrian, Mich., May 28, 1899. Ch., all b. at Rome Center, Mich.: (1) Abba Melissa, b. Dec. 29, 1835; m. Apr. 8, 1860, Oscar Todd, at Rome Center, and d. Mar. 9, 1861. (2) Adelia Maria, b. Dec. 7, 1838; m. Adrian, Mich., Nov. 27, 1867, Capt. Martin Robinson. (3) Anna Eliza, b. Jan. 27, 1840; m. at Rome Center, Mich., Dec. 5, 1860, William Morey. (4) Susan Amelia, b. July 18, 1843; m. at Adrian, Mich., May 17, 1883, Jesse Fleming. He d. at Adrian, Mich. (5) William Alonzo, b. Nov. 4, 1845; d. at Rome Center, June 29, 1859. (6) Henry Hale, b. Feb. 6, 1848; m. July 16, 1876, Julia S., dau. of Dr. Berlin, of Farmington, Minn. He d. at Lion Falls, South Dakota, Oct. 30, 1896.

2637. iv.   JAMES, b. June 8, 1815; m. Harriet Bagley (Foote), 4162-71.

2638. v.   ESTHER CEMANTHA, b. in Cayuga Co., N. Y., May 24, 1818;

m. Nov. 1, 1836, at Adrian, Mich., Lemuel Smith, son of Rev.
Joseph Bangs. He was b. May 22, 1811. She d. July 3, 1852, at
North Adams. Ch.: (1) Joseph Milton Bangs, b. Sharron, Mich.,
Aug. 10, 1837; m. June 2, 1862, Christina Webster, at College
Springs, Ia. She d. Mar., 1901, at Elmo, Mo.; m. 2nd Dec. 23,
1903, Mrs. Elizabeth Griswold, of Southern Oklahoma. Res.,
Madison, Kas. (2) James Heman Bangs, b. North Adams, June
23, 1840; m. Nov. 23, 1865, at Clarenda, Ia., Mira Jane Feltch.
Res., Olpe, Kas. (3) Mary Jane Bangs, b. North Adams, Dec. 6,
1842; m. Oct. 26, 1865, at Tecumseh, Mich., Philip Augustus
Cowley. She d. Mar. 19, 1897, at Hudson, Mich. He res. Hudson,
Mich. (4) Armenia Adelia Bangs, b. North Adams, Mar. 17, 1845;
m. Jan. 2, 1867, at Harpersfield, N. Y., David C. Buck. Res.,
Hudson, Mich. (5) Julia Peninnah Bangs, b. North Adams, Dec.
5, 1848; m. Dec. 23, 1869, at Adrian, Mich., Ezra Adams. He d.
Mar., 1896, at Westmoreland, N. Y., where she res. (6) Eli Foote
Bangs, b. North Adams, Feb. 17, 1851; m. July 10, 1869, in Nod-
away Co., Mo., Julia Sckoonover. Res., Eugene, Oregon.

2639. vi. WILLIAM B., b. Apr. 11, 1820; m. Susan A. Aylsworth, 4172-76.

2640. vii. ELIZA SABRINA, b. Dec. 14, 1821, in Villanova, Chatauqua
Co., N. Y.; m. Jan. 12, 1841, Joseph Kempton. He was b. Apr.
15, 1817. She d. Dec. 23, 1902, in Loveland, Col. Ch.: (1) Esther
Adelia Kempton, b. Oct. 28, 1841; m. June 13, 1863, at College
Springs, Iowa, Miles Leroy Stoers. He was b. June 18, 1842; d.
Dec. 24, 1866, at Winterset, Ia.; m. 2nd, Mar. 20, 1870, Jonathan
Willets. He was b. Aug. 27, 1823; d. May 9, 1902. Ch.: (a) Evalyn
Floretta Stoers, b. Jan.15, 1865. (b) Eda May Willets, b. Feb. 22, 1876.
(c) Guy Ralston Willets, b. Jan. 21, 1879; and 2 others who are
dead. (2) James B. Kempton, b. Nov. 19, 1843; m. May 20, 1869,
Maria A., dau. of Elbridge Gerry. She was b. Oct. 5, 1851. Res.,
Terry, Mont. Ch.: (a) Berney Edmond Kempton, b. July 8,
1870. (b) Henry Norman, b. Dec. 30, 1871. (c) Sarah Adelia
b. Dec. 30, 1873. (d) Sanford Smith, b. Oct. 16, 1875. (e) Asa
Sterling, b. Nov. 15, 1877. (f) James Garfield, b. Sept. 18, 1879.
(g) Mary Mable, b. Dec. 30, 1881. (h) Joseph Elbridge Kempton,
b. Dec. 22, 1892. (3) George Wellington Kempton, b. Sept. 13,
1846; m. Feb. 19, 1868, at North Adams, Mich., Mary L. Browers.
He d. May 13, 1899. Ch.: (a) James Burney Kempton, b. Sept.
19, 1869; m. Sept. 30, 1890, at Sydney, Neb., Laura Coulter. She
was b. in Aug., ——. Ch.: (i) Forest Kempton, b. Feb. 21,
1896; d. June 17, 1899. (ii) Helen Kempton, b. Aug. 15, 1900.
(b) Philinda Adelia Kempton, b. Apr. 29, 1871; m. Dec. 4, 1889,
at High Park, Col., Charlie Nash. Ch.: (i) Alice Nash, b. Nov.
30, 1890. (ii) Bernice, b. Apr. 29, 1892. (iii) Lester, b. July 8,
1894. (iv) Tendis Nash, b. Dec. 25, 1897. (c) Alice Sabina
Kempton, b. Jan. 8, 1873; m. July 3, 1889, at High Park, Montie
R. Kilburn. Ch.: (i) Beatrice Lilian Kilburn, b. Mar. 23, 1890;
d. June 10, 1890. (ii) Saville, b. Mar. 1, 1895. (iii) Miriam
Kilburn, b. May 8, 1902. (d) Geraldine Ada May Kempton, b.
Apr. 28, 1882; m. Dec. 10, 1901, Harry H. Argabrite, at Ft.
Collins, Larimer Co., Col. Ch.: (i) George Arnet Argabrite, b.

Sept. 29, 1902. (4) Wesley A. Kempton, b. Oct. 6, 1848; m. Mar. 26, 1874, at College Springs, Fannie J. Coulter. She was b. Mar. 28, 1853. Res., Loveland, Colo. Ch.: (a) Linua Mae Kempton, b. Apr. 29, 1875; m. July 3, 1893, John Dozier, at Ft. Collins, Col.; m. 2nd, July 26, 1903, at Colorado Springs, Victor Cushman. Ch.: (i) Frank Dozier, b. Nov. 9, 1894. (ii) Frave Dozier, b. Apr. 13, 1896. (b) Lois Ida Kempton, b. Oct. 12, 1876; m. Aug. 26, 1895, at Loveland, Col., Fred O. Mitchell. He was b. Nov. 19, 1873. Ch.: (i) Marie Evangeline Mitchell, b. Oct. 21, 1896. (ii) Ellen Gwendolyn Mitchell, b. June 10, 1903. (c) Lee Franklin Kempton, b. Nov. 4, 1889; d. July 9, 1890. (d) Infant Dau., b. Apr. 29, 1885. (e) Wilina Armenia, b. Jan. 13, 1886. (f) Gwendolyn, b. Nov. 4, 1889. (g) Wesley, b. Feb. 12, 1893. (h) Lester, b. Apr. 14, 1897. (5) Mary Caroline Kempton, b. Jan. 6, 1851; m. Nov. 25, 1875, at College Springs, Ia., Will H. Black. He was b. Nov. 25, 1845. Ch.: (a) Wilnia Estellia Black, b. Feb. 27, 1883. (b) Clara Adellia Black, b. Dec. 20, 1884. (6) Lucinda Melissia Kempton, b. Sept. 6, 1853; m. Feb. 15, 1877, at College Springs, Thomas Alexander Anderson. He was b. Aug. 14, 1852; d. Aug. 14, 1903. Ch.: (a) Oliver Adelbert Anderson, b. Nov. 29, 1877; m. Nov. 24, 1904, at Denver, Col., Mable, dau. of Henry and Clara Adellia (Kempton) Rough. (b) Earl James, b. Mar. 28, 1885. (c) Ethel Maude Anderson, b. Sept. 1, 1887. (7) Hannah Kempton, b. May 14, 1857; d. Oct. 5, 1857. (8) Clara Adellia Kempton, b. July 2, 1860; m. Nov. 25, 1880, at Evans, Col., Henry Rough. He was.b. June 14, 1844; d. May 8, 1884; m. 2nd, Sept. 30, 1886, at Evans, James Rowe Stevens. Ch.: (a) Mable Rough, b. Jan. 29, 1882; m. Nov. 24, 1904, at Denver, Oliver Anderson (No. 6a above). (b) Bessie Fern Stevens, b. May 8, 1890. (c) Doris Vera Stevens, b. Mar. 23, 1892.

2641. viii. AUGUSTUS N., b. Sept. 18, 1832; m. Sarah S. Parks, 4177-81.

2642. ix. ADELLIA MARIA, b.. Villanova, May 20, 1826; m. 1st, Dec. 31, 1845, Marcellus B. Darling, of Adrian, Mich.; m. 2nd, Oct., 1862, Knight Record, of Adrian, Mich. She d. Mar. 15, 1897. Res., Farmington, Minn. Ch.: (1) Lucretta Maria Darling, b. Nov. 2, 1846; d. Feb. 20, 1850. (2) Edna Ann Darling, b. July 10, 1856; m. May 18, 1881, Joseph R. Clements. Ch.: (a) Edith Louise Clements, b. July 15, 1882. (b) Joseph R. Clements, Jr., b. July 11, 1888. (3) Kate Darling, b. Nov. 10, 1858. (4) Sarah Knight Record, b. Aug., 1869; d. July 11, 1870.

2643. v. ELI SWAYZEE, b. Apr. 1, 1828; m. Mary Culter and Mary Frye, 4182-4.

1279. WILLIAM FOOTE, (453, 134, 39, 11, 3,) b. Oct. 12, 1772; m. Abiah ____. She was b. July 3, 1771.

2643¹. i. HANNAH V., b. Aug. 24, 1798; m. Mr. Conger; d. 1816.

2643². ii. MARY ANN, b. June 10, 1800; m. June 10, 1818, Birthday Cone; he was b. 1796; d. 1886. She d. June, 1881. Ch.: (1) Hannah F., b. 1819; d. 1827. (2) Crocker, b. 1820; m. ____. Ch.: (a) Mary Ann. (b) Bushday. (c) Wilbert. (d) Ella. (3) Susannah R., b. 1822; m. Lewer Strong. Res., Frederickstown. Ch.: (a)

Clayton. (4) Mary Jane, b. 1828; m. Leve Rowley. Ch.: (a)
Herma, b. (b) Etta, b. (c) Henry, b.

2643³. iii.   WILLIAM P., b. Feb. 28, 1803; m. Betsy Murphy, 4185.

2644. iv.   EPHRAIM, b. 1807; m. Abbie Dennis and Wealthy Wright, 4186-8.

2644¹. v.   LARANCE, b. 1808; m. Honor Rowley and Isabelle Long, 4189-90.

2645. vi.   ADONIJAH, b. Dec. 10, 1810; m. Elizabeth Bedell, 4191-4200.

2645¹. vii.   CORNELIA ROMSOM, b. Aug. 9, 1812; m. Nathaniel Chancey.
Ch.: (1) Paphro, b. ———; m. Ann ———. Ch.: (a) Cornelia,
b. ———. (2) James B., b. ———; m. Martha ———; res.,
Fredericktown, O. Ch.: (a) Cora. (b) Mary. (c) Hamlaton.
(d) Ella. (e) Kate. (f) Addie. (3) Coraden, b. ———; m.
Mary ———. Ch.: (a) Fred. (b) Charles. (c) Robert. (4)
Mary, b. ———; m. Bruce Ransom. Ch.: (a) Bertha. (b)
Edward. (c) Pearl. (d) Laura.

1280.   EBENEZER FOOTE, (459, 137, 39, 11, 3,) b. July 9, 1774; m. Mabel
Banks, of Redding, Ct. She d. Dec. 29, 1856, ae. 79 years. He d. Jan. 29, 1855.
Res., Unadilla, N. Y.

2645². i.   ALANSON, b. Mar., 1799; d. Sept. 5, 1822.

2646. ii.   ELIAS, b. Apr. 1, 1801; m. Harriet W., 4978-81.

2647. iii.   HYATT, b. Feb., 1804; m. 4982-5.

2648. iv.   JESSE, b. Feb., 1807; m. 4986-90.

2649. v.   EMELINE C., b. June, 1810; m. David Betts, and d. June 10, 1848.
Ch.: (1) Eben. (2) George. (3) Charlotte.

2650. vi.   CHARLES, b. Dec., 1812; 4991-3.

2650¹. vii.   PHILANDER BENJAMIN, b. July, 1815; d. Sept. 14, 1822.

2651. viii.   LEANDER BENNET, b. July 11, 1815; m. ——— Balcom, 4994.

1281.   BENAJAH ELLIS FOOTE, (459, 137, 39, 11, 3,) b. Litchfield Co., Ct.,
Apr. 18, 1777; m. 1802, Mary E. Wooden, of Oxford, Ct. She was b. Nov. 15, 1778;
d. Apr. 11, 1866; buried at North Otto, N. Y. He d. Apr. 6, 1862, in Mansfield,
Cattaraugus, N. Y.; buried at North Otto, N. Y.

2652. i.   WILLIAM D., b. Huntington, Ct., May 1, 1803; m. Mary Loveland, 4201-6.

2653. ii.   ROSWELL, b. Harwinton, Ct., Aug. 27, 1804; m. Harriet Smith,
4207-9.

2654. iii.   RANSFORD THOMAS, b. Watertown, Litchfield Co., Ct., Jan. 6,
1806; m. Susan Atwood, 4210.

2655. iv.   LINUS, b. Watertown, Ct., Dec. 13, 1807; m. 1858, Betsey Chal-
fant, of South Bend, Ind. She d. ———; m. 2nd, Aug. 21, 1878,
Losey Grey. He d. Mar. 5, in Ellicottville, N. Y.

2655¹. v.   DANIEL B., b. Plymouth, Ct., May 11, 1809; unm.

2656. vi.   LUCIUS, b. Plymouth, Ct., May 7, 1810; m. Eliza Ann Atwood
and Agnes Gallows, 4211-5.

2657. vii.   ALEXIS (named at birth Benajah L.), b. Plymouth, Ct., Aug. 11,
1812; m. Christiana Millis, 4218-23.

2658. viii.   ALBERT, b. in Watertown, Ct., Oct. 11, 1817; d. Nov. 5, 1895;
unm.; buried in Glenwood Cemetery, Colden, Erie Co., N. Y.

2659. ix.   FREDERICK, b. Oct. 11, 1817; m. Mary A. Smith, 4224-31.

2660. x.   LARMON, b. Oct. 9, 1818; m. Louisa U. Cochran, 4232-3.

2661. xi.   HENRY L., b. Sept. 2, 1820; m. Clarissa Foster, 4234-5.

1302. CAPTAIN ARNOLD FOOTE, (462, 140, 39, 11, 3,) b. ———; m. Anna Parks, of Newtown, Ct. Res., Auburn, N. Y. She d. Feb. 8, 1820, ae. 39 years.

2662. i. ROBERT P., b. July 21, 1803; d. Nov. 25, 1807.

1303. PHILO FOOTE, (464, 140, 39, 11, 3,) b. Mar. 27, 1787; m. Aug. 25, 1809, Eunice Lewis, of Derby, Ct. Res., Brookfield, Ct.

2663. i. ANN JANNETTE, b. Aug. 31, 1811; m. Feb. 8, 1829, Daniel Wildman, of Brookfield, Ct.

2664. ii. JANE, b. Oct. 3, 1813; m. Sept. 12, 1833, Isaac C. Barnum, of Bethel, Ct. She d. Oct. 27, 1848. Ch.: 3 sons and 3 daus.

2665. iii. JOHN L., b. July 22, 1815; m. Apr. 18, 1841, Hannah Blakeman, of Brookfield, Ct.

2666. iv. ABEL, b. July 19, 1817; m. Oct. 27, 1840, Abby Atkins, of Danbury, Ct.

2667. v. GRANDISON D., b. Feb. 25, 1820; m. Nov. 6, 1844, Mercy A. Porter, of Danbury, Ct.

1309. DAVID FOOTE, (473, 142, 41, 11, 3,) b. May 17, 1776; m. 1799, Sukey Underhill, of Newtown, Ct. He d. May 20, 1834.

2668. i. JOSEPH b. Nov. 9, 1799.

2669. ii. BEERS, b. July 5, 1805; m. Pamelia A. Merwin, 4236.

2670. iii. JULIA ANN, b. Feb. 25, 1810; m. May 14, 1834, J. Tooley, of Hudson, Mich.

2671. iv. SHERMAN, b. Dec. 14, 1814; m Clarena Peck, 4237-39.

2672. v. ALMIRA, b. Nov. 7, 1817; m. Sept., 1834, Sellick Boothe.

1312. ISAAC FOOTE, (473, 142, 41, 11, 3,) b. Oct. 5, 1785; m. Nov. 18, 1817, Anna, dau. of Enos Johnson, of Newtown, Ct. She was b. Apr. 5, 1788.

2673. i. POLLY MARIA, b. Feb. 19, 1809.

2674. ii. ANDREW J., b. Nov. 6, 1812.

2675. iii. HANNAH, b. May 12, 1814.

2676. iv. HEPPY ANN, b. Sept. 26, 1816.

2677. v. CHARLES SHERMAN, b. May 8, 1819.

2678. vi. MARYETTE, b. Nov. 12, 1821; d. July 19, 1822.

2679. vii. JOHN G., b. Aug. 10, 1823.

2680. viii. JOSEPH, b. May 26, 1826.

1318. STEPHEN FOOTE, (475, 142, 41, 11, 3,) b. Sept. 1, 1788; m. 1st, Mar. 30, 1811, Elizabeth Wood. She d. Apr. 3, 1812, ae. 20; m. 2nd, Apr. 24, 1813, Dorcas Barr. Res., Barker, N. Y.

2681. i. BENJAMIN FRANKLIN, b. Mar. 4, 1812; d. June 17, 1835, in Ill.

2682. ii. ELIZABETH, b. Nov. 12, 1819.

2683. iii. PETER SHEPARD, b. Aug. 29, 1824.

1319. LEMUEL FOOTE, (475, 142, 41, 11, 3,) b. July 28, 1790; m. Dec. 2, 1815, Lucretia Garnsey. He d. July 4, 1847. Res., Barker, N. Y.

2684. i. MARY M., b. Sept. 8, 1816.

2685. ii. RHODA, b. Aug. 2, 1819; d. in infancy.

2686. iii. MARIA, b. Dec. 20, 1822; d. Dec. 24, 1845.

2687. iv. JOHN MARTIN, b. Jan. 29, 1832.

1322. NIRAM FOOTE, (475, 142, 41, 11, 3,) b. Apr. 4, 1797; m. 1st, Jan. 10, 1818, Amanda Dunham. She d. July 11, 1845; m. 2nd, Dec. 31, 1848, Azubah Boardman. Res., Barker, N. Y.

2688. i. WILLIAM, b. Jan. 10, 1819.

2689. ii.   JEHIEL, b. May 2, 1821; d. 1845.
2690. iii. ADELINE, b. Mar. 8, 1825.
2691. iv.   SARAH ANN, b. Mar. 20, 1828.
2692. v.   AMY, b. Sept. 6, 1830.
2693. vi.   NIRAM, b. Oct. 12, 1832; d. Jan. 15, 1833.
2694. vii. JOHN NELSON, b. Nov. 20, 1833; d. Aug. 3, 1834.
2695. viii. JOHN, b. June 25, 1836.
2696. ix.   CHARLES HENRY, b. Jan. 31, 1838.
2697. x.   MARY JANE, b. Nov. 30, 1840.
2698. xi.   ENOS PUFFER, b. Oct. 16, 1843.

1324. WILLIAM FOOTE, (481, 142, 41, 11, 3,) b. May 20, 1790; m. Sept.
1, 1816, Marie, dau. of Joshua Bailey, of Bridgeport, Ct. She d. Sept. 11. 1872.
He d. Oct. 28, 1869. Farmer. Res., Stanford, N. Y.

2699. i.   DANIEL EDWIN, b. Mar. 30, 1818; m. Betsy Ann Griffin and
             Adelia Gould, 4249-52.
2700. ii.   HENRY B., b. Sept. 29, 1820; m. Lucretia Eells, 4253-5.
2701. iii. CHARLES A., b. Oct. 5, 1823; m. Jerusha A. Buck, 4256.
2702. iv.   ALBERT, b. Feb. 10, 1826; m. Loanda Patchen, 4257-60.
2703. v.   MINERVA, b. July 27, 1828; m. Feb. 25, 1850, James H., son of
             Daniel and Polly (Odell) Butler, of Walton, N. Y. She d. Sept.
             3, 1861, at Tompkins, N. Y. Ch.: (1) Horace Greeley. (2)
             Harvey V. (3) Laura.
2704. vi.   WILLIAM B., b. Apr. 10, 1833; m. Sarah Elizabeth Swart, 4261.
2705. vii. MARY ANN, b. Jan. 21, 1836; m. Dec. 28, 1864, Charles Edward
             Whitlock, b. Jan. 12, 1835; d. Mar. 14, 1897. Res., Hobart, N. Y.
             No ch.
2706. viii. JERUSHA M., b. Feb. 23, 1839; for 25 years she was a noted
             dressmaker of large repute, and dealer in dressmaking supplies.
             Res., Hobart, N. Y.

1325. LUTHER FOOTE, (481, 142, 41, 11, 3,) b. July 10, 1792; m. Pheba,
dau. of John B. Judson. She b. Feb. 13, 1798; d. at Oxford, N. Y., Jan. 26, 1881.
He was a mechanic of great ability; d. Feb. 10, 1878. Res., Stanford, N. Y.

2707. i.   OSCAR, b. June 3, 1822; m. Mary L. Harrison, 4262-4.
2708. ii.   ANN ELIZA, b. ———; m. George Carhart Printer, of Oxford,
             N. Y.
2709. iii. GEORGE L., b. Jan. 27, 1827; m. 4265.
2709½. iv.   CHARLES, b. ———; d. Jan. 31, 1876.

1327. HENRY FOOTE, (481, 142, 41, 11, 3,) b. Mar. 23, 1797; m. June 24,
1824, Lozina, dau. of Zolman and Hannah (Whitlock) Taylor, b. Apr. 21, 1800.
Res., Dekalb Co., Ill.

2710. i.   SALLY ANN, b. June 1, 1826; m. Oct. 9, 1844, Ira, son of
             Frederick Wager. He was b. Davenport, N. Y., July 11, 1821.
             Res., Chicago, Ill. Ch.: (1) Eugene Frederick, b. Feb. 15, 1848;
             res., Covington, Ind. (2) Henry Frederick, b. Aug. 27, 1850; d.
             Feb. 24, 1853. (3) Charles Delbert, b. Sept. 6, 1855; d. Feb. 3,
             1856. (4) Evelyn Louisa, b. Aug. 3, 1857. (5) James, b. Mar.
             10, 1862; d. Dec. 11, 1862.
2711. ii.   HANNAH, b. Sept. 2, 1829; m. Oct. 31, 1847, Richard Wilcox, b.
             Apr. 5, 1822; res., Horseheads, N. Y. Ch.: (1) Josephine, b.
             Apr. 2, 1849; m. July 3, 1865, Leman C., son of Lewis and

Rebecca (West) Palmer; res., Centerville, Pa. Ch.: (a) Roy M., b. Oct. 14, 1867. (2) Celista, b. Nov. 26, 1851; d. Sept. 19, 1852. (3) Imogene, b. Mar. 25, 1854; d. Aug. 25, 1854. (4) Celista L., b. July 4, 1855; m. Dec. 22, 1873, Levi Webb, son of Stephen and Frances (Garrison) Redfield; res., Southport, Horseheads, N. Y. Ch.: (a) Frank Wilcox, b. June 9, 1875.

2712. iii. FRANCES EMILY, b. May 5, 1831; m. May 16, 1850, Norman, son of Henry and Jane (Wagmer) Durham. He was b. 1820; d. Oct. 2, 1852; m. 2nd, 1876, Dr. Darman Cowles. He was b. July 24, 1829; res., Hazel Barrens, Mo. Ch.: (1) Clement Henry, b. June 1, 1851; d. Oct. 20, 1851. (2) Losina Jane, b. Aug. 1, 1852; d. Dec. 20, 1852. (3) Frances Emily, b. Mar. 20, 1855. (4) Ona W., b. Aug. 17, 1858.

2713. iv. EDWARD P., b. Jan. 9, 1836; m. Amanda M. Gleason, 4266-8.

2714. v. HELEN, b. July 14, 1843; m. Aug. 8, 1860, Alonzo Ed., son of Thurston and Nancy (Lockey) Carr. He was b. Nov. 5, 1832; res., Park Ave., Sycamore, Ill. Ch.: (1) Cora Eugene, b. Aug. 26, 1861. (2) Edward Alanzo, b. Oct. 31, 1866. (3) Helen Myra, b. Apr. 4, 1870.

1330. SHERMAN FOOTE, (481, 142, 41, 11, 3,) b. Newtown, Ct., Apr. 5, 1805; m. Emily Richmond. Res., Wyoming, Jones Co., Iowa.

2714¹. i. HELEN, b.

2714². ii. WILLIAM, b.

2714³. iii. LOUIS, b.

2714⁴. iv. SARAH, b.

2714⁵. v. LAURA, b.

2714⁶. vi. ANN ELIZA, b.

1331. CHARLES FOOTE, (484, 142, 41, 11, 3,) b. Sept. 30, 1802; m. Hobart, N. Y., Jan. 13, 1832, Abigail Augusta, dau. of Anthony Marvine, of Hobart, N. Y. She was b. July 10, 1810; d. Oct. 4, 1882. He was a speculator and farmer; d. May 12, 1875. Res., Hobart, N. Y.

2714⁷. i. CHARLES EDWARD, b. Jan. 20, 1833; m. June 6, 1855, Mary Leet, dau. of James Clark, of Hobart, N. Y. She was b. July 12, 1832. He was a speculator and a farmer; d. Oct. 23, 1861; s. p.

2714⁸. ii. HENRY GRIFFIN, b. June 24, 1838; d. Dec. 28, 1860.

1332. DAVID FOOTE, (484, 142, 41, 11, 3,) b. Newtown, Ct., Jan. 13, 1805; m. Stamford, Ct., Feb. 20, 1833, Julia, dau. of Kelsey Kelly. She was b. Mar. 24, 1810; d. May 18, 1854, at Harpersfield, N. Y. Methodist. Farmer. He d. June 1, 1848, at Harpersfield, N. Y.

2715. i. CHARLES L., b. Dec. 12, 1833; m. Jane Hamilton, 4270-4274.

2715¹. ii. HARRIET A., b. Oct. 23, 1835; m. in Stamford, N. Y., Apr., 1856, Stephen Odell. She d. Nov. 13, 1867.

1333. BAILEY FOOTE, (486, 145, 41, 11, 3,) b. Aug. 21, 1774; m. July 3, 1796, Jerusha Glover. She was b. in Weston, Ct., Sept. 28, 1775. He d. Apr. 26, 1822. Res., Hobart. N. Y.

2716. i. ORRIN, b. Sept. 30, 1799; m. Elizabeth T. Moore, 4275-8.

2717. ii. SALLY MARIA, b. Sept. 4, 1804; m. May 9, 1825. He was b. June 6, 1804, in Newtown, Ct. Res., Hobart, N. Y. Ch.: (1) Charles Alonzo, b. May 11, 1827. (2) Frances Elizabeth, b. June 20, 1829. (3) Delia Maria, b. Aug. 7, 1831. (4) Bailey Foote, b. Dec. 31, 1833; d. Apr. 12, 1838. (5) Julia Augusta, b. June 16, 1836.

2718. iii. GEORGE BRYANT, b. Aug. 17, 1808; m. Harriet Andrews and Maria Emma Glover, 4279-4280.

2719. iv. JANE ELIZA, b. Dec. 5, 1810.

2720. v. JULIET, b. Aug. 31, 1813; d. Apr. 27, 1838.

1334. CYRENIUS FOOTE, (486, 145, 41, 11, 3,) b. Jan. 31, 1781; m. June 27, 1819, Volusia Glover, wid. She was b. July 9, 1785, and d. Nov., 1865. He d. Sept. 27, 1830. Res., Hobart, N. Y.

2721. i. EUGENIA MARIA, b. Hobart, N. Y., July 6, 1821; m. 1847, Rev. Caleb Bailey Ellsworth, of N. Y.; d. Mar. 13, 1904. Ch.: (1) Anna Volusia, b. June 27, 1852, in N. Y.; m. Sept. 28, 1877, George Allen Williamson, of Maspeth, N. Y. City; d. Oct. 28, 1881, Maspeth, N. Y. City. Ch.: (a) Allen Ellsworth Williamson, b. Nov. 15, 1878, Maspeth, N. Y. City.

2722. ii. CORNELIA SOPHIA, b. Aug. 11, 1822; m. June, 1844, James Pierson, of New York. She d. June, 1897, Sacramento, Cal. Ch.: (1) Hobart Foote, b. Oct. 31, 1849, Lowville, N. Y.; m. 1887, Evelyn Knight. Ch.: (a) James K., b. May, 1889. (b) Elwyn, b. Mar., 1894. (c) Marjorie, b. Dec., 1896. All b. Sacramento, Cal. (2) Julia Elizabeth, b. Lowville, Feb., 1848; m. ———. One ch., unm.; res., Cleveland, O. (3) James Cyrenus, b. May, 1852, Monroe, Ct.; m. 1877, Susie Boyd, San Francisco, Cal. Res., Sacramento, Cal. Ch.: (a) Daniel Wallace, b. Sept., 1878. (b) Alice Cornelia, b. Sept., 1879; d. Sept., 1879, Sacramento, Cal. (c) Elita Eugenia, b. Nov., 1883. (d) Sue Ellinor, b. July, 1885. (e) Edith Aileen, b. July, 1889. (f) Cyr Carleton, b. Aug., 1892. (g) Claire Edwina, b. Apr., 1898. (h) Caryl Edwin, b. Apr., 1898. (i) Hobart Ellsworth, b. Jan., 1881.

2723. iii. GEORGE EDGAR, b. Jan. 1, 1824; d. Nov., 1848. Res., New York City.

2724. iv. THEODORE C., b. June 12, 1825; m. Mary Hart, 4240-2.

2725. v. DANIEL D., b. Jan. 2, 1827; m. Julia S. Amermon and Helen M. Foote and Lavinia Meeker, 4243-8.

1335. JOHN FOOTE, (486, 145, 41, 11, 3,) b. May 24, 1783; m. 1st, June 23, 1811, Sally Wainwright. She b. Sept. 10, 1792; d. Dec. 5, 1821; m. 2nd, Jan. 5, 1823, Polly Sturges. She was b. July 8, 1792, and d. Sept. 30, 1871. He d. Apr. 21, 1834. Res., Hobart, N. Y.

2726. i. HENRY WAINWRIGHT, b. Mar. 24, 1813; d. Dec. 24, 1842.

2727. ii. FREDERICK WILLIAM, b. Aug. 12, 1815; d. Mar. 23, 1885.

2728. iii. WILLIAM STURGES, b. Feb. 7, 1824; m. Mary A. Blish, 4994-7.

2729. iv. ANN ELIZA, b. Dec. 13, 1830; m. William Rollins. She d. in 1893. Ch.: (1) Helen Eliza, b. June 24, 1855; m. Oct. 20, 1886, John Marshall Bowdish. Ch.: (a) Anna Mary, b. 1891, and d. (b) Elizabeth Fuller, b. ———. (c) Charles Orin, b. ———. (d) Maude, b. in 1896; d. in 1901. (e) Frederick Foote, b. in 1894. (f) Charles Thomas, b. in 1899. (g) Elizabeth, b. in 1904.

2730. v. GEORGE T., b. Dec. 30, 1830; m. Cordelia Wakeman, 4998-9.

2731. vi. MARY CHARITY, b. Feb. 9, 1833; res., Hobart, N. Y.; unm.

1336. JABEZ BOTSFORD FOOTE, b. Oct. 13, 1785; m. Mar. 16, 1808, Lucia Foote. She d. Mar. 18, 1839, ae. 49. Res., Venango, Pa., and Stamford, N. Y.

    2732. i. CHARITY LOUIZA, b. Jan. 8, 1810, in Stamford, N. Y.; m. Jan. 18, 1829, Burrit Dunscomb. He was b. in Stamford, N. Y., Dec. 27, 1806. Ch.: (1) Betsey Louiza, b. Apr. 6, 1834. (2) Charles Henry, b. Jan. 10, 1838. Res., Venango, Pa.

    2733. ii. DAVID EDMUND, b. Jan. 17, 1812, in Stamford, N. Y. Res., Venango, Pa.

    2734. iii. MARYETT, b. Jan. 23, 1814, in Stamford, N. Y.; m. Jan. 30, 1833, John H. Bennet. He was b. in Harpersfield, N. Y. Res., Venango, Pa. Ch.: (1) Frances Adella, b. Feb. 12, 1835. (2) Helen M., b. Feb. 26, 1838.

    2735. iv. JANE ELIZABETH, b. Sept. 30, 1816, in Stamford, N. Y. Res., Erie Co., N. Y.

    2736. v. DANIEL NORTHROP, b. May 31, 1820, in Stamford, N. Y.; d. Feb. 15, 1821.

    2737. vi. FRANCES ADELLA, b. Nov. 11, 1826, in Stamford, N. Y.; d. Feb. 21, 1831.

1339. JEREMIAH FOOTE, (486, 145, 41, 11, 3,) b. June 29, 1794; m. May 17, 1826, Maria, dau. of Jethro Wood, Inventor of the Cast Iron Plow. She was b. in Scipio, N. Y., Apr. 11, 1801.

    2738. i. JETHRO WOOD, b. Jan. 8' 1827. Res., Indianapolis, Ind.

1341. ADONIRAM FOOTE, (488, 145, 41, 11, 3,) b. July 10, 1780; m. Jan. 15, 1804, Nancy Doty, in East Greenwich, N. Y. She d. June 28, 1815; m. 2nd, Jan. 28, 1817, Emily, dau. of Ezra and Mabel (Porter) Brainerd, of East Hartford, Ct. She was b. June 1, 1789; d. May 27, 1854. He d. Apr. 28, 1866, in Turin, Lewis Co., N. Y.

Elder Adoniram Foote was b. in Arlington, Vt., July 10, 1780. His youth was passed mostly in Washington Co., N. Y., where he m. Miss Nancy Doty, whose nephew, Duane Doty, a few years ago was Governor of Wisconsin. Soon afterwards he removed to Martinsburg, where the vigor of his life was expended, later he moved to Turin. His wife d. in June, 1815. In Jan., 1817, he m. Miss Emily Brainerd. A woman of intelligence, of great decision of character, and of positive piety and deep devotion, her worth to him was great and her influence upon him highly salutary, especially in leading him to embrace religion. He has also often referred with tearful emotion to the pious instructions of an aunt of his with whom he passed several of his early years, which he could never wholly forget, and which came to his mind with great freshness and force at the time he was converted. He survived his second wife a little less than eleven years. He was the father of a large family of 13 children, nine of whom lived to adult years. When he came into the county of Lewis that rich valley was but little known, and its resources were mostly undeveloped. He entered at once, and heartily, into every public enterprise calculated to promote the interests of the county. He received a military commission from Governor Tompkins, in 1812, and occupied several other offices of public trust from time to time. He was identified with those institutions whose motto speaks for the common brotherhood of mankind. He early connected himself with the anti-slavery movements of the country, as early as 1838, and in the Presidential contest of 1840 cast his vote for

James G. Birney. He was independent in expression and faithful in prayer for
the slave; yet he was not rash, not fanatical; never joined those who denounced
the church and all other institutions for not moving so rapidly in this direction
as he desired. He has often thanked God that he was permitted to live to hear
freedom proclaimed throughout all the land. His Christian life in its outward
manifestations was such as to bring honor to the name of Christ. He gave himself into God's guidance at the time of a general religious revival in 1830-31.
Mr. Foote at once joined himself to the Presbyterian Church, at Martinsburg,
and became one of the working men of the church; he was ordained an Elder in
that church, Oct. 12, 1832. He was many times member of Presbytery and Synod
and was a delegate to the General Assembly that met at Philadelphia in 1843,
and in the home work he was always diligent and faithful. His place at the
weekly prayer-meeting was seldom vacant. No day was allowed to pass without
the observance of family prayer; and on this point he was very decided and
strict, and several incidents are mentioned showing that he placed his service to
God above his earthly cares and gains. He gave liberally for the support of the
Gospel and for the great benevolent enterprises of the Christian church. Ch., all b.
in Martinsburg, N. Y., except the first three.

2739. i.   GEORGE D., b. Feb. 1, 1805; m. Sophia A. Hooker, 4281-9.
2740. ii.   NORMAN, b. Salèm, N. Y., Aug. 15, 1806; d. Feb. 20, 1815.
2741. iii. CHILD, not named, b. ———; d. in infancy.
2742. iv.   JANE, b. Oct. 9, 1809; m. May 1, 1831, Samuel Wheeler, of
             Martinsburg, N. Y. Res., Mineral Point, Wis. She d. Feb. 19,
             1877, in Ill. Ch.: (1) Jane Antoinette Wheeler, b. Apr. 23, 1833;
             m. May 8, 1852, Dr. George D. Wilber. He d. Dec., 1897. Res.,
             Elgin, Ill. Ch.: (a) George Morton Wilber, b. Feb. 1, 1853; d.
             Oct. 21, 1859. (b) Emma Gertrude Wilber, b. Jan. 13, 1854; m.
             1880, Dr. James W. Brown. Res., Col., and Grass Valley, Cal.
             No ch. (c) Frank Leon Wilber, b. Sept. 2, 1855; d. Oct. 17, 1859.
             (2) Francis Foote Wheeler, b. May 5, 1837; m. Mar. 19, 1860,
             Mendacia Reynolds. Ch.: (a) Jane Foote Wheeler, b. Jan. 19,
             1861; d. Nov., 1875. (b) Nellie Antoinette Wheeler, b. Apr.
             3, 1864; nothing further known.
2743. v.   GILES, b. June 15, 1811; m. Pamelia Lee, 4290-3.
2744. vi.   ADONIRAM, b. May 11, 1815; m. Harriet Henry, 4294-4301.
2745. vii. AMANDA, b. Oct. 6, 1817; d. Jan. 4, 1818.
2746. viii. EMILY, b. Oct. 31, 1818; m. 1st, Oct. 8, 1838, Samuel Mills,
             of Martinsburg, Lewis Co., N. Y. She d. in Martinsburg, Dec. 1,
             1846, ae. 28. He m. 2nd, Mrs. Martha M. Usher. Res., Lowville,
             N. Y. Ch.: (1) Norman Foote Mills, b. Aug. 29, 1839; m. Dec.
             10, 1862, Mary Ella Davis, of Carthage, N. Y. She d. Mar. 19,
             1882, at Parsons, Kan. He m. 2nd, July 29, 1886, Alice V.
             Millard. He d. Jan. 23, 1892, at Parsons, Kan. Ch.: (a)
             Charles Samuel Mills, b. Rome, N. Y., Sept. 15, 1863; d. Nov. 13,
             1891, at Parsons, Kan. (b) Frederick Norman Mills, b. ———;
             m. May 19, 1897, Nettie Nordyke, of Parsons, Kan. (c) Kate
             Millard Mills; nothing further known. (d) Howard Brainerd
             Mills; nothing further known. (2) Mary Emily Mills, b. May
             22, 1841; m. Apr. 18, 1865, Eugene B. Woolworth, of Turin, N. Y.
             Ch.: (a) Gertrude Mary Woolworth, b. Lyonsdale, N. Y., Mar.
             23, 1869; m. Aug. 16, 1893, Gilbert Sykes Blakely, of Worcester,

Mass. Ch.: (i) Helen Woolworth Blakely, b. Clinton, N. Y., Dec. 6, 1894. (b) Earl Eugene Woolworth, b. Lyonsdale, N. Y., Dec. 15, 1872; m. May 7, 1902, Beatrice Esmond, of Brooklyn, N. Y. He d. Feb. 5, 1903; s. p. (3) Howard Brainard Mills, b. June 18, 1843; m. Jan., 1869, Mary E. Rogers, of Lowville, N. Y. She d. May 19, 1879, at Lowville, N. Y. He d. Nov. 27, 1873, at Burlington, N. Y.; p. s. (4) Frederick E. Mills, b. July 1, 1845; m. Dec. 27, 1881, Julia Bingham, at Jesup, Iowa. He d. Feb. 8, 1900, in Buffalo, N. Y. Res., Buffalo, N. Y. Ch.: (a) Frederick Bingham Mills, b. at Jersey City, Dec. 31, 1883; d. Jan. 22, 1885. (b) Roy Procter Mills, b. Jersey City, Apr. 26, 1886. (c) Percy Bingham Mills, b. Jersey City, Sept. 14, 1889.

2747. ix. NORMAN B., b. Dec. 2, 1820; m. Maria Mills, 4302-7.

2748. x. DUANE D., b. May 13, 1822; m. Margaret A. Evans, 4308-15.

2749. xi. NANCY MARIA, b. May 27, 1824; m. May 21, 1855, Lawrence Robbins Brainard, of St. Albans, Vt. He d. Nov. 26, 1863, St. Albans, Vt. She d. Oct. 30, 1870, at St. Albans, Vt. Ch.: (1) Edward Rankin Brainard, b. St. Albans, Apr. 19, 1856; m. at Sherbrooke, Quebec, Dec. 1, 1884, Louise Florence Edwige McDonald. He is engaged in real estate and other business in the West. Res., Los Angeles, Cal. Ch.: (a) Edward Rankin Brainard, Jr., b. Los Angeles, May 10, 1888. (2) Emily (twin of Edward), b. St. Albans, Vt., Apr. 19, 1856; m. Dec. 23, 1878. Daniel Webster, son of Bolling and Sarah (Greenleaf) Abercrombie, of Montgomery, Ala. Ch.: (a) Edith Brainard Abercrombie, b. Saxtons River,. Vt., Oct. 31, 1879. (b) Ralph, b. Saxtons River, Vt., Aug. 28, 1881. (c) Esther Greenleaf, b. Worcester, Mass., Nov. 12, 1884. (d) Daniel Webster Abercrombie, b. Worcester, Mass., Oct. 30, 1886. (3) Adeliza Brainard, b. St. Albans, July 22, 1857; m. June 10, 1896, Albert Howard, son of William Henry and Charlotte Elmer Chaffee, of Providence, R. I. Albert was from Sturbridge, Mass. They were m. in Worcester, Mass. Both are artists of Boston. No ch. (4) John Bliss Brainard, M. D., b. St. Albans, June 23, 1859; m. at St. Albans, Oct. 1, 1890, Laura Nellue, dau. of John V. Barron, of Concord, N. H. Ch.: (a) Barron Brainard, b. Boston, Mass., Mar. ?, 1893. (b) John Bliss Brainard, Jr., b. Boston, Nov. 29, 1895, (5) Norman Foote Brainard, b. Feb. 2, 1861; d. Jan. 31, 1864. (6) Mary Louisa Brainard, b. St. Albans, May 27, 1862; d. Mar. 20, 1897, at Los Angeles, Cal. (7) Laura Robbins Brainard, b. Feb. 4, 1864; d. July 16, 1864.

2750. xii. JOHN BARTLIT, b. July 1, 1826; m. Mary Stiphens and Louisa Young, 4316-22.

1342. LEMUEL THOMAS FOOTE, (488, 145, 41, 11, 3,) b. June 5, 1782; m. July 3, 1806, Lucy Clark, of Greenwich, Washington Co., N. Y. She d. Apr. 8, 1863, ae. 74. He d. June 17, 1855, in Royalton, Niagara Co., N. Y.

2751. i. BETSEY, b. Feb. 25, 1808, in Salem, N. Y.; d. Aug. 15, 1809.

2752. ii. BETSEY, b. Nov. 14, 1809, in Salem, N. Y.; m. Mar. 22, 1832, Thomas Clark Edwards, of Greenwich, Washington Co., N. Y. He d. May 10, 1868. She d. June 6, 1867, ae. 58. His res.,

Pendleton, N. Y. Ch.: (1) Abner Mitchell, b. Mar. 3, 1833; d. Sept. 1, 1855. (2) Amanda Taylor, b. Sept. 27, 1834; m. July 20, 1875, Pardon Waterman Kenyon. Res., Brooklyn, N. Y. (3) Thomas Clark, Jr., b. July 24, 1837; m. Dec. 18, 1866, Elizabeth Stahl. Ch.: (a) Mary, b. May 5, 1869. (b) Christina Edwards, b. Apr. 25, 1871; m. William M. Adland, of Minneapolis, Minn., June 19, 1895. Ch.: (i) Winifred B., b. Dec. 31, 1898. (ii) Robert, b. Jan. 14, 1901; d. May 3, 1901. (c) Grace Edwards; m. Rev. Albert E. Barnes, Apr. 10, 1900; res., Anoka, Minn. Ch.: (i) Margaret Louise, b. Dec. 30, 1901. (ii) Albert Edward, b. 1904. (4) John Bartlit, b. Nov. 29, 1839. (5) William Harvey, b. Jan. 31, 1841. (6) Sarah Elvira, b. Mar. 16, 1843. (7) Mary E., b. July 19, 1844; d. Mar. 9, 1852.

2753. iii. REUBEN C., b. Dec. 15, 1811; m. Electa Taylor, 4323-9.

2754. iv. ADONIRAM, b. Mar. 17, 1814, in Salem, N. Y.; d. Dec. 9, 1815.

2755. v. AMANDA, b. July 29, 1816, in Salem, N. Y.; m. Mar. 6, 1834, Alexander Taylor, of Royalton, Niagara Co., N. Y. Res., Pendleton, N. Y. He d. Nov. 25, 1890. She d. Mar. 18, 1898. Ch.: (1) Lemuel Foote, b. May 29, 1835; d. Jan. 3, 1844. (2) Lucy A., b. June 11, 1841; m. Dec. 8, 1863, Merritt B. Fuller. Res., Sanborn, N. Y. Ch.: (a) Amanda Marcella, b. May 22, 1865; m. Charles DeLoss Dodge, Feb. 17, 1887. She d. July 20, 1905. Mr. Dodge res. at Sanborn, N. Y. Ch.: (i) Glenn Fuller, b. May 2, 1888. (ii) Ralph Wright, b. Feb. 2, 1892; d. May 6, 1904. (b) Helen Fuller, b. Nov. 1, 1872; m. Jesse F. Orton, July 25, 1895. Res., Detroit, Mich. Ch.: (i) Malcolm Fuller, b. Aug. 6, 1896. (ii) Lawrence Mitchell, b. Aug. 12, 1899. (c) Clarence Taylor, b. Jan. 2, 1876. (d) Merritt Gould Fuller, b. May 1, 1879; m. Bessie Maud Cole, Sept. 4, 1901. Res., Sanborn, N. Y. Ch.: (i) Helen Gladys, b. ――――. (ii) Grace, b. ――――. (3) L. Munroe, b. Feb. 3, 1845; m. Dec. 13, 1863, S. Vira Maryott. Ch.: (a) Frank Alexander, b. Oct. 21, 1867. (b) Julia Amanda, b. May 6, 1868. (c) Alice May, b. Aug. 17, 1874; m. Aug. 29, 1897, William Lederer. Res., Buffalo, N. Y. Ch.: (i) Dorrity, b. Sept. 18, 1898; d. May 22, 1906. (ii) Dorris, b. Mar. 23, 1901. (d) Lena, b. July 15, 1876; d. Apr. 26, 1880. ‑(4) A. Marcella, b. Apr. 17, 1851; m. Nathan Stanton, of New London, Ct., Nov. 6, 1872. Ch.: (a) Infant Son, b. Aug. 16, 1873; d. Sept. 15, 1873. (b) B. Franklin, b. June 28, 1878; m. Dec. 26, 1900, Laura B. Emmendorfer. (c) Elmer A., b. June 15, 1881. (d) George, b. Aug. 30, 1884.

2756. vi. HIRAM, b. Oct. 29, 1819, in Salem, N. Y.; m. S. Elvira Fenn, 4330-2.

2757. vii. LUCY ANN, b. July 13, 1821, in Greenwich, N. Y.; m. Feb. 24, 1841, William J. Jenkins, of Shelby, Niagara Co., N. Y. He d. Apr. 5, 1895. She d. Apr. 5, 1898. Ch.: (1) Hiram Eugene, b. May 7, 1842; d. Mar. 3, 1843. (2) Mary E., b. July 27, 1844; m. Nov. 25, 1863, Wm. Chapin. Ch.: (a) Robert M., b. Apr. 16, 1867; m. Feb. 28, 1905, Lulu Lundy. (3) Della, b. Oct. 18, 1849. (4) John Lemuel, b. Mar. 28, 1857; d. Oct. 14, 1858.

2758. viii. MARY, b. Dec. 6, 1823, in Greenwich, N. Y.; d. May 30, 1824.

2759. ix.   SENECA BRAGG, b. Dec. 13, 1825; m. Sylvia Green, 4333-8.
2760. x.   JOHN, b. May 23, 1828; m. Harriet V. Larzelier and Jane Scott, 4339-44.
2761. xi.   LEMUEL THOMAS, b. Feb. 18, 1832; m. Emily Whitney, 4345-9.

1345. BELUS HARD FOOTE, (488, 145, 41, 11, 3,) b. July 15, 1788; m. Jan. 26, 1812, Betsey Hawley. He d. Sept. 5, 1841. She d. Aug. 3, 1844, ae. 50. Lived and d. at Milford, Pa.

2762. i.   EDWIN, b. Dec. 11, 1812; m. Janette Barnes, 4350-2.
2763. ii.   NORMAN, b. Sept. 7, 1814; m. Lydia Lorenda Lathrop, 4353-6.
2764. iii.   POLLY ANN, b. Oct. 19, 1816; m. Feb. 14, 1842, Robert D. P. Montanye. Res., Madison, Wis. No ch.
2765. iv.   ELLEN BATHSHEBA, b. Oct. 16, 1818; d. Mar. 24, 1845; buried on the farm.
2766. v.   AMANDA, b. Oct. 14, 1820; m. May 30, 1853, S. U. Hamilton.
2767. vi.   FRIEND HAWLEY, b. May 26, 1823; m. Roby Reaves.
2768. vii.   JAMES RHESA, b. May 12, 1825; d. Nov. 9, 1859, in Australia; unm.
2769. viii. BETSEY ADA, b. Oct. 3, 1827; d. July 21, 1844; buried on the farm.
2770. ix.   STATIRA BARTLIT, b. Jan. 15, 1830; d. Feb. 12, 1848; buried on the farm.
2771. x.   SILAS BUCK, b. Nov. 7, 1834; m. Lydia Lorenda Lathrop, 4357-62.

1347. LINUS FOOTE, (488, 145, 41, 11, 3,) b. Nov. 26, 1793; m. Sept. 9, 1717, Laura Palmer. Res., Aurora, Ohio.

2772. i.   JOHN, b. Dec. 1818; d. Mar. 23, 1834.
2773. ii.   CHANCEY, b. 1820; d. in 1821.
2774. iii.   RUTH ANN, b. Dec. 12, 1831; m. Sept. 29, 1851, Matthias Zimmer. Res., Allerton, Iowa. Ch.: (1) Matthias, Jr., b. Oct. 15, 1853; m. July 3, 1871, Cornelia Shaffer, of Allerton, Iowa. Res., Denver, Col. (2) James, b. Sept. 20, 1859. (3) Amanda, b. Nov. 15, 1862; m. July 3, 1881, Newton O. Wilcott, b. Nov. 17, 1858, of Streetsboro. Ch.: (a) Ruth, b. Apr. 21, 1887. And 5 others who have died, names and dates not given.
2775. iv.   CHANCEY, b. Mar. 11, 1823; m. Catharine Ayers, 4363-6.
2776. v.   EDGAR, b. Sept. 13, 1825; m. Julia Payne and Miss E. T. Champlain, 4367-9.
2777. vi.   CYRUS, b. May 6, 1827; m. May 7, 1848, Minerva Loveland. He d. abt. 1896. She res. Kent, O.; p. s.
2778. vii.   ELAISA, b. July 12, 1829; m. May 6, 1848, James A. Palmer, of Aurora, Ohio. He d. Jan. 17, 1891, Res., Aurora, O. Ch.: (1) Perry Babcock, b. Mar. 6, 1849; d. June, 1850. (2) Eliza Medora, b. Streetsboro, O., June 8, 1850; m. Sept. 22, 1868, Augustus Madison Monroe, of Shalersville, O. Ch.: (a) Claton Augustus Monroe, b. Shalersville, O., July 16, 1870; m. Dec. 13, 1893, Lura Elveretta Spotberry, of Hiram, O. She was b. Jan. 4, 1874. Ch.: (i) Bernie Alfred Monroe, b. Hiram, O., May 29, 1896. (ii) Clyde Thomas Monroe, b. Hiram, O., Dec. 4, 1898. (b) Drusilla Louisa, b. Shalersville, O., Nov. 21, 1871; m. Sept. 22,

1891, Jas. Eugene Davis, of Freedom, O. He was b. Nov. 28, 1871. Ch.: (i) Martin Van Buren Davis, b. Freedom, O., Aug. 27, 1892. (c) Zetta Amelia, b. Charlestown, O., Nov. 21, 1873; m. Nov. 27, 1896, William Schibe, of Spring Prairie, Wis. He was b. Nov., 1875. Ch.: (i) Walter Julius, b. Spring Prairie, Wis., Aug. 27, 1896. (ii) Clarence Emmett, b. Spring Prairie, Wis., Aug. 13, 1902. (d) Orpha Ann, b. Shalersville, O., Nov. 15, 1875; d. Jan. 21, 1876, at Shalersville, O. (e) Clinton Winfield, b. Mantua, O., June 19, 1880; d. Apr. 5, 1881, at Mantua, O. (f) Nellie Abigail, b. Hiram, O., Sept. 16, 1884. (g) Claude Augustus, b. Hiram, O., Apr. 27, 1888. (3) General Perry, b. Streetsboro, O., Jan. 16, 1852; unm. Res., Mantua. (4) Doctor Hayes, b. Streetsboro, O., Oct. 7, 1854; m. Dec. 25, 1886, Electa Reed, of Ravenna, O. She d. Apr. 26, 1895, at Ravenna, O.; m. 2nd, Oct. 7, 1896, Maud Pease Miller, of Ravenna, O. She was b. June 20, 1881. Res., Mantua, O. Ch.: (a) Hester Elouise Palmer, b. Streetsboro, O., Sept. 18, 1898. (b) Alfred Augustus Palmer, b. Streetsboro, O., Oct. 19, 1900. (5) Oscar Major, b. Streetsboro, O., July 31, 1856; m. Apr. 13, 1878, Ida Munn, of Hiram, O. She d. Mar. 17, 1881, at Mantua, O.; m. 2nd, Apr., 1888, Neva Wilson, of Mantua, O. Ch.: (a) Maggie Bell, b. Mantua, O., Apr. 8, 1889. (b) Audry Palmer, b. Mantua, O., Nov. 12, 1890. (6) Eva Adell, b. Wooster, O., Apr. 6, 1860; m. Nov. 3, 1880, Chas. Henry Housel, of Shalersville, O. He was b. Apr. 2, 1856. Res., Mantua, O. Ch.: (a) Catharine Housel, b. Feeder Dam, Aug. 21, 1881; m. Apr. 15, 1901, Samuel Rogers, of Streetsboro, O. (b) Jennie, b. Apr. 22, 1883. (7) Colonel, b. June 8, 1865; d. Apr. 10, 1866. (8) Charles, b. Mantua, O., Feb. 23, 1867; m. Mar. 7, 1888, Bertha, dau. of Johnithan Speechley. She was b. Cambridgeshire, England, June 27, 1887. Farmer. Res., Mantua, O. Ch.: (a) Susan Isabel, b. Mantua, O., Apr. 4, 1889.

2779. viii. LINUS, JR., b. Aug. 15, 1831; m. Belinda Shurtliff and Jane Sawyer, 4370-8.

2780. ix. LAURA, b. Sept. 29, 1833; m. Oct. 7, 1850, Jeremiah Cooper, of Ravenna, Portage Co., O. Res., Streetsboro, O. Ch.: (1) Ella Amelia, b. Aurora, O., Oct. 18, 1851; m. Ravenna, O., Nov. 3, 1870, Henry B., son of William Cowley. He was b. Streetsboro, O., Apr. 17, 1845. He has filled offices of trust in the town, and has been personal property assessor, real estate assessor, trustee, and Justice of the Peace. (2) Laura Lauretta, b. Troy, O., Jan. 30, 1854; m. Edmund R. Brewster, of Streetsboro, O. He was b. Jan. 23, 1843. Ch.: (a) Bennid Cooper, b. Aurora, O., Aug. 23, 1873; m. Dec. 28, 1897, Mabel Kingsley, of Garretsville, O. (b) Edmund Randolph, b. Streetsboro, O., Jan. 27, 1876; d. Apr. 2, 1901, in the Phillipines. (c) Mary Louise, b. Urbana, O., Oct. 8, 1877. (d) Laura Ethel, b. Urbana, O., Dec. 8, 1879. (e) Elsie Ella, b. Sandusky, O., Nov. 19, 1881; m. Nov. 11, 1900, George M. Folger. (f) Eva Elizabeth, b. Sandusky, O., Dec. 10, 1883; d. Feb. 28, 1884. (g) George Gordon, b. Sandusky, Mar. 1, 1885. (h) Grace Huldah, b. Nelson, O., June 4, 1887. (i) Mark Henry,

b. Nelson, O., Aug. 14, 1889. (j) Dorothea Pearl, b. Garretsville, O., Aug. 25, 1891. (k) Ruth Beatrice, b. Garretsville, O., Sept. 5, 1893. (3) Marion Isabelle, b. Jan. 14, 1856; m. Dec. 24, 1878, Charles Granderson Harris. Ch.: (a) Lewis Guy Harris, b. Hiram, O., Jan. 4, 1880; m. July 28, 1899, Minnie L. Gunn, of Troy, O. She was b. June 17, 1880. Ch.: (i) Harland Raymond Harris, b. June 12, 1900; d. Sept. 12, 1901. (b) Paul Sheldon Harris, b. Hiram, O., Dec. 22, 1886. (4) Elsie Eloise, b. Streetsboro, O., Dec. 20, 1858; m. Streetsboro, O., Nov. 22, 1879, Ora A., son of William Frasier, of Mantua, O. He was b. Streetsboro, O., July 26, 1856. Ch.: (a) Chester Elms Frasier, b. Streetsboro, O., Oct. 26, 1882; is employed as a bill office clerk by the Erie R. R., and is also learning architecture. (b) Florence, b. Kent, O., Apr. 15, 1892. (5) Charles Everett, b. Apr. 27, 1861; m. ———. Ch.: (a) Herbert Everett Cooper, b. May 18, 1887. (b) Laura Estella, b. Hiram, O., Sept. 25, 1888. (c) Nora Dell, b. Hiram, O., Aug. 28, 1890. (d) Ida Esther, b. Hiram, O., Feb. 28, 1895. (6) Ida Rosaline, b. Streetsboro, O., Aug. 19, 1863; m. Dec. 25, 1880, Nelson O. Pierce, of Erie, Pa. He was b. Jan. 17, 1854. Ch.: (a) Elsie Luertia, b. Mantua, O., Aug. 21, 1881; m. Dec. 30, 1900, Leonard Rhodes. Ch.: (i) Theodore Nelson, b. Oct. 30, 1901. (b) Nelson Ray, b. Mar. 13, 1884. (c) George Roy, b. Nov. 11, 1885. (d) Verda Belle, b. May 25, 1901. (e) Vernon Orville, b. May 25, 1901. (7) Caroline Adell, b. Hiram, O., Jan. 30, 1866; m. Feb. 14, 1884, Victor Orson Collins, of Garretsville, O. He was b. Sept. 29, 1852. Ch.: (a) Lillian Isabelle, b. Dec. 16, 1884; m. July 27, 1902, Fred Allyn Goodell, of Charlestown, O. (b) Richard Orson, b. Dec. 8, 1887. (c) Edgar Thomas, b. Mar. 6, 1892. (d) Lulu Amelia, b. Sept. 11, 1893. (e) Victor Charles, b. Dec. 13, 1896; d. Mar. 11, 1897. (8) Arthur G., b. ———; m. May 29, 1891, Pearl Bright. She was b. Mecca, O., June 11, 1873. Ch.: (a) Etha Hazel Cooper, b. Hiram, O., July 7, 1892. (b) Jeremiah Austin Cooper, b. Hiram, O., Mar. 22, 1894. (c) Cecil Arthur Cooper, b. Troy, O., July 7, 1895. (d) Myra Elizabeth Cooper, b. Troy, O., Jan. 28, 1897. (e) Alice Theline Cooper, b. Nelson, O., Nov. 10, 1899. (9) Percy Cooper, b. Sept. 19 1876.

2781. x.   ANSEL, b. Aug. 17, 1835; d. July 23, 1858.
2782. xi.   OSCAR, b. Mar. 4, 1839; m. Aldula Shurtliff, 4379-4383.
2783. xii. CHARLES, b. Aug. 17, 1841; d. Oct. 16, 1864.

1349. CHARLES FOOTE, (488, 145, 41, 11, 3,) b. Nov. 28, 1797; m. June 13, 1820, Rebecca Wellman, of New Milford, Pa. He d. June 6, 1863. She res., New Milford, Pa.

2784. i.   BELUS H., b. Apr. 16, 1821; m. Zillah Parks, 4384-6.
2785. ii.   IRA D., b. Aug. 21, 1822; m. Charlotte A. Van Housen and Belinda Williams, 4387-95.
2786. iii. GEORGE D., b. Feb. 22, 1825; m. Marietta Stephens, 4396-4402.
2787. iv.   ORLANDO W., b. Jan. 13, 1828; m. Mary A. Chamberlain, 4403-4.
2788. v.   HATTIE A., b. Jan. 6, 1834; m. Feb. 20, 1860, Nelson B. Dorr. He d. Aug. 29, 1902, at Port Jarvis, ae. 68 years.
2789. vi.   JOHN C., b. Mar. 28, 1836; m. Catharine A. Dusenberg, 4405-7.

1354. JONATHAN FOOTE, (497, 153, 45, 13, 5,) b. Jan. 28, 1814; m. Sarah R., dau. of Newton Stevens, who was a merchant in New Haven for 40 years. Res., New Haven, Ct.

    2790. · i.   SHERMAN FRISBIE, b. Nov. 27, 1841; m. Mary H. Rice, 4408-9.

    2791. ii.   ELLSWORTH IRVING, b. New Haven, Ct., Dec. 22, 1847. Res., New Haven, Ct.

1359. JOHN FOOTE, (498, 153, 43, 13, 5,) b. Branford, Ct., Dec. 23, 1805; m. Fanny, dau. of Ralph Blackstone, of Branford, Ct., Feb. 28, 1832. Mrs. Foote was b. Apr. 10, 1806, in Branford, and d. there Dec. 11, 1880. Mr. Foote was a shoe-maker in the early part of his life and a farmer until about ten years before his death, Mar. 15, 1883. She d. Dec. 11, 1880.

    2792. i.   BETSY BLACKSTONE, b. at Branford, Apr. 3, 1842; m. William Bradley, son of Wilman Palmer, of Branford, Ct., Nov. 27, 1869. Mr. Palmer is a farmer, and they reside in Branford, Ct. No ch.

    2793. ii.   MARY, b. at Branford, Feb. 26, 1848; m. William Robbins, son of Riley O. Smith, of Branford, Ct., June 1, 1870. Mr. Smith is a machinist and they reside in Branford. Ch.: (1) Mason Foote, b. at Branford, Ct., Aug. 9, 1876; unm.; graduate of Yale Scientific School, and Astronomer at Yale Observatory, New Haven, Ct. Res., Branford, Ct.

1362. SAMUEL FOOTE, (498, 153, 43, 13, 5,) b. Sept. 18, 1812; m. Mar. 31, 1844, Sarah Elizabeth, dau. of Frederick Russell, of Branford, Ct. She was b. Feb. 3, 1817; d. Aug. 18, 1888. Mr. Foote was a farmer. He was b. at the Homestead in Branford purchased by Robert Foote, son of the first settler, June 23, 1668. Res. there all his life and d. Oct. 23, 1886.

    2794. i.   HARRISON, b. Branford, Ct., July 17, 1846; d. Aug. 6, 1848.

    2795. ii.   WILLIAM R., b. June 3, 1848; m. Nettie E. Averill, 4410-2.

    2796. iii.   ROBERT, b. Branford, Ct., Feb. 19, 1851. He was in the banking business for abt. 30 years, and retired from business in 1904, at which time he was Cashier of the National Tradesmen's Bank of New Haven, Ct. Res., 38 Howe St., New Haven, Ct.

    2797. iv.   WALTER, b. Branford, Ct., May 7, 1853; m. Caroline Delano, dau. of Capt. James G. Bragg, of Fair Haven, Mass., Mar. 1, 1877. Mrs. Caroline Foote was b. Dec. 20, 1852. Mr. Foote was a farmer, then a merchant until 1890, and Town Clerk, Town Treasurer and Judge of Probate of the town of Branford from 1891 until the time of his death, Mar. 30, 1899. No ch. Mrs. Foote res. New Haven, Ct.

    2798. v.   MARY JANE, b. Branford, Ct., Feb. 16, 1858; m. Frank Cline Bradley, a carpenter, son of Gurdon Bradley, of Branford, Ct., Oct. 18, 1882. Mr. Bradley was b. Jan. 3, 1856. Ch.: (1) Eugenia Claire, b. at Branford, Ct., Feb. 11, 1885. (2) Roberta Russell, b. at Branford, Ct., May 29, 1889.

1367. ORANGE FOOTE, (508, 168, 47, 13, 5,) b. Woodbury, Ct., Nov. 2, 1784; m. Dec. 24, 1807, Marilla Ives. Res., Clinton, N. Y.

    2799. i.   MARIETTA, b. Mar. 5, 1809; m. 1829, Isaac Archer.

    2800. ii.   LUCIUS PERRY, b. Aug. 25, 1813; m. Sept. 1, 1843, Harriet Carr, of Schenectady, N. Y.

    2801. iii.   EVELINE GRIDLEY, b. May 13, 1815; m. Oct. 9, 1843, Albert B. Fitch.

2802. iv. HARRIET MARILLA, b. June 17, 1824; m. Jan., 1846, Norman
D. Jewell.

1372. NOEL FOOTE, (508, 168, 47, 13, 5,) b. Clinton, N. Y., Sept. 28, 1797;
m. Feb. 14, 1831, Emily Gridley. He d. June 6, 1862. Res., Clinton, N. Y.

2804. i. HENRY BRONSON, b. June 24, 1836; m. Christina Maxted. He
d. May 18, 1873, leaving one ch., Ida May; m. ——— Willis, N.
Y. City.

2805. ii. MARY ELIZABETH, b. Apr. 10, 1838; m. May 9, 1860, A. W.
Mills. Res., Utica. Ch.: (1) Cora Estella, b. May 28, 1863; m.
Charles D. Larabee. Res., Clinton, N. Y. No ch. (2) Charles
Andrus, b. Oct. 22, 1869; m. Harriet Ely. Res. in Utica; graduate
of Hamilton College. Ch.: (a) Lester Foote, b. Dec. 9, 1902. (3)
Herbert Foote, b. July 20, 1879; m. Isabella Spense. Res., in New
York; graduate of Hamilton College. (4) Frederick Metmore, b.
Feb. 20, 1875; d. Apr. 4, 1900. (5) Lelia, b. 1876; d. in infancy.

2806. iii. JANE THANKFUL, b. Apr. 18, 1840; m. Sept. 14, 1859, Seth H.
Blair. She d. June 27, 1905. He d. Oct. 14, 1905. Res., Clinton,
N. Y. Ch.: (1) Frank Foote, b. Nov. 12, 1861; unm. (2) Milford
Burdette, b. May 7, 1867; m. Feb. 14, 1889, Flora Gruman. Ch.:
(a) Edith, b. 1890. (b) Delia, b. 1892; d. Apr. 22, 1903. (c)
Gertrude, b. Feb. 19, 1897. (d) Elizabeth, b. Jan. 1, 1900.

1374. DAVID FOOTE, (509, 168, 47, 13, 5,) b. ———; m. ———; d. ae. 34.

2807. i. FRANKLIN, b. ———; res., Mich.

2808. ii. DAN, b. ———.

1380. MARTIN FOOTE, (509, 168, 47, 13, 5,) b. Dec. 20, 1792; m. Sept. 12,
1812, Nancy Avery. She was b. Sept. 12, 1797. He d. 1822.

2809. i. IRA A., b. Sept. 10, 1816; m. Eliza Benjamin, 4413-4.

2810. ii. EMMA, b. June 16, 1819; m. Apr. 12, 1849, Abraham Harding
Hallock, of Westmoreland, N. Y. He was b. Aug. 17, 1800; d.
Nov. 1, 1885. She d. Nov. 27, 1879. Ch.: (1) Emma, b. Mar. 19,
1850; m. Dec. 21, 1881, Hiram K. Worden, physician, of Westmoreland, N. Y. Ch.: (a) Jessie Sylvia Hallock, b. June 29,
1883. (b) John Hallock, b. Nov. 11, 1885; Cornell University.
(c) Albert Leslie, b. July 2, 1895. (2) Mary Kingsley, b. Dec.,
1855; d. 1860. (3) Harriet, b. Aug. 17, 1869; m. 1884, Ishmael
Hughs. Ch.: (a) Mary, b. July 3, 1885. (b) Ethel, b. Jan. 10,
1889. Res., Rochester.

2811. iii. SYLVIA POWELL, b. Sept. 28, 1821; m. Apr. 15, 1841, Datus
Woodward. He was b. May 29, 1816; d. July 29, 1891. She d.
Feb. 20, 1891. Ch.: (1) Ellen Sophy, b. May 25, 1844; m. Nov.
29, 1865, Daniel D. Owen. He d. May 3, 1905. (2) Emma
Prudence, b. May 21, 1846; m. Apr. 29, Marsena P. Williams.
He d. Mar. 21, 1900. Ch.: (a) Sylvia Nell, b. Mar. 29, 1878; m.
May 17, 1905, Leslie Jacob Schuyler. (3) Charles Hallock, b.
July 1, 1858; d. Nov. 11, 1896.

1391. THOMAS MOSES FOOTE, (514, 168, 47, 13, 5,) b. Aug. 9, 1808; m.
Aug. 10, 1836, Margaret, dau. of Gamaliel and Margaret (Kineman) St. John.
She was b. Aug. 25, 1806. He was a graduate of Hamilton College and of College
P. and S. of W. N. Y. Was editor of one of the Public Journals in Buffalo, N. Y.

In June, 1849, he was appointed, by the President, United States Charge to New Granada, S. A. Res., Buffalo, N. Y.

2812. i. HELEN MARGARET, b. May 26, 1838.
2813. ii. THOMAS MOSES, b. Feb. 8, 1841.

1395. ALBERT FOOTE, (518, 170, 37, 13, 5,) b. May 18, 1796; m. 1st, Jan. 9, 1826, Mary Ann Gipson, of Galen, N. Y. She d. Mar. 21, 1839; m. 2nd, Mar. 5, 1842, Phebe, dau. of Uri B. Gillet, of Schoharie, N. Y. She was b. Feb. 5, 1821; d. Sept. 5, 1899. He d. Mar. 18, 1863. Res., Galen, N. Y.

2814. i. SARAH H., b. Feb., 1827; d. Apr, 22, 1827;
2815. ii. HANNAH, b. Galen, N. Y., Jan. 11, 1843; m. Wm. Tyler. Res., Arcade, N. Y.
2816. iii. JOSIAH, b. Galen, N. Y., July 31, 1844; m. Emma McDougal, 4415-9.
2817. iv. PHYLANDER, b. Nov. 3, 1849; m. Mary P., dau. of George Closs. She was b. Lock Berlin, N. Y., Sept., 1847. He d. Dec. 20, 1890, at Lock Berlin, N. Y.
2818. v. ALVIN JAMES, b. Galen, N. Y., Mar. 26, 1855; m. Oct. 11, 1877, Elizabeth Van Debett Hunter, a teacher. She was b. May 31, 1856. He is a farmer; Granger; Methodist. Res., Lyons, N. Y. No ch.

1396. ALVIN FOOTE, (518, 170, 37, 13, 5,) b. Nov. 3, 1797; m. June 16, 1824, Mary Ann, dau. of Stephen Palmer, of Sandisfield, Mass. Res., Lenox, Mass., and Pittsford, N. Y. She was b. Aug. 3, 1802.

2819. i. CHARLES H., b. June 17, 1825; m. Alma T. Foote (No. 1967), 4420-2.
2820. ii. CATHARINE, b. Apr. 28, 1831, in Pittsford, N. Y.; d. unm.
2821. iii. GEORGE PALMER, b. Sept. 16, 1834; m. Ann Eliza Smith and Jennie Baker, 4423-6.
2822. iv. EMELINE, b. Feb. 3, 1837; m. 1st, Audley Clark Vaughn. He was b. May 31 1837; d. July 7, 1873; m. 2nd, 1876, William Walker, of Poughkeepsie, N. Y. She d. July 11, 1906, at Pough-keepsie, N. Y. Ch.: (1) Alvin Foote, b. June 26, 1860; d. July 14, 1860. (2) Jennie Howarth, b. Aug. 21, 1861; d. Jan. 12, 1863. (3) Carrie Palmer, b. Jan. 28, 1865; d. Apr. 21, 1865. (4) Howard Clark, b. Feb. 28, 1873; d. July 15, 1873.

1398. AARON FOOTE, (518, 170, 37, 13, 5,) b. May 5, 1806; m. 1832, Isabella, dau. of Thomas McMillain, of Princeton, N. Y. She was b. Sept. 9, 1807. Res., Galen, N. Y. He d. July 7, 1889.

2823. i. WILLIAM HENRY, b. July 19, 1833, in Galen, N. Y.; d. May 4, 1851; unm.
2824. ii. SAMUEL T., b. Nov. 3, 1839; m. Kathren Rooke, 4427-30.

1400. JOHN STANLEY FOOTE, (520, 170, 37, 13, 5).

2825. i. MILO, b. ———.

1402. WALTER FOOTE, (520, 170, 37, 13, 5,) b. 1807; m. Tamezin Ford. Res., Huron, O.

2826. i. JOHN M., b. Jan. 4, 1830; m. Jan. 18, 1855, Cathrine C., dau. of Wm. Johnson, of Hartland, O. She was b. Dec. 7, 1830. He was a farmer; d. Mar. 29, 1856, at Fitchville, O.; s. p.

2827. ii. IRA, b. May 17, 1834; m. Cathrine C. Foote, 4431.

2828. iii. GEORGE W., b. June 11, 1842; m. Philena Thompson and Elizabeth Eckelbery, 4432-4.

1403. HENRY JARVIS FOOTE, (520, 170, 37, 13, 5,) b. Aug. 22, 1805; m. Apr., 1831, Maria Wilkinson. He d. July 3, 1876. Res., Fitchville, Huron Co., O. Ch. all b. at Fitchville, O.

2829. i. LUCINDA, b. Oct. 2, 1831; m. Sept. 30, 1866, Henry Hammond. She and her babe d. Feb. 29, 1872.

2830. ii. JOHN, b. Mar. 8, 1833; m. Lora Annette Talcott, 4436.

2831. iii. HANNAH, b. Dec. 23, 1834; m. abt. 1859, Prince Haskell Nye, of Peru, O. She d. Aug. 14, 1901. Res., Charlotte, Mich. Ch.: (1) Addie, b. (2) Hayden, b. (3) Irene, b. (4) Burnette, b.

2832. iv. HENRY B., b. Sept. 10, 1834; m. Lucinda Hartman, 4437-9.

2833. v. MINERVA, b. Jan. 27, 1845. Baptist. School teacher; m. Jan. 12, 1869, Gurdon Perkins Lester, Venice, N. Y. He was b. Apr. 27, 1837; d. Oct. 22, 1898, at Cherokee, O. Ch.: (1) Edna Ione, b. Nov. 11, 1870. (2) Garra Erwin, b. Sept. 23, 1872; merchant at Kinerim, Iowa.

2834. vi. MYRA, b. Feb. 1, 1847; m. abt. 1870 or 1871, George Summerton. She d. abt. 1880 or 1881. Ch.: (1) Clayton, b. (2) Lloyd Vernon, b.; d. abt. 10 years old.

2835. vii. WATSON O., b. Aug. 17, 1855; m. Augusta Bromburg, 4440-44.

1409. MOSES ROSSETER FOOTE, (520, 170, 37, 13, 5,) b. Oct. 19, 1812; m. Mary Palmer. They had five ch. She d.; m. 2nd, 1850, in Seneca Co., O., Mary Lockwood (2 ch., 2841-2). He d. Oct., 1894. She d. at Cherokee, Ia., Mar., 1875. Res., Fitchville, O., and moved to Iowa in 1855. Ch. all b. in Fitchville, O.

2836. i. SETH, b. Jan. 25, 1834; m. Amorette E. Rich, 4445-.

2837. ii. HENRY R., b. July 14, 1836; m. Julia I. Burnham, 4446-8.

2838. iii. WILLIAM HAMILTON, b. June 3, 1840; d. June 18, 1855, Huron Co., O.

2839. iv. DAVID, b. Jan. 23, 1843; m. Caroline Porter, 4449-50.

2840. v. TAMA, b. Aug. 18, 1840; d. Apr. 16, 1852.

2841. vi. ALFRED J., b. Feb. 1, 1851; traveling salesman; m. Mar. 12, 1883, Cherokee, Iowa, Emogene K. Bird. She was b. Sept. 9, 1861, Cedar Falls, Iowa. No ch.

2842. vii. MARY ELIZABETH, b. Aug. 11, 1853; m. Dec. 2, 1874, Senaiah M. Pratt, Cherokee, Iowa. Ch.: (1) Ralph D., b. Apr. 28, 1876, Cherokee, Iowa.

1411. ORVIS FOOTE, (521, 170, 37, 13, 5,) b. May 28, 1794; m. Feb. 7, 1821, Nancy D. She was b. Nov. 20, 1798; d. June 24, 1840. Res., Sheffield, Mass., Vernon, N. Y.

2843. i. CAROLINE, b. ———; m. S. E. M. Kneeland. Ch.: (1) George; res., Warren, O. (2) Edward; res., Warren, O. (3) Velina; m. A. D. Torry, of Garrettsville, O.

2843₁. ii. BRUNSON, b. Grand Rapids, Mich.

2843₂. iii. COLUMBUS, b. ———; res., Grand Rapids, Mich.

2844. iv. LEWIS, b. ———; res., Grand Rapids, Mich.

2844₁. v. JANE, b. ———; m. ——— Erwin. Ch.: 2 girls; n. f. k.

1412. MILO FOOTE, (521, 170, 37, 13, 5,) b. Dec. 19, 1796; m. Nov. 25, 1822, Eliza, dau. of David Clark, of Sheffield, Mass. She was b. Nov. 28, 1801. He d.

Aug. 12, 1838, at Freedom, O. Res., Sheffield, Mass., and Freedom, O. After his death she returned to Sheffield.

2845. i. BRADFORD CLARK, b.

2845¹. ii. MARY ANN, b. ———; m. ——— Hulbut, of Erie, Pa.

2845². iii. THERESA, b. ———; m. Nov., 1845, Dwight K. Savage, of Sheffield, Mass.

1413. WYLLYS FOOTE, (521, 170, 37, 13, 5,) b. Nov. 25, 1798; m. Nov. 8, 1825, Elizabeth S. Warner, of Sheffield, Mass. She was b. July 5, 1805; d. Nov. 11, 1885; res., Freedom, O., until 1838, and then moved to Thompson, Geauga Co., O., and d. there Jan. 2, 1869.

2846. i. CHARLES W., b. Sept. 10, 1826; m. Martha J. Freeman, Kate C. Ernot and Phebe W. Hall, 4451.

2846¹. ii. JANE E., b. Oct. 29, 1827; d. Aug. 8, 1832.

2846². iii. AMOS J., b. Dec. 12, 1829; d. Aug. 15, 1832.

2847. iv. SOPHIA ADAH, b. Feb. 27, 1832; m. Feb. 26, 1852, Correl B. Spencer. He was b. Jan. 21, 1829. Res., Chardon, Geauga Co., O. Ch.: (1) Clarence R., b. Nov. 23, 1852; m. Oct. 3, 1894, Lucy D. Strong. She was b. Oct. 31, 1861. Ch.: (a) Ann Bell Spencer, b. Mar. 1, 1903. (2) Anna Elizabeth, b. Dec. 17, 1855; m. Oct. 26, 1876, D. K. Woodward. He was b. June 8, 1851. Ch.: (a) Howard Spencer Woodward, b. Aug. 16, 1877. (b) Delbert Harrold Woodward, b. June 9, 1888.

2848. v. RALPH L., b. Nov. 3, 1834; d. Jan. 28, 1864.

2849. vi. RHODA JANE, b. Feb. 6, 1837; m. May 10, 1860, Henry C. Gurney. She d. Sept. 23, 1860. He d. from a wound received in the battle of Good Hope at Charleston, 1864.

2850. vii. MARIA E., b. July 9, 1841; d. Apr. 16, 1861.

1423. SHERMAN FOOTE, (522, 170, 37, 13, 5,) b. Adams, Mass., Sept. 21, 1804; m. July 4, 1825, Margerette D., dau. of Thaddeus and Sylvia Grey, of New Lebanon, N. Y. She was b. Sept. 12, 1802. Res., Williamstown and Pittsfield, Mass., and Batavia, O.

2851. i. ELIZABETH, b. Williamstown, Mass., May 3, 1826.

2852. ii. LEWIS, b. Pittsfield, Mass., Nov. 17, 1828.

2853. iii. AARON, b. Batavia, O., Nov. 24, 1839.

1424. JOHN BRONSON FOOTE, (522, 170, 37, 13, 5,) b. Adams, Mass., Feb. 10, 1807; m. May 12, 1840, Mary, dau. of Daniel Patten, of Westmoreland, N. Y. She was b. June 11, 1805. He graduated at Williams College. Res., Westmoreland, N. Y.

2854. i. JOHN B., JR., b. May 3, 1841; m. Gertrude Dodge, 4452-7.

2855. ii. MARY ELIZA, b. Oct. 29, 1843. Res., Clinton, N. Y.; unm.

2856. iii. NOYES, b. May 30, 1846; d. 1848.

2857. iv. SAMUEL G., b. 1849; farmer; unm.

2858. v. ADDIE L., b. May 25, 1850; m. Jan. 7, 1874, Thomas Irving. Res., Clinton, N. Y. Ch.: (1) Lena May, b. May 14, 1878. (2) Edith Ella, b. Apr. 14, 1885. Res., Clinton, N. Y.

1432. ABNER PRESTON FOOTE, (526, 171, 47, 13, 5,) b. Dec. 25, 1800; m. Nov. 6, 1824, Lucy Cluff. She was b. Oct. 20, 1805; d. Sept. 30, 1834; m. 2nd, July 3, 1836, Eunice, dau. of Philo and Ann (Hall) Mix, of Waterbury, Ct. He d. Oct. 22, 1869. Res., Oswego Co., N. Y.

2859. i. JOSEPH ELIJAH, b. Apr. 8, 1828; d. Apr. 27, 1828.

1438. EBENEZER FOOTE, (527, 171, 47, 13, 5,) b. Watertown, Ct., Dec. 15, 1789; m. Rebecca Phillips, of Alabama.

2860. i. STEPHEN PHILIPS, b.
2861. ii. OSRO, b.
2862. iii. JOHN MASON, b.
2863. iv. JONATHAN, b.
2864. v. MAHALA LOUISIANA LUCINDA, b.; nothing further known.

1441. GIDEON FOOTE, (527, 171, 47, 13, 5,) b. at Great Bend, N. Y., Apr. 17, 1799; m. Oct. 22, 1818; Lavina, dau. of Abner and Amy Gillett. Res., Guilford, N. Y., and Lenox, Pa.

2865. i. EBENEZER, b. Apr. 18, 1820; m. Martha Blanchard, 4458-65.
2866. ii. WILLIAM G., b. Sept. 23, 1821; m. Catherine Miller, 4466-9.
2867. iii. NATHANIEL H., b. May 28, 1825; m. 4470.
2868. iv. SIMEON, b. Sept. 22, 1831; m. Caroline Baker, 4471-7.
2869. v. GIDEON, b. July 10, 1835; m. Julia A. Webb, 4478-85.
2870. vi. LUCY ANN, b. Feb. 21, 1837, in Nicholson, Pa.; m. 1st, Charles Maxron; no ch.; m. 2nd, 1863, Harrison Hine, of Athens, Pa. He d. 1871; m. 3rd, 1872, John Nurse, of Elmira, N. Y. Ch.: (1) Elnora A. Hine, b. Sept. 21, 1864; m. July 29, 1880, Levi Van Kirk, of Waverly, N. Y. He d. 1884; m. 2nd, 1889, Horatio Seacord, of Newark, N. J. Ch.: (a) Susie Van Kirk, b. 1881; m. 1907, Walter Reid, of Pittston, Pa. (b) Harry Van Kirk, b. 1883. (c) Ethel May Seacord, b. 1898. (2) Mabel Hine, b. Dec. 16, 1867; m. Apr. 27, 1884, Royal Hinman, of Waverly, N. Y. He d. 1896, Waverly; she d. 1897, Niagara Falls. Ch.: (a) Royal Hinman. (3) Edith Hine, b. 1869; m. 1890, Farly Rogers, of Waverly, N. Y. (4) Mary Hine, b. 1871; d. 1871, Elmira, N. Y. (5) Willie Hine, b. ———; d. 1871, Elmira, N. Y. (6) James Nurse, b. 1874; m. 1898, Fione Hine, Elmira, N. Y. (7) Bessie Nurse, b. 1877; m. 1894, Alfred Dean, East Elmira, N. Y. She d. 1897.
2871. vii. LOVISA STATIRA, b. Nicholson, Pa., July 23, 1840; m. 1st, Birdcile Myrthe; m. 2nd, A. Ransom. Res., Lennoxville, Pa. Ch.: (1) John B. Foote Myrthe, m. Sarah Adams. Ch.: (a) Stanley. (b) Florence. (c) William. (d) Joseph. (e) Mildreth.

1442. NATHAN B. FOOTE, (527, 171, 47, 13, 5,) b. at Windsor, N. Y., Feb. 26, 1801; m. June 8, 1823, Elizabeth, dau. of Bryant and Elizabeth Robinson. Res., Lenox, Pa. She was b. Sept. 4, 1803.

2872. i. LOUVISA URSULA, b. Dec. 20, 1823; m. William Hobbs, of Lenox, Pa. Res., Port Allegany, Pa. Ch.: (1) James. (2) Alice, m. ——— Hobbs. (3) Elizabeth. (4) Freeman. (5) Susie. (6) Ella. (7) Elwin. (8) Thompson.
2873. ii. SIMEON, b. Mar. 23, 1825; m. Nancy Hodges, 4486-93.
2874. iii. NATHANIEL B., b. Dec. 4, 1828; m. Mary Hodges, 4494-4504.
2875. iv. JAMES R., b. Mar. 5' 1831; d. Dec. 28, 1844.
2876. v. ANN CLARISSA, b. Mar. 4, 1833; m. Richard Evans, of Annin, Pa. Ch.: (1) Simeon. (2) Fremont. (3) Lovisa. (4) Betsey. (5) Nathen.
2877. vi. LUCY HELEN, b. May 2, 1835; m. Alonzo Ransom, of Lenox, Pa. He m. 2nd, No. 2871. Res., Lenox, Pa. Ch.: (1) William, b. ———; m. Nelly Hobbs. Ch.: (a) Ethel. (b) Cecile. (c)

Hazel. (d) Dewey. (2) Effie, b. ———; m. Erving Ross. Ch.: (a) Lucy. (b) Eva. (c) Violet. (d) Elucious. (e) Armilla. (f) Dorris. (3) Eva, b. ———; m. Adolphus P. Barney. Ch.: (a) Hugh, b. ———; m. Martha Harrison. Ch.: (i) John Barney. (b) Maud. (c) Clifton. (d) Day. (4) Martha.

2878. vii. MARTHA MARIA, b. Feb. 17, 1837; m. Raymond Hodges. Res., Bradford, Pa. Ch.: (1) Susie Alzina, b. ———; m. Fred Buckley, of Annin, Pa.

2879. viii. ELIZABETH MARY, b. May, 1839; m. James Robinson, of Lenox, Pa.; m. 2nd, Joshua Jackson, of Greenwood, N. Y. Ch.: (1) Frank Robinson, b. (2) Elnora Jackson, b. ———; m. Freeman Hobbs. Res., Olean, N. Y. Ch.: (a) Lola Hobbs, b.

2880. ix. SUSAN AGAR, b. June, 1841; m. Andrew Jackson, of Greenwood, N. Y. Ch.: (1) Maud, b. (2) Bert, b. Res., Ridgeway, Ca.

1443. SIMEON FOOTE, (527, 171, 47, 13, 5,) b. Windsor, N. Y., Dec. 13, 1803; m. 1824, Ann Ferguson. Res., Lenox, Nicholson, and Glenwood, Pa.

2881. i. WILLIAM M., b. Mar., 1825; m. Susan Trusdale, 4505-5⁵.

2882. ii. JOHN H., b. Sept. 22, 1831; m. Juliet Rosecrans, 4506-10.

2883. iii. LYDIA ANN, b. June 7, 1834; m. Benj. Harding, of Forkston, Pa. Ch.: (1) E. E. Harding, b. Sept. 27, 1857. (2) Mrs. R. E. Sprague, b. Sept. 11, 1859. (3) Hattie, b. May 21, 1872; m. ——— Naow.

2884. iv. ALONZO, b. 1838; m. Eliza Squires. Ch. all d.

2885. v. SARAH, b. Apr. 1841; m. Chas. Watson, of Nicholson, Pa.

1454. DAVID FOOTE, (529, 171, 47, 13, 5,) b. Aug. 24, 1812; m. Nov. 27, 1833, Mary Bidwell. She was b. May 17, 1816; d. June 14, 1884, Bath, N. Y. He was a cabinet maker; d. Nov. 17, 1901. Res., Dryden, N. Y., Greenwood, N. Y., Painsville, O., Willoughby, O., and Flint, Mich. .

2886. i. HELEN PAMELIA, b. in Greenwood, N. Y., Oct. 21' 1834; d. Oct. 16, 1840, in Flint, Mich.

2887. ii. CHARLES LANE, b. Apr. 10, 1836, in Greenwood, N. Y.; d. Sept. 19, 1838, in Ypsilanti.

2888. iii. GEORGE HARVEY, b. Feb. 28, 1839, in Ypsilanti, Mich.; d. Mar. 1, 1840, in Saline, Mich.

2889. iv. DAVID BURNS, b. May 21, 1841, in Flint, Mich. Enlisted in the 8th Mich. Regt., June, 1861; was killed at Beaufort, S. C., Dec. 19, 1861, and buried in the Baptist Cemetery there.

2890. v. WARREN COOK, b. Jan. 28, 1845, in Flint, Mich.; d. Oct. 3, 1898.

2891. vi. MARY ELIZA, b. Mar. 14' 1848, in Flint, Mich.; m. July 23, 1867, Charles Adelbert, son of Philip and Mary (Clark) Muma. Res., Paris, Ontario. Ch.: (1) Maude C., b. Apr. 29, 1868, at Flint, Mich. Res., 504 Trumbell Ave., Detroit, Mich. (2) Albert Charles, b. Oct. 18, 1869, at Flint, Mich. Res., 540 Federal Building, Buffalo, N. Y. (3) Ida May, b. May 15, 1871, at Flint, Mich.; m. Aug. 24, 1898, Harrison McAllister, son of Seth Cook and Ellen (Plank) Randall. He was b. at Burr Oak, Mich., Dec. 17, 1870. Res., 1208 Prospect Street, Ann Arbor, Mich. Ch.: (a) John McAllister, b. Aug. 18, 1899; d. Aug. 19, 1899. (b) Mary Foote, b. May 14, 1901. (c) Esther McAllister, b. Dec. 19,

1902. (d) Robert Dee Bois, b. June 3, 1904. (4) Anna Estelle, b. May 12, 1873; m. Aug. 12, 1896, Rice Aner, son of Eugene E. and Rutilla (Keith) Beal. He was b. Dexter, Mich., Sept. 9, 1871. Res., Hamilton Place, Ann Arbor. Ch.: (a) Philip Muma, b. Apr. 11, 1904. (5) George Clark, b. Aug. 4, 1875, Flint, Mich.; m. May 11, 1904, Mary Irene, dau. of George and Charlotte (Paine) Parsons. She was b. Feb. 18, 1880. Res., S. Fourth Ave., Detroit, Mich. No ch.

2892. vii. ALBERT E., b. Sept. 21, 1845, Flint, Mich.; m. Sept. 22, 1881, May E. Howard. Res., Alpena, Mich. He d. Jan. 16, 1898. She was b. Apr. 26, 1858; d. Jan. 27, 1890.

2893. viii. WILLIAM H., b. June 6, 1834; m. Nettie Bristol, 4511-5.

2894. ix. ANDREW HYSLOP, b. May 15, 1856, Flint, Mich.; d. Mar. 10, 1857.

1455. DEA. GEORGE LANE FOOTE, (529, 171, 47, 13, 5,) b. Apr. 16, 1815; m. Dec. 3, 1839, Mary Ann Gillette, of Ypsilanti, Mich. Dea. of the M. E. Church, and for three years preached the Gospel at Brighton, South Lyon, and Dixborough, Mich. Since 1868 in Life Insurance business. He d. Feb. 15, 1894. She d. Feb. 19, 1894. Res., Greenwood, N. Y., Albion, and Ypsilanti, Mich.

2895. i. CHARLES E., b. May 17, 1842; m. Kate A. LaRue, 4516-20.

2896. ii. LOUISA ADELLE, b. Albion, Mich., Dec. 24, 1844; d. in infancy.

2897. iii. GEORGE E., b. Albion, Mich., July 18, 1846; m. Frances Jocklin, 4521.

2898. iv. FRANK S., b. Nov. 20, 1853; m. Bessie A. Finch, 4522.

1456. WARREN FOOTE, (529, 171, 47, 13, 5,) b. Aug. 10, 1817; m. June 8, 1843, Artemisia Sidnie Myers; m. 2nd, Mar. 2, 1856, Eliza Maria Ives. Was Justice of Peace and Postmaster in Union and Glendale, Utah; d. July 23, 1903. Res., Caldwell Co., Mo., Council Bluffs, Mo., Union, Round Valley, Utah, St. Joseph, Lincoln Co., Nevada, Long Valley, and Glendale, Utah.

2899. i. JOSEPH, b. Dec. 16, 1843; lived 14 hours.

2900. ii. DAVID, b. Aug. 23, 1845; m. Emma E. Bernett and Sarah Hall, 4523-39.

2901. iii. SARAH, b. Feb. 24, 1848, Council Bluffs, Iowa; d. Mar. 26, 1848.

2902. iv. WARREN, b. Dec. 15, 1849, Council Bluffs, Iowa; d. at St. Thomas, Nev., Feb. 22, 1867.

2903. v. NANCY, b. Oct. 11, 1852, in Union, Utah; m. July 5, 1869, Homer Arlington Bouton. Res., Glendale and Salt Lake City, Utah. Ch.: (1) Mary Artemisia, b. Sept. 22, 1873, in Glendale, Utah; m. Sept. 22, 1892, L. Wixcey, of Salt Lake City. He was b. Apr. 30, 1872. Ch.: (a) Vera, b. Aug. 1, 1893. (2) Joseph Warren, b. Oct. 14, 1876. (All b. in Glendale, Utah). (3) Harry, b. May 19, 1879. (4) Homer Arlington, b. Nov. 22, 1884. (5) William, b. May 22, 1887. (6) Louie, b. Apr. 30, 1890; d. Jan. 25, 1891. (7) Pearl, b. July 27, 1893, in Salt Lake City.

2904. vi. MARY IRENE, b. in Union, Utah, Oct. 22, 1855; m. Dec. 2, 1875, Morton, son of Royal James and Theodosia (Morton) Cutler. He was b. Sept. 18, 1853. Is engaged in the sheep business. Res., Glendale, Kane Co., Utah. Ch.: (1) Royal, b. Nov. 2, 1876; d. Aug. 24, 1878. (2) Henry, b. Sept. 20, 1877. (3) Irene, b. Aug. 17, 1879. (4) Clarence, b. Apr. 17, 1882; d.

May 29, 1882. (5) Clara, b. June 18, 1883. (6) Lucy, b. Mar.,
1885; d. Jan. 6, 1886. (7) Viola, b. Oct. 10, 1886. (8) Leona, b.
Sept. 17, 1888. (9) Lillian, b. Nov. 7, 1890. (10) Raymond, b.
Sept. 27, 1892. (11) Dau., b. June 25, 1895.

2905. vii. ARTEMISIA, b. in Union, Utah, Mar. 4, 1858; m. Feb. 18, 1880,
Brigham Cutler. He was b. Sept. 18, 1853. Res., Fredonia,
Ariz. Ch.: (1) Warren, b. July 19, 1881, in Glendale, Utah. (2)
Lewis, b. June 8, 1883. (All b. in Glendale, Utah). (3) Horace,
b. Aug. 31, 1884. (4) Artemisia, b. Aug. 13, 1886. (5) Morton,
b. Apr. 1, 1888. (6) George, b. July 11, 1891, in Fredonia, Ariz.
(7) Alvin, b. June 15, 1893, in Fredonia, Ariz. (8) Milo, b.
Oct. 16, 1896.

2906. viii. GEORGE A., b. Jan. 14, 1860; m. Leonah Bell Jones, 4540-5.

2907. ix. JACOB ALFRED, b. Jan. 10, 1863; d. Feb. 16, 1865.

2908. x. CLARISSA, b. in Scipio, Utah, Aug. 1, 1865; m. Oct. 22, 1890,
Andrew Olsen. He was b. Oct. 8, 1859. Res., Glendale, Utah.
Ch.: (1) Andrew Warren, b. Grantsville, Utah, Sept. 22, 1891. (2)
Clarence, b. Apr. 28, 1897.

2909. xi. HOMER C., b. Feb. 3, 1871; m. Olive L. Rasin, 4546-7.
Children b. by second wife.

2910. xii. JAMES FRANKLIN, b. in Mt. Pleasant, Utah, June 22, 1859;
m. Emeline Frances Minehey, 4548-55.

2911. xiii. ELIZA OLIVE, b. in Mill Creek Ward, Utah, Oct. 31, 1862; m.
Nov. 26, 1876, Benjamin Minchey; afterwards to Oscar Beebe,
Dec. 22, 1880. He was b. June 27, 1861. Res., Emery, Utah.
Ch.: (1) John Franklin, b. Oct. 29, 1878, in Salem, Utah. (2)
Joseph Oscar, b. Oct. 5, 1881; d. May 15, 1882, in Glendale,
Utah. (3) Mary Irene, b. Jan. 6, 1886, in Emery, Utah. (4)
Charles, b. Nov. 28, 1889, in Aurora, Utah. (5) Lewis Warren,
b. July 18, 1892, at Meadow Gulch, Utah.

2912. xiv. SIDNEY WALLACE, b. in Scipio, Utah, Nov. 24, 1863; d. Sept.
8, 1865.

2913. xv. JOHN A., b. Dec. 6, 1865; m. Eliza A. Merrick, 4556.

2914. xvi. CHARLES L., b. Nov. 11, 1868; m. Hannah M. Anderson,
4557-60.

2915. xvii. EDWIN MORONI, b. in Glendale, Utah, June 9, 1872; d. June
1872.

1459. REV. HORATIO FOOTE, D. D., (535, 172, 47, 13, 5,) b. Northfield,
Mass., Feb. 10, 1796; m. Feb. 15, 1826, Abigail Kirkland, of Bridgewater, N. Y.
She d. June 5, 1883. He was educated at Hartwich Academy, N. Y. Graduated at
Union College, 1820, and Auburn Theological Seminary, 1824. Ordained Pastor of
Presbyterian Church, Kingston, Ontario, Sept. 1, 1825, discharged 1828. In Montreal, Can., and Champlain, N. Y., 1828-31. Evangelist in Burlington, Vt., Hartford, Ct., Buffalo, N. Y., 1831-40. Pastor of First Congregational Church 1840-7,
in Quincy, Ill., and of Center Congregational Church 1840-60, in Quincy without
change thereafter, except that he was Hospital Chaplain during the War. Trustee
of Knox College. He d. May 10, 1886, in Ellington, Ill.

2916. i. HORATIO KIRKLAND, b. Sept. 13, 1827; d. Mar. 18, 1843.

2917. ii. ANN ELIZABETH, b. May 22, 1830; d. Mar. 12, 1832.

2918. iii. THOMAS W., b. May 23, 1832; m. Catherine Kahlenbrink,
4560²-60⁸.

(19)

2919.   iv.   WILLIAM LEWIS, b. June 18, 1836; d. July 27, 1837.

1460.   REV. LUCIUS FOOTE, (535, 172, 47, 13, 5,) b. Northfield, Mass., Aug. 3, 1798; m. 1st, Mar. 18, 1824, Electa W., dau. of Dr. Nathan Harwood, of Winfield, N. Y. She d. Sept. 15, 1865; m. 2nd, Mar. 6, 1867, Mrs. Maria Erwing, wid. of Fordyce Cutting Trowbridge, of Sheboygan, Wis. He was educated at Hartwick Academy, Auburn Seminary; ordained to ministry at Wenton, N. Y., July 30, 1827; dismissed Feb. 2, 1836. Evangelist several years, in Ohio chiefly. Pastor of Congregational Church, St. Charles, Ill., 1842-45, Orangeville, Ill., 1846, Delavan, Wis., 1847-54, without charge 1854-57, acting pastor Union Erovelirs 1857-61, without charge the rest of his life. Res., Rockport and Chicago, Ill., until 1872, then removing to Sacramento, Cal., where he res. until his death. He d. Feb. 6, 1887.

2920.   i.   LUCIUS HARWOOD, b. Apr. 10, 1826, Winfield, N. Y. Educated at Knox College and Western Reserve University. Crossed plains to California, 1853; admitted to Bar, 1856; Municipal Judge, Sacramento, 1856-60; Collector, port of Sacramento, 1861-5; Adjutant General, Cal., 1872-6; Delegate to Rep. Nat. Convention, 1876; Consul to Valparaiso, Chili, 1878-81; on special diplomatic mission in Central America, 1882; E. E. and M. P. to Corea, 1882; distinguished himself in protection of Japanese and other foreigners in Nationalist Revolt of 1883 at Seoul; received thanks of Emperor of Japan and Freedom of City of Tokio, thanks of the Government of China, and an autograph letter of thanks from the Emperor of Corea; resigned 1884 and returned to Cal.; since 1890 Secretary and Treasurer Academy of Sciences of San Francisco. M., 1862, Rose Frost Carter; she d. 1885. Author, "Red Letter Day" and other poems, 1882; "On the Heights," 1887. Res., San Francisco, Cal.

2920¹. ii.   HENRY MARTYN, b. Oct. 14, 1830; d. in Delevan, Wis., 1853.

2921. iii.   ANN ELIZA, b. June 7, 1836; m. Nov. 4, 1856, Jos. Collie, of Delevan, Wis. He was b. Nov. 4, 1824; d. July 8, 1904. Ch.: (1) George Lucius, b. Aug. 11, 1857, B. S., Beloit, College, 1881; Ph. D., Harvard, 1893; Principal, Delevan H. S. Was Professor of Geology, Beloit College, 1892. Dean, Beloit College, 1900. Acting as President, Beloit College, 1901, 1902, 1905, 1907. Member Committee of Ten. Nat. Educ. Assistant, 1892; Com. on Physical Geography for College Entrance, 1899. Fellow Geol. Soc. America; m. Mar. 26, 1896, Katherine Evalyn Burrows, at Chicago, Ill. (2) Martha Lockwood, b. July 30, 1862; d. Sept. 21, 1863. (3) Dr. Joseph Arthur, b. July 19, 1865; m. Sept. 14, 1896, Mary Drinker, at Portage, Wis. Res., Portland, O. Ch.: (a) George Cameron, b. Aug. 4, 1904, at Camp Collie, Lake Geneva, Wis.; d. Jan. 15, 1905, at Portland, O. (4) Winfred Ross, b. Apr. 24, 1869; m. Genevieve Alice Peck, June 12, 1901, at Galva, Ill. Ch.: (a) Ross Ford, b. May 25, 1902, at Camp Collie, Lake Geneva, Wis. (b) Dorothy Harwood, b. Sept. 22, 1903, at Camp Collie, Lake Geneva, Wis. (5) Henry Glenwood, b. Nov. 29, 1875; unm.

2922.   iv.   FRED E., b. Dec. 28, 1869; m. Elsie H. Ketchum, 4561¹.

1463. REV. HIRAM FOOTE, (535, 172, 47, 13, 5,) b. Burlington, N. Y., Aug.
21, 1808; m. June 27, 1839, Elizabeth Maria Becker, of Whitestown, N. Y. He
was Pastor of the Congregational Church in Rock·Prairie. Mrs. Foote was b.
Cherry Valley, Otsego Co., N. Y., Sept. 21, 1817. He graduated Oberlin College.
Mrs. Foote was educated at Clinton Seminary, N. Y. In the days when to be an
Anti-Slavery man was unpopular and dangerous, Rev. H. Foote stumped what is
now known as the Garfield district of Ohio for Joshua R. Giddings for Congress.
He removed to the West and was during his lifetime one of the prominent clergymen of that region. He held many prominent offices in the gift of the Governors
of Wis., filled many successful pastorates, and died respected and beloved by all
who knew him, at Rockford, Ill., Jan. 13, 1889. Res., Rockford, Ill.

2923. i.   ALBERT E., b. July 17, 1840; m. Mrs. Annie J. Van Dyke,
           1 ch., 4562.

2924. ii. ANTOINETTE E., b. Feb. 25, 1842; d. Sept. 24, 1845.

2925. iii. HORATIO KIRKLAND, b. Racine, Wis., Nov. 24, 1843; enlisted
           in Co. B., 1st Wis. Cavalry, Aug., 1862; d. a prisoner of war at
           Florence, S. C., Feb. 6, 1865.

2926. iv. HIRAM WELLES, b. Feb. 9, 1846; m. Eunice DeMaris Horton,
           4563.

2926¹. v. ELIZA MARIA, b. Janesville, Wis., Feb. 18, 1848; d. Oct. 26,
           1848.

2926². vi. ANTOINETTE CORNELIA, b. Janésville, Wis., Dec. 15, 1849;
           d. Rockford, Ill., Aug. 24, 1894; grad. of Rockford Female
           College; m. Hamilton H. West, of Rockford, Ill., Sept. 26, 1876.
           Ch.: (i) Clarence Hamilton West, b. Rockford, Ill., June 9, 1881.
           (2) Edna Marie West, b. Rockford, Ill., Nov. 9, 1886.

2926³. vii. LUCIUS FIELD FOOTE, b. Janesville, Rock Co., Wis., Dec. 10,
           1852; received preliminary education at Carroll College, Wis.,
           and graduated in Medicine at Medical Department of North-
           western University, Chicago, Ill. Is at present a resident of
           Minneapolis, Minn., engaged in the practice of medicine. Was
           m. to Mrs. Minnette C. Prand, of Minneapolis, Minn., dau. of
           Geo. Dowthwaite, Apr. 29, 1897.

2927. viii. CHARLES EDWARD, b. Mar. 25, 1855; m. May Pease, 4564-5.

2927¹. ix. ELLA KATHERINE, b. Janesville, Wis., Jan. 31, 1859. She
           graduated at the Rockford Female College, and has been en-
           gaged in newspaper and literary work since that time. She is
           at present residing with her mother at Rockford, Ill.

1464. HORACE FOOTE, (535, 172, 47, 13, 5,) b. Burlington, N. Y., Dec. 27,
1811; m. Feb. 2, 1843, Harriet N. Batchelder. Res., Rockford, Ill.

2927². i.   HARRIET MELINDA, b. Feb. 21, 1844; d. ———.

2927³. ii. ERASTUS HORACE, b. Aug. 21, 1846, Rockford, Ill.; d. Nov. 22,
           1869.

2927⁴. iii. FRANCIS MARIA, b. Mar. 2, 1850; d. Sept. 11, 1850.

2927⁵. iv. MARY CORNELIA, b. Aug. 8, 1853. Res., Rockford, Ill.

2927⁶. v.   ELLEN THERESA, b. Sept. 6, 1856; m. Geo. E. Smith. Ch.: (1)
           Florence, b. Jan. 9, 1882. (2) Infant, b. ———. (3) Dau., b.
           Aug. 6, 1886; d. Dec. 25, 1886. (3) Harold, b. May 10, 1888.

2928. vi. HENRY M., b. June 18, 1859; m. Oct. 11, 1881, Vina Irone,
           4566-70.

1465. ELIAL TODD FOOTE, (537, 172, 47, 13, 5,) b. Gill, Mass., May 1, 1796. Two years after his parents removed to Sherburne, N. Y., where he spent his boyhood. He was educated in the common school and under the tuition of Rev. W. M. Adams, and at Oxford Academy. He studied medicine at Sherburne with Dr. Guthrie and attended medical lectures in New York in 1814 and 1815. He was licensed by the Chenango County Medical Society, and later received the degree of M. D. He settled in Jamestown, Chautauqua Co., N. Y., in 1815, and was its first settled physician. He soon had an extensive practice, but the hardships and exposure incidental to practice in a new country led to attacks of asthma, and after a few years he gave up active practice, and turned his attention to business of a public nature.

In 1819, at the age of 23, he was elected to the Legislature, representing the counties of Chautauqua, Cattaraugus and Niagara. The county of Niagara then included what is now Erie County and Buffalo. During this session (1819-20) he was on the Canal Committee, an important one, for the State was then building the Erie Canal. In 1826 he was again elected to the Legislature, and again in 1827. In 1822 he purchased from the Holland Land Company a reserved tract of land, on which is now built a large part of the city of Jamestown. This, with its valuable water power, was speedily improved, and the growth of the new village greatly promoted. Jamestown now (1907) has 30,000 inhabitants. He was active in public improvements, aiding them liberally by his means and influence. Four of the churches were built upon land donated by him for the purpose.

In 1831, the nearest bank being at Buffalo, 90 miles distant, he secured the charter for the Chautauqua County Bank, resigning his position as director of the United States branch at Buffalo to accept the presidency of the new bank, which he resigned in 1835. He was one of the fifteen who met in 1829 to organize the Chautauqua County Temperance Society, of which he was for several years the president. He was for many years the President of the Chautauqua County Bible Society ,a life member of all the prominent religious and benevolent societies, in which he took a lively interest and to which he gave liberally. In 1818 he was appointed Associate Judge of the Court of Common Pleas, which office he held for five years until 1823, when he was appointed first judge of the County of Chautauqua, which office he continued to hold under reappointment by various governors every five years for 20 years. On his retirement, in 1843, the grand jury and the bar, without respect to party, and associate judges, joined unanimously in passing resolutions, bearing high testimony to the ability, fidelity, and impartiality with which he had for so long discharged the honorable duties of his office, and expressive of their confidence and esteem. About this time (1843) he became strongly enlisted in the anti-slavery cause, and supported the Liberty ticket in 1844. He removed to New Haven, Ct., in 1845, where he resumed the practice of medicine, and was in active practice there for some 20 years.

He was fond of historical research and collected a large amount of historical matter concerning the early history of Chautauqua, which formed the basis of the valuable history of that county, written by Mr. A. W. Young.

In 1827 he was elected a member of the Medical Society of the State of New York. He was also a member of the Massachusetts, Connecticut and Rhode Island State Medical Societies. In 1827 he was elected an honorary member of the New York Historical Society. He was a corresponding member of the Buffalo Historical Society and of the Albany Lyceum of Natural History and the New England Genealogical and Historical Society. He was one of the founders and for many years, until his death, a director of the New Haven Colony Historical Society.

Judge Foote m. at Jamestown, N. Y., Dec. 31, 1817, Anna Cheney, a native of Dover, Vt., and a dau. of·Ebenezer Cheney, a Revolutionary soldier. His wife d. July 7, 1840, and he m. for his second wife, Amelia Stiles Leavitt, wid. of Rev. Charles Jenkins, of Greenfield, Mass., in 1841. She d. at New Haven in 1867. He was again m. in 1869, to Miss Emily Stockbridge, wid. of S. W. Allis.

At the close of this biography of Judge Foote, it is fitting here to make some suitable acknowledgment for the great services which he rendered in his researches, and by his published and unpublished reminiscences concerning Sherburne. In fact, it is but simple justice to say, that no other person has done more than he did to preserve the records of all that is of value and interest in the early history of this place. The writer has already appropriated much from the treasure trove of his historical collections, while much of value still remains. In a letter which has incidentally come to the hand of the writer, Judge Foote says: "I am disposed to have a sketch of West Hill Society and neighborhood published. In this way the efforts and settlement there of Major Dixon, our father, Judge Lynde, and others, will 'be preserved for future generations.'' How much, almost unconsciously, he was then contributing to that result, by inciting others to such labors! Judge Foote was a prominent member of the Masonic fraternity, and did not withdraw from that organization even under the great stress of the Anti-Masonic excitement of 1826-31, and was for several years Master of Mt. Moriah Lodge, at Jamestown. His early political associations were with the Loco Focos, or Democrats, but his later affiliations are well shown in an incident related by Judge Stephen Holden, of Sherburne, who was at the time a student at Yale College. He says, in a communication published in ''The Sherburne News'' of Sept. 7, 1889: "Early in 1856 I attended a meeting at New Haven, Ct., held to organize the Republican party for the presidential campaign. Dr. Elial T. Foote was one of the speakers, and added greatly to the enthusiasm of the meeting. The charge was then made that the then leaders of the Democrats were preaching a new doctrine on the question of slavery in the Territories. Dr. Foote, to vindicate his right to say what the original Democratic doctrine was, against the new lights in that party, among other things, said that he was a Democrat when they 'were mewling and puking in their nurses' arms!' '' He was a man of noble presence, and, as Judge Holden says, "He was a fine looking man, of large frame and a rather broad face.'' He was nearly six feet in height, very dark hair, blue eyes, a fine face and head, and a frank, kindly way which made him very popular. In the spring of 1820, while yet in the Legislature, he was nominated unanimously by the district convention of the Western District of the State, as candidate for the State Senate. The nomination was a surprise to him, and he was strongly urged by influential members of the party to accept the same, but he felt constrained for personal and professional reasons to decline. Another candidate was presented and elected by a large majority.

Hon. Elial Todd Foote d. at New Haven, Ct., Nov. 17, 1877, in his 82nd year, and his remains were taken at his request to Jamestown for interment, among the friends to whom he was so strongly attached.

2929. i.   SAMUEL ERASTUS, b. Apr. 4, 1821; m. Elizabeth Bailey, 4571-8.

2930. ii.   MARY ANN, b. Jamestown, N. Y., July 20, 1823; m. Dec. 15, 1841, Samuel Cobb, son of Isaac and Lucy (Barrett) Crosby, of West Brattleboro, Vt. Res., Jamestown, N. Y. Ch.: (1) Florence Ellen, b. Nov. 11, 1842, Jamestown, N. Y. (2) Emmett Lawrence, b. Jan. 26, 1844, Jamestown. Res., Vance, Edwards Co., Texas. (3) Samuel Foote, b. Oct. 25, 1845, Jamestown. Res.,

DeYoung, Elk Co., Pa.; m. Ruth Cheney, 1871, dau. of Stowell Cheney, First, of Hartford, Ct. She b. in Warren Co., Pa., Jan. 3, 1853. Ch.: (a) Son, b. South West T. P., Warren Co., Pa., July, 1872; d. July 7, 1872. (b) Horace Cheney, b. in South West T. P., Warren Co., Pa., July 4, 1873. (c) Samuel Stowell, b. in South West T. P., Warren Co., Pa., May 9, 1875. (d) Clarence Almyron, b. in South West T. P., Warren Co., Pa., Feb. 9, 1877, (e) Carl Maxwell, b. in South West T. P., Warren Co., Pa., Nov. 23, 1879. (f) Willis Rea, b. in Glade T. P., Warren Co., Pa., May 26, 1884. (g) Florence Allice, b. in Mead T. P., Warren Co., Pa., Feb. 27, 1887. (h) Blanch Ruth b. in Mead T. P., Warren Co., Pa., Oct. 30, 1889. (i) Mabel Mildred, b. in Mead T. P., Warren Co., Pa., Nov. 12, 1891. (j) Paul Malcolm, b. in Highland T. P., Elk Co., Pa., Sept. 9, 1894.

2931. iii.   CHARLES CHENY, b. Sept. 5, 1825; m. Amelia Leavitt Jenkins, 4579-84.

2932. iv.   JAMES HALL, b. June 26, 1827; m. Jane Agnes Gray and Ellen Marion Harvey, 4585-9.

2933. v.   HORACE ALLEN, b. July 17, 1832; m. Emily Knevals, 4590-4.

1466. DR. SAMUEL FOOTE, (537, 172, 47, 13, 5,) b. Sherburne, N. Y., Aug. 22, 1798; m. 1822, Laura, dau. of Elijah Holbrook, at Jamestown, N. Y. She was b. Aug. 8, 1798; d. Nov. 16, 1857, at Arcadia, La. His boyhood was spent in Sherburne, where he attended the district school on the West Hill until 1816, when he spent a year at Sangerfield Academy. He was a good English scholar, with a fair knowledge of Latin. In 1818 he emigrated to Jamestown, and studied medicine with his brother, Dr. Elial T., until 1820, when he went to Fairfield, N. Y., to attend medical lectures at the College of Physicians and Surgeons. He was there two years and graduated in 1822, when he returned to Jamestown and went into practice there. Was a fine physician and surgeon, and practised his profession almost continuously in or near Jamestown till his death, May 5, 1856.

2934. i.   HORACE F., b. Mar. 18, 1823; m. Susan C. Anderson, 4593-4601.

2935. ii.   ELIZABETH J., b. Nov. 20, 1825; d. Dec. 5, 1851, at Cincinnati, Ohio.

1467. JUDGE ERASTUS FOOTE, (537, 172, 47, 13, 5,) b. Sherman, N. Y., July 1, 1800; m. Feb. 5, 1824, Aurilla, dau. of Robert Gallup, of Plymouth, N. Y. She was b. in New London, Ct., May 27, 1802; d. Harvard, Neb., 1898. He was an Attorney at Law. Res., Plymouth and Greene, N. Y. He was in practice at Greene, Chenango Co., for some 25 years, until about 1850, when he removed to Milwaukee, Wis., where he continued to practice law, and was elected Judge of one of the City Courts. He d. Feb. 16, 1875, his widow surviving him.

2936. i.   SON, not named, b. Mar. 28, 1825; d. Apr. 10, 1825, in Plymouth, N. Y.

2937. ii.   FRANCES HELLEN, b. July 3, 1826; d. Aug. 10, 1831, in Plymouth, N. Y.

2938. iii.   MARY PHILENA, b. June 24, 1828; d. Aug. 17, 1831, in Plymouth, N. Y.

2939. iv.   ROBERT ELIAL, b. Oct. 20, 1830; m. 4602-3.

2940. v.   FANNY MARIA, b. Plymouth, N. Y., June 14, 1832. Res., Milwaukee, Wis.; unm.

2941. vi. ERASTUS DEVOLSON, b. July 23, 1834; m. Cora M. Clemans, 4604-9.

2942. vii. FREDERICK SEYMOUR, b. Greene, N. Y., Oct. 22, 1837; d. Sept. 23, 1838.

1473. HON. CHARLES DOOLITTLE FOOTE, (537, 172, 47, 13, 5,) b. Sherburne, N. Y., Dec. 25, 1812; m. Aug. 25, 1834, Laura Ann Holbrook, at Waterboro, N. Y. She d. abt. 1847; m. 2nd, Sept. 18, 1849, Mary Daulton Arnold, in Covington, Ky. He res. in the vicinity of Jamestown, N. Y., until 1849, when he removed to Covington, Ky. He soon after studied law, and was for five years law partner of Hon. John G. Carlisle, Speaker of the U. S. House of Representatives. Mr. Foote served for two terms as Representative of Kenton County and four years as Senator in the Kentucky Legislature. During the cholera epidemic in 1854 he rendered heroic and philanthropic services in caring for the sick and stricken. Mary Daulton Arnold, b. Nov. 26, 1817, in Mason Co., Ky., second wife of Charles Doolittle Foote, was the dau. of James G. Arnold and Margaret Daulton. Her grandfather was Moses Daulton of the Third Vermont Cavalry of the American Revolution. Mrs. Foote was a devoted member of the Christian Church, and was possessed of many noble traits of character. She d. Nov. 29, 1883, in Covington, Ky. He d. Apr. 28, 1888. Res., Covington, Ky.

2943. i. PHILENA, b. Waterbury, N. Y., May 10, 1835; m. Harry Perrin. Ch.: (1) Harry, b.

2944. ii. STELLA ANN, b. Waterbury, N. Y., Nov. 11, 1837; d. unm.

2945. iii. CALISTA LAURA, b. Waterbury, N. Y., Oct. 1, 1839; d. unm.

2946. iv. CHARLES GALUSHA, b. Waterbury, N. Y., July 4, 1843.

2947. v. FREEMAN HOLBROOK, b. Waterbury, N. Y., Apr. 4, 1845; d. unm.

2948. vi. KETURAH, b. Covington, Ky., Aug. 18, 1850; m. Thomas Jefferson Phelps, June 25, 1878, in Covington, Ky. Ch.: (1) Isaac Jordan Phelps, b. Feb. 23, 1881. (2) Edward Casey Phelps, b. Sept. 9, 1883. Judge Phelps was the son of the late Jefferson and Elizabeth Brokenbrough Phelps. Judge Phelps served with honor in the war on the staff of Stonewall Jackson, returning to Covington after the surrender of Lee and resuming the study of the law in the office of his kinsman, John W. Stevenson. On his admission he formed a partnership with Edward Colston, of Cincinnati, but in a short time thereafter opened an office in Covington, Ky. He entered politics, an uncompromising Democrat from the day of his first vote to the day of his death, and was elected County Judge, serving eight years.

2949. vii. MARY STELLA, b. Chilo, O., Apr. 7, 1853; m. Carson B. Forse, Oct. 29, 1871, in Covington, Ky. Ch.: (1) Frances Foote Forse, b. Nov. 18, 1872; m. Robert Fulton Sutton, Oct. 4, 1904, of Newport, Ky. Ch.: (a) Mary Katherine, b. Jan. 27, 1906, in Newport, Ky. (2) Capt. William Forse, b. Mar. 2, 1875, of the U. S. Army; m. Ethel Grace Black, Feb. 7, 1901. Ch.: (a) William Black Forse, b. May 16, 1902.

2950. viii. SYBIL DOOLITTLE, b. Covington, Ky., Mar. 19, 1855; m. Edward D. Casey, Jan. 15, 1878, in Covington, Ky. Mrs. Casey was a charter member of the National Society of the Daughters of the American Revolution, and was the First Registrar of the

John Marshall Chapter of Louisville, Ky. She d. in Chicago, Ill., Dec. 14, 1900.

2951. ix.   FANNIE, b. Cincinnati, O., Apr. 29, 1858; m. Lewis Oliver Maddux, Mar. 30, 1883, in Covington, Ky. He was b. in Rushville, Ind., May 17, 1851. He is the son of William Russell and Charlotte (Posey) Maddux. Ch.: (1) Rufus Foote Maddux, b. Oct. 20, 1884. Graduated in 1906 from Yale Sheffield Scientific at the age of 21 years. (2) Louise Arnold Maddux, b. Aug. 21, 1887.

1474.   OBED HYATT FOOTE, (537, 172, 47, 13, 5,) b. Plymouth, N. Y., May 18, 1817; m. Sept. 1, 1839, Lucy Mower, dau. of Isaac Crosby, of Jamestown, N. Y. She was b. at Brattleboro, Vt., Feb. 17, 1817; d. Feb. 18, 1889. Mr. Foote was a Major, Third Mich. Cavalry (Civil War), and Deacon in the Park Congregational Church of Grand Rapids. Was Supervisor for a number of years. He d. June 2, 1870, at Grand Rapids, Mich.

2952. i.   LUCY ELIZABETH, b. Jamestown, N. Y., June 13, 1840; m. at Grand Rapids, to James Melancthon Barnett, of Grand Rapids, Dec. 5, 1865. He was b. in Brockport, N. Y., Sept. 8, 1832, and was the son of George Flint Barnett and Catherine Thorpe Barnett. Mr. Barnett is President of the Old National Bank of Grand Rapids, of which he has been successively Vice-President and President since its organization in 1863. Also interested for many years in lumber business in Michigan and in the South. Ch.: (1) George Foote, b. Apr. 23, 1867; d. Grand Rapids, ae. 5 months and 18 days. (2) James Foote, b. June 17, 1869; is a graduate of Yale (A. B.), Columbia (M. A.), and N. Y. Law School (LL.B.). Occupation, lawyer. (3) Katherine Elizabeth, b. Nov. 22, 1874. (4) Lucy, b. June 30, 1877. (5) Laura Ellen, b. Aug. 24, 1881. All b. and res. at Grand Rapids, and are unm.

2953. ii.   SIBBIL, b. June 14, 1842; d. June 14, 1842, in Jamestown, N. Y.

2954. iii.   ELLIOTT CROSBY, b. Oct. 21, 1843, at Jamestown, N. Y.; d. July 5, 1844, at Grand Rapids, Mich.

2955. iv.   SIBBIL DOOLITTLE, b. Grand Rapids, Mich., June 24, 1845.

2956. v.   ELLEN EUNICE, b. Grand Rapids, Mich., Nov. 16, 1847; m. Oct. 25, 1877, John Robertson, son of Thomas and Anne (Robertson) Smith, of Scotland. He was b. in Scotland. Res., Denver, Col. Lawyer. Ch.: (1) Margaret Robertson, b. Rosita, Col., July 23, 1885.

2957. vi.   OBED HENRY, b. Grand Rapids, Mich., June 8, 1850; d. Sept., 1850.

2958. vii.   DORA MARY, b. Grand Rapids, Mich., May 19, 1860; m. May 31, 1882, Joseph Bruff Ware; d. May 8, 1893, at Grand Rapids. He was b. May 8, 1860, Butlerville, Jennings Co., Ind. Parents, Emmor and Elizabeth Ware, who were raised Quakers, at Damascus (Garfield P. O.), Ohio. Settled in Indiana in 1859. Moved to Michigan in 1869, and to Grand Rapids in 1873. Extensive lumber dealer. Ch.: (1) Ellen Elizabeth, b. Aug. 12, 1883. (2) Joseph Emmor Ware, b. Oct. 9, 1885.

JUDGE ELIAL TODD FOOTE. No. 1465

ERASTUS FOOTE.   No. 1479

1479. ERASTUS FOOTE, (540, 172, 47, 13, 5;) son of the Hon. Erastus Foote and of Eliza Foote, his wife, dau. of Moses Carleton, of Wiscasset, Me., was b. in Wiscasset, Me., Sept. 6, 1821. He prepared for college in Augusta, Me., and graduated at Bowdoin in 1843, and afterwards practised law in Wiscasset. He m. Sarah Page Wood, dau. of Wilmot Wood, of Wiscasset, June 1, 1847. In 1868 he removed with his family to Chicago, Ill., where he engaged in business until the time of his death, Feb. 20, 1893. He was a man of singularly genial and holy character, and commanded the love and veneration of the whole community. His wife, Sarah Page Foote, b. Mar. 3, 1826; d. in Chicago, Oct. 22, 1898. They are survived by four ch., Wilmot Wood Foote, Erastus Foote, Emma Louisa Bellas, all of Chicago, and Harriette Foote Armour, of Princeton, New Jersey, and by eight grandchildren.

2959. i.   WILMOT WOOD, b. May 21, 1848; m. May 19, 1877, Mrs. Martha A. Jenks, in Chicago. She was b. Aug. 13, 1846; d. Mar. 31, 1891; m. 2nd, Nov. 30, 1893, Mae Alice Althen, in Beatrice, Neb. She was b. Mar. 15, 1870. Res., Chicago, Ill. With the ''Chicago Evening Post.''

2960. ii. ERASTUS, b. Mar. 4, 1850. President of the Dearborn Foundry Co., 1525 Dearborn St., Chicago; unm.

2961. iii. EMMA LOUISE, b. Oct. 27, 1851; m. May 11, 1880, in Chicago, Thomas H. Bellas. He d. Nov. 28, 1902. Ch.: (1) Emmeline Wood, b. Mar. 29, 1881; m. Dec. 7, 1904, Alanson, Follansbee. Res., Chicago. (2) Thomas Hunter, b. Feb. 2, 1883; d. Oct. 2, 1883. (3) Helena Mary, b. July 9, 1884. (4) Edith, b. Oct. 2, 1887.

2962. iv. ELIZA CARLETON, b. Nov. 10, 1854; d. Dec. 2, 1861.

2963. v. HARRIETTE COBB, b. Nov. 15, 1859; m. Apr. 27, 1882, in Chicago, George Allison Armour, of Chicago. Res. since July, 1895, Princeton, N. J. Ch.: (1) George, b. in Chicago, Dec. 16, 1884; d. May 30, 1893. (2) Paul, b. July 4, 1886; d. Jan. 23, 1887. (3) Norman, b. Oct. 14, 1887. (4) Barbara, b. Nov. 27, 1889. (5) William, b. Jan. 23, 1892. (6) Allison, b. Aug. 27, 1896. (7) Edmund, b. July 26, 1889. ⊰.

1483. OBED FOOTE, (543, 172, 47, 13, 5,) b. Indianapolis, Ind., Apr. 19, 1824; m. Apr. 9, 1851, Mary Grey McOuat, in Indianapolis, Ind. He d. Sept. 4, 1884, in Paris, Ill.

2964. i.   OBED, b. Apr. 19, 1854; m. Margaret Whitehall, 4610.

2965. ii. MARY, b. Sioux City, Iowa, Dec. 24, 1859; m. Harry Booth, son of Walter Booth and Caroline M. Talbot, at Paris, Ill., Oct. 9, 1879. Res., Los Angelos, Cal. Ch.: (1) Walter Booth, b. Silver City, New Mexico, June 12, 1883. (2) Gordon Foote Booth, b. Silver City, New Mexico, Jan. 1, 1886. (3) Jessie Elsie Booth, b. in Fort Bayard, New Mexico, Nov. 6, 1892.

2966. iii. JESSIE, b. Yankton, Dakota, Mar. 4, 1862; m. Apr. 20, 1885, George Gordon Peosy, Woodville, Miss. He was an Attorney at Law; d. Apr., 1891, in Silver City, New Mexico; m. 2nd, Dec. 23, 1900, William H. Jack, a ranchman and cattleman in Silver City, New Mexico.

2967. iv. GEORGE, b. Paris, Ill., May 10, 1872; d. Sept. 13, 1897, in San Diego, Cal.

1486. FOSTER FOOTE, (549, 178, 50, 16, 5,) b. 1788; m. 1812, Polly Monroe. He d. Feb. 19, 1823.

    2968. i. STEPHEN, b. 1813.

    2969. ii. MARY, b. 1815.

    2970. iii. LYDIA, b. 1823.

1493. CHESTER FOOTE, (557, 185, 53, 16, 5,) b. Woodbury, Ct., Oct. 30, 1791; m. Mar. 8, 1815, Rebecca Sherman. He moved to Alford, Berkshire Co., Mass.; served in the Mass. Legislature in 1833 and 1834. He d. Apr. 13, 1875. She d. Apr. 20, 1883, in Jonesville, N. Y. Res., Alford, Mass. Ch. all b. in Alford, Mass.

    2971. i. CHARLES SHERMAN, b. Mar. 7, 1816; m. Electa Van Deusen, 4611-3.

    2972. ii. JULIA R., b. Nov. 5, 1817; m. Rev. Edward Stout, a M. E. minister. Both d. Ch.: (1) John. (2) Edward. Res., Troy, N. Y. (3) Emily.

    2973. iii. JOHN CHESTER, b. Apr. 11, 1819; m. Jane E. Humphrey, 4614-6.

    2974. iv. FANNY R., b. Apr. 17, 1822; m. 1st, Mar. 31, 1843, William T. Hamilton. He d.; m. 2nd, Rev. Richard Wade, a M. E. minister. She d. Mar. 9, 1902, in Gloversville, N. Y.; s. p.

    2975. v. MARY E., b. July 12, 1824; m. 1849, Rev. D. B. M. Kenzie. She d. Apr. 27, 1888, in Jonesville, N. Y. Ch.: (1) Mary, b. ———; m. David Thomas; res., West Granville, N. Y. (2) Fannie, b. ———; d. ———. (3) Emily, b. ———; d. ———. (4) Mattie, b. ———. (5) David, b. ———; a physician.

    2976. vi. EMILY J., b. Jan. 12, 1828; m. Aug. 20, 1851, Asel Housinger, a M. E. minister. She d. May 14, 1885. Ch.: (1) Charles, b. (2) Sherman, b. (3) William, b.; res., Round Lake, N. Y.

    2977. vii. SAMUEL ELIJAH, b. Oct. 12, 1830; m. Clara Jane Drake, 4617-8.

    2977[1]. viii. LUCY A., b. Aug. 6, 1838; d. Dec. 15, 1838.

    2977[2]. ix. WILLIAM C., b. May 6, 1840; d. 1860; unm.

1496. CHAUNCEY FOOTE, (557, 185, 53, 16, 5,) b. in Bethlehem, Ct., May 29, 1798; m. Jan. 25, 1825, Nancy Eliza Bicknell. She was b. Jan. 20, 1800. Res., Lafayette, O.

    2978. i. CHESTER L., b. Nov. 1, 1825; Methodist minister of the No. O. Conference.

    2978[1]. ii. MARCUS B., b. Mar. 29, 1828; blacksmith in Medina, O.

    2978[2]. iii. LUCY D., b. Apr. 17, 1830.

    2978[3]. iv. HIRAM C., b. Sept. 29, 1832.

    2979. v. ANN E., b. Dec. 8, 1834.

    2979[1]. vi. GEORGE W., b. July 5, 1838.

    2979[2]. vii. JOHN F., b. Sept. 4, 1840.

    2979[3]. viii. FRANCIS M., b. May 26, 1844.

1497. ELIADEE ORTON FOOTE, (557, 185, 53, 16, 5,) b. July 4, 1806; m. Eliza Maria Wooster, of Alford, Mass. She d. July 24, 1903. He d. Dec. 12, 1903. Res., Wellington and Oberlin, O.

    2980. i. ABIGAIL LUCINDA, b. Wellington, O., Nov. 16, 1831; m. Chas. C. Smith. Their names were changed to Ponsonby in 1874.

Ch.: (1) Charles Calt Ponsoaby, b. Mar. 9, 1853. (2) Frank O. V. Ponsonby, b. Nov. 17, 1855.

2981. ii. FRANCES ALMIRA, b. July 14, 1833; d. Sept. 23, 1851.

2982. iii. GROTINS DEWEY, b. Jan. 17, 1835; d. July 10, 1882.

2983. iv. CAROLINE DEWEY, b. Apr. 11, 1837; m. Dec. 20, 1859, Charles W. Miller. Res., Norwalk, O. Ch.: (1) Agnes J., b. Oct. 11, 1861. (2) John Graham, b. Sept. 4, 1865.

2984. v. NATHAN WOOSTER, b. July 10, 1841; m. Carrie S. Lord and Mary Ross. He d. Oct. 1, 1833. Ch.: (1) Mary Bernice,

2985. vi. ELIADEE ORTON, JR., b. Oberlin, O., Oct. 1, 1845; m. Nov. 26, 1876, Emma Louise Howe. He d. Dec. 16, 1900. No ch.

2986. vii. ELLEN MARIA, b. July 21, 1848; m. Mar. 25, 1889, Arthur K. Wooster.

1505. IRA FOOTE, (561, 195, 54, 16, 5,) b. May 27, 1797; m. Dec. 25, 1822, Nancy C., dau. of Ashbel Mix, of Bristol, Ct. She d. Dec. 1, 1861. He d. Feb. 19, 1862. Res., Burlington, Ct.

2987. i. JARIUS N., b. Oct. 2, 1823; m. Emily F. Carrington, 4622-3.

2988. ii. SHUBEL DYRE, b. June 2, 1825; m. Sarah Williams, of New York. She d. 9 ch.; n. f. k.

2988¹. iii. JACOB, b. May 9, 1828; d. Sept. 11, 1830.

2989. iv. NOBLE, b. Aug. 3, 1830; m. Mary Stacy, 4624.

2990. v. SARAH ELIZA, b. Oct. 13, 1833; m. Nov. 14, 1854, Washington Upson. She d. Jan. 24, 1904. Ch.: (1) Anna Delight Upson, b. Jan. 27, 1857; m. Dec. 6, 1881, Adua North Barnes. Ch.: (a) Winslow Washington Barnes, b. Nov. 25, 1882; m. Georgia Webster. (b) Rena Alice Barnes, b. Sept., 1884; graduated at Collinsville High School, 1901, also at State Normal at New Britain in 1906, now teaching in Torrington Graded School. (c) Frank Adua Barnes, b. July 17, 1886. (d) Louis Upson, b. Mar. 14, 1888, in the great blizzard. (e) Susan Delight, b. Oct. 18, 1892. (f) Ula Marguerite, b. May 12, 1897. (g) Mildred Louise, b. Nov. 12, 1898. (2) Leuella Marua Upson, b. Nov. 22, 1866; m. June 27, 1889, John D. Horsfall. No ch.

2991. vi. SEYMAN, b. July 15, 1835; d. Feb. 22, 1860. Res., Bristol, Ct.

1509. ARIEL FOOTE, (561, 195, 54, 16, 5,) b. Burlington, Ct., May 12, 1807; m. Sept. 3, 1833, Julia Ann, dau. of Justus Webster. She was b. Nov. 3, 1809; d. Mar., 1881. He was a farmer; d. Jan. 15, 1854. Res., Hartwood, Virginia.

2992. i. MARGARETT ANN, b. Apr. 7, 1836; d. Nov. 6, 1837.

2992¹. ii. ANNIE, b. Sept. 20, 1838; d. July 14, 1859.

2992². iii. MARIAH JANE, b. Dec. 2, 1840; d. Dec. 22, 1890.

2993. iv. THOMAS ARIEL, b. Mar. 1, 1843; m. Dulcie Bella Tate, 4625-6.

2993¹. v. SARAH, b. June 20, 1845; d. Apr. 18, 1887.

2993². vi. CHARLES JACOB, b. June 18, 1848; d. Apr. 27, 1862.

1513. ABRAHAM FOOTE, (563, 195, 54, 16, 5,) b. July 2, 1797; m. Nov. 12, 1826, Mary, dau. of John Ransom, of Haddam, Ct., b. 1807; d. July 22, 1874. He d. Jan. 13, 1877. Res., Hartford and East Hartford, Ct.

2994. i. AMANDA, b. May 7, 1827; m. May 4, 1854, James Vining, at Hartford; d. June 24, 1892, at East Hartford, Ct.; buried in Zion Cemetery, Hartford, Ct. No ch. She res. with Henry.

2995. ii. JAMES, b. May 20, 1831; d. June 19, 1847.

2996. iii. HENRY, b. Nov. 24, 1838. Res., Silver Lane, East Hartford, Ct.

1516. REUBEN FOOTE, (563, 195, 54, 16, 5,) b. Dec. 31, 1808; m. Jan. 28, 1835, Elizabeth, dau. of Elisah Bebee, of Lenox, N. Y. She d. Jan. 29, 1842, ae. 33. Res., Lenox, N. Y.

2997. i. ADELIA, b. Sept. 12, 1836.

1517. EDWIN FOOTE, (565, 196, 54, 16, 5,) b. Dec. 2, 1780; m. Nov. 28, 1814, Selina, dau. of John and Elizabeth (Ives) Maltby, of Wallingford, Ct. She was b. Mar. 4, 1794; d. Sept. 5, 1884. He d. Feb. 18, 1877. Res., Northford, Ct.

2998. . i. CHARLES, b. Aug. 29, 1815; m. Selina Bunnell, 4627-32.
2999. ii. CAROLINE ELIZABETH, b. June 21, 1817; d. Feb. 10, 1837;
3000. iii. JOHN M., b. Aug. 6, 1819; m. Sarah A. Munson, 4633-5.

1519. WAREHAM WILLIAMS FOOTE, (565, 196, 54, 16, 5,) b. Aug. 20, 1798; m. Dec. 19, 1822, Lucinda Harrison. She was b. Oct. 16, 1803; d. May 12, 1875. He d. June 2, 1883. Res., Northfield, Ct. Ch. all b. in Northfield, Ct.

3001. i. ALEXANDER, b. Feb. 9, 1824; m. Sarah Kelsey, 4636-8.
3002. ii. LUCY HENRIETTA, b. Apr. 6, 1826; m. Leander Harrison, of
          Wallingford, Ct. Ch.: (1) Thern, b. ——; d. ae. 13. (2)
          Adella, b. ——. Res., Wallingford, Ct.; unm.
3003. iii. ELIHU DAVIS, b. Jan. 4, 1828; m. Jennette Ransom; d. Nov.
          12, 1863.
3004. iv. JEROME W., b. July 8, 1829; m. Ann Foote, 4639-40.
3005. v. ELIZUR H., b. Jan. 19, 1831; m. Jane Russel and —— Fowler,
          4641.
3006. vi. LUCINDA JEANETTE, b. Feb. 1, 1839; m. Sept. 23, 1859,
          Douglas Williams; d. Feb. 2, 1882. Ch.: (1) Benjamin Douglas,
          b. May 10, 1863. (2) Herman, b. Feb. 21, 1869. (3) Davis, b.
          July 18, 1871; d. Dec. 29, 1906.
3007. vii. LYNDE H., b. Oct. 15, 1835; m. Juliette Sidney, 4642.
3008. viii. LOZELLE, b. Feb. 13, 1838; m. 4643-45.
3009. ix. DELIA, b. Sept. 4, 1839; d. Sept. 18, 1840.
3010. x. HENRY FRANKLIN, b. Nov. 28, 1841; d. Feb. 20, 1845.
3011. xi. PHILO BEECHER, b. Jan. 16, 1843; enlisted in Co. K, 15th Ct.
          Vols.; d. Dec. 10, 1862.
3012. xii. MARGARET EUGENIA, b. Dec. 12, 1845; m. Sept. 23, 1883,
          Douglass Williams, b. Sept. 22, 1887.
3013. xiii. WALTER S., b. Nov. 3, 1848; m. Ida Hull, 4646-8.

1524. AUGUSTUS FOOTE, (569, 196, 54, 16, 5,) b. ——; m. July 11, 1817, Statira Whitney, of Northford, Ct. She was b. June 25, 1795; d. June 4, 1871, in Fair Haven, Ct. Res., Durham, Wallingford, and Northford, Ct.

3014. i. JOHN A., b. ——; m. Almira Grannis, 4649-50.
3015. ii. SAMUEL W., b. ——; m. Sybil Brockett, 4651-4.
3016. iii. HENRY M., b. ——; m. Juliette Barnes and Belinda Cooper,
          4655-61.
3017. iv. EMILY MARIA, b. Northford, Ct., Nov. 29, 1823; m. Sept. 7,
          1843, David Goodale. Res., Sag Harbor, L. I. She d. Apr. 17,
          1886. Ch.: (1) Emma Jane, b. Dec. 7, 1847, Sag Harbor; m. June
          18, 1862, Alexander Coburn, New Haven, Ct. Ch.: (a) Alexander
          W., b. Dec. 21, 1868. (b) Harry, b. Aug. 24, 1871. (c) John O.,

b. Apr. 1, 1873; d. Apr. 28, 1903, N. H. (d) Winfred, b. Dec. 25, 1879. (2) Edith S., b. Mar. 8, 1858, Sag Harbor; m. 1st, June 8, 1881, Edwin Pardee; m. 2nd, May 28, 1889, Homer E. Blackman; both of New Haven, Ct. Ch.: (a) Leroy Whitney Pardee, b. June 9, 1883, New Haven, Ct. (b) George A. Blackman, b. Mar. 28, 1890. (c) Ethel G. Blackman, b. July 12, 1892. (d) Josephine, b. Jan. 30, 1894; d. in infancy. (e) Austin E., b. June 26, 1896. (f) Clifford Foote, b. Apr. 6, 1897. (g) Edna, b. July 31, 1899; d. in infancy.

3018. v. MARY ANN, b. Northford, Ct., Jan. 24, 1826.

3019. vi. SARAH CELESTE, b. Northford, Ct., Jan. 17, 1830.

3020. vii. CHARLOTTE, b. Northford, Ct., June 15, 1833; d. Sept. 18, 1836.

3021. viii. GEORGE LUZERNE, b. ———; m. Lucretia Amanda Way, 4662-4.

1525. DANIEL INGRAHAM FOOTE, (569, 196, 54, 16, 5,) b. Northford, Ct., Aug. 14, 1796; m. Fair Haven, Ct., June 16, 1833, Mary, dau. of Jonathan Beers Potter, of North Branford, Ct. She was b. Mar. 28, 1816, and d. Dec. 21, 1853. Res., Fair Haven, Ct. He d. New Haven, Ct., Feb. 8, 1884. Protestant; Episcopal.

3022. i. GEORGE L., b. ———; m. Chrestina A. M. Freund, 4665-73.

3023. ii. MARY JOSEPHINE, b. June 1, 1836; m. Fair Haven, Ct., May 21, 1854, Asa Lewis, son of Asa Chamberlain. He was b. Durham, Ct., Apr. 19, 1829; d. Mar. 22, 1899, in New Haven, Ct. She was educated in the Fair Haven schools. Protestant; Episcopal. Res., New Haven, Ct. Ch.: (1) Hattie Josephine, b. Oct. 9, 1861. (2) Clarence Henry, b. Oct. 31, 1865. (3) Asa Lewis, b. May 2, 1871; m. Naugatuck, Ct., Sept. 20, 1899, Mary Edith, dau. of Joel Francis Webster. She was b. Naugatuck, Ct., Dec. 11, 1876. Protestant; Episcopal. Insurance. Res., Fair Haven, Ct.

3024. iii. JULIA ASENATH, b. Mar. 21, 1839; m. Fair Haven, Ct., May 14, 1865, Walton Silas, son of Silas Hanley. He was b. Palmer, Mass., Mar. 29, 1838; d. July 26, 1879, in New Haven, Ct. Educated at the Fair Haven schools. Protestant; Episcopal. Res., New Haven, Ct. Ch.: (1) William Arthur, b. Oct. 2, 1873; m. New Haven, Ct., May 9, 1900, Jessie Gertrude, dau. of Charles Redfield Dayton. She was b. Baltimore, Md., Feb. 12, 1877. He was educated at the Grammar School in New Haven, Ct. Is a Stationery Engineer. Protestant; Episcopal. Res., New Haven, Ct.

3025. iv. JAMES HOBART, b. Sept. 6, 1842. Res., New Haven, Ct.

1526. JACOB FOOTE, (569, 196, 54, 16, 5,) b. May 30, 1798; m. Dec. 23, 1818, Lavina, dau. of Samuel Moulthrop, North Haven, Ct. Res., North Haven, Ct.

3026. i. MARY, b. Oct. 7, 1819; m. Feb. 6, 1845, Harvey D., son of David Basset, of North Haven, Ct. He was b. Apr. 4, 1815. She d. at Meriden, Ct., Mar. 11, 1891.

1528. LUCIUS FOOTE, (569, 196, 54, 16, 5,) b. Dec. 21, 1803; m. June 27, 1828, Laura, dau. of Samuel and Eunice Hubbard, of North Guilford, Ct. She was b. Oct. 3, 1805; d. Apr. 24, 1835; m. 2nd, Nov. 2, 1835, Lois, sister of first wife. Res., Durham, Ct. Member of Ct. Legislature in 1836.

3027.   i.   GEORGE, b. May 16, 1832; d. Sept. 21, 1834.

3028.   ii.   ELLEN, b. Sept. 29, 1836; d. May·29, 1863.

3029.   iii.   MARTHA, b. Oct. 28, 1838; m. Jan. 1, 1855, Edward A., son of Jonathan Thaye. He d. Dec. 28, 1900.

3030.   iv.   EMMA JANE, b. May 16, 1842; m. Jan. 1, 1861, Joel Welles, of Stratford, Ct. Ch.: (1) Albert Foote, b. Mar. 11, 1862; m. July 1, 1903, Phebe Thomas, of New Haven, Ct. Res., New Haven, Ct. Ch.: (a) Dorothy Thomas, b. Aug., 1904.

3031.   v.   LUCIUS H., b. Dec. 30, 1844; m. Louise H. Parsons, 4674-5.

1529.   LUTHER FOOTE, (569, 196, 54, 16, 5,) b. ———; m. Jan. 3, 1830, Salina, dau. of Maltby Fowler. She was b. Jan. 2, 1810. Res., Northford, Ct.

3032.   i.   MALTBY, b. Feb. 21, 1832; d. Mar. 9, 1832.

3033.   ii.   WILLIAM, b. May 9, 1833.

3033¹.   iii.   GRACE LUCRETIA, b. Jan. 6, 1835; d. Apr. 29, 1836.

3033².   iv.   LUZERNE, b. Mar. 2, 1837; d. Apr. 17, 1837.

3034.   v.   ELEANOR SELINA, b. June 7, 1842.

3035.   vi.   THEODORE LUTHUR, b. July 6, 1847.

1531.   LUZERNE FOOTE, (569, 196, 54, 16, 5,) b. Aug. 12, 1814; m. May 20, 1838, Grace, dau. of Matthew Fowler, of Northford, Ct. She was b. June 13, 1815. Res., Northford, Ct.

3036.   i.   VICTORIA SIGOURNEY, b. Apr. 26, 1839; m. John Hall. Res., Brushy Plain, Branford, Ct.

3037.   ii.   DENIZON BROWNWELL, b. May 13, 1841. Res., Meriden, Ct.

1544.   DAVID JOHN SMITH FOOTE, (575, 196, 54, 16, 5,) b. Dec. 2, 1811; m. July 20, 1835. Res., Nappanee, Canada.

3038.   i.   ALLEN, b. July 5, 1836; m. Sarah McCray, 4676-81.

3039.   ii.   JOHN, b. Sept. 7, 1839; m. Senia Thompson, 4682-85.

3040.   iii.   ELIZABETH AMELIA, b. Jan. 2, 1842; m. Oct. 14, 1866, Thomas James McCreadie, of Buffalo, N. Y. Res., 65 Armine St., Buffalo, N. Y. Ch.: (1) Augustus James, b. Dec. 9, 1867. (2) Rhoda Eliza, b. Nov. 12, 1869. (3) Caroline Mary, b. Feb. 23, 1872. (4) Albert Earnest, b. Mar. 12, 1874. (5) Lillian Alma, b. Mar. 24, 1880.

3041.   iv.   BENJAMIN E., b. May 10, 1845; m. Almira Thompson, 4686-89.

3042.   v.   MARGARET SAPHRONIA, b. ———; m. Leonard Bailey, of Fredericksburg, Ont. No ch.

3043.   vi.   PETER ANSON, b.

1545.   BENJAMIN FOOTE, (575, 196, 54, 16, 5,) b. Mar. 6, 1815; m. July 18, 1837, Lucy Ann Briggs. She was b. May 20, 1822. Res., Nappanee, Canada.

3044.   i.   BENJAMIN SMITH, b. June 15, 1838.

3045.   ii.   MARY ELIZABETH, b. Aug. 30, 1840; m. John Shaw. Res., Salt Lake City, Utah.

3046.   iii.   JOHN WESLEY, b. May 20, 1842.

3047.   iv.   IRVINE, b. Mar. 24, 1844.

3048.   v.   DANIEL, b. Dec. 28, 1845.

1546.   ASA FOOTE, (575, 196, 54, 16, 5,) b. Sept. 3, 1817; m. Feb. 17, 1844, Mary Baldwin.

3049. i. SAMUEL, b. Feb. 22, 1854.

1547. JOHN FOOTE, (576, 196, 54, 16, 5,) b. Sept. 20, 1882; m. ———.

3049¹. i. NELSON, b.

3049². ii. WILLIAM,. b.

3049³. iii. ALICE, b.

1549. ANDREW HALL FOOTE, (576, 196, 54, 16, ·5,) b. Wallingford, Ct., Nov. 15, 1806; m. Sept. 13, 1830, Frances, dau. of Simeon and Polly (Harrison) Hoadley, of New Haven, Ct. He d. in New York abt. 1890. She was b. in New Haven, Ct., July 18, 1813; d. in New Haven, Oct. 20, 1900.

   3050. i. FRANCES MARY, b. Apr. ·9, 1832, in New Haven, Ct.; unm. Res., New Haven, Ct.

   3051. ii. ELLEN HOADLEY, b. Jan. 23, 1835, New Haven, Ct.; m. June 9, 1869, Henry W. Foster, New Haven, Ct.; d. July 3, 1903. Ch.: (1) Isabella Graham, b. Mar. 22, 1870. (2) Henry Noble, b. Dec. 4, 1873; m. Oct. 12, 1898, A. Olive Dorman, Chicago, Ill. Ch.: (a) Helen Dorman, b. Apr. 7, 1901; on Easter Sunday.

   3051¹. iii. SARAH HALL, b. Apr. 13, 1837, New Haven, Ct.; d. Apr. 6, 1842, Brooklyn, N. Y.

   3051². iv. ANDREW HALL, b. Oct. 8, 1840, Brooklyn, N. Y.; d. Dec. 12, 1841.

   3051³. v. ISABELLA GRAHAM, b. July 19, 1843, New Haven, Ct.; d. Feb. 12, 1853, New Haven, Ct.

1551. JAMES FOOTE, (576, 196, 54, 16, 5,) b. Aug. 15, 1811; m. Oct. 8, 1834, Emeline Slead; m. 2nd, Martha. Reynolds, of Wallingford, Ct. He was a manufacturer. Res., Wallingford, ·Ct.

   3052. i. ELIZA JANE, b. ———; res., Chicago, Ill.

   3053. ii. JAMES HENRY, b. ———; d. ———.

   3053¹. iii. WILLIAM P., b. ———; d. ———.

   3054. iv. EDGAR S., b. ———; res., 3824 Ridge Ave., Chicago, Ill.

1553. GEORGE BENJAMIN FOOTE, (576, 196, 54, 16, 5,) b. Oct. 18, 1817; m. Nov. 19, 1840, Sarah Ann, dau. of Hiel Hall, of Wallingford, Ct. She was b. Sept. 20, 1819; d. June 15, 1857. He was a merchant; Episcopalian; d. June 7, 1851, at his res. in Wallingford, Ct.

   3055. i. CHARLES C., b. Nov. 8, 1841; m. Martha L. Brower, 4691-3.

   3056. ii. GEORGE B., b. Apr. 23, 1844; m. Cornelia W. Ingraham and Hattie Ponseroy, 4694.

   3056¹. iii. SARAH INGRAHAM, b. Dec. 10, 1850; d. Apr. 1, 1851.

1554. HENRY CLAY FOOTE, (576, 196, 54, 16, 5,) b. Wallingford, Ct., June 19, 1820; m. Aug. 17, 1842, Cathrine Whittelsey, dau. of Hiel Hall, of Wallingford, Ct.; m. 2nd, Dec. 23, 1869, Hannah Parker Thomson. He is a merchant. Res., Philadélphia, Pa.

   3057. i. ALICE KIRTLAND, b. Aug. 21, 1843; d. Dec. 8, 1869.

   3058. ii. MARY M., b. Sept. 13, 1849; d. Sept. 25, 1851.

   3059. iii. FRANK INGRAHAM, b. Apr. 4, 1853; d. Mar. 1, 1876.

   3060. iv. SARAH MANSFIELD, b. Mar. 27, 1857; d. Oct. 18, 1875.

   3061. v. HENRY TOWNSEND, b. Jan. 29, 1863; d. Aug. 4, 1866.

   3062. vi. CHARLES THOMPSON, b. Jan. 22, 1871; d. Mar. 9, 1875.

   3063. vii. HARRY CLAY, b. Sept. 10, 1872; d. Mar. 7, 1875.

   3064. viii. MARTHA STOKES, b. June 12, 1874; m. Sept. 17, 1902, Howard Samuel Hanthorn. Res., Woodbury, Ct.

1555. CHAUNCY BISHOP FOOTE, (578, 198, 54, 16, 5,) b. May 4, 1793; m. Sept. 13, 1815, Nancy B. Ives, of Cheshire, Ct. She was b. Dec. 20, 1791. Res., North Haven, Ct.

    3065. i.   MARYETTE MARSHALL; b. Oct. 22, 1816; m. Hobart M. Cook, of Branford, Ct.
    3066. ii. HENRY HOBART, b. Oct. 9, 1818.
    3067. iii. JULIETTE JANE, b. Sept. 1, 1820; d. Jan. 10, 1843; unm.
    3068. iv. AUGUSTUS ALUTHEA, b. Aug. 25, 1822.
    3069. v.   SAMUEL STILES, b. June 25, 1824.
    3070. vi. MARIA CORNELIA, b. Mar. 28, 1831.

1561. MERWIN HARRISON FOOTE, (583, 198, 54, 16, 5,) b. Hartford, Ct.; m. Hamden, Ct., May 13, 1834, Betsey, dau. of Lyman Bradley. She was b. Hamden, Ct., Aug. 13, 1813; d. Nov. 11, 1854; m. 2nd, Hamden, Dec. 4, 1856, Harriet, dau. of Lyman Bradley. She d. Apr. 7, 1882, at Hamden, Ct. Farmer. He d. May 14, 1880, at New Haven, Ct.

    3071. i.   ADELINE BETSEY, b. Mar. 27, 1837; d. Apr. 18, 1858.
    3072. ii. WEBSTER DE F., b. May 21, 1840; m. Mary S. Ferru, 4695.
    3073. iii. EUGENE, b. Mar. 25, 1844; d. Aug. 21, 1844.
    3074. iv. ADELBERT MERWIN, b. Mar. 2, 1849; m. 4696-7.

1565. EDWIN HARRISON FOOTE, (584, 198, 54, 16, 5,) b. Feb. 9, 1806; m. Julia Ann Bancraft, of Granby, Mass. He is a merchant, and res. in North Granville, N. Y., and New Haven, Ct.

    3074¹. i. EDWARD B., b. ———; lawyer. Res., New Haven, Ct.

1566. HARRISON FOOTE, (584, 198, 54, 16, 5,) b. June 23, 1807; m. Lucy Wilcox. He was a farmer. Res., Southwick and Westfield, Mass.

    3075. i.   WILLIAM HARRISON, b.
    3076. ii. JOHN HENRY, b.
    3077. iii. ELLEN ANNETTE, b.
    3078. iv. SARAH HOLMES, b.
    3079. v.   MARGARET, WILCOX, b.

1567. COL. THADDEUS FOOTE, (584, 193, 54, 16, 5,) b. Southwick, Mass., Apr. 27, 1821; m. May 31, 1847, Harriet Maria Betts. He graduated at Yale, 1844. Col. of 10th Mich. Cavalry in the Civil War. Lawyer; d. Feb. 1, 1903. Res., Grand Rapids, Mich.

    3080. i.   HENRY WARD, b. Mar. 25, 1848; d. Dec. 13, 1871.
    3081. ii. WILLIAM T., b. May 31, 1856; m. Margaret Blanchard, 4697-99.
    3082. iii. FREDERICK BETTS, b. Oct. 31, 1858.

1573. JARED FOOTE, (588, 200, 56, 16, 5,) b. Jan. 2, 1800; m. Sept. 13, 1820, Rebecca Beecher, of Kent, Ct. She was b. Jan. 9, 1800; d. at Hamden, Ct., Oct. 27, 1876. He was a graduate of Yale College, 1820; farmer; d. July 28, 1873. Res., No. Haven, Ct.

    3083. i.   JOSEPH, b. Aug. 28, 1821; d. Nov. 21, 1840.
    3084. ii. WILFRED, b. Oct. 12, 1823; d. May 18, 1904; unm.
    3085. iii. ROBERT, b. Nov. 14, 1825; d. May 11, 1896; unm.
    3086. iv. FREDERICK JARED, b. Sept. 9, 1829. Res., Albany, N. Y.
    3087. v.   MARY BASSETT, b. Sept. 9, 1836; m. Hamden, Ct., Oct. 9, 1862, Henry Charles, son of Charles Griggs. He was b. Dec. 18, 1834; d. Apr. 17, 1886, at Waterbury, Ct. Congregationalist. She d. May 19, 1900, at Waterbury, Ct. Ch.: (1) Henry Foote,

b. Nov. 17, 1863; d. Nov. 29, 1863. (2) Charles Jared, b. Nov. 28, 1864; m. Waterbury, Ct., June 25, 1895, Elizabeth H. Bowers. He d. May 24, 1905. (3) Wilfred Elizur, b. May 2, 1866; m. Paris, France, Apr. 21, 189?, Flora Victoria Hartley. Ch.: (a) Catherine, b. Jan. 27, 1892. (4) Robert Foote, b. Feb. 22, 1868; m. Waterbury, Ct., Feb. 4, 1902, Caroline Haring White. Ch.: (a) Haring White, b. Nov. 16, 1904. (b) Caroline White, b. Dec. 1, 1906. (5) Mary Rebecca, b. May 16, 1870; d. Jan. 12, 1878. (6) David Cullen, b. June 30, 1871; m. Waterbury, Ct., June 6, 1904, Helen Trowbridge Williams. Res., Waterbury, Ct. Ch.: (a) Henry Charles, b. Jan. 27, 1907. (7) Grace, b. Aug. 1, 1873; d. Feb. 18, 1874. (8) Catherine, b. Aug. 1, 1873; d. Aug. 19, 1873.

3088.　vi.　CULLEN BEECHER, b. Nov. 28, 1838; m. Scotland, Ct., Sept. 8, 1869, Nancy Marie, dau. of Thomas L. Adams. She was b. Scotland, Ct., July 5, 1844. Protestant. Educated at North Haven Academy and at Chicago, Ill. Retired farmer.

1577.　WILLIAM CULLEN FOOTE, (588, 200, 56, 16, 5,) b. Nov. 6, 1811, at North Haven, Ct.; m. Apr. 2, 1839, Hannah Williston, dau. of George Davis, Esq., of Sturbridge, Mass. Mr. Foote was a graduate at Yale College, 1832. Studied Theology. Is a clergyman. Res., Yonkers, N. Y. Was teacher in Young Ladies' Boarding School. Presbyterian. He d. Sept. 19, 1888.

3089.　i.　HELEN S. D., b. Oct. 27, 1844; res., Yonkers, N. Y.; unm.
3090.　ii.　HENRY STERNES, b. Aug. 6, 1848; d. Aug. 15, 1854.

1585.　STEPHEN SMITH FOOTE, (597, 205, 56, 16, 5,) b. Aug. 29, 1802; m. Nov. 2, 1827, Nancy Aurilla, dau. of Roswell and Nancy (Pomeroy) Strong. She was b. June 9, 1803; d. July 1, 1851.

3091.　i.　FLORA AMELIA, b. Sept. 7, 1830; m. May 21, 1858, Chauncey S. Welton. Res., Dexter, Mich. Ch.: (1) Charles Nelson, b. July 26, 1859. Res., Bermuda Hundreds, Va. (2) Arthur Foote, b. Nov. 2, 1863. (3) George Chauncey, b. Oct. 14, 1866. Res., Fullerton, Cal.

3092.　ii.　ROSWELL SMITH, b. Mar. 12, 1833; m. 4699¹.
3093.　iii.　EMMA GRATIA, b. Aug. 1, 1837; m. Nov. 5, 1857, Levi Nelson Slocum. He d. Nov. 20, 1858; m. 2nd, June 6, 1862, David S. Bennett. Ch.: (1) Merrill Foote Slocum, b. Jan. 7, 1859.

3094.　iv.　CHARLES EGBERT, b. Sept. 6, 1840; m. Laura Gillett, 4700.
3095.　v.　GEORGE EUGENE, b. Apr. 3, 1844; d. Feb., 1857.

1594.　ALFRED FOOTE, (602, 205, 56, 16, 5,) b. Oct. 22, 1811; m. May 4, 1836, Margaret, dau. of John A. and Ann Grant, of Hobart, N. Y. She was b. Jan. 10, 1816; d. May 2, 1901. He d. 1884. Res., Franklin, N. Y.

3096.　i.　JOHN ALEXANDER, b. Catskill, N. Y., May 27, 1837; m. Adella Minerva Stoddard, 4701-3.
3097.　ii.　CHARLES WESLEY, b. Catskill, N. Y., June 8, 1843; d. Nov. 20, 1870, in New Orleans, La.

1598.　LYMAN BEECH FOOTE, (602, 205, 56, 16, 5,) b. Mar. 24, 1822; m. July 6, 1851, Sarah Amelia Gleason. She was b. Mar. 5, 1835; d. July 24, 1906. Res., Tioga, N. Y.

3098.　i.　JARED HIRAM, b. Owego, N. Y., Mar. 27, 1852; m. Alice J. Vermilya, 4704.

(20)

3099. ii. JAMES LOVELL, b Owego, N. Y., Nov. 23, 1855; m. Susan
Villeron Harding, 4705.

1602. DR. ERASTUS NELSON FOOTE, (605, 205, 56, 16, 5,) b. Jan. 3, 1819,
Franklin, N. Y.; m. Oct. 13, 1841, Maria H., dau. of Elijah White. She was b.
Aug. 12, 1820, Franklin, N. Y.; d. Feb. 28, 1905, Lockeford, Cal. He was educated
at Delaware Literary Institute and Vermont Medical College. He d. Apr. 6, 1897.
Res., Lockeford, Cal.

30991. i.   ROBERT NELSON, b. Sept. 1, 1845; d. Jan. 1, 1852.
30992. ii. GERTRUDE MARIA, b. May 13, 1847, Addison, N. Y.; m. May
20, 1863, John Andrus, of Camanche, Cal. Res., San Francisco,
Cal. Ch.: (1) Clara J. Andrus, b. Camanche, Cal., Oct. 8, 1864;
m. Dec. 6, 1883, Fernando C. Ruggles, of Woodland, Cal. Ch.:
(a) Pearl E. Ruggles, b. Nov. 2, 1884, at Galt, Cal.; m. Feb. 1,
1903, Louis C. Emetsburg, of San Francisco, Cal. Ch.: (i) Leora
C. Emetsburg, b. Jan. 8, 1904. (ii) Dorothy E., b. Dec. 31, 1906.
(b) Leta Ruggles, b. Nov. 23, 1885, Galt; d. Jan. 30, 1892, at
Stockton, Cal. (c) Stella G., b. Oct. 25, 1887, Galt, Cal. (d)
Mable C., b. Nov. 17, 1889, Galt. (e) Fred E., b. Sept. 19, 1891,
Stockton, Cal.; d. Feb. 1, 1892. (2) Mary L. Andrus, b. May 5,
1866, Camanche; m. Aug. 12, 1885, H. M. Turner, of Stockton,
Cal.; d. Apr. 30, 1895, at Galt, Cal. Ch.: (a) Zorika Turner, b.
May 11, 1891, Stockton. (3) Ann Eliza Andrus, b. Mar. 17,
1871, Galt, Cal.; m. Nov. 29, 1887, W. W. Trubody, of Stockton,
Cal.; m. 2nd, Jan. 6, 1895, Frank Thompson, of West Point, Cal.
Ch.: (a) Percy Trubody, b. Mar. 11, 1890, at Stockton, Cal.
(4) John R. Andrus, b. Galt, Cal., Aug. 15, 1881; m. June 8,
1906, Constance R. Cushman, of San Francisco, Cal.
30993. iii. GEORGE HENRY, b. Sept. 26, 1849; d. Apr. 30, 1852.
3100.   iv. FORREST, b. Mar. 5, 1852; m. Leila A. Woodworth and Laura
Agusta Coburn, 4794-4802.
31001. v.   GILBERT, b. Nov. 2, 1856; d. May 29, 1894.
31002. vi. CHAS. HARDY, b. Dec. 28, 1858. Res., Calistoga, Cal.
31003. vii. CLARA, b. Feb. 27, 1861; d. July 19, 1861.
31004. viii. GORDON MILES, b. Dec. 10, 1864. Res., Hollister, Cal.
3101.   ix. LAURA JEANETTE, b. Feb. 12, 1867, Camanche, Cal. ; m.
Julius Leonard, son of Moses Bruml. He was b. Jackson, Cal.,
Mar. 23, 1864. Res., Lockeford, Cal. Ch.: (1) Ruth, b. Nov.
8, 1896; d. Oct. 17, 1900. (2) Dorothy, b. June 11, 1898; d. Oct.
2, 1902. (3) Leonard Foote, b. Aug. 23, 1904.

1619. ROBERT ENOS FOOTE, (608, 207, 56, 16, 5,) b. Aug. 13, 1817; m.
Feb. 4, 1840, Susan Rogers. He d. Nov., 1904.
3102. i.   CHARLES, b. ——; d. Apr., 1905, at Covingtryville, N. Y.
Ch.: (1) Wm. R.
31021. ii. LEWIS R., b. ——; d. at Covingtryville, N. Y.
31022. iii. CORNELIA, b. ——; m. —— Lamar. Res., Sayre, Pa.

1621. IRA ASHEL FOOTE, (608, 207, 56, 16, 5,) b. Oct. 8, 1823; m. Oct. 31,
1844, Louisa Vickrey. He d. Jan. 12, 1854.
3103. i.   HENRY M., b. Feb. 1, 1846; m. Emma A. Watrous, 4706-8.
31031. ii. MARY B., b. Feb. 25, 1848; d. May, 1848.
31032. iii. ALICE B., b. Sept. 20, 1849; d. Jan., 1864.

1623. ERASTUS DARWIN FOOTE, (610, 208, 56, 16, 5,) b. Aug. 2, 1808; m. Mar. 14, 1833, Elizabeth Sterling, in N. Y. City. She was b. Mar. 27, 1811; d. Sept. 15, 1900, in N. Y. City. He d. Feb. 4, 1866. Res., N. Y. City.

    3103⁴. i. JAMES STERLING, b. Sept. 22, 1836; m. Mary Weightman, 4690.

1633. CHARLES NICHOLS FOOTE, (616, 208, 56, 16, 5,) b. ———; m. Grace McGregor, of Freeland, Mich. She d. Apr. 10, 1898. He is a prosperous farmer. Res., Freeland, Mich.

    3103⁵. i. AMELIA, b. July 22, 1874.

    3104. ii. GUY, b. 1880.

    3105. iii. CHARLES, b. 1883.

1634. ROBERT FOOTE, (616, 208, 56, 16, 5,) b. ———; m. Peddy Alfred. Res., Harbor Beach, Mich.

    3106. i. CHARLES A., b. 1871.

1638. DAN POLLY FOOTE, (618, 208, 56, 16, 5,) b. Aug. 18, 1831; m. Oct. 19, 1857, Elizabeth Garham. She d. Dec. 1, 1899. He was a distinguished lawyer, senator, and scholar; d. Apr. 11, 1898. Res., Saginaw, Mich.

    3107. i. GEORGE G., b. Oct. 19, 1857; m. Mary Dallas, 4709-10.

    3108. ii. CHARLES EDWIN, b. Oct. 31, 1859; m. Florence Scollard Brown. He is a noted chemist and druggist, of Jackson, Mich.

    3109. iii. LANGLEY SUTHERLAND, b. Freeland, Mich., Aug. 29, 1863. He is a noted newspaper man. Res., Saginaw, Mich.

1641. HARVEY MONROE FOOTE, (618, 208, 56, 16, 5,) b. Oct. 10, 1836; m. Elizabeth Young. Res., Oswego, N. Y.

    3109¹. i. LENA, b. ———; d. ———.

    3109². ii. HARRY J., b. ———; d. ———.

    3109³. iii. CAROLINE, b. ———; m. Fred Huxley, of N. Y. Ch.: (1) Irma, b. ———.

    3110. iv. CARRIE FRED, b. ———; res., Ontario, Wayne Co., N. Y.

1642. MAJOR-GENERAL GEORGE FRANKLIN FOOTE, (618, 208, 56, 16, 5,) b. Oct. 22, 1839; m. 1876, Mary A. Duncan. Res., Washington, D. C.

    3111. i. WILL DUNCAN, b. Sept. 14, 1878; d. May 2, 1905.

1646. CHARLES EDWARD FOOTE, (618, 208, 56, 16, 5,) b. June 30, 1847; m. Mar. 25, 1878, Harriet Maud, dau. of Hatten Beach, of Bridgeport, Mich. Mr. Foote was a teacher in his younger days; is now a fruit raiser. Res., Bridgeport, Mich.

    3112. i. EDNA LUTHERINE, b. July 30, 1879.

    3113. ii. HATTEN HENRY, b. June 23, 1883.

    3114. iii. KATHERINE POLLY, b. Jan. 25, 1885.

1650. ARCHIE HUGH FOOTE, (618, 208, 56, 16, 5,) b. Apr. 8, 1864, and d. May, 1889; m. Lila Morris, of Woodhull, Mich. Res., DeWitt, Mich.

    3114¹. i. MORRIS G., b. ———; res., Lansingburgh, Mich.

1653. HELI FOOTE, (619, 208, 56, 16, 5,) b. Feb. 18, 1842; m. Oct. 22, 1869, Helen Reid. She was b. June 16, 1848. Res., LeRoy, N. Y.

    3115. i. RICHARD, b. Sept. 5, 1870; m. June 14, 1894, Bertha Zipke.

1654. JAMES C. FOOTE, (619, 208, 56, 16, 5,) b. May 5, 1867; m. Apr. 29, 1890, Kitty R., dau. of Wilbur H. Payne, of Rochester, N. Y. She was b. Feb. 8, 1867. He is a merchant of dry goods and groceries since 1896. He was clerk of Caledonia from 1899 to 1905. Has been President, Trustee and Water Commissioner of the village of Caledonia, N. Y.

3115¹. i.   HELEN, b. Mar. 18, 1891.

3116. ii.   JAMES C., JR., b. Sept. 25, 1898.

1663. ROBERT FOOTE, (627, 209, 56, 16, 5,) b. Mar. 6, 1818; m. Feb. 11, 1846. Res., Mayfield, N. Y.

3116¹. i.   HARRIET, b. 1850; d. Jan. 18, 1872.

3116². ii.   JESSE, b. 1856; d. Jan. 23, 1877.

1666. JAMES HARVEY FOOTE, (627, 209, 56, 16, 5,) b. Aug. 23, 1824; m. July 17, 1849, Ann E. Titcomb, of Mayfield, N. Y.; m. 2nd, Sept., 1853, Helen Hogaboom, of Mayfield, N. Y. Mr. Foote studied at Union, registered at Yale, and was preparing for the Presbyterian ministry, but on account of failing health he relinquished his plans and settled in Johnstown, N. Y. He held various town offices, at one time being school commissioner of Fulton Co. The latest years of his life he was a glove manufacturer. He d. Dec. 15, 1902. Res., Johnstown, N. Y.

3116³. i.   ANN ELIZABETH, b. Aug. 28, 1854; m. Feb., 1887, Albyron Waite. He d. May, 1890; s. p. Res., Johnstown, N. Y.

3117. ii.   JENNIE S., b. Mar. 8, 1857. Res., Johnstown, N. Y.; unm.

3118. iii. EMILY GRACE, b. Oct. 15, 1863; m. May 27, 1891, Henry F. Dawes, of Milborne Port, England. Res., Johnstown, N. Y. Glove manufacturer. Ch.: (1) Denton Tavener, b. Aug. 3, 1894. (2) Helen Warfield, b. Nov. 24, 1903.

3119. iv.   FRANCES HELEN, b. May 23, 1866; m. Oct. 11, 1888, Dr. John Sand, of Brooklyn, N. Y. Res., Brooklyn, N. Y. Ch.: (1) James Harvey, b. Mar. 3, 1892. (2) John Francis, b. Feb. 21, 1899. (3) Grace Dennison, b. Jan. 30, 1900.

1668. DANIEL FOOTE, (627, 209, 56, 16, 5,) b. Feb. 24, 1828; m. Jan. 19, 1859, Ruth, dau. of Judd Hoyt, of Galway, N. Y. Mr. Foote is a farmer. He was an active member of the Presbyterian Church at Mayfield for many years, and is now Dea. of the Presbyterian Church in Johnstown, N. Y., his present res.

3120. i.   ELLA, b. Dec. 29, 1863; d. Mar. 23, 1882.

3121. ii.   EMMA, b. Aug. 25, 1865; m. Oct. 18, 1900, Edgar Hodges, of Milborne Park, Eng. No ch. Res., Johnstown, N. Y.

3122. iii. ARTHUR, b. July 17, 1872; m. Eleanor McCall, 4710-¹.

1671. WILLIAM DARIUS FOOTE, (627, 209, 56, 16, 5,) b. Sept., 1836; m. Jan. 19, 1859, Mary, dau. of Levi Shults, of Johnstown, N. Y. Mr. Foote was for many years a merchant in Johnstown, N. Y., and afterwards a glove manufacturer; d. Mar. 26, 1904. Res., Johnstown, N. Y.

3123. i.   ALICE GREY, b. Feb. 6, 1860; m. Feb. 21, 1889; Daniel Dillenbeck. Res., Johnstown, N. Y. Ch.: (1) Marion Foote, b. Mar. 6, 1890. (2) Mildred C., b. Mar. 6, 1890.

3124. ii.   CAROLINE SHULTS, b. Jan. 22, 1862; m. Apr. 15, 1891, George M. Boyant. Res., Johnstown, N. Y. Ch.: (1) Edith Murray, b. Mar. 12, 1892. (2) Ruth, b. Feb. 22, 1894; d. Feb. 26, 1894. (3) Lulu Cathrine, b. Mar. 13, 1897. (4) Marjorie, b. July 21, 1899.

3124¹. iii. MARY LOUISE, b. Aug. 6, 1864; res., Johnstown, N. Y.

3124². iv. HARRIET AGNES, b. Oct. 21, 1872; m. June 23, 1904, Daniel McMartin. Res., Johnstown, N. Y. Ch.: (1) Daniel Malcolm, b. Dec. 1, 1906.

1675. DAVID FOOTE, (630, 211, 60, 18, 5,) b. Watertown, Ct., Feb., 1780; m. 1802, Mehitabel Post, of Cornwall, Vt. She d. Sept. 16, 1872, at Crown Point, N. Y., ae. 90 years, and was buried at West Cornwall, Vt. Mr. Foote was a Selectman and was Representative of the town in 1807; d. Feb. 1, 1813, and buried at West Cornwall, Vt. He settled and built on the east part of his father's estate. The same property is now owned by his grandson and great-grandson, Rollin A. and Abram W.

3125. i. BETSEY, b. Cornwall, Vt., Apr. 2, 1803; m. Feb. 25, 1823, Truman, son of Nathan Eells, of Cornwall, Vt. He was b. Cornwall, Vt., Nov. 27, 1798; d. Mar. 30, 1877, in Quincy, Ill. She d. Mar. 12, 1855, in Cornwall, Vt. Ch., all b. in Cornwall, Vt.: (1) Nathan Murdock, b. Oct. 23, 1824; d. Mar. 28, 1847, at Cornwall, Vt. (2) David Foote, b. June 30, 1826; m. Knox Co., Ill., 1854, Anna B. Snell. He d. Aug., 1866, at Matomoras, Mexico. Ch.: (a) Benjamin H., b. Altona, Ill., Sept. 10, 1855. (b) Irene, b. Nov., 1857; m. ——— Vera, of Larado, Texas. (3) Emiline Post, b. May 18, 1829; m. Altona, Ill., Sept. 3, 1856, Joseph Culbertsan, son of Joseph and Maria (Culbertsan) Thompson. He was b. Blairsville, Pa., Sept. 18, 1826. He held the office of Probate Judge of Adams Co., Ill., four years; was a member of the (b) Culbertsan Samuel, b. Sept. 11, 1859; d. Dec. 21, 1893. (c) was attorney and farmer; also was Postmaster at the time of his death. He d. Aug. 20, 1893. Ch.: (a) Hattie Emiline, b. Macomb, Ill., Aug. 11, 1857; d. June 3, 1875, at Quincy, Ill. (b) Culbertsan Samuel, b. Macomb, Ill., Dec. 21, 1893. (c) Joseph Eells, b. Quincy, Ill., May 19, 1862. (4) Martha Ellen, b. Oct. 2, 1837; m. Altona, Ill., May, 1857, George B. Van Steenberg, of Tremont, Ill. She d. Oct., 1872, at Tremont, Ill. (5) Marcia Helen, b. Oct. 2, 1837; m. May, 1857, Amos Franklin Ward, of Altona, Ill. She d. Mar. 2, 1863, at Altona, Ill. They had 4 ch., 3 of whom d. in infancy. One dau. survives, Emma Jane, b. 1861; m. 1887, Myron Holley Mather, of Altona, Ill. Res., 287 E. Arlington Ave., Riverside, Cal. Ch.: (1) Marcia Mather, b. 1892.

3126. ii. ABRAM, b. May 5, 1805; m. Orpha Williamson and Elise Hawkins, 4711-4.

3127. iii. MARTHA M., b. Cornwill, Vt., Mar. 16, 1808; m. Henry Davis, of Crown Point, N. Y., Jan. 29, 1824. A farmer. She d. at Crown Point, N. Y., May 30, 1875. He was b. Townsend, Vt., Sept. 7, 1800; d. at Crown Point, Aug. 9, 1862. Ch.: (1) Samuel M., b. Oct. 15, 1825; d. in Almedia, Cal., Mar. 30, 1863. He was in the stage business and fancy horses, and m. Sarah Baldwin, of Crown Point, Feb. 1, 1860. (2) Mehitable P., b. Jan. 19, 1832; d. in Cal.; m. Bennett F. Benedict, of Crown Point, N. Y., Nov. 24, 1849. Ch.: Frances A., b. in Crown Point, N. Y., Dec. 7, 1854. She m. 2nd, George Mees, of Almedia, Cal. (3) Truman E., b. Crown Point, Apr. 15, 1836; m. Diantha M. McIntyre, Mar. 25, 1855. She

d. Mar. 20, 1899. Farmer and mechanic; has held town office
for several years, and is a great lover of matched
horses. Ch.: (a) Ella M., b. Crown Point, May 27,
1856; m. Orland F. Thrasher, a farmer, of Crown Point, Jan. 1,
1877. No ch. (b) Henry F., b. Crown Point, N. Y., Sept. 7, 1859;
m. Annah Heaton, of Moriah, N. Y., Sept. 24, 1885. Ch.: (i)
Violet H. Davis, b. Crown Point, N. Y., Feb. 9, 1887. He is a
merchant, formerly in the clothing business, in Crown Point,
N. Y. Now in the carriage business in Fair Haven, Vt. (c)
Sarah M., b. Crown Point, N. Y., June 17, 1862; m. Fred A.
Streeter, of Fair Haven, Vt., Sept. 26, 1887. Ch.: (i) Frank E.,
b. Saranac Lake, N. Y., Aug. 12, 1891. (ii) George A., b.
Saranac Lake, N. Y., Dec. 1, 1894; d. Apr. 28, 1895. Fred A.
Streeter was a prominent hotel-keeper in the Adirondacks; d. at
Plattsburg, N. Y., Mar. 28, 1898. (d) Elsie J., b. Crown Point,
N. Y., Apr. 3, 1868; m. Dr. J. J. Montgomery, of Luzerne, N. Y.,
Oct. 16, 1893. No ch. (e) Addie E., b. Crown Point, N. Y., June
15, 1871. (f) Fredrick A., b. Crown Point, N. Y., Oct. 24, 1874;
is a clothier in New York City; m. Anna Roberts, of New York
City, Apr. 19, 1900. Ch. b. in New York City, Apr. 28, 1902. (g)
Orra D., b. Crown Point, N. Y., Sept. 6, 1877. (4) Martha Ellen
Davis, b. Crown Point, N. Y., Apr. 6, 1839; m. Charles Hildreth,
Aug. 21, 1855. He was a soldier in the great Civil War, and was
lost in the battle of the Wilderness, Aug. 5, 1864; m. 2nd, Henry
Dunn, of White River Junction, Vt., Feb., 1866. He was a
dentist, now in the furniture and undertaking business
at White River Junction, Vt. Ch. : (a) Emma L.,
m. at Crown Point, N. Y., to John C. Hamilton. (b) Carrie
P., b. Crown Point, N. Y., Jan. 16, 1861; m. Henry Levene, of
White River Junction, Vt.; a painter. (c) Pearl H., b. Crown
Point, N. Y., June 19, 1875, and is a Post Office Assistant at
White River Junction, Vt. Martha Ellen d. at White River
Junction, Vt., Apr. 28, 1905. (5) Addelade M., b. Crown Point,
N. Y., Apr. 20, 1844; d. Aug. 27, 1847. (6) Rosella F., b. Crown
Point, N. Y., Apr. 6, 1846, and d. Feb. 19, 1901, at city of Troy,
N. Y.; m. John C. Allen, Feb. 21, 1865; he d. Apr. 20,
1905. Ch.: (a) Johnny P., b. Ulysses, N. Y., Nov. 21, 1866; d.
————. (b) Lula B., b. Crown Point, N. Y., Jan. 3, 1869. (c)
Roy A., b. Apr. 20, 1881.

3128. iv.   EMELINE, b. 1810; d. Oct. 22, 1814; buried at West Cornwall.
3129. v.   DAVID (post humous), b. Apr. 13, 1813; m. Esther Lamb, 4715.

1678. RUSSELL FOOTE, (630, 211, 60, 18, 5,) b. May 17, 1786; m. 1st, Jan.,
1809, Belinda Mead, of Cornwall, Vt. She d. Jan., 1832; m. 2nd, 1832, Huldah
Gibbs, of Middlebury, Vt. He d. May 19, 1842. Res., Cornwall, Vt.

3130. i.   RUSSEL N., b. July 4, 1810; m. Belinda Wright, 4716.7.
3131. ii.   BELINDA S., b. Aug. 21, 1813; m. Abner Ray, of Cornwall,
             Vt.; moved to Somerset, Vt., where she d. Nov. 6, 1843.
3132. iii. ORPHA AURILLA, b. Cornwall, Vt., Feb. 8, 1818; m. May 16,
             1840, Charles Granson, son of John and Catharine (Norton)
             Williams, of Lockport, N. Y.; a farmer. They lived to celebrate

their golden wedding. She d. Jan. 26, 1892, in Olean, N. Y. He
was b. Sept. 2, 1818; d. ———, at Olean, N. Y. Res., Lockport,
N. Y., Hartland, Waukusha Co., Wis., and Olean, N. Y. Ch.: (1)
Russel H. Foote, b. Lockport, N. Y., June 16, 1841; m. 1867,
Emma J. Kelsey. Ch.: (a) Linda, b. July 23, 1869. (b) Adella
Weltha, b. Jan. 23, 1870. (c) Almer H., b. Dec. 31, 1872; d.
1874. (d) Orpha Maud, b. May 4, 1879. All the rest of O. A. and
C. G. Williams' ch. b. in Hartland, Wis. (2) Belinda, S., b. Oct.
15, 1844; m. May 8, 1867, Andrew Norton Perrin, of Conesus,
Livingston Co., N. Y. Ch.: (a) William Andrew, b. Tan Fram,
Crawford Co., Pa., Mar. 1, 1868; m. May 18, 1893, Marion
Frances, dau. of B. F. Parker, of Wellesley Hills, Mass. Ch.:
(i) Marion Parker, b. Rochester, N. Y., July 5, 1899. (ii) Carol
Parker, b. Buffalo, N. Y., May 28, 1901. (b) Marion Williams,
b. Titusville, Pa., Aug. 23, 1869; m. June 14, 1898, Henry Fairfield, son of Rev. Nathan S. Benton, of Ann Harbor, Mich.
Ch., all b. at Rochester, N. Y.: (i) Andrew Perrin, b. Mar. 15,
1899. (ii) Sarah Fairfield, b. June 8, 1900. (iii) Henry Fairfield,
b. Dec. 28, 1901. (c) Mary Sybil, b. Titusville, Pa., Nov. 9,
1871; m. Sept. 19, 1905, Gage Randolph, son of Joseph H. P.
Inslee, of New York City. Ch.: (i) Gage Randolph Inslee, Jr.,
b. Oct. 19, 1906. (d) Linda Orpha, b. Titusville, Pa., Feb. 5,
1876; m. June 26, 1901, Edward Conydon, son of Edward W.
Atwater, of Batavia, N. Y. Ch.: (i) Edward Perrin, b. Rochester, N. Y., July 5, 1902. (ii) Helen Hastings, b. Rochester, N.
Y., Mar. 30, 1905. (d) Charles Norton, b. Titusville, Pa., June
8, 1879. (3) John Gould, b. Apr. 22, 1850, and d. Jan. 8, 1907;
m. Oct. 10, 1877, in St. Louis, Mo., Kate Elizabeth Foote (See
4719 for full record). (4) Charles Norton, b. Nov. 9, 1853; d.
Sept., 1877.

3133. iv.   EZRA M., b. Jan. 19, 1820; m. Sarah S. Cooke, 4718-9.
3134. v.   DAVID S., b. Dec. 24, 1821; m. Hulda D. Merritt, 4720-4.
3135. vi.   ORLIN, b. Jan. 6, 1824; d. unm.
3136. vii.   SILAS K., b. Feb. 20, 1826; m. Hetty H. Smith and A. M.
              De Wolf, 4725-34.
3137. viii. HULDA, b. Dec. 28, 1829; d. Nov. 14, 1842.
3138. ix.   JOHN S., b. May 20, 1833; m. Nancy Clapp, 4735.
3139. x.   OZIAS W., b. July 24, 1836; m. Josephine M. Phillips, 4736-38.
3140. xi.   MARY JANE, b. Cornwall, Vt., Feb. 5, 1840; m. Dec. 3, 1866,
              Alfred B., son of Alfred Wakeman, of Merton, Wis. He was b.
              Lockport, N. Y., Mar. 3, 1843. Farmer; Angus cattle a specialty. Mrs. Wakeman was
              educated at Middlebury, Vt. Ch.: (1) Frank Elmer, b. Nov. 27,
              1867; m. Nov. 27, 1895, at Bedford, Ia., Elizabeth Wilson. Ch.:
              (a) Alfred Wakeman, b. Mar. 22, 1898. (b) Newell Wakeman,
              b. Apr. 11, 1900. (c) Harold Wakeman, b. Dec. 14, 1902. (d)
              Herman Wakeman, b. Dec. 14, 1902. (2) Lillian Jane, b. Dec.
              14, 1873; m. Apr. 19, 1903, at Bedford, Ia., Francis Beck. Ch.:
              (a) Hazel Pauline Beck, b. Jan. 14, 1905.

    1679. ELIJAH FOOTE, (630, 211, 60, 18, 5,) b. May 10, 1788; m. Nov. 17,
1812, Orpha Ward, of Cornwall, Vt. She d. Dec. 29, 1815; m. 2nd, Nov. 4, 1817,

Mehitabel Gale. She was b. 1796; d. May 20, 1877. He d. Jan. 1, 1868. Res., Cornwall, Vt.

3141. i. CALVIN W., b. Mar. 8, 1814; m. Sophrona Nimlett, 4739-40.

3142. ii. JARED ABERNATHY, b. Aug. 8, 1818; m. Caroline E. Bristol and Rosaltha A. Field, 4741-6.

3143. iii. SUMMERS G., b. July 25, 1820; m. Eliza Ann Pratt, 4747-9.

3144. iv. EMELINE A., b. Sept. 29, 1832; d. Jan. 11, 1836.

3145. v. NATHAN D., b. May 15, 1829; m. Elizabeth Wilmarth, 4750-1.

3146. vi. MARIETTE, b. Jan. 23, 1832; m. Oct. 18, 1853, Victor Wright, of Cornwall, Vt. He was b. in Cornwall, Vt., July 29, 1819. Attended public schools there for a time, then helped his father on his farm. Res., Cornwall, until 1862, then at Weybridge, Vt. Farmer. Was interested in sheep raising. At one time he represented Cornwall in the State Legislature. Mr. Wright was killed Dec. 6, 1867, by being thrown from his carriage while driving down the "Ledges" in Cornwall. Mr. Wright in his lifetime was widely known because of his activity in sheep raising. At the time of his death he was President of the Addison Co. Agricultural Society, and Vice-President of the State A. S. and Wool Growers' Association. Mrs. Wright d. in Weybridge, Dec. 18, 1881. Ch.: (1) Walter Victor, b. ———; m. Bertha B., dau. of Virgil W. Blanchard, of Middlebury, Vt. Ch.: (a) Eva. (b) Leona. (2) Albert D., b. June 13, 1864; m. Nov. 19, 1887, Elida M. Spencer. She was b. Aug. 17, 1863. He owns his father's old farm in Weybridge, and is traveling salesman for Walter A. Wood Co. Res., Middlebury, Vt. Ch.: (a) Victor, b. Jan. 21, 1889; d. Mar. 11, 1893. (b) Arthur, b. Oct. 10, 1891; d. Oct. 9, 1892. (c) Evelyn E., b. Dec. 2, 1893. (d) Stanley V., b. Mar. 9, 1896.

3147. vii. MARTHA J., b. Apr. 11, 1838; m. Feb. 21, 1861, Loran, son of Samuel and Amanda Richards. Farmer. Res., New Haven, Vt., Middlebury, Vt. Ch.: (1) Elnora May, b. May 12, 1865,; d. Apr. 16, 1881, in New Haven, Vt.

1683. SAMUEL FOOTE, (633, 211, 60, 18, 5,) b. Jan. 4, 1786; m. Feb. 24, 1827, Margaret Turner. He d. June 7, 1831. Res., Crown Point, N. Y.

3148. i. JAMES, b. Apr. 27, 1828.

3149. ii. SARAH (post humous), b. Nov. 23, 1831.

1687. JAMES WENTWORTH FOOTE, (645, 215, 60, 18, 5,) b. Lebanon, N. Y., Mar. 26, 1802; m. Lovisa Lincoln. She was b. Feb. 24, 1804; d. 1872. He d. 1870, in Norwich, N. Y.

3150. i. JAMES M., b. Dec. 31, 1825; m. Ann A. Crocker, 4752.

3151. ii. LOUISA ALMIRA, b. Otselic, N. Y., Sept. 16, 1827; m. Feb. 13, 1850, Samuel B. Benedict, of Lebanon, N. Y. He was b. Mar. 5, 1825. Enlisted May 21, 1861, in the 26th Regt. N. Y. Vols.; was discharged Nov. 2, 1862. He was in the battles of Bull Run, Antietam, South Mountain, Rappahannock, Chantilly, and Slaughters Hill. He was Fife Major, and was honorably discharged when that office was abolished. He also held the office of Justice for 20 years. He d. Feb. 13, 1900. She d. Nov. 12, 1863. Res., Lebanon, Utah. Ch.: (1) Eva Amelia, b. Dec.

2, 1853; d. Mar. 4, 1854. (2) Ada Louisa, b. Feb. 10, 1855; m.
Nov. 16, 1881, Eldoras D. Squires, of Milford, N. Y. Ch.: (a)
Ida Belle, b. Oct. 11, 1883; m. Oct. 1, 1902, Edgar H. Salisbury,
of Hartwick, N. Y. Ch.: (i) Robert D., b. Hartwick, Aug. 20,
1903. (ii) Gladys Irene, b. Hartwick, May 31, 1905. (b) Lulu
Gertrude, b. Sept. 19, 1885. (c) Lucy Eldora, b. July 26, 1892.

3152. iii. LOVISA SOPHIA, b. Hamilton, N. Y., Aug. 10, 1830; m. Aug.
16, 1854, Charles Giles Adams, of Norwich, N. Y.; d. Feb. 10,
1895, at Norwich, N. Y. Ch.: (1) Florence O., b. Otselic, N. Y.,
Nov. 17, 1855; m. July 4, 1878, Warren Webb, of Beaver
Meadow, N. Y. Ch.: (a) Herbert A., b. Apr. 27, 1879; lawyer,
Beaver Meadow, N. Y. (b) Julia S., b. Feb. 6, 1885; m. June
27, 1906, Burde Gibson, at Beaver Meadow, N. Y. (c) Charles
Ivan, b. July 22, 1900. (2) Helen J., b. Sept. 7, 1857; m. Dec.
12, 1880, Wellington Davis, of Plymouth, N. Y. Ch.: (a) Homer
Grove, b. Sept. 4, 1881. (b) Erna Helen, b. Sept. 14, 1884; m. Aug.
1, 1905, Hawley Gregory, of Norwich, N. Y. (c) Flay Ruth, b. Feb. 3,
1894. (d) Ola Hazel, b. Nov. 16, 1899. (3) Alice Sophia, b. Oct. 14,
1861; m. July 22, 1879, Simeon Crumb, of Beaver Meadow, N. Y.
Ch.: (a) Simeon Aubrey, b. Aug. 1, 1896. (4) Mary E., b. June
29, 1864; m. Feb. 7, 1892, Wallace Miller, of Otselic, N. Y.
Ch.: (a) Inez, b. Sept. 12, 1895. (b) Martha Elizabeth, b. June
19, 1900. (c) Florence Minerva, b. Nov. 29, 1901. (5) Grant C.,
b. Sept. 4, 1868; d. Aug. 30, 1870. (6) Jesse D., b. Sept. 25,
1871; d. June 1, 1886.

3153. iv. ABIGAIL M., b. 1833; d. Apr. 11, 1850, at Otselic, N. Y.

3154. v. ELIZA ANN, b. Nov. 2, 1835; m. July 16, 1872, Alvah L. Snow,
of Norwich, N. Y.; d. Apr. 17, 1897. Res., Norwich, N. Y. Ch.:
(1) Lovisa F., b. Norwich, N. Y., Apr. 13, 1873; m. Sept. 4, 1895,
Corey Aldrich, of Norwich, N. Y. Ch.: (a) Lillian E., b. Apr. 23.
1897. (b) Leon Corey, b. Jan. 18, 1899. (c) Gladys Lovisa, b.
May 10, 1901. (d) Grace Jennie, b. May 10, 1901; d. May 11,
1901. (2) Warren, b. Norwich, N. Y., Aug. 15, 1878; m. 1st, Aug.
16, 1899, Rena Foote. She d. Mar. 15, 1903; m. 2nd, Hattie
Cadwell, of Norwich, N. Y. Ch.: (a) Gertrude, b. Feb. 18, 1901.
(b) Leola Eliza, b. Feb. 21, 1907.

3155. vi. LEWIS, b. June 30, 1838; m. Bethiah W. Cowels, 4753-54.

3156. vii. AMELIA CHRISTIANNA, b. Norwich, Apr. 14, 1841; m. May
26, 1858, Samuel H. Weeden, of Norwich. Res., Norwich. Ch.:
(1) Charles H., b. May 7, 1860; m. Mar. 9, 1881, Mattie Hoag,
of Norwich, N. Y. Ch.: (a) Grace, b. Apr., 1885; m. Sept. 26,
1905, Lynn Byurn. (b) Blanche, b. Oct., 1886. (c) Gladys, b.
Oct., 1895; m. Dec. 27, 1905, Elmer Stevens. (d) Otis Arnold, b.
Jan., 1904. (2) Mary L., b. Feb. 11, 1863; d. Aug., 1863, at Norwich, N. Y. (3) Horacho B., b. July 12, 1864; m. 1st, Oct 18,
1887, Josephine Reynolds. She d. Feb. 7, 1897; m. 2nd, Oct. 1,
1897, Nellie Metcalf. Ch.: (a) Edward H., b. Jan. 3, 1900. (b)
Guy, b. Feb., 1904. (4) Archie Leurs, b. Mar. 16, 1870; m. May
20, 1891, Edith Teurilligee, of Norwich. Ch.: (a) Samuel A.,
b. Dec. 13, 1898. (5) Louise H., b. Dec. 27, 1874; m. Dec. 25,

1894, David Johns. Ch.: (a) Gertrude, b. Mar. 27, 1899; d. Mar. 28, 1899. (b) Margaret, b. July 17, 1901.

3157. viii. CHARLES OLIN, b. 1814; d. Dec. 12, 1855, at Norwich, N. Y.

3158. ix. ELLEN AMELIA, b. Norwich, N. Y., June 20, 1846; m. Nov. 24, 1870, Nelson F. Willey, of Norwich; d. Nov. 26, 1901. Ch.: (1) Chester V., b. Apr. 11, 1879. (2) Ella, b. Feb. 6, 1881, at Norwich, N. Y.

1694. IRA FOOTE, (650, 216, 60, 18, 5,) b. 1786; m. ———. She d. Oct. 2, 1873, ae. 84. He d. June 30, 1869; a carpenter. Res., Malone, N. Y.

3159. i. NORMAN M., b. 1811; m. Electa Landon, 4755-65.

3160. ii. ORPHA C., b. Bangor, N. Y., July 2, 1814; m. Ira Jones, of Malone, N. Y. She d. Feb. 11, 1878, at Akron, O. Ch.: (1) Charles, m. Nancy Archer. She d. June 22, 1872, at Corry, Pa. Ch.: (a) Hattie, b. Akron, O., Aug. 1, 1868. (b) Ira, b. Corry, Pa., June 11, 1872. (2) Stafford Jones.

3161. iii. MERCY FIDELIA, b. July 6, 1816; m. 1834, Mason F. Spencer, of Malone, N. Y. He d. 1874. Ch.: (1) Byron M., b. Malone, N. Y., Aug. 18, 1840; m. Nov. 11, 1869, Olive E. Sperry. She was ·b. in Bangor, N. Y. Ch.: (a) Harry M. Spencer, b. June 27, 1875; d. Mar. 29, 1880. (b) Albert D. Spencer, b. Malone, N. Y., Apr. 9, 1877; m. Dec. 8, 1904, Nellie A. Brooks, of Hayt Corner, Seneca Co., N. Y. (c) Floyd M. Spencer, b. Malone, N. Y., June 26, 1881; m. Mar. 12, 1902, Jessie B. Lester. Ch.: (i) Harry Glenn Spencer, b. Apr. 2, 1903. (2) Angia Spencer, b. ———; m. ——— Mead, of Marion, Iowa.

3162. iv. DANIEL S., b. Apr. 10, 1823; m. Mary A. Jones, 4766-7.

3163. v. LOREN S., b. Oct. 5, 1829; m. Sina T. Bosworth, 4768-73.

3164. vi. CHARLOTTE, b. Malone, N. Y., Nov. 1, 1824; d. Dec. 23, 1891, at Grant, O.

1695. SYLVESTER SCOTT FOOTE, (650, 216, 60, 18, 5,) b. Cornwall, Vt., 1800; m. 1829, Abigail, dau. of Robert Collins, b. 1800; d. Jan., 1864, at· Weybridge, Vt. He d. Apr., 1887. Farmer. Res., Cornwall and Weybridge, Vt.

3165. i. MARY ELLEN, b. Feb. 21, 1830; m. Oct. 1, 1855, Asaph, son of David Drake, b. May 3, 1831, Weybridge; drowned June 30, 1876. She d. Apr. 4, 1901; s. p.

3166. ii. SARAH ANN, b. Apr. 29, 1837; m. Sept. 8, 1858, Samuel, son of Philo Jewett, of Weybridge, Vt. Ch.: (1) Sylvester Scott, b. Jan. 12, 1859; d. 1868. (2) Philo D., b. Nov. 3, 1861; m. Independence, Mo., 1883, Nelly Draper. Ch.: (a) Philo S. Jewett, b. Aug. 17, 1886. (3) Abigail Ellen, b. June 8, 1865; m. July 18, 1888, Charles Fuller, of Lawrence, Kansas. Ch.: (a) Jewett Charles Fuller, b. Chicago, Ill., July 10, 1889. (b) Naome Fuller, b. Chicago, Ill., Jan. 6, 1892. (c) Gladys Fuller, b. Chicago, Ill., May 10, 1895. (4) Samuel Scott, b. Mar. 21, 1872; m. Lawrence, Kan., 1895, Florence Albaugh. (5) Burt Charles, b. Sept. 12, 1874; m. Lawrence, Kan., 1897, Eudora Eaton. (6) Edson Asaph, b. Sept. 21, 1876; m. Yates Center, Kan., 1902, Lottie Cope. Ch.: (a) Samuel E. Jewett, b. Kan., Jan. 31, 1905. (7) Mary, b. Independence, Mo., Aug. 18, 1879; m. Lawrence, Kan., Oct. 16, 1895, Woodson H. Rhea.

1705. DENICE FOOTE, (657, 216, 60, 18, 5,) b. ——; m. 1831, Betsey Conroyd. He d. 1886, in Steuben Co., N. Y. She d. some years before him.

3166¹. i. WILLIAM H., b.

1709. JOSEPH HOSELEY FOOTE, (657, 216, 60, 18, 5,) b. Sept. 10, 1811; m. July 31, 1835, Rhoda Esther, dau. of Harry Mason, of Pompey, N. Y. He d. May 20, 1895. She d. Dec. 8, 1903. He was a farmer by occupation.

3167. i. MILTON M., b. June 27, 1840; m. Louise C. Coman and Clara Elizabeth Reed, 4774-8.

3168. ii. HELEN VIOLA, b. Morrisville, N. Y., Nov. 22, 1845; m. 1st, Feb. 1, 1865, Edwin G. Sanford, of Oneida Castle, N. Y. He d. Mar. 9, 1875; m. 2nd, Oct. 28, 1877, Nathaniel M. Gregg, of Munnsville, N. Y. He is a lawyer by profession. Ch.: (1) Louis E. Sanford, b. Oneida Castle, Jan. 13, 1868. (2) Mary Esther Gregg, b. Munnsville, N. Y., Dec. 23, 1880.

1711. GEORGE L. FOOTE, (657, 216, 60, 18, 5,) b. Eaton, N. Y., July 15, 1818; m. 1st, Jan. 21, 1841, Abigail A. Webb. She d. July 15, 1859; m. 2nd, Dec. 11, 1859, Lydia M. Leigh. She d. Mar. 31, 1886. Mr. Foote served in the U. S. Army in the War of the Rebellion in Company A, 176th Regt. N. Y. State Volunteers. Res., Madison, N. Y.

3169. i. WILLIAM H., b. Apr. 3, 1846; m. Anna M. Weaver, 4779-82.

3170. ii. MARY ABIGAIL, b. June 26, 1849; m. June 12, 1873, H. D. Mather. Ch.: (1) Lydia A., b. Apr. 26, 1875. (2) Gertie M., b. Apr. 9, 1876. (3) George F., b. Apr. 9, 1879.

3171. iii. GEORGE L., b. Jan. 16, 1863.

3172. iv. JAY B., b. Jan. 7, 1874.

3173. v. CHARLES L., b. Jan. 7, 1874.

3174. vi. EARL, b. Mar. 12, 1879.

1718. MAJOR ALFRED FOOTE, U. S. A. (675, 218, 60, 18, 5,) b. N. Y. City, Oct. 25, 1840; m. Oct. 31, 1865, Rebecca Foster, at Harrisburg, Pa. He d. from wounds received in the Battle of the Wilderness, Sept. 1, 1869, at Geneva, N. Y. She res., Washington, D. C.

3175. i. SAMUEL ALFRED, b. ——. Res., New Orleans, La.

1719. LAWRENCE FOOTE, (675, 218, 60, 18, 5,) b. N. Y. City, July 7, 1844; m. 1st, Oct. 2, 1872, Hannah Kenner, at Flora, Ill. She d. Nov. 5, 1880, ae. 34 years 11 months; m. 2nd, Feb. 15, 1882, Mrs. Louise Garret Morey, at New Orleans, La. Lumber dealer and President Mississippi State Bank. Res., Canton, Miss. Ch., all b. at Flora, Ill., and by first wife.

3176. i. SAMUEL ALFRED, b. Aug. 6, 1875; d. Feb. 24, 1883, at Plaquemine, La.

3177. ii. ALVIN KENNER, b. Aug. 12, 1877; m. Ada Screven Page, 4783-6.

3177¹. iii. JOHN, b. Sept. 4, 1879; d. Nov. 14, 1879, at Flora, Ill.

1720. ROBERT EBENEZER FOOTE, (675, 218, 60, 18, 5,) b. N. Y. City, Oct. 13, 1845; m. Oct. 31, 1876, Francis Hamilton. Res., Denver, Col.

3178. i. FRANCIS PASIA, b. Sept. 5, 1877; m. Jan. 15, 1904, Everett Rider. Res., Denver, Colo. Ch.: (1) Robert Everett, b. Dec. 25, 1906.

3179. ii. THOMAS, b. Aug. 21, 1879.

3180. iii. MARY HAMILTON, b. Jan. 16, 1881.

3180¹. iv. JOHN HAMILTON, b. Dec. 24, 1882; d. Jan. 22, 1886.
3181. v. ROBERT, b. Nov. 12, 1885.

1728. ANDREW NORTHRUP FOOTE, (680, 219, 60, 18, 5,) b. Jefferson, Schoharie Co., N. Y., Jan. 16, 1801; m. June 20, 1823, Amanda Matilda Phillips. After learning his trade he moved to Battle Creek, Mich., and for over ten years was foreman of Wallace Woollen Mills, after which he moved to the township of Carmel, Eaton Co., Mich., where he res. until his death, Mar. 12, 1876.

3182. i. WILLIAM, b. Mar. 13, 1824; d. Mar. 19, 1829.
3183. ii. ELEANOR, b. May 20, 1826; m. Aug. 25, 1842, Eben Stafford. He d. ———; m. 2nd, Smith Benham. He d. 1890. Ch.: (1) Child, b. ———; d. ae. 18. (2) Albert P., b. 1877; m. 1899, Laura Woodgates; a machinist; no ch. Res., Battle Creek, Mich.
3184. iii. ALBERT PORTER, b. Feb. 8, 1828; d. Mar. 30, 1829.
3185. iv. CLARK, b. Nov. 4, 1829; m. 1850, Becky Kies. She d. 1898; m. 2nd, Betsey Mains; no ch.
3186. v. ALLEN, b. Aug. 13, 1831; m. Sarah Herrick, 4803-5.
3187. vi. HENRY, b. Feb. 25, 1833; m. Mary Gaylord, 4806-7.
3188. vii. EMILY, b. Nov. 25, 1835; m. Wesley Elles; d. 1863. Ch.: (1) Emma, b. 1860; m. 1st, William Osborne; m. 2nd, John McDonald. Res., Charlotte, Mich. Ch.: (a) Harry Osborne, b. 1891. (b) Milo Osborne, b. 1893. (2) Earnest, b. 1865.
3189. viii. ALBON, b. May 23, 1837; m. Henretta Campbell, 4808-10.
3190. ix. EDWIN, b. Aug. 15, 1839; m. Aggie Vollentine, 4811-12.
3191. x. MARTIN PORTER, b. May 20, 1846; m. Delia Haughn, 4813-15.

1729. ABRAHAM HITCHCOCK FOOTE, (680, 219, 60, 18, 5,) b. Feb., 1803; m. Dec. 30, 1824, Amy, dau. of Eliphet Avery, of Schenectady, N. Y. She was b. Sept. 27, 1803; d. Apr. 15, 1881. Farmer. Presbyterian. He d. Mar. 9, 1857.

3192. i. MILES E., b. Dec. 27, 1826; m. Martha Howard, 4816-25.
3193. ii. LUCINDA, b. on Dutch Hill, Schoharie Co., N. Y., Apr. 21, 1829; m. May 28, 1856, Lewis Parker Shute. He d. Apr. 15, 1869. She m. 2nd, Oct. 15, 1872, William Garrison. He d. Apr. 3, 1883. She living with her son, Chicago, Ill. Ch.: (1) Lewis Avery, b. Mar. 23, 1857; d. Aug. 24, 1867. (2) Eliza Jane, b. Jan. 7, 1860; d. Aug. 22, 1868. (3) Rev. Abraham Lincoln, b. Feb. 15, 1865; m. June 18, 1887, Nellie, dau. of Rev. James William and Jane Elizabeth Haney. Pastor of Wesley Methodist Episcopal Church, N. Halsted St., Chicago, Ill. Ch.: (a) Lewis Harry, b. Oct. 14, 1888; d. Oct. 16, 1888. (b) Vivian Lizzie, b. June 11, 1890. (c) Zelina Luella, b. Apr. 26, 1892. (d) Harold James, b. Aug. 9, 1893; d. Dec. 15, 1893. (e) Olin Yates, b. Dec. 11, 1894. (f) Clarence William, b. July 30, 1903.
3194. iii. ANNA, b. Feb. 10, 1831; d. Sept. 15, 1833.
3195. iv. ESTHER C., b. May 10, 1833; d. Feb. 7, 1836.
3196. v. HIRAM DELONG, b. Apr. 12, 1835; m. Sabra Ann, dau. of Lewis P. Shute. He d. 1902.
3197. vi. JOHN AVERY, b. Aug. 2, 1837; unm. Res., Hillsboro, Oregon. A large farmer.
3198. vii. AMANDA, b. July, 1839; m. abt. 1861, Stephen Rector. Res., Delanson, N. Y. Ch.: (1) Ozias P., b. (2) Ervin, b. (3) Amos D., b.

3199. viii. AMOS DUEL, b. Dec. 16, 1841; d. Apr., 1864.

3200. ix. MILO P., b. Mar. 30, 1844; m. Alpharetta Kearns, 4826-8.

3201. x. ABRAM L., b. Mar. 23, 1849; m. Ida J. McCarthy and Carrie M. Morrison, 4829-37.

3202. xi. WILLIAM C., b. Apr. 30, 1851; m. Georgia Freemire, 4838-41.

1736. ALONZO DOOLITTLE FOOTE, (686, 219, 60, 18, 5,) b. Sept. 19, 1815; m. 1st, Sept. 30, 1841, Lucy R. Lum. She was b. Feb. 15, 1816; d. Sept. 28, 1860; m. 2nd, Oct. 17, 1861, Ann Louisa Lum. She was b. Jan. 7, 1823; d. Oct. 25, 1880. He d. May 22, 1896. Res., County Line, Niagara Co., N. Y.

3203. i. HARRIET A., b. Sept. 19, 1842; d. Nov. 3, 1891. Res., County Line, Niagara Co., N. Y.

3204. ii. HOMER A., b. Aug. 21, 1850; m. Nancy H. Putnam and Belle R. Ketcham, 4842-44.

1736. GEORGE AUGUSTUS FOOTE, (686, 219, 60, 18, 5,) b. Aug. 26, 1819; m. Dec. 22, 1845, Louisa M. Hubbard, b. 1824, and d. July 15, 1863; m. 2nd, Feb. 23, 1864, Emmilissa Hubbard. She was b. Aug. 3, 1832. He d. Nov. 7, 1878.

3205. i. DOTHA LEMIRA, b. June 6, 1847; m. Nov. 20, 1864, Alfred F. Burnham. She d. Jan. 11, 1871. Ch.: (1) George Almon, b. Oct. 23, 1866.

3206. ii. SHELDON A., b. June 27, 1849; m. Hattie S. Burnham, 4844¹-8.

3207. iii. JAMES ABIJAH, b. Aug. 18, 1851; m. Nellie R. Brook and Ella Kothe, 4849.

3208. iv. HARRY HUBBARD, b. Aug. 29, 1867. Res., Parkersburg, Iowa; unm.

3209. v. LOUISA AMANDA, b. Mar. 23, 1872; m. Gustavus Adolphus Pfeiffer. One ch.

1741. JACOB CHESTER FOOTE, (686, 219, 60, 18, 5,) b. June 16, 1830; m. Nov. 20, 1851, Jane Tracy, of Lone Rock, Iowa; d. Dec. 13, 1905, at Bristow, Ia. Ch. all b. at Lone Rock, Wis.

3211. i. AMANDA GIVENS, b. Feb. 7, 1857; m. C. F. Morgan, of Newton, Ia. Ch.: (1) Walter J., b. Nov. 25, 1881; unm. (2) Margaret J., b. 1889. (3) Florence, b. 1895.

3212. ii. GEORGE L., b. Dec. 24, 1858; m. Agnes Brougleton, 4850-1.

3213. iii. JENNIE MARIA, b. Aug. 2, 1862; m. Jan. 12, 1889, George W. Royer, of Lomberton, Minn. Ch.: (1) Zoe Jane. (2) Garnet.

3214. iv. HORACE A., b. Feb. 18, 1864; m. Cora A. Ray, 4852.

3215. v. CHARLES CHESTER, b. Apr. 16, 1868; m. ———. Res., Montgomery, Ia. No ch.

1742. THOMAS BRONSON FOOTE, (686, 219, 60, 18, 5,) b. Dec. 13, 1833, Johnsons Creek, Niagara Co., N. Y.; m. Dec. 3, 1857, Mary E. Von Nortwick. He d. June 8, 1876. She then m. ——— Robson, of Middleport, N. Y.

3216. i. DAU., b. July 10, 1859; d. July 10, 1859.

1745. REV. GEORGE FOOTE, (688, 220, 60, 18, 5,) b. Sept. 1, 1800; m. Dec. 19, 1825, Ann Fish, of Groton, Ct., at Lawrenceville, Ga. He was a graduate of Union College, 1823, and was a minister at Port Penn, Del. He d. at Odessa, Del., 1867. They had 6 ch., all of whom d. in infancy or childhood but one.

3217. i. HARRIET FRANCINA, b. Apr. 17, 1829. Was a member of Rutgers Institute in New York City.

1748. EZRAI ALBERT FOOTE, (688, 220, 60, 18, 5,) b. Feb. 6, 1809, at Goshen, Ct.; m. June 4, 1829, Clarissa, dau. of Julius and Eunice Beach, of Goshen, Ct. She was b. Dec. 5, 1807, and d. June 5, 1886, at Footville, Wis. In 1845 they removed to Rock Co., Wis., and settled at the point where the village now stands which bears his name. He was a man whose ability was recognized by his fellow citizens, who elected him to positions of trust and honor. In 1847 he was made a member of the Constitutional Convention, and from then until 1869 he held various public offices. He was repeatedly a member of the Wis. Legislature and of the Senate; a trustee of the State Hospital for the Insane; a director of the Beloit and Madison Railroad and of the Central Bank of Wis. He was also one of the factors in building the Evansville Seminary, and for many years was President of its board of trustees. He removed to La Cygne, Kas., in 1869, and remained there seven years, being the first Mayor of that city. Of him it was said at his death: ''He had held many positions of trust, winning for himself the high esteem of all who knew him. He was a man of good ability, energetic in the discharge of duty, and honest—a man of iron will and great force of character. His intellect was of a high order, his judgment of men and things acute and correct. His religious life was characterized by intense interest in the Master's service, and in spite of the things which enter into man's life to create discord he kept faith to the end.'' He d. Dec. 21, 1885, at Footville, Wis.

    3218. i.   RUTH ROXANA, b. Apr. 30, 1831, at Goshen, Ct.; d. unm. Res., Footville, Wis.; d. Dec. 7, 1863.

    3219. ii. JOSEPH I., b. Dec. 17, 1834; m. Emma L. Lovejoy, 4853-4.

    3220. iii. LOUISA BATTELLE, b. Sept. 28, 1839, at Goshen, Ct.; m. Dec. 23, 1860, Henry Arnold Egerton, of Northfield, Vt. Ch.: (1) Gardner Arnold, b. Nov. 3, 1864, at Footville, Wis.; d. Apr. 21, 1884. (2) Clara, b. Dec. 14, 1873; m. Mar. 10, 1898, Rev. John J. Lugg. Ch.: (a) Ruth Louise, b. July 24, 1901. (3) Jay Foote, b. Apr. 1, 1879. Since 1903 he has been connected with the First National Bank of Milwaukee, Wis.

1751. TIMOTHY BRADLEY FOOTE, (689, 220, 60, 18, 5,) b. Dec. 29, 1799; m. 1st, 1823, Jane Ann Russell, of Oswegatchie, St. Lawrence Co., N. Y. She was b. Dec. 29, 1799, at Oswegatchie, N. Y.; d. Dec. 7, 1843, in Ill.; m. 2nd, July 23, 1847, Nancy Jane Riley, of Quincy, Ill. She was b. Canada West, Dec. 17, 1830; m. 3rd, Apr. 5, 1857, Elizabeth Bessac. She was b. Candor, Tioga Co., N. Y., July 5, 1813; d. Oct., 1876, in Nephi, Juab Co., Utah. Res., Oswegatchie, St. Lawrence Co., N. Y. Mr. Foote d. Apr. 18, 1886, in Nephi, Juab Co., Utah.

    3221. i.   REUBEN RUSSELL, b. Oswegatchie, N. Y., June 14, 1824.

    3222. ii. WILLIAM, b. Oswegatchie, N. Y., Feb. 28, 1826. Res., California.

    3223. iii. STEPHEN, b. Oswegatchie, N. Y., Apr. 19, 1828.

    3224. iv. CHARLES, b. Mar. 28, 1832; m. Mariam Rollin and Hannah Mousley, 4855-67.

    3225. v.   GUY W., b. July 13, 1836; m. Eliza S. Coulson, 4868-70.

    3226. vi. VICTORIA LOUISA, b. Nauvoo, Ill., Nov. 7, 1841; m. Feb. 18, 1858, Charles Cummings. She d. June 30, 1892. Ch.: (1) George Timothy Cummings, b. July 24, 1859, Nephi, Utah; m. Nov. 14, 1878, at Salt Lake City, Frances C. Weaver. (2) Frances Louisa, b. Sept. 19, 1879, at Millville, Utah; m. May 16, 1901, at

Millville, Joseph A. Jessop. Ch.: (a) Joseph Lee Jessop, b. Apr. 26, 1903. (b) George Thomas Jessop, b. Dec. 13, 1904. (c) Charles Reed Jessop, b. Mar. 28, 1906. (3) George Timothy Cummings, b. Dec. 4, 1881; m. Oct. 8, 1902, at Salt Lake City, Lilliath Jessop. Ch.: (a) Manetta Cummings, b. Dec. 12, 1904. (4) Kater Maud, b. Oct. 20, 1884; m. June 8, 1904, at Millville, Alphia Trolson. (5) Lois Amanda, b. Sept. 15, 1886; d. June 11, 1899, at Millville, Utah. (6) Elmina, b. Sept. 16, 1888; d. Nov. 6, 1889, at Millville. (7) Frank, b. Dec. 9, 1891.

3227. vii. ELIZA JANE, b. Nauvoo, Ill., Aug. 18, 1843; d. Dec. 7, 1843, in Nauvoo, Ill.

By second wife.

3228. viii. CYRUS R., b. Sept. 16, 1848; m. Lizzie Tidwell, 4571-6.

3229. ix. SARAH, b. June 2, 1852; d. Jan. 3, 1856.

3230. x. ABNER FRANKLIN, b. Nephi, Utah, June 3, 1854; d. Apr. 5, 1865.

3231. xi. LOIS LOISA, b. Nephi, Utah, June 6, 1857; m. July 4, 1877, George W. Taylor, of St. George, Utah. Ch.: (1) Claude Hamilton, b. Salt Lake City, Utah, June 16, 1878; m. Sept. 30, 1904, Florence Balts. Ch.: (1) George Douglas, b. Feb. 9, 1905. (2) Elmira Lois, b. Salt Lake City, Oct. 13, 1887. (3) Jane, b. Salt Lake City, July 1, 1883. (4) John Marlow, b. Am. Fork, Utah, Apr. 28, 1885. (5) Bessie Ellinor, b. Kaysville, Utah, Aug. 19, 1889.

3232. xii. JOHN, b. July 19, 1859; m. Laura Young, 4877-80.

3233. xiii. TIMOTHY LESLIE, b. Nephi, Utah, Jan. 6, 1862; m. Effie Cox, Dec. 23, 1892. No ch.

3234. xiv. GEORGE W., b. July 26, 1866; m. Celestia Wilson, 4881-3.

1761. WALTER RODNEY FOOTE, (703, 222, 61, 18, 5,) b. Feb. 10, 1793; m. Sally Harrison, of North Branford, Ct.

3235. i. WILLIAM, b. 1826; m. Wealthy Sybil Stanneard, 4884-5.

3236. ii. RUSSELL, b. Aug. 16, 1833; m. Emily Conklin Dudley, 4886-9.

3237. iii. NOAH, b. ———; m. Grace Chidsey, 4890-1.

3237¹. iv. SARAH, b. ———; unm.

1762. MERRITT FOOTE, (703, 222, 61, 18, 5,) b. June 19, 1795; m. June 18, 1818, Betsey Palmer, of Branford, Ct., near Stony Creek. She was b. May 6, 1794, in Branford, Ct.; d. Apr. 25, 1837. He d. Mar. 4, 1876. Res., Branford, Ct. Ch. all b. in Branford, Ct.

3238. i. HARRIET, b. Branford, Ct., Apr. 19, 1819; m. 1842, Frederick Linsley. He was b. Branford, Ct., 1803. Ch.: (1) Charles Foote, b. Branford, Mar. 29, 1843; m. Jan. 26, 1871, Georgiana E. Gay, b. Mar. 1, 1845. Ch.: (a) Bessie Gay, b. Jan. 31, 1878; m. Oct. 19, 1904, James H. Hinsdale, of Meriden. Ch.: (i) Charles Linsley Hinsdale, b. Oct. 5, 1905. (2) Walter, b. ———; d. in infancy. (3) Wallace Frederick, b. May 13, 1848; d. unm., Mar. 24, 1877. (4) Ellen Frances, b. Sept. 11, 1850; m. Oct. 31, 1878, Franklin Nichols Hall. He was b. in Cheshire, Ct., Nov. 1, 1848. Res., Cheshire, Ct. Ch.: (a) Wallace Foote, b. Mar. 6, 1883. (b) Norman Franklin Hall, b. Cheshire, July 15, 1885. (5) Benjamin Franklin, b. Feb. 14, 1853; m. Oct. 28, 1880,

Grace E. Hosley, b. New Haven, Ct., Apr. 25, 1861. Ch.: (a) Josie Ethel, b. Branford, Mar. 3, 1882. (b) Anna Beach, b. Apr. 23, 1884; d. Apr. 4, 1891. (c) Olive Edith, b. Oct. 19, 1885. (d) David Beach, b. Sept. 20, 1889. (e) Benjamin Palmer, b. Mar. 28, 1894. (6) Bessie Foote, b. Feb. 26, 1858.

3239. ii. BENJAMIN PALMER, b. July 4, 1821; m. 1st, Emily M. Frisbe, of Branford, Ct.; m. 2nd, Sallie Page, of Branford, Ct.; m. 3rd, Nancy A. Morse, of Prospect, Ct. He d. Aug. 10, 1899; s. p. Res., Branford, Ct.

3240. iii. ELLEN AGNES, b. Dec. 14, 1823; m. May 8, 1851, Miles Talcott Merwin, of Durham, Ct. He was b. Oct. 11, 1822; d. July 29, 1904. She d. Mar. 18, 1889. Res., Durham, Ct. Ch.: (1) Ella Elizabeth, b. Apr. 17, 1852. Res., Durham, Ct. (2) Walter Lee, b. Mar. 23, 1854; m. Dec. 24, 1885, Maria Louise Moore. He d. Feb. 17, 1905. Res., Pittsburg, Pa. Ch.: (a) William Walters, b. July 11, 1887. (b) Miles Henderson, b. July 23, 1892. (c) Margaret Russell, b. July 30, 1895. (3) Benjamin Foote, b. Aug. 27, 1855; m. Feb. 22, 1883, Clara Griffin. Ch.: (a) Grace Clara, b. Feb. 24, 1884; m. Apr. 12, 1903, D. Henry Haight. Res., Copper Cliff, Ontario, Canada. Ch.: (i) Dau., b. Aug. 20, 1906. (b) Charles Benjamin Merwin, b. Nov. 15, 1885; m. ———. (c) George Barber, b. Jan. 5, 1887. (d) Emily Lottie, b. July 10, 1890. (e) Earl, b. Aug. 15, 1893. (f) Milford, b. Sept. 12, 1895. (g) Benjamin Foote, b. Apr. 12, 1897. (4) Emily Foote Merwin, b. Sept. 17, 1857. (5) Ralph Linsley Merwin, b. Apr. 22, 1860; m. Dec. 2, 1887, Mary Ella Pascoe. Res., Blue Mt. Lake, N. Y. Ch.: (a) Walter Cyrus Merwin, b. June 5, 1889. (b) Ethel May Merwin, b. Apr. 12, 1891; d. July 13, 1794. (c) Esther Russell Merwin, b. Aug. 31, 1906. (6) Agnes Dickerman, b. May 16, 1864.

3241. iv. JANE ELIZA, b. Branford, Ct., Oct. 24, 1826; m. Feb. 22, 1848, Charles Dickerman, New Haven, Ct. He was b. Sept. 10, 1816. She d. New Haven, Oct. 18, 1875. He d. New Haven, May 6, 1896. Ch.: (1) Ellen Palmer, b. Milwaukee, Wis., Nov. 12, 1848; m. 1870, Charles W. Bardeen. Ch.: (a) Charles Russell, b. 1871. (b) Bertha Foote, b. 1873. (c) Beatrice, b. 1875. (d) Norman, b. 1877. (e) Ethel, b. 1879. (2) George Lewis, b. New Haven, Ct., Apr. 12, 1852; m. 1885, Elizabeth Shoemaker, Wilkesbarre, Pa. Res., New Haven, Ct. (3) Caroline Ives, b. Sept. 23, 1856, New Haven, Ct.

3242. v. EMILY PASTORIA, b. Oct. 24, 1829; m. Chauncey R. Camp, Springfield, Mass. She d. May, 1870.

1768. AUGUSTUS FOOTE, (706, 222, 61, 18, 5,) b. Sept. 13, 1804; m. Julia A. Palmer. She d. Mar. 7, 1881, at W. Haven, Ct.

3243. i. DAVID, b. Jan. 19, 1828; m. Jane A. Rowe, 4892-4.

3244. ii. CHARLES, b. ———; d. young.

3245. iii. MARIA, b. ———; m. James Graham; d. ———. Ch.: (1) Charles. Res., West Haven, Ct.

1770. JONATHAN FOOTE, (706, 222, 61, 18, 5,) b. Feb. 16, 1815; m. Oct. 3, 1836, Abigail R. Linsley. She d. Apr. 10, 1898. He d. Aug. 12, 1882.

3246. i. MARY, b. June 26, 1836; m. Charles H. Frisbie. She d. Jan. 2, 1907; s. p.

3247. ii. HARRIET, b. Sept. 28, 1837; m. David M. Smith. No ch.

3248. iii. JANE F., b. Oct. 13, 1838; m. Levi Burr; d. Apr. 10, 1860; s. p.

3249. iv. SAMUEL, b. Dec. 11, 1842; m. Nov. 23, 1862, at No. Branford, Ct., Harriet S., dau. of Martin Hoadley. She was b. Nov. 27, 1838. He was educated at No. Branford and West Haven, Ct. Mechanic. Res., No. Branford, Ct. No ch.

3250. v. NOAH, b. Mar. 12, 1849; m. Susan Baldwin, 4895-6.

1771. DR. WILLIAM SIDNEY FOOTE, (714, 223, 61, 18, 5,) b. Nov. 21, 1802; m. Aug. 27, 1827, Mary Butler, of Branford, Ct. She was b. Sept. 23, 1803. Res., Medina, O.

3251. i. WILLIAM SCOVILLE, b. Sept. 23, 1828; m. Amanda Pope, 4897-4900.

3252. ii. EDWARD DARWIN, b. Oct. 29, 1833; d. at Pendleton, O., Apr. 30, 1852; unm.

3253. iii. SIDNEY B., b. Aug. 3, 1844; m. Alicia A. Trask, 4901-10.

1777. JOHN ALFRED FOOTE, (715, 223, 61, 18, 5,) b. Nov. 22, 1803; m. Oct. 6, 1826, Frances A., dau. of Silas and Polly (Broadley) Hitchcock, of Cheshire, Ct. She was b. June 4, 1809; d. Apr., 1855; m. 2nd, 1859, Mary Shepley (Hemperly) Caster. She was b. Sept. 12, 1816. He d. July 16, 1891.

3254. i. SAMUEL A., b. July 20, 1829; merchant; d. Apr., 1861; unm.

3255. ii. LOUISA CAROLINE, b. Cheshire, Ct., Oct. 1, 1831; m. June 19, 1854, Charles Arthur Ely, of Elyria, O. He was b. Elyria, May 2, 1829; d. Sept. 30, 1864. She d. Aug. 15, 1881. Real estate agent. Ch.: (1) William Arthur Ely, b. Elyria, July 31, 1860; m. Oct. 4, 1882, Iovia Henry, dau. of John Reed Fisher. She was b. Nov. 12, 1858, in Columbus, O. She d. Jan. 18, 1885, at Elyria, O. Ch.: (a) Arthur Ely, b. June 20, 1883, at Elyria, O.

3256. iii. MARY EUDOCIA, b. Aug. 29, 1835; m. Oct. 13, 1856, Matthew Henry Maynard, a lawyer, of Marquette, Mich. Res., Marquette, Mich. Ch.: (1) Alfred Foote Maynard, b. Aug. 17, 1857, at Marquette, Mich.; m. Helen Pickands, dau. of Wallace W. Goodwin. She was b. Oct. 22, 1861, at Cleveland, O. Res., 867 Winthrop Ave., Chicago, Ill. Ch.: (a) James Pickands Maynard, b. Nov. 20, 1887, at Marquette, Mich. (2) Cornelia Louise Maynard, b. July 21, 1860; m. Sept. 14, 1887, William D. Rees, of Cleveland, O. He is manager of iron mines. Res., 3612 Euclid Ave., Cleveland, O. Ch.: (a) Dorothy Rees, b. Dec. 15, 1888; d. Nov. 11, 1889. (b) Henry Maynard Rees, b. Nov. 17, 1890. (c) Marion Rees, b. Feb. 20, 1891. (3) Gardner Maynard, b. Mar. 3, 1863; d. Nov., 1896, in Chicago, Ill.

3257. iv. FRANCES AURELIA, b. Aug. 5, 1837; d. Nov. 10, 1838.

3258. v. CORNELIA ELIZABETH, b. Sept. 30, 1840; m. Darino Gardner Maynard, of Marquette, Mich. He d. ———; res., Weimar, Germany. Ch.: (1) Arthur Ely Maynard, b. ———; d. ———. (2) Louise Caroline, b. Feb. 16, 1865; d. Feb. 16, 1865. (3) Nellie Gardner, b. Mar. 16, 1868; m. June 25, 1890, Frederich Wilhelm Carl Heinrich Eugen von Horn Oberverwalkungsgericktsrat; b. in Berlin, Prussia, Mar. 15, 1856. Ch.: (a) Carl Gard

(21)

Eugen Hellmuth,' b. Apr. 20, 1891;' d.'Jan. 2; 1895. (b) Doris Nellie Gardie Vera, b. Nov. 22, 1893. .(c) Gard Hellmuth, b. Feb. 16, 1895.

3259.   vi.   JOHN A., b. Aug. 29, 1843, at Cleveland; O.; m. Belle Palmer, 4811-3.

3260.   vii.   ANDREW HULL, b. ———; d. ae. 9 years.

1778. ADMIRAL ANDREW HULL FOOTE, (715, 223, 61, 18, 5,) b. Sept. 12, 1806; m. June 22, 1828, Caroline, dau. of Bethuel and Elizabeth Flagg, of Cheshire, Ct. She was b. Apr. 29, 1804; d. Nov. 4, 1838; m. 2nd, Jan. 27, 1842, Caroline Augusta (his second cousin), dau. of Augustus Russell and Caroline Mary (Leffingwell) Street, of New Haven, Ct. She was b. Aug. 24, 1816; d. Aug. 27, 1863.

He was educated at the old Episcopal Academy at Cheshire, Ct. He had for a classmate Gideon Wells, afterwards Secretary of the Navy, and went immediately to sea under old Admiral Gregory. Entered the Navy in 1822 as acting midshipman, became passed midshipman in 1827, and Lieutenant in 1830. In 1833 he was Log Lieutenant of the Mediterannean Squadron and in 1838 circumnavigated the globe as First Lieutenant of the sloop of war "John Adams," participating in the attack on the pirates of Sumatra. During the cruise of the "Cumberland" he not only induced the crew to forego the use of spirits, but personally superintended their religious instruction, delivering an extemporary sermon every Sunday. In 1848, in command of the brig "Perry" off the African coast, engaged for two and one-half years in suppressing the slave trade. In command of the sloop "Portsmouth," supported by the "Sevant," he attacked the Chinese forts at Canton, massive granite structures, mounting 176 guns and garrisoned by 5,000 men, breaching the largest and strongest, and landing with a force of 280 sailors and marines, carried the work by storm.

At the beginning of the Civil War, 1861, Commander Foote was executive officer at Brooklyn Navy Yard. In July he was commissioned Captain, in Sept. he was appointed Captain, in Sept. was appointed Flag Officer of the flotilla fitting out in western waters. On Feb. 4, 1862, sailed from Cairo with a fleet of seven gunboats, of which four were iron-clad, to attack Fort Henry on the Tennessee River. He attacked the fort on the 6th without waiting for the arrival of the land forces under Gen. Grant, and in one hour compelled its surrender. On the 14th attacked Fort Donelson, on the Cumberland river. The action was sustained with great vigor on both sides for one and a quarter hours, when the fleet had to haul off because two gunboats had their steering apparatus shot away and were unmanageable. Capt. Foote was severely wounded in the ankle, his ship, the "St. Louis," was struck 61 times, but he proceeded down the Mississippi and commenced the siege of Island No. Ten, which he reduced. In July, 1862, he was appointed Rear Admiral, and in May, 1863, was ordered to the command of the South Atlantic Squadron. While preparing to leave New York City for Charleston he died. He was the author of "Abrua and the American Flag," 1854, "Letters on Japan," 1857.

Admiral Foote's sword is preserved as a sacred relic of the New Haven Historical Society. On the gold scabbard is the following inscription: "Presented by the citizens of Brooklyn to Flag Officer Andrew H. Foote as a testimonial of their high personal regard of their appreciation of his eminent professional character, distinguished public service and moral influence in a long course of active duty, and especially of his efficiency in suppressing the slave trade on the coast of Africa; his gallant conduct in the destruction of the barrier forts in China;

his masterly skill and energy in the creation of a flotilla, and of the brilliant and intrepid bombardment therewith of the fortifications of the Tennessee, the Cumberland, and the Mississippi.'' He d. at the Astor House, N. Y. City, June 26, 1863.

3261. i. JOSEPHINE, b. Cheshire, Ct., Sept. 26, 1832; d. Dec. 13, 1836.

3262. ii. JOSEPHINE, b. Cheshire, Ct., June 28, 1837; m. 1861, George L. Reese, Baltimore, Md. Ch.: 4.

3263. iii. AUGUSTUS RUSSELL STREET, b. in the Navy Yard, Boston, Mass., Apr. 4, 1847; m. Jane McNalla, 4914-5.

3264. iv. WILLIAM LEFFINGWELL, b. New Haven, Ct., Dec. 17, 1848; d. Mar. 14, 1862.

3265. v. EMILY FREDERICKA, b. Nov. 11, 1852; d. Oct. 14, 1862.

3266. vi. MARIA ENDOCIA, b. Oct. 18, 1855; d. Oct. 20, 1862.

3267. vii. JOHN SAMUEL, b. June 25, 1859; m. Anna Doolittle, 4916-20.

1783. THOMAS JEFFERSON, (718, 223, 61, 18, 5,) b. Oct. 3, 1796; m. Margaret Whitehead, of Elizabethtown, N. J. She was b. Oct. 16, 1814. He d. Aug. 23, 1865. Res., Jersey City, N. J.

3268. i. MARTHA, b. Oct. 10, 1830.

3269. ii. `LYDIA, b. Dec. 18, 1832; m. William Meeker. She is dead.

3270. iii. LOUISA, b. July 24, 1839; d. ———.

3271. iv. LUCILLA, b. Sept. 24, 1844.

3272. v. CHARLOTTE, b. Sept. 24, 1844.

3273. vi. DARWIN ROCKWELL, b. June 18, 1849; m. Minnie P. Soylor, 4921.

3274. vii. CARRIE, b. Oct. 4, 1852.

1791. DR. LYMAN FOOTE, (719, 223, 61, 18, 5,) b. Wallingford, Ct., Apr. 12, 1796; m. Aug. 26, 1821, Ann Treadwell, dau. of Isaac C. Platt, of Plattsburg, N. Y. She was b. Nov. 15, 1803; d. Oct. 6, 1832, at Ft. Winnebago, Mich.; m. 2nd, Sept. 12, 1836, Mary Morris, dau. of Isaac Cooper, of Cooperstown, N. Y. Mr. Foote graduated from Yale College, 1816. Aug., 1818, he received from Hon. John C. Calhoun (Secretary of War) an appointment as Assistant Surgeon in the Army of the United States. He was promoted to the rank of Surgeon in 1831. He was in active service during the Black Hawk, Florida and Mexican Wars, and during the last d. Oct. 24, 1846, while he was fourth in rank in the army, at Port Lavacca, Texas.

3275. i. HENRY SMITH, b. West Point, N. Y., July 7, 1823; d. Mar. 24, 1827.

3276. ii. ANN PLATT, b. Aug. 23, 1824, at Fort Brady, Mich.; d. Sept. 18, 1825.

3277. iii. ISAAC PLATT, b. Sept. 23, 1825, at Fort Brady, Mich. Grad. Geneva College, N. Y., 1847; d. Plattsburg, N. Y., Mar. 22, 1880.

3278. iv. ZEPHANIAH CHARLES, b. Feb. 1, 1827, at Plattsburg, N. Y. Grad. Geneva College, 1847; d. July 16, 1875.

3279. v. HENRY DAVIS, b. Mar. 27, 1829, at Fort Howard, Green Bay; d. June 9, 1830.

3280. vi. CAROLINE ADRIANCE, b. July 3, 1830, at Fort Howard, Green Bay; m. Oct. 10, 1849, Geo. Pomeroy Keese, of Cooperstown, N. Y. He is President of the Second National Bank. Ch.: (1) Anna Treadwell, b. Sept. 9, 1850. (2) Alice Bailey, b. Apr. 29, 1853. (3) Florence Pomeroy, b. Jan. 31, 1856. (4) Katherine

Turner, b. Feb., 1858; d. Apr. 9, 1858. (5) Theodore, b. Apr. 26, 1859. (6) Charles Platt, b. Aug. 22, 1851. (7) Caroline Merrill, b. Jan. 25, 1864. (8) Elizabeth Cooper, b. Apr. 23, 1866.

3281. vii. MARY ANN, b. Sept. 22, 1832, at Fort Crawford, Mich.

3282. viii. LYMAN, b. Aug. 30, 1837, at Fort Winnebago; d. Sept. 25, 1838.

3283. ix. MARGARET, b. Sept. 10, 1839, at Fort Winnebago; d. Dec. 20, 1839.

3284. x. FRANCIS WAITE, b. Jan. 8, 1842; m. Ann ———, 4922-3.

3285. xi. MORRIS COOPER, Sept. 16, 1843; m. Elizabeth Murphy, 4924-5.

3286. xii. JESSIE SILLIMAN, b. Aug. 1, 1846, at Madison Barracks, Sacketts Harbor, N. Y.

1794. DAVID AUSTIN FOOTE, (719, 223, 61, 18, 5,) b. Branford, Ct., May 29, 1803; m. Mary H., dau. of Tacheus Curtis, of New Lebanon, N. Y. She was b. Jan. 27, 1812; d. Aug. 11, 1892. He d. Apr. 24, 1880. Res., Branford, Ct.

3287. i. ELIZA CHARLOTTE, b. Apr. 28, 1836; m. Feb. 27, 1854, David Averill. He d. Apr. 27, 1888. Res., Branford, Ct. Ch.: (1) Emily Susan Averill, b. Branford, Ct., Mar. 13, 1855; m. Jan. 10, 1874, in Branford, Henry E. Bradley. Ch.: (a) Albert Raymond Bradley, b. Dec. 19, 1874; d. Mar. 1, 1879. (b) Charlotte LaVerne, b. Aug. 20, 1880; m. Oct. 11, 1899, Henry Clark Moore. Ch.: (i) Henry Bradley Moore, b. Mar. 22, 1902. (ii) Mary Emilie Moore, b. May 8, 1903. (iii) Josephine Moore, b. Oct. 29, 1904. (c) Robert Carlton Bradley, b. June 22, 1882; d. Mar. 11, 1886. (d) Leroy Clifton, b. Feb. 12, 1886; d. Mar. 16, 1889. (e) Sara Gertrude, b. Oct. 10, 1888. (f) Kenneth Elijah, b. Nov. 25, 1890. (g) Harold Henry, b. Sept. 17, 1892. (h) Leonard Marsden, b. July 29, 1896. (i) Emily Marion Bradley, b. May 8, 1899. (2) Alonzo Gladwin Averill, b. June 10, 1857, in Branford, Ct.; m. Annie Marshall. He d. Feb. 5, 1907. Ch.: (a) Albert Marshall Averill, b. Apr. 4, 1883. (b) Eliza Foote Averill, b. Jan. 2, 1885.

3288. ii. SAMUEL ALBERT, b. May 9, 1842; d. Jan. 7, 1865, in Havana, Cuba.

3289. iii. EDWIN JOSIAH, b. Oct. 11, 1844; m. Emily A. French, 4926-7.

1802. WILLIAM R. FOOTE, (721, 231, 72, 20, 5,) b. Durham, Ct., May, 1819; m. Amanda Jones. He d. Edgewood, Ga., 1882.

3289¹. i. FANNY, b. May, 1852, Macon, Ga.; m. Dec., 1882, R. J. Bigham, Edgewood, Ga. Ch.: (1) Eugenia, b. Sept., 1886, Edgewood, Ga. (2) Carrie S., b. Dec., 1888, Edgewood, Ga. (3) Verdie A., b. Oct., 1894, Augusta, Ga. (4) Charlotte A., b. May, 1897, Nashville, Tenn.

3289². ii. WILLIAM R., b. May, 1854; m. Maggie Whitaker, 4928.

3290. iii. JAMES G., b. Apr., 1856; m. Mary L. Stansell, 4930-37.

3291. iv. WALTER O., b. Apr., 1868; m. Laura Well, 4938-41.

1803. ISAAC HENRY FOOTE, (724, 231, 72, 20, 5,) b. July 10, 1819, in Northford, Ct.; m. Nov. 25, 1846, Marietta, dau. of Daniel Smith, of East Haven, Ct. He d. 1853.

3292. i. ISAAC FRANCIS, b. in Fair Haven, Ct., 1848; m. Addie Luddington and Mary Bidwell, 4942.

3293. ii. GEORGE, b. 1851; drowned 1858.

3294. iii. CAROLINE, b. 1853; d. 1853.

1805. GEORGE BENTON FOOTE, (724, 251, 72, 20, 5,) b. in Northford, Ct., Feb. 24, 1824; m. Sept. 10, 1851, Mary, dau. of Gilbert and Siche (Doughty) Flagler, of Beekman, Dutchess Co., N. Y. He d. Dec. 14, 1871. Res., Beekman, N. Y.

3295. i. GILBERT F., b. Apr. 27, 1859; m. Clara Williams, 4943-4.

3296. ii. GEORGE BENTON, b. in Beekman, Dutchess Co., N. Y., Jan. 10, 1866; m. June 14, 1894, Ida, dau. of Orrin A. and Josephine (Giraud) Williams. Res., Poughkeepsie, N. Y.

1810. ISAAC FOOTE, (725, 221, 60, 18, 5,) b. Oct. 17, 1844; m. Mar. 19, 1867, at Eaton, O., Mary C. Neal. She was b. Eaton, O., Nov. 23, 1844; d. Mar. ———, at Dayton, O. He was a dentist at Northford, Ct. He d. May 5, 1896, at Middletown, O. He was Captain of a Company of Vols. in the Revolutionary (Civ.) War.

3297. i. EDITH HAZEL, b. July 21, 1879.

3298. ii. DUCILLE, b. July 18, 1887; d. Mar. 20, 1892.

3299. iii. JENNIE CELESTIA, b. May 3, 1888; m. Feb. 6, 1895, William H. Pullen. Ch.: (1) Guy Foote Pullen, b. Greenwich, Ct., July 26, 1896.

1826. NATHANIEL FOOTE, (754, 235, 73, 25, 9, 3,) b. July 9, 1813; m. Apr. 28, 1847, Olivia, dau. of John and Mary Knox, of Nelson, N. Y. She was b. Aug. 16, 1814; d. Dec. 13, 1893. He was admitted to the bar in 1840, and practised law at Morrisville, N. Y. Was appointed Master and Examiner in Chancery, which office he held until the Court of Chancery was abolished by the adoption of the new State constitution in 1848. He. d. Aug. 13, 1901.

3300. i. NATHANIEL, JR., b. Nov. 15, 1849; m. Charlotte Anna Campbell, 5000-4.

3301. ii. ARTHUR ASA, b. Oct. 18; 1851; m. Kate C. Lewis, 5005-9.

3302. iii. ORLANDO KNOX, b. May 12, 1854; m. Hattie Burgess, 5010-2.

1827. ASA FOOTE, (754, 235, 73, 25, 9, 3,) b. Apr. 5, 1815; m. Jan. 28, 1846, Almedia Ann, widow of John Gale, of Goshen, Orange Co., N. Y., and dau. of John and Almedia Van Degriff, of Vernon, N. J. She was b. Sept. 1, 1813; d. May 30, 1898. He was chosen Vestryman of Christ Church, of Sherburne, N. Y., in 1853, to succeed his father, who was one of the original vestrymen when the church was founded in 1828. He was succeeded by his grandson, Asa, who is now Junior Warden. He d. Aug. 28, 1900.

3303. i. IRENE, b. Jan. 16, 1847; m. June 18, 1873, Dewitt C., son of Albert and Sylvia Case, of Norwich, N. Y. He was b. Aug. 6, 1844. She d. Apr., 1891. Ch.: (1) Harriet L., b. Apr. 11, 1868; m. Feb. 18, 1890, John M., son of Jackson L. and Mary (Rainsdell) Howard. Ch.: (a) Gertrude Irene, b. Jan. 9, 1894. (b) Robert Jackson, b. Aug. 22, 1899. (2) George Van Degriff, b. May 29, 1870; m. Oct. 20, 1891, Jessie Lyon, of Walton, N. Y. Ch.: (a) Julia Irene, b. June 18, 1892. (3) Anne Van Degriff, b. Nov. 23, 1873; m. Aug. 23, 1893, Holland Y. Burlingham. (4) Harry Edsall, b. May 13, 1878; m. Dec. 25, 1899, Jennie Blanchard, of Utica, N. Y. Ch.: (a) Anne Irene, b. Sept. 27, 1900. (b) Doris Louise, b. Mar. 19, 1903. (c) Helen Gertrude, b. 1904.

3304. ii. OLIVIA KNOX, b. Mar. 5, 1849; m. June 18, 1873, Henry Van Dyke, son of Judge Frederick A. and Mary (Jackson) Hoyt, of Goshen, N. Y. He was b. June 15, 1837; d. Feb. 2, 1906, in Goshen, N. Y. Ch.: (1) Frederick Augustus, b. Sept. 6, 1874; graduated from Columbia College in 1896. (2) Henry Foote, b. May 10, 1879; graduated from Columbia College in 1901.

3305. iii. ALMIRA WHITE, b. June 1, 1852; m. Jan. 4, 1882, Charles De Witt, son of Van Rensselaer and Melinda (Barber) Reynolds, of Sherburne, N. Y. He was b. Feb. 12, 1847; d. Mar. 1, 1904. Farmer. Res., Sherburne, N. Y. Ch.: (1) A son, b. Dec. 4, 1882; d. Dec. 4, 1882. (2) Edsall Barber, b. Dec. 7, 1884. (3) Ralph Van Rensselaer, b. Aug. 13, 1887. (4) Rhae Foote, b. Dec. 15, 1891. (5) Charles Harvey, b. Mar. 12, 1893.

3306. iv. J., b. Apr. 13, 1854; m. Ida F. Westcott, 5013-20.

1828. REV. ISRAEL FOOTE, D. D., (754, 235, 73, 25, 9, 3,) b. Feb. 1, 1817; m. Mary Louise, dau. of William and Sarah Maria Banks, of Bainbridge, Chenango Co., N. Y., May 13, 1851. She was b. Apr. 23, 1826. ' Rev. Israel Foote, D. D., graduated at Trinity College, Hartford, Ct., in the year 1842. He was ordained deacon in the year 1845, in the chapel of Jubilee College, Ill., by the rector, Rev. Philander Chase, D. D., bishop of the diocese of Ill. He was ordained priest in St. Paul's Church, Rochester, N. Y., in the year 1846, by the rector, Rev. W. H. DeLancey, D. D., L. L. D., D. C. L. The first nine years of his ministry he held the rectorship of Christ's Church, Guilford, and St. Peter's Church, Bainbridge, N. Y. He held the rectorship of Trinity Church, Fredonia, N. Y., three years, from thence was called to take charge of the mathematical department in Debeaux College, Suspension Bridge, N. Y., where he remained until May, 1859, when he received a call to St. Paul's Church, Rochester, N. Y. He held the rectorship of this church 23 years, when age and failing health made it necessary for him to resign. In accepting his resignation, the vestry conferred on him the honorary title of Rector Emeritus, with an annuity of $1,000 a year during his natural life. Rev. Israel Foote received the degree of Doctor of Divinity from the Rochester University in the city of Rochester, N. Y., in the early part of his rectorship of St. Paul's Church. He d. July 1, 1898.

3307. i. MARY ELIZABETH, b. Bainbridge, N. Y., Mar. 13, 1852; m. Nov. 5, 1878, Charles William, son of Charles Crossmon, of Rochester, N. Y., in Luzerne, Switzerland, by her father. She d. at Washington, D. C., May 8, 1902; s. p.

3308. ii. WILLIAM BANKS, b. Apr. 3, 1859; graduated in mining engineering at Lehigh University, Pa., in 1885. In charge of the Horseshoe Mine in Col. in 1888. Res., Bainbridge, N. Y.

1830. DR. EZRA FOOTE, M. D. (754, 235, 73, 25, 9, 3,) b. Apr. 5, 1821; m. Dec. 13, 1848, Rachel, dau. of John and Mary Mills, of Elgin Co., Ontario. She was b. Aug. 14, 1828. He took his degree in medicine from Geneva, N. Y., Jan., 1848. He went to King's College, of Toronto, Canada, and took his degree in Apr., 1851. He d. July 20, 1876. Res., Aylmer, Elgin Co., Ontario.

3309. i. ALMIRA VICTORIA, b. May 24, 1853; d. July, 1853.

3310. ii. MARY, b. Aug. 7, 1855; d. Oct., 1855.

3311. iii. NINA, b. Sept. 9, 1856.

3312. iv. EZRA, b. Aug. 8, 1859; d. Mar. 17, 1862.

1833. BURTON FOOTE, (754, 235, 73, 25, 9, 3,) b. Feb. 15, 1829; m. Apr. 15, 1854, Maria, dau. of William and Sarah Whithead, of Middleville, Herkimer Co., N. Y. She was b. May 16, 1883, moved to Green Lake Co., Wis., in 1861, and in 1882 to Pipestone Co., Minn., where he d. Apr. 20, 1895. She d. Oct. 24, 1903, at Atkins, Atkins Co.; Minn.

    3313. i.   HOWARD MILFORD, b. June 26, 1855; m. Nov. 10, 1895, Irena, wid. of David Rogers, and dau. of W. H. and Julia Brooks, of Madison, N. Y. Farmer. Res., Trosky, Minn. No ch.

    3314. ii. EDITH IRENE, b. Nov. 21, 1859; m. July 27, 1892, William Hubert Gordon, of Trosky, Minn. He d. June 27, 1894; m. 2nd, Charles O. Armstead, of Aitkin, Minn. A draughtsman and C. E. Ch.: (1) Thomas Burton, b. July 28, 1898. (2) Weyman Foote, b. Aug. 9, 1899. (3) Clark Gordon, b. Apr. 28, 1903.

    3315. iii. ALMIRA ELIZABETH, b. May 18, 1864; unm.

    3316. iv. ASA WATSON, b. Sept. 5, 1867; m. Chloe Myrtle Van Horsen, 5021-6.

1834. SAMUEL MILLS FOOTE, (758, 235, 73, 25, 9, 3,) b. Jan. 29, 1822; m. Sept. 28, 1852, Sarah E., dau. of Col. Samuel and Phebe Hartwell, of Plymouth, N. Y. Farmer. Res., Sherburne, N. Y.

    3317. i.   FANNIE AMELIA, b. Jan. 7, 1854; d. May 3, 1862.

    3318. ii. ANNA JOSEPHINE, b. Sept. 16, 1855. Res., Sherburne, N. Y.; unm.

    3319. iii. MINNIE CAROLINE, b. Apr. 4, 1858. Res., Sherburne, N. Y.; unm.

    3320. iv. EDWARD OTIS, b. Feb. 2, 1864. Res., Sherburne, N. Y.; unm.

    3321. v.   CLARA ELLEN, b. Dec. 6, 1865.

1840. DR. NATHANIEL FOOTE, (759, 235, 73, 25, 9, 3,) b. Aug. 8, 1831; m. Abby Jane, dau. of Guy and Nancy (Hurd) Bigelow, of Colchester, Ct., Nov. 28, 1852. She was b. Nov. 27, 1830. Nathaniel Foote took a course of study in medicine, first, with Dr. Hewel Rogers and his son George H. Rogers, M. D. He then entered the office of Professor Charles Hooker, M. D., of Yale medical department. He took a course of lectures and diploma from the Berkshire Medical College, in 1852. He held the position of Principal of Colbert Institute (in the Chickasaw Nation), under the control of the Methodist Episcopal Church, south, practising medicine also, until the spring of 1860. He then returned north and took a position with the Jersey City Insurance Company, as superintendent of agencies. In 1874 was elected Secretary of the company, and in 1879 was elected President of the company. Res., Colchester, Ct.

1843. DAN FOOTE, (765, 236, 73, 25, 9, 3,) b. Mar. 26, 1824; m. Sept. 3, 1850, Catherine Phelps, of New Berlin, N. Y. He d. June 21, 1861.

    3324. i.   EDWIN DELANCY, b. Dec. 1, 1851.

    3325. ii. TRACY PHELPS, b. Dec. 27, 1853.

    3326. iii. FRANK ISHAM, b. Aug. 18, 1856.

1844. JIRAH ISHAM FOOTE, (765, 236, 73, 25, 9, 3,) b. Colchester, Ct., Oct. 10, 1825; m. 1st, Oct. 18, 1848, Frances Maria Sherman, of Stillwater, Saratoga Co., N. Y. She d. ———; m. 2nd, Margaret M. Ray, of Albany, N. Y. He d. May 20, 1903, at Haverstraw, N. Y. Ch. of 1st marriage.

    3327. i.   HENRY WORTHINGTON, b. Haverstraw, N. Y., June 15, 1852; m. Ella P. Woodward, 5027-9.

3328. ii. AMASA FREEMAN, D. D. S., b. Washingtonville, N. Y., Nov. 24, 1853; m. Apr. 24, 1878, Mary A. King, of Middletown, N. Y. Dentist. Res., Brooklyn, N. Y. No ch.

1849. NELSON FOOTE, (765, 236, 73, 25, 9, 3,) b. May 8, 1836; m. Cornelia Lyon, of Elmira, N. Y. He d. Mar. 12, 1905. He was a veteran of the Civil War, and was buried with G. A. R. honors.

3329. i. JULIA TRACY, b. ———; m. William H. Dearborn, of Lebanon Springs, N. Y. No ch.

1865. ADRIAN FOOTE, (774, 241, 73, 25, 9, 3,) b. Dec. 4, 1882; m. Aug. 31, 1848, Mary Cornelia, dau. of Jesse and Adaline (Angell) Beardslee, a descendant of Col. Israel Angell, who commanded the second Rhode Island Regiment in the Revolutionary War. Res., Ashland, Mass.

3330. i. FREDERICK, b. May 23, 1851; m. Mary Ann Young. 5030-5.
3331. ii. MARY LOUISE, b. Pittsfield, N. Y., Sept. 11, 1853; d. Sept. 28, 1864, at New Berlin, N. Y.
3332. iii. HENRY J., b. Jan. 23, 1857; m. Cora Elizabeth Cutter, 5036-39.
3333. iv. FRANCES, b. Pittsfield, N. Y., Oct. 22, 1858; m. Nov. 30, 1886, William Townsend, son of James Townsend and Sarah Jane (Brown) Barstow, of Haverhill, N. H. He was b. Jan. 4, 1855. Grain dealer. Res., Ord, later Lincoln, Neb. Ch.: (1) Helen Jaques, b. Ord, Neb., Sept. 20, 1887. (2) Adrian Foote, b. Ord, Neb., Mar. 6, 1890. (3) Frances Isabella, b. Ord, Neb., May 8, 1895. (4) Marjorie Louise, b. Ord, Neb., Aug. 25, 1899.
3334. v. JESSIE ADALINE, b. New Berlin, N. Y., Aug. 8, 1860. Res., Ashland, Mass.
3335. vi. ELIZABETH, b. Cooperstown, N. Y., Sept. 22, 1868; d. July 13, 1869, Ashland, Mass.; buried in New Berlin, N. Y.

1873. NATHANIEL GORDON FOOTE, (781, 241, 73, 25, 9, 3,) b. June 5, 1838; m. Oct. 26, 1862, Sarah Eliza, dau. of Russell and Amanda (Ward) Dixon. She was b. Bridgewater, Oneida Co., N. Y., July 10, 1838. He served in the 114th and 90th N. Y. Vol. Infantry Regt. from Feb., 1864, to Feb., 1866; d. Sept. 21, 1876, at Delphi, N. Y.

3336. i. HATTIE ELIZABETH, b. Chittenango, N. Y., Apr. 29, 1864; d. Oct. 28, 1868.
3337. ii. JENNIE GORDON, b. Feb. 13, 1867, at Chittenango, N. Y.; m. Merwin B. Woodworth, at Chittenango Falls, N. Y., Sept. 29, 1885. He was b. at Chittenango Falls, N. Y., July 12, 1865, and d. there Aug. 7, 1886; m. 2nd, Thomas Crichton, Apr. 25, 1895, at Canastota, N. Y. He was b. at Rochester, N. Y., Apr. 15, 1853. Res., 100 Herkimer St., Syracuse, N. Y.
3338. iii. ANNA ELIZABETH, b. Dec. 18, 1868, at Chittenango, N. Y.; was graduated from Cazenovia Seminary, N. Y., in 1888, and from Syracuse University, N. Y., (A. B.), in 1902. Teacher in the New York City Training School, at Jamaica, Long Island, N. Y.
3339. iv. DR. LEWIS NATHANIEL, b. Sept. 20, 1872, Brooklyn, N. Y.; m. Mrs. Mabel Shull Ackler, dau. of Winfield Scott Shull and Libbie A. Benedict, Nov. 15, 1905. She was b. at Ilion, Herkimer Co., N. Y., Mar. 1, 1870. He was graduated from Hamilton College (A. B.), in 1894, (A. M.) in 1897, and from the N. Y. University Medical School (M. D.) in 1897. Physician in Brooklyn, N. Y.

1879. JOHN TAINTOR FOOTE, (783, 244, 74, 25, 9, 3,) b. New York City, May 27, 1819; m. Sept. 3, 1845, Jordena, dau. of Horatio Turpin and Keturah L. (Taylor) Harris, of Newport, Ky., and was a merchant in Cincinnati. She d. Nov., 1858; m. 2nd, Mary Swords, dau. of Robert and Mary (Swords) Dumont. He d. July 5, 1902; buried in Morristown, N. J.

 3340. i. WILLIAM, b. 1846; d. in infancy.

 3341. ii. LOUISE, b. Newport, Ky., Feb. 7, 1849; m. Oct. 12, 1876, John, son of Gen. David and Sarah (Benson) Stuart, of Detroit, Mich. She d. June 16, 1906. Ch.: (1) Ellen Foote, b. July 13, 1877; m. Oct. 17, 1899, Lieut.-Commander "Victor Blue," U. S. N. (2) Marion, b. July, 1879; m. 1903, Charles Terry, M. D., of Jacksonville, Fla.

 3342. iii. ELLEN, b. July 19, 1850; d. Jan. 4, 1878; unm.

 3343. iv. GEORGE WARD, b. June 16, 1852; m. Margaret Moore, 5040-42.

 3344. v. KATHARINE JORDENA, b. Cincinnati, O., Oct. 18, 1853; m. June 24, 1884, Rear Admiral Philip Henry, son of Hiram H. Cooper, U. S. N. He was b. Camden, N. Y., Aug. 5, 1844. She res. in Morristown, N. J. Ch.: (1) Geraldine, b. ———; d. Sept. 28, 1885. (2) Gerald, b. ———; d. Mar. 24, 1887. (3) Dorothy Bradford, b. Mar. 9, 1889. (4) Leslie Bradford, b. Morristown, N. J., Mar. 24, 1894.

 3345. vi. ROBERT DUMONT, b. July 19, 1862; m. Marie G. Hopkins, 5043-7.

1890. JUSTIN FOOTE, (798, 247, 76, 25, 9, 3,) b. Smyrna, N. Y., Nov. 22, 1803; m. Mar. 31, 1825, Irene, dau. of Dea. Samuel and Irene Allen Warner, of Sherburne, N. Y. She was b. May 6, 1807. Justin Foote first settled on a large farm in Otselic, but subsequently returned to Smyrna and settled on the George Bixby farm, where he lived until he was killed at the raising of a saw mill owned by a Mr. Fisher, by the falling upon him of a part of the frame, on June 19, 1834. His tragic death left a widow and five fatherless children, the youngest unborn. Of these, the eldest dau. d. at her grandfather's, Judge Foote's, in Smyrna, in 1846, ae. 20 years; Frances Irene, the next younger, d. at the residence of her mother in Alexander, N. Y., Apr. 29, 1847, ae. 17; a younger brother, Justin Hiel, d. at Belvidere, Ill., Jan. 24, 1856, ae. 24 years. Another son, Daniel E. Foote, who made his home with his grandfather, Judge Foote, in Smyrna, studied medicine with Dr. Frederick Hyde, of Cortland, and afterwards graduated from the Medical Department of the University of Buffalo, class of 1851. She m. 2nd. Aug. 12, 1847, Henry Seymore, in Batavia, N. Y. They had one son, Hervey J. Seymore, b. May 31, 1849; d. July 14, 1851. She d. Apr. 23, 1882, in Belvidere, Ill.

 3347. i. HARRIET ELIZABETH, b. Otselic, N. Y., July 24, 1826; d. July 11, 1846, in Smyrna, N. Y.

 3348. ii. DANIEL ELISHA, b. Otselic, N. Y., Apr. 7, 1828; m. Martha Elizabeth Graff, 5048-50.

 3349. iii. FRANCES IRENE, b. Smyrna, N. Y., Apr. 26, 1830; d. Apr. 29, 1847, in Alexander, N. Y.

 3350. iv. JUSTIN HIEL, b. Smyrna, N. Y., July 18, 1832; d. Jan. 24, 1856, in Belvidere, Ill.

 3351. v. SAMUEL ISAAC, b. Smyrna, N. Y., Sept. 16, 1834; m. Electa Stuphen and Laura Augusta Redington, 5051.

1893. CHARLES HENRY, (798, 247, 76, 25, 9, 3,) b. Sept. 3, 1810; m. Hulda Brooks, of New Berlin, N. Y. She d. Sept. 14, 1885. He d. July 28, 1867, at Boome, Iowa.

3352. i.   ISAAC, b. Mar. 4, 1834; m. Graty Brand, 5052-5.

3353. ii.   CHARLES H., b. July 4, 1836; m. Lucy A. Bennett, 5056-7.

3354. iii. EBENEZER HYDE, b. July 15, 1838; m. 5058-62.

3355. iv.   MARTHA MARIA, b. Howard, N. Y., Dec. 4, 1840; m. James Campbell. Res., Salt Lake City, Utah.

3355¹. v.   JULIUS AUGUSTUS, b. Howard, N. Y., Feb. 28, 1843; d. in infancy.

3356. vi.   JULIETTE AUGUSTA, b. Howard, N. Y., Feb. 28, 1843; m. Lyman Slube. She d. July 4, 1882, at Boome, Iowa. Ch.: (1) Harriet Elizabeth, b. ———; res., Springfield, Mo. (2) Martha, b. ———; res., Seattle, Wash. (3) Nellie, b. ———; res., Springfield, Mo.

3357. vii. HARRIET ALTHA, b. Smyrna, N. Y., Oct. 27, 1846; m. July 2, 1862, Robert K. Potter, of Naperville, Ill. Res., Chicago, Ill. Ch.: (1) Ella May, b. Naperville, Ill., Apr. 17, 1865; m. Dec. 23, 1886, Charles A. Rover, of Elgin, Ill. He was b. Mona, Ill., Jan. 30, 1859. Res., Waukegan, Ill. (2) Edith Well, b. Naperville, Ill., Feb. 1, 1867; m. Apr. 25, 1886, George Armstrong Hutchinson, of Boome, Iowa. Ch.: (a) Allan Grant, b. May 15, 1887; m. 2nd, Nov. 21, 1891, Edward Addison Worthington. He was b. Iroquois, Ontario, Aug. 16, 1857. Ch.: (b) Edward, b. Aug. 26, 1892; d. Feb. 5, 1893. (c) E. Llewellyn, b. Jan. 22, 1894. (d) Edith D'Elda, b. May 21, 1898. (e) Harriet Naomi, b. Jan. 25, 1904. (3) Natilie M., b. Boome, Iowa, Jan. 5, 1869. (4) Agnes L., b. Boome, Iowa, Oct. 25, 1872; m. William J. Dyer. He was b. Canton, Mo., July 9, 1872. He was adopted, at the age of five, and assumed the name of Ahern. (5) Harriet E., b. Boome, Iowa, Jan. 1, 1874; m. Allan A. Ecker. . He was b. Nov. 13, 1869. Ch.: (a) Gladys Lucille Ecker, b. Kansas City, Kansas, Nov. 10, 1895. (b) Harold William Ecker, b. Kansas City, Kansas, Nov. 2, 1898. (c) Charles Robert Ecker, b. Kansas City, Kansas, Oct. 8, 1902. (d) Mildred Ecker, b. July 23, 1906. (6) Robert K., Jr., b. Oct. 10, 1876; m. Emma Blanch Foster. She was b. Duncannon, Pa., Dec. 14, 1873. Ch.: (a) Naomi Potter, b. Apr. 3, 1904. (7) Raymond Addison, b. Boome, Iowa, May 2, 1878; m. Adelaide Eleanor Bristol. She was b. Chicago, Ill., Dec. 10, 1880. Ch.: (a) Raymond K. Y. Potter, b. July 27, 1896. (8) George Byron, d. in infancy. (9) Arthur, d. in infancy.

3358. viii. BENJAMIN IRA, b. Smyrna, N. Y., Apr. 7, 1848; d. Dec. 2, 1860.

3359. ix.   MARGARET PARSONS, b. Smyrna, N. Y., June 16, 1850; a teacher of Art and Physical Culture; m. 1873, George W., son of Dr. Robert Knight Potter, of Chicago, Ill. Res., Canton, O. Ch.: (1) Hulda May, b. May 27, 1879; m. E. Solamon Peffer, of Elgin, Ill. Corn merchant. Res., Canton, O. No ch. (2) Elizabeth Foote, b. Elgin, Ill., May 27, 1882; m. Sycamore, Ill., Sept. 3, 1900' Clarence Peoslee. He was a graduate of Effingham

College, Ill. Res., Mossillon, O. Ch.: (a) Geraldine May, b. June 25, 1902. (b) Dorithy Vivian, b. June 4, 1905.

3360. x. SARAH SIRENA, b. Smyrna, N. Y., Jan. 3, 1853; m. Addison Rodocker, of Malvern, O. Ch.: (1) Philip Henry, b. 1869; d. May 26, 1891. (2) Maud May, b. 1876; d. Aug. 16, 1897. (3) Lorena I., d. Nov. 1, 1878. (4) Addie Maria, d. Apr. 8, 1877. (5) Paul Bacon, d. Oct. 21, 1885.

3361. xi. IDA MAY, b. Oswego, Ill., Sept. 3, 1855; d. Dec. 19, 1860.

3362. xii. GAYLORD BROOKS, b. Oswego, Ill., Feb. 25, 1860; d. July 11, 1860.

1895. ISAAC FOOTE, (798, 247, 76, 25, 9, 3,) b. May 28, 1817; m. Sept. 2, 1840, Jerusha, dau. of Dr. Constant Merrick, of Lebanon, N. Y., formerly of Longmeadow, Mass. She d. at Norwich, N. Y., June 21, 1874. They moved to Norwich, N. Y., in 1860, where he d. Mar. 21, 1893.

3363. i. AMELIA, b. Aug. 7, 1841; m. Dec. 21, 1866, Henry C. Hall, of Norwich, N. Y. She d. Oct. 22, 1903. Ch.: (1) Mary Elizabeth, b. Norwich, N. Y., Mar. 3, 1868. (2) Charles Foote, b. Norwich, N. Y., Feb. 22, 1870. (3) Harry Clinton, Jr., b. Norwich, N. Y., Apr. 23, 1872; m. Apr. 30, 1894, Sarah I. Sinclair, of Norwich, N. Y. He d. Mar. 25, 1905, at Norwich, N. Y. Ch.: (a) Dorothy Hall, b. ———; d. in infancy. (b) Millicent Hall, b. ———; d. in infancy. (c) Marion Hall, b. ———; d. in infancy. (d) Donald Hall, b. ———.

3364. ii. HARRIET ELIZABETH, b. Oct. 21, 1851; d. Apr. 18, 1865.

3365. iii. CHARLES HYDE, b. June 28, 1855; d. May 22, 1856.

3366. iv. FREDERICK HYDE, b. Oct. 7, 1857; m. Mar. 10, 1896, Marietta Jarvis, dau. of Solomon Cary, of Binghamton, N. Y. No ch.

3367. v. MARGARET MERRICK, b. Dec. 10, 1860. Res., 88 Essex Ave., Orange, N. J.

1901. EDWARD WARREN FOOTE, (799, 247, 76, 25, 9, 3,) b. in Smyrna, N. Y., Mar. 5, 1820; m. 1st, Oct. 16, 1844, Phoebe, dau. of James Steere, of Hartwick, N. Y.; she was b. Mar. 23, 1822, and d. Jan. 2, 1849; m. 2nd, Aug. 27, 1851, Adeline Francis, dau. of Rufus Steere, of Laurens, N. Y. Adeline Francis Foote was b. Apr. 22, 1827, in Gloucester, R. I., and d. Feb. 8, 1864. Mr. Foote was in mercantile business. He d. May 9, 1889. Res., Hamilton, N. Y.

3368. i. ALBERT EDWARD FOOTE, b. Feb. 6, 1846; m. Augusta Mathews, 5063-6.

3369. ii. LYRA, b. in Hamilton, N. Y., May 28, 1853; m. Aug. 12, 1886, Dr. Peter Bessie, son of Dr. Peter Bessie Havens, of Hamilton, N. Y. Dr. Havens d. June 3, 1897.

3370. iii. FLORENCE, b. in Hamilton, N. Y., Feb. 8, 1856.

1903. WILLIAM SAWTRE FOOTE, (799, 247, 76, 25, 9, 3,) b. at Smyrna, N. Y., Aug. 28, 1824. Practised dentistry many years in Ct. and Ill. Moved to Belvidere, Ill., 1854, where he lived till 1891, when he moved to Chicago to live with his daughter; d. at dau.'s home in Kenilworth, Ill., Aug. 8, 1905. He m. Lucy Lovina Andrus, of Belvidere, Ill., June 1, 1858; b. Feb. 25, 1835, in N. Y. and d. June 26, 1892, in Chicago. She was a granddaughter of a Revolutionary soldier.

3371. i. FANNIE AMELIA FOOTE, b. Belvidere, Ill., Oct. 3, 1862; m. June 1, 1887, Dr. William Marion Stearns, b. June 20, 1856, at

Dale, N. Y.; graduated from Medical College in 1880; has been
for many years a Professor and Dean of the Chicago Homeopathic Medical College and a prominent physician and surgeon
of the Middle Western States. Res., Chicago, Ill. Ch.: (1)
Helen Frances, b. Jan. 24, 1891. (2) Harold William, b. July 7,
1892; d. Aug. 9, 1892. (3) Lucile Lovina, b. May 19, 1894; d.
Aug. 12, 1894. (4) Eugene Marion, b. Oct. 14, 1896. (5) Clarence
Foote, b. Nov. 14, 1897.

3372. 11. WILLIAM KELLOGG FOOTE, b. Apr. 17, 1871; m. Ella J. Downing, 5067.

1906. HON. JOHN JOHNSON FOOTE, (801, 247, 76, 25, 9, 3,) b. Hamilton,
N. Y., Feb. 11, 1816; m. Sept. 24, 1839, Mary, dau. of Hon. Amos and Mary
(Owen) Crocker, of Hamilton, N. Y. She was b. May 12, 1819, and d. Jan. 8,
1907. He was a prominent man in Central New York, and during the Civil War
was very active in the raising and organization of regiments in that portion of
the State. He was the first Central New Yorker to subscribe for Government
Bonds, and in every way an ardent patriot. Was State Senator in 1858-59;
Auditor of the New York City Post Office under Postmaster Thomas L. James;
was Acting Postmaster during Mr. James' absence in Europe. Mr. Foote's system
of rules and regulations for the reorganization and re-formation of that office have
since been adopted by the United States Post Office Department in the large
post offices in the United States.

On Saturday night, Apr. 15, 1905, just before the midnight hour,
Hon. John J. Foote, of Belvidere, Ill., gave heed to the final
summons, and folding his weary arms in token of his sub-
mission, passed to the great beyond. Long had his death been expected,
for the feebleness of old age was upon him, and the strenuousness of a well spent
life had left its mark upon the forces which for years had been the admiration of
men. Eighty-nine years had been his life allotment, while into it had been
crowded more of the important things which are included in the making of the
history of a nation than ordinarily falls to the lot of man. Since the war of
1812 little of importance has come to this continent to which he was not an
eye witness, and in which he did not participate.

Born in Hamilton, N. Y., in Feb., 1816, he there laid the foundations of his
life, to which men do not point with scorn, but direct attention to as worthy of
emulation. During the stirring times of the nation, when the cry for a division
of this government was heard, when men were carried outside the pale of reason
by their passion and love for gain, his voice was heard in the gatherings of the
wise, upholding the government, planning for the maintenance of her honor, and
struggling for the outcome, which should leave the union undivided. The guns of
Fort Sumpter aroused in him that spirit which had marked his ancestors for more
than two centuries, and crystalized into action that power and energy which made
him sought after in the councils of the nation.

The long and noble ancestry back of this man, fruitful in deeds accomplished,
good impressions made upon the public life, and in the assisting of the settlement
of questions which has greatly affected the history of our country, could not help
but accurately foreshadow the life just closed. From 1633 the line is unbroken,
and is closely identified with the stirring and important events of both England
and America. This man's family and himself have become prominent figures in
the national life of two continents. John J. Foote began life with the history of

JOHN JOHNSON FOOTE. No. 1906

REV. ELIAS JOHN FOOTE. No. 1979

a good name., He could proudly point to men whose record was one of fidelity, the maintenance of great principles, and in the crises of nation's history, were willing to give their all for that nation's integrity and welfare.

His educational training was thorough, and though he did not pursue a full classical course, later in life he received his degree from Madison—now Colgate University. In his early career he took an active part in politics as a member of the Whig party, and by reason of his personal popularity and political sagacity was many times elected to various local offices, even when his party was largely in the minority. He counted as his friends the leaders of the Republican party, and was prominently identified with such men as Roscoe Conklin and Henry Clay.

In 1857 he was elected a member of the first Republican Legislature in New York, and served as a member of the Senate with such distinguished colleagues as William A. Wheeler and General Francis B. Spinola. He was the introducer and champion of the Personal Liberty Bill, one of the most famous measures proposed in New York prior to the war, and was designed to secure for the negroes additional rights and privileges.

When the war broke out, he gained additional prominence by doing all in his power to suppress the rebellion. When Fort Sumter was fired upon, he was called into a conference in New York City with Thurlow Weed, Governor Morgan, General Wool and others to consider the situation, and devise means for putting New York on a war footing. The meeting was held on Saturday night, and the Legislature was to adjourn on the following Monday. It was imperative for the proposed adjournment to be postponed, and Mr. Foote was delegated to go to Albany and see that the adjournment resolution was rescinded. The history of his work in that connection is interesting reading.

While he was seeking to induce the Republicans to carry out the pledge outlined by the party leaders in New York, Frances B. Spinola, with whom he had often crossed swords in politics, was an interested listener. Spinola finally blurted out, "Foote, you Republicans are a pack of cowards. I am a Democrat, but I propose to vote for the reconsideration of the adjournment resolution, and for the three million dollar appropriation as you proposed, and more than that, I will raise a regiment to go down South and lick the rebels." The four years of national turmoil furnishes many records of the toil and labor of Mr. Foote in behalf of the Union cause.

In 1865, his health having become seriously impaired, he sold out his business in Hamilton, and removed with his family to Belvidere, Ill., where he settled on a large farm, giving attention mainly to agricultural pursuits. Shortly after Mr. James was made postmaster in New York by President Grant, Mr. Foote was tendered the important office of auditor, a position which had been newly created. Mr. Foote accepted the position with the understanding that as soon as he had systematized the financial affairs of the post office he should be allowed to retire. The task proved much greater than he had expected. Mr. Foote devoted the next three years of his life to that work. His work there has passed into history, every act of which in his official capacity, he credit brought to himself and profit to the government which he represented. Under his administration, abuses were corrected, the rights of the government preserved, and systems adopted for use which for years afterward placed that office at the very head of the postal department in this country. More than once was he called upon to settle questions which involved the maintaining his integrity and preserving those principles which had so distinguished his past life. To his superiors he would answer, "Very well, I have sworn to enforce these rules, and I shall do so. It is in your power to change the rules, but it is not in your power to otherwise change my obligations,'' was the keynote of his admiration. Upon his return to Belvidere, Ill., he turned his attention again to private affairs, becoming interested in the various municipal, banking and other enterprises, and proved a skillful and able financier. Only in minor offices did he again enter politics, and then only because he was practically the unanimous choice of his fellow citizens.

Such are some of the side lights of the life which has so recently ended. Some of the guide posts, which point not so much to a mere existence, as to a living tangible reality, a power that was felt, and an influence which knows no dissolution. His was the type of citizenship which increases the strength of the nation and makes her people invincible in war and progressive in times of peace; a type of citizenship injected into municipal and social life, creating aspirations for the things which tell for good, and which will bring no discredit upon their promoters when they shall pass from the stage of action.

For some years Mr. Foote lived in retirement at his home on Lincoln Ave., Belvidere, Ill. His decline was gradual, but very marked for many months. Surrounded by his loved one and the descendants of those who were in his early life associated with his public career, the ministration of love and good will has been his heritage.

Mr. Foote m. in Hamilton, N. Y., Miss Mary, dau. of Hon. Amos Crocker, of Hamilton, to whom three ch. were b., one son (John C. Foote) and two daus. (Miss Harriet Foote and Mrs. Enos Clark), the two former of Belvidere, Ill., and the last-named of St. Louis, Mo. He is survived by his wife and the 3 children. The funeral services were held on Wednesday afternoon, Apr. 15, 1905, from the residence. Rev. Dr. Pierce had charge of the service, assisted by the Rev. B. L. Brittin, of the Presbyterian Church. Interment was made in the family lot in the Belvidere cemetery.

3373. i.   MARY ANNETTE, b. Hamilton, N. Y., Sept. 9, 1840; graduated from Hamilton Female Seminary and Troy Female Seminary; m. Hamilton, N. Y., Sept. 21, 1862, Hon. Enos Clark. He was b. Oct. 19, 1834; graduated from Colgate University, and is a prominent lawyer of St. Louis, Mo.

3374. ii. JOHN CROCKER, b. Hamilton, N. Y., Sept. 20, 1841; m. Helen Garvin, 5068-71.

3375. iii. HARRIET, b. Hamilton, N. Y., May 22, 1848. She was educated at Ingham University, Troy, N. Y., and Mary's Institute, St. Louis, Mo. Is a woman of great executive ability—notably in all church work.

1912. DR. HENRY CADY FOOTE, (801, 247, 76, 25, 9, 3,) b. Aug. 28, 1825; m. Galesburg, Ill., May 27, 1851, Ann Elizabeth McKee. She was b. Elkton, Todd Co., Ky., Sept. 17, 1830; d. Oct. 2, 1880. He was educated at Hamilton College. Graduated from Albany Medical College, Jan. 22, 1850; also studied at the Ann Arbor Medical College. Settled in 1850 at Galesburg, Ill., and became one of the foremost homeopathic physicians of his time; d. May 20, 1863, at Galesburg, Ill.

3376. i. MARY ALFARETTA, b. Galesburg, Ill., Sept. 24, 1856; m. June 10, 1885, Joseph Clarence Juhinne, of Jackson, Miss. He was b. Jackson, Miss., Apr. 10, 1845.

1913. FREDERICK WILLIAM FOOTE, (801, 247, 76, 25, 9, 3,) b. Aug. 9, 1827; m. Esther Young.

3377. i. HARRIET, b. abt. 1847; res., 72 Barrows St., N. Y.

1914. GEORGE W. FOOTE, (801, 247, 76, 25, 9, 3,) b. July 4, 1829; m. Harriet Morton. He d. Sept. 2, 1892.

    3379. i. FRED ALBERT, b. July 24, 1864; m. Helen L. Soule, 5072-4.

1915. ERASTUS STRONG FOOTE, (802, 247, 76, 25, 9, 3,) b. May 16, 1818; m. Sept. 3, 1843, Mary Ann, dau. of Rev. Levi Collins, of Smyrna, N. Y. He was a land surveyor and civil engineer. In 1845 moved on to a farm at Belvidere, Boome Co., Ill., at the same time carrying on a flour mill in town. In 1862 was engaged in manufacturing lumber in Alamakee Co., Iowa, on the Mississippi. Crossed the Continent by wagon to San Francisco and returned via Isthmus of Panama, repeating the trips for several years. In 1868 settled in Toole Co., Territory of Utah. Engaged in building and operating lumber and flour mills. In 1874 was elected to the Legislature of the Territory and appointed County and Probate Judge of Toole Co. He d. Nov. 12, 1906.

    3380. i. EMILY SOPHIA, b. Belvidere, Ill., Jan. 26, 1846; m. Dec. 14, 1871, Daniel W., son of Dr. S. H. Rench, of Hagerstown, Md. He d. Nov. 30, 1893, in Salt Lake City. Ch.: (1) Joseph Dana Allen, b. Oct. 3, 1872. (2) Katherine Claire, b. Feb. 9, 1874. (3) Mary Frank, b. June 20, 1875; m. 1st, Los Angeles, Cal., Mar. 4, 1894, William B. Kinkard. Ch.: (a) Eveline Emily, b. Nov. 19, 1894; m. 2nd, July 10, 1903, Parley Phelps, of Bakersfield, Kearn Co., Cal. Ch.: (b) Herbert Hamilton, b. 1904. (4) Arthur Weisel, b. June 4, 1877. (5) Erastus Foote, b. Oct. 28, 1880; d. May 14, 1881.

    3381. ii. FRANK E., b. July 13, 1851; m. Elizabeth Ewing, 5075-7.

1919. SIDNEY FOOTE, (802, 247, 76, 25, 9, 3,) b. 1830; m. 1858, Elizabeth Flower. She d. at Madison, July 6, 1874. He graduated at Madison University, read law with Orton & Hopkins, and succeeded to their business; d. Jacksonville, Fla., Mar. 8, 1876. Res., Madison, Wis.

    3382. i. FLORENCE, b. 1859; d. at Madison, Wis.

    3383. ii. KATE, b. ———; res., Chicago, Ill.

    3384. iii. MARTHA, b. ———; res., Wyanet, Ill.

    3385. iv. ANNA, b. ———; m. Morris J. Greeley. Ch.: (1) Morris L. (2) Sidney Foote. (3) Laura May. (4) Elizabeth.

    3386. v. ELLA, b. ———.

    3387. vi. RUTH, b. ———; m. L. Holmes. Res., East Minn. and Wis.

1924. DR. HENRY EDWARD FOOTE, (808, 248, 76, 25, 9, 3,) b. June 26, 1825, Cincinnati, O.; m. Louise Agniel, May 15, 1851, at New Harmony, Ind.; d. July 12, 1871, Cincinnati, O. Assistant-Surgeon, Mexican War, 1847; enlisted Civil War, Feb. 19, 1861, for three years, Surgeon 13th Missouri (later 22nd Ohio Vols.). Received honorable discharge Nov. 18, 1864. Professor in Ohio Medical College. Professor in Miami Medical College, and one of its founders. Member of Christ Church (Episcopal), Cincinnati, O. His wife, Louise Agniel, dau. of Camille Agniel and Louise Gex, b. Dec. 25, 1828, Cincinnati, O.; d. Feb. 10, 1894, Minneapolis, Minn. Lived in New Harmony, Ind., 1837 to 1841. Went to school in Washington, D. C., 1841 to 1845.

    3388. i. LUCIEL AGNIEL, b. Jan. 10, 1853, Cincinnati, O.; m. Sept. 24, 1874, to Wm. Henry Hinkle, at Cincinnati, O. Educated in Cincinnati Public Schools; studied in Europe, 1871-1873; Miniaturist; exhibited in the Art Societies of Boston, New York, Philadelphia, and the "Salon" of Paris, France. Art student in Cincinnati

Art School; pupil of Chas. Chaplin in Paris, Douglas Volk at Minneapolis Art School; George de Forest Brush, Art Students' League, N. Y., and of Wm. Chase, at Pennsylvania Academy of Art, Philadelphia; m. William Henry, son of Anthony H. and Francis (Schillinger) Hinkle, b. Aug. 31, 1846. Graduated Yale College, 1869. With Wilson Hinkle & Co., Cincinnati, O., school book publishers (now American Book Co.), from 1869 to 1876. Moved with his family to Minneapolis, Minn., in 1877, on account of ill health. Organized and operated the Holly Flour Mill Co. and Humboldt Mill Co., 1878 to 1895. In 1887, in company with his brother, organized the Ashland Iron and Steel Co., and erected the ''Hinkle'' Charcoal Blast Furnace at Ashland, Wis. Moved to Ashland in 1895 to take active charge of the business. In 1901, erected Charcoal Works and a Wood Products Chemical Works at Ashland, in connection with the Blast Furnace. Retired and returned to Cincinnati, O., 1905. Ch.: (1) Edward Foote Hinkle, b. May 22, 1876, Cincinnati, O. Graduated from Andover, 1895. Graduated from Yale College, 1899. Student of Architecture at University of Pennsylvania, Sept., 1899, to May, 1901; Paris, France, 1901-1905. Returned to United States, July 1, 1905, to pursue profession of architecture.

3389. ii. FRANK BOND FOOTE, b. Feb. 8, 1857, Cincinnati, O.; d. Aug. 12, 1899, California; unm. Educated in Public Schools, Cincinnati, O.; Stevens Institute of Technology, Hoboken, N. J., Special Course, Class of 1878. Complete course of Mechanical Engineering in Car Shops of Texas Pacific Railway, at Marshall, Texas. Manager, Humboldt Flour Mill Co., Minneapolis, Minn., from 1880 to 1895. Retired from business on account of ill health.

3390. iii JOHN PARSONS, b. Sept. 29, 1860; d. Apr. 20, 1862, Cincinnati, O.

1930. ANDREW WARD FOOTE, (811, 248, 76, 25, 9, 3,) b. Apr. 27, 1833, of Guilford; m. May 10, 1859, Charlotte A., dau. of Orrill and Ruth (Kennedy) Wilcox, also of Guilford. She was b. Nov. 25, 1836. He was a farmer of the well-read New England type. He represented the town in the State Legislature in 1878, and d. Dec. 16, 1880. Mrs. Foote res. at the old home, Nut Plains, Guilford, Ct.

3391. i. LILY GILLETTE, b. Mar. 2, 1860.

3392. ii. ANDREW WARD, b. July 2, 1862; d. Oct. 9, 1864.

3393. iii. ANDREW WARD, b. Oct. 5, 1865; m. Winefred Burt, 5078.

3394. iv. HARRIET WARD, b. Sept. 11, 1874; m. Sept. 23, 1902, Herbert Addison, son of Dr. and Mrs. Addison Taylor, of Beverly, N. J. Miss Foote was a valued teacher of sewing and embroidery and design in Hartford Public Schools for five years before her marriage. Mr. Taylor, graduate of Cornell, is a lawyer in New York. Ch.: (1) Harriet Ward Foote, b. Nov. 3, 1903. (2) Adeline Herbert, b. Aug. 14, 1906.

1932. CHRISTOPHER SPENCER FOOTE, (811, 248, 76, 25, 9, 3,) b. May 2, 1837, of Guilford, and Mandarin, Fla.; m. May 23, 1865, Hannah J., dau. of John and Charlotte (Rose) Hubbard, of Guilford. Mrs. Foote was b. Jan. 8, 1840, and d. May 7, 1885. Mr. Foote was a farmer in Guilford and an orange grower in Florida. He d. May 28, 1880.

    3395. i.   ROBERT ELLIOTT, b. Aug. 31, 1866.

    3396. ii. GEORGE AUGUSTUS (3rd), b. Oct. 7, 1871, in Florida, and d. Aug. 30, 1872.

    3397. iii. MARY, b. Nov. 25, 1872.

    3398. iv. HARRY WARD, b. Mar. 21, 1875; m. Martha Jenkins, 5079.

    3399. v.   MARGARET SPENCER, b. June 12, 1880; adopted after her parents' death by Gen. and Mrs. Hawley.

    1934. CAPTAIN SAMUEL EDMUND FOOTE, (811, 248, 76, 25, 9, 3,) b. Jan. 20, 1843; m. Oct. 23, 1872, Lucy, dau. of Oliver and Jane (Hartwell) Bullard. Mrs. Foote was b. at West Sutton, Mass., Feb. 2, 1850. Mr. Foote was a sea captain the most of his life. He was a private in the 10th Ct. Vols., and wounded at the battle of Roanoke, N. C.; he partly recovered, and went into the Navy as a "Master's Mate." He d. May 4, 1887. Res., Brooklyn, N. Y.

    3400. i.   RAYMOND WARD, b. Aug. 19, 1873; d. Apr. 17, 1877.

    3401. ii. FLORENCE, b. Jan. 24, 1876; m. Jan. 10, 1906, John, son of William Temple and Rachel (Likens) Bell, of Franklin, Pa. He was b. July 29, 1875. She graduated from Bridgeport, Ct., High School, 1897, and New Britain (Ct.) Normal School, 1899; New Haven (Ct.) Normal School of Gymnastics, 1904. He is in the florist's business. Ch.: (1) Clarence Ward Bell, b. Oct. 31, 1906, at Franklin, Pa.

    3402. iii. HAROLD SPENCER, b. Sept. 19, 1879; res., Great Neck, N. Y.

    3403. iv. ESTHER BEECHER, b. Sept. 19, 1879.

    3404. v.   CLARENCE WARD, b. Dec. 25, 1881.

    3405. vi. JOSEPHINE HAWLEY, b. Mar. 20, 1884; res., Albany, N. Y.; unm.

    1935. WILLIAM TODD FOOTE, (811, 248, 76, 25, 9, 3,) b. Mar. 23, 1845; m. Jan. 9, 1878, Emma, dau. of George and Cornelia (Jacobs) Munger. Mrs. Emma Foote was b. Apr. 5, 1852. Mr. Foote has been a farmer the most of his life. Res., Guilford, Ct.

    3406. i.   LUCY, b. Sept. 7, 1881; m. Nov. 28, 1900, Randall Lee.

    3407. ii. KATHERINE ELIZABETH, b. Sept. 14, 1884.

    1937. ARTHUR DE WINT FOOTE, (811, 248, 76, 25, 9, 3,) of Grass Valley, Cal., b. May 24, 1849; m. Feb. 9, 1876, Mary Anna, dau. of Nathaniel and Anna (Burling) Hallock, of Milton, N. Y. Mrs. Foote was b. at Milton-on-the-Hudson, N. Y., Nov. 19, 1847, where her father's family had lived on the same land since the grant from Queen Anne to Capt. Bond, from whom the Hallocks bought their tract when it was a forest wilderness. Her parents and grandparents on both sides were of English Quaker descent. She was educated at Poughkeepsie Female Collegiate Seminary. She early showed indications of a talent for drawing, and in her 17th year was sent to New York to the School of Design in Cooper Institute. She spent three winters in New York, at Cooper Institute, and one winter in the studio of Samuel Frost Johnson, studying color. She also received special instruction in design from Dr. William Rimmer, who taught design and anatomy at the Cooper Institute; and in drawing on wood from W. J. Linton, the English artist. Her life was exceedingly simple, sheltered and quiet until her marriage of Feb. 9, 1876, with Arthur De Wint Foote, a civil engineer, who at the time of her marriage was in charge of mining work in California. When her husband's

(22)

business made.it necessary for her to travel extensively, living or stopping at New Almaden and Santa Cruz, Cal., Leadville, Colo., and other places, amid scenes very unlike those of her early home, the experience thus gained she has utilized with great judgment and rare literary ability. After Bret Harte, no one else has given more vivid and effective delineation of the wilder and rougher phases of Western life. Besides ''The Led Horse Claim,'' ''John Bodewin's Testimony,'' ''The Last Assembly Ball,'' ''In Exile and Other Stories,'' ''The Chosen Valley,'' ''Coeur d' Alene,'' ''The Cup of Trembling and Other Stories,'' she has published sundry short stories. Her too infrequent productions in the ''Century'' and other magazines are eagerly noted by discerning readers, who expect from her a higher combination of matter and treatment than they usually find elsewhere. She has illustrated her own tales, and various books and articles, always with point and force. She has also illustrated Longfellow's ''Hanging of the Crane,'' ''Skeleton in Armor,'' Whittier's ''Mabel. Martin,'' Hawthorne's ''Scarlet Letter.'' Mr. Foote entered Class of 1869 Sheffield Scientific School, but left in the second year because of trouble with his eyes. He is a member of Am. Ass. C. E., and has spent most of his life as superintendent of various mines; has contributed articles to mining periodicals, etc.

    3408. i. ARTHUR BURLING, b. Apr. 29, 1877, at New Almaden, Cal.

    3409. ii. ELIZABETH TOWNSEND, b. Sept. 9, 1883.

    3410. iii. AGNES, b. June 23, 1886; d. May 12, 1904.

    1945. CHARLES AUGUSTUS (2nd) FOOTE, (814, 253, 76, 25, 9, 3,) b. Mar. 18, 1818; d. Feb. 28, 1896. Inheriting a good competence while still a child, he erected a building during his minority, and for over 60 years conducted there a mercantile and manufacturing business, meanwhile busied with numberless outside interests. Held most of the town offices, was County Treasurer for three successive terms. One of the organizers and chief pillar of his church, like his father and grandfather, Trustee of Delaware Academy, Director of the Bank, Com. of Railroad, and for a few years in business in California, where his building was twice swept away, first by the great flood, then by fire. Always gentle and courteous, the village papers said of him at his death, ''The last gentleman of the old school in our midst has passed away.'' He m., Sept. 11, 1844, Adelia Johnson, b. Aug. 19, 1822; d. Aug. 17, 1883.

    3411. i. KATHARINE ADELIA, b. Sept. 27, 1845. Active in local affairs, and with a large social acquaintance outside Delhi. Member of D. A. R. and County Regent for a number of years. Secretary of State Charities Aid for 25 years. Secretary for Columbian Exposition, etc.

    3412. ii. CHARLES AUGUSTUS (3rd), b. Feb., 1862, and d. Feb., 1862.

    1952. WILLIAM HENRY FOOTE, (820, 254, 76, 25, 9, 3,) b. Lima, N. Y., Dec. 16, 1837; m. Grand Blanc, Mich., Dec. 29, 1858, Abbey Langton. Res., Flint, Genesee Co., Mich. Tinsmith.

    3413. i. LEWIS G., b. St. Johns, Mich., Apr. 9, 1862; d. June 30, 1862.

    3414. ii. JENNIE A., b. Flint, Mich., Oct. 3, 1866; m. Davison, Mich, Mar. 6, 1890, Seth J. McBratvrey. Ch.: (1) Earl William, b. Davison, Mich., Dec. 14, 1890. (2) Emma Melissa, b. Davison, Mich., July 20, 1892.

    3415. iii. CARRIE G., b. Flint, Mich., June 29, 1869; m. Davison, Mich., July 16, 1889, Martin T. Riecle. Ch.: (1) Hazel Maud, b. Davi-

ORPHA (FOOTE) WILLIAMS. No. 3132

REV. CHARLES C. FOOTE.   No. 1961

CHARLES FOOTE.   No. 824

CHARLES A. FOOTE.   No. 3424

MARY MYRTLE FOOTE.   No. 5081

son, Mich., Aug. 12, 1890.; (2) Cathrine Abbey, b. Davison, Mich., Feb. 11, 1892.

3416. iv. ESTELLE B., b. Flint, Mich., Mar. 27, 1877.

1954. GEORGE WESTLEY FOOTE, (820, 254, 76, 25, 9, 3,) b. Lima, N. Y., Sept. 17, 1843; m. Flint, Mich., Nov. 24, 1869, Julia Shepard. Res., Flint, Mich.

3417. i. CLARENCE W., b. Nov. 18, 1871; d. June 28, 1873.
3418. ii. NELLIE ELIZABETH, b. Oct. 23, 1873.
3419. iii. MAUD, b. Oct. 23, 1875; d. Nov. 1, 1876.
3420. iv. HAROLD OSCAR, b. May 22, 1884.
3421. v. JAMES ALFONZO, b. Apr. 7, 1887.

1955. CORIDON EDWARD FOOTE, (820, 254, 76, 25, 9, 3,) b. Grand Blanc, Mich., Jan. 9, 1894; m. Flint, Mich.; Anna Heolms. She d. at Flint, Mich.

3422. i. KATHRINE MARUNNA, b.
3423. ii. HUBERT, b. ——; d. ——.

1961. REV. CHARLES C. FOOTE, (824, 261, 80, 25, 9, 3,) of Olean, N. Y., b. Mar. 30, 1811, at Olean, N. Y.; was graduated from Oberlin College in 1840. He studied two years in Fairfield Medical School with a view to Foreign Missionary work. He was ordained to the ministry in 1840, and Sept. 10, 1840, he m. Clarissa C. Clark. He held pastorates to churches in Maume, O., Bergen, N. Y., Mt. Clemens, Mich., and White Lake, Mich. He served as Chaplain of the Detroit House of Correction for four years, 1869-73. He was candidate for Vice-President of the Gerrit Smith Liberty Party, before its consolidation with the Free-Soil Party. He was a candidate for Governor of Michigan on the ticket of the American Party in 1882. In 1854 he moved to Detroit, Mich., and was the agent for the Refuge Home Society, whose object was to provide homes for escaped slaves in Canada, which position he occupied until the war made it unnecessary for the slaves to leave the country over which floated the Stars and Stripes in order to be a free man.

He was a prominent actor in the rescue at Syracuse, N. Y., of an escaped slave, named Jerry, from the U. S. Marshal, which resulted in a broken arm for one of the deputies and the hurried departure of the others out of a second story window into the Erie Canal, and Jerry's safe arrival in Canada.

After the war he became the agent for the Freedman's Aid Society, and in that capacity did much able work. From the very inception of the Prohibition Party, Mr. Foote was one of its active spirits, and his temperance work with tongue and pen was earnest and unceasing. He devoted much time to mission work during the last 18 years of his life, and was at one time chaplain of the Seaman's Bethel. Mrs. Foote d. July 3, 1857, and was buried at White Lake, Mich. He m. 2nd, Aug. 3, 1858, Hannah E. Merritt, of Plymouth, Mich. He d. May 3, 1891, at Detroit, Mich., and was buried at White Lake, Mich. She d. Sept. 19, 1902.

3424. i. CHARLES A., b. Maume, O., Sept. 10, 1841; m. Mary E. Lincoln, 5080-87.

3425. ii. GERTRUDE H., b. Bergen, N. Y., Sept. 10, 1843; graduated from Oberlin College in 1866; taught Freedmen's Schools at Newton and Savannah, Ga. Later, teacher in Detroit, Mich., schools for four years; m. Rev. George R. Milton, Oct. 29, 1873, who d. July 23, 1892.

3426. iii. JAMES C., b. Bergen, N. Y., Apr. 10, 1845; d. Sept. 12, 1847.

3427.   iv.   EDWARD I., b. Detroit, Mich., June 29, 1861. Res., Tuolumne, Cal.

1964.   WILLIAM J. FOOTE, (824, 261, 80, 25, 9, 3,) b. ———; m. July 4, 1843, Lucy M. Alcott, of Plymouth, Ct. She d. Oct. 5, 1899. He was for many years a brick manufacturer in Medina, O., and Urbana, Ill.; d. July 2, 1888. Both were buried at Urbana, Ill.

    3428.   i.   JULIA R., b. Medina, O., Apr. 19, 1846; m. Oct. 21, 1869, Milton W. Matthews. He was an Attorney at Law and State Senator at the time of his death. He d. May 10, 1892. Ch.: (1) Loueva Mae Matthews, b. Urbana, Ill., Aug. 6, 1871; m. Aug. 19, 1895, W. A. Nicholaus, of New York. Res., Urbana, Ill. They had 3 ch.; all d. in infancy. (2) Clyde Milton Matthews, b. Dec. 22, 1878, is City Attorney. Res., Urbana, Ill.

    3429.   ii.   EVA A., b. Medina, O., Mar. 30, 1846. For more than 20 years she was a teacher in the public schools of Urbana and Champaign, Ill.

    3430.   iii.   CHARLES B., b. Medina, O., July 12, 1850; m. Elizabeth McConnell, 5088-90.

    3431.   iv.   ORLOFF W., b. Medina, O., Dec. 14, 1856; d. July 28, 1867; buried at Urbana, Ill.

    3432.   v.   CARRIE E., b. Urbana, Ill., Sept. 6, 1859; d. Mar. 23, 1860; buried at Urbana, Ill.

    3433.   vi.   FRANKLIN W., b. Urbana, Ill., Apr. 15, 1861; m. Lulu Jordan, 5091-2.

1966.   ORLOFF FOOTE, (824, 261, 80, 25, 9, 3,) b. Mendon, N. Y., July, 1822; m. Mrs. Cram. He carried on a tanning business at Michigan City, Ind. He d. Oct., 1871.

    3434.   i.   ELMER, b. ———; is a farmer, Ind.

    3435.   ii.   LOIS, b. ———; teacher, Ind.

1972.   SAMUEL FOOTE, (826, 261, .80, 25, 9, 3,) of North Bend, O., b. Feb. 2, 1822; m. Minerva A. Young, July 1, 1849; removed to Valley Center, Kansas. She d. June 28, 1890; buried at Winchester, Ind. Ch. all b. at Valley Center, Kas.

    3436.   i.   ORLENA, b. May 6, 1851.

    3437.   ii.   JOHN S., b. Oct. 2, 1854; m. Flora Parks, 5093-4.

    3438.   iii.   DAN CHARLES, b. Aug. 30, 1859; m. Anna Wolf, 5095-8.

1974.   BARNARD FOOTE, (826, 261, 80, 25, 9, 3,) b. Dec. 24, 1829, of Adams, Ind.; m. Jane F. Bridges, Mar. 15, 1855, and removed to Newton, Ill. Ch. all b. in Wade, Jasper Co., Ill.

    3439.   i.   WILLIAM F., b. Apr. 29, 1856; m. Isadore Clark, 5099-5103.

    3440.   ii.   MARY F., b. Sept. 19, 1859; d. Dec. 30, 1860; buried in Kibler Cemetery.

    3441.   iii.   HARVEY C., b. May 10, 1863; m. Nettie Bateman and Agnes Jenkins, 5112-8.

    3442.   iv.   JOHN E., b. Dec. 28, 1865; d. Nov. 23, 1875; buried in Kibler Cemetery.

    3443.   v.   FRANK V., b. Mar. 30, 1869; d. Aug. 29, 1870; buried in Kibler Cemetery.

    3444.   vi.   ARTEMICIA M., b. Sept. 6, 1871; d. Feb. 2, 1873; buried in Kibler Cemetery.

3445. vii. ELLA C. FOOTE, b. Apr. 13, 1874; m. W. D. Somers, Oct. 13, 1897. Res., Wade, Jasper Co., Ill. Ch.: (a) Lyman D., b. Aug. 3, 1898. (b) Vera A., b. Feb. 16, 1901.

1979. REV. ELIAS JOHN FOOTE, (829, 261, 80, 25, 9, 3,) b. Hinsdale, N. Y., June 22, 1824; removed with his mother to Mendon, N. Y., in 1825. He worked on a farm in his early life, and prepared for college in Lima Seminary. He studied three years in Madison University (now Colgate University), and graduated from Union College, Schenectady, in 1849; then taught school in Mendon and Honeoye, and studied law one year. In May, 1850, he sailed for California, via the Isthmus of Panama. Spent seven years in California in mining and business, returning in 1857 to enter Rochester Theological Seminary. He graduated in 1860, and in the same year received the degree of A. M. from Rochester University. While supplying the Third Baptist Church of St. Louis, Mo., he was ordained, and was called to the pastorate of that church in Feb., 1860. He m. Jan. 8, 1861, Eliza A. Spink, of Trumansburg, N. Y. After two years' service in St. Louis, he was compelled, by the disturbances of the war, to return East, where he was pastor of the following churches: East Genesee St. Baptist Church, of Syracuse, N. Y., four years; Penfield, N. Y., five years; Red Bank, N. J., four years; Middletown, N. J., seven years; Calvary Baptist Church, of Trenton, N. J., seven years. She d. in Trenton, May 5, 1885, and was buried in Trumansburg. Rev. E. J. Foote m. June 5, 1886, Mary, dau. of Ex-Lieut.-Governor Reynolds, of Wickford, R. I. Res., Trenton, N. J.

     3446. i. GEORGE T. S. FOOTE, of St. Louis; graduated from the University of Rochester in 1884; became a bank clerk in Syracuse, N. Y., and since 1889 has been teller of the Orleans County National Bank, Albion, N. Y. He m. Sara D. Field, of Albion, Sept. 14, 1887.

     3447. ii. ANNA CAMP, b. Syracuse, N. Y., Dec. 10, 1863; d. Feb. 4, 1880, and was buried in Trumansburg, N. Y.

     3448. iii. EDWARD MILTON, b. Syracuse, N. Y., Feb. 1, 1866; m. Caroline B. Cauldwell, 5111.

     3449. iv. ETHELWYNNE R., b. Trenton, N. Y., June 14, 1887.

1982. FREDERICK S. FOOTE, (831, 261, 80, 25, 9, 3,) b. Hinsdale, N. Y., Apr. 11, 1830; m. Helen R. Holcomb, Nov. 25, 1858; farmer. They removed to Jackson, Mich., and later to Athens, Mich., where she d. Nov. 11, 1901. Mr. Foote d. Apr. 7, 1903. Both were buried at Athens. Ch.: First three b. at Wakeshma, Mich., the others at Athens.

     3450. i. HESTER A., b. May 19, 1859; m. Dr. E. H. Coller, Dec. 25, 1880. He was a surgeon with rank of Major in the Civil War; d. Nov. 13, 1903, and was buried at Athens, Mich. She lives at Battle Creek. Two ch., both d. in infancy.

     3451. ii. BETSY A., b. Apr. 2, 1862; m. Frank Harrison, Jan. 25, 1884; res., near Athens, Mich. Ch.: (1) Leo. Foote, b. Aug. 14, 1886; studying pharmacy at Ann Arbor.

     3452. iii. LUNA MAY, b. Mar. 2, 1864; m. David B. Lewis, Oct. 17, 1900; res., Jackson, Mich.

     3453. iv. RALPH F., b. May 2, 1866; m. Cora L. Vaughan, 5112.

     3454. v. BARNARD ELISHA, b. Jan. 10, 1869; res., Battle Creek, Mich.

     3455. vi. IDA PEARL, b. Mar. 1, 1874; d. May 15, 1875; buried at Athens.

3456. vii. LELA VENICE, b. Oct. 22, 1879; res., Battle Creek.

1987. ELISHA FOOTE, (831, 261, 80, 25, 9, 3,) b. Leroy, N. Y., Apr. 12, 1841; m. Clara Burch, of Yates, N. Y., at Three Rivers, Mich., Sept. 4, 1864. They removed to California in 1893, and now reside in Campbell, Santa Clara Co.
3457. i. HATTIE E., of Leonidas, Mich.; m. Fleury K. Bartholomew, at San Jose, Cal., Sept. 6, 1893, and removed to Santa Clara, Cal. Ch.: (1) Max Foote, b. Santa Clara, July 11, 1899. (2) Roy Everett, b. Santa Clara, Nov. 4, 1900.
3458. ii. KATE B., b. Mendon, Mich., Dec. 25, 1873; m. Harry G. Mitchell, June 19, 1901; resides in San Francisco, Cal.

1989. GILBERT FOOTE, (831, 261, 80, 25, 9, 3,) b. Sherwood, Mich., Jan. 5, 1850; blacksmith; m. Mary F. Underwood, of Athens, Mich., Oct. 3, 1876. Res., Athens, Mich.
3459. i. DAU., b. and d. Oct. 2, 1881; buried at Athens.
3460. ii. JENNIE, b. Athens, Dec. 3, 1883.

2008. ORLO T. FOOTE, (840, 266, 80, 25, 9, 3,) b. Feb. 7, 1847; m. June 15, 1870, Julia, dau. of Austin Edwards, b. Aug. 9, 1846. Res., Franklin, N. Y.
3461. i. JENNIE, b. Feb. 1, 1874; m. Laverne, son of Samuel Lawson, Nov. 21, 1890, of North Franklin, N. Y. He d. June 12, 1902. Ch.: (1) Madge, b. Mar. 27, 1891. (2) Orlo, b. Dec. 27, 1892; d. Feb. 23, 1905. (3) Samuel, b. Aug. 20, 1896. (4) William, b. June 30, 1898. (5) Albert, b. Sept. 28, 1901.
3462. ii. ANNA, b. June 7, 1880; m. Feb. 24, 1901, I. W. Jordan, of Franklin, N. Y. Res., Margaretville, N. Y. Ch.: (1) Lawrence, b. Oct. 3, 1901. (2) Paul, b. Dec. 3, 1902.
3463. iii. MAUDE, b. Apr. 5, 1886; unm. Res., North Franklin, N. Y.

2014. CAPT. EBENEZER HALE FOOTE, (858, 273, 81, 25, 9, 3,) b. May 12, 1842; m. Apr. 18, 1880, Sarah J., dau. of William C. and Emeline Moorehouse, formerly of Warrensburgh, N. Y., at South Vineland, N. J. He was Captain in Co. K, 11th Regt. Ct. Vols. Res., South Vineland, N. J.
3464. i. EMILY SOPHIA, b. Dec. 27, 1881; m. May 20, 1902, Benjamin F., son of George and Anna Atkinson, of Millville, N. J. Ch.: (1) Claude B., b. Mar. 17, 1902.
3465. ii. ALLISON EDWIN, b. Mar. 18, 1885.
3466. iii. JOHN HALE, b. June 22, 1886.
3467. iv. ERNEST F., b. Apr. 23, 1888; d. Aug. 8, 1888.
3468. v. MARY E., b. July 25, 1893.
3469. vi. CAROLINE A., b. Oct. 29, 1896.

2016. SAMUEL SEABURY FOOTE, (858, 273, 81, 25, 9, 3,) b. Dec. 10, 1847; m. July 30, 1885, at Penryn, Cal., Delia I., dau. of James Wilson, of Iowa. He has held one term as County Commissioner for Canyon Co., is President and Manager of the Caldwell Milling Co., Middleton, Canyon Co., Idaho. Res., and ch. all b. at Middleton, Idaho.
3470. i. GEORGIA HELLEN, b. Feb. 3, 1887.
3471. ii. HAROLD EDWIN, b. Sept. 29, 1889.
3472. iii. JOY RUTH, b. Mar. 8, 1896.
3473. iv. SAMUEL STANLEY, b. Nov. 30, 1898.

2018. EDWARD LINDSLEY FOOTE, (859, 273, 81, 25, 9, 3,) b. Oct. 20, 1823; m. ———. She d. ———. He d. Nov. 30, 1893, Santa Barbara, Cal.

3474. i. BOY, b. ———; d. in infancy.

2019. JOEL FOOTE, (859, 273, 81, 25, 9, 3,) b. July 25, 1825; m. Mar. 15, 1848, Lydia Matilda, dau. of John Boyden, of Brattleboro, Vt. She was b. Nov. 28, 1826; d. May 7, 1861; m. 2nd, Nov. 13, 1862, Catherine Julia, dau. of Asa Hungerford, of Independence, O. She was b. Nov. 9, 1839. He served in a Battery of Light Artillery in the Civil War. He was a Supervisor of Roads and a Farmer. He d. Mar. 27, 1904, loved and respected by all who knew him. Res., Brooklyn, O.

3475. i. ABBY ANN, b. Mar. 5, 1849; m. Aug. 4, 1868, George D. Cutting. He d. 1881; m. 2nd, July 5, 1882, George Cooper Cassidy. He d. Apr. 5, 1901. She d. Nov. 20, 1891. Ch.:

(1) Child, b. Brooklyn, O., Feb. 19, 1871; d. Mar. 26, 1871.

(2) William Justin, b. Brooklyn, O., Jan. 9, 1872; m. Nov. 16, 1895, Ruby Janette, dau. of Thomas King, of Troy, O. She was b. Jan. 19, 1872; d. Oct. 25, 1902. He is a conductor on Cleveland Electric Railway. Res., Cleveland, O., Station H, Box 371. Ch.: (a) Forest McKinley, b. Troy, O., Oct. 8, 1896.

(3) Eliza Matilda, b. Brooklyn, O., Feb. 13, 1874; m. June 24, 1893, Samuel Bartholomew Spears, of Warren, O. He was b. Nov. 18, 1866. Operates the press in the Knitting Mill at Mentor, O. Res., East Mentor, O. Ch.: (a) Kathryn Viola, b. Mentor, O., Apr. 24, 1895. (b) Charles Booker, b. Willoughby, O., Dec. 2, 1896. (c) Lillian Belle, b. Louisville, Ky., Jan. 10, 1904. (d) Byron, b. East Mentor, O., Sept. 25, 1905.

(4) Milton Foote, b. Independence, O., Nov. 15, 1876; m. July 7, 1899, Maggie Cora, dau. of John A. Crobar, of Cleveland, O. She was b. May 14, 1882. He is a market gardener. Res., Cleveland, O., Brooklyn Station. Ch.: (a) Viola Estelle, b. South Brooklyn, O., Aug. 7, 1900; d. Nov. 2, 1900. (b) Irene Abby, b. South Brooklyn, O., July 9, 1903. (c) Howard Adelbert, b. Brooklyn, O., Aug. 5, 1905.

(5) Daisy Eunice, b. Independence, O., Sept. 14, 1878; m. Feb. 24, 1900, Henry Everett, son of Lewis A. Brott, of Willoughby, O. He was b. Sept. 18, 1876. Lumberman. Res., Willoughby, O. Ch.: (a) Harold Arvey, b. June 18, 1901. (b) Floyd Everett, b. Aug. 31, 1902. (c) Murl Stanley, b. Dec. 31, 1903. (d) Lewis Arnold, b. Feb. 9, 1905.

(6) Edgar Thompson, b. Brooklyn, O., June 11, 1883; d. July 23, 1893.

(7) Flossie May, b. Brooklyn, O., July 13, 1885.

(8) Robert Lindsley, b. Brooklyn, O., Jan. 16, 1888.

(9) Abby Ann, b. Brooklyn, O., Nov. 15, 1891; d. July, 1892.

3476. ii. EVELINE MELISSA, b. Aug., 1850; d. Aug. 27, 1857.

3477. iii. SARAH AMELIA, b. June 7, 1852; d. Sept. 21, 1888.

3478. iv. JULIA BOYDEN, b. Feb. 8, 1854; m. Aug. 4, 1874, Leroy Luther, son of John Walworth, of Algansee, Mich.; divorced; m. 2nd, June 3, 1886, James Monroe, son of Jonah Seaman, of Amboy Township, Mich. Res., Brooklyn Heights, O. Ch.: (1) Hattie Matilda, b. Brookfield, Mich., Aug. 27, 1875; m. June 8, 1897, John Ernest, son of Leroy Rovabeck, of Eaton Rapids, Mich.

He was b. Mar. 8, 1869. Farmer. Ch.: (a) Earl Leroy, b. Eaton Rapids, Mich., Oct. 27, 1905. (2) Lillie Ann, b. Brookfield, Mich., Aug. 4, 1877. (3) Bertha, b. Brookfield, Mich., July 30, 1879; d. Dec. 27, 1879. (4) Rettit Ora, b. Brookfield, Mich., Oct. 12, 1880. (5) James Marvin, b. Montgomery, Mich., Apr. 10, 1883; m. Dec. 15, 1904, Florence Amelia, dau. of Harvey Boyden, of Chicago, Ill. She was b. July 8, 1885. Carpenter. Res., Reading, Mich., R. F. D. No. 18. Ch.: (a) Harvey Austin, b. Oct. 11, 1905. (6) Clyde Fern, b. Amboy, Mich., Mar. 5, 1891. (7) Melvin Orley, b. Amboy, Mich., May 16, 1893.

3479. v. JOEL LINDSLEY, b. Feb. 22, 1856; m. Ellen Osmon, 5113-17.

3480. vi. CAROLINE MATILDA, b. Mar. 15, 1858.

3481. vii. ASA, b. Dec. 25, 1865; d. Jan. 15, 1866.

3482. viii. EDWIN, b. Dec. 25, 1865; d. Feb. 20, 1866.

3483. ix. HELEN EMILINE, b. June 8, 1868; m. July 25, 1894, Burton S., son of Francis Henry Cheater, of Brooklyn, O. He was v. Sept. 29, 1866. Clerk of the School Council of Brooklyn Heights, and a market gardener. Ch.: (1) Marion Ruth, b. Mar. 4, 1896. (2) Eveline Lucile, b. Oct. 24, 1897. (3) Luther Brainard Foote, b. Sept. 17, 1899.

3484. x. CHARLES HENRY, b. Sept. 21, 1870; m. Nellie M. Brainard, 5118-25.

3485. xi. LLOYD HUNGERFORD, b. Sept. 12, 1874; m. Clara Lucretia Hinman, 5126-8.

3486. xii. KATHERINE BIRD, b. Aug. 12, 1879. Graduated as a nurse from City Hospital of Cleveland, O., and Manhattan Hospital, New York City.

2024. EDWIN FOOTE, (859, 273, 81, 25, 9, 3,) b. Feb. 15, 1835; m. Oct. 16, 1866, Margaret, dau. of John Walsh, of Scotland. She was b. May 5, 1846; d. Feb. 5, 1899. He served nearly three years in the Civil War in Co. A, 124th O. V. I. He is a carpenter. Res., 3640 W. 32nd St., Cleveland, O.

3487. i. GEORGE, b. Cincinnati, O., Oct. 5, 1867; d. in infancy.

3488. ii. WILIAM, b. Cincinnati, O., Feb. 14, 1869; d. in infancy.

3489. iii. MARGUERITE EMELINE, b. Cincinnati, O., June 5, 1870; m. Dec. 28, 1898, Dr. Selwyn Sumner, son of John Greenly, of Waterman, Ill. He was b. June 14, 1870. He is a graduate of Ann Arbor, Mich. University, and a dentist of Collinwood, O.

3490. iv. ABBY ANN, b. Cincinnati, O., Nov. 27, 1872; m. Nov. 10, 1897, Samuel Cornin, son of Benjamin F. Killam, of Cleveland, O. He was b. May 12, 1872. Salesman. Res., 2168 E. 28th St., Cleveland, O.

3497. v. EDWIN THOMAS, b. Cincinnati, O., Nov. 8, 1874; m. Mayme Crossen, 5129-30.

3492. vi. MARY, b. Cincinnati, O., Apr. 26, 1877; d. in infancy.

3493. vii. SARAH ELIZA, b. Brooklyn Village, Dec. 25, 1884.

3494. viii. ARTHUR, b. Brooklyn Village, June 14, 1887; d. in infancy.

2025. ASA FOOTE, (859, 273, 81, 25, 9, 3,) b. Feb. 15, 1835; m. Feb. 1, 1860, Eunice Amelia, dau. of John Boyden (See 2019), of Brattleboro, Vt. She was b. Aug. 11, 1828; d. Apr. 4, 1901. He was a Christian man of sterling qualities, a carpenter, and d. May 14, 1893. Res., Cleveland, O.

3495. i. PRECY BOYDEN, b. Jan. 23, 1861; d. May, 1864.

3496. ii. MARY AMELIA, b. Sept. 27, 1865; m. Oct. 9, 1895, Zeno Lamartine, son of Julius Kent, of Bentleyville, O. He was b. June 22, 1849; is a graduate of Hillsdale College, Mich. He is Secretary and General Manager of The Deerlick Oil Stone Co., of Chagrin Falls, O., where they res. Ch.: (1) Aveline Grace, b. Cleveland, O., May 9, 1897. (2) Genevieve Martha, b. Cleveland, O., Oct. 10, 1899. (3) Lewis, b. Chagrin Falls, O., Feb. 27, 1901. (4) Malcolm, b. Chagrin Falls, O., May 23, 1903.

3497. iii. LEWIS BOYDEN, b. Nov. 21, 1866; m. June 22, 1892, Aveline, dau. of John Power Lacroix, of Delaware, O. She was b. Nov. 5, 1868; d. June 5, 1893, at Port Clinton, O.; m. 2nd, Nov. 22, 1898, Clara Blanch, dau. of Henry E. Graves, of Cleveland, O. She was b. Dec. 28, 1876; d. Feb. 19, 1900; m. 3rd, Oct. 12, 1904, Anna Bernice, dau. of Jonas Twitchell, of Custer, South Dakota. She was b. Lake City, Florida, Aug. 26, 1877. He is an alumnus of Ohio Wesleyan University, Delaware, O., Class of 1891. He was for several years Chief Clerk in the office of the City Auditor, Cleveland, O., and is with The Guardian Savings and Trust Co. of that city.

2028. GEORGE FOOTE, (859, 273, 81, 25, 9, 3,) b. Oct. 22, 1842; m. Nov. 5, 1863, Jennie T., dau. of William Howell, of Trenton, N. J. She was b. June 12, 1839, and res. at 20 Devonshire St., Cleveland, O. He was a farmer by occupation, served as a musician in the Civil War, and is now an officer at the Soldiers' Home, Sandusky, O.

3498. i. MARY, b. Brooklyn, O., May 24, 1866; m. Oct. 16, 1890, John, son of James Shankland, of Fenlon Falls, Cana. He was b. Jan. 10, 1865. Salesman. Res., 20 Devonshire St., Cleveland, O. Ch.: (1) Mary Adelle, b. South Brooklyn, O., Jan. 31, 1894. (2) Harvey Arthur, b. South Brooklyn, O., Mar. 13, 1898. (3) Earl Foote, b. Brecksville, O., Feb. 11, 1901. (4) Pearle, b. South Brooklyn, O., Aug. 20, 1905.

3499. ii. JENNIE, b. Brooklyn, O., Nov. 16, 1868; m. Oct. 16, 1888, Harvey Tuthill, son of David Bratton, of Brecksville, O. He was b. Apr. 13, 1865. Farmer and Township Trustee. Res., Brecksville, O. Ch.: (1) Harvey George, b. May 1, 1895. (2) Harry Burdette, b. Apr. 5, 1898.

3500. iii. GEORGE HOWELL, b. Brooklyn, O., Sept. 7, 1874; m. Apr. 23, 1900, Anna Catherine, dau. of Frederick Bamberger, of Cleveland, O. She was b. Sept. 19, 1878; d. Sept. 9, 1901; m. 2nd, June 1, 1904, Bertha, dau. of William Meyers, of Saginaw, Mich. She was b. Aug. 17, 1881. He is a graduate of Baldwin University, Berea, O., and is one of the firm of the F. B. Dickerson Co., of Detroit, Mich., where they reside. No ch.

2039. CHARLES BOWLER FOOTE, (868, 274, 81, 25, 9, 3,) b. Middle Haddam, Ct., Sept. 10, 1821; m. Cincinnati, O., Apr. 3, 1851, Sarah Ewing, dau. of Judge James Hall, of Cincinnati. She was b. Henderson Co., Ky., Oct. 2, 1824. Res., Cincinnati.

3500¹. i. MARY POSEY, b. Apr. 12, 1852.

3500². ii. JAMES HALL, b. Feb. 19, 1854.

3501. iii.   EDWARD K., b. Mar. 4, 1857; m. Margaret K. Ingram, 5131.
3502. iv.   CHARLES B., JR., b. June 11, 1859; m. Mollie Williams, 5132-5.
3502¹. v.   WILLIAM WHITEMAN, b. Jan. 4, 1862; d. July 23, 1873.
3502². vi.   FANNY HALL, b. Mar. 28, 1864; d. Feb. 9, 1865.
3502³. vii.   LOUISA BOWLER, b. Apr. 3, 1866.
3502⁴. viii.   ROGER, b. Aug. 10, 1869; d. Apr. 12, 1870.

2041. EDWARD AUGUSTUS FOOTE, (868, 274, 81, 25, 9, 3,) b. Oct. 22, 1827; m. Sarah Aborn, dau. of Hannah Gibbs and Charles Lee Bowler, July 16, 1861, at Fiskeville, R. I. Res., Cincinnati, O. He d. Dec. 8, 1878, Cincinnati.

3502⁵. i.   HENRY BOWLER, b. Paris, Ky., Apr. 30, 1862.
3502⁶. ii.   HANNAH ABORN, b. Cincinnati, Aug. 22, 1863; d. Aug. 8, 1865.
3502⁷. iii.   SARAH LOUISA, b. July 20, 1865; d. May 30, 1866.
3502⁸. iv.   ROBERT BONNER BOWLER, b. Mar. 15, 1867.
3503. v.   EDWARD AUGUSTUS, b. Jan. 1, 1869; m. Eloise Stettinius Urner and Mary Hills, 5136.
3503¹. vi.   SUSAN LOUISA, b. Oct. 22, 1870.
3503². vii.   AMY LEE, b. July 10, 1872.
3503³. viii.   ROGER LEE, b. June 25, 1874.
3503⁴. ix.   ALICE BRADFORD, b. Jan. 25, 1876.

2042. ROBERT BONNER FOOTE, (868, 274, 81, 25, 9, 3,) b. June 4, 1832, in Middle Haddam, Ct.; m. Apr. 30, 1861, Louisa Foote, dau. of Charles Lee and Hannah Gibbs (Aborn) Bowler. He d. Nov. 11, 1867.

3504. i.   DANIEL BOWLER, b. Oct. 8, 1862.
3504¹. ii.   SUSAN LOUISA, b. July 15, 1864; d. 1865.
3504². iii.   ROBERT BONNER, b. Sept., 1865; d. 1867.
3504³. iv.   ELIZA BOWLER, b. June 11, 1867.

2042¹. EDWARD FOOTE, (874, 274, 81, 25, 9, 3,) b. Mar. 10, 1834, Colchester, Ct.; m. Isabella, dau. of Thomas Brainard; d., Feb. 19, 1875. He was educated at Great Barrington, Mass. Merchant; d. Mar. 2, 1882. Res., Chicago, Ill.

3505. i.   CHARLES E., b. Dec. 30, 1866; m. Viola E. Smeed, 5137-8.

2056. ASA FOOTE, (891, 283, 82, 25, 9, 3,) b. Rushville, N. Y., Aug. 12, 1848; m. Ft. Atkinson, Wis., Jan. 3, 1872, Laura A., dau. of Daniel and Sophia (Whitney) Gillmore, of Danby, Vt. Sophia Whitney, dau. of Benjamin and Mary (Erumons) Whitney, b. Dec. 2, 1810. Laura A. b. June 13, 1849. Asa Foote has conducted a successful drug store for 20 years at Ft. Atkinson; has held all of the City offices of trust, Mayor, Treasurer, etc.

3506. i.   MINNIE ELLEN, b. Ft. Atkinson, Wis., Nov. 3, 1872; m. June 24, 1896, Judson W., son of John and Marriette (Royce) Gates. Res., Ft. Atkinson, Wis., where he is established in the drug business. Ch.: (1) Mildred L., b. Mar. 24, 1897.
3507. ii.   HARRIET SOPHIA, b. Aztalan, Wis., Jan. 17, 1875.
3508. iii.   AGNES FAY, b. Ft. Atkinson, Wis., May 26, 1878; m. Ft. Atkinson, Wis., May 14, 1904, Arthur R., son of ex-Governor W. D. and Elizabeth (Bragg) Hoard. Res., Ft. Atkinson, Wis., where he has large business interests. Ch.: Helen Dorothy, b. Aug. 22, 1905.
3509. iv.   LAURA GENEVIEVE, b. Ft. Atkinson, Wis., Aug. 22, 1888.

2063. JOHN FOOTE, (897, 284, 85, 26, 9, 3,) b. Feb. 9, 1801; m. Dec. 31, 1823, Eliza Partridge, of New York. She d. Sept. 11, 1871, ae. 65. He d. Nov. 29, 1883. Res., New York.

3510. i.   OLETTIA A., b. Dec. 19, 1824; d. Aug. 21, 1825.

3511. ii.   JOHN H., b. Sept. 18, 1826; m. Caroline Rhodes, 5139-40.

3512. iii. BETSEY ANN, b. Sept. 22, 1828; m. Oct. 22, 1846, William F. Wilson. Ch.: (1) Sarah Louise, b. (2) Dyle Frost, b. (3) William Francis, b.

3513. iv.   JAMES C., b. Mar. 5, 1830; m. Eliza Rhodes, 5141-6.

3514. v.   EDWARD, b. May 6, 1831.

3515. vi.   CHARLOTTE M., b. Jan. 17, 1833; m. Jan. 17, 1850, John Marshall Rockwell. She d. Apr. 16, 1905. Ch.: (1) John Marshall. (2) William Mason. (3) Dudley Hale. (4) Charlotte Maria. (5) Harriette Rebecca.

3516. vii. ALBERT W., b. July 16, 1834; m. Josephine Hussey, 5147-8.

3517. viii. SARAH E., b. Oct. 22, 1835; m. Mar. 7, 1855, John C. Smith. She d. Aug. 15, 1869. Ch.: (1) Charlotte M. (2) Sarah E.

3518. ix.   GEORGE W., b. Oct. 11, 1837; m. Elizabeth Werthword, 5149-50.

3519. x.   BENJAMIN, b. Aug. 11, 1839; d. May 11, 1841.

3520. xi.   BENJAMIN, b. Jan. 5, 1842; d. Mar., 1843.

3521. xii. MARY E., b. June 4, 1845; m. Jan. 26, 1869, Chas. T. Sheldon. Ch.: (1) Jennie E.

2083. IRA FOOTE, (919, 290, 85, 26, 9, 3,) b. Mar. 26, 1816; m. Oct. 2, 1839, Elizabeth Smith, of Parma, N. Y. She was b. Groton, Ct., Nov. 3, 1820. He d. Aug. 7, 1905, at Rochester, N. Y.

3522. i.   HENRY H., b. Jan. 29, 1844; m. Mary E. Lester, 5151-8.

3523. ii.   HARRIET ELIZABETH, b. Jan. 26, 1842; d. Mar. 27, 1843.

3524. iii. HARRIET ANNA, b. Jan. 5, 1844; m. Parma, N. Y., Aug. 28, 1864, Eugene C. Lester. Ch.: (1) Harriet Eugenia, b. Dec. 13, 1865. (2) Grace Elizabeth, b. Mar. 8, 1870.

3525. iv.   VIOLA, b. Dec. 3, 1846; m. Albion, Mich., Dec. 31, 1868, Decatur Henry Goodenow. He was b. Monell, Ill., June 29, 1844. She was educated at Brockport and Rochester, N. Y. Res., Kansas City, Mo. Ch.: (1) Fred Ira Goodenow, b. June 17, 1870; m. Elizabeth, dau. of Thomas E. Eustace. She was b. Farley, Ia., Oct. 26, 1870. He was educated at Albion College. Is a traveling salesman. Res., 3712 Main St., Kansas City, Mo. No ch. (2) Julian Frank Goodenow, b. Nov. 2, 1877; m. Caroline Brookfield, dau. of John W. Horter. She was b. Sept. 17, 1882, at Chicago, Ill. He was educated at University of Chicago, class of 1901. Ph.B. Traveling salesman. Baptist. Res., 3738 Wyandotte St., Kansas City, Mo.

3526. v.   ADA ELLEN, b. Sept. 25, 1851; m. Rochester, N. Y., Apr. 9, 1879, Orrin Todd. She d. Sept. 17, 1888.

2085. WARREN FOOTE, (919, 290, 85, 26, 9, 3,) b. Vernon, N. Y., Jan. 7, 1821; m. Phelps, N. Y., Oct. 11, 1843, Rhoda Reed. She was b. Saratoga, N. Y., Mar. 3, 1821. Res., Rush, N. Y.

3527. i.   ALICE JOSEPHINE, b. Parma, N. Y., June 2, 1845; m. Brooklyn, N. Y., William Guy Markham, of Avon, N. Y. Ch.: (1) Mary Eliza Emma, b. June 29, 1886.

3528. ii.   FRANCES S., b. Ogden, N. Y., Dec. 7, 1848; m. Addie S. Jameson, 5159-60.

3529. iii. ELLA LEORA, b. Rush, N. Y., July 4, 1850; m. Brooklyn, N. Y., Dec. 19, 1883, John H. Sanborn, of Newton Centre, Mass. No ch.
3530. iv. EMMA ELIZABETH, b. Rush, N. Y., Aug. 27, 1852; d. Nov. 26, 1902, in Brooklyn, N. Y.; unm.
3531. v. CARRIE ANTOINETTE, b. Rush, N. Y., Mar. 2, 1861; m. Brooklyn, N. Y., May 16, 1888, Rev. Francis H. Davis, of Haverhill, Mass. Ch.: (1) Warren Foote, b. Franklin Falls, N. H., Aug. 9, 1889.

2087. AVERY FOOTE, JR., (919, 290, 85, 26, 9, 3,) b. in Parma, N. Y., Nov. 19, 1853; m. June 13, 1877, Minnie Louise Spaulding, of Montour Falls, N. Y. She was b. Rochester, N. Y., Dec. 8, 1854. He is a merchant miller. Res., Newark, Wayne Co., N. Y.
3532. i. ESTELLA LOUISE, b. Parma, N. Y., Jan. 18, 1879; m. Newark, N. Y., Oct. 14, 1901, William James Harvie, of Newark. Res., Utica, N. Y. Ch.: (1) Elouise Merripine, b. June 7, 1905.

2088. LUTHER RICE FOOTE, (920, 290, 85, 26, 9, 3,) b. Apr. 30, 1819; m. Oct. 19, 1842, Mary A. Brown. She was b. Aug. 7, 1821; d. Feb. 12, 1902. He d. July 21, 1854, Vernon Center, N. Y.
3533. i. JOHN THEODOR, b. July 22, 1846; res., Oneida, N. Y.; unm.
3534. ii. CLARA E., b. Jan. 11, 1850; res., Oneida, N. Y.; unm.

2090. SEELEY TROBNDGO FOOTE, (920, 290, 85, 26, 9, 3,) b. Aug. 27, 1822; m. Mariah Chapman. He d. Sept. 5, 1875.
3535. i. BENJAMIN S., b. ———; m. Donie Grafford; res., Kansas City, Mo.

2091. JOHN FOOTE, (920, 290, 85, 26, 9, 3,) b. Oneida, N. Y., Jan. 9, 1825; m. June 19, 1855, Verginia, dau. of Reuben Jenison, of Warsaw, N. Y. She d. Feb. 12, 1904, at Traverse City, Mich. He d. Jan. 21, 1902.
3536. i. WILLIAM O., b. Apr. 17, 1859; m. Nettie E. Matteson, 5161-3.
3537. ii. JOHN NEWCOMB, b. Johnsonburgh, N. Y., Apr. 17, 1859. Is a Tanner and Hide Dealer. Res., Traverse City, Mich.; unm.
3538. iii. CORAMAY SOPHRONIA, b. Johnsonburgh, N. Y., Apr. 11, 1865; m. May 16, 1888, Willett M. Coddington, of Traverse City, Mich. Ch.: (1) Gertrude Foote, b. Sept. 13, 1885. (2) Clara Augusta, b. Jan. 3, 1893. (3) Hoyt Edward, b. June 15, 1896. (4) Homer Willett, b. July 11, 1897.
3539. iv. SYLVIA CLARISSA, b. Traverse City, Aug. 9, 1874; m. Aug. 9, 1898, Fred E. Driscal. Res., Grand Rapids, Mich. Ch.: (1) Harold F., b. July 23, 1901.

2094. CHARLES BABCOCK FOOTE, (920, 290, 85, 26, 9, 3,) b. July 25, 1831; m. Portage, Wyoming Co., N. Y., Oct. 27, 1853, Celia Buell Rogers. He d. Dec. 27, 1873. His death was caused by injuries received several years previous. She res. Batavia, N. Y.
3540. i. LUTHER RICE, b. Aug. 1, 1854; m. May Clapp, 5164.
3541. ii. CLARA ALMIRA, b. June 2, 1862; m. Rochester, N. Y., Nov. 14, 1889, George Abel Page. She was a charter member and is Corresponding Secretary of the Deo-on-go-wa Chapter of the D. A. R. Ch., all b. in Batavia, N. Y.: (1) Jerome Foote, b. Sept. 3, 1892. (2) Helen, b. Sept. 29, 1894. (3) Elizabeth, b. Sept. 28, 1896; d. Feb. 10, 1897. (4) Mary Page, b. Apr. 18, 1900; d. Dec. 25, 1902.

2096. WILLIAM A. FOOTE, (920, 290, 85, 26, 9, 3,) b. Dec. 12, 1839; m. Sept. 14, 1869, Emma D. Wood. Res., Clinton, Mo.

    3542. i. MARY LOPHIN, b. July 25, 1871; m. Oct. 20, 1897, Henry W. Kerr.

    3543. ii. SARAH ELIZABETH, b. Sept. 9, 1875; m. Apr. 21, 1898, Robert Edwin Harmon. Res., Clinton, Mo.

2097. MARK HARMON FOOTE, (921, 290, 85, 26, 9, 3,) b. Jan. 23, 1825; m. Harriet Walbridge. She was b. Nov. 22, 1835. He d. Nov. 12, 1901. Res., Lyons, Wis.

    3544. i. LUELLA, b. ———; m. Waldo Ranney. No ch. Res., Duluth, Minn. Co. Normal Dormitory.

    3545. ii. ALMIRA ELIZABETH, b. Sept. 8, 1857; d. Sept. 28, 1858.

    3546. iii. CLARA, b. ———; m. Stephen Raleigh. Res., St. Paul, Minn. Robinson, Strauss & Co. No ch.

    3547. iv. IRA ADDISON, b. Oct. 19, 1861; m. Retta Long, 5165-7.

    3548. v. ZYLPHA, b, Oct. 19, 1863; m. J. D. Buckingham. Res., Glyndon, Minn. Ch.: (1) Zella, b. ———. (2)

    3549. vi. ZELLA, b. Oct. 19, 1863; unm. Res., Lyons, Wis.

    3550. vii. HARRIET, b. Dec. 8, ———; unm.

    3551. viii. BABY, b. Feb. 25, 1876; d. Feb. 28, 1876.

2100. ADDISON OSGOOD FOOTE, (921, 290, 85, 26, 9, 3,) b. Kirkland, N. Y., Feb. 7, 1840; m. Spring Prairie, Wis., Jan. 2, 1871, Sarah Margaret, dau. of Josiah Borroughs Gleason. She was b. Spring Prairie, Wis., July 5, 1846; d Dec. 14, 1895, at Ottawa, Kas. Farmer. Res., Simpson, Kas.

    3552. i. LEON R., b. Nov. 22, 1871; m. Lizzie Creighton, 5168.

    3553. ii. ROY F., b. Jan. 5, 1874; m. Elizabeth Taylor, 5169-70.

    3554. iii. BESSIE ANNA, b. Sept. 11, 1877.

    3555. iv. EPHRAIM J., b. May 8, 1879; m. Grace Grecian, 5171.

    3556. v. JOHN ADDISON, b. Mar. 5, 1884, in Brown University, Providence, R. I.

    3557. vi. HERBERT BRANCH, b. Sept. 27, 1886.

2102. EPHRAIM SEELEY FOOTE, (921, 290, 85, 26, 9, 3,) b. Spring Prairie, Wis., July 14, 1847; m. Lyons, Wis., Dec. 27, 1871, Mattie R., dau. of R. Waite. She was b. Dec. 27, 1848, Lyons, Wis. He is a Horticulturist.

    3558. i. IRMA E., b. Feb. 18, 1875; m. Redlands, Cal., Mar. 24, 1897, Dr. W. R. Heacock.

    3559. ii. INEZ ALMINA, b. Mar. 1, 1887.

    3560. iii. WILLIARD WAITE, b. June 11, 1888; d. Feb. 6, 1890.

    3561. iv. WILFRED ROSE, b. Mar. 12, 1892.

2110. HOMER FOOTE, (935, 298, 89, 26, 9, 3,) b. July 27, 1810; m. May 6, 1834, Delia, dau. of James Scutt Dwight, of Springfield, Mass. James Scutt Dwight was a prominent merchant for many years on the corner of State and Main Streets, doing a general merchandise business, having six branch stores in the country, owning a line of boats on the river, and a distiller of good old New England rum and gin under the hill (Armory) close by. He had a large family, all of whom were prominent in business and professions one way and another. Homer Foote succeeded to this business, establishing in 1831 the hardware, iron and steel business at the old store known as the Dwight store, corner State and Main Streets. In 1845 he built the present block, corner State and Main Streets, and continued in business there for 55 years, dying a few years ago. The son,

Francis Dwight Foote, is now the proprietor of the business, succeeding to it in 1893. Homer Foote d. Apr. 6, 1898, still being the senior partner of Homer Foote & Co., Hardware, Iron and Steel.

Homer Foote was prominent in all the enterprises started in Springfield and nearby towns, was president or director of several manufacturing corporations, also director of the Pynchon Bank and Massachusetts Mutual Life Insurance Co. He res. at 201 Maple St., at the old mansion and residence until his death. He was a large public-spirited citizen, the most prominent as a good man and citizen and of the largest public interest in the welfare of Springfield, putting his efforts and his money into every good or promising enterprise. He stood high in the estimation of everyone, a man with few enemies, strong, vigorous, honorable and just.

3562. i.   EDWARD, b. May 7, 1835; m. Mary Otis Alger, 5172.

3563. ii.   EMERSON, b. Apr. 28, 1837; m. Margaret Legget Allen, 5173-5.

3564. iii. HOMER, b. Dec. 22, 1839; m. Catherine C. Bailey, 5176-8.

3565. iv.   CLEVELAND, b. Jan 1, 1842. Served nine months in the Civil War in Co. A, 46th Regt. Mass. Vols. Is a broker in scrap iron and steel and railroad material in New York City; unm.

3566. v.   MARIA SHEPARD, b. May 12, 1844; res., Springfield, Mass.; unm.

3567. vi.   FRANCIS DWIGHT, b. Nov. 19, 1845; res., Springfield, Mass.; unm.

3568. vii. DELIA DWIGHT, b. Mar. 9, 1847; unm.

3569. viii. JAMES DWIGHT, b. Feb. 14, 1850; m. Ellen B. Chandler and Louise E. Burgess, 5179-81.

3570. ix.   LAURA DWIGHT, b. Sept. 7, 1855; m. at Springfield, Mass., Jan. 7, 1880, Leonard Ware, of Boston. Ch. (all b. at Roxbury, Mass.): (1) Anna Dorr Ware, b. May 16, 1881. (2) Laura Dwight Ware, b. Feb. 28, 1883. (3) Dwight Ware, b. Sept. 4, 1885. (4) Ruth Ware, b. Oct. 28, 1887. (5) Leonard Ware, Jr., b. June 18, 1900.

3571. x.   SANFORD DWIGHT, b. Jan. 6, 1858; m. Oct. 30, 1902, Carrie, dau. of Frederick Augustus and Carrie Kitchen von Bernuth, of New York. No ch.

2113.   ADONIJAH FOOTE, (935, 298, 89, 26, 9, 3,) b. May 7, 1823; m. Julia, dau. of Samuel Bowles. She d. ———; m. 2nd, 1855, Amelia Ward, of East Port, Miss.

3572. i.   CLARA WOODWORTH, b. Nov. 22, 1856; m. Nov. 6, 1876, James Mhoon, son of Robert Campbell and Elizabeth Mhoon Brinkley, of Memphis, Tenn. He was b. Aug. 30, 1855. Ch.: (1) Robert Campbell, b. Dec. 7, 1877. (2) Mabel Caren, b. Nov. 13, 1879; m. Nov. 26, 1902, Christopher Dunkin Smithers. Ch.: (à) Christopher Dunkin Smithers, b. Sept. 4, 1903. (3) Colton Green, b. Jan. 31, 1881; d. ———. (4) Clara, b. Sept. 23, 1883; d. ———. (5) Elizabeth, b. Jan. 29, 1889. (6) James Foote, b. July 5, 1890. (7) Hugh Montgomery, b. July 23, 1893. (8) Amiel Ward, b. Jan. 10, 1896. (9) Johnstone, b. May 21, 1899.

3573. ii.   JAMES A., b. Sept. 30, 1860; m. Ruth Penn, 5182-88.

2120.   ALVIN C. FOOTE, (960, 302, 89, 26, 9, 3,) b. Mar. 7, 1833; m. Esther Eyrter.

3574. i.   MARY ESTHER, b. Aug. 6, 1859, near Oregon, Ill.; m. Feb. 20,
             1877, Marshall Thompson, Toronto, Canada; he d. Sept. 23, 1883.
             She m. 2nd, Oct. 17, 1901, Flois Allen, Hamlin, N. Y. Ch.: (1)
             Shirley Esther Thompson, b. May 25, 1879. (2) Clarence Turenne
             Thompson, b. Dec. 13, 1881. Both unm.
3574¹. ii.   LURA MAY, b. Mar. 12, 1863, Oregon, Ill.; m. Mar. 1, 1882,
             Walter A. Hinkle, Oregon, Ill.
3575. iii. FRANK MILTON, b. Aug. 20, 1865, Rockford, Ill.; m. 1895, Mary
             Kneis, of Vienna, Austria.

2126. ALONZO L. FOOTE, (962, 302, 89, 26, 9, 3,) b. Jan. 10, 1822; m. Mar.
18, 1845, Julia Smith. He d. June 5, 1888. Res., Gainesville, N. Y.
3576. i.   ELLEN L., b. Mar. 3, 1846; m. Mar. 16, 1869, Edgar F. Rugg.
             She d. Feb. 21, 1898. Ch.: (1) Essie. (2) Leden. (3) Leon.
3577. ii.   EMILY E., b. Apr. 19, 1847; m. 1st, 1873, J. Grover; m. 2nd,
             M. J. Merville.
3578. iii. KILBOURN M., b. Apr. 26, 1849; m. Eva Hurlbert, 5431-5.
3579. iv.   PHOEBE J., b. Dec. 13, 1851; d. Nov. 16, 1874.
3580. v.   FRANK E., b. Feb. 22, 1855; d. July 4, 1856.
3581. vi.   ALICE C., b. Sept. 6, 1856; m. Sept. 29, 1875, Earl W. Metcalf.
             He d. ———; m. 2nd, Aug. 5, 1901, Albert C. Gage. Res., War-
             saw, N. Y. Ch.: (1) Glenn Foote Metcalf. (2) Phoebe Metcalf.
3582. vii. FLORA C., b. Feb. 5, 1859; m. Oct. 16, 1878, Wm. Gule. Ch.:
             (1) Roy, b. ———. (2) Janet. (3) Beulah. (4) Alice.
3582¹. viii. EFFIE, b. May 28, 1864; m. Sept. 20, 1887, W. Metcalf. Ch.:
             (1) Jennie. (2) Blanche. (3) Mildred. (4) Alonzo, b. ———; d.
             June 5, 1888.

2127. DAVID L. FOOTE, (962, 302, 89, 26, 9, 3,) b. Oct. 10, 1830; m. Polly
       Frone. Res., Gainesville, N. Y.
3582². i.   MINEY, b. ———; d. ———.
3582³. ii.   MILTON, b. ———; d. ———.

2128. WILLIAM FOOTE, (962, 302, 89, 27, 9, 3,) b. Dec. 7, 1840; m. Aug.
30, 1862, Lydia Barber, b. June 16, 1845. Res., Gainesville, N. Y.
3583. i.   EDSON J., b. Sept. 24, 1863; m. Dora May Eddy, 5190-1.
3584. ii.   MARY, b. June 9, 1866; m. ——— Mead. Ch.: (1) Lydia, b. Oct.
             8, 1886. (2) Hellen, b. Feb. 22, 1889. (3) Lynn, b. Dec. 5, 1903.
3585. iii. HARVY E., b. May 12, 1868; m. Etta Couch, 5192.
3586. iv.   SETH EMERY, b. Sept. 10, 1876; m. Charlotte Hall.
3587. v.   PEARL, b. Nov. 9, 1878; m. ——— York. Ch.: (1) Frances, b.
             May 15, 1902. (2) Arthur, b. Aug. 13, 1906.
3588. vi.   AMANDA, b. Oct. 7, 1882; m. ——— Warren. Ch.: (1) Lloyd, b.
             Oct. 29, 1900. (2) Kenneth, b. July 1, 1903.

2129⁴. GEORGE FOOTE, (980, 304, 89, 36, 9, 3,) b. 1840, Bridgewater, N. Y.;
m. Aurelia Johnson, of Bridgewater, N. Y. Res., Bridgewater, N. Y.
3588¹. i.   ANNA, b. Mar. 19, 1867, Bridgewater; m. ——— Rising. Ch.: (1)
             Gladys E., b. 1900.

2129⁵. FREDERICK FOOTE, (980, 304, 89, 36, 9, 3,) b. 1843, Bridgewater,
N. Y.; m. 1st, Nellie Brown, of Bridgewater, N. Y.; m. 2nd, Zayela Conger, of
Waterville; d. 1878, Waterville, N. Y.
3588². i.   LEONARD, b. 1872; d. 1872.

3588³. ii. OLIVER, b. 1872.

3588⁴. iii. FRED, b. 1879; d. 1879, at Waterville, N. Y.

2129⁶. WILLIAM E. FOOTE, (981, 304, 89, 36, 9, 3,) b. 1840, Bridgewater, N. Y.; m. 1st, Josephine ———; m. 2nd, Emma Hall. Res., Bridgewater.

    3588⁵. i. JOSEPHINE, b. ———; m. ——— Roselands. Ch.: (1) Ethel, b. 1901, Bridgewater, N. Y.

2132. JUSTUS BATTLE FOOTE, (982, 308, 92, 27, 9, 3,) b. Lee, Mass., Jan. 25, 1801; m. Harriet Augusta, dau. of Peter Bastine. She d. Feb. 21, 1898, at Brooklyn, N. Y. He d. Nov. 28, 1878, Brooklyn, N. Y.

    3589. i. DELIA AUGUSTA, b. ———; m. Brooklyn, N. Y., June 4, 1890, James Elless Wight.

    3590. ii. AMELIA BASTINE, b.

    3591. iii. MARY, b. ———; d. in infancy.

2136. JUDGE ELISHA FOOTE (982, 308, 92, 27, 9, 3,) b. Lee, Mass., Aug. 1, 1809. Ed. Albany Institute, and studied law with Judge Daniel Cady, of Johnstown, N. Y. After being admitted to the bar he res. at Western N. Y. Was District Attorney and then Judge of the Court of Common Pleas of Seneca Co. His specialty was Patent Law, and he made several valuable inventions, two of which yielded him an ample fortune. He was a member of the National Association for the Advancement of Science, for which he contributed various papers on scientific subjects. He was also extremely fond of mathematics and wrote a work on the Calculus; m. Aug. 12, 1840, Eunice Newton. She was b. July 17, 1819; d. Sept. 30, 1888. In 1864 he was appointed to the Board of Appeals at the U. S. Patent Office, where from July, 1866, until Apr., 1869, he was Commissioner. He d. Oct. 22, 1883. Res., Seneca Falls, N. Y., and Washington, D. C.

    3592. i. MARY NEWTON, b. July 21, 1842; m. in Washington, D. C., June 25, 1868, John B. Henderson, a U. S. Senator from Mo., a man of distinguished ability and large fortune. Mrs. Henderson organized the St. Louis School of Design in 1876 and the St. Louis Exchange for Women's Work in 1879. Studied art four years in Washington University (St. Louis 1881-5) and published "Practical Cooking and Dinner Giving" (1876), "Diet for the Sick" (1883), and "Aristocracy of Health" (1904).

        Her two residences, "Boundary Castle" (Washington) and "Gleneyrie" (Bar Harbor), have been social centers where for many years the most distinguished people of the country have been entertained. Boundary Castle contains a fine picture gallery and is one of the most beautiful residence buildings at the Capital. Mrs. Henderson has taken much interest in the beautification of Washington and her influence towards its development is generally recognized. As a student of hygiene she was made a member of the "Committee of 100" organized by Prof. Irving Fisher, of Yale University, for the establishment of a National Bureau for the Advancement of Health. Ch.: (1) John Brooks Henderson, b. Feb. 18, 1870; graduate of Harvard University (1891) and the Columbian Law School (Washington, D. C.). Author of "American Diplomatic Questions" (1901). Accompanied Hon. John W. Foster to China and Japan when Mr. Foster went to conclude a treaty of peace

JUDGE ELISHA FOOTE. No. 2136

MRS. AUGUSTE FOOTE ARNOLD. No. 3593

MRS. J. B. HENDERSON, nee MARY FOOTE. ·No. 3592

JOHN B. HENDERSON, JR., SON OF MARY FOOTE HENDERSON. No. 3592

between those countries, also Civil Aide to Gen. Miles on his European trip during the Greek and Turkish War. He has been an extensive traveler and writer on biological subjects; m. Angelica Schuyler Crosby (d. July, 1907), granddaughter of Stephen Van Rensselaer, of Albany. Ch.: (a) Beatrice Van Rensselaer Henderson, b. July 5, 1906. (2) Maud, b. 1871; d. Aug. 28, 1872. (3) Frances Arnold, b. 1873; d. Dec. 5, 1875.

3592. ii. AUGUSTA, b. Oct., 1844; d. May, 1904; m. Francis B. Arnold. Mrs. Arnold was a woman of talent, beauty and social grace. She published "The Century Cook Book" (1899), "Luncheons" (1902), and a popular scientific work, "The Sea Beach at Ebb Tide" (1903). Ch.: (1) Benjamin Foote Arnold, b. 1871; d. 1897. (2) Frances Arnold, b. 1877; res., New York, N. Y. (3) Henry Newton Arnold, b. 1874; is a graduate of Harvard, also of Columbia Law School, and is now practising law at Reno, Nev.

2138. DR. GEORGE FRANKLIN FOOTE, (982, 308, 92, 27, 9, 3,) b. Albany, N. Y., Mar. 13, 1817; m. 1st, Sept. 2, 1841, Theda Louisa Steele. She was b. Jan. 13, 1817; d. Jan. 4, 1843; m. 2nd, Lyons, N. Y., Sept. 16, 1844, Anna Maria, dau. of Charles Phelps Parsons. She was b. Plattsburg, N. Y., Mar. 29, 1825; d. Feb. 16, 1884; m. 3rd; Brantford, Canada, July 26, 1884, Margaret P., dau. of Charles Phelps Parsons. She was b. Plattsburg, N. Y., May 19, 1823.

Dr. Foote was the originator and starter of the first Homeopathic Insane Asylum in this country, at Middletown, N. Y. It was all uphill work, as there was so much opposition. At last he got the Legislature to appropriate a certain amount, and he raised $600,000 by getting up a ball at the Grand Opera House in New York. After getting the building well under way there came up some political trouble, which made him feel obliged to resign, though he had always expected to be Superintending Physician. From then on till his death he was looked upon as an expert in insanity, and was frequently called in court to decide on the sanity or insanity of different people.

3594. i. FRANK HIGBY, b. Feb. 13, 1846; m. Dubuque, Iowa, 1868, Hulda Siller. She d.; m. 2nd, Stamford, Ct., Dec. 6, 1882, Annie E. Lee. She d.; m. 3rd, San Francisco, Cal., Nov. 13, 1905, Jessie L. Hawley. Res., Oakland, Cal.

3595. ii. THEODORE, b. Dec. 14, 1848; m. Laura Genung Beakes, 5193-4.

3596. iii. ANNA LOUISA, b. Nov. 2, 1852; m. Stamford, Ct., Feb. 17, 1876, Abraham Lockwood, an Englishman. Ch.: (1) Frank Arthur, b. Nov. 29, 1876; m. Dec. 8, 1903, Jessie Maud, dau. of James and Eliza Ann (Seager) Murdock. She was b. Aldershot, England, Feb. 5, 1877; res., 451 S. Sherman Ave., Denver, Cal. (2) Lizzie Juliet, b. Vineland, N. J., July 15, 1878; m. Dec. 20, 1902, Dr. George Young, an Englishman. Ch.: (a) Zoe Alice Gambia Young, b. Dec. 12, 1903.

3597. iv. GEORGE FRANKLIN, b. Sept. 23, 1857; m. Charlotte Coffin Sellick, 5195.

3598. v. JENNIE PARSONS, b. Jan. 27, 1858; m. New York, N. Y., Jan. 10, 1886, Charles Parsons Beaman. Res., Ithaca, N. Y. Ch.: (1) Anna Louisa, b. Stamford, Ct., June 22, 1883. (2) Charles Leicester, b. Stamford, Ct., May 11, 1886. (3) Margaret Parsons, b. Ithaca, N. Y., Mar. 12, 1896.

(23)

3599. vi. SARAH VORHIS, b. Feb. 27, 1859; m. Stamford, Ct., June, 1886,
           Joseph Francis Farley. She d. June 11, 1894. Ch.: (1) Otis
           Lord, b. June 22, 1887. (2) Joseph Francis, b. June 22, 1889.
           (3) John Leverett, b. 1891. (4) Mildred, b. Apr. 14, 1894.
3600. vii. CHARLES FREDERICK, b. Sept. 15, 1863; d. Aug. 14, 1864.

2141. COL. HENRY RUTGER FOOTE, (982, 308, 92, 27, 9, 3,) b. Mar. 2,
1824; m. twice, 2nd, Nov. 14, 1860, Linna Lucretia, dau. of Frank Lamar, of
Macon, Ga. She was b. Macon, Ga., Apr. 22, 1844. He d. Mar. 16, 1889, in New
York City. He was a doctor at Montequence, Tenn. Captain in 2nd N. Y. Regt.
during the Civil War. Constructing Engineer. Inventor of first method of using
coal-oil as for steam boats and many other machines, etc.
3601. i.   HARRY LAMAR, b. New York, N. Y., Sept. 22, 1861; m. 1888,
           Nellie Angus McLenan, of Scotland. He d. Apr. 6, 1896. No ch.
3602. ii. CORA LOUISE, b. New York, N. Y., June 15, 1863; d. Dec., 1863,
           in New York City.
3603 iii. FELTON MONTGOMERY, b. New York, N. Y., Feb. 3, 1865; m.
           Jacksonville, Fla., Nov. 22, 1901, Jessie May, dau. of Henry
           Dickenson, of Dansville, Va. Hotel proprietor. Res., Tampa,
           Fla., and New York City.
3604. iv. ADRIENNE NELSON, b. Franklin, Pa., Jan. 22, 1867; m. June
           23, 1897, Percy Eugene, son of Isaac Van Brunt Williamson, of
           Flatbush, Long Island. Res., New York City. Ch.: (1) Adrienne
           Linda, b. May 31, 1900. (2) Percy Eugene, b. Dec. 5, 1903. (3)
           Vivian Foote, b. Mar. 6, 1906; d. July 25, 1906.
3605. v.   JOSEPHINE JULIA, b. Detroit, Mich., Mar. 13, 1869.
3606. vi. HELEN WINDSOR, b. Corry, Pa., Sept. 5, 1873; m. Apr. 24, 1905,
           Howard Mason, son of David Henry Van Gelder, of Catskill,
           New York. He is an electrical engineer; a graduate of Brown
           University. Ch.: (1) Norman Foote, b. New York City, May 4,
           1906. Res., 545 W. 148th St., New York, N. Y.

2143. WILLIAM FOOTE, (983, 308, 92, 27, 9, 3,) b. Aug. 4, 1799; m. Mary
      Chapman, of Becket, Mass. Res., Wellington, O.
3607. i.   JULIA, b. Wellington, O., Dec. 1, 1834; m. William Dorchester,
           of Wellington, O. Ch.: (1) Frances Lucy, b. Dec. 27, 1867. (2)
           Howard Foote, b. Dec. 29, 1873.

2144. ALVAN FOOTE, (983, 308, 92, 27, 9, 3,) b. Lee, Mass, June 10, 1801;
m. May 1, 1827, Eliza Priscilla Winchell. He was b. Aug. 10, 1808; d. Sept. 11,
1844, Granville, O. Ch. all b. in Granville, O.
3608. i.   SARAH RUTH, b. Feb. 16, 1829; m. Mar. 31, 1848, Alexander
           Kerr. He d.; m. 2nd, Aug. 30, 1857, Washington Doggett. She
           d. Apr., 1876, at Hillsboro, O. Ch.: (1) Eliza Priscilla Kerr, b.
           Greenfield, O. (2) Carrie Lavinia Kerr, b. Greenfield, O. (3)
           Mary Elizabeth Doggett, b. Hillsboro, O., Dec. 18, 1862; d. Feb.
           21, 1865.
3609. ii. ANN ELIZA, b. Feb. 21, 1831; m. Granville, O., William
           McKendree Pine, Oct. 5, 1852. He was b. Aug. 1, 1827,
           Martinsburg, Va.; d. Jan. 3, 1894, Washington C. H., O. Ch. b.
           Greenfield, O.: (1) Willis McKendree, b. July 22, 1853; d. Mar.
           15, 1896, Washington C. H., O. (2) Dr. Percival Rollan Pine, b.
           Nov. 14, 1854; m. Nettie Pratt, July 28, 1880. Res., Tipton, Ia.

Ch.: (a) Genevieve, b. Sept. 19, 1882, Tipton, Ia. (3) Minne
Luella Pine, b. Nov. 26, 1856; m. Henry E. Browne, June 19,
1879, Washington C. H. He d. Jan. 5, 1881, at
Washington C. H. Ch.: (a) Alfred Henry Browne, b.
Apr. 18, 1880, Washington C. H. (4) Eliza Orlena,
b. Mar. 9, 1859; m. Thomas Henry Craig, Aug. 3, 1881,
Washington C. H., O. He was b. Mar. 30, 1859, and is a member
of the firm of Craig Bros.' Dry Goods Store, of Washington C.
H., O. Ch.: (a) Walter David, b. June 19, 1882. (b) Clarence
Eli, b. Jan. 29, 1884. (c) Mary Winchell, b. Nov. 25, 1890. (d)
Winchell McKendree, b. Apr. 27, 1892. (e) Thomas Harold, b.
Dec. 27, 1894. (f) Robert Alvan, b. June 3, 1897. (5) Ellsworth
Foote, b. Jan. 8, 1861. (6) Dr. Lucy Winchell, b. Mar. 31, 1865;
a practising physician at Washington C. H., O. (7) Edwin
Daniel Pine, b. Nov. 8, 1867, Washington C. H.; m. Nona E.
Scott, Feb. 19, 1891, Chattanooga, Tenn. Res., Dayton, Ky. Ch.:
(a) Pauline Ethel, b. July 26, 1892, Cincinnati, O. (b) Lucy
Edna, b. May 24, 1895, Newport, Ky. (8) Amy Ethel, b. Feb. 8,
1873.

3610.　iii.　AUSTA LAVINIA, b. Aug. 24, 1834; m. Judge James Harvey
Rothrock, of Cedar Rapids, Ia. He was b. Milroy, Pa., 1829,
and was Judge of the Supreme Court of Iowa for 18 years. She
d. Apr. 7, 1893. He d. Jan. 13, 1899, at Cedar Rapids, Ia. Ch.:
(1) Edward, b. (2) James Harvey, b. (3) George, b.

3611.　iv.　JULIA SOPHIA, b. Aug. 26, 1837.

2145.　ELISAH PERCIVAL FOOTE, (983, 308, 92, 27, 9, 3,) b. Lee, Mass.,
Mar. 10, 1803; m. 1st,' Roxalana, dau. of Benjamin Freeman, of
Ogden, Monroe Co., N. Y., Feb. 12, 1824; m. 2nd, Harriet Cossitt, of Oconomowoc,
Wis., Jan. 2, 1850. Mrs. Roxalana Foote was b. Mar. 17, 1808, and d. July 22,
1849, in Nepenskun, Winnebago Co., Wis. About 1826 Mr. Foote, with wife and
one child, moved from Ogden, N. Y., to the town of Wellington, Lorain Co.,
O., and located on heavily timbered land, which after several years of hard work
to clear off the timber made them a comfortable home for 20 years. Then, there
being six children to be provided for, more land was needed, so the old farm of
100 acres was sold, and in the spring of 1846 the family removed to what was then
Wisconsin Territory, where land was cheap and inhabitants few. His oldest son,
William Henry, together with an uncle and family, had preceded them the previous fall and secured sufficient land for both families, at $1.25 an acre, in a desirable
location and in what is now the town of Nepenskun, Winnebago Co., Wis., where
Mr. Foote d. Dec. 3, 1858.

3612.　i.　WILLIAM H., b. Ogden, N. Y., Dec. 6, 1824; m. Mary J. Vankirk, 5197-5204.

3613.　ii.　MARY, b. Wellington, O., July 7, 1829; m. Sept. 26, 1847, Abram
Albert Devore, in Nepenskun, Wis. He was b. in Harrison Co.,
O., Sept. 15, 1825, and was a soldier in the Civil War; was taken
prisoner at Pittsburg Landing, and kept in Andersonville Prison
several months. Res., Fulda, Murray Co., Minn. Ch.: (1) Albert
Stanley, b. July 1, 1848; m. Helen Weller, Mar. 31, 1881, in
Oshkosh, Wis. Res., Antigo, Langlade Co., Wis. Ch.: (a) Stella
May, b. June 24, 1885, in Des Moines, Minn., and d. Oct. 4,

1894. (b) Edgar Stanley, b. Mar. 28, 1887, in Des Moines, Minn. (c) Glenn Earl, b. Dec. 2, 1888, in Dovray, Minn. (d) Alvan Abram, b. Jan. 16, 1892, in Des Moines, Minn. (2) Edgar Freeman, b. Mar. 15, 1852; d. Feb. 17, 1877. (3) Mary Elizabeth, b. Feb. 28, 1854; m. Simon Peter Lambert, in Oshkosh, Winnebago Co., Wis. He was b. May 9, 1854. Ch.: (a) Mary Annette, b. July 23, 1880, in Oshkosh, Wis. (b) George Edwin, b. Nov. 8, 1882, in Oshkosh, Wis., and d. Nov. 4, 1892. (c) Herbert Alvan, b. Mar. 13, 1885, in Antigo, Wis. (4) Lillian Helentha Devore, b. Apr. 24, 1857; m. Oley Oleson, Mar. 22, 1876, in Oshkosh, Wis. She d. Mar. 10, 1891. He was employed as engineer in mills several years; was b. Nov. 14, 1851. After the death of his wife he moved to Milwaukee, Wis., and m. again to a widow with ch. Ch.: (a) Charles Abram, b. Mar. 9, 1878; d. Nov. 20, 1880, in Dovray, Minn. (b) Frederic Oliver, b. Oct. 18, 1880, and d. Oct. 18, 1901, of consumption, the day he was 21 years old, in Milwaukee, Wis. (c) Gerald, b. Mar. 7, 1883. (d) Gertrude Viola, b. Dec. 30, 1886. (5) Orlena Annette Devore, b. May 16, 1859; m. Ben Golden, Sept. 26, 1879, in Oshkosh, Wis. He was b. July 11, 1851. They now live in St. Paul, Minn., and have one dau., Lucy Clare, b. Feb. 8, 1885, in Oshkosh, Wis. (6) Harry Elmer, b. Nov. 9, 1866. These six all b. in Nepenskun, Wis. (7) George Percival, b. Oct. 12, 1861, in Berlin, Wis.; d. May 9, 1875. (8) Edith Viola, b. May 22, 1870, in Auroraville, Wis.; d. Dec. 15, 1880. (9 and 10) Twin boys, not named, b. Jan. 2, 1872; d. Jan. 19, 1872.

3614. iii.   SARAH, b. Wellington, O., July 7, 1829; now a widow living in Omro, Wis.; m. William Champlin Smith, Sept. 26, 1847, in Nepenskun, Wis. He was b. in Leroy, Genesee Co., N. Y., Feb. 29, 1824, and d. Aug. 22, 1887, falling from the roof of a barn he was repairing; killed him. Ch.: (1) Percival Henry, b. Aug. 15, 1848; d. Aug. 15, 1848. (2) Julia Orlena, b. Jan. 30, 1850; m. Samuel Justin Foss, Oct. 27, 1886, in Sherbrooke, Canada. He b. Apr. 11, 1837, and d. May 7, 1889. He was a widower, with four sons. The first wife was Mari Foote, second cousin to the last one, who had no ch. (3) William Chester Smith, b. Apr. 24, 1857; m. Clara Louise Daggett, June 30, 1877, in Berlin, Wis. She was b. Jan. 4, 1852. He graduated from the High School in Berlin when a young man, and has taught school somewhere ever since. For the last 14 or 15 years has been Principal of a High School in Kilbourn City, Wis. Ch.: (a) Ella Rosalia, b. Apr. 6, 1878, in Berlin, Wis. She is a music teacher in Downer College in Milwaukee, Wis. (b) Grace, b. July 7, 1880, in Winneconne, Wis.; a teacher. (c) Russell Lawrence, b. Mar. 22, 1884, in Winneconne, Wis. (d) Keith Daggett, b. May 16, 1892, in Kilbourn, Wis. (4) Sarah Rosalia, b. July 6, 1853; d. Aug. 20, 1859. (5) Marcellus Lathrop, b. May 25, 1855; d. Sept. 14, 1859. (6) Lucy Helen, b. Nov. 17, 1857, in Eureka, Wis.; d. Mar. 11, 1894; m. Eugene Earle, of Omro, Wis., Nov. 26, 1879. She d.; m. again after the death of first wife, and is now a merchant in Omro, Winnebago Co., Wis. Ch.: (a) Ethel, b. Apr. 10, 1881; a teacher in Omro, Wis. (b) Edna, b. June 25, 1888; d. July 3, 1888. (7) Jay Foote Smith, b. Sept. 14, 1862; m. Lizzie M. Crawford, Mar. 4, 1889, in Oshkosh, Wis. She was b. July, 1862. He is a hardware merchant in Shell Rock, Ia. Ch.: (a) Robert Crawford, b. Dec. 17, 1889; d. Dec. 31, 1889. (b) Paul Crawford, b. Mar. 24, 1899, in Shell Rock, Ia. (c) Norma Lucile, b. Sept. 16, 1904, in Shell Rock, Ia. (8) Freeman Webster Smith, b. Dec. 11, 1864; m. Blanche Quint, Nov. 15, 1885, in Omro, Wis. She was b. July 31, 1869, and d. Dec. 12, 1903. He is foreman in a printing office in Ashland, Wis. (a) Cecil Avis, b. Dec. 6, 1886, in Ashland, Wis.; she is now her father's housekeeper. (b) Percival Lathrop, b. Apr. 24, 1891, in Ashland, Wis.; living at home with his father and sister, and attending school. (9) Mark Wilmer Smith, b. May 11, 1869; m. Williettie Sage, June 8, 1889, in Omro, Wis. She was b. May 14, 1868. He works in a planing mill in Omro, Wis., and is a very steady industrious man. Ch.: (a) Edith Elizabeth, b. June 8, 1890, in Omro, Wis. (b) Lennie Cleone, b. June 6, 1894, in Omro, Wis. (c) Vera Vivian, b. Dec. 4, 1895, in Omro, Wis. (10) Earnest Stanley, b. in Omro, Wis., Mar. 27, 1874; d. Aug. 21, 1874. The first five were b. in Nepenskun, Winnebago Co., Wis.

3615. iv. ORLENA, b. Wellington, O., Dec. 6, 1831; m. Jan. 14, 1856, John Edward, son of Dea. John Sheldon, of Sheldon, Franklin Co., Vt. He d. Nov. 29, 1893, in Ripon, Wis. No ch., but an adopted dau. (1) Minnie Louise, b. Fondulac, Wis., Nov. 13, 1859; m. Grand Rapids, Mich., Sept. 14, 1887, Alonzo Nelson Hodges. He was b. Nov. 23, 1855, and d. Mar., 1905, at Hot Springs, Ark., where he had gone to solicit orders for ''The Valley City'' Desk Co., in Grand Rapids, Mich. Ch. all b. in Grand Rapids, Mich.: (a) Florence Louise, b. May 19, 1889. (b) George Edward, b. Mar. 16, 1892. (c) Ruth Elizabeth, b. Oct. 24, 1893; d. Mar. 19, 1895.

3616. v. ALVAN F., b. Wellington, O., Jan. 14, 1835; m. Martha L. Jewett, 5205-11.

3617. vi. LUCY JANE, b. Wellington, O., Dec. 14, 1842; d. Jan. 8, 1855.

3618. vii. HULDA ELIZA, b. Nepenskun, Winnebago Co., Wis., May 14, 1849; d. Dec. 14, 1854.

2146. MARSHALL FOOTE, (983, 308, 92, 27, 9, 3,) b. Lee, Mass., Nov. 28, 1805; m. 1st, Sarah, dau. of Capt. Ebenezer Cady, of Austerlitz, N. Y. She was b. July 19, 1810; d. July 13, 1851; m. 2nd, June 28, 1852, Emily Eliza Commings, of Eaton, Que. She was b. Sept. 15, 1811; d. Jan. 19, 1887. He d. Apr. 13, 1894.

3619. i. GEORGE CADY, b. Lee, Mass., Apr. 18, 1832; m. Mary Cheney, 5212-16.

3620. ii. MARI LAFLIN, b. Lee, Mass., Mar. 22, 1834; m. Samuel Justin Foss, of Sherbrooke, Que., Apr. 11, 1861. She d. Feb. 1, 1870, at Sherbrooke, Canada. Samuel Justin Foss, of Sherbrooke, was one of the most prominent citizens of that city; was Postmaster over 30 years, and one of the leading members of the Masonic fraternity in Canada. He d. May 6, 1889. Ch.: (1) Charles

Henry Foss, of Sherbrooke, Que., b. Mar. 11, 1862; m. Myrtie B. Blanchard, of Sherbrooke, Aug. 4, 1886. Mr. Foss is the local Express Agent at Sherbrooke. Ch.: (a) Frank Blanchard, b. Oct. 11, 1887. (b) Helen B., b. Sept. 17, 1895. (c) Marion, b. Sept. 13, 1897. (2) Arthur Holmes Foss, of Sherbrooke, Que., b. July 6, 1863; m. Alice J. Loomis, of Sherbrooke, Sept. 12, 1888. Mr. Foss is a hardware merchant in Sherbrooke. Ch.: (a) Percival Loomis, b. May 14, 1894; d. Feb. 5, 1902. (b) Roy Holmes, b. Jan. 19, 1896. (c) Donald Burroughs, b. Oct. 28, 1897. (3) William Justin Foss., of Pittsfield, Mass., b. Oct. 26, 1867; m. Edith Savage, of Waterloo, Que., Dec. 25, 1897. Mr. Foss is a successful merchant in Pittsfield. Ch.: (a) Ethelind, b. Nov. 15, 1900. (b) Elizabeth, b. Oct. 5, 1904. (4) Dr. Alvan Foote Foss, of Lenoxville, Que., b. Dec. 30, 1869; m. Grace L. Codd, of Waterloo, Que., May 12, 1897. Ch.: (a) Lindsay Justin, b. July 23, 1898.

3621. iii.. HENRY LYMAN, b. Lee, Mass., July 3, 1839; m. Katherine Augusta Parsons, 5217-20.

3622. iv. ELIZA JANE, b. Aug. 21, 1843; m. 1st, Oct. 22, 1872, Eugene, son of Dr. Edwin Hurlbut, of Great Barrington, Mass. He d. Apr. 28, 1887; m. 2nd, Feb. 13, 1894, Charles H. Lay, of Lee, Mass. He d. Nov. 21, 1905.

3623. v. ELLEN SOPHIA, b. Aug. 21, 1843; m. Edwin Sherrill Foss, of Sherbrooke, Que., Apr. 2, 1867. Ch.: (1) Annie Foote, b. Apr. 27, 1869. (2) Alfred Cady, b. Dec. 17, 1870; d. July 1, 1894. (3) Henry Joshua Foss, of Pittsfield, Mass., b. Sept. 8, 1874; m. Mabel Robinson, of Pittsfield, June 28, 1899. Ch.: (a) Edwin Robinson, b. Feb. 20, 1902. (b) Winthrop Henry, b. Feb. 28, 1903. (4) George Foote Foss, of Sherbrooke, Que., b. Sept. 30, 1876; m. Gertrude Maclagan, of Sherbrooke, June 25, 1902. Ch.: (a) Marshall Maclagan, b. Oct. 6, 1903. (5) Sara Cady, b. Jan. 15, 1881.

3624. vi. CHARLES NELSON, b. Dec. 14, 1848; m. Alice Belle Lathrop and Irene Pearl Morey, 5221-24.

2148. JONATHAN FOOTE, (983, 308, 92, 27, 9, 3,) b. Lee, Mass., Dec. 5, 1812; m. Carlyle, O., Oct. 12, 1841, Laura A. Howke. She was b. Tyringham, Mass., Dec. 20, 1814; d. Nov. 25, 1850; m. 2nd, Waupun, Wis., Apr. 3, 1851, Mary M. Smith. She was b. Pa., Feb. 3, 1828; d. Dec. 15, 1879. He d. Jan. 25, 1880. Res., Nepenskun, Winnebago Co., Wis.

3625. i. HARRIET EMELINE, b. Wellington, O., Apr. 2, 1844; m. Nepenskun, Wis., Apr. 24, 1872, Charles J. Davis. Ch. all b. in Aurora, Waushara Co., Wis.: (1) Franklin C., b. Mar. 7, 1876. (2) Archie F., b. May 2, 1879. (3) Mary Ella, b. Apr. 9, 1881; m. Berlin, Wis., Oct. 24, 1900, Dr. H. C. Wood. Ch.: (a) Vernon Davis, b. Dec. 1, 1901.

3626. ii. EDWARD FRANKLIN, b. Winnebago Co., Nepenskun, Wis., Nov. 3, 1847; d. July 17, 1865.

3627. iii. CHARLES SMITH, b. Nepenskun, Winnebago Co., Wis., July 21, 1854; m. Berlin, Wis., Sept. 21, 1875, Lillie Hole.

3628. iv. LESLIE MILBURN, b. Nov. 8, 1866; m. Inwood, Iowa, June 25, 1891, May Skewis.

2152. LUCIUS FOOTE, (988, 309, 92, 27, 9, 3,) b. Jan. 15, 1812; m. Lura Kilburn. He d. Jan. 2, 1889.

    3629. i. MARY JANE, b. ———; m. Henry S. Beach, of Lee, Mass. He d. 1861, at Baton Rouge, La.; m. 2nd, Henry H. Fitch, of Thetford, Vt. He d. May 2, 1905, at Pekin, Ill. Ch.: (1) Harry H. Beach, b. Lee, Mass.; m. Julia Kinsey. Ch.: (a) Linton. (b) Howard. (c) Mary. Res., Waukegan, Ill. (2) Agnes Fitch, b. Lee; d. Nov. 19, 1905, at Pekin, Ill. (3) Alice Fitch, b. Lee, Mass.

    3629¹. ii. ANJENETTE, b. Nov. 14, 1842, at Lee, Mass.; m. Dec. 17, 1861, Theodore S. Wright, of Lee, Mass. Res., Iowa Falls, Iowa, and Chicago, Ill. Ch.: (1) Georgia A., b. Oct. 30, 1862, at Pittsfield, Mass. (2) Nellie K., b. Pittsfield, May 9, 1865. (3) Charles A., b. Oct. 8, 1869, at Auburn, N. Y. Res., Iowa Falls, Iowa. (4) Albert S., b. Cato, N. Y., Apr. 4, 1871.

    3630. iii. GEORGE L., b. Apr. 23, 1843; m. Martha Littleton, 5225-9.

    3631. iv. THEODORE M., b. July 19, 1844; m. Mary E. Mesick, 5230-1.

    3631¹. v. FRANK MILLER, b. Troy, N. Y., 1852; d. 1883, at Pekin, Ill.

2155. JOEL WEST FOOTE, (988, 309, 92, 27, 9, 3,) b. Sept. 27, 1820; m. Catherine Matilda, dau. of Elijah Valentine, of Westchester, N. Y., and Catherine Matilda Schenck, of Flatbush, L. I. Elijah Valentine d. in N. Y. City, 1848. His wife, Catharine, was b. May 17, 1792; d. Oct. 17, 1873, in N. Y. City. Mrs. Foote d. Aug., 1858, at Cos Cob, Ct. Mr. Foote d. 1864, in N. Y. City.

    3632. i. JANE ARMENIA, b. N. Y. City, July 19, 1854; m. Jan. 3, 1877, in N. Y. City, Horace, son of Edward Halswell Stokes, of N. Y. City, and Nancy Stiles (his wife), of Philadelphia, Pa. Horace Stokes was b. Philadelphia, Sept. 11, 1851. Res., Hackettstown, N. J.

    3633. ii. ELEAZUR VALENTINE, b. N. Y. City, Dec. 24, 1855; res., New York City; unm.

    3633¹. iii. CATHERINE MATILDA, b. ———; d. in infancy.

2158. CHARLES S. FOOTE, (992, 309, 92, 27, 9, 3,) b. Oct. 8, 1823, at Lee, Mass.; m. Nov. 4, 1847, Jemima Schoovinaker Bevier, of Wassing, N. Y. He d. Mar. 12, 1898, at Stanleyton, Va. Res., Rochester, N. Y.

    3633². i. ELLA MAY, b. Rochester, N. Y., May 18, 1853; d. June 21, 1855, at Rochester, N. Y.

    3634. ii. CHARLES B., b. Jan. 31, 1855; m. Fannie E. Graves, 5231-2.

    3634¹. iii. JOSEPHENE, b. Oct. 16, 1857; d. July 18, 1858, at Rochester, N. Y.

    3634². iv. E. J., b. Dec. 6, 1861, at Cincinnati, O.

    3634³. v. HARRY B., b. Sept. 17, 1864, at Cincinnati, O.; d. Apr. 6, 1873, at Detroit, Mich.

2164. LESTER SYLVESTER FOOTE, (993, 309, 92, 27, 9, 3,) b. Lee, Mass., Feb. 5, 1830; m. Maria A. Williams, of Waltham, Mass. He served in Co. E, 3rd N. Y., during Civil War. He d. Nov. 27, 1906, in Bloomfield, Ct.

    3635. i. CHARLES L., b. ———. Res., Fall River, Mass.

2165. GEORGE WASHINGTON FOOTE, (993, 309, 92, 27, 9, 3,) b. Nov. 27, 1831; m. Melissa J. Cooper. He d. Mar., 1873. Res., Windsor, Ct.

    3636. i. FRED E., b. Nov. 30, 1860; d. Jan. 2, 1883, in Hartford, Ct.; unm.

3637. ii. MYRTHA ELOISE, b. Jan. 6, 1870; m. Oct. 17, 1894, at Woodstock Valley, Ct., Rev. Albert Charles, son of Geo. W. and Alona (Walker) Johnson. He was b. Aug. 29, 1857. Res., 14 Westland St., Hartford, Ct. Ch.: (1) Winfred Foote Johnson, b. Lynn, Mass., Nov. 29, 1895. (2) Wesley Albert, b. Lynn, Jan. 13, 1898. (3) Sumner Walker, b. Roxbury, Mass., May 21, 1901. (4) Alona Melissa, b. Roxbury, Nov. 28, 1902.

2173. DAVID FOOTE, (997, 311, 92, 27, 9, 5,) b. July 24, 1824; m. Jan. 1, 1844, Abigail Crans. He d. Jan. 20, 1887, Oscoda, Mich. She b. Dec. 4, 1824; d. Lorain, O., Apr. 13, 1905.

3638. i. ISABELL, b. Lorain, O., Feb. 27, 1847; m. Jan. 10, 1868, William Purcupill, of Lorain, O. He d. July 13, 1803, at Lorain, O. Ch.: (1) Eliza A., b. Mar. 18, 1869. (2) Lenorah A., b. Sept. 21, 1871. (3) Archie J., b. Mar. 20, 1875. (4) Ella A., b. Sept. 10, 1887.

3639. ii. ELLA A., b. Lorain, O., Apr. 10, 1852; m. Oct. 4, 1870, Ira B. Mansfield, of Lorain. He d. Dec. 16, 1897, at Chicago, Ill.

3640. iii. ADA E., b. Vanar, Mich., Apr. 15, 1857; m. Dec. 25, 1874, Eugene Sanborn, of Lorain. Ch. all b. at Lorain, O. Ch.: (1) Carrie W., b. Oct. 5, 1875. (2) Alice Bell, b. Sept. 4, 1879. (3) Elsie M., b. Mar. 14, 1882. (4) Elmer Eugene, b Nov. 20, 1884. (5) Hellen Ada, b. Feb. 14, 1886; d. June, 1888, at Lorain. (6) Ethel May, b. May 8, 1891. (7) Howard E., b. July 12, 1894. (8) Grace May, b. Sept. 15, 1896.

3641. iv. HERBERT P., b. Denmark, Mich., May 4, 1860; m. Mary Seinsath, 5233.

2174. LYMAN PERRY FOOTE, (997, 311, 92, 27, 9, 3,) b. Mar. 22, 1817; m. 1st, Nov. 24, 1842, Ruth Beng Smith, of Dover, O. She d. July 19, 1855. He m. 2nd, Oct. 24, 1857, Rebecca Elsie Tiedeman. He d. Nov. 23, 1889. Res., Cleveland, O.

3642. i. ROMELIA M., b. Aug. 17, 1843; m. William H. Quayle. Ch.: (1) William Foote Quayle, b. 1862; m. Feb., 1899, Frances Edwards, of Duluth, Minn. Ch. all b. in Duluth. Ch.: (a) Henry, b. (b) William, b. (c) Ruth Beng, b. (2) Helen Florence, b. 1865; m. 1897, Jay D. Tuller, of Cleveland, O. Ch.: (a) Elizabeth, b. July, 1898. (3) Charles Tod, b. 1875; m. Nov. 24, 1903, Helen R. Taylor, of LaPort, Ind. (4) Ruth Eleanor, b. 1884.

3643. ii. HIRAM S., b. June 8, 1847; d. July 30, 1854.

3644. iii. FLORENCE R., b. July 9, 1850; m. Apr. 11, 1873, Henry E. Leuer. Ch.: (1) Harry Foote, b. Feb. 18, 1874. (2) Ella Ruth, b. Aug. 7, 1876; m. July 20, 1898, Walter S. Albert. Ch.: (a) Marian Leuer, b. Oct. 6, 1899.

3645. iv. WILLIAM, b. May 15, 1855; d. Aug. 1, 1855.

3646. v. CORA ELSIE, b. Feb. 14, 1860; m. Aug. 20, 1881, Christian Narten. Res., 1979 E. 82nd St., Cleveland, O. Ch.: (1) Bertha Elsie, b. July 9, 1882; educated at Wells College. (2) Christian Carl, b. Feb. 24, 1884. Is a graduate of Williams College. (3) Lyman Foote, b. Apr. 8, 1885. Student at Williams College. (4) Peng Foote, b. Oct. 14, 1888. Student at Williams College. (5) Henry Siller, b. June 29, 1892.

3647.. vi. HELEN PENG, b. May 23, 1879; m. July 24, 1901, William Elmer
Roberts. Ch.: (1) Donald Foote, b. Dec. 14, 1902. (2) Lois
Gertrude, b. Mar. 23, 1904.

2175. THOMAS FOOTE, (997, 311, 92, 27, 9, 3,) b. Mar. 26, 1819; m. May,
1840, Candace E. Park. She was b. Sept. 23, 1822, at Dover, O.; d. Feb. 15, 1887.
He m. 2nd, Sept., 1878, Clara E. Wilford. She was b. Jan. 6, 1854, at Amherst, O.
He d. Nov., 1903. Res., Lorain, O.

3648. i. TEMPERANCE, b. 1841, at Dover, O.; m. Chas. Augustus Reed,
lawyer, of Ill. He d. · She m. 2nd, Milligan Reed (brother of
first). Ch., by 1st husband: Son, b. and d. Ch., by 2nd husband:
(2) Nellie E., b. ———; m. ———. Res., Smith Centre, Kan.
(3) Horace, b. ———. Res., Smith Centre, Kan.

3649. ii. CORWIN T., b. Apr. 11, 1847; m. Clara M. Cotton, 5234-40.

3650 iii. WALDO EMERSON, b. Dec. 22, 1880, in Amherst, O; m. June 10,
1903, Olive C. Parsons, of So. Amherst, O. Res., 'Amherst,
Lorain Co. No ch.

2177. SOLOMON R. FOOTE, (999, 311, 92, 27, 9, 3,) b. May 31,1823; m. Kingsbury, Laport Co., Ind., Nov. 9, 1846, Adaline D. Stocking. She d. Oct. 6, 1879, in
Melrose, Stearns Co., Minn. He d. Mar. 15, 1903, in San Pedro, Cal.

3651. i. EMELINE JULIA, b. Elysia, Lorain Co., O., Dec. 15, 1847; m.
Melrose, Minn., Dec. 24, 1867, Albert Garrett, son of Harvey
and Eliza Bassett Barton. He was b. Eaton, Co., July 24, 1838.
Res., San Pedro, Cal. Ch.: (1) Erminnie V., b. Melrose, Minn.,
Mar. 3, 1869; d. Apr., 1869. (2) Cora Evelyn, b. Melrose, Minn.,
May 17, 1871; m. Dec. 25, 1893, Wilber S. McIntyre. Res., Pasadena, Cal. (3) Addie Alberta, b. Birchdale, Minn., Feb. 16, 1873;
m. June 28, 1896, Frederick S. Nichols. Res., San Pedro, Cal.
(4) Ina Ozella, b. Melrose, Minn., Sept. 24, 1875; m. Mar. 16,
1904, Thomas H. Fawcett. Res., Chicago, Ill.

3652. ii. EUGENE FRANCIS, b. Elysia, Lorain Co., O., Mar. 19, 1849; d.
Mar. 12, 1852.

3653. iii. EMMA LOVETTE, b. Laport, Ind., Aug. 20, 1852; m. Minneapolis,
Minn., Oct. 22, 1874, James C., son of James B. McDonald. She
d. Jan. 29, 1882, Los Angeles, Cal. Ch.: (1) Harold Adelbert, b. Stuart, Ia., Dec. 20, 1876. (2) Ina Isabella, b. Criston,
Ia., Nov. 19, 1881.

3654. iv. LORIN SEELY, b. Sept. 25, 1854; m. Sadie Mary Trace,
5241-8.

3655. v. CAROLINE ELECTA, b. Laport, Ind., Oct. 29, 1856; m. Melrose,
Minn., Oct. 14, 1883, Amos Thomas, son of Amos Thomas Tracy
and Phebie A. (Stone), b. Hudson, Wis., Sept. 4, 1854. Res.,
Tulare, Tulare Co., Cal. Ch.: (1) Ray Amos, b. Jan. 24, 1885,
Burlington, N. Dak. (2) Pearl Adeline, b. Feb. 13, 1887, Burl-
ington, N. Dak. (3) Fred Allen, b. Oct. 8, 1888, Minot, N. Dak.;
d. June, 1906, same place. (4) Edith Alberta, b. Oct. 5, 1890,
Minot, N. Dak. (5) Chester Arthur, b. Aug. 23, 1892, San Pedro,
Cal. (6) Belle McKinley, b. Sept. 23, 1896, Compton, Cal. (7)
Mark Stanley, b. Oct. 31, 1898, Jardena, Cal.

3656. vi. MINNIE SOTA, b. Ft. Lake, Minn., Apr. 29, 1861; d. Aug. 24,
1863.

3657. vii. FRED WILLIAM, b. St. Cloud, Minn., Mar. 8, 1863; d. July 23, 1888; unm.

3658. viii. FRANCIS D., b. Aug. 25, 1867; m. Annie L. Millar, 5249-50.

2179. SILAS FOOTE, (999, 311, 92, 27, 9, 3,) b. May 11, 1826; m. Oct. 26, 1849, Julia Ann, dau. of Harvey and Eliza Bassett. She was b. Oneida Co., N. Y., June 7, 1831; d. Burlington, N. Dak., Mar. 8, 1886. Farmer and stone mason. Was killed by the Indians while driving beef cattle to soldiers at Ft. Abercrombie (May 3, 1863) at Lightening Lake, near Alexandria, Minn.

3659. i. CAROLINE ELIZA, b. Dec. 18, 1850; m. Melrose, Minn., Sept. 8, 1879, William W. Watson. He was b. Va., Aug. 15, 1844. Res., Kalispell, Montana. Ch.: (1) Julia Maria, b. Melrose, Minn., Oct. 16, 1880; d. Mar. 1, 1905, at Kalispell, Mon. (2) Mordecar Lewis, b. Melrose, Minn., Jan. 20, 1883; d. Apr. 28, 1903, at Kalispell, Mont. (3) William Wallace, Jr., b. Round Prairie, Minn., Sept. 30, 1895.

3660. ii. MARY ELLEN, b. Nov. 14, 1852; m. Harrison, Minn., Jan. 18, 1870, George W. Laflin. Res., Des Moines, Iowa.

3661. iii. CLARA ADALINE, b. Feb. 12, 1855; m. St. Cloud, Minn., Feb. 7, 1876, John Austin Masters. He was b. at St. Paul, Minn., Dec. 29, 1851. Farmer and moulder. Is an Episcopalian. Also a Modern Woodman of America. She is a member of the Lodge, Royal Neighbors of America. Ch. all b. at Harrison, Minn.: (1) Infant Dau., b. Apr. 2, 1877. (2) Maud Addie Masters, b. Oct. 5, 1878; m. Dec. 11, 1901, Samuel M. Dahl. Presbyterian. (3) Claud Austin Masters, b. May 23, 1881. Farmer. (4) Leo Arnold Masters, b. Oct. 22, 1883; m. Dec. 18, 1906, Anna Murk. Farmer. (5) May Annie Masters, b. Feb. 17, 1886. (6) Elsie Albina Masters, b. Mar. 30, 1889. (7) Winnifred Amelia Masters, b. Feb. 26, 1891. (8) Millard Arthur Masters, b. May 23, 1893. (9) Sybil Alberta Masters, b. Mar. 18, 1897.

3662. iv. EUGENE S., b. Feb. 9, 1857; m. Laura H. Hill, 5251-5.

3663. v. CHARLES H., b. May 11, 1859; n. Theresa Polley, 5256-61.

3664. vi. IDA MAY, b. Nov. 13, 1861; m. Melrose, Minn., June 5, 1884, Peter A. Anderson. Res., Belgrade, Minn.

2180. LAVIAS FOOTE, (1003, 311, 92, 27, 9, 3,) b. Dover, O., May 16, 1825; m. Dover, O., June 14, 1849, Fuetta B., dau. of Austin Lilly. She was b. Ashfield, Mass., Mar. 4, 1828. He d. July 14, 1882, at Byron, Mich.

3665. i. ALBERT A., b. Sept. 10, 1850; m. Adelaid Gibson, 5262-7.

3666. ii. FRANK B., b. June 2, 1852; m. Anna M. Brudi, 5268-70.

3667. iii. VARUS R., b. May 9, 1854; m. Rosa M. Narregang, 5271-2.

3668. iv. EARNEST C., b. July 10, 1856; m. Jessie C. Buruger, 5273-7.

2182. RANSOM L. FOOTE, (1003, 311, 92, 27, 9, 3,) b. Dover, O., July 22, 1828; m. Dover, O., Oct. 1, 1853, Julia B., dau. of Algenon and Sophrons (Smith) Farr, of Dover, O. She was b. Dover, O., June 23, 1833; d. Mar., 1907; buried at Royalton, Minn. Res., Long Beach, Cal.

3669. i. RICHARD, b. Oct. 22, 1854; d. in infancy.

3670. ii. HARRIET S., b. May 3, 1856; m. Jan., 1881, J. M. Gould. She d. Mar. 9, 1883.

3671. iii. IDA B., b. July 3, 1857; m. Aug. 10, 1887, J. M. Black. He d. Feb. 13, 1888. Res., Royalton, Minn.

3672. iv. CORA DELL, b. Feb. 28, 1862; m. Dec. 3, 1890, George Ames Savory, of Royalton, Minn. He was b. May 9, 186—. Ch.: (1) Edwin Farr, b. Nov. 8, 1891. (2) Edith B., b. Apr. 7, 1893. (3) Edna D., b. Apr. 7, 1893.

3673. v. CHARLES R., b. Dec. 22, 186—; m. Mattie Rictor, 5278-81.

3674. vi. ALPHONSO E., b. Nov. 22, 1865; m. Ellen Rictor, 5282-6.

3675. vii. HENRY P., b. July 22, 1867; m. Anna Shambrock, 5287-9.

2186. ASAHEL P. FOOTE, (1003, 311, 92, 27, 9, 3,) b. May 2, 1836; m. 1880, Ann Sutherland. She was b. July 20, 1861, Bangor, Me.; d. 1889, in Minn.

3676. i. ELDORA BELLE, b. Oct. 19, 1882.

3677. ii. WALTER ERWIN, b. Apr 27, 1885.

3678. iii. ETHEL BEATRICE, b. Apr. 30, 1887.

2191. EDWARD FOOTE, (1008, 312, 92, 27, 9, 3).

3679. i. EDWARD HUBERT, b. Oct. 13, 1850; m. Georgiana Frances Woodard, 5290-2.

3680. ii. EMILY ELIZABETH, b. Smithtown Br., L. I., Apr. 3, 1852; m. Oct. 13, 1875, Elisha Gilman, son of E. L. Woodard, of Somerville, b. Feb. 20, 1848. Ch.: (1) Margaret, b. Aug. 15, 1881; d. Aug. 15, 1881. (2) Beatrice, b. Nov. 19, 1882. Res., Somerville, Mass.

3681. iii. CLARA FRANCES, b. May 13, 1854; d. Somerville, Aug. 1, 1865.

3682. iv. THERON ELLIOTT, b. Feb. 16, 1860; d. Somerville, Mass., Aug. 11, 1865.

2194. THERON LYMAN FOOTE, (1008, 312, 92, 27, 9, 3,) b. in Lee, July 9, 1835; m. Sept. 18, 1860, Abigail Lucelia, dau. of Jason and Rhoda Langdon, b. in Great Barrington, Mass., Jan. 23, 1832, and d. in Lee, Feb. 11, 1903. He d. May 11, 1900.

3683. i. WILLIAM BRYANT, b. July 26, 1861; m. Mary Louise Peirson, 5293-7.

3684. ii. JESSIE ELIZABETH, b. Lee, Mass., Feb. 10, 1863; m. June 9, 1886, Edward S., son of Samuel Shepard and Lydia Rogers. He was b. Lee, Mass., Apr. 27, 1864. Ch.: (1) Edward Foote, b. July 4, 1887. (2) Mary Barlow, b. Dec. 22, 1888. (3) Arthur Lyman, b. July 12, 1893. (4) Donald Sheldon, b. Jan. 1, 1898.

3685. iii. ANNIE BUTLER, b. Lee, Mass., Dec. 14, 1864; m. Oct. 13, 1886, Augustus R., son of Wellington and Mary Shannon Smith. He was b. Lee, Mass., Apr. 1, 1863. Ch.: (1) Juliet Shannon, b. Oct. 8, 1887. (2) Elsie Waldron, b. July 19, 1890. (3) Lucille Foote, b. Nov. 26, 1891.

2197. WALTER BLAIR FOOTE, (1009, 312, 92, 27, 9, 3,) b. Dec. 5, 1833; m. Rochester, O., Oct. 4, 1858, Jane, dau. of Hiram and Esther Dunn Tanner. She was b. May 17, 1834. She was a teacher in the public schools in Buffalo, N. Y. Was present at the organization of the National W. C. T. U. in 1874. Was President of the Cayuga Co. W. C. T. U. for 11 years, and is State Supt. of Dep. of School Savings Bank. He was a farmer in Wellington, O., moving to Cleveland, O., in 1866, where he d. July 2, 1904.

3686. i. MARY, b. Aug. 14, 1859; m. June, 1887, Franklin Sanborn Atwater. He d. Aug. 7, 1901. Ch.: (1) Edgar Foote, b. Cleveland, O.,

June 19, 1893. (2) Walter Sanborn, b. Cleveland, O., Mar. 8, 1897. (3) Emma A., b. Auburn, Geauga Co., O., Sept. 16, 1898.

3687. ii. CLAYTON HUNTER, b. Aug. 2, 1863; m. Maud C. Wentworth and Elizabeth Miller, 5298-5300.

3688. iii. EMMA LILLIAN, b. Cleveland, O., Mar. 28, 1868; m. Jan. 12, 1889, Edmund Howard Jones, of Cleveland, O. Ch.: (1) Clayton Ernest, b. Lakeside, O., July 13, 1890. (2) Paul Vincent, Lowell, Mass., Dec. 6, 1894.

3688¹. iv. ALICE MEDORA, b. Jan. 23, 1873; unm. Sec. of the C. H. Foote Lumber Co.

2202. CHARLES R. FOOTE, (1011, 312, 92, 27, 9, 3,) b. June 2, 1838; graduate Williams College, 1859; m. 1873, Sarah Caroline, dau. of Harvey Taroner and Caroline (Watterman) Cole, b. Whitehall, N. Y., Apr. 18, 1842.

3689. i. HAROLD, infant son, d. 1874.

3690. ii. ETHELWYN, b. Feb. 17, 1875.

2204. WILLIAM DOW FOOTE, (1015, 314, 92, 27, 9, 3,) b. Jan. 22, 1836, Rutland, Vt.; m. Mary Frances Leggett. She was b. Mar. 4, 1852, near Des Moines, Ia.; d. Apr. 29, 1888, Toronto, Canada.

3691. i. EMILY NASH, b. Dec. 14, 1873, Des Moines, Ia.; res., 1150 25th St., Des Moines, Ia.; m. June 15, 1904, Des Moines, John E. Hood. Ch.: (1) Helen, b. Des Moines, May 26, 1905.

3692. ii. CLARA, b. Aug. 28, 1876, Des Moines, Ia.; m. Mar. 16, 1904, Edward B. Hazen. Res., Astoria, Oregon.

3692¹. iii. VINNIE ELIZABETH, b. Nov. 6, 1878, Des Moines; d. Oct. 24, 1880.

3692². iv. FANNIE FERN, b. Oct. 30, 1882, Des Moines; d. Feb. 21, 1883.

3692³. v. MARY FLORENCE, b. Mar. 11, 1884, Des Moines; d. Oct. 4, 1884.

3692⁴. vi. RUTH, b. Mar. 29, 1886; d. May 7, 1887, Des Moines, Ia.

2205. HENRY SOLOMON FOOTE, (1015, 314, 92, 27, 9, 3,) b. ———.

3693. i. DAU., b. ———; m. Hugh McGrandle; d. July, 1902.

2212. SEWARD ALLEN FOOTE, (1016, 314, 92, 27, 9, 3,) b. Port Henry, N. Y., May 31, 1844; m. July 19, 1875, Flora E. Hall. She was b. Nov. 10, 1851; d. Feb. 17, 1901, at Port Henry, N. Y.

3694. i. MARY FLORA, b. Apr. 29, 1877; res., Port Henry, N. Y.

3695. ii. WILLIAM HARRIS, b. Oct. 12, 1878; d. Aug. 22, 1879.

3696. iii. SEWARD HALL, b. Jan. 2, 1880; m. Nov., 1905, Marriea Lurean Broughton.

3697. iv. THEODORE BREESE, b. Sept. 10, 1884.

3698. v. HENRY HODGMAN, b. Dec. 29, 1887; d. Jan. 2, 1888.

3699. vi. EDITH HODGMAN, b. Apr., 1893.

2215. HENRY FOOTE, (1046, 339, 104, 28, 9, 3,) b. May 22, 1818; m. Mary Ann Lamb. She was b. 1826, and d. 1886. He d. July 29, 1884. Res., Colchester, Ct.

3700. i. JAMES STEPHEN, b. 1851; m. Jane G. Goodrell, of Hartford, Ct. He graduated from Yale, 1877; College of Physicians and Surgeons, N. Y., in 1881. Res., Wichita, Kan., in 1887; Chicago. Ill., in 1891; Omaha, 1893. Professor of Hist. and Path., Creighton Med. College, since 1893; s. p.

3700¹. ii. CLARA E., b. 1853; d. 1865.

3700². iii. JENNIE A., b. 1859; m. Walter J. Holbrook. Res., The Buckingham, St. Louis; s. p.

3700³. iv. MARTHA L., b. 1863; d. 1877.

2217. WILLIAM FOOTE, (1049, 339, 104, 28, 9, 3,) b. in Colchester, Ct., Nov. 17, 1816; m. Sept. 1, 1843, Emeline Brown, of Columbia, Ct. He was engaged in farming and store keeping for a few years, and then entered the employ of the Haywood Rubber Co. of his native town, where he remained in different capacities as overseer of the shoe room and packing room, also shipping clerk for over 30 years as a faithful and trustful employee. He d. Jan. 10, 1893. She d. Aug., 1896.

3701. i. EMMA JANE, b. Apr. 5, 1847; d. Sept. 11, 1865.

3702. ii. ANNETTE JULIA, b. Oct. 4, 1848; d. Aug. 23, 1869.

3703. iii. JAMES C., b. Sept. 25, 1852; m. Fannie Avery, 5301-4.

3704. iv. FRED W., b. Nov. 1, 1854; m. Annie King, 5305-6.

3705. v. MARY, b. May 17, 1860; m. Dec. 25, 1882, Dr. C. N. Gallup, of Columbia, Ct. Res., Long Hill, Ct. Ch.: (1) Edna May, b. June 29, 1886. (2) Mabel Emeline, b. Mar. 19, 1889.

2219. ALBERT FOOTE, (1049, 339, 104, 28, 9, 3,) b. July 22, 1821; m. Mary Ann, dau. of Arnold and Hannah (Douglass) Chase, of Amherst, Mass. She d. Apr. 10, 1905, ae. 76 years. He d. Sept. 30, 1869.

3706. i. ALBERT H., b. Jan. 1, 1853; m. Ella Payson, 5307-8.

3707. ii. JENNIE R., b. Nov. 22, 1855; m. C. B. Lyman, of Columbia, Ct. She d. May 18, 1903. Ch.: (1) Albert E. Lyman, b. Sept. 30, 1876. (2) Fannie E., b. Apr. 24, 1878; m. H. P. Collins, of Columbia. (3) Marion H. Lyman, b. June 16, 1892; d. May 18, 1904.

3708. iii. LOTTIE E., b. Aug. 11, 1857; m. Fred Brown. Ch.: (1) Minnie A. Brown, b. ———; m. J. A. Masterson, of 79 Wilson St., Providence, R. I.

3709. iv. EDWARD E., b. Sept. 4, 1860; m. Alice E. Hills, 5309-11.

3710. v ANNIE B., b. Sept. 20, 1862; m. Dec. 16, 1866, Geo. B. Miller, of Colchester, where they res. Ch.: (1) Florence A. Miller, b. Dec. 18, 1889. (2) Clayton G. Miller, b. Nov. 16, 1890. (3) May A. Miller, b. Jan. 30, 1892. (4) Amy Foote Miller, b. Feb. 2, 1894; d. Mar. 13, 1899.

2225. HORACE FOOTE, (1050, 339, 104, 28, 9, 3,) b. Nov. 14, 1822; m. Oct. 10, 1849, Lucy A. Webster. He d. Jan. 31, 1888.

3711. i. HORACE, b. Feb. 7, 1867; m. Mar. 29, 1888, Mary E. Shepard. No ch. Res., Liberty Hill, Ct.

3712. ii. ROGER, b. Aug. 29, 1860; m. 5312-15.

2228. RALPH CLARK FOOTE, (1050, 339, 104, 28, 9, 3,) b. Oct. 22, 1828; m. Mar. 3, 1858, Lydia Newton Harvey. She was b. Colchester, Ct., Oct. 8, 1833. Res., Colchester, Ct.

3713. i. SALLY MARIA, b. Dec., 1857.

3714. ii. ELIAS HARVEY, b. Jan. 25, 1860.

3715. iii. SYDIA CLARK, b. Jan. 14, 1862.

3716. iv. ESTHER CLARK, b. Jan. 16, 1864.

3716¹. v. MARY ELEANOR, b. May 6, 1866.

3717. vi. AMELIA JANE, b. May 14, 1868.

3717¹. vii. FANNIE MINERVA, b. July 25, 1870; d. Nov. 10, 1876.

3718. viii. HARRIET HARVEY, b. Oct. 20, 1872.
3719. ix.   BETSEY MINERVA, b. May 26, 1876.
3720. x.   ETHEL WILHEMINA, b. Oct. 25, 1877.

2233. DAN FOOTE, (1062, 347, 105, 28, 9, 3,) b. Colchester, Ct., Feb. 27, 1808; m. 1st, Eliza Foote; m. 2nd, Lucretia, dau. of Russell Kellogg. Res., Colchester, Ct. Ch. by first wife all d. in infancy.
3720¹. i.   SUSAN, b. Apr. 23, 1840; d. abt. 1845.
3721. ii.   CHARLES, b. Colchester, Ct., Feb. 17, 1843. Is a carriage maker. unm.
3722. iii. HARRIET, b. Colchester, Ct., Feb. 17, 1847; m. 1st, John R. Buell, of Colchester. He was a carpenter; d. Jan., 1872; m. 2nd, Apr. 29, 1880, Edwin R., son of Benjamin Hills, of East Hampton. Farmer. Res., Colchester, Ct. No ch.
3723. iv. KATE, b. Colchester, 1849; unm.

2235. DANIEL T. FOOTE, (1069, 347, 105, 28, 9, 3,) b. July 25, 1816, Colchester, Ct.; m. Jan. 2, 1839, Martha, dau. of Aaron Burr, of Great Barrington, Mass. She was b. June 16, 1814; d. Jan. 23, 1907. He was a cabinet maker; d. Feb. 22, 1899.
3724. i.   JANE ALMIRA, b. Aug. 15, 1840; d. Nov. 17, 1862.
3724¹. ii. LOIS ELLEN, b. July 12, 1842; d. Mar. 4, 1843.
3725. iii. JOSEPH F., b. Aug. 20, 1845; m. Lucy Lewis, 5316.
3726. iv. EDWARD Y., b. June 7, 1850; m. Addie F. Smith, 5317-8.

2237. EDWARD Y. FOOTE, (1069, 347, 105, 28, 9, 3,) b. May 31, 1819; m. Lucy A. Mason. She d.; m. 2nd, Mary E., dau. of William Cliff, of Mystic. Real Estate Agent. He d. Dec. 8, 1881.
3727. i.   EMMERSON Y., b. ———; m. and d. Left 2 ch. Res., Downers Grove, Ill.
3728. ii.   WILLIAM C., b. ———; m. ———. With Fire Department, New Haven, Ct.

2238. JOSEPH A. FOOTE, (1069, 347, 105, 28, 9, 3,) b. Jan. 18, 1821; m. Frances J., dau. of Stephen Foote, of Colchester, Ct. Hotel proprietor; d. Oct. 6, 1868.
3729. i.   GEORGE W., b. ———; m. ———; 2 ch. Res., New Haven, Ct.

2239. JOHN C. FOOTE, (1069, 347, 105, 28, 9, 3,) b. June 28, 1823; m. Nov. 7, 1855, Sarah, dau. of George Clark, b. June 13, 1791, and Sophia Taylor Clark. Sarah Foote was b. Sept. 9, 1831. A soldier in the Civil War; in the Battle of Cold Harbor. He d. Sept. 24, 1900. Res., Colchester, Ct.
3730. i.   GEORGE C., b. Sept. 1, 1856; m. Lillian M. Chapman, 5319.
3731. ii.   WALLACE E., b. Oct., 1860; d. Jan., 1861.
3732. iii. ELISABETH C., b. July 30, 1868; d. Nov. 14, 1890.

2242. SALMON C. FOOTE, (1069, 347, 105, 28, 9, 3,) b. Jan. 23, 1828; m. Oct. 16, 1851, Julia A., dau. of Joseph A. and Julia A. Williams, of Mystic, Ct. She was b. June 29, 1832. (8 ch., 4 d. young.) He d. July 6, 1905. Res., Mystic, Ct.
3733. i.   FRANK HOWARD, b. Nov. 19, 1852; m. Alice Curtiss, 5320-1.
3734. ii.   JULIA GALLOP, b. May 18, 1867; unm.
3735. iii. CHARLES WARREN, b. Dec. 10, 1871; m. Mary Avery, 5322-5.
3736. iv. SALMON STANTON, b. Mar. 17, 1875; res., Baltimore, Md.

2245. FRANK FOOTE, (1069, 347, 105, 28, 9, 3,) b. Aug. 14, 1832; m. Lydia (Crippen), of Great Barrington, Mass.

3737. i. MARY T., b.
3738. ii. BERTHA, b.
3739. iii. MARGARET, b.

2448. JOHN LAWRENCE FOOTE, (1495, 557, 185, 53, 16, 5,) b. Oct. 11, 1825; m. Oct. 15, 1848, Ann Morgan Brighton. He d. Sept. 10, 1885, Wellington, O. Res., Wellington.

3740. i. CHAS. DEVILLE, b. Jan. 23, 1853; m. Jan. 1, 1904, Mary Kennedy, Oberlin, O. Res., Cleveland, O.
3741. ii. WALTER EBER, b. Feb. 10, 1858; m. Katherine Warner. Res., Wellington, O.
3742. iii. FRANK HAVLY, b. May 18, 1861; m. Elizabeth Walker. Res., Covington, Tenn.
3743. iv. ANNIE E., b. Nov. 1, 1865, Wellington; m. Fred W. Mueller. Res., Wellington, O.

2255. FREDERICK MANFRED FOOTE, (1082, 362, 113, 36, 10, 3,) b. Nov. 11, 1849; m. June 23, 1880, Frankie, dau. of Wm. Langworthy, of Middlebury. She d. Feb. 24, 1907. Mr. Foote has been Street Commissioner and Trial Justice of the Peace for many years. Res., Middlebury, Vt.

3744. i. MADELINE, b. Sept. 28, 1882; grad. Middlebury High School, June, 1901.
3745. ii. WILLIAM, b. Feb. 19, 1887.

2288. STEPHEN·FOOTE, (1097, 374, 115, 37, 10, 3,) b. Skaneateles, N. Y., Mar. 11, 1807; m. 1st, Skaneateles, Nov. 13, 1832, Nancy Watson. She d. Mar., 1886, at Auburn, N. Y.; m. 2nd, 1844, Elenor Tenure; m. 3rd, Oct. 28, 1847, Mary J. Shaw, of Stafford, N. Y. Res., Fairfield, O. Ch. all b. at Skaneateles, N. Y.

3746. i. EDGAR W., b. Apr. 24, 1842; d. Feb 18, 1847, at Skaneateles, N. Y.
3747. ii. JAMES I., b. Nov. 27, 1837; d. Nov. 3, 1856, at Skaneateles, N. Y.
3748. iii. BURDETTE M., b. Oct. 7, 1850; d. July 9, 1871, at Auburn, N. Y.
3749. iv. WILLIS S., b. June 17, 1853; m. Lellie L. Taylor, 5326-30.

2290. ASA .CHILDS FOOTE, (1097, 374, 115, 37, 10, 3,) b. Skaneateles, N. Y., June 20, 1811; m. 1st, Jan. 19, 1842, Lydia, dau. of Francis Hollister, of Genoa, N. Y. She d. Dec. 1, 1852; m. 2nd, Jan. 19, 1854, Rhoda Fuller, dau. of Daniel Rooks, of Kelloggsville, N. Y. He was Dea. of the Skaneateles Baptist Church over 30 years. His farm was on the west shore of the lake, about two miles from the village. He was one of the best men that ever lived. He d. May 16, 1884.

3750. i. JAY, b. 1844; d. Jan. 26, 1849.
3751. ii. CHARLES, b. ———; d. Jan. 31, 1852; abt. two years old.
3752. iii. LYDIA LILLIAN, b. June 29, 1852; ed. at Auburn and taught school there; m. Sept. 7, 1880, Charles Jefferies Hughes. He was b. India, Aug., 1850. Baptist. Ch.: (1) Lillie Ellen Hughes, b. Skaneateles, Oct. 26, 1881; d. Oct. 7, 1900, at Skaneateles, N. Y. (2) Asa Malcolm Hughes, b. Penn Yan, N. Y., Nov. 6, 1883. (3) Charles Edmund Hughes, b. Penn Yan, Jan. 13, 1886;

d. Mar. 24, 1888. (4) John Ralph Hughes, b. Chicago, Ill., Aug. 28, 1888; d. Jan. 25, 1892, at Skaneateles, N. Y. (5) Ruth Grey Hughes, b. Chicago, Ill., Aug. 28, 1888. (6) Albert William Hughes, b. Skaneateles, Jan. 21, 1891.

3753. iv. EMMA, b. Mar. 19, 1856; res., Skaneateles, N. Y.; umn.

3754. v. EDWARD L., b. June 29, 1860; m. Julia Elster, 5331-3.

3755. vi. JESSIE ANN, b. May 21, 1863; m. Mar. 1, 1893, at Skaneateles, Samuel Nelson Allen, Baptist. Ch.: (1) Joseph Eugene Allen, b. Oct. 1, 1896.

3756. vii. ADDIE MAY, b. Sept. 24, 1865; d. June 29, 1885.

2291. PERRY FOOTE, (1097, 374, 115, 37, 10, 3,) b. Skaneateles, Dec. 24, 1813; m. Skaneateles, Nov. 21, 1844, Lodema, dau. of Eli Benedict. She was b. in Brookfield, Ct.; d. in Skaneateles. He d. Apr. 18, 1888, in Skaneateles, N. Y. Ch. all b. at Skaneateles, N. Y.

3757. i. CHATTIE VIRGINIA, b. Sept. 25, 1851; m. Oct. 22, 1874, Albert Hatch. Res., Scranton, Pa. Ch.: (1) Frank Howard Hatch, b. Oct. 8, 1879. (2) Annie Lodema Hatch, b. Nov. 3, 1880. (3) Jeanette Allen Hatch, b. July 27, 1883.

3758. ii. FRANK B., b. July 31, 1853; m. Emma Marie Abbott, 5334-.

3759. iii. MARY REBECCA, b. Jan. 20, 1861; m. Feb. 8, 1888, Frederick Grow, of Glenwood, Pa. Res., Stamford, Pa.

3760. iv. FRED G., b. Dec. 8, 1863; m. Katherine Rawson, 5335-6.

2293. WILLIAM FOOTE, (1097, 374, 115, 37, 10, 3,) b. Skaneateles, Aug. 30, 1819; m. Owasco, N. Y., Sept. 12, 1841, Jane, dau. of John Stoner. She was b. Skaneateles, Oct. 6, 1822; d. May 18, 1903, at Skaneateles. He was bap. 1858, at Ira, N. Y., by Judson Davis. Baptist; farmer. He d. Apr. 30, 1895, at Skaneateles.

3761. i. M. AUGUSTA, b. Oct. 24, 1842; m. Ira, N. Y., Mar. 25, 1873, Edward E. Wells. Ch.: (1) Mabel Wells, b. ———; m. Ernest Terpening. Ch.: (a) Winnifred Terpening, b. ———. (b) Gladys Terpening, b. ———.

3762. ii. OSCAR A., b. Jan. 13, 1844; m. Rose M. Doratt, 5337-8.

3763. iii. SARAH FRANCES, b. Apr. 19, 1845; m. Ira, N. Y., Jan. 3, 1882, Benjamin E. Duckett. Ch.: (1) Elma E. Duckett, b. Jan. 24, 1883.

3764. iv. WILLIAM HENRY, b. Mar. 29, 1847; d. May 9, 1865.

3765. v. OZIAS INSDRO, b. Nov. 8, 1848; m. Clara Kilburn and Janete P. Bull, 5339-41.

3766. vi. STELLA, b. Jan. 24, 1851; m. Ira, N. Y., Dec. 28, 1869, Walter Phelps. Ch.: (1) Maud Phelps, b. May 25, 1872. (2) Raymond Phelps, b. Sept. 7, 1889.

3767. vii. CORA E., b. June 24, 1858; m. Ira, N. Y., May 14, 1879, Lofton L. Dudley. Ch.: (1) Una, b. Oct. 31, 1881. (2) Edwin, b. Dec. 19, 1882. (3) Leland, b. Jan. 20, 1895.

2294. CHAUNCEY FOOTE, (1097, 374, 115, 37, 10, 3,) b. Skaneateles, N. Y., Mar. 23, 1823; m. Mich., Apr., 1852, Charity, dau. of Mrs. Marion (Stark) Brinkerhoff; a relative of Gen. Stark of Revolutionary fame. She was b. in Owasco, N. Y.; d. Dec. 30, 1905, at Elmira, N. Y. Mr. Foote was a teacher, later a farmer. He d. Aug. 30, 1903, at Elmira, N. Y.

3768. i. CHARLES BENSON, b. Feb. 13, 1851; m. Edith May Moses, 5342.

3769. ii. ADELLA, b. June, 1855; m. Ed. S. Buettess, at Owasco, N. Y.

2296. SAMUEL FOOTE, (1099, 374, 115, 37, 10, 3,) b. Dec. 22, 1798; m. July 2, 1818, Eliza, dau. of Henry Hunsiker, of Owasco, N. Y. Res., Fairfield, O.

 3770. i. HENRY, b. ———; d. Cleveland, O. Had wife and 2 girls. Was a sutler in the Civil War.

 3771. ii. DELILAH, b. ———; d. ———; was m. Ch.

 3772. iii. FRANKLIN, b. ———; unm.; d. in N. Y.

 3773. iv. HERCELIA, b. ———; m. Dr. Langworthy; d. ———. Ch.

 3774. v. MARIA, b. ———; m. Dr. Langworthy. Ch.

 3775. vi. LYNDON, b. ———; m. Frances Benson. Now living in ———. Two ch.

2300. LUCUS FOOTE, (1099, 374, 115, 37, 10, 3,) b. Mar. 27, 1813; m. May 21, 1834, Mary, dau. of Alexander Price, of Fairfield, O. She was b. Apr. 14, 1817; d. Jan. 14, 1892. He d. June 22, 1894. Res., North Fairfield, O.

 3776. i. OSCAR DARWIN, b. Aug. 31, 1835; m. Mindana Eunice Kellogg, 5343-.

 3777. ii. MARY AMANDA, b. June 19, 1837; d. May 13, 1893.

 3778. iii. WILLIAM FRANKLIN, b. July 10, 1840; m. Louise Underhill, 5344-7.

2301. MARCUS FOOTE, (1099, 374, 115, 37, 10, 3,) b. Mar. 27, 1813 (twin to Lucus); m. Lora Kinney Gere. He d. Apr. 13, 1889.

 3779. i. LYDIA, b. No. Fairfield, O., Mar 9, 1840; m. Alexander Kirtland, of Plymouth, O. Ch.: (1) Lulu, b. North Fairfield, O., Nov. 30, 1856; m. J. Howard Vinton, Mound Prairie, Walworth Co., Wis., Nov. 30, 1874; d. July 4, 1886. Ch.: (a) Maud, b. Oct. 2, 1878; m. Delta I. Jarrett, Chicago, Ill., b. ———. Ch.: (i) Alice, b. Nov. 17, 1901. (ii) Evelyn Maud, b. Mar. 30, 1903 (iii) Gladys Ruth, b. Oct. 14, 1904. (iv) Enid Martha, b. Feb. 22, 1906. Lydia m. 2nd, Geo. W. Eldredge, Richmond, Ill. Ch.: (2) Charles M., b. No. Fairfield, O., Aug. 26, 1866; m. ———; has ch. Res., Chicago, Ill. (3) G. Earle, b. Hillsdale, Mich., Mar. 15, 1869; unm. (4) George, b. Richmond, Ill., Apr. 15, 1880; unm.

 3780. ii. MARK ALPHA, b. North Fairfield, O., Apr. 10, 1858; m. Kate E. St. Clair, Crystal Lake, Ill., Jan. 1, 1881. Lives in Chicago, Ill. No ch.

2309. NOBLE FOOTE, (1113, 375, 115, 37, 10, 3,) b. Feb. 16, 1804; m. Dec. 31, 1829, Emily Barrett Smith. She was b. Oct. 14, 1807; d. Jan. 19, 1885. He d. Dec. 23, 1873.

 3781. i. NANCY SMITH, b. Jan. 19, 1832; m. Oct. 29, 1863, James P. Fenn. She d. Nov. 23, 1889. Ch.: (1) Noble C., b. May 4, 1865; m. Lottie Elmer. Ch.: (a) Elmer Fenn, b. (b) Florence Fenn, b. (2) Franklin E., b. Aug. 6, 1872; m. Jan. 11, 1898, Inez Brown. He was shot by Eastwood, Aug. 14, 1899.

 3782. ii. EDMUND N., b. July 17, 1838; m. Harriet Bates Stowell, 5348.

 3783. iii. MARY ELECTA, b. June 2, 1835; d. June 26, 1836.

 3784. iv. ALLEN R., b. Apr. 22, 1837; m. Helen A. Jenkins, 5349-52.

 3785. v. MARY JANE, b. Jan. 12, 1844; d. Mar. 15, 1844.

 3786. vi. ELSEY VELDANAE, b. Mar. 17, 1845; d. Oct. 18, 1848.

2311. ELIJAH FOOTE, (1113, 375, 115, 37, 10, 3,) b. in Canton, N. Y., May 28, 1810; m. Jan. 1, 1834, Olivia Luce, of Hubbardton, Vt. She was b. at

(24)

Hubbardton, Vt., May 25, 1809; d. July 3, 1883, at Goshen, Ind.' He d. July 8, 1863, at Grand Rapids, Mich.

    3787. i. AARON LUCE, b. Kempville, N. Y., Dec. 11, 1834; m. Orpha Viola Watson, 5353-56.

    3788. ii. LUCY AMELIA, b. Kempville, N. Y., Apr. 8, 1837; m. May 22, 1861, Alfred Pew, of New York City. Res., Washington, D. C. Ch.: (1) Lillie Amelia Foote Pew, b. at Grand Rapids, Mich., May 4, 1865; m. Mar. 18, 1886, Alvin Dings, of. Huntersland, N. Y. Res., Milwaukee, Wis. Ch.: (a) Fred Alvin, b. Grand Island, Neb., May 26, 1887. (b) Marshall Edgar, b. in Chicago, Ill., Nov. 13, 1888. (c) Mable Grace, b. Milwaukee, Wis., Nov. 30, 1898. (2) Della Antenetta Pew, b. Lowell, Mich., Nov. 1, 1867; m. Dec. 25, 1884, Harlow Street Rice, of Pocahontas, Ill. Res., Grand Island, Neb. Ch.: (a) Zora Rice, b. New York City, Dec. 17, 1890; d. in infancy. (b) Ward Harlow Rice, b. Hiland, N. C., Jan. 2, 1892. (c) Lewis Sidney Rice, b. Newport News, Va., July 13, 1887. (3) Frederick W. Pew, b. Grand Rapids, Apr. 5, 1871; m. Dec. 26, 1893, Helen M. Hood, of Barbados, B. W. I. Res., Buffalo, N. Y. Ch.: (a) Gladys Hood Pew, b. No. Plainfield, N. J., May 4, 1898.

    3788¹. iii. OLIVIA CLEMENTINE, b. Kempville, N. Y., July 26, 1839; d. Mar. 24, 1841, at Kempville.

    3788². iv. ALLEN R., b. Jan. 26, 1842; m. Emma L. Hayte, 5356¹.

    3789. v. ELIJAH H., b. Mar. 24, 1845; m. Frances A. Howe, 5357-60.

    3790. vi. DELLA ANNETTE, b. Olcott, N. Y., Aug. 24, 1848; m. Sept. 20, 1877, Cyrus Edward Perkins, of Lawrence, Mass. Res., Grand Rapids, Mich. Ch.: (1) Mabel Helen Perkins, b. Grand Rapids, July 26, 1880. (2) Edward Foote Perkins, b. Grand Rapids, Nov. 19, 1883.

    2313. WILLIAM HENRY FOOTE, (1113, 375, 115, 37, 10, 3,) b. May 20, 1815; m. 1st, May 12, 1842, Almira G. Goodrich. She d. Nov. 9, 1855; m. 2nd, in LaSalle, Mich., Mrs. Rebecca Dunlap Miller; m. 3rd, Feb. 22, 1871, in Vt., Mrs. Lenora Holley. He d. June 12, 1899, at Cross Village, Mich.

    3791. i. WILLIAM WALTER, b. Mar. 9, 1843; m. Anna H. Green and Jane Allison, 5361-3.

    3792. ii. CHARLES HENRY, b. Oct. 30, 1844; m. Maria Rose, 5363¹.

    3793. iii. MATTHEW TAYLOR, b. Sept. 6, 1847; m. Anna C. Ellsworth, 5364-67.

    3794. iv. EDWARD RUSSELL, b. Aug. 25, 1851; m. Alice Agard, 5368-70.

    3795. v. WARREN MILO, b. at Osseo, Mich., Aug. 11, 1855; m. Nettie Stetson Parker, 5371-73.

    3796. vi. STEPHEN MILLER, b. LaSalle, Mich., Feb. 19, 1859; m. Sara Brooks, 5374-75.

    3797. vii. LILLIAN VIOLA, b. LaSalle, Mich., June 9, 1861; m. St. Albans, Vt., May 1, 1888, John H. Doody, of Middlebury, Vt. He was b. Middlebury, Aug. 30, 1855. Res., Middlebury, Vt. Ch.: (1) Stephen Allen Doody, b. Middlebury, Mar. 26, 1891; graduated from Middlebury High School, in class of 1907. (2) Hazel Grace Doody, b. Middlebury, July 4, 1896.

    3798. viii. ARTHUR, b. Feb. 25, 1863; m. Jennie Wood, 5376-7.

DR. GEORGE FRANKLIN FOOTE, No. 2138

JULIUS MERRILL FOOTE. No. 3800

3799. ix. CARRIE R., b. LaSalle, Mich., Feb. 9, 1866; m. Dec. 8, 1882,
Joseph Rhines. He was b. Watertown, N. Y., Mar. 2, 1846.
Ch.: (1) Jesse M., b. Midland, Mich., June 11, 1884. (2) Paul
W., b. Chase, Mich., Feb. 16, 1887. (3) Irma B., b. Northfield,
Minn., Dec. 4, 1888. (4) Joseph R., b. Burnside, Minn., Nov. 22,
1890. (5) Nellie A., b. Burnside, Minn., Sept. 16, 1892. (6)
Herbert R., b. Burnside, Minn., June 30, 1894. (7) Minnie L.,
b. Burnside, Minn., Feb. 8, 1896. (8) Andrew M., b. Haugen,
Wis., Oct. 12, 1900.

2316. JULIUS DANA FOOTE, (1114, 375, 115, 37, 10, 3,) b. Hinsdale, N. H.,
Aug. 17, 1817; m. Castleton, Vt., Sept. 14, 1840, Jane Eliza Merrill. She was b.
Castleton, Vt., Nov. 7, 1818; d. May 22, 1897. He d. Nov. 3, 1886, at Sherman,
N. Y.

3800. i. JULIUS MERRILL, b. Wayne, Pa., Oct. 30, 1843; m. Newark, N.
J., Oct. 30, 1870, Cornelia Elizabeth, dau. of Rev. M. E. Strieby,
D. D., of Newark, N. J. She b. Mt. Vernon, O., Dec. 5, 1845.
Mr. Foote served in the Civil War as First Sergeant, Co. H,
176th N. Y. Vols., and later in U. S. Navy in the squadron
of Admiral Farragut. He is a member of "The Order of the
Founders and Patriots of America" by virtue of the Foote
ancestors, and was the Treasurer General of the Order, and is
now a member of the General Court. He is President of the
Strieby & Foote Drop Forging Co., of Newark, N. J.   No ch.

3801. ii. MARY ELIZA, b. Hydeville, Vt., Feb. 20, 1847; d. Apr. 5, 1862,
at Syracuse, N. Y.

3802. iii. FREDERICK G., b. Mar. 17, 1853; m. Alice L. Beals, 5378.

2321. JOHN GRAHAM FOOTE, (1115, 375, 115, 37, 10, 3,) b. Middlebury,
Vt., Apr. 21, 1814; m. 1st, Burlington, Ia., Aug. 20, 1845, Eliza Lane Ewing. She
d. Aug. 5, 1853; m. 2nd, Burlington, Ia., June 27, 1855, Mary Eliza Merrill. Mr.
Foote came to Burlington, Ia., in 1843, and entered the mercantile business. In
1861 he was nominated and elected by the Republican party for the State Senate,
serving from 1862-1865 inclusive. He was appointed and served for twelve years
as one of the Commissioners for the Construction of the State Capitol of Iowa.
He d. Mar. 4, 1896. Res., Burlington, Ia.

3803. i. JOHN GRAHAM, b. Burlington, Ia., July 24, 1847; d. Feb. 2,
1848.

3804. ii. HARRIET MOSEBY, b. Burlington, Ia., Nov. 13, 1848; m. in
Burlington, Ia., Frank Reese Dunham. He d. June 31, 1901, in
Burlington, Ia. Ch.: (1) Clark, b. Sept. 28, 1870; d. Aug. 10,
1871. (2) Harriet Foote, b. Dec. 22, 1871. (3) John Graham, b.
July 3, 1874. (4) George Foote, b. Sept. 17, 1876.

3805. iii. JOHN EWING, b. Burlington, Ia., Apr. 4, 1850; d. Apr. 15,
1850.

3806. iv. MARY ELIZA, b. Burlington, Ia., July 26, 1851; d. Feb. 12,
1857, in Burlington, Ia.

3807. v. GRAHAM MERRILL, b. Oct. 13, 1856; m. Anna W. Joy, 5379-80.

3808. vi. HENRY GEAR, b. Burlington, Ia., Dec. 21, 1857; d. Aug. 10,
1858.

3809. vii. CHARLES RUSSELL, b. Burlington, Ia., June 4, 1859; d. Dec.
8, 1861.

2322. CHARLES KING FOOTE, (1115, 375, 115, 37, 10, 3,) b. Middlebury, Vt., Aug. 5, 1816; m. Mobile, Ala., July 12, 1843, Sarah B. Lyon. He d. Aug. 30, 1901, in Mobile, Ala. Ch. all b. in Mobile, Ala. She lives in Englewood, N. J.

3810. i. MARY LYON, b. ——; m. L. H. Konerly.

3811. ii. ROSA FISHER, b. ——; m. Hiram H. Smith.

3812. iii. CHARLES GRAHAM, b. ——.

3813. iv. HELEN GAINES, b. ——; m. Richard H. Clark. Res., 956 Government St., Mobile, Ala.

3814. v. SALLIE B., b. ——; m. —— Waller.

3815. vi. ANNIE LYON, b. ——.

2325. MOSES SCOTT FOOTE, (1115, 375, 115, 37, 10, 3,) b. Middlebury, Vt., June 11, 1822; m. 1st., Burlington, Ia., Dec. 13, 1853, Laura Amba Fletcher. She d. May 18, 1857, in St. Louis, Mo.; m. 2nd, Mobile, Ala., Dec. 4, 1860, Louisa J. Hunter. She d. in Minn. He d. Jan. 2, 1884, in Pensacola, Fla.

3816. i. SARAH GRAHAM, b. Burlington, Ia., Nov. 23, 1854. Her mother d. when she was two years old, and she was adopted by her aunt (No. 2320). She is Corresponding Secretary of the Academy of Science at Davenport, Ia.

3817. ii. CHARLES SHELDON, b. Burlington, Ia., Jan. 18, 1857; d. June 4, 1857.

3818. iii. ANN TOULMIN, b. Mobile, Ala., Feb. 10, 1862.

3819. iv. FRANK ROSS, b. Mobile, Ala., Mar. 4, 1865; d. Dec., 1865.

2326. MARK SYLVESTER FOOTE, (1115, 375, 115, 37, 10, 3,) b. Middlebury, Vt., Aug. 21, 1823; m. St. Louis, Mo., Mary Stella Mauro. He d. Feb. 13, 1904, in Burlington, Ia.

3820. i. CLARA GRAHAM, b. Burlington, Ia., Sept. 1, 1852. She was educated at St. Mary's Academy, Notre Dame, Ind., graduating in 1871. She m. Burlington, Ia., Oct. 21, Henry D. Squires, residing there for a number of years, and afterwards in St. Paul, Minn., and St. Louis, Mo., where she d. Apr. 15, 1904. Ch.: (1) Charles Foote, b. Burlington, Ia., Oct. 6, 1874.

3821 ii. MARK MAURO STANISLAUS, b. Burlington, Ia., Apr. 15, 1854; m. Miza Elizabeth Brenner.

3822. iii. HELEN SHELDON, b. Burlington, Ia., Sept. 13, 1856; graduated St. Mary's, Notre Dame, Ind., 1876; m. Sept. 8, 1880, Harold Vincent Hayes, of Chicago, Ill., where they res. Ch.: (1) Gear Sheldon, b. Chicago, Ill., Aug. 3, 1881; d. Feb. 23, 1886. (2) Mark Snowden, b. Chicago, Ill., Dec. 18, 1883; d. Feb. 19, 1886. (3) Vincent Butler, b. Chicago, Feb. 2, 1887. (4) Marguerite Foote, b. Chicago, Oct. 21, 1888; d. July 27, 1889. (5) Dana Anthony, b. Chicago, June 8, 1891.

3823. iv. ELIZA WHARTON, b. Burlington, Ia., Apr. 18, 1861; m. Jan. 17, 1900, Frank D. H. Lawlor, of St. Johns, New Brunswick, who res. for a short time in Canada, but afterwards returned to Burlington, Ia., having since then been engaged as Supt. of the Burlington Water Works. She was educated at Mt. St. Joseph's Academy, Dubuque, Ia., graduating in 1883. Ch.: (1) Mary Josephine, b. Port Coburn, Can., Oct. 4, 1902.

3824. v. MOSES LATIMER, b. Nov. 21, 1863; m. Lillian R. Bruns, 5385.

3825. vi. HENRY GEAR, b. Burlington, Ia., Nov. 8, 1865. He was educated at the University of Notre Dame, Ind., after which he was engaged in mercantile pursuits until his death. He d. Apr. 11, 1894, in St. Louis, Mo.

3826. vii. MARY ALICE, b. Burlington, Ia., Apr. 8, 1869; d. Nov. 10, 1873.

3827. viii. SUSAN WILEY, b. Burlington, Ia., July 12, 1871; d. Dec. 22, 1876.

2328. HOLMES FOOTE, (1117, 375, 115, 37, 10, 3,) b. Apr. 19, 1817; m. Sept. 17, 1843, Hester Iverson. She was b. in Asgath, England, Apr. 8, 1816; came to this country when she was six years old; d. July 24, 1896. He was a farmer; d. May 24, 1886. Res., Fairfield, Vt.

3828. i. JOAN E., b. Oct. 30, 1845; m. 1st, Oct. 27, 1875, George A. Fox. He d. Nov. 11, 1881; m. 2nd, Oct. 27, 1902, John Tagul. Res., E. Fairfield, Vt. No ch.

3829. ii. ELIZABETH A., b. Dec. 9, 1848; m. 1st., July 10, 1871, Frank McIntyre. He d. Feb., 1878; m. 2nd, Aug. 10, 1884, Noel B. Blair. Res., Fairfield, Vt. No ch.

3830. iii. GENEVRA C., b Oct. 9, 1854; m. Jan. 1, 1879, Bernard J. Moran. They res. on the old Foote Homestead at Fairfield, Vt. Ch.: (1) Hester Ann Moran, b. Jan. 22, 1883. (2) Hazel May, b. May 8, 1885. (3) Holmes Peter, b. July 8, 1888. (4) Halcyon Fabolia Moran, b. July 20, 1895.

2330. ORANGE FOOTE, (1117, 375, 115, 37, 10, 3,) b. Jan. 7, 1821; m. Sept. 9, 1847, Charlotte L. Buckley. She d. May 22, 1887. When about 14 years old Mr. Foote learned the saddlers' trade, which he continued through life. His words were few; they were never wasted on trifles or contentions. He d. Mar. 14, 1870. Res., Cambridge, Vt.

3831. i. IRA, b. 1851; d. 1860, at Cambridge, Vt.

3832. ii. CHARLES P., b. 1855.

2331. IRA L. FOOTE, (1117, 375, 115, 37, 10, 3,) b. Dec. 10, 1822; m. 1st, Feb., 1849, Ann I. Albee; m. 2nd, Jane Stevens. She d. Feb. 17, 1902. He went west when young and settled in West Point, Ill. Res., Stronghurst, Ill.

3833. i. CH., by his first wife.

2333. OSCAR FOOTE, (1117, 375, 115, 37, 10, 3,) b. May 5, 1826; m. 1st, Sept. 13, 1853, Francis Perley. He went to Boston, 1849; engaged in the pork business. The Lakeman Market was established and successfully conducted by him. He d. Aug. 24, 1894.

3834. i. O. PERLEY, b. ———; res., Boston, Mass.

3835. ii. ETTA A., b. ———; m. ——— Rich. Res., 425 Mass. Ave., Boston, Mass.

3836. iii. MARY F., b. ———; res., Boston, Mass.

2339. SOLON FOOTE, (1118, 375, 115, 37, 10, 3,) b. May 18, 1818; m. Mar. 22, 1849, Lovice R. Bailey. She d. June 3, 1850; m. 2nd, Dec. 18, 1852, Mary Sturges. He was a farmer; d. Oct. 22, 1888. Res., Fairfield, Vt.

3837. i. LOVISA BAILEY, b. ———; res., Fairfield; unm.

3838. ii. LEWIS, b. ———; res., Oklahoma.

2341. MERRITT FOOTE, (1118, 375, 115, 37, 10, 3,) b. Feb. 12, 1823; m. Dec. 12, 1846, Emily I. Stevens. She d. June 25, 1857; m. 2nd, Sept. 20, 1859, Lizzie (Maynard) Snow. He was a farmer. Res., Johnson, Vt.

3839. i. HERMAN EUGENE, b.
3840. ii. HATTIE, b.
3841. iii. LYNDA, b.

2356. AMBROSE FOOTE, (1124, 377, 115, 37, 10, 3,) b. Romeo, Mich., Dec. 22, 1827; m. June 17, 1856, Ann Rebekah, dau. of Elizabeth Sheets (widow), of Fredericktown, Knox Co., O. Res., Fenton, Genesee Co., Mich.

3842. i. CHARLES HENRY, b. Fenton, Mich., Mar. 25, 1857. Res. with his parents in Fenton; unm.

3843. ii. IDA ALICE, b. Ionia, Mich., Oct. 18, 1858. Has succeeded to her aunt's millinery business. Res., Fenton, Mich.; m. Oct. 8, 1906, to George Faulkner, by Rev. Seth Reed in Methodist Church, Flint.

3844. iii. FREDERICK, b. Fenton, Mich., Mar. 15, 1862; res., Lansing, Mich.; unm.

3845. iv. DEWIT, b. Ionia, Mich., Jan. 26, 1866; d. Mar. 8, 1871, of scarlet fever, in Fenton, Mich.

3846. v. MARY JANE, b. Fenton, Mich., Mar. 16, 1868; d. Mar. 9, 1871, of scarlet fever, in Fenton, Mich. Both buried in one casket.

3847. vi. JEANETTE, b. Fenton, Mich., May 29, 1872; m. Dec. 24, 1890, John M. Norton, of Fenton, Mich. Res., Flint, Mich. Ch.: (1) Hazel, b. Fenton, Mich., Mar. 17, 1900.

3848. vii. GEORGE M., b. May 4, 1876; m. Myra Gerow, 5386-7.

2357. PE YU FOOTE, (1124, 377, 115, 37, 10, 3,) b. Romeo, Mich., May 19, 1830; m. July 23, 1854, Sarah Ellen, dau. of Thomas Carran, of Clarkson, Oakland Co., Mich. Res., Bay City, Mich.

3849. i. FLORINE ESTELLA, b. Pontiac, Mich., Oct. 2, 1855; res. with her parents in Bay City, Mich.; unm.

3850. ii. JOHN R., b. Sept. 13, 1857; m. Emma C. Ludwig, 5388-92.

3851. iii. WILLIAM P., b. Fenton, Mich., Sept. 26, 1860; d. Aug. 6, 1861, of scarlet fever.

3852. iv. THOMAS EDWARD, b. Fenton, Mich., Oct. 27, 1862; d. Nov. 10, 1883, of typhoid fever, in San Antonio, Texas.

3853. v. FREDERICK D., b. Fenton, Mich., Nov. 27, 1864; d. Apr. 19, 1865, in Fenton, Mich.

3854. vi. HORACE L., b. Mar. 19, 1866; m. Alice M. Davie, 5393.

2359. HENRY C. FOOTE, (1125, 377, 115, 37, 10, 3,) b. Troy, N. Y. He enlisted in the army and served as Lieutenant in a colored Regt. to the end of the Civil War; m. Hannah, dau. of Elizabeth Sheets (widow), of Fredericktown, Knox Co., O. He d. Feb. 6, 1905, overcome by smoke and flames in rescuing an old lady, who was an invalid, from a burning building; he was taken to a hospital and d. two days later. She res. in Chicago, Ill.

3855. i. JOHN, b. in Chicago; res., Chicago, Ill.
3856. ii. MARY, b. ———; m. ——— Adams.

2363. DANIEL FOOTE, (1133, 380, 117, 37, 10, 3,) b. Aug. 3, 1802; m. Mar. 17, 1825, Laura, dau. of Appleton Tracy, of Pittsfield, Mass. She d. June 11, 1891. He d. Jan. 21, 1870. Res., Dalton, Mass.

3857. i. DANIEL, b. Dec. 27, 1825; m. Sarah Hubbard, 5394.

3858. ii. JAMES A., b. Dec. 25, 1827; m. Roxanna Mickels, 5395-7.

3859. iii. ELIZABETH, b. Washington, Mass.; m. Justin Barrett, of Pitts-field, Mass. She d. in Springfield, Mass. Ch.: (1) Marten Van Buren, b. Pittsfield, Mass., 1851; d. in infancy. (2) William, b. Pittsfield, Mass.; d. in Springfield, Mass. (3) Everett, b. Pitts-field, Mass.; d. in Springfield, Mass. (4) Laura, b. Pittsfield, Mass.; d. Springfield, Mass. (5) Carrie, b. Pittsfield, Mass.

3860. iv. LAURA AMANDA, b. Washington, Mass.; m. George Sprague, of Pittsfield, Mass. Ch.: (1) Harriett, b. Dalton, Mass. (2) Eugene, b. Dalton, Mass.

3861. v. MARTEN VAN BUREN, b. Washington, Mass., Oct. 3, 1832; d. 1841.

3862. vi. CHARLOTTE, b. Dalton, Mass.; m. Chas. Morey, of Troy, N. Y. Ch.: (1) Elmer Elsworth, b. Noosack, N. Y.; d. in childhood. (2) Clarence, b. Noosack, N. Y.; d. in childhood. (3) A son, b. ———; d. in infancy.

3863. vii. SUSAN, b. Dalton, Mass.; m. Manly Morey, of Troy, N. Y. Ch.: (1) Clara, b. Noosack, N. Y. (2) Charlotte, b. Noosack, N. Y.

3864. viii. CYNTHIA, b. Dalton, Mass.; m. Martin Sprague, of Pittsfield, Mass. Ch.: (1) Fred, b. Pittsfield, Mass. (2) Charlotte, b. Pitts-field, Mass.; d. in childhood.

3865. ix. ANDREW J., b. Dalton, Mass.; m. Ermina Brown, 5398-9.

2366. JAMES FOOTE, (1133, 380, 117, 37, 10, 3,) b. May 1, 1807; m. Nov. 13, 1835, Eliza, dau. of Luther Brown, of Pittsfield, Mass. She d. Mar. 25, 1899. He d. Feb. 18, 1882. He was a farmer.

3866. i. EMMA JANE, b. Pittsfield, Mass., June, 1836; d. Dec., 1839.

3867. ii. LUCY, b. Pittsfield, Mass., Aug. 4, 1838; m. Aug. 4, 1857, Emery N. Nash, of Pittsfield, Mass. She d. June 3, 1873.

2373. JOSEPH FOOTE, (1133, 380, 117, 37, 10, 3,) b. Apr. 24, 1820; m. 1st, Aug. 14, 1844, Martha Maria, dau. of Appleton Tracy, of Pittsfield, Mass. She d. Feb. 14, 1882, at Pittsfield, Mass.; m. 2nd, Jan. 16, 1884, Sarah, dau. of Warren Barrows, of Pittsfield, Mass. Mr. Foote was a member of the City Council at the time of his death. He d. Nov. 26, 1891, at Pittsfield, Mass.

3868. i. JOSEPH M., b. Oct. 1, 1845; m. Ellen M. Goodell, 5400-6.

3869. ii. ASAPH S., b. May 26, 1847; m. Fannie A. Strong, 5407.

2381. GEORGE FOOTE, (1135, 380, 117, 37, 10, 3,) b. ———; m. Oct. 14, 1833, Lucy Mack, dau. of John Talcott and granddaughter of Col. David Mack, of Middlefield, Mass. He d. July 3, 1859.

3870. i. MARY, b. Feb. 13, 1836; m. G. S. Donahue, of Manitowoc, Wis. She d. Sept., 1859. Ch.: (1) Charlotte, b. (2) John W., b.

3871. ii. SARAH MACK, b. Apr. 29, 1837; m. Albert N. Baker, of South Bend, Ind. She d. Feb. 22, 1904, at South Bend. Ch.: (1) George Albert, b. Oct. 10, 1859; m. May 1, 1904, Bessie Agnes Chapen. (2) Helen M., b. ———. Both res. in South Bend, Ind.

3872. iii. HARRIET, b. Feb. 17, 1839; m. N. W. Faulk, of Preston Hollow, N. Y. She d. Feb. 22, 1904. Ch.: (1) Carrie, b Mar. 16, 1859; d. Aug. 28, 1880.

3873. iv. JOHN H., b. Jan. 2, 1849; m. Lena Glass, 5407[1-72].

3874. v.   CHARLOTTE, b. Mar. 19, 1852; m. Sept. 12, 1893, John M. Russell.
He is proprietor of Pine Bluff Farm, Middleburgh, N. Y. Ch.:
(1) Burchard Foote Russell, b. June 21, 1894.

2382. CHARLES RICE FOOTE, (1139, 381, 117, 37, 10, 3,) b. Oct. 30, 1816;
m. Phebe Loper. He was a merchant, of Boston, Mass.; d. Nov., 1891.

3875. i.   ELLEN WARNER, b. 1854; m. Edwin Southwick. She d. 1891.

3876. ii. CLARA RICE, b. ———; m. Edwin Smith. She d. 1894.

2383. GEORGE FOOTE, (1139, 381, 117, 37, 10, 3,) b. Burlington, Vt.,
May 4, 1818; m. at Montreal, Canada, July 31, 1844, Phebe Gelston Dwight, b.
Montreal, Canada, Oct. 24, 1823. She d. Jan. 8, 1858; m. 2nd, Sept. 12, 1860, at
Wolcottville, Ct., Ellen Louisa Hungerford, b. July 13, 1838. He d. Jan. 6, 1897.
Presbyterian. Grocer. Res., Detroit, Mich.

3877. i.   HELEN ELIZABETH, b. Detroit, Mich., May 4, 1845; m. 1st,
June 5, 1867, George A. Stanley. He was b. Wallingford, Ct.,
Oct. 5, 1818; d. Dec. 13, 1883, at Cleveland, O.; m. 2nd, Edward
Payston, son of Wilmot Williams. He was b. New York City,
N. Y.; d. Apr. 29, 1900, at Atlantic City, N. J. She was edu-
cated at Detroit Schools and Seminary, Cleveland, O. Presby-
terian. Res., 1101 Pacific Ave., Atlantic City, N. J. Ch.: (1)
George Foote, b. Apr. 29, 1870; d. Nov. 5, 1874. (2) Clara Eliza-
beth, b. Mar. 11, 1875; d. Feb. 12, 1903.

3878. ii.   HORACE LOOMIS, b. Nov. 4, 1840; d. Feb. 8, 1850.

3879. iii.   GEORGE ALVAN, b. Apr. 12, 1850; d. May 16, 1853.

3880 iv.   MARY DWIGHT, b. Detroit, Mich., Apr. 16, 1853; m. 1st, Detroit,
Mich., June 4, 1873, Charles A. Marvin. He d. 1875; m. 2nd,
Burlington, Vt., Apr. 14, 1879, Col. Albert Simpson, son of
Thomas Cummins. He was b. Tecumseh, Mich., July 19, 1851.
He is Lieutenant-Colonel of General Staff, U. S. A., at present
assigned on duty at the Army War College, Washington, D. C.
She was educated at the Detroit Female Seminary, Detroit.
Mich. Episcopalian. Ch.: (1) Stanley Foote Marvin, b. and d.
in 1875. (2) Esther Ruth Gelston Cummins, b. Dec. 11, 1882.

3881. v.   CAROLINE SANGER, b. Detroit, Mich., Feb. 15, 1856; m. George
Foote Marsh, son of No. 2384. He went to the Alaskan Gold
Fields, and d. July 26, 1900, at Cape Nome, Alaska. Mrs. Marsh
early showed aptitude in the art of entertaining, and after many
successful private efforts, was persuaded by the urgent requests
of some of her prominent friends to appear before the public in
a series of lectures on Colonial Life and Times. Mrs. Marsh res.
at Claremont-on-the-James, in Virginia, for a number of years,
and made a special study of the early records and relics of the
Old Dominion. Her opportunities for acquiring information from
the inside have been exceptional, and the result of her diligent
use of them is a most entertaining lecture on ''Colonial Homes
on the James; Interiors and Exteriors.'' She is now interested
in the sale of Architects Bronze, a metal that adheres so closely
to the base that the two are practically homogeneous. Office at
9, E. 22nd St., N. Y. Ch.: (1) Caroline Edwards Leavett Marsh,
b. Detroit, Mich., Oct. 28, 1879; m Harold Clyde, son of Samuel
R. Kinsey. He was b. Philadelphia, Pa., Nov. 4, 1883. She was

educated at the Woman's College, Richmond.   Episcopalian.
Res., 17 Livingston Place, N. Y. C.   (2) Charlotta Foster, b.
May 1, 1880.   (3) Helen Elizabeth, b. Jan. 21, 1892.

3882. vi.   JANE ALLYN, b. Detroit, Mich., Nov. 8, 1857; m. Fortress
Monroe, Va., Apr. 25, 1883, James Jared, son of Gardiner Tracy.
He was b. Lansingburg, N. Y., Dec. 3, 1819. She was educated
at the Detroit Seminary and Cleveland Seminary. Res., 3535
Euclid Ave., Cleveland, O.   James Jared Tracy was b. in
Lansingburg, N. Y., Dec. 3, 1819. His father was for many years
a printer and publisher at Lansingburg, editing the ''Lansingburg Gazette'' for many years. In 1825 the family moved to
Utica, N. Y., where he lived until his death. James J. received
a common school education, and at the early age of 14 began to
earn his own living. He moved to Cleveland at the age of 16
(1836) when it was a village of less than 5,000. He has lived in
Cleveland all these years, amassing, by careful attention to
business, a comfortable fortune. He is hale and hearty at the
age of 87 years, attending daily to his business affairs. He was
63 years old before marrying for the first time, and his wife was
many years his junior. His son is now a Senior at Harvard
College, and expects, after taking a mechanical engineering
course at Harvard, to return and make his home in Cleveland.
His dau. is at school in Bryn Mawr, Pa. Ch.: (1) James Jared
Tracy, Jr., b. Feb. 27, 1884.   (2) Catharine Lancing Tracy, b.
Feb. 20, 1888.

3883. vii. GEORGE HUNGERFORD, b. Detroit, Mich., July 1, 1861; m.
at White Pigeon, Mich., Oct. 14, 1891, Josephine Hyde. She was
b. Mar. 5, 1866. He was educated at Detroit; is a traveling salesman with Standart Bros., Detroit, Mich. Res., Detroit, Mich.
No. ch.

3884. viii. CHARLOTTE AUSTIN, b. Aug. 1, 1865; m. Dec. 10, 1885, at
Detroit, Mich., Augustus Torrey, Beverly, Mass. He d. Aug. 19,
1902. Res., 20, Kirby Ave. West, Detroit, Mich. Ch.: (1) Dana
Hungerford Torrey, b. Aug. 3, 1887. (2) Helen Cutler Torrey, b.
Aug. 12, 1888.   (3) Charlotte Foote Torrey, b. Aug. 17, 1896.

3885. ix.   FREDERICK JOY, b. Mar. 22, 1869; President, William Wright
& Co., Detroit, Mich.; unm.

2388. GEORGE LUTHER FOOTE, (1144, 381, 117, 37, 10, 3,) b. in Windsor,
Vt., Mar. 26, 1827; m. Esther Mamton, dau. of James Young. She was b. Aug. 28,
1854, in Boston, Mass. He was educated at Cambridge, Mass. Banker at Boston,
Mass. He d. Nov. 24, 1887, at his res., Cambridge, Mass.

3886. i. GEORGE LUTHER, b. Feb. 19, 1886; is a student in Harvard
College.

2395. JAMES FOOTE, (1148, 383, 117, 37, 10, 3,) b. Middlebury, Vt., July
25, 1822; m. Grandville, Mich., Oct. 8, 1848, Eliza Freeman. She d. Aug. 8, 1900.
He moved to Mich. 1843; is a farmer. Res., Grandville, Mich.

3887. i.   HENRY O., b. July 25, 1850; m. Rilla Mills, 5408.

3888. ii. HARLOW H., b. Apr. 3, 1854; m. Etta Hooper, 5409-10.

3889. iii. FREEMAN, b. May 29, 1858; d. Jan. 9, 1874.

3890. iv. ABIAH H., b. July 23, 1860; m. Sept., 1888, Chas. Barbey. Res.,
            905 Quigley Ave., Grand Rapids, Mich. Ch.: (1) Guy, b. Apr.
            10, 1890. (2) Frank, b. Mar. 27, 1892. (3) James, b. Aug.,
            1894.
3891. v. GEORGE H., b. June 18, 1865; m. Ella Atkinson.

2396. JOHN BERTHONG FOOTE, (1148, 383, 117, 37, 10, 3,) b. Middlebury,
Vt., July 25, 1822; m. at Poultney, Vt., 1848, Sarah Louisa, dau. of Hiram Kilbourn. She was b. St. Albans, Vt., July 9, 1830; d. May 27, 1900, at Middlebury,
Vt. He was educated at Middlebury, Vt. Carpenter. He d. June 24, 1904, •
at Worcester, Mass. Res., Middlebury, Vt.
3892. i. CHARLES W., b. July 13, 1849; m. Ida M. Wheeler, 5411-14.
3893. ii. CARRIE W., b. Sept. 25, 1851; m. at Salisbury, Vt., Joseph Nash.
            Res., Middlebury, Vt.
3894. iii. CASWELL WILLIAM, b. Mar. 18, 1867, at Middlebury, Vt.; m.
            June 15, 1901, Elizabeth, dau. of Gilbert and Matilda Goker, at
            Worcester, Mass.

2400. HORACE BOARDMAN FOOTE, (1150, 387, 117, 37, 10, 3,) b. June 21,
1819; m. Nov. 11, 1847, Delia Minerva Havens. She b. N. Y., 1847; d. Nov. 30,
1896, at Tompkins, Mich., their res.
3895. i. ALBERT HAVENS, b. Aug. 8, 1848; m. Mar. 18, 1868, Georgianna
            Jackson. She d. Aug. 22, 1868, at Tompkins, Mich. He was
            killed in a mine, May 9, 1882, in Idaho.
3896. ii. CAROLINE FRANCES, b. May 19, 1851; m. Jan. 20, 1870, Frank
            D. Hyde. She d. Apr. 30, 1904. Ch.: (1) Durward M., b. Jan.
            6, 1872; m. 1890, Caroline Bishop. Ch.: (a) Blanch, b. Aug.,
            1891. (b) Roylston, b. ———. (2) Mayme, b. Jan., 1874. (3)
            Charles, b. Jan., 1876. (4) Royce, b. Nov., 1879.
3897. iii. WALLACE H., b. June 9, 1853; m. Etna Green, 5415-8.
3898. iv. HARRIET ELIZA, b. June 23, 1855; m. Dec. 24, 1875, Riley
            C. Rhines. She d. May 14, 1878.
3899. v. JOHN C., b. Sept. 23, 1857; m. Kate M. Wenman, 5419.
3900. vi. CHARLES H., b. Sept. 26, 1861; m. Octavia F. Saturlee, 5420-22.
3901. vii. KATE ERUETTE, b. Oct. 22, 1869; m. Sept. 12, 1888, William
            Carpenter. Ch.: (1) Clair, b. Aug. 29, 1891. (2) Lyda, b. June
            2, 1893.

2402. WALLACE TURNER FOOTE, (1150, 387, 117, 37, 10, 3,) b. in Middlebury, Vt., Mar. 18, 1825; m. Oct. 13, 1853, Hilah Eliza, dau. of Lucius Archibald
(No. 1016) and Emily Pamelia Foote, of Port Henry, N. Y. She d. May 8, 1907.
Wallace T. Foote d. Oct. 19, 1904. He was b. in Middlebury, Vt., Mar. 18, 1825,
and moved to Port Henry, N. Y., in 1847. From that time until his retirement
from active business in 1885 he was conspicuously identified with the iron business. In later years he was successful in other lines, being interested in the pulp
and paper industry, and also for years president of the First National Bank of
Wyoming, Iowa. His home for 57 years was in Port Henry, where he maintained
a wise and generous interest in everything that affected the welfare of the community. He was one of the promoters and directors of the first railroad that ran
into the Upper Champlain Valley on the New York side.
    Mr. Foote was one of the last of those pioneers of the iron industry in our
country who helped in the laying of its foundation and aided its growth to the

WALLACE TURNER FOOTE. No. 2402

DAVID THOMPSON FOOTE.   No. 2532

JOHN FOOTE.   No. 2516

present enormous proportions. When he entered the business in 1850 the square stone stack, with its inefficient superimposed ovens, the blast driven through its open top by some nearby water power, producing from 6 to 10 tons of pig iron per day, was but a feeble prophecy of our 500-ton modern furnace. In 1852 he took charge of the Port Henry Furnace Company, a corporation of Boston gentlemen, with B. T. Reed as president, whose property consisted of two stone stack furnaces, Nos. 1 and 2, located on the shores of Lake Champlain at Port Henry. In Nov., 1854, he inaugurated the modern furnace by blowing in the "new No. 2" at that place, which was described by a historian of about that time as follows:

This furnace was constructed on a new plan, having an outer case or shell of boiler iron riveted together and standing upon plates, supported by cast iron columns. This is the first erection of the kind built in the country, and so far as I am aware in the world, although some have been constructed in Europe with a boiler iron shell supported by brick arches. The furnace is 46 feet high, 16 feet diameter at the top of the boshes, 8 feet high at the top of the furnace, and is blown through five tuyeres by a vertical steam engine having a steam cylinder 30 inches in diameter, 6 feet stroke, and a wind cylinder 84 inches diameter, 6 feet stroke. In 1860 another furnace was commenced, but not completed until 1862. This furnace is propelled by machinery similar to the other, but somewhat enlarged in its proportions and power. The furnace built by Powell & Lansing was taken down in 1855, and that erected by Gray was demolished in 1865. During the last five years these furnaces have produced 58,100 tons of pig iron.

The English method of working a high furnace with a closed top has been recently adopted, and each of the furnaces has been raised 20 feet, giving them an elevation of 66 feet. One of them, after an operation of three months under this charge, shows a very satisfactory result by an increased production of iron with a less consumption of coal per ton of iron made. The company obtains lime from a quarry upon its own property a short distance from the furnaces. Anthracite coal is exclusively used and is principally transported in return boats from Rondout.

The adoption of the "closed top" referred to in the foregoing extract marked the first introduction of that device in American iron making. At about the same time Mr. Foote introduced the "closed front" in this country, and applied the use of chemistry as an aid in burdening a furnace.

Mr. Foote's brother, Charles H., former vice-president of the Illinois Steel Company, Chicago, and Mr. Foote's sons, Fred H., also a former vice-president of the Illinois Steel Company; George C., superintendent of the Zenith Furnace Company, Duluth, and Wallace T., of Witherbee, Sherman & Co., Incorporated, Port Henry, N. Y., all received their training under him. He was a man of strong character, showing the marks of his Puritan ancestry in his high sense of justice, his inflexible will and energy, his grasp of affairs and his broad Christianity, while the high position which he held in his home community speaks eloquently of the regard of those who knew him best. Ch. all b. in Port Henry, N. Y.

3902. i. FREDERICK HODGEMAN, b. Sept. 29, 1854; m. Nettie A. Chamberlain, 5423-6.

3903. ii. HARRIET, b. Oct. 26, 1856; d. Apr. 10, 1859.

3904. iii. CHARLES SEWARD, b. Feb. 7, 1860; m. Mary Cecilia Wentworth, 5427-8.

3905. iv. MARY ELLEN, b. Sept. 21, 1861; was educated at Smith College.

3906. v. WALLACE TURNER FOOTE, JR., was b. at Port Henry, N. Y.,
Apr. 7, 1864. He was educated in the Port Henry public schools,
Williston Seminary, Union College, and the Columbia Law School.
Upon being admitted to the New York bar he entered upon the
practice of his profession at Port Henry, and shortly thereafter
became interested in politics. On June 3, 1891, he m. Mary S.
Witherbee, of Port Henry, who d. in New York City, May 28,
1896, without ch. He was a member of the U. S. House of Representatives in the 54th and 55th Congresses, and continues his
interest in politics in an advisory capacity. Mr. Foote is a
director of Witherbee, Sherman & Co. (Inc.), the extensive and
well known iron ore and iron dealers and mine owners, and is
President of the Lake Champlain and Moriah Railroad Company,
and largely interested in other iron ore and industrial enterprises. He maintains his residence in his native town.

3907. vi. THOMAS HEERMANS, b. Apr. 14, 1866; grad. at Union College,
1886; electrical engineer, Pasadena, Cal.; m. June 14, 1893,
Minerva May Barton, of Attleboro, Mass. No ch.

3908. vii. DAISY, b. May 8, 1869; d. July 3, 1870.

3909. viii. SUSAN EMILY, b. Port Henry, N. Y., Mar. 31, 1874; grad.
Smith College, and Post Grad. at Barnard; m. June 30, 1904,
Grosvenor Hyde Backus, of Brooklyn, N. Y., lawyer, N. Y. City.
Ch.: (1) Wallace Freeman, b. Jan. 4, 1907, at Brooklyn, N. Y.

3910. ix. GEORGE CLARK, b. July 7, 1878; grad. Union College in 1899,
and has since been connected with the iron business; unm.

2406. CHARLES HOWARD FOOTE, (1150, 387, 117, 37, 10, 3,) b. Aug. 26,
1842; m. Apr. 19, 1865, Sarah Catherine Murdock, of Crown Point, N. Y. She d.
Aug., 1865, in Tompkins, Mich.; m. 2nd, June 30, 1869, Mary Trueman Smith, of
Whitehall, N. Y., retired ironmaster. Res., Spear St., Burlington, Vt., formerly
of Chicago.

3911. i. MARY T., b. May 12, 1871; d. Sept. 12, 1871.

3912. ii. CHARLES H., b. May 6, 1872; d. Aug. 31, 1872.

3913. iii. HENRY C., b. Feb. 5, 1874; m. Evelyn A. Williams, 5429-30.

3914. iv. HARRIET ELIZA, b. Feb. 19, 1876; m. Nov. 28, 1900, Capt.
Willard H. McCornack. Res., Ft. Riley, Kas. Ch.: (1) Margaret Anna, b. Manila, P. I., Nov. 2, 1902; d. Ft. Riley, Kas.,
Nov. 21, 1904. (2) Willard Foote, b. Ft. Riley, Kas., Dec. 16,
1905.

3915. v. KATHARINE HILAH, b. Nov. 12, 1878; m. June 19, 1899, Joseph
B. Card, of Chicago, Ill. Ch.: (1) Mary Foote, b. June 13, 1900.
(2) Katharine Bartow, b. Jan. 3, 1902. (3) Joseph B., Jr., b.
Nov. 12, 1904.

3916. vi. THOMAS WEATHERBEE, b. May 8, 1880; m. Aug. 16, 1905,
Florence A. Hunn. No ch.

2407. ALLEN FREEMAN FOOTE, (1153, 387, 177, 37, 10, 3,) b. ———; m.
Oct. 11, 1853, Elvira L. Fenn. Always lived on the old homestead at Middlebury,
Vt.; d. Nov. 18, 1884.

3917. i. FREEMAN ALLEN, b. Nov. 11, 1863; d. unm.

2413. CHAUNCY D. FOOTE, (1163, 389, 117, 37, 10, 3,) b. Apr. 29, 1833;
m. Nov. 25, 1861, Mary J. Northrup.

3918. i. ANNA N., b. Sept. 27, 1867; d. Aug. 29, 1868.

3919. ii. GUELA BIRD, b. May 31, 1869.

3920. iii. HENRY N., b. Oct. 9, 1875.

2419. GEORGE B. FOOTE, (1164, 389, 117, 37, 10, 3,) b. ———; res., Helena, Mont.

3920¹. i. HENRY, b. ———; res., Butte, Mont.

3920². ii. EDNA, m. Harvey Freeman, Helena, Mont.

3920³. iii. KATHERINE, b. ———; res., Butte, Mont.

2429. CHARLES HENRY FOOTE, (1182, 391, 117, 37, 10, 3,) b. Feb. 24, 1831; m. Isabel McLane, of New Sweden, N. Y. He d. 1889. Res., Plattsburgh, N. Y.

3921. i. WILLIAM McLANE, b. ———; res., Plattsburgh, N. Y.

3922. ii. HARTWELL, b. ———. Res., Cala.

3923. iii. JOHN M., b. New York.

2432. HENRY VAN RENSELAER FOOTE, (1182, 391, 117, 37, 10, 3,) b. Oct. 24, 1840; m. Sept. 21, 1863, Henrietta A., dau. of Wm. T. and Marietta A. Hubbard. He is a railroad machinist. Res., Malone, N. Y.

3924. i. GERTRUDE M., b. June 20, 1864; d. June 13, 1871.

2435. ASA FOOTE, (1183, 392, 118, 37, 10, 3,) b. Aug. 15, 1807; m. Johnson, Trumbull Co., O., Nov. 12, 1840, Mary, dau. of Philip Dickinson. She was b. Bridgeport, Ct., Apr. 22, 1817; d. Mar. 15, 1872, Fowler, O. He d. Nov. 12, 1884, in Fowler, O. He was a farmer.

3925. i. LEVI, b. Mar. 7, 1842. He was a soldier in Co. K, 41st Ohio Infantry; d. Jan. 23, 1862, in a hospital in Louisville, Ky.

3926. ii. PHILIP, b. May 21, 1849; m. Orrell Baldwin.

3927. iii. CURTIS, b. July 7, 1846. He was a soldier in Co. D, 177th Ohio Vol. Infantry; d. Feb. 27, 1865, at Nashville, Tenn.

3928. iv. LAVILLA, b. June 25, 1849; d. Mar. 5, 1850.

3929. v. HELEN, b. Aug. 24, 1852; m. Fowler, O., June 1, 1872, Lloyd G., son of Horace Spencer. He was b. Hartford, O., May 5, 1851; is a farmer. Res., Warren, O. Ch.: (1) Benjamin F., b. Apr. 16, 1874; m. Lillian dau. of Lewis Clark. She was b. Hartford, O., Dec. 25, 1873. Ch.: (a) Reed Clark, b. Apr. 21, 1901 (b) Asa Lee, b. Jan. 15, 1903. (c) Benj. V., b. Sept. 21, 1905. (2) Byron H., b. June 9, 1876.

3930. vi. AURIE DELANY, b. Sept. 27, 1857; m. Youngstown, O., Feb. 5, 1879, Frank E. Clark. Ch.: (1) Mary Blanche, b. Feb. 25, 1882. (2) Ward Elmer, b. June 8, 1890. (3) Mabel Dorris, b. Mar. 3, 1903.

2458. GILES WESLEY FOOTE, (1186, 392, 118, 37, 10, 3,) b. Mt. Morris, N. Y., July 11, 1818; m. Nov. 1, 1842, Harriet, dau. of George W. Bump. She was b. Lynn, Ct., Nov. 14, 1822; d. Mar. 17, 1881. He was Postmaster and Assessor of Mt. Morris for several years. He d. Oct. 24, 1885. Res., Mt. Morris, N. Y.

3931. i. GILES, b. July 31, 1843; m. Nellie Whitenack, 5440-5.

3932. ii. JOHN B., b. July 18, 1844; unm.

3933. iii. ASA E., b. Sept. 4, 1846; m. Lucy Hubbard, 5446-50.

3934. iv. ELIZABETH, b. July 30, 1850; m. Jan. 22, 1890, William Holmes. Res., Dalton, N. Y. Ch.: (1) Harrison, b. Nunda, N. Y., May 22, 1893.

3935. v. LILLIE L., b. June 5, 1856; m. Jan. 13, 1876, George Devinney. Res., Mt. Morris, N. Y. Ch.: (1) Edith L., b. Mt. Morris, N. Y., Nov. 4, 1876; m. Jan 8, 1896, George Coffin Ch.: (a) Leon Coffin, b. June 27, 1898. (b) Howard Coffin, b. Nov. 12, 1901. (2) Clifford E., b. Mt. Morris, N. Y., July 30, 1880; m. Apr. 5, 1905, Clara Wright. (3) Floyd W., b. Mt. Morris, N. Y., Oct. 12, 1885. (4) LaVerne, b. Mt. Morris, N. Y., May 24, 1894. (5) Roy, b. Mt. Morris, N. Y., Nov. 20, 1896.

3936. vi. FRANCIS S., b. Feb. 28, 1853; m. Nancy Wallace, 5451.

3937. vii. GEORGE W., b. Feb. 24, 1862; m. Belle Burnap, 5452.

3938. viii. FANNIE JANE, b. Aug 2, 1865; m. Oct. 15, 1890, Walter E. Wainman. Res., Bolivar, N. Y. Ch.: (1) Earl Foote, b. Eldred, Pa., May 5, 1892.

2459. CHARLES FOOTE, (1186, 392, 118, 37, 10, 3,) b. Sparta, N. Y., Oct. 15, 1822; m. Mt. Morris, Dec. 19, 1843, Sarah Mitchael. He d. Apr. 8, 1885, at Des Moines, Ia.

3939. i. ELIZA, b. ———; d. ———.

3940. ii. EMMA, b. ———; d. ———.

3941. iii. FRANCIS, b. ———; d. ———.

2460. NORMAN FOOTE, (1186, 392, 118, 37, 10, 3,) b. Sparta, N. Y., Sept. 16, 1824; m. Mt. Morris, N. Y., June 7, 1854, Emily Jane, dau. of Thomas Jarrad, who was b. in England, Dec. 21, 1799. She was b. Avon, N. Y., June 10, 1831. Mr. Foote was a farmer; he was also actively interested in political matters and filled many minor town offices. He d. Apr. 21, 1891. Res., Mt. Morris, N. Y.

3942. i. FRED J., b. Feb. 12, 1856; m. Mary B. Ott, 5453-4.

3943. ii. CHARLES E., b. Feb. 9, 1858; m. Sadie M. McCurdy, 5455.

3944. iii. CLARENCE A., b. May 12, 1860; m. Stella M. Olney, 5456-8.

3945. iv. CHESTER THOMAS, b. Mt. Morris, N. Y., Mar. 28, 1863; m. Nunda, N. Y., Jan. 12, 1905, Helen Maria, dau. of John M. Cooper, of Nunda, N. Y. She was b. Apr. 16, 1873. He is engaged in manufacturing the Foote Concrete Mixers; also interested as one of the inventors and patentee.

3946. v. FRANK J., b. Mt. Morris, N. Y., June 1, 1868; m. Sarah Ann Marsh and Harriet Marsh, 5459-61.

2469. ELISHA F. FOOTE, (1187, 396, 118, 37, 10, 3,) b. Feb. 26, 1826; m. May 5, 1856, Lucy Prindle.

3947. i. CAROLINE PAMELIA, b. May 15, 1857; d. Dec. 22, 1861.

3948. ii. FRANK E., b. Oct. 2, 1859; d. Dec. 28, 1861.

3949. iii. LILLIAN, b. Sept. 21, 1861, in Nebraska City; m. Nov. 28, 1888, Charles Hursted Moore (No. 446 in Moore Gen.). She d. May 8, 1892. Ch.: (1) Carl Newton Moore, b. June 25, 1890, at Ft. Dodge, Ia.

3950. iv. JENNIE M., b. Sept. 5, 1863; m. President Crawford.

3951. v. LYLE M., b. Aug. 18, 1865.

3952. vi. JAMES E., b. Aug. 12, 1869; d. Oct. 31, 1870.

3953. vii. MARY P., b. Aug. 28, 1871; m. ——— Cooley.

3954. viii. CHARLES N., b. Jan. 15, 1874; d. May 3, 1877.

2473. AARON S. FOOTE, (1190, 396, 118, 37, 10, 3,) b. Apr. 19, 1816; m 1st, Jan. 13, 1840, Caroline Gifford; m. 2nd, Feb. 11, 1863, Susan Haren. She d.

Dec. 8, 1863; m. 3rd, Feb., 1864, Cordelia Hill. He was a carpenter and mill-wright. Res., Hope, Hamilton Co., N. Y.

3955.   i.   CHARLOTTE, b. Mar. 6, 1841; m. Apr. 1, 1862, Isaac H. Brownell, of Hope Valley, N. Y. Ch.: (1) Lizzie, b. May 12, 1862. (2) Alphia, b. (3) Raymond, b. (4) David, b. (5) Henry, b. (6) David, b.

3956.   ii.   NELSON B., b. Mar. 29, 1843.

3957.   iii.   BENJAMIN L., b. May 10, 1848; m. J. Adalaide Skimm, 5462.

3958.   iv.   SYBIL MARGUERITE, b. May 11, 1851, at Hope, N. Y.; m. John Harris. She d. Dec. 13, 1901. Ch.: (1) James, b. (2) Peter, b. (3) Charlotte, b. ———; m. Chas. Williams. (4) Florence, b. ———; m. Edwin Duheme.

3959.   v.   HENRY, b. June 28, 1853; m. Emma Brennell, 5463-4.

3960.   vi.   WILLARD, b. May 15, 1856; d. May 29, 1856.

3961.   vii.   WILLIE, b. May 15, 1856; d. May 29, 1856.

3962.   viii.   SARAH ELLEN, b. Feb. 8, 1857; d. Feb. 27, 1857.

3963.   ix.   WILLIAM A., b. July 2, 1859; m. Maria ———, 5465.

3964.   x.   SUSAN E., b. Feb. 27, 1865.

3965.   xi.   MARY, b. Apr. 19, 1866.

3966.   xii.   JESSIE, b.

2476.   CHARLES WESLEY FOOTE, (1190, 396, 118, 37, 10, 3,) b. Northville, N. Y., July 1, 1823; m. Emma Jane Brookes, Oct. 28, 1851. In 1861 he moved to Juda, Wis.; d. and was buried there, July 18, 1866. Mrs. Foote was b. 1822, and with her children lives at Emerald Grove, Wis. P. O., Janesville.

3968.   i.   FRANKLIN DARIUS, b. Dec. 7, 1852; unm.

3969.   ii.   HARRIET ANN, b. Dec. 11, 1855; unm.

2480.   ORRIN FREEMAN FOOTE, (1190, 396, 118, 37, 10, 3,) b. July 31, 1832; m. May 21, 1853, Mary Ann, dau. of Abraham Failing, b. Dec. 17, 1832. He was nicknamed Commodore. He was a carpenter and builder, and in this section built many of the most prominent houses, etc. Then bought flour and grist mill, to which was added a large cider and vinegar mill. He also owned a fruit and poultry farm. Was the father of high license in this town; a prominent business man here; a Freemason; a member of the First Church of Christian Scientists in Utica, N. Y. He d. July 21, 1898. Res., Deansboro, N. Y.

3970.   i.   LAWRENCE AMY, b. Oct. 18, 1855; m. Hattie Elvira De Land.

3971.   ii.   ADELAIDE SELECTA, b. Sept. 8, 1869. She is a florist. Res., Deansboro, N. Y.; unm.

3972.   iii.   MINERVA M., b. Sept. 16, 1871; m. Jan. 10, 1894, John Bristol Baker, a descendant of Perigin White, b. in the "Mayflower" and m. Gov. Winthrop's widow. Also a descendant of Robert Treat Payne. Ch.: (1) John Oren, b. May 8, 1904.

3973.   iv.   MYRON OREN, b. Feb. 26, 1874; d. Apr. 29, 1902.

2484.   JAMES EDWIN FOOTE, (1195, 396, 118, 37, 10, 3,) b. July 21, 1833; m. Mary F., dau. of James H. and Abigail (Wells) Kennicott, of Mayfield, N. Y. He was among the first settlers of Otoe Co., Neb., in 1856. The Otoe Indians had not moved to their reservation, but gave no trouble. He enjoyed pioneer life on the broad prairies, and remained with his father until he was m., Jan. 4, 1860. His present res. is on his preemption.

3974.   i.   JOHN W., b. Oct. 30, 1860; m. Myrta C. Todd, 5466.

3975.   ii.   EDITH M., b. Sept. 16, 1862.

3976.   iii.   CLARA E., b. Oct. 24, 1869.

3977.   iv.   ANGIE R., b. Nov. 7, 1874; d. Feb. 2, 1895.

2487.   MELVILLE B. FOOTE, (1197, 386, 118, 37, 10, 3,) b. Jan. 7, 1840, at Northville, N. Y. Educated at the New York Conference Seminary, Charlotteville, N. Y. Enlisted Aug. 6, 1862, in Co. E, 115th Regt. N. Y. Infantry. Mustered into service, Aug. 26, 1862. Discharged at Albany, N. Y., July 3, 1865. Participated in 31 skirmishes and engagements; m. June 17, 1866, Betsey M., dau. of Alanson Trowbridge, Edinburgh, Saratoga Co., N. Y. Res., Delta, Fulton Co., O., Neb. City, and Ayr, Adams Co., Neb.

3978.   i.   HARRIET BELL, b. June 23, 1869, at Camp Creek, Otoe Co., Neb.; m. Feb. 21, 1894, Albert E. Eastwood. Res., Long Beach, Cal. Ch.: (1) Pauline A., b. Dec. 29, 1894.   (2) Harold, b. June 4, 1896, in Ayr, Neb.

3979.   ii.   CHARLES W., b. Mar. 3, 1872; m. Lena M. Boyd, 5467.

3980.   iii.   ARTHUR, b. Apr. 28, 1875; d. Aug. 30, 1875.

3981.   iv.   EUGENE C., b. Sept. 6, 1879; m. Bessie E. Byrne, 5468-9.

3982.   v.   FANNIE EVELYN, b. Mar. 11, 1882; d. Feb. 8, 1900, at Ayr, Neb.

2487¹.   DR. CHARLES E. FOOTE, (1197, 396, 118, 37, 10, 3,) b. Oct. 19, 1855; m. Feb. 7, 1880, Clara J. Whitman. Dentist. Res., Ballston Spr., N. Y.

3983.   i.   C. RAY, b. June 17, 1882.

3984.   ii.   RALPH E., b. Jan. 24, 1885.

3985.   iii.   MAY BEATRICE, b. Nov. 12, 1890.

2489.   HENRY FOOTE, (1201, 404, 119, 37, 10, 3,) b. Sept. 15, 1815; m. 1836, Lemira Woodruff, of Avon, Ct. Res., in 1856, Half Day, Lake Co., Ill., and d. there in 1886. Ch. all of Canton, Ct.

3986.   i.   GEORGE H., b. 1844; m. Lottie L. Doty, 5470-4.

3987.   ii.   STANLEY T., b. 1848; m. Frances Hertel, 5475-6.

3988.   iii.   FRANK H., b. 1850; m. Martha Wilson, 5477-9.

3989.   iv.   JOHN MARTIN, b. 1853; m. Savilla Woodruff, 5481.

3990.   v.   LOUISA, b. 1859; d. in infancy.

2490.   LUCIUS FOOTE, (1201, 404, 119, 37, 10, 3,) b. Apr. 5, 1817; m. Sarah Barber, of Canton, Ct., and d. there in 1863.

3991.   i.   ELLEN M., b. 1850; m. Orrin Wilcox, of Farmington, Ct.; d. in Garretsville, O., in 1886. Ch.: (1) Emma. (2) Henry; res., Farmington, Ct.

2492.   JOHN MILLS FOOTE, (1201, 404, 119, 37, 10, 3,) b. Feb. 9, 1827; m. Savilla Woodruff, of Avon, Ct., May 13, 1851. In 1866 he removed to West Hartford, Ct., and located at what is now known as "Foote's Corners." Throughout his life he carried on the meat business, and was a large dealer in horses and cattle, buying large droves in Northern New York, Vermont, Ohio, and Canada. During the latter part of the Civil War he was employed by the U. S. Government buying horses and mules for use in the Army. He d. at his home in West Hartford, Ct., June 16, 1899, and is buried in Spring Grove Cemetery, Hartford, Ct.

3992.   i.   JOHN MILLS, JR., b. Jan. 12, 1858; m. Helen A. Stanley, 5482-4.

2495. CHARLES THORNTON FOOTE, (1202, 404, 119, 37, 10, 3,) b. Oct. 12, 1818, in Canton Center, Ct.; m. Dec. 8, 1847, Lydia Eglintine Boardman. She was b. Feb. 15, 1823, at Bristol, Ct. He d. in Brooklyn, N. Y., Apr. 26, 1892.

3993. i. CHARLES CHAUNERY, b. Nov. 25, 1848; d. July 22, 1850.

3994. ii. ELLEN ELIZABETH, b. Oct. 3, 1851; unm.

3994¹. iii. GEORGE LAMEL, b. July 28, 1858; d. Mar. 28, 1878.

3995. iv. MARY WILSON, b. Mar. 8, 1865; unm.

2496. ARTHUR WELLINGTON FOOTE, (1202, 404, 119, 37, 10, 3,) b. Aug. 1, 1820; m. in Geneva, N. Y., Elizabeth, dau. of Daniel Rieggles. Res., ——.

3996. i. LILLIE CORTELYOU, b. Oct. 5, 1852; m. June, 1876, Hon. Dwight B. Backenstose, of Geneva, N. Y. No ch.

3997. ii. GRACE HUMPHREYS, b. Mar. 6, 1854; m. Oct. 24, 1877, Lornell Mason Palmer, of N. Y. He served four years in the Civil War. Was made Captain. Was a member of the Loyal Legion, and a most successful business man. Ch.: (1) Lowell Melvin, b. Brooklyn, N. Y., Nov. 9, 1878; m. Dec. 20, 1899, Amy Jameson Burnham. She was b. July 20, 1878. Ch.: (a) Eleanor Burnham Palmer, b. Oct. 5, 1900. (b) Elizabeth Cortelyou Palmer, b. Feb. 24, 1905. (2) Arthur Wellington, b. Sept. 19, 1879. Was a student at Columbia Law School; d. Aug. 31, 1903; mourned by his class-mates and the Law Faculty of Columbia. (3) Harold Irving, b. Dec. 14, 1880; d. Feb. 28, 1889. (4) Florence Edith, b. Brooklyn, N. Y., Feb. 1, 1882; m. Jan. 21, 1901, Theodore Weicker. He was b. in Darmstadt, Germany, June 6, 1862. Ch.: (a) Theodore Weicker, Jr., b. Jan. 15, 1902, in Stamford, Ct. (b) Lowell Palmer Weicker, b. Stamford, Ct., Oct. 4, 1903. (5) Grace Marion, b. Sept. 25, 1883. (6) Lily Cortelyou, b. Brooklyn, N. Y., Mar. 19, 1885; m. Dec. 14, 1904, John Gibson McIlfain, Jr. He was b. Philadelphia, Pa., July 4, 1882. No ch. (7) Ethel Josephine, b. Oct. 18, 1889. (8) Carleton Humphreys, b. Mar. 21, 1891.

3997¹. iii. ANNA JOSEPHINE, b. Apr. 11, 1856; d. Dec. 24, 1859.

2497. ELIZUR LANCEL FOOTE, (1202, 404, 119, 37, 10, 3,) b. Oct. 6, 1822, at Canton Center, Ct.; m. June 2, 1855, Mary E. Wilson, of Cambridge, Maryland. She was b. May 22, 1837. She d. in Brooklyn, N. Y., Sept. 24, 1896. He d. in Chicago, Ill., May 15, 1868.

3998. i. HOWARD W., b. Aug. 31, 1856; m. Josephine Ross, 5485-9.

3998¹. ii. CHARLES WELLINGTON, b. Nov. 17, 1859; d. Jan. 30, 1877.

3999. iii. CLARENCE, b. Mar. 29, 1862; m. Carrie A. Burt, 5490-1.

4000. iv. LAURA HUMPHREYS, b. Aug. 20, 1864; m. May 5, 1886, Charles Reuben Pitts. He was b. Mar. 5, 1857, in Brooklyn, N. Y. She d. Apr. 16, 1904, in Brooklyn. Ch.: (1) Marjorie, b. Mar. 4, 1887; m. Sept. 9, 1905, Robert Samuel Bliss. (2) Marion, b. Aug. 21, 1888. (3) Laura Humphreys, b. Sept. 4, 1893.

2499. EDWARD HUBERT FOOTE, (1202, 404, 119, 37, 10, 3,) b. May 18, 1827, at Canton Center, Ct.; m. Oct. 18, 1853, Frances Witter. She was b. Jan. 10, 1830. He d. Nov. 3, 1854.

4001. i. FANNIE HUBERTA, b. July 17, 1855.

(25)

2500. JOHN HOWARD FOOTE, (1202, 404, 37, 10, 3,) b. Nov. 11, 1833, at Canton Center, Ct.; m. 1st, Jan. 11, 1860, Eliza Cook. She was b. June 30, 1836, in New York City, and d. Nov. 21, 1875; m. 2nd, Jan. 29, 1879, Bessie C. Perrine. She was b. in Brooklyn, N. Y., Jan. 27, 1856. He d. in Brooklyn, N. Y., May 17, 1896.

John Howard received a good academic education and afterward learned the art of clock making in one of the large factories in Bristol, Ct. He was gifted by nature with a mechanical turn of mind and soon mastered the intricacies of the trade. He afterward found employment in the extensive machine shops of Woodruff & Beach, at Hartford, Ct., as a journeyman machinist. He continued until the autumn of 1851, and in Jan., 1852, went to New York City, where he was employed for about two years as clerk in a hardware store. In Dec., 1853, he entered the employ of Rohe & Leavitt, importers of musical instruments. He was a born musician, and learned to play while a mere lad of seven years. This, added to his practical knowledge of mechanics, enabled him to readily adapt himself to his new occupation, and he soon became thoroughly familiar with the various instruments and a recognized expert in the trade. This firm, established in 1835, was not only the oldest in the trade, but recognized as the representative house in this line in America. Mr. Foote continued his connection with them until their retirement in 1863, when he bought out their interest and became their successor. He enlarged and developed the business greatly, and in 1868 established a branch house in Chicago, under the management of his brother. The business of the house extended to every part of the United States, and to every part of the globe, and included every variety of brass, stringed and other instruments, some of the best makers in Europe having made Mr. Foote their sole representative in America. In 1883 Mr. Foote was invited by the directors and managers of the United States National Museum, attached to the Smithsonian Institution, in Washington, D. C., to make a permanent exhibit of musical instruments, showing the progress in this line during the past century. He accepted the invitation and donated everything connected with the exhibit, thus making it perpetual, being the only one of its kind admitted to the Museum.

In 1890, Mr. Foote presented to Congress a ''Plea for Uniform or Specified Duties on Behalf of the Manufacturers and Importers of Musical Instruments, with an Argument and a Series of Tables Illustrating the Proposed Rates of Duty, under the House Bill 9416, and the Senate Bill then under Discussion, as Compared with Existing and Former Rates of Duty.'' The Arguments presented by Mr. Foote were the result of many years of experience and an intimate knowledge of all the materials that entered into the manufacture of musical instruments. He was not successful in his efforts, as the Senate Committee on Finance had determined on a certain course of action and declined to make any change.

In early life Mr. Foote displayed considerable poetic and literary talent, and was a frequent contributor of poems to the ''Journal of Commerce,''·the New York ''Evening Post,'' and other papers. He wrote under the *nom-de-plume* of ''Pearlfisher.'' Since 1872, Mr. Foote had spent his summers in Canton (formerly West Simsbury), where he erected a large and elegant house, with all the modern improvements, on the property which has been in the possession of the Foote family for 250 years. The place to which he gave the name of ''Bel-Air'' is one of the finest in that part of the country. In 1882 he assisted in forming the Farmington Valley Agricultural Corporation of Canton, Ct., of which, up to the time of his death in 1896, he was annually elected its president. Mr. Foote was a man of strong and decided opinions, amounting almost to obstinacy, characteristics peculiar to the Foote family, and exemplified in a marked degree in Admiral Foote of the United States Navy during the Civil War. He was nevertheless kind and pleasing in his manners, and a man of large-hearted liberality, a notable instance of which was shown in the repairing and remodeling of the old Church at Canton Centre, to which he was not only the principal contributor, but the virtual architect, designer and builder as well, devoting over three months of his time during the summer of 1874 to the work.

4002. i. ELLEN HOWARD, b. Oct. 29, 1860; m. 1st, Henry Martyn Strieby, of Newark, N. J.; m. 2nd, Edward Rombey, M. D., of Germany.

4003. ii. HUBERT PORTER, b. Sept. 28, 1862; m. Apr. 19, 1890, Louise Josephine Van Meter. She was b. Kane, Ill., Apr. 29, 1865. No ch.

4004. iii. LILLIE HOLBROOK, b. Nov. 26, 1864.

4004¹. iv. DAUGHTER, b. Feb. 12, 1869; d. Feb. 15, 1869.

4004². v. FREDERICK LANERL, b. Dec. 14, 1872; d. Oct. 19, 1876.

4004³. vi. BESSIE LA RUE, b. Dec. 25, 1879; d. Dec. 14, 1881.

4005. vii. JOHN HOWARD, Jr., b. Sept. 20, 1881; res., New York City.

4006. viii. STELLA HUMPHREYS, b. Apr. 6, 1883.

4007. ix. AGNES ELIZABETH, b. June 7, 1885.

4007¹. x. CLARA, b. Oct. 18, 1887; d. Aug. 28, 1888.

4008. xi. LANCEL HUMPHREYS, b. July 15, 1890.

4009. xii. DELANO PERRINE, b. Oct. 22, 1893.

4010. xiii. EDITH, b. May 22, 1896.

2501. ALFRED MILLER FOOTE, (1203, 404, 119, 37, 10, 3,) b. Mar. 16, 1826; m. 1st, Aug. 9, 1848, at Euclid, O., Ruth L., dau. of Ezekiel and Orpha Adams. She d. Jan. 14, 1853; m. 2nd, Sept. 17, 1861, Sarah Evertson, dau. of Isaac Elbert and Delia (Wisner) Brush. Res., Euclid, O., and New York City. He d. Oct. 28, 1906.

4011. i. EDWARD HERSCHEL, b. May 19, 1850; d. July 28, 1851.

4012. ii. ALFRED ADAMS, b. Jan. 11, 1853; d. Mar. 9, 1867.

2502. DR. EDWARD BLISS FOOTE, (1203, 404, 119, 37, 10, 3,) b. Feb. 20, 1829; m. at Watertown, Mass., Sept. 6, 1853, Catherine Goodno, dau. of John and Anna (Champney) Bond.

Dr. Edward Bliss Foote spent the first 15 years of his life at the parental residence, seven miles east of the city of Cleveland, on Euclid Avenue, where he attended what was then known as Shaw Academy, and now East Cleveland High School. Leaving school, he entered the printing office of the Cleveland "Herald," then owned by J. A. Harris, where he learned the trade of printer, and was given employment in the job printing office of Smead & Coles, the latter (Edwin Coles) afterwards founding the Cleveland "Leader" and eventually uniting the Cleveland "Herald" with the same publication. From there he went to New Haven, Ct., and accepted a position as compositor on the New Haven "Journal." Remaining there for a brief period, he removed to New Britain, Ct., where he became the editor of the New Britain "Journal," which became the largest weekly in the State. Two years later we find him associated as co-editor with J. W. Heighway, editor and proprietor of the Brooklyn "Morning Journal," the first morning paper published on Long Island. It was while thus engaged that Dr.

Foote began the study of medicine. He entered the office of a specialist of New York City, and after he had completed his reading under him, he began to practice under the directions of his preceptor. He matriculated in the Penn Medical University in Philadelphia, from which he graduated in 1860. The same year he located at Saratoga Springs, N. Y., and began the practice of his profession, but soon moved to New York City, where a wider field was open to him. His office in the city, for over 30 years, has been 120 Lexington Avenue, and his practice may be said to be world wide and lucrative. His patients may be found wherever the English and German languages are spoken. His name is not alone known here, where he has practised so successfully, but he has achieved a wide fame as the author of several books and monographs upon medicine, which have met a popular demand—the first one, "Medical Common Sense," next, "Plain Home Talk," and, finally, "Science in Story," in five volumes. These, as well as numerous monographs upon medicine, hygiene, and the human temperaments, have found their way to nearly every part of the world. The late Stephen Massett, the extensive traveler, litterateur, and song writer, remarked that he had met with "Plain Home Talk" in every clime that he had visited, even so far away as South Africa. An address by Dr. Foote before the Medical Congress Auxiliary of the Columbian Exposition in 1893, on "The Causes of Disease, Insanity, and Death," received much favorable comment from the Chicago press, and awakened lively discussion in the body of physicians before which it was delivered. He edited "Dr. Foote's Health Monthly" for 20 years, and also contributed articles to different magazines and medical journals from time to time. In the year 1853 Dr. Foote was joined in matrimony to Miss Catherine G. Bond, dau. of John Bond, of Watertown, Mass., in which State she grew to womanhood. To Dr. and Mrs. Foote have been born three sons—E. B. Foote, Jr., Hubert T., and Alfred Herschel, the latter, a promising youth, dying of appendicitis at the age of twelve years. The Junior and Hubert have followed their father in medical practice. Dr. E. B. Foote, Jr., was a graduate of the College of Physicians and Surgeons of New York City, of the class of 1876, carrying off the Seguin prize for the best report of the lectures on nervous diseases. The second son, Dr. Hubert T., a resident of New Rochelle, in Westchester Co., was graduated at the Eclectic Medical College of the City of New York. Dr. Foote accumulated a sufficient competency to enable him to pass the sunset years of a very busy life in comfort and ease. He has been a resident of Larchmont Manor for nearly a quarter of a century, his residence being, in its location, one of the most commanding in the village, and so situated as to afford a magnificent view of Long Island Sound, and the various inlets between Larchmont and New Rochelle. He d. Oct. 5, 1906.

4013. i.   EDWARD BOND, b. at Collamers, O., Aug. 15, 1854; m. 1900, May Emily, dau. of John and Martha (Livermore) Bond, of Watertown, Mass. She is a graduate of the New York Medical College and Hospital for Women, and filled the chair of Materia Medica of that Institution for eight years. She is a member of the Sorosis Club and the National Society of New England Women. Dr. Edward Bond Foote continues the practice of medicine at his father's old office, 120 Lexington Ave., New York.

4014. ii. HUBERT T., b. Jan. 18, 1859; m. Annie E. Thomas, 5492-3.

4015. iii. ALFRED HERSCHEL, b. in New York City, May 16, 1871; d. Feb. 22, 1883.

No. 2502

No. 4013

No. 4014

2510. ORLIN FOOTE, (1208, 405, 119, 37, 10, 3,) b. Mar. 10, 1836; m. Jan. 24, 1867, in Harbor Creek, Rachel, dau. of William and Susan (Hope) Cooper, of Cooperstown, Pa. She was b. Dec. 31, 1838. Farmer. Res., Belleville, Pa.

4015[1]. i. LILY, b. Nov. 30, 1867; d. Feb. 6, 1886.

4016. ii. SARAH ROSE, b. Mar. 21, 1871; m. Sept. 17, 1891, John W. Wynkoop. Res., Erie, Pa. Ch.: (1) Linnie, b. Mar. 27, 1893; d. Feb. 6, 1894. (2) Florence M., b. Apr. 12, 1896. (3) Orlin Foote, b. Oct. 31, 1898. (4) Ruth Alice, b. Mar. 8, 1903. (5) Edward J., b. Oct. 27, 1906.

4016[1]. iii. ELLA, b. Sept. 24, 1874; d. May 29, 1902.

4016[2]. iv. LAURA, b. July 18, 1880.

2511. LESTER FOOTE, (1208, 405, 119, 37, 10, 3,) b. Jan. 25, 1840; m. Susan, dau. of William and Emily Scott. Res., Kansas.

4017. i. CALVIN, b.

4017[1]. ii. MEDA, b.

4017[2]. iii. JESSIE, b.

2516. JOHN FOOTE, (1212, 405, 119, 37, 10, 3,) b. Austinburg, O., June 28, 1820, now living at Pasadena, Cal.; m. Oct., 1848, to Elmina Fisher, of Vienna, Wis. She d. Aug. 15, 1868. His father d. when he was a mere child, and a few of the early years of his life were spent in the home of his grand-parents in Ct. Later he was a student of Grand River Institute in Ohio, and taught school in Ohio and Kentucky. In 1844 and 1845 he taught near Navoo, Ill., and was in that section at the time the famous Mormon leader, Joe Smith, was killed. In 1845 he went to Wisconsin, and took Government land in Lodi, Columbia Co. He lived here from that date until 1897, when he came to Pasadena, Cal., where he now lives with his daughters. He was a radical Abolitionist, and later a great worker in the Prohibition cause. He was not noted for his orthodox religious belief, but he was noted for his honesty, his morality, and his hatred of injustice and hypocrisy. Ch. all b. at Lodi, Wis.

4018. i. LAURA REBECCA, b. Aug. 29, 1849.

4018[1]. ii. MARY ELMINA, b. Nov. 5, 1851; d. Feb., 1852.

4019. iii. JOHN WILLARD, b. Jan. 26, 1853; m. Martha Hyslop, 5494-95.

4020. iv. EMILY BERTHA, b. Dec. 11, 1854; res., Pasadena, Cal.

4020[1]. v. FLORENCE MARIA, b. Sept. 4, 1857; d. May 17, 1876, at Lodi, Wis.

4021. vi. FRANK FISHER, b. June 23, 1860; m. Lizzie McDonald, 5496-7.

4021[1]. vii. AGNES MILLS, b. Apr. 20, 1862; res., Pasadena, Cal.

4022. viii. EDITH VIOLA, b. Dec. 9, 1864; d. Sept. 20, 1865, at Lodi, Wis.

4022[1]. ix. VIRGIL ORSON, b. Mar. 27, 1868; d. Sept. 5, 1868, at Lodi, Wis.

2517. LUTHER FOOTE, (1212, 405, 119, 37, 10, 3,) b. Austinburg, O., Oct. 8, 1823. He was a farmer, and followed that business until 1882, when he came to Santa Ana, Cal. From there he moved to Pasadena, Cal., in 1884. He was a sincere, devout follower of John Campbell, and, in truth, the founder of the First Christian Church in Pasadena, Cal., now a very large and flourishing organization. He m. Aug. 29, 1850, Lurana Hall, of Austinburg, O.; she d. Jan. 11, 1895, at Pasadena, Cal. He d. Sept. 12, 1886. Ch. b. at Austinburg, O.

4023. i. LAURA ISABELLE, b. Dec. 10, 1851; m. Sept. 6, 1870, Phillip Shoemaker, Kellogg, Ia. She d. Sept. 22, 1871.

4024. ii. FRANK ARTHUR, b. Mar. 25, 1856; m. May 15, 1895, Julia DeLong, and Jessie Foster, 5498-9.

2518. JOSEPH B. FOOTE, (1219, 415, 126, 38, 11, 3,) b. Mar. 23, 1813; m. Maria L. Taylor.

    4025. i. KATE, b. ———; m. ——— Mackey, New York.

2523. DAVID AUGUSTUS FOOTE, (1219, 415, 126, 38, 11, 3,) b. in Danby, Ct., Mar. 13, 1823; m. Dec. 25, 1845, Eliza Moore Trowbridge, of Danbury, b. Jan. 27, 1823. Living at Mt. Vernon, N. Y. He d. Dec. 27, 1881.

    4026. i. CHARLES B., b. Oct. 26, 1846; m. Abbie M. Bigelow, 5500-1.

    4027. ii. FRANK TROWBRIDGE, b. Apr. 22, 1849; d. Jan. 1, 1881, Chicago.

    4028. iii. NELLIE GERTRUDE, b. Apr. 17, 1852; d. Mar. 8, 1905; m. Edward W. Speck, Winona, Minn., Dec. 24, 1868. Mr. Speck d. Nov. 29, 1894. Ch.: (1) Walter Wellington, b. Nov. 27, 1875, Chicago. (2) Charles Edward, b. Feb. 26, 1874; d. Sept. 6, 1874. (3) Mildred Foote, b. May 16, 1881, Chicago.

    4029. iv. HERBERT AUGUSTUS, b. Mar. 10, 1854; d. Oct. 10, 1859.

    4030. vi. CARRIE ELIZA, b. July 17, 1856; d. Sept. 28, 1857.

    4031. vii. JENNIE SARAH, b. Dec. 5, 1858; d. Oct. 5, 1859.

    4032. viii. JESSIE SUSAN, b. July 15, 1862, Chicago; m. in Chicago, Ill., to William A. Trowbridge, Mar. 23, 1881. Mr. Trowbridge was b. July 28, 1859. Now living in Mt Vernon, N. Y. Ch.: (1) Douglas Stanley, b. Sept. 16, 1888.

2524. JOHN FOOTE, (1219, 415, 126, 38, 11, 3,) b. May 22, 1825; m. Martha ———. Both lived and are buried at Darien, Ct.

    4033. i. MARIE ANTOINETTE; res., Brooklyn, N. Y.; unm.

    4034. ii. HERBERT; m. ———; res., Stamford, Ct.

    4035. iii. ALICE; unm.; res., Brooklyn, N. Y.

    4036. iv. STELLA; unm.; res., Brooklyn, N. Y.

2525. LEANDER PERRY FOOTE, (1219, 415, 126, 38, 11, 3,) b. Danbury, Ct., Jan. 5, 1828; m. 1st, Catherine Ann, dau. of Epaphraz and Drusilla (Ely) Holmes, of N. Y., Apr. 26, 1849. She was b. Jan. 19, 1829; d. Dec. 29, 1878; m. 2nd, 1881, Jennie Dawson, of South Norwalk, Ct. She d. Mar., 1883. He is a hatter. Res., S. Norwalk, Ct.

    4037. i. DRUSILLA ELY, b. in Danbury, Ct., Jan. 19, 1850.

    4038. ii. IDA ISABELLA, b. in Danbury, Ct., Dec. 12, 1854; d. Sept. 22, 1855.

    4039. iii. FANNIE ISABELLE, b. in Danbury, Ct., Apr. 4, 1858.

2527. CHARLES E. FOOTE, (1219, 415, 126, 38, 11, 3,) b. June 2, 1833; m. Mary ———; d. ———. Res., Omaha, Neb.

    4040. i. WALTER, m.

    4041. ii. PAULINE, b. ———; d. ———; res., Rockford, Ill.

    4042. iii. GERTRUDE.

2530. CHARLES BENJAMIN FOOTE, (1223, 418, 126, 38, 11, 3,) b. Sept. 6, 1837; m. Sept. 16, 1863, Charlotte L. Ames. She d. Jan. 24, 1871; m. 2nd, Sept. 30, 1875, Mary De G., dau. of Rev. Thomas S. Hastings, D. D., of New York City. Res., Bridgeport, Ct.

Mr. Foote was vestryman of St. Bartholomew's Church, New York, also member of the Union League, Metropolitan, Century and Groller Clubs, Metropolitan Museum of Art, and the New England Society. He was a member of the New York Stock Exchange, and also held the office of Vice-President. He was a member of the firm of Hatch & Foote, who were in business on Wall Street, New York, for over 30 years. He d. Sept. 20, 1900.

4043. i. FANNY HASTINGS, b. Aug. 21, 1876; m. Apr. 30, 1902, Frank Huntington Bosworth, Jr., of New York City. Ch.: (1) Mary Hastings, b. Apr. 29, 1903. (2) Eleanor, b. Sept. 27, 1905.

4044. ii. STERLING THOMPSON, b. Apr. 26, 1880.

4045. iii. HASTINGS, b. Sept. 13, 1887.

4046. iv. ISABEL ELEANOR, b. Apr. 6, 1890.

2531. WILLIAM HENRY FOOTE, (1223, 418, 126, 38, 11, 3,) b. Aug. 24, 1839; m. Nov. 15, 1871, Ida Augusta Hayes. She was b. Oct. 11, 1852. Res., Bridgeport, Ct.

4047. i. CHARLES MERRITT, b. Sept. 21, 1872; m. Grace Jelliffe, 5502.

4048. ii. STANLEY CLIFFORD, b. Feb. 15, 1876.

2532. DAVID THOMPSON FOOTE, (1223, 418, 126, 38, 11, 3,) b. July 17, 1841; m. May 22, 1872, Mary Alice, dau. of Capt. Henry B. Gould. She was b. July 31, 1848. Res., Bridgeport, Ct. He has held the office of Selectman of the town for two years, and is also a Vestryman of Trinity Church. He is now and has been connected with the Adams Express Company for over 25 years.

4049. i. HENRY GOULD, b. May 22, 1874; m. Jessie M. Queal, 5503-4.

4050. ii. DAVID FREDERICK, b. July 14, 1876; d. Nov. 16, 1885.

4051. iii. ENOCH THOMPSON, b. Sept. 14, 1883; d. Nov. 17, 1885.

4052. iv. EARL WHITE, b. Sept. 14, 1883; d. Dec. 17, 1885.

4053. v. HOWARD GOULD, b. Feb. 18, 1886; d. Dec. 17, 1886.

2537. SPAULDING FOOTE, (1225, 419, 128, 38, 11, 3,) b. New Fairfield, Ct., abt. 1852; m. St. Albans, Vt., abt. 1838, Elizabeth Oaks, of Enosburgh, Vt. He was Colonel of Militia, lumberman and farmer. He d. abt. 1844 at Enosburgh, Vt.

4054. i. HERBERT, b. Enosburgh, Vt., abt. 1839.

4055. ii. A GIRL, b. abt. 1841; d. in infancy.

4056. iii. OSCAR, b. Enosburgh, Vt., abt. 1843.

2542. ISAAC FOOTE, (1225, 419, 128, 38, 11, 3,) b. Fairfield, Vt., Feb. 2, 1823; m. Feb. 15, 1846, Lucy Luciena, dau. of Sheldon Gillette, of Baptist Corners, Charlotte, Vt. She was b. Baptist Corners, Vt., Sept. 24, 1828; d. Feb. 15, 1867, at Port Perry, Ontario, Canada. He was a carpenter and contractor; d. Jan. 1, 1906, at Louisville, Ky.

4057. i. ISAAC NEWTON CHARLES, b. Highgate Springs, Vt., Sept. 16, 1847; m. Grace Elizabeth Johnston, 5505-7.

4058. ii. LAURA ABIGAIL, b. Baptist Corners, Charlotte, Vt., June 22, 1850; m. Aug. 1, 1870, Dr. James Alexander, dentist, son of John Murray, of Ingersoll, Ontario. Ch.: (1) Newton Harnden, b. Port Perry, Ont., June 1, 1871. (2) Florence May, b. Port Perry, Ont., July 3, 1873; m. Dec. 22, 1896, Herbert Edward, son of Chas. McKenzie, Port Perry, Ont. (3) James Wallace, b. Port Perry, Ont., Feb. 6, 1876; m. June 21, 1897, Alma Whitney; d. Apr. 1, 1899, at Toronto, Ont. (4) Frederick Foote, b. Port Perry, Ont., Apr. 29, 1878; m. Dec. 17, 1900, Callie K. Ruby. (5) Clarence Norman, b. Port Perry, Ont., Dec. 26, 1882.

2543. TRUMAN SHERMAN FOOTE, (1229, 421, 128, 38, 11, 3,) b. Albany, N. Y., Feb. 11, 1845; m. Jane Foote Mix, dau. of Ashbel Mix and Olive Eliza Foote, of Bristol, Ct., Oct. 27, 1868.

After the death of Mr. Foote's parents in Albany, N. Y., he went to Bristol, Ct., where he lived with his guardian until he was 15 years of age, when he removed to New Haven, Ct., and resided here until his death. On coming to New Haven he secured a position as bookkeeper with the firm of Tyler & Frost, but his adeptness for his business was soon recognized and in 1868 he was made a member of the firm under the name of Tyler, Frost & Company.

He was prominent in local and State politics and served as a member of the Common Council, was also Town Clerk and Chairman of the Democratic Town Committee. It is said of Mr. Foote that he could look defeat in the face with as genial a smile as when victory rewarded the efforts of his party.

In secret society affairs, Mr. Foote confined his enthusiasm to the Masonic order, having been a member of Wooster Lodge No. 79, A. F. and A. M.; Franklin Chapter No. 2, R. A. M.; New Haven Commandery No. 2, Knights Templar, and was one of the first New Haven Masons to be raised to the Ancient Accepted Scottish Rite.

Mr. Foote's happiest moments were when with his family. There the gentle sweetness of voice and manner had full play, there the devoted husband and tender affectionate father lived. He was esteemed in social and business life alike, and of a most genial nature, none knew Mr. Foote but to value his friendship. He was aggressive in business, positive in his convictions, generous in his treatment of others, he made firm friends and won the confidence of his associates. Despising hypocrisy, none more quick to pull the veil from falsehood or more quick to entrust confidences to those in whom he believed. He was one who allowed the cares of business to unduly burden him, and when, on June 16, 1887, he died suddenly, twenty good working years were cut off from what might have been expected for him.

> " Formed on the good old plan,
> A true and brave and downright honest man,
> Loathing pretense, he did with cheerful will,
> What others talked of, while their hands were still."

Mrs. Foote m. twice, her second husband being George Edward Hoadley, son of George Hoadley, of New Haven, Ct., Feb. 5, 1890, b. in New Haven, Ct., July 18, 1832; d. Mar. 11, 1893 (No. 257, Hoadley Genealogy). No ch. second marriage.

4059. i. EDWARD ASHBEL, b. in New Haven, Ct., Nov. 27, 1869; m. Hellen Adams Payne, 5508.

4060. ii. TRUMAN SHERMAN, b. in New Haven, Ct., June 11, 1871; m. Geordia Hardy, 5509.

4061. iii. MARY DANA, b. in New Haven, Ct., Mar. 2, 1874; m. Bennett William Farnham, son of William Henry Farnham and Helen Jane Smith, of New Haven, Ct., Nov. 27, 1895. They were m. in Bridgeport, Ct. Ch. all b. in New Haven, Ct.: (1) William Foote, b. Jan. 8, 1898. (2) Benett Dana, b. July 24, 1907. The youngest member of the family in this book.

4062. iv. BABY BOY, b. in New Haven, Ct., May 2, 1878; d. May 2, 1878.

4063. v. HERRICK ORVILLE, b. in New Haven, Ct., Dec. 13, 1882. Res., New Haven, Ct.

TRUMAN SHERMAN FOOTE. No. 2543

HERRICK ORVILLE FOOTE. No. 4063

2547. HARLOW FOOTE, (1240, 432, 130, 39, 11, 3,) b. Jan. 31, 1804; m. Nov. 29, 1827, Euretta Rockwell.

4064. i. MARY MARIA, b. Jan. 21, 1830; m. Jerry K. Harris, of Chester, Mass.; d. abt. 1880, in Chester, Mass. Ch.: (1) Aston Foote, b. ———; is an engineer; res., Irving St., West Springfield, Mass.

2550. DAVID AUSTIN FOOTE, (1240, 432, 130, 39, 11, 3,) b. Dec. 10, 1810; m. Nov. 13, 1839, Esther E., dau. of Luke and Philena (Ingraham) Hill. She was b. in Amherst, Mass., Dec. 27, 1817, and d. Jan. 1, 1858; m. 2nd, July 8, 1858, Lucetta Felton. She d. Feb. 26, 1896. He d. Dec. 18, 1869. Farmer. Res., Conway, Mass.

4065. i. FRANCES E., b. Dec. 13, 1840; d. July 28, 1841.

4066. ii. BESSIE P., b. Nov. 26, 1843; m. Nov. 11, 1868, Daniel, son of Daniel and Dulcenia (Brown) Ballard. He was b. in Wendell, Franklin Co., Mass., Jan. 16, 1840. He is a farmer in the town of New Salem, Mass., also insurance agent, Chairman of the Board of Selectmen, and School Committee. He represented his district in the Legislature in 1882. He is the seventh in line of descent from William Ballard, who came from England in 1634, and settled in Andover, Mass. Ch.: (1) Frederick Foote Ballard, b. Jan. 3, 1872; m. June 10, 1897, Geneva Siey. Ch.: (a) Bessie Belle, b. Mar. 25, 1903. (2) Mae Elvira Ballard, b. July 14, 1873; m. Oct. 5, 1904, Arland E. Murray. Res., Lincoln, Vt. (3) Bessie Jane, b. Sept. 10, 1876; d. Apr. 30, 1893. (4) Lottie Louise, b. May 22, 1879; d. Dec. 19, 1885.

4067. iii. DAVID A., b. Dec. 2, 1847; d. Sept. 13, 1849.

4068. iv. MARY E., b. May 27, 1852; m. Aug. 16, 1876, Albert Ballard. Ch.: (1) Annie Frances, b. Nov. 5, 1877. (2) Walter Milton, b. Feb. 27, 1879; d. Mar. 12, 1879. (3) Harold Foote, b. July 12, 1886.

4069. v. ETTA E., b. Dec. 31, 1857; d. Dec. 15, 1878.

4070. vi. ELIZA F., b. Apr. 10, 1861; d. Nov. 5, 1879.

2553. EMERSON COGSWELL FOOTE, (1240, 432, 130, 39, 11, 3,) b. June 10, 1818; m. Feb. 15, 1841, Abigail B. Field. He d. June 11, 1899. Was an undertaker.

4071. i. ZERVIAH, b. May 19, 1843; m. Mar. 22, 1864, John B. Packard; d. May 21, 1872.

4072. ii. WILLIAM HARLOW, b. Mar. 1, 1848; d. Aug. 6, 1851.

4073. iii. GEORGE F., b. May 28, 1853; d. Mar. 2, 1856.

4074. iv. JOSEPHINE L., b. Nov. 24, 1856; m. Mar. 10, 1875, Wm. K. Batchelder.

4075. v. ANNA R., b. May 9, 1859; m. Dec. 30, 1880, Fred Holcomb.

4076. vi. FANNIE R., b. May 9, 1865; d. May 23, 1865.

2554. ALDEN AURELIUS GAY FOOTE, (1240, 432, 130, 39, 11, 3,) b. Peru, Mass., Sept. 9, 1820; m. Whately, Mass., Jan. 5, 1848, Julia Elvira, dau. of Calvin Wells. She was b. Whately, Mass., Sept. 15, 1824; d. Aug. 30, 1858, at Whately, Mass. He d. June 2, 1858, at Whately, Mass.

4077. i. LUCY ELLEN, b. June 24, 1850; m. June 27, 1872, Myron M. Lloyd, of Northampton, Mass. Res., 25 Vassar St., Springfield, Mass. Ch.: (1) Harry Rogers, b. Westfield, Mass., June 21,

1873. Assistant City Editor, Springfield "Republican." (2) Marshall Foote, b. Westfield, June 16, 1876; d. Mar. 29, 1879.

4078. ii. FRANCES ERMINA, b. Aug. 6, 1855; d. Mar. 20, 1858.

4079. iii. JULIA ALDEN, b. July 28, 1858; m. Greenfield, Mass., Oct. 2, 1882, Charles F. Austin. Res., 8 Woronoco Ave., Westfield, Mass. Ch.: (1) Helen Margerum, b. Westfield, Mass., Apr. 18, 1887. (2) Robert, b. Westfield, June 30, 1892; d. Westfield, Sept. 1, 1894.

2558. DAVID FOOTE, (1241, 432, 130, 39, 11, 3,) b. ———; m. Mary Ann Gleason.

4079¹. i. RUAH, b.

4079². ii. MARY, b.

4079³. iii. LEAMON, b.

2559. CHARLES FOOTE, (1241, 432, 130, 39, 11, 3,) b. Greenfield, N. Y., Feb. 19, 1809; m. Jan. 11, 1843, Bethiah Gleason. She was b. Jan. 22, 1824. She res. with her dau. at Ballston Spr., N. Y. He d. July 23, 1870.

4079⁴. i. LAURA A., b. 1844; m. Oct. 1, 1866, Burton St. John; d. 1867. No ch.

4080. ii. SARAH M., b. 1846; m. Oct. 18, 1870, R. I. Towle, of Corey, Pa. Res., Newport, Wash. Ch.: (1) Sarah, b. (2) Grace, b.

4081. iii. ALBERT G., b. 1848; m. Ada Weller, 5954-7.

4082. iv. DANIEL A., b. Sept. 9, 1850; m. Frances L. Slade, 5958-9.

4083. v. LEAMON R., b. Dec. 26, 1852; m. Mary Warring, 5960-6.

4084. vi. EDSON G., b. Nov. 6, 1854; m. Emma Hovey, 5967-70.

4084¹. vii. LIZZIE A., b. Jan. 27, 1857; m. Feb. 12, 1874, Emerson G. Wicks. Res., Saratoga Sprs., N. Y. No ch.

4084². viii. ELLA G., b. Sept. 21, 1859; d. Aug. 10, 1878.

4084³. ix. ELMIRA E., b. Oct. 20, 1863; d. 1884.

4084⁴. x. LOLA V., b. Oct. 10, 1866; m. Oct. 10, 1888, Fred James. Res., Orchard Farm, Ballston Spr., N. Y. Ch.: (1) Raymond, b.

2573. DANIEL BAILEY FOOTE, (1244, 432, 130, 39, 11, 3,) b. Milton, Saratoga Co., N. Y., May 31, 1825; m. Mt. Palatine, Ill., Nov. 11, 1848, Euphemia Powell. He d. Tonica, Ill., June 21, 1865.

4085. i. EUPHEMIA LOUISE, b. Eden LaSalle Co., Ill., Nov. 21, 1849; m. Ottawa, Ill., Dec. 7, 1870, Sherman Leland. He is the owner of the LaSalle Co. Abstract Books Firm, Sherman Leland & Son. Res., Ottawa, Ill. Ch.: (1) Margaret G., b. Aug. 30, 1871; d. Nov. 6, 1886. (2) Edwin Sherman, b. Nov. 23, 1872; m. June 25, 1901, Mabel Anna Hood. Ch.: (a) George Sherman, b. Sept. 20, 1902. (b) Howard Dixon, b. Dec. 26, 1905. (3) Dauphin Foote, b. Sept. 7, 1874; d. May 10, 1889. (4) Robert McArthur, b. July 12, 1876; was a soldier in the Spanish War; d. May 16, 1898. (5) Elizabeth Day, b. Jan. 26, 1879; m. Feb. 15, 1905, Octavius R. White.

4086. ii. MARY ELIZA, b. Aug. 17, 1851; d. Sept. 27, 1856.

4087. iii. FRANCIS ANNA, b. Nov. 28, 1853; d. Feb. 11, 1857.

2574. JAMES S. FOOTE, (1244, 432, 130, 39, 11, 3,) b. May 6, 1833; m. Jan. 8, 1857, Caroline A. Crandell, of Milton, Saratoga Co., N. Y. Mr. Foote came to Tonica, LaSalle Co., Ill., in 1849, and settled there, where his ch. were all b. and still res. there.

4088. i. EDWARD J., b. Jan. 25, 1858; m. S. Luella Bayley, 5510-3.

4089. ii. HENRIETTA E., b. Oct. 7, 1859.

4090. iii. EMMA M., b. Mar. 5, 1861; m. Oct. 20, 1887, Clarence Ong. Ch.: (1) Ralph W., b. July 17, 1891. (2) Fred L., b. Feb. 10, 1896. (3) Harry A., b. Oct. 15, 1897.

4091. iv. FRED L., b. July 3, 1865.

2584. ISAAC SALMON FOOTE, (1247, 433, 130, 39, 11, 3,) b. Washington, Ct., June 28, 1805; m. Feb. 18, 1846, Mary L. Baisley, of Brooklyn, N. Y. She was b. May 10, 1812; d. Dec. 1, 1854. He d. Mar. 16, 1857, in Brooklyn, N. Y.

4092. i. ISAAC OTIS, b. Brooklyn, N. Y., Dec. 20, 1847; m. and enlisted in 14th Ct. Vols., Sept. 2, 1862, and served during the Civil War. Discharged, July 6, 1865.

4093. ii. ROBERT V., b. Sept. 21, 1851; m. Juliette A. Hitchcock, 5514-16.

2586. CHARLES PARKER FOOTE, (1247, 433, 130, 39, 11, 3,) b. June 20, 1809; m. Apr. 19, 1838, Lucy Ann, dau. of Williams Barton, of Charlotte, Vt.

4094. i. WILBUR, b. Charlotte, Vt., Oct. 3, 1839; m. Emma Witherwax. Ch.: (1) Charles P. (2) Gillman Williams.

4095. ii. CAROLINE, b. Charlotte, Vt., Sept. 13, 1841; d. Feb. 9, 1849.

4096. iii. DEA. WILLIAMS, b. Charlotte, Vt., Dec. 9, 1843; m. Sept. 23, 1868, Henrietta, dau. of Henry Stebbens.

4097. iv. SUSAN IDA, b. Charlotte, Vt., Aug. 10, 1850; m. Sept. 12, 1877, Amos Jay, son of Dea. Homer Clarke. Ch.: (1) Carolyn Elsie, b. Charlotte, Vt., Sept. 26, 1878; m. Aug. 10, 1899, Edwin Hewett Prindle. (2) Homer Foote, b. Hinesburg, Vt., May 5, 1880; m. Dec. 8, 1903, Eleanor Fletcher. He is Dea. of the Baptist Church, and res. on the home farm. (3) Fay Edmund, b. Hinesburg, Vt., July 4, 1883; m. Oct. 13, 1904, Lulu Fletcher.

2587. PHILO PARKER FOOTE, (1247, 433, 130, 39, 11, 3,) b. Washington, Ct., Oct. 17, 1811; m. New York, N. Y., Apr. 13, 1836, Sarah, dau. of Abram Van Wyke. She was b. at New Hamburg, N. Y., May 4, 1815; d. Oct. 25, 1890, at Brooklyn, N. Y. Res., Washington, Ct., and Brooklyn, N. Y. Ch. all b. in Brooklyn, N. Y., but No. 4098.

4098. i. GEORGE LEWIS, b. New York, N. Y., Feb. 2, 1837; d. Oct. 4, 1881, in Brooklyn, N. Y.

4099. ii. ABIGAIL ANN, b. Aug. 20, 1839; d. Nov. 26, 1843, in Brooklyn, N. Y.

4100. iii. SARAH FRANCES, b. Aug. 16, 1842; m. Dec. 12, 1867, George Gein, of New York City. Res., Brooklyn, N. Y. Ch.: (1) Marie Frances, b. Brooklyn, N. Y., Sept. 23, 1868; m. Dec. 31, 1900, Irving Jerome Allen. Res., Hasbrouck Heights, N. J. (2) William, b. Brooklyn, N. Y., Aug. 12, 1870; m. Dec. 2, 1903, Anna Maria Theiss. (3) George, Jr., b. Brooklyn, N. Y., Mar. 13, 1872; m. Sept. 25, 1905, Helen Moock. (4) Emma Ida, b. Brooklyn, N. Y., Aug. 22, 1874. (5) Sarah, b. Brooklyn, N. Y., May 28, 1877.

4101. iv. EMMA AMELIA, b. June 19, 1843; m. May, 1865, Ephraim Smith. She d. Sept. 12, 1886, in Brooklyn, N. Y. Ch.: (1) George, b. (2) Jennie Parker, b.

4102. v. JAMES LENOX WINFIELD, b. Dec. 17, 1847; m. Jane E. Areson, 5517-9.

4103. vi. SUSAN IDA, b. Nov. 29, 1850; res., Fishkill, N. Y.; unm.
4104. vii. CHARLES PHILO, b. Sept. 7, 1856; m. Alida Edna Loucks, 5520.
4105. viii. EDWARD FRANKLIN, b. Dec. 3, 1858; m. Susan Maud Billings, 5521-2.

2589. JOHNSON H. FOOTE, (1248, 433, 130, 39, 11, 3,) b. 1802; m. Sarah, dau. of Elisha Alexander. She was b. May 17, 1803; d. 1875. He d. May 30, 1875. Res., Charlotte, Vt.
4106. i. CELINDA A., b. 1826; m. D. W. Hazard, of Ferrisburg, Vt. He was b. 1819; d. Oct. 8, 1888. She d. Jan. 4, 1899. Farmer; s. p.
4107. ii. HENRY A., b. 1827; d. Apr. 2, 1894. Res., Charlotte, Vt.; unm.
4108. iii. LUCY ANN, b. 1832; m. Eli B., son of Dea. Homer Clark. He was b. 1827; d. Sept. 5, 1874. She d. Sept. 22, 1877.
4109. iv. FLORA J., b. 1836; d. July 10, 1902; unm. Res., Charlotte, Vt.
4110. v. GEORGE A., b. July 24, 1839; m. Martha A. Clark, 5523-4.

2591. SAMUEL FOOTE, (1248, 433, 130, 39, 11, 3,) b. Charlotte, Vt., Feb. 25, 1804; m. Mary Ann Hawley, of Ogdensburg, N. Y. She was b. Dec. 19, 1802. Ch. all b. in Crawford, O.
4111. i. CHARLES M., b. Aug. 6, 1828; m. 5525.
4111¹. ii. MARTHA L., b. Oct. 13, 1830; m. ——— Murril. Res., Preston, Minn.
4112· iii. SIMEON, b. Jan. 22, 1832; m. 5526-31.
4112¹. iv. ANN ELIZA, b. Nov. 7, 1837; m. William Fife; she d. Preston, Minn.
4113. v. IRA, b. Apr. 22, 1835; m. Sarah W. Thompson, 5532-36.
4114. vi. ALFRED H., b. Apr. 22, 1840; m. Rebecca J. Stowe and Luella Sweete, 5537-42.
4115. vii. JAMES A., b. Feb. 19, 1843; m. Luecinda B. Fox, 5543-46.
4115¹. viii. LUCY A., b. Jan. 18, 1848; m. C. H. Woodford. Res., Council Bluffs, Iowa.

2593. MILO FOOTE, (1248, 433, 130, 39, 11, 3,) b. ———; m. ———; lived at Savanna, Ill., and moved with family to Cal. abt. 1860; n. f. k.
4116. i. WILLIAM, b.
4116¹. ii. ALFRED, b.
4116². iii. GILES, b. G. B. Foote, Dubuque, Iowa.
4116³. iv. HELEN, b.

2599. MYRON FOOTE, (1249, 433, 130, 39, 11, 3,) b. Madrid, N. Y., Aug. 10, 1815; m. Mary L. Gate. Both d. abt. 1889. Res., St. Lawrence Co., N. Y.
4117. i. MYRON G., b. Aug. 9, 1839; m. Marcia C. Hepburn, 5546¹-7.
4118. ii. MARY, b. ———; m. Byron Kelsey. Res., Centralia, Wash.
4119. iii. MARTHA, b. ———; m. John B. Horsford. He d. abt. 1887, in Salt Lake City, Utah. She res. with her sons in Oakland, Cal. Ch.: (1) Clarence E., b. (2) Berton J., b.; drowned in a lake abt. 1890 in Utah. (3) Myron B., b. (4) Starr C., b. The three boys are in business in San Francisco, Cal.

2600. HORACE FOOTE, (1249, 433, 130, 39, 11, 3,) b. Madrid, N. Y., Oct. 29, 1816; m. Apr. 20, 1848, Rosanna, dau. of Asaph and Verta Whittlesey, of Tallmadge, O., and shortly thereafter, with his bride, sailed as a missionary for Syria. He was assigned to a new station at Tripoli, and there he remained engaged in his chosen work a period of six years. At that time the dangerously impaired health of Mrs. Foote, coupled with the hope of medical aid to be secured in France or England, led them thither, only to find that nothing further could be done for her relief. An effort was made to reach America, but Mrs. Foote d. Dec. 24, 1854, just before entering New York harbor, and her body lies buried in the graveyard of her childhood's home at Tallmadge.

Though never able physically to return to the missionary field and labor, there is no doubt that his unremitting and zealous efforts produced a remarkable impress upon the entire community. The keynote of his teaching was ever the upbuilding of character. Religious belief, important however it might and should be, was to him the means only to the still more important end, right living, righteousness. Broadening and brightening in spirit and belief to the last day of his life, he inculcated and marvelously illustrated one of his favorite passages —''And the greatest of these is love.'' He graduated at Western Reserve College, 1846. Pastor, Middlebury, O., 1846-7. Ordained, Hudson, O., Apr. 6, 1848. Missionary, A. B. C. F. M., Triple Lyres., 1848-54. Released, 1856. He d. Oct. 17, 1887. Res., Tallmadge, O.

    4120. i. CHARLES WHITTLESEY, b. ——; m. Harriet Mason Hosford, 5547-52.

2602. ORSON MERRILL FOOTE, (1250, 433, 130, 39, 11, 3,) b. Dec. 21, 1847; m. Mar. 4, 1885, Senna S. Jones. She was b. July 26, 1830.

    4121. i. LEWIS A., b. May 1, 1858; m. Estella Wilson, 5553-4.

    4122. ii. CLARK MERRILL, b. Jan. 26, 1860; m. 5555-6.

    4123. iii. JESSE J., b. Feb. 9, 1867; m. Grace Eastman, 5557.

2604. GILBERT L. FOOTE, (1252, 433, 130, 39, 11, 3,) b. Nov. 17, 1832; m. 1st, May 21, 1852, Welthia G., dau. of Roswell P. Smith, b. Apr. 29, 1834; d. July 10, 1885; m. 2nd, Margaret Emerson. She d. Feb. 24, 1902. Farmer and cattle drover. Res., Potsdam, N. Y.

    4124. i. CHARLES, b. Nov. 13, 1854; m. Ida Allison, 5558.

    4125. ii. NELLIE, b. Sept. 19, 1857; m. Feb. 14, 1878, at Morley, N. Y., William Moyer, son of Samuel Moyer. He was b. Apr. 1, 1853. Ch.: (1) Charley, b. June 5, 1882. (2) Louis, b. June 13, 1886.

    4126. iii. GILBERT A., b. July 31, 1859; m. Clara Spotswood, 5559.

2607. AMOS C. FOOTE, (1262, 433, 130, 39, 11, 3,) b. Nov. 4, 1801; m. Lydia Tallman, of Perrington, N. Y.

    4127. i. ANDREW T. MELANCTON, b.

    4128. ii. DAU.

2613. ALBERTUS B. FOOTE, (1262, 433, 130, 39, 11, 3,) b. Manlius, N. Y., Nov. 3, 1818; m. Dec. 24, 1840, Caroline Wellman, dau. of Zalmon Goodsell, of Brookfield, Ct.

    4129. i. MARY FRANCES, b. New Milford, Ct., June 12, 1842.

    4130. ii. ELIZABETH ANN, b. New Milford, Ct., July 26, 1844; d. Dec. 12, 1844, at Kent, Ct.

    4131. iii. CAROLINE ELIZABETH, b. Bridgeport, Ct., Jan. 24, 1847.

2617. REV. GEORGE LEWIS FOOTE, (1270, 447, 134, 39, 11, 3,) b. Newtown, Ct., Mar. 4, 1812; m. Minerva, dau. of Wm. and Luella (Steel) Tuttle. She was b. Windham, N. Y., Sept. 22, 1815. He d. Nov. 2, 1863, at Morris, N. Y.

    4132. i. GEORGE, b. Roxbury, Ct., Apr. 25, 1840; d. Nov. 4, 1840.

4133. ii.   HARRIET MINERVA, b. Roxbury, Ct., Aug. 18, 1841; m. Bishop
            D. L. Tuttle. Res., 74 Vandeventer Place, St. Louis, Mo. Ch.:
            (1) George A., b. (2) Herbert, b. (3) Arthur, b. (4) Christine,
            b.; m. Stanley M. Ramsey, Cincinnati, O.; has two ch.

4134. iii. REV. GEORGE WILLIAM, b. Mar. 17, 1843; m. Sarah E. E.
            Pidsley, 5560.

4135. iv.   HENRY LEWIS b. Roxbury, Ct., May 2, 1845; m. July 15, 1868,
            Christine Carr. She d. Sept. 27, 1869; s. p.; m. 2nd, Oct. 30,
            1873, Ellen M. Wiggin. She d. Aug. 14, 1889; s. p.; m. 3rd,
            June 18, 1891, Harriet E. Rieley; no ch. Rector of the Episcopal
            Church in Marblehead, Mass.

4136. v.   MARY TUTTLE, b. Roxbury, Ct., Feb. 6, 1847; m. Rev. D. B.
            Miller. Res., St. Louis, Mo.

4137. vi.   SARAH MARIA, b. Roxbury, Ct., 1852; m. A. W. White. He
            d. ———. She res., St. Louis, Mo.

4137¹. vii. FRED RHEIA, b. McLean, N. Y., June 20, 1850; d. in infancy.

4137². viii. SARAH CATHERINE, b. McLean, N. Y., Apr. 5, 1852; d. ———.

4137³. ix.   CHARLES, b. McLean, N. Y., June 22, 1854; d. ———.

2620. FREDERICK WILLIAM FOOTE, (1270, 447, 134, 39, 11, 3,) b. Oct. 23,
1816; m. Dec. 27, 1816, Vashti Butler Thompson, of Madison, N. J.; d. abt. 1879,
at Elizabeth, N. J. Mrs. Foote res. in Elizabeth.

4138. i.   JULIA MAGIE, b. Dec. 31, 1841. Res., Elizabeth, N. J.; unm.

4139. ii.   FREDERICK WILLIAM, JR., b. Elizabeth, N. J., Dec. 6, 1844;
            m. Sara Randolph de Puy, 5561-5.

4140. iii. FRANCES MEEKER, b. Sept. 15, 1846; m. Apr. 21, 1875, William
            Boyce Eakin. He d. Res., Elizabeth, N. J. Ch.: (1) Elizabeth
            Butler, b. Apr. 27, 1877. (2) William Boyce, Jr., b. July 24,
            1868. (3) Frederick Foote, b. Nov. 25, 1879. (4) Constant
            Mathien, b. Jan. 18, 1886.

4141. iv.   LOUIS THOMPSON, b. Aug. 24, 1848; d. Dec. 15, 1874.

4142. v.   GEORGE RHESA, b. Nov. 19, 1850; d. Mar. 1, 1852.

4143. vi.   ANNA BUTLER, b. July 11, 1853; res., 433 Westminster Ave.,
            Elizabeth, N. J.

4144. vii. HARRIET, b. May 7, 1850; m. June 19, 1889, William Pebnington
            Loler; no ch.

4145. viii. MARY ROBERTS, b. Oct. 13, 1858; m. June 17, 1884, John
            Burnside Value. Ch.: (1) Burnside Rini, b. Aug. 10, 1888. (2)
            Mary Foote, b. July 6, 1894.

4146. ix.   HENRY H., b. Apr. 30, 1862; m. Ada S. Henderson, 5566.

2627. CHARLES HOMER FOOTE, (1273, 447, 134, 39, 11, 3,) b. Newtown,
Ct., May 18, 1812; m. Sept. 17, 1835, Mary, dau. of Joseph and Mary French, of
Randolph, Vt., at Chardon, O. She d. May 4, 1883. He d. Oct. 15, 1874; both at
Chardon, O.

4147. i.   MARY LOUISE, b. Mar. 15, 1848; d. Mar. 29, 1848.

4148. ii.   MARY S., b. May 14, 1850, at Chardon, O.; m. May 20, 1880,
            Albert D. Hovey, at Chardon, O. Ch. all b. at Chardon, O.: (1)
            Charles Albert Hovey, b. Sept. 7, 1884. (2) Ralph Foote Hovey,
            b. May 24, 1891.

4149. iii. JULIA CONVERSE, b. Dec. 20, 1854; d. June 15, 1875, at Char-
            don, O.

2629. JUSTIN FOOTE, (1273, 447, 134, 39, 11, 3,) b. at Newtown, Ct., May 19, 1816; m. 1st, Sarah Ann Edgecomb. She d.; m. 2nd, Annie M. Hickey. He d. Apr. 26, 1857.

4150. i. ERASTUS BAILEY, b. Barton, N. Y., July 4, 1841; m. 1866, Ruth A. King, of Waverly, N. Y.; d. 1880, in Oxford, Kas.; s. p.

4151. ii. GILBERT E., b. June 8, 1843; m. Isadore W. Davis, 5567¹-8.

4152. iii. HOBART J., b. Groton, N. Y., Dec. 5, 1844; d. July 19, 1882, at Waverly, N. Y.

4153. iv. SARAH ANN, b. abt. 1846; d. 1851, at McLean, N. Y.

4154. v. CHARLES H., b. abt. 1848; m. Ida Stark, 5569-71.

4155. vi. JAMES H., b. McLean, N. Y., abt. 1853; m. Isabel Morrow, 5572-3.

2635. JOHN MILTON FOOTE, (1274, 447, 134, 39, 11, 3,) b. Sept. 19, 1811; m. Oct. 1, 1835, Allida Ann Jackson. She was b. June 11, 1817; d. Nov. 12, 1885. He d. June 16, 1885. Ch. all b. in Adams Township, Hillsdale Co., Mich.

4155¹. i. LUCY A., b. Sept. 24, 1836; d. Dec. 23, 1836.

4156. ii. ABIGAIL S., b. Oct. 16, 1838; m. Eli A. Fuller. She d. Oct. 28, 1899. Res., Hillsdale, Mich. Ch.: (1) Augustus N., b. Aug. 30, 1859; m. Josaphine Loomis. (2) William Elmer, b. June 20, 1861; m. in N. Y. City. (3) Carrie A., b. May 4, 1863; m. Byron S. Everkast. (4) Hattie A., b. July 16, 1866; m. Joseph W. Houghton. (5) Myron G., b. Mar. 24, 1868; m. Mary Walsh. (6) Reuben J., b. Dec. 10, 1869. (7) Gertrude A., b. July 9, 1874. (8) Della A., b. June 11, 1876. (9) Lula A., b. June 12, 1878.

4157. iii. WILLIAM HENRY, b. Jan. 6, 1841; m. Melissa A. Fuller. Res., North Adams, Mich.

4158. iv. DELILA M., b. Dec. 22, 1842; d. Aug. 18, 1844.

4159. v. MILTON, b. Jan. 17, 1845; m. Fedelia A. Farley and Kathern Alzina Lane, 5574.

4160. vi. AUGUSTUS, b. Feb. 25, 1854; d. Sept. 1, 1855.

4161. vii. JOHN B., b. May 4, 1857; m. Anna L. Payne, 5575-6.

2637. JAMES FOOTE, (1274, 447, 134, 39, 11, 3,) b. Lock, Cayuga Co., N. Y., June 8, 1815; m. Nov. 16, 1837, Harriet M. Bagley, b. Metz, Cayuga Co., Sept. 7, 1818. She d. Sept. 16, 1872. He d. Mar. 16, 1880. He was Treasurer of the town of Adams for 20 years and Supervisor for eight years. Republican; farmer. Res., North Adams, Mich. Ch. all b. at North Adams, Mich.

4162. i. DAVID MILTON, b. Oct. 6, 1838; m. Myra Barker and Alice Yawger. He d. Nov. 21, 1893, at Charlotte, Mich.

4163. ii. HESTER MARIA, b. Feb. 25, 1840; m. Anson Barker. She d. Oct. 2, 1904, at Cambria, Mich.

4164. iii. HELEN AMELIA, b. Feb. 20, 1842; m. Norman Collins. Ch.: 2 daus.

4165. iv. CHARLES ROBERT, b. Apr. 11, 1844; d. Sept. 13, 1852, in North Adams, Mich.

4166. v. LOUISA MATILDA, b. Jan. 16, 1846; m. Charles H. Randolph. She d. June 4, 1894, at Addison, Lenawee Co., Mich.

4167. vi. RUFINA ADEL, b. June 10, 1848; m. Feb. 1, 1868, Eliphalet D. Barber. He was b. Wheatland, Mich., 1854; was a soldier in the Civil War; enlisted at the age of 17 years in Co. A, 11th Mich. Cavalry. Res., 57 Corwin St., Battle Creek, Mich. Ch.: (1) Flora Estelle, b. Moscow, Mich., Sept. 15, 1870; m. June 25, 1896,

Almond Burt Holcomb, at Battle Creek, Mich. He is engineer and steam fitter. (2) Edgar Foote, b. Fayette, Mich., Oct. 15, 1874; m. Apr. 3, 1897, Hetta Belle Henry, at Battle Creek, Mich. He is Traffic Manager of Citizens' Tel. Co., Traverse City, Mich. (3) Frank Eliphalet, b. Dec. 4, 1876, Wheatland, Mich.; d. Oct. 29, 1878, at Ogden, Kan. (4) Hester Belle, b. Ogden, Kan., Nov. 21, 1878; m. Dec. 25, 1897, Albert Schumacher, at Battle Creek, Mich. He is a carpenter and architect. (5) Inez Delle, b. Wheatland, Mich., May 13, 1881; m. Dec. 25, 1904, Fritz Buchholtz, at Albion, Mich. He is a cigar maker. (6) Don Demeloin, b. Battle Creek, Mich., June 23, 1891.

4168. vii. ELIZABETH ADELIA, b. Feb. 10, 1850; d. Sept. 30, 1852, in Adams, Mich.

4169. viii. MARY LYDIA, b. Feb. 1, 1853; d. Aug. 5, 1872, in Adams, Mich.

4170. ix. JULIA EVA, b. Sept. 18, 1855; d. same day.

4171. x. ESTELLE MINERVA, b. Jan. 18, 1857; m. Frank Dean and D. English. She d. Mar. 21, 1904, in Montpelier, O.

2639. WILLIAM BRISCOE, (1274, 447, 134, 39, 11, 3,) b. Apr. 11, 1820; m. Dec. 15, 1842, Susan Adelaide, dau. of Warner Aylsworth. She was b. Mar. 20, 1823, in N. Y. She d. Feb. 9, 1888; he d. Sept. 5, 1852.

4172. i. MYRON HOLLEY, b. Jan. 9, 1844; d. Aug. 7, 1854.

4173. ii. FRANCIS MARRION, b. June 21, 1846; d. Jan. 16, 1851.

4174. iii. CELIA MARIA, b. Apr. 19, 1848; m. June 21, 1870, Lucius A. Martin, at Muscatine, Iowa. He d. May 9, 1902, at New London, Wis.

4175. iv. WILLIAM WARNER, b. Apr. 9, 1850; d. Apr. 9, 1851.

4176. v. WILLARD L., b. May 16, 1852; d. May 16, 1853.

2641. AUGUSTUS NORMAN, (1274, 447, 134, 39, 11, 3,) b. Sept. 18, 1823; m. June 2, 1853, Sarah Susan, dau. of Abijah Parks. Res., Jackson, Mich. Commonwealth Power Co.

4177. i. WILLIAM A., b. June 9, 1854; m. Ida E. Westerman, 5577-80.

4178. ii. DELLA ELEANOR, b. ———; m. Adrian, Mich., Aug. 31, 1876, Prof. James Lent Holmes, of Farrington, Minn. He d. May 18, 1878; m. 2nd, Apr. 6, 1881, John L. Schoolcraft, at Adrian, Mich. He d. Oct. 1, 1891, at Adrian, Mich. Ch.: (1) Nettie Maria, b. Adrian, Mich., July 25, 1883. (2) Dell E., b. Adrian, Mich., Dec. 8, 1885. (3) James Edward, b. Adrian, Mich., Feb. 6, 1887. (4) John L., b. Battle Creek, Mich., Sept. 28, 1888.

4179. iii. NETTA AUGUSTA, b. Adrian, Mich., Sept. 25, 1855; m. Dec. 12, 1882, James Bayard Gibbons. He was b. Schuyler Co., N. Y., Nov. 27, 1853. Ch.: (1) Charles Bayard, b. Balaton, Minn., Feb. 28, 1884. (2) Helen M., b. Balaton, Minn., Aug. 28, 1885. (3) Norman Edward, b. Marshall, Minn., Oct. 16, 1888; d. Dec. 22, 1888.

4180. iv. JAMES B., b. Mar. 16, 1867; m. Rebecca E. Tuttle, 5581-4.

4181. v. CATHERINE AMELIA, b. Adrian, Mich., Feb. 25, 1869; m. William Pierson, son of John Church Darling. He was b. Kalamazoo, Mich., Apr. 25, 1869. Ch.: (1) Willard Foote, b. Kalamazoo, Mich., Feb. 25, 1894. (2) Florence Ella, b. Sept. 23,

1895, Kalamazoo, Mich. (3) Alta Louise, b. Kalamazoo, Mich., Sept. 23, 1895.

2643· ELI SWAYZEE FOOTE, (1274, 447, 134, 39, 11, 3,) b. Villanova, Chautauqua Co., N. Y., Apr. 1, 1828; m. North Adams, Mich., Apr. 8, 1854, Mary Culter. She d. Mar. 18, 1863, at Adrian, Mich.; m. 2nd, Apr. 7, 1867, Mary Frye, Laporte, Ind. She d. Oct. 2, 1905, at Asbury Park, N. J. At the time of his death he was in the employ of the San Antonio and Arkansas Pass R. R. Co. as foreman of the Car Department, which position he had held for many years, and was held in high esteem by that Company. He d. Feb. 18, 1902, in Yoakum, Texas.

    4182. i. FREDERICK, b. Adrian, Mich., June 7, 1856; m. Jeanette Sprague, 5585.

    4183. ii. MARY, b. Adrian, Mich., Mar. 18, 1863; d. Sept. 15, 1863, at Adrian, Mich.

    4184. iii. CLIFFORD AUGUSTUS, b. Laporte, Ind., Aug. 22, 1868. Res., Yoakum, Texas.

2643¹. WILLIAM P. FOOTE, (1279, 453, 134, 39, 11, 3,) b. Feb. 28, 1803, in Mass.; m. in Milan, N. Y., July 17, 1828, Betsy Murphy. She was b. June 5, 1806, just 101 years before the Foote Family Association was formed, and still living on the old Foote home, two miles north of Fredericktown, O. He d. Jan. 18, 1895. Res., N. Y. and Knox Co., O.

    4185. i. JOHN M., b. Apr. 15, 1829; m. Eva L. Payne, 6151-6.

2644. EPHRAIM FOOTE, (1279, 453, 134, 39, 11, 3,) b. 1807; m. Abbie Dennis; m. 2nd, Welthy Wright.

    4186. i. HENRY R., b. ———; m. Sarah Ann ———, 6157-9.

    4187. ii. WILBERT D., b. ———; m. Sarah ———, 6160-1.

    4188. iii. GEORGE W., b. ———.

    4188¹. iv. HELLEN, b. ———.

    4188². v. JULIA, b. ———.

2644¹. LARANCE FOOTE, (1279, 453, 134, 39, 11, 3,) b. 1808; m. Honor Rowley; m. 2nd, Isabelle Long.

    4189. i. WILLIAM, b. ———; m. Mary ———, 6167-68.

    4190. ii. ABIAH, b. ———; m. Cyrus Hosak. Ch.: (1) Earnest, b. (2) Fred, b. (3) William, b.

    4190¹. iii. MARY B., b. ———.

2645. ADONIJAH FOOTE, (1279, 453, 134, 39, 11, 3,) b. Auburn, N. Y., Dec. 10, 1810; m. Fredericktown, O., Jan. 31, 1839, Elizabeth Bedell. She was b. Newton, N. J., Jan. 18, 1821; d. Aug. 5, 1888, near Fredericktown, O. He d. Mar. 2, 1873, near Fredericktown, O.

    4191. i. LOIS D., b. Oct. 18, 1839; m. Jan. 16, 1862, Alexander Austen.

    4191¹. ii. HELEN M., b. Dec. 24, 1841; d. Feb. 21, 1891.

    4192. iii. WILBERT V., b. Oct. 25, 1843; m. Lydia A. Hill, 6169-75.

    4193. iv. WILLIAM H., b. Oct. 10, 1845; m. Mary A. Foote, 6176-82.

    4193¹. v. ABBIE R., b. Jan. 25, 1847; m. Nov. 20, 1877, David Bryant.

    4193². vi. THOMAS R., b. Oct. 9, 1849.

    4193³. vii. CORNELIA J., b. Oct. 25, 1851; m. Isam Reynolds.

    4194. viii. HOMER P., b. Oct. 18, 1853; m. Harriet E. Brown, 6183-7.

    4195. ix. MARY E., b. Oct. 4, 1855; m. Nov. 20, 1877, Lewis Dickey. Ch.: (1) Omer, b. (2) Bessie, b. (3) Ida, b. (4) Samuel, b. (5) Lula, b. (6) John, b.

(26)

4196. x.   M. CELIZA, b. Oct. 3, 1857; m. Feb. 21, 1900, Leander Black-
            ledge. Res., Fredericktown, O.
4197. xi. OLIVE ABIAH, b. Dec. 23, 1859; m. Dec. 25, 1883, George
            Wright. Ch.: (1) Elworth, b. (2) Walter, b. (3) Victor, b.
4198. xii. HATTIE, b. June 22, 1862; d. Mar. 23, 1883.
4199. xiii. JAMES BEDELL, b. Feb. 24, 1865; m. May 29, 1895, Anna L.
            Maple. He is one of Fredericktown's most prominent business
            men, the owner of the Bell Foundry, and the founder of the
            Foote addition, a man full of energy and business, and has much
            interest in all public affairs for the helping of mankind; donated,
            with his sister Herma, grounds for water works for the city of
            Fredericktown.
4200. xiv. HERMIE ELIZABETH, b. Feb. 21, 1869; d. in the hospital at
            Pittsburg, Jan. 30, 1907, after an illness of two years. She was
            b. and spent her early years on the old home farm, one and a
            half miles north of Fredericktown. The bright, summer days of
            her childhood were spent in roaming over fields and through the
            woodlands and enjoying the beauties of nature. With persistent
            energy and ambition her artistic ability developed into a profit-
            able business, which was established with her brother in 1892.
            She continued in that business for eight years. For the past
            seven years she has been engaged with her brother in the J. B.
            Foote Foundry Co. During the last two years her failing health
            has made it impossible to continue in active business. Her un-
            usual ability made her rank among the first of the business
            people of the town. She had a deep and earnest motive back of
            her work, which was the elevation and prosperity of the working
            class.

    2652. WILLIAM D. FOOTE, (1281, 459, 137, 39, 11, 3,) b. Watertown, Ct.,
May 1, 1803; m. twice; 2nd, Jan. 8, 1836, Maria Loveland. She was b. in Ct.,
May 17, 1817; d. Aug. 27, 1897. Mr. Foote was an industrious farmer in St.
Joseph Co., 38 years; d. Apr. 22, 1890.
4201. i.   MARGARET ANN, b. Erie Co., N. Y., Nov. 25, 1836; m. Mar. 20,
            1856, Lucius, son of Samuel Treadwell, of South Bend, Ind. He
            was b. Apr. 9, 1831; d. Apr. 7, 1886. Ch.: (1) Mary E., b. South
            Bend, Ind., June 20, 1858; m. Oct. 3, 1882, Andrew Jackson, son
            of David Rudduck, of South Bend, Ind. Ch.: (a) Darwin, b.
            South Bend, Ind., Mar. 6, 1884; d. Nov. 27, 1884. (2) Marilla
            S., b. South Bend, Ind., Oct. 3, 1860; d. Mar. 6, 1864. (3) Effie
            M., b. South Bend, Ind., Aug. 23, 1863; m. Nov. 6, 1895, Frank,
            son of Thomas Bowen. (4) William E., b. South Bend, Ind., May
            27, 1867; d. Mar. 13, 1868.
4202. ii. SUSAN, b. Erie Co., N. Y., Nov. 14, 1839; m. Apr. 6, 1857, Orlando,
            son of Lewis Wheelock, of Glenwood, N. Y. He was b. July 30,
            1834; d. Nov. 7, 1900. Ch.: (1) Flora Belle, b. Glenwood, N. Y.,
            Feb. 22, 1867; m. Aug. 2, 1887, Orlando, son of John M. Asire, of
            South Bend, Ind. Ch.: (a) Horace W., b. South Bend, Ind., Mar.
            7, 1891.
4203. iii. RUTH, b. Erie Co., N. Y., Nov. 17, 1845; m. Dec. 31, 1863, Har-
            rison, son of Thomas Robbins, of Morgan Co., Ind. Ch.: (1)

Carrie May, b. South Bend, Ind., Dec. 4, 1866; m. Dec. 20, 1883, Evaw, son of Zechariah Garrett, of South Bend, Ind. Ch.: (a) Myrtle, b. South Bend, Ind., Mar. 16, 1886. (b) Delbert, b. South Bend, Ind., Sept. 24, 1893. (c) Walter, b. South Bend, Ind., Nov. 22, 1899. (2) George, b. South Bend, Ind., Jan. 4, 1869; m. Sept. 20, 1888, Carrie, dau. of Samuel Hawkins, of South Bend, Ind. Ch.: (a) Ray, b. South Bend, Ind., Mar. 20, 1891. (b) Ruth, b. South Bend, Ind., Sept. 16, 1901. (3) Glen, b. South Bend, Ind., June 10, 1886. (4) Walter, b. South Bend, Ind., Dec. 19, 1888; d. Aug. 30, 1889.

4204. iv. LINUS, b. Jan. 20, 1848; m. Melissa Rupe, 5586.

4205. v. MARY, b. Erie Co., N. Y., July 22, 1852; m. Sept. 11, 1870, Osborne, son of Daniel Keeley, of South Bend, Ind. He was b. Apr., 1847; d. Aug. 10, 1872; m. 2nd, Jan. 29, 1874, William, son of Samuel Rupe, of South Bend, Ind. Ch.: (1) Millie B., b. South Bend, Ind., Oct. 6, 1871; d. Aug. 22, 1873.

4206. vi. CYRUS, b. Apr. 25, 1857; m. Carrie Hayes, 5587-8.

2653. ROSWELL FOOTE, (1281, 459, 137, 39, 11, 3,) b. Watertown, Ct., Aug. 24, 1804; m. 1828, Harriet Smith. She was b. May 13, 1810; d. Apr. 15, 1866. Res., Woodbury, Ct.

4207. i. SARAH MARIA, b. July 15, 1829; m. June 1, 1851, Charles Manville. Ch.: (1) Jane, b. Aug. 10, 1853. (2) Henry, b. June 8, 1855. (3) Wallace, b. Jan. 5, 1857. (4) Charles, b. Sept. 14, 1860. (5) Hattie, b. Mar. 16, 1862.

4208. ii. GEORGE SMITH, b. Apr. 19, 1831; m. Mar. 25, 1869, Louisa Ward. She d. Jan. 27, 1896.

4209. iii. ELIZABETH MARY, b. May 3, 1834; m. May 4, 1860, Augustus Thompson. He was b. Oct. 12, 1819; d. Feb. 28, 1875. She res. Milldale, Ct. Ch.: (1) Elsworth Elmer Thompson, b. Feb. 2, 1861; m. Apr. 16, 1883, Ervillia Lewis. He d. Mar. 20, 1887. Ch.: (a) Elmer Ives, b. May 20, 1884. (b) Cora, b. Apr. 28, 1886. (2) Augustus Thompson, b. July 22, 1866; d. July 25, 1889. (3) Elsie Netta Thompson, b. June 11, 1868; m. 1st, May 12, 1889, Matthew A. Trewhella; m. 2nd, Charles I. Parker. Ch. by 1st husband: (a) Julia Elizabeth, b. June 1, 1890. (b) Clifford Thompson, b. Jan. 25, 1892. (c) Jennie, b. Jan. 23, 1894. (4) Belle Louise Thompson, b. May 7, 1870; m. Oct. 17, 1894, Henry Allen North, in Meriden. Ch.: (a) Elsie Parker North, b. Feb. 23, 1903. (5) William Richard Thompson, b. Jan. 22, 1873.

4209¹. iv. CHARLES EDWARD, b. Dec. 27, 1852.

2654. RANSFORD THOMAS FOOTE, (1281, 459, 137, 39, 11, 3,) b. Watertown, Litchfield Co., Ct., Jan. 6, 1806. He was a man of marked integrity and always willing to extend a helping hand to his fellow men. He met the vicissitudes of pioneer life manfully, and by indefatigable perseverance he ultimately hewed out a comfortable home amidst the primeval wilderness of the Holland Land Purchase of Western New York. His wife, Susan, dau. of Wheeler and Susannah (Stoddard) Atwood, was b. in Woodbury, Litchfield Co., Ct., Dec. 2, 1805; they were m. Nov. 16, 1828, in Ct.; moved to Unadilla, N. Y., in 1829; in 1830 came to Otto, Cattaraugus Co., N. Y., where they lived for six years, moving from there to Colden, Erie Co., N. Y. At the latter place Mr. Foote engaged in the boot and shoe manufacturing business, which he conducted for three years. In Mar., 1839, he moved with his family to Concord, Erie Co., N. Y., where he res. until his decease on Apr. 6, 1891, having lived on the same farm for 52 continuous years. She d. Sept. 12, 1890.

4210. i. HARRY, b. Cattaraugus Co., Mar. 22, 1832, and was educated in the common schools of those times, attending the district school in winter and working on the farm in summer. He alternated teaching with farming and mechanical pursuits for a few years, but for the past 40 years has made farming the primary avocation of life. After living on the old homestead in Concord, Erie Co., N. Y., 53 years, or from Mar., 1839, to Oct. 7, 1892, he moved to Springville, N. Y., where he now res., a retired farmer. Feb. 11, 1864, he m. Jennie Rollo Calkins, b. Aug. 23, 1838, dau. of William A. and Eliza Fitz (Rollo) Calkins, of Colden, N. Y. No ch. The memories of a pleasant life on the farm associated with father and mother, come back to the writer with responsive emotions. The same silver streams go purling on their courses, the ripples will ripple on just as happily, the sunshine will kiss the hills and valleys just as warmly and lovingly, the herds of cattle will be ruminating on the green pastures just as meekly and quietly; but other eyes will be looking upon them, other hearts will throb and burn with hopes, ambitions, loves, joys and sorrows as of old.

2656. LUCIUS FOOTE, (1281, 459, 137, 39, 11, 3,) b. Plymouth, Ct., May 7, 1810; m. 1st, Jan., 1842, Eliza Ann, dau. of Oliver Atwood, of Watertown, Ct.; m. 2nd, 1856, Agnes Galloway. She d. in South Dakota, Mar. 20, 1886. He d. in Mansfield, Cattaraugus Co., N. Y., Mar. 27, 1861.

4211. i. LARMON, b. in Ct., 1842; m. Angelia Foster, 5589-90.
4212. ii. HENRY C., b. in Ct., 1844; m. Josephene Salsbury, 5591-2.
4213. iii. GIRL, d. five weeks old.
4214. iv. FRANK, b. Apr. 19, 1859; m. Alice Abel and Mrs. Libby Riley, 5593-7.
4215. v. MARY L., b. Apr. 27, 1861; m. Sept. 9, 1882, Ransom Nourse, of Hebron, Ill., and now live in Stettler, Alberta, Canada. Ch.: (1) Mabel, b. July 12, 1884; m.; lives in Indian Territory. (2) Clara May, b. Oct. 14, 1886; d. Aug. 29, 1906. (3) Frank, b. June 10, 1888. (4) Asa, b. May 8, 1890. (5) Flossie Agnes, b. Jan. 16, 1892. (6) Lester, b. in Indian Territory, July, 1900.

1820. FRANCIS E. FOOTE, (942, 298, 89, 26, 9, 3,) b. Aug. 26, 1826, Chardon, O.; m. July 14, 1849, Harriet Eldridge, at Chardon, O.

4216. i. EUGENE, b. June 24, 1850, Chardon; d. Aug. 31, 1863, Chardon.
4217. ii. JAMES, b. Feb. 4, 1853; m. Nellie Markel, 5189.
4218. iii. MARY, b. May 18, 1856, Chardon; m. Oct. 21, 1874, Nathan Harvey. Res., Chardon, O.

2657. ALEXIS FOOTE, (1281, 459, 137, 39, 11, 3,) b. Aug. 11, 1812; m. Sept. 4, 1843, Christiana Millis, b. at Saratoga, N. Y., Feb. 22, 1826. She d. Mar. 22, 1900. He d. Oct. 15, 1859. Res., South Bend, Ind. Ch. all b. at South Bend, Ind.

4219. i. FRANK MILLES, b. May 26, 1846; m. Ida Lucy Duel, 5598-5601.
4220. ii. WILLIAM A., b. June 6, 1848; m. Florence E. Frazier, 5602-5.
4221. iii. JAMES E., b. June 13, 1851; m. Georgia Clawson, 5606-11.
4222. iv. MARY EMELINE, b. Jan. 9, 1853.
4223. v. MARK W., b. Dec. 18, 1854; m. Rose M. Wells, 5612-16.
4224. vi. MATTIE EVA, b. South Bend, Ind., Oct. 2, 1856; m. at South Bend, Ind., Apr. 10, 1881, Ralph Samuel Tarbell, b. Sept. 19, 1853; d. Mar. 11, 1901. Ch.: (1) Ozmun Ami Tarbell, b. at South Bend, Ind., Feb. 8, 1883; m. Francis Evelyn Walker, b. at Manchester, Tenn., Aug. 24, 1883. They were m. at South Bend, Ind., Jan. 17, 1905. (2) Horace William Tarbell, b. at South Bend, Ind., Jan. 31, 1886. (3) Fred. Foote Tarbell, b. at South Bend, Ind., Nov. 26, 1887.

2659. FREDERICK FOOTE, (1281, 459, 137, 39, 11, 3,) b. Oct. 11, 1817; m. Oct., 1841, Mary Ann, dau. of Edward Smith, of Middlebury, Ct. She was b. May 28, 1820. She d. Feb. 18, 1899. He d. Apr. 2, 1891.

4225. i. HARRIET CORNELIA, b. in Watertown, Ct., Sept. 13, 1842; m. William Henry Bassette, of Burlington, Colorado, son of William and Maria Bassette, of Watertown, Ct., May 26, 1886. Harriet C. Bassette was from the years 1864 to 1874 a teacher to the Freedmen in Georgia and South Carolina under the auspices of the American Missionary Association of New York City.

4226. ii. URANIA URSULA FOOTE was m. in Watertown, Ct., Jan. 1, 1874, to George Wellman, of Woodbury, Ct., son of Jacob Wellman. Was b. in Maine, Apr. 15, 1846. She d. in Bethany, Ct., Feb. 10, 1887.. Ch.: (1) Martha Wellman, b. Oct. 12, 1878; m. Feb. 1, 1900, Myron Wheeler, Watertown, Ct., b. Jan. 4, 1872, son of Eli Wheeler, of Watertown, Ct. Myron Wheeler is a prosperous farmer. Ch.: (a) Mary, b. Nov. 25, 1900. (b) Loren William, b. Jan. 27, 1902. (c) Ernest, b. July 18, 1904. (2) Frederick Amos Wellman, b. Nov. 1, 1879, Plymouth, Ct., mechanic; m. Apr. 15, 1903, to Nellie Prince Tolles, dau. of Hattie Ellen and Henry Tolles, of Plymouth, Ct. (3) Susan Urania Wellman, b. May 28, 1886; teacher, Watertown, Ct.

4227. iii. PRESTON ATWOOD, b. Oct. 13, 1851; mechanic, Chicago, Ill.

4228. iv. ELLIS BENAGER, b. Sept. 14, 1856. Many years an invalid; d. in Watertown, Ct., Feb. 3, 1891.

4229. v. ABBIE E., b. Oct. 29, 1859, of Watertown, Ct. A popular and successful teacher in this and adjoining towns.

4230. vi. HENRY LYMAN, b. Jan. 4, 1863, of Des Moines Iowa.

4231. vii. WILLIAM SKILTON, b. Oct. 23, 1865; m. Feb. 14, 1887, Grace, dau. of David M. Ward, of Watertown, Ct. She was b. Nov. 23, 1870. Mr. Foote is a very successful farmer, Res., Watertown, Ct.

2660. LARMON FOOTE, (1281, 459, 137, 39, 11, 3,) b. Oct. 9, 1818, in Watertown, Ct.; m. Louisa Urania Cochran. She was b. Nov. 4, 1832; d. Dec. 28, 1882. He d. Mar. 24, 1892. Res., Great Valley, Cattaraugus Co., N. Y.

4232. i. ALICE A., b. Dec. 12, 1853; d. July 15, 1889; m. 1873, Ambros W. Markham. He was b. May 16, 1849. He d. Ch.: (1) Alida. (2) Ethel.

4233. ii. LUCY LUELLA, b. Oct. 3, 1855; m. Dec. 25, 1872, Lyman Jones. He was b. Mar. 23, 1850, and d. Jan. 24, 1897. She d. June 10, 1885. Ch.: (1) Willber, b. in Great Valley, Cattaraugus Co., N. Y., Jan. 24, 1881. Res., Perry, Wyoming Co., N. Y.

2661. HENRY L. FOOTE, (1281, 459, 137, 39, 11, 3,) b. Sept. 2, 1820; m. Apr. 7, 1853, Clarisa Foster. She was b. July 31, 1831, and d. July 31, 1882, in Mansfield, Cattaraugus Co., N. Y. He d. Sept. 1, 1898.

4234. i. ELLA S., b. Nov. 16, 1854; m. Nov. 11, 1874, Charles A. Locke. Ch.: (1) Harry, b. May 4, 1877; m. (2) Hattie, b. July 24, 1880. (3) Mildred, b. 1890.

4235. ii. ATTY E., b. May 12, 1863; m. Feb. 29, 1888, Geo. G. Rasey. Ch.: (1) Ralph L., b. Dec. 1, 1888. (2) Henry J., b. Mar. 13, 1889. (3) Harry D., b. Feb. 11, 1890.

2669. BEERS FOOTE, (1309, 473, 142, 41, 11, 3,) b. July 5, 1805; m. Apr. 9, 1829, Pamelia A. Merwin, of Newtown, Ct. Res., Brookfield, Ct.

4236. i. SAMUEL, b. May 29, 1830; d. Apr. 18, 1833.

2671. SHERMAN FOOTE, (1309, 473, 142, 41, 11, 3,) b. Dec. 14, 1814; m. Oct. 11, 1835, Clarena, dau. of John A. Peck, of Brookfield, Ct.

4237. i. CORNELIA EVELYN, b. Dec. 29, 1837; m. Oct. 22, 1857, Samuel S. Dunning, of Bethel, Ct.

4238. ii. HENRY L., b. Brookfield, Ct., July 18, 1841; m. 1st, Oct. 12, 1864, at Brookfield, Jennie Maria, dau. of Benjamin Hawley. She was b. Feb. 5, 1843, in Brookfield; d. Jan. 14, 1904, in Brookfield; m. 2nd, Oct. 21, 1905, at Bayonne, N. J., Fannie Foster Allaine (widow), dau. of Daniel Foster. She was b. Peekskill, N. Y., Mar. 15, 1866. Farmer. Congregationalist. Res., Brookfield, Ct. No ch.

4239. iii. WILLIAM WORTH, b. Sept. 22, 1846; m. Jean Lewis, of N. Y. Res., Mt. Kisco, N. Y.

2724. THEODORE CYRENIUS, (1334, 486, 145, 41, 11, 3,) b. June 12, 1825; m. Mary Elizabeth Hunt, of New York, N. Y. She d. Apr. 10, 1907. He d. Jan. 27, 1905, at Cleveland, O.

4239¹. i. HERBERT CARRINGTON, b. Mar. 15, 1852; m. Eva Victoria Withycombe, of Cleveland; d. Aug. 27, 1888, at Cleveland, O.; s. p.

4240. ii. WILLIE H., b. July 11, 1855; m. Fannie E. Roberts, 5651-3.

4241. iii. THEODORE C., b. July 26, 1857; m. Leila M. Wilson, 5654-5.

4242. iv. HARRY M., b. Sept. 20, 1863; m. Mary Withycombe, 5655-6.

4242¹. v. ARTHUR SPENCER, b. Apr. 19, 1873; d. Aug. 7, 1873, in Cleveland, O.

2725. DANIEL DELAZON FOOTE, (1334, 486, 145, 41, 11, 3,) b. Hobart, N. Y., Jan. 2, 1827; d. in Tarrytown, N. Y., on Aug. 20, 1905. Merchant and pioneer American silk manufacturer. Protectionist. Advocate, writer and speaker for American industrial independence. Mr. Foote was m. three times, 1st to Julia Seaman Amerman, who d. in 1850; 2nd to Helen Morilla Foote, who d. in 1863, and last to Lavinia Meeker on Sept. 6, 1865, who survives him.

4243. i. JULIA AUGUSTA, b. New York, May 12, 1850.

4244. ii. HENRY WAINWRIGHT, b. in New York, Aug. 28, 1852. Merchant and glass manufacturer; speaker and writer on Protective

Political Economy. Author of the "Principle of Protection"; promoter of glass industry and farmer. Res., 156 Broadway, N. Y.

4245. iii. FREDERICK S., b. June 27, 1858; m. Anna Griebel, 6142-7.

4246. iv. BENJAMIN LINCOLN, b. Tarrytown, N. Y., June 7, 1866.

4247. v. HELEN LAVINIA, b. Tarrytown, N. Y., Dec. 22, 1869.

4247¹. vi. CLARA WIBERT, b. Tarrytown, N. Y., Apr. 1, 1871.

4247². vii. WILLIAM, b. Tarrytown, N. Y., Apr. 23, 1873; d. Aug. 1, 1873.

4248. viii. CATHERINE LOUISE, b. Tarrytown, N. Y., Mar. 24, 1878.

2699. DANIEL EDWIN FOOTE, (1324, 481, 142, 41, 11, 3,) b. Mar. 30, 1818, in Stamford, N. Y.; m. 1st, June 7, 1842, Betsy Ann Griffen. She d. Apr. 22, 1857; m. 2nd, Feb. 23, 1859, Adelia Gould. Both were of Stamford, N. Y. Farmer. He d. Apr. 6, 1897. Res., Stamford, N. Y., and after 1850, Medina, O.

4249. i. FRANCIS MARIA, b. June 6, 1846; d. Oct. 22, 1848.

4250. ii. SAMUEL G., b. July 17, 1850; m. Henrietta Cole, 5616-9.

4251. iii. WILLIAM C., b. June, 1868; m. Carrie Perkins, 5620-1.

4252. iv. FAYETTE DANIEL, b. Nov., 1870; m. Lydia Weible, Feb. 14, 1901. Res., Medina, O. Farmer.

2700. HENRY BAILEY FOOTE, (1324, 481, 142, 41, 11, 3,) b. Sept. 29, 1820; m. Jan. 30, 1856, Lucretia, dau. of Horace and Eliza Eels, of Walton, N. Y. She was b. June 3, 1827, and d. Feb. 28, 1875. He d. Aug. 24, 1889. Farmer. Res., Stamford, N. Y.

4253. i. EDWIN B., b. Feb. 6, 1857; m. Lizzie Ross, 5622-4.

4254. ii. EMMA ADELIA, b. Mar. 11, 1863; m. Oct. 20, 1885, Burr Brockway, of Stamford, N. Y. Ch.: (1) Florence, b. Jan. 20, 1888. (2) Orrin Burr, b. Sept. 21, 1889.

4255. iii. FRANK S., b. May 1, 1866; m. Dora C. Dayton, 5625-7.

2701. CHARLES AUSTIN, (1324, 481, 142, 41, 11, 3,) b. Oct. 5, 1823; m. Jarusha Ann Buck, Mar. 12, 1845. She d. Oct. 10, 1896. He d. May 23, 1899. Farmer and cattle dealer. Res., Stamford, N. Y.

4256 i. ORLANDO B., b. Feb. 27, 1846; m. Ella E. Stevens, 5628-37.

2702. ALBERT FOOTE, (1324, 481, 142, 41, 11, 3,) b. Feb. 10, 1826; m. Sept. 25, 1850, Loanda, dau. of David Patcher. She d. 1886. He moved with his family to Medina, O., in 1857. Dealer in real estate.

4257. i. DAVID, b. Harpersfield, N. J., 1853; m. Frances Caroline Barlow and Mary White, 5638-40.

4258. ii. FRANCES, b. Stamford, N. Y., Jan. 10, 1855; m. Jan. 25, 1878, Augustus Waltz. She d. Dec. 29, 1890. Farmer. Res., Lafayette, Ohio.

4259. iii. HARRIET, b. Medina, O., July 26, 1861; m. Mar. 12, 1884, Miles Dorman. She d. Jan. 6, 1891.

4260. iv. STATIRA, b. Medina, O., Sept. 24, 1867; m. Jan. 17, 1900, John W. Whitehead.

2704. WILLIAM BAILY FOOTE, (1324, 481, 142, 41, 11, 3,) b. Apr. 10, 1833; m. Mar. 14, 1866, Sarah Elizabeth Swart. She was b. Nov. 22, 1841; d. May 16, 1885. Farmer, living on the old Foote Homestead until his death; the Homestead then passed out of the Foote family. He d. Dec. 23, 1884. Res., Stamford, N. Y.

4261. i. BERTHA ADALINE, b. Dec. 9, 1866; m. Apr. 6, 1886, John J.
Clark. Farmer. Ch.: (1) William J., b. Nov. 1, 1888. (2) Alida
Jerusha, b. June 6, 1893. (3) Randall E., b. Aug. 20, 1897.

2707. OSCAR FOOTE, (1325, 481, 142, 41, 11, 3,) b. June 3, 1822; m. Mary
L. Harrison, of New York City. She was b. June 24, 1831, and d. Nov. 3, 1882.
Mr. Foote held the office of Supervisor of L'Anse, Mich., for eleven years; he was
also Clerk of Baraga Co., Mich. He d. June 14, 1897.

4262. i. ROBERT WALLACE, b. June 26, 1860. Proprietor of Hotel,
Breckinridge, Col.

4263. ii. FRANK W., b. Aug. 10, 1862. Is Supervisor of L'Anse, Mich.;
unm.

4264. iii. NELEA, b. Feb. 10, 1869; m. W. R. Harris. Res., Mass. City,
Mich. Ch.: (1) Adeline J., b. July 22, 1895. (2) Mary Louise, b.
May 9, 1898. (3) Robert Foote, b. Nov. 25, 1903.

2709. GEORGE L. FOOTE, (1325, 481, 142, 41, 11, 3,) b. Oxford, N. Y.,
Jan. 27, 1827; m. ———. He was a soldier in the Civil War; d. just after the
battle of Winchester, Va., Sept. 20, 1864.

4265. i. CARRIE, b. Wyoming, Ia., Dec. 6, 1861; m. June 12, 1888, Frank
B. Newkirk, of Oxford, N. Y. R. R. Engineer. Ch.: (1) George
Frederick, b. Oxford, N. Y., Sept. 20, 1893.

2713. EDWARD PETER FOOTE, (1327, 481, 142, 41, 11, 3,) b. Jan. 9, 1836;
m. Aug. 28, 1864, Amanda M., dau., of Samuel and Lucina (Shepard) Gleason.
She was b. Nov. 9, 1844; d. July 12, 1873. Res., Genoa, Ill.

4266. i. FREDERICK, b. Apr. 28, 1866.

4267. ii. WILLARD, b. July 8, 1868.

4268. iii. JENNIE LOUISA, b. July 26, 1871.

2715. CHARLES L. FOOTE, (1332, 484, 142, 41, 11, 3,) b. Dec. 12, 1833; m.
at Stamford, N. Y., Feb. 22, 1855, Jane, dau. of Eurial Hamilton. She was b. at
Harpersfield, N. Y., July 24, 1834; d. Jan. 11, 1906, at Harpersfield, N. Y. Methodist.
Farmer and carpenter. He d. Apr. 10, 1906, at Bloomville, N. Y. Ch. all b. at
Harpersville, N. Y.

4270. i. FRANK A., b. Mar. 24, 1856; m. Alice Pierce, 5641-43.

4271. ii. JULIA L., b. Sept. 8, 1857; m. Nov. 6, 1889, in Hobart, N. Y.,
William H., son of Aleck Forman. He was b. Sept. 23, 1844; d.
July 23, 1905; s. p. Res., Bloomville, N. Y.

4272. iii. ADALINE H., b. Dec. 12, 1859; m. at Harpersfield, N. Y., Dec.
19, 1888, William Dyer. Res., Jefferson, N. Y.

4273. iv. JOHNSON E., b. Feb. 26, 1826; m. Adaline Crowe, 5644-8.

4274. v. ALBERT E., b. Oct. 8, 1870; m. in Delhi, N. Y., Oct. 18, 1904,
Anna Burdick (widow), dau. of Leon H. Every. She was b. at
Bloomville, N. Y., Sept. 27, 1883. He was educated at Harpers-
field, N. Y. Methodist. Carpenter. Res., South Gilboa, N. Y.
No ch.

2716. ORRIN FOOTE, (1333, 486, 145, 41, 11, 3,) b. Harpersfield, N. Y., Sept.
30, 1799; m. Oct. 18, 1826, Elizabeth, dau. of John T. and Eleanor Moore. She
was b. in Roxbury, N. Y., Oct. 30, 1794; d. Nov. 5, 1886. He was a member of
the House of Representatives of the Legislature of the State of New York in
1846. Merchant and manufacturer. He was a great business man. He lived on

the old Foote Homestead in New York until 1852, and then moved to Alexander, Va., then to Brooklyn, N. Y., where he d. July 18, 1873.

4275. i. BAILEY, b. June 20, ——; d. July 3, 1832.

4276. ii. ELEANOR ELIZABETH, b. Sept. 4, 1834; d. Oct. 24, 1835.

4277. iii. CHARLOTTE ELIZABETH, b. July 19, 1836, in Stamford, N. Y.; m. Sept. 15, 1859, Joseph Merrill. She d. July 1, 1902, in Brooklyn, N. Y.; s. p.

4278. iv. JOHN MOORE, b. Nov. 4, 1840; m. Mary Francis Cromwell and Ella A. Flindt, 5649-60.

2718. GEORGE BRYANT FOOTE, (1333, 486, 145, 41, 11, 3,) b. Aug. 17, 1808; m. Sept. 10, 1833. She was b. Stamford, N. Y., May 2, 1809; d. June 15, 1835, in Hobart, N. Y.; m. 2nd, June 12, 1836, Maria Emma Glover. She was b. Newtown, Ct., Feb. 1, 1813.

4279. i. BAILEY, b. Sept. 28, 1834.

4280. ii. MARY JANE, b. Mar. 23, 1837; m. Samuel H. Stevens. Ch.: (1) Cassie Englina, b. ——; m. Mar. 29, 1893, Bruce S. Preston, b. Oct. 13, 1863. Res., Roxbury, N. Y.

2739. GEORGE DENSMORE FOOTE, (1341, 488, 145, 41, 11, 3,) b. Salem, N. Y., Feb. 1, 1805; m. Sept. 20, 1828, Sophia Ann Hooker. She d. Oct. 8, 1886. He d. Oct. 10, 1846, at Pleasant Prairie. *w.i.*

4281. i. JOHN H., b. Aug. 22, 1829; m. Emeline Eastman, 5657-64.

4282. ii. RACHEL ANN, b. Martinsburg, N. Y., Aug. 28, 1831; m. Oct. 1852, John Reynolds, of Pleasant Prairie, Wis. Ch.: (1) George Foote, b. Pleasant Prairie, Wis., July 12, 1853; m. Jan. 22, 1876, Eliza Griffin. Res., Argos, Ind. No ch. (2) Philip Henry, b. Jan. 6, 1857; m. Feb. 25, 1886, Margaret Doyle. Ch.: (a) Theresa, b. Dec. 15, 1886. (b) John, b. June 22, 1890. (3) Frank Minot, b. Jan. 6, 1857; d. Sept. 28, 1859. (4) Phebe Ann, b. Oct. 6, 1858; d. Feb. 13, 1860. (5) Charlotte Ann, b. Jan. 2, 1861; m. July 24, 1895, E. Bememderfer. No ch. Res., Chicago, Ill. (6) Margaret Sophia, b. Oct. 31, 1862. Res., Ranney, Wis. P. O., Pleasant Prairie, R. D. 33; unm. (7) Alfred Churchill, b. Jan. 2, 1865; m. Mar. 4, 1890, Helen E. King. (8) Justin B., b. Dec. 5, 1866; unm. (9) Richard A., b. July 5, 1869; m. Nov. 28, 1894, Alice E. Closby. Ch.: (a) Richard A., Jr., b. July 14, 1896. (b) William Delos, b. Sept. 13, 1898. (c) John Lowell, b. Oct. 11, 1901. (10) Arthur Leon, b. June 24, 1872; m. June 28, 1894, Tina J. Threster. Ch.: (a) Helen Margaret, b. Jan. 27, 1895. (b) Esther Rachel, b. Jan. 15, 1900. (11) Josephine L., b. May 15, 1874; m. Nov., 1901, Richard A. Selway. Res., Alzada, Montana. Ch.: (a) Vera, b. Aug. 18, 1903.

4283. iii. CHARLOTTE AMANDA, b. Martinsburg, N. Y., June 17, 1833; she res. with her sister Rachel's dau. at the home farm in Ranney, Pleasant Prairie, Wis., R. D. 33.

4284. iv. GEORGE WILLIAM, b. Martinsburg, N. Y., July 13, 1835; m. Jan. 22, ——, Eliza Griffin; no ch.

4285. v. EMMA CHURCHILL, b. Pleasant Prairie, Wis., Sept. 8, 1837; m. Feb. 23, 1862, Henry Kirke White. He d. Sept., 1905. Ch.: (1) George Henry, b. Dec. 8, 1862; m. Apr. 20, 1887, Florence Dabbs. Ch.: (a) Edna Gladys, b. (b) Kenneth George, b. (2)

Clara Philena, b. Aug. 26, 1865; m. Nov. 21, 1887, Edwin Leroy Adams. Ch.: (a) James Kirke, b. May 11, 1888. (b) Alta May, b. Apr. 29, 1889. (c) Dorothy Emma, b. May 7, 1894. (d) Francis, b. July 14, 1895. (e) Edwin Leroy, b. Jan. 31, 1897. (f) Bert, b. (g) Ward, b. (3) Dallas Ward, b. Dec. 8, 1867. (4) Clarence Walter, b. Nov., 1868. (5) Carrie Ann, b. Dec., ——; d. ——. (6) Alma.

4286. vi. HENRY M., b. Oct. 28, 1839; m. Alphonsine Platt, 5665-7.

4287. vii. JANE, b. Pleasant Prairie, Aug. 31, 1842; m. Arthur Frederic Jones, of Hebron, Ill. Ch.: (1) Jessie M., b. Oct. 17, 1877; d. Nov. 14, 1877. (2) Charles Frederic, b. Oct. 28, 1878; d. Nov. 22, 1878. (3) Arthur Henry, b. Mar. 13, 1880; m. Feb., 1902, Edith Temple. (4) Sophia Ann, b. Sept. 9, 1884; d. Mar. 8, 1885. (5) Henry Samuel, b. Dec. 8, 1885. (6) Alice M., b. May 25, 1889.

4288. viii. CHARLES P., b. Nov. 25, 1844; m. Ella Silliman, 5668-75.

4289. ix. EMILIE MILLS, b. Pleasant Prairie, Wis., Dec. 25, 1846; m. Mar. 4, 1870, James Ward White, of Pleasant Prairie, Wis. Res., Charles City, Iowa. Ch.: (1) Ward C., b. Douseman, Wis., Jan. 16, 1876. (2) Louise J., b. Pleasant Prairie, Wis., Mar. 6, 1880. (3) Mabel E., b. Charles City, Iowa, Dec. 31, 1886.

2743. GILES FOOTE, (1341, 488, 145, 41, 11, 3,) b. June 15, 1811; m. Dec. 20, 1835, Pamelia Lee, of Martinsburg, N. Y. Res., Glendale, N. Y.

4290. i. CHARLES L., b. July 1, 1837; m. Helen A. Lee, 5676-80.

4291. ii. WARREN G., b. Mar. 16, 1842; m. Lydia A. Powell, 5681-6.

4292. iii. ADONERAM L., b. Jan. 25, 1844; m. Cornelia Benedict, 5687-90.

4293. iv. IRA HUBBARD, b. Dec. 5, 1847; m. Agnes Charlotte Lee and Annie Louise McGuire, 5691-2.

2744. ADONIRAM FOOTE, (1341, 488, 145, 41, 11, 3,) b. May 11, 1815; m. Jan. 1, 1839, Harriet Henry, of Martinsburg, N. Y. She was b. 1819; d. Apr. 8, 1865, Port Leyden, Lewis Co., N. Y. He d. 1874, in Ohio, and was buried in Martinsburg, N. Y. Ch. all b. in Martinsburg, N. Y.

4294. i. JANE HARRIET, b. May 27, 1840; m. Feb. 7, 1866, E. Perry Woolworth, of Port Seyden, Lewis Co., N. Y. He d. Aug. 11, 1876, at Norwick, N. Y. She m. 2nd, Aug. 8, 1880, A. E. Mason, of Racine, Wis. Ch.: (1) Eugene Henry Woolworth, b. Port Seyden, N. Y., Mar. 1, 1867. Res., Buckley, Pierce Co., Wash.; unm. (2) Hattie Nancy Woolworth, b. Port Seyden, N. Y., Feb. 28, 1868; m. Aug., 1886, Wilber B. Morehouse, of Weston, Ct. She d. Oct. 12, 1889, at Weston, Ct. Ch.: (a) Herbert Cornwall, b. (3) Grace Ethel Mason, b. Lockport, N. Y., Dec. 5, 1882. Res., Buckley, Pierce Co., Wash.

4295. ii. FRANCIS A., b. Apr. 9, 1842; m. Thera Kugg, of Kenoska, Wis., and Jennie Henry, of Lowville, N. Y.; n. f. k.

4296. iii. ELVIRA ELIZA, b. Sept. 14, 1843; m. Nov. 11, 1875, Frederick Crandall, of Glenfield, N. Y. She d. June 9, 1886, at Glenfield, N. Y. Ch.: (1) Ray Wayne, b. Dec. 4, 1876; m. Oct. 25, 1899, Maude May Burnham, at Lowville, N. Y. Ch.: (a) Florence Elizabeth Crandall, b. June 18, 1900. (b) Bernice Adele, b. Feb. 21, 1902. (2) Roy Wilson, b. Dec. 3, 1880; m. Sept. 21, 1898,

Lottie May Houghton, at Carthage, N. Y. Ch.: (a) Walter Wallace Crandall, b. Sept. 2, 1900; d. Feb. 15, 1901. (b) Ralph Merril Crandall, b. Mar. 21, 1902.

4297. iv. GEORGE H., b. May 15, 1845; m. Sarah J. Reynolds, 5693-97.

4298. v. JAMES A., b. Oct. 6, 1847; m. Jennie Amsdell, 5698.

4299. vi. AMY MARIA, b. Oct. 10, 1849; m. Jan. 9, 1868, Leonard Dean, of West Leyden, N. Y. Ch.: (1) Leon Foote, b. May 24, 1869, at Turin, N. Y.; m. May 15, 1901, Lillian Wakefield, of Hubbard, O. He is a tailor. Res., Blairsville, Pa. (2) Harold Everett, b. Feb. 26, 1873, at Talcottville, N. Y.; m. Mar. 20, 1895, Jennie Pike, of Passaic, N. J. Ch.: (a) Eleanor M., b. Sept. 14, 1895, at Butler, Pa. (b) Amy May, b. May 7, 1898, at Newton Falls, O. (c) Harold P., b Jan. 12, 1900, at Zelienople, Pa. (d) Miles E., b. July 2, 1902, at Zelienople, Pa. Harold Everett Dean is a merchant tailor. Res., Zelienople, Pa. (3) Leroz, b. Jan. 1, 1877, at Dayonsville, N. Y.; d. Mar. 8, 1877. (4) Cora Maud, b. Mar. 17, 1878, at Dayonsville, N. Y.; m. June 18, 1902, Leander Stewart Doutt, of Zelienople, Pa. (5) Elvie Florence, b. Jan. 13, 1882, at West Lyden, N. Y. (6) Emily Gertrude, b. Oct. 21, 1887, at Petrolia, Pa. (7) Ralph Glenford, b. Nov. 20, 1893, at Petrolia, Pa.

4300. vii. EMILY AMANDA, b. Oct. 31, 1852; m. Oct. 31, 1873, John H. Wilson, of Lockport, N. Y. He d. Sept. 12, 1885. Res., Lockport, N. Y. Ch.: (1) Gertrude, b. Lockport, N. Y., Aug. 17, 1875. (2) Harriet Amy, b. Jan. 23, 1884; m. Wm. H. Granty, Dec. 6, 1903. Ch.: (a) Gertrude Lena, b. July 5, 1905. (b) Wm. Elliott, b. Nov. 22, 1906.

4301. viii. ELVIE ANTOINETTE, b. Nov. 20, 1855; m. July 3, 1884, Andrew Morrison, of Passaic, N. J. Ch. all b. in Passaic, N. J. Ch.: (1) Harriet Elvie, b. Aug. 10, 1885. (2) Louisa Foote, b. Jan. 12, 1891. (3) Amy Dean, b. Jan. 18, 1895.

2747. NORMAN BRAINARD FOOTE, (1341, 488, 145, 41, 11, 3,) b. Dec. 2, 1820; m. Oct. 31, 1848, Maria Mills, of Lowville, N. Y. He carried on a wholesale grocery business for many years. He d. Sept. 6, 1900, in Rome, N. Y. She d. Jan. 15, 1901. Res., Rome, N. Y.

4302. i. EMILY MILLS, b. Adams, N. Y., Nov. 26, 1849. Bookkeeper in her brother's store in Rome; unm.

4303. ii. FREDERICK N., b. July 23, 1852; m. Nora F. Thompson, 5699-5708.

4304. iii. JOHN R., b. Jan. 23, 1854; m. Mary F. Kirkland, 5709-12.

4305. iv. EDWARD HIBBARD, b. Dec. 31, 1858. Res., Rome, N. Y.; unm. Was Sec. of Y. M. C. A. in Brooklyn, N. Y. Afterwards in business at Dallas, Texas. Now in Manila, P. I.

4306. v. WILLIAM A., b. Sept. 7, 1863; m. Mary D. Smith, 5713-16.

4307. vi. SUSAN COWAN, b. ———. Is a librarian. At present engaged in cataloguing a library in Wilkesbarre, Pa. Res., New York.

2748. DUANE DOTY, (1341, 488, 145, 41, 11, 3,) b. May 13, 1822; m. Feb. 27, 1849, Margaret Ann Evans, of New Bremen, Lewis Co., N. Y. After several years spent in farming he moved to Lowville, where he dealt in agricultural implements until he d. He was an Elder in the Presbyterian Church many.

years. A man of influence and highly respected. He d. Oct. 4, 1902. She d. July 13, 1905.

4308. i.   ELLIS E., b. Jan. 25, 1850; m. Emma Shoemaker, 5717-26.
4309. ii. EZRA BRAINARD, b. Sept. 8, 1851; unm.
4310. iii. ALDIS DUTCHER, b. Apr. 7, 1853, at Turin, N. Y.; unm. A grocer at Lowville, N. Y., for several years.
4311. iv. FLORENCE ELLEN, b. Apr. 3, 1855, at Turin, N. Y.; m. Mar. 13, 1894, Sylvester Schoolcraft, of Whitesboro, N. Y. He d. July 12, 1895. She still res. in Lowville, N. Y.
4312. v.   ROBERT DUANE, b. Aug. 26, 1856, at Turin, N. Y.; d. at Lowville, Feb. 28, 1883.
4313. vi. KATIE JANE, b. Oct. 16, 1858; d. Mar. 14, 1861.
4314. vii. JOHN BARTLIT, b. Oct. 16, 1860; m. May 10, 1892, Ada Florence Mansel, of Utica, N. Y. Agent for Standard Dictionary. Res., Sacramento, Cal. No ch.
4315. viii. EMILY MARGARET, b. Oct. 7, 1862; m. Oct. 1, 1890, Rev. John Newton Forman. She was a missionary teacher in India in 1887. Ch.: (1) Florence Dorothy, b. July 28, 1891, at Futagurh, India.

2750. JOHN BARTLIT FOOTE, D. D., (1341, 448, 145, 41, 11, 3,) b. July 1, 1826; m. 1st, May 19, 1851, Mary Stilphen, of Bartlett, N. H. She was b. Sept. 12, 1826. She d. Aug. 24, 1859, in Syracuse, N. Y. Mr. Foote was Pastor there of the M. E. Church; m. 2nd, Nov. 8, 1860, Louisa, dau. of Rev. Seth and Elizabeth (Crossett) Young, of Dewitt, N. Y.

Rev. John Bartlit Foote, D. D., was b. in Martinsburg, N. Y., July 1, 1826. He was the youngest son of Adoniram Foote, who was of the seventh generation from Nathaniel Foote.the Settler. His mother was Emily Brainard, a descendant of Daniel Brainard, who was b. in England and came to this country, settling in Haddam, Ct., about 1662. The early years of Mr. Foote's boyhood were spent in the home of his parents, attending school at the village academy and helping in such work as a boy can do on the farm or in the shop; his father conducting a shoe shop and tannery, as also a farm.

He was converted at the age of thirteen in Revival Services conducted by Rev. Isaac Puffer in the Methodist Stone Church in Martinsburg in Mar., 1839, and later became a student in Lowville Academy, where under able instructors he was prepared to enter an Advanced Class at Wesleyan University, Middletown, Ct. This it was his purpose to do, but, attending a session of Conference, an address of Bishop Janes on "Christian Perfection" and a sermon by Dr. Scott on "The very God of Peace Sanctify you wholly," so impressed him that in the class meeting on the evening of the day of his return he received the experience of perfect love and at once decided to take a course in the School of Theology, which had just been opened at Concord, N. H., by Dr. John Dempster. This he did, and was graduated from that school in Nov., 1850, being the first student to receive a diploma from the Concord Biblical Institute, now the Boston School of Theology. This diploma was given by request some ten years ago to the Boston Institution, where it is preserved. During the years of his student life he taught at intervals, of a term each, in various places in the vicinity of his home, and while at Concord, N. H., he taught at East Concord and at Osterville, Mass. After serving a pastorate of six months at Ballard Vale, Mass., Mr. Foote was m. in the spring of 1851 to Miss Mary Stilphen, of Lower Bartlett, N. H., and, returning to New York State, he joined the Black River Conference, which was in session in Oswego the first week in July of that year. After serving some churches in the northern part of the State, Belleville, Sackets Harbor, Watertown and Ogdensburg, he was appointed to the First M. E. Church in Syracuse. While pastor there his wife d. The following year he was appointed to the church at Potsdam, and in Nov., 1860, he was m. to Louisa Young, of Dewitt, N. Y., the youngest dau. of Rev. Seth Young, who was one of the early circuit preachers of central New York, and who d. in 1835, when his dau. was but eight years old.

After a pastorate of two years each in the churches of Rome and Oswego, Mr. Foote was appointed in the spring of 1865 Presiding Elder of the Rome District. During the four years in this relation, he, in union with one of the pastors on the district, secured a forest at Trenton Falls, N. Y., for a permanent camp ground for the District. This beautiful and romantic spot has become a favorite summer resort for families in that section, while still serving the original purpose of a camp meeting ground for one or two weeks each summer.

During the year 1866, called the Centenary of American Methodism, an unusual interest was awakened on the subject of Education, and the Conference of that year appointed a Commission, of which Mr. Foote was chairman, to investigate the feasibility of removing the Genesee College at Lima to a more central location as a nucleus for the building up of a great University.

A good deal of money was raised for this object throughout the Conference, the larger part of which was from the Rome district.

In 1869 he was appointed Presiding Elder of the Syracuse district, and owing to a division of Conference boundaries about this time, he came to be a member of the Central New York instead of the Black River Conference.

In Feb., 1870, a Methodist State Convention, of which he was Secretary, was held in Syracuse, which culminated in the founding of Syracuse University and the removal of Genesee College.

In 1871 Mr. Foote became a member of the National Holiness Association, and in that connection assisted in conducting camp meetings in twenty-four States, from Maine to Nebraska.

The number of camp meetings of which he has had charge, or has assisted in conducting, in the course of his ministerial work was 140.

After the close of his work as Presiding Elder, he served several charges as pastor until 1894, when, after a protracted illness, he was retired from active work in Conference relations, though he has since held the position of Chaplain of the Onondaga Penitentiary for ten years.

At the celebration of "Old Home Week" in the city of Oswego during the first week of July, 1906, Mr. Foote was invited to conduct the lovefeast on Sunday morning, July 1. By a singular coincidence it was his 80th birthday and the 55th anniversary of the week in which he joined the Conference in that same church.

4316.   i.   OSMON C. BAKER, b. Mar. 22, 1852, in Belleville, N. Y.; d. at Wesleyan University, Middletown, Ct., Nov. 10, 1870, in second year of College.

4317.   ii.   MARTHA EMILY, b. May 28, 1854, at Sacketts Harbor, N. Y. Ph.B., Syracuse University, 1876; Ph.D., 1885. Engaged in educational work continuously from the time of her graduation until 1905. The following year was spent mostly in giving lectures. In 1891 she was sent abroad by the National Bureau of Education to investigate conditions of higher education of women in Great Britain and other European countries. She attended lectures while abroad at Oxford, Cambridge, Leipzig and Zurich. On her return she was connected with the University of Chicago as Assistant Professor of English Literature from 1892 to 1900, and with Northwestern University at Evanston, Ill., from 1900 to 1905 as Assistant Professor of English and Dean of Women. She was m. Aug. 7, 1884, to John M. Crow, Ph.D., Archaeologist and Educator. He was Professor of Greek in Iowa College at Grinnell, Iowa, from 1884 to the time of his death, Sept. 28, 1890. Mrs. Crow was Lady Principal in the College during the same time. They had one dau., Agatha, b. Sept., 1888, at Grinnell, Iowa; d. at Colorado Springs, Aug. 22, 1890.

4318. iii. JOHN STILPHEN, b. Aug. 23, 1859, at Syracuse, N. Y.; d. Sept. 15, 1859.

4319. iv. WILLIAM YOUNG, b. Feb. 1, 1863, in Rome, N. Y. B. A., graduate of Syracuse University, class of 1887. Engaged for a time in teaching. He was for some years Professor of Latin in Syracuse High School, but resigned the position to engage in business. He is now conducting a successful book trade in Syracuse, N. Y. He m. Dec. 25, 1900, Cecilia Von Schiller Heire. Mrs. Foote d. Jan. 14, 1903. He m. 2nd, Dec. 1, 1906, Mrs. Maie Streight Becker, of Brooklyn, N. Y.

4320. v. MARY LOUISE, b. Jan. 19, 1865, in Oswego, N. Y.; d. Aug. 2, 1866, in Rome, N. Y.

4321. vi. ELIZABETH LOUISA, b. Aug. 23, 1866, in Rome, N. Y. B. A., Syracuse University, 1888; B. L. S., N. Y. State Library School, 1892. Is at present, and for some years past, Instructor of Training Class in N. Y. Public Library, New York City.

4322. vii. MABEL WINIFRED, b. Oct. 17, 1869, in Rome, N. Y.; youngest child in the ninth generation of the line of Adoniram Foote; res. with her parents in Syracuse, N. Y., and has charge of the Reading Club department in the Book Store of her brother, W. T. Foote.

2753. REV. REUBEN CLARK FOOTE, (1342, 488, 145, 41, 11, 3,) b. Salem, N. Y., Jan. 28, 1834; m. Royalton, N. Y., Electa Taylor. He was a Methodist preacher and a member of the Genesee Conference; d. Pendleton, N. Y., Mar. 8, 1898. She d. Pendleton, May 31, 1891.

4323. i. REUBEN CLARK, b. Dec. 6, 1834; m. Louisa Ames and Sophia Dillworth, 5727-8.

4324. ii. OLIVER T., b. Jan. 28, 1836; m. Amelia C. Whipple, 5729-32.

4325. iii. ALVIN W., b. Aug. 6, 1839; m. Jane Actxley, 5733-5.

4326. iv. SARAH ANN, b. Nov. 25, 1841; m. Mar. 14, 1861, Charles McNall, McNall Corners, Niagara Co., N. Y. Ch.: (1) Ameila, b. Sept. 2, 1868; m. Chas. M. D. Sheldon, Nov. 21, 1889. (2) Alma A., b. ———; d. Mar. 20, 1871.

4327 v. MARY EMILINE, b. Mar. 22, 1846; m. Sept. 27, 1866, W. Bennett. She d. Aug., 1906. Res., Middleport, N. Y.

4328. vi. AMANDA E., b. Jan. 9, 1848; m. Luther Davis, Jan. 1, 1870. She d. May 18, 1875. Ch.: (1) Cora E., b. Feb. 29, 1872.

4329. vii. HIRAM E., b. May 8, 1851; m. Hattie Dixon, 5736-8.

2756. HIRAM FOOTE, (1342, 488, 145, 41, 11, 3,) b. ———; m. Jan. 12, 1842,
S. Elvira Fenn, of Royalton, N. Y. He d. Royalton, June 5, 1850. She m. 2nd,
Edward Beeby. She d. Mar. 22, 1880.

    4330. i.   JAMES HENRY, b. July 17, 1843. Enlisted in 21st Mich. Vol.
             Infantry, Sept. 3, 1862; d. Jan. 27, 1863, in Hospital No. 4, Nash-
             ville, Tenn.

    4331. ii. LUCY P., b. Dec. 1, 1844; m. May 21, 1873, Amos R. Morehouse.
             Res., Big Rapids, Mich. Ch.: (1) Lyman Foote, b. Oct. 21, 1874.
             Electrical engineer; m. June 25, 1903, Mary Cornelia Wyman.
             Ch.: (a) Ruth Ellen, b. Sept. 10, 1904; d. Sept. 18, 1904. (2)
             Hiram Robinson, b. Mar. 8, 1876; m. Nov. 23, 1901, Iva MacGriffin,
             of Charlotte, Mich. R. R. Mail Clerk. Ch.: (a) Robert Griffin,
             Aug. 7, 1903. (b) Lowell James, b. Dec. 2, 1904. (3) Grace, b.
             Sept. 15, 1878; Grad. Univ. of Mich., 1902; Teacher at Big Rapids,
             Mich. (4) James Amos, b. Oct. 10, 1880; Grad. Univ. of Mich.
             Is a doctor at Idaho Spr., Col.

    4332. iii. HIRAM ELROY, b. Jan. 21, 1848; d. Oct. 14, 1858.

2759. SENECA BRAGG FOOTE, (1342, 488, 145, 41, 11, 3,) b. Dec. 13, 1825; m.
Jan. 10, 1849, Sylvia Green, of Royalton, N. Y. She d. Aug. 17, 1899. He d.
Dec. 16, 1896. Ch. all b. Royalton, N. Y.

    4333. i.   STEPHEN W., b. Oct. 8, 1850; m. Alice Garrett, 5739-46.

    4334. ii. ARVILLA, b. Jan. 26, 1853; d. Apr. 20, 1880.

    4335. iii. SENECA BRAGG, Jr., b. Aug. 3, 1857; d. Aug. 28, 1874.

    4336. iv. JOHN L., b. Jan. 1, 1860; m. Emeline Gantt, 5747-50.

    4337. v.   BETTA, b. Nov. 29, 1862; m. Aug. 19, 1890, John H. Harris,
             Duluth, Minn. Ch: (1) Robert Foote, b. Apr. 19, 1895.

    4338. vi. ROBERT, b. Aug. 22, 1865.

2760. DR. JOHN FOOTE, (1342, 488, 145, 41, 11, 3,) b. May 23, 1828; m.
Apr. 16, 1851, Harriet V. Larzelier. She d. Aug. 26, 1855; m. 2nd, Jane Scott, Dec.
17, 1857. She d. Nov. 4, 1889. He is a physician. Res., Kansas City, Mo.

    4339. i.   HARRIET SOPHIA, b. June 29, 1852; m. May 29, 1870, Charles
             J. Wright. He d.; m. 2nd, Solomon Green. Ch.: (1) Lillian
             Wright, b. Apr. 1, 1871; m. Apr. 1, 1888, John C. Stanbrough.
             No ch. (2) Marion, b. Nov. 8, 1872; m. Geo. P. Knight, Dec. 27,
             1893. Ch.: (a) Alice, b. July 27, 1893. (b) Kenneth Keith, b.
             Mar. 22, 1899.

    4340. ii. MARGARET LUCY, b. Jan., 1855; d. 1865.

    4341. iii. DR. EDGAR JOHN, b. July 25, 1859; m. Agnes Gowans, Apr. 12,
             1883; m. 2nd, Ida E. McGorman, Aug. 15, 1899. He is a physician
             residing in Buffalo, N. Y.

    4342. iv. MELVINA, b. Aug. 25, 1860; m. July 15, 1886, Justus Wilfred
             Brown. They reside in Kansas City, Mo.

    4343. v.   JENNIE AMANDA, b. Apr. 23, 1863; m. William Newman Patt,
             Aug. 11, 1891. They reside at Creston, Ia. Ch.: (1) Roscoe, b.
             July 1, 1893. (2) Luella, b. May 2, 1896.

    4344. vi. EDNA MAY, b. Sept. 10, 1870; m. Antone Houston, Nov. 11, 1897.
             They reside in Kansas City, Mo. Ch.: (1) John Raymond Hous-
             ton, b. Mar. 8, 1900.

2761. REV. LEMUEL THOMAS FOOTE, (1342, 488, 145, 41, 11, 3,) b. in
Greenwich, N. Y., Feb. 18, 1832, and was the youngest of eleven children. When

he was one year old his family moved to Royalton, Niagara Co., N. Y. His early
life was spent on the farm. He obtained his education at Lima Seminary, N. Y.,
and Alleghany College, Meadville, Pa. He was m. Oct. 27, 1857, to Emily A.
Whitney, of Pike, Wyoming Co., N. Y. In 1860 he joined the Genesee Conference
of the Methodist Episcopal Church. The first appointment was Middleport, N. Y.
From his second appointment, Cambria, he was mustered in as Lieutenant (1862)
of Co. H, 151st Regt. N. Y. State Volunteers. He was afterwards appointed
Chaplain of the 151st Regt. N. Y. S. V., which office he held until the close of the
Civil War. After the war, he resumed his work as minister of the Methodist
Episcopal Church. His appointments were, successively, Collins, Evans, Pekin,
Lyndonville, Buffalo, Rochester. In the last-named place he held pastorates at
three different churches, and was Presiding Elder of the Rochester District for
six years. His last charge was Penfield, N. Y. He retired in 1895, and resides at
Rochester, N. Y.

4345.　i.　FRANK WHITNEY, b. Aug. 3, 1858, Royalton, N. Y.; m. Laura
N. Hyde.

4346.　ii.　JULIA BETSEY, b. May 11, 1860, Middleport, N. Y.; teacher in
the Rochester (N. Y.) Schools.

4347.　iii.　MARY LUELLA, b. Jan. 14, 1862; m. June 15, 1887, Henry
Tobias Conklin, of Binghamton, N. Y. Res., Schenectady, N. Y.
He is the General Freight Agent, D. & H. R. R. Co. Ch.: (1)
Mable, b. Feb. 9, 1891 (an adopted child).

4348.　iv.　SYLVIA, b. Mar. 15, 1866, Collins, N. Y.; m. Sept. 8, 1891, Rev.
James Gosnell. He d. Oct. 15, 1900, Lockport, N. Y. He was a
member of the Genesee Conference, and at the time of his death
he was pastor of the First M. E. Church at Lockport, N. Y. Res.,
Rochester, N. Y. Ch.: (1) Frank Lemuel, b. Sept. 22, 1892. (2)
Arthur James, b. Nov. 5, 1894. (3) Harold Foote, b. Dec. 24,
1896. (4) Ralph Whitney, b. Mar. 8, 1900.

4349.　v.　ADELAIDE, b. Feb. 6, 1870, Pekin, N. Y. Teacher in Public
Schools, Rochester, N. Y.

2762. EDWIN FOOTE, (1345, 448, 145, 41, 11, 3,) b. Dec. 11, 1812, at New
Milford, Pa.; m. 1st, Sept. 5, 1840, Janette Barnes. She d. Apr. 24, 1845; m. 2nd,
Oct. 10, 1850, Adelia Adelaide Lyon. She d. Sept. 15, 1888, at Brenham, Texas.
He d. May 31, 1854, at San Antonio, Texas.

4350.　i.　FRANCES MARIA, b. Feb. 3, 1844; d. Aug. 7, 1846.

4351.　ii.　FRANCES AMANDA, b. Jan. 21, 1853. Res., Brenham, Texas;
unm.

4352.　iii.　EDWIN, Jr., b. Aug. 27, 1854; m. Nellie Hoard, 5756-8.

2763. NORMAN FOOTE, (1345, 448, 145, 41, 11, 3,) b. Sept. 7, 1814; m. July
13, 1843, Lydia Lorenda Lathrop. Res., New Milford, Pa. He d. Dec. 31, 1894.

4353.　i.　ADA JANETTE, b. Aug. 22, 1844; d. Sept. 3, 1850.

4354.　ii.　LESLIE, b. Mar. 3, 1846; m. Mary C. Harper, 5759-62.

4355.　iii.　ELMER W., b. Aug. 6, 1852; m. Julia Cooper Ray, 5763-4.

4356.　iv.　BYRON, b. Feb. 4, 1856; m. Ida May Reynolds and Julia Cooper
Raynor Foote, 5765.

2771. SILAS BUCK FOOTE, (1345, 448, 145, 41, 11, 3,) b. at New Milford,
Pa., Nov. 7, 1834; m. July 9, 1858, Lydia Lorana Park. She d. Jan. 30, 1903.
His father, Belus H. Foote, a native of Vt., was a shoe manufacturer and farmer,
and d. in the year 1841. He, then seven years of age, was educated in a log

SILAS B. FOOTE. No. 2771

REV. DR. J. B. FOOTE. No. 2750

schoolhouse in New Milford, and was reared by an elder brother, proprietor of a general store, in which Silas Foote remained until his nineteenth year. His brother then sold his business in Prompton, Pa., and, accompanied by his wife and Silas, went to San Antonio, Texas, where, in 1853, he embarked in the mercantile business. His death there occurred in May, 1854, and Silas B. Foote afterward returned to Pa. with his brother's widow. For some time he engaged in the sale of patent rights with the former partner of his brother, and they traveled extensively in this connection throughout the country.

In 1857, Mr. Foote arrived in Red, Wing, Minn., and having a stock of goods shipped to him at that point, he embarked in general merchandise on his own account. Later he traded his business for lots and other real estate, and subsequently exchanged his property interests for a stock of shoes and opened a shoe store in Red Wing under the firm style of Foote & Sweeney. A year later George R. Sterling purchased Mr. Sweeny's interest, and the firm of Foote & Sterling was thereby organized This firm was succeeded by Foote, Johnson & Company, and a year later T. A. Schulze, Gustave Schurmeier and Constantine Henry were admitted to a partnership, while in 1881 the firm became Foote, Schulze & Company, carrying on business in St. Paul. Mr. Foote has been a manufacturer of and wholesale dealer in shoes in St. Paul for 25 years. The company occupies immense buildings, which are constantly being enlarged, and they employ between six and seven hundred operatives in the manufacture of boots and shoes.

On July 6, 1858, Mr. Foote was m. to Miss Lydia Lorana Park, a dau. of Dr. Ezra Park, of Montrose, Pa. There are four sons and a dau. of this marriage. Ezra P., a fine musician, who is leader of a large orchestra in Portland, Oregon; Fred W., a lawyer, of Red Wing, Minn.; Edwin H., who is engaged in business in Red Wing as a member of the firm of S. B. Foote & Company, dealers in shoes; Bessie Park, at home; and Robert M., a student at Faribault.

For many years Mr. Foote has been a useful and earnest worker in Christ's Episcopal Church of Red Wing, in which he has long served as vestryman, while at the present writing he is now churchwarden. He erected a very beautiful and costly chapel as a memorial to his deceased wife. In community affairs he has ever been deeply and helpfully interested. In 1882-3 he was Mayor of Red Wing, acceding to the request of the temperance element to become chief executive. He enforced the law in regard to temperance so strictly that he aroused the opposition of the saloon element and those who do not entertain strong temperance principles, and in consequence was retired from the office at the end of his term. He has, however, never ceased his activity in behalf of Red Wing, where he maintains his residence, and of St. Paul, to which city he goes daily for the supervision of his business. He is Thirty-second Degree Mason, belonging to the Consistory of the Scottish Rite and the Chapter and Commandery of the York Rite and also to the Mystic Shrine. He likewise belongs to the St. Paul Jobbers' Union and to various commercial bodies. Although 73 years of age he is still an active business man, possessing the vigor and energy of many a much younger man, while in spirit and interests he seems yet in his prime. Constantly enlarging the scope of his activities through the close application and earnest effort which are the indispensable concomitants to success, he stands to-day as one of the foremost manufacturers and merchants of St. Paul.

4357. i. ROBERT MONTANYE, b. June 13, 1859; d. Dec. 26, 1860.

4358. ii. EZRA PARK, b. Sept. 12, 1866.

4359. iii. FREDERICK W., b. Feb. 11, 1872; m. Sarah O'Brien, 5766.7.

(27)

4360. iv. EDWIN HAWLEY, b. Jan. 6, 1876; m. Evalyn Thersa Lawther, 5768-70.

4361. v. BESSIE AMANDA, b. Dec. 11, 1877.

4362. vi. ROBERT M., b. May 12, 1889.

2775. CHANCEY FOOTE, (1347, 488, 145, 41, 11, 3,) b. Mar. 11, 1823; m. Sept. 1, 1856, Catherine Ayers. He d. July 29, 1865. She d. at New Milford, Pa., Mar. 19, 1900.

4363. i. EVA FRANCES, b. Dec. 8, 1857; m. Jan. 3, 1877, Frank Gardner. She d. Feb. 12, 1894. Ch.: (1) Nicholas Passmore, b. Nov. 19, 1877; d. Nov. 11, 1878. (2) Margaretta A., b. Apr. 9, 1881. (3) John Wallace, b. Apr. 5, 1885. (4) Susan Eva, b. Dec. 29, 1891.

4364. ii. LAURA ELEANOR, b. Aug. 12, 1861; m. May 25, 1881, Leanard Seaman, of Upsonville, Pa. Ch.: (1) Mabel F., b. Aug. 2, 1890.

4365. iii. WILLIAM GRANT, b. May 20, 1863; m. Alice Boatle Chapin, 5771-2.

4366. iv. DORA ELLEN, b. Apr. 12, 1865.

2776. EDGAR FOOTE (1347, 488, 145, 41, 11, 3,) b. Sept. 13, 1825; m. Nov. 15, 1847, Julia Payne. She d. Mar. 29, 1857, in Streetsboro, O.; m. 2nd, Feb. 14, 1858, Emma T. Chaplain; res., Streetsboro, O.

4367. i. AMANDA, b. Nov. 25, 1851.

4368. ii. FRANK ELWOOD, b. Aurora, O., Nov. 21, 1860; d. Apr. 7, 1878, in Streetsboro, O.

4369. iii. EVERETT CHALFONT, b. Aurora, O., May 3, 1864; m. Carrie Lorrain, 5773-75.

2779. LINUS FOOTE, JR. (1347, 488, 145, 41, 11, 3,) b. Aug. 15, 1831; m. Jan. 31, 1855, Belinda Shurtliff. She d. Sept. 20, 1865, at Randolf, O.; m. 2nd, Sept. 15, 1866, Jane Sawyer Green, of Solon, O. She d. Dec. 23, 1875; m. 3rd, Aurora, O., Aug. 3, 1879, Sarah Jane Zimmer. She was b. Louisville, Ky., Nov. 15, 1849.

4370. i. ALMA DEAN, b. Aurora, O., Mar. 12, 1853; d. May 11, 1854, Aurora, O.

4371. ii. JUSTIN HAYES, b. Portage, O., Sept. 28, 1854; m. Helen Maria Munn, 5776-7.

4372. iii. EDGAR CHARLES, b. Aurora, O., Jan. 9, 1859; m. Mary Van Della Thompson, 5778-9.

4373. iv. EGBERT BURTON, b. Aurora, O., Jan. 29, 1862; m. Suella Haskins, 5780.

4374. v. LEONARD ALLEN, b. Aurora, O., July 8, 1867; m. Anna Snedacar.

4375. vi. JENNIE BELLE, b. Aurora, O., June 1, 1869; m. Aug. 20, 1887, William Kiser, of Chardon, O. He was b. Apr. 25, 1866; res., 462 So. Pierce St., Milwaukee, Wis. Ch.: (1) Linus Egbert, b. Fargo, N. Dak., May 19, 1891. (2) William Carroll, b. Fargo, N. Dak., June 29, 1893.

4376. vii. JOHN A., b. Aurora, O., Nov. 15, 1872; m. Belle Sippert, 5781-2.

4377. viii. ALMA RUTH, b. Aurora, O., Jan. 17, 1881; m. Sept. 29, 1898, Herman Kurth, of Cumberland, Md. Ch.: (1) Robert Adolph, b. Cleveland, O., Mar. 3, 1900. (2) Charles Arthur, b. Cleveland, O., May 13, 1902.

4378. ix. FRANK ARTHUR, b. Portage, O., Aug. 6, 1886.

2782. OSCAR FOOTE, (1347, 488, 145, 41, 11, 3,) b. Mar. 4, 1839; m. Jan. 4, 1860, Aldula Shurtliff. She d. Sept. 28, 1881. M. 2nd, May 13, 1889, Flavilla Foster Foote. She was b. Oct. 13, 1842; res., Kent, O.

    4379. i.   ADDIE LAURA, b. Streetsboro, O., Jan. 8, 1861; m., Jan. 25, 1877, Robinson Lewis. He was b. Feb. 7, 1848; m. Apr. 2, 1889, Richard N. Pattern. Ch.: (1) Freddie Vienna, b. Streetsboro, O., Sept. 10, 1877. (2) Lulu May, b. Kent, O., Mar 29, 1881.

    4380. ii.   ZYLPHIA, b. Streetsboro, O., Aug. 30, 1864; d. Nov. 3, 1881.

    4381. iii.   CHARLES, b. Streetsboro, O. Feb. 18, 1868; m. Mary Abel, 5783-86.

    4382. iv.   NINA MAY, b. Streetsboro, O., Aug. 5, 1872; m. May 10, 1888, Wilson Dudley Pratt, of Kent, O. He was b. Dec. 25, 1870. Ch.: (1) Roy Oscar, b. Kent, O., Dec. 30, 1891. (2) Ray Noble, b. Massilon, O., Dec. 31, 1893.

    4383. v.   NETTIE, b. Kent, O., July 27, 1881; d. Sept. 2, 1881, at Kent, O.

2784. BELUS HARD FOOTE (1349, 488, 145, 41, 11, 3,) b. Apr. 16, 1821; m., July 3, 1850, Zillah Ann Parks of Binghamton, N. Y. She d. Sept. 30, 1876. He d. Apr. 13, 1894; res., Franklin, Pa.

    4384. i.   ARTHUR WILLIS, b. Apr. 27, 1851; m. Mary Aurilla Wood, 5787-8.

    4385. ii.   IDA ELIZABETH, b. May, 23, 1853; d. Sept. 1, 1862.

    4386. iii.   LETA FRANCELIA, b. Apr. 30, 1855; d. July 12, 1902; unm.

2785. IRA DUANE FOOTE, (1349, 488, 145, 41, 11, 3,) b. Aug. 21, 1822; m. Feb. 14, 1846, Charlotte A. Van Housen, of New Milford, Pa. She d. ———; m. 2nd, Nov. 28, 1884, Belinda Williams, of Susquehanna, Pa. Res., Binghamton, Pa.

    4387. i.   ESTELLA ANN, b. May 19, 1848; m. New Milford, Pa., Jan. 31, 1874, Herbert Hamilton.

    4388. ii.   ANNIS ELIZA, b. Oct. 5, 1849.

    4389. iii.   WILLIAM HERBERT, b. Sept. 3, 1851; m. Florence Weed Berthron, 5789-90.

    4390. iv.   HENRY E., b. Mar. 28, 1854; d. Oct. 26, 1866.

    4391. v.   HATTIE A., b. July 30, 1855; b. Dec. 26, 1860.

    4392. vi.   ADA ORRILLA, b. July 24, 1857; m. New Milford, Pa., Nov. 25, 1879, Ulric Byrd Rice. Ch.: (1) George Perry, b. Feb. 17, 1882.

    4393. vii.   ALVIN DUANE, b. Nov. 12, 1859; d. Apr. 10, 1877.

    4394. viii.   IRENE ANTOINETTE, b. Jan. 26, 1862; m. New Milford, Pa., Oct. 4, 1885, Daniel Dexter Foster.

    4395. ix.   VERNA MAY, b. ———; m. Binghamton, Pa., May 14, 1898, George Henry Brown. Ch.: (1) Clarence Melvin, b. Jan. 30, 1900.

2786. GEORGE DUNMORE FOOTE, (1349, 488, 145, 41, 11, 3,) b. Feb. 22, 1825; m. Nov. 29, 1856, Marietta S., dau. of Harvey S. Stephens. She was b. Bridgewater, Pa., Oct. 7, 1833. He d. Aug. 22, 1886. Farmer. Res., Bridgewater, Pa.

    4396. i.   FLORA CORNELIA, b. Apr. 4, 1861; m. Conkins, Pa., Jan. 12, 1890, Samuel C. Warner. Ch.: (1) Warren, b. ———; d. in infancy.

    4397. ii.   HENRY FRANCIS, b. Feb. 17, 1863; m. Alice Devine, 5791-2.

    4398. iii.   HARRIET LOUISE, b. Sept. 4, 1864; m. Mar. 11, 1882, Edward Cooley, of Montrose, Pa. She d. Mar. 23, 1890. Ch.: (1) Beatrice, b. July 25, 1883. (2) Teddy, b. Apr. 17, 1888.

4399. iv. EMMA LOWELLA, b. Apr. 20, 1867; m. Mar. 6, 1887, Frank Gifford, of Great Bend, Pa. Ch.: (1) Glen Nelson, b. May 15, 1888.
4400. v. EDWIN GEORGE, b. Apr. 20, 1867; m. Emma Rice.
4401. vi. CHARLES NELSON, b. Feb. 26, 1869; d. Oct. 19, 1869.
4402. vii. LILLIAN ALICE, b. May 23, 1873; m. Dec. 25, 1894, Lavelle Gifford, of Conkin, Pa. She d. Mar. 25, 1895.

2787. ORLANDO WILLIAMS FOOTE, (1349, 488, 145, 41, 11, 3,) b. Susquehanna, Pa., Jan. 13, 1828; m. Mary Ann Chamberlin. He was a traveling salesman. He d. Mar., 1890, in New York. Res., Brooklyn, Pa.
4403. i. WILLIAM CHAMBERLIN, b. Mar. 13, 1862; m. 1884, Minnie Harden Albins, of New Milford, Pa. Traveling salesman. Res., Scranton, Pa.
4404. ii. GRACE LEONA, b. Nov. 21, 1875.

2789. JOHN CHASE FOOTE, (1349, 488, 145, 41, 11, 3,) b. at New Milford, Pa., Mar. 28, 1836; m. Mar. 10, 1864, Catherine Augusta Dusenberg, of Binghamton, N. Y. First Lieutenant, 50th Regt. Pa. Vols., from Sept. 6, 1861, to Feb. 17, 1863. He d. Dec. 31, 1876, at his res., Binghamton, N. Y.
4405. i. LEWIS H., b. Aug. 8, 1865; m. Sarah Fitsgerald, 5793-5.
4406. ii. MINNIE D., b. Dec. 6, 1866; m. Nov. 26, 1896, Whitney V. Parker.
4407. iii. HENRY S., b. ———; m. Oct. 21, 1894, Lillian Goulden.

2790. SHERMAN FRISBIE FOOTE, (1354, 497, 153, 45, 13, 5,) b. Nov. 27, 1841, in New Haven, Ct.; m. Oct. 25, 1871, Mary Hutton, dau. of George Rice. She was b. Dec. 4, 1846.
4408. i. ARTHUR ELLSWORTH, b. Jan. 3, 1874; m. Edith Burr Palmer, 5808-9.
4409. ii. HENRY LYMAN, b. Mar. 11, 1881. Grad. of Yale, class of '04. Res., Dayton, O.

2795. WILLIAM RUSSELL FOOTE, (1362, 498, 153, 43, 13, 5,) b. June 3, 1848, of Branford, Ct.; m. Nettie Elizabeth, dau. of Samuel Averill, of Branford, Ct., Dec. 17, 1873. Mrs. Nettie Foote was b. in Branford, Ct., Aug. 22, 1854. Mr. Foote was a farmer until 1895. He has been Town Clerk, Town Treasurer and Judge of Probate of the Town of Branford, and Treasurer of the Branford Savings Bank since 1899.
4410. i. WALLACE HARRISON, b. at Branford, Ct., May 17, 1875.
4411. ii. MABLE LEE, b. at Branford, Ct., Aug. 20, 1876.
4411¹. iii. ADA, b. at Branford, Ct., Nov. 10, 1877; d. July 10, 1878.
4412. iv. ROLAND TREMAINE, b. at Branford, Ct., Nov. 30, 1883; d. Feb. 16, 1885.

2809. IRA AVERY FOOTE, (1380, 509, 168, 47, 13, 5,) b. Sept. 10, 1816; m. May 30, 1839, Eliza Benjamin. She d. Mar. 17, 1865. He d. Nov. 26, 1880. Both buried at Chagrin Falls, O.
4413. i. CHARLES MARTIN, b. at Chagrin Falls, O., June 20, 1842; m. Mary, dau. of Daniel and Mary Philips, 1864, at Bainbridge, Geauga Co., O. After her death he m. Louise Christian, of Cleveland, O. He was killed by the electric cars in Cleveland, O., Dec. 13, 1903. No ch.
4414. ii. SARAH NANCY, b. in Bainbridge, O., Apr. 2, 1850; m. Nov. 30, 1871, Delaville L., son of George and Hannah Fenkell, of Cha-

grin Falls, O. Ch.: (1) George Harrison, b. Feb. 4, 1873; m. Feb. 22, 1897, Jeanie, dau. of Charles and Susan Harris, of Rocky River, O. Res., Erie, Pa. He is Chief Engineer of the City Water Works. Ch.: (a) Neal Harris, b. in Detroit, Mich., Apr. 18, 1898. (b) Margaret Susan, b. in Erie, Pa., Dec. 18, 1902. (2) Neal Charles, b. Apr. 30, 1880. Grad. Ann Harbor University in Mechanical Engineering. Res., Detroit, Mich. Employ of Detroit City Water Works.

2816.   JOSIAH FOOTE, (1395, 518, 170, 37, 13, 5,) b. July 31, 1844; m. Dec. 4, 1870, Emma, dau. of S. Nelson McDougall, Galen, N. Y. She was b. Aug. 19, 1848.

4415.   i.   CORA B., b. Dec. 21, 1871; m. Mar. 19, 1890, Christopher Hiller, 484 Frost Ave., Rochester, N. Y. Ch.: (1) Marvin L., b. July 7, 1891. (2) Walter Carroll, b. Feb. 10, 1894, and d. Jan. 22, 1896. (3) Gertrude, b. Oct. 10, 1895. (4) Ethel, b. Dec. 31, 1896. (5) Emma, b. Nov. 28, 1899. (6) Bertha, b. June 17, 1905.

4416.   ii.   LILLIAN, b. Oct. 12, 1873.

4417.   iii.   ALBERT J., b. Feb. 28, 1876; m. Clara Latsch, 5810-11.

4418.   iv.   GERTRUDE M., b Feb. 5, 1878; living at home; unm.

4419.   v.   FLORENCE E., b. June 4, 1880; m. Nov. 3, 1903, Edward P. Goetzmann, Clyde, N. Y. Ch.: (1) Louie Jason Goetzmann, b. Dec. 11, 1894.

2819.   REV. CHARLES HENRY FOOTE, D. D., (1396, 518, 170, 37, 13, 5,) b. June 17, 1825; m. June 15, 1854, Alma T. Foote (No. 1967). Res., New Brunswick, N. J., Jerseyville, Ill., St. Louis, Mo., Evansville, Ind., and Ionia, Mich., he being the pastor of Presbyterian Churches in the places named. Mr. Foote d. June 27, 1880, and was buried at Ionia, Mich. Mrs. Foote res. in Muskegon, Mich., with her dau., Mrs. Sessions.

The following inscription is on a bronze tablet in the Presbyterian Church at Ionia, Mich.:

In Memoriam.

CHARLES H. FOOTE, D. D.

Born June 17, 1825.

Ordained May 23, 1854.

Died June 27, 1880.

An able and faithful Minister of Christ.
The beloved Pastor of this Church from 1878 to 1880.
Intellectually, Vigorous and Original.
Emotionally, Generous and Genial.
Spiritually, Earnest and Energetic.

"Remember the Word that I said unto you, being yet present with you."

4420.   i.   BESSIE G., b. in New Brunswick, N. J., Aug. 10, 1855; d. Jan. 17, 1856; buried at New Brunswick.

4421.   ii.   CARRIE P., b. in New Brunswick, N. J., June 11, 1857; d. Oct. 16, 1859; buried in Jerseyville, Ill.

4422.   iii.   MARY SCOTT, b. in Jerseyville, Ill., Aug. 19, 1861; m. Clarence W. Sessions, July 5, 1882, in Ionia, Mich. Res., Muskegon, Mich., where Mr. Sessions held the office of City Attorney for a number of years, and is now Circuit Judge. Ch.: (1) Marjorie Foote, b. in Ionia, Mich., Dec. 25, 1883. (2) Clarence Nathaniel, b. in Muskegon, Mich., Apr. 2, 1890.

2821.   GEORGE PALMER FOOTE, (1395, 518, 170, 37, 13, 5,) b. Sept. 16, 1834, in Pittsford, N. Y.; m. Nov. 13, 1864, Ann Elizabeth Smith, of Pittsford, N. Y. She d. June 1, 1870; m. 2nd, 1872, Jennie Baker, of Hamilton, N. Y. He d. Oct., 1880. She res. McLeansboro, Ill.

     4423.   i.   ANNA LOUISE, b. Aug. 9, 1867, in Pittsford, N. Y.; m. Sept. 14, 1893, John Douglas Chickering, of Brockport, N. Y. Res., Spokane, Wash. Ch.: (1) Katharine Louise, b. Nov. 14, 1896.
     4424.   ii.   CHARLES SMITH, b. Pittsford, N. Y., May 8, 1870; d. June 3, 1899; unm.
     4425.   iii.   GEORGE B., b. Mar. 20, 1874; m. Mattie Hyatt, 5812.
     4426.   iv.   JOHN PALMER, b. July 24, 1879, in McLeansboro, Ill.; m. 1906, in St. Louis, Mo. Res., St. Louis, Mo. No ch.

2824.   SAMUEL THOMAS FOOTE, (1398, 518, 170, 37, 13, 5,) b. Nov. 3, 1839; m. Kathren Rooke, of Salem, N. Y.

     4427.   i.   WILLIAM H., b. Jan. 29, 1869; m. Emma Fink, 5813-5.
     4428.   ii.   ELMER R., b. Apr. 25, 1872; unm. Res., Lyons, N. Y.
     4429   iii.   ELDON J., b. Apr. 25, 1872; m. Emma Duedey, 5816.
     4430.   iv.   DELIA ELIZABETH, b. July 1, 1879; unm.

2827.   IRA FOOTE, (1402, 520, 170, 37, 13, 5,) b. May 17, 1834; m. Sept. 7, 1858, Catharine C. Foote, of Hartland, O. She d. Feb. 8, 1877.

     4431.   i.   CORA EVA, b. Jan. 30, 1860; m. Oct. 12, 1876, Emery F., son of William Porter. Res., New London, O. Ch.: (1) Willie C., b. Aug. 10, 1877; d. Sept. 23, 1877. (2) Maude L., b. June 12, 1879. (3) Ona E., b. June 2, 1883. (4) Willard Foote, b. Dec. 29, 1887.

2828.   GEORGE W. FOOTE, (1402, 520, 170, 37, 13, 5,) b. June 11, 1842, in Fitchville, O.; m. 1st, 1863, Philena, dau. of William Thompson; m. 2nd, Mar. 21, 1869, Elizabeth Eckelberry, of New London, O. She was b. Jan. 8, 1849. He d. 1897, at Hillsdale, Mich. She and two sons res. South Howell St., Hillsdale, Mich.

     4432.   i.   WALLACE, b. Dec. 30, 1869.
     4433.   ii.   FORD, b. 1875. Res., Hillsdale, Mich.
     4434.   iii.   ROBERT, b. 1886. Res., Hillsdale, Mich.

2830.   JOHN FOOTE, (1403, 520, 170, 37, 13, 5,) b. Mar. 8, 1833; m. Oct. 13, 1855, Lora Anette, dau. of Rev. Joel Talcott, of Wakeman, O. He was a carpenter and farmer; also an active member of the Baptist Church at Hartford, O.; d. May 26, 1872. Mrs. Foote m. 2nd, Henry Hammond, Oct. 13, 1874. He d. Dec. 23, 1899. She d. May 20, 1905.

     4436.   i.   MILO, b. Sept. 4, 1862; m. Ella E. Eshenroder, 5817.

2832.   HENRY BRONSON FOOTE, (1403, 520, 170, 37, 13, 5,) b. Sept. 10, 1837, Fitchville, O.; m. 1st, Feb. 15, 1863, Lucinda, dau. of Solomon Hartman; m. 2nd, Feb. 6, 1867, Mary S., dau. of Amos and Ruth Ann Clark, Townsend, O. She was b. Dec. 5, 1838. Res., Homer, Mich.

     4437.   i.   LUELLA E., b. Mar. 5, 1864. Res., Homer; unm.
     4438.   ii.   SARAH LOUISA, b. Feb. 23, 1866, Ramona, Indian Territory; m. Oct. 24, 1890, James B. Seeley.
     4439.   iii.   JOHN CLARK, b. Mar. 24, 1870.

2835. WATSON ORVIS FOOTE, (1403, 520, 170, 37, 13, 5,) b. Aug. 17, 1855; m. Dec. 24, 1882, Augusta J. Bromburg. Res., Tekonsha, Mich.

    4440. i. SON, b. and d. Oct. 22, 1883.

    4441. ii. EZRA LEON, b. June 16, 1885.

    4442. iii. MYRA LORENA, b. Apr. 10, 1887.

    4443. iv. CHRISTA ADELL, b. July 31, 1893.

    4444. v. SOPHIA DOROTHY, b. Aug. 9, 1901; d. Oct. 15, 1901.

2836. SETH FOOTE, (1409, 520, 170, 37, 13, 5,) b. Jan. 25, 1834; m. Amorette E. Rich. Seth Foote held various company and regimental offices as a member of the 8th Kansas Volunteers during the Civil War. Was Aide-de-camp to Colonel Heg, commanding a brigade at the battle of Chickamauga. Was Ordnance Officer at the battle of Mission Ridge, where he was mortally wounded. Res., Westfield, O.

    4445. i. DELLIZON A., b. Apr. 14, 1860; m. Milla H. Baird, 5818-20.

2837. HENRY R. FOOTE, (1409, 520, 170, 37, 13, 5,) b. July 14, 1836, Huron Co., O.; m. Feb., 1871, Julia Isabelle, dau. of Benjamin Burnham, at Farnersburg, Ia. She was b. June 20, 1847, Orange Co., Vt.; d. Jan. 8, 1904, at Castana, Ia. He d. July 5, 1891, at Monona, Ia.

    4446. i. THERON A., b. Apr. 6, 1872; m. Alma C. Meier, 5821-3.

    4447. ii. FLAVILLA SALOME, b. July 18, 1873; unm. Res., McGregor, Ia.

    4448. iii. VIOLA JANETTE, b. July 21, 1876; d. Nov. 22, 1878.

2839. DR. DAVID FOOTE, (1409, 520, 170, 37, 13, 5,) b. Jan. 23, 1843, Huron Co., O.; m. July 4, 1860, Caroline Porter. Res., 366 Champion St., Battle Creek, Mich.

    4449. i. MERRILL, b. Aug., 1863.

    4450. ii ALICE, b. Apr., 1865.

2846. CHARLES W. FOOTE, (1413, 521, 170, 37, 13, 5,) b. Sept. 10, 1826; m. 1st, May 19, 1850, Martha J. Freeman. She was b. Dec. 1, 1827; d. Sept. 1, 1872; m. 2nd, Mar. 12, 1874, Kate C. Ernot. She was b. Aug. 23, 1844; d. Oct. 14, 1890; m. 3rd, Oct. 27, 1892, Phebe W. Hall. She was b. Mar. 30, 1826. He d. Apr. 13, 1897. Res., Thompson, Geauga Co., O.

    4451. i. WYLLIS J., b. May 8, 1851; m. Adelia R. Bower, 5824.

2854. JOHN BRONSON FOOTE, Jr., (1424, 522, 170, 37, 13, 5,) b. May 3, 1841; served 2 years and 10 months in Civil War; m. 1871, Gertrude E. Dodge, of Vernon, N. Y. He d. Jan. 31, 1903, at Clinton, N. Y.

    4452. i. ORVILLE D., b. ——; m. Estelle Dunn. Res., 141 Albany St., Utica, N. Y.

    4453. ii. CLAYTON E., b. ——; m. Floy Christward. Res., Ilion, N. Y.; d. Aug 26, 1906. Ch.: (1) Irma M., b. June 21, 1899; d. Sept. 14, 1903, at Utica, N. Y.

    4454. iii. LOUISA D., b. Aug. 28, 1877; m. Walter M. Seeyle. Res., 288 Oneida St., Utica, N. Y. Ch: (1) Gertrude E., b. June 8, 1906.

    4455. iv. FANNY, b. Jan. 13, 1875; d. Apr. 7, 1882, at Clinton, N. Y.

    4456. v. GERTRUDE, b. Aug. 28, 1877; d. May 18, 1883, at Clinton, N. Y.

    4457. vi. JOHN, b. May 6, 1891; d. Sept. 11, 1891, at Clinton, N. Y.

2865. EBENEZER FOOTE,, (1441, 527, 171, 47, 13, 5,) b. at Guilford, N. Y., Apr. 18, 1819; m. June 1, 1839, Martha Blanchard, dau. of Jacob and Mary Shiffer, of Plains, Pa. She was b. Feb. 10, 1821. She d. May 7, 1900. He d. Sept. 18, 1902. Res., Duryea, Luzerne Co., Pa. Both were members of the M. E. Church.

4458. i.   ANDREW JACKSON, b. in Pittsboro Township, Mar. 19, 1840; d. Feb. 7, 1863, by accident.

4459. ii.   WILLIAM LEBANOUS, b. Apr. 16, 1842. Mr. Foote lived with grandparents, Jacob and Mary Skiffer, on a farm until the War of '61 to '65; then enlisted in U. S. Service; served until the close of the War. Since then has followed the occupation of General Outside Supt. of Coal Mines, Wilkesbarre Division of the Delaware and Hudson Co. Res., 22 S. Wells St., Wilkesbarre, Pa.; m. Emma Louise, dau. of Thomas and Nancy Burch, of Dundaff, Susquehanna Co., Pa., b. Apr. 24, 1845, Clifford, Susquehanna Co., Pa. Public school education. Member of the M. E. Church. No ch.

4460. iii.   HARRIET LYDIA, b. Apr. 16' 1842; m. Jan. 30, 1862, Daniel Harwood Knapp, of Lackawanna, Pa. He d. Mar. 8, 1884. Ch.: (1) Blanche, b. Apr. 13, 1864; m. Dec. 18, 1890, John Wood, Lackawanna, Luzerne Co., Pa. Ch.: (a) Myrtle, b. Apr. 16, 1892, Old Forge, Pa. (b) Clarence, b. Apr. 10, 1894. (c) Helen, b. May 15, 1897. (2) Harvey, b. Mar. 10, 1866; d. July 25, 1876. (3) Cora, b. Oct. 31, 1868; m. Sept. 6, 1895, Lyman W. Hoffecter, Jeryman, Lackawanna Co., Pa. Res., Duryea, Luzerne Co., Pa. Contractor and builder. Ch.: (a) Merl, b. June 26, 1896. (4) Martha, b. June 12, 1870; d. July 29, 1876. (5) Delbert, b. Mar. 26, 1877; m. Nov. 26, 1901, Elizabeth Williams, of Scranton, Pa. Iron worker. Present res., 120 Spaulding St., Buffalo, N. Y. Ch.: (a) Howard, b. Jan. 15, 1903. (b) Margaret, b. July 13, 1904. (6) Bruce, b. Mar. 25, 1879; m. Apr. 30, 1900, Carrie Gless, of Scranton, Pa. Carpenter. Res., Scranton, Pa. Ch.: (a) Janice, b. El Paso, Texas, Aug. 5, 1901. (b) Theo, b. El Paso, Texas, Jan. 24, 1903.

4461. iv.   JEREMIAH, b. Dec. 2, 1846; d. Mar. 10, 1852.

4462. v.   NANCY ELIZABETH, b. Nov. 19, 1850; d. Mar. 10, 1852.

4463. vi.   NETTIE, b. June 17, 1854; m. Jan. 6, 1877, Robert Bruce Lamont. of Old Forge, Pa. A physician. Res., 22 So. Wells St., Wilkesbarre, Pa.

4464. vii.   CLARA, b. May 10, 1856; m. May 25, 1881, John A. Wood, of Old Forge, Pa. She d. July 11, 1889. Res., 22 So. Wells St., Wilkesbarre, Pa. Ch.: (1) Jessie, b. Mar. 2, 1882.

4465. viii.   ALICE, b. Mar. 4, 1858; m. Henry Lewis Edsall, of Duryea, Luzerne Co., Pa. Merchant. Res., 11 Luzerne Ave., West Pittston, Pa. Ch.: (1) Muzette, b. Moosic, Pa., June 13, 1884. (2) Rena Clara, b. Duryea, Pa., Sept. 24, 1891.

2866. WILLIAM FOOTE, (1441, 527, 171, 47, 13, 5,) b. Paris, N. Y., Sept. 23, 1821; m. Catherine Miller.

4466. i.   MARY, b. ——; m. —— Madison. Res., 2 Laurel St., Wilkesbarre, Pa.

4467. ii.   EMMA, b. ——; m. E. C. Martin. Res., Meshoppen, Pa.

4468. iii.   JAMES, b. ——; m. ——. Res., Topeka, Kas.

4469. iv.   GEORGE, b. ——.

2867. NATHANIEL HIBBARD FOOTE, (1441, 527, 171, 47, 13, 5,) b. May 28, 1825, in Cherry Valley; m. ——. Res., Scranton, Pa.

4470. i.   POLLY, b. ——.

2868. SIMEON FOOTE, (1441, 527, 171, 47, 13, 5,) b. Sept. 22, 1831, in Cherry Valley, N. Y.; m. Feb. 1, 1854, Caroline Baker. She was b. Feb. 4, 1836. He d. Jan. 11, 1888. Res., Sugar Run, Pa.

4471. i   EUGENE, b. Dec. 5, 1852; m. Alice Steel, 5825-35.

4472. ii.   EDITH, b. July 12, 1857; m. June 5, 1872, O. A. Wandell, of Wyalusing, Pa.; m. 2nd, Mar. 30, 1877, Edgar Ely. Res., 821 Anthiscite Ave., Wilkesbarre, Pa. Ch.: (1) Curtis Wandell, b. Dec. 5, 1874; m. Clara Allen, of Dushore, Pa. Ch.: (a) Francis. (b) Rodney. (2) Mabel Wandell, b. Feb. 9, 1876; m. A. J. Barnhart, of Wyalusing, Pa. She d. Dec. 22, 1892, at Lopes, Pa. (3) Aaron Ely, b. Oct. 15, 1878, at Wyalusing; m. Lillian Evans, of Vernon, Pa. Ch.: (a) Emery Lester Ely, b. (4) Edgar C. Ely, b. Feb. 28, 1880; d. May 26, 1880. (5) Herman, b. July 12, 1881; m. Dec. 24, 1898, Jennie Pereast, of Bath, Maine. Ch.: (a) Victor, b. Bath, Me.; d. at Noxen, Pa. (6) Beulah, b. Feb. 28, 1883; m. June, 1898, Thomas J. Vanhorn, of Lopes, Pa. Ch.: (a) Lionel, b. (b) Richard, b. (c) Charlie, b. (d) Howard, b. (7) Floyd, b. June 15, 1885; unm. (8) Inez, b. Mar. 18, 1886; d. Apr. 1, 1887. (9) Venetia, b. Mar. 12, 1887; m. Mar. 10, 1905, Arthur Beahm, of Noxen, Pa. Ch.: (a) Verona, b. Sept. 10, 1906. (10) Frank, b. May 28, 1888, at Wyalusing, Pa.; d. July 27, 1899, at Noxen, Pa. (11) Betsey, b. Apr. 9, 1891, at Lopes; d. Nov., 1891. (12) Beatrice, b. at Lopes, May 27, 1892. (13) Evallie, b. Aug. 14, 1893. (14) Vivian, b. Oct. 28, 1894. (15) Iva, b. Feb. 29, 1896. (16) Bretta, b. Feb. 4, 1898; d. July 7, 1899. (17) Andrey, b. Apr. 22, 1899; d. July 23, 1899, at Noxen. (18) Foy Dale, b. July 19, 1902; d. Mar. 16, 1903.

4473. iii.   HIBBARD, b. Sept. 5, 1858, at Falls, Pa.; m. 5836-8.

4473¹. iv.   PARLEY, b. Oct. 28, 1861; killed by a tree, May 15, 1873.

4473². v.   EBENEZER, b. Apr. 26, 1864; unm. Res., Alleghany, Pa.

4473³. vi.   ELIAS, b. May 17, 1866, at Schultzville, Pa.; d. Sept. 7, 1866.

4473⁴. vii.   NELLIE, b. Aug. 11, 1867; d. Jan. 13, 1868.

4473⁵. viii.   NELSON, b. Aug. 11, 1867; d. Jan. 11, 1868.

4474. ix.   ELLNORA, b. May 25, 1869; m. William Henson, of Dushore, Pa. She d. Apr., 1897.

4475. x.   CLARENCE, b. July 15, 1873; m. Clara Merritt, of Laceyville, Pa.

4476. xi.   WASH STELLA, b. Feb. 20, 1876; m. J. M. Vanover, of Wyalusing, Pa. Res., Barclay, Pa. Ch.: (a) Rodney, b. (b) Clara, b. (c) Francis, b. (d) Hattie, b.

4477. xii.   MAUD, b. Jan. 12, 1879; m. George Merritt, of Laceyville, Pa. Ch.: (a) Dewey. (b) Floyd. (c) Fred.

2869. GIDEON O. FOOTE, (1441, 527, 171, 47, 13, 5,) b. July 10, 1834, in Lenox, Pa.; m. Julia A. Webb. She was b. July 20, 1840. He d. May 5, 1907. Res., Lestershire, N. Y.

4478. i.   JOHN MILO, b. June 17, 1861; m. Etna C. ———, 5839-42.

4479. ii.   ZEBULON, b. July 11, 1861; d. May 8, 1864.

4480. iii.   FLORENCE A., b. at Newton, Pa., Feb. 17, 1865; m. Aug. 7, 1882, Charles F. Knickerbocker. He was b. in Madison, Pa., Oct. 14, 1860. He is Constable and Deputy Sheriff. Res., Elm-hurst, Pa. Ch.: (1) Elizabeth, b. (2) Arthur, b. (3) Pearl, b. (4) William, b. (5) Charlotte, b. (6) Myrtle, b. (7) Stanley R., b. (8) Florence M., b. (9) Kenneth, b. (10) Charles, Jr., b. (11) Carlisle, b.

4481. iv. FRANK C., b. May 21, 1867; unm.

4482. v. JOSEPH H., b. Feb. 24, 1870; d. Dec. 6, 1872.

4483. vi. EMERY C., b. Nov. 16, 1873; m. Helen Lunger. No ch.

4484. vii. AUGUSTA L., b. Feb. 7, 1877; m. Frank A., son of Rev. Fayette A. and Caroline A. Matteson. Rev. Fayette is a retired Baptist minister. Res., Binghamton, N. Y. Rev. Frank is Pastor of M. E. Church, No. Sanford, N. Y. Ch.: (1) Leode A. (2) Truman F. (3) Raymond E.

4485. viii. BERT L., b. Dec. 11, 1880.

2873. SIMEON FOOTE, (1442, 527, 171, 47, 13, 5,) b. Nov. 23, 1825; m. Nancy A. Hodges, of Ceres, Pa. She d. Apr. 16, 1905. He d. Jan. 17, 1903. Res., Port Allegany, Pa.

4486. i. JOSEPH H., b May 4, 1849; m. Mary M. Sheldon, of Coudersport, Pa. She d. Apr. 16, 1905; s. p.

4487. ii. NANCY E., b. Oct. 7, 1851; m. Edwin Holcomb, of Annin, Pa. Ch.: (1)Kittie L., b. Apr. 19, 1871; m. 1st, Delvs Marsh; m. 2nd, Herman Plummer, of Corryville, Pa. She d. Apr. 10, 1894. Ch.: (a) Hazel Marsh, b. June 5, 1889. (b) Flossie Plummer, b. July 13, 1893. (2) Reginald L. Holcomb, b. July 6, 1881; d. Nov. 27, 1898.

4488. iii. ROSALIA, b. Jan. 17, 1854; m. John Bessie, of Annin, Pa. Res., Portville, Pa. Ch.: (1) Henry N. Bessie, b. July 29, 1873. (2) Lell Bessie, b. Jan. 16, 1879. (3) Daisy Bessie, b. Feb. 7, 1886. (4) Henrietta Bessie.

4489. iv. ROSELTHA, b. ———; m. William Austin, of Belle Run, Potter Co., Pa. Res., Shingle House, Pa. Ch.: (1) Senith Austin, b. ———; m. Ward Cole. (2 and 3) Boys; n. f. k.

4490. v. LEWIS K., b. ———; m. Ina Spencer, 5843.

4491. vi. FRANK, b. ———; m. Minnie Crandell, 5844.

4492. vii. HATTIE, b. Feb. 29, 1865; m. William B. Cleveland. Ch.: (1) William Lyle Cleveland, b. Oct. 7, 1891. (2) Lyona Belle Cleveland, b. Apr. 26, 1903.

4493. viii. CARRIE, b. Oct. 13, 1869; m. Cyrus Austin, of Belle Run, Pa.; m. 2nd, Merle Plummer, of Carryville, Pa. Ch.: (1) Frankie Austin, b. Mar. 12, 1892. (2) Carl Austin, b. Mar. 23, 1894. (3) Leslie Austin, b. Dec. 7, 1898. (4) Paul Plummer, b. Jan. 25, 1906.

2874. NATHANIEL BACON FOOTE, (1442, 527, 171, 47, 13, 5,) b. Dec. 4, 1828; m. Sept. 11, 1849, Mary E., dau. of Joseph and Nancy Hodges, of Ceres, McKean Co., Pa.

4494. i. WILLIAM H., b. July 1, 1850; m. Ida Terry, 5845-6.

4495. ii. MARY MARIA, b. Oct. 1, 1852, at Annin, Pa.; m. Aug. 12, 1871, George W. Taft, of Jasper, Steuben Co., N. Y. Res., Ceres, Pa. Ch.: (1) Mary E. Taft, b. Apr. 12, 1878, in Barron Co., Wis.; m. Sept. 8, 1897, Edward E. Patchen, of Canisteo, N. Y.

4496. iii. NATHAN, b. Apr. 17, 1854; m. Mary Parks, 5847-51.

4497. iv. MARTHA, b. Ceres, Pa., Apr. 3, 1856; m. May 25, 1874, John B. Newell, of Hedgesville, N. Y. Res., Ashton, S. Dak. Ch.: (1) Mary Idella, b. Oct. 15, 1875; m. May 12, 1896, Thos. Magee, of Wis. She d. Apr. 26, 1903. Ch.: (a) Milton Eugene Magee, b. Aug. 13, 1897. (b) Thos. Oliver Magee, b. Feb. 3, 1900. (c) Lola Mal Magee, b. July 15, 1902; d. Mar. 14, 1903. (2) Pearl Newell, b. July 20, 1877; m. Sept. 25, 1893, A. M. Grover, of Wis. Ch.: (a) Chester H. Grover, b. July 22, 1895. (b) Leslie Lyle Grover, b. Aug. 25, 1896. (c) Vivian Viva Grover, b. May 26, 1901. (3) Martha Newell, b. Apr. 20, 1879; m. Nov. 11, 1896, Thos. Ziglar, of S. Dak. Ch.: (a) George W. Zigler, b. Aug. 22, 1898. (b) Pearl Ilene Ziglar, b. Apr. 15, 1900. (c) Leslie Britton Ziglar, b. Dec. 15, 1902. (4) Tennie Newell, b. Sept. 20, 1884; m. May 7, 1902, William Ziglar, of S. Dak. (5) Minnie Newell, b. Feb. 2, 1892. (6) J. Britton Newell, b. Sept. 26, 1893. (7) Vera May Newell, b. Oct. 9, 1897.

4498. v. OLIVE, b. at Annin, Feb. 7, 1858; d. Mar. 17, 1859.

4499. vi. RAYMOND HODGES, b. Mar. 4, 1860, at Annin; m. Oct. 20, 1897, Bessie Hooker, of Port Allegeny. Res., Port Allegeny, Pa. No ch.

4500. vii. IDELLA E., b. in Ceres, Sept. 5, 1862; m. July 4, 1881, James Black, of Greenwood, N. Y. Ch.: (1) Grace Idella, b. Apr. 1, 1882, at Carryville, Pa.; d. 1889. (2) James J., b. Dec. 7, 1889, at Carryville, Pa. (3) Frank K., b. Mar. 30, 1891, at Carryville. (4) Earle E., b. at Ceres, Pa., Sept. 22, 1896. (5) Martha, b. in Ceres, Nov. 26, 1900.

4502. viii. ULYSSES H., b. Sept. 17, 1867; m. Rose Plummer, 5852-4.

4503. ix. JAMES R., b. Dec. 27, 1871, at Annin, Pa.

4504. x. SIMEON M., b. Apr. 2, 1874; m. Ina Warden, 5855-61.

2881. WILLIAM MILLER FOOTE, (1443, 527, 171, 47, 13, 5,) b. Lenox, Pa., Mar., 1825; m. May 7, 1842, at Lenox, Susan, dau. of Samuel Perce Truesdale. She was b. Nov. 11, 1829, at Lenox, Pa. He was a salesman; d. Dec., 1887.

4505. i. WILLIAM SIMEON, b. Lenox, Pa., July 31, 1858; m. Olive Susan Marcy, 5857.

4505¹. ii. JENNIE, b. 1846; m. Leon St. John, of Mansfield, O. She d. 1870, Nicholson, Pa.

4505². iii. LIFFIE, b. 1848; m. Joseph William Umphred, of Oakland, Cal. She d. 1880, Lenox, Pa.

4505³. iv. ANNIE, b. 1850; m. Orin William Titus, of Alford, Pa. She d. 1872, Waverley, Pa.

4505⁴. v. IDA, b. 1862; d. 1879, Scranton, Pa.

4505⁵. vi. JENNIE, b. 1864; d. 1873.

2882. JOHN HENRY FOOTE, (1443, 527, 171, 47, 13, 5,) b. Sept. 22, 1831; m. Juliet Rosecrams, of Tunkhannock, Pa. He d. 1901.

4506. i. ALONZO, b. Res., Kasson Brook, Pa.

4507. ii. THOMAS, b. Res., Kasson Brook, Pa.

4508. iii. WILLIAM, b. Res., Kasson Brook, Pa.

4509. iv. URBAN, b. Res., Kasson Brook, Pa.

4510. v. GEORGE D., b. Res., Elmira, N. Y.

4510¹. vi. MRS. GEORGE SLATER, b. Res., Kasson Brook, Pa.

4510². vii. MRS. E. E. HARDING, b. Res., Kasson Brook, Pa.

4510³. viii. MRS. CLINT McCARROLL, b. Res., Kasson Brook, Pa.

2893. WILLIAM HARRISON FOOTE, (1454, 529, 171, 47, 13, 5,) b. June 6, 1834; m. in Flint, Mich., Dec. 24, 1874, Nettie J., dau. of Newell G. and Mary J. (Derby) Bristol. She was b. Flint, Mich., Jan. 30, 1857. He is a photographer. Res., Flint, Mich. Ch. all b. in Flint, Mich.

4511. i. AMY GRACE, b. Mar. 30, 1876.

4512. ii. WILLIAM HARRISON, b. Jan. 31, 1881.

4513. iii. MARY B., b. Mar. 20, 1883.

4514. iv. ROYAL G., b. Oct. 10, 1885.

4515. v. FRED D. W., b. Dec. 16, 1891.

2895. CHARLES EMERY FOOTE, (1455, 529, 171, 47, 13, 5,) b. at Saline, Mich., May 17, 1842; m. Ypsilanti, Mich., Apr. 19, 1866, Kate, dau. of Othniel Gordon and Hannah (Bowell) La Rue. She was b. Mt. Morris, N. Y., July 30, 1845. He served in the 1st Mich. Vol. Infantry and the 22nd Mich. Vol. Infantry in the Civil War. He was wounded at the battle of Chickamauga, Sept. 20, 1863. Res., Detroit, Mich.

4516. i. WARREN GEORGE, b. Ypsilanti, Mich., July 7, 1867.

4517. ii. GUY CHARLES, b. Ypsilanti, Mich., Aug. 15, 1869.

4518. iii. ADAH LOUISE, b. Ypsilanti, Mich., Mar., 1872.

4519. iv. EDWARD LA RUE, b. Battle Creek, Mich., Sept. 10, 1874.

4520. v. FREDERIC LA RUE, b. Battle Creek, Mich., July 28, 1883.

2897. GEORGE EVERLYN FOOTE, (1455, 529, 171, 47, 13, 5,) b. Albion, Mich., July 18, 1846, Frances, dau. of Henry and Jenette (Siminson) Joslin. She was b. July 14, 1839. He served in the 22nd Mich. Infantry in 1864, and is engaged in the Life Insurance business in Detroit, Mich.

4521. i. RALPH ADAIR, b. Dexter, Mich., Mar. 11, 1873.

2898. FRANKLIN SHELDON FOOTE, (1455, 529, 171, 47, 13, 5,) b. Ypsilanti, Mich., Nov. 20, 1853; m. 1st, Apr. 3, 1878, Alfaretta M. Finch. She was b. Green Springs, O.; d. Aug. 12, 1888, at Clyde; m. 2nd, Locust Point, O., Dec. 22, 1888, Melvina Amanda, dau. of Geo. W. and Mary L. (Meeker) Long. She was b. Locust Point, O., Oct. 9, 1863.

4522. i. EDGAR LONG, b. Indianapolis, Ind., Oct. 12, 1890.

2900. DAVID FOOTE, (1456, 529, 171, 47, 13, 5,) b. Hancock Co., Ill., Aug. 25, 1845; m. St. Joseph, Nev., Apr., 1866, Emma E. Bennett; m. 2nd, Apr. 30, 1876, Sarah Rebecca, dau. of Job and Elizabeth (Jones) Hall She was b. Sept. 24, 1860. Farmer. Res., Glendale, Utah.

4523. i. DAVID ALMA, b. St. Thomas, Nev., Mar. 23, 1867; d. 1868, at St. Thomas, Nev.

4524. ii. WARREN N., b. Feb. 26, 1869; m. Ruth E. Maxwell, 5858-64.

4525· iii. GEORGE A., b. Jan. 29, 1872; m. Rosa C. Wanslee, 5865-70.

4526. iv. ORSON F., b. July 2, 1877; m. Matilda T. Parker, 5871-4.

4527. v. JOB, b. Oct. 7, 1878; d. Oct. 7, 1878.

4528. vi. WILLIAM ARTHUR, b. Oct. 15, 1879; res., Lovell, Wyoming.

4529. vii. SARAH LOVINIA, b. Aug. 29, 1881; m. ——— Black; res., Emery, Utah.

4530. viii. SAMUEL COLEMAN, b. Aug. 13, 1884; m. Dec. 30, 1906, Emily Jane, dau. of Geo. W. Hicks, b. May 12, 1884, at Mt. Carmel, Kane Co., Utah. Res., Safford, Graham Co., Ariz.

4531. ix. MARY IRENE, b. Esclanta, Utah, Nov. 14, 1886; m. Dec. 27, 1905, Melburn Crandall. He was b. Jan. 18, 1882, Huntington, Utah. Res., Safford, Ariz. Ch.: (1) Merlin David Crandall, b. Safford, Ariz., Sept. 14, 190—.

4532. x. ROBERT, b. Aug. 6, 1887.

4533. xi. DAVID, b. July 18, 1889.

4534. xii. NANCY, b. July 19, 1891.

4535. xiii. HOMER HAROLD, b. July 4, 1893.

4536. xiv. RHODA, b. Mar. 28, 1896.

4537. xv. GERALD, b. Apr. 5, 1898.

4538. xvi. MARTIN ORVILL, b. Aug. 23, 1900.

4539. xvii. GLEN, b. July 3, 1902.

2906. GEORGE ALBERT FOOTE, (1456, 529, 171, 47, 13, 5,) b. Union, Utah, Jan. 14, 1860; m. May 27, 1891, at Aurora, Utah, Leanah Bell, dau. of John F. and Sarah Alice (Beebe) Jones. She was b. Oxford, Idaho, Aug. 2, 1875. Farmer. Res., Glendale and Emery, Utah.

4540. i. ALICE, b. Glendale, Utah, Apr. 10, 1892.

4541. ii. DELILAH, b. Glendale, Utah, Sept. 16, 1893.

4542. iii. ARTEMISIA, b. Oct. 1, 1898.

4543. iv. ARVILLIA, b. Oct. 17, 1900.

4544. v. GEORGE ALBERT, b. Dec. 11, 1902·

4545. vi. FLORANCE, b. Sept. 23, 1904.

4545¹. vii. LOUISA, b. Mar. 12, 1907.

2909. HOMER CLARENCE FOOTE, (1456, 529, 171, 47, 13, 5,) b. St. Thomas, Nev., Feb. 3, 1871; m. Olive Lucretia Rasix. Res., Glendale, Utah.

4546. i. CLARENCE WILLIAM, b. Oct. 20, 1903.

4547. ii. HAZEL, b. Apr. 27, 1905.

2910. JAMES FRANKLIN FOOTE, (1456, 529, 171, 47, 13, 5,) b. Mt. Pleasant, Utah, June 22, 1859; m. Hillsdale, Utah, Dec. 25, 1876, Emiline Frances, dau. of Pleasant and Emiline (Degraw) Manchey. She was b. Fountain Green, Utah, Mar. 14, 1859. Farmer. Res., Emery, Utah.

4548. i. CHARLES FRANKLIN, b. Hillsdale, Utah, Dec. 1, 1877.

4549. ii. JACOB, b. Hillsdale, Utah, Feb. 2, 1880.

4550. iii. AMMON, b. Glendale, Utah, Jan. 23, 1882.

4551. iv. SARAH FRANCES, b. Emery, Utah.

4552. v. ELIZA EMILINE, b. Emery, Utah, Aug. 22, 1886; d. Mar. 25, 1888.

4553. vi. IRINE, b. Emery, Utah, Mar. 23, 1889.

4554. vii. OLIVE, b. Glendale, Utah, Jan. 31, 1892.

4555. viii. WARREN, b. June 5, 1894.

2913. JOHN AMMON FOOTE, (1456, 529, 171, 47, 13, 5,) b. St. Joseph, Nev., Dec. 6, 1865; m. Emery, Utah, Mar. 2, 1886, Eliza Ann, dau. of George and Hannah Merrick. He d. of typhoid fever, Dec. 6, 1887.

4556. i. JOHN AMMON, Jr., b. Emery, Utah, Jan. 29, 1887.

2914. CHARLES L. FOOTE, (1456, 529, 171, 47, 13, 5,) b. Nov. 11, 1868, at St. Joseph, Nev.; m. Feb. 17, 1897, Hannah M., dau. of Niels and Martina Anderson. She was b. Ephraim, Utah, Jan. 13, 1874. Res., Emery Utah.

4557. i. LUCILLE, b. Mar. 11, 1898.

4558. ii. LOREEN, b. Aug. 22, 1899.

4559. iii. GRANT LANE, b. July 25, 1901.
4560. iv. CHARLES HORACE, b. Apr. 19, 1903.
4560¹. v. REED ALLON, b. Feb. 28, 1905.

2918. THOMAS WHITESIDE FOOTE, (1459, 535, 172, 47, 13, 5,) b. May 23, 1832; m. Sept. 25, 1850, Catherine Kathlenbrink. She was b. Prussia, Germany, Apr. 15, 1830. He d. June 6, 1900. Res., Quincy, Ill.
4560². i. HORATIO K., b. Res., Melrose, Wis.
4560³. ii. PAUL K., b. Res., Melrose, Wis.
4560⁴. iii. THOMAS M., b. Res., Melrose, Wis.
4560⁵. iv. DAU., b.; m. C. A. E. Gantert. Res., Quincy, Ill.
4560⁶. v. DAU., b.; m. H. F. Weingartner, of Belvidere, Ill.

2922. FRED EMERY FOOTE, (1460, 535, 172, 47, 13, 5,) b. Dec. 28, 1869, Rockford, Ill. Res., 480 E. Carruthers St., Portland, Oregon; m. Aug. 10, 1899, Elsie Harriet, dau. of Ernest Byron Ketchem, Arroy Grande, Cal. He was educated at Sacramento, Cal. Merchant. She was b. Sept. 10, 1873, at Arroy Grande, Cal.
4561. i. LUCIUS KETCHUM, b. May 23, 1900.
4561¹. ii. ERNEST EMERY, b. May 8, 1902; d. Oct. 3, 1903.
4561². iii. HAROLD STANLEY, b. Mar. 14, 1905.

2923. ALBERT EUGENE FOOTE, (1463, 535, 172, 47, 13, 5,) b. Joliet, Ill., July 17, 1840; m. June 1, 1885, Mrs. Annie Jarratt VanDyke, of Milwaukee, Wis. He d. Mar. 4, 1903, at Milwaukee, Wis.
4562. i. ALBERT HIRAM, b. Milwaukee, Wis., June 11, 1886.

2926. HIRAM WELLS FOOTE, (1463, 535, 172, 47, 13, 5,) b. Janesville, Wis., Feb. 9, 1846; m. Milwaukee, Wis., 1873, Eunice DeMaris Horton. Educated at Carroll College, Wis. Res., Los Angeles, Cal.
4563. i. CLARA DEMARIS HORTON, b. St. Paul, Minn., Oct. 29, 1876; d. July 29, 1901, in Minneapolis, Minn.

2927. CHARLES EDWARD FOOTE, (1463, 537, 172, 47, 13, 5,) b. at Janesville, Wis., Mar. 25, 1855; m. May Pease, of Cumberland, Barron Co., Wis., in 1883. She d. at Cumberland, Nov. 4, 1901. Charles Edward Foote received his preliminary education at Carroll College, and is now practising the profession of dentistry at Cumberland, Wis., of which city he is the Mayor.
4564. i. FLORENCE MAY, b. at Cumberland, Wis., Nov. 12, 1883; graduated from the High School of her home city and the School of Pharmacy of the University of Minnesota, and is now practising her profession at Baraboo, Wis.
4565. ii. ELSIE DEMARIS, b. at Cumberland, Wis., July 13, 1890; d. at Cumberland, Oct. 9, 1892.

2928. HENRY MARTIN FOOTE, (1464, 535, 172, 47, 13, 5,) b. June 18, 1859, Rockford, Ill.; m. Oct. 11, 1881, Vina Irone. Res., Oregon City, Ore.
4566. i. EURA, b. Aug. 13, 1882, Rockford, Ill.
4567. ii. EARL G., b. Sept. 6, 1885, Rockford, Ill.
4568. iii. HAZEL, b. Oct. 10, 1886, Rockford, Ill.; d. Feb., 1899.
4569. iv. BENNIE, b. Apr., 1888, Ashland, Oregon; d. Feb., 1890, Oregon.
4570. v. BERNEITA, b. Feb. 2, 1891, Oregon City, Oregon.

2929. SAMUEL ERASTUS FOOTE, (1464, 537, 172, 47, 13, 5,) b. Jamestown, N. Y., Apr. 4, 1821; m. in Jamestown, N. Y., Oct. 20, 1842, Elizabeth Lee, dau. of Rev. Winthrop and Martha Stanwood Bailey, of Berlin, Mass. She was

b. Pelham, Mass., Nov. 21, 1822. He d. July 7, 1884, in St. Louis, Mo. Res., Milwaukee, Wis., Erie, Pa. She res., St. Louis, Mo.

4571. i. FRANCIS BAILEY, b. Grand Rapids, Mich., July 24, 1844; d. Aug. 23, 1851, in Milwaukee, Wis.

4572. ii. CHARLES STANWOOD, b. Milwaukee, Wis., Mar. 7, 1847; d. Aug. 15, 1847.

4573. iii. EMERSON L., b. Milwaukee, Wis., Nov. 25, 1848; m. Julia C. Chase, 5875-8.

4574. iv. ANNIE CHENEY, b. Milwaukee, Wis., Mar. 10, 1851. Res., St. Louis, Mo.

4575. v. ELIZABETH, b. Milwaukee, Wis., Sept. 26, 1854; d. Sept. 31, 1854, in Milwaukee, Wis.

4576. vi. MARY ISABELLA, b. Milwaukee, Wis., July 23, 1856; d. Sept. 27, 1857, in Wauwatoosa, Wis.

4577. vii. ARTHUR H., b. July 28, 1858; m. Gertrude E. McGill, 5879-81.

4578. viii. EMILY KNEVALS, b. Milwaukee, Wis., Jan. 18, 1862; m. St. Louis, Mo., Oct. 11, 1893, Dr. Edward C. Runge, of St. Petersburg, Russia. Since 1898 he has been Supt. of the St. Louis Insane Asylum. Res., St. Louis, Mo.

2931. DR. CHARLES CHENEY FOOTE, (1465, 537, 172, 47, 13, 5,) b. Sept. 5, 1825; m. New Haven, Ct., Apr. 22, 1852, Amelia Leavitt, dau. of Rev. Charles and Amelia Stiles (Leavitt) Jenkins (his step sister), of New Haven, Ct., where he practised medicine until his death. He d. Nov. 9, 1871. She res. 26 Elm St., New Haven, Ct. Ch. all b. in New Haven, Ct.

4579. i. ANNA ELIZA, b. Apr. 25, 1853; d. June 12, 1861.

4580. ii. AMELIA LEAVITT, b. New Haven, Ct., Mar. 26, 1855; m. New Haven, Ct., Apr. 30, 1878, Edward Bruce, son of J. Henry Hill, b. Petersham, Mass., Aug. 2, 1818, and Sarah Bruce (Jenkins) Hill, b. Barre, Mass., Feb. 12, 1822. He was b. Worcester, Mass.; June 2, 1853. She d. Dec. 7, 1900, New York, N. Y. Ch.: (1) Amelia Leavitt Hill, b. New York, N. Y., Jan. 4, 1884. Res., New York City.

4581. iii. MARY LOUISA, b. Oct. 24, 1856; d. Sept. 8, 1857.

4582. iv. SARAH WELLS, b. Feb. 14, 1859. Res., New Haven, Ct.; unm.

4583. v. CHARLES JENKINS, b. Aug. 28, 1867. Now a practicing physician in New Haven, Ct.

4584. vi. HORACE KNEVALS, b. Apr. 1, 1867; d. Sept. 14, 1871.

2932. JAMES HALL FOOTE, (1465, 537, 172, 47, 13, 5,) b. Jamestown, Chautauqua Co., N. Y., June 26, 1827; m. Jamestown, N. Y., Nov. 5, 1850, Jane Agnes, dau. of Dr. Alfred W. and Valeria Elizabeth Dodd Gray, of Jamestown, N. Y. She was b. Brownville, Jefferson Co., N. Y., July 31, 1831; d. Oct. 24, 1862, in Kilbourn City, Wis. Her remains were interred in the Foote Plot in Lake View Cemetery, Jamestown, N. Y., Lot 18, in Olevet Section. He m. 2nd, New York City, Sept. 16, 1863, Ellen Marion, dau. of Col. Charles Rufas and Rebecca Hayward Harvey, of New York, N. Y. She was b. Poughkeepsie, N. Y., Jan. 11, 1839. Her parents removed to New York when she was an infant. She d. Dec. 1, 1901, in Canaan, Ct. Mr. Foote followed the sea for many years in a whaling vessel; later engaged in the wholesale hardware business and also interested in a book bindery. Like his father and brother, Horace Allen, he has always been interested in preserving the family records. He has not only gathered the records of his own branch, but in his travels to California, in 1906-7, interested many others in the work.

4585. i. MARY EVELYN, b. Jamestown, N. Y., Dec. 1, 1851; m. Apr. 20, 1875, in St. James M. E. Church, Madison Ave., New York City, Dr. George E. Morgan. He was b. Peninsula, O., Apr 13, 1848. Is a graduate of the Hanneman Medical College, Philadelphia, Pa., in 1871, and has been a practising physician in New York and connected with Manhattan Hospital in New York. He served his full time in the 5th Iowa Infantry during the Civil War. Res., New York City. Ch.: (1) Evelyn Foote, b. New York City, Jan. 13, 1878; m. New York City, Jan. 11, 1898, Alexander, son of William and Jane Von Wartz, of New York City. He was b. Dec. 1, 1875, New York City. Ch.: (a) Isibella Britton, b. Heartnellville, Vt. (2) Rollin Kedzie, b. New York City, June 8, 1881; m. Oakland, Cal., Jan. 1, 1904, Dr. Alice, dau. of David and Ellen Morgan Bush, of San Francisco, Cal. (3) Marion, b. New York City, July 2, 1887.

4586. ii. VALERIA GRAY, b. Milwaukee, Wis., Mar. 30, 1854; m. New York City, Jan. 19, 1881, Harry Hayden, son of David Benjamin and Jerusia Bogue Treadwell, of New York City. He was b. Treadwell, Delaware Co., N. Y., Apr. 6, 1856. He was mustered into the Regular U. S. Army 1898, and served as Adjutant, with rank of Captain, 22nd Regt. N. G. S. N. Y., New York City, throughout the war with Spain, and was unanimously elected Lieutenant-Colonel at its close, having served in that regiment 21 consecutive years. He was also appointed Aide-de-Camp on Theodore Roosevelt's Military Staff, Jan. 8, 1899, and retained during his term of service as Governor of New York State. Ch.: (1) Florence, b. New York City, Nov. 11, 1881; d. Feb. 5, 1890. (2) Harry Gray, b. New York City, Aug. 28, 1884; in Princeton University. (3) Jennie, b. New York City, July 29, 1889; in Briarcliff Seminary, Briarcliff, N. Y.

4587. iii. HATTIE, b. Kilbourn City, Wis., Aug. 16, 1860; m. New York City, July 23, 1879, William Bebee, son of David Benjamin and Jerusia Bogue Treadwell, of New York City. He was b. Andes, Delaware Co., N. Y., Feb. 5, 1860. Ch.: (1) William Bebee, Jr., b. New York City, May 21, 1880. He was a member of the 22nd Regt. National Guards of the State of New York. Was mustered into the Regular Army in 1898 and served throughout the war with Spain in said Regt. (2) James Foote, b. New York City, Nov. 26, 1882; d. Apr. 29' 1902. (3) John Charles, b. New York City, Mar. 17, 1885. (4) George Morgan, b. New York City, May 22, 1889; d. June 9, 1889, in New York City.

4588. iv. ELIAL TODD, Jr., b. New York City, Aug. 25, 1865; unm. With Vacuum Cleaning Co.

4589. v. JAMES HARVEY, b. Pittsfield, Mass., Apr. 7, 1868; m. Sarah Phelps Gaylord, 5882-3.

2933. HORACE ALLEN FOOTE, (1465, 537, 172, 47, 13, 5,) b. Jamestown, N. Y., July 17, 1832; m. Jan. 23, 1862, at New Haven, Ct., Emily, dau. of Sherman

JAMES HALL FOOTE.   No. 2932

HORACE ALLEN FOOTE. No. 2933

Wakefield and Lucy Miles Knevals, of New Haven, Ct. When his father moved to New Haven, Ct., Horace entered the Hopkins Grammar School, to prepare for Yale, but his inclination for business being so decided he did not enter college, but went to Milwaukee, Wis., in the early 60's he returned east, and engaged in business in N. Y. City, having been senior member, for more than 25 years, of the firm of Foote and Knevals, wholesale dealers in molasses, coffees, and sugars. He was a member of the N. Y. Chamber of Commerce, the N. Y. Historical Society, the Sons of the Revolution, and the Society of Colonial Wars. He d. Apr. 23, 1903, in N. Y. City.

4590. i.   CALEB KNEVALS, b. New Haven, Ct., Aug. 23, 1866; d. Feb. 23, 1867, in N. Y. City.

4591. ii. HORACE CHENEY, b. June 11, 1868; m. Doris Kristensson, 5884.

4592. iii. DR. SHERMAN KNEVALS, b. N. Y. City, Jan. 5, 1874. A graduate of Yale University, and of the College of Physicians and Surgeons in N. Y. A practising physician and a member of the Board of Health in N. Y., with Hospital connections.

2934. DR. HORACE FREEMAN FOOTE, (1466, 537, 172, 47, 13, 5,) b. Jamestown, N. Y., Mar. 18, 1823; m. Woodville, La., Oct. 11, 1846, Susan C., dau. of W. C. Anderson. She was b. Greensboro, Ala, Jan. 1, 1832. He was a fine physician and practised medicine for many years both in La. and Texas. He d. Mar. 1, 1902, at Yoakum, DeWitt Co., Texas.

4593. i.   HORACE K., b. Jackson, La., May 30, 1848; m. Missouri Anderson, 5885-91.

4594. ii. GERTRUDE E., b. Jackson, La., Apr. 13, 1850; m. Nov. 20, 1873, Jefferson Davis, son of B. F. Carroll, of Dresden, Texas, at Blooming Grove, Texas. He was b. Landerdale Co., Miss., Sept. 16, 1847. Has been a retail lumber dealer in Corsicana, Texas, for many years, and is now engaged in drilling for oil. Res., Corsicana, Texas. Ch.: (1) Carl F., b. Blooming Grove, Sept. 25, 1874. (2) Ernest, b. Dresden, Feb. 14, 1878; m. Hanna, dau. of Dr. Miller Bond, of Missouri, Oct. 25, 1900, at Corsicana, Texas. He is with the Standard Oil Co. Res., Jennings, La. Ch.: (a) Ernest Bond, b. Corsicana, Aug. 3, 1901. (b) Geraldine, b. Dalta, Nov. 16, 1902. (c) William Arthur, b. Jennings, La., Mar. 21, 1905. (3) Guy, b. Oct. 31, 1881. (4) Fred, b. Sept. 13, 1889. (5) Gertrude, b. Oct. 9, 1891.

4595. iii. CHARLES, b. Arcadia, La., June 25, 1852; d. Feb. 15, 1853.

4596. iv. OBED, b. Arcadia, La., Dec. 17, 1854; d. July 19, 1858.

4597. v. JAMES A., b. Arcadia, La., Dec. 8, 1856; d. Nov. 15, 1859.

4598. vi. SAMUEL D., b. Arcadia, La., Jan 9, 1859; m. Pursley, Texas, Mar. 25, 1886, Camilla Isabelle, dau. of Samuel L. Coker. He was a bright laywer, a forcible writer, and a splendid citizen. He d. Nov. 4, 1903, at El Paso, Texas; s. p.

4599. vii. LAURA ESTELLE, b. Arcadia, La., Apr. 13, 1861.

4600. viii. WILLIAM C., b. Centralia, Ill., Aug. 3, 1864.

4601. ix. CLARENCE C., b. Arcadia, Texas, Feb. 7, 1869.

2939. ROBERT ELIAL FOOTE, (1467, 537, 172, 47, 13, 5,) b. in Plymouth, N. Y., Oct. 20, 1830; m. ———. He d. July 26, 1904. Res., Harvard, Neb.

4602. i.   FRANK E., b. Dec. 31, 1867; m. Estella Wilson and Ida M. Larson, 5892-3.

(28)

4603.   ii.   LILLIE C., b. Mar. 31, 1874, in Milwaukee, Wis.; m. Mar. 18,
             1900, William T. Linder, of Lincoln, Neb. Res., Lincoln. Neb.
             No ch.

2941. ERASTUS DEVOLSON FOOTE, (1467, 537, 172, 47, 13, 5,) b. Ply-
mouth, N. Y., July 23, 1834; m. Sept. 8, 1861, Cora M., dau. of Rev. S. W.
Clemans, of Gloversville, N. Y. She was b. Hyde Park, Vt., June 13, 1844. He d.
Apr. 26, 1899, at Waupun, Wis.

4604.   i.   FRANCES HELENA, b. Iron Ridge, Wis., June 24, 1862; d. Jan.
             23, 1863.
4605.   ii.   WILLIAM ERASTUS, b. Sept. 18, 1863; d. Dec. 3, 1892, at
             Waupun, Wis.
4606.   iii. FRED LOVELL, b. Foxlake, Wis., Nov. 8, 1869; d. Apr. 4, 1873,
             at Waupun, Wis.
4607.   iv.   ROBERT CLEMANS, b. Waupun, Wis., Jan. 18, 1872; m. Sept. 11,
             1902, Louisa Rhirn Kendosf, of Milwaukee, Wis.
4608.   v.   BERRU BELLE, b. Waupun, Wis., Feb. 23, 1873; d. Apr. 12,
             1873.
4609.   vi.   MILDRED, b. Waupun, Wis., Mar. 13, 1876; m. Aug. 9, 1898,
             Edgar A. Pratt, of Worcester, Mass. Res., Watertown, Wis.

2964. OBED FOOTE, (1483, 543, 172, 47, 13, 5,) b. Indianapolis, Ind., Apr.
10, 1854; m. Sept. 26, 1889, Margaret Whitehill.

4610.   i.   MARY MARGUERITE, b. Apr. 4, 1892.

2971. CHARLES SHERMAN FOOTE, (1493, 557, 185, 16, 5,) b. Alford,
Mass., Mar. 7, 1816; m. Feb., 1840, Electa Van Deusen. She d. 1896. He d. at
Sandusky, O., Apr. 13, 1906. Res., Cleveland, O., Daytona, Fla., and Sandusky, O.

4611.   i.   MARK ALONZO, b. Sept. 17, 1842; d. June 15, 1843.
4612.   ii.   MARY LOUISA, b. June 3, 1844; m. 1864, Isaac Foster Mack.
             Res., Sandusky, O. He is editor of the local paper. Ch.: (1)
             Cora E., b. in Brodhead, Wis., July, 1865; m. Sept., 1887, John
             Cooley Robinson, of Westfield, Mass. Ch.: (a) Mary Foote
             Robinson, b. at Westfield, Mass., June 1, 1888. (b) Richard
             Mack Robinson, b. at Sandusky, O., Aug. 3, 1894. (2) Charles
             Foote Mack, b. at Broadhead, Wis., Sept., 1868; m. Jan. 4, 1893,
             Anna DeWolfe, of Vincennes, Ind. No ch.
4613.   iii. GEORGE HENRY, b. Apr. 4, 1846; m. Lydia Purdy and Mary
             Baker. 5901-4.

2973. JOHN CHESTER FOOTE, (1493, 557, 185, 16, 5,) b. Alford, Mass.,
Apr. 11, 1819; m. Torringford, Ct., July 22, 1851, Jane E. Humphrey. She d. Feb.
11, 1902. He d. Aug. 31, 1898. Res., Lawrence, Mass.

4614.   i.   CHARLES HENRY, b. Torringford, Ct., Apr. 15, 1852; d. Sept.
             15, 1852.
4615.   ii.   MARTHA ELIZA, b. Derby, Ct., Nov. 29, 1853; m. June 4, 1879,
             Rev. A. W. Stafford. He has been pastor of Bocornanville Cong.
             Church, Chicago, Ill., for ten years. Ch.: (1) George Chester,
             b. Darlington, Wis., May 6, 1880. He graduated from Beloit
             College in 1902. Is now with the Peterson Nursery Co., of
             Chicago, Ill. (2) Clara Mildred, b. Darlington, Wis., Apr. 14,
             1882. She graduated from Wheaton College in 1905. (3) Helen
             Louise, b. Rock Falls, Wis., Dec. 3, 1890.

4616. iii. CLARA JANE, b. Bunville, Ct., June 29, 1856. Res., Milburn, Ill.

2977. SAMUEL ELIJAH FOOTE, (1493, 557, 185, 53, 16, 5,) b. Alford, Mass., Oct. 12, 1830; m. West Milton, Saratoga Co., N. Y., 1855, Clara Jane Drake. He d. 1866. She m. 2nd, E. H. Swift, 1887. He d. 1893.

4617. i. SHERMAN D., b. May 3, 1858; m. Emma Whitman, 5905.
4618. ii. WILLIAM C., b. 1862; m. Jennie Gregory, 5906.

2987. JARIUS NEWELL FOOTE, (1505, 561, 195, 54, 16, 5,) b. Oct. 2, 1823; m. Dec. 31, 1848, Emily F. Carrington.

4622. i. CHILD, b. ———; drowned in a kettle of hot water, ae. 2 years.
4623. ii. JENNIE, b. ———; m. Fred Champlain. He d. Ch.: 2 daus., one m. and the other res. with her mother in Waterbury, Ct.

2989. NOBLE FOOTE, (1505, 561, 195, 54, 16, 5,) b. Aug. 3, 1830; m. 1860, Mary M. Stacy. She d. May 14, 1888. Owned and operated grist and sawmill at Whigville, Ct. Afterwards became a village blacksmith. He was a very strong man; d. Mar. 13, 1903.

4624. i. GRACE, b. July 28, 1866. Is a clerk at the Bristol (Ct.) Post Office; formerly post-mistress at Whigville.

2993. THOMAS ARIEL FOOTE, (1509, 561, 195, 54, 16, 5,) b. Hartwood, Va., Mar. 1, 1843; m. Dec. 4, 1884, Dulcie Bella, dau. of James Tate. She was b. Bealeton, Va., Apr. 30, 1849. Is a farmer; d. Sept. 13, 1906. Res., Hartwood, Va.

4625. i. VIOLA POCAHONTAS, b. Feb. 9, 1888; m. Mar. 22, 1905, Thomas Baker, son of Robert Brigham. He was b. in Thrying, Yorkshire, England, June 24, 1873. He is a farmer and veterinary surgeon. Educated at Bridlington and London. Episcopalian. She was educated at Hartwood, Va. Res., Hartwood, Va.
4626. ii. JENNIE BEATRICE. b. Nov. 14, 1890.

2998. DEA. CHARLES FOOTE, (1517, 565, 196, 54, 16, 5,) b. Aug. 29, 1815; m. Apr. 24, 1843, Selina, dau. of Jacob and Polly Rogers Bunnell, of North Branford, Ct. She was b. Oct. 26, 1826. He entered Yale College with a view of preparation for the ministry, but after two years' study his health and eyes failed and he was obliged to relinquish the attempt. He spent several years in teaching, and was Deacon of the Cong. Church in Northford, Ct., 40 years. He d. Mar. 1, 1886.

4627. i. CHARLES, b. June 11, 1846; m. Estelle E. Allen, 5907-8.
4628. ii. CAROLINE SELINA, b. Aug. 12, 1848; d. Sept. 7, 1851.
4629. iii. DWIGHT M., b. Mar. 8, 1852; m. Inez J. Williams, 5909-10.
4630. iv. WILLIAM M., b. July 20, 1854; m. Lois Rossites, 5911-2.
4631. v. ELIZABETH IMOGENE, b. May 19, 1857; m. Nov. 27, 1879, Jonathan Edward, son of Dea. Roger Watson and Cynthia (Huntington) Newton. Res., Durham and Higganum, Ct. She d. Mar. 27, 1889. Ch.: (1) Charles, b. Feb. 3, 1886; d. Oct. 3, 1904.
4632. vi. MARY ROGERS, b. May 7, 1867; d. Jan. 14, 1884.

3000. JOHN MALTBY FOOTE, (1517, 565, 196, 54, 16, 5,) b. Northford, Ct., Aug. 6, 1819; m. Nov. 18, 1846, Sarah Ann, dau. of Roswell and Julia Ann (Hall) Monson. She was b. Aug. 3, 1823; d. Apr. 15, 1889. Res., No. Branford, Ct.

4633. i. JOHN MALTBY, b. Feb. 17, 1851; d. Aug. 22, 1851.

4634.   ii.   SERENO M., b. Apr. 22, 1853; m. Roso J. Cooper, 5913-6.

4635.   iii. IDA SELINA, b. May 29, 1858; d. Sept. 22, 1858.

3001.   ALEXANDER FOOTE, (1519, 565, 196, 54, 16, 5,) b. Feb. 9, 1824; m. Feb. 28, 1853, Sarah Kelsey, of Northford, Ct. He was Selectman and for many years a fish merchant. He d. Jan. 1, 1894. Res., New Haven, Ct.

4636.   i.   CARLTON A., b.; res., 559 Howard Ave., New Haven, Ct.

4637.   ii.   ANNETTE MARIA, b.; d. Mar. 1, 1890, at New Haven, Ct.; unm.

4638.   iii. MYRON PHILO, b.

3004.   JEROME WILLIAMS FOOTE, (1519, 565, 196, 54, 16, 5,) b. July 8, 1829; m. Nov. 24, 1853, Ann Foote, dau. of Abiatha Foote. He d. Nov. 17, 1866. She m. 2nd, Douglass Williams, Oct. 1, 1888.

4639.   i.   JULIA, b. Dec. 8, 1856; m. Dec. 8, 1885, Nelson W. Hull. Res., Woodville, Ct.

4640.   ii.   HATTIE, b. Feb. 28, 1858; m. July, 1879, Henry E. Smith. Res. Suffield, Ct.

3005.   ELIZUR HARRISON FOOTE, (1519, 565, 196, 54, 16, 5,) b. Jan. 19, 1831; m. 1st, Jane Russell; m. 2nd, —— Fowler. Ch. by first wife.

4641.   i.   EDWARD, b. ——. Res., New Haven, Ct. With A. Foote & Co.

3007.   LYNDE HARRINGTON FOOTE, (1519, 565, 196, 54, 16, 5,) b. Oct. 15, 1835; m. Juliette Gidney, wid. of Benjamin Dourd.

4642.   i.   FLORA, b. ——; m. Arthur A. Blakeslee. Res., Wallingford, Ct. Ch. 2.

3008.   LOZELLE FOOTE, (1519, 565, 196, 54, 16, 5,) b. Feb. 13, 1838; m. twice. Ch.: 2 by first wife, 1 by second.

4643.   i.   FRANK L., b.

3014.   JOHN AUGUSTUS FOOTE, (1524, 569, 196, 54, 16, 5,) b. Durham, Ct., Apr. 29, 1818; m. Northford, Ct., May 29, 1842, Almira Linsley Granniss. She d. May 19, 1888. He d. May 10, 1867, in Fair Haven, Ct.

4649.   i.   HARRIET EMMA, b. Sept. 2, 1846; m. Fair Haven, Ct., June 10, 1874, Tyler Gedney. Res., Wallingford, Ct. Ch.: (1) Minnie Almira, b. Feb. 18, 1881.

4650.   ii.   HENRY H., b. Mar. 16, 1850; m. Carrie Fowler Cook, 5928-32.

3015.   SAMUEL WHITNEY FOOTE, (1524, 569, 196, 54, 16, 5,) b. Wallingford, Ct., Sept. 29, 1819; m. No. Haven, Ct., Oct. 1, 1848, Sybil, dau. of Jared Brockett. She was b. No. Haven, Ct.; d. May 13, 1903, at No. Haven, Ct. He d. Mar. 22, 1887, at No. Branford, Ct.

4651.   i.   CHARLES B., b. Sept. 28, 1849; m. Elizabeth Thompson, 5933-5.

4652.   ii.   FRANK W., b. Apr. 10, 1857; m. Ada C. Robinson, 5936-9.

4653.   iii. ELLA CORNELIA, b. Sept. 10, 1861; res., Montrose, Ct.

4654.   iv.   LUCY ANNETTE, b. Nov. 19, 1852; m. No. Branford, Ct., June, 1882, Harry E. Barnett. She d. Feb. 17, 1883.

3016.   HENRY MARTIN FOOTE, (1524, 569, 196, 54, 16, 5,) b. Wallingford, Ct., Aug. 25, 1820; m. 1843, No. Haven, Ct., Juliette, dau. of Hibbard Barnes. She d. Nov. 18, 1845; m. 2nd, 1846, Belinda, dau. of David Cooper. She was b. No. Haven, Ct., Mar. 15, 1818; d. Nov. 18, 1894. He was a shoemaker and farmer.

4655.   i.   EMMA AUGUSTA, b.

4656.   ii.   NETTIE G., b. May 27, 1847; m. Fair Haven, Ct., May 28, 1898, Herman Robinson.

4657. iii. NINA A., b. Aug. 7, 1849.

4658. iv. MARY E., b. Feb. 20, 1851.

4659. v. ELBERT H., b. Aug. 25, 1852; d. Mar. 23, 1881.

4660. vi. EMMA H., b. Feb. 25, 1854; d. Oct. 4, 1887.

4661. vii. JUDSON D., b. Feb. 13, 1856; m. Louise A. Hill, 5940-1.

3021. GEORGE LUZERNE FOOTE, (1524, 569, 196, 54, 16, 5,) b. Northford, Ct., July 18, 1835; m. ———.

4662. i. FREDERICK W., b. Fair Haven, Ct., Nov. 22, 1860; m. Doda Ives, 5942-3.

4663. ii. G. CLIFFORD, b. Fair Haven, Ct., Oct. 17, 1869; m. Matilda A. Bostwick, 5944-7.

4664. iii. LEA STATIRA, b. Fair Haven, Ct., Dec. 13, 1877; m. Dec. 21, 1899, Herbert, son of Charles William Kannahan. He was b. Feb. 7, 1876. Ch.: (1) Helen Foote, b. (2) Esther Leah, b.

3022. GEORGE LAWSON FOOTE, (1525, 569, 54, 16, 5,) b. Aug. 1, 1834; m. Baltimore, Md., Oct. 14, 1866, Chrestina Anna Margaret, dau. of Wilhelm Freund. She was b. Saxony, Germany. He was educated at the Fair Haven Schools. Is a watchman. Protestant Episcopal. Res., Baltimore, Md.

4665. i. MARY ALICE, b. June 18, 1868; m. Baltimore, Md., Oct. 6, 1889, William Edward, son of James Edward Stewart. He was b. St. George, Del., Dec. 8, 1856. Protestant Episcopal. Res., Baltimore, Md. Ch.: (1) Clark Foster, b. Aug. 18, 1890. (2) George Ruley, b. July 23, 1892. (3) Frank Carroll, b. Apr. 17, 1895. (4) Robert Foote, b. Oct. 25, 1902.

4666. ii. GEORGE H., b. Apr. 29, 1870; m. Mary A. Rebstock, 5948-50.

4667. iii. JANUS S., b. Nov. 15, 1872; m. Helen S. Menskaw, 5951-2.

4668. iv. WALTER ANDERTON, b. Jan. 7, 1875.

4669. v. ARTHUR OSBORN, b. Jan. 23, 1877; d. June 7, 1879.

4670. vi. ROBERT M., b. Dec. 18, 1879; m. Mary M. Clark, 5953.

4671. vii. CLARENCE MILES, b. Mar. 25, 1882.

4672. viii. ELLA REGINA, b. Aug. 26, 1884; m. Baltimore, Md., May 16, 1906, Daniel Lawson, son of Henry Clifton Eames. He was b. Rutland, Jefferson Co., N. Y., May 20, 1884. He is a cashier. Protestant Episcopal. Res., Bridgeton, N. J.

4673. ix. LEWIS HENRY, b. Feb. 17, 1888; d. July 15, 1888.

3031. LUCIUS HUBBARD FOOTE, (1528, 569, 196, 54, 16, 5,) b. Dec. 30, 1844; m. May 3, 1866, Louise H., dau. of Clement M. and Sarah Hill Parsons. She was b. May 3, 1846. Res., Northford, Ct.

4674. i. MARTHA THAYER, b. Apr. 10, 1868; m. Nov. 6, 1889, Benjamin J., son of Chas. and May Linsly Maltby, of Northford, Ct. Ch.: (1) Lucius Foote, b. Jan. 15, 1891. (2) Catharine Linsley, b. Aug. 14, 1893.

4675. ii. ALICE PARSONS, b. Sept. 18, 1878; m. Oct. 21, 1903, Albert W. Foote. (See No. 5909 for complete record).

3038. ALLEN FOOTE, (1544, 575, 196, 54, 16, 5,) b. July 5, 1836; m. Sarah McCray, of Deseronto, Ont.

4676. i. EDWARD, b.

4677. ii. ISABELLE, b.

4678. iii. MARY JANE, b.

4679. iv. DONALD, b.
4680. v. MARGARET, b.
4681. vi. ALEX, b.

3039. JOHN FOOTE, (1544, 575, 196, 54, 16, 5,) b. Sept. 7, 1839; m. Senia Thompson, of Napanee, Ont.
4682. i. ELIZA, b.; d.
4683. ii. LUCY, b.; d.
4684. iii. LUMAN, b.
4685. iv. LENA, b.; d.

3041. BENJAMIN E. FOOTE, (1544, 575, 196, 54, 16, 5,) b. May 10, 1845; m. Almira Thompson, of Selba, Ont.; d. in Violet, Ont., in 1900.
4686. i. JOSEPHINE, b.
4687. ii. SALOME, b.
4688. iii. GEORGE ALLEN, b.
4689. iv. FRANK, b.

3103⁴. JAMES STERLING FOOTE, (1623, 610, 208, 56, 16, 5,) b. N. Y. City, Sept. 22, 1836; m. Sept. 13, 1870, Mary Weightman, of N. Y. City. She was b. Apr. 15, 1841.
4690. i. JAMES STERLING, b. June 28, 1871; d. Aug. 20, 1876, at Brooklyn, N. Y.
4690¹. ii. CHARLOTTE ELIZABETH, b. May 8, 1874, at Brooklyn, N. Y.; d. Apr. 24, 1907.

3055. CHARLES CONSTANT FOOTE, (1553, 576, 196, 54, 16, 5,) b. Nov. 8, 1841, at Wallingford, Ct.; m. Jan. 1, 1873, at Meriden, Ct., Martha Louise Brower. She was b. July 27, 1848. He was educated at Wallingford, Ct., and Bastrop, Tex. Res., Hamilton, Ontario, Canada.
4691. i. FRED F., b. Oct. 6, 1873, at Meriden, Ct.; d. Sept. 2, 1881, at Hamilton, Ont.
4692. ii. SARAH K., b. Wallingford, Ct., Jan. 28, 1877.
4693. iii. ELSIE C., b. Hamilton, Ont., Oct. 5, 1881; m. June 8, 1902, in Hamilton, Ont., R. B. McLeeland.

3056. GEORGE BENJAMIN FOOTE, (1553, 576, 196, 54, 16, 5,) b. Apr. 23, 1844, at Wallingford; m. 1st, Jan. 8, 1868, at South Hadley, Mass., Cornelia W., dau. of Warren Ingraham. She was b. Aug. 2, 1844; d. Feb. 12, 1883; m. 2nd, Jan. 5, 1885, at Meriden, Ct., Hattie, dau. of Noah Pomeroy. She was b. May 6, 1858. He was educated at Wallingford and Meriden, Ct. Is Supt. of Silver Plating. Res., Meriden, Ct.
4694. i. LILLIAN W., b. Jan. 12, 1870.

3072. WEBSTER DE FORREST FOOTE, (1561, 583, 198, 54, 16, 5,) b. May 21, 1840; m. New Haven, Ct., Sept. 26, 1878, Mary Seward Ferru. Res., 121 Lawrence St., New Haven, Ct.
4695. i. ARTHUR FERRU, b. Apr. 5, 1884.

3074. ADELBERT MERVIN FOOTE, (1561, 583, 198, 54, 16, 5,) b. May 2, 1849; m. ——.
4696. i. OLIVER D., b. Res., Exchange St., Fair Haven, Ct.
4697. ii. ADELBERT M., b. Res., Main St., Wallingford, Ct.

3081. WILLIAM TAYLOR FOOTE, (1567, 584, 198, 54, 16, 5,) b. Grand

Rapids, Mich., May 31, 1856; m. May 4, 1898, Margaret Blanchard. Res., Rialto, Cala.

4697¹. i. WILLIAM BLANCHARD, b. July 4, 1900; d. July 13, 1900.

4698. ii. FREDERICK BETTS, b. June 11, 1903.

4699. iii. PHILIP BLANCHARD, b. July 9, 1906.

3092. ROSWELL SMITH FOOTE, (1585, 597, 205, 56, 16, 5,) b. Mar. 12, 1833; m. ———; d. 1905. Res., Los Angeles, Cal.

4699¹. i. JESSIE, b. ———; m. ——— Browning.

3094. CHARLES EGBERT FOOTE, (1585, 597, 205, 56, 16; 5,) b. Sept. 6, 1840; m. Jan. 9, 1868, Laura, dau. of George and Caroline (Wiswell) Gillett. Res., Cobleskill, N. Y., and Kalamazoo, Mich.

4700. i. MELVIN, b. May 9, 1869.

3096. JOHN ALEXANDER FOOTE, (1594, 602, 205, 56, 16, 5,) b. Catskill, N. Y., May 27, 1837; m. N. Y. City, Jan. 25, 1865, Adella Minerva, dau. of Benjamin B. and Minerva E. Stoddard. She was b. Unionville, O., Dec. 23, 1843. He is a lumber merchant and has a fruit farm. Res., Catskill, N. Y.

4701. i. MARY ADELLA, b. Catskill, N. Y., Mar. 20, 1868; m. Jan. 11, 1893, Robert, son of Robert and Emma C. Harding, of Brooklyn, N. Y. Ch.: (1) Mary Adella Harding, b. Brooklyn, N. Y., Feb. 22, 1894. (2) Robert Harding, b. Catskill, N. Y., Apr. 21, 1897. (3) Helen Foote Harding, b. Brooklyn, N. Y., Feb. 24, 1907.

4702. ii. FLORENCE STODDARD, b. Catskill, N. Y., Jan. 24, 1872.

4703. iii ALFRED GRANT, b. Catskill, N. Y., Feb. 9, 1873; m. June 7, 1905, Lillian Ray, dau. of William R. Peet, of Brooklyn, N. Y.

3098. JARED HIRAM FOOTE, (1598, 602, 205, 56, 16, 5,) b. Owego, N. Y., Mar. 27, 1852; m. Sept. 2, 1873, Alice J. Vermilya. He was a miller and traveling salesman.

4704. i. WILLIAM A., b. Mar. 18, 1875; m. Edith L. Ferguson, 5976-7.

3099. JAMES LOVELL FOOTE, (1598, 602, 205, 56, 16, 5,) b. Owego, N. Y., Nov. 23, 1855; m. Sept. 22, 1875, Susan Villeron Harding. Res., Owego, N. Y.

4705. i. JESSIE F., b. Feb. 2, 1877.

3102. CHARLES A. FOOTE, (1619, 608, 207, 56, 16, 5,) b. Oxford, N. Y., Oct. 23, 1843; m. Dec. 25, 1864, Ruth E. Laman. He d. Apr. 21, 1905, at Oxford, N. Y.

4705¹. i. MINNIE A., b. Oxford, May 15, 1867; m. Feb. 21, 1889, at Oxford, N. Y., Judson A. Burton. Ch.: (1) Ruth H., b. 1891; d. Oct. 11, 1894. (2) Granville J., b. Nov. 3, 1895.

4705². ii. WILLIAM R., b. Coventryville, N. Y., Feb. 10, 1872; m. Franklin, N. Y., June 10, 1897, Harriett Morrison. Ch.: (1) Ruth Sarah, b. June 3, 1904.

4705³. iii. FRED L., b. Oxford, Sept. 5, 1879; m. Franklin, N. Y., Dec. 26, 1900, Agnes Edgerton.

4705⁴. iv. MARY M., b. Coventryville, N. Y., Mar. 4, 1882; m. Oxford, N. Y., Dec. 23, 1903, Olin P. Pierce. Ch.: (1) Helen Ida, b. Oct. 12, 1906.

3103. HENRY M. FOOTE, (1621, 608, 207, 56, 16, 5,) b. Green, N. Y., Feb. 1, 1846; m. Feb. 14, 1867, Emma A., dau. of Jas. S. and Betsey A. Watrous. He served during Civil War in Co. A, 187th Regt. Pa. Vols. District Attorney of

Tioga County, Pa. Member of the Legislature of the State from said County. Appointed Assistant Attorney U. S. Department of Justice, July, 1889, four years; since has been engaged in the practice of law at Washington, D. C.

4706. i. IDA A., b. July 20, 1868; m. Oct. 10, 1896, A. C. Gibbs.

4707· ii. MAUD E., b. Nov. 21, 1880; m. Nov. 23, 1904, M. G. Gibbs.

4707¹. iii. MORTIMER, b. Nov. 21, 1880; d. in infancy.

4708. iv. MABEL L., b. Dec. 26, 1884.

·3107· GEORGE GRAHAM FOOTE, (1638, 618, 208, 56, 16, 5,) b. Oct. 19, 1857; m. Mary Dallas. He is a lawyer. Res., Paonia, Col.

4709. i. ELIZABETH G., b. Sag City, Mich., Mar. 17, 1899.

4710. ii. BARBARA, b. Paonia, Col., Oct., 1901.

3122. ARTHUR FOOTE, (1668, 627, 209, 56, 16, 5,) b. July 17, 1872; m. Feb. 9, 1897, Eleanor McCall, of Gloversville, N. Y. Res., Johnstown, N. Y.

4710¹. i. HELEN, b. Jan. 24, 1898.

3126. COL. ABRAM FOOTE, (1675, 630, 211, 60, 18, 5,) b. in Cornwall, Vt., May 5, 1805, at the homestead of his father, and lived on the same farm nearly all his life. A man of strong convictions and fearless in his expression. He was Lieutenant-Colonel of Militia. He held nearly all of the town offices at different times, including Constable for 30 years. Represented the town in the General Assembly in 1845, 1846 and 1853. Was Deacon of the Baptist Church at West Cornwall for many years; m. 1st, Nov. 25, 1827, Orpha, dau. of Abraham Williamson, of Cornwall, Vt. She was b. July 18, 1804; d. Apr. 24, 1851; m. 2nd, Aug. 27, 1851, Elsie Hawkins (wid.), dau. of Rev. Jehiel Wright, of Cornwall. Dea. Foote d. June 10, 1876; buried at West Cornwall, Vt.

4711. i. MARSHALL WILLIAMSON, b. Apr. 12, 1828; d. July 30, 1852, at Norwich, Ct. Buried at W. Cornwall, Vt.

4712. ii. ROLLIN A., b. Jan. 9, 1832; m. Julia A. Sampson, 5978-80.

4713. iii. GARRISON W., b. Mar. 8, 1834; m. Harriet A. Sperry, 5981.

4714. iv. EMMA ORPHA, b. May 5, 1843; m. Cornwall, Vt., Jan. 18, 1866, Alverton Stockwell, son of Alonzo Bingham, of Cornwall, Vt. Ch.: (1) Roy Alverton, b. Aug. 13, 1870, in Pomfret, Vt.; m. Cornwall, Vt., Mar. 4, 1896, Olive Annis, dau. of James Edwin and Harriet (Goodspeed) Weston, of Cornwall, Vt. She was b. Aug. 31, 1872, at Vermontville, N. Y. Res., Cornwall, Vt. Ch.: (a) Maud Weston, b. Jan. 11, 1897. (b) Edwin Alverton, b. Mar. 13, 1898. (c) Albert Roy, b. Mar. 4, 1901. (d) Frederick Milton, b. Oct. 12, 1904. (2) Jessie Emma, b. Oct. 11, 1875, in Cornwall, Vt.; d. June 25, 1892; killed by a train at Hartsdale, Ind., while crossing the track during a terrible storm; buried at West Cornwall, Vt.

3129. DAVID FOOTE, (1675, 630, 211, 60, 18, 5,) b. Apr. 13, 1813; m. Esther Lamb, of Middlebury, Vt. He graduated from Middlebury College in 1838, and the following year was Principal of the Academy at Moriah, N. Y. Was from 1840 to 1843, Pastor of the Baptist Church in Nassau, N. Y. Was four years Pastor in Hannibal, N. Y., and in 1847-48 was Pastor of a new Church formed from the Church in Hannibal, to which he had previously ministered. He received a call to settle in La Grange, N. Y. Preached there the last Sabbath in May, and d. of brain fever the next Thursday, June 1, 1848.

4715. i. ADDIE, b. Apr. 21, 1845; m. Jan. 3, 1865, Dr. Myndert Van Patten, of Sterling, Kansas. He is the oldest physician in age and length of residence in Sterling, and is connected with the

COL. ABRAM FOOTE. No. 3126   EMMA ORPHA (FOOTE) BINGHAM.
No. 4714

ROLLIN ABRAM FOOTE. No. 4712   GARRISON WILLIAM FOOTE. No. 4713

House built by David Foote (No. 630) in Cornwall, Vt., in 1807.
Always owned by his descendants.

26 ft. in circumference, 150 ft. broad and 125 ft. high.
On the Lot owned by Robert Foote. No. 5

Sterling Hospital. Has been Mayor of Sterling. Is a cancer specialist. Mrs. Van Patten took special interest in Church work. She d. Feb. 1, 1885. Ch.: (1) Lutrede Isabella, b. June 17, 1866; m. in Sterling, Feb. 10, 1885, Cassius M. Clay, son of W. L. Elliott, of Sterling. He was b. July 19, 1862. Mail contractor and rancher. Res., Farmington, New Mexico. Ch.: (a) Adalaide Rebecca, b. May 4, 1886; d. July 2, 1887. (b) Frances Lutrede, b. Sept. 30, 1888. Grad. Farmington High School 1907. (c) Lena Elizabeth, b. Mar. 7, 1890. Grad. Farmington High School 1907. (d) Preston Greene, b. Jan. 6, 1892. (e) Ansel Cassius, b. Feb. 24, 1894; d. Sept. 6, 1894. (f) Saretta Lillian, b. Nov. 30, 1895. (All above were b. in Sterling, Kan.) (g) John Paul, b. Dec. 25, 1897, in Cedar Edge, Colo. (h) Faith Theresa, b. Sept. 22, 1899, in Durango, Colo. (i) Henry Lewis, b. Farmington, N. Mexico. (j) Eddy Wilbur, b. Apr. 26, 1904, at Durango, Colo. (k) Grace Winifred, b. Oct. 12, 1906, in Farmington, N. Mexico. (2) Carrie Melissa, b. Dec. 21, 1869; d. Feb. 25, 1870. (3) George Foote, b. Jan. 3, 1878. Res., Farmington, N. Mexico. (4) Mary Elizabeth, b. Dec. 18, 1874; m. May 25, 1898, Charles R. Peterson. He was b. Dec. 15, 1873. She d. Sept. 30, 1906. She was an earnest Christian. Res., Rice Co., and Hanstan, Hodgeman Co., Kan. Ch.: (a) Fernette Estelle, b. Mar. 6, 1899. (b) Alice Mae, b. Dec. 14, 1900. (c) Bessie Adalaide, b. Jan. 16, 1903. (5) Fernette Adelaide, b. ———. (6) Winifred Estelle, b. Sept. 5, 1881; m. Will Heimer, of Hanston, Kan. Res., Hanston, Kan.

3130. RUSSELL NELSON FOOTE, (1678, 630, 211, 60, 18, 5,) b. July 4, 1810; m. Dec. 1, 1831, Belinda, dau. of Daniel Wright, in Cornwall, Vt. She was b. Oct. 10, 1810; d. Apr. 10, 1870, at Laramie, Kan. He d. Apr. 22, 1886, at Kansas City, Mo.

 4716. i. MYRON E., b. Apr. 13, 1838; m. Sarah G. Jackson, 5982-5.

 4717. ii. HARRIET BELINDA, b. May 12, 1842; m. May 12, 1861, Aquila James Reid. He was b. Nov. 7, 1834. She is Principal of N. Y. College of Dresscutting, Ladies' Tailoring and Millinery, 806 E. 11th St., Kansas City, Mo. Ch.: 6 sons, 4 d. in infancy. Ch.: (1) Myron Lleuelly Reid, b. Feb. 19, 1863; m. Hattie Ethel Wren. She was b. Apr. 9, 1866, near Paola, Miami Co., Kan. Res., 2304 Bellefontaine Ave., Kansas City, Mo. Ch.: (a) Hattie Eudura Reid, b. Jan. 11, 1889. (b) Frederick Bertrand, b. Aug. 1, 1892. (c) Thomas Ethelbert, b. Nov. 16, 1894. (d) Kenneth Myron, b. Oct. 14, 1898. (e) Luther James, b. Oct. 5, 1900. (f) Louise Reid, b. June 28, 1903. (2) Ethelbert Courtney Reid, b. Dec. 24, 1872; m. Aug. 19, 1903, Rachel Cheaunan. He is agent of Wells Fargo and Co., Muskogee, Indian Ter. Ch.: (a) Allen Courtney Reid, b. Muskogee, Apr. 1, 1906.

3133. PROF. EZRA MEAD FOOTE. (1678, 630, 211, 60, 18, 5,) b. Shoreham, Vt., Jan. 19, 1820; m. Lewiston, N. Y., May 11, 1846, Sarah Smith, dau. of Judge Lothrop Cooke, of Lewiston, N. Y. She d. Jan. 14, 1906, at Ypsilanti, Mich.

At the age of 16 years he started out to make his own fortune, at first studying for a doctor, at Lockport, N. Y., but soon giving that up for music, being endorsed with a marvelous voice and great personal magnetism; a fine stage presence.

He studied in Boston, and soon after took his place as a concert and church singer, besides leading choruses of large size. In 1858 he went to Michigan to take the chair of Music and Elocution in the State Normal School, till 1866. Wishing a wider field he went to Chicago, and was engaged to lead the singing in the Presbyterian Churches, besides teaching music and elocution in the Chicago University. He engaged to make a tour of California and England with Dwight L. Moody, but the Chicago fire broke up that plan, and soon after he went to Louisville, Ky. In 1874, he took charge of the music in Topeka and Lawrence (Kan.) Schools. He remained there till 1878, when he accepted the position of musical director of the Ypsilanti Public Schools, where his home was. He resigned at the age of 70 years, amid the regrets of all. He sent eight thousand dollars to the Sanitary Commission at St. Louis for the Soldiers of the Civil War. He d. July 12, 1896, at Ypsilanti, Mich.

    4718. i.   ANNA STOWE, b. Aug. 14, 1847; m. Aug. 23, 1866, Tubal Cain
                 Owen, of Marine City, Mich. Ch.: (1) Eber Ward, b. June 13,
                 1868.. Graduate of Ann Harbor, University Mich. Law Depart-
                 ment. Res., Ypsilanti, Mich. (2) Richard Lawrence, b. May 29,
                 1870. (3) Abba Esrene, b. July 30, 1872. Graduate of Musical
                 Conservatory, Ypsilanti, State Normal College.   Teacher in
                 Violin Department. All res. in Ypsilanti, Mich.

    4719. ii. KATE ELIZABETH, b. ———; m. St. Louis, Mo., Oct. 10, 1877,
                 John Gould Williams (son of No. 3132), of St. Louis, Mo.
                 He was b. Merton, Wis., Apr. 22, 1850, and d. Jan. 8, 1907. She
                 graduated from Ypsilanti High School and Mich. State Normal
                 School. Is an artist. He was in the oil business in Pa. and
                 West Va., and later in the real estate business. Res., Los
                 Angeles, Cal. Ch.: (1) Mabel Claire, b. Apr. 20, 1879; m. June
                 27, 1901, Dr. Raymond A. Clifford. He was Assistant Surgeon in
                 Mich. State Univ., Ann Harbor. Graduate of Jefferson Medical
                 College, Philadelphia, and Michigan Universities. She d. Aug.
                 23, 1905, of typhoid fever. Hers was a beautiful sunny life.
                 She was a beautiful woman. She died full of Christian love and
                 faith—one more beautiful singer gone to join the chorus above.
                 Ch.: (a) Phyllis de Harr Clifford, b. Nov. 10, 1903. (2) John
                 Gould, b. May 20, 1886; d. June 11, 1887. (3) Charles Ezra, b.
                 Nov. 15, 1887. (4) Andrew Norton Perrin, b. May 13, 1903.

    3134. DAVID S. FOOTE, (1678, 630, 211, 60, 18, 5,) b. Cornwall, Vt., Dec.
24 1821; m. Apr. 24, 1850, Hulda D. Merritt. She d. Jan. 14, 1904, at Dallas,
Texas. He d. Feb. 9, 1864, at Merton, Wis.

    4720. i.   MERRITT S., b. July 6, 1851; m. June 25, 1879, Emma Foster.
                 He d. Oct. 14, 1892; s. p.

    4721. ii. MORRIS D., b. May 11, 1853; m. Ella Adams, 5986-7.

    4722. iii. WILLIS ORLIN, b. Mar. 20, 1856; m. Myra L. Mulliner, 5988-9.

    4723. iv. EDWARD DAVID, b. Mar. 9, 1858; d. Sept. 25, 1896, at Houston,
                 Texas; unm.

    4724. v.   HATTIE HANNAH, b. May 8, 1861; m. Apr. 12, 1882, John C.
                 Allendorph. Res., Kansas City Ch.: (1) Shirley H., b. Jan. 11,
                 1887.

    3136. SILAS K. FOOTE, (1678, 630, 211, 60, 18, 5,) b. Cornwall, Vt., Feb.
20, 1826; m. July 1, 1847, Hetty H., dau. of Moses Smith, of Merton, Wis. She

was b. Meadville, Pa., Dec. 20, 1829; d. Feb. 28, 1869; m. 2nd, A. Malvina De Wolf, of Cleveland, O. He d. Jan. 6, 1896. She res. Hot Springs, Ark. He was general insurance agent at Louisville, Ky., for many years.

4725. i. SARAH ELLA, b. Hartland, Wis., July 7, 1849; m. Oct. 16, 1873, William Loomis Perrin, of Conesus Center, N. Y. She d. Apr. 11, 1901, in Rochester, N. Y. Ch.: (1) Hetty Foote, b. Conesus Center, N. Y., Nov. 5, 1874. Res., Rochester, N. Y.; unm. (2) William, b. Conesus Center, N. Y., Jan. 1, 1876; m. Aug. 14, 1901, Elsie Curtiss Brooks, of Rome, N. Y. (3) Arthur Fuller, b. Olean, N. Y., Sept. 17, 1882. (4) Margurete, b. Rochester, N. Y., June 23, 1892.

4726. ii. ORLIN C., b. Hartland, Wis., Oct. 2, 1851; d. Jan. 3, 1852.

4727. iii. LINNA L., b. Hartland, Wis., Apr. 18, 1856; m. Geo. P. Weller, of Louisville, Ky. Ch.: (1) George L., b. Louisville, Ky., Oct. 15, 1875. Graduate of Cornell, Ithaca, N. Y.; m. Jan. 24, 1899, Melville Minge Bolling, of Louisville, Ky. Ch.: (a) La Rue Bolling, b. Louisville, Ky., Dec. 30, 1899.

4728. iv. DON C., b. Oct. 3, 1857. Res., Kane, Pa.; unm.

4729. v. FLORENCE ORPHA, b. Hartland, Wis., Sept. 23, 1859; m. Aug. 29, 1879, Charles B. Williams, of Stillman Valley, Ill. Res., 150 N. 64th Ave., Oak Park, Chicago, Ill. Ch.: (1) Dora Julia, b. Dec. 27, 1880; m. Nov. 5, 1903, Carl C. Clererdon, of Austin, Ill. Ch.: (a) Vernon Williams Clererdon, b. Apr. 6, 1905. (2) Alice May, b. Aug. 27, 1882. (3) Linna Linwood, b. Oct. 19, 1884. (4) Nellie Gertrude, b. Dec. 2, 1885. (5) Luther Foote, b. May 16, 1888. (6) Ruth Sarah, b. July 22, 1891; d. Mar. 26, 1894. (7) Mary Florence, b. May 25, 1893.

4730. vi. HARRY, b. Quincy, Ill., Feb. 9, 1862; d. Dec. 24, 1862.

4731. vii. CARRY, b. Quincy, Ill., Feb. 9, 1862; d. Sept. 9, 1862.

4732. viii. SILAS K., b. Quincy, Ill., Apr. 10, 1864; m. Mary V. Smith. Banker. Res., Kane, Pa.

4733. ix. HETTY H., b. Louisville, Ky., Feb. 27, 1869; d. June 19, 1869.

4734. x. JOHN BURTON, b. Louisville, Ky., Dec. 28, 1871; m. Chaffar L. Darby, 5990-3.

3138. JOHN SANFORD FOOTE, (1678, 630, 211, 60, 18, 5,) b. May 20, 1833; m. Nancy Clapp, of Lowell, Mass.

4735. i. EMMA J. Res., So. Walker St., Lowell, Mass.

3139. OZIAS W. FOOTE, (1678, 630, 211, 60, 18, 5,) b. Cornwall, Vt., July 24, 1836; m. Nov. 29, 1860, Josephine M. Phillips, of Westfield, Melina Co., O. He was Lieutenant in the Civil War, and on Guard Duty at Johnson Island. He d. Sept. 17, 1888, at San Jacinto, Riverside Co., Cal.

4736. i. ELULIO L., b. July 15, 1863; d. Sept. 28, 1871, in Granger, Medina Co., O.

4737. ii. FICHA F., b. Granger, O., Aug. 5, 1873; m. San Jacinto, Cal., Sept. 28, 1898, A. G. Eadie, of Ottawa, Ont., Canada, where they reside.

4738. iii. LINNA B., b. Granger, O., July 22, 1879. Res., San Jacinto, Cal.

3141. CALVIN WARD FOOTE, (1679, 630, 211, 60, 18, 5,) b. Cornwall, Vt., Mar. 8, 1814; m. Dec. 24, 1835, Sophronia, dau. of Daniel Nimblet, of Bristol, Vt.

4739. i.   MARY ELLEN, b. Cornwall, Vt., Oct. 18, 1836; d. Aug. 3, 1870, in
           Middlebury, Vt.
4740. ii. HARRISON A., b. July 23, 1840; m. Mary J. Powell, 5994-5.

3142. JARED ABERNATHY FOOTE, (1679, 630, 211, 60, 18, 5,) b. Cornwall,
Vt., Aug. 8, 1818; m. 1st, Apr. 21, 1847, Caroline E., dau. of Aaron and Mary
Bristol. She was b. Jan. 13, 1824; d. Jan. 13, 1857; m. 2nd, Oct. 30, 1860, Rosaltha
A., dau. of Joshua and Lucinda W. Field. She was b. Apr. 1, 1838. He d. May 15,
1893. Jared Foote always lived on the original farm bought by his grandfather,
and for many years in the house built in 1807, and later occupied by his uncle,
Russell Foote. This house is well preserved, as will be seen by the picture taken
in 1907. It is only a few rods south of the original log house built in 1795-6.
The frame of the house has never been changed since it was built, and was considered the best built house in town at that time. Three Foote generations have
since been born in this residence. The farm has always been in the Foote family,
and is now owned by F. E. Foote, third descendant of David Foote.

4741. i.   ELIJAH B., b. May 23, 1852; m. Carrie E. Raine, 5996-9.
4742. ii. ALICE MONICA, b. Cornwall, Vt., Oct. 29, 1855; m. Judson H.,
           son of Philo Bristol, of Vergennes, Vt. He owns and operates
           a large ranch at Ft. Collins, Col. Ch.: (1) Addie Stone, b. Ft.
           Collins, Col., Dec. 30, 1887. Graduated from Colorado State
           Agricultural College, Class of 1901; m. Jan. 21, 1902, Clyde H.,
           son of J. A. Brown, hardware merchant, Ft. Collins, Col. Ch.:
           (a) Lawrence Bristol, b. Ft. Collins, Col., Nov. 13, 1903. (b)
           Blanche Margaret, b. Sept. 26, 1905. (2) Warren Judson, b. Ft.
           Collins, Col., Dec. 22, 1883. Is clerk at Langham Hotel, San
           Francisco, Cal. (3) Ralph Foote, b. Ft. Collins, Col., Sept. 2,
           1885. Is foreman in the Great Western Sugar Company, Ft.
           Collins, Col. (4) Alice Mildred, b. Ft. Collins, Col., Dec. 16,
           1895.
4743. iii. CAROLINE ELIZABETH, b. Jan. 13, 1859. Graduated at Ran-
           dolph, Vt., Normal School; m. Apr. 22, 1884, John S., son of
           William Proctor, of Loveland, Col. Ch. all b. at Loveland, Col.
           Ch.: (1) Emily Louise, b. Feb. 18, 1885. (2) Roy Simpson, b.
           Sept. 8, 1886. (3) Lola Blanche, b. Mar. 20, 1888. (4) Edith
           Alice, b. Dec. 2, 1890. (5) Jared Foote, b. Oct. 11, 1892. (6)
           Ruth Mary, b. Jan. 20, 1895. (7) Charles William, b. Dec. 19,
           1896. (8) Adeline Lydia, b. Dec. 27, 1898. (9) Willie S., b.
           Sept. 11, 1905.
4744. iv. ADELINE LYDIA, b. Jan. 13, 1859. Graduated at Randolph
           Normal. Taught until the fall of 1905; m. Dec. 5, 1905, Willard
           Colton, a widower, having two ch. Ch.: (1) Mabel, b. July 3,
           1895. (2) Frank, b. Jan. 20, 1899.
4745. v.   FRANKLIN E., b. Dec. 4, 1862; m. Una R. Sanford, 6000-2.
4746. vi. FLORA GERTRUDE, b. Dec. 10, 1864; m. Mar. 1, 1894, Edwin
           Allen, son of Moses and Rosanna Lee. He was b. Leicester, Vt.
           Feb. 11, 1857. Res., Cornwall, Rutland and Vergennes, Vt. Ch.:
           (1) Marjorie Ruth, b. Cornwall, Vt., Jan. 9, 1895. (2) Helen
           Mary, b. Rutland, Vt., Jan. 8, 1897. (3) Maurice Foote, b. Rut-
           land, Vt., Feb. 28, 1900.

3143. SUMMERS G. FOOTE, (1679, 630, 211, 60, 18, 5,) b. July 25, 1820; m.
Eliza Pratt, of Bridport, Vt. Res., Westfield, O.

4747. i.   EDNA, b. Cornwall, Vt., Oct. 13, 1849; m. Bowling, O., Nov., 1874, Earl Huestin. Ch.: (1) Nellie Imogene, b. Bowling, O., Oct. 2, 1876; m. Bowling, O., Mar., 1884, A. E. Shuleon.

4748. ii. GERTRUDE, b. Westfield, O., Feb. 15, 1860; m. Feb. 3, 1886, Bowling, O., George Munshowere.

4749. iii. AMMIE HETTY, b. Westfield, O., Sept. 27, 1866; m. Bowling, O., 1877, J. D. Bolles. Res., Boston, Mass. Ch.: (1) Dr. J. Ralph, b. Jan. 18, 1875; m. Florida, O., July, 1905, Jennie Lowery. (2) Gertrude L., b. Dec. 30, 1880. (3) Frank, b. Dec. 30, 1883. (4) Edith, b. Oct. 27, 1885. (5) Gale, b. Apr. 17, 1888. (6) Howard, b. Feb. 6, 1892; pharmacist. (7) Ada Mabel, b. Sept. 9, 1894. (8) Lueile, b. Sept. 9, 1896. (9) Julius Harold, b. Apr. 10, 1895.

3145. NATHAN D. FOOTE, (1679, 630, 211, 60, 18, 5,) b. May 15, 1829; m. Elizabeth Willmarth, of Addison, Vt.; moved to Wis., being one of the earliest settlers of Palmyra; d. Mar. 20, 1867.

4750. i.   GEORGE E., b. June, 1855; m. Allie Lothrop, 6003-5.

4751. ii. EMELINE G., b. Mar., 1858; d. Jan. 18, 1866.

3150. JAMES MONROE FOOTE, (1687, 645, 215, 60, 18, 5,) b. Hamilton, N. Y., Dec. 31, 1825; m. Ann Amelia Crocker. He d. Mar. 1, 1857, at Norwich, N. Y.

4752. i.   LUCINDA, b. Oct. 12, 1851; m. —— Buckhed. Res., No. Brookfield, N. Y.

4752¹. ii. CORNELIA, b. July 18, 1854; d. Feb., 1855.

3155. LEWIS FOOTE, (1687, 645, 215, 60, 18, 5,) b. Otselic, N. Y., June 30, 1838; m. Homer, N. Y., Oct. 17, 1865, Bithiah Wilkins Cowles. She was b. June 2, 1841. She graduated from Homer Academy in 1863, completing two courses. He graduated from Univ. of Mich., 1886; Degree, C. E. Res., Wellsville, Kan.

4753. i.   LEWIS L., b. Dec. 5, 1869; m. Belle A. Harter, 6006.

4754. ii. CHARLES C., b. Oct. 9, 1875; m. Isabella A. McKay, 6007-8.

3159. NORMAN M. FOOTE, (1694, 650, 216, 60, 18, 5,) b. 1811; m. Sept. 10, 1835, Electa, dau. of Thomas Landon. She was b. Jan. 27, 1817. He d. 1890, in Malone, N. Y.

4755. i.   BUEL, b. ——; d. in infancy.

4756. ii.   BUEL L., b Oct. 14, 1839; m. Louise Ayhes, 6009-11.

4757. iii. WILLIAM W., b. July 7, 1841; m. Ophelia Lewis, 6012-3.

4758. iv.   JEWETT J., b. Dec. 11, 1844; m. Mrs. Carrie Hutchinson, 6014-6.

4759. v.   ISAAC L., b. June 2, 1846; m. Libby Drury and Kate Spaulding, 6017-9.

4760. vi.   WATSON E., b. ——.

4761. vii. HENRY M., b. June 21, 1850; m. Etta L. Baker, 6020-3.

4762. viii. ALBERT N., b. May 26, 1854; m. Julia E. Larkin, 6024-5.

4763. ix.   NATHAN E., b. June 30, 1856; m. Ella Burhans, 6026-7.

4764. x.   ARETTA, b. 1858; d. young.

4765. xi.   FRED F., b. June 9, 1860; m. Jessie K. Alvord, 6028-9.

3162. DANIEL SYLVESTER FOOTE, (1694, 650, 216, 60, 18, 5,) b. Bangor, N. Y., Apr. 10, 1823; m. Braceville, O., June 13, 1840, Mary Ann Jones. She was b. Malone, N. Y., Apr. 29, 1822; d. Mar. 19, 1906, at Akron, O.

4766. i.   FRANCES MARION, b. May 13, 1852; d. Nov. 6, 1852.

4767. ii. IDA BELLE, b. May 24, 1854; m. Sept. 14, 1886, Thos. Craighead Reynolds. Res., 21 S. Walnut, Akron, O.

3163. LOREN SHELDON FOOTE, (1694, 650, 216, 60, 18, 5,) b. Malone, N. Y., Oct. 5, 1829; m. Braceville, O., Sept. 3, 1854, Sina T., dau. of Ancil Bosworth. She was b. Braceville, O., Oct. 30, 1833. Farmer and stock dealer. He d. Mar. 2, 1898, at Grant, Montgomery Co., Iowa.

4768. i. CHARLOTTE AMY, b. Apr. 25, 1856; m. Dec. 25, 1873, at Red Oaks, Iowa, Anson Loomis. Ch.: (1) Marie V., b. Feb. 17, 1877; m. ——— Holden. Ch.: (a) Angelic Holden, b. Mar. 8, 1906. (2) Maude H., b. May 20, 1880; m. ——— Brown. (3) Ella S.. b. Aug. 8, 1891.

4769. ii. IRA ANCIL, b. Oct. 23, 1857; m. Jessie Taylor, 6030-2.

4770. iii. ALICE F., b. Mar. 20, 1859; d. Jan. 3, 1862.

4771. iv. JENNIE G., b Dec 13, 1862; m. Red Oaks, Ia., Mar. 7, 1888, Henry Murphy. Ch.: (1) Mamie G., b. July 2, 1889. (2) Earl L., b. Mar. 4, 1891. (3) Sharon, b. Mar. 2, 1897. (4) Lola Louise, b. Dec. 23, 1898. (5) Austin L., b. Sept. 2, 1900.

4772. v. LORENZO D., b. Jan. 8, 1869; m. Katherine Olcorn, 6033.

4773. vi. GERTRUDE PALMER, b. Feb. 2, 1878; m. Grant, Ia., Oct. 30, 1901, Frank Galloway. Res., Carson, Ia.

3167. MILTON MASON FOOTE, (1709, 657, 216, 60, 18, 5,) b. Morrisville, N. Y., June 27, 1840; m. Dec. 12, 1866, Louise C., dau. of Orvilliers Coman, of Eaton, N. Y. She d. Mar. 17, 1869; m. 2nd, Mar. 21, 1870, Clara Elizabeth, dau. of Josiah Reed, of De Ruyter, N. Y. He is a printer.

4774. i. COMAN M., b. Feb. 13, 1868; m. Etta M. Brown, 6034.

4775. ii. HARRY R., b. Mar. 12, 1874; m. Elma Hull, 6035-9.

4776. iii. ALICE LOUISE, b. Oswego, N. Y., Apr. 4, 1876; m. Dec. 8, 1897, Frank C. Wiltsie, of Marcellus, N. Y. He is a farmer and poultry fancier. Ch.: (1) Hazel Georgette, b. Marcellus, N. Y., Apr. 4, 1899. (2) Mabel Alice, b. Marcellus, N. Y., Aug. 16, 1903.

4777. iv. FRED GEORGE, b. Watertown, N. Y., Aug. 25, 1878; m. June 4, 1903, Cora E., dau. of George H. Smith, of Syracuse, N. Y. He is a photographer artist in Syracuse, N. Y.

4778. v. ELMER MASON, b. Syracuse, N. Y., Apr. 8, 1866. Is a printer pressman, of Rochester, N. Y.

3169. WILLIAM H. FOOTE, (1711, 657, 216, 60, 18, 5,) b. Apr. 3, 1846; m. Feb. 25, 1875, Anna Mariah Weaver, of Stockbridge, N. Y. She d. Dec. 26, 1905. He is a carpenter and joiner. He served in the Northern Army during the Rebellion. Res., Madison, N. Y.

4779. i. CLARENCE E., b. Madison, N. Y., Feb. 21, 1876; d. Mar 4, 1880.

4780. ii. CLARA E., b. Oct. 29, 1878.

4781 iii. GEORGE H., b. Jan. 17' 1881; m. Sept. 16, 1903, Alice Henry. Res., Madison, N. Y.

4782. iv. NELLIE, b. June 10, 1884; m. June 18, 1901, Maurice O'Connell. Ch.: (1) Helen, b. Apr. 4, 1902. Res., Madison, N. Y.

3177. ALVIN KENNER FOOTE, (1719, 675, 218, 60, 18, 5,) b. Flora, Ill., Aug. 12, 1877; m. Mar. 6, 1900, Ada Screven Page, at the University of Virginia. Res., Canton, Miss.

4783. i. JANE CAMPBELL, b. Feb. 1, 1901, at Univ. of Va.

4784. ii. DELIA BRYAN, b. Oct. 16, 1902; d. Jan. 8, 1905, at Canton, Miss.

4785. iii. ANNE PAGE, b. June 18, 1905; d. Sept. 13, 1905, at Canton, Miss.

4786. iv. LAWRENCE, b. Aug. 26, 1906, at Canton, Miss.

2545. WILLIAM S. FOOTE, (1234, 422, 128, 38, 11, 3,) b. Jan. 3, 1862; m. Feb. 10, 1885, Nora L. Raymond. Res., Bridgeport, Ct.

4787. i. WILLIAM C., b. abt. 1885; m. Sept. 12, 1905, Catherine Vagel, of Baltimore, Md. He is a contractor and builder in Milford, Ct.

4788. ii. JENNIE LOUISE, b. abt. 1887.

4789. iii. MABEL E., b. abt. 1888.

4790. iv. FLORENCE ISABEL, b. abt. 1890.

4791. v. RAYMOND STARR, b. abt. 1891.

4792. vi. HENRY GORDON, b. abt. 1895.

4793. vii. GEORGE L., b. abt. 1900.

3100. FORREST FOOTE, (1642, 618, 208, 56, 16, 5,) b. Mar. 5, 1852, Steuben Co., N. Y.; m. Jan. 18, 1876, Leila Ada Woodworth, Nova Scotia. She was b. Aug. 28, 1856; d. Apr. 20, 1889; m. 2nd, Mar. 24, 1891, Laura Augusta Coburn, of Amandor Co., Cal. She was b. Nov. 4, 1861. Farmer. Res., Stockton, Cal.

4794. i. LEILA JEANETTE, b. Oct. 19, 1876; d. June 8, 1878.

4795. ii. ROBERT NELSON, b. Sept. 23, 1878; m. Nov. 24, 1905, Margaret Isabelle Hughes.

4796. iii. MYRTLE LOUISA, b. Jan. 3, 1881; m. Feb., 1902, Ezra Clampits. No ch.

4797. iv. RALPH MILES, b. Mar. 23, 1883.

4798. v. EDNA MARIE, b. Aug. 28, 1885.

4799. vi. FRANK JENNINGS, b. Mar. 22, 1893.

4800. vii. EDWIN FORREST, b. Sept. 6, 1896.

4801. viii. GERTRUDE LOIS, b. Mar. 11, 1900.

4802. ix. VIVIAN EMESTINE, b. Jan. 28, 1904.

3186. ALLEN FOOTE, (1728, 680, 219, 60, 18, 5,) b. Aug. 13, 1831; m. Dec. 15, 1850, Sarah Herrick. He was an engineer, and for many years was foreman in the round house at St. James, Minn. Res., LeSure Co., St. James, and St. Paul, Minn.

4803. i. EMMA JANE, b. Williams Co., O., June 17, 1855; m. R. Hodgden. Res., St. Paul, Minn. Three ch.

4804. ii. GEORGE E., b. Sept. 22, 1857; m. Hattie Gardner, 6040-43.

4805. iii. CHARLES W., b. June 25, 1864; m. Emma B. Ceagen, 6044-6.

3187. HENRY FOOTE, (1728, 680, 219, 60, 18, 5,) b. Feb. 25, 1833; m. Nov., 1854, Mary Gaylord. He was a farmer; d. 1899. Res., near Olivet, Mich.

4806. i. MELVILLE, b. 1860; m. 6047-8.

4807. ii. MATTIE, b. 1868; m. John Gardner. Res., Ashland, O.

3189. ALBON FOOTE, (1728, 680, 219, 60, 18, 5,) b. May 23, 1837; m. 1858, Henretta Campbell. She d. in 1863; m. 2nd, Jan. 28, 1864, Sarah P. Soutwick. He was a prosperous farmer. Res. on the old home farm in Carmel, Eaton Co., Mich., until his death, Jan. 19, 1905.

4808. i. FRANK M., b. Jan. 28, 1861; m. Cora Ella Tefft, 6049-50.

4809. ii. CLARA HENRIETTA, b. Dec. 18, 1863; m. 1879, John Tanner, farmer. Res., near Charlotte, Mich. Ch.: (1) Mabel G., b. Carmel, Mich., Jan. 11, 1883. (2) Berton A., b. Sept. 30, 1884. (3) Edna E., b. Mar. 30, 1889. (4) Maud, b. Aug. 18, 1891. (5) Hortence, b. Jan. 11, 1901. (6) Stanley J., b. Sept. 12, 1904.

4810. iii. PEARL, b. Carmel, Mich.; Apr. 2, 1876; d. 1888.

3190. EDWIN FOOTE, (1728, 680, 219, 60, 18, 5,) b. Aug. 15, 1839; m. 1863, Aggie Vollentine. He is a carpenter. Res., St. James, Minn.

4811. i. ELLA, b. 1864; d. 1905.

4812. ii. WALTER, b. 1870; m. ———.· Liveryman. Res., St. James, Minn.

3191. MARTIN PORTER FOOTE, (1728, 680, 219, 60, 18, 5,) b. May 20, 1846; m. 1879, Delia Haughn. He is a farmer.

4813. i. FRED J., b. Aug. 16, 1881; unm. Res., Battle Creek, Mich.

4814. ii. LOREN, b. Sept. 1, 1883; m. Miss Cronk, 6051.

4815. iii. NINA, b. Jan. 17, 1886; m. David Newcomb. He runs a grocery store at Battle Creek, Mich. No ch.

3192. MILES ELIPHELET FOOTE, (1729, 680, 219, 60, 18, 5,) b. Dec. 27, 1826; m. Sept. 26, 1849, Martha Howard. He d. Mar. 15, 1897.

4816. i. HARRIET, b. Jan. 18, 1852; m. Sept. 19, 1868, Edward P. Brown; d. Feb. 4, 1886. Ch.: (1) William J., b. July 29, 1870; m. Nov. 29, 1897, Eliza Homewood. Res., Fayette, Iowa. Ch.: (a) Clara May, b. Sept. 7, 1894. (b) Albert J., b. Aug. 15, 1896. (2) Mary L., b. Sept. 16, 1872; m. June 4, 1889, James Smiley. Res., Green Brier, Tenn. Ch.: (a) Frank, b. Sept. 29, 1891. (b) Bessie, b. Mar. 28, 1894. (c) Corbett, b. Mar. 15, 1900. (d) William P., b. Sept. 21, 1902. (3) Fred, b. Oct. 5, 1875; d. Aug. 19, 1892. (4) Martha E., b. Aug. 23, 1879; m. May 29, 1893, George Helwig. Ch.: (a) Harriet, b. Nov. 3, 1899. (5) Miles E., b. Oct. 2, 1881. (6) Henry M., b. Dec. 27, 1883.

4817. ii. VICTORIA, b. Aug. 9, 1854; m. Dec. 22, 1872, William H. Conover. Ch.: (1) Sherman, b. Feb. 17, 1873; m. June 22, 1898, Linnie Brook. Res., Telocaset, Oregon. Ch.: (a) Leslie J., b. July 3, 1899. (b) Elver G., b. Aug. 10, 1901; d. July, 1906. (2) Maud, b. Dec. 13, 1874; m. Dec. 21, 1898, Fayette D. Winslow. Res., Esperance, N. Y. Ch.: (a) Blanche E., b. Jan. 9, 1900. (b) John W., b. Apr. 13, 1902. (c) Child, b. 1906. (3) Floyd C., b. Apr. 29, 1876; m. Dec. 5, 1901, Fannie N. Picket. No ch. Res., Esperance, N. Y. (4) Frank, b. Apr. 23, 1877; m. Aug. 21, 1901, Elizabeth Shattuck. Ch.: (a) Glen, b. ———. Res., Hillsboro, Oregon. (5) Flora, b. Mar. 14, 1882; m. Jan. 2, 1900, Herman E. Vanhatta. Res., Esperance, N. Y. (6) Harry L., b. July 19, 1884. (7) William H., Jr., b. Jan. 16, 1887. (8) J. G. Blaine, b. Feb. 23, 1889; d. Dec. 3, 1893. (9) James A., b. May 4, 1893.

4818. iii. GEORGE W., b. July 10, 1856; m. May 18, 1881, Urana M. Howe. No ch.

4819. iv. FRANK, b. July 18, 1858; d. Feb. 6, 1875.

4820. v. CORWIN, b. Sept. 26, 1860; m. Ellen Anderson, 6052.

4821. vi. SARAH, b. Sept. 23, 1862; m. Oct. 4, 1882, John Easton. Res., Esperance, N. Y. Ch.: (1) Mabel, b. Nov. 26, 1888. (2) Walter, b. 1891. (3) George W., b. Apr. 30, 1902.

4822. vii. JOHN, b. Sept. 19, 1864; m. Hattie N. Young, 6053-55.

4823. viii. EDGAR, b. July 11, 1866; m. Nov. 7, 1888, Orvilla S. Parkes. No ch. Res., Esperance, N. Y.

4824. ix. ANNIE, b. Sept. 5, 1868.

4825. x. ALVA, b. June 29, 1873.

3200. MILO PERRY FOOTE, (1729, 680, 219, 60, 18, 5,) b. Mar. 30, 1844; m. 1870, Alphrema Hearns. Res., Amsterdam, N. Y.

4826. i. SCHUYLER P., b. 1872; m. Julia Lyons, 6053-6.

4827. ii. AMY A., b. 1877; m. Dec. 20, 1893, George Overlaugh. Ch.: (1) Alie May, b. 1895. (2) Charles Perry, b. 1897. (3) Maud Ella, b. 1898. (4) Raymond Jefferson, b. 1903.

4828. iii. JOHN H., b. 1885; unm.

3201. ABRAM LARKIN FOOTE, (1729, 680, 219, 60, 18, 5,) b. Mar. 23, 1849; m. 1st, Sept. 27, 1871, Ida J. McCarthy, at Decorah, Iowa. She d.; m. 2nd, Sept. 24, 1879, at West Union, Fayette Co., Iowa, Carrie M. Morrison. Res., Fayette, Iowa.

4829. i. ALVA, b. Sept. 10, 1873; d. Jan. 23, 1876.

4830. ii. JENNIE, b. June 14, 1875; m. ———.

4831. iii. WILLIAM AVERY, b. June 26, 1880.

4832. iv. RUTH AMANDA, b. Feb. 28, 1882; m. Dec. 7, 1904, Ralph Eels Metzgar. Ch.: (1) Veda Veryl, b. Oct. 18, 1906.

4833. v. AMY EDNA, b. June 1, 1884; d. Apr. 27, 1896.

4834. vi. ROBERT ASA, b. Nov. 16, 1885; d. Aug. 2, 1887.

4835. vii. AMOS LARKIN, b. Apr. 6, 1888.

4836. viii. CHARLES HOMER, b. Aug. 17, 1891.

4837. ix. DEETTA, b. Apr. 1, 1895; d. Jan. 1, 1903.

3202. WILLIAM CHAUNCY FOOTE, (1729, 680, 219, 60, 18, 5,) b. Apr. 30, 1851; m. Dec. 9, 1871, at Eden, Iowa, Georgia Anna Freemire. She was b. Jan., 1856. Moved to Iowa in 1880. Res., Esperance, N. Y.

4838. i. AMOS D., b. Nov. 12, 1872; m. Frances M. Davis, 6057-9.

4839. ii. CELESTIA ELIZABETH, b. Aug. 15, 1874, Heron Lake, Minn.; m. France E. Nelson. Res., Kimbra, Minn. Ch.: (1) Clara, b. Sept. 28, 1902. (2) ———, b. Apr. 1, 1906.

4840. iii. OZIAS PEARL, b. Sept. 26, 1880, at Mankato, Minn.; m. Oct. 9. 1904, Ora Belle Blason. Carpenter. Res., Springfield, Mo. No ch.

4841. iv. NELLIE MAY, b. Oct. 18, 1884, Mankato, Minn.; m. P. C. Morgan. Res., Washatuna, Wash.

3204. HOMER ALONZO FOOTE, (1736, 686, 219, 60, 18, 5,) b. Aug. 21, 1850; m. Jan. 5, 1871, Nancy Putnam. She was b. Apr. 22, 1852; d. Jan. 16, 1874, at County Line, N. Y.; m. 2nd, Dec. 7, 1875, Belle R. Ketcham. She was b. May 10, 1852. Res., Barkers, Niag. Co., N. Y.

4842. i. GLENN H., b. Feb. 19, 1878; m. June 27, 1906, Bernice L. Brace.

4843. ii. MARGARET B., b. Dec. 20, 1880; d. Mar. 4, 1898.

4844. iii. HARRY A., b. June 11, 1890. Res., Barkers, N. Y.

3206. SHELDON ALONZO FOOTE, (1737, 686, 219, 60, 18, 5,) b. June 27, 1849; m. Dec. 11, 1871, Hattie S. Burnham, b. Aug. 6, 1849, and d. Oct. 2, 1904.

(29)

He is in partnership with his son, George A., dealers in hardware, furniture and implements, at Parkersburg, Iowa. Was a farmer until 1879. Ch. all b. at Parkersburg.

4841. i.   JENNIE ROMELIA, b. Oct. 11, 1876; d. Dec. 22, 1876.
4845. ii. DOTHA LOUISA, b. Oct. 26, 1878; m. Sept. 3, 1901, Harry H. Reader. Banker.
4846. iii. GEORGE A., b. Feb. 17, 1881; m. Lena M. Hull, 6060.
4647. iv. EDWARD JAMES, b. June 14, 1884. Traveling salesman, St. Louis.
4847. v.   EDNA JANE, b. June 14, 1884; d. Mar. 10, 1886.
4848. vi. SHELDON BURNHAM, b. Sept. 18, 1890.

3207. JAMES ABIJAH FOOTE, (1737, 686, 219, 60, 18, 5,) b. Aug. 18, 1851; m. Nov. 25, 1873, Nellie R. Brook,. b. Dec. 16, 1854; m. 2nd, Oct. 3, 1889, Ella Kothe. He is a land owner; formerly bought grain, stock, etc. Res., Parkersburg, Iowa.

4849. i.   MAUD LOUISA, b. Dec. 1, 1879; m. Mar. 28, 1907, Edmund W. Miller. Res., Waterloo, Ia.
4849. ii. EVELYN, b. Nov. 24, 1895.

3212. GEORGE L. FOOTE, (1741, 686, 219, 60, 18, 5,) b. Dec. 24, 1858; m. Feb. 3, 1885, Agnes Broughton. She was b. Jan. 11, 1859. He is a cashier in the Bank of Montgomery, Montgomery, Ia.

4850. i.   DORA A., b. Mar. 28, 1885.
4851. ii. FRANK B., b. Feb. 19, 1887.

3214. HORACE A. FOOTE, (1741, 686, 219, 60, 18, 5,) b. Feb. 18, 1864; m. June 10, 1896, Cora A. Ray, of Bristow, Ia. Mr. Foote is cashier of "The Citizens Bank," Bristow, Iowa.

4852. i.   RAY CHESTER, b. Nov. 2, 1906, at Bristow, Ia.

3219. REV. JOSEPH IVES FOOTE, (1748, 688, 220, 60, 18, 5,) b. in Goshen, Ct., Dec. 17, 1834; m. Emma Frances, dau. of Wm. C. and Emily (Abbott) Lovejoy, Oct. 28, 1860. His boyhood days were spent at Footville, Wis., on his father's farm, until he was sent to college. There he took a five years' classical course, graduating with honors from Lawrence University. He also took a course of civil engineering, and the course required of teachers of the State Normal Schools of Wisconsin. He has been Regent of the State Normal Schools of Wisconsin and Superintendent of Schools of Rock County. He was called to the Presidency of a Spanish-American College in Chili; was Professor of Elocution in Avoca Ladies' Seminary; Professor of Languages and Civil Engineering in Austin College, Texas; and President of the Literary and Agricultural Departments of Polytechnic College at Houston, Texas. In 1879 he was admitted to the bar in Kansas City, with license to practice law in the Courts of the State of Missouri. He was Chaplain of the 13th Wis. Vols. and Veteran Vol. Infantry, serving three years, until the close of the war. In 1858 he entered the ministry of the Methodist Episcopal Church, serving 35 years. In 1886, on account of ill health, he and his wife removed to California, where he was appointed pastor of a church at Coronado Beach. He d. in San Diego, July 18, 1899.

4853. i.   IDAHO, b. Apr. 3, 1863, at Footville, Wis.; d. Oct. 16, 1864.
4853. ii. IVAH, b. Nov. 4, 1866, at Footville, Wis.; d. Oct. 25, 1870.
4854. iii. RUTH, b. Dec. 4, 1867, at Evansville, Wis.; d June 6, 1868.

3224. CHARLES FOOTE, (1751, 689, 220, 60, 18, 5,) b. Mar. 28, 1832; m. Mariam Rollin and Hannah Mousley. Mariam was b. June 24, 1835. Hannah was b. Feb. 29, 1840. He d. Mar. 26, 1900.

4855. i.   MERCY A., b. Feb. 12, 1856; dau. of Mariam.
4856. ii.   CHARLES W., b. Nov. 20, 1859; m. Caroline Pitts, 6061-70.
4857. iii. TIMOTHY B., b. Sept. 7, 1861; m. Mary Jane Sketchley, 6071-9.
4858. iv.   JOHN F., b. Oct. 11, 1863; m. Elsie Bowers, 6080.
4859. v.   THOMAS A., b. Feb. 6, 1866; m. Lizette Marsh, 6081.
4860. vi.   MARY ELLEN, b. Sept. 4, 1868; d. Jan. 24, 1889; m. Charles
             Hyde, of Nephi. Ch.: (1) Nellie, b. Jan. 16, 1889. (2) Mary
             Ellen, b. Jan. 12, 1888; d. Jan. 24, 1889.
4861. vii. HARRISON, b. July 23, 1871; m. Ida May Wright, 6082-83.
4862. viii. GEORGE A., b. June 11, 1873; m. Minnie Carter, 6084.
4863. ix.   LOIS JANE, b. Feb. 21, 1876; d. Mar. 2, 1891.
4864. x.   ARTHUR, b. Aug. 11, 1878.
4865. xi.   CHARLES BERTIAN, b. Dec. 19, 1880; d. Feb. 16, 1896.
4866. xii. SUSAN PEARL, b. Mar. 17, 1886.
4867. xiii. VICTORIA MOUSLEY, b. Sept. 24, 1887.

3225. GUY WESTFIELD FOOTE, (1751, 689, 220, 60, 18, 5,) b. July 13, 1836;
m. Sept. 18, 1864, Eliza S. Coulson. She was b. Sept. 16, 1848. He d. at Halbrook,
Ariz., Mar. 1, 1889, and she d. May 6, 1903.
4868. i.   LYDIA JANE, b. June 24, 1866; m. Dec. 25, 1882, A. E. Maupin,
             of Nephi, Utah. Ch.: (1) George Henry, b. Jan. 28, 1884. (2)
             Cora M., b. Apr. 2, 1886. (3) Rebecca, b. Feb. 21, 1888; d. Feb.
             24, 1888.
4869. ii.   IDA LOUISE, b. Feb. 21, 1868; m. June 14, 1885, Oscar McGee, of
             Almieda, Cal. Ch.: (1) Alice S., b. June 8, 1886. (2) George W.,
             b. Jan. 18, 1888. (3) James, b. June 17, 1890, and d. Sept. 17,
             1891. (4) Luella, b. Feb. 8, 1893.
4870. iii. VICTORIA, b. Mar. 19, 1870; m. Sept. 13, 1886, Charles G. Testen-
             man, Nephi, Utah. Ch.: (1) Guy, b. June 17, 1891.

3228. CYRUS RILEY FOOTE, (1751, 689, 220, 60, 18, 5,) b. Sept. 15, 1848; m.
June 23, 1871, Lizzie Tidwell, Salt Lake City, Utah. She was b. Dec. 7, 1853.
Proprietor of Opera House, Nephi, Utah.
4871. i.   ERNEST, b. Nov. 15, 1872.
4872. ii.   EFFIF, b. Feb. 25, 1874; m. Sept., 1904, Wm. Miller, at Nephi,
             Utah. Ch.: (1) Charles Orlando, b. May 13, 1906.
4873. iii. LUCIA BERNETTA, b. Apr. 9, 1876; m. Sept. 25, 1902, John
             Albert Cotterll.
4874. iv.   LESLIE, b. July 2, 1878.
4875. v.   JOHN LOUIS, b. Aug. 17, 1880.
4876. vi.   CHARLES, b. June 17, 1883.

3232. JOHN FOOTE, (1751, 689, 220, 60, 18, 5,) b. July 19, 1859; m. Feb.
21, 1884, Laura Young, at Provo, Utah. She was b. June 17, 1867. Res., Provo,
Utah.
4877. i.   SAMUEL, b. Jan. 10, 1891.
4878. ii.   JOHN M., b. Sept. 27, 1896.
4879. iii. NORMAN, b. Jan. 29, 1902.
4880. iv.   LENORE, b. Nov. 28, 1905.

3234. GEORGE WASHINGTON FOOTE, (1751, 689, 220, 60, 18, 5,) b. Nephi,
Utah, July 26, 1866; m. Nov. 28, 1894, Celestia Wilson. Res., Nephi, Utah.
4881. i.   GEORGE CLARENCE, b. July 22, 1896.

4882. ii. BERTRAND WILSON, b. Apr. 1, 1898.

4883. iii. EMERSON RILEY, b. Apr. 14, 1902.

3235. WILLIAM FOOTE, (1761, 703, 222, 61, 18, 5,) b. 1826; m. Wealthy Sybil Stannard, of Westbrook, Ct.

4884. i. SYBIL WEALTHY, b. July 22, 1869, in Stony Creek, Ct.; m. 1898, William Beazley; d. Nov. 20, 1897. Ch.: (1) Edward Foote Beazley, b. ———.

4885. ii. WILLIAM RODNEY, b. in Stony Creek, Ct., Dec. 25, 1873; m. July 22, 1901, Albutina Katherina Yehle, of Germany. No ch.

3236. RUSSELL FOOTE, (1761, 703, 222, 61, 18, 5,) b. Aug. 16, 1833; m. May 25, 1858, Emily Conklin Dudley.

4886. i. MARION ELIZABETH, b. May 17, 1859; m. Apr. 18, 1888, Jesse L. Harrison. Ch.: (1) Robert Russell Harrison, b. Oct. 11, 1889. (2) Sallie Linsley Harrison, b. Sept. 4, 1891. (3) Lloyd Dudley Harrison, b. Mar. 25, 1898.

4887. ii. SARAH TALCOTT, b. Jan. 1, 1867; m. Nov. 7, 1894, E. H. Rose. Res., Branford, Ct. Ch.: (1) Kenneth Dudley Rose, b. Jan. 4, 1896.

4888. iii. MABEL ELVIRA DUDLEY, b. July 10, 1876; m. May 23, 1906, Walter Fayette Rossiter. Res., Guilford, Ct.

4889. iv. BESSIE ARNOLD, b. May 24, 1878; d. Apr. 28, 1885.

3237. NOAH FOOTE, (1761, 703, 222, 61, 18, 5,) b. ———; m. Grace Chidrey. Res., Branford, Ct.

4890. i. GEORGE, b. ———; m. Carrie Hale and Miss Palmer, 6085-6.

4891. ii. FRANK, b. ———; m. Nellie, dau. of Martin Bishop, of N. Branford. Ch.: (1) Martin Bishop Foote.

3243. DAVID FOOTE, (1768, 706, 222, 61, 18, 5,) b. Jan. 19, 1828; m. Sept. 3, 1854, Jane A. Rowe. He d. May 25, 1903. Res., Baltimore, Md.

4892. i. IDA MARION, b. Aug. 11, 1855; m. Hugh S. Oren, of Baltimore, Md. Res., Roland Park, Baltimore, Md.

4893. ii. JULIA SMITH, b. Feb. 16, 1858; m. Howard M. Somers, of Baltimore, Md. Res., 2032 Fairmount Ave., Baltimore, Md.

4894. iii. JENNIE ROWE, b. Jan. 21, 1861; m. Harry Sloan, of Baltimore, Md. Res., 1844 W. Saratoga St., Baltimore, Md.

3250. NOAH FOOTE, (1770, 706, 222, 61, 18, 5,) b. Mar. 12, 1849; m. May 3, 1868, at Guilford, Ct., Susan dau. of George Baldwin. She was b. in Branford, July 19, 1846. He was educated at No. Branford, Ct., and in New York. Teamster. He d. May 14, 1874. Res., No. Branford, Ct.

4895. i. JONATHAN ROBERT, b. Mar. 15, 1869; m. Sept., 1901. No ch.

4896. ii. GEORGE HERBERT, b. May 30, 1871; m. Oct. 24, 1900. No ch.

3251. WILLIAM SCOVILLE FOOTE, (1771, 714, 223, 61, 18, 5,) b. Sept. 23, 1828; m. Jan. 1, 1857, Amanda M. Pope. Res., Ottawa, Ohio.

4896[1]. i. WILLIAM HENRY, b. Oct. 29, 1857; d. Aug. 18, 1858.

4897. ii. LAURA CATHERINE, b. July 10, 1859; m. Apr. 11, 1880, Edward M. Wilkins. Ch.: (1) Ethel A., b. Apr. 30, 1881; m. May 16, 1907, George Long. (2) Charles A., b. Feb. 18, 1882. (3) Sadie L., b. Dec. 4, 1886. (4) Mary E., b. Feb. 5, 1889. (5) Edna B., b. Apr. 11, 1895. (6) Edward L., b. Mar. 25, 1904.

4897[1]. iii. MARY ABIGAIL, b. July 14, 1861; d. Mar. 10, 1903.

4898. iv. PRICELLA FRANCES, b. Jan. 21, 1865; m. Feb. 1, 1885, John S.
Hart; d. May 22, 1907. Ch.: (1) Samuel Louis, b. Dec. 3, 1885; d.
Mar. 25, 1888. (2) Clarence A., b. Mar. 31, 1889. (3) Sidney
B., b. Apr. 18, 1892. (4) Esther, b. Dec. 21, 1894. (5) Harold
P., b. June 20, 1897. (6) Doris Leon, b. Sept. 13, 1900; d. June
10, 1901. (7) Franklin D., b. May 10, 1902.

4898¹. v. EDWARD D., b. Aug., 1867; d. Mar. 29, 1868.

4898². vi. CHARLES HERBERT, b. Jan. 29, 1869; d. Oct. 6, 1896.

4899. vii. HARLAND POPE, b. ———; m. Oct. 11, 1905, Jane P. Rothman.

4899¹. viii. EDWIN B., b. Aug. 8, 1871; d. Oct. 23, 1872.

4900. ix. CLARISSA ADELIA, b. May 4, 1875; m. Mar. 7, 1896, William
Rice. She d. Oct. 12, 1900. Ch.: (1) Freda Grace, b. Aug. 23,
1896. (2) Leslie Ray, b. Mar. 24, 1898.

3253. SIDNEY B. FOOTE, (1771, 714, 223, 61, 18, 5,) b. Aug. 3, 1844; m.
Jan. 2, 1869, Alicia A. Trask. She was b. Dec. 9, 1853. He d. Nov. 29, 1896.

4901. i. WILSON A., b. July 14, 1869; m. Altha L. Lyon, 6087-90.

4902. ii. JOHN E., b. Aug. 18, 1871; m. Addie L. Hatch, 6091.

4903. iii. SIDNEY SCOVILLE, b. Dec. 21, 1873.

4904. iv. ALFRED NATHANIEL, b. May 7, 1876.

4905. v. FLORENCE LEONIA, b. Feb. 6, 1879; m. Michael Hein.

4906. vi. LOIS IRENE, b. June 3, 1883; m. Dec. 4, 1901, Jeston Chapman.
He was b. Dec. 26, 1879. Ch.: (1) Madge Marie, b. July 6, 1903.
(2) Joice Elane, b. Oct. 1, 1905.

4907. vii. CHARLES LESLIE, b. Apr. 28, 1886.

4908. viii. MILTON CLIFFORD, b. Aug. 16, 1889.

4909. ix. MARY FREELOVE, b. Feb. 23, 1892.

4910. x. ALICIA ALTHEA, b. Feb. 2, 1896; d. Aug. 24, 1906.

3259. JOHN A. FOOTE, (1777, 715, 223, 61, 18, 5,) b. Aug. 29, 1843; m. Dec.
4, 1873, Belle Palmer. She was b. Dec. 7, 1851. Res., 215 W. 80th St., N. Y. City.
Formerly of Cleveland, O.

4911. i. FRANCES HITCHCOCK, b. Jan. 18, 1875.

4912. ii. SOPHIE PALMER, b. Mar. 23, 1877.

4913. iii. LOUISE CAROLINE, b. Mar. 4, 1882.

3263. AUGUSTUS RUSSELL STREET FOOTE, (1778, 715, 223, 61, 18, 5,)
b. in the Navy Yard, Boston, Mass., Apr. 4, 1847; m. Kate Shepard, dau. of Horace
A. and Elizabeth (Fitch) Nunnally. He is employed in the Government offices at
Washington. Res., 1712 22nd St., N. W., Washington, D. C.

4914. i. LULA JOHNSON, b. May 6, 1880, at Washington, D. C.; m. June
25, 1906, Francis Elmon Cady, of Brookline, Mass.

4915. ii. MARGUERITE NESBETT, b. Feb. 13, 1890.

3267. JOHN SAMUEL FOOTE, (1778, 715, 223, 61, 18, 5,) b. in the Brooklyn
Navy Yard, June 25, 1859; m. Sept. 8, 1885, Anne Doolittle, of New Haven,
Ct. She was b. Oct. 26, 1862. Res., Denver, Colo., Philadelphia, Pa.

4916. i. ANDREW HULL, b. Oct. 31, 1887.

4917. ii. ANNA MODJESKA, b. Feb. 13, 1889.

4918. iii. ALICE GERTRUDE, b. Feb. 9, 1893.

4919. iv. ROBERT NATHANIEL, b. Aug. 27, 1894.

4920. v. ELEANOR ISABELL, b. Jan. 20, 1896.

3273. DARWIN ROCKWELL FOOTE, (1783, 718, 231, 72, 5,) b. June 18,
1849; m. Minnie P. Soylor. Res., 158 Stiles St., Elizabeth, N. J.

4921. i. ARCHIE W., b. May 22, 1882.

3284. FRANCIS WAITE FOOTE (1791, 719, 231, 72, 20, 5,) b. Jan. 8, 1842, at St. Francis Barracks, St. Augustine, Fla.; m. Oct. 15, 1872, Love L. Bursley, of Me. He d. Oct. 4, 1878. Mrs. Foote is living with her sons in Washington, D. C.

4922. i. LIEUT. MORRIS COOPER, b. Feb. 26, 1874.

4923. ii. RICHARD FRANCHOT, b. June 18, 1875.

3285. BRIG.-GENERAL MORRIS COOPER FOOTE, (1791, 719, 231, 72, 20, 5,) b. Sept. 16, 1843; m. Apr. 29, 1891, Annie Elizabeth Murphy. His great-grandfather was William Cooper, the founder of Cooperstown, N. Y., and his maternal great-grandfather was Jacob Morris, who served as an officer in the Revolutionary War, whose father was Lewis Morris, of Morrisania, a signer of the Declaration of Independence. His father died during the Mexican War in 1846 and his mother moved to Cooperstown, with her children, where he attended school for a time, later going to Plattsburg, N. Y., and to a Commercial College in Syracuse, N. Y.

In September, 1861, he enlisted as a private in the 44th New York Volunteer Infantry and served until June, 1862, when he was appointed Second Lieutenant of the 92nd New York Volunteer Infantry, and First Lieutenant 121st New York Volunteers, Mar., 1865. Appointed Second Lieutenant, 9th U. S. Infantry, May, 1866, in which regiment he served for 36 years through all the grades of First Lieutenant, Captain, Major and Lieutenant-Colonel. Apr. 15, 1902, he was appointed Colonel of the 28th U. S. Infantry, in which regiment he served until Feb. 18, 1903, when he was appointed Brigadier-General, at which grade he was retired, at his own request, after a service of over 40 years.

General Foote was a typical specimen of the American soldier. He devoted his whole life to the service of his country. He served throughout the entire Civil War, and was present at the surrender of Lee at Appomattox. He was taken prisoner Apr. 20, 1864, at Plymouth, N. C., while serving as aide on the staff of Brigadier-General H. W. Wessells, at the time of the capture of that place by overwhelming odds. He was a prisoner at Libby, Macon, Charleston and Columbia, escaping from the latter place after thrilling adventures before arriving at the mouth of the Santee River and taking refuge on board the U. S. gunboat "Nipsic."

In Dec., 1864, he was among the 600 officers, prisoners of war, placed under fire, in an effort to prevent the batteries on Morris Island from shelling the city of Charleston. He was the only officer hit, receiving a slight flesh wound from a piece of shell. He was brevetted captain of volunteers in 1865 for gallant and meritorious services before Petersburg and in the battle of Little Sailor's Creek, Va. He commanded one of the two companies of the 9th U. S. Infantry that received the Territory of Alaska from Russia in 1867, and was present when the Russian flag was hauled down at Sitka.

He was adjutant of the Black Hills Expedition, under Col. Richard I. Dodge, in 1875, and was in charge at the Brule Sioux Indian Agency in 1876. He was in the field against hostile Sioux in 1877, and in the Geronimo Campaign in 1886.

When the war with Spain broke out, he went to Cuba with his regiment, the 9th U. S. Infantry, and commanded a battalion at San Juan, and was at the surrender of the Spanish Army in the city of Santiago in July, 1898.

In June, 1900, he went to the Philippines, and subsequently to China with his regiment. He was present at the battle of Tien-Tsin, and marched with the

Allied Armies to the relief of the Legations at Pekin, taking part in all the engagements en route. In Oct., 1900, he was ordered to return to Tien-Tsin in command of the United States forces, and represented the United States in the "Conseil" or provisional government of that city.

He returned with his regiment to the Philippines, May, 1901, and served at Basey, Samar, for some months. Later, as Colonel of the 28th U. S. Infantry, he served in Cavite Province, near Manila, and also on the Island of Mindanao.

General Foote returned from the Philippines in Apr., 1903, and after spend-ing a year in California he went to Europe to enjoy a few years' travel and well-earned rest. He d. at Geneva, Switzerland, Dec. 6, 1905. His remains were brought back to the United States and buried in the U. S. National Cemetery at Arlington, Va., near Washington, D. C.

    4924. i. WILLIAM COOPER, b. Jan. 10, 1892.

    4925. ii. FRANCIS CHANDLER, b. Mar. 20, 1894.

    3289. EDWIN JOSIAH FOOTE, (1794, 719, 223, 61, 18, 6,) b. Branford, Ct., Oct. 11, 1844; m. Dec. 20, 1874, Emily Adams, dau. of Joseph and Martha French, of New Gretna, N. J. Edwin Josiah Foote followed the sea in early life. Served in the Rebellion of States, and commander of steam vessels coastwise after war. Also manufacturer of fertilizers and oils for 22 years in the States of Maine, New Jersey and Virginia. Retired from manufacturing 1894, and engaged in the mercantile business and oyster culture. Res., Wachapreague, Va.

    4926. i. CLARA MARY, b. Oct. 5, 1876, at New Gretna, N. J.; m. Apr. 22, 1896, at Wachapreague, Va., George Thos., son of L. J. and Bittie Hyslop, of Keller, Va. Ch.: (1) Sadie French Hyslop, b. Jan. 31, 1897. (2) Luther Carlton, b. Mar. 5, 1899; d. Aug. 22, 1902. (3) Edwin James Hyslop, b. Dec. 2, 1902. (4) Rooker White, b. Dec. 24, 1904.

    4927. ii. SAMUEL C., b. Apr. 27, 1879; m. Myrle Smith, 6092.

    3289². WILLIAM R. FOOTE, (1802, 721, 231, 72, 20, 5,) b. May, 1854, West Point, Ga.; m. Nov., 1878 Maggie Whitaker, Milledgville, Ga. Res., West Point, Ga.

    4928. i. WALTER W., b. Jan., 1892, West Point, Ga.

    3290. JAMES G. FOOTE, (1802, 721, 231, 72, 20, 5,) b. Apr., 1856, Sparta, Ga.; m. Aug., 1883, Mary L. Stansell, Dalton, Fla. Res., Edgewood, Ga. Ch. all b. at Edgewood, Ga.

    4930. i. JAMES J., b. Nov., 1888.

    4931. ii. MARY M., b. Mar., 1890.

    4932. iii. FANNY, b. July, 1892.

    4933. iv. LEOLIN, b. June, 1895.

    4934. v. MARSHALL, b. June, 1897.

    4935. vi. JULIA, b. Oct., 1896.

    4936. vii. CATHERINE, b. Nov., 1899.

    4937. viii. MILDRED, b. Sept., 1901.

    3291. WALTER O. FOOTE, (1802, 721, 231, 72, 20, 5,) b. Apr., 1868, Madison, Ga.; m. Oct. 1889, Laura Well, Marietta, Ga. Res., Edgewood, Ga., and Atlanta, Ga.

    4938. i. MAGGIE M., b. Apr., 1891, Edgewood, Ga.

    4939. ii. ELISE, b. Aug., 1898, Atlanta, Ga.

    4940. iii. ANNE, b. Feb., 1901, Atlanta, Ga.

    4941. iv. WALTER O., b. July, 1903.

3292. ISAAC FRANCIS FOOTE, (1803, 724, 231, 72, 20, 5,) b. Fair Haven, Ct., 1848; m. 1st, 1872, Addie Luddington, of Baltimore, N. Y.; m. 2nd, 1882, Mary Bidwell, of New Haven, Ct. He d. 1901, in Aurora, Ill.

 4942. i. GEORGE LUDDINGTON, b. Fair Haven, Ct., 1873; d. 1902; unm.

3295. GILBERT FLAGLER FOOTE, (1805, 724, 231, 72, 20, 5,) b. Beekman, Dutchers Co., N. Y., Apr. 27, 1859; m. Dec. 6, 1893, Clara, dau. of Orren A. and Josephine (Giraud) Williams, of Poughkeepsie, N. Y. Res., Poughkeepsie, N. Y.

 4943. i. ANDREW GIRAUD, b. Feb. 2, 1895.
 4944. ii. GILBERT FLAGLER, Jr., b. Sept. 1, 1896.

2257. ZEPHENIAH FOOTE, (1090, 367, 114, 36, 10, 5,) b. June 9, 1827; m. 1850, Desire Brown, of Pittsfield, N. Y. He d. 1863. Res., Morris, N. Y.

 4945. i. CHARLES M., b. Morris, N. Y., July 18, 1855. Res., Walton, N. Y.
 4946. ii. ELLEN M., b. Morris, N. Y., Jan. 25, 1860; m. Elias Howland, Mar. 24, 1894. Res., Walton, N. Y. Ch.: (1) Ralph, b. Apr. 15, 1895; d. Oct. 8, 1895.

2258. LUCIUS FOOTE, (1090, 367, 114, 36, 10, 5,) b. Dec. 18, 1829; m. 1st, 1855, Lavina Cass. She d. 1879; m. 2nd, 1882, Amanda M. Clark. He d. 1904, at Morris, N. Y.

 4947. i. DAVID M., b. May 11, 1856; m. Lillie B. Williams, 6093-5.
 4948. ii. PERRY D., b. Dec. 18, 1859; m. Mary L. Thomas, 6096.
 4949. iii. SEDATE S., b. Morris, May 28, 1862; d. Aug. 20, 1881, at Colorado.

2260. MOSES W. FOOTE, (1090, 367, 114, 36, 10, 5,) b. June 8, 1833; m. 1864, Mary Crimby. He d. 1890, in Morris, N. Y.

 4950. i. GERTRUDE ELIZABETH, b. Jan. 8, 1866. Res., Morris, N. Y.; unm.

2261. DANIEL H. FOOTE, (1090, 367, 114, 36, 10, 5,) b. Aug. 15, 1834; m. 1855, Catharine Crawford, of New Berlin, N. Y. He d. 1903, Morris, N. Y.

 4951. i. GEORGE HENRY, b. Aug. 11, 1857, Morris, N. Y.; unm.
 4952. ii. DEVILLE, b. Jan. 7, 1859; m. Margaret L. Tiffany, 6097-8.
 4953. iii. HERBERT, b. Sept., 1860, Morris, N. Y.; d. Sept. 16, 1865.

2262. SEDATE FOOTE, (1090, 367, 114, 36, 10, 5,) b. June 29, 1846; m. 1868, Elizabeth Taylor, of Morris, N. Y. Res., Morris, N. Y.

 4954. i. STEPHEN A., b. Apr. 3, 1869; m. Clara Van Dusen, 6099-6102.
 4955. ii. HENRY DANIEL, b. Dec. 25, 1874; m. 1903, Katherine M. Foster. Res., Morris, N. Y.

2264. ALBERT FOOTE, (1090, 367, 114, 36, 10, 5,) b. Jan. 15, 1840; m. 1863, Amelia Palmatier, of Morris, N. Y. Res., Morris, N. Y.

 4956. i. CORA D., b. Feb. 6, 1864; m. 1891, Melvin C. Gardner.
 4957. ii. FLOYD W., b. Dec. 31, 1866; m. 1900, Ella Wood.
 4958. iii. F. MAY, b. Sept. 11, 1871; m. 1891, Nelson Houghtaling. Res., Morris, N. Y.
 4959. iv. NELLIE R., b. June 3, 1876. Res., Morris, N. Y.; unm.

2267. JOHN JAY FOOTE, (1093, 367, 114, 36, 10, 3,) b. Sept. 27, 1839; m. Jan. 1, 1863, Affia Sophia Johnson, of Garrattsville, N. Y.; m. 2nd, Dec. 11, 1889, Emeline E. Perry, of Hardwick, N. Y. He d. Dec. 31, 1790. Res., Garrattsville, N. Y.

 4960. i. GEORGE CLAYTON, b. Sept. 1, 1867; m. Dec. 10, 1891, Adda M. Sherman. Res., Garrattsville, N. Y. No ch.

4961. ii.   LYDIA ESTHRE, b. Dec. 10, ——; m. Oct. 2, 1889, Elmer C.
             Talbot. Ch.: (1) Dau. Res., Garrattsville, N. Y.
4962. iii. WILLIAM N., b. July 25, 1874; m. Rose A. Lasher, 6103-4.

2269. ALVA EUGENE FOOTE, (1093, 367, 114, 36, 10, 3,) b. Dec. 24, 1847,
Garrattsville, N. Y.; m. Feb. 3, 1874, of same place, Emily Porter. He d. Sept. 10,—
1891.
4963. i.   CORA, b. Apr. 24, 1878.

2270. SAMUEL FOOTE, (1095, 370, 115, 37, 10, 3,) b. Morgan, O.
4963¹. i.   SAMUEL, b. ———; m. Miss Powers, of Pa. Several ch. Res.,
             Morgan, O.

2271. ROGER FOOTE, (1095, 370, 115, 37, 10, 3,) b. Morgan,, O.; m. Chloe
Mather. He d. abt. 1866 at Morgan, O.
4964.   i.   NATHANIEL G., b. ———; m. Minerva Coon, 6105-10.
4964¹. ii. REBECCA.
4964². iii. ALVIN.
4964³. iv. FIDELIA.
4965.   v.   EUNICE LOUISE, b. ———; m. —— Bailey. Ch.: (1) Charles,
             b. ———. Res., Rock Creek, O.
4966.   vi. WILLIAM W., b. Nov. 7, 1831; m. Emeline Brooks, 6111-16.
4967.   vii. RUFUS.
4967¹. viii. ELMINA, b. ———. Res., Rock Creek, O.
4967². ix. FRANKLIN, b.

2272. ROSWELL FOOTE, (1095, 370, 115, 37, 10, 3,) b. ———; m. 1st,———;
m. 2nd, Jan., 1840, Sabra Emeline, dau. of Thomas and Huldah Holman, and wid.
of Jerry Van Wormer. She was b. Apr. 11, 1809; d. Trumbald, O., Mar. 27, 1860.
He d. Morgan, Ashtabula Co., O., Mar. 31, 1841.
4968. i.   AMANDA, b.
4968¹. ii. LUTHER, b.
4969. iii. ROSWELL JERRY, b. Morgan Township, O., Apr. 4, 1841. Was
             in the Union Army, and a member of Co. C, 1st. Regt. Ohio Volun-
             teer Artillery; d. Nashville, Tenn., Jan. 21, 1864; unm.

2273. JOHN FOOTE, (1095, 370, 115, 37, 10, 3,) b. ———; m. ———. Res.,
Rock Creek, O.
4970. i.   ARTEMISIA, b. ———; m. ———. One dau.
4970¹. ii. ———; m. David Sullivan. Res., Cleveland, O.
4970². iii. ———; m, Hiram Latimer. Res., Rock Creek, O.

2275. LAUREN BRADFORD FOOTE, (1095, 370, 115, 37, 10, 3,) b. Torringford, Ct., Nov. 13, 1802; m. 1st, Apr. 8, 1829, Abigail Moses. She was b. Oct. 12,
1810, and d. July 24, 1842; m. 2nd, O'ct. 5, 1843, Cornelia M. Ballard. She was b.
Jan. 11, 1824; d. Jan. 10, 1907. He d. Sept. 27, 1881. Res., Footville, Ashtabula
Co., O.
4970³. i.   SARAH, b. Mar. 8, 1830; d. Dec. 18, 1901; unm.
4970⁴. ii. JEROME, b. Aug. 29, 1832; d. Jan. 9, 1833.
4971.   iii. IRENEUS M., b. Mar. 4, 1834; m. Dorinda E. Mills, 6117-20.
4972.   iv. DERRIN, b. June 11, 1837; m. Ellen Hawkings, 6188-90.
4972¹. v.   EMMERSON, b. Aug. 12, 1846; d. Jan. 1, 1847, Footeville, O.
4972². vi. ELLEN E., b. Sept. 14, 1848, Footville; m. June 5, 1870, in Austin-
             bury, O., T. F. Van Leuven, Lime Springs, Ia. Ch.: (1) Alice

M., b. Apr. 22, 1871; m. May 15, 1889, C. A. Searles. Ch.: (a) Maud B. Searles, b. Apr. 30, 1890. (b) Neva M., b. July 28, 1891; d. Sept. 16, 1893. (c) Lincoln D., b. Feb. 12, 1896; d. Sept. 16, 1897. (d) Mildred M. Searles, b. Aug. 18, 1889. (2) L. Madge, b. Aug. 22, 1874; m. Sept. 9, 1897, W. U. Smith, St. Paul, Minn. (3) Nettie C., b. July 22, 1896; d. July 16, 1891. (4) Lucy G., b. Jan. 1, 1881; d. Mar. 11, 1888.

4973. vii. HOWARD S., b. 1852; m. Abbie Lottie Tourgee, 6121-2.
4974. viii. CHARLES E.; b. 1856; m. Jennie Lick, 6123-7.
4975. ix.   ABBIE M., b. 1858; m. 1883, V. J. Metcalf, of Ashtabula, O.

2276. JULIUS FOOTE, (1095, 370, 115, 37, 10, 3,) b. Morgan, O.; m. Mary Hazet.

4976. i.   MORRIS J., b. Jan. 26, 1838; m. Ellen J. Holman, 6128-30.
4977. ii. LOUISA, b. ———; m. Arthur Henderson. Res., Cleveland, O. Ch.: (1) Charles A., b. ———; m. ———. Two daus.

2646. ELIAS W. FOOTE, (1280, 459, 137, 39, 11, 3,) b. Apr. 1, 1801; m. Harriet W. She d. May 11, 1867, ae. 57. He d. Oct. 25, 1851.

4978. i.   SARAH JANE, b. Apr. 2, 1837. Res., Oaksville, N. Y.; unm.
4979. ii.   LAWRENCE W., b. Oct. 29, 1838; d. Mar. 24, 1890. Two ch.
4980. iii. BENJAMIN A., b. Sept. 21, 1843; m. ———. Four ch. Res., Highmore, South Dak.
4981. iv.   E. JOSEPHINE, b. Oct. 6, 1847. No ch.

2647. HYATT FOOTE, (1280, 459, 137, 39, 11, 3,) b. Feb., 1804.

4982. i.   CHARLES HENRY, b. Nov. 17, 1845; d. June, 1869.
4983. ii.   LYDIA L., b. June 27, 1848; m. ———. No ch.
4984. iii. EMELINE C., b. Oct. 11, 1850; m. Geo. Ulman. Ch.: One son.
4985. iv.   C. JANE, b. June 21, 1857.

2648. JESSE FOOTE, (1280, 459, 137, 39, 11, 3,) b. Feb., 1807; m. Margaret Boalt, Nov. 24, 1833. She b. May. 1, 1811; d. May 14, 1854. He d. Feb. 25, 1863.

4986. i.   GEORGE B., b. Mar. 30, 1835; m. Clarissa Sisson, 6131-3.
4987. ii.   THEODORE L., b. Sept. 23, 1838; d. Jan. 29, 1867; unm.
4988. iii. NORMAN A., b. Jan. 8, 1842; d. Feb. 1, 1852.
4989. iv.   URIAH H., b. Oct. 6, 1845; m. Melissa Lilley, 6134-8.
4990. v.   CORA I., b. June, 1853; m. June 18, 1877, Berdeth Holley; d. Nov. 12, 1887.

2650. COL. CHARLES FOOTE, (1280, 459, 137, 39, 11, 3,) b. at Unadilla, Feb. 12, 1812; m. Jan. 20, 1842, Eliza Clark. She was b. Mar. 4, 1819; d. Feb. 14, 1900, in Guilford, N. Y. He d. Dec. 10, 1868, in Guilford, N. Y.

4991. i.   CHARLES RILEY, b. Nov. 10, 1843, Unadilla; d. 1864, Rochester.
4991¹. ii. RANSOM EUGENE, b. 1846, Guilford; d. 1849, Guilford.
4992. iii. ALBERT CLARK, b. July 9, 1849; m. Frances M. Myers, 6139-41.
4992¹. iv. MARY ELIZA, b. 1853; d. 1863, Guilford.
4993. v.   RUTH ELLA, b. Dec. 13, 1855, Guilford; m. June 5, 1878, William E. Utter, Guilford, N. Y.

2651. LEANDER BENNET FOOTE, (1280, 459, 137, 39, 11, 3,) b. July 11, 1815; m. Oxford, N. Y., Aug. 15, 1848, Sarah Lynn, dau. of Henry Balcom, of Oxford, N. Y. She was b. Oxford, Apr. 4, 1828, and d. Bath, N. Y., Apr. 26, 1901. He d. Oxford, N. Y., Sept. 27, 1863. Res., Oxford, N. Y.

4994. i. MARY BANKS, b. Sycamore, Ill.

EDWARD FOOTE. No. 3562

MAY DWIGHT FOOTE WENDELL (No. 5172), and her Son,
TEN EYCK WENDELL, JR.

JUDGE NATHANIEL FOOTE. No. 3300

2728. WILLIAM STURGES FOOTE, (1335, 486, 145, 41, 11, 3,) b. Feb. 7, 1824; m. Sept. 12, 1849' Mary Adelaide Blish. She was b. Dec. 20, 1826; d. Dec. 13, 1893. He d. in 1880. Res., Hobart, N. Y.

    4994¹. i. FREDERICK MORTIMER, b. June 1, 1851; d. Nov. 30, 1867.

    4995. ii. HARRIET AUGUSTA, b. Apr. 11, 1856; m. Sept. 23, 1873, George D. Ostrom. Ch.: (1) Frederick, b. 1872; d. 1893'

    4996. iii. CHARLES PARSHALL, b. Mar. 25, 1860; m. Vida Stevens.

    4997. iv. FRANCES MARY, b. June 5, 1870; m. Oct. 18, 1905, Stoddard Stevens. Ch.: (1) Mary Lucinda; b. Mar. 8, 1907.

2730. GEORGE THOMAS FOOTE, (1335, 486, 145, 41, 11, 3,) b. Dec. 13, 1830; m. Dec. 26, 1859, Cordelia Wakeman. She was b. May 22, 1833, and d. July 18, 1888. He d. May 10, 1891.

    4998. i. CORINNE, b. June 19, 1861; m. Jan. 30, 1884, Merritt C. Borst. She d. Dec. 21, 1893, at Jersey City. Ch.: (1) Althea, b. Sept. 16; 1886.

    4999. ii. JULIE ELIZABETH, b. Aug. 3, 1866. Res., New York; unm.

2979¹. GEORGE W. FOOTE, (1496, 557, 185, 53, 16, 5,) b. July 4, 1838, Lafayette, O.; m. Feb. 19, 1860, Ruth A. Green, Independence, O. Architect, Inman Building, Atlanta, Ga.

    4999¹. i. EMMA L., b. Apr. 13' 1861; m. Oct. 31, 1888, Elmer R. Kirk, of Port Clinton, O. Res., E. Pine St., Atlanta, Ga. Ch.: (1) Hazel, b. Mar. 19, 1892, Atlanta, Ga. (2) Dorothy, b. May 11, 1901, Atlanta, Ga.

    4999². ii. CHAUNCEY L., b. June 4, 1866; m. Daisy E. Post, 6191-4.

3300. JUDGE NATHANIEL FOOTE, LL.D., (1826, 754, 235, 73, 25, 9, 3,) b. Morrisville, N. Y., Nov. 15, 1849; m. Rochester, N. Y., Jan. 10, 1872, Charlotte Ann, dau. of James C. and Jeanette M. (Armitage) Campbell. She was b. Rochester, N. Y., May 18' 1849. He was baptized about 1858 by Rector of Christ Church, Sherburne, N. Y. Educated at the Morrisville Union School, Cazenovia Seminary, Cazenovia, N. Y., and Hamilton College, Clinton, N. Y., Class of 1870. Studied law in the office of his father at Morrisville, N. Y., and admitted to the bar as attorney and counsellor-at-law at Binghampton, N. Y., Dec. 8, 1870; m. Jan. 10, 1872, at St. Paul's Church, Rochester, N. Y., by the Rev. Israel Foote, D. D., to Charlotte A. Campbell, dau. of James C. Campbell and Jeanette M. Armitage. practised law at Morrisville, N. Y., with John E. Smith, Esq., under the firm name of Smith & Foote, until July, 1873. Removed to Rochester, N. Y., July, 1873, and engaged in the practice of law in that city until Jan. 2, 1905. On that date was appointed by the Governor Justice of the Supreme Court of New York to fill a vacancy for one year. Elected a Justice of the Supreme Court, Nov., 1905, for a full term of 14 years, and is now serving as such in the Seventh Judicial District of the State of New York. Was a delegate to the New York State Constitutional Convention in 1894, which prepared the revised Constitution adopted by vote of the people in Nov. of that year, served as Chairman of the Committee on Revision and Engrossment, member of the Committee on the Judiciary, Privileges and Elections and Civil Service. Was elected first President of the Rochester Bar Association on its organization in 1892, re-elected the following year. Member of the New York State Bar Association, Rochester Bar Association, Rochester Historical Society, American Society of International Law, National Geographic Society and American Institute of Civics. Episcopalian; Vestryman of St. Paul's Church, Rochester. Hamilton College conferred the degree of LL.D., June, 1907.

5000. i. NATHANIEL FREDERICK, b. Nov. 3, 1872; m. Mabel Norton Toole, 7000.
5001. ii. FRANC ESTELLE, b. Jan. 13, 1875.
5002. iii. LOUISE KNOX, b. Sept. 24, 1877; m. Rochester, N. Y., Apr. 7, 1906, John Colegate Jessup, Jr. Ch.: (1) John Knox Jessup, b. at Rochester, N. Y., Mar. 5, 1907.
5003. iv. CHARLOTTE CAMPBELL, b. June 24, 1881; m. Rochester, N. Y., June 2, 1906, Jerome Babcock Chase.
5004. v. OLIVIA JEANNETTE, b. Feb. 5, 1886.

3301. ARTHUR ASA FOOTE, (1826, 754, 235, 73, 25, 9,) b. Morrisville, N. Y., Oct. 18, 1851; m. June 13, 1877, Kate C., dau. of Alfred C. and Eusebia N. Lewis. She was b. July 29, 1858. He, after receiving an academic education, entered the Albany Law School, N. Y., and in 1874 graduated and commenced the practice of law at Morrisville, N. Y., where he still res.
5005. i. MILLIE ALTHIA, b. June 20, 1878; m. Sept. 3, 1901, Clifford Stark, of Elutira, N. Y. Ch.: (1) David Foote, b. June 2, 1902. (2) Lewis Clifford, b. June 30, 1903.
5006. ii. LEWIS ARTHUR, b. Nov. 19, 1879.
5007. iii. ETHEL KATE, b. Oct. 22, 1881.
5008. iv. ROBERT NATHANIEL, b. Dec. 9, 1883; d. Aug. 24, 1895.
5009. v. LEON LAENTES, b. Feb. 28, 1888.

3302. ORLANDO KNOX FOOTE, (1826, 754, 235, 73, 25, 9,) b. in Morrisville, N. Y., May 12, 1854; m. June 2, 1887, Hattie Adella, dau. of William and Jane Elsie Burgess, of Rochester, N. Y. She was b. May 15, 1858. He was educated at Cazenovia Seminary, Cazenovia, N. Y., and at the Massachusetts Institute of Technology, Boston, Mass., where he graduated in the course of architecture. He was engaged about five years with some of the leading architectural firms in New York and Boston, and is now senior member of the firm of Foote & Headley, architects, Rochester, N. Y.
5010. i. EDWARD BURGESS, b. July 23, 1889.
5011. ii. HAROLD POOLE, b. July 1, 1892.
5012. iii. ALICE KNOX, b. Apr. 16, 1896.

3306. J. FOOTE, (1827, 754, 235, 73, 25, 9, 3,) b. Apr. 13, 1854; m. Dec. 15, 1875, Ida F., dau. of Eli R. and Abigail (Wescott) Wescott, by J. L. Barnes, rector of the Church of the Evangelist, at Oswego, N. Y. She was b. May 12, 1853. He is a farmer and keeps a livery stable. Res., Sherburne, N. Y.
5013. i. ASA, b. Sept. 26, 1879.
5014. ii. ELIZABETH, b. Sept. 26, 1879; d. Jan. 5, 1883.
5015. iii. IDA OLIVIA, b. May 11, 1881; d. Jan. 11, 1883.
5016. iv. ALMEDA, b. Dec. 29, 1884.
5017. v. SUSAN MORRISS, b. Nov. 25, 1886.
5018. vi. OLIVIA WESTCOTT, b. Dec. 16, 1889.
5019. vii. IDA HENRIETTA, b. May 19, 1893.
5020. viii. J. WESTCOTT, b. July 4, 1896.

3316. ASA WATSON FOOTE, (1833, 754, 235, 73, 25, 9, 3,) b. Sept. 5, 1867; m. June 1, 1895, Chloe Myrtle Van Horsen, of Willow Springs, Missouri. He operates a farm and saw mill plant. Res., Waldeck, Atkin Co., Minn.
5021. i. NINA MYRTLE, b. Mar. 10, 1896.
5022. ii. ASA ERNEST, b. Sept. 15, 1897.
5023. iii. GLEN HAZEL, b. Oct. 25, 1898.

5024. iv. ROBERT HOWARD, b. Mar. 8, 1900.

5025. v. FRANCIS ERTLE, b. Oct. 20, 1903.

5026. vi. WELLS BURTON, b. Nov. 24, 1906.

3327. HENRY WORTHINGTON FOOTE, (1844, 765, 73, 25, 9, 3,) b. Haver-straw, N. Y., June 15, 1852; m. Nov. 25, 1879, Ella P. Woodward, of Royalton, N. Y. He studied Law. Res., San Diego, Cal.

    5027. i. LESLIE FRANCES, b. Middletown, N. Y., Aug. 26, 1880; m. San Diego, Cal., May 21, 1901, John Rumsey Barrows. Res., Los Angeles, Cal. Ch.: (1) Eleanor Woodward, b. San Diego, Cal., June 5, 1902.

    5028. ii. FRIEDA PHILENA, b. Helena, Montana, Nov. 25, 1884; m. San Diego, Cal., Nov. 30, 1904, James Lincoln Chapman, of National City, Cal. He is a civil engineer. Res., Kenosha, Wis.

    5029. iii. DORIS WOODWARD, b. Helena, Montana, Oct. 13, 1889. Res., San Diego, Cal.

3330. FREDERICK FOOTE, (1865, 774, 241, 73, 25, 9, 3,) b. Pittsfield, N. Y., May 23, 1851; m. Turnersville, Texas, Dec. 30, 1885, Mary Ann Young. She was b. July 8, 1861; dau. of William Ewing Young and Mary Jane Caulfield; b. on shipboard, parents emigrating from Ireland. He was educated in the School of Industrial Science, Worcester, Mass. Res., Turnersville, Texas. Ch. all b. at Turnersville, Texas.

    5030. i. FREDERICK, b. Jan., 1888.

    5031. ii. CLARENCE DEAN, b. Dec. 25, 1888.

    5032. iii. RUBY MAE, b. Dec. 27, 1890.

    5033. iv. HAZEL EVELYN, b. Oct. 12, 1892.

    5034. v. ADRIAN, b. Jan. 22, 1895.

    5035. vi. NATHANIEL, b. Mar. 10, 1901.

3332. HENRY J. FOOTE, (1865, 774, 241, 73, 25, 9, 3,) b. Pittsfield, N. Y., Jan. 23, 1857; m. Cora Elizabeth Cutter, Ashland, Mass., June 27, 1892. She b. Nov. 13, 1858; dau. of Elam Cutter and Myra Elizabeth Bell. Res., Ashland, Mass. Ch. all b. Ashland, Mass.

    5036. i. GLADYS MYRA, b. Oct. 12, 1892.

    5037. ii. EDITH LOUISE, b. June 19, 1895.

    5038. iii. KATHERINE, b. Dec. 23, 1897.

    5039. iv. RAYMOND HENRY, b. June 9, 1901.

3343. GEORGE WARD FOOTE, (1879, 783, 244, 74, 25, 9, 3,) b. Cincinnati, O., June 16, 1852; m. June 16, 1879, Margaret Gilsen Moore, of Cleveland, O. Res., 34 Bull St., Newport, R. I.

    5040. i. JOHN TAINTOR, b. Mar. 29, 1880; m. Ada Bridge Curtis. Res., Mt. Vernon, Knox Co., O.

    5041. ii. HAROLD GODWIN, b. Aug. 6, 1881. Res., Cleveland, O.

    5042. iii. KENNETH MOORE, b. Dec. 10, 1885. Res., Cleveland, O.

3345. ROBERT DUNMONT FOOTE, (1879, 783, 244, 74, 25, 9, 3,) b. Cincinnati, O., July 19, 1862; m. Madison, N. J., July 7, 1866, Marie Gilmour, dau. of Henry Hopkins. She was b. Apr. 27, 1864. He was educated in Europe and Harvard University. Mr. Foote is a banker. Res., Morristown, N. J.

    5043. i. MARIE NATALIE, b. Oct. 23, 1887.

    5044. ii. ALICE DUNMONT, b. Aug. 25, 1891.

    5045. iii. MARIANNE LATHROP, b. Nov. 10, 1895.

5046. iv. ROBERT DUNMONT, Jr., b. July 30, 1898.

5047. v. JOHN TAINTOR, b. July 31, 1902.

3348. DANIEL ELISHA FOOTE, (1890, 798, 247, 76, 25, 9, 3,) b. Otselic, N. Y., Apr. 7, 1828; m. July 19, 1853, Martha Elizabeth, dau. of William B. and Nancy (Morse) Up De Graff (sometimes written Up De Grove), of Newark Valley, Tioga Co., N. Y. She was b. Vestal, Broome Co., N. Y., June 14, 1830. He studied medicine and surgery with Dr. Frederick Hyde, of Cortland, N. Y., and graduated from the University of Buffalo in 1851. In 1852 he went to Newark Valley, N. Y., where he remained until 1854, when he removed to Belvidere, Ill. He is a member of the Ill. State Medical Society and also of the American Medical Association. Res., Belvidere, Ill.

    5048. i.. STELLA ELIZABETH, b. Belvidere, Ill., May 24, 1856; m. Jan. 28, 1885, Edwin William, son of Henry and Rebecca Warren, of Belvidere, Ill. He was b. Akron, N. Y., Sept. 4, 1856. He is a farmer and res. on the farm formerly owned by his father. She is a graduate from Rockford Seminary (now Rockford College), in Rockford, Ill. Res., Belvidere, Ill. Ch.: (1) Frederick Foote, b. Feb. 10, 1886. (2) Daniel Edwin, b. Feb. 11, 1887. (3) Henry Russell, b. May 10, 1890. (4) Arthur Richard, b. Jan. 9, 1892.

    5049. ii. HARRIET LOUISA, b. Belvidere, Ill., May 5, 1859; m. Apr. 3, 1907, David Dickey Sabin, of Belvidere, Ill.

    5050. iii. MARY IRENE, b. Belvidere, Ill., Nov. 13, 1866.

3351. SAMUEL ISAAC FOOTE, (1890, 798, 247, 76, 25, 9, 3,) b. Smyrna, N. Y., Sept. 16, 1834; m. 1st, Electa Sutphen; m. 2nd, June 18, 1868, Laura Augusta, dau. of Deacon John Wales Redington, of Norwich, N. Y. About 1865 Mr. Foote settled in Norwich, N. Y., where he continued to live until 1883. During his residence there he filled some of the town offices, and was for many years a Deacon in the Congregational Church. In 1883 Mr. Foote removed with his family to Scranton, Pa. During his residence in Scranton Mr. Foote was a Ruling Elder in the First Presbyterian Church of that place. Mr. Foote d. June 22, 1896. He led a quiet life, respected by all and loved by his many friends and especially by little children. Mrs. Foote was b. at Lawyersville, N. Y., May 9, 1845.

    5051. i. ARTHUR R., b. May 7, 1870; m. Emma W. Burns, 7021.

3352. ISAAC FOOTE, (1893, 798, 247, 76, 25, 9, 3,) b. Otselic, N. Y., Mar. 4, 1834; m. Oct., 1854, Gratey Brand. She d. July, 1859; m. 2nd, Sept. 12, 1885, Minnie Barry, of Nashua, N. H. Res., Chanute, Kan.

    5052. i. ARTINNRIA, b. Sept. 18, 1855; m. Robert Murry, of Syracuse, N. Y. Ch.: 4.

    5053. ii. SAMUEL ISAAC, b. Sept. 19, 1857; d. Dec., 1863.

    5054. iii. EVA N., b. Aug. 18, 1886; m. Elmer Sherman, of Neodesha, Kan. Ch.: (1) Victor.

    5055. iv. COL. GANE, b. Mar. 11, 1888, Superior, Mich.

3353. CHARLES HENRY FOOTE, Jr., (1893, 798, 247, 76, 25, 9, 3,) b. Sherburne, N. Y., July 4, 1836; m. 1855, Lucy Adalaid Bennett, at Oswego, Ill. She d. Jan. 28, 1907. He d. June, 1905, in El Paso, Texas.

    5056. i. HATTIE L., b.

    5057. ii. CHARLES H., b.

3354. EBENEZER HYDE FOOTE, (1893, 798, 247, 76, 25, 9, 3,) b. Howard, Steuben Co., N. Y., July 15, 1838; m. 1870, Ada Knapp, of Sycamore, Ill. She d. Jan. 29, 1893, at Wymore, Neb. Res., Beatrice, Neb.

5058. i. JESSIE, b. Jan. 29, 1873, Beatrice, Neb.; unm.
5059. ii. ISAAC, b. Feb., 1879; m. Lillie McRight, 7022.
5060. iii. LULU M., b. Jan. 29, 1878, Beatrice, Neb.
5061. iv. ELIZABETH, b. May 29, 1881, Hanover, Kan.
5062. v. PURL LEVAN, b. Jan. 6. 1883, Wymore, Neb.

3368. ALBERT EDWARD FOOTE, (1901, 799, 247, 76, 25, 9, 3,) b. Hamilton, N. Y., Feb. 6, 1846; m. Jan. 11, 1872 Augusta,, dau. of Hon. James Mathews, of Knoxville, Ia. He prepared for college at Cortland Acad., Homer, N. Y., and graduated from the University of Michigan in 1867 with the degree of M. D. He was deeply interested in natural history, especially in botany and mineralogy. On graduating, he had won so high a rank in his scientific studies that he was chosen out of a large class as assistant in the University laboratory. From this position he was called, in a year, to the Professorship of Chemistry in the Iowa State College at Ames, Iowa. Here he remained as a successful instructor for five years, with the exception of one year spent in Europe, under leave of absence, when he studied chemistry under the celebrated Hoffman in Berlin. In 1875 he removed to Philadelphia, Pa. Here he turned his attention to mineralogy as a business in connection with that of dealing in scientific books. In the development and prosecution of this work his services to science were many and important. His explorations after minerals extended to all parts of America and to many foreign countries. He was one of the most widely known representatives of the science of mineralogy in this country. Contributions from his pen were published in the leading scientific journals. Mrs. Foote res. in Philadelphia. Dr. Foote d. Oct. 10, 1895, at Atlanta, Ga.

5063. i. WARREN M., b. Dec. 27, 1872; m. Florence W. Grugan, 7032-3.
5064. ii. LYRA ADELAIDE, b. Ames, Ia., June 5, 1874; d. St. Louis, Mo., Dec. 23, 1875.
5065. iii. ALBERT EDWARD, b. Philadelphia, Pa., Jan. 27, 1877.
5066. iv. GENEVIEVE AUGUSTA, b. Philadelphia, Pa., Nov. 18, 1880.

3372. DR. WILLIAM KELLOGG FOOTE, (1903, 799, 247, 76, 25, 9, 3,) b. Belvidere, Ill., Apr. 17, 1871; m. May 19, 1897, Ella Josephine Downing, of Belvidere, Ill. She was b. June 16, 1873. They settled in Joliet, near Chicago, Ill., where they res. until 1905, when they moved to Omaha, Neb. Dr. Foote graduated from Medical College in 1893, with highest honors; soon afterwards became a lecturer, and later Professor in the Chicago Homeopathic Medical College, which position he honorably filled until he moved to Omaha.

5067. i. FRANCES ESTHER, b. July 11, 1900.

3374. JOHN CROCKER FOOTE, (1905, 801, 247, 76, 25, 9, 3,) b. Hamilton, N. Y., Sept. 20, 1841; m. New York City, Apr. 24, 1867, Helen, dau. of Judge Samuel Bostwick and Julia Maria (Mitchell) Garvin, of New York City. She was b. Utica, N. Y., Jan. 18, 1847. Is a graduate of Miss Wadleigh's 12th St. School, of New York City, and is a member of the Society, D. A. R. He graduated from Madison (now Colgate) University in 1864. He is a merchant. Is a member of the Ill. Society of Sons of the Revolution, of the Mo. Society of Colonial Wars, of the N. Y. Society of Founder and Patriots of America, of the Ct. Society of Mayflower Descendants, and of the Society of Pilgrim John Howland of the Mayflower. He res. in Hamilton, N. Y., until Sept., 1869, when the family moved to Belvidere, Boone Co., Ill.

5068. i. MARY HELEN, b. Hamilton, N. Y., Apr. 11, 1868; m. Belvidere, Ill., July 21, 1897, by Rev. George R. Pierce, D.D., to Rev. Harry

Edward Purinton, of Chicago, Ill. He was b. Cuba, N. Y., Dec. 23, 1867; graduated from Colgate University in 1894 and from Theological Department of Chicago University in 1897. Has preached in Denver, Col., and Marquette, Mich. In 1905 was Pastor of Presbyterian Church at Victor, Col. She attended Belvidere High School and Rockford Female College. Is a member of the Society of Mayflower Descendants and the Society of the D. A. R. Ch.: (1) Raymond Foote Purinton, b. Denver, Col., Nov. 17, 1898.

5069. ii.   MARIA GARVIN, b. Belvidere, Ill., Sept. 21, 1870; attended Waterman Hall Female Seminary. Is a member of the Society of the Mayflower Descendants and of Society of D. A. R. Was m. in Belvidere, Ill., June 22, 1905, to Alfred A. Engstrom. He attended North Western University, and is a member of the firm of Engstrom Brothers, Rockford, Ill.

5070. iii.   FLORENCE ANNETTE, b. Belvidere, Ill., Oct. 24, 1875; m. Belvidere, Ill., June 12, 1901, by Rev. Harry Edward Purinton, to Prof. Ebenezer Washington Engstrom.   She graduated from Belvidere High School and attended Northwestern University. Is a member of the Society of Mayflower Descendants and the Society of the D. A. R. He graduated from the Northwestern University, and has filled the chairs of English, Elocution and Oratory in Dakota University, and at Albion College, Albion, Mich. Res., Evanston, Ill. Ch.: (1) Helen Wilhelmina Engstrom, b. Albion, Mich., Aug. 9, 1902.

5071. iv.   JOHN GARVIN, b. Belvidere, Ill., Feb. 7, 1877; m. Hampshire, Kane Co., Ill., July 2, 1901, by Rev. Harry Edward Purinton, Mary Adeline, dau. of B. T. Watrous.

John Garvin Foote was a graduate of Belvidere High School, and also attended Colgate University (his father's "Alma Mater"). He left college in the Junior Collegiate year. After leaving college he completed a course in banking, and was for a while with Merchants Loan and Trust Company Bank, Chicago, Ill. On account of ill health he left the bank, and later went to Phoenix, Ariz. He reached his home in Belvidere, Ill., from Phoenix, Ariz., on the evening of May 16, 1903, and d. at his home about one o'clock in the morning of May 17. He was a young man of sterling qualities, as George R. Pierce, D. D., said of him: "Never was memory fairer, purer, sweeter, more precious, than of this son, brother, husband, friend." He was a member of the Society of Mayflower Descendants and of the Society of Sons of the Revolution.

Amid beautiful flowers and in the sunshine of a perfect summer day, the funeral services for the late John G. Foote were held at his parents' home. A large company of friends filled the house, while many others stood upon the lawn. Prayer was offered by Rev. Mr. Brittin. Rev. Geo. R. Pierce, D. D., read the Scripture and spoke. Dr. Pierce had been Mr. Foote's pastor for seven years.

He spoke as follows: Friends and neighbors, it is borne in upon me, that we are each and all gathered in this home to-

No. 3374

John Brocker. Foote

JOHN GARVIN FOOTE. No. 5071

day, asking ourselves a question, as old as grief; the question
that underlies all our little life,—the question, Why? No voice
from the blue immensity about us has ever answered that heart-
breaking cry, going up since men were; so we, like the men of
old, go on seeking reasons, when Death comes for the young, the
fair, the good. They, those pagan men of old, said reverently in
their tears, "The Gods loved him. It was their love that took
him from the stress of this world to the violet carpeted peace
of their immortal glory." We in our bewilderment, forgetting
that he who is prepared to die is most well equipped to live, say,
"He was prepared," and we repeat the cry of Job: "The Lord
gave, and the Lord hath taken away; blessed be the name of the
Lord!" And we strain our eyes, trying to read between the
lines of the transcendent vision, which tells us, of "A City, not
made with hands, whose gates of pearl are never closed day or
night, whose light is the Lord, where His servants serve Him,
and see His face, where is neither pain, nor tears, nor parting,
any more."

It has been my privilege to know the son of this home in a
peculiar and intimate way. When I came to Belvidere he was a
slender stripling scarce 17. I went in and out of this house
for nearly four months before I could be settled in the parsonage.
I not only knew his parents, and his grandparents, but I remembered his great grandfather as a notable man in bowery
Hamilton, New York, when I, a boy, went there to enter college.
That great grandfather, by the way, stood for all things that
make for righteousness. How could a man be other than noble,
springing from such a stock? I was the boy's pastor. More, I
was the next door neighbor. A pastor may not know his flock,
but spite of brick, and wood, and walling conventions, we come
to know our neighbors. We know if they be good, if they be
true, and of what stuff their pretentions are made, so across
this stretch of grass between this home and the place I called
home, I watched this young son and brother, and friend, come
and go,—come and go for seven years or more and saw as the
days ran into years the genial, generous, gentle boy become a
genial, generous gentleman. To a fine eye it was enough to see him
with his mother and sisters. To a fine ear it was enough to
hear him addressing the dear home folk, at this house, or at
that other home down the street where dwell the grandparents
and the aunts, who was to him as a second mother.

And beyond this home group were hosts of friends, and one
especially dear with whom the intimacy was close and brotherly,
for this was a symmetrical character, round, full, harmonious,
perfect so far as we know it in every human tie. Refined to
distinction, he was of course reserved, but it was easy to guess
the springs of his actions, and the character of his feelings by
his conduct. So as I stand here, words seem paltry before the
overwhelming bereavement of this home, bereavement so deep
I venture that every parent in Belvidere sympathizes with these
parents and these grandparents, that every wife in Belvidere

feels for this girl wife, for whom long years and many changes will never efface the memory of this moment, and of the two years that have preceded it. When I think of her, and her great love and loss, I am reminded of Shelley's immortal lament, in which he says:

"Out of the day and night,
A Joy has taken flight.
Fresh Spring, and Summer and Winter hour
Move my faint heart with grief,—but with delight,—
No more,—O—never more!"

When I think of his sisters I am reminded of Eugenie de Guerin's wail above the bier of her brother Maurice, "What name so dear as brother!" And always I wonder, what this life might have become had it been as we say "finished" here. That it would have been a joy, a stay, a comfort, it is easy to conjecture. So, friends, is it not easy to believe that in the larger economy of God, this life and power, with others like it, have uses somewhere,—beautiful, necessary, transcendant, beyond our comprehending.

Never was memory fairer, purer, sweeter, more precious, than of this son, brother, husband, friend,—who "Gladly did live, And gladly did die, And laid him down with a will,"—like a good soldier. Up to the last the fine high courage lasted. He reached his father's house we cannot imagine at what cost of weakness, weariness, and will. He looked once more into the dear eyes, then went quietly on to the All Father, at whose City you may be sure he was met and is welcomed, even as he was met and is welcomed here at yonder gate.

Be glad, dear friends, that you, that we, had him so long. Be comforted in that gladness and, believe that in him, the vision is fulfilled; servant of God here, he shall serve Him forever, and he, the dear lad we knew, and love, and miss so sorely, shall see the Master's Face.

3379. FRED ALBERT FOOTE, (1914, 801, 247, 76, 25, 9, 3,) b. July 24, 1864; m. June 16, 1889, Helen L. Soule. She was b. Sept. 27, 1865; d. Nov. 22, 1905. Res., 1464 Broad St., St. Paul, Minn.
5072. i. WALTER MORTEN, b. Nov. 8, 1890; d. Aug. 22, 1899.
5073. ii. LILLIAN ROWENA, b. Aug. 23, 1900.
5074. iii. MARION, b. Apr. 8, 1903.

3381. FRANK ERASTUS FOOTE, (1915, 802, 247, 76, 25, 9, 3,) b. July 13, 1851; m. July 3, 1879, Elizabeth Ewing, of Pittsburg, Pa. She d. Mar. 26, 1886; m. 2nd, May 15, 1887, Mary E. Samberson, of Portland, Oregon. She d. Jan. 4, 1900, at Warrens, N. Y. He was an assayer of great reputation throughout all the Western mining States. He d. Mar. 5, 1889, at Salt Lake City, Utah.
5075. i. FRANK COLLINS, b. Dec. 4, 1880.
5076. ii. ALICE EWING, b. Dec. 2, 1882.
5077. iii. ELIZABETH M., b. Mar. 19, 1886; d. July 27, 1886.

3393. ANDREW WARD FOOTE, Jr., (1930, 811, 248, 76, 25, 9, 3,) b. Oct. 5, 1865; m. Oct. 26, 1892, Winifred dau. of Pitts and Katherine (Thompson) Burt, of Cincinnati, O. Mr. Foote is maker of machinists' machinery; educated in public schools, and entered Pratt & Whitney Co., at Hartford, for "special instruction." Mrs. Foote was b. June 18, 1866. Res., Cleveland, O.

    5078. i. KATHERINE WINIFRED, b. Nov. 18, 1902.

    3398. HARRY WARD FOOTE, (1932, 811, 248, 76, 25, 9, 3,) b. Mar. 21, 1875; m. June 22, 1904, Martha, dau. of William and Katherine (Babcock) Jenkins, of Brookline, Mass. Mr. Foote is a graduate of Sheffield Scientific School, 1895; degree of Ph.D. in 1898, and studied in Leipsic and Munich, Germany, 1898 and 1899; is Assistant Professor Physiological Chemistry in Sheffield Scientific School. Mrs. Foote was b. Oct. 6, 1879. Graduate of Bryn Mawr, 1902. Res., New Haven, Ct.

    5079. i. WILLIAM JENKINS, b. Apr. 27, 1905.

    3424. CHARLES A. FOOTE, (1961, 824, 261, 80, 25, 9, 3,) b. Sept. 10, 1841, Maumee, O.; enlisted in June, 1861, in the 7th Regiment of Infantry of the Michigan Volunteers. He was in the siege of Yorktown, Va.; in the battles of Ball's Bluff, West Point and Fair Oaks. In the last named contest he was left on the field as mortally wounded, but he recovered, and was honorably discharged in 1862. He re-enlisted in the 146th New York Regiment of Volunteers in Aug., 1864. He was in the Fifth Corps during the siege of Petersburg; participated in the battles of People's Farm, Hatcher's Run, White Oaks' Road, Quaker Road, Five Forks, and Appomattox Court House, and was also engaged in the raid to Belfield, and the destruction of 16 miles of railroad. He saw the white flag when it left the Confederate Lines for General Grant's Headquarters. He marched through Richmond and Petersburg to Washington, and was there mustered out at the close of the war, and has since been a farmer at Washington, Ia. He m. Mary E. Lincoln, of Quincy, Ia., Mar. 1, 1866. Res., Corning, Ia.

    5080. i.   CLARISSA FOOTE, b. Feb. 17, 1869, in Washington, Ia.; m. Albert Homan, Dec., 1895. Res., Corning, Ia. Ch., all b. at Corning: (1) Charles F., b. Sept. 7, 1897. (2) Edith M., b. Nov. 8, 1898. (3) Edmund, b. Sept. 16, 1900.

    5081. ii.   MARY MYRTIE, b. May 15, 1870; now a Missionary to Turkey under the American Board. Her present station is Erzroom, Turkey in Asia.

    5082. iii.   ANNA M., b. Feb. 27, 1872; d. Oct. 12, 1877.

    5083. iv.   CHARLES L., b. Apr. 16, 1875, and d. Sept. 16, 1875. The last of a long line of first born sons.

    5084. v.   GEORGE E., b. Apr. 16, 1877; d. Oct. 12, 1877.

    5085. vi.   RUBY T., b. June 19, 1880; d. July 3, 1889.

    5086. vii.   GERTRUDE E., b. Dec. 31, 1881; d. June 29, 1889.

    5087. viii.   LAURA E., b. June 28, 1884; d. June 27, 1889.

    3430. CHARLES B. FOOTE, (1964, 824, 261, 80, 25, 9, 3,) b. June 12, 1850, of Medina, O.; m. Elisabeth McConnell, Oct. 21, 1886. He is an engineer on the Ill. Cent. R. R. Res., Champaign, Ill.

    5088. i.   CHARLES W., b. in Champaign, Feb. 17, 1889; d. Oct. 31, 1890.

    5089. ii.   JOHN HILAND, b. in Champaign, Feb. 1, 1893.

    5090. iii.   RALPH MATTHEWS, b. in Champaign, Nov. 1, 1895.

    3433. FRANKLIN W. FOOTE, (1964, 844, 261, 80, 25, 9, 3,) b. Urbana, Ill., Apr. 15, 1861; m. Oct. 4, 1902, Lulu Jordan, of Waterbury, Ct. He is a news dealer. Res., Urbana, Ill.

    5091. i.   EDITH LOUEVA, b. Urbana, Ill., July 29, 1903.

    5092. ii.   WILLIS BRONSON, b. Urbana, Ill., Oct. 25, 1905.

3437. JOHN S. FOOTE, (1972, 826, 261, 80, 25, 9, 3,) b. Valley Center, Kas., Oct. 2, 1854; m. Dec. 24, 1881, Flora Parker. They lost three ch., dying in infancy. Res., Valley Center, Kas.

    5093. i.   ETHEL L., b. Sept. 19, 1882, Valley Center, Kas.; m. Clarence Woods, 190—.

    5094. ii. GLADYS F., b. Oct. 11, 1889, Valley Center, Kas.

3438. DAN CHARLES FOOTE, (1972, 826, 261, 80, 25, 9, 3,) b. Aug. 30, 1859, of Valley Center, Kas.; m. Anna Wolf, Jan. 7, 1890. She d. July 17, 1902; buried in Elkens, Oklahoma.

    5095. i.   ORLENA ANNA, b. Jan. 18, 1891.

    5096. ii. AMELIA S., b. Feb. 3, 1893.

    5097. iii. CHARLES F., b. Dec. 21, 1894.

    5098. iv. EDNA MAY, b. May 21, 1902.

3439. WILLIAM F. FOOTE, (1974, 826, 261, 80, 25, 9, 3,) b. Apr. 29, 1856, Wade, Jasper Co., Ill.; m. Isadore Clark, Apr. 22, 1880. Res., Champaign, Ill. Ch. all b. in Wade, Ill.

    5099. i.   HARRY, b. Jan. 29, 1881; d. Aug. 16, 1882; buried in Slait Point Cemetery, Jasper Co., Ill.

    5100. ii. RUBEN C., b. Nov. 13, 1882.

    5101. iii. HOMER G., b. Nov. 19, 1886.

    5102. iv. ROSCO B., b. Oct. 8, 1888.

    5103. v.   MABEL C., b. Dec. 12, 1891.

3441. HARVEY C. FOOTE, (1974, 286, 261, 80, 25, 9, 3,) b. May 10, 1863, Wade, Ill.; m. Nettie Bateman, Dec. 22, 1885. She d. Dec. 19, 1886; m. 2nd, Mar. 12, 1889, Agnes Jenkins. Ch. all b. in Wade, Ill.

    5104. i.   DASHIA, b. Dec. 19, 1886.

    5105. ii. ALMA C., b. Jan. 4, 1890.

    5106. iii. ROY H., b. Dec. 23, 1891.

    5107. iv. OLIN M., b. Apr. 8, 1894.

    5108. v.   GRACE W., b. Sept. 17, 1896.

    5109. vi. VERNON R., b. Dec. 10, 189—.

    5110. vii. HARVEY C., b. June 13, 1901.

3448. EDWARD MILTON FOOTE, (1979, 829, 261, 80, 25, 9, 3,) b. Syracuse, N. Y., Feb. 1, 1866; m. Oct. 26, 1899, Caroline B. Cauldwell, of New York. He graduated from the University of Rochester in 1886, and from the Harvard Medical School in 1890. After two years' service in the New York Hospital and two years' study abroad, he took up the practice of his profession in New York at 136 W. 48th St. Is Instructor of Surgery, Columbia University, and Visiting Surgeon, N. Y. City Hospital and St. Joseph's Hospital, N. Y.

    5111. i.   MILTON, b. New York, Nov. 6, 1901; d. July 26, 1902.

3453. RALPH FOOTE, (1982, 831, 261, 80, 25, 9, 3,) b. Athens, Mich., May 2, 1866; m. Jan. 19, 1902, Cora L. Vaughan. Res., Midland, Mich.

    5112. i.   ——.

3479. JOEL LINDSLEY FOOTE, (2019, 859, 273, 81, 25, 9, 3,) b. Feb. 22, 1856; m. Oct. 24, 1889, Ellen, dau. of Aaron James Osmon, of Lima, O. She was b. July 14, 1869. He is a market gardener and a Councilman, of Brooklyn Heights, O. Ch. all b. at Brooklyn, O.

    5113. i.   MILLIE OSMON, b. Oct. 21, 1892.

    5114. ii. JOEL LINDSLEY, b. Sept. 26, 1894.

5115. iii. MABEL ESTELLE, b. Apr. 23, 1896.

5116. iv. AARON JAMES, b. Dec. 13, 1901.

5117. v. KENNETH JEROME, b. Nov. 3, 1906.

3484. CHARLES HENRY FOOTE, (2019, 859, 273, 81, 25, 9, 3,) b. Sept. 21, 1870; m. Sept. 21, 1892, Louise Brainard, of Brooklyn Heights, O. She was b. Apr. 9, 1874. He is marshal of Brooklyn Heights, O., and a market gardener. Ch. all b. at Brooklyn Heights, O.

    5118. i. FLORENCE MARIE, b. July 19, 1893.

    5119. ii. HAZEL HELEN, b. Oct. 27, 1894.

    5120. iii. LOUIS BRAINARD, b. Aug. 18, 1896.

    5121. iv. CLINTON THEODORE, b. May 8, 1898.

    5122. v. WILLARD EDWIN, b. Oct. 29, 1899; d. July 5, 1902.

    5123. vi. FOREST AVERY, b. July 23, 1901.

    5124. vii. CHARLES HUNGERFORD, b. June 4, 1903.

    5125. viii. MYRON EVERETT, b. Feb. 10, 1905.

3485. LLOYD HUNGERFORD FOOTE, (2019, 895, 273, 81, 25, 9, 3,) b. Sept. 12, 1870; m. Sept. 30, 1899, Clara Lucretia, dau. of Asa Hinman, of Brooklyn Heights, O. She was b. Apr. 20, 1876. He is a market gardener. Has served as Road Supervisor and is now a Councilman of Brooklyn Heights, O.

    5126. i. GLADYS EVELYN, b. Brooklyn Heights, O., Oct. 17, 1901.

    5127. ii. ALICE VIOLA, b. Brooklyn Heights, O., May 26, 1904.

    5128. iii. FERN LUCILE, b. Dec. 27, 1906.

3491. EDWIN THOMAS FOOTE, (2024, 895, 273, 81, 25, 9, 3,) b. Cincinnati, O., Nov. 8, 1874; m. May 11, 1898, Mayme Crossen. She was b. Feb. 22, 1878; d. Aug. 14, 1903. Res., Cleveland, O.

    5129. i. FLORENCE MARGUERITE, b. Cleveland, O., Mar. 24, 1899.

    5130. ii. IRENE ESTELLE, b. Cleveland, O., Mar. 25, 1901; d. July 15, 1902.

3501. EDWARD KILBOURNE FOOTE, (2039, 868, 274, 81, 25, 9, 3,) b. Mar. 4, 1857; m. in St. Andrew's Ch., Aberdeen, Scotland, Aug. 30, 1886, Margaret Knight, dau. of John Ingram, of Oldmeldrum, Scotland. Both artists, and res. abroad.

    5131. i. REGINALD CHARLES, b. Sept. 28, 1889; d. Jan., 1890, and buried in Venice, Italy.

3502. CHARLES BOWLER FOOTE, Jr., (2039, 868, 274, 81, 25, 9, 3,) b. June 11, 1859; m. Feb. 6, 1889, Mollie Williams, of Cincinnati, O. Res., Walnut Hills, Cincinnati, O.

    5132. i. ELEANOR WILLIAMS, b. May 31, 1890.

    5133. ii. ELLIS BURDETTE, b. June 17, 1892.

    5134. iii. NATHANIEL, b. Oct. 20, 1894.

    5135. iv. MARY ELLIS, b. Sept. 17, 1900.

3503. EDWARD AUGUSTUS FOOTE, Jr., (2041, 868, 274, 81, 25, 9, 3,) b. Cincinnati, O., Jan. 1, 1869; m. Dec. 28, 1899 Eloise Stettinius Urner, of Cincinnati, O. She d. Aug. 17, 1900, in Cleveland, O.; m. 2nd, Apr. 9, 1904, Mary Hills, of Cleveland, O.

    5136. i. EDWARD ADDISON, b. Cleveland, O., Mar. 19, 1905.

3505. CHARLES EDWARD FOOTE, (2042[1], 874, 274, 81, 25, 9, 3,) b. Dec. 30, 1866, Geneseo, N. Y. Educated at Geneseo Normal School. Stenographer. Epis.

copalian; m. Viola E., dau. of William Smeed. He d. Jan. 6, 1901, Rochester, N. Y. She was b. Nov. 6, 1864. Res., Rochester, N. Y.

 5137. i. EDWARD BARNARD, b. Jan. 26, 1894.
 5138. ii. HOWARD ANSCOMB, b. Sept. 2, 1896.

 3511. JOHN H. FOOTE, (2063, 897, 284, 85, 26, 9, 3,) b. Sept. 18, 1826; m. May 24, 1852, Caroline Rhodes. Res., New York City.

 5139. i. ADELAIDE L., b. May 11, 1856; m. Mar. 12, 1877, Grassett L. Byrnes, of Brooklyn, N. Y. He was b. June 9, 1849. Ch.: (1) John H. Byrnes, b. Brooklyn, N. Y., Nov. 23, 1878; m. Feb. 21, 1903, Elizabeth R. Kenney. She was b. Brooklyn, N. Y., Aug. 20, 1884. Ch.: (a) Thelma Regina, b. Brooklyn, N. Y., Nov. 5, 1903. (b) John H., b. Aug. 3, 1905; d. Aug. 12, 1905. (c) Elizabeth Loraine, b. Aug. 27, 1906.
 5140. ii. ALBERT L., b. Aug. 23, 1863; m. Annie M. Martin, 7063-9.

 3513. JAMES C. FOOTE, (2063, 897, 284, 85, 26, 9, 3,) b. Mar. 5, 1830; m. New York City, July 6, 1858, Eliza Rhodes. Res., Brooklyn, N. Y.

 5141. i. CHARLES ALONZA, b. Brooklyn, N. Y., Aug. 2, 1854; d. Sept. 4, 1859, at Brooklyn, N. Y.
 5142. ii. MINNIE, b. Brooklyn, N. Y., July 31, 1861; d. Nov. 9, 1862, in Brooklyn, N. Y.
 5143. iii. STILL BORN (not named).
 5144. iv. NETTIE, b. Brooklyn, N. Y.; d. Apr. 9, 1865.
 5145. v. COL. JOHN HENRY, b. July 10, 1866; m. at Camp Black, Hemstead Plains, N. Y., May 12, 1898, Hattie L. Silkworth. He served in the war with Spain with the 14th Regiment Infantry National Guard, N. Y., as Captain, and now holds the position of Colonel in the same regiment. Res., Brooklyn, N. Y.
 5146. vi. ANNIE ELIZA, b. Brooklyn, N. Y., Feb. 23, 1869; d. Apr. 8, 1871, in Brooklyn, N. Y.

 3516. ALBERT W. FOOTE, (2063, 897, 284, 85, 26, 9, 3,) b. July 16, 1834; m. Aug. 30, 1858, Josephine Hussey.

 5147. i. ALBERT, b.
 5148. ii. LILLIAN, b.

 3518. GEORGE W. FOOTE, (2063, 897, 284, 85, 26, 9, 3,) b. Oct. 11, 1837; m. Nov. 30, 1864, Elizabeth Werthworth.

 5149. i. FRANK W., b.
 5150. ii. WALTER, b.

 3522. HENRY H. FOOTE, (2083, 919, 290, 85, 26, 9, 3,) b. Jan. 29, 1844; m. North Parma, N. Y., Sept. 29, 1864, Mary E. Lester. She was b. North Parma, N. Y., Sept. 17, 1845; d. May 29, 1884. Res., Gates, N. Y.

 5151. i. J. ADELE, b. Dwight, Ill., July 4, 1865; m. Rochester, N. Y., Oct. 28, 1890, George L., son of Henry M. and Susan (Sargent) Street. Ch.: (1) William S. Street, b. Dec. 12, 1892. (2) Mary E. Street, b. Nov. 22, 1898. (3) George S. Street, b. Feb. 19, 1905.
 5152. ii. CLARA B., b. Albion, Mich., Dec. 10, 1867; m. Rochester, N. Y., June 15, 1893, Frank, son of Adam Bosche. She d. Apr. 24, 1905. Ch.: (1) Clarence E. Bosche, b. Rochester, N. Y., Oct. 11, 1894.

5153. iii. ADDIE, b. Gates, N. Y., Nov. 30, 1869; m. Rochester, N. Y., Dec. 18, 1888, Henry B. Horndorf. Ch.: (1) Lester N., b. Sept. 16, 1889. (2) Elliott, b. Mar. 21, 1891. (3) Hobart, b. Jan. 13, 1896.

5154. iv. BABY, b. Gates, N. Y., Mar. 3, 1872; d. Apr. 27, 1872.

5155. v. ELLEN E., b. Gates, N. Y., Oct. 2, 1873; m. Rochester, N. Y., Sept. 15, 1896, Herman P., son of John Monroe. Ch.: (1) Marion E. Monroe, b. Rochester, N. Y., Apr. 24, 1898. (2) Gladys E. Monroe, b. Rochester, N. Y., Nov. 22, 1901.

5156. vi. VIOLA E., b. Gates, N. Y., Nov. 25, 1875; m. Rochester, N. Y., June 14, 1898, Charles N., son of Geo. C. and Mary (Potter) Clark.

5157. vii. IRA L., b. June 15, 1880; m. Nellie Drury, 7070.

5158. viii. HENRY H., Jr., b. Rochester, N. Y., June 19, 1882. Res., Rochester, N. Y.; unm.

3528. FRANCIS SEELY FOOTE, (2085, 919, 290, 85, 26, 9, 3,) b. Ogden, N. Y., Dec. 7, 1848; m. Brooklyn, N. Y., June 8, 1882, Addie Sarah Jameson. She was b. July 5, 1857. Res., 67 Myrtle Ave., Montclair, N. J.

5159. i. FRANCIS SEELY, Jr., b. Brooklyn, N. Y., Mar. 31, 1883. A graduate of Columbia.School of Mines in Class of 1905.

5160. ii. EDNA AMORY, b. Brooklyn, N. Y., Jan. 30, 1888.

3536. WILLIAM ORSON FOOTE, (2091, 920, 290, 85, 26, 9, 3,) b. Johnson-burgh, N. Y., Apr. 17, 1859; m. Mar. 5, 1882, Nettie E., dau. of Abner L. Matteson, of Manton, Mich. She was b. Avon, O., Mar. 15, 1860. He has held various offices. Merchant, and member of the Board of Education of Traverse City, Mich.

5161. i. WILLIAM REUBEN, b. Manton, Mich., Jan. 16, 1883. Merchant. Res., Traverse City, Mich.

5162. ii. HARRISON CARD, b. Traverse City, Mich., June 17, 1889.

5163. iii. MAURINE VIRGINIA, b. Traverse City, Mich., Oct. 23, 1896.

3540. LUTHER RICE FOOTE, (2094, 920, 290, 85, 26, 9, 3,) b. Aug. 1, 1854; m. New York City, June 2, 1897, by Rev. Edward Huntington Rudd, to May Clapp. He is engaged in the wholesale shoe manufacturing business. Res., 6-8 Woodlawn St., Rochester, N. Y.

5164. i. ELSIE MARGARET, b. Sept. 1, 1898.

3547. IRA ADDISON FOOTE, (2097, 921, 290, 85, 26, 9, 3,) b. Oct. 19, 1861, at Spring Prairie, Wis.; m. Mar. 25, 1886, Retta Long. She was b. at Lone Jack, Mo., Sept. 30, 1860. In 1883 they moved to Simpson,, Kan., where he was engaged in the mercantile and grain business for 22 years; moved to Colorado City, Colo., 1905, engaged in general merchandise business; elected Mayor of that city, 1907. Res., 418 Colorado Ave., Colorado City, Colo. Ch. all b. at Simpson, Kan.

5165. i. FLOYD, b. Jan. 1, 1888.

5166. ii. DONALD FOREST, b. Apr. 11, 1889.

5167. iii. MARK HENRY, b. Jan. 9, 1892.

5167¹. iv. WYBORN, b. Apr. 17, 1899.

3552. LEON RUSSELL FOOTE, (2100, 921, 290, 85, 26, 9, 3,) b. Nov. 22, 1871; m. Butte, Montana, June 27, 1900, Lizzie, dau. of David James Creighton. She was b. Aug. 24, 1878. He is Principal of Beaverhead County High School, Dillon, Montana.

5168. i. LEON CREIGHTON, b. Sept. 23, 1901.

3553. ROY FLETCHER FOOTE, (2100, 921, 290, 85, 26, 9, 3,) b. Jan. 5, 1874; m. Ottawa, Kas., May 26, 1903, Elizabeth Taylor. Res., Colorado City.

5169. i. JAMES HERBERT, b. Mar. 12, 1904.

5170. ii. SARAH MARGARET, b. June 2, 1905.

3555. EPHRAIM JOSIAH FOOTE, (2100, 921, 290, 85, 26, 9, 3,) b. May 8, 1879; m. Asherville, Kas., Oct. 6, 1903, Grace Grecian.

5171. i. ROY EPHRAIM, b. Jan. 18, 1905.

3562. EDWARD FOOTE, (2110, 935, 298, 89, 26, 9, 3,) b. Springfield, Mass., May 7, 1835; m. Jan. 10, 1865, Mary Otis Alger Tyler, of Boston. He was in Co. K, 7th N. Y. Regt., which defended the Capitol at the time of the war. He was a distinguished railroad contractor and a bright business man. He was a very handsome man, and during the Civil War was noted for his beautiful voice, which his dau. inherited. He d. July 27, 1885. Res., New York.

5172. i. MAY DWIGHT, b. New York City, July 12, 1868; m. June 1, 1898, Ten Eyck, son of Benjamin Rush and Margaret Ten Eyck (Burr) Wendell, of Albany, N. Y. He was b. Nov. 7, 1857. Besides her voice, Mrs. Wendell is a composer of children's songs; one of her best being "Visitors," which Mrs. Payne Whitney, dau. of the late Secretary Hay, wrote the words of, for Mrs. Wendell's music. Mrs. Wendell is a member of the Mayflower Society and of the Colonial Dames of America. Res., Cazenovia, N. Y., and Washington, D. C. Ch.: (1) Ten Eyck Wendell, b. Boston, Mass., July 19, 1899.

3563. EMERSON FOOTE, (2110, 935, 298, 89, 26, 9, 3,) b. Springfield, Mass., Apr. 28, 1837; m. Dec. 28, 1863, Margaret Legget, dau. of Judge William M. and Catherine Maria (Legget) Allen, of New York City. Her grandfather was the Hon. Stephen Allen, whose life record is printed in Hunt's "Merchants of New York City." Res., New York City.

5173. i. ALICE, b. Mar. 2, 1867; m. Allan MacDougall, of New York City. Ch.: (1) Gladys, b. Mar. 1, 1891. (2) Allan, b. June 3, 1894. (3) Donald, b. Feb. 26, 1897.

5174. ii. EMERSON, b. Oct. 12, 1876. Res., New York City; unm.

5175. iii. HENRY, b. Jan. 16, 1881. Res., New York City; unm.

3564. HOMER FOOTE, (2110, 935, 298, 89, 26, 9, 3,) b. Springfield, Mass., Dec. 22, 1839; m. Oct. 22, 1863, Catherine C., dau. of John Bailey, of New York. She was b. N. Y. City, June 7, 1844; d. Aug. 26, 1905. Res., Springfield, Mass.

5176. i. HOMER, Jr., b. July 5, 1865; m. Margaret H. Williams, 7071.

5177. ii. RUSSELL STURGIS, b. Dec. 5, 1868.

5178. iii. AUGUSTUS RICHARD, b. Feb. 13, 1872.

3569. JAMES DWIGHT FOOTE, (2110, 935, 298, 89, 26, 9, 3,) b. Springfield, Mass., Feb. 14, 1850; m. New York, N. Y., Oct. 20, 1880, Ellen B. Chandler. She d. May 28, 1886, at 33 E. 37th St., N. Y.; m. 2nd, New York, Apr. 18, 1891, Louise E., dau. of George Burgess. Res., New York.

5179. i. NATHAN CHANDLER, b. New York City, July 27, 1881.

5180. ii. JAMES DWIGHT, b. New York City, May 16, 1886.

5181. iii. VALERIA DEANE, b. New Rochelle, N. Y., Apr. 18, 1891.

3573. JAMES ADONIJAH FOOTE, (2116, 935, 298, 89, 26, 9, 3,) b. Sept. 30, 1860; m. Humboldt, Tenn., Nov. 23, 1886, Ruth, dau. of Dr. James W. Penn.

She was b. Gibson Co., Tenn., Aug. 19, 1862. He was bap. at Rome, Ga., Apr. 8, 1867, by Rev. Wm. C. Williams. Is an Episcopalian. Educated at Eula, Miss., and Springfield, Mass. Is a wholesale grain dealer. Res., Sheffield, Alabama.

5182. i. CLARA MAY, b. Oct. 2, 1887.

5183. ii. HAROLD, b. June 23, 1889.

5184. iii. ROSA, b. Feb. 6, 1891; d. Aug. 20, 1892.

5185. iv. STANLEY, b. Jan. 12, 1893.

5186. v. JAMES ADAIR, b. Mar. 2, 1896; d. Dec. 29, 1898.

5187. vi. FRANCIS PENN, b. Feb. 16, 1901.

5188. vii. EMERSON ADONIJAH, b. Dec. 13, 1906.

4217. JAMES FOOTE, (1820, 942, 298, 89, 26, 9, 3,) b. Feb. 4, 1853, at Chardon, O.; m. Aug. 12, 1879, Nellie Markle. He d. Aug. 30, 1889. Res., Chardon, O.

5189. i. LOU E., b.

3583. EDSON J. FOOTE, (2128, 962, 302, 89, 27, 9, 3,) b. Gainesville, N. Y., Sept. 24, 1863; m. Dora May Eddy. Res., Gainesville, N. Y.

5190. i. GLENN, b. Apr. 25, 1892.

5191. ii. GUY, b. Oct. 23, 1893.

5191¹. iii. ROY, b. Feb. 25, 1899.

3585. HARVEY ELBERT, (2128, 962, 302, 89, 27, 9, 3,) b. Gainesville, N. Y., May 12, 1868; m. Etta Couch. Res., Gainesville, N. Y.

5192. i. HOWARD, b. Oct. 24, 1900.

3595. DR. THEODORE FOOTE, (2138, 982, 308, 92, 27, 9, 3,) b. Dec. 14, 1848; m. Feb. 28, 1877, Laura Genung, dau. of William Lewis and Martha (Sayer) Beakes. She was b. Aug. 28, 1875. Her father was b. Nov. 12, 1824; d. Feb. 26, 1886. Her mother b. May 5, 1835; d. Mar. 14, 1883. A practising physician of Vineland, N. J., for many years.

5193. i. GEORGE WILSON, b. Vineland, N. J., Mar. 29, 1879.

5194. ii. THEODORA, b. Vineland, N. J., Oct. 22, 1893.

3597. GEORGE FRANKLIN FOOTE, (2138, 982, 308, 92, 27, 9, 3,) b. Sept. 23, 1857; m. 1st, New Haven, Ct., May 28, 1878, Charlotte Coffin Selleck; m. 2nd, Aug. 1, 1906, Jeannette Gault. Mr. Foote has been the business manager of Sage College, Cornell University, Ithaca, N. Y., for the past 14 years.

5195. i. EDWARD THADDEUS, b. July 23, 1884. Grad. Cornell, 1906. Electrical engineer; with Cutler Hammer Co. of Milwaukee, Wis.

3612. WILLIAM HENRY FOOTE, (2145, 983, 308, 92, 27, 9, 3,) b. Ogden, N. Y., Dec. 6, 1824; m. Mary Jane, dau. of John Vankirk, of Rome, Oneida Co., N. Y., Sept. 28, 1848. Mrs. Foote was b. May 12, 1831, in Rome, N. Y. Mr. Foote is a farmer and has held various town offices. Res., Nepenskun, Wis.

5196. i. ADELAIDE ARVILLA, b. Dec. 2, 1849; m. Adelbert Warren Pingrey, of Winneconne, Wis., Mar. 11, 1880. He b. Sept. 16, 1850, and now lives in Jenkins, Iowa. Is a farmer. She d. Apr. 19, 1900. Ch.: (1) Mary Adelia, b. June 16, 1882, in Jenkins, Iowa, and m. Frank Runkle, Dec. 20, 1900. He was b. Mar. 26, 1872. Ch.: (a) Harold Adelbert, b. Apr. 18, 1902. (2) William Gary, b. Nov. 6, 1886, in Jenkins, Iowa; living at his father's home. (3) Avis Belle, b. Oct. 8, 1887, in Jenkins, Iowa.

5197. ii. EUCELIA ROXALANA, b. Dec. 1, 1851; m. James Henry
Brewer, Oct. 6, 1874. He was b. June 5, 1846, and is now a
well-to-do farmer in the town of Nepenskun, Wis. Had one son
by a former wife named Jay. Ch. by 2nd wife: (1) Cora Edna,
b. Apr. 22, 1876, in town of Nepenskun, Wis., and m. Aug. 21,
1902, William Michaels, a merchant in Berlin City, who was b.
Sept. 10, 1871. They res. in the city of Berlin, Wis., and have
one ch., Grace Winifred, b. Dec. 5, 1903. (2) Burt Foote, b.
Jan. 25, 1879, in town of Nepenskun, Wis. He has attended
the Agricultural School in the University in Madison.

5198. iii. ARTHUR PERCIVAL, b. Sept. 29, 1854; m. Avis Anna Holt,
7072-5.

5199. iv. ELLA MINERVA, b. Nov. 6, 1856; m. John Kolb, Mar. 23, 1887.
He is a prosperous farmer in town of Nepenskun, and was b.
Jan. 28, 1856. Ch.: (1) John Harrison, b. Apr. 18, 1888. (2)
Edwin Siegel, b. Feb. 21, 1899.

5200. v. EUPHEMA IONE, b. May 10, 1859; d. Mar. 12, 1862.

5201. vi. JENNIE IONE, b. Aug. 13, 1862; m. Will Kolb, Dec. 25, 1889.
He is John's brother, and also a well-to-do farmer in town of
Nepenskun, Wis.; b. Feb. 20, 1863. Ch.: (1) William Earl, b.
Dec. 25, 1894, in Nepenskun, Wis. (2) Carl Arthur, b. Oct. 18,
1900, in Nepenskun, Wis.

5202. vii. WILLIS HENRY, b. Sept. 19, 1867; d. Apr. 26, 1869.

5203. viii. EVELYN RUTH, b. Sept. 10, 1870; d. Jan. 26, 1872.

5204. ix. LUCY BELLE FOOTE, b. Dec. 21, 1872; m. David Henry
Shepardson, Dec. 25, 1895. He was b. Aug. 10, 1873. Graduated from
Oshkosh Normal School, and is now Principal of High School in
Unity, Clark Co., Wis. Ch.: (1) Hugh Albion, b. Oct. 13, 1898,
in Oshkosh, Wis. (2) Kenneth Foote, b. July 29, 1903, in
Nepenskun, Wis.

3616. ALVAN FREEMAN FOOTE, (2145, 983, 308, 92, 27, 9, 3,) b. Wellington, O., Jan. 14, 1835; m. Appleton, Ontagamie Co., Wis., Jan. 25, 1859, Martha
Love, dau. of Frederick Augustus Jewett. She was b. Waukesha, Wis., Mar. 4,
1840. He is in the bee business, while his oldest son runs the farm. Res.,
Jenkins, Mitchell Co., Ia.

5205. i. ALVAN FRED, b. Nepenskun, Wis., Aug. 5, 1860; d. Oct. 18,
1863.

5206. ii. LUA BELL, b. Nepenskun, Wis., Sept. 12, 1862; d. Mar. 18,
1863.

5207. iii. EDWIN H., b. June 27, 1864; m. Metahbel McRorie, 7076-7.

5208. iv. MYRTIE MAY, b. Nepenskun, Wis., July 2, 1866; m. Feb. 26,
1889, John A. Mason, of Wasioja, Minn. He was b. Jan. 25,
1858. Res., Wasioja, Dodge Co., Minn. Ch.: (1) Berkley Alvan,
b. Wasioja, Minn., Sept. 18, 1891.

5209. v. HARLEY B., b. Feb. 1, 1869; m. Emma E. Millington, 7078-80.

5210. vi. ALICE MABEL, b. Berlin, Wis., Nov. 17, 1874; m. Mar. 8, 1904,
Raymond, son of William Minnis. A prosperous farmer. Res.,
Jenkins, Ia. Raymond, the son, is a farmer also, and they
own and live on a farm near their parents. Ch.: (1) Alice, b.
Jan. 22, 1906.

5211. vii. PERCY BERNARD, b. Jenkins, Ia., May 2' 1884; attends a college in Neb. during the winter, and in summer he works for his brother on the farm.

3619. GEORGE CADY FOOTE, (2146, 983, 308, 92, 27, 9, 3,) b. Lee, Mass., Apr. 18, 1832; m. Jan. 1, 1863, Mary, dau. of Elias Cheney, of Sherbrooke, Quebec, Canada. She was b. Nov. 6, 1843; d. June 9, 1892, in Lee, Mass. He d. Jan. 6, 1892. Res., Sherbrooke, Que.

5212. i. GEORGE SHERRIEL, b. July 22, 1864; d. Feb. 27, 1870, in Sherbrooke, Que.

5213. ii. WILLIAM HENRY, b. Oct. 20' 1867; d. Nov. 25, 1867, at Sherbrooke, Que.

5214. iii. MARIA FOSTER, b. June 27, 1868; m. June 3, 1897, Arthur Chester, son of Dr. Chester Cowles, of Derby Line, Vt. Ch. all b. at Derby Line, Vt.: (1) Edith Marie, b. Apr. 22, 1899. (2) Chester Foote, b. Mar. 30, 1900. (3) George Arthur, b. May 8, 1901.

5215. iv. MARY EDITH, b. Oct. 11, 1871; m. Aug. 15, 1896, Conrad, son of Daniel Upham, of Trmo, Nova Scotia. Ch.: (1) Kent, b. Providence, R. I., Sept. 19, 1901.

5216. v. CHARLES STOCKWELL, b. Mar. 20, 1874; d. July 22, 1874, at Sherbrooke, Que.

3621. HENRY LYMAN FOOTE, (2146, 983, 208, 92, 26, 9, 3,) b. Lee, Mass., July 9, 1837; m. Oct. 2, 1860, Katherine Augusta, dau. of Joel Beruan and Frances (Lovell) Parsons, of St. Louis, Mo. She was b. Sept. 6, 1840. He d. Jan. 8, 1875. Res., Memphis, Tenn., St. Louis, Mo., and Omaha, Neb.

5217. i. MARI LAFLIN, b. Feb. 13, 1862; m. Nov. 24, 1880, James Boyd, at St. Louis. Res., Laramie, Wy.

5218. ii. FRANCES ELLEN, b. June 18, 1865. She has taught school since 1882, in the public schools, part of the time in Mass. Res., Chicago, Ill.

5219. iii. GEORGE HENRY, b. Feb. 27, 1873.

5220. iv. ANNIE PARSONS, b. July 17, 1875; m. 1899, Harry R. Harris. Res., Idaho. Ch.: (1) Mildred Leontine Harris, b. Nov. 29, 1900.

3624. CHARLES NELSON FOOTE, (2146, 983, 208, 92, 26, 9, 3,) b. Dec. 14, 1848; m. Dec. 31, 1874, Alice Belle, dau. of Ralph H. Lathrop, of Rochester, N. Y. She was b. Dec. 18, 1853; d. Mar. 23, 1900; m. 2nd, June 26, 1901, Irene Pearl, dau. of Albert G. Morey, Esq., of La Grange, Ill. He is a farmer, occupying the old homestead of his ancestors at Lee, Mass. Was Town Clerk of Lee for many years and a member of the State Legislature of 1889. Has also held various town offices and positions in local organizations.

5221. i. CLARA AMELIA, b. Jan. 14, 1876.

5222. ii. RALPH MARSHALL, b. Apr. 6, 1877; d. Apr. 7, 1879.

5223. iii. JENNIE ALICE, b. Sept. 15, 1881.

5224. iv. LEON CHARLES WINTHROP, b. June 17, 1890.

3630. GEORGE LUCIUS FOOTE, (2152, 988, 309, 92, 27, 9, 3,) b. Troy, N. Y., Apr. 23, 1843; m. Apr. 25, 1870, Martha Littleton, who was b. Delaware, Dec. 18, 1844.

5225. i. GEORGE L., b. Feb. 3, 1871; m. Grace Bunnell, 7081.

5226. ii. FLORENCE MAY, b. Brooklyn, N. Y., Feb. 8, 1874; m. Oct. 5, 1892, Joseph H. Swan, of Brooklyn, N. Y. Ch.: (1) Edith.

5227. iii. GRACE LITTLETON, b. Aug. 20, 1876, Brooklyn; unm.
5228. iv. FRANK MILLER, b. Brooklyn, Sept. 15, 1880; unm.
5229. v. EDMUND WILLARD, b. Sept. 15, 1880, Brooklyn; unm.

3631. THEODORE MARSHALL FOOTE, (2152, 988, 309, 92, 27, 9, 3,) b. at Stockbridge, Mass., July 19, 1844; m. Mary Emma, dau. of Robert Graves Mesick, of Brooklyn, N. Y., Oct. 15, 1874. Mr. Foote is an advanced inventor and electrical engineer. Res., Brooklyn, N. Y., and Boston, Mass.
5230. i. THEODORE M., Jr., b. Jan. 16, 1876; m. Alfa M. Price, 7082-3.
5231. ii. EMMA LURA, b. Rutherford, N. J., July 28, 1881.

3634. CHARLES B. FOOTE, (2158, 992, 309, 92, 27, 9, 3,) b. Rochester, N. Y., Jan. 31, 1855; m. Feb. 15, 1883, Fannie E. Graves, of Page Co., Va. He is a hardware dealer at Stanleyton, Va.
5231¹. i. BEULAH ESTELLE, b. Feb. 15, 1884; d. at Stanleyton, Va.
5232. ii. HARRY AURISS, b. July 9, 1886.

3641. HERBERT P. FOOTE, (2173, 997, 311, 92, 27, 9, 5,) b. Denmark, Mich., May 4, 1860; m. Dec. 25, 1882, Mary Seinsath, of Tiffin, O.
5233. i. FRANK E., b. Apr. 28, 1883.

3649. CORWIN THOMAS FOOTE, (2175, 997, 311, 92, 27, 9, 3,) b. Apr. 11, 1847, at Dover, O.; m. Feb. 8, 1870, Clara May Cotton, of Sheffield, O. She was b. Jan. 12, 1854. Res., "The Oaks," Lorain, O.
5234. i. LOTTA T., b. Amherst, O., Apr. 13, 1873; m. Sept. 15, 1897, Frank Lovejoy, machinist. Res., Lorain, O.
5235. ii. ROBERT S., b. Amherst, Sept. 26, 1875; m. 1904. Res., Los Angeles, Cal.
5236. iii. CAROLINE A., b. Amherst, July 19, 1877; m. Nov. 25, 1899, Arthur Berge, farmer. Res., Toledo, O.
5237. iv. ALICE LEONE, b. Amherst, Sept. 29, 1884; m. Sept. 1, 1904, Roland Davis, shoe dealer. Res., Elyra, O.
5238. v. GEORGE W., b. Amherst, June 29, 1886. Res., Goldfield, Nev.
5239. vi. TEMPERANCE R., b. Amherst, Mar. 6, 1888. Res., Lorain, O.
5240. vii. GERALD THOMAS, b. Lorain, O., Jan. 19, 1891. Res., Lorain, O.

3654. LORIN SEELY FOOTE, (2177, 999, 311, 92, 27, 9, 3,) b. La Porte Co., Ill., Sept. 25, 1854; m. Aug. 11, 1878, Sadie Mari, dau. of Ferdinand Trace. She was b. Crawford Co., Penn., Sept. 19, 1855. He was educated in the Normal School, St. Cloud, Minn. Is a stockman, ranchman and butcher. Res., Minot, N. D.
5241. i. ETHEL MAY, b. Dec. 19, 1881; d. Sept. 8, 1882.
5242. ii. LEROY ALBERT, b. Sept. 9, 1882.
5243. iii. MABEL EVLYN, b. Jan. 30, 1884; m. May 10, 1906, William, son of Chris. Tiller.
5244. iv. HAROLD LORIN, b. Apr. 4, 1887; d. Apr. 12, 1887.
5245. v. MINNIE AGNES, b. June 25, 1888.
5246. vi. STANLEY RALPH, b. July 27, 1890.
5247. vii. JESSIE ADALINE, b. Apr. 18, 1894.
5248. viii. MYRTLE CHARLOTTE, b. Jan. 31, 1895; d. Apr. 19, 1898.

3658. FRANCIS DANE FOOTE, (2177, 999, 311, 92, 27, 9, 3,) b. Melrose, Minn., Aug. 25, 1867; m. Burlington, Ward Co., N. D., Dec. 4, 1885, Annie Lyle, dau. of William L. Miller. He is a contractor, transfer line, livery. Res., San Pedro, Cal.

5249. i. CLYDE HARRISON, b. Gardena, Cal., June 9, 1892.

5250. ii. ETTA MAY, b. Burlington, N. D., May 11, 1900; d. Aug., 1900, in Burlington, N. D.

3662. EUGENE SILAS FOOTE, (2179, 999, 311, 92, 27, 9, 3,) b. Feb 9, 1857, at Blackearth, Wis.; m. Sept. 2, 1880, St. Cloud, Minn., Laura Helen, dau. of Joseph and Joanna Balch (Hill) Stewart, b. at Bellevue, Minn., Oct. 26, 1862. He was a teacher and farmer, lived in Kandiyohi Co., Minn., from 1858 to 1862, and from 1868 to 1875; at St. Cloud, Minn., 1862 to 1868, and 1875 to 1880, and 1883 to 1895; at Belle Prairie, Minn., 1880 to 1883; at Rice, Minn., since 1895. A Republican in politics, a member of Anchor Lodge 178, A. F. and A. M., and Longola Camp 3896, M. W. A. She is a member of Royalton Chapter 111, O. E. S., and Burr Oak Camp 1120, R. N. A. Ch. all b. at St. Cloud, Minn.

5251. i. GUY KAREL, b. Oct. 28, 1883.

5252. ii. PAUL, b. Aug. 4, 1888.

5253. iii. HAROLD STEWART, b. May 25, 1890.

5254. iv. CHARLES EUGENE, b. Nov. 20, 1892.

5255. v. WAITE LOREN, b. July 5, 1895.

3663. CHARLES HENRY FOOTE, (2179, 999, 311, 92, 27, 9, 3,) b. Willmar, Minn., in Kandiyohi Co., May 11, 1859; m. Apr. 28, 1890, at St. Cloud, Minn., Theresa, dau. of John Cutter and Amanda (Korn) Polley. She b. Winnebago, Minn., Jan. 21, 1862. Mr. Foote is a lawyer; lived in Willmar, Minn., until 1862; at St. Cloud, from 1862 to 1868, and from 1878 to 1891; at Harrison, Minn., 1868 to 1878; at Kalispell, Montana, since 1891. A member of Lake Tent 22, K. O. T. M., Kalispell, and B. A. Y. of Kalispell. Unitarian; she Episcopalian, and member of L. O. T. M.

5256. i. DOROTHY, b. Nov. 12, 1891.

5257. ii. EUGENE BARTON, b. Feb. 19, 1895.

5258. iii. JESSIE, b. July 8, 1897.

5259. iv. KATHARINE, b. Jan. 22, 1899.

5260. v. ISABEL, b. July 27, 1900.

5261. vi. HELEN, b. Dec. 22, 1901.

3665. ALBERT A. FOOTE, (2180, 1003, 311, 92, 27, 9, 3,) b. Sept. 10, 1850; m. Sept. 14, 1871, Adelaide M., dau. of William Gibson. She was b. Detroit, Mich., Dec. 6, 1846; d. Sept. 16, 1898, at Clarion, Charlevoix Co., Mich. Episcopalian; m. 2nd, June 3, 1902, Mrs. Delia Smith, dau. of Charley Potvin. She was b. Canada, May 6, 1866. Catholic. He is a millwright. Episcopalian. Res., Randolph, Ind. Ter.

5262. i. ERNEST GIBSON, b. Sept. 1, 1872; d. Mar. 29, 1873.

5263. ii. LOUIS H., b. Sept. 21, 1873; m. Effie C. Culpepper, 7084.

5264. iii. ALBERTA WADE, b. Feb. 2, 1875; m. James, son of Duncan Stewart. He was b. Sept. 3, 1862, in Ontario, Canada. Is an Episcopalian. Res., Germfask, Mich. Ch.: (1) Duncan McDermot Stewart, b. Apr. 1, 1900, in Gulliver. (2) Lachlan McKenzie Stewart, b. Nov. 22, 1902, at Germfask, Mich. (3) James Donald Stewart, b. Aug. 19, 1904, at Germfask.

5265. iv. GRACE ADELAID, b. Dec. 27, 1876.

5266. v. FAETTA LILLY, b. Menominu Co., Mich., Apr. 5, 1903.

5267. vi. ELFREDA, b. Schodercraft Co., Mich., Feb. 9, 1906.

3666. FRANK B. FOOTE, (2180, 1003, 311, 92, 27, 9, 3,) b. Dover, O., June 2, 1852; m. Grandville, Mich., Mar. 2, 1881, Anna M., dau. of John C. Brush. She was b. Byron, Kent Co., Mich., Mar. 17, 1862. He was bap. Allegan, Mich., Mar., 1878, by Rev. Scott. Is an Episcopalian. Lumberman. Res., Grand Rapids, Mich.

5268. i.   LEON L., b. Mar. 5, 1882.
5269. ii. HARTLEY B., b. Feb. 11, 1884.
5270. iii. ALANSON F., b. Feb. 27, 1886.

3667. DR. VARUS R. FOOTE, (2180, 1003, 311, 92, 27, 9, 3,) b. May 9, 1854; m. at Grand Rapids, Mich., July 17, 1877, Rose M., dau. of Owen Narregang, of Rochester, N. Y. She was b. Sept. 22, 1852. He was educated at Chicago College of Medicine, Bennett Eclectia. Res., Wiggins, Miss.

5271. i.   PEARL BERTHA, b. Jan. 28, 1879; m. at Waynesboro, Miss., Jan. 7, 1897, Ward H. Davis. Ch.: (1) Ward Foote Davis, b. Dec. 17, 1897. (2) Josie Pearl, b. July 11, 1900; d. July 6, 1901. (3) John Linton, b. Dec. 3, 1901. (4) Nelda May Davis, b. Oct. 5, 1904.
5272. ii. LINTON VARUS, b. Feb. 7, 1881; m. June 17, 1904, Kate Kremble.
5273. iii. JAMES MONROE, b. Mar. 30, 1884; m. at St. Joseph, Mich., Aug. 14, 1905, Lillian May Congdon.

3668. ERNEST C. FOOTE, (2180, 1003, 311, 92, 27, 9, 3,) b. July 10, 1856; m. Jessie C. He d. She res. with ch. at Palmer, Oregon.

5273¹. i.   LOTTIE B., b.
5274. ii. WALTER C., b.
5275. iii. RAY G., b.
5275¹. iv. NEVA M., b.
5276. v.   BERNEY C., b.
5277. vi. VIRGIL E., b.

3673. CHARLES R. FOOTE, (2182, 1003, 311, 92, 27, 9, 3,) b. St. Cloud, Minn., Dec. 22, 1863; m. Royalton, Minn., Mar. 19, 1896, Mattie Rictor. Ch. all b. at Royalton, Minn.

5278. i.   FERN, b. Oct. 7, 1897.
5279. ii. NORMAN CHARLES, b. May 25, 1899.
5280. iii. PERSIS, b. July 23, 1901.
5281· iv. CONSTANCE, b. Nov. 5, 1903.

3674. ALPHONSO E. FOOTE, (2182, 1003, 311, 92, 27, 9, 3,) b. Lasock, Minn., Nov. 22, 1865; m. Wis., June 26, 1894, Ellen Rictor. Res., Royalton, Minn. Ch. all b. Royalton, Minn.

5282. i.   MATTIE ELLEN, b. July 13, 1895.
5283. ii. MAY LUCILE, b. Sept. 22, 1897.
5284. iii. ALPHONSO EVINGSTON, b. Oct. 16, 1900.
5285. iv. IVAN LEWIS, b. July 19, 1902.
5286. v.   IRENE, b. Mar. 26, 1905.

3675. HENRY P. FOOTE, (2182, 1003, 311, 92, 27, 9, 3,) b. Two Rivers, Minn., July 22, 1867; m. Little Falls, Minn., Mar. 25, 1889, Anna Shambrock. Res., Royalton, Minn.

5287. i.   MYRTLE ELNORA, b. June 2, 1890.
5288. ii. GENEVA HARRIET, b. Aug. 5, 1892.
5289. iii. MILDRED BURRETTA, b. July 12, 1894; d. July 6, 1896.

3679. EDWARD HERBERT FOOTE, (2191, 1008, 312, 92, 27, 9, 3,) b. Lee, Mass., Oct. 13, 1850; m. Sept. 3, 1879, Georgiana Frances, dau. of Elisha Gilman Woodward, of Somerville, Mass. She was b. Somerville, Mass., Apr. 13, 1850. He was a member of the class of 1871, Mass. Inst. Technology, graduating as a civil engineer, which profession he followed about three years and then entered the employ of his father's firm, where he remained as employe and member until the incorporation of the business in 1904, when he retired from active business. Res., Somerville, Mass.

    5290.   i.   HAROLD, b. Aug. 13, 1880; d. Aug. 13, 1880.

    5291.   ii.   MARGUERITE, b. Oct. 23, 1881.

    5292.   iii.   KATHERINE, b. Nov. 27, 1889.

    3683. WILLIAM BRYANT FOOTE, (2194, 1008, 312, 92, 27, 9, 3,) b. Lee, Mass., July 26, 1861; m. Oct. 9, 1889, Mary Louise, dau. of Deacon Henry M. Peirson, of Pittsfield, Mass. She was b. Pittsfield, Mass., Jan. 26, 1861. Res., Pittsfield, Mass.

    5293.   i.   THERON PEIRSON, b. Apr. 26, 1892.

    5294.   ii.   ALBERT PEIRSON, b. Feb. 12, 1894; d. Feb. 14, 1895.

    5295.   iii.   HAROLD PEIRSON, b. Dec. 1, 1895.

    5296.   iv.   EDWARD PEIRSON, b. Apr. 19, 1897.

    5297.   v.   ENSIGN PEIRSON, b. Nov. 16, 1903.

    3687. CLAYTON HUNTER FOOTE, (2196, 1009, 312, 92, 27, 9, 3,) b. Aug. 2, 1863, Rochester, O.; m. Dec. 18, 1889, Maud Cushman, dau. of Nathaniel and Sarah (Cushman) Wentworth. She was b. Mar. 23, 1868, in Canfield, O.; d. Sept. 26, 1897; m. 2nd, Aug. 24, 1904, Anna Elizabeth, dau. of Frank Miller. She was b. Jan. 2, 1874. Wholesale lumber dealer. Res., 1271 E. 114th St., Cleveland, O.

    5298.   i.   FLORENCE MEDORA, b. Apr. 21, 1891.

    5299.   ii.   MARJORIE GRACE, b. Aug. 24, 1893.

    5300.   iii.   MABEL WENTWORTH, b. Dec. 28, 1895.

    5301.   iv.   ELIZABETH MILLER, b. Sept. 19, 1906.

    3703. JAMES C. FOOTE, (2217, 1049, 339, 104, 28, 9, 3,) b. Sept. 25, 1852; m. Fannie Avery, of Preston, Ct. Res., Athol, Mass.

    5301¹.   i.   GRACE A., b.

    5302.   ii.   AMETTA F., b.

    5303.   iii.   WILLIAM, b.

    5304.   iv.   EDITH, b.

    3704. FRED W. FOOTE, (2217, 1049, 339, 104, 28, 9, 3,) b. Nov. 1, 1854; m. Annie King, of Colchester, Ct. He is a Superintendent of the Union Rubber Co., of Providence, R. I.

    5305.   i.   EMMA, b.

    5306.   ii.   CHARLES, b. ———; d. young.

    3706. ALBERT HARRISON FOOTE, (2219, 1049, 339, 104, 28, 9, 3,) b. Jan. 1, 1853; m. Apr. 6, 1881, Ella L. Payson, of Hebron. Res., Colchester, Ct. Lives on the old home farm.

    5307.   i.   FRANK EDWARD, b. May 20, 1891.

    5308.   ii.   ELMER HARRISON, b. Nov. 11, 1893.

    3709. EDWARD ERASTUS FOOTE, (2219, 1049, 339, 104, 28, 9, 3,) b. Sept. 4, 1860, in Colchester, Ct.; m. Oct. 3, 1889, Alice Elizabeth, dau. of Julius and Elizabeth (Mitchel) Hills, of Gilead, Ct. Res., Gilead, P. O., Andover, Ct.

5309. i.   ROBERT ERASTUS, b. May 27, 1891.   Student at Bacon Academy, Colchester.

5310. ii. HELEN ELIZABETH, b. Apr. 7, 1893. Attending school at Manchester, Ct.

5311. iii. ARNOLD CHASE, b. Jan. 25, 1899.

3712. ROGER FOOTE, (2225, 1050, 339, 104, 28, 9, 3,) b. Aug. 29, 1860; m. Res., Colchester, Ct.

5312. i.   ROGER S., b.

5313. ii. IDA M., b.

5314. iii. IRVING W., b.

5315. iv. ETHEL A., b.

3725. JOSEPH FISH FOOTE, (2235, 1069, 347, 105, 28, 9, 3,) b. Aug. 20, 1845; m. Lucy A. Lewis, of Norwich, Vt. He is a mechanic by trade. Res., 301 Locust St., Holyoke, Mass.

5316. i.   WILLIAM L., b. 1881; m. Gertrude Ford, 7085.

3726. EDWARD YOUNG FOOTE, (2235, 1069, 347, 105, 28, 9, 3,) b. June 7, 1850, New Marlboro, Mass. Res., 77 Castle St., Great Barrington, Mass. Printer. Educated at Public School, Great Barrington, Mass.; m. July 4, 1883, Addie F., dau. of Timothy A. Smith, of Becket, Mass. Res., Great Barrington, Mass.

5317. i.   OLIVE BERNICE, b. Dec. 24, 1884.

5318. ii. RUTH MARTHA, b. Aug. 1, 1900.

3730. GEORGE CLARK FOOTE, (2239, 1069, 347, 105, 28, 9, 3,) b. Sept. 1, 1856; m. Lillian M. Chapman. Res., Danielson, Ct.

5319. i.   RUBY C., b. May 26, 1889. Res., Danielson, Ct.

3733. FRANK HOWARD FOOTE, (2240, 1069, 347, 105, 28, 9, 3,) b. Nov. 19, 1852; m. Alice Curtis, who was b. Sept. 26, 1857.

5320. i.   HENRY C., b.

5321. ii. MARY ELIZABETH, b.

3735. CHARLES WARREN FOOTE, (2240, 1069, 347, 105, 28, 9, 3,) b. Dec. 10, 1871, at Mystic, Ct.; m. Sept. 25, 1901, New London, Ct., Mary Avery, b. July 21, 1872. He was educated at Mystic, Ct. Machinist. Congregationalist.

5322. i.   OSCAR AVERY, b. Apr. 19, 1903.

5323. ii. DOROTHY STANTON, b. Aug. 10, 1904; d. Aug. 20, 1904.

5324. iii. JOSEPHINE STANTON, b. July 9, 1905.

5325. iv. CHARLES MORGAN, b. Oct. 10, 1906.

3749. WILLIS S. FOOTE, (2288, 1097, 374, 115, 37, 10, 3,) b. June 17, 1853, Skaneateles, N. Y.; m. July 16, 1877, Lellie L. Taylor, of Auburn, N. Y. Res., Auburn, N. Y.

5326. i.   H. BURDETTE, b. Nov. 26, 1878, Auburn, N. Y.; electrical engineer, with The General Electric Co. at Schenectady, N. Y.

5327. ii. J. FAYE, b. Dec. 22, 1881, Syracuse, N. Y.

5328. iii. LURA M., b. June 24, 1886, Auburn, N. Y.

5329. iv. PAUL A., b. Feb. 27, 1891, Auburn, N. Y.

5330. v.   MARGERY L., b. Feb. 12, 1893, Auburn, N. Y.; d. Aug. 8, 1893.

3754. EDWARD LINCOLN FOOTE, (2290, 1097, 374, 115, 37, 10, 3,) b. June 29, 1860; m. Sept. 7, 1888, Julia Elster, of Niles, N. Y. Res., Skaneateles, N. Y.

5331. i.   WALTER ASA, b. June 30, 1894.

5332. ii. ADDIE LOUISE, b. Mar. 19, 1896.

5333. iii. ELSTER, b. Dec. 6, 1903.

3758. FRANK BENEDICT FOOTE, (2291, 1097, 374, 115, 37, 10, 3,) b. July 31, 1853; m. Emma Marie Abbott. Res., Skaneateles, N. Y., and Scranton, Pa.

5334. i. MYRTIS ABBOT, b. Dec. 10, 1879; Scranton, Pa., and Skaneateles.

3760. FRED GRANT FOOTE, (2291, 1097, 374, 115, 37, 10, 3,) b. Dec. 8, 1863; m. Katherine Rawson. Res., Scranton, Pa.

5335. i. RAWSON WARD, b. Mar. 18, 1886, at Skaneateles.

5336. ii. KATHRYN LOUISE, b. Jan. 29, 1895, at Skaneateles.

3762. OSCAR A. FOOTE, (2293, 1097, 374, 115, 37, 10, 3,) b. Jan. 13, 1844; m. at Catskill, N. Y., Nov. 7, 1872, Rose M. Daratt.

5337. i. DAU., b. ———; d. Feb., 1882.

5338. ii. NORDIE, b. ———; m. 1901, Lewis Adams. She d. Feb. 3, 1906.

3765. OZIAS INSDRO FOOTE, (2293, 1097, 374, 115, 37, 10, 3,) b. Nov. 8, 1848; m. at Rockford, Ill., Oct. 18, 1876, Clara Kilburn; m. 2nd, in Rockford, Jan. 20, 1892, Jeanette P. Bull. He d. Feb. 19, 1896.

5339. i. CAMILLA, b. Nov. 8, 1877; m. Oct. 21, 1897, E. A. Camlin.

5340. ii. MARGARET, b. Nov. 28, 1892.

5341. iii. HELEN, b. Apr. 7, 1894.

3768. CHARLES BENSON FOOTE, (2294, 1097, 374, 115, 37, 10, 3,) b. Feb. 13, 1851; m. Jan. 5, 1887, Edith May Moses. She was b. at Skaneateles, N. Y., 1864. Res., 510 Henick St., Elmira, N. Y.

5342. i. CLARA ADELLE, b. Dec. 9, 1887.

3776. OSCAR DARWIN FOOTE, (2300, 1099, 374, 115, 37, 10, 3,) b. Aug. 31, 1835; m. July 4, 1855, Mindana Eunice, dau. of Ashu Porter and Polly M. Kellogg. Engineer. Res., Port Clinton, O.

5343. i. MIDORA AMANDA, b. at No. Fairfield, O., July 20, 1857; m. Nov., 1877, Benjamin Alepanda Borden, of Elmore, O. Merchant. Ch.: (1) Bertha Lucille, b. at Rocky Ridge, O., Aug. 10, 1878. (2) Alexander, b. Rocky Ridge, Jan. 29, 1883. (3) Howard Kellogg, b. Francis, N. Dak., July 15, 1888. (4) Alice Adelia, b. Rocky Ridge, July 15, 1894.

3778. WILLIAM FRANKLIN FOOTE, (2300, 1099, 374, 115, 37, 10, 3,) b. July 10, 1840; m. Louise Underhill.

5344. i. MARY LOUISA, b. at Cleveland, O.; m. ———. Ch.: (1) Mrs. J. T. Barnum.

5345. ii. ANNA, b. ———; m. ——— Sherwin. Res., 36 Newark Ave., Jersey City, N. J.

5346. iii. LAURA, b. Sept. 29, 1866; m. ——— Boyer. She d. Oct. 1, 1905. Ch.: (1) Blanche, b. July 9, 1882; d. July 9, 1882, Rocky Ridge. (2) Gertrude J., b. Aug. 28, 1883, Rocky Ridge, O.; m. May 29, 1900, A. G. Zimmer, Chicago, Ill. He d. Mar. 23, 1905, at Denver, Col.; m. 2nd, Oct. 14, 1905, J. Jameson. Ch.: (a) George Zimmer, b. Jan. 18, 1902, Chicago, Ill. (3) Grace W., b. Apr. 9, 1889, Ashland, O.; d. Sept. 8, 1889, Ashland, O.

5347. iv. EULETTA, b. Jan. 24, 1875; m. Aug. 4, 1904, at Kenmore, N. Y., Leroy Nathaniel Mattoon. She is a ladies' hatter. Res., 5645 West Lake St., Chicago, Ill.

(31)

3782. EDMUND NOBLE FOOTE, (2309, 1113, 375, 115, 37, 10, 3,) b. East Middlebury, Vt., July 17, 1833; m. Sept. 22, 1856, Harriet Bates, dau. of Milton and Susan Stowell, of Middlebury, Vt. She was b. in Middlebury, Apr. 18, 1830; d. at Rockville, Ct., Feb. 20, 1903. Res., Rockville, Ct.

    5348. i. EDMUND WARNER, b. in Middlebury, Vt., May 18, 1858. Res., Rockville, Ct. He is a newspaper reporter.

–3784. ALLEN RUSSEL FOOTE, (2309, 1113, 375, 115, 37, 10, 3,) b. Apr. 22, 1837; m. July 4, 1857, Helen A. Jenkins. He was a farmer and lived near the old Foote homestead in Middlebury, Vt. He d.

    5349. i. BERTHA JANE, b. May 13, 1861; d. Oct. 13, 1862.

    5350. ii. WILLIAM MANLEY, b. Apr. 3, 1864; m. Marguerite Blume.

    5351. iii. CORA EMMA, b. Mar. 29, 1872; m. July 1, 1891, Henry C. Walker. Res., Middlebury, Vt. Ch.: (1) Faith Grace, b. July 25, 1892. (2) Helen Ruth, b. Dec. 26, 1897. (3) Dorothy Foote, b. Sept. 22, 1902.

    5352. iv. GRACE ANNA, b. June 19, 1876. Grad. Castleton Normal School, and teacher in the Middlebury Graded School; m. July 3, 1907, in New York City, Michael Halpin. He is a graduate of Middlebury College. Res., Middlebury, Vt.

3787. AARON LUCE FOOTE, (2310, 1113, 375, 115, 37, 10, 3,) b. in Kempville, N. Y., Dec. 11, 1834; m. Nov. 17, 1857, Orpha Viola Watson, of Grand Rapids, Mich. She d. Feb. 21, 1900. He d. Feb. 21, 1904. Both at Grand Rapids, Mich.

    5353. i. WILLIE E., b. Apr. 17, 1862; m. Carrie E. Fuller, 7101-3.

    5354. ii. FRANK WALLACE, b. June 11, 1868, at Grand Rapids, Mich., and d. there May 2, 1872.

    5355. iii. LORA V., b. Nov. 28, 1871, at Grand Rapids, Mich.

    5356. iv. ROY J., b. Sept. 23, 1879, Grand Rapids, Mich.

3788[1]. ALLEN RIPLEY FOOTE, (2311, 1113, 375, 115, 37, 10, 3,) b. Jan. 26, 1842; m. Emma L. Hoyte, of St. Louis, Mo. Res., Columbus, O.

    5356[1]. i. ISABELLA SOUTHWORTH, b. St. Louis, Mo.

3789. ELIJAH HEDDING FOOTE, (2311, 1113, 375, 115, 37, 10, 3,) b. Mar. 24, 1845, Olcott, N. Y.; m. June 16, 1869, Frances Amelia Howe, of Ravenna, O. Res., Grand Rapids, Mich. He served two years in the War of 1861-65. Was appointed Commissioner to the Pan-American Exposition at Buffalo, by Gov. Bliss, in 1900. Was appointed on the Board of Managers of the Mich. Soldiers' Home in 1905 by Gov. Warner, and is still on that Board. He is on the Board of Directors of the State Bank of Mich., and a life member and director of the Board of Trade of Grand Rapids, and Secretary and General Manager of the Grand Rapids Chair Co., and President of the Imperial Fur Company, both cf Grand Rapids. Frank Stuart Foote is Secretary and Treasurer and General Manager of the Imperial Fur Co.

    5357. i. FRANK S., b. June 29, 1872; m. Florence E. Zorus, 7104-6.

    5358. ii. WILL HOWE, b. June 29, 1874, at Grand Rapids, Mich.

    5359. iii. IDA CELESTIA, b. July 15, 1883, at Grand Rapids, Mich.; m. June 16, 1904, Louis Seal Reynolds. Res., Grand Rapids, Mich.

    5360. iv. EMMA HOWE, b. Feb. 3, 1885, Grand Rapids, Mich.

3791. WILLIAM WALTER FOOTE, (2313, 1113, 375, 115, 37, 10, 3,) b. May 20, 1815; m. Aug. 11, 1870, in Deerfield, Mich., Amy H. Green. She d. Dec. 16, 1886, in Good Hart, Mich.; m. 2nd, July 27, 1890, in Albion, N. Y., Jane Allison.

5361. i.   THRESSA A., b. Nov. 17, 1871, in Deerfield, Mich.

5362. ii. HERBERT W., b. Deerfield, Apr. 3, 1873; d. June 28, 1896.

5363. iii. GRACE G., b. Deerfield, May 14, 1875; m. Bird W. Glerydum,
            of Petoskey, Mich.

3792. CHARLES HENRY FOOTE, (2313, 1113, 375, 115, 37, 10, 3,) b. Oct.
30, 1844; m. 1866, Maria Rose, of Casseo, Hillsdale Co., Mich. He d. on the railroad 1868, in Osseo, Mich.

5363¹. i.   DAU. Res., Big Rapids, Mich. (1884).

3793. MATTHEW TAYLOR FOOTE, (2313, 1113, 375, 115, 37, 10, 3,) b.
Sept. 6, 1847, in Middlebury, Vt.; m. 1876, at Lansing, Mich., Anna S. Ellsworth,
of Bradford, Pa. She d. Apr. 20, 1902, at Howard City, Mich.

5364. i.   RALPH E., b. Lansing, 1878.

5365. ii. MAUD J., b. 1881, in Kent Co., near Grand Rapids, Mich.; d.
            1891, in Harrison, Tenn.

5366. iii. ALMYEA, b. Big Rapids, Mich., 1882; d. 1886, in Big Rapids,
            Mich.

5367. iv. GRACE M., b. Harrison, Tenn., 1896.

3794. EDWARD RUSSELL FOOTE, (2313, 1113, 375, 115, 37, 10, 3,) b. Aug.
25, 1851; m. 1st, 1872, Alice Agard, of Lansing, Mich. She d.; m. 2nd, ———
Lawrence. Res., Dallas, Texas. Ch. by 1st wife.

5368. i.   IDA, b. in Greenville, Mich.

5369. ii. GEORGE W., b. in Lansing.

5370. iii. LORA, b. in Big Rapids, Mich.

3795. WARREN MILO FOOTE, (2313, 1113, 375, 115, 37, 10, 3,) b. Osseo, Mich.,
Aug. 11, 1855, adopted and named Trude; m. Aug. 2, 1882, Nettie Stetson Parker,
of Portland, Me. On her grandfather's side she was descended from Commodore
Perry. In the winter of 1868 and 1869 he went to Saginaw, Mich., where he lived
until 1901. He graduated from the High School in June, 1877, and for several
years engaged in the business of contractor and builder. After studying
stenography, he went into the office of W. R. Burt, then president of the Home
National Bank, in 1887, where he remained for ten years, working up from
stenographer to bookkeeper and confidential secretary. In 1897 he went into the
fire insurance business for himself, and in 1901 he went to Wausau, Wis., to take
an office position, where he now resides.

5371. i.   EDNA MAUD, b. May 26, 1883; d. Oct. 1, 1892.

5372. ii. WARREN DWIGHT, b. Aug. 10, 1884.

5373. iii. JESSIE ELIZABETH, b. Sept. 7, 1896.

3796. MAJOR STEPHEN MILLER FOOTE, (2313, 1113, 375, 115, 37, 10, 3,)
b. LaSalle, Mich., Feb. 19, 1859; m. Apr. 24, 1889, Sara, dau. of Major John and
Esther (Willing) Brooke, Surgeon, U. S. Army, at Fortress Monroe, Va. Mrs.
Foote is a D. A. R. Major Foote's younger days were spent in the vicinity of
Middlebury, Vt., attending Beeman Academy at New Haven, Vt., teaching school
in Cornwall, and two years at Middlebury College, receiving his appointment to
West Point in 1880. A thorough student and hard worker, he has won several
prizes for essays on modern warfare since entering the army. He graduated from
the U. S. Military Academy, West Point, N. Y., in 1884, and was commissioned
Second Lieutenant in the 4th U. S. Artillery; commissioned First Lieutenant in
the same regiment in 1889; Captain in the 6th U. S. Artillery in 1899; Major,
Artillery Corps, U. S. A., in 1906. Was a Major of the 3rd U. S. Vol. Engineers in

1898-99. Served in the Santiago Campaign in the Spanish War, and served in the Philippine Islands from 1899 to 1901. At present (1907) in command of the Artillery District of New Orleans. Res., Jackson Barracks, La.

    5374. i.   ESTHER WILLING BROOKE, b. Media, Pa., Apr. 8, 1893.

    5375. ii. ELIZABETH LOIS, b. Radnor, Pa., Oct. 1, 1896.

    3798. ARTHUR FOOTE, (2313, 1113, 375, 115, 37, 10, 3,) b. at La Salle, Mich., Feb. 25, 1863; m. Mar. 20, 1890, Jennie Wood. She was b. at Mt. Clemens, Mich., Nov. 26, 1858. Res., Harbor Springs, Mich.

    5376. i.   LETHA IRENE, b. Jan. 20, 1891, in Good Hart, Mich.

    5377. ii. ZOLA, b. May 23, 1900, at Harbor Springs, Mich.

    3802. FREDERICK GUERNSEY FOOTE, (2316, 1114, 375, 115, 37, 10, 3,) b. Mar. 17, 1853, at Buffalo, N. Y.; m. June 9, 1881, Alice Laura Beals, at Galva, Ill. She was b. Oct. 24, 1856. He is in business with the Meriden Cutlery Co., N. Y. City. Res., Ridgefield Park, N. Y.

    5378. i.   MABEL MARY, b. at New York City, Dec. 7, 1883; d. June 7, 1900, at Hackensack, N. J.

    3807. GRAHAM MERRILL FOOTE, (2321, 1115, 375, 115, 37, 10, 3,) b. in Burlington, Ia., Oct. 13, 1856; m. in Burlington, Nov. 9, 1881, Anna W. Joy, of Muscatine, Ia. Res., 225 W. 8th St., Long Beach, Cal.

    5379. i.   SON, b. and d. Feb. 10, 1883.

    5380. ii. GRAHAM MERRILL, b. in Kewanee, Ill., Mar. 17, 1889.

    3821. MARK MAURO STANISLAUS FOOTE, (2326, 1115, 375, 115, 37, 10, 3,) b. Burlington, Iowa, Apr. 15, 1854; m. Oct. 23, 1888, Miza Elizabeth Brenner, of Philadelphia, Pa., who was b. in New Orleans, La., Apr. 5, 1855. He was educated, receiving the degree of Bachelor of Arts, at the University of Notre Dame, Ind., and remained two or three years teaching at the same University, receiving also the degree of Master of Arts. He embraced the faith of the Catholic Church at the University, receiving the name of Stanislaus in baptism. Since then he has followed the profession of accounting, now holding the position of General Accountant of the City Comptroller's Office in Chicago.

    5381. i.   MARGARET MARY FOOTE, b. Chicago, Ill., Feb. 13, 1890; d. Feb. 14, 1890.

    5382. ii. REGINA MARY DORING, b. Chicago, Ill., Aug. 2, 1891.

    5383. iii. CECELIA ELISABETH FLETCHER, b. Chicago, Ill., Oct. 17, 1895.

    5384. iv. MARK ANTONY BRENNER, b. Chicago, Ill., June 9, 1900.

    3824. MOSES LATIMER FOOTE, (2326, 1115, 375, 115, 37, 10, 3,) b. Burlington, Ia., Nov. 21, 1863; m. Dec. 29, 1886, Lillian Raymond Bruns, of Kewanee, Ill. He was educated at the University of Notre Dame, Ind. Engaged in business in Columbus, O.

    5385. i.   PHILIP MAURO, b. Kewanee, Ill., July 18, 1897.

    3848. GEORGE M. FOOTE, (2356, 1124, 377, 115, 37, 10, 3,) b. Fenton, Mich., May 4, 1876; m. Feb., 1898, Myra, dau. of Sarah Gerow (widow), of Fenton, Mich. Res., Flint, Mich.

    5386. i.   HARRY, b. Mar. 17, 1900.

    5387. ii. GEORGIA BERYL, b. Nov. 10, 1901; d. Nov. 3, 1902.

    3850. JOHN RANDOLPH FOOTE, (2357, 1124, 377, 115, 37, 10, 3,) b. Fenton, Mich., Sept. 13, 1857; m. June 26, 1883, Emma C., dau. of Franz Joseph Ludwig, of San Antonio, Texas. Res., San Antonio, Texas.

5388. i. MARY ESTELLA, b. San Antonio, Texas, Apr. 2, 1884; m. at St. Mark's Episcopal Church, San Antonio, Tex., July 2, 1906, to Edward Eiflor, of San Antonio, by Rev. Dean Richardson. Res., San Antonio, Texas.

5389. ii. ELLEN JANE, b. Bay City, Mich., June 20, 1885; d. July 28, 1898, at Grand Rapids, Mich.

5390. iii. WILHELMINA, b. Bay City, Mich., Mar. 17, 1887.

5381. iv. EDNA MARGARET, b. Bay City, Mich., Jan. 26, 1892.

5392. v. ALICE RUTH, b. Slater, Mo., Mar. 2, 1894.

3854. HORACE LEROY FOOTE, (2357, 1124, 377, 115, 37, 10, 3,) b. Fenton, Mich., Mar. 19, 1866; m. May 21, 1890, Alice M., dau. of Isaac Davie, of Grand Rapids, Mich. Res, Grand Rapids, Mich.

5395. i. THOMAS EDWARD, b. Mar. 4, 1904.

3857. DANIEL FOOTE, (2363, 1133, 380, 117, 37, 10, 3,) b. Washington, Mass., Dec. 27, 1825; m. Sarah, dau. of Enoch Hubbard, of Pittsfield, Mass.

5394. i. EMMA, b. May 20, 1856; d. Dec. 24, 1880, at Pittsfield, Mass.

3858. JAMES APPLETON FOOTE, (2363, 1133, 380, 117, 37, 10, 3,) b. Washington, Mass., Dec. 25, 1827; m. Dec. 25, 1855, Roxanna, dau. of Nicholas Mickels, of Cicero, N. Y. She d. Feb. 18, 1867.

5395. i. MILTON J., b. Apr. 29, 1859; d. Aug. 22, 1859.

5396. ii. FANNIE A., b. Pittsfield, Mass., Feb. 26, 1861.

5397. iii. MARY JANE, b. May 19, 1866; d. Jan. 26, 1867.

3865. ANDREW J. FOOTE, (2363, 1133, 380, 117, 37, 10, 3,) b. Dalton, Mass.; m. Ermina, dau. of Henry Brown, of Worthington, Mass. She d. in Pittsfield, Mass.

5398. i. SUSAN, b. Dalton, Mass.; d. Aug., 1885, in Pittsfield, Mass.

5399. ii. WALTER, b. Pittsfield, Mass., 1870. Res., Boston, Mass.

3868. JOSEPH MERRICK FOOTE, (2373, 1133, 380, 117, 37, 10, 3,) b. Pittsfield, Mass., Oct. 1, 1845; m. June 12, 1872, Ellen M., dau. of Peter Goodell, Jr., of Lanesboro, Mass. He is a farmer. Ch. all b. at Pittsfield, Mass.

5400 i. CHARLES NEWMAN, b. Nov. 30, 1874.

5401. ii. JOSEPH EUGENE, b. Nov. 20, 1876.

5402. iii. ADA MARIA, b. Feb. 24, 1878.

5403. iv. ARTHUR JOHN, b. Apr. 28, 1880.

5404. v! EARL BOWEN, b. Mar. 24, 1882.

5405. vi. ALTA BERTHA, b. Apr. 5, 1884.

5406. vii. HERBERT AUSTIN, b. Oct. 14, 1888.

3869. ASAPH SANFORD FOOTE, (2273, 1133, 380, 117, 37, 10, 3,) b. Pittsfield, Mass., May 26, 1847; m. Sept. 8, 1874, Fannie Adeline, dau. of Cyrus Strong, of No. Egremont, Mass. He is a farmer. Res., Pittsfield, Mass.

5407. i. MILTON HOWARD, b. July 22, 1875; m. June 2, 1897, Anna H., dau. of George F. Read, of Pittsfield, Mass. He is a market gardener.

3873. JOHN H. FOOTE, (2381, 1135, 380, 117, 37, 10, 3,) b. Jan. 2, 1849; m. Aug. 4, 1872, Lena Glass. Res., South Bend, Ind.

5407[1]. i. SARAH B., b.

5407[2]. ii. JOHN H., b.

3887. HENRY O. FOOTE, (2395, 1148, 383, 117, 37, 10, 3,) b. July 25, 1850; m. Dec. 31, 1873, Rilla Mills. Res., Granville, Mich.

5408. i. ABBIE I., b. Apr. 20, 1881.

3888. HARLOW H. FOOTE, (2395, 1148, 383, 117, 37, 10, 3,) b. Apr. 3, 1854; m. Jan. 11, 1883, Etta Hooper. Res., Granville, Mich.

5409. i. NELLIE E., b. Mar. 28, 1885.
5410. ii. CHARLES H., b. Dec. 31, 1904.

3892. CHARLES WALTER FOOTE, (2396, 1148, 383, 117, 37, 10, 3,) b. July 13, 1848, at West Rutland, Vt.; m. Jan. 23, 1877, Ida Martilla, dau. of Bryant and Mary E. (Wakefield) Wheeler, at Newport, N. H. She d. Mar. 15, 1900. He d. Mar. 16, 1907. Res., Middlebury, Vt., and Worcester, Mass.

5411. i. HARRY WALTER, b. at Worcester, Mass., Mar. 17, 1878; m. Oct. 24, 1896, Lena Julia, dau. of George and Ellen (Pryor) Brown, at Charlton, Mass.
5412. ii. EDGAR WHEELER, b. at Worcester, Mass., Sept. 20, 1879.
5413. iii. ERNEST W., b. Oct. 9, 1881; m. Mary A. Mahan, 7119-20.
5414. iv. ALBERT WAGNER, b. at Worcester, Mass., Mar. 24, 1884; d. at Worcester, Aug. 10, 1884.

3897. WALLACE HENRY FOOTE, (2400, 1150, 387, 117, 37, 10, 3,) b. June 9, 1853; m. June 5, 1875, Etna Green, of Iowa. Res., Estherville, Iowa.

5415. i. ARTHUR CLYDE, b. Mar. 6, 1876.
5416. ii. GRACIE FIDELIA, b. Mar. 24, 1878; m. Jack A. Cain, Sept. 26, 1900.
5417. iii. WALLACE CLYDE, b. Dec. 31, 1881.
5418. iv. CLAIRE IDEL, b. Nov. 28, 1888.

3899. JOHN CLARK FOOTE, (2400, 1150, 387, 117, 37,10, 3,) b. Sept. 23, 1857; m. Dec. 24, 1877, Kate M. Wenman, of Tompkins, Mich. She d. Nov. 8, 1892; m. 2nd, Dec. 22, 1897, Mrs. Young.

5419. i. FRANK, b. June 7, 1892.

3900. CHARLES HOWARD FOOTE, (2400, 1150, 387, 117, 37, 10, 3,) b. Sept. 26, 1861; m. July 10, 1884, Octavia Frances Saturlee. She d. July 30, 1889; m. 2nd, July 24, 1890, Anna L. Cooper. He was assistant overseer of furnaces; d. Feb. 17, 1907. Res., Delray, Mich.

5420. i. HORACE H., b. Aug. 10, 1885. Res., Delray, Mich.
5421. ii. HARROLD, b. June 26, 1894.
5422. iii. FRANCES L., b. June 14, 1898.

3902. FREDERICK HODGEMAN FOOTE, (2402, 1150, 387, 117, 37, 10, 3,) b. Port Henry, N. Y., Sept. 29, 1854; m. Nov. 7, 1877, Jeanette Armory Chamberlain, of Wyoming, Iowa. He was educated at Yale. Ironmaster. Res., Chicago, Ill.

5423. i. WALLACE PARK, b. Port Henry, N. Y., May 31, 1879; m. Ethel Ada Baldwin, of Decatur, Ill, on Apr. 24, 1906. Grad. Cornell Univ. Followed the iron business.
5424. ii. HILAH REBECCA, b. Port Henry, N. Y., June 23, 1882.
5452. iii. WILLIAM HENRY, b. Port Henry, N. Y., June 9, 1884.
5426. iv. ELSIE, b. Mayville, Wis., Apr. 12, 1889; d. Aug. 14, 1896, at Chicago, Ill.

3904. CHARLES SEWARD FOOTE, (2402, 1150, 387, 117, 37, 10, 3,) b. Feb. 7, 1860; m. June 6, 1891, Mary Cecilia Wentworth, of Strafford, Pa. Grad. Yale, 1883, and Albany Law School, 1885. Member of Assembly, N. J., 1900 and 1901. Lawyer, N. Y. City.

    5427. i. THOMAS WENTWORTH, b. Plainfield, N. J., Mar. 23, 1892.

    5428. ii. ROBERT SEWARD, b. Plainfield, N. J., Aug 17, 1893.

3913. HENRY CRAWFORD FOOTE, (2406, 1150, 387, 117, 37, 10, 3,) b. Feb. 5, 1874; m. Feb., 1898, Evelyn Augusta Williams.

    5429. i. EVELYN AUGUSTA, b. Feb., 1900.

    5430. ii. CHARLES H., b. Dec., 1901; d. Sept., 1902.

3578. KILBOURN M. FOOTE, (2126, 962, 302, 89, 26, 9, 3,) b. Apr. 26, 1849; m. Eva Hurlbert. Res., Harrold, Hughs Co., South Dakota.

    5431. i. FRED A., b.

    5432. ii. PLYRM, b.

    5433. iii. MERLE, b.

    5434. iv. ALICE, b.

    5435. v. FERN, b.

3931. GILES FOOTE, (2458, 1186, 392, 118, 37, 10, 3,) b. July 31, 1843; m. Dec. 5, 1866, Nellie, dau. of Thomas Whitenack, of Mt. Morris, N. Y. She was b. Jan. 13, 1845, at Ovid, N. Y. He is a veteran of the Civil War. Now retired. Res., Philadelphia, Pa.

    5440. i. ALICE MAY, b. at Mt. Morris, N. Y., Aug. 31, 1867.

    5441. ii. EMMA LORENA, b. at Mt. Morris, N. Y., Jan. 12, 1869.

    5442. iii. HAZEL MABEL, b. at Smyrna, Del, June 4, 1873.

    5443. iv. T. LEROY, b. at Juniata, Neb., Jan. 16, 1875.

    5444. v. GILES WESLEY, b. at Juniata, Neb., Apr. 11, 1879. Res., Philadelphia, Pa.

    5445. vi. THERON DEVERE, b. at Harrington, Del., Aug. 5, 1881.

3933. ASA E. FOOTE, (2458, 1186, 392, 118, 37, 10, 3,) b. Sept. 4, 1846; m. Dec. 28, 1870, Lucy Hubbard, of Belvidere, Ill. Mrs. Foote was b. May 27, 1846. Mr. Foote is a farmer and stock raiser.

    5446. i. CHESTER R., b. Dec. 8, 1874; m. Sarah C. Walker, 7121.

    5447. ii. FRANCIS E., b. Dec. 27, 1877; m. Nora E. Caster, 7122.

    5448. iii. JAMES WRAY, b. at Juniata, Neb., Sept. 16, 1880; m. Mar. 28, 1904, Amelia, dau. of Daniel F. Mather. She was b. Alleghany, Va., Nov. 22, 1885.

    5449. iv. HARRIET, b. at Nevada, Mo., Oct. 12, 1882.

    5450. v. NELLIE, b. at Kingsley, Kan., July 7, 1886.

3936. FRANCIS S. FOOTE, (2458, 1186, 392, 118, 37, 10, 3,) b. Feb. 28, 1853; m. Sept. 15, 1882, Nancy Wallace, of Tennessee. She was b. July 15, 1854. Farmer, stock raiser.

    5451. i. GEORGE, b. Sept. 18, 1883; m. Lenna E. Sever, 7123.

3937. GEORGE W. FOOTE, (2458, 1186, 392, 118, 37, 10, 3,) b. Feb. 24, 1862; m. Mar. 16, 1892, Belle, dau. of Milton Burnap, of Mt. Morris. He d. Jan. 15, 1893. Res., Mt. Morris, N. Y.

    5452. i. GEORGE, b. Mt. Morris, N. Y., Apr. 25, 1893.

3912. FRED JARED FOOTE, (2460, 1186, 392, 118, 37, 10, 3,) b. Mt. Morris, N. Y., Feb. 12, 1856; m. Jan. 8, 1878, Mary B., dau. of Darius Ott. She was b. Sept. 20, 1857. Mr. Foote is a farmer and resides on the old homestead settled by his grandfather in 1823-1825.

5453. i. EMMA L., b. Nov. 19, 1879, at Mt. Morris, N. Y.; m. Fred, son of Avery Gardner, Mar. 6, 1895. Ch.: (1) Marie G., b. May 3, 1899. (2) Ethel L., b. Dec. 1, 1900. (3) Mabel B., b. Oct. 9, 1902.

5454. ii. EDWIN C., b. at Mt. Morris, N. Y., Aug. 27, 1881.

3943. CHARLES EDWARD FOOTE, (2460, 1186, 392, 118, 37, 10, 3,) b. Mt. Morris, N. Y., Feb. 9, 1858; m. at Rochester, N. Y., July 21, 1893, Sadie M., dau. of Hugh McCurdy, of Antrim, Ireland. Mrs. Foote was b. Mar. 11, 1868. Mr. Foote is interested as one of the inventors and manufacturers of the Foote Concrete Mixers, Nunda, N. Y.

5455. i. OLNEY JARED, b. Oct. 29, 1904.

3944. CLARENCE ARTHUR FOOTE, (2460, 1186, 392, 118, 37, 10, 3,) b. Mt. Morris, N. Y., May 12, 1860; m. Apr. 16, 1884, Stella M., dau. of Newell Olney, Dalton, N. Y. She was b. at Grange, Alleghany Co., N. Y., Mar. 16, 1861. Mr. Foote is engaged in the lumber business at Mt. Morris, N. Y.

5456. i. OLNEY N., b. at Nunda, N. Y., Mar. 20, 1886.

5457. ii. DORIS EMILY, b. at Mt. Morris, N. Y., Nov. 27, 1887.

5458. iii. LEONE MAY, b. at Mt. Morris, N. Y., Dec. 18, 1892.

3946. FRANK J. FOOTE, (2460, 1186, 392, 118, 37, 10, 3,) b. Mt. Morris, N. Y., June 1, 1868; m. 1st, Sarah Ann, at Mt. Morris, N. Y., Nov. 10, 1889, and 2nd to Harriet, at Mt. Morris, N. Y., Oct. 3, 1905, both daus. of Fred Marsh, Mt. Morris, N. Y. Mrs. Sarah Foote was b. at Mt. Morris, N. Y., Aug. 2, 1871; d. Sept. 24, 1901. Mrs. Harriet Foote was b. Aug. 23, 1869, at Mt. Morris, N. Y. Mr. Foote is engaged in contracting. Res., Nunda, N. Y.

5459. i. RISSA M., b. Aug. 18, 1890; d. Nov. 2, 1890.

5460. ii. MURIEL LOUISE, b. July 14, 1895.

5461. iii. RUTH IRENE, b. Oct. 6, 1898.

3957. BENJAMIN L. FOOTE, (2473, 1190, 396, 118, 37, 10, 3,) b. May 10, 1848; m. J. Adalaide Skimm. Res., Deansboro, N. Y.

5462. i. CARRIE, b.

5462¹. ii. CHARLOTTE, b.

3959. HENRY FOOTE, (2473, 1190, 396, 118, 37, 10, 3,) b. June 28, 1853; m. Emma Burnell.

5463. i. JENNIE, b.

5463¹. ii. HARRY, b.

5464. iii. MILDRED, b.

5464¹. iv. FANNIE WOODS, b.

3963. WILLIAM A. FOOTE, (2473, 1190, 396, 118, 37, 10, 3,) b. July 2, 1850; m. Maria ———, of Williamsport, Pa.

5465. i. WILLIAM A., b.

3974. JOHN W. FOOTE, (2484, 1195, 396, 118, 37, 10, 3,) b. Nebraska City, Neb., Oct. 30, 1860; m. Myrta C. Todd. She was b. Pine Rock, Ill., 1862. Res., Nebraska City, Neb.

5466. i. EARLE, b. May 9, 1890.

3979. CHARLES W. FOOTE, (2487, 1197, 386, 118, 37, 10, 3,) b. Mar. 3, 1872; m. Aug. 21, 1902, at Juniata, Neb., Lena M. Boyd. Mr. Foote is Registrar of Deeds for Adams Co. Res., Hastings, Neb.

5467. i. DOROTHY EVELYN, b. Nov. 13, 1905, at Hastings, Neb.

3981. EUGENE C. FOOTE, (2487, 1197, 386, 118, 37, 10, 3,) b. Sept. 6, 1879, Ayr, Adams Co., Neb.; m. Aug. 29, 1903, at Council Bluffs, Iowa, Besse Ellyn Byrne. He is a graduate of Highland Park College, of Des Moines, Iowa; also of Creighton Medical College, Omaha, Neb., Class of 1905. A practicing physician at Pauline, Neb.

5468. i. EUGENIA CLARE, b. Casey, Iowa, Dec. 19, 1904.

5469. . ii. MERRIE GWENDOLYN, b. Pauline, Neb., Mar. 13, 1907.

3986. GEORGE H. FOOTE, (2489, 1201, 404, 119, 37, 10, 3,) b. Canton, Ct., 1844; m. Oct. 20, 1869. He served three years with an Illinois Regiment in the Civil War. Ch. all b. in Half Day, Ill. Res., Elgin, Ill.

5470. i. GEORGE H., b. Sept. 29, 1874; d. Apr. 20, 1875.

5471. ii. MYRA M., b. June 13, 1876; d. Sept. 27, 1903.

5472. iii. WARREN W., b. Sept. 22, 1877.

5473. iv. BELLE L., b. Aug. 4, 1879; d. Apr. 13, 1883.

5474. v. GEORGE M., b. June 21, 1887.

3987. STANLEY T. FOOTE, (2489, 1201, 404, 119, 37, 10, 3,) b. Canton, Ct., 1848; m. 1878, Frances Hertel, of Half Day, Ill.

5475. i. CHARLES H., b. Half Day, Ill., Sept., 1879.

5476. ii. DORA M., b. Half Day, Ill., May 17, 1886.

3988. FRANK H. FOOTE, (2489, 1201, 404, 119, 37, 10, 3,) b. Canton, Ct., 1850; m. 1897, Martha Wilson, of Half Day, Ill. Res., Half Day, Ill.

5477. i. CORA, b. 1900.

5478. ii. VIOLA, b. 1902.

5479. iii. LEOLA, b. 1904.

3989. JOHN MARTIN FOOTE, (2489, 1201, 404, 119, 37, 10, 3,) b. Canton, Ct., 1853; m. Apr. 27, 1887, Anna Wells, of Half Day, Ill. After completing his education he taught in the public schools of Half Day, Ill., for a number of years. He then became a partner with his brother, Stanley T., in the grocery and provision business in Half Day, Ill. He became one of the leading citizens of the town, holding the office of Treasurer of the Schools for ten years, Supervisor for eight years, and was also Town Clerk for several years. On being elected County Treasurer of Lake Co., he was obliged to remove to Waukegan, the county seat, where he d. Apr. 27, 1901, during his second term as Treasurer of the County.

5481. i. LELA E., b. Half Day, Ill., Jan. 8, 1891.

3992. JOHN MILLS FOOTE, Jr., (2492, 1201, 404, 119, 37, 10, 3,) b. Canton, Ct., Jan. 12, 1858; m. Oct. 12, 1882, Helen Annetta Stanley, of West Hartford, Ct. He received his education in the public schools of West Hartford and the West Hartford High School. After leaving school he was associated in business with his father until 1888, when he was appointed a Deputy Sheriff for Hartford County, which office he has held continuously, his present term expiring in June, 1911. In 1882, he was appointed a constable of his town, which office he has held continuously since. In 1885, he was appointed Tax Collector of the town of West Hartford, and he has held this office continuously since. He was a Messenger in the House of Representatives, in 1891 to 1905. He has been a State Deputy Game and Fish Warden, and Fish and Game Warden for Hartford County, since 1890. In fraternal circles he is a Knight Templar and a thirty-second degree mason, becoming a mason in 1879, the year he reached his majority. Is a member of the Masonic Veteran Association of Ct., and also a member of the order, Nobles of the Mystic Shrine. Ch. all b. in West Hartford, Ct.

    5482. i. EDWARD MILLS, b. Oct. 25, 1885.
    5483. ii. ELLIOTT STANLEY, b. Apr. 20, 1889.
    5484. iii. HELEN SELDEN, b. May 30, 1892.

    3998. HOWARD WILCOX FOOTE, (2497, 1202, 404, 119, 37, 10, 3,) b. Aug. 31, 1856, at Cambridge, Md.; m. Nov: 9, 1880, Josephine Ross. She was b. May 1, 1862, in Brooklyn, N. Y.

    5485. i. SHIRLEY, b. Aug. 10, 1881.
    5486. ii. LAUREL ROSS, b. Feb. 17, 1884.
    5487. iii. MARGUERITE HOWARD, b. Sept. 18, 1887.
    5488. iv. FREDERIC LE BARON, b. Oct. 2, 1894.
    5489. v. KENNETH, b. Aug. 22, 1897; d. May 23, 1898.

    3999. CLARENCE FOOTE, (2497, 1202, 404, 119, 37, 10, 3,) b. Mar. 23, 1862, at Orange, N. J.; m. Oct. 6, 1886, Carrie Burt. She was b. July 6, 1867, at Orange, N. J. He is cashier of the Greenwich Bank, New York City.

    5490. i. CLARENCE RUSSELL, b. June 5, 1889.
    5491. ii. HAROLD EUGENE, b. Oct. 2, 1895.

    4014. HUBERT TOWNSAND FOOTE, (2502, 1203, 404, 119, 37, 10, 3,) b. Saratoga Spr., N. Y., Jan. 18, 1859; m. May 29, 1884, Annie Elroy Thomas, of New Haven, Ct.

    5492. i. ELROY BERTHA, b. New York City, Dec. 11, 1886; m. June 13, 1906, John Colby Winch. Res., 126 N. Ave., New Rochelle, N. Y.
    5493. ii. IRENE, b. New Rochelle, N. Y., Apr. 7, 1892.

    4019. JOHN WILLARD FOOTE, (2516, 1212, 405, 119, 37, 10, 3,) b. Lodi, Wis., Jan. 26, 1853; m. Oct., 1882, Martha Hyslop, of Vienna, Wis. Now living at Redondo, Cal.

    5494. i. JOHN ROBERT, b. Mar. 13, 1889, at Pasadena, Cal.
    5495. ii. AGNES MARTHA, b. Feb. 2, 1894, at Fall River, Kansas.

    4021. FRANK FISHER FOOTE, (2516, 1212, 405, 119, 37, 10, 3,) b. Lodi, Wis., June 23, 1860; m. May, 1888, Lizzie McDonald, of Arlington, Wis. He d. Oct. 30, 1894. Widow lives at Lodi, Wis.

    5496. i. FRANK McDONALD, b. Mar. 21, 1889, at Racine, Wis.
    5497. ii. LAURA MABEL, b. Aug. 19, 1892, at Racine, Wis.; d. 1905, Lodi, Wis.

    4024. FRANK ARTHUR FOOTE, (2517, 1212, 405, 119, 37, 10, 3,) b. Austinburg, O., Mar. 25, 1856; m. 1st, May 15, 1895, Julia DeLong; m. 2nd, July 12, 1900, Jessie Foster. Now living in Pasadena, Cal.

    5498. i. LUTHER, b. Mar. 13, 1897, Los Angeles, Cal.
    5499. ii. JOHN ARTHUR, b. Mar. 6, 1905, Pasadena, Cal.

    4026. CHARLES BENEDICT FOOTE, (2523, 1219, 415, 126, 38, 11, 3,) b. Bridgeport, Ct., Oct. 26, 1846; m. East Somerville, Mass., July 7, 1874, Abbie Maria Bigelow. Res., Evanston, Ill.

    5500. i. SIDNEY BIGELOW, b. May 28, 1875; m. Sept. 6, 1906, Julia, dau. of C. M. Schenck, of Denver, Col. Mrs. Foote was b. June 21, 1876, at Burlington, Ia. Res., Denver, Col.

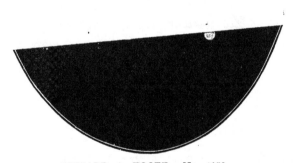

EDWARD A. FOOTE. No. 4059

the year he reached his majority. Is a member of the Masonic Veteran Association of Ct., and also a member of the order, Nobles of the Mystic Shrine. Ch. all b. in West Hartford, Ct.

    5482. i.   EDWARD MILLS, b. Oct. 25, 1885.
    5483. ii. ELLIOTT STANLEY, b. Apr. 20, 1889.
    5484. iii. HELEN SELDEN, b. May 30, 1892.

    3998. HOWARD WILCOX FOOTE, (2497, 1202, 404, 119, 37, 10, 3,) b. Aug. 31, 1856, at Cambridge, Md.; m. Nov. 9, 1880, Josephine Ross. She was b. May 1, 1862, in Brooklyn, N. Y.

    5485. i.   SHIRLEY, b. Aug. 10, 1881.
    5486. ii. LAUREL ROSS, b. Feb. 17, 1884.
    5487. iii. MARGUERITE HOWARD, b. Sept. 18, 1887.
    5488. iv. FREDERIC LE BARON, b. Oct. 2, 1894.
    ~~5489.~~ ~~—~~ KENNETH, b. Aug. 22, 1897; d. May 23, 1898.

186
Ora

5493 — Irene, married 1st Vernon Castle Blythe. As Mr and Mrs Vernon Castle they achieved a notable success as dancers. He was a Captain in the Air Service in the World War and was killed when his plane fell Feb 15, 1918. She married 2nd, May 3, 1919 to Capt Robert Elias Tremain, of Ithaca, New York. They were divorced at Paris July 23, 1923 and she married 3rd, Nov 28, Maj. Frederic McLaughlin, of Chicago. She now (1929) lives.

Sai
Ne·

Wi
at

W: *by J.W. Sherborne J. 1-4-1929*

Oct. 30, 1894. Widow lives at Lodi, Wis.

    5496. i.   FRANK McDONALD, b. Mar. 21, 1889, at Racine, Wis.
    5497. ii. LAURA MABEL, b. Aug. 19, 1892, at Racine, Wis.; d. 1905, Lodi, Wis.

    4024. FRANK ARTHUR FOOTE, (2517, 1212, 405, 119, 37, 10, 3,) b. Austinburg, O., Mar. 25, 1856; m. 1st, May 15, 1895, Julia DeLong; m. 2nd, July 12, 1900, Jessie Foster. Now living in Pasadena, Cal.

    5498. i.   LUTHER, b. Mar. 13, 1897, Los Angeles, Cal.
    5499. ii. JOHN ARTHUR, b. Mar. 6, 1905, Pasadena, Cal.

    4026. CHARLES BENEDICT FOOTE, (2523, 1219, 415, 126, 38, 11, 3,) b. Bridgeport, Ct., Oct. 26, 1846; m. East Somerville, Mass., July 7, 1874, Abbie Maria Bigelow. Res., Evanston, Ill.

    5500. i.   SIDNEY BIGELOW, b. May 28, 1875; m. Sept. 6, 1906, Julia, dau. of C. M. Schenck, of Denver, Col. Mrs. Foote was b. June 21, 1876, at Burlington, Ia. Res., Denver, Col.

EDWARD A. FOOTE.　No. 4059

TRUMAN SHERMAN FOOTE. No. 4060

5501. ii. EDNA BIGELOW, b. June 8, 1878. Res., Evanston, Ill.

4047. CHARLES MERRITT FOOTE, (2531, 1223, 418, 126, 38, 11, 3,) b. Sept. 21, 1872; m. Jan. 30, 1895, Grace Jellife, of New York, N. Y.

5502. i. STUART MORRELL, b. Oct. 8, 1895.

4049. HENRY GOULD FOOTE, (2532, 1223, 418, 126, 38, 11, 3,) b. May 22, 1874; m. Jan. 8, 1902, Jessie Margaret, dau. of John Henry Queal, of Minneapolis, Minn. He spent his early days in Bridgeport, Ct., graduating from the High School in the Class of 1893. Was a prominent member of Masonic and Odd Fellows' Lodges of that city. In the year 1899 he entered business in Boston,. Mass., but soon after moved to the West. Is President and General Manager of the H.. G. Foote Lumber Co., wholesale and retail lumber dealers of Minneapolis, Minn. Mrs. Foote was b. at Ames, Iowa, Sept. 24, 1880.

5503. i. JANE QUEAL, b. Oct. 11, 1904.

5504. ii. HENRY GOULD, b. Mar. 16, 1906.

4057. ISAAC NEWTON CHARLES FOOTE, (2542, 1225, 419, 128, 38, 11, 3,) b. Highgate Spr., Vt., Sept. 16, 1847; m. Sept. 14, 1887, Grace Elizabeth, dau. of James Johnson, of Louisville, Ky. She was b. Louisville, Ky., Sept. 30, 1850. He is a machinist and tool sharpener. Is at the head of the saw, tool and belt department of the Kentucky Wagon Manufacturing Co. at Louisville, Ky., which position he has held for over twenty years. Ch. all b. in Louisville, Ky.

5505. i. EDITH FLORENCE, b. Nov. 9, 1888.

5506. ii. MURRY KOSIOL, b. July 10, 1890.

5507. iii. RUTH GILLETTE, b. Jan. 24, 1893.

4059. EDWARD ASHBEL FOOTE, (2543, 1229, 421, 128, 38, 11, 3,) b. New Haven, Ct., Nov. 27, 1869; m. Helen Adams, dau. of William Henry Payne, of Sag Harbor, Long Island, N. Y., Sept. 5, 1898, in New York, N. Y. Mrs. Foote was b. Aug. 20, 1875.

Mr. Foote spent his early boyhood days in New Haven, Ct., where he. was educated. He was exceedingly public-spirited and was foremost in any movement or enterprise for the public good. He was one of the organizers of a volunteer fire company in Westville, Ct., a suburb of New Haven, and his unceasing efforts in any enterprise in which he took part were not spared until the coveted end had been gained. During his business career his name was a guarantee of sound business principles, justice and integrity, as was his father's before him, in whatever connection it was used.

Mr. Foote resided in New Haven until Sept. 5, 1898, when he started for the West. He went to Albert Lea, Minn., where he took charge of the city lighting plant, but finding the opportunities for a young man more extensive in a mercantile way, he purchased a laundry plant in that city, which he conducted successfully. Wishing to extend his field, he sold the plant in Albert Lea in Oct., 1903, and purchased a laundry plant in Fairmont, Minn., which he conducted until his death, Nov. 23, 1904. Mr. Foote d. a comparatively young man, and was buried in New Haven, Ct. He was prominent in fraternal affairs, having been a member of the Knights of Pythias, Elks, Woodmen of the World, and several other organizations.

5508. i. EDWARD ASHBEL, b. in Albert Lea, Minn., Nov. 17, 1902.

4060. TRUMAN SHERMAN FOOTE, (2543, 1229, 421, 128, 38, 11, 3,) b. New Haven, Ct., June 11, 1871; m. Feb. 17, 1897, Georgia, dau. of Capt. John Aaron and Georgianna Hayden Hardy, of New Haven, Ct. She was b. New Haven, Ct., Dec. 2, 1868. Res., 51 Fountain St., New Haven, Ct.

5509. i. TRUMANIA, b. Fair Haven, Mass., June 21, 1906.

4088. EDWARD J. FOOTE, (2574, 1244, 432, 130, 39, 11, 3,) b. Jan. 25, 1858; m. Oct. 10, 1888, S. Luella Bayley. Res., Tonica, La Salle Co., Ill.
5510. i. JAY W., b. Feb. 20, 1890.
5511. ii. CELIA JANETTE, b. June 20, 1892.
5512. iii. ELMER B., b. Apr. 15, 1896.
5513. iv. RALPH, b. June 12, 1899.

4093. ROBERT VICTOR FOOTE, (2584, 1247, 433, 130, 39, 11, 3,) b. Brooklyn, N. Y., Sept. 21, 1851; was adopted by Jason Parker, of Woodbury, Ct., and thereafter known as Parker. He m. June 5, 1884, Juliette A. Hitchcock, dau. of George Hitchcock, of Woodbury, Ct. Mrs. Parker was b. in Woodbury, Ct., Mar. 23, 1854.
5514. i. HERBERT FOOTE, b. Naugatuck, Ct., Feb. 12, 1886.
5515. ii. ESTHER ELIZABETH, b. Naugatuck, Ct., Apr. 21, 1889.
5516. iii. MARION LOUISE, b. Naugatuck, Ct., Jan. 24, 1893.

4102. JAMES LENOX WINFIELD FOOTE, (2587, 1247, 433, 130, 39, 11, 3,) b. Brooklyn, N. Y., Dec. 17, 1847; m. May 10, 1871, Jane E., dau. of John Tallman Areson, of Brooklyn, N. Y. She was b. Jamaica, L. I., June 27, 1844. Mr. Foote received his elementary education at a private school in Woodbury, Ct., and Williston, Vt., afterwards reading law with Judge George Reynolds, of King's Co., N. Y., when he was admitted to the Bar, May 20, 1872, and practiced law in New York and Brooklyn. He was a man of strong personality, a devoted husband and father, and greatly beloved by his family and friends. He d. Mar. 21, 1902, at Brooklyn, N. Y. Mrs. Foote res. at Brooklyn, N. Y.
5517. i. LOUISE EVERETT ARESON, b. Brooklyn, N. Y., Oct. 28, 1873; m. Feb. 8, 1898, William Wallace Walsh, Jr., of Brooklyn, N. Y. He was b. Elizabeth, N. J., Nov. 2, 1871. Res., Brooklyn, N. Y.
5518. ii. JOHN VAN WYCK, b. Brooklyn, N. Y., Oct. 6, 1877; d. July 6, 1878, in Red Oak, Ia.
5519. iii. ALICE, b. Brooklyn, N. Y., Dec. 17, 1882; d. Dec. 21, 1882, in Brooklyn, N. Y.

4104. CHARLES PHILO FOOTE, (2487, 1247, 433, 130, 39, 11, 3,) b. Brooklyn, N. Y., Sept. 7, 1856; m. Saratoga, N. Y., July 23, 1896, Alida Edna Loucks. She was b. Sharon, Ct., 1874.
5520. i. EARL VAN WYCK, b. Marion, Ct., Apr. 15, 1898.

4105. EDWARD FRANKLIN FOOTE, (2587, 1247, 433, 130, 39, 11, 3,) b. Brooklyn, N. Y., Dec. 3, 1858; m. Cohoes, N. Y., Sept. 18, 1883, Susan Maud Billings. She was b. Bergen, N. J., Jan. 3, 1861. Res., Goshen, Orange Co., N. Y.
5521. i. PAULINE MAY, b. Brooklyn, N. Y., Sept. 27, 1886.
5522. ii. EDITH FRANCES, b. Brooklyn, N. Y., Apr. 16, 1892; d. Mar. 12, 1893.

4110. GEORGE ALEXANDER FOOTE, (2589, 1248, 433, 130, 39, 11, 3,) b. July 24, 1839; m. Martha Ann, dau. of Dea. Homer Clark. He has held many of the town offices and represented the town of Charlotte in the General Assembly at Montpelier, Vt. Had care of the poor farm and inmates at Charlotte, in Charlotte Center. He did successful business in a store several years. At the death of his sister, Celinda, he moved to Charlotte village, to care for his sister, Flora, and now res. there in comfortable retirement.

JAMES LENOX WINFIELD FOOTE.   No. 4102

JAMES A. FOOTE.   No. 4115

ALFRED H. FOOTE.   No. 4114

5523. i. DARWIN O., b. May 6, 1862; m. Florence G. Gove, 7144-6.

5524. ii. PEARLY ELI, b. Aug. 5, 1879; d. May 5, 1893.

4111. CHARLES M. FOOTE, (2591, 1248, 433, 130, 39, 11, 3,) b. Aug. 6, 1828. He was a Private in the 8th Minn. Infantry. Marched with Sherman to the sea; m. ——. Res., Preston, Minn.

5525. i. NELLIE, b. ——. Res., Preston, Minn.

4112. SIMEON FOOTE, (2591, 1248, 433, 130, 39, 11, 3,) b. Jan. 22, 1832, in N. Y. State, and d. at Orion, Minn., Nov. 25, 1876; m. ——. Served in 2nd Minn. Vols. Res., Orion, Minn.

5526. i. PHILANDER H., b. Jan., 1859; m. Susie E. M. Foster, 7147-52.

5527. ii. JOSEPH C., b. Sept. 15, 1862; m. Geneva Wilkins, 7153-4.

5528. iii. FLORENCE AMELIA, b. ——; m. Earnest V. Lombard, at Chatfield, Minn. Res., Lake City, Minn. No ch.

5529. iv. SAMUEL E., b. ——; m. Annabel McGill, 7155.

5530. v. MARY L., b.

5531. vi. CHARLES W., b.

4113. IRA FOOTE, (2591, 1248, 433, 130, 39, 11, 3,) b. Apr. 22, 1835; m. 1857, Sarah M. Thompson. Res., West Union, Iowa.

5532. i. HENRY, b. 1858; m. Clara Henderson, 7156-63.

5533. ii. JOHN C., b. 1860; m. 7164-7.

5534. iii. SYLVESTER, b. 1862; m. 7168-70.

5535. iv. MINNIE, b. 1864; m. 1883, —— Shroud. Ch.: (1) Laken, b. 1886. (2) Grace, b. 1895.

4114. ALFRED H. FOOTE, (2591, 1248, 433, 130, 39, 11, 3,) b. Apr. 22, 1840. He was First Lieutenant, Company A, Brackette Battalion, Minn. Cavalry. Mustered out, May, 1866, at which time he was holding the position of Ordnance Officer of the District of the Upper Mo., at Sioux City, Ia.; m. June 7, 1866, Rebecca J. Stowe. She d. May 3, 1872; m. 2nd, June 29, 1874, Luella Sweet. He is now Clerk of the District Court, Washington, Kansas.

5537. i. HARRY E., b. Feb. 20, 1867, Preston, Minn.; m. Feb. 14, 1906, in Greenleaf, Kansas, Thressa Mans.

5538. ii. HATTIE E., b. Sept. 6, 1869, Preston, Minn.; m. June 22, 1893, W. H. Springle. Res., Seattle, Wash.

5539. iii. CHARLES E., b. Jan. 3, 1877, Washington; m. Feb. 6, 1895, Minnie Barber.

5540. iv. DANFORD E., b. Dec. 10, 1879, Washington; m. Oct., 1903, Clara Paradise, at Concorda, Kansas.

5541. v. LAWRENCE E., b. July 18, 1888, Washington, Kansas.

5542. vi. FLORENCE E., b. July 18, 1888, Washington, Kansas.

4115. JAMES A. FOOTE, (2591, 1248, 433, 130, 39, 11, 3,) b. Chatfield, Ohio, Feb. 19, 1843. Moved with parents to Mt. Carroll, Ill., in 1852; to Chatfield, Minn., in 1855, in which state he res. until Oct., 1902; m. Oct. 21, 1869, Lucinda B. Fox, a school teacher, of Pike, Wyoming Co., N. Y. Ch. all b. at Anoka, Minn. He was First Lieutenant, Co. H, 1st Regiment Minn. Heavy Artillery, in Civil War. Was converted in 1865, while attending Pike Seminary, N. Y., and joined Baptist Church. Filled positions of Senior Bible Class teacher, Trustee, and Secretary to Trustees. Belongs to First Baptist Church, Pasadena, Cal. Also, in 1860, left his father's home at Chatfield, Minn., and went to Preston, Fillmore Co., and attended school until he enlisted. Res., Pasadena, Cal.

5543. i.   ARTHUR MERTON, b. Mar. 14, 1873.

5544. ii. WILLIS DE WITTE, b. Feb. 15, 1876; m. Mamie Fendly, 7171-2. 7173.

5545. iii. RAYMOND HAWLEY, b. June 19, 1879.

5546. iv. JESSIE ADELLA, b. Feb. 22, 1881; d. June 19, 1901.

4117. MYRON GALE FOOTE, (2599, 1249, 433, 130, 39, 11, 3,) b. Potsdam, N. Y., Aug. 9, 1839; m. 1866, Marcua C. Hepburn. She d. May 15, 1890. He worked on a farm with his father in N. Y. until about 21 years of age, when he left for California. He became a mechanical and mining engineer, and through his proficiency became associated with many of the mines of the famous Comstock lode, in Virginia City, Nev. He remained in Virginia City and Gold Hill, Nev., until 1883, when he accepted temporary employment in Butte, Montana, and from there went to Park City, Utah, where he became chief engineer of the Ontario and Daly Mines and the Ontario Mill and Marsac Mill. The Ontario and Daly were at that time the chief producers in Utah. He was killed in a runaway accident at Park City, May 7, 1888.

5546¹. i.   WILLIAM, b. ———; d. in infancy.

5547. ii.   HENRY G., b. Nov. 23, 1877; m. 1900, Vera M. Foote. He was educated at the University of Cal. Is in the Railway Mail Service (Eighth Division), in San Francisco. Res., 1444 Chestnut St., Oakland, Cal.

5547¹. iii. MILLIE E., b. ———. Res. with her brother at Oakland, Cal.

4120. CHARLES WHITTLESEY FOOTE, (2600, 1249, 433, 130, 39, 11, 3,) b. Jan. 1, 1853, at Tripoli, Syria; m. Harriet Mason Hosford, b. Sept. 12, 1857, dau. of Professor Henry B..Hosford, at Hudson, O., July 31, 1879. He graduated from Western Reserve College, with first honors, in 1874. Received degree M. A. from Cornell University, June, 1876, and from the same institution, Ph.D., in June, 1877. Practised law at Akron, O., about ten years; then became electrical engineer and engaged in electric railway construction. In 1894, because of menacing ill health, removed to Southern California. Is now Secretary of Citrus Protective League of California, with headquarters at Los Angeles, Cal. Res., Claremont, Cal.

5548. i.   FRANCES ROSANNA, b. May 26, 1880. Librarian, Pomona College, Claremont, Cal.

5549. ii. CHARLES RAYMOND, b. Aug. 8, 1883. Grad. Pomona College 1907.

5550. iii. ROBERT HOSFORD, b. July 29, 1886; d. Feb. 27, 1888.

5551. iv. HARRIET RUTH, b. Jan. 10, 1889.

5552. v.   HELEN MARJORIE, b. Apr. 2, 1894.

4121. LEWIS A. FOOTE, (2602, 1250, 433, 130, 39, 11, 3,) b. May 1, 1858, at Madrid, N. Y. Educated at Potsdam Normal School; m. Estelle Isabelle, dau. of Valorus Wilson, b. 1858. Banker. Congregationalist. Res., 313 13th St., Sioux City, Iowa.

5553. i.   ORSON MERRILL, b. Sept. 3, 1885.

5554. ii. FRED WILSON, b. July 24, 1889.

4122. CLARK MERRILL FOOTE, (2602, 1250, 433, 130, 39, 11, 3,) b. Jan. 26, 1860; m. ———. Druggist. Res., San Diego, Cal.

5555. i.   SHILA, b.

5556. ii. CLARK, b.

4123. DR. JESSE JACOB FOOTE, (2602, 1250, 433, 130, 39, 11, 3,) b. Feb.

9, 1867; m. June 11, 1890, Grace, dau. of Howard Eastman. Res., Parishville, N. Y.

    5557. i. HOWARD E., b. Aug. 12, 1893.

    4124. CHARLES FOOTE, (2604, 1252, 433, 130, 39, 11, 3,) b. Nov. 13, 1854; m. July 4, 1881, Ida, dau. of Wm. Allison. She was b. Nov. 14, 1854. Farmer. Methodist.

    5558. i. GRACE, b. Jan. 17, 1884; m. Nov. 14, 1902, Judson Todd. Ch.:
        (1) Don, b. Apr. 12, 1904. (2) Charles Wm., b. June 10, 1905.

    4126. DR. GILBERT A. FOOTE, (2604, 1252, 433, 130, 39, 11, 3,) b. July 31, 1859; m. July 17, 1890, at Norfolk, N. Y., Clara, dau. of George Spotswood. Educated at St. Lawrence University and N. Y. University Medical College. She was b. Nov. 3, 1870. Presbyterian. Res., Dexter, N. Y.

    5559. i. MARJORIE, b. May 20, 1890.

    4134. REV. GEORGE WILLIAM FOOTE, (2617, 1270, 447, 134, 39, 11, 3,) b. at Roxbury, Ct., May 2, 1845; m. Apr. 3, 1867, Sarah Ellen Elizabeth, dau. of Rev. Edward Pidsley, of Pottersville, N. Y. He was ordained minister of the Episcopal Church in New York City in 1864. Res., San Jose, Cal.

    5560. i. CHRISTINE, b. Mar. 31, 1871; d. Aug. 8, 1871.

    4139. FREDERICK WILLIAM FOOTE, Jr., (2620, 1270, 447, 134, 39, 11, 3,) b. at Elizabeth, N. Y., Dec. 6, 1844; m. Apr. 14, 1864, Sara Fitz Randolph, dau. of Rev. Ephraim and Isabelle (Randolph) de Puy, of Burlington, N. J. He was a prominent banker in New York City for many years; d. May 13, 1889, at Far Rockaway, N. Y.

    5561. i. NATHANIEL (NILES), b. Feb. 21, 1865; m. Katherine Andrews,
        7173.
    5562. ii. ISABELLE DE PUY, b. Jan. 5, 1867; m. Holmes Agnew.
    5563. iii. SARA RANDOLPH, b. Nov. 28, 1868; m. Nov. 11, 1886, Robert
        Sale Hill; d May 8, 1891. Ch.: (1) Robert, Jr., b. Sept. 19, 1888.
    5564. iv. FLORENCE BUTLER, b. May 28, 1870; d. Oct. 10, 1889; unm.
    5565. v. JULIA DE PUY, b. ———; d. in infancy.

    4146. HENRY HAWLEY FOOTE, (2620, 1270, 447, 134, 39, 11, 3,) b. Apr. 30, 1862; m. Oct. 12, 1886, Ada Scruier Henderson.

    5566. i. MAUD BUYAN, b. Nov. 23, 1889.

    4151. GILBERT E. FOOTE, (2629, 1273, 447, 134, 39, 11, 3,) b. Barton, N. Y., June 8, 1843; m. Sept. 28, 1870, Isadore W. Davis, of Waverly, N. Y. Res., Waverly, N. Y.

    5567. i. CHRISTIANA, b. Feb. 12, 1872, at Waverly.
    5568. ii. WILLIAM J., b. Jan. 21, 1874; d. May 29, 1879, at Waverly, N. Y.

    4154. CHARLES H. FOOTE, (2629, 1273, 447, 134, 39, 11, 3,) b. Groton, N. Y., July 21, 1851; m. Dec. 16, 1877, Ida Stark. Res., Cortland, N. Y.

    5569. i. FLORENCE, b. Groton, Apr. 27, 1879.
    5570. ii. FRANK, b. Spencer, Jan. 26, 1881.
    5571. iii. ANNA, b. Groton, Apr. 27, 1885.

    4155. JAMES H. FOOTE, (2629, 1273, 447, 134, 39, 11, 3,) b. ———; m. Isabel Morrow.

    5572. i. PHILIP M., b.
    5573. ii. DONALD B., b.

4159. MILTON FOOTE, (2635, 1274, 447, 134, 39, 11, 3,) b. Jan. 17, 1845; m. 1st, July 13, 1871, Fidelia A. Farley, of Speedsville, N. Y.; m. 2nd, May 30, 1876, Kathern Alzina Lane. Res., 72 Manhattan St., Rochester, N. Y.

    5574. i. MYRTIA A., d. in infancy.

4161. JOHN BRISCOE FOOTE, (2635, 1274, 447, 134, 39, 11, 3,) b. May 4, 1857; m. July 3, 1876, Anna L. Payne, of Napoleon, Mich. Res., St. Charles, Ill.

    5575. i. CARRIE L., b. Oct. 6, 1878; m Dec. 6, 1899, Walter Stevens, of Jackson, Mich.

    5576. ii. ALDA, b. Sept. 6, 1882; m. Charles H. Barnes; d. Nov. 26, 1902. Ch.: (1) Madeline, b. July 26, 1900. (2) Carolyn, b. Apr. 17, 1902.

4177. WILLIAM A. FOOTE, (2641, 1274, 447, 134, 39, 11, 3,) b. June 9, 1854; m. Feb. 28, 1878, Ida E., dau. of Hon. George W. Westerman, of Adrian, Mich. She was b. Nov. 15, 1857. He was creator and is principal owner and president of the Commonwealth Power Co., Jackson, Mich.

    5577. i. RAYMOND AUGUSTUS, b. in Minneapolis, Minn., Mar. 1, 1880; d. Aug. 13, 1880.

    5578. ii. ETHEL LUCILE, b. Sept. 25, 1881.

    5579. iii. EDNA TIRZAH, b. June 8, 1883, at Adrian, Mich.

    5580. iv. ELSIE GRACE, b. Apr. 6, 1885; d. Nov. 11, 1889.

4180. JAMES BERRY FOOTE, (2641, 1274, 134, 39, 11, 3,) b. at Adrian, Mich., Mar. 16, 1867; m. Oct. 22, 1890, Rebecca Eliza Tuttle, of Jackson, Mich. She was b. June 4, 1868. Res., Jackson, Mich. General Supt. of the Commonwealth Power Co.

    5581. i. JAMES HAROLD, b. Nov. 21, 1891.

    5582. ii. ELEANOR GRACE, b. Apr. 16, 1893.

    5583. iii. MARGARET LUCILE, b. Feb. 1, 1898.

    5584. iv. KENNETH MILLMAN, b. Oct. 20, 1901.

4182. FREDERICK FOOTE, (2643, 1274, 447, 134, 39, 11, 3,) b. June 7, 1856; m. at Salt Lake City, Utah, July 15, 1886, Jeanette Sprague. Res., Salt Lake City.

    5585. i. LEONE, b. Salt Lake City, Jan. 28, 1893.

4204. LINUS FOOTE, (2652, 1281, 459, 137, 39, 11, 3,) b. in Erie Co., N. Y., Jan. 20, 1848; m. Jan. 22, 1870, Melissa, dau. of Daniel Rupe, of South Bend, Ind. He has held the various town offices. Farmer. Res., South Bend, Ind.

    5586. i. LARIMON H., b. Apr. 6, 1872; m. Barbara Culler, 7176-8.

4206. CYRUS FOOTE, (2652, 1281, 459, 137, 39, 11, 3,) b. St. Joseph Co., Ind., Apr. 25, 1857; m. Jan. 14, 1876, Carrie, dau. of James H. Hayes, of Washington, N. Y. He has held the various town offices. Farmer. Res., South Bend, Ind.

    5587. i. MABEL ROSE, b. at South Bend, Ind., June 2, 1881; m. Apr. 23, 1904, Alonzo Miller. Res., South Bend, Ind.

    5588. ii. VERNA, b. at South Bend, Ind., Sept. 24, 1888; d. Sept. 24, 1890.

4211. LARMON FOOTE, (2656, 1281, 459, 137, 39, 11, 3,) b. in Ct., 1842; m. 1866, Angelia Foster. Res., Little Valley, N. Y.

    5589. i. NELLIE, b. 1868.

    5590. ii. HARLON, b. 1872; d. 1896.

4212. HENRY C. FOOTE, (2656, 1281, 459, 137, 39, 11, 3,) b. in Ct., 1844; m. 1871, Josephine Salisbury. Res., Little Valley, N. Y.

5591. i. JENNIE, b. in 1872; d. in 1878.

5592. ii. FLOSSIE, b in 1879; m. ———. Res., Newark, N. J. Ch., Girl, 8 years.

4214. FRANK FOOTE, (2656, 1281, 459, 137, 39, 11, 3,) b. Apr. 19, 1859; m. 1st, 1891; m. 2nd, 1895, Alice Abel, of Buffalo, N. Y.; m. 3rd, Mrs. Libby Riley. One of the leading business men of Bradford, Pa. Portrait opposite p. 160.

5593. i. HAZEL, b. Aug. 9, 1896, in Buffalo, N. Y.

5594. ii. ALICE, b. in Bradford, Pa., July 7, 1898.

5595. iii. CECIL, b. in Bradford, Pa., Oct. 29, 1901.

5596. iv. HERBERT, b. in Bradford, Pa., Nov. 27, 1903.

5597. v. HARRY, b. in Bradford, Pa., Mar. 13, 1906.

4219. MAJOR FRANK MILLES FOOTE, (2657, 1281, 459, 137, 39, 11, 3,) b. at South Bend, Ind., May 26, 1846; m. Nov. 3, 1873, Ida Lucy Deuel, at Waterloo, N. Y. She was b. Aug. 24, 1850. He was raised on a farm and received a common school education. In 1871 came to Wyoming and was connected with the Union Pacific Railroad for 19 years. During that time served a term in the Territorial Legislature in 1875 and 1876; four years as Probate Judge and County Treasurer of Uinta Co., Wyoming (1877-1880); two years as Under Sheriff of Uinta Co., Wyoming; four years as Penitentiary Commissioner for the State of Wyoming, and member of the Evanston School Board for nine years.

In 1890, was appointed by President Harrison, Receiver of Public Moneys of the U. S. Land Office at Evanston, Wyoming, which position he has held since, with the exception of three years in the Cleveland Administration and one and one-half years that he was in the Army. In 1894 was elected Colonel of the National Guard of the State of Wyoming, and re-elected in 1897. In the spring of 1898 went to the Philippines in command of the troops from the State of Wyoming. Was at the taking and surrender of Manila, Aug. 13, 1898. Was on the firing line for six months during the war with the Insurgents. His command took part in a good share of the battles with the Insurgents, and returned to the United States in the fall of 1899.

Was Grandmaster of the Independent Order of Odd Fellows in 1879 and 1880; Grand Master of Masons of the State of Wyoming in 1880 and 1881. Grand Commander of Knights Templar of the State of Wyoming in 1895 and 1896; elected to the 33rd Degree in 1884, and an active member of the Supreme Council 33rd Degree, of the United States of America, for the States of Wyoming and Utah. See p. 160 for portrait.

5598. i. FRANK ALEXIS, b. at Evanston, Wyoming, July 4, 1876; d. Oct. 8, 1881.

5599 ii. MARY EMELINE, b. at Evanston, Wyoming, Feb. 6, 1878; m. Dec. 30, 1903, Daniel E. Rathbun. Res., Evanston, Wyoming.

5600. iii. GRACE SERAT, b. Evanston, Wyoming, July 10, 1884.

5601. iv. ROBERT PARKS, b. Evanston, Wyoming, Oct. 1, 1887.

4220. WILLIAM ALEXIS FOOTE, (2657, 1281, 459, 137, 39, 11, 3,) b. South Bend, Ind., June 6, 1848; d. at South Bend, Ind., Sept. 10, 1886; m. Dec. 31, 1874, at Warsaw, Ind., Florence E. Frazier, b. Lagrange, Ind., Apr. 3, 1851. Farmer, merchant, and flour milling.

5602. i. BLANCH EVA, b. at South Bend, Ind., Feb. 3, 1877; d. Jan. 28, 1879.

5603. ii. HELEN CHRISTINE, b. at South Bend, Ind., Jan. 29, 1880.

5604. iii. FRANK FRAZIER, b. at South Bend, Ind., Apr. 11, 1883; d. Dec. 22, 1889.

5605. iv. ATHOL MARION, b. at South Bend, Ind., Jan. 13, 1885.

4221. JAMES EDWIN FOOTE, (2657, 1281, 459, 137, 39, 11, 3,) b. at South Bend, Ind., June 13, 1851; d. at Rock Springs, Wyoming, Dec. 12, 1903; m. Mar. 15, 1881, at Salt Lake City, Utah, Georgie Clawson, b. at Salt Lake City, Utah, Apr. 20, 1860. Farmer, liveryman, and miner.

5606. i. JAMES HAZEL, b. at Salt Lake City, Utah, Jan. 11, 1882.

5607. ii. SYBIL, b. at Salt Lake City, Utah, May 5, 1887.

5608. iii. CLAIRE, b. at Salt Lake City, Utah, Aug. 23, 1888.

5609. iv. DALE, b. at Salt Lake City, Uath, June 28, 1893.

5610. v. JULIAN EDWIN, b. Salt Lake City, Utah, Feb. 20, 1901.

5611. vi. MAX MILBURN, b. at Salt Lake City, Utah, June 16, 1902.

4223. MARK WALLACE FOOTE, (2657, 1281, 459, 137, 39, 11, 3,) b. at South Bend, Ind., Dec. 18, 1854; m. Mar. 1, 1877, at South Bend, Ind., Rose M. Wells, b. Nov. 25, 1859. Farmer, liveryman, and miner.

5612. i. IDA DEUEL, b. at South Bend, Ind., Nov. 13, 1879.

5613. ii. JAMES WALTER, b. at South Bend, Ind., Nov. 8, 1881.

5614. iii. LANSING MILLIS, b. at South Bend, Ind., Sept. 19, 1883.

5615. iv. DONALD CHESTER, b. at South Bend, Ind., Jan. 19, 1888.

4250. SAMUEL GRIFFEN FOOTE, (2699, 1324, 481, 142, 41, 11, 3,) b. Stamford, N. Y., July 17, 1850; m. May 7, 1879, Henrietta Cole, of Medina, O. She was b. Mar. 9, 1856. Farmer. Res., Medina, O.

5616. i. MYRON T., b. Medina, O., May 17, 1880. Graduated from Medina High School in June, 1899. Entered the Ohio State University, Sept., 1901. Civil engineer.

5617. ii. BESSIE ANN, b. Medina, O., July 4, 1881. Graduated at Medina High School in June, 1900; m. Apr. 7, 1904, H. F. Clevedon. He is a telegraph operator.

5618. iii. EARL H., b. Medina, O., Sept. 30, 1882. Graduated from Medina High School, June, 1900. Entered Denison University, Sept., 1904.

5619. iv. MARIA ADELA, b. Apr. 5, 1888.

4251. WILLIAM CELLIC FOOTE, (2699, 1324, 481, 142, 41, 11, 3,) b. Medina, O., June, 1868; m. June 2, 1897, Carrie Perkins, of Medina, O. Educated at the Medina High School. He runs a flour mill in Wellington, O.

5620. i. MARVIN, b. Wellington, O., Aug. 16, 1899.

5621. ii. BESSIE A., b. Wellington, O., 1902.

4253. EDWIN BAILEY FOOTE, (2700, 1324, 481, 142, 41, 11, 3,) b. Stamford, N. Y., Feb. 6, 1857; m. 1885, Lizzie Ross. Went to California in the spring of 1885. Res., Ceres, Cal.

5622. i. HUGH, b. 1892.

5623. ii. HARRY, b. 1899.

5624. iii. HAZEL, b. 1899.

4255. FRANK SEYMOUR FOOTE, (2700, 1324, 481, 142, 41, 11, 3,) b. Stamford, N. Y., May 1, 1866; m. Aug., 1888, Dora C. Dayton, of Jefferson, N. Y. He moved to Orlando, Oklahoma, Dec. 1, 1899 Farmer.

5625. i. WARD H., b. Dec. 25, 1890.

5626. ii. ANNA P., b. Oct. 28, 1893.

5627. iii. BURR D., b. Feb. 10, 1895; d. Oct. 1, 1895.

4256. ORLANDO BAILEY FOOTE, (2701, 1324, 481, 142, 41, 11, 3,) b. Feb. 27, 1846; m. June 11, 1873, Ella Eudora, dau. of Samuel and Alvisa (Sherman) Stevens. Farmer, and an extensive stock dealer. Res., Stamford, N. Y.

5628. i. CHARLES STEVENS, b. Nov. 27, 1874; d. Nov. 20, 1875.

5629. ii. LIZZIE MAY, b. Nov. 20, 1875; m. June 14, 1900, William Henry Sheffield.

5630. iii. EDWARD LIVINGSTON, b. July 9, 1877; m. Ethel P. Irwin, 7179.

5631. iv. HELEN EUDORA, b. July 1, 1879.

5632. v. HATTIE ANNA, b. Mar. 9, 1883.

5633. vi. KATE, b. Sept. 1, 1885.

5634. vii. JOHN AUSTIN, b. Nov. 28, 1889.

5635. viii. FREDERICK BAILEY, b. Nov. 17, 1891.

5636. ix. ANSTIS ALVIRA, b. Aug. 9, 1894.

5637. x. ORLANDO BAILEY, Jr., b. Mar. 17, 1898.

4257. DAVID FOOTE, (2702, 1324, 481, 142, 41, 11, 3,) b. Harpersfield, N. J., 1853; m. 1st, 1878, Frances Caroline Barlow, of Medina, O. She was b. Oct. 9, 1853; d. Feb. 8, 1883; m. 2nd, Feb., 1886, Mary White. He moved to Oregon in 1905. Farmer.

5638. i. FRANCES CAROLINE, b.

5639. ii. ARTHUR, b. Sept. 3, 1891.

5640. iii. ALBERT, b. Mar. 26, 1896.

4270. FRANK A. FOOTE, (2715, 1332, 484, 142, 41, 11, 3,) b. Harpersville, N. Y.. Mar. 24, 1856; m. at Jefferson, N. Y., Feb. 5, 1879 Alice, dau. of Electus Pierce. She was b. in Blenheim Hill, N. Y. He was educated at Harpersfield. Methodist. Carriage maker. Res., So. Jefferson, N. Y. Ch. all b. in Jefferson, N. Y.

5641. i. CLYDE L., b. Oct. 15, 1880; m. Jan. 4, 1905, at Gilboa, N. Y., Harriet, dau. of Leander Van Hosen. She was b. So. Gilboa, N. Y., Apr. 28, 1880. Farmer. Res., So. Gilboa, N. Y. No ch.

5642. ii. FREDERICK H., b. May 28, 1884.

5643. iii. ELLA J., b. Apr. 14, 1898.

4273. JOHNSON E. FOOTE, (2715, 1332, 484, 142, 41, 11, 3,) b. Harpersfield, N. Y., Feb. 26, 1862; m. in Stamford, N. Y., Aug. 12, 1886, Adaline, dau. of David Crowe. She was b. at Summit, N. Y., Nov. 8, 1860. He was educated at Harpersfield, N. Y. Farmer. Res., Summit, N. Y.

5644. i. D. AUSTEN, b. June 5, 1887.

5645. ii. AUGUSTA J., b. May 7, 1891.

5646. iii. MILDRED R., b. Nov. 24, 1892.

5647. iv. AGNES N., b. May 16, 1896.

5648. v. CHARLES L., b. Jan. 16, 1904.

4278. JOHN MOORE FOOTE, (2716, 1331, 486, 145, 41, 11, 3,) b. Nov. 4, 1840; m. Dec. 16, 1873, Mary Frances, dau. of Jacob and Mary Cromwell. She was b. Sept. 29, 1848, in Wellington, N. Y.; d. Aug. 7, 1883. He m. 2nd, Oct. 23, 1902, Ella Amanda, dau. of William and Marie Flindt. She was b. in Brooklyn, N. Y., Nov. 6, 1856. He d. Jan. 3, 1903, in Brooklyn, N. Y. Res., Brooklyn, N. Y.

5649. i. CHARLOTTE ELIZABETH, b. Oct. 27, 1879, and d. Dec. 26, 1880, in Brooklyn, N. Y.

5650. ii. MARY ELSIE, b. Dec. 27, 1881; d. Nov. 28, 1884.

4240. WILLIE HUNT FOOTE, (2724, 1334, 486, 145, 41, 11, 3,) b. July 11, 1855, at Dobbs Ferry, N. Y.; m. June 18, 1884, Fannie Elizabeth Roberts, of Cleveland, O. Res., 2166 E. 89th St., Cleveland, O.

5651. i. LIDA ELIZABETH, b. Nov. 5, 1887.
5652. ii. HERBERT CARRINGTON, b. Apr. 14, 1892.
5653. iii. HELEN SCAIFE, b. Apr. 14, 1892.

4241. REV. THEODORE CLINTON FOOTE, Ph.D., (2724, 1334, 486, 145, 41, 11, 3,) b. July 26, 1857; m. Sept. 19, 1892, Leila M. Wilson, of Cleveland, O. He is Ph.D. of John Hopkins' University. Res., Baltimore, Md.

5654. i. AGNES W., b. 1894, Cleveland, O.
5655. ii. ESTHER E., b. 1905, in Balto, O.

4242. HARRY MORTIMER FOOTE, (2724, 1334, 486, 145, 41, 11, 3,) b. Dobbs Ferry, N. Y., Sept. 20, 1863; m. June 19, 1894, Mary Withycombe, of Cleveland, O. Res., Cleveland, O.

5655¹. i. DOUGLAS, b. July 17, 1895; d. July 18, 1895, Cleveland, O.
5656. ii. LEONARD WITHYCOMBE, b. Nov. 26, 1896, at Cleveland, O.

4281. JOHN HOOKER FOOTE, (2739, 1341, 488, 145, 41, 11, 3,) b. Martinsburg, N. Y., Aug. 22, 1829; m. Mar. 4, 1858, Emeline Eastman. Res., Pleasant Prairie, Wis. Ch. all b. in Pleasant Prairie, Wis., but No. 5664.

5657. i. MARY, b. Mar 2, 1859; d. May 14, 1862.
5658. ii. HELEN, b. Jan. 2, 1861; d. Feb. 18, 1861.
5659. iii. ALLENE, b. May 19, 1863; m. Jan. 30, 1883, Frank Silliman, of Woodstock, Ill. Ch.: (1) Harry Foote, b. Woodstock, Ill., Nov. 1, 1883. (2) Eva, b. Woodstock, Ill., May 31, 1885. (3) Nellie Winifred, b. Woodstock, Ill., Dec. 11, 1887.
5660. iv. MYRA, b. Feb. 27, 1865; m. Nov. 25, 1887, F. G. Hibbard, of Woodstock, Ill. Ch.: (1) Gladys Elizabeth, b. Dundee, Ill., May 21, 1889. (2) Donald Foote, b. Elgin, Ill., Feb. 24, 1892. (3) Elvira, b. Elgin, Ill., Jan. 21, 1894. (4) Doris, b. Elgin, Nov. 20, 1896. (5) Helen, b. Jan. 9, 1901. (6) Margaret, b. June 7, 1902, at Bellefourche, S. D. (7) Russell Goodwin, b. Boyes, Montana, Dec. 2, 1904.
5661. v. LAURA, b. Apr. 27, 1867; m. Jan. 30, 1889, F. T. Barnes, of Woodstock, Ill. Ch.: (1) Lois, b. Woodstock, Ill., Jan. 4, 1890. (2) Fayette, b. Woodstock, Ill., June 18, 1892. (3) Erma, b. Woodstock, Ill., July 8, 1897.
5662. vi. LELIA, b. Apr. 27, 1867; m. Oct. 28, 1896, W. H. McConnell, of Omaha, Neb.
5663. vii IDELLA, b. Aug. 20, 1868; m. Oct. 9, 1895, Wallace Cowen, of Fort Scott, Kas. Ch.: (1) John Harold, b. Fort Scott, Kas., Sept. 11, 1897. (2) Helen Dinsmore, b. Sept. 11, 1897, Fort Scott, Kas.; d. July 9, 1898. (3) Ellen Avice, b. Oct. 5, 1898; d. July 23, 1899. (4) Melvin Willard, b. Aug. 29, 1900. (5) Ethleen, b. Sept. 12, 1901; d. Oct. 21, 1901.
5664. viii. JOHN H., Jr., b. Nov. 23, 1871; m. Josephine Wiggin, 7180-1.

4286. HENRY MARTYN FOOTE, (2739, 1341, 488, 145, 41, 11, 3,) b. Pleasant Prairie Wis., Oct. 28, 1839; m. 1st, Nov. 14, 1866, Alphonsine Platt. She

d. 1902, at Norman, Oklahoma; m. 2nd, Oct. 22, 1905, Mrs. M. E. Preston, of Oklahoma City. Res., Oklahoma City.

5665.   i.   NORMAN D., b. Sept. 18, 1867; m. Minnie Robertson, 7182.

5666.   ii.   ARTHUR L., b. Sept. 15, 1872; m. Emma Gilbert, 7183-4.

5667.   iii.   HENRY CLIFTON, b. Woodstock, Ill. Graduate from Sulphur Springs College, Sulphur Springs, Texas, B. A.; m. Jan., 1903, Susie Amos. In business in Norman, Oklahoma.

4288.   CHARLES PHILLIP FOOTE, (2739, 1341, 488, 145, 41, 11, 3,) b. Pleasant Prairie, Wis., Nov. 25, 1844; m. Sept. 29, 1868, Ella Silliman, of Woodstock, Ill. He was in the 1st Wis. Vols. during the Civil War; was wounded in the hip at the battle of Perryville, which crippled him for life. Res., Woodstock, Ill., and Merna, Neb.

5668.   i.   CORA E., b. Woodstock, Ill., Nov. 23, 1874.

5669.   ii.   BERTHA G., b. Woodstock, Ill., Feb. 10, 1876; m. Mar. 28, 1906, Joseph J. Ashley. Ch.: (1) Cecil Ira, b. June 19, 1907.

5670.   iii.   SOPHIA ANN, b. Woodstock, Ill., Apr. 20, 1877; m. Nov. 19, 1903, Harry Sweeney. Ch.: (1) Ella Beatrice, b. June 30, 1904.

5671.   iv.   STYLES S., b. Mar. 20, 1879; d. Apr. 21, 1891, at Merna, Neb.

5672.   v.   CARLOS, b. June 5, 1881; m. Anna R. Amsberry, 7185.

5673.   vi.   REX, b. Woodstock, Ill., Nov. 30, 1882.

5674.   vii.   MARTHA, b. Woodstock, Ill., Dec. 25, 1884.

5675.   viii.   ROSCOE CONKLING, b. Woodstock, Ill., Aug. 16, 1887.

4290.   CHARLES LEE FOOTE, (2743, 1341, 488, 145, 41, 11, 3,) b. Rome, N. Y., July 1, 1837; m. Jan. 1, 1866, Helen Amelia Lee, of Turin, N. Y. Farmer. Res., Glenfield, N. Y. Ch. all b. in Turin, N. Y.

5676.   i.   JULIA FLORENCE, b. July 16, 1869; m. Apr. 26, 1887, George Elmer Young, of Martinsburg, N. Y. Ch. all b. at Martinsburg, N. Y.: (1) Mary Leone, b. Jan. 9, 1890. (2) George Bernard, b. May 12, 1895. (3) Gilmore Bryant, b. May 26, 1897.

5677.   ii.   FREDERICK C., b. June 20, 1871; m. Katherine E. Berk, 7186-9.

5678.   iii.   LAFAYETTE, b. May 16, 1876; m. Elanora Emerson, 7190.

5679.   iv.   EARL A., b. Jan. 19, 1880; m. Ella Louise Powell, 7191-2.

5680.   v.   BERTHA C., b. Mar. 25, 1887.

4291.   WARREN G. FOOTE, (2743, 1341, 488, 145, 41, 11, 3,) b. Martinsburg, N. Y., Mar. 16, 1842; m. Nov. 10, 1864, Lydia A. Powell, of Marcy, Oneida Co., N. Y. He d. June 22, 1900, at West Martinsburg, N. Y.

5681.   i.   CLARA FRANCES, b. Aug. 23, 1865; m. Feb. 15, 1888, Lee H. Salmon. Ch.: (1) Ella Mildred, b. May 6, 1889. (2) Lydia Mabel, b. Apr. 14, 1891. (3) Clara Amanda, b. May 23, 1893. (4) Leo M., b. Nov. 1, 1898. (5) Muriel, b. June 28, 1901.

5682.   ii.   ELLA AMELIA, b. Apr. 2, 1867; m. Dec. 3, 1884, Dennison Tiffany. Ch.: (1) Roscoe C., b. Nov. 29, 1885. (2) Gladys M., b. Sept. 19, 1887. (3) Warren F., b. Sept. 12, 1892. (4) Elfreda, b. Feb. 21, 1900.

5683.   iii.   GEORGE P., b. July 19, 1870; m. Lillian Carpenter, 7193.

5684.   iv.   DANIEL W., b. Mar. 11, 1875; m. Martha A. Stiles, 7194-5.

5685.   v.   MABEL LYDIA, b. June 28, 1877; m. May 17, 1899, William E. Dekin. Ch.: (1) Margery, b. Mar. 8, 1900.

5686.   vi.   MAYNARD W., b. June 28, 1877; m. Jessie Kelly, 7196.

4292. ADONIRAM J. FOOTE, (2743, 1341, 488, 145, 41, 11, 3,) b. Martinsburg, N. Y., Jan. 25, 1844; m. Sept. 8, 1868, Jane Cornelia, dau. of James and Jenette (Doig) Benedict, b. Apr. 15, 1845, in Turin, N. Y. Res., Rome, N. Y.

5687. i. JAMES BENEDICT, b. Rome, N. Y., Aug. 2, 1873. He is a civil engineer.

5688. ii. DOIG, b. Aug. 5, 1875; d. Dec. 1, 1875.

5689. iii. BESSIE, b. Apr. 4, 1877; d. Jan. 8, 1878.

5690. iv. CORNELIA, b. June 5, 1880; d. Jan. 30, 1881.

4293. IRA HUBBARD FOOTE, (2743, 1341, 488, 145, 41, 11, 3,) b. Martinsburg, N. Y., Dec. 5, 1847; m. Agnes Charlotte Lee, of Turin, N. Y. She d. Mar. 4, 1881, at Ogdensburg, N. Y.; m. 2nd, Jan. 17, 1882, Annie Louisa McGuire, of Ogdensburg, N. Y. Res., 51, N. Y. Ave., Ogdensburg, N. Y.

5691. i. AGNES CALISTA, b. Ogdensburg, N. Y., Jan. 15, 1871; m. Dec. 2, 1890, Jay Eston Leonard, at Ogdensburg, N. Y. Res., 32 Gould Ave., Newark, N. J. Ch.: (1) Ira Jay Leonard, b. Nov. 6, 1891. (2) Stanley Hoerle, b. Aug. 29, 1895. (3) Harold William, b. Apr. 12, 1899. (4) Lauretta Lee, b. Sept. 14, 1901.

5692. ii. RALPH JAMES, b. July 30, 1884, in Ogdensburg, N. Y.; graduate of the University of Illinois; member of the Sigma Nu fraternity. In the real estate business for a short time in Los Angeles, Cal.; m. July 9, 1906, Claudia Mowrey, of Seattle, Washington, in Los Angeles, Cal. Secretary and member of the Board of Trustees of the Puget Sound Freight and Storage Company of Seattle. Manager and owner of the West Coast Advertising Bureau of Seattle, 354 Arcade Annex, Seattle, Washington.

4297. GEORGE HENRY FOOTE, (2744, 1341, 488, 145, 41, 11, 3,) b. May 15, 1845; m. Mar. 17, 1869, Sarah Jane Reynolds. Res., Farnam, Dawson Co., Neb.

5693. i. SUSAN AGNES, b. June 1, 1871; m. Dec. 24, 1891, Joseph O. Tillotson. Res., about two miles from Farnam, Neb. Ch.: (1·) Hazel Agnes, b. Sept. 28, 1892. (2) Leroy Merrell, b. Aug. 7, 1896. (3) Leon Orville, b. Feb. 2, 1900. (4) Emery Alfred, b. Nov. 25, 1901.

5694. ii. BENJAMIN, b. Feb. 26, 1873; d. Sept. 14, 1873.

5695. iii. EMILY GERTRUDE, b. Nov. 7, 1875.

5696. iv. GEORGE WASHINGTON, b. July 3, 1879. Kicked by a horse, July 3, 1891; d. July 4, 1891.

5697. v. GROVER THURSMAN, b. Nov. 7, 1889.

4298. JAMES ALBERT FOOTE, (2744, 1341, 488, 145, 41, 11, 3,) b. Oct. 6, 1847; m. 1874, Jennie Amsdell, of Pleasantville, Pa. Pharmacist. He d. Mar. 29, 1892, at Petrolia, Pa.

5698. i. FRANK AMSDELL, b. Mar. 6, 1882.

4303. FREDERICK NORMAN·FOOTE, (2747, 1341, 488, 145, 41, 11, 3,) b. Rome, N. Y., July 23, 1852; m. Mar. 2, 1887, Nora French Thompson. He is employed by J. H. Allen & Co. as Department Manager at St. Paul, Minn.

5699. i. CARRIE THOMPSON, b. Dallas, Texas, Jan. 3, 1888.

5700. ii. RUTH SEARL, b. Dallas, Texas, July 24, 1889.

5701. iii. GERTRUDE MARY, b. Dallas, Texas, July 28, 1891.

5702. iv. EMILY BRAINARD, b. Dallas, Texas, July 3, 1892.

5703. v. FREDERICK NORMAN, b. Dallas, Texas, May 1, 1894; d. June 3, 1894.

5704. vi. JAMES EDWARD, b. Dallas, Texas, Sept. 18, 1895.

5705. vii. MABEL BRAINARD, b. Dallas, Texas, May 11, 1897; d. Mar. 6, 1898.

5706. viii. WILLIAM OLIVER, b. Dallas, Texas, Sept. 30, 1898; d. June 13, 1899.

5707. ix. JOHN HERBERT, b. St. Paul, Mich., Dec. 16, 1902.

5708. x. HARRIET EVANS, b. St. Paul, Mich., Oct. 21, 1905.

4304. JOHN ROGERS FOOTE, (2747, 1341, 488, 145, 41, 11, 3,) b. Rome, N. Y., Jan. 23, 1854; m. Sept. 22, 1887, Mary Frances Kirkland. He carries on a 5 and 10 cent store in Rome, N. Y.

5709. i. HENRIETTA MARIA, b. Dec. 1, 1888.

5710. ii. MARY LOUISE, b. Feb. 20, 1893.

5711. iii. ELIZABETH KIRKLAND, b. Mar. 20, 1896.

5712. iv. FRANK KIRKLAND, b. June 25, 1898; d. Feb. 10, 1900.

4306. WILLIAM ADAMS FOOTE, (2747, 1341, 488, 145, 41, 11, 3,) b. Sept. 7, 1863, in Rome, N. Y.; m. Aug. 13, 1897, Mary D. Smith, of Brooklyn, N. Y. Res., 1475 70th St., Brooklyn, N. Y.

5713. i. NATHANIEL BRAINARD, b. Brooklyn, July 27, 1898.

5714. ii. DOROTHEA SHAFTSBURY, b. New York, May 11, 1901.

5715. iii. MILTON ST. JOHN, b. New York, Apr. 12, 1903; d. Aug. 3, 1904, at Ocean Grove, N. J.

5716. iv. NORMAN MILLS, b. Brooklyn, May 29, 1905.

4308. ELLIS EVANS FOOTE, (2748, 1341, 488, 145, 41, 11, 3,) b. Martinsburg, N. Y., Jan. 25, 1850; m. Aug. 14, 1872, Emma Shoemaker, of Herkimer. She was b. Oct. 20, 1850. Dealer in agricultural implements and wind mills. Res., Lowville, N. Y.

5717. i. LEIGH SNELL, b. Apr. 15, 1874; unm. Res., Lowville, N. Y.

5718. ii. DUANE CHRISTIAN, b. Dec. 2, 1875.

5719. iii. MARGARETTA, b. July 1, 1877; d. July 9, 1894.

5720. iv. ROLF ELLIS, b. June 25, 1880.

5721. v. FRED DUANE, b. Sept. 18, 1882; d. Jan. 12, 1883.

5722. vi. ANNA E. SHOEMAKER, b. Jan. 1, 1885.

5723. vii. JUDSON MAX, b. July 23, 1886.

5724. viii. EMILY MABEL, b. Feb. 24, 1887.

5725. ix. HAROLD HARRISON, b. Dec. 28, 1888.

5726. x. JAMES TIMOTHY, b. Mar. 29, 1893.

4323. REUBEN CLARK FOOTE, (2753, 1342, 488, 145, 41, 11, 3,) b. Dec. 6, 1834; m. Mar. 5, 1855, Louisa Ames. She was b. Sept. 27, 1834, and d. Jan. 5, 1890, at Pendleton Center, N. Y.; m. 2nd, Sophia Dillworth.

5727. i. MINNIE ELIZABETH, b. Apr. 17, 1858; m. Feb. 20, 1884, Henry M. Treichler. Res., North Tonawanda, N. Y. Ch.: (1) John Clark, b. June 19, 1885. (2) Florence Louise, b. Oct. 13, 1888.

5728. ii. BURT AMES, b. Mar. 7, 1866; unm. Res., Buffalo, N. Y.

4324. OLIVER T. FOOTE, (2753, 1342, 488, 145, 41, 11, 3,) b. Jan. 28, 1838; m. Dec. 24, 1864, Amelia C. Whipple. She was b. Jan. 26, 1843. He d. May 11, 1891. Res., Appleton, N. Y.

5729. i. CHARLEY O., b. Dec. 3, 1865; d. Nov. 22, 1872.

5730. ii.   LILLIE E., b. May 31, 1873; m. Jan. 11, 1893, Alexander, son of John and Janet Gow. He was b. Apr. 7, 1866. She d. July 29, 1893. No ch.

5731. iii.   CHANCEY W., b. Feb. 9, 1878; m. Lottie M. Blacklock, 7201-3.

5732. iv.   NELLIE A., b. Oct. 26, 1881; m. Oct. 22, 1902, Robert F., son of Charles and Ella Duncan. He was b. Sept. 11, 1876. Ch.: (1) Carl Foote Duncan, b. June 14, 1904.

4325. ALVIN WALLOW FOOTE, (2753, 1342, 488, 145, 41, 11, 3,) b. Aug. 6, 1839; m. Oct. 27, 1864, Jane Ackley. Farmer. Res., Barker, N. Y.

5733. i.   LOREN A., b. Oct. 26, 1866; m. Carrie Bidleman and Clara Mudge, 7204.

5734. ii.   REUBEN C., b. Dec. 22, 1869; m. Minnie A. Hoffman, 7205-6.

5735. iii.   GEORGE W., b. Feb. 2, 1877; m. 1st, Margaret Pease; m. 2nd, Mabel A. Nye. Res., Somerset, Niagara Co., N. Y. No ch.

4329. HIRAM ELROY FOOTE, (2753, 1842, 488, 145, 41, 11, 3,) b. May 8, 1850; m. Dec. 1, 1875, Harriet E. Dixon, of Westwood, Erie Co., N. Y. She was b. Sept. 9, 1857, at Westwood, N. Y. He d. May 7, 1890, at Pendleton Center, N. Y.

5736. i.   SENECA B., b. Sept. 21, 1876; m. Kathryn Denigan, 7207.

5737. ii.   CHARLES D., b. Aug. 9, 1879; d. May 8, 1880, at Pendleton, N. Y.

5738. iii.   ADA K., b. Pendleton, May 3, 1882; m. ———. He d. She and ch. res. Tonawanda, Erie Co., N. Y.

4333. STEPHEN WILBUR FOOTE, (2759, 1342, 488, 145, 41, 11, 3,) b. Oct. 8, 1850; m. Sept. 19, 1876, Alice Gantt, of Lockport, N. Y. Res., 28 Franklin Ave., Lockport, N. Y.

5739. i.   BETSY, b. Jan. 22, 1878; m. Jan. 16, 1902, William Sherman Silsby, of Lockport, N. Y. Res., Royalton, N. Y. Ch.: (1) Julia Elizabeth, b. July 7, 1903. (2) Alice Ruth, b. Dec. 6, 1905.

5740. ii.   VINCEY, b. Nov. 29, 1879.

5741. iii.   WILBUR EPHRAIM, b. Aug. 3, 1881; m. May Manley, of Dannemora, N. Y., July 1, 1907. P. O., Dannemora, N. Y.

5742. iv.   SYLVIA, b. Aug. 15, 1883; d. Aug. 2, 1905.

5743. v.   ROGER BRUCE, b. Mar. 12, 1885.

5744. vi.   SENECA JOHN, b. Sept. 26, 1887.

5745. vii.   BENJAMIN FLAGLER, b. Dec. 31, 1889.

5746. viii.   ELEANOR MARGARET, b. July 1, 1897.

4336. JOHN LEMUEL FOOTE, (2759, 1342, 488, 145, 41, 11, 3,) b. Jan. 1, 1860; m. Oct. 15, 1884, Emeline Flagler Gantt, of Lockport, N. Y. Res., Duluth, Minn.

5747. i.   CHARLES SYLVESTER, b. July 16, 1885.

5748. ii.   ALICE DOROTHY, b. Dec. 29, 1889.

5749. iii.   JOHN LEMUEL, Jr., b. Sept. 23, 1891.

5750. iv.   ABIGAIL REMMINGTON, b. May 12, 1905.

4338. ROBERT FOOTE, (2759, 1352, 488, 145, 41, 11, 3,) b. Aug. 22, 1865; m. June 10, 1898, Jessie Ann Church of Duluth, Minn. She d. Mar. 2, 1904. P. O., Ohio, Col.

5751. i.   DONALD CHURCH, b. Oct. 20, 1899.

4345. FRANK WHITNEY FOOTE, (2761, 1342, 488, 145, 41, 11, 3,) b. Aug. 3, 1858; m. Nov. 17, 1886, at Cawnpore, India, Laura North Hyde, M. D., a

Missionary of the Woman's Foreign Missionary Society. He graduated from the University of Rochester in 1883. In the following winter he entered the ranks of Methodist missionaries, taking up the educational work at Cawnpore, where he was Principal of the Memorial School. Four years later he became Principal of the English Boys' High School at Naini Tal, which has recently become a part of Philander Smith College. They were connected with the North India Methodist Episcopal Mission. In 1893 they returned to America. He d. Jan. 15, 1907. Res., 20 Emma St., Rochester, N. Y.

    5752. i. LEMUEL HIBBARD, b. Aug. 20, 1887, Cawnpore, India.

    5573. ii. ELLEN MARTHA, b. Feb. 27, 1889, Naini Tal, India.

    5754. iii. SYLVIA HERA, b. Dec. 17, 1891, Naini Tal, India.

    5755. iv. GRACE ELDORE, b. Feb. 16, 1893, Naini Tal, India.

    4352. EDWIN FOOTE, JR., (2762, 1345, 488, 145, 41, 11, 3,) b. Aug. 27, 1854; m. Red Wing, Minn., Jan. 14, 1880, Nellie Hoard. Res., New Milford, Pa.

    5756. i. LAURA ADELIA, b. Feb. 13, 1881.

    5757. ii. MARGUERITE, b. Aug. 27, 1886.

    5758. iii. FRANCES MARIA, b. Feb. 13, 1888.

    4354. LESLIE FOOTE, (2763, 1345, 488, 145, 41, 11, 3,) b. Mar. 3, 1848; m. Mar. 10, 1869, Mary C. Harper. She was b. Jan. 31, 1850. Res., New Milford, Pa., and St. Paul, Minn.

    5759. i. LILLIE, b New Milford, Ct., Feb. 13, 1870; m. St. Paul, Minn., Apr. 21, 1895, Harry Ottway. Res., Shawnee, Oklahoma. Ch.: (1) Merton Gerard, b. St. Paul, Minn., May 13, 1896. (2) Leonard Vincent, b. Mandau, N. Dak., Aug. 29, 1897. (3) Jessie Jeanette, b. West Superior, Wis., Sept., 1899. (4) Elmer W., b. Elizabeth, N. J., Apr. 22, 1902. (5) Le Roy A., b. Little Rock, Ark., May 19, 1904.

    5760. ii. JESSE, b. Aug. 14, 1874; m. Edna Smith and Mrs. George Seibert, 7210-1.

    5761. iii. ADA J., b. Red Wing, Minn., Feb. 5, 1882; m. Aug. 5, 1902, Frank T. Benson. Ch.: (1) Donald Theodore, b. St. Paul, Minn., June 12, 1903. (2) Dorothy Martha, b. St. Paul, Minn., May 16, 1904.

    5762. iv. ROLLAND R., b. St. Paul, Minn., July 5, 1890.

    4355. ELMER WELLINGTON FOOTE, (2763, 1345, 488, 145, 41, 11, 3,) b. New Milford, Pa., Aug. 6, 1851; m. Montrose, Pa., Sept. 10, 1878, Julia Cooper, dau. of Rev. J. W. Raynor, a Presbyterian minister, of Montrose, Pa. She was b. Springville, Pa., Sept. 7, 1857. He was educated at New Milford, Pa. Mechanic. He d. Oct. 25, 1879, at New Milford, Pa.

    5763. i. MINNIE LOVINA, b. Bridgewater, July 2, 1879; m. New Milford, Pa., June 6, 1900, James Franklin Tingley. He was b. Sept. 11, 1860. Ch.: (1) Clara Belle, b. May 5, 1903.

    5764. ii. LOTTIE MAY, b. Bridgewater, July 2, 1879; m. New Milford, Pa., June 6, 1900, Harry Ransom. Ch.: (1) Dorothy Frances, b. New Milford, Pa., Oct. 6, 1901.

    4356. BYRON FOOTE, (2763, 1345, 488, 145, 41, 11, 3,) b. Feb. 4, 1856; m. Montrose, Pa., Sept. 6, 1882, Ida May Reynolds. She d. June 22, 1888; m. 2nd, Binghampton, N. Y., June 8, 1892, Julia Cooper Raynor Foote, wid. of No. 4375. He d. June 12, 1899. She m. 3rd, Mr. Towner. They res. on the old Foote homestead in New Milford, Pa.

5765.	i.	FLORENCE, b. May 26, 1884; d. Nov. 29, 1884.

4359.	FREDERICK WARNER FOOTE, (2771, 1345, 488, 145, 41, 11, 3,) b. Red Wing, Minn., Feb. 11, 1872; m. Apr. 26, 1899, Sadie O'Brien, St. Paul, Minn.
5766.	i.	FREDERICK CHRISTOPHER, b. Feb. 4, 1900; d. Aug. 22, 1903.
5767.	ii.	MARY LORANA, b. Nov. 25, 1901·

4360.	EDWIN HAWLEY FOOTE, (2771, 1345, 488, 145, 41, 11, 3,) b. Red Wing, Minn., Jan. 6, 1876; m. Nov. 8, 1898, Evalyn Thersa, dau. of William Lawther. He is engaged in business in Red Wing as a member of the firm of S. B. Foot & Co., dealers in shoes.
5768.	i.	EVALYN MARYNEA LAWTHER, b. Sept. 29, 1899.
5769.	ii.	THEODOSIA VERNON LAWTHER, b. Feb. 24, 1901.
5770.	iii.	SILAS BUCK, Jr., b. Sept. 25, 1906.

4365.	WILLIAM GRANT FOOTE, (2775, 1347, 488, 145, 41, 11, 3,) b. Standing Stone, Bradford Co., Pa., May 20, 1863; m. Binghampton, N. Y., Dec. 4, 1890, Alice B., dau. of R. C. Chapin, of Binghampton, N. Y. She was b. Binghampton, N. Y., Nov. 9, 1874. Farmer. Res., Heart Lake, Pa.
5771.	i.	CHANCEY WILLIAM, b. Mar. 23, 1892; d. June 13, 1902.
5772.	ii.	JOHN TRACY, b. Oct. 8, 1901; d. Jan. 1, 1903.

4369.	EVERETT CHALFANT FOOTE, (2775, 1347, 488, 145, 41, 11, 3,) b. Aurora, O., May 3, 1864; m. Oct. 30, 1890, Carrie Lorain. She was b. Jan. 23, 1869. Res., Streetsboro, O.
5773.	i.	RUTH HAZEL, b. Streetsboro, Aug. 27, 1892.
5774.	ii.	CORNELIA EMMA, b. Mar. 7, 1898.
5775.	iii.	EVERET LIONEL, b. Sept. 8, 1900.

4371.	JUSTIN HAYES FOOTE, (2779, 1347, 488, 145, 41, 11, 3,) b. Portage, O., Sept. 28, 1854; m. Feb. 21, 1879, Helen Maria Munn, of Hiram, O. She was b. Apr. 10, 1860.
5776.	i.	JUSTIN WADE, b. Hiram, O., Feb. 11, 1879; d. May 7, 1892, in Cleveland, O.
5777.	ii.	BERTHA MAY, b. Streetsboro, O., Mar. 19, 1886.

4372.	EDGAR CHARLES FOOTE, (2779, 1347, 488, 145, 41, 11, 3,) b. Aurora, O., Jan. 9, 1859; m. Apr. 2, 1884, Mary Van Della Thompson, of Huntsburg, O. She was b. Shalerville, O., July 15, 1860. Res., Warrensville, O.
5778.	i.	GEORGE HARRY, b. Hampden, O., Nov. 15, 1886.
5779.	ii.	EGBERT CHARLES, b. Warrensville, O., June 3, 1892.

4373.	EGBERT BURTON FOOTE, (2779, 1347, 488, 145, 41, 11, 3,) b. Aurora, O., Jan. 29, 1862; m. Aug. 25, 1886, Luella Haskins, of Mantua, O. He d. Aug., 1889, at Auburn, O.
5780.	i.	NELLIE MAUD, b. Nov. 16, 1888.

4376.	JOHN A. FOOTE, (2779, 1347, 488, 145, 41, 11, 3,) b. Aurora, O., Nov. 15, 1872; m. Apr. 4, 1894, Belle Lippert, of Warrensville, O. She was b. Apr. 21, 1875. Res., Cleveland, O.
5781.	i.	DELLA MAUD, b. Cleveland, O., Jan. 23, 1895.
5782.	ii.	CLARENCE HENRY, b. Cleveland, O., Mar. 26, 1901.

4381.	CHARLES FOOTE, (2782, 1347, 488, 145, 41, 11, 3,) b. Streetsboro, O., Feb. 18, 1868; m. Apr. 24, 1893, Mary Abel, of Ravenna, O. She was b. June 18, 1869. Res., Kent, O.

5783. i. ZILPHA EDITH, b. Kent, O., Apr. 14, 1894.

5784. ii. ROBERT, b. Ravenna, O., July 27, 1895.

5785. iii. CATHARINE, b. Kent, O., Nov. 24, 1896.

5786. iv. OSCAR, b. Kent, O., Jan. 24, 1898.

4384. ARTHUR WILLIS FOOTE, (2784, 1349, 488, 145, 41, 11, 3,) b. Franklin, Pa., Apr. 27, 1851; m. June 20, 1872, Mary Aurilla Wood, of Bridgewater, Ct.

5787. i. ERNEST, b. May 30, 1873; d. Feb. 9, 1875.

5788. ii. MABEL, b. Aug. 3, 1889; d. Sept. 19, 1892.

4389. WILLIAM HERBERT FOOTE, (2785, 1349, 488, 145, 41, 11, 3,) b. Sept. 3, 1851; m. New Milford, Ct., Oct. 21, 1879, Florance Weed Berthrop.

5789. i. CHARLES WEED, b. May 4, 1881.

5790. ii. ALVIN WARD, b. July 6, 1890.

4397. HENRY FRANCIS FOOTE, (2786, 1349, 488, 145, 41, 11, 3,) b. Feb. 17, 1863; m. Binghamton, N. Y., Jan. 28, 1885, Alice Devine.

5791. i. GEORGE JAMES, b. Apr. 13, 1886.

5792. ii. HARRY, b. Oct. 9, 1887.

4405. LEWIS HARPER FOOTE, (2789, 1349, 488, 145, 41, 11, 3,) b. Aug. 8, 1865; m. Aug. 2, 1890, Sarah Fitzgerald.

5793. i. AUGUSTA, b. July 18, 1891; d.

5794. ii. HARPER DUSENBURY, b. Jan. 25, 1893; d.

5795. iii. CHARLES ALDEN, b. Mar. 18, 1895; d.

4408. ARTHUR ELLSWORTH FOOTE, (2790, 1354, 497, 153, 45, 13, 5,) b. Jan. 3, 1874; m. May 5, 1900, Edith Burr, dau. of Rev. Charles Ray Palmer, of New Haven, Ct. He graduated Yale, 1896. Res., New York City.

5808. i. RAY PALMER, b. at Dongan Hills, Staten Island, N. Y., May 16, 1901.

5809. ii. MARGARET ELLSWORTH, b. at Dongan Hills, Staten Island, N. Y., Oct. 29, 1903.

4417. ALBERT J. FOOTE, (2816, 1395, 518, 170, 37, 13, 5,) b. Feb. 28, 1876; m. Syracuse, N. Y., Clara E., dau. of Wm. Latsch, of Syracuse, N. Y., b. July 27, 1879. Res., Lyons, N. Y.

5810. i. GEORGE A., b. June 30, 1904.

5811. ii. WILBERT, b. Dec. 22, 1905.

4425. GEORGE B. FOOTE, (2821, 1395, 518, 170, 37, 13, 5,) b. Pittsford, N. Y., Mar. 20, 1874; m. 1898, Mattie Hyatt, of McLeansboro, Ill.

5812. i. ALBERT GEORGE, b. Apr. 14, 1901, McLeansboro, Ill.

4427. WILLIAM H. FOOTE, (2824, 1398, 518, 170, 37, 13, 5,) b. Jan. 29, 1869; m. Jan. 17, 1891, Emma Fink.

5813. i. FRANCES S., b. Aug. 13, 1892.

5814. ii. SAMUEL, b. Feb. 8, 1903.

5815. iii. BLANCHE E., b. Nov. 28, 1895.

4429. ELTON T. FOOTE, (2824, 1398, 518, 170, 37, 13, 5,) b. Apr. 25, 1872; m. Nov. 28, 1893, Emma Dudley, of Lyons, N. Y.

5816. i. IRVING E., b. Mar. 8, 1895.

4436. MILO TALCOTT FOOTE, (2830, 1402, 520, 170, 37, 13, 5,) b. Sept. 4, 1862; m. Apr. 4, 1886, Ella E., dau. of William Eshenroder, of Milan, O. She was b. Oxford, Erie Co., O., Aug. 17, 1863. He is a graduate of the Business Department of the Western Reserve Normal School of Milan, O. He acted as teacher in above department, and taught district schools. Farmer and Delaine sheep breeder. Res., New London, O. P. O., Collins, O.

5817. i. EDNA LENORA, b. Hartland, O., Mar. 22, 1887. Music teacher.

4445. DELLIZON ARTHUR FOOTE, A. M., M. D., (2836, 1409, 520, 170, 37, 13, 5,) b. Westfield, O., Apr. 14, 1860; m. 1891, Millie Harriet Baird. She was b. Lima, N. Y., Sept. 27, 1861. Ch. all b. in Omaha, Neb. Office at 216-221, Paxton Block, Omaha, Neb.

5818. i. MARJORIE BAIRD, b. Oct. 14, 1892.
5819. ii. ARTHUR NEWMAN, b. May 10, 1894.
5820. iii. MILDRED AMORETTE, b. Mar. 20, 1897.

4446. PROF. THERON ADOLPHUS FOOTE, (2837, 1409, 520, 170, 37, 13, 5,) b. Apr. 6, 1872; m. Aug. 29, 1899, Alma C. Meier. He is interested in the Colesburg Pottery Co., Colesburg, Ia.

5821. i. SALOME FLAVILLE, b. Colesburg, Ia., Sept. 9, 1900.
5822. ii. SPENCER THERON, b. Castana, Ia., July 15, 1902.
5823. iii. HOLLIS LENORE, b. July 23, 1904.

4457. WYLLIS JESSE FOOTE, (2846, 1413, 521, 170, 37, 13, 5,) b. May 8, 1851; m. May 21, 1871, Adelia R. Bower. She was b. Oct. 21, 1853. Res., Thompson, O.

5824. i. MAUDE B., b. Oct. 6, 1878; m. Sept. 22, 1900, Charles G. Leslie. He was b. Mar. 7, 1876. Ch.: (1) Doris Elizabeth Leslie, b. Dec. 6, 1904.

4471. EUGENE FOOTE, (2868, 1441, 527, 171, 47, 13, 5,) b. Dec. 5, 1852; m. Oct. 8, 1875, Alice R. Steele. She was b. Mar. 16, 1853. Res., Colley, Pa.

5825. i. JOSEPH, b. Nov. 23, 1876.
5826. ii. EVA L., b. Sept. 25, 1877; m. July 4, 1893, D. L. Erle, of Colley, Pa. She d. 1899, at Colley, Pa. Ch.: (1) Louisa, b. July 29, 1894. (2) M. Stanley, b. Feb. 29, 1896. (3) Byron F., b. Oct. 2, 1898.
5827. iii. BYRON, b. Sept. 19, 1878, Scranton, Pa.
5828. iv. NEWTON, b. May 27, 1880, Colley, Pa.
5829. v. CARRIE T., b. May 28, 1882; m. Nov. 8, 1899, D. L. Erle, of Colley, Pa., her sister's husband. Ch.: (1) Miles G., b. June 5, 1900. (2) Orvin L., b. Dec. 10, 1901.
5830. vi. CHESTER, b. Jan. 18, 1884, Wilkesbarre, Pa.
5831. vii. MYRTLE, b. Sugar Run, Pa., May 11, 1886.
5832. viii. PEARL, b. May 16, 1888; d.
5833. ix. HENRIETTA, b. Mar. 27, 1892, Colley, Pa.
5834. x. AGNES, b. June 22, 1895, Colley, Pa.
5835. xi. EMMA, b. Mar. 10, 1898, Colley, Pa.

4473. HIBBARD FOOTE, (2868, 1441, 527, 171, 47, 13, 5,) b. Sept. 5, 1858, at Falls, Pa.; m.

5836. i. MILDRED, b.
5837. ii. FRANCIS, b.
5838. iii. LOLA, b.

4478. JOHN MILO FOOTE, (2869, 1441, 527, 171, 47, 13, 5,) b. June 17, 1861; m. Etna C. ———. Res., Dunsmore, Pa.

5839. i. MINNIE MAY, b. Mar. 7, 1885.

5840.   ii.   CLARENCE EDWARD, b. Feb. 19, 1887.

5941.   iii. ANNIE L., b. Apr. 26, 1889.

5942.   iv.   OLIVER JOHN, b. Jan. 26, 1893.

4490.   LEWIS K. FOOTE, (2873, 1442, 527, 171, 47, 13, 5,) b. Jan. 27, 1860;
m. Ina Spencer, of Eleven Mile, Pa. Res., Roulette, Pa.

5843.   i.   MARION N., b.

4491.   FRANK FOOTE, (2873, 1442, 527, 171, 47, 13, 5,) b. Apr. 29, 1862; m.
Minnie Crandell, of Turtle Point, Pa. Res., Little Genesee, N. Y.

5844.   i.   RONALD E., b. July 17, 1901.

4494.   WILLIAM HOBBS FOOTE, (2874, 1442, 527, 171, 47, 13, 5,) b. July
1, 1850; m. Dec. 21, 1874, Ida Terry, of Augusta, Wis. She d. Nov. 21, 1891. He
d. Oct. 29, 1892. Res., Barron Co., Wis.

5845.   i.   WILLIAM, b. ———; d. ———.

5846.   ii.   NATHAN L., b. June 19, 1877; m. Agatha Warden.

4496.   NATHAN FOOTE, (2874, 1442, 527, 171, 47, 13, 5,) b. at Annin, Pa.,
Apr. 17, 1855; m. Sept. 7, 1879, Mary, dau. of Daniel Parks. She was b. at Fon-
du-lac, Wis., June 21, 1861. Res., Foote, Sask., Ont., Canada. As he was the
first settler there, the people voted to have it called after him.

5847.   i.   L. T., b. July 26, 1880; d. Sept. 8, 1880, Sumner, Wis.

5848.   ii.   WILLIAM GEORGE, b. Nov. 15, 1881; d. Jan. 30, 1882, Barron
                Co., Wis.

5849.   iii. RALPH L., b. May 14, 1883; m. Hannah Boe, 7212.

5850.   iv.   GERTRUDE, b. at Canton, Wis., May 6, 1888; m. Aug. 17, 1906,
                Alvin McLillan, of Quebec.

5851.   v.   RAYMOND WALTER, b. at Minneapolis, Minn., Mar. 19, 1896.

4502.   ULYSSES H. FOOTE, (2874, 1442, 527, 171, 47, 13, 5,) b. at Annin,
Pa., Sept. 17, 1867; m. Rose Plummer, of Corryville, Pa. Res., Smithport, Pa.

5852.   i.   MARY S., b.

5853.   ii.   HARRY, b.

5854.   iii. KEITH, b.

4504.   SIMEON M. FOOTE, (2874, 1442, 527, 171, 47, 13, 5,) b. at Annin,
Pa., Apr. 2, 1874; m. May 20, 1896, Ina Warden, of Ceres, Pa. Res., Ceres, Pa.

5855.   i.   EVA MAY, b. Mar. 8, 1897.

5856.   ii.   REGGIE, b. Dec. 15, 1899.

5856¹.   iii. LOLA, b. May 29, 1901; d. Mar. 27, 1904.

4505.   WILLIAM SIMEON FOOTE, (2881, 1443, 527, 171, 47, 13, 5,) b. Lenox,
Pa., July 31, 1858; m. Olive Susan, dau. of Simeon Marcy. She was b. June 12,
1879, at Lenox, Pa. Salesman. Res., 805 Harrison Ave., Scranton, Pa.

5857.   i.   WILLIAM OSCAR, b. Susquehanna, Pa., Mar. 15, 1892.

4524.   WARREN RODOLPHUS FOOTE, (2900, 1456, 529, 171, 47, 13, 5,) b.
Feb. 26, 1869, St. Thomas; m. Jan. 5, 1892, Ruth Elizabeth Maxwell. Res.,
Safford, Ariz.

5858.   i.   EUPHRASIA, b. Oct. 23, 1892.

5859.   ii.   CLARENCE, b. Aug. 25, 1894.

5860.   iii. ELLA MAUD, b. Nov. 19, 1896; d. Mar. 21, 1897.

5861.   iv.   WARREN R., b. June 14, 1898; b. Dec. 20, 1906.

5862.   v.   PEARL, b. Sept. 14, 1900.

5863.   vi.   VIOLA, b. Dec. 29, 1902.

5864. vii. GRACE, b. Aug. 7, 1905.

4525. GEORGE ARLINGTON FOOTE, (2900, 1456, 529, 171, 47, 13, 5,) b. Glendale, Utah, Jan. 29, 1865; m. Nov. 15, 1892, Rosa Cooper, dau. of Jessie and Malinda Wanslee, b. Feb. 9, 1874, at Ozark, Ark. Res., Emery, Utah.

5866. i. EMMA MILINDA, b. May 1, 1894.
5867. ii. GEORGE VERNON, b. Aug. 25, 1896.
5868. iii. DAVID RAY, b. June 10, 1898.
5869. iv. WALTER, b. Aug. 16, 1899.
5870. v. ELIZABETH MAUD, b. Nov. 4, 1904.

4526. ORSON FRANKLIN FOOTE, (2900, 1456, 529, 171, 47, 13, 5,) b. Glendale, Utah, July 2, 1877; m. Sept. 12, 1900, at Safford, Ariz., Matilda Tennessee Parker. She was b. May 5, 1883, at Tenoke, Ark. Res., Safford, Ariz.

5871. i. DAVID ARTHUR, b. July 28, 1901; d. Mar. 30, 1903, at Safford, Ariz.
5872. ii. LAURA RHODA, b. Dec. 19, 1902.
5873. iii. LEWIS BERRY, b. Jan. 10, 1904.
5874. iv. HOMER ERVIN, b. Oct. 5, 1906.

4573. EMERSON LEE FOOTE, (2929, 1465, 537, 172, 47, 13, 5,) b. Milwaukee, Wis., Nov. 25, 1848; m. June 28, 1887, Julia Crawford Chase, of St. Louis, Mo. She is a direct descendant of John Alden, who came to America in the "Mayflower" in 1620. Res., St. Louis, Mo., where he has recently connected with Missouri Iron Co., at Sligo, Mo. Ch. all b. Sligo, Mo., but 5878.

5875. i. EDWARD CHASE, b. Oct. 5, 1890.
5876. ii. JOHN ALDEN, b. Sept. 2, 1892.
5877. iii. SAMUEL ERASTUS, b. Nov. 22, 1895.
5878. iv. JULIA STANWOOD, b. St. Louis, Mo., Nov. 3, 1901.

4577. ARTHUR HOYT FOOTE, (2929, 1465, 537, 172, 47, 13, 5,) b. Wauwatoosa, Wis., July 28, 1858; m. Nov. 7, 1882, Gertrude Emily, dau. of Owen and Sarah (Oliver) McGill, of Waterford, Pa. She was b. Waterford, Pa., Oct. 20, 1857. Res., St. Louis, Mo.

5879. i. ELEANOR BAILEY, b. St. Louis, Mo., Sept. 21, 1883. She is a graduate from St. Louis High School, and now a student in Domestic Science, normal course, at Pratt Institute, Brooklyn, N. Y.
5880. ii. LUCY DODDS, b. Eureka Spr., Ark., Feb. 20, 1885. Graduated from St. Louis High School, June, 1905.
5880¹. iii. ARTHUR McGILL, b. Eureka Spr., Ark., Oct. 24, 1889; d. Apr. 12, 1891, at Erie, Pa.
5881. iv. HORACE STANWOOD, b. St. Louis, Mo., Dec. 28, 1891.

4589. JAMES HARVEY FOOTE, (2932, 1465, 537, 172, 47, 13, 5,) b. Pittsfield, Mass., Apr. 7, 1868; m. Norfolk, Litchfield Co., Ct., Jan. 4, 1899, in the Congregational Church, Sarah Phelps, dau. of Edward Lewis and Sarah Gaylord.

5882. i. SIBYL, b. Readsboro, Vt., Dec. 23, 1899.
5883. ii. HARVEY, b. Caanan, Ct., Aug. 3, 1902.

4591. HORACE CHENEY FOOTE, (2933, 1465, 537, 172, 47, 13, 5,) b. N. Y. City, June 11, 1868; a graduate of Yale University, studied law, and since in book business and also with his father's company; m. Dec. 1, 1903, Doris Kristensson. She d. June 1, 1905. Res., 207 W. 103rd St., N. Y. City.

5884. i. HORACE ALLEN, b. June 1, 1905.

4593. HORACE K. FOOTE, (2934, 1466, 537, 172, 47, 13, 5,) b. Jackson, La., May 30, 1848; m. Oct. 10, 1875, Missouri, dau. of John W. Anderson, of Nacogdoches, Texas. She was b. Nacogdoches, Texas, Sept. 12, 1855. He has taught school for many years. Res., Cotton Gin, Texas.

    5885. i.   JUNIUS TALCOT, b. Nacogdoches, Texas, Aug. 16, 1876; m. Corsicana, Texas, July 25, 1901, Mary Belle, dau. of Joseph H. Sims, of Cotton Gin, Texas. Res., Dublin, Texas. No ch.

    5886. ii.   GERTRUDE E., b. Nacogdoches, Texas, Feb. 23, 1878; m. Nov. 13, 1898, Arthur Andrew, son of Dr. John Roger Johnson, of Cotton Gin, Texas. Ch.: (1) Carl Wendell, b. Cotton Gin, Texas, Aug. 21, 1902. (2) Leroy Alston, b. Cotton Gin, Texas, July 13, 1904.

    5887. iii.   ELLEN ESTELLE, b. Nacogdoches, Texas, Sept. 7, 1879; m. Cotton Gin, Texas, Dec. 29, 1903, John Griffin, of Navarro Co., Texas. Ch.: (1) Horace L., b. Cotton Gin, Texas, Oct. 15, 1904.

    5888. iv.   CORA EDNA, b. Nacogdoches, Texas, Feb. 5, 1881; m. Mar. 19, 1902, James Keys, of Cotton Gin, Texas. No ch.

    5889. iv.   GROVER HOUSTON, b. Corsicana, Texas, Nov. 12, 1884.

    5890. v.   ADA ELMA, b. Navarro, Texas, Dec. 15, 1887.

    5891. vi.   HORACE BRILEY, b. July 25, 1889; d. Sept. 12, 1891.

4602. FRANK E. FOOTE, (2939, 1467, 537, 172, 47, 13, 5,) b. Dec. 31, 1867; m. 1st, Estella Wilson; m. 2nd, Mar. 24, 1899, Ida M. Larson. Res., Burlington, Ia.

    5892. i.   VIVIAN IZENE, b. Aug. 19, 1887; m. Harry Chapman Prichard, of St. Louis. Ch.: (1) Robert Chapman.

    5893. ii.   ROBERT FOOTE, b. Nov. 27, 1900.

4613. GEORGE HENRY FOOTE, (2971, 1493, 557, 185, 16, 5,) b. Apr. 4, 1846; m. Nov. 24, 1875, Lydia Purdy. She d. Dec. 13, 1890; m. 2nd, Feb. 8, 1893, Mary T. Baker, of Cleveland, O. Res., Cleveland, O., and Daytona, Fla.

    5901. i.   HELEN D., b. Mar. 26, 1878.

    5902. ii.   CHARLES SHERMAN, b. May 2, 1880; d. May 8, 1888.

    5903. iii.   MARY LOUISE, b. Mar. 26, 1886.

    5904. iv.   GEORGE HENRY, b. Dec. 25, 1889.

4617. SHERMAN D. FOOTE, (2977, 1493, 557, 185, 53, 16, 5,) b. Bacon Falls, Ct., May 3, 1858; m. Emma Whitman, of Jersey City, N. J. Is engaged with Manhattan Rubber Co., New York, N. Y.

    5905. i.   GRACE V., b. Aug., 1879; m. 1901, Edwin Lapronx. He d. 1902.

4618. WILLIAM C. FOOTE, (2977, 1493, 557, 185, 53, 16, 5,) b. So. Norwalk, Ct., 1862; m. 1885, Jennie Gregory. He graduated from Ann Arbor College in 1884. He has been Superintendent of Schools in So. Norwalk since 1891.

    5906. i.   DAU., b. Sept. 15, 1899.

4627. CHARLES FOOTE, (2998, 1517, 565, 196, 54, 16, 5,) b. June 11, 1846; m. Apr. 24, 1872, Estella Evelyn, dau. of Marcus Leavitt Camp and Susan Atkins Allen. She was b. June 6, 1847; d. Feb. 6, 1883. Res., Northford, Ct.

    5907. i.   FRANK CHARLES, b. May 21, 1875; m. Sadie Louise Foster.

    5908. ii.   GEORGE LEAVITT, b. May 3, 1881. Ch.: (1) Frank George, b. Jan., 1907.

4629. DWIGHT MALTBY FOOTE, (2998, 1517, 565, 196, 54, 16, 5,) b. Mar. 8, 1852; m. Apr. 24, 1877, Inez Julia, dau. of Dwight and Sarah Ann (Samphier) Williams. She was b. May 12, 1851. Res., Wallingford and Branford, Ct.

5909. i.   ALBERT W., b. June 2, 1879; m. Alice P. Foote, 7222.

5910. ii. GRACE A., b. Feb 7, 1882.

4630. WILLIAM MALTBY FOOTE, (2998, 1517, 565, 196, 54, 16, 5,) b. July 20, 1854;' m. July 27, 1882, Lois, dau. of Dea. John Ruggles and Frances Cleora (Cruttenden) Rossiter, of No. Guilford, Ct. She was b. Oct. 3, 1857. He d. Aug. 26, 1892.

5911. i.   BENJAMIN ROSSITER, b. Mar. 23, 1886.

5912. ii. MARY SELINA, b. Oct. 8, 1887.

4634. SERENO MALTBY FOOTE, (3000, 1517, 565, 196, 54, 16, 5,) b. Apr. 22, 1853; m. Sept. 10, 1877, Roso Jane Cooper. She was b. Feb. 9, 1854. Res., No. Branford, Ct.

5913. i.   LAURA COOPER, b. Jan. 30, 1879.

5914. ii. SERENO SCOTT, b. June 21, 1885.

5915. iii. HERBERT JOHN, b. Mar. 21, 1888.

5916. iv. SARAH MONSON, b. Apr. 2, 1894·

4650. HENRY H. FOOTE, (3005, 1519, 565, 196, 54, 16, 5,) b. Mar. 16, 1850; m. New Haven, Ct., Mar. 27, 1870, Carrie Fowler Cook. She d. July 8, 1882.

5928. i.   VERNON HENRY, b. Apr. 25, 1871; d. Nov. 28, 1893.

5929. ii. FEFFIE LEE, b. Nov. 25, 1872; d. Feb. 9, 1889.

5930. iii. HAROLD LINSLEY, b. Dec. 24, 1876; m. Alice Hovey.

5931. iv. ROY WHITNEY, b. May 15, 1878.

5932. v.   BROWNIE, b. Jan. 18, 1881.

4651. CHARLES BROCKETT FOOTE, (3015, 1524, 569, 196, 54, 16, 5,) b. Sept. 28, 1849; m. No. Branford, Ct., Nov. 25, 1880, Elizabeth Thompson, granddaughter of Julia (Foote) and John H. Thompson. Res., New Haven, Ct.

5933. i.   CLARENCE WHITNEY, b. May 23, 1882.

5934. ii. ETHEL ANNETTE, b. Oct. 27, 1885.

5935. iii. WESLEY THOMPSON, b. May 21, 1894.

4652. FRANK WHITING FOOTE, (3015, 1524, 569, 196, 54, 16, 5,) b. Apr. 10, 1857; m. N. Branford, Ct., June 16, 1886, Ada C. Robinson. Res., Montowese, Ct.

5936. i.   CHARLOTTE ADA, b. July 16, 1887.

5937. ii. ERNEST BURDETTE, b. Aug. 8, 1889.

5938. iii. MILTON ROBINSON, b. Oct. 21, 1897.

5939. iv. IRMA MILDRED, b. Sept. 22, 1901.

4661. JUDSON D. FOOTE, (3016, 1524, 569, 196, 54, 16, 5,) b. Montowese, Ct., Feb. 13, 1856; m. Montowese, Ct., June 6, 1883, Louisa A., dau. of Rev. E. S. Hill. She was b. Brewster, Mass., Oct. 4, 1862. He is Postmaster; manager Grocery Store. Res., Montowese, Ct.

5940. i   ELBERT JUDSON, b. Apr. 3, 1885; d. Jan. 18, 1887.

5941. ii. FLORENCE LOUISE, b. Mar. 7, 1888.

4662. FREDERICK WHITNEY FOOTE, (3021, 1524, 569, 196, 54, 16, 5,) b. Fair Haven, Ct., Nov. 22, 1860; m. Nov. 19, 1884, Doda, dau. of Chauncey Ives. Res., New Haven, Ct.

5942. i.   AUGUSTA WHITNEY, b. Feb. 1, 1886.

5943. ii. GEORGE CHAUNCEY, b.

4663. G. CLIFFORD FOOTE, (3021, 1524, 569, 196, 54, 16, 5,) b. Fair Haven, Ct., Oct. 17, 1869; m. May 29, 1893, Matilda Amelia, dau. of Rev. William Lewis Bostwick. She was b. Wilton, Ct., May 23, 1870. He is an oyster grower. Res., New Haven, Ct.

    5944. i. RUTH BOSTWICK, b. July 21, 1894.
    5945. ii. BERNICE GENEVIEVE, b. Oct. 18, 1896.
    5946. iii. MARION ISABELLE, b. Oct. 5, 1899.
    5947. iv. DORATHY MATILDA, b. Dec. 3, 1901.

4666. GEORGE HOWARD FOOTE, (3022, 1525, 569, 196, 54, 16, 5,) b. Baltimore, Md., Apr. 29, 1870; m. Baltimore, Md., Dec. 25, 1895, Mary Ann, dau. of Charles Rebstock. She was b. Baltimore, Md., June 16, 1874. Res., Baltimore, Md.

    5948. i. VELMA ASBORN, b. Aug. 29, 1896.
    5949. ii. GLADYS ROBERTA, b. Nov. 16, 1900; d. Mar. 13, 1904.
    5950. iii. HAZEL REBSTOCK, b. Nov. 9, 1904.

4667. JANUS SOMUS FOOTE, (3022, 1525, 569, 196, 54, 16, 5,) b. Baltimore, Md., Nov. 15, 1872; m. Baltimore, Md., Nov. 28, 1895, Helen Sophia, dau. of Zachariah Menskaw. She was b. Baltimore, Oct. 25, 1877. He is a machinist. Res., Baltimore, Md.

    5951. i. ARTHUR SOMUS, b. Nov. 5, 1896; d. Aug. 26, 1897.
    5952. ii. HELEN TRYPHENA, b. Sept. 15, 1898.

4670. ROBERT MALCOLM FOOTE, (3022, 1525, 569, 196, 54, 16, 5,) b. Baltimore, Md., Dec. 18, 1879; m. Baltimore, Md., Mary Magdalene, dau. of Robert McSham Clark. She was b. Baltimore, Oct. 21, 1883. He is a designer. Res., Baltimore, Md.

    5953. i. LEONA REGINA, b. June 18, 1904.

4081. ALBERT G. FOOTE, (2559, 1241, 432, 130, 39, 11, 3,) b. 1848; m. Ada Weller. Res., Buffalo, N. Y.

    5954. i. MALLEY, b.
    5955. ii. MAUD, b.
    5956. iii. CHARLES, b.
    5957. iv. FRANK, b.

4082. DANIEL A. FOOTE, (2559, 1241, 432, 130, 39, 11, 3,) b. Sept. 9, 1850; m. Oct. 10, 1881, Frances L. Slade. Res., Ballston Spa., N. Y.

    5958. i. GEORGE L., b. Sept. 13, 1883; m. Feb. 1, 1906, Sarah J. Holmes.
    5959. ii. GLADYS F., b. Sept. 20, 1898.

4083. LEAMON R. FOOTE, (2559, 1241, 432, 130, 39, 11, 3,) b. Dec. 26, 1852; m. Mary Warring.

    5960. i. EDITH, b.
    5961. ii. LILLY, b.
    5962. iii. CLARA, b.
    5963. iv. ROY, b.
    5964. v. ANNA, b.

4084. EDSON G. FOOTE, (2559, 1241, 432, 130, 39, 11, 3,) b. Nov. 6, 1854; m. Emma Hovey.

    5967. i. MINA, b.
    5968. ii. WALTER, b.
    5969. iii. GRACE, b.
    5970. iv. BETHIA, b.

(33)

4704. WILLIAM A. FOOTE, (3098, 1598, 602, 205, 56, 16, 5,) b. Mar. 18, 1875; m. July 23, 1898, Edith L. Ferguson. Miller.

5976. i. ALICE MARGUERITE, b. Sept. 11, 1900.
5977. ii. DOROTHY MAY, b. June 4, 1903.

4712. ROLLIN ABRAM FOOTE, (3126, 1675, 630, 211, 60, 18, 5,) b. Cornwall, Vt., Jan. 9, 1832; m. Mar. 1, 1854, Julia Arabella, dau. of William and Arabella (Wilcox) Sampson, of Weybridge, Vt. She was b. Aug. 7, 1833; d. Sept. 28, 1898, in Cornwall, Vt. Mrs. Foote's greatgrandfather, William Sampson, of Londonderry, N. H., was one of the first settlers of Cornwall, Vt. (See History of Cornwall), and a Deacon of the Congregational Church for many years. Among his ten children was Eliphalet, who m. Amanda Post. To them were b. twelve ch., the sixth being William, b. June 20, 1801. He m. Arabella Wilcox, of Bridport, Vt., Jan. 7, 1824. Ch.: (1) Mary, m. Loyal Huntington, of Weybridge, Vt. (2) Sarah, m. Ira Twitchell, of Weybridge, Vt. (3) Annette, unm. (4) Julia, m. Rollin Foote. (5) Angeline, m. George Waldron, of Addison, Vt. Mr. Foote is specially interested in horses and merino sheep. Farmer. He has held the various town offices. Always lived in Cornwall, Vt., and on the old homestead nearly all of his life.

5978. i. ORPHA ARABELLA, b. Feb. 15, 1859; d. Nov. 3, 1860.
5979. ii. ABRAM W., b. Oct. 24, 1862; m. Kate D. Nichols, 7251-8.
5980. iii. FRANK S., b. May 16, 1869; m. Hila R. Wolcott, 7259-63.

4713. GARRISON WILLIAM FOOTE, (3126, 1675, 630, 211, 60, 18, 5,) b. Cornwall, Vt., Mar. 8, 1834; m. Cornwall, Jan. 6, 1859, Harriet Augusta, dau. of Kinney and Direxa (Hapgood) Sperry, of Cornwall, Vt. He has been Town Clerk of Crown Point, N. Y., for 28 years, and Associate Judge from Essex Co. two years. She d. Oct. 27, 1904. He d. Jan. 22, 1907. Both buried at Crown Point. Res., Pomfret, Vt., and Crown Point, N. Y.

5981. i. WILLIAM GARRISON, b. Cornwall, Vt., Sept. 24, 1862; d. Apr. 12, 1888, at Crown Point, N. Y.; unm.

4716. MYRON EZRA FOOTE, (3130, 1678, 630, 211, 60, 18, 5,) b. Apr. 13, 1838; m. Nov. 1, 1865, Sarah G. Jackson. She was b. in Kansas City, Mo., Dec. 6, 1847. He is a real estate agent, Hannibal, Mo.

5982. i. SILAS N., b. Aug. 4, 1866; m. Eleanor O. Farnsworth, 7264-5.
5983. ii. SARAH ANNETTE, b. in Holton, Kansas, Apr. 16, 1868. Res., Chicago, Ill.
5984. iii. CHARLIE E., b. in Holton, Kansas, Feb. 4, 1870. Res., Attica, Ind.
5985. iv. HERBERT A., b. in Holton, Kansas, Jan 19, 1872. Res., Hiawatha, Kansas.

4721. MORRIS D. FOOTE, (3134, 1678, 630, 211, 60, 18, 5,) b. May 11, 1853; m. Sept. 13, 1882, Etta Adams. He d. July 31, 1900, at Houston, Texas.

5986. i. HAZEL, b. June 20, 1883.
5987. ii. DONALD MERRITT, b. July 1, 1897.

4722. WILLIS ORLIN FOOTE, (3134, 1678, 630, 211, 60, 18, 5,) b. Mar. 20, 1856; m. Dec. 15, 1887, Myra L. Milliner. Mr. Foote is one of the leading horsemen of the southwest. At his extensive stables at No. 280 Exposition Ave., Dallas, Texas, is always to be found a fine string of horses. Gov. Francis (3), 2m. 11½s., now stands at the head of the stud. Willis is a natural horse trainer.

5988. i. RACHEL M., b. Mar. 2, 1892.

5989. ii. JOHN M., b. Dec. 4, 1893.

4734. JOHN BURTON FOOTE, (3136, 1678, 630, 211, 60, 18, 5,) b. Louisville, Ky., Dec. 28, 1871; m. Apr. 10, 1893, Chaffar L. Darby. She was b. Marianna, Fla., Nov. 29, 1891. Res., Hot Springs, Ark.

5990. i. ANNA MALVINA, b. Mar. 26, 1894.

5991. ii. WILBURT WADE, b. June 12, 1897.

5992. iii. EMILY CHAFFER, b. Apr. 10, 1900.

5993. iv. JANE BOSWELL, b. Sept. 22, 1904.

4740. HARRISON ALMANSON FOOTE, (3141, 1679, 630, 211, 60, 18, 5,) b. Cornwall, Vt., July 23, 1840; m. Jan. 1, 1863, Mary Jane, dau. of Henry Powell, of Middlebury, Vt. She was b. Weybridge, Vt., Nov. 4, 1843. He is a speculator, contractor and builder, in New Castle, Col.

5994. i. ELLA CORAL, b. May 8, 1864; m. Nov. 23, 1892, Harvey B.
Hazelton, of Strafford, Vt. Farmer, later in the shoe business in Keene, N. H. Res., Long Beach, Cal. Ch.: (1) Cecil Powell, b. White River Junction, Vt., May 8, 1894; d. May 12, 1894. (2) Earle Foote, b. Bethel, Vt., Feb. 19, 1896.

5995. ii. WALLACE C., b. July 25, 1867; m. Mattie M. Langworthy, 7266-7.

4741. ELIJAH BRISTOL FOOTE, (3142, 1679, 630, 211, 60, 18, 5,) b. Cornwall, Vt., May 23, 1852; m. Oct. 18, 1876, Carrie Elizabeth, dau. of James Raine, of Crown Point, N. Y. She was b. Crown Point, N. Y., Aug. 7, 1855. Farmer and interested in the cattle and dairy business. Res., Greeley, Col.

5996. i. ELMER STAFFORD, b. Cornwall, Vt., Sept. 5, 1878. Civil engineer.

5997. ii. ANNA BELLE, b. Cornwall, Vt., Aug. 20, 1880; d. Mar. 11, 1882.

5998. iii. HERBERT LEON, b. Ft. Collins, Col., Dec. 24, 1887.

5999. iv. HOWARD LAWRENCE, b. Ft. Collins, Col., Dec. 24, 1887; d. Aug. 21, 1888, at Littleton, Col.

4745. FRANKLIN EDWARD FOOTE, (3142, 1679, 630, 211, 60, 18, 5,) b. Cornwall, Vt., Dec. 4, 1862; m. Cornwall, Vt., Oct. 13, 1897, Una Rockwell, dau. of Harrison Edgar and Cornelia (Rockwell) Sanford, of Cornwall, Vt. She was b. Cornwall, Vt., Jan. 9, 1874. Mr. Foote is a farmer, Selectman of Cornwall, and an extensive dealer in apples and hay. Senior member of the firm of Foote & Hemingway. Res., Cornwall, Vt., on the old R. J. Jones' farm. Also owns the old homestead.

6000. i. SANFORD ROCKWELL, b. Jan. 7, 1899, in Cornwall, Vt.

6001. ii. WINFIELD ELLSWORTH, b. July 17, 1901, in Cornwall, Vt.

6002. iii. CORNELIA GERTRUDE, b. Dec. 18, 1905, in Cornwall, Vt.

4750. GEORGE E. FOOTE, (3145, 1679, 630, 211, 60, 18, 5,) b. June, 1855; m. Alice, dau. of Rev. H. F. Lothrop, of Palmyra, Wis. Res., Palmyra, Wis. Moved on a farm near Lincoln, Neb. Was taken with consumption and returning to Palmyra d. Apr. 18, 1882.

6003. i. ALFRED W., b. Nov. 17, 1878; m. Minnie Detloff, 7268-70.

6004. ii HERBERT L., b. Lincoln, Neb., Apr. 4, 1880. Farmer. Res., Palmyra, Wis.; unm.

6005. iii. JESSIE, b. Lincoln, Neb., Mar. 29, 1881; m. Dec. 24, 1902, N. J. Cony, of Palmyra, Wis. Farmer. She d. Aug. 26, 1903, of consumption.

4753. LEWIS LINCOLN FOOTE, (3155, 1687, 645, 215, 60, 18, 5,) b. Detroit, Mich., Dec. 5, 1869; m. Baker, Iowa, Oct. 23, 1892, Belle A., dau. of Daniel and Samiah (Clapp) Harter. She was b. Mar. 30, 1868, and d. July 14, 1907. He graduated from State University of Iowa, Mar. 10, 1891, D. D. S. Graduated from Northern Ill. College of Opthalmology and Otology, June 1, 1904, Oph. D. Res., Richland, Iowa.

6006. i.   KARL HARTER, b. Traer, Iowa, July 25, 1893.

4754· CHARLES COWLES FOOTE, (3155, 1687, 645, 215, 60, 18, 5,) b. Detroit, Mich., Oct. 9, 1875; m. Worthington, Minn., May 24, 1898, Isabella A., dau. of George C. and Margrete (Boice) McKay. She was b. Coatbridge, Scotland, July 23, 1876.

6007. i.   ISABELLE COWLES, b. July 15, 1899.
6008. ii. GEORGE LEWIS, b. Apr. 2, 1903.

4756. BUEL L. FOOTE, (3159, 1694, 650, 216, 60, 18, 5,) b. Oct. 14, 1839; m. Mar. 19, 1862, Louise Ayhes. Res., Malone, N. Y.

6009. i.   MYRON M., b. Feb. 11, 1866; m. Gertrude L. Allen, 7271-3.
6010. ii. ORETTA E., b. May 1, 1870; d. Dec. 4, 1878.
6011. iii. ANSON B., b. Apr 9, 1872; d. Jan. 12, 1889.

4757. WILLIAM W. FOOTE, (3159, 1694, 216, 60, 18, 5,) b. July 7, 1841; m. Mar. 21, 1866, Ophelia Lewis. She was b. June 18, 1840. Res., Whipperville, N. Y.

6012. i.   LYMAN L., b. Feb. 2, 1869; m. Libbie J. Dougherty and Bridget Daly, 7274-6.
6013. ii. NELLIE O., b. May 25, 1880; m. Oct. 27, 1904, Cloyton A. Westcott. Ch.: (1) Edna Mae, b. Sept. 23, 1905.

4758. JEWETT JAMES FOOTE, (3159, 1694, 216, 60, 18, 5,) b. Dec. 11, 1844; m. May 4, 1867, Caroline Hutchins. She was b. Aug. 9, 1840. Res., Malone, N. Y.

6014. i.   WILLIAM W., b. Constable, N. Y., Aug. 24, 1868. Farmer.
6015. ii. NEWTON F., b. Aug. 4, 1875; m. Rebecca Rutler, 7277-8.
6016. iii. EVA V., b. Constable, N. Y., Oct. 31, 1881; m. June 30, 1903, John E. Seach. Ch.: (1) Dorothy Foote Seach, b. June 17, 1904. (2) Edgar Berdell Seach, b. March 26, 1906.

4759. ISAAC L. FOOTE, (3159, 1694, 650, 216, 60, 18, 5,) b. June 2, 1846; m. Dec. 24, 1872, Libby Drury. She d. Oct. 12, 1885; m. 2nd, Mar. 2, 1887, Kate L. Spaulding, b. at Bangor, N. Y., July 4, 1859. Res., Malone, N. Y.

6017. i.   J. HOLLIS, b. Apr. 30, 1888.
6018. ii. RAYMOND P., b. Sept. 9, 1891.
6019. iii. RALPH D., b. Oct. 12, 1894.

4761. HENRY M. FOOTE, (3159, 1694, 650, 216, 60, 18, 5,) b. June 21, 1850; m. Charlotte, Vt., Nov. 22, 1875, Etta L., dau. of Joseph M. and Miranda Baker. Mr. Baker was b. July 14, 1806. Mrs. Baker was b. Mar. 31, 1810. Mrs. Foote was b. July 27, 1848. They always lived in Cornwall, Vt.

6020. i.   CHAUNCEY P., b. Feb. 18, 1879. Is employed in the General Electric Co. in Schenectady, N. Y.
6021. ii. NORMAN S., b. Jan. 15, 1883. Real estate broker, fire insurance agent, and publisher of Foote's Farm Record and Account Book, Middlebury, Vt.

6022. iii. LESLIE B., b. Sept. 4, 1885. Student at Burlington Business College.

6023. iv. RUTH ELIZABETH, b. Aug. 10, 1890. Student in High School, Middlebury, Vt.

4762. ALBERT NORMAN FOOTE, (3159, 1694, 650, 216, 60, 18, 5,) b. May 26, 1854; m. July 22, 1880, Julia Elizabeth Larkin. Res., Malone, N. Y.

6024. i. ELTON ALBERT, b. Dec. 4, 1882.

6025. ii. ETHEL MAY, b. Sept. 5, 1886; m.

4763. DR. NATHAN E. FOOTE, (3159, 1694, 650, 216, 60, 18, 5,) b. Malone, N. Y., June 30, 1856; m. Carthage, Jefferson Co., N. Y., Apr. 16, 1879, Ella, dau. of John S. Burnham. She was b. Evans Mills, Jefferson Co., N. Y., Sept. 26, 1859. He graduated from the University of Maryland at Baltimore in 1884, D. D. L. Has been in practice in Whitehall, N. Y., since 1886.

6026. i. LEROY H., b. Apr. 1, 1883. Is practising dentistry at Cambridge, N. Y.

6027. ii. LEON B., b. Sept. 20, 1886. Student in Union College, Schenectady, N. Y.

4765. FRED F. FOOTE, (3159, 1694, 650, 216, 60, 18, 5,) b. June 9, 1860; m. Malone, N. Y., Dec. 24, 1884, Jessie K. Alvord, by Rev. C. S. Richardson. She was b. Dec. 19, 1866. Res., Malone, N. Y.

6028. i. LULU MARGUERITE, b. Jan. 29, 1887; m. Malone, N. Y., Sept. 28, 1901, Edgar M. Barse.

6029. ii. GRACE REYNOLDS, b. Aug. 27, 1891; d. Jan. 25, 1892.

4769. IRA ANCIL FOOTE, (3163, 1694, 650, 216, 60, 18, 5,) b. Grant, Ia., Oct. 23, 1857; m. Aug. 12, 1891, at Red Oaks, Ia., Jessie Taylor.

6030. i. MERRIL A., b. June 15, 1892.

6031. ii. LEILA DARLE, b. Dec. 11, 1893.

6032. iii. MAURICE, b. Nov. 21, 1898.

4772. LORENZO D. FOOTE, (3163, 1694, 650, 216, 60, 18, 5,) b. Grant, Ia., Jan. 8, 1869; m. Jan. 30, 1901, Katherine Alcorn, at Grant, Ia.

6033. i. LOREN, b. July 4, 1903.

4774. COMAN MILTON FOOTE, (3167, 1709, 657, 216, 60, 18, 5,) b. Morrisville, N. Y., Feb. 13, 1868; m. Nov. 24, 1897, Etta M., dau. of Lucius T. Brown, of Syracuse, N. Y. Printer. Res., Syracuse, N. Y.

6034. i. LUCIUS COMAN, b. Aug. 27, 1899.

4775. HARRY REED FOOTE, (3167, 1709, 657, 216, 60, 18, 5,) b. Oswego, N. Y., Mar. 12, 1874; m. Elma, dau. of Seymore Hull, of Marietta, N. Y. Printer pressman. Res., Scranton, Pa.

6035. i. CLARA ERMINA, b. Syracuse, N. Y., Feb. 19, 1898.

6036. ii. SEYMORE MILTON, b. Adams, N. Y., Aug. 27, 1900.

6037. iii. MAURICE EARL, b. Adams, N. Y., Dec. 1, 1901'

6038. iv. FRANK HARRY, b. Adams, N. Y., Sept. 15, 1903.

6039. v. RUTH AMARETTE, b. Syracuse, N. Y., Jan 8, 1906.

4804. GEORGE EDWARD FOOTE, (3186, 1728, 680, 219, 60, 18, 5,) b. LeSure, Mich., Sept. 22, 1857; m. Dec. 24, 1881, Hattie Gardiner. He is a locomotive engineer.

6040. i. HARRY W., b. Dec. 4, 1882; res., St. Paul, Minn.

6041. ii. GRACE RUTH, b. Jan. 22, 1885; res., St. James, Minn.

6042. iii. HELEN ALICE, b. Feb. 4, 1889; res., St. James, Minn.

6043. iv. RAY GARDINER, b. Dec. 18, 1896; res., St. James, Minn.

4805. CHARLES WALLACE FOOTE, (3186, 1728, 680, 219, 60, 18, 5,) b. LeSure, Mich., June 25, 1864; m. Sept. 24, 1884, Emma Bessie Cragen. Dealer in real estate and fire insurance. Res., St. James, Minn.

6044. i. LLOYD CRAGEN, b. Apr. 24, 1884; res., St. Paul, Minn.

6045. ii. RALPH HERRICK, b. Apr. 22, 1886; res., St. James, Minn.

6046. iii. RAY ALLEN, b. Oct. 8, 1892; res., St. James, Minn.

4806. MELVIN FOOTE, (3187, 1728, 680, 219, 60, 18, 5,) b. 1860; m. ———. Farmer. He d. 1897. Res., near Olivet, Mich.

6047. i. FLORENCE, b. Feb. 23, 1882; m. John Tenny. Res., near Bellevue, Mich.

6048. ii. FRANK, b. 1884.

4808. FRANK MARION FOOTE, (3189, 1728, 680, 219, 60, 18, 5,) b. Carmel, Eaton Co., Mich., Jan. 28, 1861; m. Nov. 16, 1885, Cora Ella Tefft. He is a physician and surgeon. Health Officer for seven years. In 1901 was elected Mayor of Marshall, Mich., at the expiration of which term was re-elected. Res., Marshall, Mich.

6049. i. GRACE ELLA, b. Lansing, Mich., Jan. 25, 1888. Res., Marshall, Mich.

6050. ii. PEARL CELIA, b. Marshall, Mich., June 18, 1892. Res., Marshall, Mich.

4814. LOREN FOOTE, (3191, 1728, 680, 219, 60, 18, 5,) b. Sept. 1, 1883; m. 1902, Miss Cronk. Res., Vermontville, Mich.

6051. i. FLOYD H., b. Feb. 4, 1904.

4820. CORWIN FOOTE, (3192, 1729, 680, 219, 60, 18, 5,) b. Sept. 26, 1860; m. Sept. 30, 1903, Ellen Anderson. Res., Esperance, N. Y.

6052. i. CORWIN, JR., b. July, 1904.

4822. JOHN FOOTE, (3192, 1729, 680, 219, 60, 18, 5,) b. Sept. 19, 1864; m. Sept. 25, 1889, Hattie N. Young. Res., Delanson, N. Y.

6053. i. CHARLES H., b. Aug. 11, 1890; d. Dec. 6, 1891.

6054. ii. CLARENCE, b. July 20, 1892.

6055. iii. FRANK, b. June 27, 1894.

4826. SCHUYLER P. FOOTE, (3200, 1729, 680, 219, 60, 18, 5,) b. Dec. 16, 1896; m. Julia Lyons. Res., Amsterdam, N. Y.

6056. i. HAROLD, b. 1901.

4838. AMOS DUEL FOOTE, (3202, 1729, 680, 219, 60, 18, 5,) b. Nov. 12, 1872, Jackson Jct, Winnisheik Co., Iowa; m. 1st, Oct. 19, 1893, at Epworth, Ia., Frances May Davis. She was b. Oct. 19, 1873; d. July 28, 1903, at Brighton, Mo.; m. 2nd, 1906, Josephine Dell Bohnsack. He is a carpenter, contractor and house mover. In 1873 he moved to Jackson Co., Minn., then in 1879 to Mankota, Minn., then to Marion, Iowa, in 1888. Present res., Springfield, Mo.

6057. i. WILLIAM HOMER, b. Aug. 5, 1895, at Marion, Ia.

6057¹. ii. CHARLES FREDERICK, b. Jan. 17, 1897; d. Nov. 28, 1902.

6058. iii. ZELMA BELLE, b. Jan. 27, 1899, Epworth, Iowa; d. Mar. 17, 1899.

6059. iv. HELEN MAY, b. Mar. 5, 1900, Epworth, Iowa.

4846. GEORGE ANSON FOOTE, (3206, 1737, 686, 219, 60, 18, 5,) b. Feb. 17, 1881; m. Sept. 9, 1903, Lena M. Hull. She was b..July 30, 1880. A partner with his father in the hardware store at Parkersburg, Ia.

6060. i. DOREEN HULL, b. June 16, 1905.

4856. CHARLES WILLIAM FOOTE, (3224, 1751, 689, 220, 60, 18, 5,) b. Nov. 20, 1859; m. Dec. 9, 1883, Caroline Pitts. She was b. June 10, 1861. Res., Nephi, Utah.

6061. i.   BYRON C., b. Sept. 4, 1884.
6062. ii.   RUDGER, b. Feb. 20, 1886.
6063. iii. CAROLINE SEA, b. Oct. 7, 1887.
6064. iv.   ROSCOE PITT, b. May 9, 1891.
6065. v.   RALPH BERTRAN, b. Aug. 28, 1892.
6066. vi.   RUTH, b. June 10, 1894.
6067. vii. CHESTER FRANKLIN, b. Feb. 27, 1897.
6068. viii. LOIS, b. May 2, 1899.
6069. ix.   LILLIAN ERMA, b. Feb. 17, 1903.
6070. x.   CLARENCE ARTHUR, b. June 10, 1905.

4857. TIMOTHY BRADLEY FOOTE, (3224, 1751, 689, 220, 60, 18, 5,) b. Sept. 7, 1861; m. Nov. 4, 1884, Mary Jane Sketchley. She was b. London, England, Oct. 18, 1861. Res., Nephi, Utah.

6071. i.   MARY HANNAH, b. Oct. 3, 1885.
6072. ii.   VERA FERN, b. Dec. 3, 1886.
6073. iii. SUELLA, b. May 4, 1888.
6074. iv.   TIMOTHY B., b. Aug. 9, 1889.
6075. v.   HULDA VICTORIA, b. May 20, 1891.
6076. vi.   JANE L., b. Mar. 14, 1893.
6077. vii. SUSAN PEARL, b. Feb. 11, 1897.
♦ 6078. viii. DAVID EMERSON, b. Dec. 30, 1898.
6079. ix.   CHARLES BERTRAN, b. Mar. 28, 1903.

4858. JOHN FRANKLIN FOOTE, (3224, 1751, 689, 220, 60, 18, 5,) b. Oct. 11, 1861; m. Oct. 12, 1888, Elsie Bowers. He d. Nov. 9, 1899. Res., Nephi, Utah.

6080. i. FRANKLIN, b. Aug. 9, 1899; d. Nov. 9, 1899.

4859 THOMAS ALMA FOOTE, (3224, 1751, 689, 220, 60, 18, 5,) b. Aug. 18, 1891; m. Lizette Marsh.

6081· i. MADA LIZETTE, b. July 1, 1904.

4861. HARRISON FOOTE, (3224, 1751, 689, 220, 60, 18, 5,) b. July 23, 1871; m. 1895, May Wright.

6082. i.   IDA TABITHA, b. Jan. 6, 1896.
6083. ii. CHARLES HARRISON, b. Sept. 7, 1904.

4862. GEORGE ABNER FOOTE, (3224, 1751, 689, 220, 60, 18, 5,) b. June 11, 1873; m. Nov. 18, 1897, Minnie Carter.

6084. i. HANNAH F., b. Apr. 12, 1906.

4890. GEORGE FOOTE, (3237, 1761, 703, 222, 61, 18, 5,) b. ———; m. 1875, Carrie, dau. of Samuel and Jane (Bunnell) Hale, of N. Bradford, Ct. She d.; m. 2nd, Miss Palmer, of Fair Haven, Ct.

6085. i.   GRACE, b.
6086. ii. BERTHA, b.

4901. WILSON ADELBERT FOOTE, (3253, 1771, 714, 223, 61, 18, 5,) b.

July 14, 1869; m. 1st, Dec. 7, 1892, Altha L. Lyon. She was b. Nov. 19, 1876; d. Dec. 10, 1902; m. 2nd, June 2, 1907, Abbie M. Claggett, b. June 24, 1871. Res., Princeton, Minn.

    6087. i.   JASON L., b. Oct. 11, 1893.
    6088. ii.   GLADYS L., b. June 23, 1895.
    6089. iii. VERNON L., b. Sept. 1, 1899.
    6090 iv. RITA L., b. Nov. 28, 1901; d. Sept. 14, 1902.

    4902. JOHN EDWARD FOOTE, (3253, 1771, 714, 223, 61, 18, 5,) b. Aug. 18, 1871; m. Mar. 26, 1893, Addie Laura Hatch. She was b. July 2, 1872. Res., Princeton, Minn.

    6091. i.   LOLA IRENE, b. Aug. 13, 1894; d. July 31, 1895.

    4927. SAMUEL CARLTON FOOTE, (3289, 1749, 719, 223, 61, 18, 6,) b. New Gretna, N. J., Apr. 27, 1879; m. Dec. 20, 1905, at Wachapreague, Va., Myrle, dau. of Edgar and Julia Smith, of Wachapreague, Va. He is a marine engineer in the U. S. Life Saving Service.

    6092. i.   MIRIAN EMILY, b. Nov. 25, 1906, at Wachapreague, Va.

    4947. DAVID M. FOOTE, (2258, 1090, 367, 114, 36, 10, 5,) b. Morris, N. Y., May 11, 1856; m. Nov. 28, 1895, Lillie Belle Williams, b. Sept. 17, 1875. Res., Montrose, Colo.

    6093. i.   LAVINA LUELLA, b. July 22, 1898; d. Apr. 22, 1907.
    6094. ii.   MARIAN IVA, b. Nov. 22, 1901.
    6095. iii. ALBERTA MAE, b. Aug. 24, 1904; d. Feb. 4, 1907.

    4948. PERRY D. FOOTE, (2258, 1090, 367, 114, 36, 10, 5,) b. Morris, N. Y., Dec. 18, 1859; m. Mar. 17, 1887, Mary L. Thomas. Res., Morris, N. Y.

    6096. i.   BLANCHE MARY, b. May 23, 1892, Morris, N. Y.

    4952. DEVILLE FOOTE, (2261, 1090, 367, 114, 36, 10, 5,) b. Morris, N. Y., Jan. 7, 1859; m. Feb. 21, 1894, Margaret Leone Tiffany. Res., Scranton, Pa.

    6097. i.   BEATRICE LEONE, b. Mar. 7, 1895.
    6098. ii.   ERRICSON CUSHING, b. Dec. 14, 1897.

    4954. STEPHEN A. FOOTE, (2262, 1090, 367, 114, 36, 10, 5,) b. Apr. 3, 1869, Morris, N. Y.; m. Feb. 4, 1891, Clara Van Dusen. Res., Morris, N. Y.

    6099. i.   FLORENCE E., b. Apr. 12, 1896.
    6100. ii.   FRANCIS B., b. Feb. 3, 1898.
    6101. iii. ANDREW L., b. Nov. 21, 1899.
    6102. iv. STANLEY S., b. May 3, 1904.

    4962. WILLIAM NATHAN FOOTE, (2267, 1093, 367, 114, 36, 10, 3,) b. July 25, 1874; m. Jan. 3, 1895, Rose A. Lasher. Res., Garrettsville, N. Y.

    6103. i.   CURTIS C., b. May 16, 1896.
    6104. ii.   FANNIE E., b. Aug. 14, 1901. Res., Burlington, N. Y.

    4964. NATHANIEL GIBBS FOOTE, (2271, 1095, 370, 115, 37, 10, 3,) b. ———; m. Minerva Coon. Res., Morgan and Rock Creek, Ohio.

    6105. i.   THALIA ANN, b. ———; m. E. A. Kellogg, of Rock Creek. Res., Jefferson, Ohio.
    6106. ii.   ORLO ALANSON, b. June 22, 1850; m. Sarah Young, 7086-90.
    6107. iii. ERNEST NATHANIEL, b. ———; m. Angie Huxley, of Akron, O. Res., Cleveland, O.
    6108. iv. CHLOE REBECCA, b. ———; m. Arthur Rummel, of New Castle. Res., New Castle, O.

6109. v. FRANCES MINERVA, b. ———; m. Arthur Brown, of Jefferson, O. Res., Greenville, Pa.

6110. vi. OLIVE MATILDA, b. ———; m. Chas. Fry, of Greenfield, Pa. Res., Franklin, Pa.

4966. WILLIAM W. FOOTE, (2271, 1095, 370, 115, 37, 10, 3,) b. Nov. 7, 1831, Morgan, Ohio; m. Emeline Brooks, Laporte, Ohio. He d. July 5, 1894, Kidder, Mo.

6111. i. MINNIE E., b. May 11, 1857, Oberlin, O.; unm. Res., Oberlin, O.

6112. ii. DELIA, b. May 24, 1862, Laporte, O.; unm. Res., Oberlin, O.

6113. iii. MARY M., b. May 8, 1864, Morgan, O.; m. June 23, 1892, Dr. J. W. Cannon, Kidder, Mo. Ch.: (1) Eunice, b. Mar. 30, 1893. (2) Mary, b. Dec. 7, 1894. (3) Willson, b. Jan. 1, 1897. (4) Marguerite, b. Nov. 22, 1898. (5) Harold, b. Dec. 5, 1900. (6) Robert, b. Sept. 23, 1903. All b. in Kidder, Mo.

6114. iv. ALICE M., b. May 16, 1866, Lafayette, O.; unm. Res., Oberlin, O.

6115. v. EUNICE L., b. Apr. 21, 1868, Gustavus, O.; unm.

6116. vi. WILLIAM W., b. June 30, 1870, Cleveland, O.; m. July 20, 1898, Ethel, only dau. of John B. Healy, of Oberlin, O. No ch.

4971. IRENEUS MOSES FOOTE, (2275, 1095, 370, 115, 37, 10, 3,) b. Mar. 4, 1834, at Morgan Township, O.; m. Sept. 14, 1859, Dorinda E. Mills, at Mentor, O. She was b. May 20, 1830. Res., 802 N. Division St., Creston, Ia. He d. Apr. 20, 1899, at Creston, Ia.

6117. i. SON, b. Dec. 17, 1860; d. Jan. 5, 1861.

6118. ii. CLARA IRENE, b. Footville, O., Mar. 19, 1862; m. Dec. 19, 1883, Geo. H. Bickford, Creston, Ia. He was b. July 26, 1858. Res., Corning, Ia. Ch.: (1) Walter Isaac, b. Corning, Ia., Nov. 28, 1884. (2) Vernard Ralph, b. Corning, Ia., Aug. 1, 1886. (3) Frank E., b. Corning, Ia., Sept. 21, 1887. (4) Carlton, b. Creston, Ia., Aug. 25, 1890. (5) Lauren Ireneus, b. Creston, Ia., Aug. 8, 1892. (6) Miriam, b. Creston, Ia., Feb. 28, 1895; d. Aug. 20, 1905. (7) Paul, b. Lovimor, Ia., Oct. 20, 1899.

6119. iii. ARTHUR ERNEST, b. Mechanicsville, O., Mar. 29, 1866. Res., Creston, Ia.

6120. iv. MAY ROSE, b. Warren Co., Ia., May 1, 1868. Res., Creston, Ia.

4973. HOWARD S. FOOTE, (2275, 1095, 370, 115, 37, 10, 3,) b. Footville, O., June 1, 1852; m. 1886, Abbie Lottie Tourgee, of Andover, O. He is Superintendent of Schools of Jefferson, O.

6121. i. PAUL D., b. Mar. 22, 1888.

6122. ii. RALPH L., b. Oct. 10, 1891.

4974 CHARLES E. FOOTE, (2275, 1095, 370, 115, 37, 10, 3,) b. Footville, O., Aug. 1, 1856; m. 1877, Jennie Lick, of Lime Springs, Ia. Res., Sanborn, Ia.

6123. i. LORIN ALONZO, b. June 10, 1879.

6124. ii. ALFRED KNOWLTON, b. May 19, 1881.

6125. iii. HELEN CORNELIA, b. Oct. 29, 1883.

6126. iv. GEORGE VAN LEUVEN, b. May 7, 1886.

6127. v. BERNICE C., b. Apr. 2, 1889.

4976. MORRIS JULIUS FOOTE, (2276, 1095, 370, 115, 37, 10, 3,) b. Morgan, O., Jan. 26, 1838; m. Feb. 19, 1868, Ellen J., dau. of Archibald and Nancy (Warner) Holman, of Jefferson, O. He enlisted May, 1861, in a Mich. Co. that joined the 70th N. Y. Vols. Served with his regiment in all the engagements of the Army of the Potomac until May 6, 1864, when he was wounded in the right shoulder, but remained on duty until June 17, 1864, when he was shot in his right knee, causing amputation of the leg. Enlisted as a private soldier. Promoted, first Sergeant, then Second Lieutenant May 5, First Lieutenant in Sept., and Captain in Dec., 1863. Detailed Acting-Adjutant of regiment. Acted Field Officer, and part of the time in command of regiment. After the war he was elected Treasurer of Ashtabula Co., O., for two terms of four years. In 1874 he came to Washington, and graduated from the National Law University of Washington, and is a member of the Washington Bar. He is a member of the Loyal Legion, National Geographical Society, and many other organizations. A man highly considered in civil, military and legal circles. Res., Berwyn Heights, Md.

6128.   i.   EGBERT WARREN, b. Apr. 22, 1869; d. Sept. 12, 1870, in Jefferson, O.

6129.   ii.   KATHARINE LUCILE, b. Adrian, Mich., June 29, 1871; m. 1st. Oct. 28, 1892, Frank Perry, of Sydney, Australia; m. 2nd, Nov. 26, 1896, S. E. C. Newton, of Hull, England; m. 3rd, Nov. 20, 1906, Isidor I., son of Martin Maas, of Durkheim, Germany. She was educated at the Norward Institution at Washington, D. C. Went to Paris, Oct. 1890, studied elocution at Rudy Inst. Made debut on the London stage with Mr. Wilson Barrett in 1891; starred in Australia in 1892; toured the Provinces with her own company, and retired from the stage in 1906. Res., Elgin Ave., London, Eng.

6130.   iii. CHARLES E., b. July 23, 1873; m. Conchita Astol, 7091-3.

4986.   GEORGE B. FOOTE, (2648, 1280, 459, 137, 39, 11, 3,) b. Mar. 30, 1835; m. Feb. 18, 1857, Clarissa Sisson. He d. Aug. 22, 1902. Res., Wells Bridge, Otsego Co., N. Y.

6131.   i.   JESSE L., b. ——; m. ——. No ch. Res., Wells Bridge.

6132.   ii.   NORMAN A., b. ——; d. Feb. 1, 1904; unm.

6133.   iii. CLARISSA MARION, b. ——; m. Thaddeus Covey. Res., Wells Bridge.

4989.   URIAH H. FOOTE, (2648, 1280, 459, 137, 39, 11, 3,) b. Oct. 6, 1845; m. Dec. 25, 1867, Melissa Lilly. Res., Unadilla, N. Y.

6134.   i.   J. ARTHUR, b. Oct. 31, 1868; m. Nellie Ames, 7174-5.

6135.   ii.   MINNIE JANE, b. Dec. 3, 1872; d. Apr 21, 1902; m. Charles Codington, b. Sept. 29, 1868. Res., Unadilla. Ch.: (1) C. Earl, b. Sept. 26, 1892. (2) Lee Albert, b. June 14, 1895. (3) Ethel May, b. Nov. 7, 1897. (4) Myrtle Iva, b. Sept. 13, 1899.

6136.   iii. BERTHA IRENE, b. Oct. 18, 1875; m. Frank L. Searles. Res., Bainbridge, N. Y. Ch.: (1) Alta Lorene, b. July 28, 1895. (2) Lena Mae, b. Apr. 16, 1900.

6137.   iv.   CORA BELL, b. Apr. 14, 1879; m. George R. Burlison. Res., Unadilla, N. Y. Ch.: (1) Lina Irene, b. June 30, 1899.

6138.   v.   ORA ADELLA, b. Apr. 14, 1879; m. Clarence B. Fancher. Res., Otsego, N. Y Ch.: (1) Nina Belle, b. Dec. 2, 1903.

4992.   ALBERT CLARK FOOTE, (2650, 1280, 459, 137, 39, 11, 3,) b. July 9, 1849; m. Apr. 12, 1876, Frances Mayrilla Myers, of Sidney, N. Y. Res., Guilford, N. Y.

6139.   i.   ASA B., b. Apr. 29, 1880.

6140. ii. R. WILBUR, b. Apr. 18, 1892.

6141. iii. ARTA MAE, b. May 6, 1895.

4245. FREDERICK SHERMAN FOOTE, (2725, 1334, 486, 145, 41, 11, 3,) b. June 27, 1858, in Dobbs Ferry, N. Y. Inventor and manufacturer; m. Dec. 22, 1895, Anna Griebel. Res., 780 8th Ave., N. Y. City.

6142. i. HENRY GRIEBEL, b. in N. Y., Nov. 14, 1896.

6143. ii. EUGENE ELLSWORTH, b. in Lyme, Ct., Jan. 22, 1899.

6144. iii. FREDERICK GLOVER, b. in N. Y., Sept. 16, 1900.

6145. iv. HELEN, b. in N. Y., Aug. 12, 1902.

6146. v. JULIAN RICHMOND, b. in N. Y., Sept. 28, 1903; d. Apr. 23, 1906.

6147. vi. CHARLES NATHANIEL, b. Aug. 11, 1906.

4185. JOHN M. FOOTE, (2643³, 1279, 453, 134, 39, 11, 3,) b. Apr. 15, 1829; m. Oct. 18, 1854, Eva L, Payne. She d. Sept. 28, 1892. He d. June 28, 1903. Res., Fredericktown, O.

6151. i. MATILDA A., b.

6152. ii. LUCRETIA L., b.

6153. iii. PHEBE J., b.

6154. iv. WILLIAM C., b.

6155. v. WELTHA E., b.

6156. vi. JOHNNIE M., b.

4186. HENRY R. FOOTE, (2644, 1279, 453, 134, 39, 11, 3,) b. ———; m. Sarah Ann ———.

6157. i. ABBIE, b.

6158. ii. EPHRAIM, b.

6159. iii. JAMES H., b.

4187. WILBERT D. FOOTE, (2644, 1279, 453, 134, 39, 11, 3,) b. ———; m. Sarah ———.

6160. i. GERTRUDE, b.

6161. ii. ELIZABETH, b.

4189. WILLIAM FOOTE, (2644, 1279, 453, 134, 39, 11, 3,) b. ———; m. Mary ———.

6167. i. BYRON D., b.

6168. ii. WILLIAM H., b.

4192. WILBERT V. FOOTE, (2645, 1279, 453, 134, 39, 11, 3,) b. Oct. 25, 1843; m. July 2, 1875, Lydia Ann Hill.

6169. i. LIBBIE, b.

6170. ii. ROBERT, b.

6171. iii. MAGGIE, b.

6172. iv. JENNIE, b.

6173. v. PEARL, b.

6174. vi. WILBERT, b.

6175. vii. GOLDIA, b.

4193. WILLIAM HENRY FOOTE, (2645, 1279, 453, 134, 39, 11, 3,) b. Oct 10, 1845; m. Jan. 17, 1885, Mary Ann Foote.

6176. i. RUBY, b.

6177. ii. OLIVE, b.

6178. iii. BENJAMIN, b.

6179. iv. JAY B., b.
6180. v. PEARL, b.
6181. vi. GEORGE, b.
6182. vii. HENRIETTA, b.

4194. HOMER P. FOOTE, (2645, 1279, 453, 134, 39, 11, 3,) b. Oct. 18, 1853; m. Nov. 15, 1879, Harriet E. Brown.
6183. i. BERTHA, b.
6184. ii. EARL, b.
6185. iii. HOMER, b.
6186. iv. HELEN, b.
6187. v. DARWIN, b.

4972. DERRIN FOOTE, (2275, 1095, 370, 115, 37, 10, 3,) b. Morgan, O., June 11, 1837; m. Apr. 4, 1867, Ellen Hawkings. He d. May 7, 1903, in Fairfield, Neb. Ch. all b. in Geneva, O.
6188. i. CHARLES A., b. Nov. 20, 1869; d. Oct. 12, 1895, in Fairfield, Neb.
6189. ii. ETTA D., b. July 14, 1875; d. Oct. 25, 1895.
6190. iii. GUY O., b. July 13, 1877; d. Oct. 24, 1895.

4992[2]. CHAUNCEY L. FOOTE, (2979[1], 1496, 557, 185, 53, 16, 5,) b. June 4, 1866, Breckersville, O.; m. Dec. 24, 1885, Daisy E. Post, Cleveland, O. Served in U. S. Army through Spanish-American War and through Philippine-American War. Evangelist. Res., Atlanta, Ga.
6191. i. DAISY EMMA, b. Dec. 11, 1886; d. Feb. 18, 1887.
6192. ii. VERA, b. May 13, 1888; d. Jan. 17, 1889.
6193. iii. RUTH, b. Nov. 6, 1891; d. Jan. 30, 1892.
6194. iv. GEORGE POST, b. Mar. 19, 1896, Atlanta, Ga.

1499. WILLIAM CLAYBOURNE FOOTE, (557, 185, 53, 16, 5,) b. Nov. 9, 1803; m. Sarah P. Bromley. She was b. Aug., 1803, at Johnstown, N. Y.; d. Feb. 8, 1867, at Oxford, Wis. He d. 1886, at Oxford, Wis.
6195. i. JAMES, b. ——; d. 1863, at Chattanooga, Tenn.
6196. ii. WILLIAM HENRY, b. 1831. Res., Oxford, Wis.
6197. iii. ELIDA NORTON, b. ——. Served in the War; d. Neillsville, Wis., 1871.
6198. iv. FRANK DUNLERY, b. May 17, 1836; m. June 19, 1860, Mary A. Caughlin, Wellington, O. He d. Mar. 10, 1903. Res., Sparta, Wis. Ch.: (1) Mary L., b. July 6, 1864; d. Jan. 18, 1900. (2) Clarence E., b. Nov. 23, 1868; d. Sept. 6, 1906. (3) Sarah Louise, b. Oct. 20, 1874; m. Apr. 19, 1905, D. Bernard Barton, of Mason City, Iowa.
6199. v. ANDREW JACKSON, b. June, 1843; d. 1865.
6200. vi. MARY A., b. ——; d. in infancy, at Owego, N. Y.

2978. REV. CHESTER LUCIUS FOOTE, (1496, 557, 185, 53, 16, 5,) b. Nov. 1, 1825; m. Oct., 1851, Cynthia M. Baker, of Florence, O. She d. Jan.. 9, 1899. He was a minister in the M. E. Church from his 25th year to his death, Jan. 6, 1899, at. Los Angeles, Cal. Husband and wife were buried in the same grave at Seattle, Wash.
6201. i. GEORGE B., b. Oct., 1852; d. 1866.
6202. ii. CORA, b. 1856; d. 1874.
6203. iii. NELLY BAKER, b. 1861; m. Dec. 24, 1890, Chas. A. Kilbourne, Seattle, Wash. Several ch.
6204. iv. JOHN, b. 1878; d. 1879.

2978³. HIRAM C., (1496, 557, 185, 53, 16, 5,) b. Sept. 2, 1832; m. 1856, Caroline Ray, Berea, O.; d. Feb., 1858.

6205. i. FRED M., b. 1857. Res. with his mother in Kansas.

2979³. FRANCIS M., (1496, 557, 185, 53, 16, 5,) b. May 26, 1844; m. 1883, Mary Watterson, Cleveland, O. Res., Sandusky, O.

6206. i. JESSIE b. 1884, Cleveland, O.

6207. ii. MAY, b. 1886, Cleveland, O. Res., Cleveland; unm.

3741. WALTER EBER FOOTE, (2448, 1495, 557, 185, 53, 16, 5,) b. Feb. 10, 1858; m. May 15, 188—, Katherine Warner, Penfield, O. She was b. Sept. 25, 1870. Res., Cleveland, O.

6208. i. GRACE DOROTHY, b. Feb. 12, 1896.

5000. NATHANIEL FREDERICK FOOTE, (3300, 1826, 754, 235, 73, 25, 9, 3,) b. Nov. 3, 1872; m. Nov. 11, 1902, at Brooklyn, N. Y., Mabel Norton Toole.

7000. i. ELEANOR NORTON, b. at Brooklyn, N. Y., Apr. 20, 1905.

5051. CAPT. ARTHUR REDINGTON FOOTE, (3351, 1890, 798, 247, 76, 25, 9, 3,) b. Norwich, N. Y., May 7, 1870; m. Dec. 29, 1903, Emma Ward, dau. of Dr. Reed Burns, of Scranton, Pa. She was b. at Honesdale, Pa., Oct. 11, 1877. He served through the Spanish-American War as Second Lieutenant, 13th Regiment Pa. Vol. Infantry. Served 17 years in the National Guard of Pa., retiring in 1903 with the rank of Captain. In Sept., 1903, Capt. Foote removed to Charleston, W. Va., and is General Manager of the Blue Creek Coal and Land Co., and the Kanawha and W. Va. R. R. Co. He is a Ruling Elder in the Presbyterian Church.

7021. i ARTHUR REDINGTON, b. Scranton, Pa., Aug. 17, 1906.

5059. ISAAC FOOTE, (3354, 1893, 798, 247, 76, 25, 9, 3,) b. Feb., 1879, Beatrice, Mich.; m. Sept. 25, 1904, Lillie McRight, of Formoso, Kan.

7022. i. ORA MAY, b. Sept. 4, 1905, Beatrice, Mich.

5063. WARREN MATHEWS FOOTE, (3368, 1901, 799, 247, 76, 25, 9, 3,) b. Ames, Ia., Dec. 27, 1872; m. May 14, 1896, Melanie, dau. of Florence and William Grugan of 1317 Arch St., Phil., Pa. She was b. Philadelphia, Pa., Feb. 14, 1873. He graduated from the University of Pa. in 1894, with the degree of B. S. He is manager of the Foote Mineral Co. at Philadelphia, Pa.

7032. i. ELEANOR JUSTICE, b. Philadelphia, Nov. 18, 1902.

7033. ii. FLORENCE MELANIE, b. Nov. 23, 1906.

5140. ALBERT L. FOOTE, (3511, 2063, 897, 284, 85, 26, 9, 3,) b. Aug. 23, 1863; m. June 20, 1888, Annie M. Martin, of Brooklyn, N. Y. She was b. Mar. 10, 1864. Res., Brooklyn, N. Y.

7063. i. CATHERINE V., b. Dec. 4, 1887.

7064. ii. JOHN H., b. Aug. 15, 1889.

7065. iii. WILLIAM, b. Oct. 21, 1891; d. Apr. 29, 1892.

7066. iv. THOMAS A., b. Feb. 27, 1893.

7067. v. MATTHEW M., b. Aug. 1, 1895.

7068. vi. FLORENCE C., b. Oct. 29, 1897.

7069. vii. JEROME J., b. Oct. 29, 1903.

5157. IRA L. FOOTE, (3522, 2083, 919, 290, 85, 26, 9, 3,) b. Rochester, N. Y., June 15, 1880; m. June 15, 1904, Nellie Drury. Res., Oswego, N. Y.

7070. i. DONALD H., b. Oswego, N. Y., Oct. 7, 1905.

5176. HOMER FOOTE, JR., (3564, 2110, 935, 298, 89, 26, 9, 3,) b. Spring-field, Mass., July 5, 1865; m. June 28, 1893, Margaret H., dau. of David Williams. She was b. New York City, Sept. 8, 1869. Res., Tarrytown-on-the-Hudson, N. Y.

7071. i. ELIOT BROOKS, b. Hackensack, N. J., Apr. 1, 1894.

5198. ARTHUR PERCIVAL FOOTE, (3612, 2145, 983, 308, 92, 27, 9, 3,) b. Sept. 29, 1854; m. Nov. 9, 1881, Avis Anna,, dau. of John Holt, of Nepenskun, Wis. She was b. July 19, 1854, and d. May 18, 1907. Farmer. They live with and care for his aged parents in Nepenskun, Wis.

7072. i. ERMA, b. Feb. 20, 1888.
7073. ii. ARTHUR CLAIR, b. Oct 8, 1889.
7074. iii. JOHN HENRY, b. May 30, 1893.
7075. iv. CHARLES LYNDON, b. June 28, 1895.

5207. EDWIN HAROLD FOOTE, (3616, 2145, 983, 308, 92, 27, 9, 3,) b. Nepenskun, Wis., June 27, 1864; m. May 18, 1892, in Riceville, Ia., Mehitable, dau. of Henry McRorie. She was b. Nov. 28, 1871, in Douglas, Iowa. Farmer. Res., Jenkins, Ia.

7076. i. CECIL EDWIN, b. Oct. 23, 1901, in Jenkins, Ia.
7077. ii. ALICE LORENA, b. July 23, 1904, in Jenkins, Ia.

5209. HARLEY BENJAMIN FOOTE, (3616, 2145, 983, 308, 92, 27, 9, 3,) b. Berlin, Wis., Feb. 1, 1869; m. in Cresco, Ia., Dec. 7, 1899, Emma E. Millington. She was b. Apr. 24, 1876. He is editor and publisher of a paper in Stewartville, Minn. Ch. all b. in Stewartville, Minn.

7078. i. OLIVE MARIE, b. Jan. 7, 1902.
7079. ii. LUCILE ELLEN, b. Feb. 8, 1903.
7080. iii. EDITH MARTHA, b. Nov. 17, 1904.

5225. GEORGE LUCIUS FOOTE, (3630, 2152, 988, 309, 92, 27, 9, 3,) b. Brooklyn, N. Y., Feb. 3, 1871; m. Oct. 24, 1894, Grace Bunnell, of Brooklyn, N. Y.

7081. i. MARJORIE, b. June 12, 1896, in Brooklyn, N. Y.

5230. THEODORE MARSHALL, JR., (3631, 2152, 988, 309, 92, 27, 9, 3,) of Danville, Ill.; m. Alfa May, dau. of A. S. Price, of Danville, Ill., June 30, 1901. Mr. Foote is an electrical expert.

7082. i. MADGE EVELYN, b. at Danville, Ill., May 1, 1902.
7083. ii. EMMA ELEANOR, b. at Danville, Ill., Apr. 7, 1905.

5263. LOUIS HOWARD FOOTE, (3665, 2180, 1003, 311, 92, 27, 9, 3,) b. Sept. 21, 1873; m. Effie Caviness Cuepepper, dau. of Jonathan H. Caviness. She was b. Sept. 1, 1869. Lumberman. Res., Tishomingo, Ind. Ter.

7084. LOUIS HOWARD, b. Jan. 6, 1904.

5316. WILLIAM LEWIS FOOTE, (3725, 2235, 1069, 347, 105, 28, 9, 3,) b. 1881; m. Gertrude Ford. Res., Holyoke, Mass.

7085. i. LEWIS FORD, b. 1905.

6106. ORLO ALANSON FOOTE, (4964, 2271, 1095, 370, 115, 37, 10, 3,) b. June 22, 1850; m. Oct. 16, 1871, Sarah J. Young, of Rock Creek, O. Res., Cleveland, O.

7086. i. FRANCIS NATHANIEL, b. June 7, 1873, Akron, O.; m. June 6, 1901, Maud Mull Maxson, of Ravenna, O. Secretary of the Foote-Howard Co., Cleveland, O.

7087. ii. KATHERINE MINERVA, b. Aug. 16, 1874; d. Mar. 9, 1893, in Cleveland, O.

7088. iii. ANNA MARIA, b. Mar. 11, 1880, Cleveland; m. Nov. 21, 1906, Edward H. Ruck, of Cleveland, O.

7089. iv. ORLO ALANSON, b. Mar. 3, 1887. Res., Cleveland, O.

7090. v. RUTH LLEWELLEN, b. Aug. 30, 1889. Res., Cleveland, O.

6130. JUDGE CHARLES EUGENE FOOTE, (4976, 2276, 1095, 370, 115, 37, 10, 3,) b. Jefferson, O., July 23, 1873; m. Conchita Astol, of Ponce, Porto Rico. He was educated in Washington, D. C. Graduated at the Columbia University Law School. Was admitted to the Washington Bar in 1893. Practised law in Washington, and two years in New York, N. Y. Went to Porto Rico, Apr., 1899, as Supervisor of Schools. Appointed Associate Judge of Humacao District. When laws were changed was appointed District Judge of Guayama District, and afterwards, by request, appointed Judge of the Humacao District, Porto Rico.

7091. i. MORRIS EUGENE, b. Humacao, Porto Rico.

7092. ii. ANN ELLEN, b. Guayama, Porto Rico.

7093. iii. KATHARINE LUCILE, b. Humacao, Porto Rico.

5353. WILLIE EDWARD FOOTE, (3787, 2311, 1115, 375, 115, 37, 10, 3,) b. Apr. 17, 1862, at Grand Rapids, Mich.; m. Nov. 17, 1885, Carrie E. Fuller, of Grand Rapids, Mich.

7101. i. FRANK LEROY, b. July 18, 1887, Grand Rapids, Mich.

7102. ii. NINA L., b. Nov 5, 1891, Grand Rapids, Mich.

7103. iii. WILLIE EDWARD, b. Oct. 12, 1893, Grand Rapids, Mich.

5357. FRANK STUART FOOTE, (3787, 2311, 1115, 375, 115, 10, 3,) b. June 29, 1872, Grand Rapids, Mich.; m. Apr. 20, 1897, Florence Edna Zorus, of Homer, Ill. Res., Grand Rapids, Mich.

7104. i. VERNON STUART, b. Feb. 14, 1900.

7105. ii. EUGENE HOWARD, b. Oct. 22, 1902.

7106. iii. MARGARET ELLEN, b. June 22, 1904, and d. Apr. 30, 1905, at Grand Rapids, Mich.

5413. ERNEST WILLIAM FOOTE, (3892, 2396, 1148, 383, 117, 37, 10, 3,) b. at Worcester, Mass., Oct. 9, 1881; m. Jan. 10, 1903, Mary Agnes, dau. of Patrick and Catherine (O'Leary) Mahan, at Worcester, Mass. Res., Worcester, Mass.

7119. i. VIOLA MARIE, b. Dec. 22, 1803; d. Jan. 17, 1904.

7120. ii. ELIZABETH ROSE, b. Apr. 4, 1905.

5446. CHESTER R. FOOTE, (3933, 2458, 1186, 392, 118, 37, 10, 3,) b. Sumner Co., Kan., Dec. 8, 1874; m. Oct. 18, 1899, Sarah C. Walker. She was b. Barry Co., Mo., June 17, 1871. Res., May, Oklahoma.

7121 i. ETHEL R., b. Feb. 28, 1902.

5447. FRANCIS EARL FOOTE, (3933, 2458, 1186, 392, 118, 37, 10, 3,) b. Hunewell, Kan., Dec. 27, 1877; m. Jan. 1, 1902, Nora E. Caster, of Woodward, Oklahoma. She was b. Osage, Kan., Jan. 1, 1878. Res., May, Oklahoma.

7122. i. MABEL V., b. Feb. 14, 1903, at May, Oklahoma.

5451. GEORGE FOOTE, (3936, 2458, 1186, 392, 118, 37, 10, 3,) b. Nevada, Mo., Sept. 18, 1883; m. Feb. 17, 1904, Lenna E. Sever. She was b. Sept. 19, 1883. Res., Stockholm, Oklahoma.

7123. i. ADRIAN E., b. Stockholm, Feb. 5, 1905.

5523. DARWIN ORSON FOOTE, (4110, 2589, 1248, 433, 130, 39, 11, 3,) b. May 6, 1862; m. Mar. 5, 1885, Florence Gertrude, dau. of Moses Franklin and Electa Maria Gove, of East Charlotte, Vt. She was b. Lincoln, Vt., June 20, 1866. He is a farmer on the large farm formerly owned by Dennis Hazard, and now by George Foote, and has held several town offices. Res., East Charlotte, Vt. Ch. all b. in Charlotte, Vt.

    7144. i. STELLA RACHEL, b. Oct. 6, 1887. Graduated from Castleton Normal, June, 1905.

    7145. ii. CLARENCE FLOYD, b. Dec. 24, 1890.

    7146. iii. RUTH HAZEL, b. June 20, 1899.

5526. PHILANDER HANFORD FOOTE, (4112, 2591, 1248, 130, 39, 11, 3,) b. Jan., 1859; m. Susie E. M. Foster, June, 1884. Res., Ortonville, Minn.

    7147. i. GRACE M., b. Rochester, Minn., Nov., 1885.

    7148. ii. WALTER, b. Ortonville, Minn., Aug. 15, 1887.

    7149. iii. BESSIE, b. Ortonville.

    7150. iv. BERNICE, b. Ortonville.

    7151. v. RAY, b. Ortonville.

    7152. vi. MARY, b. Ortonville.

5527. JOSEPH CLARENCE FOOTE, (4112, 2591, 1248, 130, 39, 11, 3,) b. Sept. 15, 1862; m. Geneva B. Wilkins. Res., Goodhue, Minn.

    7153. i. MARGARET LUCILLA, b. July 11, 1904, St. Paul Park, Minn.

    7154. ii. FLORENCE GERTRUDE, b. Feb. 1, 1907, Goodhue, Minn.

5529. REV. SAMUEL E. FOOTE, (4112, 2591, 1248, 130, 39, 11, 3,) b. ———; m. June, 1900, at Barlow, O., Annabell McGill. Res., Barlow, O.

    7155. i. ALEEN S., b. Nov., 1903.

5532. HENRY FOOTE, (4113, 2591, 1248, 130, 39, 11, 3,) b. 1858; m. 1886, Clara Henderson. She was b. 1868. Res., West Union, Fayette Co., Ia.

    7156. i. BLANCHE, b. 1888.

    7157. ii. MELVA, b. 1890.

    7158. iii. FERN, b. 1892.

    7159. iv. HARRY, b. 1894.

    7160. v. RUTH, b. 1896.

    7161. vi. ALFRED, b. 1898.

    7162. vii. HAZEL, b. 1900.

    7163. viii. CLARA, b. 1906.

5533. JOHN FOOTE, (4113, 2591, 1248, 130, 39, 11, 3,) b. 1860; m. 1st, 1881, ———; m. 2nd, 1904, ———. Res., Hawkeye, Ia.

    7164. i. WILL R., b. 1883.

    7165. ii. LETA V., b. 1893.

    7166. iii. JOHN C., b. 1898.

    7167. iv. JENTRA E., b. 1905.

5534. SYLVESTER FOOTE, (4113, 2591, 1248, 130, 39, 11, 3,) b. 1862; m. 1891. Res., West Union, Ia.

    7168. i. VICTOR, b. 1893.

    7169. ii. MARION, b. 1898.

    7170. iii. EUGENE, b. 1903.

5544. WILLIS DE WITT FOOTE, (4115, 2591, 1248, 433, 130, 39, 11, 3,) b. Anoka, Minn., Feb. 15, 1876; m. Mamie Fendly, of Woodburg, Ga. Res., Pasadena, Cal.

7171. i. DOROTHY BRYANT, b. Aug. 27, 1905.

7172. ii. FENDLY D., b. Dec. 3, 1906.

5561. NATHANIEL FOOTE, (4142, 2620, 1270, 447, 134, 39, 11, 3,) b. New York City, Feb. 21, 1865; m. June 10, 1886, Katherine, dau. of John R. and Cornelia Andrews. She d. Mar. 24, 1895, in N. Y. City. Res., 987 Madison Ave., N. Y. City, and Englewood, N. J.

7173. i. FREDERICK WILLIAM, b. N. Y. City, Feb. 2, 1892.

6134. J. ARTHUR FOOTE, (4989, 2648, 1280, 459, 137, 39, 11, 3,) b. Oct. 31, 1868; m. Nov. 21, 1889, Nellie Ames, b. Aug. 7, 1864. Res., Meadville, N. Y.

7174. i. FLOYD AMES, b. Jan. 20, 1892.

7175. ii. STUART ARTHUR, b. June 20, 1904.

5586. LARIMON HENRY FOOTE, (4204, 2652, 1281, 459, 137, 39, 11, 3,) b. Apr. 6, 1872; m. Nov. 24, 1890, Barbara Cullar, of South Bend, Ind. Res., South Bend, Ind.

7176. i. MYRTLE BLANCHE, b. July 11, 1892.

7177. ii. DORATHY DEAN, b. Aug. 7, 1894.

7178. iii. HELEN MARGARET, b. May 3, 1902.

5630. EDWARD LIVINGSTON FOOTE, (4256, 2701, 1324, 481, 142, 41, 11, 3,) b. July 9, 1877; m. Sept. 23, 1903, Ethel Pauline Irwin, of Poland, N. Y. She was b. Nov. 26, 1877. He graduated at Lee Center High School in 1892, from Oneonta Normal in 1902. Cattle dealer and butcher. Res., Stamford, N. Y.

7179. i. ELINOR, b. Sept. 27, 1904.

5664. JOHN HOOKER FOOTE, JR., (4281, 2739, 1341, 488, 41, 11, 3,) b. Benton, Ill., Nov. 23, 1871; m. 1st, Nov. 18, 1896, Josephine Wiggin, of Ft. Scott, Kan. She d. Sept. 26, 1897, at Ft. Scott; m. 2nd, Aug. 19, 1905, Julia Eugenia Hamlin.

7180. i. WALTER, b. Aug. 21, 1897; d. Jan. 12, 1898.

7181. ii. WILMA EUGENIA, b. Mar. 20, 1907.

5665. NORMAN DENSMORE FOOTE, (4306, 2739, 1341, 488, 145, 41, 11, 3,) b. Kenosha, Wis., Sept. 18, 1867; m. Mar. 28, 1888, Minnie Robertson. Res., Norman, Okla.

7182. i. ALICE LILLIAN, b. Tupelo, Miss., Feb. 1, 1889.

5666. ARTHUR LEON FOOTE, (4306, 2739, 1341, 488, 145, 41, 11, 3,) b. Woodstock, Ill., Sept. 15, 1872; m. Dec. 23, 1896,. Emma Gilbert, of Sulphur Springs, Texas. Res., Winsboro, Texas.

7183. i. HENRY GILBERT, b. Sulphur Springs, Nov. 9, 1897.

7184. ii. ARTHUR LEON, Jr., b. Sulphur Springs, Sept. 8, 1900.

5672. CARLOS FOOTE, (4288, 2739, 1341, 488, 145, 41, 11, 3,) b. Monna, Neb., June 5, 1881; m. Nov. 30, 1904, Anna R. Amsberry. Res., Monna, Neb.

7185. i. STILES CHARLES, b. Nov. 10, 1905.

5677. FREDERICK CHARLES FOOTE, (4310, 2743, 1341, 488, 145, 41, 11, 3,) b. in Turin, June 20, 1871; m. Sept. 17, 1893, Katherine Elizabeth Berk, of Greig. Res., Turin, N. Y.

7186. i. CHARLES LEON, b. May 27, 1895, at Turin, N. Y.

7187. ii. HELEN GLADYS, b. Lowville, N. Y., Feb. 10, 1897.

7188. iii. GEORGE DEWEY, b. Martinsburg, N. Y., Apr. 24, 1899.

7189. iv. AGNES MYRTLE, b. Turin, N. Y., Mar. 21, 1902.

(34)

5678. LAFAYETTE FOOTE, (4310, 2743, 1341, 488, 145, 41, 11, 3,) b. in Turin, N. Y., May 16, 1876; m. Jan. 4, 1905, at Watertown, Eleanora Emerson.

7190. i. ELMER BERNARD, b. Apr., 1906.

5679. EARL ADONIRAM FOOTE, (4310, 2743, 1341, 488, 145, 41, 11, 3,) b. in Turin, Sept. 2, 1902; m. Ella Louise Powell. Res., Glenfield, N. Y.

7191. i. JAMES LYNN, b. Glenfield, Oct. 7, 1904.

7192. ii. MERRILL THEODORE, b. Mar. 9, 1906; d. May 8, 1906.

5683. GEORGE POWELL FOOTE, (4311, 2743, 1341, 488, 145, 41, 11, 3,) b. July 19, 1870; m. Nov. 25, 1897, Lillian Carpenter. Res., Martinsburg, N. Y. Manager of Holbrook Hunt Co.'s Store.

7193. i. THELMA FRANCES, b. Apr. 15, 1899.

5684. DANIEL WHITAKER FOOTE, (4311, 2743, 1341, 488, 145, 41, 11, 3,) b. Mar. 11, 1875; m. Sept. 7, 1898, Martha A. Stiles. Res., Martinsburg, N. Y.

7194. i. RALPH STILES, b. Aug. 13, 1899.

7195. ii. RONALD E., b. Oct. 14, 1901.

5686. MAYNARD WARREN FOOTE, (4311, 2743, 1341, 488, 145, 41, 11, 3,) b. June 28, 1877; m. Oct. 12, 1898, Jessie Kelly.

7196. i. HAROLD M., b. May 18, 1900.

5731. CHANCEY WELLINGTON FOOTE, (4323, 2753, 1342, 488, 145, 41, 11, 3,) b. Feb. 9, 1878; m. Feb. 9, 1899, Lottie May, dau. of George and Laura Blacklock. She was b. Oct. 26, 1881. Res., North Hartland, N. Y.

7201. i. LILLIAN WINFRED, b. May 9, 1900.

7202. ii. EDITH LAURA, b. Apr. 18, 1903.

7203. iii. ETHEL BEATRICE, b. Apr. 10, 1905.

5733. LOREN ALLEN FOOTE, (4325, 2753, 1342, 488, 145, 41, 11, 3,) b. Oct. 26, 1866; m. 1st, Carrie Bidleman; m. 2nd, Clara Mudge. Res., Somerset, Niagara Co., N. Y.

7204. i. STANLEY A., b. May 3, 1897. By 1st wife.

5734. REUBEN C. FOOTE, (4325, 2753, 1342, 488, 145, 41, 11, 3,) b. Dec. 22, 1869; m. Minnie A. Hoffman. Res., Wilson, Niagara Co., N. Y.

7205. i. ELMA, b. Nov. 26, 1887; m. S. D. Plumb.

7206. ii. LESTER, b. Jan. 28, 1890.

5736. SENECA B. FOOTE, (4329, 2753, 1342, 488, 145, 41, 11, 3,) b. Pendleton, N. Y., Sept. 21, 1876; m. June 18, 1902, Kathyrin Denigan, of Buffalo, N. Y. Res., Tonawanda, N. Y.

7207. i. MARGARET, b. in Tonawanda, N. Y., Nov. 24, 1904.

5760. JESSE FOOTE, (4354, 2763, 1345, 488, 145, 41, 11, 3,) b. Montrose, Pa., Aug. 14, 1874; m. Feb. 15, 1893, Edna Smith. She d. Apr. 23, 1903; m. 2nd, Apr. 9, 1905, Mrs. George Seibert. Res., St. Paul, Minn.

7210. i. JAMES LESLIE, b. Sept. 16, 1894.

7211. ii. MELVIN, b. Sept. 23, 1898.

5849. RALPH LEROY FOOTE, (4496, 2874, 1442, 527, 171, 47, 13, 5,) b. May 14, 1883; m. Nov. 22, 1905, Hannah Boe, of Monte Video, Minn.

7212. i. CLAYTON EARL, b. Sept. 6, 1906.

5909. ALBERT WILLIAM FOOTE, (4629, 2998, 1517, 565, 196, 54, 16, 5,) b. Northford, Ct., June 2, 1879; m. Oct. 21, 1903, Alice Parsons (No. 4629), dau.

COL. MORRIS JULIUS FOOTE. No. 4976

No. 5989   No. 5988
FAMILY OF WILLIS ORLIN FOOTE. No. 4722

No. 7253   No. 7257   No. 7255   No. 7253   No. 7251
No. 7252   No. 7258   No. 7251

of Lucius Foote. She was b. Sept. 18, 1878, at Durham, Ct. He was educated at Wallingford High School, Ct. Farmer. Res., Northford, Ct.

    7222. i. LOUISE SELINA, b. Jan. 15, 1905.

    5979. ABRAM WILLIAM FOOTE, (4712, 3126, 1675, 630, 211, 60, 18, 5,) b. Cornwall, Vt., Oct. 24, 1862; m. Bridport, Dec. 18, 1883, Kate Dodge, dau. of John Darwin and Maria Alzina (Johnson) Nichols, of Bridport, Vt. Mr. Nichols was b. in Peru, N. Y., June 27, 1827; d. in Granville, Vt., Aug., 1894. Mrs. Nichols was b. July 17, 1836; d. in Cornwall, Vt., Mar. 23, 1903. Both buried at Bridport, Vt. Mrs. Foote was b. at Peru, N. Y., Nov. 14, 1864. Mr. Foote has held the usual town offices, representing the town in the General Assembly of 1900, and was elected Assistant Judge of Addison County Court in 1902, re-elected in 1904. Is President and Manager of the Rutland Co. Tel. & Tel. Co., and Manager of the Cornwall Tel. & Tel. Co. Res., Cornwall. P. O., Middlebury, Vt.

    7251. i. WILLIAM ROLLIN, b. Nov. 2, 1884. Educated at Middlebury High School and Vermont Academy, Saxtons River, Vt. Inspector for N. E. Tel. & Tel. Co., Burlington, Vt., in 1905, and now (1907) Assistant Manager of The Rutland Co. Tel. & Tel. Co.

    7252. ii. EVA GERTRUDE, b. Aug. 30, 1886. Educated at Vermont Academy, Saxtons River, Vt. Graduated from Castleton Normal School in June, 1905. Has taught continuously since then in the public schools in Cornwall, Vt.

    7253. iii. ARABELLA WILCOX, b. Sept. 5, 1888. Educated at Middlebury High School. With her sister's help, she did the typewriting of the copy for this book.

    7254. iv. KATHLEEN MARIA, b. Oct. 24, 1889. Graduated from Middlebury High School in June, 1907. Entered Middlebury College, Sept., 1907

    7255. v. CHARLES NICHOLS, b. Jan. 2, 1891. Student in Middlebury High School.

    7256. vi. JESSIE EMMA, b. Apr. 4, 1892. Student in Middlebury High School. Helped her sister in typewriting the copy for this book.

    7257. vii. RALPH ABRAM, b. Sept. 19, 1894.

    7258. viii. ESTELLE JULIA, b. Aug. 19, 1899.

    5980. FRANK SAMPSON FOOTE, (4712, 3126, 1675, 630, 211, 60, 18, 5,) b. Cornwall, Vt., May 16, 1869; m. June 6, 1893, Hila Rosebella, dau. of Samuel and Julia (Washburne) Wolcott. She was b. Feb. 17, 1876. Mr. Foote is an artist, painter and musician, and Organist in the Memorial Baptist Church at Middlebury, Vt. Res., Cornwall, Vt.

    7259. i. HAROLD, b. and d. Aug., 1894.

    7260. ii. INEZ JULIA, b. July 4, 1895.

    7261. iii. REGINALD ROLLIN, b. Mar. 7, 1898.

    7262. iv. IRIS MARY, b. Aug. 5, 1901.

    7263. v. BEATRICE DOROTHY, b. Mar. 28, 1906.

    5982. SILAS N. FOOTE, (4716, 1678, 630, 211, 60, 18, 5,) b. Aug. 4, 1866; m. Nov. 24, 1897, Eleanor O. Farnsworth, of Alton, Ill. Res., 448 Hartford Ave., Los Angeles, Cal.

    7264. i. SILAS EVERETT, b. in Topeka, Kansas, Mar. 1, 1901.

    7265. ii. EDNA MAY, b. in Topeka, Kansas, Jan. 25, 1903.

5995. WALLACE CALVIN FOOTE, (4740, 3141, 1679, 630, 211, 60, 18, 5,) b. Middlebury, Vt., July 25, 1867; m. Aug. 12, 1891, Mattie May, dau. of Henry T. Langworthy, of Middlebury, Vt. He is a dry goods merchant of Vergennes, Vt.

    7266. i. HAROLD MAURICE, b. Middlebury, Vt., Oct. 11, 1895.

    7267. ii. ELSIE LANGWORTHY, b. Vergennes, Vt, Apr. 15, 1898.

6003. ALFRED W. FOOTE, (4750, 3145, 1679, 630, 211, 60, 18, 5,) b. Ottawa, Wis., Nov. 17, 1878; m. Minnie, dau. of Angnsl Detloff, of Eagle, Wis. Educated at Milton, Wis. Taught school. Served as a private in Co. C, 1st Regt. Wis. Vols., during the Spanish-American War. Farmer. Res., Palmyra, Wis.

    7268. i. ELMER RAYMOND, b. Palmyra, Wis., May 19, 1901.

    7269. ii. BESSIE MAY, b. Palmyra, Oct. 15, 1903.

    7270. iii. MYRTLE FRANCES, b. Palmyra, Aug. 16, 1905.

6009. MYRON M. FOOTE, (4756, 3159, 1694, 650, 216, 60, 18, 5,) b. Feb. 11, 1866; m. Apr. 4, 1894, Gertrude L. Allen. Res., Malone, N. Y.

    7271. i. CHARLES LEROY, b. May 20, 1896; d. Sept. 20, 1896.

    7272. ii. KENNETH M., b. Mar. 20, 1900.

    7273. iii. DAYTON DONALD, b. Nov. 11, 1905.

6012. LYMAN L. FOOTE, (4757, 3159, 1694, 216, 60, 18, 5,) b. Feb. 2, 1869; m. Nov. 25, 1889, Libbie J. Dougherty. She d. Jan. 17, 1897, ae. 31; m. 2nd, Sept. 25, 1901, Bridget Daly. Res., Malone, N. Y.

    7274. i. ELLA A., b. Aug. 15, 1893.

    7275. ii. LEWIS DESMOND, b. Jan. 11, 1904.

    7276. iii. MARION KATHARINE, b. Aug. 21, 1905.

6015. DR. NEWTON F. FOOTE, (4758, 3159, 1694, 216, 60, 18, 5,) b. Constable, N. Y., Aug. 4, 1875; m. Sept. 22, 1897, Rebecca Rutler. She was b. Feb. 23, 1876.

    7277. i. LELAND F., b. Apr. 19, 1899.

    7278. ii. JEWETT J., b. Aug. 19, 1902.

2157. WILLIAM E., (992, 309, 92, 27, 9, 3,) b. Nov. 9, 1820; m. Lucy Ann Foote. He d.

    7279. i. SAMUEL M., b. Oct. 9, 1851.

    7280. ii. CHARLES, b. ———; d. ———.

    7281. iii. WILLIAM, Jr., b. Nov. 24, 1855.

    7282. iv. CALVIN .M., b. Sept. 20, 1862; d. ———.

ADDITIONS AND CORRECTIONS.

P. 25, No. 7, (5) Mercy Judson, m. Solomon Burton; g.-g.-g.-grandfather of Bishop Lewis W. Burton, of Lexington, Ky.

P. 44, No. 233, (7) Asa Bigelow, was a merchant at Malden, N. Y. Ch.: Hon. John Bigelow, of Gramary Park, N. Y. President of Library Association at Bryant Square and 42nd St., N. Y. No. 234, Hon. W. H. Richmond, of Scranton, Pa., is a descendant of Ann and Joshua Bailey.

P. 47, No. 238, Rev. Caleb Frank Gates, D. D., President of Roberts College, Constantinople, Turkey, is a descendant of Esther and Caleb Gates.

P. 129, No. 418, Enoch Foote was a General of the State Militia, also represented Bridgeport, Ct., in the State Legislature in 1822 and 1831; d. Mar. 14, 1856.

715. GOV. SAMUEL AUGUSTUS FOOTE, (223, 61, 18, 5,) b. Nov. 8, 1780, Cheshire, Ct. (For family record see page 188. Portrait opposite page 185.) Though of a delicate constitution in childhood and youth, he prepared for and graduated at Yale College before he was 17 years of age. He subsequently pursued the study of law with the late Judge Reeve, at Litchfield, until declining health compelled him to relinquish the cherished purpose of entering the legal profession. He commenced business at New Haven, in the West India trade, in 1803. In this business he continued, occasionally taking a voyage, for the double purpose of benefiting his health and his pecuniary affairs, until about the year 1813, when the war and the declining health of his father induced him to retire to Cheshire, where he resided upon the estate where he was born until the period of his own death, which occurred Sept. 16, 1846.

From the early part of the year 1817 to the year 1835, he was in public life. During this time he was repeatedly a member and Speaker of the House of Representatives of Connecticut, elected to the Senate of that State, a member of the House of Representatives of the United States, Governor of the State, and subsequently, in 1844, one of her Presidential Electors. When a member of the Senate of the United States, he introduced the resolution which still bears his name, and on which Webster and Hayne made the splendid efforts which signalized themselves and the American Senate. While Governor of the State, Mr. Foote received the degree of LL.D. from the College where he graduated, and in his last protracted illness he enjoyed the like filial attention which, under similar circumstances, he had bestowed upon his own father.

The Rev. Edward Bull, formerly a tutor in Yale College, who had resided at Cheshire, and been familiar with Governor Foote for several years previous to his decease, thus speaks of his public and private character:

Governor Foote was for a long period employed almost constantly in the service of the public: There is scarcely any office in the gift of his fellow citizens which they did not confer on him. He was successively a member of the House of Representatives, Speaker, and Governor of the State, and occupied seats in both Houses of Congress. In all the important business of his native town, he was sure to be employed whenever his services could be obtained, and they were never declined to save his own time or labor, when his exertions could advance the interest of the public or individuals.

That which specially strikes us as characteristic and distinguishing in Gov. Foote as a public man, is his integrity, industry, decision and perseverance. These qualities are the foundation of his success, and of the confidence which he secured in the community. He was eminently, in all his views and aims, a practical statesman. What he decided to be right and expedient he ever firmly adhered to. What he aimed to accomplish he labored at as a working man, systematically and perseveringly. His measures might not always be approved, but the honest convictions by which he held, and the fearless fidelity and honest zeal with which he pursued them, was never questioned by any one who knew him.

He was, at least a portion of his life, a warm party man, but no party drill could ever bring him to give his vote for a measure which he had denounced as unwise and inexpedient. No man ever more utterly repudiated the doctrine that offices are the mere spoils which are acquired by the successful competitor. The principle to which he ever adhered is that those who receive the honors and emoluments of office are debtors to their constituents to the full amount of a faithful devotion of their time and talents to their official duties. To this principle he conscientiously conformed his own conduct, both in the general business of legislation and in prosecuting and securing the rights of such as entrusted him with their claims. To this last remark, I doubt not, some who read this will bear testimony by the recollection of such services, gratuitously rendered to themselves or their friends.

Governor Foote was an exemplary and consistent member of the Congregational Church and Society of Cheshire, of which (embracing a period of nearly a century), his father and grandfather were successively pastors. Here, as well as in all his social relations, his influence was extensive and exerted to promote the ends of the Gospel,—truth, order, harmony, Christian morality and true Godliness.

In his family everything was conducted by a uniform system of order, and a frank and generous hospitality maintained towards his friends. As a father, though he gave no countenance to that laxness of parental restraint which is so common at this day, yet no one ever made home more pleasant and dearer to his children, nor received from them more unequivocal tokens of their love and reverence.

P. 227, No. 2159, iii, JOSEPHINE CHARLOTTE, b. Dec. 18, 1828; m. Col. Wm. Ladew, of Ulster Co., N. Y. She d. May 25, 1907, N. Y. City. He d. Apr. 26, 1880. Ch.: (1) Frances Antoinette, b. Feb. 3, 1848, Ulster Co.; m. June 4, 1873, Louis Van Graveness, of Kingston, N. Y. Ch.: (a) Josephine, b. June 12, 1874, Kingston, N. Y. (b) Flora, b. Sept. 19, ——, Rhinebeck, N. Y. (c) Mary, b. Mar. 9, 1881, Brooklyn, N. Y. (d) Lulu, b. Nov. 8, 1893, Kingston, N. Y. (2) Charles Henry Clay, b. May 30, 1850; m. Emma Barber, Rhinebeck, N. Y. (3) Flora Estella, b. Feb. 19, 1852, Herkimer Co., N. Y.; m. Edwin Boxter, of Jersey City, N. J. (4) Ella Della, b. Oct. 21, 1855; m. Henry Covert, of Jersey City, N. J. (5) William Phillips, b. Nov. 11, 1858; m. Isabella Pratt, of Rhinebeck, N. Y.

P. 227, No. 2161, v, ISABELLA, b. May 8, 1837; m. Alfonso Phillips. Ch.: (1) William Ladew. Res., Rochester, N. Y.

P. 243, No. 2378, John. Ch.: Mary E. Miller. Res., Lafayette, Colo.

P. 265, Bishop Frederick Foote Johnson, of Sioux Falls, S. D., is a descendant of Rhesa, No. 1270.

P. 298, No. 1496, Chauncey Foote, d. Feb., 1872, Wellington, O. Mrs. Foote d. Apr. 10, 1899, at Wellington, O. Was a member of the M. E. Church for 88 yrs.

No. 2978[1], Marcus B., b. Mar. 29, 1828; d. Apr. 7, 1854.

No. 2978[2], Lucy D. Foote, m. 1850, Shubel Coy. Res., Lafayette, O. Ch.: (1) Ferdinand, b. 1852; was murdered, together with both parents, in Medina, O., July 2, 1862.

No. 2979, Ann E. Foote, b. Dec. 8, 1834; m. 1852, John A. Titus, Berea, O. She d. Feb. 1, 1907. He d. Feb. 5, 1907. Both buried at the same time. Ch.: (1) Ada Eliza, b. 1858; m. 1st, 1880, Charles Baker, of Painesville, O. He d. Oct. 1, 1889. She m. 2nd, Samuel Phelps, of Wellington, O. Ch.: (a) George Baker, b. Aug., 1881, Wellington, O. (b) Mildred Phelps, b. 1896, Wellington, O. (2) Frances, b. 1866; d. 1876.

No. 2979², John F. Foote. Res., San Francisco, Cal., in 1890; n. f. k.

P. 325, No. 3299, Jennie C., b. May 6, 1868.

P. 327, No. 1840, DR. NATHANIEL FOOTE'S ch. were: 3322, i, ARTHUR N., b. Feb. 1, 1865; d. Feb. 1, 1865. 3323, ii, JENNIE A., b. Jan. 8, 1872; d. Sept. 17, 1874.

P. 346, No. 2063, JOHN C. FOOTE, b. Nov. 29, 1802.

P. 363, No. 2191, EDWARD FOOTE, b. Lee, Mass., Oct. 12, 1824; m. Oct. 25, 1849, Mrs. Emily (Curtis) Chapin, dau. of David and Eliza Curtis, of Stockbridge, Mass. She was b. Stockbridge, Oct. 30, 1822; d. Apr. 20, 1898, in Somerville, Mass. In the spring of 1851 Mr. Foote went to Smithtown Branch, L. I., N. Y., where he engaged in farming until the fall of 1864, when he moved to Somerville, where he became a member of the firm of Skilton, Foote & Co., manufacturers of Bunker Hill Pickles, in which business he continued until his death, which occurred May 31, 1898, in Somerville. He was for over 25 years a Deacon in the Broadway Congregational Church of Somerville, Mass.

P. 367, No. 3737, i, MARY TAYLOR, b. Oct. 30, 1868, N. Y. C.; m. Feb. 27, 1892, at Mystic, Ct., Charles W. Noyes, florist. Res., Mystic, Ct. Ch.: (1) Berton Frank, b. Prophetstown, Ill., Aug. 18, 1901. (2) Morgan Foote, b. Prophetstown, July 3, 1904.

No. 3738, ii, BERTHA W., b. Jan. 29, 1871, at S. Norwalk, Ct., unm.

No. 3739, iii, FRANCES MARGARET, b. Oneida, N. Y., Jan. 12, 1874; m. Charles H. Hoxie, at Mystic, Ct., Nov. 21, 1899. Insurance agent. Res., Arlington, Mass. Ch.: (1) Elizabeth Foote, b. Nov. 9, 1900. (2) Frances Van Ripper, b. July 30, 1905.

No. 3742, iii, FRANK HARLEY, b. May 18, 1861; m. Nov. 16, 1892, Elizabeth Neoma Walker, Covington, Tenn. She was b. Feb. 18, 1875, Covington. Res., Obion, Tenn. Ch. (by adoption), Nannie John Abbott, b. June 27, 1891, Glass, Tenn.

No. 3743, iv, ANNA ELIZABETH, m. Apr. 23, 1884, Prof. Frederick William Mueller, at Wellington, O. He was b. Sept., 1863, Sandusky, O. Res., Tarkio, Mo., Tarkio College. Ch.: (1) Lillian Vischer, b. Feb. 12, 1885, Wellington. (2) Helen Margaret, b. Apr. 3, 1892, Galeburg, Ill. (3) Merry Christmas, b. Dec. 25, 1897, Galesburg. (4) Frederick William, Jr., b. Apr. 8, 1900, Galesburg, Ill.

P. 398, No. 4144, HARRIET, m. Wm. Pennington Toler. He is dead.

P. 400, No. 4178, b. Sept. 25, 1855, and No. 4179, b. Aug. 17, 1856.

P. 409, No. 4284, GEORGE W., m. Oct. 4, 1866, Jane F. Husted.

P. 468, No. 3448, Dr. EDWARD M. FOOTE. Ch.: 5112, ii, Priscilla, b. at Greenwich, Ct., Sept., 1907; the youngest in the family.

DESCENDANTS OF PASCO FOOTE

OF SALEM, MASS.

To any who are connected with this branch, and not here recorded, if they will send their family record to A. W. Foote, Middlebury, Vt., the data will be recorded for future publication.

1. PASCO FOOTE, of Salem, Mass., (First record in 1636, when he had a grant of land), joined the Church about 1652-3, when his eight ch. were all baptized, Feb. 6. He d. Nov. 28, 1670. His will was dated Sept. 20, 1670, probated June 30, 1671, by his son Isaac.

   2.   i.   JOHN, b.; probably d. young.
   3.   ii.   MALACHI, b.; probably d. young.
   4.   iii. . SAMUEL, b.; m. Hannah Currier.
   5.   iv.   ELIZABETH, b.; m. ———— Birtch; living in 1670.
   6.   v.   MARY, b.; name Foote in 1670.
   7.   vi.   ISAAC, b.; m. Abigail Ingalls, 6811-17.
   8.   vii.   PASCO, b.; m. Martha Ward and Margaret Stallion, 6818-21.
   9.   viii. ABIGAIL, b.; m. Oct. 15, 1670, George Early, Salem. Ch.: (1)
            Abigail, b. July 1, 1671.

4. CAPT. SAMUEL FOOTE, of Amesbury, "Planter," m. June 23, 1659, Hannah, dau. of Richard and Ann Currier. She was b. July 8, 1843, He received land in Amesbury in 1659-60-62 and 68; was made a townsman in 1660; had seat in meeting-house 1667; oath of allegiance, 1677; Representative, 1689-90. His house was called Capt. Foote's Fort. He was taken by the Indians in the assault on Amesbury and tortured to death July 7, 1690. His son, John, was appointed administrator of the estate in Sept., 1690. Widow Hannah was living 1691. One Hannah Foote was dismissed from Salisbury to Amesbury Church May 5, 1700.

  10.   i.   JOHN, b. July 9, 1660; m. Bathsheba ————, 22-4.

7. ISAAC FOOTE, (1), b. ————; m. Oct. 2, 1668, Abigail, dau. of Thomas Ingalls, Salem, Mass. She was b. in Salem, July 21, 1648.

  11.   i.   ISAAC, b. Feb. 4, 1670; d. in June, 1670.
  12.   ii.   ABIGAIL, b. Sept. 21, 1671.
  13.   iii. SAMUEL, b. Apr. 29, 1673; m. Mary Palmer, 25-8.
  14.   iv.   ELIZABETH, b. Apr., 1675; m. June 29, 1698, Nathaniel, son of
            John and Mary (Tompkins) Felton, of Salem, Mass. He was
            b. June 8, 1672; d. July, 1732. Ch.: (1) Abigail, b. May 12, 1699;
            m. Aug. 25, 1737, James Taylor. (2) Samuel, b. Aug. 7, 1701;
            d. Feb. 2, 1717. (3) Malachi, b. May 14, 1705; m. Feb., 1735,
            Abigail Jacobs. (4) Mary, b. Mar. 16, 1707; m. Nov. 20, 1753,
            Caleb Balah, of Danvers. (5) Elizabeth, b. May 17, 1709. (6)
            Nathaniel, b. Dec. 29, 1710; d. Apr. 3, 1712. (7) Benjamin, b.
            Sept. 9, 1712; m. Joanna ————. (8) Nathaniel, b. May 9,
            1714; m. July 174—, Anna Jacobs. (9) Isaac, b. Mar. 6, 1716.
            Res., Salem, 1748. (10) Samuel, b. May 20, 1721.
  15.   v.   MALACHI, b. Apr. 11, 1680.
  16.   vi.   MARY, b. May 7, 1682; d. in infancy.
  17.   vii. MARY, b. Jan., 1691.

8 PASCO FOOTE, (1,) b. ———; m. 1st, Oct. 2 1668, Martha Ward, in Salem, Mass.; m. 2nd, Nov. 30, 1678, Margaret Stallion. He d. Margaret m. 1688, James Haynes, of New London, Ct.

    18. i. MALACHI, b. Aug. 18, 1668; m. Elizabeth Masters, 29-30.
    19. ii. MARTHA, b. Dec. 14, 1671.
    20. iii. PASCO, b. Sept. 1, 1677.
    21. iv. ISAAC, (by 2nd wife), b. ———.

    10. CAPT. JOHN FOOTE, (4, 1,) b. July 9, 1660; bap. June 22, 1699, at Salisbury; m. Bathsheba ———. She d. Sept. 3, 1727, at Amesbury, Mass. Oath of allegiance, 1677; "Training Band," 1680; "Snow shoe man," 1708; freeman, 1690. Captain of militia. He d. abt. 1737. His son John administered estate June 6, inventory of estate June 25, 1737. Res., Amesbury, Mass. (Old Families of Salisbury and Amesbury, Vol. I., p. 161.)

    22. i. SAMUEL, b. Mar. 3, 1691; m. Dorothy Colby, 31-6.
    23. ii. MEHITABLE, b. Mar. 30, 1694, at Amesbury.
    24. iii. JOHN, b. Dec. 20, 1697, at Amesbury; m. Mary ———, 37.

    13. SAMUEL FOOTE, (7, 1,) b. Apr. 29, 1673; m. Nov. 12, 1696, Mary, dau. of Richard Palmer, of Salem, Mass. She was b. July 8, 1673, in Salem; d. ———. He d. 1741. His wife Mary was appointed administrator of his estate, July 17, 1741. Res., Salem, Mass.

    25. i. ISAAC, b. Aug. 18, 1697; m. Mary Fowler, 38-39.
    26. ii. SAMUEL, b. May 13, 1700; m. Aug. 1, 1723, Elizabeth Britton. Ch.: (1) Samuel.
    27. iii. MARY ELIZABETH, b. Oct. 29, 1701; m. ——— Short.
    28. iv. ABIGAIL, b. Mar. 15, 1704; m. ——— Mansfield.

    18. MALACHI FOOTE, (8, 1,) b. Aug. 18, 1668; m. Dec. 13, 1710, Elizabeth Masters.

    29. i. MALACHI, b. Sept. 18, 1711.
    30. ii. JOHN, b. Aug. 13, 1715; m. Jan. 12, 1745, Mary Turner.

    22. SAMUEL FOOTE, (10, 4, 1,) b. Mar. 3, 1691-2; m. Jan. 29, 1711-2, Dorothy, dau. of Thomas and Mary (Powell) Colby. Res., Amesbury, Mass.

    31. i. PASCO, b. Mar. 17, 1711-2; m. Jemima Colby, 40.
    32. ii. THEOPHILUS, b. Mar. 2, 1714; m. Sarah Challis, 41-49.
    33. iii. BATHSHEBA, b. Apr. 27, 1717.
    34. iv. PELTIAH, b. Jan. 27, 1721.
    35. v. ENOCH, b. Sept. 11, 1725.
    36 vi. SARAH, b. Aug. 29, 1727.

    24. JOHN FOOTE, (10, 4, 1,) b. Dec. 20, 1697; m. Mary ———. Res., Amesbury, Mass., 1737. Inventory of the estate of Capt. John Foote, of Amesbury, returned June 27, 1737.

    37. i. WILLIAM, b. ———; m. Ruth Smith, 49-55.

    25. ISAAC FOOTE, (13, 7, 1,) b. Aug. 18, 1697; m. Oct. 17, 1722, Mary Fowler, of Salem, Mass., Aug. 20, 1741. Administration on the estate of Isaac Foote, late of Salem, granted to his grandson, Samuel Foote, Mariner. Res., Salem, Mass.

    38. i. ENOCH, b. ———; m. Ruth Ingalls, 56-58.
    39. ii. MARY, b. ———.

    31. PASCO FOOTE, (22, 10, 4, 1,) b. Mar. 17, 1711-2; m. Jemima Colby. Res., Amesbury, Mass.

40. i.   JACOB, b. Aug. 11, 1754; m. Sarah Carr, 59-67.

32. THEOPHILUS FOOTE, (22, 10, 4, 1,) b. Mar. 2, 1714; m. 1736, Sarah Challis. Res., Amesbury, Mass.
41. i.   ELIZABETH, b. Dec. 18, 1738.
42. ii.   CHALLIS, b. Apr. 22, 1740. Res., N. H.
42¹. iii. THOMAS, b. Jan 21, 1743; d. young.
43. iv.   SARAH, b. Jan. 21, 1743.
44. v.   ANNA, b. Sept. 22, 1745.
45. vi.   THEOPHILUS, b. Sept. 22, 1747; m. ———; d. 1830; 68-73.
46. vii. THOMAS, b. July 22, 1749; m. Elizabeth Lowell, 74-80.
47· viii. PASCO, b. May 19, 1751.
48. ix.   SAMUEL, b. Mar. 27, 1756. Res., Maine.

37. WILLIAM FOOTE, (24, 10, 4, 1,) b. 1754, Boston; m. Ruth, dau. of Abner Smith. He d. Mar. 27, 1823, ae. 69 years. She d. Mar. 13, 1813, ae. 59 years.
49. i.   EUNICE, b. Nov. 8, 1778; m. Warham Sackett.
50. ii.   RUTH, b. Nov. 26, 1780; m. ——— Weller.
51. iii. ASA W., b. Aug. 4, 1786; m. Lucy Johnson and Betsey E. Rice, 81-96.
52. iv.   CHESTER, b. Apr. 3, 1790; m. Amanda Winchell.
53. v.   ALVA THOMAS, b. Jan 12, 1792; m. Asenath Belden, 97-106.
54. vi.   ARBA, b. July 27, 1793; m. Ann Northam.
55. vii. ELECTA, b. Aug. 2, 1797; m. Josiah Pomeroy.

38. ENOCH FOOTE, (25, 13, 7, 1,) b. ———; m. Mar. 8, 1748, Ruth, dau. of Daniel Ingalls. She d. Sept., 1770. He d. Aug., 1764.
56. i.   ENOCH, b. Andover, June 10, 1748, 107-9.
57. ii.   CALEB, b. Andover, July 6, 1750; m. Mary Dedman, 110-4.
58. iii. SAMUEL, b. Mar. 2, 1759. Res., Newburyport, Mass.; d. at sea, unm., abt. 1780.

40. JACOB FOOTE, (31, 22, 10, 4, 1,) b. Aug. 11, 1754, Amesbury, Mass. (Old Families of Salisbury and Amesbury, Mass., Vol. II., p. 530); m. Mar. 19, 1775, Kingston, N. H., Sarah, dau. of Silvanus and Sarah (Elliott) Carr. She was b. July 6, 1753. She d. Dec. 8, 1832. He d. Jan. 29, 1828.
59. i.   JOHN, b May 27, 1775; m. Elizabeth M. Morse, 115-21.
60. ii.   MARY, b. June 25, 1777; d. Oct. 5, 1846, in Ohio.
61. iii. ELIAS, b. Sept. 7, 1779; d. Sept. 27, 1844.
62. iv.   SARAH, b. Sept. 9, 1781; d. May 25, 1859.
63. v.   BETTY, b. May 18, 1784; d. Feb. 22, 1800.
64. vi.   JACOB, b. Mar. 12, 1787; m. Fanny ———, 122-9.
65. vii. DOROTHY, b. Oct. 10, 1789; d. Dec. 5, 1853, in Ohio.
66. viii. LEVI, b. Apr. 3, 1792; m. Caroline Ferris, 130.
67. ix.   LEURETIA, b. May 11, 1797.

45. THEOPHILUS FOOTE, (32, 22, 10, 4, 1,) b. Sept. 22, 1747. Res., Amesbury, Mass.
68. i.   EPHRAIM.
69. ii.   LOWELL, b. Aug., 1785.
70. iii. ROBERT, m. Dec. 6, 1818, Susan Goodrich, of Haverhill, Mass. In 1839 his estate was settled. Res., Amesbury, Mass.
71. iv.   JOHN.

72. v. JAMES, b. Aug. 28, 1789; m. Susan Woodman, 131-8.
73. vi. WILLIAM, b. Sept. 2, 1795; d. Aug. 11, 1862.

46. THOMAS FOOTE, (32, 22, 10, 4, 1,) b. July 22, 1749, in Amesbury; m. Elizabeth, dau. of Capt. Abner and Elizabeth (Eaton) Lowell.

74. i. THOMAS, b. June 5, 1772.
75. ii. ABNER, b. May 4, 1774.
76. iii. SALLY, b. 1779.
77. iv. LEWIS, b. 1784; 139-42.
78. v. LUKEY, b. 1786.
79. vi. JAMES, b. 1789.
80. vii. WILLIAM, b. 1794.

51. ASA WILLIAM FOOTE, (37, 24, 10, 4, 1,) b. Aug. 4, 1786, Chester, Mass.; m. 1st, Lucy Johnson; m. 2nd, Betsey Rice, of Waterford, Maine. She was b. Feb. 19, 1790; d. Dec. 3, 1864. Lucy Johnson Foote was b. May 18, 1784; d. 1816. He was a farmer. Res., Chester, Mass.; d. May 16, 1845.

81. i. CHARLES, b. Sept. 2, 1808, Chester, Mass.; m. Ann Card, of New York. He d. Ch.: (1) Henrietta, b. ———; m. Gustavus Baylies. She d. (2) Mary, b. ———. Res., Newtown, L. I. (3) Anna.

82. ii. SARAH, b. Dec. 25, 1810, Chester, Mass.; m. Dea. Alex. Ingham, Middlefield, Mass. She d. July 25, 1848. Ch.: (1) Sarah, b. ———; m. N. G. Bonney. He d. Res., Norwich, Ct. Ch.: (a) Thurston. (b) Jennie. (2) Samuel, b. ———; d. ———. (3) Diantha, b. ———; d. ———.

83. iii. ALLEN, b. June 16, 1812; m. Harriet A. Renne, Pittsfield, Mass. He d. May 16, 1848. Ch.: (1) Edwardetta, b. Oct. 7, 1838, Oregon, Ogle Co., Ill.; m. Oct. 26, 1856, Rufus B. Artz, b. Aug. 16, 1834, Williamsport, Md. Ch.: (a) Oscar Allen, b. Aug. 10, 1857, Oregon, Ill. (b) Francis, b. Apr. 29, 1860, Rochelle, Ill. (c) Harriet, b. Jan. 12, 1862, Mt. Morris, Ill.

84. iv. LEWIS, b. Feb. 24, 1814; m. 1st, Delia Paul; m. 2nd, Mrs. Mary Buck Miller; d. Nov. 25, 1865. Ch.: (1) Clark; res., Chicago. (2) Alice, b. ———; m. ——— Wilcoxon; res., Belle Plaine, Iowa. (3) Viola, b.; d. (4) Anna, b. ———; m. Charles M. Brag; res., Chicago. (5) Clara, b. ———; m. ——— Stone; res., Torrance, Cal. (6) Albert, b.; res., Chicago. (7) Lucy, b.; m. Adam Ringlep; res., Maquoketa, Ia.

85. v. DWIGHT, b. Dec. 13, 1815; m. Emily Hughs. He d. Jan. 14, 1879. Ch.: (1) Elias; res., Eldora, Ia. (2) Sarah; b.; res., Eldora, Ill.

86. vi. LUCY ANN, b. May 12, 1818; d. Jan. 27, 1833; unm.

87. vii. EBER RICE, b. May 19, 1819; m. Francis Loomis, Southwick, Mass. He d. Mar. 30, 1853.

88. viii. SAMUEL BUDD, b. Nov. 6, 1820; m. Catherine Foss, Huntington, Mass. He d. Apr. 14, 1883. Ch.: (1) Sarah. (2) Frank. (3) Isabel. (4) Georgianna. (5) Hattie. (6) Eliza. (7) Andrew. (8) David.

89. ix. FRANCIS BURR, b. Jan. 13, 1822; m. Amanda Corning, Stepney, Ct. He d. Sept. 13, 1877. Ch.: (1) Franklin W. (2) Sarah E. (3) Hattie A.

90. x. FANNY BURTON, b. Jan. 13, 1822; d. July 16, 1898; unm.

91. xi. ASA SPRONT, b. Aug. 25, 1823; m. Mary E. Daniels, 142-3.
92. xii. FRANK ERASTUS, b. Mar. 4, 1825; m. Eugenia Whipple and Frances M. Noble, 144-7.
93. xiii. WILLIAM LAFAYETTE, b. Mar. 31, 1827; d. Dec. 24, 1851; unm.
94. xiv. MARY ANN, b. Oct. 15, 1828; d. Feb. 18, 1850; unm.
95. xv. GEORGE WASHINGTON, b. Apr. 28, 1830; m. Mary Dewey and Alice Dean, 148-52.
96. xvi. ELIZA CAROLINE, b. Jan. 31, 1833; m. Reuben Noble, Westfield, Mass., b. Oct. 26, 1820; m. Mar. 29, 1854; d. June 2, 1890. Was a manufacturer of whips. Was Postmaster of Westfield, 1858-61. State Senator, 1872. House of Representatives, 1874-76. In 1868, he was the Democratic Candidate for Lieutenant-Governor, and in 1870 Democratic Candidate for Congress, Henry L. Davis, of Pittsfield, being the opposing candidate.

53. DEA. ALVA THOMAS FOOTE, (37, 24, 10, 4, 1,) b. Jan. 12, 1792; m. Asenath Belden. She was b. Mar. 17, 1795, at Wethersfield, Ct.; d. July 24, 1870. He was Deacon of the Congregational Church of Chester Centre, Mass. He d. Apr. 21, 1878.

97. i. CORINTH E., b. Chester, Mass., Sept. 2, 1817; m. Dec. 6, 1843, Samuel Bartlett, of Northampton, Mass. Ch.: (1) Alvah L. Bartlett, b. Aug. 11, 1844; m. Aug. 15, 1865, Mary Claflin, of Northampton. Ch.: (a) Louis Bartlett, b. Aug. 25, 1867; m. Dec. 3, 1889, Bertha Smith, of Northampton. Ch.: (i) Ada Louise Bartlett, b. Jan. 7, 1891. (ii) Virginia Fay Bartlett, b. Dec. 27, 1906.
98. ii. ALVAH, JR., b. Mar. 4, 1819; m. Sarah Elder and Elizabeth Taylor, 153.
99. iii. ALFRED S., b. Jan. 22, 1821; m. Helen Maria Burnham, 154-6.
100. iv. MERCY, b. ———; d. ae. 3 years.
101. v. JANE L., b. Chester, Mass., July 15, 1825; m. Sept. 15, 1846, Oliver H. Thayer. He was b. Williamsburgh, Mass, Feb. 9, 1824. She d. July 27, 1888, in Hadley, Mass. Ch.: (1) Henry M., b. Jan. 22, 1848; m. Feb. 16, 1871, Helen A. Cook, of Hadley, Mass. She d. Nov., 1893; m. 2nd, Sept., 1894, Lottie Warfield. Ch.: (a) Frank Herbert, b. Nov. 22, 1871; m. Nellie Bissell. Ch.: (i) Mildred, b. (ii) Howard, b. (b) Edith, b. (c) Daisy, b. (twins); d. in infancy. (d) Helen M., b. Feb. 10, 1886. (2) Edward C. Thayer, b. Oct. 3, 1851; m. Nov. 10, 1883, Lillian G. Barkalow, of Holyoke, Mass. Ch.: (a) Frank C., b. July 20, 1886. (b) Bessie G., b. Aug. 21, 1891. (3) Harriet L., b. Aug. 22, 1856; m. Oct. 16, 1879, Samuel D. Smith, of Hadley, Mass. (4) Jennie H., b. Sept. 19, 1859; m. Oct. 24, 1879, Clesson Wood. Ch.: (a) Grace, b. Aug. 20, 1885; d. Apr. 12, 1886. (b) Marion, b. Jan. 17, 1887. (5) Lizzie E., b. Aug. 18, 1863.
102. vi. HARRIETT L., b. Jan. 1, 1829; m. Benjamin Kyle. He d. Ch.: (1) Alice, b. ———; m. William Lonza. Ch.: (a) John Lonza, b. ———; m. Rose Deming. (2) William P. Kyle, b. ———; m. Alice Lane and Mattie ———.
103. vii. REBECCA W., b. Chester, Mass., Mar. 19, 1831; m. Jan. 24, 1885, Ezra Thayer, of Hadley, Mass. He d. Ch.: (1) Charles H.

Thayer, b. Oct. 13, 1858; m. Jan. 19, 1882, Annie Carter. of
Northampton, Mass. Ch.: (a) Bessie Thayer, b. Aug. 25, 1884.

104. viii. EDWARD N., b. Mar. 27, 1833; m. Mary E. Bartlett, 157-8.

105. ix. MONROE B., b. May 12, 1835; d. May 28, 1874; unm.

106. x. CORNELIUS, b. Jan. 29, 1837; d. Jan. 3, 1863; unm.

56. ENOCH FOOTE, (38, 25, 7, 1,) b. Andover, Mass., June 10, 1748. Res.,
Newburyport, Mass.; d. in the West Indies.

107. i. ENOCH, b. Oct. 2, 1775; m. Sally George, 159-61.

108. ii. SAMUEL, b. Dec. 13, 1777; d. at sea, Oct. 20, 1799.

109. iii. JOSEPH, b. Apr. 5, 1781. Went south in 1812; n. f. k.

57. CALEB FOOTE, (38, 25, 13, 7, 1,) b. Andover, Mass., July 6, 1750. Res.,
Salem, Mass.; m. Feb. 13, 1775, Mary, dau. of William Dedman. She was b. Mar.
27, 1751. He d. in the West Indies, May 10, 1787. She d. Nov. 2, 1834.

110. i. MARY, b. Sept. 19, 1776; m. 1794, Wm. Newhall, who d. 1797;
m. 2nd, John Southwick, b. 1776; d. 1854. She d. June 19,
1866. Ch.: (1) Gorham. (2) William. (3) John. (4) Martha.
(5) Mary Sedman, m. Henry L. Reed. Ch.: (a) Henry Alonzo.
(b) Nathaniel. (c) Charles Ferdinand, m. Christina M. Pearson.
Ch.: (i) Charles Albert. (ii) Mary.

111. ii. CALEB, b. July 15, 1778; m. Martha West and Mary West, 162-3.

112. iii. WILLIAM LUCAS, b. ———; d. in infancy.

113. iv. ALEXANDER, b. ———; d. in infancy.

114. v. JOHN, b. Oct. 2, 1786. Clergyman. Res., Conewango, N. Y.; m.
———; d. Oct. 2, 1880. Ch.: (1) Mary L., 164.

59. JOHN FOOTE, (40, 31, 22, 10, 4, 1,) b. May 27, 1775; m. Elizabeth
May, dau. of Daniel Morse, a Revolutionary soldier. Res., Sudbury, Vt., and
Small Point, Georgetown, Me.

115. i. JACOB, b. Aug. 25, 1796; m. Hannah Lowell, 165-7.

116. ii. JAMES M., b. July 13, 1798; m. Lydia Nason. Both d. No ch.

117. iii. JOHN WYMAN, b. June 16, 1804; m. Nancy Lowell, 168-72.

118. iv. MARY, b. Apr. 21, 1807; m. Nichols Blandell. He was a steam
engineer. Both d. Portland, Me.; s. p.

119. v. JANE, b. Apr. 5, 1809; m. Capt. James DeBreman.

120. vi. FRANCIS M., b. Jan. 20, 1813; m. Sarah Fogg, 173-4.

121. vii. SARAH ANN, b. ———; m. Capt. John F. Liscomb. Cn.: (1)
John Francis. (2) William. (3) Hattie.

64. JACOB FOOTE, (31, 22, 10, 4, 1,) b. Mar. 12, 1787; m. Oct. 18, 1810,
Fanny ———. She was b. Haverhill, N. H., May 21, 1787. He d. Oct. 26, 1865.
She d. Nov. 4, 1851.

122. i. BETSEY, b. Warren, Vt., Nov. 28, 1811.

123. ii. POLLY, b. Warren, Apr. 2, 1813; d. Aug. 20, 1814, of dropsy.

124. iii. LEVI B., b. Mar. 8, 1815; d. Aug. 18, 1862.

125. iv. ELIAS, b. May 19, 1817; m. Angeline T., 175.

126. v. JASON, b. Barnet, Vt., July 6, 1819.

127. vi. JACOB, b. Peacham, Apr. 13, 1822; d. Sept. 4, 1823, of dysentery.

128. vii. LAVANDA, b. Peru, N. Y., June 16, 1824.

129. viii. LOUISA, b. Shelburne, Vt., July 24, 1826.

66. LEVI BARTLETT FOOTE, (31, 22, 10, 4, 1,) b. Apr. 3, 1792, Kingston,
N. H.; m. Caroline Ferris. He d. Feb. 20, 1855.

130.. i.   ADELINE, b. Peru, N. Y., Dec. 31, 1823; m. Gilbert Thayer. Res. 2253 Morgan Ave., Morgan Park, Ill.

131. ii.   WILLIAM EDWIN, b. May 16, 1826; m. Elizabeth Crandall, 176.

72. JAMES L. FOOTE, (45, 32, 22, 10, 4, 1,) b. Aug. 28, 1789; m. Susan Woodman, Sept. 4, 1814. She was b. Oct. 5, 1793. He d. Nov. 26, 1872. She d. Oct. 6, 1870. Res., Newburyport, Mass.

131¹. i.   SARAH ANN, b. Nov. 25, 1815; m. May 9, 1836, Benjamin F. Leavitt; d. July 4, 1878.

132. ii.   JAMES HENRY, b. Oct. 6, 1817; m. Apr. 21, 1844, Julia Morriss; d. at sea, Jan. 7, 1864.

133. iii.   SUSAN DAY, b. Jan. 29, 1820; m. Apr. 7, 1847, George W. Robbins. She d. Jan. 2, 1875. Ch.: (1) Harriett H., b. 1848; m. Apr. 19, 1901, Edward Woebus. (2) Susan, b. 1851; d. 1872.

134. iv.   NATHANIEL GREELEY, b. Apr. 11, 1822; m. Aug. 31, 1847, Mary A. Eastman; d. July 17, 1873.

135. v.   JANE BROCK, b. Mar. 29, 1824; m. J. Dudley Lyford, Feb. 24, 1852. She d. Oct. 19, 1865.

136. vi.   WILLIAM THOMAS, b. Jan. 11, 1827; m. Joanna Smith; d. Aug. 2, 1854.

137. vii.   MARTHA ELLEN, b. Aug. 21, 1829; m. Oct. 3, 1850, Albert P. Pierce. Ch.: (1) Frank A., b. Aug. 8, 1851; d. Nov., 1872. (2) Jennie M., b. July 30, 1853; m. Chas. E. Leavitt, 1875. He d. 1891. Ch.: (a) Mabel F., b. 1876; m. 1901, Alexander M. Walt. Ch.: (i) Bernice, b. July, 1902. (b) Chas. A., b. 1878; d. 1879. (c) Herbert P., b. 1880. (d) Lucy H., b. 1889; d. 1890.

138. viii.   JOHN HARROOD, b. July 31, 1833; m. Mary A. Hoffatt, 177-9.

77. LEWIS FOOTE, (46, 32, 22, 10, 4, 1,) b. 1784; m. Apr., 1810, Mary Swett. He was lost at sea on the privateering brig, "Mars," which sailed from Portsmouth, N. H., Sept., 1814, and was never heard from.

139. i.   GEORGE W., b. Jan. 24, 1811.

140. ii.   THOMAS, b. Mar. 14, 1813; m. Lydia Tabor, 180-5.

141. iii.   BETSEY, b. Mar. 14, 1813.

142. iv.   LEWIS, b. DDec. 16, 1814.

91. ASA SPROUT FOOTE, (51, 32, 22, 10, 4, 1,) b. Chester, Mass., Aug. 25, 1823; m. Mary E. Daniels, b. July 10, 1824.

143. i.   HOMER, b. Feb. 5, 1851; m. Mary E. Morgan, 186-8.

144. ii.   EBER, b. Nov. 13, 1853; m. Flora C. Ostorn, 189.

92. FRANK ERASTUS FOOTE, (51, 32, 22, 10, 4, 1,) b. Mar. 4, 1825. Res., Springfield, Mass., and Chester Center, Mass.; m. 1st Eugenia Whipple. She d.; m. 2nd, Francis Noble. He d. May 16, 1905.

144. i.   HELEN E., b.

145. ii.   ANNA B., b.

146. iii.   FRANK C., b.

147. iv.   THURMAN L., b. ———. Res., Springfield, Mass.

95. GEORGE WASHINGTON FOOTE, (51, 32, 22, 10, 4, 1,) b. Chester, Mass., Apr. 28, 1830. Res., 73 Bradford St., Pittsfield, Mass.; m. 1st, Sept. 11, 1855, Mary C., dau. of Erastus and Matilda (Millard) Dewey, of New Lenox, Mass. She was b. Apr. 27, 1833; d. Dec. 3, 1873; m. 2nd, Nov. 24, 1875, Alice B. C., dau. of Benjamin and Jerusha (Dewey) Dean, of Midland City, Mich.

148. i. GEORGE DEWEY, b. Oct. 21, 1861; m. Mina E. Gale, 190-1.
149. ii. CHARLES RICE, b. July 9, 1865; m. Martha E. Webster, 192-3.
150. iii. BENJAMIN DEAN, b. Mar. 13, 1880, Pittsfield, Mass. Grad. High School in Pittsfield and grad. Worcester Polytechnic Institute, 1903. Been in General Electric Works in Schenectady, N. Y. Present res., Schenectady.
151. iv. NELSON ALLEN, b. July 24, 1882, Pittsfield, Mass. Grad. Pittsfield High School. Is in Albany Business College.
152. v. MARY ALICE, b. Apr. 11, 1885, Pittsfield, Mass. Grad. Pittsfield High School, 1903. Smith College, Northampton, Mass., '07.

98. ALVAH FOOTE, JR., (53, 37, 24, 10, 4, 1,) b. Mar. 14, 1819, Chester, Mass.; d. June 11, 1905; m. Sarah Elder. She d.; m. 2nd, Elizabeth Taylor.

153. i. EDWARD PAYSON, b. Dec. 16, 1853; m. Carrie Anna Weld, 194-6.

99. ALFRED SMITH FOOTE, (53, 37, 24, 10, 4, 1,) b. Jan. 22, 1821, Chester, Mass.; m. Oct. 1, 1850, Helen Maria Burnham, South Egremont, Mass. She was b. Sept. 29, 1827; d. Nov. 22, 1894.

154. i. FLORENCE ESTELLE, b. Nov. 29, 1854. Teacher.
155. ii. FRANK MONROE, b. Nov. 1, 1857; m. Mrs. Mary Knowlton. Res., Chester, Mass.
156. iii. HELEN BURNHAM, b. Sept. 10, 1859; m. Chas. Andrews Montgomery, East Boothbay, Me. Ch.: (1) Florence Isabelle, b. May 24, 1891. Res., Northampton, Mass.

104. EDWARD NEWTON FOOTE, (53, 37, 24, 10, 4, 1,) b. Mar. 27, 1833, Chester, Mass.; m. June 6, 1857, Mary E., dau. of Theodore and Eunice (Noble) Bartlett, Northampton, Mass. Res., Medford, Mass.

157. i. JENNIE L., b. June 3, 1860; m. May 22, 1890, Charles H. Park, Sunderland, Eng. Res., Eugene, Oregon. Ch.: (1) Kenneth B., b. Ariz., June 1, 1891.
158. ii. CHARLIE, b. 1864; d. 1867.

107. ENOCH FOOTE, (56, 38, 25, 7, 1,) b. Oct. 2, 1775, Newburyport, Mass.; m. Nov. 25, 1802, Sarah (Sally) George, Haverhill, Mass. She d. Nov. 10, 1809; m. 2nd, Dolly Ingers, Oct. 4, 1810. She d. Mar. 10, 1843; m. 3rd, Oct. 17, 1844, Ann Cushing. He d. Dec. 30, 1849.

159. i. GEORGE B., b. Haverhill, Oct. 13, 1804; m. Josephine Breck Whittier, 197-9.
160. ii. ABIGAIL (ABBY) b. June 30, 1807, Haverhill, Mass.; m. Nov. 29, 1829, Christopher Tompkins. He d. Sept. 28, 1873. She d. Apr. 10, 1887. Ch.: (1) Enoch Foote, b. Nov. 4, 1830, Middleboro, Mass.; m. June 18, 1856, Kate H. Shurtleff, Haverhill, Mass. Ch.: (a) Abbie Hayden, b. Jan. 9, 1858, Haverhill. (2) Sarah Whitwell, b. Dec. 16, 1832, Middleboro; d. 1836, Middleboro. (3) Charles Chase, b. Aug. 3, 1837, New Bedford; d. Oct. 28, 1857, Haverhill. (4) George Henry, b. July 9, 1841, New Bedford. (5) Mary Chase, b. Feb. 9, 1848, Haverhill.
161. iii. CAROLINE GREENLEAF, b. Aug. 2, 1811; m. July 3, 1834, Warren Ordway. Res., Bradford, Mass. Ch.: (1) George Warren, b. May 8, 1835; m. Abbie Fiske. He d. Oct., 1886. (2) Enoch Foote, b. Sept. 21, 1836; d. May 20, 1874. (3) Caroline Frances, b. Dec. 9, 1838; m. Walter Everett, of Charles-

town. She d. Oct. 31, 1901. Ch.: (a) Carrie Foote, m. Peter Weeks. (b) Ellen L., b. ———; m. Eber Keys. (c) Mary E. (4) Mary Emery, b. June 22, 1841; m. Eugene Carter, of Bradford, Mass. She d. Aug. 2, 1898. Ch.: (a) Warren Carter. (b) George H. Carter. (5) David Leighton, b. Aug. 5, 1844; d. Mar. 17, 1869, at Florence, Italy. (6) Ellen Bradstreet, b. Dec. 31, 1845; d. Nov. 14, 1860. (7) Herbert Ingersol, b. Nov. 21, 1851; m. S. Alice Fitts, of Haverhill, Mass.

111. CALEB FOOTE, (57, 38, 25, 13, 7, 1,) b. July 15, 1778; m. 1st, Martha, dau. of Samuel Massey West, b. Nov. 17, 1781; d. Dec. 28, 1805; m. 2nd, Mary, dau. of Samuel Massey West. She was b. 1786; d. June 17, 1808.

162. i. CALEB, b. Feb. 28, 1803; m. Mary Wilder White, 200-6.

163. ii. SAMUEL, b. June 1, 1805; d. Sept. 22, 1805.

115. JACOB FOOTE, (59, 40, 31, 22, 10, 4, 1,) b. Aug. 25, 1796; m. Nov. 21, 1822, Hannah, dau. of Stephen and Prudence (Blinwell) Lowell. She d. May 15, 1809. He d. Apr. 10, 1864. Res., Phipsburg, Me. Now Baltimore.

165. i. ABNER LOWELL, b. Aug. 20, 1823; m. Ellen J. Barr, of Portland, Me. He was a steam engineer. Settled at Baltimore, Md.; d. there Nov. 27, 1902, leaving a wife and ch.

166. ii. ALPHEUS H., b. June 30, 1826; m. Nancy F———. She d. May 22, 1901. Res., 330 Washington St., Bath, Me.

167. iii. CYRUS MORSE, b. May 10, 1828; m. Jane E. Arris, 217-23.

117. JOHN WYMAN FOOTE, (59, 40, 31, 22, 10, 4,) b. June 16, 1804; m. Nancy Lowell, of Phipsburg.

168. i. EMELINE, b.

169. ii. CONSTANT EPHRAIM, b. Ret. steamboat captain. Res., Norwich, Ct.

170. iii. ELIZABETH.

171. iv. WILLIAM.

172. v. JULIA.

120. FRANCIS FOOTE, (59, 40, 31, 22, 10, 4, 1,) b. Jan. 20, 1813; m. Sarah, dau. of Capt. Jeremiah Fogg, of Bath, Me. He was a steam engineer.

173. i. LENDAL LITCHFIELD, b.

174. ii. DRUGELLA, b. ———; m. A. Pierce, Portland. Ch.: (1) A son.

125. ELIAS FOOTE, (64, 31, 22, 10, 4, 1,) b. Peacham, Vt., May 19, 1817; m. Angeline T———; d. 1860, ae. 44.

175. i. WILLIAM W., b. Sept. 12, 1858; m. 224-9.

131. WILLIAM EDWIN FOOTE, (66, 31, 22, 10, 4,) b. Peru, N. Y., May 16, 1826; m. ———. Res., Davenport, Iowa.

176. i. CAROLINE CRANDALL, b. Feb. 20, 1869. Res., Chicago, Ill.

138. JOHN HARWOOD FOOTE, (72, 45, 32, 22, 10, 4, 1,) b. July 31, 1833; m. Mary A. ———.

177. i. ANNIE M., b. May 24, 1858.

178. ii. CHARLES S., b. Dec. 25, 1864; m. Amelia Higgins, 230.

179. iii. CARRIE M., b. Dec. 25, 1864.

140. THOMAS FOOTE, (77, 46, 32, 22, 10, 4, 1,) b. Mar. 14, 1813, Amesbury, Mass.; m. Nov. 26, 1835, Lydia Tabor b. Bristol R. I., Aug. 13, 1813. He d. Dec. 17, 1887. She d. Mar. 14, 1899.

180. i. MARY ELIZA, b. Sept. 1, 1837; d. Aug. 26, 1840.
181. ii. CHARLES E., b. June 5, 1840; m. Mary F. Smith, 231-2.
182. iii. FREDERICK W., b. Apr. 21, 1843; d. Apr. 23, 1844.
183. iv. HENRY T., b. Sept. 27, 1845; m. Charlotte E. Ainsworth, 233.
184. v. ALFRED W., b. Feb. 21, 1848; m. Fanny S. Randall, 234-5.
185. vi. JAMES LEWIS, b. Apr. 15, 1856; m. Arats Platt, of Manchester,
N. H. She d. Jan. 19, 1907. He is a successful manager and
treasurer of The Slatington, Bangor Syndicate, miners, shippers and
exporters of roofing slate, Slatington, Pa.

143. HOMER FOOTE, (91, 51, 32, 22, 10, 4, 1,) b. Feb. 5, 1851, North Castle,
N. Y.; m. Feb. 22, 1872, Mary E. Morgan, North Wilton. She was b. Apr. 15,
1849. Res., Bridgeport, Ct.
186. i. FLORA B., b. Feb. 8, 1873, Wilton, Ct.; m. July 22, 1894, Chas.
McPherson, Norwalk, Ct. Ch.: (1) H. Eloise, b. Nov. 29, 1895,
Bridgeport, Ct.
187. ii. PERCY A., b. Dec. 11, 1876; m. June 9, 1906, Helen McIntosh,
Bridgeport, Ct.
188. iii. EBER L., b. Aug. 31, 1879; d. Aug. 27, 1880, Norwalk, Ct.

144. EBER FOOTE, (91, 51, 32, 22, 10, 4, 1,) b. Nov. 13, 1853; m. Dec., 1874,
Flora C. Osborne. Res., Bridgeport, Ct.
189. i. RAYMOND W., b. Apr. 17, 1885, Norwalk, Ct.

148. GEORGE DEWEY FOOTE, (95, 51, 32, 22, 10, 4, 1,) b. Oct. 21, 1861;
m. Sept. 3, 1884, Mina E., dau. of William F. and Chloe (Webster) Gale. She was
b. May 4, 1864, West Stockbridge, Mass.
190. i. DEWEY GALE, b. Aug. 5, 1886, Pittsfield, Mass.
191. ii. ANNA LOUISE, b. Apr. 19, 1888, Pittsfield, Mass.

149. CHARLES RICE FOOTE, (95, 51, 32, 22, 10, 4, 1,) b. July 9, 1865.
Res., 81 Bradford St., Pittsfield, Mass. Was Councilman in Ward 7, 1902-3. Is
Alderman in same; m. Martha E., dau. of Nelson and Theresa (Warden) Webster,
b. May 22, 1868, at East Nassau, N. Y.
192. i. EDNA WEBSTER, b. Jan. 12, 1891, Pittsfield, Mass.
193. ii. HERBERT NELSON, b. Jan. 6, 1894; d. June 23, 1903.

153. EDWARD PAYSON FOOTE, (98, 53, 37, 24, 10, 4, 1,) b. Dec. 16,
1853, Blandford, Mass.; m. Aug. 13, 1889, Carrie Anna Weld.
194. i. HAZEL LUCILE, b. Nov. 21, 1890.
195. ii. DORIS ELIZABETH, b. Dec. 8, 1893.
196. iii. CLAUDE KENNETH, b. July 21, 1898.

159. GEORGE B. FOOTE, (107, 56, 38, 25, 13, 7, 1,) b. Haverhill, Mass., Oct.
13, 1804; m. Dec., 1856, Josephine Breck, dau. of Richard and Harriet (Swan)
Whittier of Methuen, Mass. He d. May 19, 1870.
197. i. GEORGE WHITTIER, b. Sept. 23, 1857; m. Adelaide Elizabeth
Pierce, 236-40.
198. ii. ENOCH WARREN, b. June 25, 1859; m. Julia Manter Cleveland.
241-44.
199. iii. CHARLES LINCOLN, b. Feb., 1864; d. Dec., 1864.

162. CALEB FOOTE, (111, 57, 38, 25, 13, 7, 1,) b. in Salem, Mass., Feb. 28,
1803. When he was 14 years of age he was apprenticed in the printing-office of
the Salem ''Gazette,'' of which paper he became editor and proprietor in less

(35)

than a score of years. Under his able guidance it became one of the leading papers of Eastern Massachusetts. He continued his active connection with this paper until he was 84 years old, a period of 70 years, which can hardly be paralleled in the history of American journalism. He was also at different times a member of the State Legislature and of the Governor's Council, and Postmaster of Salem. He was a man whose long life of integrity, wisdom and courtesy gave him a large influence in the community. He m. Oct. 31, 1835, Mary, dau. of Hon. Daniel Appleton White and Mary Wilder, of Salem. She was b. Dec. 12, 1810; d. Dec. 24, 1857. He d. June 17, 1894, at Milton, Mass.

    200. i. ELIZA DWIGHT, b. July 20, 1836; d. Sept. 3, 1837.

    201. ii. HENRY WILDER, b. June 2, 1838; m. Frances Ann Eliot, 245-48.

    202. iii. WILLIAM OME WHITE, b. Mar. 31, 1841; d. Sept. 29, 1842.

    203. iv. MARTHA WEST, b. Mar. 20, 1842; d. May 15, 1842.

    204. v. MARY WILDER, b. Aug. 20, 1843; m. Sept. 25, 1865, John Boies Tileston. He was b. Sept. 30, 1834; d. Jan. 24, 1898. She res., 99 Mt. Vernon St., Boston, Mass. Ch.: (1) Mary Wilder, b. July 7, 1866. (2) Margaret Harding, b. Nov. 1, 1867; m. Dec. 22, 1899, David Linn Edsall. He was b. July 6, 1869. Ch.: (a) John Tileston, b. Nov. 2, 1902. (b) Richard Linn, b. Nov. 16, 1905. (3) Roger Edmund, b. Aug. 7, 1869; m. Sept. 15, 1897, Maria Regina Gordon. Ch.: (a) Maria Regina, b. Aug. 1, 1898. (b) Roger Gordon, b. Jan. 14, 1901. (c) John Boies, b. Dec. 22, 1902. (4) Amelia Peabody, b. Oct. 30, 1872. (5) Wilder, b. Jan. 22, 1875; m. Nov. 18, 1903, Clare Williams. She d. Jan. 14, 1905. (6) Edith, b. Nov. 25, 1880. (7) Eleanor Boies, b. June 9, 1886.

    205. vi. ARTHUR WILLIAM, b. Mar. 5, 1853; m. Katherine G. Knowlton, 249.

    167. CYRUS MORSE FOOTE, (115, 59, 40, 31, 22, 10, 4,) b. May 10, 1828; m. Jane E. Arris. He d. Aug. 20, 1894.

    217. i. ALIEDA, b. Pittsburg, 1851; d. 1852.

    218. ii. CHARLES T., b. 1853; m. Susie L. Miller, 260.

    219. iii. EUGENE C., b. 1855. Killed in a railroad accident.

    220. iv. ANNE S., b. 1858; m. William Sparks. Ch.: (1) Grace. (2) Mabel. (3) Lillian. (4) Frank A. (5) Herbert E. (6) Florence.

    221. v. FRANCIS A., b. 1860; m. Farenholtz Lottee Annie, 261-3.

    222. vi. JACOB W., b. Portland, Me., 1860; d. 1863.

    223. vii. JENNIE MAY, b. Portland, Me., 1866; m. —— Wallace. Ch.: (1) Harry F., b.

    175. WILLIAM W. FOOTE, (125, 64, 31, 22, 10, 4,) b. Sept. 12, 1858; m. ——. Res., Burlington, Vt.

    224. i. EDGAR H., b. Feb. 18, 1884, in Burlington, Vt.

    225. ii. HARRY E., b. Burlington, Jan. 8, 1887.

    226. iii. GLENNA E., b. Feb. 18, 1889.

    227. iv. MAUD E., b. Jan. 7, 1891.

    228. v. MABLE E., b. Sept. 21, 1896, in Burlington, Vt.

    229. vi. GLADYS E., b. Burlington, Nov. 25, 1903.

    178. CHARLES S. FOOTE, (138, 72, 45, 32, 22, 10, 4,) b. Dec. 25, 1864; m. June 15, 1898; Amelia Higgins, of Hyde Park, Mass. Res., Hyde Park, Mass.

CALEB FOOTE.   No. P 162

REV. HENRY WILDER FOOTE. No. P 201

230. i. DAVID H., b. May 25, 1899.

181. CHARLES E. FOOTE, (140, 97, 46, 32, 22, 10, 4,) b. June 5, 1840; m. June 11, 1860, Mary F. Smith, of Salisbury, N. H. She d. Sept. 2, 1901. He is a senior member of the firm of Foote, Brown & Co., dealers in dry goods, groceries, hardware, crockery, room paper, paints and oil, Penacook, N. H.

    231. i. HELEN L., b. July 20, 1863; m. James Farrand. Res., Penacook, N. H.

    232. ii. CHARLES SMITH, b. ———; d. in infancy.

183. HENRY T. FOOTE, (140, 97, 46, 32, 22, 10, 4,) b. Sept. 27, 1845; m. Apr. 13, 1876, Charlotte E. Ainsworth, of Vt. Res., Penacook, N. H.

    233. i. WALTER A., b. ———; m. ———. Is in the employ of John B. Narick Co., hardware, Manchester, N. H.

184. ALFRED W. FOOTE, (140, 97, 46, 32, 22, 10, 4,) b. Feb. 21, 1848; m. Fanny S. Randall, of Hampstead, N. H. He d. Apr. 11, 1891.

    234. i. CHARLES T., b. Res., Haverhill, Mass.

    235. ii. GUY H., b. Res., Hampstead, N. H.

197. GEORGE WHITTIER FOOTE, (159, 107, 56, 38, 25, 13, 7, 1,) b. Sept. 23, 1857; m. Nov. 23, 1880, Adelaide Elizabeth Pierce, of Athol, Mass. She d. Mar., 1901.

    236. i. GEORGE LESLIE, b. Oct. 12, 1881.

    237. ii. JOSEPHINE ELLEN, b. Aug. 7, 1884; d. Dec. 30, 1884.

    238. iii. HERBERT WHITTIER, b. Oct. 10, 1885.

    239. iv. WILLIAM PIERCE, b. Feb. 14, 1888; d. Apr. 17, 1888.

    240. v. JULIA HARRIET, b. Aug. 21, 1890.

198. ENOCH WARREN, (159, 107, 56, 38, 25, 7, 1,) b. June 25, 1859; m. Nov. 25, 1884, Julia Manter Cleveland, of Middletown, Ct.

    241. i. WARREN CLEVELAND, b. June 26, 1886.

    242. ii. RICHARD WHITTIER, b. Feb. 8, 1890.

    243. iii. CHARLES LINCOLN, b. May 15, 1893.

    244. iv. ROBERT, b. Feb. 14, 1901.

201. HENRY WILDER FOOTE, (162, 111, 57, 38, 25, 13, 7, 1,) b. Salem, Mass., June 2, 1838. He was educated at Fiske Latin School, and at Harvard, from which he graduated in 1858. Three years later he graduated from Harvard Divinity School. After declining calls to two important pulpits he was installed as minister of King's Chapel, Boston, Dec. 22, 1861, where he remained until his death, May 29, 1889. As pastor of this historic church he necessarily took a conspicuous position in the community, though his broad culture, scholarly attainments, and spirit of self-forgetting service would have brought him distinction in any case. His chief literary work was the compilation of the "Annals of King's Chapel," a work of great importance in the New England history. Many of his sermons were published in pamphlet form, and a volume of them was collected after his death under the title, "Thy Kingdom Come." The inscription upon his monument at King's Chapel describes him as "a man of thorough learning, broad charity, and clear unswerving faith; gentle, pure, strong; wise in judgment, tender in sympathy, rich in holy thought and work; revering justice he loved mercy and walked humbly with his God. His ever present sense of duty inspired a life whose joy was to strengthen and to cheer. With victorious faith and abiding peace he lived among us blessing and blessed." He m. July 9, 1863, Frances Anne, dau. of

Hon. S. A. Eliot, of Boston, a woman of saintly character, who is also commemorated by a tablet in King's Chapel.

245.   i.   MARY, b. Boston, Nov. 6, 1864; d. Dec. 10, 1885.
246.   ii. FRANCES ELIOT, b. Feb. 2, 1875, in Boston; m. June 14, 1906, Louis Craig Cormish.
247.   iii. HENRY WILDER, b. Feb. 2, 1875, Boston; m. Eleanor Tyson Cope, 264-5.
248.   iv. DOROTHEA, b. Boston, Nov. 3, 1880; m. June 2, 1904, at Boston, Roger Bigelow Merriman. He was b. May 24, ·1876· Ch.: (1) Roger Bigelow Merriman, b. Apr. 29, 1905.

205. ARTHUR WILLIAM FOOTE, (162, 111, 57, 38, 25, 13, 7, 1,) b. Salem, Mass., Mar. 5, 1853; m. July 7, 1880, Katherine Grant, dau. of Chas. W. and Kate A. Knowlton. Res., Dedham, Mass. A dramatical composer of distinction. Graduated at Harvard 1874. Has composed over forty pieces of music for orchestra, piano and violin. Organist of the First Unitarian Church of Boston since 1878.

249.   i.   KATHERINE, b. Boston, Mass., Sept. 26, 1881.

218. CAPT. CHARLES T. FOOTE, (167, 115, 40, 31, 22, 10, 4,) b. 1853; m. Susie L. Miller. Res., Boston, Mass.

260.   i.   CHARLES F., b. 1883.

221. CAPT. FRANCIS A. FOOTE, (167, 115, 59, 40, 31, 22, 10, 4,) b. Portland, 1860; m. Farenholtz Lottee Annie.

261.   i.   CHARLES F., b.
262.   ii. HENRY A.
263.   iii. GEORGE A.

247. HENRY WILDER FOOTE, (201, 162, 111, 57, 38, 25, 13, 7, 1,) b. Feb. 2, 1875, Boston; m. June 22, 1903, Eleanor Tyson, dau. of Alexis T. and Elizabeth S. Cope, b. Nov. 9. 1879, Germantown, Pa. He graduated at Harvard, A. B., 1897, A. M., 1900, S. T. B., 1902 (from Harvard Divinity School). Minister of the First Unitarian Church of New Orleans, Oct. 1, 1902, to June 1, 1906; of the First Unitarian Church of Ann Arbor, Mich., Sept. 1, 1906.

264.   i.   HENRY WILDER, b. Aug. 30, 1905.
265.   ii. AGNES COPE, b. Ann Arbor, Mich., Mar. 11, 1907.

A NEW YORK BRANCH.

JOHN FOOTE was b. in England in 1757, but at the age of 19 he, with his one sister and widowed mother, were living in Holland. His mother owned a grist mill and John was the miller. At this time John was seized by a British boat crew, and though he protested that he was not a native of that province, they would not release him or allow him to say good-bye to his mother, but hurried him to the vessel. He was brought over to America and served in the British Army until the surrender of Burgoyne, when he managed to join the American Army, in which he served until peace was declared. The rolls at Washington have him registered in Col. Robt, Van Rensselaer's Regiment. When the war was finished, John Foote married and settled in New York City, where he engaged in the trucking business until 1800, when, selling out his business and most of his household effects, he moved by means of two teams and covered wagons, his family, now consisting of himself, wife, and eight children, to Cayuga Co. in Central New York, settling in "Indian Fields," now is town of Genoa. Here they became acquainted with the family of Christopher Jansen, who had recently moved there from Easton, Penna.—but previously from Holland. Three of John Foote's sons eventually married three of the Jansen girls. The Jansen name was evidently of Danish origin. In 1812, John Foote sold his real estate in Genoa and moved to Odessa, Schuyler Co., near Watkins' Glen, where he owned 300 acres of land, which he bought in 1800, paying for it £300. Here he d. in 1817. His widow survived him nearly 20 years, and most of the foregoing facts were given by Mrs. Foote to her grandson, Jacob Jansen Foote. John Foote was of medium height, strongly built, and had blue eyes. The majority of his descendants have dark eyes. The Jansens had very dark brown, almost black, eyes. John Foote was m. to Catherine Miller, Mohawk Valley, N. Y.

1. i. JOHN, b. in New York City, 1784; m. Molly, dau. of Christopher Jansen, of Genoa, N. Y. Res., Genoa, N. Y.

2. ii. PHILIP, b. in New York City, Oct. 4, 1786; m. Barbara Jansen, 9-15.

3. iii. DANIEL, b. in New York City, 1788; m. Mary Jansen, 16.

4. iv. ADAM, b. in New York City, 1790.

5. v. CATHERINE, b. in N. Y. City, 1792; m. John Conrad.

6. vi. ESTHER, b. in New York City, 1794; m. Richard Mann.

7. vii. SUSAN, b. in New York City, 1796; m. Thomas Smith.

8. viii. ELIZABETH, b. in New York City, 1798; m. Eben Adams.

2. PHILIP FOOTE, b. Oct. 4, 1786; m. Barbara, dau. of Christopher Jansen, of Genoa, N. Y. He d. at Ithaca, N. Y., Sept. 3, 1858. She d. there, 1861, ae. 74.

9. i. JOHN, b. in Genoa, N. Y., 1807; m. Mary Anne Consen.

10. ii. CHRISTOPHER JANSEN, b. in Genoa, N. Y., Apr. 4, 1810; m. Abigail Stout, 20-24.

11. iii. SARAH, b. in Genoa, N. Y., 1812; m. 1829, Philip Sisson, of Genoa Falls, N. Y. Ch. all b. in Seneca Falls: (1) Frances, b. (2) Franklin. (3) Augustus. (4) Josephine, m. May 6, 1863, William J., son of John C. Thayer, of Seneca Falls. He was in the Civil War. Was a corporal of Co. A, 33rd N. Y. Infantry. - Was honorably discharged at Philadelphia, May 22, 1862. He was b. June 29, 1839. She d. June 4, 1889. Ch.: (a) Ermina Josephine, b. at Seneca Falls, Mar. 5, 1864; m. Sept. 16, 1885, Loren L. Quigley. Res., Auburn, N. Y. She d. Aug. 9, 1897. Ch. all b. in Auburn, N. Y.: (i) Frank, b. Sept. 12, 1886. (ii) Harold, b. May 29, 1891. (iii) Josephine V., b. Apr. 11, 1893. (iv) Loren, b. Apr. 19, 1895. (v) Bertha, b. Feb. 23, 1897. (b) Bertha, b. Apr. 10, 1866. (c) Nellie H., b. Aug. 5, 1870; m. June 22, 1892, Frank B., son of William Carlton, of Dunkirk, N. Y. He was b. Sept. 26, 1866. Grad. Hamilton College. Is Pastor of Bethlehem Presbyterian Church, Buffalo, N. Y. Ch.: (i) Josephine Thayer, b. Feb. 14, 1894. (ii) Frank William, b. Dec. 15, 1895; d. Feb. 7, 1898. (iii) William Gilchrist, b. July 15, 1897. (iv) Lester Thayer, b. July 15, 1897; d. May 23, 1903. (v) Kathryn Lester, b. Sept. 5, 1904. (d) R. Lester, b. June 16, 1872; m. Oct. 25, 1900, Gertrude Pauline Muchmore, of Shelbyville, Ind. He is an electrical engineer. Res., Peoria, and Chicago, Ill.

12. iv. MARY, b. in Genoa, N. Y., 1814; m. Nov., 1834, William, son of Thomas Pollard, of Seneca Falls, N. Y. Ch.: (1) Sarah Adeline, m. Charles A., son of Augustus Wetmore. Ch.: (a) Edith May.

(2) William Frederick, b. ———; m. Cora, dau. of Elijah Thomas, of Seneca Falls, N. Y.
13. v.   HIRAM, b. 1816; m. Esther Harding, 25-26.
14. vi. MORGAN, b. 1822.
15. vii. PHILIP, b. Ithaca, N. Y., 1824.

3. DANIEL FOOTE, b. 1788; m. Mary, dau. of Christopher Jansen, of Genoa, N. Y.
16. i.   JACOB JANSEN, b. at Genoa, 1812; m. ———.
9. JOHN FOOTE, b. 1807; m. Mary Anne Cousen. Res., Golconda, Ill.
17. i.   IRVING.
18. ii. MARY.
19. iii. JOHN.

10. CHRISTOPHER JANSEN FOOTE, b. Ithaca, N. Y.; m. Jan. 28, 1838, Abigail Stout, dau. of M. Blue, of Ithaca, N. Y. She was b. in Dryden, N. Y., June 25, 1816; d. at Ithaca, N. Y. He d. at Ithaca, May 30, 1879, ae. 70. Ch. all b. at Ithaca, N. Y.
20. i.   NELSON WEART, b. Oct. 28, 1838; m. Mary E. Goodrich, 27-29.
21. ii. GEORGE WASHINGTON, b. Jan. 8, 1841; m. Addie S. Holten, 30-32.
22. iii. WILLIAM JANSEN, b. Sept. 28, 1843; m. Ruth Bradbury and Charlotte Swayne, 33-36.
23. iv. PHILIP LAFAYETTE, b. Apr. 20, 1850; m. Sarah Frances Van Kirk, 37-40.
24. v.   FRANCIS EDGAR, b. June 16, 1857; m. Apr. 15, 1880, Ida May, dau. of Mrs. J. K. Massey, of Ithaca, N. Y. Res., Dillon, Montana. He was educated in public schools of Ithaca, N. Y. City Editor of a prominent paper in Ithaca. Is Editor and Publisher of the Dillon ''Tribune,'' Dillon, Montana. She was b. in Rome, N. Y., June 28, 1860.

13. HIRAM FOOTE, b. 1816; m. Esther Harding.
25. i.   MARY.
26. ii. FRANK.

16. JACOB JANSEN FOOTE, b. ———. Res., Mich., and Black Creek, Wis., in 1887. Had five ch. Two boys and three girls. One dau. m. Res., 1883, Texas. Eldest son was an expert miller, and at one time was employed in Minneapolis Mills.

20. NELSON WEART FOOTE, b. Oct. 28, 1838; m. Jan. 18, 1876, Mary E., dau. of Orvill Goodrich, of Olney, Ill. He was in service of U. S. Government during Civil War, having charge of 120 men, who rebuilt bridges in Tennessee which had been burned by the Confederates. They were guarded by U. S. troops while at work, and the task was no sinecure. After the war ended, he went in business with his brother, George Washington Foote, in Scranton, Pa., selling out after two years and moving to Lockport, N. Y., and later to Decatur, Ill. After living there a number of years, he moved to Lincoln, Neb. Res., also, Greenville, Texas. Mrs. Foote was b. in White Co., Ill., Oct. 15, 1841.
27. i.   ABBIE, b. Oct. 12, 1876; m. Sept. 28, 1898, Peter J., son of Patrick Cain, of Montgomery, Mo.
28. ii. JENNIE GOODRICH, b. Sept. 27, 1878; m. Nov. 5, 1901, John G., son of Daniel Wolf, of Hammond, Ind.

29. iii. ETTA BILLY, b. in Jasper Co., Ill., Dec. 25, 1880; m. May 6, 1903, Harry B., son of Charles Servier, of Bristol, Tenn.

21. GEORGE WASHINGTON FOOTE, b. Jan. 8, 1841; m. Feb. 8, 1866, Addie S., dau. of Jeptha Holten, of Jersey City, N. J. He was living in Jersey City during the early part of the Civil War, and went into the U. S. Service until peace was declared. After the war he and his brother were in business at Scranton, Pa. Res., Jersey City. He went into the service of the Pullman Car Co. Res., Chicago. Superintendent of Pullman Car Dining Service. Mrs. Foote was b. Mar. 28, 1837, and d. at Lake Bluff, Ill., Mar. 25, 1902.

30. i. CARRIE H., b. in Jersey City, N. J., Jan. 5, 1868; d. Jan. 28, 1870.
31. ii. ADA S., b. Jan. 30, 1871, in Jersey City, N. J.; m. May 2, 1903, Dr. Emory West, son of Stephen Reeves, of Plymouth, Ind. He was b. Nov. 12, 1878. Res., Lake Bluffs, Ill. Ch.: (1) Helen Ada, b. Dec. 11, 1904. (2) Alma May, b. Sept. 26, 1906.
32. iii. LULU M., b. Jan. 30, 1871, in Jersey City, N. J.

22. WILLIAM JANSEN FOOTE, b. Sept. 28, 1843; m. 1st, Ruth, dau. of Cornelius Bradbury, Ithaca, N. Y., and 2nd, Oct. 29, 1870, Charlotte, dau. of W. M. Swayne, of Lockport, N. Y. He enlisted during the Civil War in Co. D, 137th Regt. N. Y. S. V. Enrolled Aug. 19, 1862. Honorably discharged, June 9, 1865. He was in battles of Gettysburg and Chancellorsville, and with Hooker in Tennessee. At the battle of Lookout Mountain, Corp. Wm. J. Foote was wounded while up the mountain. He was supporting the color-bearer, when a bullet struck him over the right eye, which did not penetrate the skull, but made an ugly wound, for which he was furloughed. He returned to his regiment and marched with "Sherman to the Sea." After passing through the dangers of war, he was destined to end his life through an accident, occurring 23 years after peace was declared. While working on a railroad bridge in Scranton, Pa., he fell, striking on a pile of iron, injured beyond recovery. He lingered for several weeks; d. Oct. 13, 1888. He was buried with military honors at Scranton, Pa. Mrs. Foote was b. Eunis Co., Ireland, Oct. 19, 1849.

32. i. JOHN, b. at Lockport, N. Y., May 15, 1872.
33. ii. NELSON S., b. at Buffalo, N. Y., May 15, 1872; m. Jennie M. Leadbetter.
34. iii. CLYDE M., b. Ithaca, N. Y., Sept. 23, 1881.
35. iv. MALVERN HILL, b. Scranton, Pa., Sept. 15, 1886.

23. PHILIP LAFAYETTE FOOTE, of Poughkeepsie, N. Y.; m. Oct. 17, 1877, Sarah Frances, dau. of Daniel Alfred Van Kirk, of Jacksonville, N. Y. He was educated at Ithaca, N. Y., passing through the public schools and finishing at the Ithaca Academy. At 17 years of age, he commenced the study of dentistry. Is a graduate of Philadelphia Dental College, of Ithaca, N. Y. Res., Poughkeepsie, N. Y., in 1880. Is a dentist there. Mrs. Foote was b. at Jacksonville, N. Y., Oct. 31, 1849, and is a descendant of a brother of Sir Francis Drake, through Esther Drake, her great-grandmother.

36. i. SADIE ANNA, b. in Jacksonville, N. Y., Aug. 19, 1878; m. June 27, 1885, William Edwin, son of Charles Bussing, of Brooklyn, N. Y. She was educated at Lyndon Hall, Poughkeepsie High School, of Ithaca and Vassar College.
37. ii. ALFRED VAN KIRK, b. in Ithaca, N. Y., Mar. 10, 1880; m. Mary Gertrude Waechter.
38. iii. PERCY LAFAYETTE, b. Poughkeepsie, N. Y., Dec. 20, 1882.

39.   iv. HAROLD STOUT, b. Poughkeepsie, N..Y., Sept. 22, 1884.

33. NELSON S. FOOTE, b. at Buffalo, N. Y., May 15, 1872; m. Nov. 1, 1884, Jennie M., dau. of Ebenezer Leadbetter, of Beckwith, Nova Scotia.

40.   i. CHARLOTTE P., b. at Haverhill, Mass., May 19, 1905.

37. ALFRED VAN KIRK FOOTE, b. in Ithaca, N. Y., Mar. 10, 1880; m. Jan., 1904, Mary Gertrude, dau. of Godfrey Waechter, of Poughkeepsie, N. Y. He was educated in public schools of Poughkeepsie. Studied dentistry with his father, and afterward graduated from the Philadelphia Dental College, 1902. Res., Ill., 1904, and practicing dentistry in Welden, Ill. She was b. Apr. 7, 1883.

41.   i. LAURA ELIZABETH, b. at Welden, Ill., Dec. 3, 1904.

THE VIRGINIA BRANCH.

I have followed the record as given by Gov. H. S. Foote. I shall be very glad to make any addition to this record, to be published in the next volume of this work. If you have definite information, send it at once to A. W. Foote Co., Middlebury, Vt.

The first Foote we have any record of in this branch was born at Cardenham, in the county of Cornwall, Aug. 10, 1632. His name was Richard Foote, son of John Foote. He was m. Dec. 19, 1657, to Hester, dau. of Nicholas Hayward, of London, Grocer. Nicholas Hayward, the father of Mrs. Foote, carried on an extensive trade with Virginia.

1. SUSANNAH, b. Aug. 13, 1658, and d.

2. SAMUEL, b. Jan. 25, 1659-60; d. Mar. 27, 1697; buried at Windsor.

3. MARY, b. Oct. 1, 1662; was buried May 19, 1664, in St. Bennett Sherehog Church.

4. JOHN, b. Mar. 27, 1665; d. Oct. 20, at Jamaica.

5. RICHARD (the first of the family to settle permanently in Virginia), b. Jan. 31, 1666.

6. ELIZABETH, b. Oct. 27.

7. MARY, b. Jan. 18, 1670; d. Oct. following.

8. HESTER, b. Dec. 8, 1672; d. Dec. 18, 1672.

9. GEORGE, b. Oct. 22, 1673.

10. SARAH, b. Oct. 22, 1675; bap. Oct. 23; buried at St. Bennetts Sherehog Church, 1675.

11. SARAH, b. June 27; bap. July 9, 1676.

12. FRANCIS, b. Jan. 8, 1678; bap. Jan. 23; d. Apr. 1, 1697, and buried Apr. 3.

13. HENRY, b. July 5; bap. July 15, 1680.

14. MATTHIAS, b. Dec. 13, 1683; bap. the same day; d. July 20, 1684.

5. RICHARD FOOTE, the younger, b. Jan. 31, 1666, came to Virginia towards the end of the seventeenth century and settled in Stafford County, where he d. Mar. 21, 1729 (St. Paul's Church Register). Owing to the destruction of the records of that county, but little can be learned concerning him. His will was dated Apr. 15, 1724, and though it was destroyed, is cited in a deed from Thomas Booth, Jr., of Gloucester, and Richard Foote, of Stafford, Prince William County,

Sept. 8, 1734, and in another dated Nov., 1762, and recorded in Fauquier County, from Richard Foote, of Stafford.

15. i. RICHARD, b. 1702; m. Katharine Fossaker, 18-22.
16. ii. GEORGE, b. ——; m. —— Berryman and Ann Janes, 23-9.
17. iii. JOHN, b. ——; d. unm.

15. RICHARD FOOTE, (5), b. 1702; m. Aug. 6, 1726, Katherine Fossaker. He was Justice of Stafford in 1745, and was living there in 1762.

18. i. SARAH, b. Jan. 29, 1732; m. Nov. 26, 1750, Rev. William, son of Rev. David Stuart. The Rev. David Stuart came to this country from Scotland in 1716 or 1717, after the defeat at Culloden. He was a minister and settled here at St. Paul's Church. He was its Rector and continued so until his death in 1749, when he was succeeded by his son, William Stuart, who was probably his father's assistant for some time before his death. The Rev. Wm. Stuart was educated at William and Mary, and was sent by his father to London in 1745, where he was ordained by Edmond, Lord Bishop of London, and preached in St. Paul's Church until age and infirmity compelled him to resign. Richard Foote, at his death, gave "Cedar Grove," in King George Co., to h:s daughter Sarah, and the Stuarts have always owned and occupied the property. Rev. Wm. Stuart d. 1799, ae. 75 years. Ch.: (1) Jane, b. Dec. 1, 1751; d. (2) David, b. Aug. 3, 1753. (3) William, b. Oct. 21, 1761. (4) Henry Foote, b. Apr. 25, 1763; d. (5) Richard, b. Sept. 4, 1770. · (6) Henry Foote, b. Oct. 18, 1772; d. June 8, 1793. (7) Jane, b. 1774; m. her cousin, Richard Helm Foote (see No. 31 for complete record). (8) Ann, b. (9) Hellen, b.
19. ii. JOHN, b. Nov. 30, 1735; m.
20. iii. KATHERINE, b. Nov. 24, 1740.
21. iv. RICHARD, b. Oct. 3, 1743.
22. v. GEORGE, b. 1748; m. Helen Helm, 31-32.

16. GEORGE FOOTE, (5,) b. ——; m. 1st, —— Berryman. She d.; m. 2nd, Ann Janes. Ch. by 1st wife.

23. i. GEORGE, b. ——; m. 33-34.
24. ii. GILSON, b. ——; m. ——; went south; d. s. p.
25. iii. HENRY, b.
26. iv. ——, m. Benjamin Pope. Res., Louisville, Ky., where she d., leaving ch.
27. v. ——, m. James Butler, of So. Carolina. Ch.: (1) Major Butler, late member of Congress from So. Carolina.
28. vi. ——, m. Mr. Savage, of So. Carolina. Ch.: (1) Son, res., near Florence, Ala.
Ch. by 2nd wife.
29. vii. RICHARD, b. ——; was Lieutenant of Marines in the Revolution, and was killed in battle off the Capes of Chesapeake.
30. viii. WILLIAM, b. ——; m. 35-46.

22. GEORGE FOOTE, (15, 5,) b. 1748; m. Helen, dau. of Capt. Lenaugh Helm, of Prince William Cove, Va. Mr. Foote d. 1775.

31. i. RICHARD HELM, b. 1773; m. Jane Stuart, 47-51.
32. ii. HESTER, b. ——; m. Captain William Edwards, of Fauquier, Va.

23. GEORGE FOOTE, (16, 5,) b. ———; m. ———. Moved to So. Carolina, and d. there.

    33. i. WILLIAM, b. ———. Clerk of Noxubée Co., Miss.
    34. ii. JOHN.

30. WILLIAM FOOTE, (16, 5,) b. ———; m. ———; d. Fauquier Co., Va.. 1833.

    35. i. GEORGE, b. ———; m. 52-55.
    36. ii. JOHN, b. ———; d. New Orleans; s. p.
    37. iii. ANNE, b. ———; m. Judge Taylor, Vicksburg, Miss.
    38. iv. WILLIAM, b. Noxubee Co., Miss.
    39. v. GILSON, b. Noxubee Co., Miss.
    40. vi. PHILIP, b. ———; m. 56-9.
    41. vii. MARY, b. ———; m. John Massie, Alexandria.
    42. viii. SIGISMUND, b. ———; m. 1st, John Ashton; m. 2nd, Dr. Charles Stuart, of Prince William Co., Va.
    43. ix. RICHARD, b. Fauquier Co., Va.
    44. x. ALEXANDER, b. ———; m. 60.
    45. xi. FREDERICK, b. Prince William Co., Va.
    46. xii. EDWIN, b. Breckenridge Co., Ky.; m. 61-.

31. RICHARD HELM FOOTE, (22, 15, 5,) b. 1773; m. Dec. 16, 1795, Jane, dau. of No. 18. He d. Mar., 1818, at his res., "Spring Hill," Fauquier Co., Va.

    47. i. GEORGE WILLIAM, b. ———; m. Esther Edmunds.
    48. ii. CELIA JANE STUART, b.
    49. iii. RICHARD H., b. ———; d. 1823.
    50. iv. HENRY S., b. Feb. 28, 1804; m. Elizabeth Winters.
    51. v. SARAH CATHERINE, b. ———; m. Francis H. Hereford, and emigrated to Alabama in 1825, then to Hillsboro, Ill. She had had several sons; one, Francis Hereford, was a United States Senator.

35. GEORGE FOOTE, (30, 16, 5,) b. ———; m. ———; d. abt. 1820. Ch.: all b. in Alabama.

    52. i. WILLIAM.
    53. ii. GEORGE.
    54. iii. MARY.
    55. iv. LEVIN.

40. PHILIP FOOTE, (30, 16, 5,) b.; m.; d. Ch. all b. in Alabama.

    56. i. ANN.
    57. ii. MARY.
    58. iii. PHILIP.
    59. iv. CHARLES.

44. ALEXANDER FOOTE, (30, 16, 5,) b.

    60. i. STEPHEN, of Fairfax Co., Va.

50. GOV. HENRY S. FOOTE, (31, 22, 15, 5,) b. Fauquier Co., Va., Feb. 28, 1804; m. Elizabeth Winters, of Nashville, Tenn. He was educated at Georgetown College, District of Columbia, and Washington College, now Washington and Lee University, during 1817-19, and after studying law at Warrentown, Va., was admitted to the bar in 1823. He emigrated the same year to Tuscumbia, Ala., where he edited a Democratic newspaper, and in 1827 removed to Jackson, Miss., and formed a law partnership with Andrew Hutchinson. In Jan., 1847, he was

elected to the U. S. Senate for the term beginning Mar. 4, and was Chairman of the Committee on Foreign Relations; was an earnest advocate of the compromise of 1850. He resigned from the Senate to assume the duties of Governor of Miss., to which office he had been elected in 1851, over Jefferson Davis, and served from Jan., 1852, until Jan., 1854. Upon the expiration of his term, Governor Foote removed to California, but returned to Miss. in 1858 and resumed the practice of law in Vicksburg in 1860, and was strongly in favor of the preservation of the Union. He was bitterly opposed to secession, and quit Mississippi territory when secession was about to become a reality, removing to Tennessee. He, however, gave his adhesion to the Confederate Government, became a member of the Confederate House of Representatives, and served from Feb., 1862, until Jan., 1865, when he resigned and went abroad. In the Confederate Congress he was noted particularly for his opposition to Jefferson Davis and to the continuation of the War, and he favored a suspension of hostilities on the terms offered by Lincoln in 1863 and 1864. After the war he became identified with the administration of Grant, and was appointed by him Superintendent of the U. S. Mint, at New Orleans, which post he held until his death. He was an author of note, his publications including "Texas and the Texans" (Philadelphia, 1841, 2 vols.), "The War of the Rebellion" or "Scylla and Charybdis" (New York, 1866), "The Bench and Bar of the South and Southwest"*(1876), "Personal Recollections," and various speeches and literary addresses. He d. May 20, 1880, in Nashville, Tenn.

   61. i. HENRY STUART, b.

   62. ii. ANNIE E., b.; m. 1855, Hon. William Morris Stewart, U. S. Senator from Nevada for many years.

ADDITIONS AND CORRECTIONS

P. 44, No. 234, (4) Nathaniel Bailey, b. Sept. 6, 1768. His dau., Clarissa, b. Apr. 19, 1800; m. William W. Richmond. Their son is Hon. W. H. Richmond, of Scranton, Pa., b. Oct. 23, 1821; m. June 5, 1849, Lois Roxanna Morse. For complete Family Record see Richmond Genealogy, No. 5060.

P. 62, No. 505, (2) Sarah Mallory, b. Jan. 1, 1788; m. John B. Larkin. They had 12 ch. The 7th was Jerusha, b. Feb. 14, 1820; m. Oct. 24, 1834, Elam Sanford. Ch.: (1) Jane Anna, b. July 10, 1836; m. Henry Overington; 3 ch. and 4 g.-ch. (2) Elam Miles, b. Sept. 24, 1838; m. Elizabeth Gregory; 4 ch. (3) Medora, b. Mar. 24, 1842; m. Louis Lorenzo Todd. (4) Augusta Melinda, b. May 15, 1844; m. Capt. Chas. Crowell; 2 ch. (5) Edward Swanzey, b. Dec. 20, 1846; m. Katherine Kingsley; 6 ch. (6) Chas. Henry, d.

P. 269, No. 2649. (2) George Samuel Betts, b. Sept. 21, 1845; unm. (3) Charlotte Elizabeth, b. May 25, 1843; m. in Unadilla, N. Y., Jan. 23, 1863, Aurelius Thatcher Hurd. Ch.: (a) Frances Amelia, b. Mar. 21, 1863. (b) George Eben, b. Oct. 12, 1867; d. Mar. 6, 1888.

P. 309, Line 24, should read, "State Constitutional Convention, in 1861, at Springfield, Ill.," and the line there printed is the proper substitute for line 28.

P. 372, No. 3810, MARY LYON FOOTE, b. 1844; m. 1867, Lewis Hancock Kennerly. Ch.: (1) Sarah. (2) Charles. (3) Louis. (4) Alzina.

No. 3811. ROSA FISHER FOOTE, b. 1846; m. 1867, Hinson H. Smith. Ch.: (1) Mary. (2) William. (3) Charles.

No. 3812. CHARLES G. FOOTE, b. 1851; unm.

No. 3813. HELEN GAINES FOOTE, b. 1854; m. 1877, Richard Henry Clark. Ch.: (1) Helen Gaines. (2) Mary Morris. Res., New York City.

No. 3814. SALLIE BERNARD FOOTE, b. 1859; m. 1882, Charles James Waller. No ch.

No. 3815. ANNIE L. FOOTE, b. 1861; m. 1885, Osborn H. Parker; d. 1890. Ch.: (1) Sallie Foote.

P. 400, No. 4178, was b. Sept. 25, 1855, and No. 4179, b. Aug. 17, 1856.

P. 423, No. 2836, SETH FOOTE, m. July 1, 1859; d. May 14, 1864, at Farmersburgh, Ia.

P. 489, No. 3986, m. Charlotte Dotey, b. 1846.

P. 494, No. 5547, m. Vera E. Merrill. No. 5547, Millie E. Foote was b. Sept. 25, 1868.

No. 4122, C. M. FOOTE, m. Aug. 9, 1885, Fannie Adelia Cook. Mrs. Foote was b. Feb. 26, 1865. Ch.: (1) Gertrude Helen, b. Sept. 28, 1891; d. Sept. 11, 1892.

No. 5555, SHEILA LENA, b. Mar. 30, 1894.

No. 5556, CLARK MERRIL, Jr., b. Feb. 14, 1897.

P. 505, No. 4352, EDWIN FOOTE, Jr. Present res. (1907), Red Wing, Minn.

P. 516, No. 6021, NORMAN STEWART FOOTE, m. Oct. 9, 1907, Jessie Crane, of Bridport, Vt.

P. 528. No. 7144, STELLA RACHEL FOOTE, m. Oct. 23, 1907, Alfred Lyman Payne, of Cornwall, Vt.

P. 531, No. 7251, WILLIAM ROLLIN FOOTE, m. Oct. 23, 1907, Claribel Hulett, of Pawlet, Vt.

No. 7252, EVA GERTRUDE FOOTE, m. Oct. 30, 1907, Leslie Earl, son of Allen L. and Nellie (Howard) Mott, of Hubbardton, Vt.

P. 535. The last line but one should read: P. 468, No. 3448, DR. EDWARD M. FOOTE.

P. 544, No. 131, Mrs. Foote was b. Aug. 31, 1841, at Scranton, Pa.; dau. of Dr. W. H. H. Crandall; m. Wm. E. Foote, Dec. 22, 1867, in Des Moines, Ia.; d. July 2, 1889.

P. 547, No 184, ALFRED WARREN FOOTE, m. Mar. 22, 1871, Sarah Frances Randall. She was b. Dec. 18, 1855, at Chester, N. H. Ch.: 2331, OLA MAY, b. June 16, 1872; d. Oct. 7, 1894. 234, CHARLES THOMAS, b. Nov. 20, 1874; res., Haverhill, Mass. 2341, ESTHER ALICE, b. Jan. 27, 1878; d. Feb. 12, 1898. 235, GUY LEWIS, b. June 9, 1881; res., Haverhill Mass. 2351, MARK RANDALL, b. Feb. 8, 1889; d. Nov. 9, 1901.

P. 64, No. 510. (3) Miss Sarah B. Hammond, of Rome, N. Y., is a granddaughter of Julius C. Pond.

P. 108, No. 298. JESSE FOOTE went to Lexington at the first call. He was afterwards in the War of the Revolution, and fought at Brandywine and Monmouth.

P. 134, No. 1230. (2) After the death of Mr. Fenn, Martha Eliza (Mix) Fenn m. 2d Wilson Dewey of Haydenville, Mass.

P. 135, No. 1230. (3) Mary L. Mix d. March 17, 1906, in New Haven, Ct., and was buried in Evergreen cemetery.

P. 135, No. 1230. (7) read JANE FOOTE MIX, not Jennie.

P. 145, No. 1297. Dr. WINTHROP FOOTE (M. D. University of New York), d. at Bedford, Indiana, 1856, his son was Dr. Ziba (M. D. University of New York,) b. at Bedford, Ind., 1824, and d. 1907; his son is Judge Oscar Foote, (B. L. Columbia of Washington, D. C.,) b. at Bedford, Ind., 1859. Res. 804 Summit Ave., Seattle, Wash. Ch.: 3 sons, all d. in childhood.

P. 243, No. 2379. DANIEL SAMUEL FOOTE, m. F. Emeline Goodwin. He was a farmer. Ch.: (1) Mrs. C. E. Herrick, res. 311 Waverly Ave., Syracuse, N. Y. (2) Delevan S. Foote, m. Minnie Isabel, dau. of Orlando and Mary E. (Goodrich) Curtis. Ch.: (a) Delevan Curtis Foote. (b) Walter Curtis Foote, b. Aug. 5, 1875, at Chicago, Ill., m. Kathryn G. Miller of Muskegon, Mich; educated at the Normal Training School, and two years at the Medical Department of the Northwestern University, at Chicago, and then went into the Street Car advertising business with his father.

P. 223, No. 2114. HARRIET FOOTE was b. in Granville, N. Y., July 23, 1813; d. Aug. 22, 1896. (1b) Frank E. Harkness, b. Aug. 10, 1874, L. L. B., Harvard, 1900. (1c) Stanley B. Harkness, b. Jan. 7, 1880.

P. 237, No. 2287. HANNAH, m. Dec. 30, 1821, William Cherry. He was b. Oct. 20, 1793, in Elizabethtown, N. J.; d. Dec. 19, 1859, N. Fairfield, O. She d. Mar. 7, 1881, N. Fairfield, O. Ch.: (1) Adaline, b. Sept. 29, 1822, Sempronius, N. Y.; m. 1844, Homer J. Austin, of Ripley, O.; d. ———. Ch.: (a) Augusta Ummethun; res., Kansas City, Mo. (b) Leona; m. Mr. Conover, of Kansas City, Mo. (c) Frank; res., Mobile, Ala. (d) Homer, Jr.; res., Ga. (2) Timothy T., b. June 18, 1827; d. Feb. 14, 1828, N. Fairfield, O. (3) Edgar, b. Mar. 1, 1830; d. Sept. 14, 1838, N. Fairfield, O. (4) Vinton, b. Apr. 28, 1832; m. Elizabeth Terry, of Peru, O.; d. May 28, 1894. Ch.: (a) Cecetia. (b) Ada, m. Morrow; res., Buffalo, Mo. (c) Inez O., b. ———; m. Bannon; res., Buffalo, Mo. (5) Byron Harrison, b. Feb. 11, 1840; m. Emma J. Boughton, May 11, 1870, N. Fairfield, O.; res., Oberlin, O. Ch.: (a) Luella, b. Mar. 17, 1871, N. Fairfield, O.;m. Rettig. (b) Alice L., b. Apr. 16, 1874,

N. Fairfield, O.; m. Bishop. (c) Florence, b. Aug. 6, 1881, N. Fairfield, O.; m. Giles. (d) Amy L., b May 13, 1894, E Norwalk, O. (e) Fern A., b. Mar. 16, 1890, Oberlin, O.

No. 2289. RUTH, m. Darius Cherry. Ch.: (1) Lucy Ann, b. Olena, O.; m. Dr. David Wood; res., Norwalk, O. (2) Corydon, m. Carry Forbes.

P. 272, No. 2715. Ch.: (1) Ida Odell, m. Henness. Res. Stamford, N. Y.

P. 273, No. 2717. SALLY M. FOOTE, m. Charles Walker Booth.

P. 326, No. 3305. (2) Edsall B. Reynolds, m. Aug. 22, 1906, Anna Bell Lottridge.

P. 325, No. 1810., fought in the Civil War, not the Revolution.

P. 334, No. 3375. HARRIET FOOTE, m. Apr. 1, 1907, at Belvidere, Ill., David D. Sabin.

P. 360, No. 3646. (4) is Perry Foote Narten, and No. 3647 is HELEN PERRY FOOTE.

P. 392, No. 4059 m. Helen A. Payne and No. 4060 m. Georgia Hardy.

No. 4061, (2) is Bennett Dana Farnham.

P. 412, No. 4310. ALDIS D. FOOTE, d. Oct. 23, 1896, at Lowville. No. 4314, MRS. ADA F. FOOTE, d. July 24, 1907.

P. 413, No. 4317. Mrs. Martha (Foote) Crow, is now engaged in writing and lecturing in New York City and elsewhere.

P. 415, No. 4331. (3) Grace Morehouse, m. Oct. 9, 1907, Thurman S. Rogers.

P. 416, No. 4346. JULIA B. FOOTE, m. Dec. 25, 1907, (D. V.) George W. Pye. Res. 240 Rutger St., Rochester, N. Y.

P. 436, No. 3014. Mrs. Almira L. Foote; d. March 11, 1888.

P. 492, No. 5509. TRUMANA FOOTE, not Trumania.

No. 4110. GEORGE A. FOOTE, had a store at Charlotte Center several years.

P. 444, No. 4742. JUDSON H. BRISTOL, d. Oct. 7, 1907, at Ft. Collins, Colo.

P. 504, No. 5738. ADA K. is unm. Res. with her mother at Tonawanda.

P. 512, No. 5930. Ch.: 7223, i, HAWLEY HAROLD; 7224, ii, ELEANOR HOVEY, b. Feb. 18, 1905.

P. 513, No. 5954. MALLY ADA, b. Aug. 22, 1875; m. Oct. 30, 1901, Albert M. Grigg. No. 5955. CARRIE MAUDE, b. Oct. 14, 1877; m. Dec. 3, 1902, Wm. D. Gibby. No. 5955¹. ANNA MABEL, b. Feb. 10, 1880; d. Jan., 1882. No. 5956. CHARLES MORTIMER, b. Sept. 28, 1881; m. Nov. 20, 1901, Mae Elizabeth Wheeler Ch.: (1) Norman Charles, b. July 19, 1906. No. 5956¹. GEORGE ALBERT, b. Sept. 12, 1883; d. No. 5957. FRANCES M., b. July 22, 1891; unm.

No. 4083. Leamon R. Foote, m. Nov. 26, 1877, Mary Waring.

No. 5960. EDITH, b. Sept. 18, 1878; m. June 12, 1902, Arthur Darron. Ch.: (1) Dorothy, b. Sept. 26, 1903. No. 5961. LILLIAN, b. Feb. 5, 1880; m. Nov. 5, 1903, Marshall Potter. Ch.: (1) Louise, b. Dec. 11, 1905. No. 5962. CLARA, b. July 17, 1882; m. Dec. 21, 1900, William Campbell. Ch., (1) Edith, b. Oct. 26, 1901. (2) Grace, b. July 26, 1903. (3) Florence, b. Aug. 10, 1905. No. 5963. ROY, b. July 8, 1884. No. 5964. ANNA, b. Dec. 18, 1886; m. Fred Styles, Mar. 25, 1906. No. 5965. WILHELMINA, b. Feb. 26, 1891. No. 5965¹. MARIAN, b. Mar. 26, 1893; d. Sept. 1, 1893. No. 5965². ELMER, b. Apr. 25, 1895; d June 22, 1896. No. 5966. DOROTTY, b. Mar. 21, 1897. No. 5966¹. JEANNIE, b. Oct. 7, 1898. No. 5966². HELENE, b. Feb. 20, 1900; d. Mar. 10, 1900. No. 5967 MINA, b. Jan. 12, 1886. No. 5968. WALTER, b. Oct. 20, 1891. No. 5969. GRACE, b. June 12, 1896. No. 5970. BETHIA, b. Nov. 16, 1902.

Index of Christian Names of Persons by the Name of FOOTE

THE FIGURES REFER TO PAGES.

Christine, 495.
C. Jane, 458.
Claire, 498.
Claire I., 486.
Clara, 127, 178, 306, 349, 364, 387, 424,
  513, 528, 539.
Clara A., 348, 362, 475, 481.
Clara B., 470.
Clara D. H., 430.
Clara E., 327, 348, 364 384, 446, 517.
Clara F., 363, 501.
Clara G., 372.
Clara I., 521.
Clara J., 435.
Clara M., 455, 473.
Clara R., 376.
Clara W., 350, 407.
Clarence, 385, 425, 490, 509, 518.
Clarence A., 382, 488, 519.
Clarence C., 433.
Clarence D., 461.
Clarence E., 446, 509, 524.
Clarence F., 528.
Clarence H., 178, 506.
Clarence M., 437.
Clarence R., 490.
Clarence W., 337, 339, 429, 512.
Clarinda E., 179.
Clarissa, 60, 62, 70, 100, 108, 117, 122,
  155, 161, 176, 220, 222, 233, 237, 264,
  289, 467.
Clarissa A., 236 453.
Clarissa L. 151.
Clarissa M., 522.
Clarissa P., 117.
Clark, 122, 245, 316, 494, 539.
Clark M., 397, 494, 556.
Clarke, 218, 219.
Claude K., 545.
Clayton E., 423, 530.
Clayton H., 364, 479.
Cleveland, 350.
Clifford A., 401.
Clinton, 153.
Clinton T., 469.
Clotilda, 60, 61.
Clyde H., 477.
Clyde L., 499.
Clyde M., 551.
Columbus, 284.
Coman M., 446, 517.
Comfort, 63.
Constance, 478.
Constant E., 544.
Cora, 457, 488, 524.
Cora B., 421, 522.
Cora D., 363, 456.
Cora E., 360, 368, 422, 482, 501, 511.
Cora I., 458.
Cora L., 354.
Coramay S., 348.
Coridon E., 205, 339.
Corinne, 459.
Corinth E., 540.

Cornelia, 175, 222, 306, 445, 502.
Cornelia E., 321, 406, 506.
Cornelia G., 515.
Cornelia J., 401.
Cornelia M., 236, 263.
Cornelia R., 269.
Cornelia S., 273.
Cornelius, 108, 220, 264, 541.
Corwin, 448, 518.
Corwin T., 361, 476.
C. Ray, 384.
Cullen B., 305.
Culver D., 178.
Curtis, 381.
Curtis C., 520.
Cynthia, 66, 166, 246, 263, 264, 375.
Cynthia A., 165, 228.
Cynthia M., 236.
Cyrene, 64, 154.
Cyrenius, 147, 273.
Cyrus, 109, 111, 228, 278, 403, 496.
Cyrus M., 544, 546.
Cyrus R., 319, 451.
Daisy, 380.
Daisy E., 524.
Dale, 498.
Damaris, 70.
Dan, 47, 81, 83, 98, 118, 153, 192, 193,
  209, 234, 282, 327, 366.
Dan C., 340, 468.
Dan P., 177, 307.
Danford E., 493.
Daniel, 28, 31, 32, 33, 37, 38, 40, 48,
  56, 57, 58, 60, 61, 62, 67, 72, 84, 108,
  111, 119, 120, 121, 139, 141, 145, 146,
  167, 168, 169, 176, 179, 181, 182, 205,
  222, 242, 243, 261, 302, 308, 374, 375,
  485, 549, 550.
Daniel A., 262, 394, 513.
Daniel B., 262, 269, 346, 394.
Daniel D., 273, 406.
Daniel E., 271, 329, 407, 462.
Daniel H., 124, 235, 247, 456.
Daniel I., 301.
Daniel N., 274.
Daniel P., 197.
Daniel S., 314, 445.
Daniel T., 234, 366.
Daniel W., 205, 501, 530.
Daraxo, 122.
Darius, 64, 155, 156.
Darwin, 218, 524.
Darwin O., 493, 528.
Darwin R., 323, 453.
Dashia, 468.
Dauphin K., 262.
D. Austin, 499.
David, 36, 37, 39, 49, 54, 56, 59, 60,
  62, 65, 66, 67, 70, 80, 94, 99, 102, 111,
  117, 128, 137, 145, 146, 147, 153, 156,
  161, 169, 179, 180, 191, 192, 218, 229,
  260, 261, 270, 272, 282, 284, 287, 288,
  309, 320, 360, 394, 407, 423, 428, 429,
  440, 452.

Hobart J., 399.
Hollis L., 508.
Holmes, 241, 259, 373.
Homer, 222, 227, 349, 350, 472, 524, 526, 542, 545.
Homer A., 317, 449.
Homer C., 289, 429.
Homer E., 510.
Homer G., 468.
Homer H., 429.
Homer P., 401, 524.
Horace, 102, 121, 136, 153, 161, 233, 259, 264, 291, 365, 396.
Horace A., 294, 317, 432, 450, 510.
Horace B., 221, 245, 378, 511.
Horace C., 433, 510.
Horace F., 294, 433.
Horace G., 242.
Horace H., 486.
Horace K., 431, 433, 511.
Horace L., 374, 376, 485.
Horace S., 510.
Horatio, 161, 289.
Horatio K., 289, 291, 430.
Hosea, 36, 55, 56, 117, 118.
Howard, 473.
Howard A., 470.
Howard E., 495.
Howard G., 391.
Howard L., 515.
Howard M., 327.
Howard S., 458, 521.
Howard W., 385, 490.
Hubert, 339.
Hubert P., 387.
Hubert T., 388, 490.
Hugh, 498.
Hulda V., 519.
Huldah, 38, 58, 70, 78, 79, 144, 181, 186, 237, 243, 311.
Huldah E., 357.
Huldah J., 227.
Hunn B., 219.
Huron, 109.
Hyatt, 269.
Ichabod, 32. 40, 68, 69, 172, 174.
Ida, 427, 483.
Ida A., 374, 440.
Ida B., 362, 446.
Ida C., 482.
Ida E., 419.
Ida H., 460.
Ida I., 390.
Ida L., 451.
Ida M., 362, 331, 452, 480.
Ida O., 460.
Ida P., 341.
Ida S., 436.
Ida T., 519.
Ida V., 214.
Idaho, 450.
Idella, 500.
Idella E., 427.
Inez A., 349.

Inez J., 531.
Ira, 63, 108, 121, 147, 153, 166, 182, 220, 241, 284, 299, 314, 347, 373, 396, 422, 493.
Ira A., 175, 282, 306, 349, 420, 446, 471, 517.
Ira D. 280, 419.
Ira H., 410, 502.
Ira L., 241, 373, 471, 525.
Irene, 34, 160, 325, 429, 478, 490.
Irene A., 419.
Irene E., 469.
Ireneus M., 457, 521.
Iris M., 531.
Irma E., 349.
Irma M., 512.
Irvine, 302.
Irving, 480, 550.
Irving E., 507.
Isaac, 29, 33, 41, 44, 48, 60, 61, 67, 75, 76, 78, 84, 89, 120, 140, 145, 169, 186, 188, 189, 190, 196, 197, 223, 259, 270, 325, 331, 391, 462, 463, 525, 536, 537.
Isaac F., 324, 456.
Isaac H., 189, 324.
Isaac L., 445, 516.
Isaac N., 129, 259.
Isaac N. C., 391, 491.
Isaac O., 395.
Isaac P., 323.
Isaac S., 140, 262, 263, 395.
Isaac W., 223.
Isabel, 477, 539.
Isabel E., 391.
Isabell, 360.
Isabell A., 244.
Isabella, 83, 227, 534.
Isabella S., 482.
Isabelle, 437.
Isabelle C., 516.
Isabelle D. P., 495.
Isabelle G., 303.
Israel, 32, 48, 80, 83, 84, 191, 196, 326.
Israel O., 192.
Ivah, 450.
Ivan L., 478.
J., 326, 460.
J. Adele, 470.
Jabez, 70, 179.
Jabez B., 147, 274.
Jacob, 33, 40, 41, 66, 67, 74, 108, 166, 168, 169, 186, 299, 301, 429, 538, 541, 544, 550.
Jacob A., 289.
Jacob C., 186, 317.
Jacob J., 220,, 550.
Jacob W., 546.
James, 60, 62, 74, 109, 121, 140, 141, 146, 170, 219, 242, 243, 244, 258, 266, 299, 303, 375, 377, 399, 404, 424, 473, 524, 539.
James A. 317, 350, 375, 396, 411, 433, 450, 472, 473, 485, 493.

(37)

Vivian I., 511.
Volney, 228.
Waite L., 477.
Wallace, 233, 244.
Wallace C., 486, 515, 532.
Wallace E., 366.
Wallace H., 378, 420, 486.
Wallace P., 486.
Wallace T., 245, 378, 380.
Waldo E., 361.
Walter, 54, 55, 154, 281, 283, 390, 448, 470, 485. 510, 513, 528, 529.
Walter A., 437, 480, 547.
Walter B., 232, 363.
Walter C., 478, 557.
Walter E., 363, 367, 482, 525.
Walter G., 418.
Walter M., 466.
Walter O., 324, 455.
Walter R., 187, 319.
Walter S., 300.
Walter W., 482, 455.
Waltham W., 196.
Wareham W., 168, 300.
Ward N., 498.
Warren, 108, 161, 220, 288, 347, 429.
Warren C., 287, 457.
Warren D., 483.
Warren G., 410, 428, 501.
Warren M., 370, 463, 483, 525.
Warren N., 428.
Warren R., 509.
Warren W., 489.
Wash. S., 425.
Watson, 284.
Watson E., 445.
Watson O., 423.
Wealthy, 54, 119, 235, 266.
Wealthy A., 122.
Wealthy C., 191.
Webster DeF., 304, 348.
Welles B., 461.
Weltha E., 523.
Weriban. 250.
Wesley T., 512.
Wilbert, 523.
Wilbert D., 401, 523.
Wilbert V., 401, 523.
Wilbur, 395.
Wilbur E., 503.
Wilburt W., 515.
Wilfred, 304.
Wilfred R., 349.
Wilhelmina, 485, 558.
Will D., 307.
Will H., 482.
Will R., 528.
Willard, 383, 408.
Willard E., 469.
Willard L., 400.
Willard P.. 172.
Williard W., 349.

William, 49, 51, 61, 70, 72, 78, 100, 107, 120, 122, 141, 146, 178, 182, 183, 185, 189, 209, 219, 220, 224, 226, 233, 236, 237, 244, 250, 268, 270, 271, 272, 302, 303, 316, 318, 319, 329, 344, 351, 354, • 360, 365, 367, 368, 396, 401, 407, 424, 427, 452, 479, 494, 509, 523, 525, 532, 537, 538, 539, 544, 553, 554.
William A., 116, 221, 227, 244, 247, 249, 383, 400, 405, 411, 428, 439, 449, 488, 496, 497, 503, 514.
William B., 125 267, 271, 326, 363, 400, 407, 411, 439, 449, 479.
William C., 166, 172, 252, 298, 305, 317, 366, 407, 420, 433, 435, 447, 449, 455, 511, 523, 524.
William D., 179, 232, 269, 308, 364, 402.
William E., 224, 262, 352, 434, 494, 532, 542 544 557.
William F., 340, 369, 468, 481.
William G., 196, 286, 506, 509, 514.
William H. 93, 95, 188, 194, 205, 259, 262, 283, 284, 288, 304, 315, 338, 355, 364, 368, 370, 391, 393, 399, 401, 419, 422, 426, 428, 446, 452, 473, 475, 486, 507, 509, 518, 523, 524.
William J., 200, 207, 340, 467, 495, 550, 551,
William K., 332, 463.
William L., 75, 101, 187, 217, 290, 323. 424, 480, 526, 540, 541.
William M., 287, 381, 427, 435, 483, 512.
William N., 457, 520.
William O., 348, 471, 503, 509.
William O. W., 546.
William P., 269, 303, 374, 401, 547.
William R., 189, 281, 324, 420, 439, 452, 455, 471, 509, 531, 556.
William S., 187, 198, 247, 260, 273, 321, 331, 405, 427, 447, 452, 459, 509.
William T., 204, 304, 337, 438, 542.
William W., 346, 370, 400, 406, 457, 445, 482, 516, 521, 544, 546.
William Y., 414.
Williams, 395.
Willie, 383.
Willie E., 482, 527.
Willie H., 406, 474, 500.
Willis B., 467.
Willis D. W., 494, 528.
Willis O., 422, 514.
Willis S., 367, 480.
Willmot W., 297.
Wilma E., 529.
Wilson A.. 453, 519.
Winfield E., 515.
Winfred R.. 349.
Winthrop, 145, 557.
Wyborn, 471.
Wyllis J., 423, 508.
Wyllys, 155, 285.
Zebulon. 425.
Zella, 349.

Index of Other Names

FOOTE HISTORY AND GENEALOGY

2776. EDGAR FOOTE (1347, 488, 145, 41, 11, 3,) b. Sept. 13, 1825; m. Nov. 15, 1847, Julia Payne. She d. Mar. 29, 1857, in Streetsboro, O.; m. 2nd, Feb. 14, 1858, Emma T. Chaplain; res, Streetsboro, O.

4367. i. AMANDA, b. Nov. 25, 1851.

4368. ii. FRANK ELWOOD, b. Aurora, O., Nov. 21, 1860; d. Apr. 7, 1878, in Streetsboro, O.

4369. iii. EVERETT CHALFONT, b. Aurora, O., May 3, 1864; m. Carrie Lorrain, 57-75.

2779. NJS FOOTE, JR. (347, 488, 145, 41, 11, 3,) b. Ag. 15, 1831; m. Jan. 31, 1855, Belinda Shurtliff. She d. Sept. 20, 1865, at Ralf, O.; m. 2nd, Sept. 15, 1866, Jane Sawyer ., of Solon, O. She d. Dec. 23, 1875; m. 3rd, Aurora, O., Aug. 3, 1879, Sarah Jane Zimmer. She was b. ... Ky., ... 15, 1849.

4370. i. MA DEAN, b. Aurora, O., Mar. 12, 1853; d. May 11, 1854, Aurora, O.

4371. ii. IRN HAYES, b. Portage, O., Sept. 28, 1854; m. Helen Maria ..., 5776-7.

4372. iii. EDGAR CHARLES, b. Aurora, O., Jan. 9, 1859; m. Mary Van Della ..., 5778-9.

4373. iv. E EBT BURTON, b. Aurora, O., Jan. 29, 1862; m. Salla Haskins, 5786.

4374. v. LEONARD LN, b. Aurora, O., July 8, 1867; m. Ana Sdar.

4375. vi. JENNIE BELLE, b. Aurora, O., June 1, 1869; m. Ag. 20, 1887, William Kiser, of Chardon, O. He was b. Apr. 25, 1865; res. 462 So. Pierce St., ... Wis. Ch.: (1) Linus Egbert, b. ... N. Dak., May 19, 9?. (2) Wm Carroll, b. Fargo, N. Dak., June 29, 1893.

4376. vii. JOHN A., b. ... O., Nov. 15, 1872; m. Belle Sippert 3781-2.

4377. viii. MA RUTH, b. Aurora, O., Jan. 17, 1881; m. Sept. 29, 19?, ... Md. Ch.: (1) Robert dlph,